Connecting to the Source

Excerpts from the
Wisdom of Kabbalah

LAITMAN
KABBALAH
PUBLISHERS

Connecting to the Source
Excerpts from the Wisdom of Kabbalah
Copyright © 2021 by Michael Laitman
All rights reserved
Published by Laitman Kabbalah Publishers
Contact Information
E-mail: info@kabbalah.info
Website: www.kabbalah.info
Toll free in USA and Canada: 1-866-LAITMAN
1057 Steeles Avenue West, Suite 532, Toronto,
ON, M2R 3X1, Canada
Tel. 1-416-274-7287
No part of this book may be used or reproduced
in any manner without written permission of the publisher,
except in the case of brief quotations embodied
in critical articles or reviews.

Editors: Roy Akoka, Margalit Ventura, Ronit Shye, Dudi Aharony
Excerpt Collection and Sorting: Orly Goldman, Orly Shimon, Eyal Oz, Osnat Bernstein, Ben Zion Girtz, David Menichuck, Dafna Bar, Hilda Yaniv, Vered Schwartz, Hoter Ben Hur, Yovav Hoffenberg, Yaniv Si, Madonna Chen, Michal Levi Shor, Maayan Akoka, Nir Krevner, Sigal Ratz, Ofer Nakash, Ilay Nisim, Inbal Gvili, Tzipi Bar, Moti Bar, Kaya Nevifur, Ruhama Rosenzweig, Shabtai Kalabrino, Shuli Oren, Tahel Shadmon

ISBN: 978-1-77228-036-4

Translation: Chaim Ratz

Editing: Mary Pennock, Mary Miesem, Joseph Donnelly,
Michael Kellogg, Debbie Wood

Proofreading: Haya Fleury

Printing and Post Production: Uri Laitman

FIRST EDITION: March 2021
First Printing

Table of Contents

Part 1: The Essence of the Wisdom of Kabbalah.........................7
    1. What Is the Wisdom of Kabbalah about? 8
    2. The Purpose of Creation 12
    3. The Thought of Creation 29
    4. The Essence of Man 33
    5. The Awakening of the Point in the Heart 43
    6. The Soul of Adam HaRishon 45
    7. All the Wisdoms in the World Are Included in the Wisdom of Kabbalah 51
    8. The Origin of Resistance to the Wisdom of Kabbalah 54

Part 2: Studying the Wisdom of Kabbalah..............................65
    1. The Merit of the Study – The Reforming Light 66
    2. Preparation for the Study 95
    3. A Path of Torah and a Path of Suffering 98
    4. The Language of Kabbalah Is a Language of Branches 103
    5. Who Is a Kabbalist? 110
    6. Kabbalists and the Writings of Kabbalah 122
    7. The Necessity to Study Kabbalah 130

Part 3: Dissemination of the Wisdom of Kabbalah 149
    1. Israel and the Nations of the World 150
    2. The Role of Israel 160
    3. The Importance of Disseminating the Wisdom of Kabbalah 176
    4. Our Generation – The Last Generation 184
    5. The Society in the Last Generation 190

Part 4: Man's Relation to the Creator..................................195

   1. If I am Not for Me, Who Is for Me?................................ 196
   2. There Is None Else Besides Him................................... 200
   3. Adhesion.. 213
   4. By Your actions, We Know You.................................... 263
   5. The Greatness of the Creator.................................... 267
   6. Contentment to the Creator...................................... 279

Part 5: Man's Work on the Spiritual Path..............................297

   1. Faith Above Reason.. 298
   2. From Not for Her Sake to For Her Sake........................... 329
   3. Two Opposites in the Same Carrier............................... 342
   4. Love Will Cover All Crimes...................................... 346
   5. Make for Yourself a Rav [Teacher/Great One]..................... 350
   6. Labor... 361
   7. Intention... 376
   8. Yearning.. 385
   9. Devotion.. 395
  10. Overcoming.. 399
  11. Prayer.. 402
  12. A Prayer of Many.. 450
  13. Gratitude... 457
  14. The Perception of Reality....................................... 463

Part 6: States on the Spiritual Path 485

   1. The Preparation Period.. 486
   2. Concealment and Revelation...................................... 489
   3. Recognition of Evil... 509
   4. The Burdening of the Heart...................................... 523
   5. Fear.. 543
   6. Shame... 547
   7. Ascents and Descents.. 549
   8. Despair with One's Own Strength................................. 574
   9. Impregnation.. 584

Part 7: The Society as a Cause of Spiritual Attainment 593
  1. The Choice of the Environment 594
  2. From Love of People to Love of the Creator 600
  3. The Influence of the Environment on a Person 609
  4. The Ten 619
  5. The Center of the Group 624
  6. The Power in Connection 632

Part 8: The Principles of Spiritual Work in the Group 647
  1. The Purpose of the Society 648
  2. The Importance of the Goal 654
  3. Love of Friends 656
  4. Annulment and Subjugation 674
  5. *Hitkalelut* [Incorporation] 700
  6. *Arvut* [Mutual Responsibility] 711
  7. The Agenda of the Assembly of Friends 717
  8. The Covenant 724
  9. They Helped Every Man His Friends 731
  10. Envy, Lust, and Honor 734
  11. Buy Yourself a Friend 741
  12. Seeing the Friend's Merit 747
  13. Joy on the Path 750
  14. Judge Every Person to the Side of Merit 773

PART 1
The Essence of the Wisdom of Kabbalah

1

What Is the Wisdom of Kabbalah about?

1. Baal HaSulam, "The Essence of the Wisdom of Kabbalah"

What the Wisdom Is About?

This question comes to the mind of every right-minded person. To properly address it, I will provide a reliable and lasting definition: This wisdom is no more and no less than a sequence of roots that hang down by way of cause and consequence, following fixed, determined laws that interweave into a single, exalted goal described as "the revelation of His Godliness to His creatures in this world."

2. Baal HaSulam, "The Teaching of the Kabbalah and Its Essence"

What is the wisdom of Kabbalah? As a whole, the wisdom of Kabbalah concerns the revelation of Godliness, arranged on its paths in all its aspects—those that have been revealed in the worlds and those that are destined to be revealed, and in all the manners that can ever be revealed in the worlds, to the end of time.

3. Baal HaSulam, *The Study of the Ten Sefirot*, Part 1, Chapter 1, *Ohr Pnimi*, Item 1

Bear in mind, that the entire wisdom of Kabbalah is founded on spiritual matters that do not take up time or space.

4. Baal HaSulam, "The Essence of the Wisdom of Kabbalah"

There is no other wisdom in the world where matters are so fused and intertwined by way of cause and effect, primary and consequential, as is the wisdom of Kabbalah, connected from top to bottom just like a long chain. Therefore, upon the temporary loss of but a small cognizance, the entire wisdom darkens before our eyes, for all its matters are tightly connected to one another, literally fusing into one.

5. Baal HaSulam, "The Essence of Religion and Its Purpose"

Many are mistaken and compare our holy Torah to ethics. But this has come to them because they have never tasted religion in their lives. I call upon them: "Taste and see that the Lord is good." It is true that ethics and religion both aim at the same thing—to raise man above the filth of the narrow self-love and bring him to the apex of love of others.

But still, they are as far one from the other as the distance between the thought of the Creator and the thought of people. For religion extends from the thoughts of the Creator, and ethics comes from thoughts of flesh and blood and from their life's experiences. Hence, there is an evident difference between them, both in practical aspects and in the final aim.

6. Baal HaSulam, "Introduction to The Study of the Ten Sefirot," Item 8

This explains the great difference between the wisdom of the Torah and the rest of the teachings in the world: Acquiring the other teachings in the world does not improve life in this world whatsoever, since they do not even render mere gratification for the torments and suffering one experiences during one's life. Hence, one need not correct one's body, and the labor that he gives in return for them is quite sufficient, as with all other worldly possessions acquired in return for labor and toil.

However, the sole purpose of engagement in Torah and *Mitzvot* is to make a person worthy of receiving all the goodness in the intention of creation, "to do good to His creations."

7. Baal HaSulam, "The Wisdom of Israel Compared to External Wisdoms"

The value of any wisdom in the world is according to the purpose that it yields. This is the goal to which all the scrutinies aim. Therefore, a wisdom without some purpose is inconceivable except for infants playing games, since to pass the time they come and this is their purpose, according to their value. For this reason, a wisdom is not evaluated by keenness and proficiency, but according to the merit of the purpose that it yields.

You therefore find that any external wisdom is only for the purpose of corporeality, which is sure to be gone today or tomorrow. In that case, it is sufficient for the subject to be as the predicate.

Although the wisdom has many advantages over these subjects, for wherever it is, it is nonetheless a spiritual object, but we have already said that it is evaluated by the purpose, which is its persistence for eternity. If the purpose is transitory and fleeting, it is lost along with it.

Now we have a standard by which to gauge the significance of the wisdom of Israel compared to an external wisdom. It concerns only the understanding of the ways of the Creator over His creations and adhering to Him. It follows that the very essence of this wisdom relies on the Creator. And because the importance of the Creator compared to His creations, which He has created, is inconceivable, the merit of the wisdom of Israel compared over external wisdoms is also inconceivable.

Because the very essence of our wisdom is ever valid and eternal, our entire wisdom will also remain eternal. And because it concerns being favored and approaching the Creator, which is the finest goal that can be perceived, one who engages in it, and certainly one who is rewarded with it, is the finest among the speaking species.

8. *Zohar for All*, *Toldot* [Generations], "These Are the Generations of Isaac," Item 190

There are several secrets of the Torah in each and every action that is written in the Torah, and there is wisdom and true law in every single word. Hence, the words of the Torah are holy words, to show wonders from them, as it is written, "Open my eyes, that I may behold wonderful things from Your law."

9. *Zohar for All*, BeHaalotcha [When You Mount the Candles], Passover in Its Time and Second Passover, Item 58

Woe unto one who says that the Torah comes to tell literal tales and the uneducated words of such as Esau and Laban. If this is so, even today we can turn the words of an uneducated person into a law, and even nicer than theirs. And if the Torah indicates to mundane matters, even the rulers of the world have among them better things, so let us follow them and turn them into a law in the same way. However, all the words of the Torah have the uppermost meaning.

10. *Zohar for All*, VaEtchanan, "Leather Gowns," Item 35

The Creator is destined to open eyes that were not wise to gaze in the upper wisdom and attain what they did not attain in this world so they would know their Master. Happy are the righteous who will be rewarded with that wisdom, for there is no wisdom like that wisdom, and no knowledge like that knowledge, and no *Dvekut* [adhesion] like that *Dvekut*.

11. Ramchal, 138 Doors to Wisdom

Only this is the wisdom of Kabbalah: to know the guidance of the Upper Desire, why It created all those creations, what It wants from them, and what the end of all the cycles of the world will be.

12. RAMAK, Know the God of Your Father

There is one who look at the Torah and the matters only literally, but those are in disgrace for the next world for the matters there are not the literal, but their meaning.

13. RAMAK, Know the God of Your Father

The secrets of the Torah clothe in allegories and riddles in the Torah because of the expansion of the Torah and their descent from the highest degrees down to this corporeal world.

14. Raaiah Kook, *Orot HaKodesh*

The wisdom of truth teaches us the global unity, the equal side that must be found in all of creation to the very top, to similarity of the form to its Maker, and how to walk by its light without failing.

15. Ramchal, Zeal for the Lord of Hosts

The true and genuine definition of the wisdom of truth is the wisdom of the procession of the operations of the Emanator, who acted to create His world and operates by sustaining it. The thing is that the Emanator wanted to arrange His actions according to one intention that came up in His thought to follow it in His work. The collection of all those processions and their ordinances is called "the wisdom of truth."

2

The Purpose of Creation

1. Baal HaSulam, "What the Wisdom Is About"

General—the whole of humanity, obligated to eventually come to this immense development, as it is written, "For the earth shall be full of the knowledge of the Lord, as water covers the sea" (Isaiah 11, 9). "And they shall teach no more every man his neighbor, and every man his brother, saying, know the Lord, for they shall all know Me, from the least of them to the greatest of them" (Jeremiah 31, 33), and he says, "Your Teacher will no longer hide Himself, and your eyes will behold your Teacher" (Isaiah 30).

2. Baal HaSulam, "Introduction to The Book of Zohar," Item No. 39

The Creator's desired goal for the creation He had created is to bestow upon His creatures, so they would know His truthfulness and greatness, and receive all the delight and pleasure He had prepared for them.

3. Baal HaSulam, "The Teaching of the Kabbalah and Its Essence"

All the conducts of creation, in its every corner, inlet, and outlet, are completely prearranged for the purpose of nurturing the human species from within it, to improve its qualities until it can sense the Creator as one feels one's friend.

These ascents are like rungs of a ladder, arranged degree by degree until it is completed and achieves its purpose.

4. Baal HaSulam, "Matan Torah" [The Giving of the Torah]

The aim of the Creator from the time He created His creation is to reveal His Godliness to others, since the revelation of His Godliness reaches the creature as pleasant bounty that is ever growing until it reaches the desired measure.

By this, the lowly rise with true recognition and become a *Merkava* [chariot/structure] to Him, and to cling unto Him until they reach their final completion: "The eye has not seen a God besides you."

5. Baal HaSulam, "The Shofar of the Messiah"

The purpose of creation is invaluable, for a tiny spark such as man's soul can rise in its attainment higher than the ministering angels.

6. Baal HaSulam, "The Essence of Religion and its Purpose"

His guidance is purposeful and aims to eventually bring us to *Dvekut* [adhesion] with Him, so He would reside within us

7. Baal HaSulam, Letter No. 17

"The purpose of the soul when it comes in the body is to be rewarded with returning to its root and with *Dvekut* [adhesion] with Him while clothed in the body, as it is written, "To love the Lord your God, to walk in all His ways, to keep His commandments, and to adhere to Him."

8. Baal HaSulam, "Introduction of The Book of Zohar," Item No. 39

This purpose does not apply to the still and the great spheres, such as the earth, the moon, or the sun, however luminous they may be, and not to the vegetative or the animate, for they lack the sensation of others, even from among their own species. Therefore, how can the sensation of the Godly and His bestowal apply to them?

Humankind alone, having been prepared with the sensation of others of the same species, who are similar to them, after working in Torah and *Mitzvot*, when they invert their will to receive to a desire to bestow and achieve equivalence of form with their Maker, they receive all the degrees that have been prepared for them in the upper worlds, called NRNHY. By this they become qualified to receive the purpose of the thought of creation. After all, the purpose of the creation of all the worlds was for man alone.

9. Baal HaSulam, "The Acting Mind"

Every person is obliged to attain the root of his soul.

10. Baal HaSulam, "Matan Torah" [The Giving of the Torah]

The purpose of the whole of creation is for the lowly creatures to be able, by observing Torah and *Mitzvot*, to rise ever upward, ever developing until they are rewarded with *Dvekut* with their Creator.

But here came the sages of *The Zohar* and asked why we were not created in this high stature of *Dvekut* with Him to begin with. What reason did He have to burden us with this labor and burden of creation and the Torah and *Mitzvot*? They replied, "He who eats that which is not his is afraid to look at his face." This means that one who eats and enjoys the labor of one's friend is afraid to look at his face because by doing so he becomes increasingly humiliated until he loses his human form.

Because that which extends from His wholeness cannot be deficient, He gave us room to earn our exaltedness by ourselves, through our work in Torah and *Mitzvot*.

11. Baal HaSulam, Introduction to "From the Mouth of a Sage"

The meaning of the souls of the children of Israel is that they are a part of God above. The soul cascaded by way of cause and consequence and descended degree by degree until it was suitable to come into this world and clothe the filthy corporeal body. It ascends degree by degree until its stature is completed by keeping the Torah and observing its *Mitzvot*. Finally, it is worthy of receiving its complete reward, which has been prepared for it in advance, meaning attaining the holy Torah as the names of the Creator, which are the 613 *Pekudin*.

12. Baal HaSulam, "The Love of God and the Love of Man"

The purpose of creation applies to the entire human race, none excluded.

13. Baal HaSulam, "The Arvut" [Mutual Guarantee], Item 23

The purpose of creation lies on the shoulders of the whole of the human race, black, or white, or yellow, without any essential difference.

14. Baal HaSulam, "The Love of God and the Love of Man"

If the whole purpose of the Torah and all of creation is but to raise the base humanity to become worthy of that wonderful sublimity, and to adhere to Him, He should have created us with that sublimity to begin with instead of troubling us with the labor of creation, and the Torah and *Mitzvot*.

We could explain this with the words of our sages: "One who eats that which is not his is afraid to look at his face." This means that anyone who feeds on the labor of others is afraid (ashamed) to look at his own form, for his form is inhuman.

Because no deficiency comes from His wholeness, He has prepared for us this work, so we may enjoy the labor of our own hands. This is why He created creation in this base form. The work in Torah and *Mitzvot* lifts us from the baseness of creation, and through it we achieve our sublimity by ourselves. Then we do not feel the delight and pleasure that comes to us from his generous hand as a gift, but as the owners of that pleasure.

15. Baal HaSulam, "The Study of the Ten Sefirot," Part One, "Inner Observation"

If the purpose of the creation of the worlds was to delight His creatures, why did He create this corporeal, turbid, and tormented world? Without it, He could certainly delight the souls as much as He wanted; so why did He bring the soul into such a murky and filthy body?"

They explained it with the verse, "He who eats that which is not his own is afraid to look at his face." This means there is a flaw of shame in any free gift. To spare the souls this blemish, He created this world where there is work. And they will enjoy their labor, for they take their full pay in return for their work and are thus spared the blemish of shame.

16. Baal HaSulam, "Introduction to The Book of Zohar," Item 4

The only tactic is to examine the end of the act, that is, the purpose of creation, for nothing can be understood in the middle of the process, but only at its end.

17. Baal HaSulam, "The Essence of Religion and Its Purpose"

The Creator is the absolute good. He watches us in complete benevolence without a hint of evil and in a purposeful guidance. This means that His guidance compels us to undergo a series of phases, by way of cause and effect, preceding and resulting, until we are qualified to receive the desired benefit. At that time, we will arrive at our purpose as a ripe and fine-looking fruit.

18. Baal HaSulam, "The Essence of Religion and Its Purpose"

His guidance over the reality that He has created is in the form of purposeful guidance, without taking into consideration the order of the phases of development, for they deceive us and prevent us from understanding their purpose, being always opposite to their final shape.

It is about such matters that we say, "There is none so wise as the experienced." Only one who is experienced has the opportunity to examine creation in all its phases of development, all the way through its completion, and can calm things down so as to not to fear those spoiled images that creation undergoes in the phases of its development, but believe in its fine and pure end.

19. Baal HaSulam, "The Essence of Religion and Its Purpose"

We understand that any being of the four types—still, vegetative, animate, and speaking—as a whole and in particular, are under a purposeful guidance, meaning a slow and gradual growth by way of cause and effect, as a fruit on a tree, which is guided well toward its final outcome of becoming a sweet and fine-looking fruit.

Go and ask a botanist how many phases the fruit undergoes from the time it becomes visible until it is completely ripe. Not only do its preceding phases show no evidence of its sweet and fine-looking end, but as if to anger, they show the opposite of the final outcome. That is, the sweeter the fruit is at its end, the more bitter and unsightly it is in the earlier phases of its development.

20. Baal HaSulam, "The Peace"

The corrupt conducts in the states of humanity are the very ones that generate the good states. And each good state is nothing but the fruit of the work in the bad state that preceded it. Indeed, these values of good and bad do not refer to the value of the state itself, but to the general purpose: Each state that brings humanity closer to the goal is considered good, and one that deflects them from the goal is considered bad.

By this standard alone is the "law of development" built—the corruption and the wickedness that appear in a state are considered the cause and the generator of the good state, so that each state lasts just long enough to grow the evil in it to such an extent that the public can no longer bear it. At that time, the public must unite against it, destroy it, and reorganize in a better state for the correction of that generation.

And the new state, too, lasts just as long as the sparks of evil in it ripen and reach such a level that they can no longer be tolerated, at which time it must be destroyed and a more comfortable state is built in its stead. And so the states clear up one by one and degree by degree until they come to such a corrected state that there will be good without any sparks of evil.

21. Baal HaSulam, "Introduction to The Study of the Ten Sefirot," Item 155

Why then did the Kabbalists obligate every person to study the wisdom of Kabbalah? Indeed, there is a great thing about it, which should be publicized: There is a wonderful, invaluable remedy to those who engage in the wisdom of Kabbalah. Although they do not understand what they are learning, through the yearning and the great desire to understand what they are learning, they awaken upon themselves the lights that surround their souls.

This means that every person from Israel is guaranteed to finally attain all the wonderful attainments with which the Creator contemplated in the thought of creation to delight every creature. And one who has not been awarded in this life will be granted in the next life, etc., until one is awarded completing His thought, which He had planned for him, as it is written in *The Zohar*.

And while one has not attained perfection, the lights that are destined to reach him are considered surrounding lights. This means that they stand ready for him but are waiting for him to purify his vessels of reception, and then these lights will clothe the able vessels.

Hence, even when he does not have the vessels, when he engages in this wisdom, mentioning the names of the lights and the vessels related to his soul, they immediately illuminate upon him to a certain extent. However, they illuminate for him without clothing the interior of his soul, for lack of vessels able to receive them. Yet, the illumination one receives time after time during the engagement draws upon him grace from above, and imparts him with abundance of sanctity and purity, which bring him much closer to achieving his wholeness.

22. Baal HaSulam, "Introduction to the Book Panim Meirot uMasbirot," Item 22.

One does not live for oneself, but for the whole chain. Thus, each and every part of the chain does not receive the light of life into itself, but only distributes the light of life to the whole chain.

23. "The Arvut" [Mutual Guarantee]

It is upon the Israeli nation—through Torah and *Mitzvot*—to qualify itself and all the people of the world to develop until they take upon themselves that sublime work of the love of others. This is the ladder to the purpose of creation, which is *Dvekut* with Him.

24. Baal HaSulam, "Emanation of the Soul"

Every person was created only to obtain a complete and illuminating soul from the Creator, worthy of perpetual and eternal *Dvekut* [adhesion].

25. Baal HaSulam, "Peace in the World"

Everything in reality, good or bad, and even the most harmful in the world, has a right to exist and must not be destroyed and eradicated from the world. We must only mend and reform it because any observation of the work of creation is enough to teach us about the greatness and perfection of its Operator and Creator. Therefore, we must understand and be very careful when casting a flaw on any item of creation, saying it is redundant and superfluous, as that would be slander about its Operator.

26. Baal HaSulam, "Introduction to The Book of Zohar," Item 14

Thus you necessarily find that on the whole, there are three states to the soul:

The First State is their presence in *Ein Sof*, in the thought of creation, where they already have the future form of the end of correction.

The Second State is their existence during the six thousand years, which were divided by the above two systems into a body and a soul. They were given the work in Torah and *Mitzvot* in order to invert their will to receive and turn it into a desire to bestow contentment upon their Maker, and not at all for themselves.

During the time of that state, no correction will come to the bodies, only to the souls. This means that they must eliminate from within them any form of self-reception, which is considered the body, and remain with but a desire to bestow, which is the form of the desire in the souls. Even the souls of the righteous will not be able to rejoice in the Garden of Eden after their demise, but only after their bodies have completely rotted in the dust.

The Third State is the end of the correction of the souls after the revival of the dead. At that time, the complete correction will come to the bodies, too, for then they will turn reception for themselves, which is the form of the body, to take on the form of pure bestowal, and they will become worthy of receiving for themselves all the delight, pleasure, and pleasantness in the thought of creation.

And with all that, they will attain strong *Dvekut* by the force of their equivalence of form with their Maker, since they will not receive all this because of their desire to receive, but because of their desire to bestow contentment upon their Maker, since He derives pleasure when they receive from Him. For purposes of brevity, from now on I will use the names of these three states, namely "first state," "second state," and "third state," and you will remember all that is explained here in every state.

27. Baal HaSulam, "Introduction to The Book of Zohar," Item 6

Our sages have already said that the Creator created the world for no other reason but to delight His creatures. And here is where we must place our minds and all our thoughts, for it is the ultimate aim of the act of the creation of the world.

28. Baal HaSulam, "The Teaching of the Kabbalah and Its Essence"

Since there is no act without some purpose, it is certain that the Creator had a purpose in the creation set before us. The most important thing in this whole diverse reality is the sensation given to the animals—that each of them feels its own existence. And the most important sensation is the noetic sensation, given to man alone, by which one also feels what is in the other—others' pains and comforts. Hence, it is certain that if the Creator has a purpose in this creation, its subject is man. It is said about this, "All of the Lord's works are for him."

But we must still understand what was the purpose for which the Creator created this lot. Indeed, it is to elevate him to a higher and more important degree, to feel his Creator like the human sensation, which is already given to him. And as one knows and feels one's friend's wishes, so he will learn the ways of the Creator, as it is written about Moses, "And the Lord spoke to Moses face to face, as a man speaks to his friend."

Any person can be as Moses. Undoubtedly, anyone who examines the evolution of the creation before us will see and understand the great pleasure of the Operator, whose operation evolves until it acquires that wondrous sensation of being able to converse and deal with one's Creator as one speaks to one's friend.

29. Baal HaSulam, "Introduction to the Preface to the Wisdom of Kabbalah," Item 1

It is written in *The Zohar*, *Vayikra*, Portion *Tazria*, "Come and see: All that exists in the world exists for man, and everything exists for him, as it is written, 'Then the Lord God formed man,' with a full name, as we have established, that he is the whole of everything and contains everything, and all that is above and below, etc., is included in that image."

Thus, it explains that all the worlds, upper and lower, are included in man. And also, the whole of reality within those worlds is only for man.

30. Baal HaSulam, "The Arvut" [Mutual Guarantee], Item 20

The end of the correction of the world will only be by bringing all the people in the world under His work, as it is written, "And the Lord will be King over all the earth; in that day, the Lord will be one and His name one." The text specifies, "on that day," and not before.

31. Baal HaSulam, "Introduction to The Study of the Ten Sefirot," Items 68-69

To understand this we must first acquire a genuine understanding of the nature of the love of the Creator itself. We must know that all the inclinations, tendencies, and properties instilled in man, with which to serve one's friends, all these tendencies and natural properties are required for the work of the Creator.

To begin with, they were created and imprinted in man only because of their final role—the ultimate purpose of man, as it is written, "No outcast shall be cast out from Him." One needs them all so as to complement oneself in the ways of reception of the abundance and to complete the will of the Creator.

This is the meaning of "Everyone who is called by My name, I have created him for My glory" (Isaiah 43:7), and also "All that the Lord has worked was for His sake" (Proverbs 16:4). However, in the meantime, man has been given a whole world to develop and complete all these natural inclinations and qualities in him by engaging in them with people, thus yielding them suitable for their purpose.

It is as our sages said, "One must say, 'The world was created for me,'" for all the people in the world are required for a person, as they develop and qualify the attributes and inclinations of every individual to become a fit tool for His work.

Thus, we must understand the essence of the love of the Creator from the properties of love by which one person relates to another. The love of the Creator is necessarily given through these qualities, since they were only imprinted in man for His sake to begin with.

32. Baal HaSulam, "The Essence of Religion and Its Purpose"

When one comes to love others, he is in direct *Dvekut*, which is equivalence of form with the Maker, and along with it man passes from his narrow world, filled with pain and impediments, to an eternal and broad world of bestowal upon the Creator and upon people.

33. Baal HaSulam, *Shamati*, Article No. 42 "What Is the Acronym Elul in the Work?"

We must understand the purpose of creation, which is said to be because He wishes to do good to His creations. And because of the *Tikkun* [correction], so there will not be a matter of the "bread of shame," a *Tzimtzum* [restriction] was made. And from the *Tzimtzum* extended the *Masach* [screen] by which the vessels of reception are turned into bestowal.

When the vessels are prepared to be in order to bestow, we immediately receive the light that is hidden and treasured for His creatures. It means that one receives the delight and pleasure that was in the thought of creation, to do good to His creations.

34. Baal HaSulam, *The Study of the Ten Sefirot*, Part 8, *Ohr Pnimi*, Item 88

All our work in prayers and practical *Mitzvot* [commandments] is to sort once more and raise all those souls that fell from *Adam HaRishon* into the *Klipot* [shells] until they are brought to their first root as they were in it before he sinned with the tree of knowledge.

35. RABASH, Article No.6 (1984), "Love of Friends"

The purpose of creation is not necessarily for a select group. Rather, the purpose of creation belongs to all creations without exception. It is not necessarily the strong and skillful, or the brave people who can overcome. Rather, it belongs to all the creatures.

(Examine the "Introduction to The Study of the Ten Sefirot," Item 21, where it quotes *Midrash Rabba*, Portion, "This is the Blessing": "The Creator said unto Israel: 'Regard, the whole wisdom and the whole of Torah are easy: Anyone who fears Me and does the words of Torah, the entire wisdom and the whole of the Torah are in his heart.'")

36. RABASH, Article No. 267. "Man Was Created in the Torah"

It is known that the purpose of creation is to do good to His creations. For this reason, a nature has been imprinted in man that he will want to receive pleasure for his own delight. This is called the "evil inclination" (as explained in the introduction to the *Sulam* [Ladder commentary on *The Zohar*]), as it is written, "For the inclination of man's heart is evil from his youth."

It is called the "evil inclination" because by wanting to receive pleasure, a person becomes removed from the real pleasure because he has no equivalence of form. However, through the Torah, he will have a correction where through the Torah, it will be possible for him to receive the real pleasures, as our sages said, "I have created the evil inclination; I have created the Torah as a spice" (Baba Batra 16).

The spice is as our sages said, "I wish they left Me and kept My Torah [law], for the light in it reforms them" (Jerusalem Talmud, *Hagigah*, Chapter 1, Rule No. 7). It therefore follows that the Torah has the power to reform a person, referring to the evil within man, meaning the will to receive, that it will work in order to bestow.

In this manner, he will have *Dvekut* [adhesion] and will be able to receive the real pleasures and will not be considered a receiver. Thus, through the Torah, it will be possible to sustain man in this world, for the Torah will reform him.

This is the meaning of "Let us make man," which they explained, "I and you will establish him in the world." That is, from the Creator comes the will to receive and from the Torah comes the desire to bestow, and from those two, man will be able to exist in the world. That is, through those two, he will be able to receive abundance yet remain in *Dvekut*.

37. RABASH, Article No. 12 (1988), "What are Torah and Work in the Way of the Creator?"

We should make several discernments in the Torah: 1) one who learns Torah in order to know the rules, to know how to observe the *Mitzvot* of the Torah, 2) one who learns Torah in order to observe the *Mitzva* of learning Torah, as it is written (Joshua 1), "This book of Torah shall not move from your mouth, and you shall contemplate it day and night." RASHI interprets "contemplate it" as "looking in it," every thought in the Torah is in the heart, as he said, "The contemplation of my heart is before You." 3) He learns Torah in order to be rewarded with the light of the Torah, as it is written, "I have created the evil inclination; I have created the Torah as a spice because the light in it reforms him." By this he will be rewarded with faith, and to adhere to the Creator, and then he will become "Israel" for he believes in the Creator in complete faith. 4) Once he has been rewarded with faith, he is rewarded with the "Torah, as in the names of the Creator." In *The Zohar*, this is called "The Torah and Israel and the Creator are one." At that time he is rewarded with the purpose of creation, which is to do good to His creations, when the creatures receive what the Creator wants to give to the creatures.

38. RABASH, Article No. 12 (1988), "What are Torah and Work in the Way of the Creator?"

What are Torah and work, in the work? The answer is that he learns Torah in order to be able to do the work, which is called "which God has created to do." That is, the creatures must do the work of turning the will to receive into a desire to bestow, by which they will have *Dvekut*, which is equivalence of form, and they will also be able to receive the delight and pleasure, which is the purpose of creation.

39. RABASH, Article No. 1 (1984),"Purpose of Society – 2"

Since man is created with a *Kli* called "self-love," where one does not see that an act will yield self-benefit, one has no motivation to make even the slightest motion. And without annulling self-love, it is impossible to achieve *Dvekut* [adhesion)] with the Creator, meaning equivalence of form.

And since it is against our nature, we need a society that will form a great force so we can work together on annulling the will to receive, called "evil," as it hinders the achievement of the goal for which man was created.

For this reason, society must consist of individuals who unanimously agree that they must achieve it. Then, all the individuals become one great force that can fight against itself, since everyone is integrated in everyone else. Thus, each person is founded on a great desire to achieve the goal.

To be integrated in one another, each person should annul himself before the others. This is done by each seeing the friends' merits and not their faults. But one who thinks that he is a little higher than his friends can no longer unite with them.

40. RABASH, Article No. 12 (1988), "What are Torah and Work in the Way of the Creator?"

The creation of the worlds and souls was primarily with one intention—to correct everything so that it works in order to bestow, which is called *Dvekut*, equivalence of form. The Creator said about the Torah, "I have created the evil inclination; I have created the Torah as a spice." That is, once man receives the Torah as a spice, the evil inclination will be corrected to work in order to bestow, as it is written in *The Zohar*, "The angel of death is destined to be a holy angel."

A person cannot see all this because he takes after the majority, called "the whole of Israel." It was said that the beginning of the education everyone receives is in *Lo Lishma*, meaning that the engagement in Torah and *Mitzvot* is in order to receive reward in *Kelim* [vessels] of self-benefit, and the *Lishma* is forbidden to reveal to a person upon the admission of a person into the observance of Torah and *Mitzvot*, as mentioned in the words of Maimonides.

This causes a person to understand with his intellect that he needs to learn Torah only in order to know the rules, how to observe the *Mitzvot*, as our sages said, "An uneducated person is not a *Hassid*." Although they also learn Torah that does not pertain to practical *Mitzvot*, learning that part of the Torah is because of the commandment to learn Torah, as it is written, "And you shall reflect on it day and night." That is, he learns because it is a *Mitzva*, just like the rest of the *Mitzvot*.

41. RABASH, Article No. 13 (1988), What Is "The People's Shepherd Is the Whole People" in the work?

He must believe in the sages, who said that the purpose of creation is to do good to His creations.

When a person begins to examine creation with his eyes, meaning which form of good and doing good he sees that the creatures are receiving from Him, the opposite view appears to man. He sees that the whole world suffers torments, and it is hard to find one person who can say that he feels and sees how His guidance is in the form of good and doing good.

In that state, when he sees a dark world, and he wants to believe above reason that the Creator behaves with the world in Private Providence as good and doing good, he remains standing on this point, and all kinds of foreign thoughts come into his mind. Then, he must overcome above reason, that Providence is good and does good. At that time he receives a need for the Creator to give him the power of faith that he will have the strength to go above reason and justify Providence.

42. RABASH, Article No. 496, "The Path of Truth"

Those who walk on the path of truth, who want to bring contentment to the Maker, see that everything they do is not for the sake of the Creator, so they pray to the Creator to see that they can work for the sake of the Creator.

At that time, the Creator says, "Wherever I mention My name," meaning that you will give me the possibility to attribute My name to your actions. In other words, there will be an awakening from below, where I, says the Creator, will attribute My name to the actions. So how will you know that I am already attributing My name to them? You will see this if I "come to you and bless you."

In other words, the whole purpose of creation, which is to do good to His creations, cannot be revealed before you correct the matter of the bread of shame, meaning that you work in order to bestow. At that time, the purpose of creation will come true, which is to do good to His creations.

43. RABASH, Article No. 10 (1989) "What Does it Mean that the Ladder Is Diagonal, in the Work?"

The two lines are needed, for by both, we achieve the middle line, for there cannot be a middle line unless there are two lines before it. Therefore, when there is a dispute, it can be said that "the third one comes and decides between them and makes peace." But if there is no dispute, there is no need to make peace. That is, if we want to have peace, we must first produce a dispute, or there is no room for peace.

Yet, the question is, Why do we need peace? It would be better, so we understand, if there were no dispute and no need for peace. This is common sense.

The answer is that since we have these two opposites in our nature, it follows that this dispute is the reality, for nature has made us this way. That is, from the perspective of the purpose of creation, we have a nature that the Creator gave a desire to receive delight and pleasure. And from the perspective of the correction of creation, we must go in the opposite direction, namely to bestow, like the Creator, "As He is merciful, so you are merciful."

It follows that those two extremes are in us. And what we say is that a dispute is required, as our sages said, "One should always vex the good inclination over the evil inclination." As RASHI interpreted, "He should make war with it." This means that one should reveal the evil in him. He does not produce evil through the dispute. Rather, the evil within us is concealed, and if light of *Kedusha* [holiness] enters there, the will to receive in us promptly awakens and receives everything for itself. This will immediately go to the side of *Tuma'a* [impurity] and *Klipot* [shells/peels].

For this reason, we must wage war, by which the evil will come out of its hiding and fight with the good inclination.

It follows that specifically through war it becomes revealed, since it wants to fight with the good inclination. When it shows its real face, the person sees what a "high mountain" it is and realizes that the only way is to ask the Creator to help him subdue the evil and to be able to work only with the aim to bestow.

44. RABASH, Article No. 10 (1987), "Purim, and the Commandment: Until He Does Not Know"

Our sages said (*Kiddushin* 40b), "If he performs one *Mitzva* [good deed/correction], happy is he, for he has sentenced himself and the entire world to the side of merit." Therefore, since he is in a state where he has no concern for self-love but rather for love of others, it follows that by wanting to receive delight and pleasure from the Creator, he wants to keep the love of others between man and God, and between man and man.

This is as it is written in *The Zohar* ("Introduction of the Book of Zohar," Item 67): "'And to say to Zion, 'You are My people.'' ...Do not pronounce 'You are My people [*Ami*]' with a *Patach* in the *Ayin*, but "You are with Me [*Imi*]," with a *Hirik* in the *Ayin*, which means partnering with Me. ... Happy are they who exert in the Torah."

Although there it speaks of between man and the Creator, but the matter of interpretation of a partner can also be applied between man and man, since this implies that later, the whole world will receive the side of merit. It follows that he did good between man and man by causing the entire world to receive the delight and pleasure that exist in the purpose of creation.

It follows that he has become a partner of the Creator in that through him will come the assistance by which everyone will achieve the purpose of creation. Thus, he has become a partner of the Creator, as it is written, "I started creation by wanting to give delight and pleasure, and Israel exert to realize the goal by making *Kelim* [vessels] that are fit to receive the upper abundance without any flaw, called 'bread of shame.' Rather, even when they receive the delight and pleasure, they will not lose the *Dvekut* [adhesion], called 'equivalence of form,' for this was the reason for the *Tzimtzum* [restriction]."

45. RABASH, Article No. 22 (1985), "The Whole of the Torah Is One Holy Name"

We must always consider the goal, which is to "do good to His creations." If the evil inclination comes to a person and asks him all of Pharaoh's questions, he should not reply with lame excuses, but say, "Now, with your questions, I can begin with the work of bestowal."

This means that we should not say about the questions of the evil inclination that it came to us in order to lower us from our degree. On the contrary, now it is giving us a place to work, by which we will ascend on the degrees of wholeness. That is, any overcoming in the work is called "walking in the work of the Creator," since each penny joins into a great amount." That is, all the times we overcome accumulate to a certain measure required to become a *Kli* for the reception of the abundance.

Overcoming means taking a part of a vessel of reception and adding it to the vessels of bestowal. It is like the *Masach* [screen], which we must put on the *Aviut* [thickness/will to receive]. It follows that if one has no will to receive, one has nothing on which to place a *Masach*. For this reason, when the evil inclination brings us foreign thoughts, this is the time to take these thoughts and raise them above reason.

This is something one can do with everything one's soul desires. He should not say that now he has received rejection from the work. Rather, he should say that he was given thoughts and desires from above so as to have room to admit them into *Kedusha* [holiness]. It therefore follows that it is to the contrary: because he is brought closer from above, he was sent work.

It was said about this: "The ways of the Lord are straight; righteous walk in it and transgressors fail in it."

46. *Zohar for All*, "Introduction of The Book of Zohar," "On the Night of the Bride," Item 138

The complete benefit, in the great measure that He had contemplated for us, is only in bestowal, which is pleasure without any boundary and limitation. But reception for oneself is limited and highly restricted because the satiation promptly puts out the pleasure. It is written, "The Lord has made everything for His own purpose," meaning that everything that occurs in the world was created from its inception only to bestow contentment upon Him. Thus, people engage in worldly affairs in complete contrast to how they were initially created, since the Creator is saying, "The whole world was created for Me," as it is written, "The Lord has made everything for His own purpose," and "Everyone who is called by My name, I have created for My glory."

And we say the complete opposite because we are saying, "The whole world was created only for us." We want to devour all the abundance of the world into our bellies, for our own delights, and for our own glory. Thus, it is no wonder that we are still unworthy of receiving His complete benefit. For this reason, His guidance of good and evil has been prescribed for us, with guidance of reward and punishment, for they are interdependent because reward and punishment result from good and evil. When we use the vessels of reception contrary to how they were created, we necessarily sense evil in the operations of Providence in relation to us.

47. *Zohar for All, Toldot* [Generations], "These Are the Generations of Isaac," Item 2

When He wished to create man, the Torah said to Him, "If man is created and later sins, and You will sentence him, why should Your deeds be in vain? After all, he will never be able to tolerate Your judgments." The Creator told her, "But I have created repentance before I created the world. If he sins, he will be able to repent and I will forgive him."

The Creator said to the world when He created it and created man, "World, you and your nature persist only by the Torah. This is why I have created man within you, to engage in Torah. If he does not engage in Torah, I will revert you back to chaos." Thus, all is for man and the Torah stands and calls before people to engage and exert in the Torah, but no one lends an ear.

48. *Zohar for All, VaYechi* [Jacob Lived], Four Species, Item 212

It is written about it, "Every one that is called by My name ... for My glory," so that I will be respected. "Whom I have created," to unify Me. "I have formed him" to do good deeds unto Me, and "I have made him" to evoke the upper force through it.

49. *Zohar for All, VaYera* [The Lord Appeared], "Who shall ascend into the mountain of the Lord," Item 76

"Who shall ascend into the mountain of the Lord, and who shall stand in His holy place?" All the people in the world do not see why they are in the world. They do not observe so as to know for what purpose they are living in the world, and the days go by and never return. And all those days that people live in this world rise and stand before the Creator, for they were all created and they are real.

50. *Zohar for All, Zohar Hadash,* Song of Songs, "The Wisdom One Must Know," Items 482-483.

The wisdom that one should know: to know and to observe the secret of his Master, know himself, know who he is, how he was created, where he comes from and where he is going, how the body is corrected, and how he will be judged by the King of all.

To know and to observe the secret of the soul. What is this soul within him? Where does it come from, and why does it come into this body, which is a foul drop that is here today, and in the grave tomorrow? To know the world one is in, and for what will the world be corrected. Afterward, one should observe the sublime secrets of the upper world, to know one's Master. And one observes all that from within the secrets of the Torah.

51. Raaiah Kook, *Me'orot HaRaaiah*

The Creator wanted the correction of the whole world. This is why our sages said (*Shabbat* 88b), "Each and every word that came forth from the Creator is divided into seventy languages," indicating to the preparation that there is in the Torah to complement all the nations.

52. Rav Shneur Zalman of Liadi, *The Tanya*

The purpose of the creation of the world is the revelation of His kingship, that there is no king without a people.

53. Rav Chaim Vital, Introduction of Rav Chaim Vital to *Shaar HaHakdamot*

The Creator delights in all that He has created in His world only when His children engage in the secrets of the Torah, to know His greatness, His beauty, and His merit.

54. Ramchal, "The Rules of Opening Wisdom and Knowledge"

The first rule that we know about the intention of the Emanator is that since He wants to do good, He wanted to create created beings that would receive His goodness. In order for the goodness to be complete, it must be received by merit, and not by charity, so that shame will not blemish it, as one who eats that which is not his.

In order to be able to be rewarded, He created one reality for them to correct, which He does not need, and when they correct it, they will be rewarded.

55. Ramchal, *Daat Tevunot*

The rule is that the Creator seemingly refrained, meaning that when He created His creations, He refrained from making them according to His capability, but rather according to what He wanted and aimed for in them. He created them deficient so they would complete themselves, and their completion will be their reward thanks to what they had exerted to obtain. And all this, only by His will to do complete good.

56. Ramchal, *Daat Tevunot*

The first foundation upon which the entire building stands is that the Upper Will desired that man should complete himself and all that was created for him, and this itself will be his merit and reward. His merit, since he engages and labors to obtain this wholeness, when he obtains it, he will enjoy only his labor and part in all his toil. His reward, for in the end, he will be the one who is complete and will delight in abundance forever and ever.

57. *Likutey Moharan*, First Edition, Mark 5

Every person should say, "The whole world was created only for me" (Sanhedrin 37). It follows that if the whole world has been created for me, I have to look and delve into the correction of the world at all times, satisfy the needs of the world, and pray for them.

58. Ramchal, *Daat Tevunot*

God is certainly the absolute good, and indeed, it is the conduct of the Good to do good. This is why He wanted to create created beings, so He could do good to them, for if there is no recipient of the good, there is no doing good. Indeed, in order for the doing good to be complete, He knew, with His sublime wisdom, that those who receive it should receive it through their own labor, for then they will be the owners of that good, and they will have no shame left when they receive the good, as one who receives almsgiving from another.

59. The Holy Shlah, *Toldot Adam*

The name Adam implies *Adame LaElyon* [I will be like the upper one]. This is the core purpose.

60. Rabbi Meir Even Gabai, *Avodat HaKodesh*

The purpose of all the created beings is the complete man, and the man's purpose is unification, which is knowing the Creator.

61. *Likutey Halachot* [Assorted Rules], "Blessings on Seeing and Personal Blessings," Rule No. 4

The vitality is mainly through unity, by all the changes being included in the source of the unity. For this reason, "Love your friend as yourself" is the great rule of the Torah, to include in unity and peace. The vitality, sustenance, and correction of the whole of creation is mainly by people of differing views becoming included together in love, unity, and peace.

62. Ramchal, *Mesilat Yesharim*

The basis and root of the work is for one to clarify and verify one's duty in one's world and on what one should focus wherever he toils his whole life. Our sages instructed us that man was created only in order to delight in the Lord and enjoy the luster of His *Shechina* [Divinity], that this is the real delight and the greatest of all the delights that can be.

The place of that delight is actually the next world, since this is what was created with the required preparation for it. However, the way to get to our destination is this world, and the means that bring one to that purpose are the *Mitzvot* [commandments] that the Creator has commanded us, and the place for performing the *Mitzvot* is only this world. For this reason, initially, man was placed in this world so that through the means available for him here he will be able to reach the place that has been prepared for him, which is the next world, to satiate himself there with the good that he had acquired through those means.

63. Rabbi Menachem Mendel of Kotzk, *A Bush Burns in Kotzk*

Man was made so as to lift the heavens!

3

The Thought of Creation

1. Baal HaSulam, "Preface to the Wisdom of Kabbalah" Item 4

There is a great rule concerning the *Kelim* [pl. of *Kli*]: The expansion of the light and its departure make the *Kli* fit for its task. This means that as long as the *Kli* has not been separated from its light, it is included in the light and is annulled within it like a candle before a torch. This annulment is because they are completely opposite from one another, on opposite ends. This is so because the light extends from His self, existence from existence. From the perspective of the thought of creation in *Ein Sof* [infinity], it is all toward bestowal and there is no trace of a will to receive in it. Its opposite is the *Kli*, the great will to receive that abundance, and is the root of the initiated creature, in which there is no bestowal whatsoever. Hence, when they are bound together, the will to receive is annulled in the light within it.

2. Baal HaSulam, "Introduction to The Book of Zohar," Item 13

By the very thought to create the souls, His thought completed everything, for He does not need an act, as do we. Instantaneously, all the souls and worlds that were destined to be created emerged filled with all the delight and pleasure and the gentleness that He had planned for them, in the final perfection that the souls were destined to receive at the end of correction, after the will to receive in the souls has been fully corrected and has turned into pure bestowal, in complete equivalence of form with the Emanator.

3. Baal HaSulam, "Introduction to the Preface to the Wisdom of Kabbalah," Item 1

It is written in *The Zohar*, *VaYikra*, Portion Tazria, "Come and see: All that exists in the world exists for man, and everything exists for him, as it is written, 'Then the Lord God formed man,' with a full name, as we have established, that he is the whole of everything and contains everything, and all that is above and below, etc., is included in that image." Thus, it explains that all the worlds, upper and lower, are included in man. And also, the whole of reality within those worlds is only for man.

4. Baal HaSulam, "Foreword to The Book of Zohar," Item 34

Take our sense of sight, for example: We see a wide world before us, wondrously filled. But in fact, we see all that only in our own interior. In other words, there is a sort of a photographic machine in our hindbrain, which portrays everything that appears to us and nothing outside of us. He has made for us there, in our brain, a kind of polished mirror that inverts everything seen there, so we will see it outside our brain, in front of our faces. Yet, what we see outside of us is not a real thing. Nevertheless, we should be so grateful to His Providence for having created that polished mirror in our brains, enabling us to see and perceive everything outside of us, for by this He has given us the power to perceive everything with clear knowledge and attainment, and measure everything from within and from without. Without it, we would lose most of our perception. The same is true with the Godly will, concerning Godly perceptions. Even though all these changes unfold in the interior of the receiving souls, they nevertheless see it all in the Giver Himself since only in this manner are they awarded all the perceptions and all the pleasantness in the thought of creation. You can also deduce this from the above parable. Even though we see everything as being in front of us, every reasonable person knows for certain that all that we see is only in our own brains. So are the souls: Although they see all the images in the Giver, they have no doubt that all those are only in their own interior and not at all in the Giver.

5. RABASH, Article No. 12 (1985), "Jacob Dwelled in the Land Where His Father Had Lived"

A person should work only for the Creator, meaning without any reward. This means that he is ready for complete devotion without any reward, without any return being born out of his devotion. Rather, this is the core—his purpose, that he wants to annul his self before the Creator, meaning (cancel) his will to receive, which is the existence of the creature. This is what he wants to annul before the Creator. It follows that this is his goal, meaning his goal is to give his soul to the Creator. This is not so in corporeality with respect to love of others. Although this is a great degree, and not all the people can work for the general public, still, devotion is only a means and not a goal, and he would be happier if he could save the public without giving up his life. Let us ask all those who volunteer to go to war for their country. If someone could advise them how to save their country without losing their lives, they would certainly be happy. But when there is no choice, they are willing to go, for the public, so that the public will receive the reward, while they are giving up everything. Although this is a great force, it has nothing to do with devotion to the Creator, where devotion is the goal, and what comes out as a result is not their purpose, as this was not their intention. Therefore, devotion in spirituality is worthless to corporeal people, since for them devotion is a means and not the goal, while in spirituality it is the opposite: devotion is the goal. By this we will understand the meaning of receiving in order to bestow. Man's purpose is only to bestow upon the Creator, for this is the meaning of equivalence of form, "As He is merciful, so you are merciful." When he achieves the degree of devotion to the Creator because he wants to annul himself in order to delight the

Creator, he sees that the purpose of the Creator, as it was in the thought of creation, is to do good to His creations. At that time he wants to receive the delight and pleasure that was in the purpose of creation—to delight His creatures.

6. *Zohar for All*, "Introduction of The Book of Zohar," "On the Night of the Bride," Item 140

Prior to the end of correction, before we qualified our vessels of reception to receive only in order to give contentment to our Maker and not to our own benefit, *Malchut* is called "the tree of knowledge of good and evil." This is so because *Malchut* is the guidance of the world by people's actions. And since we are unfit to receive all the delight and pleasure that the Creator had contemplated in our favor in the thought of creation, we must receive the guidance of good and evil from the *Malchut*. This guidance qualifies us to ultimately correct our vessels of reception in order to bestow and to be rewarded with the delight and pleasure He had contemplated in our favor.

7. *Zohar for All*, "Introduction of The Book of Zohar," "Two Points," Item 121

The thought of creation is to delight His creatures and no pleasure is perceived by the creature while he must be separated from the Creator. Moreover, we learn that the Creator craves to dwell in the lower ones.

The common thing in understanding those two matters, which deny each other, is that the world was created in complete oppositeness from the Creator, from one end to the other, in every single point. This is so because this world was created with a desire to receive, which is the opposite form of the Creator's, in whom there is not even a shred of this desire, as it is written, "And man is born the foal of a wild donkey."

In that respect, all the issues of the governance of His guidance in this world are in total contrast to the thought of creation, which is only to delight His creatures, for it is according to the desire to receive in us, which is our standard and our tastefulness.

This is the meaning of the locks on the gates. First, all the many contradictions to His uniqueness, which we taste in this world, separate us from the Creator. Yet, when exerting to keep Torah and *Mitzvot* with love, with our soul and might, as we are commanded—to bestow contentment upon our Maker—all those forces of separation do not affect us into subtracting any of the love of the Creator with all our souls and might. Rather, in that state, every contradiction we have overcome becomes a gate for attainment of His wisdom. This is so because there is a special quality in each contradiction—revealing a special degree in attaining Him. And those worthy ones who have been rewarded with it turn darkness into light and bitter into sweet, for all the powers of separation—from the darkness of the mind and the bitterness of the body—have become to them gates for obtainment of sublime degrees. Thus, the darkness becomes a great light and the bitter becomes sweet.

8. *Zohar for All*, *Shemot* [Exodus], "My Beloved Is Mine and I Am His, He Pastures among the Lilies"

When a thought came before the Creator to create His world, all the worlds rose in one thought, and in that thought they were all created, as it is written, "In wisdom have You made them all." And in that thought, which is wisdom [*Hochma*], this world and the world above were created.

9. *Zohar for All*, Noah, "And the House, While It Was Being Built"

That thought expanded even more, in order to be revealed, and that voice knocked and struck the lips. Then the speech came out, which complemented everything and disclosed everything. It means that everything is that concealed thought that was inside, and all is one.

4

The Essence of Man

1. Baal HaSulam, "Introduction to The Book of Zohar," Item 20

Our essence is as the essence of all the details in reality, which is no more and no less than the will to receive.

2. Baal HaSulam, "The Writings of the Last Generation"

Egoism is embedded in the nature of every person, as in any animal.

3. Baal HaSulam, "A Speech for the Completion of The Zohar"

One cannot make a single movement without any benefit for himself.

4. Baal HaSulam, "The Freedom"

The primary innovation, from the perspective of creation, which He has created existence from absence, applies to one and only aspect, defined as the "will to receive."

5. Baal HaSulam, "The Freedom"

All the corporeal entities in our world, that is, everything within that space, be it still, vegetative, animate, a spiritual object or a corporeal object, if we want to distinguish the unique self of each of them, how they differ from one another, even in the smallest particle, it amounts to no more than that "desire to receive."

6. Baal HaSulam, *Shamati*, Article No. 241. "Call Upon Him When He Is Near"

Adam (people), as in *Adame LaElyon* [I will be like the Most High]

7. Baal HaSulam, "The Freedom"

All the vessels and the bodies, from spiritual worlds and from physical worlds, are deemed spiritual or corporeal substance whose nature is to want to receive.

8. Baal HaSulam, "Introduction to the preface to the Wisdom of Kabbalah," Items 2-3.

The Creator's intention in creation was to delight His creatures. Certainly, as soon as He contemplated creating the souls and delighting them abundantly, they immediately emerged from before Him, complete in form and with all the delights He had planned to bestow upon them. This is because in Him, the thought alone completes, and He does not need actions as we do. Accordingly, we should ask, "Why did He create the worlds restriction after restriction down to this murky world, and clothed the souls in the murky bodies of this world?

The answer to this is written in *The Tree of Life*—"to bring to light the perfection of His deeds" (*The Tree of Life*, Branch 1). Yet, we must understand how it is possible that incomplete operations would stem from a complete Operator, to the point that they would require completion through an act in this world.

The thing is that we should distinguish between light and *Kli* [vessel] in the souls. The essence of the souls that were created is the *Kli* in them, and all the bounty that He had planned to impart them with and delight them is the light in them. This is because since He had planned to delight them, He necessarily made them as a desire to receive His pleasure, since the pleasure and delight increase according to the measure of desire to receive the abundance.

Know that that will to receive is the very self of the soul with regard to the generation and elicitation existence from absence. This is considered the *Kli* of the soul, while the joy and the abundance are considered the light of the soul, extending existence from existence from His self.

9. Baal HaSulam, "Introduction to The Book of Zohar," Item 21

The very essence of the soul is a will to receive, as well. And the only difference we can tell between one object and another is only by its desire, for the desire in any essence creates needs, and the needs create thoughts and concepts so as to obtain those needs, which the will to receive demands.

10. Baal HaSulam, "A Speech for the Completion of The Zohar"

Man's very essence is only to receive for oneself. By nature, we are unable to do even the smallest thing to benefit others. Instead, when we give to others, we are compelled to expect that in the end, we will receive a worthwhile reward

11. Baal HaSulam, "Introduction to the Preface to the Wisdom of Kabbalah," Item 4

Creation refers to appearance of something that did not exist before. This is considered existence from absence. Yet, how do we picture something that is not included in Him, since He is almighty and includes all of them together? Also, one does not give what is not in Him.

As we have said, the whole creation that He created is only the *Kelim* [plural for *Kli*] of the souls, which is the will to receive. This is clear, since He necessarily does not have a will to receive, as from whom would He receive? Hence, this is truly a new creation, not a trace of which existed previously, and is therefore considered existence from absence.

12. Baal HaSulam, "Introduction to The Book of Zohar," Item 18

We must not ponder the state of rest of the beings in the world besides man, since man is the center of creation. All other creatures do not have any value in themselves, but to the extent that they help man achieve his wholeness. Hence, they rise and fall with him without any consideration of themselves.

13. Baal HaSulam, *Shamati*, Article No. 153, "A Thought Is a Result of the Desire"

A thought is a result of the desire. A person thinks of what he wants. He will not think of what he does not want. For example, a person never thinks of his day of death. On the contrary, he will always contemplate his eternity, since this is what he wants. Thus, one always thinks of what is desirable for him.

However, there is a special role to the thought: It intensifies the desire. The desire remains in its place; it does not have the strength to expand and perform its action. Yet, because one thinks and contemplates a matter, and the desire asks the thought to provide some counsel and advice to carry out the desire, the desire grows, expands, and performs work in actual practice.

It turns out that the thought serves the desire, and the desire is the "self" of the person. Now, there is a big self or a small self. A big self controls the small selves.

He who is a small self and has no control at all, the advice to magnify the self is through the persistent thought of the desire, since the thought grows to the extent that one thinks of it.
And so, "His law will he contemplate day and night," for by persisting in it, it grows into a big self until it becomes the actual ruler.

14. Baal HaSulam, "The Nation"

The measure of egoism inherent in every creature is a necessary condition in the actual existence of the creature. Without it, it would not be a separate and distinct being in itself. Yet, this should not at all deny the measure of altruism in a person. The only thing required is to set distinct boundaries between them: The law of egoism must be kept in all its might, to the extent that it concerns the minimum existence. And with any surplus of that measure, permission is granted to waive it for the well-being of one's fellow person.

Naturally, anyone who acts in this manner is to be considered exceptionally altruistic. However, one who relinquishes one's minimal share, too, for the benefit of others, and thus risks one's life, this is completely unnatural.

15. Baal HaSulam, "Matan Torah [The Giving of the Torah]," Item 12

"A wild ass will be turned into man," since when one emerges out of the bosom of creation, one is in utter filth and lowliness, meaning a multitude of self-love that is imprinted in him, and his every movement revolves solely around himself without a shred of bestowal upon others.

Thus, then one is at the farthest distance from the Root, on the other end, 1) since the root is all bestowal without a hint of reception, 2) whereas the newborn is in a state of complete self-reception without a hint of bestowal. Therefore, his situation is regarded as being at the lowest point of lowliness and filth in our human world.

16. Baal HaSulam, "This Is for Judah"

The absence that precedes man's existence is the form of the beast. This is why it is written, "a wild ass's colt is born a man," as it is necessary for every person to begin in the state of a beast. The writing says, "Man and beast You save, O Lord." As a beast is given all that it needs for its sustenance and the fulfillment of its purpose, He also provides man with all that is necessary for his substance and the fulfillment of his purpose.

Therefore, we should understand where is the advantage of man's form over the beast, from the perspective of their own preparation. Indeed, this is discerned in their wishes, since man's wishes are certainly different from those of a beast. And to that extent, God's salvation of man differs from God's salvation of a beast.

17. Baal HaSulam, "Introduction to the Preface to the Wisdom of Kabbalah," Item 9

All the worlds, upper and lower and everything within them, were created only for man. This is so because all these degrees and worlds came only to complement the souls in the measure of *Dvekut* they lacked with respect to the thought of creation.

In the beginning, they were restricted and hung down degree by degree and world after world, down to our material world, to bring the soul into a body of this world, which is entirely to receive and not to bestow, like animals and beasts. It is written, "A wild ass' colt is born a man." This is considered the complete will to receive, which has nothing in terms of bestowal. In that state, one is regarded as the complete opposite of Him, and there is no greater remoteness than this.

Afterward, through the soul that clothes within one, he engages in Torah and *Mitzvot*. Gradually and slowly, from below upward, he obtains the same form of bestowal as his Maker, through all those qualities that hung down from above downward, which are but degrees and measures in the form of the desire to bestow.

Each higher degree means that it is farther from the will to receive and closer to being only to bestow. In the end, one is awarded being entirely to bestow and not to receive anything for himself. At that time, one is completed with true *Dvekut* with Him, for man was created only for this. Thus, all the worlds and everything in them were created only for man.

18. Baal HaSulam, "This Is for Judah"

We find that the only need in man's wishes, which does not exist in the whole of the animate species, is the awakening toward Godly *Dvekut* [adhesion]. Only the human species is ready for it, and none other.

It follows that the whole issue of presence in the human species is in that preparation imprinted in him to crave His work, and in this he is superior to the beast.

19. Baal HaSulam, "Introduction to the Book Panim Meirot uMasbirot," Item 6

And now sons do hear me: The wisdom cries aloud outside; she calls you from the streets, "Whoso is on the Lord's side, let him come to me," "For it is no vain thing for you; because it is your life, and the length of your days."

"You were not created to follow the act of the grain and the potato, you and your asses in one trough." And as the purpose of the ass is not to serve all its contemporary asses, man's purpose is not to serve all the bodies of the people of his time, the contemporaries of his physical body. Rather, the purpose of the ass is to serve and be of use to man, who is superior to it, and the purpose of man is to serve the Creator and complete His aim.

20. Baal HaSulam, "Introduction to The Study of the Ten Sefirot," Items 68-69

All the inclinations, tendencies, and properties instilled in man, with which to serve one's friends, all these tendencies and natural properties are required for the work of the Creator.

To begin with, they were created and imprinted in man only because of their final role—the ultimate purpose of man, as it is written, "No outcast shall be cast out from Him." One needs them all so as to complement oneself in the ways of reception of the abundance and to complete the will of the Creator.

This is the meaning of "Everyone who is called by My name, I have created him for My glory" (Isaiah 43:7), and also "All that the Lord has worked was for His sake" (Proverbs 16:4). However, in the meantime, man has been given a whole world to develop and complete all these natural inclinations and qualities in him by engaging in them with people, thus yielding them suitable for their purpose.

It is as our sages said, "One must say, 'The world was created for me,'" for all the people in the world are required for a person, as they develop and qualify the attributes and inclinations of every individual to become a fit tool for His work.

Thus, we must understand the essence of the love of the Creator from the properties of love by which one person relates to another. The love of the Creator is necessarily given through these qualities, since they were only imprinted in man for His sake to begin with.

21. Baal HaSulam, "The Essence of Religion and Its Purpose"

The crass, undeveloped person does not recognize egoism as bad at all. Therefore, he uses it openly, without any shame or restraint, stealing and murdering in broad daylight wherever he can. The somewhat more developed sense some measure of their egoism as bad and are at least ashamed to use it in public, stealing and killing openly. But in secret, they still commit their crimes, but are careful that no one will see them.

The even more developed sense egoism as so loathsome that they cannot tolerate it in them and reject it completely, as much as they detect of it, until they cannot, and do not want to enjoy the labor of others. Then begin to emerge in them sparks of love of others, called "altruism," which is the general attribute of goodness.

But that, too, evolves gradually. First develops love and desire to bestow upon one's family and kin, as in the verse, "Do not ignore your own flesh." When one develops further, one's attribute of bestowal expands to all the people around him, being one's townspeople or one's nation. And so one adds until he finally develops love for the whole of humanity.

22. Baal HaSulam, "Matan Torah [The Giving of the Torah]," Item 13

It is a natural law for any being that anything outside one's own body is regarded as unreal and empty. And any movement that a person makes to love another is performed with a reflected light and some reward that will eventually return to him and serve him for his own benefit. Thus, such an act cannot be considered "love of others" because it is judged by its end. It is like rent that pays off only in the end. However, the act of renting is not considered love of another.

But making any movement only as a result of love for others, without any spark of reflected light or hope for any kind of reward in return is completely impossible by nature.

23. Baal HaSulam, "Peace in the World"

The nature of each and every person is to exploit the lives of all other people in the world for his own benefit, and all that he gives to another is only out of necessity. Even then, there is exploitation of others in it, but it is done cunningly, so his friend will not notice it and concede willingly.

The reason for this is that the nature of every branch is close to its root. Because man's soul extends from the Creator, who is one and unique, and everything is His, likewise, man, who extends from Him, feels that all the people in the world should be under his own governance and for his own private benefit. This is an unbreakable law. The only difference is in people's choices: One chooses to exploit people by obtaining lowly lusts, and one by obtaining governance, while the third by obtaining respect. Furthermore, if one could do it without much effort, he would agree to exploit the world with all three together—wealth, governance, and respect. However, he is forced to choose according to his possibilities and capabilities.

This law can be called "the law of singularity in man's heart." No person escapes it (rather each and every one takes his share in that law), the great according to his size, and the small according to his size.

Thus, the above law of singularity in the nature of every person is neither condemned nor praised, as it is a natural reality and has a right to exist like all parts of reality. And there is no hope to eradicate it from the world or even slightly blur its form, just as there is no hope to eradicate the entire human race from Earth. Therefore, we will not be lying at all if we said about this law that it is the absolute truth.

Since it is undoubtedly so, how can we even try to ease one's mind by promising him equality with all the people in the collective? Nothing is further from human nature than this, while one's sole inclination is to soar higher, above the whole collective.

24. Baal HaSulam, "Peace in the World"

Attribute of singularity, which exists in each of us, whether less or more.

Although we have clarified that it comes from a sublime reason, that this attribute extends to us directly from the Creator, who is singular in the world and the Root of all creations, still, since the sensation of singularity has settled in our narrow egoism, it affects ruin and destruction until it became the source of all the ruins that were and will be in the world.

Indeed, there is not a single person in the world who is free from it, and all the differences are only in the ways it is used—for the desires of the heart, for governance, or for honor—and this is what separates people from one another.

But the equal side in all the people of the world is that each of us stands ready to exploit all the people for his own private benefit with every means at one's disposal without taking into any consideration that he is going to build himself on the ruin of his friend.

25. Baal HaSulam, "The Nation"

By the term, "egoism," I am not referring to the original egoism. Rather, I am referring to "narrow egoism." That is, the original egoism is nothing but self-love, which is all of one's positive, individualistic power of existence. In that respect, it is not at odds with the altruistic force, although it does not serve it.

However, it is the nature of egoism that the manner of using it makes it very narrow, since it is more or less compelled to acquire a nature of hatred and exploitation of others in order to make one's own existence easier. Also, it is not abstract hatred, but one that appears in acts of abusing one's friend for one's own benefit, growing murkier according to its degrees, such as deceiving, stealing, robbing, and murdering. This is called "narrow egoism," and in that respect it is at odds with—and the complete opposite from—love of others. It is a negative force that destroys the society.

Its opposite is the altruistic force. This is society's constructive force, since all that one does for another is done only by the altruistic force.

26. RABASH, Article No. 14 (1991), "What Does It Mean that Man's Blessing Is the Blessing of the Sons, in the Work?"

Man's main purpose is to cling to "I am the Lord your God." In other words, wanting to be rewarded with "I" being as "the Lord your God,"

27. RABASH, Article No. 18 (1987),"What Is Preparation for Reception of the Torah? – 1"

After all the work that a person has put into awakening to achieve the truth, meaning to really know why he was born and what goal he should achieve, so now the Creator disclosed to him that the inclination of a man's heart, which is the receiver, is evil from his youth. That is, it cannot be said that now he sees that the inclination has become bad. Rather, it is evil from his youth. However, until now he could not determine that it was really evil; therefore, the person was in states of ascent and descent. In other words, at times he would listen to the inclination and say that from now on I will know that this is my enemy and everything it advises me to do is to my detriment.

But afterwards, the esteem of the inclination rises again and once again he listens to it and works for it wholeheartedly, and so on and so forth. He feels that he is as "a dog returning to its vomit." That is, he has already determined that it was unfit for him to listen to it because all the nourishments that the inclination gives him are but food fit for beasts and not for man. But all of a sudden, he returns to animal food and forgets all the decisions and views he had before.

Afterward, when he regrets, he sees that he has no other way but for the Creator to make him see that the inclination that is called "evil" really is evil. Then, once the Creator has given him this knowledge, he does not go astray again but asks the Creator to give him the strength to overcome it each and every time the inclination wants to fail him, so he will have the strength to overcome it.

It therefore follows that the Creator should give him both the *Kli* [vessel] and the light, meaning both the awareness that the inclination is evil and there is a need to emerge from under its reign, and the correction for this is the Torah, as it is written, "I have created the evil inclination, I have created the Torah as a spice." Accordingly, the Creator gave him both the need for the Torah, as well as the Torah. This is regarded as the Creator giving him the light, as well as the *Kli*.

28. RABASH, Article No. 268, "One Learns Only Where One's Heart Desires"

Man was created with a nature that he wants to delight only himself.

29. RABASH, Article No. 760," The Material of the Soul"

Concerning the soul, which is a part of God above, the kabbalists compared it to a stone that is carved from a mountain. The question is, How can it be said that it is the same material as the mountain, for it is from His essence?

We should interpret that they mean that it is discerned as existence from existence. This is why they made a comparison to a stone from a mountain. The difference is that it is a part of the matter, which He divided, to be called a "soul." This is the will to receive, meaning that this part is called "Creation," meaning existence from absence.

30. RABASH, Article No. 487, "Concerning the Will to Receive"

The will to receive is man's essence, which is called something innovated existence from absence. However, the rest of the things, meaning all the fillings, extend existence from existence. Every kind of fulfillment in the world extends existence from existence since the Creator contains them. But the negative things, meaning deficiencies and suffering, are something new.

31. *Zohar for All*, *VaYera* [The Lord Appeared], "A Calculation of the Time of the Messiah," Item 453

Man is created in utter wickedness and lowliness, as it is written, "When a wild ass's foal is born a man." And all the vessels in one's body, meaning the senses and the qualities, and especially the thought serve him only wickedness and nothingness all day. And for one who is rewarded with adhering unto Him, the Creator does not create other tools instead, to be worthy and suitable for reception of the eternal spiritual abundance intended for him. Rather, the same lowly vessels that have thus far been used in a filthy and loathsome way are inverted to become vessels of reception of all the pleasantness and eternal gentleness.

Moreover, each *Kli* whose deficiencies had been the greatest has now become the most important. In other words, the measure that they reveal is the greatest.

32. *Zohar for All, Zohar Hadash,* Song of Songs, "The Wisdom One Must Know, 482-483.

The wisdom that one should know: to know and to observe the secret of his Master, know himself, know who he is, how he was created, where he comes from and where he is going, how the body is corrected, and how he will be judged by the King of all.

To know and to observe the secret of the soul. What is this soul within him? Where does it come from, and why does it come into this body, which is a foul drop that is here today, and in the grave tomorrow? To know the world one is in, and for what will the world be corrected. Afterward, one should observe the sublime secrets of the upper world, to know one's Master. And one observes all that from within the secrets of the Torah.

33. *Zohar for All, BeHaalotcha* [When You Mount the Candles], "God Has Not Empowered Him to Eat From Them," Item 140

How hard-hearted are people, for they do not watch over the words of that world at all. The evil in the heart, which clings to all organs of the body, does that to them. "There is an evil which I have seen under the sun, and it is heavy upon men." This evil is the force of the evil in the heart that wishes to dominate the worldly matters and does not watch over the matters of that world at all.

34. *Zohar for All, Toldot* [Generations], Association of the Quality of Rachamim with Din

The evil inclination is needed in the world like the rain is needed in the world. Without the evil inclination there would be no joy of studying in the world. But then it will not be defiling as before, to sin by it. "My holy mountain" is the heart, the place where the evil inclination dwells.

A good heart is the structure of the body and the soul. This is why it is written, "And you shall love the Lord your God with all your heart," for the heart is the core of everything.

35. *Zohar for All, VaYishlach* [And Jacob Sent], "And Jacob Sent Messengers," Item 1-4

When a person arrives in the world, the evil inclination immediately comes along with him and always complains about him, as it is written, "sin crouches at the door." Sin crouches—this is the evil inclination. "At the door"—the door of the womb, meaning as soon as one is born.

David called the evil inclination by the name, "sin," as it is written, "and my sin is ever before me," because it makes man sin before his Master every day. And this evil inclination does not leave man from the day he is born and for all time. And the good inclination comes to a person from the time he comes to be purified.

And when does one come to be purified? When he is thirteen years of age. At that time, a man connects in both the good inclination on the right, and the evil inclination on the left. And these are really two appointed angels, and they are always with man.

If a man comes to be purified, the evil inclination surrenders before him and the right governs the left. And both the good inclination and the evil inclination join to keep man in all the roads he travels, as it is written, "For He will give His angels charge over thee, to keep thee in all thy ways."

36. *Zohar for All*, *VaYeshev* (And Jacob Sat), "And Jacob Sat," Items 1-2

How many slanderers are there to a person from the day the Creator gives him a soul in this world? And because he came into the world, the evil inclination immediately appears to partake with him, as it is written, "Sin crouches at the door," for then the evil inclination partakes with him.

A beast watches over itself from the day it is born, and runs from fire and from any bad place. When man is born, he immediately comes to throw himself into the fire, since the evil inclination is within him and promptly incites him to the evil way.

37. Maimonides, *Commentary on Mishnah*

Man's purpose to eat, drink, and have intercourse, or to build a wall, all those recurring happenings do not add to his inner strength. And also, in that, he partakes with most created beings. But the wisdom is what adds to his inner strength and shifts him from the level of contempt to the level of glory. Before one learns and knows, he is regarded as a beast, no different from the rest of the animals except in logic, that he is an animal with logic. He wants to say with logic that he depicts to himself the concepts. And the most distinguished concept is to depict to himself the oneness of the Creator and all that accompanies that matter from the Creator, that the rest of the teachings are only in order to grow accustomed through them until they achieve Godly knowledge.

5

The Awakening of the Point in the Heart

1, Baal Sulam, *Shamati*, Article No, 199, "To Every Man of Israel"

Every man of Israel has an internal point in the heart, which is considered simple faith. This is an inheritance from our fathers, who stood on Mount Sinai. However, it is covered by many *Klipot* [shells], which are all kinds of dresses of *Lo Lishma* [not for Her sake], and the *Klipot* must be removed. Then his basis will be called "faith alone."

2. RABASH, Article No. 34, TANTA [Taamim, Nekudot, Tagin, Otiot]

Taamim [flavors] means one who wants to taste a good taste in life should pay attention to his point in the heart.

Every person has a point in the heart, except it does not shine. Rather, it is like a black dot. The point in the heart is a discernment of *Nefesh* [soul] of *Kedusha* [holiness], whose nature is a vessel of bestowal.

However, she is in a state of *Shechina* [Divinity] in the dust, meaning that a person regards her as nothing. Instead, to him she is as important as dust. This is called *Nekudot* [dots/points].

The solution is to increase her importance and make its importance as *Tagin* [crowns], like a "Crown on his head." That is, instead of being dust, as before, he should raise her importance to be as a *Keter* [crown] on his head.

At that time, the *Nefesh* of *Kedusha* expands in *Otiot* [letters], meaning in the *Guf* [body], for the *Guf* is called *Otiot*. In other words, the *Kedusha* spreads from potential to actual, called *Otiot* and *Guf*.

3. RABASH, Article No. 940, "The Point in the Heart"

When the Temple was ruined, it is written, "And let them make Me a Temple and I will dwell within them." This pertains to the point in the heart, which should be a Temple where the light of the Creator dwells, as it is written, "And I will dwell within them." Hence, one should try to build his structure of *Kedusha* [holiness], and the structure should be able to contain the upper abundance called "abundance poured from the Giver to the receiver." However, according to the rule, there must be equivalence of form between the Giver and the receiver so the receiver, too, must have the aim to bestow like the Giver.

This is called "action," as it is written, "Let them make Me a Temple," where the acting applies to the *Kli* [vessel] and not the light, since the light pertains to the Creator and only the action pertains to the creatures.

4. RABASH, Article No. 6 (1991), "What Is, 'The Herdsmen of Abram's Cattle and the Herdsmen of Lot's Cattle,' in the Work?"

In this work there are ascents and descents. A person must believe that he has a point in the heart, which is a spark that shines. But sometimes, it is only a black dot and does not shine. We must always awaken that spark because at times that spark awakens by itself and reveals a lack in a person, where he feels that he needs spirituality, that he is too materialistic and he sees no purpose that enables him to emerge from these states.

That spark gives him no rest. That is, as a corporeal spark cannot illuminate, but using the spark, a person can light up things, so that through the things that the spark touches, a great fire can ignite. Likewise, the spark within man's heart cannot shine, but that spark can light up his actions so they will illuminate because the spark pushes him to work.

However, sometimes the spark quenches and does not shine. This can be in the middle of the work, and this is regarded as a person having a road accident. In other words, in the middle of the work, something happened to him and he descended from his state and was left unconscious. Now he does not know that there is spirituality in reality, he has forgotten everything, and he has entered the corporeal world with all of his senses.

Only after some time does he recover and sees that he is in the corporeal world and he begins to climb up once again, meaning to feel the spiritual lack. Then, once again, he receives a drive to approach the Creator.

Afterward, he descends from his degree once more, but he must believe that each time he raises his spark to *Kedusha* [holiness]. Although he sees that he has descended from his state and fell back to the place where he was at the beginning of his work, each time he nonetheless raises new sparks. That is, each time, he raises a new spark.

In the "Introduction to The Book of Zohar" (Item 43), he says, "When man is born, he immediately has a *Nefesh* [soul] of *Kedusha*. But not an actual *Nefesh*, but the *Achoraim* [posterior] of it, its last discernment, which, during its *Katnut* [smallness/infancy], is called a 'point,' and it dresses in man's heart."

We should interpret that this "point," which is still in the dark, reveals and shines each time according to one's work on purifying his heart. At that time, the point begins to shine. This means that each time a person begins to ascend once more after the descent, he should believe that this is a new discernment from what he had during the previous ascent, for he has already elevated it to *Kedusha*. Thus, each time he begins a new discernment.

5. RABASH, Letter No. 21

Therefore, this is the only point on which we must make every effort that one has acquired from the point in the heart, since each point in the heart gives strength to work, but if this force is used to serve the environment...

6

The Soul of Adam HaRishon

1. Baal HaSulam, "Introduction to the Book Panim Meirot uMasbirot," Item 22

The eternal soul of life that the Creator had blown into his nostrils, only for the needs of *Adam HaRishon*, has departed because of the sin of the Tree of Knowledge. It acquired a new form, called "Sweat of Life," meaning the general has been divided into myriad parts, tiny drops, divided between *Adam HaRishon* and all his progeny through the end of time.

It follows, that there are no changes whatsoever in the acts of the Creator, but there is rather an additional form here. This common light of life, which was packed in the nose of *Adam HaRishon*, has expanded into a long chain, revolving on the wheel of transformation of form in many bodies, body after body, until the necessary end of correction.

2. Baal HaSulam, "600,000 Souls"

The whole is found within each item, since in the end, all the souls will unite into one discernment, returning to their spiritual root.

3. Baal HaSulam, *The Study of the Ten Sefirot*, Part 8, "Inner Light," Item 88

All our work in prayers and practical *Mitzvot* [commandments] is to sort once more and raise all those souls that fell from *Adam HaRishon* into the *Klipot* [shells] until they are brought to their first root as they were in it before he sinned with the tree of knowledge.

4. Baal HaSulam, "600,000 Souls"

It is said that there are 600,000 souls, and each soul divides into several sparks. We must understand how it is possible for the spiritual to divide, since initially, only one soul was created, the soul of *Adam HaRishon*.

In my opinion, there is indeed only one soul in the world, as it is written (Genesis 2:7), "and breathed into his nostrils the soul [also "breath" in Hebrew] of life." That same soul exists in all the children of Israel, complete in each and every one, as in *Adam HaRishon*, since the spiritual is indivisible and cannot be cut—which is rather a trait of corporeal things.

Rather, saying that there are 600,000 souls and sparks of souls appears as though it is divided by the force of the body of each person. In other words, first, the body divides and completely denies him of the radiance of the soul, and by the force of the Torah and the *Mitzva* [commandment], the body is cleansed, and to the extent of its cleansing, the common soul shines on him.

For this reason, two discernments were made in the corporeal body: In the first discernment, one feels one's soul as a unique organ and does not understand that this is the whole of Israel. This is truly a flaw; hence, it causes along with the above-mentioned.

In the second discernment, the true light of the soul of Israel does not shine on him in all its power of illumination, but only partially, by the measure he has purified himself by returning to the collective.

The sign for the body's complete correction is when one feels that one's soul exists in the whole of Israel, in each and every one of them, for which he does not feel himself as an individual, for one depends on the other. At that time, he is complete, flawless, and the soul truly shines on him in its fullest power, as it appeared in *Adam HaRishon*, as in "He who breathed, breathed from within Him."

This is the meaning of the three times of a person:

A spark of a soul, the act by way of sparkling, as in prohibiting and permitting.

A particular soul, one part out of 600,000. It is permanently completed, but its flaw is with it. This means that his body cannot receive the whole of the soul, and feels himself as being distinct, which causes him a lot of pains of love.

Subsequently, he approaches wholeness, the common soul, since the body has been cleansed and is entirely dedicated to the Creator and does not pose any measures or screens and is completely included in the whole of Israel.

5. Baal HaSulam, Letter No. 4

You lack nothing but to go out to a field that the Lord has blessed, and collect all those flaccid organs that have drooped from your soul, and join them into a single body.

In that complete body, the Creator will instill His *Shechina* incessantly, and the fountain of intelligence and high streams of light will be as a never ending fountain. Each place on which you cast your eye will be blessed, and all will be blessed because of you, for they will bless you constantly.

6. Baal HaSulam, "Emanation of the Soul"

Every person was created only to attain a complete and illuminating soul from the Creator, worthy of eternal and everlasting *Dvekut* [adhesion].

7. Baal HaSulam, Letter No. 17

The purpose of the soul when it comes in the body is to be rewarded with returning to its root and with *Dvekut* [adhesion] with Him while clothed in the body, as it is written, "To love the Lord your God, to walk in all His ways, to keep His commandments, and to adhere to Him."

8. Baal HaSulam, "The Meaning of Conception and Birth"

Kabbalists have attainment and attain a matter in full. That is, they are rewarded with attaining all those degrees in reality that one can attain. This is considered that they have attained a matter in full, and that complete matter is called a "soul."

9. Baal HaSulam, "The Acting Mind"

Every person is obliged to attain the root of his soul.

10. Baal HaSulam, "The Writings of the Last Generation"

The will to receive imprinted in every creature, and which is disparity of form to the Creator. Thus, the soul has separated from Him as an organ is separated from the body, since disparity of form in spirituality is like a separating axe in corporeality. It is therefore clear that what the Creator wants from us is equivalence of form, at which time we adhere to Him once more, as before we were created.

This is the meaning of the words, "Adhere to His attributes; as He is merciful, etc." It means that we are to change our attribute, which is the will to receive, and adopt the attribute of the Creator, which is only to bestow, so that all our actions will be only to bestow upon our fellow persons and benefit them as best as we can.

By this we come to the goal of adhering to Him, which is equivalence of form

11. Baal HaSulam, "Introduction to the preface to the Wisdom of Kabbalah," Items 2-3

The Creator's intention in creation was to delight His creatures. Certainly, as soon as He contemplated creating the souls and delighting them abundantly, they immediately emerged from before Him, complete in form and with all the delights He had planned to bestow upon them. This is because in Him, the thought alone completes, and He does not need actions as we do. Accordingly, we should ask, "Why did He create the worlds restriction after restriction down to this murky world, and clothed the souls in the murky bodies of this world?

The answer to this is written in *The Tree of Life*—"to bring to light the perfection of His deeds" (*The Tree of Life*, Branch 1). Yet, we must understand how it is possible that incomplete operations would stem from a complete Operator, to the point that they would require completion through an act in this world.

The thing is that we should distinguish between light and *Kli* [vessel] in the souls. The essence of the souls that were created is the *Kli* in them, and all the bounty that He had planned to impart them with and delight them is the light in them. This is because since He had planned to delight them, He necessarily made them as a desire to receive His pleasure, since the pleasure and delight increase according to the measure of desire to receive the abundance.

Know that that will to receive is the very self of the soul with regard to the generation and elicitation existence from absence. This is considered the *Kli* of the soul, while the joy and the abundance are considered the light of the soul, extending existence from existence from His self.

12. Baal HaSulam, "From My Flesh I Shall See God"

It is impossible to sustain one's body in the world without a certain amount of knowledge about the corporeal nature, such as knowing which drugs are lethal and what things burn or harm, as well as knowledge and assessment of what is in one's friend's heart, without which it is impossible to exist in the material world.

Just so, man's soul cannot exist in the next world until it has acquired a certain amount of the nature of the systems of the spiritual worlds, their changes, couplings, and generations.

Likewise, concerning the soul, a person reincarnates until one acquires the wisdom of truth in full. Without them, the soul cannot reach its full level. But it is not that the knowledge one has acquired raises the level of the soul. Rather, it is the soul's inherent nature that it will not grow by its own effort before it has acquired the knowledge of the spiritual nature. Its growth depends on the measure of its knowledge.

The reason this is so is that if it could grow without knowing, it would be harmed, like an infant who is ignorant and cannot walk. If it could walk on its feet, it would throw itself into a fire.

However, the growth comes primarily through good deeds which depend on attaining the wisdom of truth. And both the knowledge and the good deeds depend on attaining the wisdom of truth. And for the above reason, both come together.

13. Baal HaSulam, "From My Flesh I Shall See God"

Each complete soul attains all the souls from *Adam HaRishon* to the end of correction, as one perceives one's acquaintances and neighbors, and according to one's knowledge guards oneself from them, or connects and lives with them. And it is not surprising that one attains all the souls, since spirituality does not depend on time or place, and there is no death there.

14. Baal HaSulam, "Man's Actions and Tactics"

After all the actions of the creatures unite, all the souls in the world must unite and merge into one soul, truly one, which emerges out of all the souls and they truly become one, as in the beginning of creation, when only one man [Adam] was created, and from his *Zivugim* [couplings], he engendered sons, and the sons follow in his ways, making *Zivugim* until this world is made, with seventy nations, and from within them, the seed of Israel. At the end of correction, they will merge in one another until all of them will become one man like *Adam HaRishon*

15. RABASH, Article No. 10 (1984), "What Is the Degree One Should Achieve in Order Not to Have to Reincarnate?"

We have to know that all of the souls extend from the soul of *Adam HaRishon*, for after he sinned in the sin of the Tree of Knowledge, his soul divided into 600,000 souls. This means that the one light that *Adam HaRishon* had, which the Holy *Zohar* called *Zihara Ila'a* [upper brightness], which he had in the Garden of Eden at once, spreads into numerous pieces.

16. RABASH, Article No. 353, "Abraham Arose"

The *Kli* [vessel] in which the light of the Creator can reside is regarded as a soul.

17. RABASH, Article No. 17, "Concerning the Shechina" [Divinity]

The meaning of "soul" is that there is a revelation of His Godliness here to a certain extent, which the lower ones can receive.

18. RABASH, Article No. 17, "Concerning the Shechina" [Divinity]

A soul is called "part of the *Shechina*," meaning a part that the lower one can attain according to the measure of the purity.

19. RABASH, Article No. 13 (1984), "Sometimes Spirituality Is Called a 'Soul'"

The body is born with a nature of self-love, which is disparity of form from the Creator, whom we attain as only giving. Thus, one should cleanse one's body and come to equivalence of form so he, too, will want to do things that are only to bestow. By that, he will be able to reach this high degree called *Neshama*.

20. RABASH, Article No. 13 (1984), "Sometimes Spirituality Is Called a 'Soul'"

We must understand why spirituality is sometimes called "a soul" [Heb: *Neshama*], as it is written, "Body and soul," and sometimes spirituality is called "soul" [Heb: *Nefesh*], as in, "And you shall love the Lord your God with all your heart and with all your soul."

Usually, when speaking of spirituality, we speak of its highest discernment, which is *Neshama*, so that one will know that a high degree has been made ready for him, which is *Neshama*, to evoke in his heart the desire to achieve it and to think what is the reason that he has not achieved it yet. Then he will come to know that all we need in order to attain spirituality is equivalence of form.

21. *Zohar for All*, Pinhas, "Israel Are Organs of the Shechina," Item 491

The *Shechina* [Divinity] is a testimony to Israel, who are her organs, and she is a soul upon them.

22. *Zohar for All, VaYeshev* (And Jacob Sat), Come to Your Brother's Wife, #156

The Creator made man as it is above, all in wisdom. And there is not an organ in a man that does not stand in sublime wisdom, for each organ implies a unique degree. And after the whole body is properly corrected in its organs, the Creator partakes with it, and instills a holy soul within it, to teach man the ways of Torah and to keep His commandments so that man will be corrected appropriately, as it is written, "the soul of man shall teach him."

23. *Zohar for All. Toldot* [Generations], These Are the Generations of Isaac, #3

Also, there is not an organ in a man's body that does not have a corresponding creation in the world.
    This is so because as man's body divides into organs and they all stand degree over degree, established one atop the other and are all one body, similarly, the world, meaning all creations in the world are many organs standing one atop the other, and they are all one body.

24. Raaiah Kook, *Letters of the Raaiah*

The light of the soul of each individual is connected to the common soul of all of creation, from which the entire universe draws the light to complement all its details. We can add light to our soul through Torah, wisdom, *Mitzvot* [commandments], work, and good qualities every single moment. Any time we add light to our soul, if we only notice that we fear not only for ourselves but for all of creation, then we add complementation and life in everything.

25. Raaiah Kook, *Orot*

Our soul is great. It is strong and mighty. It shatters iron walls, blasts mountains and hills. It is infinitely broad; it must spread and cannot contract … Our soul will spread in everyone, embrace everyone, sustain and encourage everyone, and will bring everyone back to the place of our house of life.

7

All the Wisdoms in the World Are Included in the Wisdom of Kabbalah

1. Baal HaSulam, "The Teaching of the Kabbalah and its Essence"

The wisdom of truth is contingent upon all the teachings, and all the teachings are contingent upon it. This is why we do not find a single genuine Kabbalist without comprehensive knowledge in all the teachings of the world, since they acquire them from the wisdom of truth itself, as they are included in it.

2. Baal HaSulam, "The Essence of the Wisdom of Kabbalah"

As the emergence of the living species in this world and the conduct of their existence are a wondrous wisdom, the appearance of the Godly abundance in the world, the degrees and the conduct of their actions, unite to create a wondrous wisdom far more than the science of physics. This is so because the science of physics is merely knowledge of the arrangements of a particular kind existing in a particular world. It is unique to its subject, and no other science is included in it.

This is not so with the wisdom of truth. Because it is knowledge of the whole of the still, vegetative, animate, and speaking in all the worlds, in all their instances and conducts, as they were included in the thought of the Creator, that is, in the purposeful subjects, for this reason, all the teachings in the world, from the least of them to the greatest of them, are wondrously included in it, as it equalizes all the various teachings, the most different and the most remote from one another, as the east from the west. It makes them all equal, meaning until the orders of each teaching are compelled to come by its ways.

3. Baal HaSulam, "The Freedom"

They have no scientific solution as to how a spiritual object can have any contact with physical atoms in the body, to bring it into any kind of motion. All their wisdom and delving did not help them find a sufficient bridge to cross that wide and deep crevice between the spiritual entity and the corporeal atom. Hence, science has gained nothing from all these metaphysical methods.

To move a step forward in a scientific manner here, all we need is the wisdom of Kabbalah. This is because all the teachings in the world are included in the wisdom of Kabbalah.

4. Baal HaSulam, "The Essence of the Wisdom of Kabbalah"

There is no other wisdom in the world where matters are so fused and intertwined by way of cause and effect, primary and consequential, as is the wisdom of Kabbalah, connected from top to bottom just like a long chain. Therefore, upon the temporary loss of but a small cognizance, the entire wisdom darkens before our eyes, for all its matters are tightly connected to one another, literally fusing into one.

5. Baal HaSulam, "The Teaching of the Kabbalah and its Essence"

Since the whole of the wisdom of Kabbalah speaks of the revelation of the Creator, naturally, there is none more successful teaching for its task.

6. Baal HaSulam, "The Teaching of the Kabbalah and its Essence"

The greatest wonder about this wisdom is the integration in it: All the elements of the vast reality are incorporated in it until they come into a single thing—the Almighty, who contains them together.

7. Baal HaSulam, "The Teaching of the Kabbalah and its Essence"

The wisdom of medicine, or any other wisdom, could be interpreted according to the wisdom of Kabbalah no less than the wisdom of philosophy. This is so because all the teachings are included in it and were imprinted by its seal.

8. Nahmanides, "The Teaching of the Lord Is Whole"

All the sages of the nations do not know about creation what the smallest one in Israel knows. The benefit of the rest of the teachings is to be a ladder for the wisdom of knowing the Creator.

9. Rabbi Tzvi Hirsh Eichenstein of Ziditshov, *Sur Mera Ve'aseh Tov* [*Depart from Evil and Do Good*]

There is no other wisdom in the world like the wisdom of the depth of the secrets of the flavors of Torah. Without it, all other teachings are regarded as nothing and as emptiness.

10. The Maharal of Prague, *Derech Chaim*

The Torah is a Godly wisdom, and the Torah is not a human teaching. Therefore, the Godly Torah requires much founding and strengthening. Otherwise, the Torah, the degree of the Torah, is unsustainable. Likewise, the soul requires much preparation, to receive the wisdom of the Godly Torah. But a human teaching, like the teachings of the nations, does not relate to this, since the teaching is indeed suitable for the man. Moreover, the rest of the teachings certainly do not reach the Creator, for their home and foundation to be there. Rather, this pertains only to the Torah.

11. Rabbi Nachman of Breslov, *Talks of the Moharan*

Where the wisdom of all sciences ends, there begins the wisdom of Kabbalah.

12. Rabbi Shimon Bar Tzemach Duran, *TASHBETZ*

The inner wisdom, in which there is no deceit, and whose merit is far greater than all other teachings, is the wisdom of truth, the wisdom of Kabbalah.

13. Rabbi Nachman of Breslov, *Talks of the Moharan*

Where the wisdom of philosophy ends, there begins the wisdom of Kabbalah. This means that philosophers searched only through the wheels, but from there and above, they know nothing. And even in teachings from the wheels and below, they are also very bewildered, almost all of them, as they themselves know. And the wisdom of Kabbalah begins where their teaching ends, meaning from the wheels and above.

14. Raaiah Kook, *Orot HaKodesh*

The theory of evolution, which is currently overtaking the world, is aligned with the secrets of the world of Kabbalah more than all other philosophical teachings.

8

The Origin of Resistance to the Wisdom of Kabbalah

1. Baal HaSulam, "Introduction to The Book of Zohar," Item 70

Woe unto those people who make the spirit of Messiah leave and depart from the world, and not be able to return to the world. They are the ones who make the Torah dry, without any moisture of sense and reason. They confine themselves to the practical part of the Torah and do not want to try to understand the wisdom of Kabbalah, to know and to understand the secrets of the Torah and the flavors of *Mitzva*. Woe unto them, for they cause poverty and ruin, looting and killing, and destruction in the world.

2. Baal HaSulam, "Introduction to The Book of Zohar," Item 69

If, God forbid, it is to the contrary, and a person from Israel degrades the merit of the internality of the Torah and its secrets, which deals with the conducts of our souls and their degrees, and the intellectual part and the reasons for the *Mitzvot* compared to the advantage of the externality of the Torah, which deals only with the practical part, and even if one does occasionally engage in the internality of the Torah, and dedicates a little of one's time to it, when it is neither day nor night, as though it were redundant, by this one disgraces and degrades the internality of the world, which are the children of Israel, and raises the externality of the world over them, meaning the nations of the world. They will humiliate and disgrace the children of Israel, and will regard Israel as redundant, as though the world has no need for them.

Furthermore, by this they make even the externality in the nations of the world overpower their own internality, for the worst among the nations of the world, the harmful and the destructors of the world, rise above their internality, who are the righteous of the nations of the world. Then they make all the ruin and the heinous slaughter that our generation had witnessed.

3. Baal HaSulam, "Introduction to The Book of Zohar," Item 57

The darkness that have befallen us in this generation, such as we have never seen in all the generations preceding us. It is so because even the servants of the Creator have abandoned the engagement in the secrets of the Torah.

Maimonides has already given a true allegory about that. He said that if a line of a thousand blind people walks along the way and there is at least one leader amongst them who can see, they are guaranteed to walk on the right path and not fall in pits and obstacles since they follow the sighted one who leads them. But if that person is missing, they are certain to stumble over every hurdle on the way and will all fall into the pit.

So is the matter before us. If the servants of the Creator had, at least, engaged in the internality of the Torah and extended a complete light from *Ein Sof*, the whole generation would have followed them, and everyone would be certain of their way, that they would not fall. But if even the servants of the Creator have distanced themselves from this wisdom, it is no wonder the whole generation is failing because of them. And because of my great sorrow, I cannot elaborate on that!

4. Baal HaSulam, "Introduction to The Book of Zohar," Item 69

The redemption of Israel and the whole of Israel's merit depend on the study of *The Zohar* and the internality of the Torah. And vice-versa, all the destructions and the decline of the children of Israel are because they have abandoned the internality of the Torah, degraded its merit, and made it seemingly redundant.

5. Baal HaSulam, "Introduction to the Book From the Mouth of a Sage"

It is known from books and from authors that the study of the wisdom of Kabbalah is an absolute must for any person from Israel. If one studies the entire Torah and knows the Mishnah and the Gemara by heart, if one is also filled with virtues and good deeds more than all his contemporaries, but has not learned the wisdom of Kabbalah, he must incarnate once more into this world to study the secrets of Torah and wisdom of truth. This is brought in several places in the writings of our sages.

6. Baal HaSulam, Letter No. 39

Indeed, that which I dreaded came to me, and the hands of illiterate have betrayed me, doing what I did not order, after my stern warning not to disclose my secret to any person, whoever he may be. And now they have defamed me in the eyes of the generation and have failed me on the path of my exalted work to bring contentment to my Maker. Who can forgive them this? Heaven will testify to my labor in all my strength to extend His holiness to that generation.

And yet, the *Sitra Achra* [other side] always finds her people, doers of her missions, setting obstacles before me wherever I turn to benefit others. Thus far are my words. "Those who are with us are more than those who are with them," and the Creator does not deny my reward. Bit by bit, I am paving the way, at times less, at times more, but always with profit (reward), until I am rewarded with taking down all the enemies of the Creator with the help of His great and terrible name.
As for you, do not fear the fear of fools. Those who slander, my little finger is bigger than their waist. So the Creator desired, and so He made me, and who will tell Him what to do and what to work? The merit of my law is greater than the merit of their fathers. Similarly, the contemporaries of Prophet Amos defamed him and said that the Creator had no one on whom to instill His *Shechina* [Divinity] but that stutterer, as it is written in the *Psikta* [a Midrash].

However, it is written, "A truthful lip shall be established forever, and a lying tongue is only momentary," for in the end, the truthful people are the winners. Amos remains alive and existing forever, and who has heard or knows what had happened to his adversaries?

So it is here. The sayers can harm only their own kind, so it follows that the storm swirls on the head of the wicked, the truth lives on and does not weaken by all the lies. Instead, it grows even stronger by them, like a sown field that is strengthened by the manure and dung that are thrown in. With the Creator's will, the blessing of the field increases and multiplies by them.

I still do not feel the harm that will come to me through them concerning the dissemination of my teaching, so I do not know how to calculate a way to instill light and save it from their evil. And yet, it is certain that if I feel any harm, I will take my revenge against them, as is the law of Torah, and I will contend forcefully with them. I will do all that is within the power of my hand to do, as it is the Creator I fear, and there is no other force but Him.

7. Baal HaSulam, "Introduction to The Study of the Ten Sefirot," Items 1-3

At the outset of my words, I find a great need to break an iron wall that has been separating us from the wisdom of Kabbalah, since the ruin of the Temple to this generation. It lies heavily on us and arouses fear of being forgotten from Israel.

However, when I begin to speak to anyone about engaging in this study, his first question is, "Why should I know how many angels are in the sky and what their names are? Can I not keep the whole Torah in all its details and intricacies without this knowledge?"

Second, he will ask, "The sages have already determined that one must first fill one's belly with Mishnah and Gemara, and who can deceive himself that he has already completed the whole of the revealed Torah, and lacks only the wisdom of the hidden?"

Third, he is afraid that he will turn sour because of this engagement. This is because there have already been incidents of deviation from the path of Torah because of engagement in Kabbalah. Hence, "Why do I need this trouble? Who is so foolish as to place himself in danger for no reason?"

Fourth: Even those who favor this study permit it only to holy people, servants of the Creator, and not all who wish to take the Lord may come and take.

Fifth, and most important, "There is a conduct in our midst that, when in doubt, keep this: Do as the people do," and my eyes see that all those who study Torah in my generation have one view, and refrain from studying the hidden. Moreover, they advise those who ask them that it is undoubtedly preferable to study a page of Gemara instead of this engagement.

Indeed, if we set our hearts to answer but one very famous question, I am certain that all these questions and doubts will vanish from the horizon, and you will look unto their place to find them gone, meaning this indignant question that the whole world asks, namely, "What is the meaning of my life?" In other words, these numbered years of our life that cost us so heavily, and the numerous pains and torments that we suffer for them, to complete them to the fullest, who is it who enjoys them? Or even more precisely, whom do I delight?

It is indeed true that historians have grown weary contemplating it, and particularly in our generation, no one even wishes to consider it. Yet the question stands as bitterly and as vehemently as ever. Sometimes it meets us uninvited, pecks at our minds and degrades us to the ground before we find the famous ploy of flowing mindlessly in the currents of life as always.

Indeed, it is to resolve this great riddle that the verse says, "Taste and see that the Lord is good." Those who keep the Torah and *Mitzvot* [commandments] correctly are the ones who taste the taste of life. They are the ones who see and testify that the Lord is good, as our sages say, that He created the worlds to do good to His creations, since it is the conduct of The Good to do good.

8. Baal HaSulam, *Shamati* Article No. 181, "Honor,"

Honor is something that stops the body, and to that extent it harms the soul. Hence, all the righteous who became famous and respected, it was a punishment. But the great righteous, when the Creator does not want them to lose by being famous as righteous, the Creator guards them from being honored, so as not to harm their souls.

Hence, to the extent that they are honored on one hand, on the other hand, they are faced with dissenters who degrade them with all kinds of degradations. To the extent that creates an equal weight to the honor given to a righteous, to that very extent the other side gives disgrace.

9. Baal HaSulam, "Remembering"

This is the meaning of the declining merit of the generations until they arrived at the final shrinkage in our generation, when authors' wisdom is foul and they who fear sin are loathed. In that state the crowd feels content and are not obliged to God's work at all, nor feel any lack in its absence. Even those who do engage in work, it is merely out of habit. They have no thirst or aspiration to finding any speck of knowledge in their work.

And should a sage tell them, "Come, let me teach you wisdom, to understand and to instruct in the word of God," they already know their reply: "I already know that I will not be as Rashbi and his friends, and let things stay as they are, and I wish I could observe the literal in full." However, it is said about them, "The fathers have eaten sour grapes, and the children's teeth grow blunt," for they engage in Torah and *Mitzvot* [commandments] that are unripe, and their children's teeth will grow utterly blunt, and they wonder why they need this work. It is for you, and not for Him, and you, too, blunt its teeth. This is the form of our generation, with which we are dealing.

10. Baal HaSulam, Letter No. 10

An exiled disciple, his rav [teacher] is exiled with him." This was perplexing to our sages, for how can there be slandering in the Torah and work of the disciple to the point of expelling him from the domain of the Creator, especially once he is clung to a true teacher? They explained that when the disciple descends, it seems to him that the rav has descended, too. And because it is so, it really is so, meaning that he can enjoy his rav only to the extent that he assumes in his heart. Therefore, all he has is a low and inferior rav, as much as he values him. Thus, his rav is exiled with him.

11. RABASH, Letter No. 8

Although among themselves they are very remote and so different from one another that they can never agree on anything. They might even hate each other to such an extent that they cannot bear being in the same room with one another, and all wish to kill each other. Still, against us they all unite.

And since they are biased because of the will to receive in them, and "Bribe blinds the eyes of the wise," they promptly see the opposite of what they thought of us. And after all the praises and virtues that they found in us—that each of us is praiseworthy and honorable—once they have made their resolution, they quickly execute the verdict passionately and zealously, since we spoil their reputation with our views. Thus, on the one hand, they see that truth is on our side; on the other hand, our way is burdensome to them.

To excuse themselves, they have no other choice but to destroy us and obliterate our name from the face of the earth. They toil and strain for that, to disperse us to every direction, and they plot and conspire how to fail us and place stumbling blocks on our way, using all sorts of means—legitimate and illegitimate alike, even if these means contradict the human spirit and the spirit of Torah. They do not care because they see that there will be no persistence to their will if we have any domination and expansion of our goal to wholehearted and honest people, for then we will have the power to show them the truth.

And this is bad for them, for it is better for them to do what their hearts wish and at the same time be "the face of the generation"—influential and spiritual leaders. For this, they conspire plots of ruin and destruction for our future and say, "The sooner the better; it is better to degrade them while they are still small, so not a trace of them remains."

Still, we should be very grateful to them for respecting us and for appreciating our view by saying that at least they joke, mock, despise, and slander us. In other words, at least we have a reality in the world and it is not so easy for them to resolve to obliterate our name from the face of the earth.

12. *Zohar for All*, *Nasso*, "Mixed Multitude," Items 103-104

"Strong men and those who fear sin roam from city to city without favor," and the mixed multitude boycott them among them. In many places, they are given only rationed things, so there will be no resurrection to their fall, not even worldly life. And all the sages and the strong men and those who fear sin are in sorrow, distress, and grief, and they are regarded as dogs, as it is written, "The precious sons of Zion, weighed against fine gold, how are they regarded as earthen jars, the work of a potter's hands, at the corner of every street. They find no boarding among them.

And those mixed multitude are rich, tranquil, joyful, without sorrow and without any grief. They are robbers and bribers, and they are the judges, the heads of the people, for the earth is filled with robbery because of them. It is written about them, "Her enemies have become the masters."

13. Rav Chaim Vital, "Introduction of Rav Chaim Vital to Shaar HaHakdamot"

Woe unto people from the affront of Torah. When they engage only in the literal and in its stories, it wears its widow-garments, covered with the buttocks-bag, and all the nations shall say unto Israel:

"What is thy Beloved more than another beloved? Why is your Torah more than another Torah? After all, your Torah, too, is stories of the mundane." And there is no greater affront to the Torah than that.

Hence, woe unto those people from the affront of the Torah. They do not engage in the wisdom of Kabbalah, which honors the Torah, for they prolong the exile and all the evils that are about to come to the world.

14. Rabbi Shimon Ben Levi, *Ketem Paz*

Here is an answer to the wiseacre fools whose wisdom is little, who speak out against those who engage in the wisdom of Kabbalah, and say about them that they hear words but see no picture. Woe unto them and to their misfortune for their folly and wantonness, for they will not gain from this. Rather, they prevent the people of the Lord from rising to the mountain of His holiness.

15. Rabbi Baruch Ben Avraham of Kosov, *Pillar of the Work*

The great obligation to study the wisdom of truth, which is the wisdom of Kabbalah and the secrets of Torah, is well known to all, as is explained in ancient books. I am surprised at the people of our generation, whose humble ones refrain from learning the wisdom of truth.

16. The Holy Shlah, *In Ten Utterances*

The wisdom of Kabbalah makes the fool wise. Also, one who did not see the light of this wisdom has never seen lights in his life, for then he will understand and learn the meaning of His uniqueness, blessed be He, and the meaning of His governance ... and all who retire from it retire from the spiritual, eternal life.

17. Raaiah Kook, *Letters of the Raaiah*

While the orthodoxy continues to insist solely on Gemarah and Mishna, rejecting Agada [legend] and ethics, Kabbalah and research ... it impoverishes itself, and all the means that it applies to protect itself, without taking the real potion of life, the inner light of the Torah, the matter is revealed and felt. The revealed in Torah and *Mitzvot* [commandments] alone, can never, under any circumstances bring one to one's goal, in any generation, and all the more so in ours. It is possible only alongside the expansion of one's many spiritual roots.

18. Rabbi Pinchas Eliyahu Ben-Meir, *Sefer HaBrit*, Part 2, Article No. 12, Chapter 5

The crown of the Torah is the wisdom of Kabbalah, from which the majority of the world retires, saying, "Observe what you were permitted to observe, and you have no engagement in the hidden." You, if you are fit for this teaching, reach out your hand, hold it, and do not move from it, since one who did not taste the flavor of this wisdom has never seen lights in his life, and he walks in the dark. Woe unto the people from the affront of this Torah.

19. Rav Yitzhak Yehuda Yehiel of Komarno, *Notzer Hesed (Keeping Mercy)*, Chapter 4, Teaching 20

Many fools escape from studying the secrets of our teacher the Ari and *The Book of Zohar*, which are our lives. Had my people heeded me at the time of the Messiah, when evil and heresy increase, they would have delved all their lives in the study of *The Book of Zohar* and the *Tikkunim* [corrections], and the writings of the ARI. They would revoke all the harsh decrees and would extend abundance and light.

20. RAMAK, *Know the God of Your Father*

Many thought it was in correct to engage in the secret too much, since the practical Torah would be forgotten from Israel, meaning the permitted and forbidden, the kosher and non-kosher, and what shall become of this law if we all delve in the secrets of Torah? However, those who loath it are not among the servants of the Creator.

21. Rabbi Tzvi Hirsh Eichenstein of Ziditshov, *Sur Me'ra Ve'aseh Tov* [*Depart from Evil and Do Good*]

Without knowing the wisdom of Kabbalah, one is like a beast, since he performs the *Mitzva* [commandment] without reason, only going through the motions. He is like beasts that eat fodder, in which there is no flavor of man's food. Even if he is a great businessman with many occupations, he should not excuse himself from engaging in this wisdom.

22. Raaiah Kook, *Letters of the Raaiah*

All the great kabbalists unanimously cry out that as long as its secrets are removed from the Torah and they do not engage in its secrets, they are ruining the world.

23. Rabbi Yosef Eliezer Rosenfeld, *Havat Yair*

Anyone who refrains from learning Kabbalah is rejected from the presence of the righteous, loses his world, and he is not rewarded with seeing that the light of a king's face is life.

24. Rav Chaim Vital, "Introduction of Rav Chaim Vital to Shaar HaHakdamot"

When one is occupied with the wisdom of the Mishnah and Babylonian Talmud, but does not dedicate a part to the secrets of Torah and its concealments, too, it is like a body that sits in the dark without a human soul, in a way that the body is dry, not drawing from the source of life.

This is the meaning of what he says elsewhere, which is mentioned above and goes as follows: They are the ones who make the Torah dry and do not want to exert in the wisdom of Kabbalah.

25. Rabbi Pinchas Eliahu Ben-Meir, *Sefer HaBrit* [*The Book of the Covenant*], Part 2, Article No. 12, Chapter 5

One who did not engage in the wisdom of truth, who did not want to learn it when his soul wanted to rise to the Garden of Eden, is rejected from there with disgrace.

26. Rabbi Nahman of Breslov, *Likutey Halchot*

Now we must draw near to the true righteous in this generation, so as to clarify for us the faith according to the current time, since faith must be scrutinized each day anew. This is the essence of the intensification of the evil inclination, which grows in each and every generation specifically to conceal and hide the true righteous in that generation. As we evidently see, the dispute is mainly over the righteous in that generation. But after some time, they admit that he, too, was righteous. And they say that he was certainly righteous, but dispute the righteous in the next generation. Thus, in the days of the ARI, there was a great dispute over the ARI and they would not admit that in that generation there was such an innovation that had such spirit of holiness as presented in the writings of the ARI. But after several generations, the ARI was accepted and everyone admits that his were wondrous innovations and he was a Godly man. Nevertheless, they dispute other righteous in the generations following his. Finally, not long before our time, there was The Baal Shem Tov, who was a wondrous, awesome light, but there was a big dispute over him. In the days of The Baal Shem Tov, the majority of dissenters admitted concerning the ARI but disputed The Baal Shem Tov. So it is in every generation, and it has already been written in books (see end of the book *Noam Elimelech* where he speaks of it). All this is because the main scrutiny, which is the scrutiny of faith, is done precisely by the true righteous in that generation, for you have only "the judge of your days," since faith must be scrutinized each day anew, to the extent of the renewal of the work of creation on that day. This is clarified specifically through the righteous in that generation. For this reason, the one whom it concerns himself toils to conceal and hide that righteous and increase dispute and doubt over him so people would not come near him, since faith, which is the essence of the holiness of Israel, depends specifically on that righteous.

27. Rabbi Yosef Yitzchak Schneersohn, *Sefer Hasichot*

It is known that the fiercest resistance to the teaching and guidance of our teacher, The Baal Shem Tov, was from Lithuania in general and from the capital, Vilnus, in particular. Its beginning was back in the year 1754 or prior to that, meaning six years while our teacher The Baal Shem Tov was still alive.

When the teaching of our teacher, The Baal Shem Tov, grew strong through disciples who have mastered the Torah were strong in fear of God, the war grew fierce by those great in Torah from among the sect of the opposers whose intention was for the sake of the Creator.

The reason for the fear of the opposers was certain occurrences of the new philosophy of Spinoza, the expansion of tokens through practical Kabbalah, the abomination of Shabtai Tzvi, the Frank Sect, in addition to the isolation of those great in Torah in Lithuania, their remoteness from life, and their faith in those who spoke falsely about our teacher, The Baal Shem Tov, and his disciples. All this wreaked havoc within Israel.

28. Rabbi Baruch Ben Abraham of Kosov, *Amud HaAvoda* [*Pillar of the Work*]

I saw in many books of kabbalists, the great and bitter punishment for those who avoid studying the wisdom of Kabbalah, and the magnitude of the reward and the pleasure in the next world for those who study it.

29. Meshulam Feibush Heller, *Yosehr Divrey Emet*

Indeed, in this generation, the inverted *Klipa* [shell/peel] that is swirling in the blazes of the blade of the swirling sword from *Haver* [friend] to *Herev* [sword], as it is written, "Mighty men of evil have grown old." Some are as righteous and wise disciples, and pious wrapped in white, only their heart is not purified from respect and envy. And from their envy, they cast a flaw on the holy ones through the lies and falsehood, and slander the true servants of the Creator. It is all because they were seduced by the enticing of the serpent, that he who is greater than his friend, his inclination is greater than him (*Sukkah* 52), which the sayer rav said. He wanted to say that anyone who is greater than his friend, it follows that he has pride in the heart. In this one, his inclination is greater than him.

He wished to say that his inclination grows by itself due to the pride and envy that they feel when they see those wise ones, who in our time have a good reputation, and distinguished people from the masses who are pure admire them as true righteous and sages should be admired, to be dusted by the dust of their feet, while no one turns to them. It seems to them that they are righteous and pious, and better wise disciples than they are, so they cast a flaw in them and fabricate inconceivable lies and falsehood as has happened in our time in order to derogate their reputation, as it is written about it in *Duty of the Hearts*, that the evil inclination entices a person in this matter.

Also, one in whom no flaw or blemish is found, as was Rabbi Menachem Mendel, of whom the mockers would say that he was truly righteous but very proud, and as was said similarly about the sayer rav. It was all because of the above mentioned enticement, for those who know the truth about themselves, that they have not begun to serve the Creator whatsoever, for had they been rewarded with fear even for one minute, much less other degrees, they would have chased those righteous ones to teach them the path of the Creator as those true eternal great ones who acknowledged it and submitted before the righteous.

30. Rabbi Nachman of Breslov, *Likutey Edut HaMeshulash*

In each and every generation, the dispute over the righteous increases and becomes more provoked. For the most part, the dispute is mainly over those righteous who engage in bringing the farthest souls from Creator closer since the quality of judgment provokes his souls a great deal. Hence, resentment enters the heart of the world. Also, it sometimes enters the heart of the greatest righteous to dispute the righteous who bring them closer until it seems to them that they are not behaving properly. This follows and extends from the dispute that the tribes had with Joseph the righteous.

31. RAMAK, *Know the God of Your Father*

We saw that those who depart from this wisdom divide into three parts: One part are those who depart from it saying that it is not necessary to believe in the hidden in the Torah for many reasons. If they think of the matters literally and have no interest in the hidden, who would force them to believe in ten *Sefirot* and the rest of the parts in this wisdom? They want to believe only in the wondrous oneness, and when even a little bit of this wisdom comes to them, and especially when they hear of *Ein Sof* [infinity] and the form of the Torah, they gasp lawlessly to slander the knowledgeable, and they regard them almost as heretics.

There is a second sect that departs from this wisdom. They share many complaints and they all agree about the great merit of the wisdom. Some say that it is a sublime wisdom and not everyone is worthy of entering it, to the point that he considers punishing those who engage in it saying that he is zealous for the Lord and for His law, seeing that they stretched out their hand to a high place to engage in Godliness. Then there is a third sect that departs from this wisdom saying that one is close to erring in these matters and it is possible to come to sin and fall into one of the mistakes that concern a high place. The intention of this sect is desirable but their actions are undesirable. Even if a person does not find someone to teach him properly, he should not refrain from engagement in the Torah because of it, for in the end, the reward for learning is in his hand, and by this he will be rewarded with the truth.

PART 2
Studying the Wisdom of Kabbalah

1

The Merit of the Study – The Reforming Light

1. Baal HaSulam, "Introduction to The Study of the Ten Sefirot," Item 11

We find and see in the words of the sages of the Talmud that they have made the path of Torah easier for us than the sages of the Mishnah. This is because they said, "One should always practice the Torah and *Mitzvot*, even *Lo Lishma*, and from *Lo Lishma* he will come to *Lishma*, since the light in it reforms him."

Thus, they have provided us with a new means instead of the penance presented in the above-mentioned Mishnah, Avot: the "light in the Torah." It bears sufficient power to reform one and bring him to practice Torah and *Mitzvot Lishma*.

They did not mention penance here, but only that engagement in Torah and *Mitzvot* alone provides one with that light that reforms, so one may engage in Torah and *Mitzvot* in order to bring contentment to his Maker and not at all for his own pleasure. And this is called *Lishma*.

2. Baal HaSulam, "Introduction to The Study of the Ten Sefirot," Items 12-13

The light in the Torah shines only to those with faith. Moreover, the measure of that light is as the measure of the force of one's faith. Yet, to those without faith it is the opposite, as it is written, "To the left leaning in it — a potion of death" (Shabbat 88), for they receive darkness from the Torah and their eyes darken.

Sages have already presented a nice allegory about this matter regarding the verse, "Woe unto you who desire the day of the Lord! Why do you need the day of the Lord? It is darkness and not light" (Amos 5). There is an allegory about a rooster and a bat that were awaiting the light. The rooster said to the bat, "I await the light for the light is mine. But you, why do you need the light?" (Sanhedrin 98b).

3. Baal HaSulam, "Introduction to The Study of the Ten Sefirot," Item 155

Why then did the Kabbalists obligate every person to study the wisdom of Kabbalah? Indeed, there is a great thing about it, which should be publicized: There is a wonderful, invaluable remedy to those who engage in the wisdom of Kabbalah. Although they do not understand what they are learning, through the yearning and the great desire to understand what they are learning, they awaken upon themselves the lights that surround their souls.

This means that every person from Israel is guaranteed to finally attain all the wonderful attainments with which the Creator contemplated in the thought of creation to delight every creature. And one who has not been awarded in this life will be granted in the next life, etc., until one is awarded completing His thought, which He had planned for him, as it is written in *The Zohar*.

And while one has not attained perfection, the lights that are destined to reach him are considered surrounding lights. This means that they stand ready for him but are waiting for him to purify his vessels of reception, and then these lights will clothe the able vessels.

Hence, even when he does not have the vessels, when he engages in this wisdom, mentioning the names of the lights and the vessels related to his soul, they immediately illuminate upon him to a certain extent. However, they illuminate for him without clothing the interior of his soul, for lack of vessels able to receive them. Yet, the illumination one receives time after time during the engagement draws upon him grace from above, and imparts him with abundance of sanctity and purity, which bring him much closer to achieving his wholeness.

4. Baal HaSulam, "Introduction to The Study of the Ten Sefirot," Item 18

The Creator, Who created it and gave the evil inclination its strength, evidently knew to create the remedy and the spice liable to wear off the power of the evil inclination and eradicate it altogether.

And if one practices Torah and fails to remove the evil inclination from himself, it is either that he has been negligent in giving the necessary labor and exertion in the practice of Torah, as it is written, "I did not labor and found, do not believe," or perhaps he did put in the necessary amount of labor, but has been negligent in the quality.

This means that while practicing Torah, they did not set their minds and hearts to draw the light in the Torah, which brings faith to one's heart. Rather, they have been absent-minded about the principal requirement demanded of the Torah, namely the light that yields faith. And although they initially aimed for it, their minds went astray during the study.

5. Baal HaSulam, *Shamati*, Article No. 235, "Looking in the Book Again"

After one sees some words of Torah in a book and memorizes them, since what enters the mind is already blemished, hence, when looking in the book again, he can elicit the light so as to receive illumination from what he is seeing now. This is already considered new and unblemished.

6. Baal HaSulam, "Introduction to The Study of the Ten Sefirot," Item 141

You can understand the words of our sages about the words, "Leave Me and keep My law." They interpreted, "I wish that they left Me and kept My Torah—the light in it reforms them" (Jerusalem Talmud, *Hagigah*, Chapter 1, *Halacha* 7).

This is perplexing. They mean that they were fasting and tormenting to find the revelation of His face, as it is written, "They desire the nearness of God" (Isaiah 58:2). Yet, the text tells them in the name of the Creator, "I wish you would leave Me, for all your labor is in vain and futile, for I am nowhere but in the Torah. Hence, keep the Torah and look for Me there, the light in it will reform you, and you will find Me," as it is written, "Those who seek Me shall find Me."

7. Baal HaSulam, *Shamati*, Article No. 68, "Man's Connection to the Sefirot"

One cannot correct one's thought, but should only aim the heart—make one's heart straight to the Creator. Then all of his thoughts and actions will naturally be to bestow contentment upon his Maker. When he corrects his heart to be a heart and desire of *Kedusha*, the heart will then be the *Kli* in which to place the upper light. And when the upper light shines in the heart, the heart will grow stronger and he will add and supplement continuously.

Now we can interpret our sages' words, "Great is the learning that yields action." It means that through the light of the Torah he is led into action, as the light in it reforms him. This is called "an act." This means that the light of the Torah builds a new structure in his heart.

8. Baal HaSulam, "Concealment and Disclosure of the Face of the Creator-1"

One's request to become stronger in believing in His guidance over the world during the concealment brings one to contemplate the books, the Torah, and to draw from there the illumination and understanding how to strengthen his faith in His guidance. These illuminations and observations that one receives through the Torah are called "the Torah as a spice." When they accumulate to a certain amount, the Creator has mercy on him and pours upon him the spirit from above, that is, the higher abundance.

But once he has completely discovered the spice—the light of Torah that one inhales into one's body—through strengthening in faith in the Creator, one becomes worthy of guidance with His face revealed. This means that the Creator behaves with him as is fitting to His name, "The Good Who Does Good."

9. Baal HaSulam, *Shamati*, Article No. 218, "The Torah and the Creator Are One"

The Torah is called "the light" in it. This means that during the study, when we feel the light, and want to give to the Creator with this light, as it is written, "One who knows the commandment the Master will serve Him." Hence, he feels that he exists, that he wants to bestow upon the Creator, and this is the sensation of oneself.

However, when one is awarded the discernment of "the Torah and the Creator are one," one finds that all is one. At that time, one feels the Creator in the Torah. One should always yearn for the light in it; and the light we can with what we learn, although it is easier to find the light in words of Kabbalah.

10. Baal HaSulam, "The Teaching of the Kabbalah and Its Essence"

The Torah is the only spice to annul and subdue the evil inclination, as our sages said, "The light in it reformed them."

11. Baal HaSulam, "Introduction to The Study of the Ten Sefirot," Item 17

The student pledges, prior to the study, to strengthen himself in faith in the Creator and in His guidance in reward and punishment, as our sages said, "Your employer is liable to pay you the reward for your work." One should aim one's labor to be for the *Mitzvot* of the Torah, and in this way, he will be rewarded with enjoying the light in it, and his faith will strengthen and grow through the power in this light, as it is written, "It shall be health to your navel, and marrow to your bones" (Proverbs 3:8).

Then one can be certain that from *Lo Lishma* he will come to *Lishma*, in a way that even one who knows about himself that he has not been rewarded with faith still has hope through the practice of Torah, for if he sets his heart and mind to attain faith in the Creator through it, there is no greater *Mitzva* than this. It is as our sages said, "Habakkuk came and stressed only this: 'A righteous shall live by his faith'" (*Makkot* 24).
Moreover, there is no other counsel but this.

12. Baal HaSulam, "Introduction to the Book Panim Meirot uMasbirot," Item 5

It is written in *The Zohar*: "With this composition, the children of Israel will be redeemed from exile." Also, in many other places, only through the expansion of the wisdom of Kabbalah in the masses will we obtain complete redemption.

Our sages also said, "The light in it reforms him." They were intentionally meticulous about it, to show us that only the light enclosed within it, "like apples of gold in settings of silver," in it lies the *Segula* [power/cure] that reforms a person. Both the individual and the nation will not complete the aim for which they were created, except by attaining the internality of the Torah and its secrets.

13. Baal HaSulam, *Shamati*, Article No. 6, "What Is Support in the Torah, in the Work?"

Torah refers to the light clothed in the Torah, as our sages said, "I have created the evil inclination; I have created the Torah as a spice." This refers to the light in it, since the light in it reforms him.

14. Baal HaSulam, *Shamati*, Article No. 34, "The Advantage of a Land"

What should one do in order to come to love the Creator? For this purpose we are given the remedy of engaging in Torah and *Mitzvot* [commandments], for the light in it reforms him. There is light there which lets him feel the severity of the state of separation. Bit by bit, as one aims to acquire the light of Torah, hatred for separation is created in him. He begins to feel the reason that causes him and his soul to be separated and far from the Creator.

15. Baal HaSulam, "Introduction to The Study of the Ten Sefirot," Item 22

It is easier to draw the light in the Torah while practicing and laboring in the wisdom of truth than in laboring in the revealed Torah. The reason is very simple: The wisdom of the revealed Torah is clothed in external, corporeal clothes, such as stealing, plundering, torts, etc. For this reason, it is difficult and heavy for any person to aim his mind and heart to the Creator while learning, so as to draw the light in the Torah.

It is even more so for a person for whom learning the Talmud itself is heavy and arduous. How can he remember the Creator during the study, since the scrutiny concerns corporeal matters, and cannot come in him simultaneously with the intention for the Creator?

Therefore, he advises him to engage in the wisdom of Kabbalah, as this wisdom is clothed entirely in the names of the Creator. Then he will certainly be able to easily aim his mind and heart to the Creator during the study, even if it is very difficult for him to study, for the study of the issues of the wisdom and the Creator are one and the same.

16. Baal HaSulam, "Introduction to The Study of the Ten Sefirot," Item 35

Even though they do not succeed through the practice in the revealed Torah, since there is no light in it and it is dry due to the smallness of their minds (see Item 16), they could still succeed by engaging in the study of Kabbalah, for the light in it is clothed in the clothing of the Creator—the Holy names and the *Sefirot*. Thus, they could easily come to that state of *Lo Lishma* that brings them to *Lishma*.

17. Baal HaSulam, "The Teaching of the Kabbalah and Its Essence"

There is another magnificent power in it: All who engage in it, although they still do not understand what is written in it, are purified by it, and the upper lights draw closer to them.

18. Baal HaSulam, Matan Torah [The Giving of the Torah], Item 12

Through the natural remedy of engagement in Torah and *Mitzvot Lishma*, which the Giver of the Torah knows, as our sages said (*Kidushin* 30b), "The Creator says, 'I have created the evil inclination; I have created for it the Torah as a spice.'" Thus, that creature develops and marches upward in degrees of the above-said exaltedness until he loses all remnants of self-love and all the *Mitzvot* in his body rise, and he performs all his actions only to bestow, so even the necessity that he receives flows in the direction of bestowal, meaning so he can bestow.

19. RABASH, Article No. 218, "Israel Are the Sons of Kings"

Wherever one retires from enjoying and causes unification, you find in it *Kedusha* [holiness], since the upper light can be there because the *Kelim* [vessels] can receive the light of the Creator called *Kedusha*, for the *Kedusha* is present only in a place of purity. "Purity" means purity of qualities, and then the *Kedusha* is present in a place of purity.

However, sometimes, "I the Lord, who dwells with them in the midst of their *Tuma'a* [impurity]," meaning that even when they still do not have *Kelim* that are ready to be in equivalence, in order to assist a person in achieving this, he must be aided from above. This is the meaning of *Lo Lishma*, that the light in it reforms him. That light is called "The Lord, who dwells with them in the midst of their *Tuma'a*."

This pertains specifically to one who wants to achieve *Lishma* but cannot overcome his body. Hence, he is given that light so he can defeat the will to receive and walk in the way of the Creator, which is bestowal.

20. RABASH, Article No. 12 (1988), "What Are Torah and Work in the Way of the Creator?"

The Torah reveals something new to a person, which he did not know before. This is so because man is born with a nature of wanting to receive. When told to work with a desire to bestow, it is to him unimportant and despicable. The body wants to run away from such desires, since it can only lose if it uses the vessels of bestowal.

However, when a person learns Torah with the aim to be rewarded with the light of Torah because this light reforms him, this light of Torah reveals something new to him, which he did not know before. That is, now he knows the complete opposite of what he thought before. Before he was rewarded with the light of Torah, he knew that what is important to man is primarily the vessels of reception, for with the vessels of reception he can receive the joys of life in this world. Conversely, with acts of bestowal he can only do good to others, that they, too, will enjoy the world through his help.

However, this is only for the purpose of *Mitzva*, because he feels sorry for others who cannot provide for themselves, and he is helping them. Certainly, he expects those people whom he benefits not to be ungrateful and respect him.

But now, by being rewarded with the light of Torah, which reforms him, something new has been revealed to him: By using the vessels of reception, he loses life and delight and pleasure for himself. If he uses the vessels of bestowal for the sake of others, he will receive *true* delight and pleasure for himself. Only through vessels of bestowal does he gain for himself delight and pleasure, whereas with vessels of reception he loses delight and pleasure. This secret has now been revealed to him through the light of the Torah.

21. RABASH, Article No. 721, "The Segula of Torah and Mizvot"

There is a *Segula* [power/cure] in *Torah and Mitzvot* [commandments] that if he learns with this intention, although his heart disagrees with it, and all that he does with this intention is against his will and heart, yet through compulsory work, he is rewarded with inverting his desire from self-love to love of others.

We should understand what is written, that it is harder to attain the concept of bestowal upon others as this is against nature. Nevertheless, through the power of *Torah and Mitzvot* in order to bestow, we can be rewarded with inverting our nature into aiming to bestow.

There is a question: When one is immersed in the nature of self-love, how can he engage in *Torah and Mitzvot* in order to bestow, since he has no desire or ability whatsoever to do anything unless it is for his own sake? Thus, how can one be educated into engaging in *Torah and Mitzvot* in order to bestow?

We should say that although man's nature is only self-love, and that which is against it is hard for him to do, to the point that all his organs go against him, but there is the matter of coercion, meaning that when he engages in *Torah and Mitzvot*, he learns against his will, meaning that he wants it to be only for the sake of the Creator, and then he learns and thinks only about things that speak of the matter of bestowal.

And although the body disagrees, through the labor in which he exerts himself, forcing his body to work with this intention, although his heart's desire disagrees with this intention, the light in it reforms him.

22. RABASH, Article No. 16 (1984), "Concerning Bestowal"

This means that first, one must see if he has the strength to come to be able to act with the aim to bestow contentment upon the Creator. Then, when he has already come to realize that he cannot achieve it by himself, that person focuses his Torah and *Mitzvot* on a single point, which is that "the light in it reforms him," that this will be the only reward that he wants from the Torah and *Mitzvot*. In other words, the reward for his labor will be for the Creator to give him this strength called "the power of bestowal."

There is a rule that one who makes an effort, meaning cancels his rest, it is because he wants something, since he knows that without labor he will not be given, so he must toil. For this reason, a person who exerts to keep Torah and *Mitzvot* must certainly be missing something, and this is why he exerts in Torah and *Mitzvot*, to obtain what he wishes through it.

Accordingly, one must pay attention and contemplate what he wants—what is the reward that he wants for his work—before he begins his work in serving the Creator. Or, put simply, what is the reason that compels him to engage in Torah and *Mitzvot*? Then, when he determines what he needs, for which he must toil, a person begins to think very hard until it is difficult for him to know what he really wants.

23. RABASH, Article No. 12, (1988), "What Are Torah and Work in the Way of the Creator?"

The meaning of "Torah and work" is that he learns Torah in order for the Torah to bring him the light of Torah. By this, he will be able to invert the vessels of reception to work in order to bestow, and with these *Kelim* he will be rewarded with *Dvekut* with the Creator, called "learning Torah *Lishma*."

24. RABASH, Article No. 267, "Man Was Created in the Torah"

It is known that the purpose of creation is to do good to His creations. For this reason, a nature has been imprinted in man that he will want to receive pleasure for his own delight. This is called the "evil inclination" (as explained in the introduction to the *Sulam* [Ladder commentary on *The Zohar*]), as it is written, "For the inclination of man's heart is evil from his youth."

It is called the "evil inclination" because by wanting to receive pleasure, a person becomes removed from the real pleasure because he has no equivalence of form. However, through the Torah, he will have a correction where through the Torah, it will be possible for him to receive the real pleasures, as our sages said, "I have created the evil inclination; I have created the Torah as a spice" (*Baba Batra* 16).

The spice is as our sages said, "I wish they left Me and kept My Torah [law], for the light in it reforms them" (Jerusalem Talmud, *Hagigah*, Chapter 1, Rule 7). It therefore follows that the Torah has the power to reform a person, referring to the evil within man, meaning the will to receive, that it will work in order to bestow.

In this manner, he will have *Dvekut* [adhesion] and will be able to receive the real pleasures and will not be considered a receiver. Thus, through the Torah, it will be possible to sustain man in this world, for the Torah will reform him.

This is the meaning of "Let us make man," which they explained, "I and you will establish him in the world." That is, from the Creator comes the will to receive and from the Torah comes the desire to bestow, and from those two, man will be able to exist in the world. That is, through those two, he will be able to receive abundance yet remain in *Dvekut*.

25. RABASH, Article No. 12, (1988), "What Are Torah and Work in the Way of the Creator?"

We engage in the Torah in order to subdue the evil inclination, meaning to achieve *Dvekut* [adhesion] with the Creator, so that all our actions will be only in order to bestow. That is, by ourselves, we will never be able to go against nature, since the mind and heart that we must acquire require assistance, and the assistance is through the Torah. It is as our sages said, "I have created the evil inclination; I have created the Torah as a spice. By engaging in it, the light in it reforms them."

26. RABASH, Article No. 12 (1988), "What Are Torah and Work in the Way of the Creator?"

Feeling the vitality in the Torah requires great preparation to prepare his body to be able to feel the life in the Torah. This is why our sages said we must begin in *Lo Lishma*, and through the light of Torah he obtains while still in *Lo Lishma*, it will bring him to *Lishma*, since the light in it reforms him. Then, he will be able to learn *Lishma*, meaning for the sake of the Torah, which is called "Torah [law] of life," as he has already attained the life in the Torah, for the light in the Torah will have given such qualification to a person as to be able to feel the life that is in the Torah.

27. RABASH, Article No. 12 (1988), "What Are Torah and Work in the Way of the Creator?"

We should make several discernments in the Torah: 1) one who learns Torah in order to know the rules, to know how to observe the *Mitzvot* of the Torah, 2) one who learns Torah in order to observe the *Mitzva* of learning Torah, as it is written (Joshua 1), "This book of Torah shall not move from your mouth, and you shall contemplate it day and night." RASHI interprets "contemplate it" as "looking in it," every thought in the Torah is in the heart, as he said, "The contemplation of my heart is before You." 3) He learns Torah in order to be rewarded with the light of the Torah, as it is written, "I have created the evil inclination; I have created the Torah as a spice because the light in it reforms him." By this he will be rewarded with faith, and to adhere to the Creator, and then he will become "Israel" for he believes in the Creator in complete faith. 4) Once he has been rewarded with faith, he is rewarded with the "Torah, as in the names of the Creator." In *The Zohar*, this is called "The Torah and Israel and the Creator are one." At that time he is rewarded with the purpose of creation, which is to do good to His creations, when the creatures receive what the Creator wants to give to the creatures.

28. RABASH, Article No. 12 (1988), "What Are Torah and Work in the Way of the Creator?"

RASHI interpreted about the verse, "You shall contemplate it day and night," he says "look in it. Every thought in the Torah is in the heart." We should understand what he means by saying that the thought is in the heart, since when we learn Torah, it is in the mind and not in the heart, so why does he tell us, "Every thought in the Torah is in the heart"?

We should interpret that this does not pertain specifically to the Torah that relates to rules he learns in order to know how to observe the *Mitzvot*. Instead, he wishes to say that the Torah also includes the last two discernments just mentioned: 1) that he learns in order to receive the light of Torah, 2) that he is then rewarded with the Torah, called "the names of the Creator."

Those two belong specifically to the heart, as Rabbi Abraham ibn Ezra says (in the "Introduction to the book Panim Masbirot," Item 10), "Know that all the *Mitzvot* that are written in the Torah or the accepted ones, which the forefathers have established, although the majority of them are in deed or utterance, they are all in order to correct the heart. This is because the Lord wants all the hearts, and He understands the inclination of every thought. It is written, 'To those whose hearts are straight,' and conversely, 'a heart filled with thoughts of transgression.' Know that the Torah was given only to men of heart."

29. RABASH, Article No. 12 (1988), "What Are Torah and Work in the Way of the Creator?"

It is our inability to do anything for the sake of the Creator. Only the light of Torah will correct the heart, for the heart is called "desire," and by nature, it is a desire only to receive. But how can a person go against nature?

This is why the Creator said, "I have created the evil inclination; I have created the Torah as a spice." It follows that he is not learning Torah for the intellect, to understand, but he is learning in order to understand so as to achieve *Dvekut* with the Creator, who is clothed in the Torah, and this pertains to the heart. Through the light he will receive, it reforms him, meaning that the will to receive for his own sake can receive strength from above that enables it to work for the sake of the Creator.

30. RABASH, Article No. 12 (1988), "What Are Torah and Work in the Way of the Creator?"

If a person wants to work and observe Torah and *Mitzvot* without any reward, only because he wants to serve the King, then he needs to know the greatness of the King, for the measure of his work depends on the extent of his faith in the greatness of the King, for only the greatness and importance of the King gives him fuel for work.

It is as it is written in *The Zohar* about the verse, "Her husband is known at the gates." It means that each according to what he assumes in his heart. By this, he tells us that to the extent that a person assumes in his heart the greatness and importance of the Creator, to that extent he dedicates himself to serving the King.

For this reason, people of this kind, who want to work only in order to bestow, and the whole reason that compels them to engage in Torah and *Mitzvot* is the importance and greatness of the Creator, as it is written in *The Zohar* that "The essence of fear is to work because He is great and ruling," when these people believe that the Creator is clothed in the Torah, and believe what the Creator said to Israel, "I sold you My Torah; it is as though I have been sold with it," when they learn Torah they want to elicit the light of the Torah that reforms him. This is the meaning of what our sages said, "He who comes to purify," through the Torah, "is aided," since the Creator is clothed in the Torah.

31. RABASH, Letter No. 62

Man's primary work is to examine the greatness of the Creator. That is, one should delve in books that speak of the greatness of the Creator, and while delving, one should depict to oneself to what extent our sages, the Tanaaim and Amoraim, felt the greatness of the Creator.

One should pray to the Creator to shine so he may feel His greatness, so he can subdue his heart and annul before the Creator, and not follow the currents of the world, which is pursuing only the satisfaction of beastly lusts, but that the Creator will open his eyes so he may engage all his life in Torah and work, and "In all your ways, know Him." That is, even when engaging in corporeal matters, it will be for the purpose of *Kedusha* [holiness], as well.

But from *Lo Lishma*, we come to *Lishma*. That is, *Lishma* is already a high degree, and one must begin from *Lo Lishma*. In other words, one should be fully aware that pleasure is found primarily in Torah and work, and not in corporeality.

Although at the moment he feels more pleasure in corporeal things, more than he feels in spiritual things, it is because he lacks the qualification in Torah and work, which also depends on faith in the Creator. At that time, through Torah and faith in the Creator, one feels the light in the Torah, and that light reforms him.

32. RABASH, Article No. 12 (1988), "What Are Torah and Work in the Way of the Creator?"

A person must make a great effort before he comes to learn so that his learning will bear fruit and good results, meaning so the learning will bring him the light of Torah, by which it will be possible to reform him. Then, through the Torah, he becomes a wise disciple.

What is a "wise disciple"? Baal HaSulam said that it is a student who learns from the wise. That is, the Creator is called "wise," and a person who learns from Him is called a "disciple of the wise." What should one learn from the Creator? He said that a person should learn only one thing from the Creator. It is known that the Creator wishes only to bestow. Likewise, man should learn from Him to be a giver. This is called a "wise disciple."

33. RABASH, Article No. 12 (1988), "What Are Torah and Work in the Way of the Creator?"

If in the beginning of his study, when a person comes to study, there is no desire to thereby achieve complete faith, which he can achieve through the light in the Torah by wanting to adhere to the one who wears it, who is clothed in the Torah and gives the light of Torah and none other, it follows that he is learning Torah, which is the clothing of the Creator. Through it, he wants to achieve complete faith, adhere to the one who wears it, who is the giver of the Torah.

Here there is unification of three discernments: 1) the Torah, which is the clothing of the Creator, 2) the Creator, who is clothed in the Torah, and 3) Israel, the person who is learning Torah with the above intention.

This is called "unification," called "the Torah and the Creator and Israel are one." Although *The Zohar* speaks to those who have already been rewarded with "the names of the Creator," which is called that they have been rewarded with a "hand *Tefillin*," called "faith," and a "head *Tefillin*," called "Torah," yet, those who walk on the path of achieving Torah and faith also receive a surrounding from this unification.

34. RABASH, Article No. 22 (1985), "The Whole of the Torah Is One Holy Name"

During the study we must always pay attention to the purpose of the study of Torah, meaning what we should demand from the study of Torah. At that time we are told that first we must ask for *Kelim*, meaning to have vessels of bestowal, called "equivalence of form," by which the restriction and concealment that were placed on the creatures are removed. To the extent that this is so he begins to feel the holiness and begins to have a taste for the work of the Creator. At that time he can be happy because *Kedusha* [holiness] yields joy, for the light of doing good to His creations shines there.

But if he has not yet decided that he should always walk on the path of bestowal, as our sages said, "all your works will be for the Creator," this is regarded as "preparation of the *Kelim*" to be fit for reception of the upper abundance. He wants to be rewarded with vessels of bestowal through the study, as our sages said, "The light in it reforms him."

And once he has been rewarded with vessels of bestowal, he comes to a degree called "attainment of the Torah," which is the "names of the Creator," as *The Zohar* calls it: "The Torah, the Creator, and Israel are one."

35. RABASH, Article No. 12 (1988), "What Are Torah and Work in the Way of the Creator?"

It is beneficial to elicit the light from the Torah—if he aims while engaging in the Torah, to learn in order to receive the reward of the Torah, called "light." At that time, the learning of Torah is good for him. But when he is distracted from the purpose of studying Torah, the Torah does not help complete the work of making the vessels of bestowal and not using the vessels of reception for one's own sake. Otherwise, his Torah vanishes from him. That is, the force of Torah and that should have subdued the evil inclination is cancelled. This is the meaning of the words, "Any

Torah with which there is no work," meaning when he does not aim for the Torah to do the work of turning the vessels of reception to work in order to bestow, "is finally cancelled," meaning that that force is cancelled.

36. RABASH, Article No. 22 (1985), "The Whole of the Torah Is One Holy Name"

We should discern two things in the Torah: 1) the light of Torah, which comes in order to reform him. This is the correction of the *Kelim* [vessels]. 2) Obtaining the light of Torah, which is the "holy names," called the "revelation of His Godliness to His creatures in this world" (see in the essay *Matan Torah* ["The Giving of Torah"]).

It therefore follows that when we study Torah we should discern the two above matters: 1) to extend light so it will create for us vessels of bestowal. It is impossible to obtain these *Kelim* [vessels] without the light of Torah. Therefore, what does he expect? To be rewarded for studying Torah. His only desire is to obtain that *Kli*, called "vessel of bestowal." This is precisely once he has begun the work of bestowal and has made great efforts to be able to do things only with the intention to bestow.

Only then can he come to know that the will to receive that was installed in him by nature cannot be cancelled. At that time he begins to understand that he needs "heaven's mercy," and only the Creator can help him be rewarded with vessels of bestowal, and this help comes from the light of Torah.

37. RABASH, Article No. 21 (1988), "What Does It Means that the Torah Was Given Out of the Darkness in the Work?"

The Torah is given specifically to the deficient, and that deficiency is called "darkness." This is the meaning of the words, "The Torah was given out of the darkness." That is, one who feels darkness in his life because he has no vessels of bestowal is fit to receive the Torah, so that through the Torah, the light in it will reform him and he will obtain the vessels of bestowal. Through them, he will be fit to receive the delight and pleasure, for those two are included in the Torah: 1) The *Kli*—that he wants to bestow. 2) Then he receives the delight and pleasure into the vessels of bestowal.

Conversely, the nations of the world did not receive the Torah, since it was given out of the darkness. In the work, "the nations of the world" means that the body comprises seventy nations that want the Torah not because they feel darkness when they have no vessels of bestowal. Rather, their only desire is the vessels of reception and they have no desire to emerge from that control. They want the Torah in order to add more light to themselves, meaning more pleasure than they receive from corporeal matters. That is, they also want the next world, as it is written in *The Zohar*, "They howl as dogs *Hav, Hav* [give, give], give us the wealth of this world, and give us the wealth of the next world." That is, the wealth of this world is not enough for them, but they also want the wealth of the next world.

It follows that the Torah was given specifically to those who feel that their will to receive controls them. They cry out from the darkness that they need the Torah in order to deliver them from the darkness that is the control of the vessels of reception, on which there was a *Tzimtzum* [restriction] and concealment so that no light will shine in that place. But that place is the cause for the need to receive the Torah.

38. RABASH, Article No. 21 (1988), "What Does It Means that the Torah Was Given Out of the Darkness in the Work?"

Since the Torah came because of the darkness, the Torah did two things: 1) "The light in it reforms him." Then, the *Tzimtzum* and concealment depart from his vessels of reception because where he had vessels of reception, he has now been rewarded with vessels of bestowal. This is the meaning of the words, "And the Lord will shine upon you." That is, as the Creator wants to bestow, so man will be rewarded with a desire to bestow. 2) After he has been rewarded with vessels of bestowal, meaning he was granted the ability to work *Lishma* [for Her sake], which is called "learning Torah *Lishma*," then he is shown the secrets of the Torah, as Rabbi Meir says (in the Mishnah, *Avot*). This is the meaning of the words, "And His glory will be seen upon you," meaning the glory of the Creator, which is the revelation of Godliness. It "will be seen upon you," for then one is rewarded with "The Torah, and Israel, and the Creator are one."

39. RABASH, Article No. 21 (1990), What Is, "As I Am for Nothing, so You Are for Nothing, in the Work?"

They said, "I have created the evil inclination; I have created the Torah as a spice," meaning the light spices the evil inclination. In other words, the Creator gives the power to want to do everything for the sake of the Creator.

40. RABASH, Article No. 12 (1988), "What Are Torah and Work in the Way of the Creator?"

A person should examine with which purpose does he want to observe the *Mitzva* [commandment] of learning Torah? That is, does he engage in Torah because of the Torah itself, in order to know how to observe the rules of doing the *Mitzvot*, or is the learning of Torah itself his whole intention, and knowing the rules of doing the *Mitzvot* is a completely different matter for him? meaning he is learning Torah for two reasons.

However, even while learning Torah for the sake of learning Torah, he should still distinguish with which intention he is learning. Is it to observe the commandments of the Creator, as it is written, "And you shall reflect on Him day and night," or is he learning in order to receive the light of Torah because he needs the light of Torah in order to cancel the evil within him, as our sages said, "I have created the evil inclination; I have created the Torah as a spice"? It turns out that he is learning in order to obtain the spice, as our sages said, "The light in it reforms him."

Certainly, prior to learning Torah, a person should examine the reason for which he is learning Torah, for any act needs to have some purpose that causes him to do the act. It is as our sages said,

"A prayer without an aim is as a body without a soul." For this reason, before he comes to learn Torah he must prepare the intention.

41. RABASH, Article No. 12 (1988), "What Are Torah and Work in the Way of the Creator?"

A person who is born with the will to receive and wants to correct it into working in order to bestow, since this is against nature, he has only one counsel: Only the light of Torah can invert him into working in order to bestow, as it is written, "I have created the evil inclination; I have created the Torah as a spice," and the light in it reforms the heart. It is said that "evil" is receiving for one's self, and "good" is when his heart is only about bestowal and not about reception.

For this reason, those who engage in Torah not necessarily in order to know the rules and customs how to observe the *Mitzvot*, but have another, exalted role, that they are learning Torah in order to correct the heart, these are called "wise-hearted," since everything is named after its action. For this reason, the Torah they learn with this intention is called "wise-hearted" and not "wise-minded," since they need the Torah in order to correct the heart.

42. RABASH, Article No. 875, "Three Lines – 4"

Before one is rewarded with emerging from self-love and doing everything in order to bestow, called *Lishma*, although he learns all these matters as they are, they are only names without any clarification, meaning that he has no attainment in those things that he is learning, since he has no knowledge about the material of the upper roots, called "the holy names," or *Sefirot* and *Partzufim* [pl. of *Partzuf*].

We can learn the upper matters, called "the wisdom of Kabbalah," only by way of *Segula* [remedy/power], since they can bring a person desire and yearning to adhere to the Creator because of the *Kedusha* [holiness] of the matters that speak of the holy names. Conversely, in the revealed Torah, he must believe that the whole Torah is the names of the Creator. It follows that these matters are more capable (as explained in the essay, "The Giving of the Torah").

When a person learns the upper matters in order for it to bring him closer to *Kedusha*, it causes a nearing of the lights. This means that this learning will cause him to thereby be rewarded with aiming all his actions in order to bestow. This is called "work in the manner of preparation," where he prepares himself to be worthy of entering the King's palace and to adhere to Him.

43. RABASH, Article No. 10 (1987), "What Is the Substance of Slander and Against Whom Is It?"

The important thing is to be rewarded with *Dvekut* with the Creator, which is called "a vessel of bestowal," meaning equivalence of form. This is why the remedy of Torah and *Mitzvot* was given, so that through it we would be able to exit self-love and reach love of others.

44. RABASH, Article No. 10 (1987), "What Is the Substance of Slander and Against Whom Is It?"

The main work we must do, to achieve the purpose for which the world was created—to do good to His creations—is to qualify ourselves to acquire vessels of bestowal. This is the correction for making the King's gift complete, so they will feel no shame upon reception of the pleasures. And all the evil in us removes us from the good that we are destined to receive.

We were given the remedy of Torah and *Mitzvot* so as to achieve those *Kelim*. This is the meaning of what our sages said (*Kidushin* 30), "The Creator says, 'I have created the evil inclination; I have created for it the spice of Torah,' by which he will lose all the sparks of self-love within him and will be rewarded with his desire being only to bestow contentment upon his Maker."

45. *Zohar for All*, New Zohar, "Song of Songs," "The Wisdom that One Needs," Item 484

Anyone who walks into that world without knowing the secrets of the Torah will be sent out of all the gates of that world even if he has acquired many good deeds.

46. *Zohar for All*, "On the Night of the Bride," Item 125

Rabbi Shimon was sitting and studying the Torah on the night when the bride, *Malchut*, unites with her husband. On that night, after which—on the day of *Shavuot*—the bride is to be with her husband under the *Huppah* [wedding canopy], all the friends, who are the members of the bridal chamber, must be with her on that night and rejoice with her in the corrections that she is corrected, meaning to engage in Torah, from Torah to Prophets, from Prophets to Hagiographa, the interpretations of the texts, and the secrets of the wisdom, for these are her corrections and adornments.

The Bride and her maidens come and stand on their heads, and she is corrected in them and rejoices in them all through that night. On the next day, the day of *Shavuot*, she comes to the *Huppah* only with them. And these friends, who engage in the Torah all night long, are called "members of the *Huppah*." And when she comes to the *Huppah*, the Creator asks about them, blesses them, and crowns them with the crowns of the bride. Happy are they.

Explanation: There are two meanings to it, which coincide.

1) The days of the exile are called "night," since this is the time of the concealment of His face from the children of Israel. At that time, all the powers of separation of the servants of the Creator dominate, and yet, precisely at that time the bride bonds with her husband—through Torah and *Mitzvot* of the righteous, who at that time are regarded as those who hold the Torah. All the sublime degrees called, "secrets of the Torah," are revealed by them, since this is why they are called "those who make them," for they seemingly make the Torah. It follows that the days of the exile are called "night," in which the bride bonds with her husband, and all the friends, who are the members of the bridal chamber, are those who hold the Torah.

After the end of correction and the complete redemption, it is written, "For there shall be one day, which is known to the Lord, neither day nor night, when in the evening time there will be light." This is why it is written that on the next day, the bride is to be with her husband under the *Huppah*, for then *BON* will return to being *SAG*, *MA* will be *AB*, and *AB* is regarded as the next day and a new *Huppah*.

At that time, the righteous are called "members of the *Huppah*," who engage in Torah, in whom there is no action, for then it is said, "And the earth shall be full of the knowledge of the Lord." And since those righteous—through their good deeds—raise *BON* to being *SAG* by their extension of the fear from the past, they are regarded as making this new *Huppah*, and this is why they are called "members of the *Huppah*."

2) The night of *Shavuot* is called "the night in which the bride bonds with her husband." This is so because on the next day, she is destined to be with her husband under the *Huppah*, on the day of *Shavuot*, the day of the reception of the Torah. However, it is the same matter as the first explanation because on the day of the reception of the Torah it was already the end of correction, in the form of "He will swallow up death forever, and the Lord God will wipe away tears from all faces." It is as it is written in the verse, "*Harut* [carved] on the tablets"; do not pronounce it *Harut*, but *Herut* [freedom], since freedom from the angel of death has come.

47. Zohar for All, Lech Lecha [Go Forth], "Night and Midnight" Items 363-367

At midnight, when the roosters awaken, the north side awakens in *Ruach* [wind], meaning the left line in illumination of *Shuruk*, meaning illumination of *Hochma* with absence of *Hassadim*, *GAR de Ruach*. The scepter, the south side—right line, *Hassadim*—rises and mingles with that *Ruach* of the left line, and they mingle with one another. At that time, the *Dinim* of the left line rest and it is mitigated in *Hassadim*. Then the Creator awakens in His custom to play with the righteous in the Garden of Eden.

At that time, happy is a man who rises to play in the Torah, since the Creator and all the righteous in the Garden of Eden listen to his voice, as it is written, "You who dwells in the gardens, the friends are listening to your voice; let me hear it."

Moreover, the Creator draws upon him a thread of grace, to keep him in the world so that the upper ones and lower ones will guard him, as it is written, "By day the Lord will command His grace; and in the night, His song is with me."

Anyone who engages in Torah at that time will certainly have a permanent part in the next world. What is permanent? These *Mochin* extend from *YESHSUT*, whose *Zivug* is intermittent and not permanent. But each midnight, when the Creator awakens in the Garden of Eden, all those plantings—the *Sefirot* in the Garden of Eden, the *Nukva*—will be watered abundantly from that stream, which is called "a primordial stream," "a stream of delights," "upper *AVI*," whose waters never stop, meaning that the *Zivug* of *AVI* never stops. And one who rises and engages in the Torah, it is as though that stream pours down on his head and waters him inside the plantings in the Garden of Eden. Hence, he has a permanent share in the *Mochin* of the next world, too, meaning *YESHSUT*, since the *Mochin de AVI* contain the *Mochin de YESHSUT* within them, too.

Moreover, since all the righteous in the Garden of Eden listen to him, they put a share for him in that potion of the stream, which are the *Mochin* of upper *AVI*. It turns out that he has a perpetual part for the next world, which are included in *Mochin de AVI*.

48. *Zohar for All*, *Toldot* [Generations], "These Are the Generations of Isaac," Item 14

Bless the Lord all the servants of the Lord. Who are they who are worthy of blessing the Creator? All of the Creator's servants. Even though all the people in the world are from Israel, they are all worthy of blessing the Creator.

But blessings for which upper and lower are blessed, who are they who bless Him? It is the servants of the Creator. And who are they whose blessing is a blessing? It is them who stand in the house of God at night, those who rise at midnight and awaken to read in the Torah. They are the ones who stand in the house of God at night. And they need both: to be servants of the Creator, as well as to rise at midnight, for then the Creator comes to entertain with the righteous in the Garden of Eden.

49. *Zohar for All*, *New Zohar*, *VaYetze*, "Behold, a Ladder Was Placed on the Earth," Items 44-47

Rabbi Aba fell asleep and Rabbi Yosi was sitting. He saw that Rabbi Aba's face was growing red and he was laughing, and he saw a great light in the house.

Rabbi Yosi said, "This means that the *Shechina* [Divinity] is here." He lowered his eyes, sat there until the dawn rose in the morning and light shone in the house. When he raised his eyes, he saw the dawn and the darkness of the house.

Rabbi Aba woke up; his face was shining and his eyes laughing. Rabbi Yosi held him. Rabbi Aba said, "I know what you want. Indeed, I saw sublime secrets. When Matat, minister of the *Panim* [face] held my soul, he raised her to high and sublime chambers.

"And I saw the souls of the rest of the righteous go up to there, and the minister of the *Panim* told them, 'Happy are you, righteous, for thanks to you I am built in a holy building of the honorable name,'" for the lights of the holy name are extended to him, to answer, to bestow upon the hosts of the upper King.

And I saw the Torah that I had learned, that it was placed there pile over pile, like a big tower. And because of it, I was happy with my share and my eyes laughed.

50. *Zohar for All*, *BeShalach* [When Pharaoh Sent], "And the Lord Walks before Them by Day," Items 46-51

The Creator and all the righteous in the Garden of Eden, all listen to His voice. It is written, "You who sit in the gardens, friends listen to your voice; let me hear it." "You who sit in the gardens" is the assembly of Israel, *Malchut*. At night, she praises the Creator with the praise of the Torah. Happy is he who partakes with her in praising the Creator in the praise of the Torah.

When the morning comes, the assembly of Israel, *Malchut*, comes and plays with the Creator, and He gives her the scepter of *Hesed* [grace/mercy]. But not only to her, but to her and to all those who partake with her. One who engages in Torah at night, the Creator draws to him a thread of *Hesed* during the day. This is why *Malchut* is called "The morning star," for she praises the Creator at night with the praise of the Torah.

When the morning should rise, the light darkens and grows black, and the blackness is present. Then a woman clings to her Husband, which is the third watch, when a woman tells with her husband, meaning ZON, to tell with Him, and she comes to His palace.

Afterwards, when the sun should set, the night shines and comes and takes the sun. Then, all the gates close, donkeys bray, and dogs bark. When half the night is through, the King begins to rise and the queen, *Malchut*, begins to sing. The King, ZA, comes and knocks on the palace's gate and says, "Open for me, my sister, my wife." And then He plays with the souls of the righteous.

Happy is he who has awakened at that time with words of Torah. For this reason, all the children of the queen's palace must rise at that time and praise the King. All praise before Him and the praise rises from this world, which is far from Him, and this is more favorable to the Creator than anything.

When the night departs and the morning comes and dawns, the King and queen are in joy, in a coupling, and He gives her presents, as well as to all the dwellers of the palace. Happy is he who is numbered among the dwellers of the palace.

51. *Zohar for All, VaYikra* [The Lord Called], "Behold, Bless the Lord, All You Servants of the Lord," Items 200-203

"Bless the Lord, all you servants of the Lord." This is a praise for all those with faith. Who are those with faith? They are the ones who engage in Torah and know how to unite the Holy Name properly. And the praise of those with faith is that they stand at midnight to engage in Torah and adhere to the assembly of Israel, *Malchut*, to praise the Creator with words of Torah.

When one rises at midnight to engage in Torah, a Northern wind—meaning illumination of the left—awakens at midnight, which is the deer and *Malchut*, and stands and praises the Creator, ZA. And when she stands, several thousands and several tens of thousands stand with her in their existence, and they all begin to praise the holy King.

The Creator listens to he who was rewarded and rose at midnight to engage in Torah. It is written, "You who dwell in the gardens, friends listen to your voice; let me hear it." And all that multitude above and those who praise their Master in song keep silent for the praises of those who engage in Torah. They declare and say, "Bless the Lord, all servants of the Lord." In other words, you who engage in Torah, bless the Lord. You—praise the holy King; you—crown the King.

And the deer, *Malchut*, is crowned in that man. She rises before the King and says, "See in what son I have come to You, in what son I have awakened toward You." And who are those that all their merit is before the King? It is they who stand in the house of the Creator in the nights. They are the ones who are called "servants of the Creator"; they are the ones who are worthy of blessing the King and whose blessing is a blessing, as it is written, "Lift up your hands to the sanctuary, and bless the Lord." You, who merit the holy King being blessed by you, the blessing through you is a blessing.

52. *Zohar for All, VaYikra* [The Lord Called], "The Morning Doe," Items 367-372.

"For the Leader upon the morning doe ["deer" or "the morning star"], a psalm of David." The morning doe is the assembly of Israel, called "A lovely hind and a graceful doe." But is the doe of the dawn, meaning *Malchut*, not through the whole day? A doe is from that place which is called "A lovely hind and a graceful doe." She comes from a place called "dawn," as it is written, "Is sure as the morning," meaning *Hesed*. King David said that about the assembly of Israel, which means that what is written about the morning doe, *Malchut*, is when she clothes in *Hesed*.

When the night falls, the upper and lower doors shut, and all the outer ones awaken and roam throughout the world, turning people's bodies and surrounding their places and beds. They see the shape of the holy King who watches over them, and they are afraid to do harm because the people strengthen themselves in their beds with the words of the holy Name and they are kept. And the souls of people rise each as it should. Happy are the righteous, whose souls rise while they sleep and do not detain in a place where they needn't.

At half the night, a herald stands and declares and the doors are opened. At that time, a spirit of the north side awakens, meaning illumination of *Hochma* in the left line, and strikes the harp of David, meaning *Malchut*. It plays by itself and praises the King, ZA, and the Creator entertains Himself with the righteous in the garden.

Happy is he who awakens from his sleep at that time and engages in Torah. Also, anyone who rises at that time and exerts in Torah is called "a friend of the Creator and of the assembly of Israel." Moreover, they are called "His brothers and friends," as it is written, "For the sake of my brothers and friends I will say, 'Peace be within you.'" They are considered friends of the upper angels and upper camps, as it is written, "The friends listen to your voice."

When the day rises, a herald stands and declares, and the doors on the south side open. Then the stars and signs awaken and the doors of *Rachamim* [mercy] open, and the King sits and receives praises from the friends who rose at night. At that time, the assembly of Israel takes these words of praise and rises to the King, ZA, and all the friends who rose at night grip to the wings of *Malchut*. Their words of praise come and reside in the King's bosom, and then the King commands to write down all those words.

In the book, all the sons of His palace who rise at night are written down, and a thread of grace extends over them during the day, and from that thread of grace, the man is crowned with the crown of the King, which is *GAR*. Then upper and lower fear him, he enters all the King's gates and there is no one to protest against him. Even when the litigants are poised to sentence the world, they do not sentence him because he was registered in the King's list, and it is known that he is from the King's palace. For this reason, they do not pass judgment on him. Happy are the righteous who engage in Torah, especially when the Creator longs for words of Torah, at midnight.

53. *Zohar for All, VaYikra* [The Lord Called], "A Flame Under the Wings of the Rooster," Item 394

Torah that is studied at night is purer than Torah that is studied during the day, since the purity of the written Torah is in the oral Torah, in *Malchut*, which is called "night." The oral Torah, *Malchut*, governs at night and awakens more than at daytime, and when *Malchut* governs, she is the purity in the Torah.

54. *Zohar for All, VaYikra* [The Lord Called], "A Flame Under the Wings of the Rooster," Items 397-399

When the rooster calls and people sleep in their beds and do not awaken, the rooster calls, strikes his wings and says, "Woe unto so and so; he is cursed by his Master, he is abandoned by his Master," since his spirit has not awakened and he did not observe the King's honor.

At the rise of day, a herald declares about him and says, "But no one says, 'Where is God my Maker, who gives songs in the night,'" to help him with those praises so that all will be in one assistance. The *Malchut* sings to ZA at night, to help man so he, too, will awaken with these praises. And when one praises and engages in Torah, she raises MAN, he helps the *Malchut*, and they are both in one assistance.

What is "My Maker"? When a person rises at midnight, he engages in the song of the Torah, since the song of the Torah is read only at night, when he engages in the Torah. When the day rises, the Creator and the assembly of Israel correct him with a single thread of grace that was saved from all, to illuminate him among the upper ones and lower ones.

"Where is God my Maker." It should have said, "Makes for me"; why "My Maker"? When he rises at midnight to engage in Torah, when the day rises, Abraham awakens with his thread of grace and the Creator and the assembly of Israel correct him. They make him a new creation every day, as it is written, "God, my Maker."

55. *Zohar for All, Metzorah* [The Leper], "When the Night Grows Dark," Items 5-9

"As birds trapped in a snare, so the sons of men are ensnared." People do not know and do not hear and do not observe their Master's will. And the announcer calls before them daily, and there is no one to listen and no one to awaken one's spirit to the work of his Master.

When the night grows dark and the gates close, the *Nukva* of the great abyss awakens and several armies of damagers are in the world. At that time, the Creator puts all the people in the world to sleep. He puts to sleep even all those who have awakening of life, meaning the righteous. And the spirits roam the world and announce things to people in their dreams. Some of them are lies and some of them are true. And people become connected in their sleep.

And when the north wind awakens and the night divides, a flame bursts out and strikes under the wings of the rooster, and he calls. Then the Creator enters the Garden of Eden to play with the righteous, and an announcer comes out and calls, and all the people in the world awaken in their beds. And those with awakening of life rise up from their beds to the work of their Master, and engage in Torah and in praising the Creator until the morning comes.

When the morning comes, all the armies and camps above praise the Creator. Then, several gates open to all sides, and Abraham's gate, *Hesed* [mercy], opens in the assembly of Israel, *Malchut*, to summon all the people in the world to enjoy the *Hassadim* [mercies]. It is written, "And Abraham planted a tamarisk tree in Beersheba," since *Malchut* is called Beersheba, and Abraham planted the tree of *Hesed* in it.

And one who cannot awaken his spirit to serve his master, with what face will he rise before the King when judgment is evoked upon him, and he is caught and chained, meaning when he is imprisoned so as to be brought to judgment? He will not have the merit to be saved. It is written about that, "As birds trapped in a snare." As they, "So the sons of men are ensnared." And before a person leaves this world, the soul with the body are sentenced to several judgments before they part, and there is no one to watch over it.

56. *Zohar for All*, *Shmini* [On the Eighth Day], "Man Was Created in the Torah," Item 8

All those who engage in Torah cling to the Creator and are crowned in the decorations of Torah. They are loved above and below, and the Creator offers them His right hand, mercy. It is even more so with those who engage in Torah at night, as well, for they have established that they partake in Divinity and join together. And when the morning comes, the Creator decorates them with a single string of grace, so they will be among the higher and among the lower.

57. *Zohar for All*, *Aharei Mot* [After the Death], "The Poets, Heyman, Yedutun, and Asaf," Items 152-154

When the night comes, the angels outside the curtain awaken. They are drawn from the *Achoraim de Malchut* and from her externality. At that time everything quiets down and there is no opening of a door. The *Dinim* below, of *Malchut*, who is below all the *Sefirot*, awaken all of them until half the night. After midnight, when all the angels that extend from the middle line gather, an appointee is appointed over them and collects all the camps, as it is written, "Which was the rearward of all the camps and their hosts." His name is Asaf [*Me'asef* means "in the rear" or "gathering"], corresponding to the Asaf of above, introduced in Psalms. *Malchut* is called Asaf because the illuminations of all the *Sefirot* gather in her for she receives from everyone. And since that minister extends from *Malchut*, his name is called Asaf.

Until the morning comes. When the morning comes, the boy Matat, who suckles from his mother's breasts, *Malchut*, rises to purify the angels of the night and enter the sun. When the morning rises, it is a time of good will, when the queen is speaking with the king, ZA. The king stretches from Himself a thread of blessings, *Hassadim*, and spreads over the queen and those who bond with her, those who engage in Torah at night, when it is divided.

Happy is he who comes with the queen when she comes to welcome the king, ZA, to speak with him, and he is with her when the king sends forth his right hand, the light of *Hassadim*, to welcome the queen.

58. *Zohar for All*, *Aharei Mot* [After the Death], "The Poets, Heyman, Yedutun, and Asaf," Items 155-156

All those who engage in Torah when half the night is through unite with the *Shechina* [Divinity]. When the morning comes and the queen, the *Shechina*, bonds with the king, ZA, they are with the king and the king spreads his wings over all of them, as it is written, "By day the Lord will command grace [*Hesed*], and at night, His song is with me."

When the morning rises, the patriarchs, *HGT de ZA*, come with the queen and rush to speak with her and bond with her. And in them the Creator, *ZA*, speaks with her and calls her to spread His wings over her.

59. *Zohar for All, Kedoshim*, "Oh Land of Whirring Wings," Item 18

One who wants to be sanctified with the will of his Master will engage only from midnight onward or at midnight, since at that time, the Creator, *ZA*, is in the Garden of Eden, in *Malchut*, and upper *Kedusha* [holiness] awakens, and that is the time to be sanctified. This is so for the rest of the people. For wise disciples, who know the ways of Torah, midnight is their time to rise and engage in Torah, to connect to the assembly of Israel, *Malchut*, and praise the holy name, *Malchut*, and the holy King, *ZA*.

60. *Zohar for All, Emor*, "He Gives Prey to Those Who Fear Him," Item 31

Anyone who engages in Torah at night and rises at midnight, when the assembly of Israel, *Malchut*, awakens to correct the King's house, to extend illumination of *Hochma* [wisdom] for Him, as it is written, "The house will be built with wisdom," that man partakes with her. This is considered that he is from the King's house, and each day he is given from those corrections of the house.

61. *Zohar for All, Miketz* [At the End], "They Brought Him Hastily out of the Dungeon," Items 32-33

"The Lord favors those who fear Him." Oh how the Creator desires the righteous, since the righteous make peace above, in *AVI*, and make peace below, in *ZON*, and bring the bride to her husband. And for this reason, the Creator desires those who fear Him and do His will. Through the MAN that they raise to *ZON*, *ZON*, too, raise MAN to *AVI*, and a *Zivug* occurs above, in *AVI*, and below, in *ZON*. And they bring the bride, *Nukva*, to her husband, *ZA*, to mate. For this reason, the Creator, *ZA*, desires only them, for without them there would be no peace, which is a *Zivug*, neither above in *AVI* nor below in *ZON*.

"Them that await His mercy." "Them that await His mercy" are those who engage in Torah at night and partake with Divinity. And when the morning comes, they await His mercy.

When a person engages in Torah at night, a thread of mercy extends upon him during the day, as it is written, "By day the Lord will command His mercy, and in the night His song shall be with me."

62. *Zohar for All, Aharei Mot* [After the Death], "Nefesh and Ruach" [Soul and Spirit], Item 217

"Even my spirit within me seeks You," that I may cling to You with great love in the night. One should rise each night out of love of the Creator to engage in His work until the morning rises and draws upon him a thread of grace [*Hesed*]. Happy is one who loves the Creator with this love. Those true righteous who love the Creator so, the world exists because of them and they govern all the harsh decrees above and below.

63. *Zohar for All*, *VaYikra* [The Lord Called], "When the Morning Stars Sang Together," Items 379-380

"When the morning stars sang together, and all the sons of God shouted for joy." When the Creator comes to entertain with the righteous in the Garden of Eden, all things, meaning degrees in the lower world, *Malchut*, and all the upper ones and lower ones awaken toward Him. And all the trees, meaning degrees, in the Garden of Eden begin to praise before Him, as it is written, "Then shall all the trees of the wood sing for joy before the Lord, for He has come." And even the birds in the land all utter praise before Him.

At that time, a flame comes out and strikes the wings of the rooster, who calls and praises the holy King. He calls upon people to exert in Torah, in praising their Master, and in His work. Happy are those who rise from their bed to engage in Torah.

When the morning comes, the doors on the south, meaning *Hesed*, open and the gates of healing come out to the world. And Eastern wind, ZA, awakens and *Rachamim* are present. And all those stars and signs, meaning degrees, which are appointed under the governance of that morning, which is *Yesod* that shines *Hassadim*, they all begin to praise and to sing for the High King. It is written about that, "When the morning stars sang together, and all the sons of God shouted for joy."

But what do the sons of God, who are *Din*, want here, summoning a shout on this morning, which is the time of *Hesed*? After all, all the *Dinim* [judgments] are removed when the *Hesed* awakens in the world. However, "And all the sons of God shouted for joy" means that the authority of the harsh *Dinim* has been broken, their strength has been shattered, since "Shout" means that they broke, as it is written, "The earth is broken, broken down."

64. *Zohar for All*, *VaYigash* [And Judah Approached], "Sixty Breaths," Items 34-39

King David would sleep as a horse; he slept little. Thus, how did he rise at midnight? After all, this measure of sixty breaths of the horse's sleep is little and he would not rise even at a third of the night.

However, when the night came, he would sit with all the great ones of his house and he would sentence judgments and engage in words of Torah. This means that he did not go to sleep in the beginning of the night, but close to midnight. Afterwards, he would sleep his sleep until midnight, rise at midnight, awaken, and engage in the work of his Master, in song and in praise.

King David lives and exists forever and ever. King David kept himself all his life from tasting the taste of death, since sleep is one part of sixty of death. And David, because of his place, which is "alive," slept only sixty breaths, since he lived only through sixty breaths, minus one, and from there on, man tastes the taste of death and the side of the spirit of impurity governs him.

This is why King David kept himself from tasting the taste of death and from being governed by the side of the other spirit. This is because sixty breaths minus one means that the life above—up to sixty breaths—are sixty high breaths, and life depends on them. And from there down it is death.

This is why King David was measuring the night until midnight, so he would remain alive and the taste of death would not govern him. And when half the night was through, David would exist in his place, in his degree, living and existing, since he had woken up from his sleep and sang and praised. This is so because when he awoke at midnight and the holy *Keter*—the *Nukva*, awakened—it must not find David connected to another place, the place of death.

When half the night was through and the upper holiness awakened, if a person who sleeps in his bed does not rise from his sleep to observe the glory of his Master, by that he connects to death and clings to another place, to the *Sitra Achra*. This is why King David would always rise at midnight to observe the glory of his Master, living in a living, and he would not sleep in slumber to the point of tasting the taste of death. This is the reason why he would sleep as a horse, sixty breaths, but not in completeness, for they lacked one.

Sleeping means shutting of the eyes, meaning the *Mochin*. This is as one who is lying mindlessly with his eyes shut. Its root extends from the domination of the illumination of the left line, *Hochma*, when it is in dispute with the right line, *Hassadim*, where because the *Hochma* cannot shine without *Hassadim*, the *Mochin* are blocked out.

Awakening from sleep extends from the middle line, since the state of sleep continues until the ascent of the middle line with the *Masach de Hirik* in it. This is the point of *Man'ula* [lock], which diminishes the left line and includes it in the right, when the *Hochma* in the left is included in the *Hassadim* in the right. At that time, the *Mochin* open and the *Hochma* can shine.

65. *Zohar for All*, *VaYigash* [And Judah Approached], "Sixty Breaths," Item 39

But the *Nukva*, which is called "night," receives the construction of her *Sefirot* from ZA. For this reason, she, too, is divided at the point of *Chazeh*, like him. From the point of midnight, from the *Chazeh* and above—in the first six hours through the middle of the night—there is no force of *Din* and death there from the point of *Man'ula* at all. Rather, from the point of *Chazeh* down, in the second six hours, they, too, become life and holiness like the HGT above, if there is the correction of awakening in them.

However, if there is no correction of awakening in them—the sentencing in the middle line—and the dominion of the left without the right continues, meaning sleep, then the force of death in *Man'ula* at the point of *Chazeh* awakens and the NHY from the *Chazeh* down, the second six hours—after midnight—are dominated by death and the *Sitra Achra*.

66. *Zohar for All*, *VaYigash* [And Judah Approached], "Sixty Breaths," Items 46-47

Thus, these are sixty breaths indeed, the six hours preceding midnight, which are of life, both above in the upper worlds, from *Chazeh* of the *Nukva* and above, and below in this world. And past the point of midnight, there are sixty other breaths, HGT NHY from the *Chazeh* down, all of which are from the side of death, and the degree of death is upon them, meaning the point of *Man'ula* at the point of

Chazeh, which causes every death in the world. And those sixty breaths from the *Chazeh* and below are called "sleep," and they are all the taste of death.

This is the reason why King David clung to those sixty breaths of life on the six hours preceding midnight, from the *Chazeh* and above, since the force of *Din* and death at the point of *Chazeh* cannot reach them. And from then on he would not sleep at all, as it is written, "I will not give sleep to my eyes."

67. *Zohar for All, VaYigash* [And Judah Approached], "Sixty Breaths," Items 48-52

"O Lord, the God of my salvation, I have cried out by day and in the night before You." At midnight, King David would rise and engage in Torah, in songs and praises for the joy of the King and the mistress. This is the joy of faith in the land, since this is the merit of faith, Divinity, which is seen in the land.

This is so because above, several high angels begin with joy and singing in several ways, praising at night on all the sides, even in illumination of the left side. This is so because at that time it is the dominion of the *Nukva*, as it is written, "She rises while it is still night." It is similar below, on earth. He who praises the Creator in the night on earth, the Creator desires him, and all the holy angels that praise the Creator listen to the one who praises the Creator on earth at night, since this singing is in perfection, to enhance the glory of the Creator from below and to sing of the joy of unification.

King David wrote, "O Lord, the God of my salvation." When is the Lord the God of my salvation? He is my salvation on that day when I first sing for You in the night, for then He is my salvation in the day.

This is so because he who praises his Master in the song of Torah at night grows stronger in *Gevura* during the day, on the right side, *Hesed*. The *Hochma* that he received in the night from the left side dresses in *Hesed* from the right side during the day because a thread of grace comes out from the right side, and then it extends on him and he is strengthened in it. This is why David said, "O Lord, the God of my salvation, I have cried out by day."

And this is also why he said, "It is not the dead who praise the Lord." "It is not the dead" because the living should bless the living, and not the dead toward the living, as it is written, "It is not the dead who praise the Lord." Rather, we bless the Creator because we are alive and we have no part whatsoever in the side of death. King David is alive and close to the One who lives forever. And one who is close to Him, to the One who lives forever, is alive, as it is written, "But you that adhere unto the Lord your God are alive everyone of you this day." And it is also written, "And Benaiah the son of Jehoiada, the son of a valiant man of Kabzeel."

68. Rav Kook, *Lights of Torah*, Chapter 10, Item 10

One of the wonders of learning the secrets of Torah is that when a person learns these sublime matters out of love and internal feeling, although he cannot grasp the matters clearly with his intellect, they still elevate his entire being. If this is so, the matters shine their light upon him.

69. Ramchal, *Adir BaMarom*

Rashbi [Rabbi Shimon bar Yochai] composed *The Book of Zohar* according to the illumination that came to him when he was corrected in the cave. It is a great and terrible composition that reveals the depth of the secrets in great clarity about the Torah itself. This is "revealing the Torah in its interior."

70. RAMAK, Know the God of Your Father, 2

This book will be called *The Book of Zohar* because of the influence of that light from the upper radiance. Through its light, all who engage in it are influenced by Godly Providence, since upper light and abundance from *Daat* is poured in the secrets of the Torah. Since it flowed from there, that composition was called *The Book of Zohar* [*Book of Radiance*], meaning it streamed that radiance.

71. RAMAK, *Ohr Yakar*, Gate 1, Mark 5.

When we engage in this composition, we awaken the power of the souls with the power of Moses, since when they engage in it, they renew and renewed light that was innovated at the time of composing it. The *Shechina* [Divinity] shines and illuminates from that light as when it was first engendered, and all who engage in it reawaken that benefit and first light that Rabbi Shimon bar Yochai and his friends revealed while composing it.

72. Raaiah Kook, *Orot* [*Lights*]

Now the time obligates to increase possession of the inner Torah. *The Book of Zohar*, which breaks new paths, sets a trail in the desert, a track in the wilderness, it and all its crops, is ready to open the gates of redemption.

73. The HIDA, *The Name of the Greats*

Learning *The Zohar* is a great correction to illuminate the soul and sanctify it.

74. Rabbi Tzvi Hirsh of Ziditshov, *Ateret Tzvi*

One who has not seen the Light of *The Book of Zohar* has never seen light in his life.

75. Rabbi Tzvi Hirsh Eichenstein of Ziditshov, *Depart from Evil and Do Good*

Hear me, my brothers and friends, who are craving and seeking the truth, the truth of the work of the heart—to behold the pleasantness of the Lord and to visit His hall. My soul shall bow and cling unto *The Book of Zohar*, as the power of engaging in the holy book is known from our ancient sages.

76. Rabbi Moshe Chaim Ephraim of Sudilkov, *Degel Mahaneh Ephraim*, Assortments

The words of *The Zohar* are capable for the soul. Even though he does not understand what he is saying whatsoever, it is akin to one who enters a perfumery. Even if he takes nothing, he still absorbs the fragrance.

77. Rav Yitzhak Yehuda Yehiel Safrin of Komarno, *Notzer Hesed*, Chapter 4, Teaching 20

Each and every letter in *The Book of Zohar* and the writings of our great teacher by Rav Chaim Vital … are great corrections for the soul, to correct all the incarnations.

78. Rabbis of Jerusalem

The merit of learning *The Zohar* is known, that it revokes all kinds of calamities and harsh and bad decrees.

79. RAMAK, *Know the God of Your Father*

We would never have the power to undress the Torah from its clothes were it not for Rabbi Shimon bar Yochai and his friends.

80. "Introduction to The Zohar," Livorno Press, 1892

The virtue of the study of *The Book of Zohar* is already known, as the ARI said, "A single day of studying *The Book of Zohar* and the secrets of Torah equals an entire year of studying the literal.

81. Rav Raaiah Kook, *Love of Israel in Sanctity*, 232

There is no measurement or value to the virtue of one who contemplate the words of the living God, *The Book of Zohar*, all that accompany it, the words of true sages, and especially the clear writings of the Ari … By constant engagement, the gates of light and the openings of wisdom will be revealed to all who walk on the path of the Creator wholeheartedly, whose soul yearns to approach the hall of the honorable King. Hence, all who volunteer to engage in the wisdom even an hour or two each day, and with a good thought, are blessed. The Creator adds it to an act, and it will be regarded as though he is standing all day long forever in the court of the Creator and His dwelling place is in the secrets of the Torah.

82. Rabbi Yitzhak Maltzan, "A Commentary on the Vilna Gaon Prayer Book"

It was testified in the name of the GRA (Vilna Gaon) that he said, "The order of the study is from below upward, and the attainment will guide him from above downward, for when one fully understands the secret, he will also understand the literal, and as long as he does not understand the secret, the literal will also not be clear." It therefore follows that by meriting being among those who know His name, which is the internality of the Torah, by this we will also fully understand the literal meaning.

83. Rabbi Chaim of Voluzhin, *Nefesh HaChaim*

The reason that our sages wrote that learning *The Zohar* is awesome and very sublime although he does not know what he is saying (reading) is that in the whole of the Torah there is PARDES, and in every study, the secret is not apparent whatsoever. On the contrary, the mind of one who reads and learns is only on the literal, without understanding if there is even a secret in the Torah at all. Conversely, in *The Book of Zohar*, the secrets are revealed and the learner knows that it speaks wonders and secrets of the Torah, and he does not know. This is very helpful for correcting the soul.

84. Rabbi Eliyahu Di Vidash, *Resheet Hochma*

Learning according to the literal is called "slave," and according to the secret, it is called "son." When one knows one's Master only according to the literal, he is usually called a "slave." When he is a son, who knows the secrets of Torah in *Atzilut*, like a son searching through his father's treasures, he is called a "son."

85. The HIDA, *The Name of the Greats*

Precisely the study of *The Zohar* has more *Segula* [power/merit] than learning the Bible, the Mishnah, and the Talmud. This is surprising for in what is its power greater than all of the Torah? Whether for the Bible or for the Mishnah, meaning that the Bible, the Mishnah, and the Talmud are very clothed and the secret is not at all apparent in them. Not so is *The Zohar*, which speaks of the secrets of the Torah explicitly, and there is not a fool who will read and not understand that its words are in the depth of the secrets of the Torah. Hence, since the secrets of Torah are revealed without clothing, they brighten and illuminate the soul.

86. RAMAK, *Know the God of Your Father*

There is no part of the Torah that causes such unification as the secrets of the Torah.

87. Simcha Bonim of Pshischa, A *Torah of Joy*, p 57

Previously, the evil inclination was not so strong, and the revealed Torah was sufficient as a spice against it. But now, before the redemption, the evil inclination is intensifying and requires strengthening through the hidden, too.

88. RAMAK, *Know the God of Your Father*

The merit of this composition is such that one who engages willingly, the love of the Creator will draw him like a magnet pulls the iron. It will permeate him to save his *Nefesh* [soul], *Ruach* [spirit], and *Neshama* [soul], and his correction.

89. The Holy Shlah, *In Ten Utterances*

The wisdom of Kabbalah makes the fool wise, and one who has not seen the light of this wisdom has never seen lights in his life, for then he will understand and learn the meaning of His uniqueness and the meaning of His governance ... and all who retire from it, retire from the spiritual, eternal life.

90. Rabbi Chaim of Voluzhin, *Nefesh HaChaim*

One who engages in Torah, even if he initially becomes soiled with enormous iniquities and sins, and terribly submerged in mire and sludge, the abyss of evil, nevertheless, by engaging in Torah he can be certain that the light in it will surely reform him, the good will overcome the evil in him bit by bit, until finally, the good will prevail and spread through all of him completely.

91. Rav Yitzchak Safrin of Komarno, *The Path of Unification*

When you aim, with submission and fear, to awaken the surrounding lights and the *Mochin* above, although you do not know any essence or the surrounding lights or the *Mochin* of anything, still, by your knowledge, you awaken their existence. And although you do not know their essence, a great light is drawn over to you.

2

Preparation for the Study

1. Baal HaSulam, "Introduction to The Study of the Ten Sefirot, Item 17

Hence, the student pledges, prior to the study, to strengthen himself in faith in the Creator and in His guidance in reward and punishment, as our sages said, "Your employer is liable to pay you the reward for your work." One should aim one's labor to be for the *Mitzvot* of the Torah, and in this way, he will be rewarded with enjoying the light in it, and his faith will strengthen and grow through the power in this light, as it is written, "It shall be health to your navel, and marrow to your bones" (Proverbs 3:8).

2. RABASH, Article No. 12 (1988), "What Are Torah and Work in the Way of the Creator?"

A person should examine with which purpose does he want to observe the *Mitzva* [commandment] of learning Torah? That is, does he engage in Torah because of the Torah itself, in order to know how to observe the rules of doing the *Mitzvot*, or is the learning of Torah itself his whole intention, and knowing the rules of doing the *Mitzvot* is a completely different matter for him? meaning he is learning Torah for two reasons.

However, even while learning Torah for the sake of learning Torah, he should still distinguish with which intention he is learning. Is it to observe the commandments of the Creator, as it is written, "And you shall reflect on Him day and night," or is he learning in order to receive the light of Torah because he needs the light of Torah in order to cancel the evil within him, as our sages said, "I have created the evil inclination; I have created the Torah as a spice"? It turns out that he is learning in order to obtain the spice, as our sages said, "The light in it reforms him."

Certainly, prior to learning Torah, a person should examine the reason for which he is learning Torah, for any act needs to have some purpose that causes him to do the act. It is as our sages said, "A prayer without an aim is as a body without a soul." For this reason, before he comes to learn Torah he must prepare the intention.

3. RABASH, Article No. 29 (1986), "Lishma and Lo Lishma"

One must try to remember the goal while studying Torah, so it will always be before his eyes what he wants to receive from the study, that the study will impart greatness and importance of the Creator.

Also, while observing the *Mitzvot*, not to forget the intention that thanks to observing the *Mitzvot*, the Creator will lift the concealment on spirituality from him and he will receive a feeling of the greatness of the Creator.

However, it is hard work observing Torah and *Mitzvot* with the intention to thereby be rewarded with approaching the Creator—to obtain the greatness of the Creator so he can bring Him contentment because of the importance of the Creator, that this will be his reward and he has no desire for any other reward for his work.

4. RABASH, Article No. 12 (1988), "What Are Torah and Work in the Way of the Creator?"

A person must make a great effort before he comes to learn so that his learning will bear fruit and good results, meaning so the learning will bring him the light of Torah, by which it will be possible to reform him. Then, through the Torah, he becomes a wise disciple.

What is a "wise disciple"? Baal HaSulam said that it is a student who learns from the wise. That is, the Creator is called "wise," and a person who learns from Him is called a "disciple of the wise."

5. RABASH, Article No. 875, "Three Lines – 4"

Before one is rewarded with emerging from self-love and doing everything in order to bestow, called *Lishma*, although he learns all these matters as they are, they are only names without any clarification, meaning that he has no attainment in those things that he is learning, since he has no knowledge about the material of the upper roots, called "the holy names," or *Sefirot* and *Partzufim* [pl. of *Partzuf*].

We can learn the upper matters, called "the wisdom of Kabbalah," only by way of *Segula* [remedy/power], since they can bring a person desire and yearning to adhere to the Creator because of the *Kedusha* [holiness] of the matters that speak of the holy names. Conversely, in the revealed Torah, he must believe that the whole Torah is the names of the Creator. It follows that these matters are more capable (as explained in the essay, "The Giving of the Torah").

When a person learns the upper matters in order for it to bring him closer to *Kedusha*, it causes a nearing of the lights. This means that this learning will cause him to thereby be rewarded with aiming all his actions in order to bestow. This is called "work in the manner of preparation," where he prepares himself to be worthy of entering the King's palace and to adhere to Him.

6. Ramchal, *Derech HaShem*

One who purifies and sanctifies himself by his actions will draw through his learning bestowal to the extent of the preparation that he had prepared himself. And the more he prepares, the more precious and powerful becomes the study.

7. *Pri Tzadik*, *VaYeshev*, Item 3

The first *Hassidim* [adherents of the *Hassidut* movement] would spend one hour in prayer so as to aim their hearts to their Father in heaven. The word "aim" means the directness of the heart; it is to direct the heart so it is not scattered into the passions and lusts of worldly matters, but only to aim directly to his Father in heaven.

8. Rav Chaim Vital, *Pri Etz Chaim*, Gate "Conducts of Learning," Chapter 1

My teacher would say that the heart of the intention of reading in the Torah depends on aiming to connect one's heart to its root through the Torah in order to complete the upper tree and complete the upper *Adam* [man] and correct him, for this is the whole purpose of man's creation and the purpose of his engagement in the Torah.

3

A Path of Torah and a Path of Suffering

1. Baal HaSulam, "The Essence of Religion and Its Purpose"

Bear in mind that two forces serve to push us up the rungs of the aforementioned ladder, until we reach its head in the sky, which is the purposeful point of equivalence of form with our Maker. The difference between these two forces is that the first pushes us involuntarily, meaning not of our own choice. This force pushes us from behind, and it is called "from behind." We defined it as "the path of pain" or "the way of the earth."

From that path stems the philosophy of morality called "ethics," which is based on empirical knowledge, through examination of the practical reason. The essence of that teaching is but a summary of the evident damages that result from the nucleons of egoism.

These experiences come to us by chance, not as a result of our conscious choice, but they are certain to lead us to their goal, for the image of evil grows ever clearer to our senses. And to the extent that we recognize its damages, to that extent we remove ourselves from it and climb to a higher rung on the ladder.

The second force pushes us voluntarily, meaning of our own choice. That force pulls us from before and is called "from before." This is what we defined as "the path of Torah and *Mitzvot*," for engaging in *Mitzvot* and the work to bring contentment to our Maker rapidly develops in us that sense of recognition of evil, as we have shown in "Matan Torah," Item 13.

Here we benefit twice:

1) We do not have to wait for life's ordeals to push us from behind, whose measure of goading is measured only by the amount of agony and destruction inflicted upon us by finding the evil within us. Rather, as we work for the Creator, that recognition develops in us without any prior suffering or ruin. On the contrary, through the subtle pleasantness we feel when working solely for Him, to bring Him contentment, there develops within us a relative recognition of the lowliness of these sparks of self-love—that they are obstacles on our way to receiving that subtle taste of bestowal upon the Creator. Thus, the gradual sense of recognition of evil evolves in us through times of delight and great tranquility, through reception of the good while serving the Creator out of our sensation of the pleasantness and gentleness that reach us due to the equivalence of form with our Maker.

2) We save time, for He operates according to "our own volition," thus enabling us to increase our work and hasten time as we please.

2. Baal HaSulam, "Introduction to the Book Panim Meirot uMasbirot," Item 6

You can understand their words about the verse, "I, the Lord, will hasten it in its time." The Sanhedrin (98) interpreted, "Not rewarded—in its time; rewarded—I will hasten it."

Thus, there are two ways to attain the above-mentioned goal: through their own attention, which is called a "path of repentance." If they are rewarded with it, "I will hasten it" will be applied to them. This means that there is no set time for it, but when they are rewarded, the correction ends, of course.

If they are not awarded the attention, there is another way, called "path of suffering," as our sages said, Sanhedrin 97, "I place upon them a king such as Haman, and they will repent against their will," meaning in its time, for in that there is a set time, and they will want it.

By this, they wanted to show us that His ways are not our ways. For this reason, the case of the flesh-and-blood king who had troubled so to prepare those great things for his beloved son and was finally tormented in every way, and all his trouble was in vain, bringing contempt and wrath, will not happen to Him.

Instead, all the works of the Creator are guaranteed and true, and there is no fraud in Him. This is as our sages said, "Not rewarded—in its time." What the will does not do, time will do, as it is written in Panim Masbirot, end of Branch 1, "Can you send forth lightning that they may go and say to you, 'Here we are'?"

There is a path of pain that can cleanse any defect and materialism until one realizes how to raise one's head out of the beastly trough in order to soar and climb the rungs of the ladder of happiness and human success, for one will cleave to one's root and complete the aim.

3. Baal HaSulam, "Peace in the World"

The end is certain to come to Israel by the above-mentioned law of gradual development, and it is called "in its time," meaning tied to the chains of time. And Israel's guaranteed end, by taking the development of their qualities under their own authority is called "I will hasten it," meaning completely independent of time.

4. Baal HaSulam, *Shamati*, Article No. 50, "Two States"

There are two forces that contradict one another, an upper force and a lower force. The upper force is, as it is written, "Every one who is called by My Name, I have created him for My glory." This means that the whole world was created only for the glory of the Creator. The lower force is the will to receive, which claims that everything was created for it—both corporeal things and spiritual things—all is for self-love.

The will to receive claims that it deserves this world and the next world. Of course, the Creator is the winner, but this is called "the path of suffering," and it is called "a long way." But there is a short way called "the path of Torah," and this should be everyone's intention—to shorten time.

This is called "I will hasten it." Otherwise, it will be "in its time," as our sages said, "rewarded—I will hasten it; not rewarded—in its time," "when I place upon them a king such as Haman, and he will force you to reform."

5. Baal HaSulam, *Shamati*, Article No. 195, "Rewarded – I will Hasten It"

"Rewarded—I will hasten it," meaning the path of Torah; "not rewarded—through suffering," an evolutionary path that will finally lead everything to utter perfection. The path of Torah means that an ordinary person is given virtues by which he can make for himself *Kelim* [vessels] that are ready for it. And the *Kelim* are made through the expansion of the light and its departure.

A *Kli* [vessel] is specifically called "the will to receive." This means that he lacks something, and "there is no light without a *Kli*," for the light must be caught in some *Kli*, so it would have a hold.

But an ordinary person cannot have desires for sublime things, since it is impossible to have a need before there is fulfillment, as it is written, "the expansion of the light, etc." For example, when a person has a thousand pounds, he is rich and content. However, if he subsequently earns more, up to five thousand pounds, and then loses until he is left with two thousand, he is then deficient. Now he has *Kelim* [vessels] for three thousand pounds, since he had already had it. Thus, he has actually been canceled.

And there is a path of Torah for this. When one is accustomed to the path of Torah, to regret the scantiness of attainment, and every time he has some illuminations, and they are divided, they cause him to have more sorrow and more *Kelim*.

This is the meaning of every *Kli* needing light, that it is not filled, that its light is missing. Thus, every deficient place becomes a place for faith. Yet, were it filled, there would be no existence of a *Kli*, existence of a place for faith.

6. Baal HaSulam, "The Writings of the Last Generation"

There are two ways to discover the completeness: the path of Torah or the path of suffering.

Hence, the Creator has given humanity technology, until they have invented the atom and the hydrogen bombs. If the total ruin that they are destined to bring upon the world is still not evident to the world, they can wait for a third world war, or a fourth one. The bombs will do their thing, and the relics who remain after the ruin will have no other choice but to take upon themselves this work where both individuals and nations will not work for themselves more than is necessary for their sustenance, while everything else they do will be for the good of others. If all the nations of the world agree to it, there will no longer be wars in the world, for no person will be concerned with his own good whatsoever, but only with the good of others.

This law of equivalence of form is the law of the Messiah. It was said about this, "But in the end of days, it shall come to pass, etc., and many nations shall go and say, 'Come, and let us go up, etc., for out of Zion shall go forth the law, etc., and He shall judge between many nations.'" That is, the Messiah will teach them the work of the Creator in equivalence of form, which is the teaching and the law of the Messiah. "And shall prove to mighty nations," meaning He will prove to them that if they do not take upon themselves the work of the Creator, all the nations will be destroyed by wars. But if they do accept His law, it is said about it, "And they shall beat their swords into shovels."

If you take the path of Torah and receive the spice, very well. And if you do not, you will tread the path of suffering, meaning that wars will break out with atom and hydrogen bombs, and all the nations of the world will seek advice how to escape the wars. Then they shall come to the Messiah, to Jerusalem, and He will teach them this law.

7. Baal HaSulam, "The Freedom"

Man's imagination uses the mind just as the microscope serves the eyes: Without the microscope, we would not see anything harmful, due to its smallness. But once we see the harmful being through the microscope, we distance ourselves from the noxious element.

Thus, it is the microscope that brings man to distance himself from the harm, and not the sense, for the sense did not detect the harm-doer. And to that extent, the mind fully controls man's body, to push it away from bad and pull it toward the good. Thus, in all the places where the attribute of the body fails to recognize the beneficial or the detrimental, it needs only the mind's knowledge.

Furthermore, since man knows his mind, which is a true conclusion from life's experiences, he can therefore receive knowledge and understanding from a trusted person and take it as law, although his life's events have not yet revealed these concepts to him. It is like a person who asks the advice of a doctor and obeys him even though he understands nothing with his own mind. Thus, one uses the mind of others no less than one uses one's own.

As we have clarified above, there are two ways for Providence to make certain that man achieves the good, final goal: The path of suffering and the path of Torah. All the clarity in the path of Torah stems from this. For these clear conceptions that were revealed and recognized after a long chain of events in the lives of the prophets and the men of God, there comes a man who fully utilizes them and benefits from them, as though these concepts were events of his own life. Thus, you see that one is exempted from all the ordeals one must experience before he can develop that clear mind by himself. Thus, one saves both time and pain.

8. Baal HaSulam, "The Peace"

Nature, like a skillful judge, punishes us according to our development. For we can see that to the extent that humankind develops, the pains and torments obtaining our sustenance and existence also multiply.

Thus you have a scientific, empirical basis that His Providence has commanded us to observe with all our might the *Mitzva* of bestowal upon others in utter precision, in such a way that no member from among us would work any less than the measure required to secure the happiness of society and its success. As long as we are idle performing it to the fullest, nature will not stop punishing us and take its revenge.

And besides the blows we suffer today, we must also consider the drawn sword for the future. The right conclusion must be drawn—that nature will ultimately defeat us and we will all be compelled to join hands in following its *Mitzvot* with all the measure required of us.

9. Baal HaSulam, "Peace in the World"

There are two authorities here acting in the above-mentioned conduct of development: One is the authority of heaven, which is sure to turn anything harmful and evil to good and useful, but it will come in its time, in its own way, heavily, and after a long time. Then there is the authority of the earth. When the "evolving object" is a living, feeling being, it suffers horrendous torments and pains while under the "press of development" which carves its way ruthlessly.

The "authority of the earth," however, consists of people who have taken this above-mentioned law of development under their own government and can free themselves entirely from the chains of time, and who greatly accelerate time, namely the completion of the ripeness and correction of the object, which is the end of its development.

10. Baal HaSulam, "The Freedom"

It can be compared to a sick man who does not wish to obey the doctor's orders before he understands by himself how that advice would cure him, and therefore begins to study medicine by himself. He could die of his illness before he learns medicine.

So is the path of suffering compared to the path of Torah. One who does not believe the concepts that the Torah and prophecy advise him to accept without self-understanding must come to these concepts by himself by following the chain of cause and effect from life's events. These are experiences that greatly rush and can develop the sense of recognition of evil in them, as we have seen, without one's choice, but because of one's efforts to acquire a good environment, which leads to these thoughts and actions.

4

The Language of Kabbalah Is a Language of Branches

1. Baal HaSulam, "The Essence of the Wisdom of Kabbalah"

Each lower world is an imprint of the world above it. Hence, all the forms in the higher world are meticulously copied, in both quantity and quality, to the lower world.

Thus, there is not an element of reality or an occurrence of reality in a lower world that you will not find its likeness in the world above it, as identical as two drops in a pond. And they are called "root and branch." That means that the item in the lower world is deemed a branch of its pattern found in the higher world, which is the root of the lower element, as this is where that item in the lower world has been imprinted and made to be.

That was the intention of our sages when they said, "You have not a blade of grass below that has not a fortune and a guard above that strike it and tell it, 'Grow'!"

2. Baal HaSulam, "The Essence of the Wisdom of Kabbalah"

All the words and utterances our lips pronounce cannot help us clarify even a single word from the spiritual, Godly matters above the imaginary time and space. Instead, there is a special language for these matters, the language of the branches, according to their relation to their upper roots.

However, this language, though very suitable for its task of delving into the studies of this wisdom, more than other languages, is only so if the listener is wise in his own right, meaning that he knows and understands the way the branches relate to their roots.

3. Baal HaSulam, "Introduction to The Study of the Ten Sefirot," Item 156

There is a strict condition during the engagement in this wisdom not to materialize the matters with imaginary and corporeal issues. This is because thus they breach, "You shall not make unto you a statue or any image."

In that event, one is rather harmed instead of receiving benefit.

4. Baal HaSulam, "The Freedom"

The *Mitzvot* [commandments] in the Torah are but laws and conducts set in higher worlds, which are the roots of all of nature's conducts in this world of ours. Hence, the laws of the Torah always match the laws of nature in this world as two drops of water.

5. Baal HaSulam, "The Teaching of the Kabbalah and Its Essence"

The language of the Kabbalists is a language in the full sense of the word: very precise, both in terms of root and branch and concerning cause and consequence. It has the unique merit of being able to express subtle details in this language without any limits. Also, through it, it is possible to approach the desired matter directly, without the need to connect it with what precedes it or follows it.

6. Baal HaSulam, "The Teaching of the Kabbalah and Its Essence"

Four languages are used in the wisdom of truth:

1. The language of the Bible, its names, and appellations.
2. The language of laws. This language is very close to the language of the Bible.
3. The language of legends, which is very far from the Bible, since it has no consideration of reality. Strange names and appellations are attributed to this language, and it also does not relate to concepts by way of root and its branch.
4. The language of *Sefirot* and *Partzufim*. In general, sages had a strong tendency to conceal it from the ignorant, since they believed that wisdom and ethics go hand in hand. Hence, the first sages hid the wisdom in writing, using lines, dots, tops, and bottoms. This is how the [Hebrew] alphabet was formed with the twenty-two letters before us.

7. Baal HaSulam, *The Study of the Ten Sefirot*, "Inner Light," Part One, Chapter One, Item 1

It is difficult for novice, for they perceive matters by means of corporeal boundaries of time, space, change and exchange. However, the authors only used those as signs to point to their Upper Roots.

8. Baal HaSulam, "The Essence of the Wisdom of Kabbalah"

Kabbalah uses only names and appellations that are concrete and real. It is an unbending law for all Kabbalists that "Anything we do not attain, we do not define by a name and a word."

Here you must know that the word "attainment" [Heb: *Hasagah*] means the ultimate degree of understanding. It derives from the phrase, *Ki Tasig Yadcha* ["Your hand shall attain"]. That means that before something becomes utterly lucid, as though gripped in one's hand, Kabbalists do not consider it attained, but by other names such as understanding, comprehension, and so on.

9. Baal HaSulam, "The Essence of the Wisdom of Kabbalah"

Kabbalists have found a set and annotated vocabulary sufficient to create an excellent spoken language. It enables them to converse with one another of the dealings in the spiritual roots in the upper worlds by merely mentioning the lower, tangible branch in this world, which is well defined to our corporeal senses.

The listeners understand the upper root to which this corporeal branch points because it is related to it, being its imprint. Thus, all the beings of the tangible creation and all their instances have become to them like well-defined words and names, indicating the high spiritual roots. Although there cannot be a verbal expression in their spiritual place, as it is above any imagination, they have earned the right to be expressed by utterance through their branches, arranged before our senses here in the tangible world.

This is the nature of the spoken language among Kabbalists by which they convey their spiritual attainments from person to person and from generation to generation by word of mouth and in writing. They fully understand one another, with all the required accuracy needed for negotiating in a research of wisdom, with precise definitions one cannot fail in. This is so because each branch has its own natural, unique definition, and this absolute definition indicates its root in the higher world.

10. Baal HaSulam, "The Teaching of the Kabbalah and Its Essence"

Each of the manifold still, vegetative, animate, and speaking in this world has its corresponding part in the world above it, without any difference in its form but only in its substance. Thus, an animal or a rock in this world is a corporeal matter, and its corresponding animal or rock in the higher world is a spiritual matter, occupying no space or time. However, their quality is completely the same.

And here we should certainly add the matter of relation between matter and form, which is naturally conditioned on the quality of form, too. Similarly, with the majority of the still, vegetative, animate, and speaking in the upper world, you will find their similitude and likeness in the world above the upper. This continues through the first world where all the elements are completed, as it is written, "And God saw everything that He had made, and behold, it was very good."

11. Baal HaSulam, "The Freedom"

The wisdom of Kabbalah mentions nothing of our corporeal world.

12. Baal HaSulam, "The Essence of the Wisdom of Kabbalah"

It follows that the root, called "fortune," compels it to grow and assume its attribute in quantity and quality, as with the seal and its imprint. This is the law of root and branch that applies to every detail and occurrence in reality, in every single world, in relation to the world above it.

13. Baal HaSulam, "The Essence of the Wisdom of Kabbalah"

The substance of the elements of reality in the first, uppermost world, is finer than in all the ones below it. And the substance of the elements of reality in the second world is thicker than in the first world, but finer than all that is of a lower degree.

This continues similarly down to this world before us, whose substance of the elements of its reality is coarser and darker than in all the worlds preceding it. However, the shapes and elements of reality and all their occurrences come unchanged and equal in every world, both in quantity and quality.

They compared it to the conduct of a seal and its imprint: All the shapes in the seal are perfectly transferred in every detail and intricacy to its imprinted object.

14. Baal HaSulam, "The Essence of the Wisdom of Kabbalah"

There is nothing in the reality of the lower world that does not stem from its superior world. As with the seal and the imprint, the root in the upper world compels its branch in the lower one to reveal its entire form and attribute, as our sages said, that the fortune in the world above, related to the grass in the world below, strikes that grass and forces it to complete its growth. Because of this, each and every branch in this world well defines its mold situated in the higher world.

15. Baal HaSulam, "The Teaching of the Kabbalah and Its Essence"

The internality of the wisdom of Kabbalah is no different from the internality of the Bible, the Talmud, and the legends. The only difference between them is in their explanations.

This is similar to a wisdom that has been translated into four languages. Naturally, the essence of the wisdom has not changed at all by the change of language. All we need to think of is which translation is the most convenient for conveying the wisdom to the reader.

16. Baal HaSulam, "The Teaching of the Kabbalah and Its Essence"

The names, appellations, and *Gematrias* belong entirely to the wisdom of Kabbalah. The reason they are found in the rest of the languages, too, is that all the languages are included in the wisdom of Kabbalah, since they are all particular cases that the other languages must be assisted with.

But one should not think that these four languages, which serve to explain the wisdom of the revelation of Godliness, evolved one at a time, over time. The truth is that all four appeared before the sages of truth simultaneously.

In truth, each consists of all the others. The language of Kabbalah exists in the Bible, such as the standing on the *Tzur* [rock], the thirteen attributes of mercy in the Torah and in *Micah*. To an extent, it is sensed in each and every verse. There are also the *Merkavot* [chariots/structures] in Isaiah and Ezekiel, and atop them all *The Song of Songs*, which is purely the language of Kabbalah in its entirety. It is similar in laws and in legends, and all the more so with the matter of the unerasable holy names, which bear the same meaning in all the languages.

17. Baal HaSulam, *The Study of the Ten Sefirot*, Part One, "Inner Observation"

Those whose eyes have not been opened to the sights of heaven, and have not acquired the proficiency in the connections of the branches of this world with their roots in the upper worlds are like the blind scraping the walls. They will not understand the true meaning of even a single word, for each word is a name of a branch that relates to its root.

Only if they receive an interpretation from a genuine sage who makes himself available to explain the matter in the spoken language, which is necessarily like translating from one language to another, from the language of the branches to the spoken language, only then will he be able to explain the spiritual term as it is.

18. Baal HaSulam, *Ohr HaBahir*

The corporeal mountain before us in this world, which is called Mt. Olives, also has a borrowed relation to this name. This is the meaning of the words, "And his legs stood in that day on the Mount of Olives." Therefore, it is clear that if one who attained named that mountain, he surely understood the complete meaning of this name. And if someone ignoble (named that mountain), it must be that by chance, he saw that its soil was good for olives, or that he saw many olives were growing on it, etc.

19. Baal HaSulam, "Introduction to The Book of Zohar," Item 58

1) faith has diminished in general, 2) faith in the holy ones, the sages of the generations in particular, and 3) the books of Kabbalah and *The Zohar* are full of corporeal parables. Hence, people are afraid lest they will lose more than they will gain since they could easily fail with materializing. This is what prompted me to compose a sufficient interpretation on the writings of the Ari, and now on *The Zohar*. And I have completely removed that concern, for I have evidently explained and proven the spiritual meaning of every thing, that it is abstract and devoid of any corporeal image, above space and above time, as the readers will see, to allow the whole of Israel to study *The Book of Zohar* and be warmed by its sacred light.

20. Baal HaSulam, "The Essence of the Wisdom of Kabbalah"

Kabbalists have found that the form of the four worlds named *Atzilut*, *Beria*, *Yetzira*, and *Assiya*, beginning with the first, highest world, called *Atzilut*, down to this corporeal, tangible world, called *Assiya*, is exactly the same in every item and event. This means that everything that eventuates and occurs in the first world is found unchanged in the next world, below it, too. It is likewise in all the worlds that follow it, down to this tangible world.

There is no difference between them, but only a difference of degree perceived in the substance of the elements of reality in each and every world.

21. Baal HaSulam, "The Essence of the Wisdom of Kabbalah"

From the higher. Thus, one must first attain the upper roots the way they are in spirituality, above any imagination and with pure attainment, And once he has thoroughly attained the upper roots with his own mind, he may examine the tangible branches in this world and know how each branch relates to its root in the upper world, in all its orders, in quantity and quality.

22. Baal HaSulam, "The Freedom"

The whole of reality seen in the nature of this world is only because they are extended and taken from laws and conducts of upper, spiritual worlds.

23. RABASH, Letter No. 19

All those who attained the light of the Creator through their work wanted all those who follow them to benefit from their discoveries, too. Therefore, they named each and every attainment, so they might understand the intentions and attainments they had attained. This would create a common language between them.

24. *Zohar for All*, *BeHaalotcha* [When You Mount the Candles], "Passover in its Time and Second Passover," Item 60

This story in the Torah is a clothing of the Torah. And one who considers this clothing as the actual Torah and nothing else, damned will be his spirit and he will have no share in the next world. This is the reason why David said, "Open my eyes, that I may behold wondrous things out of Your law," that is, gaze upon what lies beneath the clothing of the Torah.

25. *Zohar for All*, *BeHaalotcha* [When You Mount the Candles], "Passover in its Time and Second Passover," Item 62

Such is the Torah. It has a body, which is the *Mitzvot* of the Torah, which are called "the bodies of the Torah." This body clothes in dresses, which are mundane stories, and the fools in the world consider only that clothing, which is the story of the Torah. They do not know more and do not consider what exists underneath that clothing.

26. *Zohar for All*, *BeHaalotcha* [When You Mount the Candles], "Passover in its Time and Second Passover," Item 58

Woe unto one who says that the Torah comes to tell literal tales and the uneducated words of such as Esau and Laban. If this is so, even today we can turn the words of an uneducated person into a law, and even nicer than theirs. And if the Torah indicates to mundane matters, even the rulers of the world have among them better things, so let us follow them and turn them into a law in the same way. However, all the words of the Torah have the uppermost meaning.

27. Zohar for All, BeHaalotcha [When You Mount the Candles], "Passover in its Time and Second Passover," Item 64

Woe unto the wicked ones who say that the Torah is nothing more than fables and consider only the clothing. Happy are the righteous who consider the Torah as they should. As wine sits only in a jar, the Torah dwells only in that clothing. Hence, one needs to regard what is found under the clothing, which is why all these tales are dresses.

28. RAMAK, *Know the God of Your Father*

The secrets of the Torah clothe in allegories and riddles in the Torah because of the expansion of the Torah and their descent from the highest degrees down to this corporeal world.

29. Raaiah Kook, *Orot HaKodesh*

The depth of the Godly secrets is simple and cannot be understood clearly with the human mind, but rather by reception from wondrous people that the Godly light has permeated into their souls.

30. Raaiah Kook, *Letters of the Raaiah*

In the entry *Adam Kadmon*, I was startled to see how they depicted a corporeal shape to the Kabbalistic concept of *Adam Kadmon*, which is only a metaphysical concept, as the Godly intellect. God forbid that we should allow ourselves to materialize such sacred concepts even in the learning.

31. RAMAK, *Know the God of Your Father*

Through the clothing on the Torah, you enter its interior. There is nothing in the revealed in the Torah that the concealed did not cause. It is like a seal that is imprinted by wax, and there is no addition or deduction in the imprint that does not exist in the seal.

5

Who Is a Kabbalist?

1. Baal HaSulam, Letter No. 46

Anyone who receives the abundance from the Creator boasts with the crowns of the Creator, and one who is rewarded with feeling during the act how the Creator, too, boasts about having found him ready to receive His giving is called "a Kabbalist."

2. Baal HaSulam, "The Wisdom of Kabbalah and Philosophy"

The word "spirituality" has nothing to do with philosophy. This is because how can they discuss something that they have never seen or felt? What do their rudiments stand on?

If there is any definition that can tell spiritual from corporeal, it belongs only to those who have attained a spiritual thing and felt it. These are the genuine Kabbalists; thus, it is the wisdom of Kabbalah that we need.

3. Baal HaSulam, "A Speech for the Completion of The Zohar"

The merit of one who has been rewarded with adhering to Him once more, meaning rewarded with equivalence of form with the Creator by inverting the will to receive imprinted in him through the power in Torah and *Mitzvot*. This was the very thing that separated him from His self. He turned it into a desire to bestow, and all of one's actions are only to bestow and to benefit others, as he has equalized his form with the Maker. It follows that he is just like the organ that was once cut off from the body and has reconnected to the body: It knows the thoughts of the rest of the body once again, just as it did prior to the separation from the body.

So is the soul: After it has acquired equivalence with Him, it knows His thoughts once more, as it knew prior to the separation from Him due to the will to receive's disparity of form. Then the verse, "Know the God of your father," comes true in him, as then he is rewarded with complete knowledge, which is Godly knowledge, and he is rewarded with all the secrets of the Torah, as His thoughts are the secrets of the Torah.

4. Baal HaSulam, "The Meaning of Conception and Birth"

Kabbalists have attainment and attain a matter in full. That is, they are rewarded with attaining all those degrees in reality that one can attain. This is considered that they have attained a matter in full, and that complete matter is called a "soul."

5. Baal HaSulam, "Introduction the Book Panim Meirot uMasbirot," Item 8

Come and see how grateful we should be to our teachers, who impart us their sacred lights and dedicate their souls to do good to our souls. They stand in the middle between the path of harsh torments and the path of repentance. They save us from the netherworld, which is harder than death, and accustom us to reach the heavenly pleasures, the sublime gentleness and the pleasantness that is our share, ready and waiting for us from the very beginning, as we have said above. Each of them operates in his generation, according to the power of the light of his teaching and sanctity.

Our sages have already said, "You have not a generation without such as Abraham, Isaac, and Jacob."

6. Baal HaSulam, "Remembering"

Our sages and their teachings have given us in Kabbalah, but in that, they are as faithful witnesses, eyewitnesses, and nothing more. Instead, they teach us the way by which they were awarded being eyewitnesses. When we understand, our wisdom will be as theirs, and we will attain a true and real foundation, and upon a glorious, eternal building.

7. Baal HaSulam, "The Freedom"

Since the more developed in the generation is certainly the individual, it follows that when the public wants to relieve themselves of the terrible agony and assume conscious and voluntary development, which is the path of Torah, they have no choice but to subjugate themselves and their physical freedom to the discipline of the individual, and obey the orders and remedies that he will offer them.

8. Baal HaSulam, "The Freedom"

In spiritual matters, the authority of the collective is overturned and the law of taking after the individual is applied, that is, the developed individual. For it is plain to see that the developed and the educated in every society are always a very small minority. It follows that the success and spiritual well-being of society is bottled and sealed in the hands of the minority.

Therefore, the collective is obliged to meticulously guard all the views of the few, so they will not perish from the world. This is because they must know for certain, in complete confidence, that the truer and more developed views are never in the hands of the collective in authority, but in the hands of the weakest, that is, in the hands of the indistinguishable minority. This is because every wisdom and everything precious comes into the world in small quantities. Therefore, we are cautioned to preserve the views of all the individuals due to the collective's inability to sort them out.

9. Baal HaSulam, "The Teaching of the Kabbalah and Its Essence"

Adam ha Rishon was the first to receive a sequence of sufficient knowledge by which to understand and to successfully utilize the maximum of everything he saw and attained with his eyes.

The order of this knowledge is given only from mouth to mouth. And there is also an order of evolution in them, where each can add to his friend

10. Baal HaSulam, "A Speech for the Completion of The Zohar"

Rashbi and his generation, the authors of *The Zohar*, who were granted all 125 degrees in completeness, even though it was prior to the days of the Messiah. It was said about him and his disciples: "A sage is preferable to a prophet." Hence, we often find in *The Zohar* that there will be none like the generation of Rashbi until the generation of the Messiah King. This is why his composition made such a great impression in the world, since the secrets of the Torah in it occupy the level of all 125 degrees.

This is why it is said in *The Zohar* that *The Book of Zohar* will be revealed only at the End of Days, the days of the Messiah. This is so because we have already said that if the degrees of the examiners are not at the full measure of the degree of the author, they will not understand his intimations since they do not have a common attainment.

Since the degree of the authors of *The Zohar* is at the full level of the 125 degrees, they cannot be attained prior to the days of the Messiah. It follows that there will be no common attainment with the authors of *The Zohar* in the generations preceding the days of the Messiah. Hence, *The Zohar* could not be revealed in the generations before the generation of the Messiah.

11. Baal HaSulam, "A Bastard Wise Disciple Precedes a Commoner High Priest"

Through adhering to wise disciples, it is possible to receive some support.

In other words, only a wise disciple can help him, and nothing else. Even if he is great in the Torah, he will still be called "a commoner," if he has not been rewarded with learning from the Creator's mouth.

Hence, one must surrender before a wise disciple and accept what the wise disciple places on him without any arguments, but by way of above reason.

12. Baal HaSulam, *Shamati*, Article No. 99, "He did Not Say Wicked or Righteous"

A person has the choice of going to a place where there are righteous. One can accept their authority, and then he will receive all the powers that he lacks by the nature of his own qualities. He will receive it from the righteous. This is the benefit in "planted them in each generation," so that each generation would have someone to turn to, adhere to, and from whom to receive the strength required to rise to the degree of a righteous. Thus, they, too, subsequently become righteous.

13. Baal HaSulam, Letter No. 55

And the Lord said unto Abram, 'Go forth from your country,'" etc. This proximity is perplexing and bewildering, for the first appearance of the Creator to the first father, who is the root and the kernel of all of Israel, and the entire correction containing all the hoped for abundance and happiness to be revealed to us, and the abundance in the worlds to all the righteous and the prophets from beginning to end.

It is so because the law in *Kedusha* [holiness] and spirituality is that the root contains within it all the offspring that come and appear because of it, as it was said about *Adam HaRishon* that he included all the souls that would appear in the world.

14. Baal HaSulam, "Introduction to The Book of Zohar," Item 57

If a line of a thousand blind people walks along the way and there is at least one leader amongst them who can see, they are guaranteed to walk on the right path and not fall in pits and obstacles since they follow the sighted one who leads them. But if that person is missing, they are certain to stumble over every hurdle on the way and will all fall into the pit.

15. Baal HaSulam, "The Teaching of the Kabbalah and its Essence"

The most successful way for one who wishes to learn the wisdom is to search for a genuine Kabbalist and follow all his instructions, until one is rewarded with understanding the wisdom in one's own mind, meaning the first discernment. Afterward, one will be rewarded with its conveyance mouth to mouth, which is the second discernment, and after that, understand in writing, which is the third discernment. Then, one will have inherited all the wisdom and its instruments from his teacher with ease and will be left with all his time to develop and expand.

However, in reality there is a second way: Through one's great yearning, the sights of heaven will open before him and he will attain all the origins by himself. This is the first discernment. Yet, afterward, one must still labor and exert extensively until he finds a Kabbalist sage before whom he can bow and obey, and from whom to receive the wisdom by way of conveyance face to face, which is the second discernment.

Then comes the third discernment. Since he is not attached to a Kabbalist sage from the outset, the attainments come with great efforts and consume much time, leaving little time to develop in it. Also, sometimes the knowledge comes after the fact, as it is written, "and they shall die without wisdom." These are ninety-nine percent and what we call "entering but not exiting." They are as fools and ignorant in this world, who see the world set before them but do not understand any of it, except for the bread in their mouths.

Indeed, in the first way, too, not everyone succeeds, since after being rewarded with attainment, the majority of them become complacent and cannot subjugate themselves to their teacher sufficiently, as they are not worthy of the conveyance of the wisdom. In this case, the sage must hide the essence of the wisdom from them, and "they shall die without wisdom," "entering but not exiting."

This is so because there are harsh and strict conditions in conveying the wisdom, which stem from necessary reasons. Hence, very few are regarded highly enough by their teachers for them to find them worthy of this thing, and happy are the rewarded.

16. Baal HaSulam, Letter No. 43

Allegorically, you can say the words of our sages about the verse, "Leave Me and keep My law"—"I wish they would leave Me" means that they were proud of the exaltedness. And although "he and I cannot dwell in the same place," still, "Keep My law," be attached to a genuine righteous with proper faith in the sages. Then there is hope that the righteous will reform them and will sentence them to the side of merit as is appropriate for the presence of the Creator. What could come out of their humbleness and lowliness so the Creator does not move His abode from them, if they have no genuine righteous [person] to guide them in His law and prayer, and lead them to a place of Torah and wisdom?

17. Baal HaSulam, *Shamati*, Article No. 187, "Choosing Labor"

The matter of the lower *Hey* in the *Eynaim* [eyes] means that there was a *Masach* [screen] and a cover over the eyes. The eyes mean Providence, when one sees hidden Providence.
A trial means that a person cannot decide either way, when one cannot determine the Creator's will and the will of his teacher. Although one can work devotedly, he is unable to determine if this devoted work is appropriate or not, that this hard work would be against his teacher's view, and the view of the Creator.

To determine, one chooses that which adds labor. This means that one should act according to one's teacher. Only labor is for man to do, and nothing else. Hence, there is no place for doubt in one's actions and thoughts and words. Instead, he should always increase labor.

18. Baal HaSulam, *Shamati*, Article No. 40, "What Is the Measure of Faith in the Rav?"

One must trust the opinion of his rav and believe what his rav tells him. It means that one should go as his rav told him to do.

And although he sees many arguments and many teachings that do not go hand in hand with the opinion of his rav, he should nevertheless trust the opinion of his rav and say that what he understands and what he sees in other books that do not coincide with his rav's opinion, he should say that as long as he is in multiple authorities, he cannot understand the truth, and he cannot see what is written in other books, the truth that they say.

It is known that when one is still not rewarded, his Torah becomes to him a potion of death. And why does it say, "Not rewarded, his Torah becomes to him a potion of death"? This is because all the teachings that one learns or hears will not bring him any benefit to make one able to be imparted with life, which is *Dvekut* [adhesion] with the Life of Lives. On the contrary, one is constantly drawn farther from the Life of Lives, since all that he does is only for the needs of the body, called "receiving for oneself," and this is considered separation.

This means that through his actions he becomes more separated from the Life of Lives, and this is called "the potion of death," since it brings him death and not life. It means that one becomes ever farther from bestowal, called "equivalence of form with the Creator," by way of "As He is merciful, so are you merciful."

19. Baal HaSulam, Letter No. 45

A student should be in true annulment before the teacher, in the full sense of the word, for then he unites with him and he can perform salvations in his favor.

20. Baal HaSulam, *The Study of the Ten Sefirot*, Part One, "Inner Observation"

Those whose eyes have not been opened to the sights of heaven, and have not acquired the proficiency in the connections of the branches of this world with their roots in the upper worlds are like the blind scraping the walls. They will not understand the true meaning of even a single word, for each word is a name of a branch that relates to its root.

Only if they receive an interpretation from a genuine sage who makes himself available to explain the matter in the spoken language, which is necessarily like translating from one language to another, from the language of the branches to the spoken language, only then will he be able to explain the spiritual term as it is.

21. Baal HaSulam, *Shamati*, Article No. 25, "Things that Come from the Heart"

Regarding things that come from the heart, enter the heart. Hence, why do we see that even if things have already entered the heart, one still falls from his degree?

The thing is that when one hears the words of Torah from his teacher, he immediately agrees with his teacher and resolves to observe the words of his teacher with his heart and soul. But afterward, when he comes out to the world, he sees, covets, and is infected by the multitude of desires roaming the world. Then, he and his mind, his heart, and his will are annulled before the majority.

As long as he has no power to sentence the world to the side of merit, they subdue him, he mingles with their desires, and he is led like sheep to the slaughter. He has no choice; he is compelled to think, want, crave, and demand everything that the majority demands. Then he chooses their foreign thoughts and their loathsome lusts and desires, which are alien to the spirit of the Torah. In that state, he has no strength to subdue the majority.

Instead, there is only one counsel then: to cling to his teacher and to the books. This is called "From the mouth of books and from the mouth of authors." Only by clinging to them can he change his mind and will for the better. However, witty arguments will not help him change his mind, but only the remedy of *Dvekut* [adhesion], for this is a wondrous cure, as the *Dvekut* reforms him.

22. RABASH, Article No. 4 (1987) "It Is Forbidden to Hear a Good Thing from a Bad Person"

In truth, we always need a guide who knows how to lead a person, so as to tell between truth and falsehood, since one cannot scrutinize alone.

23. RABASH, Article No. 424, "The Dispute between Korah and Moses"

With the intellect, it is impossible to understand the Torah, since the view of landlords is opposite from the view of Torah, and we need only faith in the sages.

24. RABASH, Article No. 1 (1990), What Does "May We Be the Head and Not the Tail" Mean in the Work?

All the work of the created beings, that they must work above reason. It is impossible to do anything without faith in the sages, who arranged for us the order of the work. Once a person has accepted his work as "a tail to the lions," he follows the sages, to walk only as they had arranged for us. This is as our sages said (*Avot*, Chapter 1:4), "Be dusted by the dust of their feet (of the sages)." The Bartenura interprets that you should follow them, for one who walks kicks up dust with his feet, and one who follows him fills up with the dust that they raise with their feet.

We should understand what our sages imply to us with this allegory. We should interpret that one who goes after faith in the sages looks at their way, and they say that we must go above reason. Then, a person begins to be as spies, to see if it is truly worthwhile to follow their path. This is regarded as the feet of the sages kicking up dust, which goes into the eyes of their followers. That is, when a person wants to understand the path of the sages, they tell us that we must follow them with our eyes shut, or dust will enter. Something unimportant is called "dust," meaning that there cannot be greater lowliness than this.

Since man was given the reason and intellect in order to understand everything according to the intellect, and here we are told to walk by accepting faith in the sages, and a person wants to understand this path, and since as long as one is placed under the governance of the will to receive for himself, he cannot know what is good and what is bad, but must accept everything the way the sages determined for us, or dust and dirt will enter his eyes and he will not be able to move forward, but when we do not criticize the words of the sages and do not want to accept their words within reason, specifically by this we are rewarded with knowledge [reason] of *Kedusha* [holiness].

This is so because the whole reason why we need to go above reason is that we are immersed in self-love. Hence, through faith above reason, we are rewarded with vessels of bestowal.

25. RABASH, Article No. 10 (1989), "What Does It Mean that the Ladder Is Diagonal, in the Work?"

Is written (*Moed Katan* 17a), "If the Rav is similar to an angel of the Creator, let them seek to learn from him. If he is not, let them not seek to learn from him. They ask about it, Must one who wants to learn from a rav first see the angel of the Creator and then, after he has seen the form of the angel of the Creator, this is the time to go seek a rav who is similar to an angel of the Creator?"

According to the above, we should interpret that if the rav teaches the disciples the work that must be done in order to bestow, meaning why a person comes into this world, to do God's mission, to work for the sake of the Creator, that person is a messenger of the Creator and not a landlord in this world, but is a servant of the Creator. The meaning of "messenger of the Creator" is "angel of the Creator." This is the meaning of "If the rav is similar to an angel of the Creator, let them seek to learn from him."

26. RABASH, Article No. 680, "Annulment—the Baal Shem Tov Way"

The way to annul the body used to be through abstention. But there is another way, which is annulment before the rav [great one, teacher]. This is the meaning of "Make for yourself a rav." "Making" is clarified by force, without any intellect.

As abstention revokes the body only through action and not through the mind. Likewise, annulment before the rav is by force and not through intellect. That is, even in a place where one does not understand the view of one's rav, he annuls himself and the Torah and the work, and comes to the rav so he will guide him.

There is guidance in the manner of the general public, called *Ohr Makif* [surrounding light], which is light that shines only from outside, and is without words, but only by coming to the rav and sitting in front of him, sitting at his table during the meal or during the service. Yet, there is another way, which is internal, and this is specifically through "mouth-to-mouth."

27. RABASH, Article No. 4 (1989), "What Is a Flood of Water in the Work?"

There is the matter of above reason. This is regarded as wanting to walk with his eyes shut, meaning that although reason and the senses do not understand what our sages tell us, they assume upon them faith in the sages and say that we must take upon ourselves faith in the sages, as it is written, "And they believed in the Lord and in His servant, Moses." Without faith, nothing can be achieved in spirituality.

28. RABASH, Article No. 7 (1984), "According to What Is Explained Concerning 'Love Your Friend as Thyself'"

The meaning of "righteous"? It is those who want to keep the rule, "Love your friend as thyself." Their sole intention is to exit self-love and assume a different nature of love of others.

29. *Zohar for All*, *Beresheet*-1 [Genesis], "This Is the Book of the Generations of Adam," Item 472

They lowered a book for *Adam HaRishon*, and in it he knew and attained the upper wisdom. It is written about it, "This is the book of the generations of Adam." That book comes to the children of the gods, the sages of the generation, and anyone rewarded with looking in it knows in it sublime wisdom. They look in it and attain in it, and that book lowered the owner of the secrets, Angel Raziel, to *Adam HaRishon* in the Garden of Eden.

30. *Zohar for All, Shemot* [Exodus], "And a New King Arose," Item 84

Were it not for sages, people would not know what is Torah and what are the *Mitzvot* [commandments] of the Creator, and there would be no difference between man's spirit and the spirit of a beast.

31. Rabbi Elimelech of Lizhensk, *Noam Elimelech* [*The Pleasantness of Elimelech*]

The righteous, by his righteousness, installs his good desires and thoughts in others, so they, too, will have the good desire to adhere to the Creator with all their heart. By installing the desire in others, it is already regarded as an act, since an act in others was made of the desire that he has. This is the meaning of the verse, "You open Your hand and satisfy every living thing with desire," since the righteous extends abundance to the worlds and to every person. And how does he do that? By installing his desire in others. It follows that they have all become righteous through him. By this he can extend upon them great abundance for the righteous is the one who seemingly opens his arms to the Creator in order to bestow upon the world. And with what does he open? The verse interprets, "and satisfy every living thing with desire," by satisfying everyone with the desire to love the Creator.

32. Rabbi Yehuda HaLevi, *The Kuzari*

God created *Adam HaRishon* in a template of a man who completed his adolescence whole in body and qualities. He received from God the complete vital soul and the highest level possible of intellect for man according to his human quality, as well as the Godly power beyond the intellect, namely the degree that when he reaches it, man will adhere to God and to the spiritual, and will attain the truth in the beginning of the thought without delving or learning. This is why we refer to *Adam HaRishon* as "the son of God," and all those who are like him, his descendants, were called "sons of God."

33. Nehunya ben HaKanah, *Sefer HaPliah*

Kabbalists are the sons of the prophets and their disciples, who received from the kabbalists generation after generation through Moses, the master of all prophets, for Moses received the Torah from Sinai and passed it on to Joshua, and Joshua to the elders, and the elders to the prophets, and the prophets passed it onto to the members of the Great Assembly, and they are the beginning of wisdom. They are the true sages who receive from the prophets. They are the authors of the Talmud, and from them we know the wisdom of Kabbalah, prophecy included, for they and all their words are profound secrets.

34. GRA, Vilna Gaon, *Aderet Eliyahu*

It is a grave warning not to learn the wisdom of Kabbalah by yourself from the books, for it is impossible to attain the depth of the intention of the Godly matters, which highly prevail over the human intellect, but rather through much sanctity and purity through a giver, an honest, faithful Kabbalist who had received from a renown Kabbalist.

35. *The Book of Education, Parashat Teruma*

All the matters, for we will be lost even in the literal without assistance from the Kabbalists. To them we will bow down, and it will be revealed to us with all those eyes.

36. Rabbi Shmuel Di Ozida, *Midrash Shmuel, Avot 1, 16*

It is written "Make for yourself a Rav," meaning accept him as your Rav. In order to benefit from the Rav, the student must believe in him and trust his words, as was said, "Depart from doubt," namely do not doubt your Rav's words, but rather trust him, for without it, he will not help you.

37. Babylonian Talmud, Sanhedrin

Rav Hasda said, "Anyone who disputes his rav is as one who disputes the *Shechina* [Divinity]." Rabbi Hama, son of Rabbi Hanina, said, "Anyone who quarrels with his rav is as one who does with the *Shechina*." Rabbi Hanina bar Papa said, "Anyone who is angry with his rav is as one who is angry with the *Shechina*." Rabbi Abbahu said, "Anyone who doubts his rav is as one who doubts the *Shechina*."

38. Martin Buber, *Ohr HaGanuz*

Rabbi David Leykas, a disciple of the Baal Shem Tov, asked followers of his father-in-law, Rabbi Motel of Chernobyl: "Do you have complete faith in your Rav?" They kept silent, for who would dare to say that he has complete faith? "In that case," said Rabbi David, "I'd like to tell you what faith is. One Shabbat [Sabbath], the third meal [closing Sabbath meal] with the Baal Shem Tov stretched on until late in the evening, as would often happen. Afterwards, we said grace for the food and immediately proceeded to the evening service, did *Havdala* [marking the end of Shabbat and beginning of the week], and sat down for the *Melave Malka* [post Shabbat] meal. We were all very poor and did not have a penny, certainly not on Shabbat [when it's forbidden to carry money]. Even so, when the Baal Shem Tov told me after the *Melave Malka* meal, 'David, give money for mead [alcoholic beverage made of fermented honey and water],' I placed my hand in my pocket, although I knew I had nothing, and took out a *Zahuv* [coin]. I gave the coin to buy mead."

39. Rabbi Shlomo Rabinowicz of Radomsk, *Tifferet Shlomo*

To explain according to the Mishnah (*Pirkei Avot*, 2:8): "Rabbi Yohanan Ben Zakkai had five disciples, and he would praise them." It seems as though we should reflect on this. A great rav, the leader of the generation such as Rabbi Yohanan Ben Zakkai had only five disciples? After all, he was the leader of all of Israel!

In truth, he had several, but those five disciples were low-spirited and lowly in their own eyes, and did not know about their merit whatsoever. This is why he praised specifically them, and they were the ones from among all the disciples who were worthy of receiving from him. This is so because the heart of the preparation to receive the Torah is the lowliness of being a "receiver," as it is written in the name of Rav Moshe Leib of Sasov about the verse (Gen. 44:17), "The man in whose possession the cup has been found, he shall be my slave." The cup, which is a receptacle, must stand below the vessel from which it is poured into it since if it is above, it cannot pour into it. Likewise, the disciple must be low in his mind compared to the rav who bestows upon him, and then he will be suitable for receiving from him.

40. The Raaiah Kook, *Orot HaKodesh* [*Lights of Sanctity*], 3, p 153

The souls of the great righteous contain everything: They have all the good and evil of everything. They suffer torments for all and receive pleasure from all, as they transform the evil of all into good.

41. Rav Chaim Vital, Introduction of Rav Chaim Vital to *Gate to Introductions*

Indeed, there is no generation without chosen ones who have been instilled with the spirit of holiness. Elijah the prophet was revealed to them and teaches them the secrets of this law.

42. Raaiah Kook, *Orot HaKodesh*

The depth of the Godly secrets is simple and cannot be understood clearly with the human mind, but rather by reception from wondrous people that the Godly light has permeated into their souls. When we learn their words with the appropriate preparation comes the inner conclusion and settles the matters in the heart to the point that they are similar to what is attained in the natural and simple mind. We must always join the power of truth of Kabbalah to this science, and then the matters become illuminated and joyful as when they were given from Sinai, to each one according to his degree.

43. Rabbi Eliyahu Eliezer Desler, *A Letter from Eliyahu*

Rabbi Shlomo Elkabetz asked in the book *Brit HaLevi* why the disciples of Rabbi Akiva died specifically in the days of the [Omer] count. He explained that any rav who learns with the disciples gives them of his soul, meaning of his very spiritual essence. This is why disciples were called "sons." If the disciples unite properly, his bestowal achieves its goal, since only when all come together does all his bestowal illuminate in all of them. It is known that each disciple takes only one spark of the giving of his rav, the spark that pertains to the essence of the soul of the disciple. Naturally, only when they are all included together is his giving complete.

However, if the disciples part from one another in their conduct, they lose the bestowal of their rav and there remains a lone giving without achieving its goal. This is a dangerous situation. The disciples of Rabbi Akiva, for all their greatness, did not treat each other with respect, and by that they parted from each other. Naturally, they did not let the bestowal of Rabbi Akiva, their teacher, achieve its goal. When the days of the count arrived, in which the lights of the preparation for the giving of the Torah sparkle, they were put at risk and died, for one who sees the light of *Kedusha* [holiness] sparkles and does not exert to be rewarded with it and ascend by it, but rejects it and remains in his *Katnut* [smallness/infancy], it is certainly a great complaint that puts one in harm's way.

6

Kabbalists and the Writings of Kabbalah

1. Baal HaSulam, "The Teaching of the Kabbalah and Its Essence"

Know that the names, appellations, and Gematrias belong entirely to the wisdom of Kabbalah. The reason they are found in the rest of the languages, too, is that all the languages are included in the wisdom of Kabbalah, since they are all particular cases that the other languages must be assisted with. But one should not think that these four languages, which serve to explain the wisdom of the revelation of Godliness, evolved one at a time, over time. The truth is that all four appeared before the sages of truth simultaneously. In truth, each consists of all the others. The language of Kabbalah exists in the Bible, such as the standing on the Tzur [rock], the thirteen attributes of mercy in the Torah and in Micah. To an extent, it is sensed in each and every verse. There are also the Merkavot [chariots/structures] in Isaiah and Ezekiel, and atop them all The Song of Songs, which is purely the language of Kabbalah in its entirety. It is similar in laws and in legends, and all the more so with the matter of the unerasable holy names, which bear the same meaning in all the languages.

2. Baal HaSulam, "Disclosing a Portion, Covering Two"

We did not find a single book in the wisdom of truth that precedes Rashbi's The Book of Zohar, since all the books in the wisdom prior to his are not categorized as clarifications of the wisdom, but are mere intimations, without an order of cause and consequence, as it is known to those the knowledgeable ones.

3. Baal HaSulam, "Disclosing a Portion, Covering Two"

Rabbi Shimon Bar-Yochai's soul was of the surrounding light kind. Hence, he had the power to clothe the words and teach them in a way that even if he taught them to many, only the worthy of understanding would understand. This is why he was given "permission" to write *The Book of Zohar*. The permission was not "granted" to write a book in this wisdom to his teachers or to the first ones who preceded them in writing in this wisdom, even though they were certainly more knowledgeable in this wisdom than he. But the reason is that they did not have the power to dress the matters as did he.

4. Baal HaSulam, "A Speech for the Completion of The Zohar"

Rashbi and his generation, the authors of *The Zohar*, were granted all 125 degrees in completeness, even though it was prior to the days of the Messiah. It was said about him and his disciples: "A sage is preferable to a prophet." Hence, we often find in *The Zohar* that there will be none like the generation of Rashbi until the generation of the Messiah King. This is why his composition made such a great impression in the world, since the secrets of the Torah in it occupy the level of all 125 degrees. This is why it is said in *The Zohar* that *The Book of Zohar* will be revealed only at the End of Days, the days of the Messiah. This is so because we have already said that if the degrees of the examiners are not at the full measure of the degree of the author, they will not understand his intimations since they do not have a common attainment. Since the degree of the authors of *The Zohar* is at the full level of the 125 degrees, they cannot be attained prior to the days of the Messiah. It follows that there will be no common attainment with the authors of *The Zohar* in the generations preceding the days of the Messiah. Hence, *The Zohar* could not be revealed in the generations before the generation of the Messiah.

5. Baal HaSulam, "Disclosing a Portion, Covering Two"

Predecessors were not given permission from above to disclose the interpretations of the wisdom, and the ARI was given this permission. This does not distinguish any greatness or smallness at all, since it is possible that the merit of the ARI's predecessors was much greater than his, but they were not given permission for it. For this reason, they refrained from writing commentaries that relate to the essence of the wisdom, but settled for brief intimations that were not in any way linked to one another.

Therefore, since the books of the ARI appeared in the world, all who study the wisdom of Kabbalah have left their hands from all the books of the RAMAK, and all the first and the great ones who preceded the ARI, as it is known among those who engage in this wisdom. They have attached their spiritual lives solely to the writings of the ARI in a way that the essential books, considered proper interpretations in this wisdom, are only The Book of Zohar, the *Tikkunim*, and following them, the books of the ARI.

6. Baal HaSulam, "Introduction to the Book Panim Meirot uMasbirot," Item 8

Indeed, that Godly man, Rav [teacher/great one] Isaac Luria [the ARI], troubled and provided us the fullest measure. He did wondrously more than his predecessors, and if I had a tongue that praises, I would praise that day when his wisdom appeared almost as the day when the Torah was given to Israel. There are not enough words to measure his holy work in our favor. The doors of attainment were locked and bolted, and he came and opened them for us. Thus, all who wish to enter the King's palace need only purity and sanctity, and to go and bathe and shave their hair and wear clean clothes, to properly stand before the upper Kingship. You find a thirty-eight-year-old who subdued with his wisdom all his predecessors through the Ge'onim [pl. for genius] and through all times. All the elders of the land, the gallant shepherds, friends and disciples of the Godly sage, the RAMAK, stood before him as disciples before the Rav. All the sages of the generations following them to this day, none missing, have abandoned all the books and compositions that precede him: the Kabbalah of the RAMAK, the Kabbalah of the Rishonim [first], and the Kabbalah of the Ge'onim, blessed be the memory of them all. They have attached their spiritual life entirely and solely to his Holy Wisdom.

7. Baal HaSulam, Letter No. 39

Know for certain that since the time of the ARI to this day, there has not been anyone who understood the method of the ARI to the fullest, as it was easier to attain a mind twice as great and twice as holy than the ARI's than to understand his method in which many hands fiddled—from the one who first heard and wrote them through the last compilers, while they still did not attain the matters as they are in their upper root. Thus, each inverted and confused the matters. And now, by the Creator's will, I have been rewarded with a conception [impregnation] of the soul of the ARI, not because of my good deeds but by a higher will. It is beyond me, too, why I have been chosen for this wonderful soul, with which no one has been granted since his passing until today. I cannot elaborate on this matter as it is not my way to discuss the concealed.

8. Baal HaSulam, "A Speech for the Completion of The Zohar"

We can see that all the interpretations of *The Book of Zohar* before ours did not clarify as much as ten percent of the difficult places in *The Zohar*. Even in the little they did clarify, their words are almost as abstruse as the words of *The Zohar* itself. But in our generation, we have been rewarded with the *Sulam* [Ladder] commentary, which is a complete interpretation of all the words of *The Zohar*. Moreover, not only does it not leave an unclear matter in the whole of *The Zohar* without interpreting it, the clarifications are based on a straightforward analysis, which any intermediate examiner can understand. And since *The Zohar* appeared in our generation, it is a clear proof that we are already in the days of the Messiah, at the outset of that generation of which it was said, "for the earth will be full of the knowledge of the Lord."

9. Baal HaSulam, *The Study of the Ten Sefirot*, Part One, "Inner Observation"

This is what I have troubled to do in this interpretation, to explain the *Eser Sefirot*, as the Godly sage the Ari had instructed us, in their spiritual purity, devoid of any tangible terms. Thus, any novice may approach the wisdom without failing in any materialization and mistake. With the understanding of these *Eser Sefirot*, one will also come to examine and know how to comprehend the other issues in this wisdom.

10. Baal HaSulam, "The Shofar of the Messiah"

And who better than I knows that I am not at all worthy of being even a messenger and a scribe for disclosing such secrets, much less to understand them down to their roots. So why has the Creator done so to me? It is only because the generation is worthy of it, as it is the last generation, which stands at the threshold of complete redemption. For this reason, it is worthy of beginning to hear the voice of the Shofar of the Messiah, which is the revealing of the secrets.

11. Baal HaSulam, "Introduction to the Study of the Ten Sefirot," Item 30

There is no greater disclosure than writing a book, whose author does not know who reads his book. It is possible that complete wicked will scrutinize it. Hence, there is no greater uncovering of secrets of Torah than this. And we must not doubt these holy and pure (the greatest of the nation), that they might infringe even an iota of what is written and explained in the Mishnah and the Gemara, that they are forbidden to disclose, as it is written in the prohibition to learn (in *Masechet Hagigah*).

Rather, all the written and printed books are necessarily considered the Taamim of the Torah, which Atik Yomin first covered and then uncovered, as it is written, "the palate tastes food." Not only are these secrets not forbidden to disclose, but on the contrary, it is a great *Mitzva* [commandment] to disclose them (as it is written in Pesachim 119).

And one who knows how to disclose and discloses them, his reward is plentiful. This is because by disclosing these lights to many, particularly to the many, depends the coming of the Messiah, soon in our days, Amen.

12. Baal HaSulam, "Foreword to The Book of Zohar," Item 1

The depth of wisdom in The Book of Zohar is enclosed and locked behind a thousand locks, and our human tongue is too poor to provide us with sufficient, reliable expressions to interpret one thing in this book to the fullest. Also, the interpretation I have made is but a ladder to help the examiner rise to the height of the matters and examine the words of the book itself. Hence, I have found it necessary to prepare the reader and give him a route and an inlet in reliable definitions concerning how one should contemplate and study the book.

13. Baal HaSulam, "Introduction to The Study of the Ten Sefirot," Item 103

Indeed, there is a profound intention here. The concealed Torah implies that the Creator hides in the Torah, hence the name, "the Torah of the hidden." Conversely, it is called "revealed" because the Creator is revealed by the Torah. Therefore, the Kabbalists said, and we also find it in the prayer book of the Vilna Gaon [GRA], that the order of attainment of the Torah begins with the concealed and ends with the revealed. This means that through the appropriate labor, where one first delves in the Torah of the hidden, he is thus granted the revealed Torah, which is the literal. Thus, one begins with the concealed, called Sod [secret], and when he is rewarded, he ends in the literal.

14. Baal HaSulam, "Introduction to The Book of Zohar," Item 58

It is mainly because 1) faith has diminished in general, 2) faith in the holy ones, the sages of the generations in particular, and 3) the books of Kabbalah and *The Zohar* are full of corporeal parables.

Hence, people are afraid lest they will lose more than they will gain since they could easily fail with materializing. This is what prompted me to compose a sufficient interpretation on the writings of the Ari, and now on *The Zohar*. And I have completely removed that concern, for I have evidently explained and proven the spiritual meaning of every thing, that it is abstract and devoid of any corporeal image, above space and above time, as the readers will see, to allow the whole of Israel to study *The Book of Zohar* and be warmed by its sacred light. I have named that commentary The *Sulam* (Ladder) to show that the purpose of my commentary is as the role of any ladder: If you have an attic filled abundantly, all you need is a ladder to climb. And then, all the bounty in the world is in your hands. But the ladder is not a purpose in and of itself, for if you pause on the rungs of the ladder and do not enter the attic, your goal will not be achieved. So it is with my commentary on *The Zohar*, for the way to fully clarify these most profound of words has not yet been created. Nonetheless, with my commentary, I have constructed a path and an entrance for any person by which to rise and delve and scrutinize *The Book of Zohar* itself, for only then will my aim with this commentary be completed.

15. RABASH, Article No. 75 "The Work of the Greatest in the Nation"

Baal HaSulam made it so that if an ordinary person follows his way, he can achieve *Dvekut* [adhesion] with the Creator just like a dedicated wise disciple. Before him, one had to be a great wise disciple in order to be rewarded with *Dvekut* with the Creator. Before the Baal Shem Tov, one even had to be among the greatest in the world, or he would not be able to attain Godliness.

16. *Zohar for All*, VaYetze, "Upper Righteous and Lower Righteous," Item 139

The Zohar speaks nothing of corporeal incidents, but of the upper worlds, where there is no sequence of times as it is in corporeality. Spiritual time is elucidated by change of forms and degrees that are above time and place.

17. *Zohar for All*, BeHaalotcha, "Passover in Its Time and Second Passover," Items 59-60

The Torah created the angels and all the worlds, and they exist for it. Moreover, when it came down to this world, the world could not tolerate it if it had not clothed in these clothes of this world, which are the tales and words of the uneducated. Hence, this story in the Torah is a clothing of the Torah. One who considers this clothing as the actual Torah and nothing else, damned will be his spirit and he will have no share in the next world. This is why David said, "Open my eyes, that I may behold wondrous things from Your law," that is, gaze upon what lies beneath the clothing of the Torah.

18. *Zohar for All*, BeHaalotcha, "And the Ark Rested in the Seventh Month," Item 14

It is written, "And the ark rested in the seventh month, on the seventeenth day of the month, upon the mountains of Ararat." This verse has certainly been set apart from the rest of the Torah and has become simply a story. But why should we mind if it rested on this mountain or on that? After all, it had to rest somewhere! Happy are Israel, for they were given the superior law, the law of truth. And one who says that that story in the Torah [in Hebrew, Torah means law, too] points only to that story, damned be he, for if this is so, then the Torah is not the superior Torah, the law of truth. Certainly, the holy, superior Torah is a true law.

19. *Zohar for All*, *BeHaalotcha*, "And the Ark Rested in the Seventh Month," Items 15-16

It is dishonorable for a flesh and blood king to speak words of an illiterate person, much less write them. Can you even conceive that the High King, the Creator, had no holy things to write and to turn them into a law, but that He rather collected words of such common people as the words of Esau, the words of Hagar, the words of Laban concerning Jacob, the words of the mare, the words of Balaam, the words of Balak, and the words of Zimri, and assembled all those written stories and turned them into the law? If this is so, why is it considered "The law of truth," "The law of the Lord is complete," "The testimony of the Lord is sure," "The precepts of the Lord are right," "The commandment of the Lord is pure," "The fear of the Lord is pure," and "The ordinances of the Lord are true"? It is also written, "They are more desirable than gold, than much fine gold." These are the words of Torah. Indeed, the holy, upper Torah is certainly the law of truth, the complete law of the Creator, and each and every word indicates the uppermost things, for that thing in the story does not indicate only itself, but rather points to the whole.

20. *Zohar for All*, *Nasso*, "He Who Strays," Item 90

The enlightened will understand, since they are from the side of *Bina*, *Tree of Life*, of whom it is written, "And the enlightened will shine as the brightness of the firmament," in this composition of Rabbi Shimon, *The Book of Zohar*, from *The Zohar* [brightness/shining] of upper *Ima*, who is called *Teshuva* [repentance]. These do not need experience, and because Israel are destined to taste from the tree of life, which is *The Book of Zohar*, through it, they will come out of exile in mercy and it will exist in them.

21. *Zohar for All*, *BeHaalotcha*, "The Raven and the Dove," Item 88

"And the enlightened shall shine as the brightness of the firmament." These are the authors of the Kabbalah. They are the ones who exert in this brightness, called *The Book of Zohar*, which is like Noah's ark, gathering two from a town, and seven kingdoms, and sometimes one from a town and two from a family, in whom the words, "Every son that is born you shall cast into the Nile" come true. The Torah is called "a son." The newborn is the attained. "Into the Nile" means the light of Torah. "Cast" is like "You will study it" [it's an anagram in Hebrew], where you study each insight that is born in you by the light of Torah and by its soul. This is the light of this *Book of Zohar*, and it is all because of you.

21. Rav Yitzhak Yehuda Yehiel Safrin of Komarno, *Heichal HaBerachah* [*The Hall of Blessing*],

In this last generation, it is possible to draw the upper *Shechina* [Divinity] only through *The Zohar* and the writings of Rav Chaim Vital, which were said in the spirit of holiness. In this generation, one who desires life, loves days, does not spend a day without *Kedusha* [holiness], to see the good of the next world in this world, should cling only to *The Book of Zohar* and the writings of Rav Chaim Vital, which were said in the spirit of holiness.

23. The HIDA, *The Name of the Greats*

Precisely the study of *The Zohar* has more *Segula* [power/merit] than learning the Bible, the Mishnah, and the Talmud. This is surprising for in what is its power greater than all of the Torah? Whether for the Bible or for the Mishnah, meaning that the Bible, the Mishnah, and the Talmud are very clothed and the secret is not at all apparent in them. Not so is *The Zohar*, which speaks of the secrets of the Torah explicitly, and there is not a fool who will read and not understand that its words are in the depth of the secrets of the Torah. Hence, since the secrets of Torah are revealed without clothing, they brighten and illuminate the soul.

24. Rabbi Pinchas Eliyahu Ben Meir, *Sefer HaBrit* [*Book of the Covenant*], Part 2, Essay No. 12, Chapter 5

Know for certain, my brother, that the previous generations and the early days that were in the fifth millennium are not as these generations and these days. In those days, the gates of wisdom were closed and locked. Hence, Kabbalists were few then. Conversely, in this sixth millennium, when the gates of light, the gates of mercy, have been opened, since it is near the end of days, and there is joy of *Mitzva* [commandment] and great contentment in the eyes of the Creator to make the glory of His kingdom known forever. Especially now that the holy writings of the ARI have been printed, who opened for us the gates of light that have been sealed and locked by a thousand keys since days of old, and all his words are words of the living God, based on Prophet Elijah, and by whose permission he revealed what he revealed. Now there is no obstacle or peril before us, just as in the revealed.

25. Rabbi Avraham Ben Mordechai Azulai, Introduction to the Book *Ohr HaChama*, 81

Permission has been given to engage in *The Book of Zohar*. It is a select commandment to engage in it in public, great and small, as is said in *Raaiah Meheimana* [the Faithful Shepherd].

26. Raaiah Kook, *Orot* [*Lights*]

Now the time obligates to increase possession of the inner Torah. *The Book of Zohar*, which breaks new paths, sets a trail in the desert, a track in the wilderness, it and all its crops, is ready to open the gates of redemption.

27. Raaiah Kook, "For the Third of Elul"

There is nothing in my views and thoughts whose source is not in the writings of the ARI.

28. Rav Raaiah Kook, Love of Israel in Sanctity, 232

There is no measurement or value to the virtue of one who contemplate the words of the living God, *The Book of Zohar*, all that accompany it, the words of true sages, and especially the clear writings of the Ari.

29. RAMAK, *Know the God of Your Father*

We would never have the power to undress the Torah from its clothes were it not for Rabbi Shimon bar Yochai and his friends.

30. RASHASH, *The Light of the RASHASH*, p 159

I know that by merit of *The Book of Zohar* and the writings of Kabbalah that will spread out in the world, the people of Israel will be freed. Our redemption depends on this learning.

7

The Necessity to Study Kabbalah

1. Baal HaSulam, "Introduction to The Study of the Ten Sefirot," Item 155.

Why then did the Kabbalists obligate every person to study the wisdom of Kabbalah? Indeed, there is a great thing about it, which should be publicized: There is a wonderful, invaluable remedy to those who engage in the wisdom of Kabbalah. Although they do not understand what they are learning, through the yearning and the great desire to understand what they are learning, they awaken upon themselves the lights that surround their souls.

This means that every person from Israel is guaranteed to finally attain all the wonderful attainments with which the Creator contemplated in the thought of creation to delight every creature. And one who has not been awarded in this life will be granted in the next life, etc., until one is awarded completing His thought, which He had planned for him.

2. Baal HaSulam, "Introduction to the Book From the Mouth of a Sage"

It is known from books and from authors that the study of the wisdom of Kabbalah is an absolute must for any person from Israel. If one studies the entire Torah and knows the Mishnah and the Gemara by heart, if one is also filled with virtues and good deeds more than all his contemporaries, but has not learned the wisdom of Kabbalah, he must incarnate once more into this world to study the secrets of Torah and wisdom of truth. This is brought in several places in the writings of our sages.

3. Baal HaSulam, "Introduction to The Study of the Ten Sefirot," Item 36

It is impossible for the whole of Israel to come to that great purity except through the study of Kabbalah, which is the easiest way, suitable even for commoners.

Conversely, while engaging only in the revealed Torah, it is impossible to be rewarded through it, except for a chosen few and after great efforts, but not for the majority of people.

4. Baal HaSulam, "The Essence of the Wisdom of Kabbalah"

The whole of humanity, obligated to eventually come to this immense development, as it is written, "For the earth shall be full of the knowledge of the Lord, as water covers the sea" (Isaiah 11, 9). "And they shall teach no more every man his neighbor, and every man his brother, saying, know the Lord, for they shall all know Me, from the least of them to the greatest of them" (Jeremiah 31, 33), and he says, "Your Teacher will no longer hide Himself, and your eyes will behold your Teacher" (Isaiah 30).

5. Baal HaSulam, Letter No. 55

All the people of the world will unite and be qualified for His work.

6. Baal HaSulam, "The Acting Mind"

Every person is obliged to attain the root of his soul.

7. Baal HaSulam, "Introduction to the Book Panim Meirot uMasbirot," Item 1

Great merit is required in order to understand the *Peshat* of the texts, since first we must attain the three parts of the internality of the Torah, which the *Peshat* robes, and the *Peshat* will not be parsed. If one has not been rewarded with it, one needs great mercy, so it will not become a potion of death for him.

It is the opposite of the argument of the negligent in attaining the internality, who say to themselves, "We settle for attaining the *Peshat*. If we attain that, we will be content." Their words can be compared to one who wishes to step on the fourth step without first stepping on the first three steps.

8. Baal HaSulam, Letter No. 38

I will tell you as I heard from the ADMOR of Kalshin. In earlier times, one had to first obtain all seven external teachings, called "the seven maidens that serve the king's daughter," as well as terrible mortification. And yet, not many gained favor in the eyes of the Creator. But since we have been rewarded with the teachings of the ARI and the work-ways of the Baal Shem Tov, it is truly possible for anyone, and the above preparations are no longer necessary.

9. Baal HaSulam, "Introduction to The Book of Zohar," Item 71

Now it is upon us, relics, to correct that dreadful wrong. Each of us remainders should take upon himself, heart and soul, to henceforth intensify the internality of the Torah and give it its rightful place according to its merit over the externality of the Torah.

10. Baal HaSulam, "The Writings of the Last Generation"

Now, distinguished readers, this book lays here before you in a closet. It states explicitly all the wisdom of statesmanship and the conducts of private and public life that will exist at the end of days, meaning the books of Kabbalah [in the manuscript, next to the text beginning here, it was written, "They are the perfection preceding the imperfection"]. In it, the corrected worlds that emerged with the perfection are set, as it says, perfection emerges first from the Creator, then we correct it and come to the perfection that exists in the upper world, emerging from *Ein Sof*, as in "the end of an act is in the preliminary thought." Because the incomplete extends gradually from the complete, and there is no absence in the spiritual, they all remain existing and depicted in their complete perfection, in particular and in general, in the wisdom of Kabbalah.

Open these books and you will find all the good orders that will appear and the end of days, and you will find within them the good lesson by which to arrange mundane matters today as well, for we can learn from the past and by this correct the future.

11. Baal HaSulam, "Introduction to The Book of Zohar," Item 69

The redemption of Israel and the whole of Israel's merit depend on the study of *The Zohar* and the internality of the Torah.

12. Baal HaSulam, "The Teaching of the Kabbalah and Its Essence"

Since the whole of the wisdom of Kabbalah speaks of the revelation of the Creator, naturally, there is none more successful teaching for its task. This is what the Kabbalists aimed for—to arrange it so it is suitable for studying.

And so they studied in it until the time of concealment (it was agreed to conceal it for a certain reason). However, this was only for a certain time, and not forever, as it is written in *The Zohar*, "This wisdom is destined to be revealed at the end of days, and even to children."

13. Baal HaSulam, "Introduction to The Study of the Ten Sefirot," Item 97

During the practice of Torah, every person must labor in it, and set his mind and heart to find "the light of the King's face" in it, meaning attainment of open Providence, called "light of the face." Any person is capable of it, as it is written, "those who seek Me shall find Me," and as it is written, "I labored and did not find, do not believe."

Thus, one needs nothing in this matter except the labor alone.

14. Baal HaSulam, "The Shofar of the Messiah"

The disclosure of the wisdom of the hidden in great masses; it is a necessary precondition that must be met prior to the complete redemption.

15. Baal HaSulam, "Introduction to the Book Panim Meirot uMasbirot," Item 5

Is written in *The Zohar*: "With this composition, the children of Israel will be redeemed from exile." Also, in many other places, only through the expansion of the wisdom of Kabbalah in the masses will we obtain complete redemption.

Our sages also said, "The light in it reforms him." They were intentionally meticulous about it, to show us that only the light enclosed within it, "like apples of gold in settings of silver," in it lies the *Segula* [power/cure] that reforms a person. Both the individual and the nation will not complete the aim for which they were created, except by attaining the internality of the Torah and its secrets.

16. Baal HaSulam, "Introduction to the Book Panim Meirot uMasbirot," Item 5

It is the great expansion of the wisdom of truth within the nation that we need first, so we may merit receiving the benefit from our Messiah. Consequently, the expansion of the wisdom and the coming of our Messiah are interdependent.

Therefore, we must establish seminaries and compose books to hasten the distribution of the wisdom throughout the nation.

17. Baal HaSulam, "Introduction to The Study of the Ten Sefirot," Item 30

Not only are these secrets not forbidden to disclose, but on the contrary, it is a great *Mitzva* [commandment] to disclose them (as it is written in *Pesachim* 119).

And one who knows how to disclose and discloses them, his reward is plentiful. This is because by disclosing these lights to many, particularly to the many, depends the coming of the Messiah, soon in our days, Amen.

18. Baal HaSulam, "The Shofar of the Messiah"

There is a precondition for redemption—for all the nations of the world to acknowledge Israel's law, as it is written, "And the land will be full of knowledge," as in the example of the exodus from Egypt, where there was a precondition that Pharaoh, too, would acknowledge the true God and His laws, and would allow them to leave.

This is why it is written that each one from the nations will hold a Jewish man and lead him to the holy Land. It was not enough that they could leave by themselves. You must understand from where the nations of the world came by such a will and idea. Know that this is through the dissemination of the true wisdom, so they will evidently see the true God and the true law.

The dissemination of the wisdom in the masses is called a *"Shofar."* Like the *Shofar*, whose voice travels a great distance, the echo of the wisdom will spread the world over, so even the nations will hear and acknowledge that there is Godly wisdom in Israel.

19. Baal HaSulam, "Time to Act"

For a long time now, my conscience has burdened me with a demand to come out and create a fundamental composition regarding the essence of Judaism, religion, and the knowledge of the authentic wisdom of Kabbalah, and spread it among the nation, so people will come to know and properly understand these exalted matters in their true meaning.

20. Baal HaSulam, *Shamati*, Article No. 38, "The Fear of God Is His Treasure"

One should always remember the reason that obligates him to engage in Torah and *Mitzvot*. This is the meaning of what our sages meant by "that your *Kedusha* will be for My Name." It means that I will be your cause, meaning that all your work is in wanting to delight Me, meaning that all your actions will be in order to bestow.

Our sages said (*Berachot* 20), "Everything there is in keeping, there is in remembering." This means that all those who engage in observing Torah and *Mitzvot* with the aim to achieve "remembering," by way of "When I remember Him, He does not let me sleep." It follows, that the keeping is primarily in order to be awarded remembering.

Thus, one's desire to remember that the Creator is the cause for observing Torah and *Mitzvot*. This is so because it follows that the reason and the cause to observe the Torah and *Mitzvot* is the Creator, as without it one cannot adhere to the Creator, since "He and I cannot dwell in the same abode" due to the disparity of form.

21. Baal HaSulam, "Introduction to The Study of the Ten *Sefirot*," Item 22

It is easier to draw the light in the Torah while practicing and laboring in the wisdom of truth than in laboring in the revealed Torah. The reason is very simple: The wisdom of the revealed Torah is clothed in external, corporeal clothes, such as stealing, plundering, torts, etc. For this reason, it is difficult and heavy for any person to aim his mind and heart to the Creator while learning, so as to draw the light in the Torah.

It is even more so for a person for whom learning the Talmud itself is heavy and arduous. How can he remember the Creator during the study, since the scrutiny concerns corporeal matters, and cannot come in him simultaneously with the intention for the Creator?

Therefore, he advises him to engage in the wisdom of Kabbalah, as this wisdom is clothed entirely in the names of the Creator. Then he will certainly be able to easily aim his mind and heart to the Creator during the study, even if it is very difficult for him to study, for the study of the issues of the wisdom and the Creator are one and the same.

22. Baal HaSulam, "Introduction to the Book From the Mouth of a Sage"

The entire part of the revealed Torah is but a preparation to become worthy and merit attaining the concealed part. It is the concealed part that is the very wholeness and the purpose for which man is created.

Hence, clearly, if a part of the concealed part is missing, although one may keep the Torah and observe its *Mitzvot* in the revealed part, he will still have to come to this world again to receive what he should receive, namely the concealed part in the form of the 613 *Pekudin*. Only in this is the soul completed, as the Creator had predetermined for it.

You can therefore see the utter necessity for anyone from Israel, whomever he may be, to engage in the internality of the Torah and its secrets. Without it, the intention of creation will not be completed in man.

This is the reason that we reincarnate, generation after generation, to our current generation, which is the residue of the souls upon which the intention of creation has not been completed, as they did not attain the secrets of the Torah in past generations.

This is why it was said in *The Zohar*: "The secrets of Torah are destined to be revealed at the time of the Messiah." It is clear to anyone who understands since they will be completing the intention of creation, and therefore merit the coming of the Messiah. Hence, inevitably, the secrets of the Torah will be revealed among them openly since if the correction is prevented.

23. Baal HaSulam, "Introduction to the Book Panim Meirot uMasbirot," Item 4

We should thoroughly understand that this matter of redemption and the coming of the Messiah that we hope will be soon in our days, Amen, is the uppermost wholeness of attainment and knowledge, as it is written, "and they shall teach no more every man his neighbor, saying: 'Know the Lord,' for they shall all know Me, from the greatest of them unto the least of them." And with the completeness of the mind, the bodies are completed, too, as it is written (Isaiah 65), "The youth, a hundred years old, shall die."

When the children of Israel are complemented with the complete knowledge, the fountains of intelligence and knowledge shall flow beyond the boundaries of Israel and water all the nations of the world, as it is written (Isaiah 11), "For the earth shall be full of the knowledge of the Lord," and as it is written, "and shall come unto the Lord and to His goodness."

The proliferation of this knowledge is the matter of the expansion of the Messiah King to all the nations. Yet, it is the opposite with the crude, materialistic plebs. Since their imagination is attached to the complete power of the fist, the matter of the expansion of the kingdom of Israel over the nations is engraved in their imagination only as a sort of dominion of bodies over bodies, to take their full fee with great pride, and boast over all the people in the world.

What can I do for them if our sages have already rejected them, and the likes of them, from among the congregation of the Creator, saying, "All who is proud, the Creator says, 'he and I cannot dwell in the same abode.'"

24. Baal HaSulam, "Introduction to The Book of Zohar," Item 57

The aridity and the darkness that have befallen us in this generation, such as we have never seen in all the generations preceding us. It is so because even the servants of the Creator have abandoned the engagement in the secrets of the Torah.

Maimonides has already given a true allegory about that. He said that if a line of a thousand blind people walks along the way and there is at least one leader amongst them who can see, they are guaranteed to walk on the right path and not fall in pits and obstacles since they follow the sighted one who leads them. But if that person is missing, they are certain to stumble over every hurdle on the way and will all fall into the pit.

So is the matter before us. If the servants of the Creator had, at least, engaged in the internality of the Torah and extended a complete light from *Ein Sof*, the whole generation would have followed them, and everyone would be certain of their way, that they would not fall. But if even the servants of the Creator have distanced themselves from this wisdom, it is no wonder the whole generation is failing because of them. And because of my great sorrow, I cannot elaborate on that!

25. Baal HaSulam, "Introduction to The Study of the Ten Sefirot," Item 23

From the words of the Gemara: "A disciple who has not seen a good sign in his study after five years will also not see it." Why did he not see a good sign in his study? Certainly, it is only due to absence of the intention of the heart, and not for any lack of aptitude, as the wisdom of Torah requires no aptitude.

Instead, as it is written in the above *Midrash*: "The Creator said to Israel, 'Regard, the whole wisdom and the whole Torah are easy: Anyone who fears Me and observes the words of the Torah, the whole wisdom and the whole Torah are in his heart.'"

Of course, one must accustom oneself in the light of Torah and *Mitzvot*, and I do not know how much. One might remain in waiting all his years. Hence, the Braita warns us (*Hulin* 24) not to wait longer than five years.

Moreover, Rabbi Yosi says that only three years are quite sufficient to be granted the wisdom of the Torah (*Hulin* 24). If one does not see a good sign after this long, he should not fool himself with false hopes and deceit, but know that he will never see a good sign.

Hence, one must immediately find himself a good tactic by which to succeed in achieving *Lishma* and to be rewarded with the wisdom of the Torah. The Braita did not specify the tactic, but it warns not to remain in the same situation and wait longer.

This is the meaning of the Rav's words, that the surest and most successful tactic is the engagement in the wisdom of Kabbalah. One should leave one's hand entirely from engagement in the wisdom of the revealed Torah, since he has already tested his luck in it and did not succeed. And he should dedicate all his time to the wisdom of Kabbalah, where his success is certain

26. Baal HaSulam, "Introduction to the Book Panim Meirot uMasbirot"

Who would dare extract it from the heart of the masses and scrutinize their ways, when their attainment is incomplete in both parts of the Torah called *Peshat* [literal] and *Drush* [interpretation]? In their view, the order of the four parts of the Torah, PARDESS, begins with the *Peshat*, then the *Drush*, then *Remez* [insinuated], and in the end the *Sod* [secret] is understood.

However, it is written in the Vilna Gaon prayer book that the attainment begins with the *Sod*. After the *Sod* part of the Torah is attained, it is possible to attain the *Drush*, and then the *Remez*. When one is granted complete knowledge of these three parts of the Torah, one is awarded the attainment of the *Peshat* of the Torah.

27. Baal HaSulam, "The Arvut" [Mutual Guarantee], Item 20

The end of the correction of the world will only be by bringing all the people in the world under His work.

28. RABASH, Article No. 456, "Small Talents"

If a person is born with small talents, how can it be said that he will be a wise disciple? After all, his brain is too small to understand words of Torah.

Midrash Rabbah says about this (portion, "This Is the Blessing"), "The Creator said to Israel, 'Be sure, the whole wisdom and the whole Torah are easy. Anyone who fears Me and performs the words of Torah, all the wisdom and all of the Torah are in his heart.'"

He interpreted this in the "Introduction to The Study of the Ten Sefirot" as follows: There is no prerequisite for excellence here, for only by the *Segula* [merit/power/cure] of fear of heaven and observance of the *Mitzvot* [commandments] we are rewarded with all the wisdom of the Torah. This is the meaning of "Everything is in the hands of heaven but the fear of heaven," for only in fear of heaven is there choice, and everything else, the Creator gives.

29. RABASH, Article No. 75, "The Work of the Greatest in the Nation"

Baal HaSulam made it so that if an ordinary person follows his way, he can achieve *Dvekut* [adhesion] with the Creator just like a dedicated wise disciple. Before him, one had to be a great wise disciple in order to be rewarded with *Dvekut* with the Creator. Before the Baal Shem Tov, one even had to be among the greatest in the world, or he would not be able to attain Godliness.

30. RABASH, Article No. 6 (1984), "Love of Friends – 2"

The purpose of creation is not necessarily for a select group. Rather, the purpose of creation belongs to all creations without exception. It is not necessarily the strong and skillful, or the brave people who can overcome. Rather, it belongs to all the creatures.

(Examine the "Introduction to The Study of the Ten Sefirot," Item 21, where it quotes *Midrash Rabba*, Portion, "This is the Blessing": "The Creator said unto Israel: 'Regard, the whole wisdom and the whole of Torah are easy: Anyone who fears Me and does the words of Torah, the entire wisdom and the whole of the Torah are in his heart.'")

31. *Zohar for All*, VaYera, "A Calculation of the Time of the Messiah," Item 460

And when it is near the days of the Messiah, even infants in the world are destined to find the secrets of the wisdom, and know in them the ends and calculations of redemption, and at that time, it will be revealed to all.

32. *Zohar for All*, New Zohar, Song of Songs, "The Wisdom One Should Know," Item 484

Anyone who goes to that world without knowing the secrets of Torah is ejected from all the gates of that world, even if he has many good deeds.

33. *Zohar for All*, *Shemot* [Exodus], "Come with Me from Lebanon, My Bride," Items 60-61

Woe unto people who do not know and are not careful with the work of their Creator. This is so because each day, a voice comes out of Mount Horeb and says, "Woe unto people, for they slight the works of their Creator. Woe unto people from desecrating the glory of the Torah."

Anyone who engages in Torah in this world and acquires good deeds inherits a whole world. And anyone who does not engage in Torah in this world and does not do good deeds, inherits neither this world nor the next world. He asks, "Either one inherits a whole world or loses both worlds? But there is he who inherits his world according to his place and according to what he deserves. Thus, there is a middle way." Only one who does not have any good deeds is devoid of both worlds. But if he has good deeds, even if they are incomplete, he inherits his world according to what he deserves, both in this world and in the next world.

If people knew the Creator's love for Israel they would roar as lions and chase Him in order to adhere to Him.

34. *Zohar for All*, *Toldot* [Generations], "He called – I Do Not Know the Day of My Death," Item 125

One should engage in the Torah for the name of the Creator. Divinity is called "Name" because anyone who engages in the Torah and does not exert for her name is better off not being created.

"In whose heart are the highways." "Lift up a song for Him who rides through the deserts, whose name is the Lord." Extolling the rider of the deserts means that one should engage in the Torah with the aim to extol the Creator and make Him respected and important in the world.

He tells us the meaning of Torah *Lishma* [for her name], which is highways in their hearts: to aim one's heart so his engagement in the Torah will draw abundance of knowledge for him and for the whole world. Thus, the name of the Creator will grow in the world, as it is written, "And the earth shall be filled of the knowledge of the Lord." Then the words, "And the Lord shall be king over all the earth"

35. *Zohar for All*, *BeShalach* [When Pharaoh Sent], "And the Lord Walks before Them by Day," Items 43-45

"For the Leader upon the morning star. A Psalm of David." How beloved is the Torah before the Creator. Anyone who engages in the Torah is loved above, loved below, and the Creator listens to his words, does not leave him in this world, and does not leave him to the next world.

One should engage in Torah day and night, as it is written, "You shall meditate upon it day and night," and as it is written, "If My covenant is not with you day and night." During the day, it is the time of work for all. But at night, the time of rest, why is it necessary to engage in Torah? It is so that there will be a complete name in him. As there is no day without a night, and one is incomplete without the other, the Torah must be with the person day and night, and wholeness will be with man day and night.

Day is ZA and night is the *Nukva*. When one engages in the Torah day and night, he unites ZA and *Nukva*, and this is the entire wholeness, as it is written, "And there was evening and there was morning, one day."

Night is primarily from midnight onward. And even though the first half of the night is included in the night, at midnight, the Creator comes to the Garden of Eden to play with the righteous who are there, and then one must rise and engage in Torah.

36. RAMAK, *Know the God of Thy Father*

The wisdom of the secret is not given to one person, for each one has a part in the Torah and it is impossible for one person to attain all the wisdom, and if not all the people of the world.

37. Raaiah Kook, *Arfiley Tohar*

Turning the hearts and engaging the minds in noble thoughts whose origin is the secrets of Torah has become an absolute must for the existence of Judaism in the last generation.

38. The Baal Shem Tov, *Me'irot Eynayim*

All the more so, with all of our heart, spirit, and might, we should pursue the wisdom of faith, which is the wisdom of the path of Kabbalah, the path of truth.

39. The ADMOR of Zidichov

It is impossible to be purified and sanctified in the last generations without the wisdom of *The Zohar* and the Kabbalah.

40. Raaiah Kook, "The Generations of the Rav"

It is no coincidence, but the very essence of my soul, that I feel delight and pleasure when engaging in the Godly secrets extensively and freely. This is my main purpose. All the duties of the rest of the skills, the practical and intellectual, are secondary compared to my essence. I must find my happiness within me, not in people's approval or in any career, whatever it is.

41. Ramchal, "The Gates of Ramchal"

The Creator is commanding us to know His guidance, and we do want to know what this guidance teaches us. What this guidance teaches us is but the wisdom of truth, which is delving in His Godliness. It follows that we undoubtedly see it as mandatory to learn the wisdom of truth.

42. Rabbi Chaim Vital, *Otzrot Chaim*, p 18

The resulting rule is that one must know the Creator, and one who has not seen this wisdom has never seen lights in his life, and the fool walks in the dark.

43. Rabbi Yitzhak Ben Tzvi Ashkenazi, *Taharat HaKodesh*, 147

The Torah was given to learn and to teach so that everyone will know the Creator, from small to great. Also, we found in many books of Kabbalist that they warn about the study of this wisdom—that everyone must learn it.

44. Rabbi Tzvi Hirsh Horovitz of Backshwitz, *Hanhagot Yesharot*

The words of *The Zohar* are good for the soul, and are approachable for everyone in Israel. Small and great belong there, each according to one's understanding and the root of one's soul.

45. Rav Yitzhak Yehudah Yehiel of Komarno, *Notzer Hesed (Keeping Mercy)*, Chapter 4, Teaching 20

Had my people heeded me in this generation, when heresy increases, they would have studied *The Book of Zohar* and the *Tikkunim* [corrections], and contemplated them with nine-year-old children, his fear of wisdom would precede his wisdom, and he would persist.

46. Rabbi Shabtai Ben Yaakov Yitzhak Lifshitz (1845-~1910), *Segulat Israel* [*The Merit of Israel*], System 7, Item 5

May it be that the holy flock would begin their study of *The Book of Zohar* when they are still small, nine and ten years old … and redemption would certainly come without any Messiah labor-pains.

47. Raaiah Kook, *Orot HaKodesh*

The tendency to reveal the secrets of Torah is the ideal goal in life and in reality.

48. Rabbi Yosef Chaim of Bagdad, *The Son of the Living Man, Benaiahu*, introduction

Since the time the precious light of the two great lights, *The Book of Corrections* and *The Book of Zohar* has shone, the Jews, the congregation of Israel, have taken it upon themselves to maintain the sacred study of the *Tikkunim* [corrections] and *The Zohar*, alone and with others, young and old. And although they are unable to attain and to understand the meaning of the pure sayings in these holy books, nevertheless, they drink their words with thirst and read with great enthusiasm.

49. Raaiah Kook, *The Writings of Rav Kook*

The intention of the wisdom of the secrets, throughout its scope, is to develop the power of the soul, to the point of acknowledging its inner strength, drawing from its source without needing any medium teaching.

50. The Vilna Gaon (GRA), *Even Shlemah (A Perfect and Just Weight)*, Chapter 11, Item 3

Redemption will come only by studying Torah, and redemption depends primarily on the study of Kabbalah.

51. The HIDA, *The Name of the Greats, Maarechet Gedolim*, 1, 219

In proximity to the generations approximately a thousand years after the ruin, the light of *The Zohar* appeared, to protect the generations. If we are rewarded with engaging in the secrets of Torah and do it properly, by this the salvation of Israel will spread.

52. Raaiah Kook, *Orot*

The secrets of Torah bring the redemption; they return Israel to its land.

53. Raaiah Kook, *Letters of the Raaiah*

The young, or those who find in themselves heaviness and little yearning for the inner light, must dedicate at least an hour or two a day to the wisdom of Kabbalah. Then, over time, their minds will broaden.

54. Rav Moshe Cordovero (RAMAK), *Know the God of Thy Father*, 5

There is no doubt that of all the teachings in the world, none is more important than learning the secrets of Torah, for they concern Godliness, since the very fact that He has given the Torah to Israel is the intention to know God and serve Him.

55. Rav Yitzhak Yehuda Yehiel Safrin of Komarno, *Heichal HaBerachah* [*The Hall of Blessing*], *Devarim* [Deuteronomy], 208

At the time of the Messiah, evil, insolence, and vices will increase, led by the heads of the mixed multitude. Then the hidden light will appear out of Heaven—*The Book of Zohar* and the *Tikkunim* [Corrections]—followed by the writings of our teacher, the ARI. Through this study, one uproots the thistles and evil in one's soul, he will be rewarded with adhering to the upper light, and will be rewarded with all the virtues in the world.

56. Rav Raaiah Kook, *Treasures of the Raaiah*, 2, 319

As long as the inner soul is deprived of its natural nourishment, it gradually wanes, withers, and degenerates. Therefore ... we must bring in the light and assertively determine consistent and organized study as an unbreakable law ... of the spiritual learning ... until one reaches the boundary of the Godly wisdom at the source of Israel—the wisdom of truth and the Kabbalah and all its details.

57. Rav Yitzhak Yehuda Yehiel of Komarno, *Notzer Hesed* [*Keeping Mercy*], Chapter 4, Teaching 20

Many fools escape from studying the secrets of our teacher the Ari and *The Book of Zohar*, which are our lives. Had my people heeded me at the time of the Messiah, when evil and heresy increase, they would have delved all their lives in the study of *The Book of Zohar* and the *Tikkunim* [corrections], and the writings of the ARI. They would revoke all the harsh decrees and would extend abundance and light.

58. Rabbi Shabtai Ben Yaakov Yitzhak Lifshitz, *Segulat Israel* [*The Virtue of Israel*], Set No. 7, Item 5

And Rabbi Shem Tov had already written in *The Book of Faiths* that Judah and Israel will be redeemed forever only through the wisdom of Kabbalah, since only this is a Godly wisdom given to the sages of Israel since days and years of old. By its merit, the glory of God and the glory of His sacred law will be revealed.

59. Rav Yitzhak Yehuda Yehiel Safrin of Komarno, *Netiv Mitzvotecha* [*The Path of Your Commandments*], Introduction, "The Path of Unification," 1, Item 4

But most importantly, know, my brother, that this study has been revealed so brightly and expansively at this time because the evil is greatly increasing and the assembly of Israel is falling. Through this study, the soul is purified. Indeed, while studying the secrets, and particularly *The Book of Zohar* and the *Tikkunim* [corrections], the soul illuminates.

60. Rabbi Baruch Ben Avraham of Kosov, *Pillar of the Work*

The great obligation to study the wisdom of truth, which is the wisdom of Kabbalah and the secrets of Torah, is well known to all, as is explained in ancient books. I am surprised at the people of our generation, whose humble ones refrain from learning the wisdom of truth.

61. Rabbi Baruch Ben Abraham of Kosov, *Amud HaAvoda* [*Pillar of the Work*]

I saw in many books of kabbalists, the great and bitter punishment for those who avoid studying the wisdom of Kabbalah, and the magnitude of the reward and the pleasure in the next world for those who study it.

62. Rabbi Pinchas Eliahu Ben-Meir, *Sefer HaBrit* [*The Book of the Covenant*], Part 2, Article No. 12, Chapter 5

One who did not engage in the wisdom of truth, who did not want to learn it when his soul wanted to rise to the Garden of Eden, is rejected from there with disgrace.

63. Rav Raaiah Kook, *Orot HaTorah* [*Lights of the Torah*] 10, 5

Since the secrets of Torah come from a superior source—from the great concealment of the internality of the soul, a part of God above—they can enter all the hearts, even those hearts that have not reached the extent of expanded knowledge for acquiring a broad and deep science. When they use their gift—the inclination toward the secrets of the upper one, along with acknowledging their scientific weakness, which fills them with humility—they bring blessing to the world and reveal, with their pure desire, a great light of the knowledge of the sages.

64. Rabbi Avraham Ben Mordechai Azulai, "Introduction to the Book Ohr HaChama," 81

What has been decreed above, not to engage openly in the wisdom of truth, was only for a time—until the end of the year, 1490. From then on it will be called "the last generation," the sentence has been lifted, and permission has been given to engage in *The Book of Zohar*. And from the year, 1540, it is has become praiseworthy to engage in public, great and small. And since it is by virtue of this that the Messiah King will come, and not by another virtue, we must not be negligent.

65. Rav Yitzhak HaCohen Kook (the Raaiah), *Otzrot HaRaaiah* [*Treasures of the Raaiah*], 2, 317

Before us is an obligation to expand and establish the engagement in the inner side of the Torah, in all its spiritual issues, which, in its broader sense, includes the broad wisdom of Israel, whose apex is the knowledge of God in truth, according to the depth of the secrets of Torah. These days, it requires elucidation, scrutiny, and explanation, to make it ever clearer and ever more expansive among our entire nation.

66. Raaiah Kook, *Letters of the Raaiah*

Have strength my friend to shine the light of the wisdom of the hidden in the world. Now the days are nearing when everyone will recognize and know that the salvation of Israel and the salvation of the whole world depend only on the emergence of the wisdom of Kabbalah in a clear language.

67. Raaiah Kook, *Ikvey HaTzon* [*Footsteps of the Flock*], 54

The great spiritual questions that were previously known only to the greatest and most excellent, must know be known, in various degrees, to all the people. Sublime and lofty words must be brought down from their high fort to the depth of the common, ordinary level. This requires great wealth of spirit and constant practice. Only then will the mind expand and the language be clarified sufficiently to express even the deepest mattes in a light and popular style, to satiate thirsty souls.

68. Raaiah Kook, *Letters of the Raaiah*

I have agreed to disclose the secrets of the world since the time requires it. Greater and better than me have suffered the libel of the people for such matters, who pressed their pure spirits, for the correction of the generation, to say new things and reveal the concealed, to which the common mind has not been accustomed.

69. Raaiah Kook, *Eight Collections*

The correction will come through the light of the Messiah. To this, the expansion of the learning of the secrets of Torah and revealing the lights of God's wisdom in all the forms worthy of being revealed will help a lot.

70. Raaiah Kook, *Me'orot HaRaaiah*

The Creator wanted the correction of the whole world. This is why our sages said (*Shabbat* 88b), "Each and every word that came forth from the Creator is divided into seventy languages," indicating to the preparation that there is in the Torah to complement all the nations.

71. Raaiah Kook, *Orot HaKodesh*

The illumination of the Messiah, his teaching can and must spread to all the nations and the organization of their governance, and on all the ways of life.

72. RASHASH, *The Light of the RASHASH*, p 159

I know that by merit of *The Book of Zohar* and the writings of Kabbalah that will spread out in the world, the people of Israel will be freed. Our redemption depends on this learning.

73. GRA, Vilna Gaon, *Aderet Eliyahu*

It is a grave warning not to learn the wisdom of Kabbalah by yourself from the books, for it is impossible to attain the depth of the intention of the Godly matters, which highly prevail over the human intellect, but rather through much sanctity and purity through a giver, an honest, faithful Kabbalist who had received from a renown Kabbalist.

74. Rav Chaim Vital, Introduction of Rav Chaim Vital to *Shaar HaHakdamot*

One does not complete one's duty by engagement only in the Bible, the Mishna, the legends, and the Talmud. Rather, one must engage as much as one can with the secrets of Torah the work of the *Merkava* [the wisdom of Kabbalah], for the Creator delights in all that He has created in His world only when His children engage in the secrets of the Torah, to know His greatness, His beauty, and His merit.

75. Rabbi Tzvi Hirsh Eichenstein of Ziditshov, *Sur Me'ra Ve'aseh Tov* [*Depart from Evil and Do Good*]

Without knowing the wisdom of Kabbalah, one is like a beast, since he performs the *Mitzva* [commandment] without reason, only going through the motions. He is like beasts that eat fodder, in which there is no flavor of man's food. Even if he is a great businessman with many occupations, he should not excuse himself from engaging in this wisdom.

76. Maimonides, "Commentary on Mishnah Portions"

Man's purpose to eat, drink, and have intercourse, or to build a wall, all those recurring happenings do not add to his inner strength. And also, in that, he partakes with most created beings. But the wisdom is what adds to his inner strength and shifts him from the level of contempt to the level of glory. Before one learns and knows, he is regarded as a beast, no different from the rest of the animals except in logic, that he is an animal with logic. He wants to say with logic that he depicts to himself the concepts. And the most distinguished concept is to depict to himself the oneness of the Creator and all that accompanies that matter from the Creator, that the rest of the teachings are only in order to grow accustomed through them until they achieve Godly knowledge.

77. Rav Chaim Vital, Introduction of Rav Chaim Vital to *Shaar HaHakdamot*

Had we engaged in the wisdom of Kabbalah, redemption would have drawn closer, for everything depends on the study of this wisdom, and refraining from engaging in it postpones and delays the building of our Temple.

78. Ramchal, *Derech Etz Chaim*

Learning the wisdom of truth, which is the wisdom of Kabbalah, is the beginning of all the corrections, as Rabbi Shimon Bar Yochai said openly: By merit of learning the wisdom of Kabbalah, Israel will be redeemed from exile.

79. The Vilna Gaon (GRA), *Even Shlemah* [*A Perfect Weight*]

Redemption and the coming of the Messiah depend only on the study of Kabbalah.

80. Raaiah Kook, *Letters*

It is precisely during big crisis and great danger that we have to take the best remedy. We must be radical. Compromise with half, third or a quarter of the nation we will not correct anything.

81. Raaiah Kook, *Letters*

All the great Kabbalists unanimously cry out like cranes that as long as we deny the Torah of its secrets and do not engage in its secrets, we are destroying the world. The water has run out in the sea and the river is parched and dried up. They are the ones who remove the secret and the wisdom from the Torah and make the Torah dry.

82. The HIDA, *The Name of the Greats*

Precisely the study of *The Zohar* has more *Segula* [power/merit] than learning the Bible, the Mishnah, and the Talmud. This is surprising for in what is its power greater than all of the Torah? Whether for the Bible or for the Mishnah, meaning that the Bible, the Mishnah, and the Talmud are very clothed and the secret is not at all apparent in them. Not so is *The Zohar*, which speaks of the secrets of the Torah explicitly, and there is not a fool who will read and not understand that its words are in the depth of the secrets of the Torah. Hence, since the secrets of Torah are revealed without clothing, they brighten and illuminate the soul.

83. Rabbi Yaakov Tzvi Yalish, *The Congregations of Jacob*

Through Israel's engagement in the secrets of the Torah, the Messiah will come soon in our days, Amen.

84. Rav Yitzhak Yehuda Yehiel Safrin of Komarno, *Heichal HaBerachah* [*The Hall of Blessing*],

In this last generation, it is possible to draw the upper *Shechina* [Divinity] only through *The Zohar* and the writings of Rav Chaim Vital, which were said in the spirit of holiness. In this generation, one who desires life, loves days, does not spend a day without *Kedusha* [holiness], to see the good of the next world in this world, should cling only to *The Book of Zohar* and the writings of Rav Chaim Vital, which were said in the spirit of holiness.

85. Raaiah Kook, *Letters*

The revealed in the Torah and *Mitzvot* is utterly incapable of leading to one's goal in all the generations, and especially in our generation, but only along with expanding one's many spiritual roots.

86. Simcha Bonim of Pshischa, *A Torah of Joy*, p 57

Previously, the evil inclination was not so strong, and the revealed Torah was sufficient as a spice against it. But now, before the redemption, the evil inclination is intensifying and requires strengthening through the hidden, too.

PART 3
Dissemination of the Wisdom of Kabbalah

1

Israel and the Nations of the World

1. *Zohar for All*, Shemot [Exodus], "Who Send Out Freely the Ox and the Donkey," Item 67

"Happy are you who sow beside all waters, who send out freely the ox and the donkey." Happy are Israel, whom the Creator desires more than all the nations and brought them close to Him, as it is written, "The Lord your God has chosen you." It is also written, "For the portion of the Lord is His people, Jacob the lot of His inheritance." And Israel adhere to the Creator, as it is written, "But you who cling unto the Lord your God."

2. *Zohar for All*, Emor, "I was Sanctified in Three Degrees," Item 92

In what place does one sanctify himself in *Kedusha* [holiness], to include himself in it? When one comes to write, the Lord of Hosts, mentioned after the third *Kadosh* [third "Holy," said during a prayer], *Netzah* and *Hod*, in which there is the matter, "I the Lord sanctify you." After the three times *Kadosh*, we say only "the Lord of Hosts," meaning we do not include ourselves there.

Afterwards, when one comes to the verse, "The whole earth is full of His glory," when *Kedusha* is extended to *Malchut*, he should include himself in *Kedusha*, to be sanctified below, within that glory below, *Malchut*, as it is written, "And was sanctified by My glory." Afterwards he should work in particular, first including himself in *Malchut*, in the glory below, in the verse, "The whole earth is full of His glory," containing the whole earth and all the nations, and then he will extend *Kedusha* in particular, only to Israel, so that everything will be sanctified. And from Israel, *Kedusha* will extend to the whole world.

3. *Zohar for All*, Ki Tazria [When a Woman Inseminates], "He Shall Be Brought Unto the Priest," Item 138

I see the people in the world who do not observe and do not know the glory of their Master. It is written about Israel, "I have set you apart from the peoples to be Mine," and it is written, "Sanctify yourselves and be holy; for I am holy." And if they part from the Creator, where is their sanctity? After all, it is their desire that turns away from Him.

The writing declares and says, "Do not be as the horse or as the mule which have no understanding." Indeed, what is the difference between a human and a horse or a mule? Only their sanctity—to be whole and marked above all.

4. Zohar for All, Tetzaveh [Command], "And You, Bring ... Near You," Item 39

"From among the children of Israel," since everything is called "one" being one, as it should be, only from among the children of Israel. This is so because the children of Israel stand below to open ways, to illuminate paths, to light the candles, which are the upper *Sefirot*, and to bring everything from below upwards so all will be one. This is why it is written, "But you that cleave unto the Lord."

5. Zohar for All, Pekudei [Accounts], "And Moses Established the Tabernacle," Item 393

The Creator chose Israel for His lot and portion, and brought them near Him. He made of them certain degrees in this world, the patriarchs, such as above, to perfect all the worlds as one, above and below, as it is written, "The heaven is My throne, and the earth is My footstool," to perfect above and below into being one.

6. Zohar for All, Pekudei [Accounts], "The Hair in the Tefillin," Item 337

The holy Israel, which is a single nation in holy unification, the Creator gives them a counsel by which to be saved from everything.

7. Zohar for All, Ki Tazria [When a Woman Inseminates], "Infected Houses," Item 145

Happy are Israel who adhere to the Creator and whom the Creator loves, as it is written, "I have loved you, says the Lord." And for His love, He brought them into the holy land to instill His Divinity among them and to dwell with them, so Israel will be holier than all the people in the world.

8. Zohar for All, Kedoshim, "Oh Land Of Whirring Wings," Item 20

The Creator did not want all the nations of the world but only Israel. He made them a single nation in the world and called them "One nation," as His name. He crowned them with several crowns and with several *Mitzvot* [commandments] to crown in.

9. Zohar for All, Kedoshim, "Oh Land Of Whirring Wings," Item 25

These are the ones who are called, "the sons of the Creator." And for this reason, it is written, "You shall be holy for I the Lord am holy." Happy are Israel for not placing this thing in another place, for not wanting anything in return for their holiness, except to truly adhere to Him, to Him and not to another. Hence, "You shall be holy for I, the Lord your God am holy."

10. Zohar for All, Emor, "So That He Will Not Profane His Offspring among His People," Item 36

Happy are Israel in this world and in the next world, for it is written about them, "And I will distinguish you from the nations to be unto Me." How distinguished are Israel from everyone in *Kedusha* [holiness], to serve the Creator, as it is written, "Sanctify and be holy for I am the Lord your God."

11. Zohar for All, On the Eighth Day, "That You Should Be Defiled by Them," Item 117

The Creator is destined to purify Israel. With what will He purify them? With what is written, "And I will sprinkle clean water upon you, and you shall be pure." These are the waters of mercy, which clothe and include the illumination of the left, from which the purity comes. And since they are purified, they are sanctified, for they cling to the sanctity of ZA, which has the *Mochin* of AVI, called, "holiness." And Israel, who cling to the Creator, are called, "holiness," as it is written, "Israel is the Lord's sacred portion, the first of His harvest." It is also written, "And you shall be holy men unto Me." Happy are Israel, for the Creator says about them, "You shall be holy, for I am holy," since it is written, "and to Him shall you cling," and, "He has not dealt so with any nation; and as for His ordinances, they have not known them, halleluiah."

12. Zohar for All, Aharei Mot [After the Death], "And Aaron Shall Cast Lots upon the Two Goats," Item 115

Happy are Israel more than all the idol-worshipping nations, for the Creator wishes to purify them and have mercy on them, for they are His lot and inheritance, as it is written, "For the portion of the Lord is His people, Jacob the lot of His inheritance." It is also written, "He made him ride on the high places of the earth." They grip above, in ZA, hence the love of the Creator clings to them, as it is written, "I have loved you, says the Lord."

And out of the great love that He loves them, He has given them one day in the year to purify and cleanse themselves of all their iniquities, as it is written, "For on this day shall atonement be made for you, to cleanse you," so they are worthy in this world, in the next world, and there will be no sin among them. For this reason, on that day Israel are crowned and rule over all the seekers of *Din* and over all the spirits.

13. Zohar for All, Kedoshim, "Oh Land Of Whirring Wings," Item 22

Let one come and exert in the one. The Creator, who is one, will exert in the one, which is Israel, for the King exerts only in what is worthy of Him. This is why it is written, "He is in the one, and who will turn Him?" The Creator dwells and is present only in the one. "And He is in the one," as one who has been established in upper *Kedusha* [holiness] to be one, in Israel. Then He is in the one, and not in another nation.

14. *Zohar for All*, Emor, "Every Letter of the Name Is the Wholeness of the Whole Name," Item 70

Israel ascend from below upward, as it is written, "And your descendants will be as the dust of the earth." It is also written, "I will multiply your descendants as the stars of the heaven." They will rise from the dust of the earth to the stars of the heaven. Afterwards, they rise above everything and adhere to the uppermost place, as it is written, "And you who adhere to the Lord your God."

15. *Zohar for All*, Emor, "So That He Will Not Profane His Offspring among His People," Item 37

"Salvation is the Lord's, Your blessing is upon Your people, Selah." Happy are Israel, for wherever they are exiled, the *Shechina* [Divinity] is exiled with them. Thus, when Israel come out of exile, the *Shechina* will also come out of exile. To whom will be the redemption, to the Creator or to Israel? Salvation is certainly the Lord's. When? When "Your blessing is upon Your people, Selah," when the Creator watches over Israel with blessings, to bring them out of exile and do good to them. At that time, salvation is certainly the Lord's, for the *Shechina* will come out of exile. For this reason, the Creator will bring the people of Israel back from the exile, as it is written, "And the Lord your God will bring you back from captivity and have mercy on you," where "bring" means that He, too, will return with Israel from the exile.

16. *Zohar for All*, Pinhas, "Let Israel Rejoice in Those who Make Him," Item 118

Oh how Israel are loved by the Creator. Their joy and their praises are only about Him, for any joy of Israel in which they do not include the Creator is not joy.

17. *Zohar for All*, Haazinu, "An Apple and a Lily," Item 9

Israel's fate is better than that of all the idol-worshipping nations for the rest of the nations were given to appointed ministers to govern them while the fate of holy Israel is good in this world and in the next world since the Creator did not give them to an angel or to another ruler, but took them for His lot, as it is written, "For the lot of the Lord are His people," and as it is written, "For the Lord chose Jacob for Himself."

18. *Zohar for All*, Haazinu, "As an Eagle Stirs Up Its Nest," Item 240

Happy are Israel for the Creator leads them. It is written about them, "For the Lord chose Jacob for Himself, Israel for His treasure." It is also written, "The Lord will not abandon His people because of

His great name," since they have adhered to one another because Israel adhered to His great name. For this reason, the Creator will not leave them, as wherever they are, the Creator is with them.

19. *Zohar for All, Ki Tetze*, "Ten *Shofarot* [festive horns]," Item 142

It is written, the mother broods on the chicks. Israel tweet to her with several tweets of the prayers and she does not want to come down to them, to shine from above downward. She does not want to change from *Katnut* [infancy], when she lays and illuminates only from below upward.

What do Israel do? They take with them the mother, *Shechina* [Divinity] and tie her in a knot of *Tefillin*. When they reach the *Shema* reading, her sons call by the six words of unification, "Hear, O Israel, the Lord our God, the Lord is one," which are HGT NHY of ZA from *Gadlut* [adulthood].

They come down to their mother, the *Shechina*, and tie themselves to her in the unification of "Blessed is the name of His kingdom forever and ever." This is the meaning of the verse, "The appointed times of the Lord which you shall call." You shall call the VAK of *Gadlut* of ZA to illuminate in the *Shechina*, as then she will shine the *Hassadim* from above downward. This is her season, the time of her *Zivug*, as it is written, "My special times," that you will call them on My times, on My season.

20. *Zohar for All, VaYelech* [And Moses Went], "And Moses Went," Item 1

Happy are Israel, whom the Creator desires. And because He desired them, He called them, "Holy firstborn sons," brothers, as though He came down to live with them, as it is written, "And let them make Me a sanctuary, that I may dwell among them." He wished to correct them such as above, placed seven clouds of glory over them, and His Divinity walks before them.

21. *Zohar for All, New Zohar*, Song of Songs, "The Incense," Item 357

All the camps of all the other nations spread and divide from one another. This is why Israel are called "one nation," since they are in unity and in one connection. This is why they are called "connected flock," unlike the rest of the nations.

22. *Zohar for All, BeShalach* [When Pharaoh Sent], "When Moses Entered the Cloud," Item 305

Why was the land lost? The Creator said, "For abandoning My law." As long as Israel engaged in Torah, the power and courage of all the idolaters was broken, as it is written, "Your right hand, O Lord, shatters the enemy." As long as the voice of Israel was heard in synagogues and seminaries

23. *Zohar for All, BeShalach* [When Pharaoh Sent], The Enemy Said, "I Will Pursue," Items 313-314

"The enemy said, 'I will pursue, I will overtake.'" "The enemy said" is the great appointee over Egypt. When he was given dominion over Israel he contemplated obliterating them under his government. But the Creator remembered the greatest in the generation, the patriarchs, who were protecting them. And do not say that only he wished to obliterate them. Rather, all those ministers appointed over all the idol worshipping nations wish to obliterate Israel under them when they are given authority and governance over Israel.

Hence, all those peoples that are governed by those appointees inflict laws to destroy Israel, but the Creator remembers the greatest in the generation, the patriarchs, and protects them. When Moses saw that, he began to praise the Creator and said, "Who is like You among the gods, O Lord?"

24. *Zohar for All*, *Aharei Mot* [After the Death], "It Is Forbidden to Teach Torah to One Who Was Not Circumcised," Items 300-302

Anyone who has been circumcised and inscribed in the holy name is given in the revealed words in the Torah. He is informed in acronyms, in summaries, and the strict caution of the *Mitzvot* of the Torah is placed on him. And not more, until he rises to another degree, as it is written, "He declares His words to Jacob." However, "His statutes and His ordinances are to Israel." This is a higher degree, as it is written, "Your name shall no longer be called Jacob, but Israel shall be your name."

Thus, Israel is more important than Jacob. This is why it is written, "His statutes and His ordinances to Israel," which are the secrets of the Torah, the laws of the Torah, and the concealed matters of the Torah. This should be revealed only to one who is at a higher level, as it should be.

And as it is with Israel, that only to those who are at a high level is the Torah revealed, it is even more so to idol worshipping nations. And anyone who has not been circumcised, but is given even one small letter in the Torah, it is as though he ruined the world and is lying in the name of the Creator, for everything depends on the circumcision, and one is connected to the other. The Torah is tied to the circumcision, as it is written, "If My covenant is not day and night, I have not appointed the ordinances of heaven and earth."

It is written, "This is the law [Torah] that Moses placed before the children of Israel." He placed it before the children of Israel, but he did not place it before the rest of the nations. This is why it is written, "Speak to the children of Israel," and it is written, "And to the children of Israel you will say," And likewise all of them: only to Israel.

25. *Zohar for All*, *Aharei Mot* [After the Death], "And You Came and Defiled My Land," Item 295

Happy are Israel, whom the Creator desires more than all the idol-worshipping nations. Out of His love for them, He has given them true laws, planted among them the tree of life, ZA, and placed the *Shechina* among them. It is because Israel are inscribed in a holy inscription in their flesh, and it is apparent that they are His, from the dwellers of His palace.

26. *Zohar for All*, Balak, "And the Donkey Saw the Angel of the Lord," Items 439-441

"Go forth, daughters of Zion, and gaze on King Solomon, on the crown with which his mother crowned him on the day of his wedding." King Solomon is ZA; his mother is *Bina*.

At that time, she rejoices with all the King's sons, who are those who come from the side of Israel. They do not connect with the *Zivug* of ZA and *Malchut*, and only Israel stand with them, as they are the household who serve them. They raise MAN through their Torah and prayer, which awaken for the *Zivug*. For this reason, the blessings that come out from the *Zivug* of ZA and *Malchut* are Israel's.

Israel take everything, all the blessings that come out from the illumination of the *Zivug* of ZA and *Malchut*, and send a part of them to the rest of the nations, and the rest of the nations are nourished by that part. From the side of the portion of the appointees over the rest of the nations, a very thin trail comes out. From there extends the part of the external ones and the nations of the world, and from there it divides into several sides. This is what we call the "extract," which comes from the holy land, *Malchut*.

For this reason, the whole world drinks from the extract of the land of Israel, as the land of Israel is *Malchut*. Whether above or below, all other idol-worshipping nations are nourished only by that extract, and even the bottom *Sefirot* are nourished from that extract.

27. *Zohar for All*, Balak, "And the Donkey Saw the Angel of the Lord," Item 441

Great illuminations come out from the *Zivug* of ZA and *Malchut* through the unification of the three lines. Israel take everything because they are adhered to the middle line while the nations of the world and all the external ones, which are adhered to the left line without the right, cannot receive from the illuminations of that *Zivug*.

For this reason, Israel receive the whole illumination of the *Zivug*, since they are adhered to the middle line, which includes everything, and because they raised MAN and caused that *Zivug*.

28. *Zohar for All*, Balak, "And the Donkey Saw the Angel of the Lord," Item 441

The whole world drinks from the extract of the land of Israel since only Israel were chosen from the whole world to adhere to the middle line. Hence, they take all the illumination of the *Zivug*, and the rest of the world only the extract, as in, a thin trail, called the "lane in the vineyards." It is a trail from the ministers of the rest of the nations that are blessed from it, since the ministers of the nations of the world are called "vineyards," and that thin trail from the left line, from which they are blessed, is called the "lane in the vineyards."

29. *Zohar for All*, Balak, "And Dawned on Them from Seir," Items 150-151

Before he notifies the ministers of the nations, each day they would chase Israel for her and kill them. But He made it that He invited them and they did not want. They gave Him gifts and presents so that Israel would receive it, and Moses received all of them to give to Israel, as it is written, "You have ascended on high, You have led captive Your captives; You have received gifts among men." This is why Israel inherited the Torah without objections and without any complaints at all.

The witnesses of the children of Israel are the gifts and presents they had received from the ministers of the nations. For this reason, death did not govern, and nor did the *Sitra Achra* [other side]. And not only did they receive the Torah without any objections, they also received gifts and presents from everyone.

30. *Zohar for All*, *Lech Lecha* [Go Forth], "Bless the Lord, You His Angels," Items 315-318

"Bless the Lord, you His angels… hearing unto the voice of His word." Happier are Israel than all the other nations of the world, for the Creator has chosen them from among all nations, and has made them His share and His lot. Hence, He has given them the holy Torah, since they were all in one desire at Mount Sinai and preceded doing to hearing, as they said, "We shall do and we shall hear."

And since they preceded doing to hearing, the Creator called upon the angels and told them: "Thus far, you were the only ones before Me in the world. Henceforth, My children on the earth are your friends in every way. You have no permission to sanctify My name until Israel bond with you in the earth, and all of you together will join to sanctify My name, since they preceded doing to hearing, as the high angels do in the firmament," as it is written, "Bless the Lord, you His angels … They do His word," first. And then it is written, "Hearing the voice of His word."

"Bless the Lord, you His angels" are the righteous in the land. They are as important before the Creator as the high angels in the firmament, since they are mighty and powerful, for they overcome their inclination like a hero who triumphs over his enemies. "Hearing the voice of His word" means being rewarded hearing a voice from above every day and at any time they need.

Who can stand with them, these high, holy ones? Happy are they for they can stand before them. Happy are those who can be saved from them. The Creator's guidance is over them each day. How can we stand before them? This is why it is written, "Choose, and bring near, so he may dwell in Your courts," as well as, "Happy is the man whose strength is in You."

31. *Zohar for All*, Noah, "That Jew," Items 108-110

And when the moon is properly filled with blessings above, Israel come and nurse from her alone. This is why it is written, "On the eighth day you will have an assembly." An assembly is a gathering, since all that was gathered from the upper blessings, other nations do not nurse from her but Israel. This is why it is written, "You will have an assembly," you, and not the rest of the nations; you and not the rest of the appointees.

For this reason, Israel appease the Creator with water that they pour over the altar to give to the appointees of the nations some of the blessings, so they will engage in it and avoid mingling with the joy of Israel as they suckle the upper blessings. It is written about that day, "My beloved is for me, and I am for him," for none other mingles with us.

There is an allegory about a king who invited his loved one for a meal that he was having on a certain day, so the one who loves the king would know that the king favors him. The king said, "Now I want to rejoice alone with the one who loves me, yet I fear that when I am at the meal with the one who loves me, all those appointed officers will come and sit with us at the table to join the meal of joy together with the one who loves me."

What did the lover do? First, he made stews of vegetables and ox meat, and gave it to those appointed officers to eat, and then the king sat alone with the one who loves him for that sublime meal with all the delicacies in the world. And while he was alone with the king, he asks him for all his needs, and he gives him. And the king rejoices alone with the one who loves him, and no foreigners will interfere between them. Such are Israel with the Creator. This is why it is written, "On the eighth day you will have an assembly."

32. *Zohar for All*, Balak, "Fear Not, My Servant Jacob," Items 56-57

There has not been a day since the world was created when the Creator had to be with Israel as that time when Balaam wanted to obliterate Israel's enemies from the world. The Creator said about this, "Balaam wanted to obliterate you from the world but I will not do so. Rather, as it is written, 'For I will destroy completely all the nations where I have scattered you, only I will not destroy you completely.' If all the nations of the world come, they will not be able to obliterate you from the world." Laban came first and wanted to uproot only Jacob from the world. The Creator came and protected him. Pharaoh came and wanted to obliterate them from the world. The Creator came and protected them. Haman came and wanted to obliterate them from the world. The Creator came and turned everything on its head. Likewise, in each and every generation, the Creator always protects Israel.

33. Raaiah Kook, *Orot* [*Lights*]

The love of Israel must be nourished. It is unlike the natural love in every nation, which is found in its members. The basis of every nation is natural and simple, a necessity of life and congregation, the satisfaction of natural and convenient desires through a group that has close ties to one another. That desire does not need to be awakened by means of education and learning.

However, connecting the assembly of Israel is built primarily on common spiritual aspirations, which themselves require much spiritual strengthening and reinforcement in the heart of every individual, and even more so in the life of the whole public.

34. *Zohar for All*, *BeShalach* [When Pharaoh Sent], "When Moses Entered the Cloud," Items 305-306

There is nothing in the world that breaks the force of idol worshipping nations as when Israel engage in Torah. As long as Israel engage in Torah, the right strengthens and the power and courage of the idol worshipping nations breaks. This is why the Torah is called "strength," as it is written, "The Lord will give strength to His people."

When Israel do not engage in Torah, the left intensifies and the power of the idol worshipping nations grows. They suckle from the left, rule over Israel, and inflict upon them laws that they cannot endure. Because of that, Israel were exiled and scattered among the nations.

35. *Zohar for All, Truma* [Donation], "Who Is She Who Looks Forth Like the Dawn," Item 1

"For Jacob has chosen *Koh* [the Lord] for himself, Israel for his merit." How beloved are the children of Israel before the Creator, who desires them, and who wishes to cling unto them and to bond with them, and who has made them a single nation in the world, as it is written, "And what one nation on the earth is like Your people Israel," and they desired Him and bonded with Him. It is written, "For Jacob has chosen *Koh* [the Lord] for himself," and it is written, "For the Lord's portion is His people." And to the rest of the nations He has given ministers to rule over them, while He took Israel into His portion.

2

The Role of Israel

1. Baal HaSulam, "The Arvut" [Mutual Guarantee], Item 24

The Israeli nation had been constructed as a sort of gateway by which sparks of purity would flow onto the entire human race throughout the world.

And these sparks multiply daily, like one who gives to the treasurer until they are filled sufficiently, meaning until they develop to such an extent that they can understand the pleasantness and tranquility that are found in the kernel of love of others, for then they will know how to shift the balance to the side of merit, and will place themselves under His burden, and the side of sin will be eradicated from the earth.

2. Baal HaSulam, "The Arvut" [Mutual Guarantee], Item 21

The role of the Israeli nation to qualify the world for a certain measure of purity, until they are worthy of taking upon themselves His work, no less than Israel were worthy at the time they received the Torah.

3. Baal HaSulam, "The Love of God and the Love of Man"

Why the Torah was given to the Israeli nation without the participation of all the nations of the world. The truth is that the purpose of creation applies to the entire human race, none excluded. However, because of the lowliness of the nature of creation and its power over people, it was impossible for people to be able to understand, determine, and agree to rise above it. They did not demonstrate the desire to relinquish self-love and come to equivalence of form, which is *Dvekut* with His attributes, as our sages said, "As he is merciful, so you are merciful."

Thus, because of their ancestral merit, Israel succeeded, and over 400 years they developed and became qualified, and sentenced themselves to the side of merit. Each and every member of the nation agreed to love his fellow man.

Being a small and single nation among seventy great nations, when there are a hundred gentiles or more for every one of Israel, when they had taken upon themselves to love their fellow person, the Torah was then given specifically to qualify the Israeli nation, to qualify itself.

4. Baal HaSulam, "The Writings of the Last Generation"

We must set a good example to the world because we are better qualified than all other nations. It is not because we are more idealistic than they are, but because we suffered from tyranny more than all other nations. For this reason, we are more prepared to seek counsel that will end tyranny from the land.

5. Baal HaSulam, *Shamati* Article No. 144, "There Is a Certain People"

"There is a certain people scattered abroad and dispersed among the peoples." Haman said that in his view, we will succeed in destroying the Jews because they are separated from one another; hence, our power against them will certainly prevail, as it causes separation between man and the Creator. And the Creator will not help them anyway, since they are separated from Him. This is why Mordecai went to correct that flaw, as it is explained in the verse, "the Jews gathered," etc., "to gather and to stand up for their lives." This means that they saved themselves by uniting.

6. Baal HaSulam, "The Arvut" [Mutual Guarantee], Item 19

Rabbi Elazar, son of Rashbi, clarifies the matter of *Arvut* even further. It is not enough for him that all of Israel be responsible for one another, but the whole world is included in the *Arvut*. Indeed, there is no dispute here, for everyone admits that initially, it is enough to begin with one nation for the observance of the Torah, meaning for the beginning of the correction of the world, as it was impossible to begin with all the nations at once. It is as they said, that the Creator went with the Torah to every nation and tongue and they would not receive it. In other words, they were immersed in the filth of self-love up to their necks, some in adultery, some in robbery and murder and so on, until it was impossible to even conceive, in those days, to even ask if they agreed to retire from self-love.

Therefore, the Creator did not find a nation or a tongue qualified to receive the Torah, except for the children of Abraham, Isaac, and Jacob, whose ancestral merit reflected upon them, as our sages said, "The fathers observed the whole Torah even before it was given." This means that because of the exaltedness of their souls, they could attain all the ways of the Creator with respect to the spirituality of the Torah, which stems from their *Dvekut* with Him without first needing the ladder of the practical part of the Torah, which they had no possibility of observing at all, as written in "Matan Torah," Item 16.

Undoubtedly, both the physical purity and the mental exaltedness of our holy fathers greatly influenced their sons and their sons' sons, and their righteousness reflected upon that generation, whose members all assumed that sublime work, and each and every one stated clearly, "We will do and we will hear." Because of this, we were chosen, out of necessity, to be a chosen people from among all nations. Hence, only the members of the Israeli nation were admitted into the required *Arvut*, and not the nations of the world at all, since they did not participate in it. This is the plain reality.

7. Baal HaSulam, "The Arvut" [Mutual Guarantee], Item 20

The end of the correction of the world will only be by bringing all the people in the world under His work, as it is written, "And the Lord will be King over all the earth; in that day, the Lord will be one and His name one." The text specifies, "on that day," and not before. And there are several more verses, "For the earth will be full of the knowledge of the Lord…" "…and all the nations will flow unto him."

But the role of Israel toward the rest of the world resembles the role of our holy fathers toward the Israeli nation: As the righteousness of our fathers helped us develop and cleanse until we became worthy of receiving the Torah, for were it not for our fathers, who observed the whole of the Torah before it was given, we would certainly not be any better than the rest of the nations, as mentioned in Item 12, so it is upon the Israeli nation—through Torah and *Mitzvot*—to qualify itself and all the people of the world to develop until they take upon themselves that sublime work of the love of others. This is the ladder to the purpose of creation, which is *Dvekut* with Him.

Thus, each and every *Mitzva* that each person from Israel performs in order to bring contentment to one's Maker, and not for any reward and self-love, helps, to some extent, with the development of all the people of the world. This is because it is not done at once, but by a slow, gradual development, until it increases to such a degree that it can bring all the people in the world to the desired purity.

8. Baal HaSulam, "The Shofar of the Messiah"

There is a precondition for redemption—for all the nations of the world to acknowledge Israel's law, as it is written, "And the land will be full of knowledge," as in the example of the exodus from Egypt, where there was a precondition that Pharaoh, too, would acknowledge the true God and His laws, and would allow them to leave.

This is why it is written that each one from the nations will hold a Jewish man and lead him to the holy Land. It was not enough that they could leave by themselves. You must understand from where the nations of the world came by such a will and idea. Know that this is through the dissemination of the true wisdom, so they will evidently see the true God and the true law.

The dissemination of the wisdom in the masses is called a "Shofar." Like the Shofar, whose voice travels a great distance, the echo of the wisdom will spread the world over, so even the nations will hear and acknowledge that there is Godly wisdom in Israel.

9. Baal HaSulam, "Introduction to The Book of Zohar," Item 71

In such a generation, all the destructors among the nations of the world raise their heads and wish primarily to destroy and to kill the children of Israel, as it is written (*Yevamot* 63), "No calamity comes to the world but for Israel." This means, as it is written in the above *Tikkunim*, that they cause poverty, ruin, robbery, killing, and destructions in the whole world.

After, through our many faults, we have witnessed all that is said in the above-mentioned *Tikkunim*, and moreover, the judgment struck the very best of us, as our sages said (*Baba Kama* 60), "And it begins with the righteous first," and of all the glory Israel had had in the countries of

Poland and Lithuania, etc., there remains but the relics in our holy land, now it is upon us, relics, to correct that dreadful wrong. Each of us remainders should take upon himself, heart and soul, to henceforth intensify the internality of the Torah and give it its rightful place according to its merit over the externality of the Torah.

Then, each and every one of us will be rewarded with intensifying his own internality, meaning the Israel within him, which is the needs of the soul over his own externality, which is the nations of the world within him, being the needs of the body. And that force will come to the whole of Israel until the nations of the world within us recognize and acknowledge the merit of the great sages of Israel over them and will listen to them and obey them.

And the internality of the nations of the world, the righteous of the nations of the world, will overpower and submit their externality, who are the destructors. The internality of the world, too, who are Israel, will rise in all their merit and virtue over the externality of the world, who are the nations.

Then, all the nations of the world will recognize and acknowledge Israel's merit over them, and they will follow the words (Isaiah 14), "And the peoples will take them and bring them to their place, and the house of Israel will possess them in the land of the Lord." And also (Isaiah 49), "And they will bring your sons in their arms, and your daughters will be carried on their shoulders." This is the meaning of what is written in *The Zohar* (Nasso, p 124b), "Through your composition, which is *The Book of Zohar*, they will be redeemed from exile with mercy."

10. Baal HaSulam, "A Handmaid Who Is Heir to Her Mistress"

Know that a branch that extends from the internality are the people of Israel, who have been chosen as the operators of the correction and the general purpose. They contain the preparation required for growing and developing until they come to move the nations to achieve the general goal.

The branch that extends from the externality is the rest of the nations. They have not been imparted the qualities that make them worthy of receiving the conducts of development of the purpose one at a time. Rather, they are fit to receive the correction at once and to the fullest, according to their upper root.

11. Baal HaSulam, "The Arvut" [Mutual Guarantee], Item 20

Each and every *Mitzva* that each person from Israel performs in order to bring contentment to one's Maker, and not for any reward and self-love, helps, to some extent, with the development of all the people of the world. This is because it is not done at once, but by a slow, gradual development, until it increases to such a degree that it can bring all the people in the world to the desired purity.

12. Baal HaSulam, "Exile and Redemption"

I hereby propose to the House of Israel to say to our troubles, "Enough!" and at the very least make a human calculation regarding those adventures that they have inflicted on us time and time again, and here in our country, as well. We wish to start our own policy, as we have no hope of clutching at the ground as a nation as long as we do not accept our holy Torah without any allowances, to the last condition of the work *Lishma*, and not for one's own sake, with any residue of selfishness, as I have proven in the article "Matan Torah."

If we do not establish ourselves accordingly, then there are classes among us, and we will undoubtedly be pushed, once to the right and once to the left, like all the nations. And much more so, since the nature of the developed is that they cannot be restrained, for any important notion that comes from an opinionated person will not bow its head before anything and knows no compromise. This is why our sages said, "Israel is the fiercest among the nations," as one whose mind is broader is most obstinate.

This is a psychological law, and if you do not understand me, go and study this lesson among the contemporary members of the nation: While we have only begun to build, time has already disclosed our fierceness and assertiveness of the mind, and that which one builds, the other ruins.

…This is known to all, but there is only one innovation in my words: They believe that in the end, the other side will understand the danger and will bow his head and accept their view. But I know that even if we tie them up together, one will not surrender to the other even a little, and no danger will interrupt anyone from carrying out his ambition.

In a word: As long as we do not raise our goal above the corporeal life, we will have no corporeal resurrection, for the spiritual and the corporeal in us cannot dwell together. We are the children of the idea, and even if we are immersed in forty-nine gates of materialism, we will still not give up the idea. Hence, it is the holy purpose of for His sake that we need.

13. Baal HaSulam, "The Arvut" [Mutual Guarantee], Item 28

"Now, if you surely listen to My voice and keep My covenant," meaning make a covenant on what I am telling you here: to be My *Segula* from among all peoples. This means that you will be My *Segula*, and sparks of purification and cleansing of the body will pass through you onto all the peoples and the nations of the world, for the nations of the world are not yet ready for this, and at any rate, I need one nation to start with now, so it will be as a remedy for all the nations. For this reason, He ends, "for all the earth is Mine," meaning all the peoples of the earth belong to Me, as do you, and are destined to adhere to Me, as written in Item 20.

But now, while they are still incapable of performing that task, I need a virtuous people. If you agree to be the remedy for all the nations, I command you to "be unto Me a kingdom of priests," which is the love of others in its final form of "Love your friend as yourself," the axis of all the Torah and *Mitzvot*. And "a holy nation" is the reward in its final form of *Dvekut* with Him, which includes all the rewards that can even be conceived.

14. Baal HaSulam, *Shamati* Article No. 69, "First Will Be the Correction of the World"

He said that first will be the correction of the world, then there will be the complete redemption, the coming of the Messiah. This is the meaning of "And your eyes shall see your Teacher," etc., "And the whole earth shall be full of knowledge." This is the meaning of what he wrote, that first the interior of the worlds will be corrected, and subsequently the exterior of the worlds. But we must know that the correction of the externality of the worlds is a higher degree than the correction of the internality.

And the root of Israel is from the internality of the worlds. This is the meaning of "for you are the least of all the peoples." However, by correcting the internality, the externality will be corrected, too, though in small pieces. And the externality will be corrected each time (until many pennies accumulate into a great sum), until all the externality is corrected.

The main difference between the internality and the externality is, for example, when one performs a certain *Mitzva* [commandment], not all the organs agree to it. It is like a person who fasts. We say that only his internality agreed with the fast, but his externality is feeling discomfort by the fast, since the body is always in opposition to the soul. Thus, the difference between Israel and the nations of the world should only be made concerning the soul; but concerning the body, they are the same, for the body Israel, too, cares only for its own benefit.

Hence, when individuals in the whole of Israel are corrected, the whole world will naturally be corrected. It follows that the nations of the world will be corrected to the extent that we correct ourselves. This is the meaning of what our sages said, "Rewarded—he sentences himself and the whole world to the side of merit." They did not say, "he sentences the whole of Israel," but "the entire world to the side of merit," meaning that the internality will correct the externality.

15. Baal HaSulam, "Introduction to the Book Panim Meirot uMasbirot," Item 4

This matter of redemption and the coming of the Messiah that we hope will be soon in our days, Amen, is the uppermost wholeness of attainment and knowledge, as it is written, "and they shall teach no more every man his neighbor, saying: 'Know the Lord,' for they shall all know Me, from the greatest of them unto the least of them." And with the completeness of the mind, the bodies are completed, too, as it is written (Isaiah 65), "The youth, a hundred years old, shall die."

When the children of Israel are complemented with the complete knowledge, the fountains of intelligence and knowledge shall flow beyond the boundaries of Israel and water all the nations of the world, as it is written (Isaiah 11), "For the earth shall be full of the knowledge of the Lord," and as it is written, "and shall come unto the Lord and to His goodness."

The proliferation of this knowledge is the matter of the expansion of the Messiah King to all the nations.

16. Baal HaSulam, "The Writings of the Last Generation"

Judaism must present something new to the nations. This is what they expect from the return of Israel to the land! It is not in other teachings, for in that we never innovated. In them, we have always been their disciples. Rather, it is the wisdom of religion, justice, and peace. In this, most nations are our disciples, and this wisdom is attributed to us alone.

17. Baal HaSulam, "The Writings of the Last Generation"

It is a fact that Israel is hated by all the nations, whether for religious, racial, capitalist, communist, or for cosmopolitan reasons, etc. It is so because hatred precedes all reasons, but each one resolves the loathing according to one's own psychology. No counsel will help here, except to initiate international, moral, and altruistic communism among all nations.

18. Baal HaSulam, "The Writings of the Last Generation"

The egoistic communism, based on waves of envy and hate, will never be rid of them. Rather, when there are no bourgeois, they will cast their hate on Israel. We must not be mistaken that egoistic communism will cure the hatred of Israel from the nations. Only altruistic communism can be expected to heal it.

19. Baal HaSulam, "The Writings of the Last Generation"

Israel must be the first among the nations to assume the international, altruistic communism. It must be a model demonstrating the good and beauty of this government because they suffer and will suffer from the tyranny of the nations more than all other nations. They are like the heart that burns before all the other organs. Hence, they are better suited to adopt the proper government first.

20. Baal HaSulam, "The Love of God and the Love of Man"

The Israeli nation was to be a "passage." This means that to the extent that Israel cleanse themselves by observing the Torah, so they pass their power on to the rest of the nations. And when the rest of the nations also sentence themselves to the side of merit, the Messiah will be revealed, whose role is not only to qualify Israel to the ultimate goal of *Dvekut* with Him, but to teach the ways of the Creator to all the nations, as it is written, "And all nations will flow unto Him."

21. RABASH, Letter No. 18

Through the people of Israel, who are more capable than all the nations to approach the Creator, He will then bestow the abundance upon the rest of the nations.

22. *Zohar for All*, *Beresheet*-1 [Genesis], "A Prayer for the Poor," Item 198

Sons, life, and nourishments are drawn to the lower ones only from the middle pillar, called "My son, My firstborn, Israel." He is also called "the tree of life," and in Daniel, he is called "A tree in which there is food for all." For Divinity, who is only in the lower ones, Israel below are considered her life, Divinity's, and the Torah is considered her nourishments. The prayer, regarded as the offering that brings Divinity to a *Zivug* with ZA, it is said about her in exile that she says to ZA her husband, "Give me sons."

23. *Zohar for All*, *Beresheet*-1 [Genesis-1], "And the Lord God Built the Rib" Item 280

It is known that the Emanator started creation and established creation in a way that the children of Israel could finish it, as we learn, "You are in partnership with Me, I started creation and you finish it."

24. *Zohar for All*, Shlach Lecha, "Man in the World as Above," Item 83

Israel's lot is better than that of all the nations in the world, for the Creator wanted them and called His name in them and took pride in them, for the world was created only for Israel to engage in Torah, since One connects to one, ZA and *Malchut*. Israel below, in this world, are His existence, as through their good deeds, they raise MAN for their *Zivug*. They are also the existence of all other nations that exist thanks to Israel, but this is when they do their Master's will.

25. *Zohar for All*, Shlach Lecha, "Man in the World as Above," Item 83

Israel's lot is better than that of all the nations in the world, for the Creator wanted them and called His name in them and took pride in them, for the world was created only for Israel to engage in Torah, since One connects to one, ZA and *Malchut*. Israel below, in this world, are His existence, as through their good deeds, they raise MAN for their *Zivug*. They are also the existence of all other nations that exist thanks to Israel, but this is when they do their Master's will.

26. *Zohar for All*, Pinhas, "Why Israel Are More in Sorrow than the Rest of the Nations," Items 152-153

Israel were made by the Creator, the heart of the whole world. And so are Israel among the nations, like a heart among the organs. And as the organs of the body cannot exist in the world even a minute without the heart, all the other nations cannot exist in the world without Israel. And so is Jerusalem among the rest of the countries, like a heart among the organs. Hence, it is in the middle of the whole world, like a heart, which is in the middle of the organs.

Also, Israel are lead within the rest of the nations as the heart within the organs. The heart is soft and weak, and it is the sustenance of all the organs, and all the organs do not feel any sorrow, trouble, and grief, but only the heart, in which there are sustenance and intelligence. Sorrow and grief do not come near the rest of the organs whatsoever because there is no sustenance in them, and they do not know anything.

All the other organs are not close to the king, who is wisdom and intelligence that are in the brain, except the heart. The rest of the organs are far from it and do not know of it at all. So are Israel—close to the holy king, while the rest of the nations are far from Him.

27. *Zohar for All*, Zohar Hadash, Hukat, "To the Conductor [also: Winner] of Lilies," Items 107-108

It is written, "How good and how pleasant it is for brothers to also sit together." Brothers sitting together means the connection of the brother, ZA, in *Tzedek* [justice], *Malchut*. "Also" comes to include Israel, who are the *Merkava* [structure/chariot] for this unification. This is why she said to him, "Where do you pasture? Where do you make it lie down?" Where do you pasture yourself? Where do you make those herds of Jacob lie down? "The oil of gladness from your friend" are the upper patriarchs, who have first connected in you.

Israel are the brothers and friends of ZA, anoint him with oil of gladness on their heads with their prayer. Oil of gladness are the twelve rivers of pure persimmon that illuminate in her from the twelve *Behinot* [discernments] in ZA. At that time, there is gladness in the worlds, good will in the worlds, and the anger departs from the world.

28. *Zohar for All*, *VaYetze* [And Jacob Went Out], "Prophecy, Vision, and Dream," Item 53

"And behold the angels of God ascending and descending on it." Those are the appointees of all the nations, which ascend and descend on this ladder. And when Israel sin, the ladder is lowered down and those appointees rise. When Israel improve their actions, the ladder rises and all the appointees come down, and their governance is cancelled. It all depends on this ladder. Here in his dream, Jacob saw the governance of Esau and the governance of all the other nations.

29. *Zohar for All*, *Zohar Hadash*, *Hukat*, "To the Conductor [also: Winner] of Lilies," Items 99-100

Rabbi Shimon started and said, "The song of songs that is for Solomon." Several times the Creator admonished Israel, to bring them back in repentance to Him, so they would walk on the straight path, in order to rise among them. When Israel are worthy and walk on the straight path, it is as though the ascent is for the Creator with them from among all the nations of the world. This is so because when Israel are worthy and walk on the straight path, the Creator raises them above all the people in the world, and everyone thanks and praises Him.

And not only they, but even the upper ones above thank Him because of Israel. Moreover, He truly ascends in His glory because of Israel. And moreover, even Israel truly ascend in the glory of the Creator above and below.

When Israel merit, the throne above, *Malchut*, rises ever upward in several joys, several love, and the worlds, ZA and *Malchut*, connect in gladness. Then everyone is blessed from the depth of the streams, *Bina*, and all the worlds are watered and blessed and sanctified in several blessings, several *Kedushot* [pl. of *Kedusha* (holiness)], and the Creator rejoices with them in joy in wholeness.

30. *Zohar for All*, *Lech Lecha* [Go Forth], "And the Lord Said to Abram, After Lot Had Separated," Item 191

This is the difference between the souls of Israel and the nations of the world. Israel extend from *Kelim de Panim* [anterior *Kelim*], which are fit for reception of complete lights even prior to the end of correction. But the nations of the world extend from the external *Kelim*, which cannot receive completion prior to the end of correction.

Similarly, the worlds divide into internality and externality. The land of Israel are *Kelim de Panim* with respect to the world, and abroad are the *Kelim* of externality. Thus, there is no wholeness abroad before the end of correction, for then it is said, "And the Lord shall be King over all the earth," and

"For the earth shall be full of the knowledge of the Lord." However, before the end of correction, there is no wholeness except in the *Kelim de Panim* of the world, which are the land of Israel.

Also, the Creator alone governs over the land of Israel. Since the land of Israel is made of *Kelim de Panim*, it received a correction at that time, too, as it is written, "A land which the eyes of the Lord your God are always upon it," and in which Divinity appears. However, abroad, dominion is given to the seventy ministers, which are also the externality of *Kedusha* [holiness], extending from the external *Kelim*, and which have no wholeness prior to the end of correction. Hence, "And the Lord shall be King over all the earth" did not come true except in the land of Israel.

This is why it is written that as Divinity appears only in its proper place, in the land of Israel, she appears and is revealed only to a man who is worthy of her, who will keep from evoking the *Zivug* in the externality of the *Nukva*, in the place below the *Chazeh*. This is so because then he separates the *Nukva* from ZA and the abundance goes abroad to the seventy ministers of the nations of the world, which are the owners of the external *Kelim* that yearn for that abundance.

When Israel sinned and were burning incense to other gods inside the land, they evoked a *Zivug* in *Nukva's* external *Kelim*, extending the abundance from above downwards, and then the abundance goes to other gods. At that time the rest of the nations reign because the abundance reached their seventy nations. Hence, all suck from Divinity, which drew near them because the external *Kelim* of Divinity were close to the nations of the world, for only they receive from them.

31. *Zohar for All*, Ruth, "They Both Went," Item 418

As maggots and worms rise in the body, when Israel are bad, the nations of the world, the children of Esau and Ishmael, who are called "Maggot and Worm," control them and the body splits so that Israel will be killed. It is written about that, "His flesh pains him and his soul," the *Shechina* [Divinity], "mourns him." What is "His flesh pains him and his soul mourns him"? The flesh of Israel pains them and the soul of Israel mourns. At that time, she yearns for the upper soul, which is called Naomi, *Bina*.

32. *Zohar for All*, Pekudei [Accounts], "Calculation and a Number," Items 93-94

When the sea raises its waves in anger and the waves come up to wash the world over, when they come and see the sand of the sea, they promptly break and turn back quiet, and cannot rule and wash the world over.

Similarly, Israel are like the sand of the sea. When the rest of the nations, the waves of the sea—angry, with harsh *Dinim*—see that Israel are connected to the Creator, they turn back and break before them, and cannot rule over the world.

33. *Zohar for All*, Zohar Hadash, Hukat, "To the Conductor [also: Winner] of Lilies," Item 97

Corresponding to that verse, the words "calculation and number," is the verse in Song of Songs, "Do not see me that I am black," for I dressed in judgment to judge the world. At that time, she is regarded as black. She says to her children who approach her into the house, "Do not see me that I am black." Certainly, if you engaged in the Torah that I gave you, do not fear. But if you did not engage, you will make me make the nations of the world vengeful because of you, where you will be scattered, as it is written, "My mother's sons were angry with me, made me a caretaker of the vineyards."

They commented about that, "If Israel are sentenced, if they repent, the Creator brings down that sentence on the other nations. If they do not repent, they go down among the nations, who eat them bone and flesh."

34. *Zohar for All, VaYechi* [Jacob Lived], "Do Not Remember the Iniquities of Our Forefathers against Us" 412-413

Had Israel gathered good deeds before the Creator, the idol worshipping nations would never have risen against them. But Israel cause the rest of the nations to raise their heads in the world, for if Israel had not sinned before the Creator, the rest of the idol worshipping nations would have surrendered before them.

If Israel had not extended bad deeds to the other side in the land of Israel, the rest of the idol worshipping nations would not have ruled in the land of Israel and they would not be exiled from the land. It is written about that, "For we are very poor" because we have no good deeds as we should.

35. *Zohar for All, Truma* [Donation], "You Shall Make a Table," Items 485-488

"And you shall eat and be satisfied, and you shall bless the Lord your God." How happy are Israel because the Creator favored them and brought them near Him from among all the nations. For Israel, He gives His food and satiation to the whole world. Were it not for Israel, the Creator would not have given nourishment to the world. And now that Israel are in exile, it is all the more so: the world receives sevenfold twice the nourishment and satiation so that an extract of that will suffice for Israel.

When Israel were in the holy land, nourishments would come down to them from a high place, they gave an extract to the idol-worshipping nations, and all the nations were feeding on the extract. Now that Israel are in exile, the matter has been turned around in a different way: the food comes to the nations of the world and Israel receive an extract from them.

There is an allegory about a king who made a meal for his household. As long as they do his will, they eat at the meal with the king and give the part of the bones for the dogs to chew on. When his household do not do the king's will, he gives the entire meal to the dogs and the bones to his household.

As long as Israel do their Master's will, they eat at the King's table and the entire meal is prepared for them. They give the bones of their joy, which is the extract, to the idol-worshipping nations. And as long as Israel do not do their Master's will, they are exiled and the meal is given to the dogs, while they are given the extract, as it is written, "Thus will the sons of Israel eat their bread: unclean among the nations," for they eat the extract of their abomination, their loathsome food. Woe unto a king's son who sits and waits for the servant's table, who eats what is left of his table.

36. Zohar for All, VaYishlach [And Jacob Sent], "Fear Not, You Worm of Jacob," Item 254

Israel is the tree of life, ZA. And because the children of Israel clung to the tree of life, they will have life, and they will rise from the dust and exist in the world, and they will become one nation, serving the Creator.

37. Zohar for All, VaEra [And I Appeared], "And I Appeared—In God Almighty [Shadai], and My Name Is HaVaYaH, I Am Not Known to Them," Item 15

"A Psalm of David. The land is the Lord's, and all it contains; the world and those who dwell in it." "The land" is the holy land of Israel, which is destined to be watered by the Creator and to be blessed with Him first. And from it, the whole world will be watered. "The world and those who dwell in it" is the rest of the lands, which drink from it.

38. Raaiah Kook, *Hadarav*

This nation was created and came for the whole world, to prepare it for its future.

39. *Midrash Rabbah*, Song of Songs

Israel bring Light to the world, as was said (Isaiah 60), "And nations will follow your light."

40. Yitzhak Isaac Hever, *Siach Yitzhak*, Part 2, Assortments 1

Creation and choice, and the correction and corruption of the world are all dependent upon Israel.

41. Raaiah Kook, *Orot*

Israel, as a unique nation, was blessed in the depth of its sanctity and Godly aspiration. It influences the whole extent of the nations, to refine the national soul in each nation and bring all the nations closer through its power to a more sublime and noble status.

42. Rav Kook, "Whisper to Me the Secret of the Lord"

The purpose of Israel is to unite the entire world into a single

43. *Midrash Tana'im*, *Devarim* [Deuteronomy], Chapter 14

Israel is the Creator's virtue, as it is said, "To be a virtuous nation unto Him."

44. Rabbi Shmuel Bornstein of Sochatchov, *Shem MiShmuel* [*A Name Out of Samuel*],

The name "Israel" means *Li-Rosh* [I am the head]. One should see oneself as the head and beginning of creation, and his vocation as bringing all the people in the world under the wings of the *Shechina* [Divinity].

45. Raaiah Kook, *Orot HaKodesh*

In Israel is the secret to the unity of the world.

46. Raaiah Kook, *Orot HaKodesh*

You should know that although for themselves, Israel are already chosen, sanctified, and crowned with the crowns of the Creator, as long as the whole world, with all its parts, is not corrected, Israel, too, will not reach their final sublimity. However, when His kingship is revealed in the world and the good governs and properly suppresses the bad, Israel will inherit their complete sublimity.

47. Raaiah Kook, *Orot HaTshuva* [*Lights of Repentance*]

The revival of the nation is the foundation for the construction of the great repentance, the repentance of the upper Israel and the repentance of the whole world which will follow.

48. Raaiah Kook, *Ein Ayah*

When Israel ascends according to his true, internal quality, to give to the entire world a new and corrected form, not only Israel will ascend, but the entire world. At that time, a new era will begin, in which there will be no admixture of the filth of evil, and wickedness and uprising will not affect it in the least, and anger and sadness will not be able to reign within it. Then, oppression will become obsolete and the sword will lose its status and will become complete abomination.

49. Raaiah Kook, *Orot*

The Assembly of Israel is the essence of the entire reality. In this world, this essence is poured out in the actual Israeli nation, in its corporeality and spirituality, in its genealogy and its faith. The Israeli history is the essence of the ideal of the general history, and there is no movement in the world, in all the nations, whose similitude is not found in Israel. Its faith is the finest essence and the source that imparts the good and the idealism unto all the faiths. Naturally, it is the force that questions all the terms of faith until it leads them to the degree of a clear language, for all to call out the name of the Creator, "And your God is the Holy One of Israel, who is called the 'God of the whole earth.'"

50. Raaiah Kook, *Orot HaKodesh*

The revealed unity of the moral, spiritual, and intellectual world, along with the material, technical, and social world is expressed in the world through Israel. The skill of the land of Israel is to establish in the world the revelation of this unity, which gives a new face to the entire human culture.

51. Rav Kook, *Letters of the Raaiah*, 1966

Great is my belief that all this global uproar of a time of the shifting world in which we live in has come essentially, only for Israel. We are now called upon to carry out a great task willingly and mindfully: to build ourselves and the entire ruined world along with us.

52. Raaiah Kook, *Orot*

The construction of the world, which is currently collapsing under the dreadful storms of a blood-filled sword requires the construction of the Israeli nation. The construction of the nation and the revelation of its spirit are one and the same, and all of it is united with the construction of the world, which is crumbling and awaits a force full of unity and sublimity. All this is present in the soul of the assembly of Israel. The spirit of the Creator is filled with it, and the spirit of one in whose sensation of the soul pulsates cannot be still in this great hour without calling on all the forces in the nation, "Wake up and arise for your duty."

53. Rav Kook, *The Purpose of Israel and Its Nationality* [*Israel's Vocation and Nationhood*]

The Creator's service that is given to Israel, its purpose is the ascent of all of humanity, which cannot ascend if not through the ascent of the people of Israel, such that the blessing will manifest in it and enable it to provide the blessing to the world, in turn.

54. Raaiah Kook, *Letters*

We are called upon to unite the world. But before we unite the living, material world, we are called upon to reveal the plan of spiritual unity, which is our own secret.

55. Rav Kook, *Letters of the Raaiah*

Have strength my friend to shine the light of the wisdom of the hidden in the world. Now the days are nearing when everyone will recognize and know that the salvation of Israel and the salvation of the whole world depend only on the emergence of the wisdom of Kabbalah in a clear language.

56. *Midrash Rabbah*, Song of Songs

Israel bring Light to the world.

57. *Likuta Halachot*, "The Blessing for the Scent, and a Blessing of Thanksgiving," Rule No. 4

There is a medium between all the worlds and the Creator, and it is the Israeli soul, which is very high at its root and is truly a Godly part. It is the medium that connects all the worlds with the Creator, and through it, the abundance and vitality and existence are drawn to all the worlds. For this reason, everything depends on Israel.

58. Rav Yaakov HaCohen Shakira, *A Well of Living Water*

Israel are the first to receive all the abundance, and from them it is dispensed to all the worlds. This is why they are called *Li-Rosh* [I am the head], meaning that they are regarded as the *Rosh* [head/first], the first to receive the blessing, and then to the rest of the people in the world.

59. Rabbi Kalonymus Kalman Halevi Epstein, *Maor VaShemesh*

When it came up in His simple will to create the world, Israel were the first to come up in the thought, as the Creator anticipated that the Israeli nation would be in the world and that through their great passion to adhere to their Creator and their great yearning and longing they would raise *MAN*, by which they would bring down abundance to all the worlds. The intention of creation was that abundance would come down only through an awakening from below. Through the raising of *MAN* that Israel awaken, and through the *MAN* that they raise, all the worlds ascend and add passion to adhere to their root. This is the Creator's main delight, when Israel refine themselves from the depth of corporeality and yearn to adhere to their Creator.

60. *Sefat Emet*, *Shemot* [Exodus], Portion Yitro [Jethro]

The children of Israel became responsible for the correction of the entire world by the power of the Torah. This is the meaning of what was said to them, "For all the earth is Mine, and you will be unto Me a kingdom of priests and a holy nation." Everything depends on the children of Israel. As they correct themselves, so are all creations drawn after them.

61. Rav Kook, *Israel's Vocation and Nationhood*

Israel's vocation is to be a light to the world, to pull all the people in the world out of the darkness of ignorance and vanity of false views, which have brought about the disorder of the material world and the decline of the human spirit. For this reason, the Master of all the deeds chose His people Israel as the one by whom the truth of the oneness of the Creator will be revealed in the world and the Private Providence will be revealed. This is the most instrumental knowledge for straightening of the ways and views of the entire human race.

62. *Shem MiShmuel*, Portion *Haazinu*

The intention of creation was for all to be one bundle, to do the Creator's will. But the matter was spoiled because of the sin of *Adam HaRishon*, until even the best in those generations could not unite together in order to serve the Creator. Rather, they were individuals, alone. The correction of this matter began in the generation of Babylon, when separation occurred in the human race, meaning the beginning of the correction of gathering and assembling people to serve the Creator, which started with Abraham and his descendants. Abraham would roam and call out the name of the Creator until a great community gathered unto him, who were called "the people of the house of Abraham." Thus, the matter grew until it became the assembly of the congregation of Israel. In the future, the end of correction will be when all become one bundle to do the Creator's will wholeheartedly.

63. Rabbi Moshe Chaim Ephraim of Sudilkov, *Degel Mahaneh Ephraim*

It is good for the people of the children of Israel to always unite together in one bundle. Then, even those who are of lesser degree help their friends sanctify with more *Kedusha* [holiness] and attain more. The upper one needs the one below it, and the lower one needs the one above it. Likewise, you should always be bundled in one bundle, and then your roots will unite, as well. This is the meaning of "You will be unto Me a *Segula* [virtue/remedy]," meaning that you will be a *Segula* in the upper world, as well, when you are in one unity below.

64. Raaiah Kook, *Orot*

All the cultures in the world will be renewed through the renewal of our spirit. All the views will be set straight, all of life will be illuminated by the joy of a new birth when we rise, and all the faiths will wear new clothes. The blessing of Abraham to all the nations of the Earth will begin its operation firmly and openly, and on its foundation, our building in the land of Israel will begin anew. The current ruin is a preparation for a new revival for the name of the Creator which will become increasingly revealed.

3

The Importance of Disseminating the Wisdom of Kabbalah

1. Baal HaSulam, "The Freedom"

While most of humanity is undeveloped, and the developed ones are always a small minority, if you always determine according to the will of the majority, which are the undeveloped and the reckless, the views and desires of the wise and developed in society, which are always the minority, will never be heard and be taken into consideration. Thus, you seal off humanity's fate to regression, for it will not be able to make even a single step forward.

2. Baal HaSulam, "The Shofar of the Messiah"

There is a precondition for redemption—for all the nations of the world to acknowledge Israel's law, as it is written, "And the land will be full of knowledge," as in the example of the exodus from Egypt, where there was a precondition that Pharaoh, too, would acknowledge the true God and His laws, and would allow them to leave.

This is why it is written that each one from the nations will hold a Jewish man and lead him to the holy Land. It was not enough that they could leave by themselves. You must understand from where the nations of the world came by such a will and idea. Know that this is through the dissemination of the true wisdom, so they will evidently see the true God and the true law.

The dissemination of the wisdom in the masses is called a "Shofar." Like the Shofar, whose voice travels a great distance, the echo of the wisdom will spread the world over, so even the nations will hear and acknowledge that there is Godly wisdom in Israel.

3. Baal HaSulam, "Introduction to The Book of Zohar," Item 67

When a person from Israel enhances and dignifies his internality, which is the Israel in him, over the externality, which are the nations of the world in him, that is, he dedicates the majority of his efforts to enhance and exalt his internality, to benefit his soul, and gives little efforts, the mere necessity, to sustain the nations of the world in him, meaning the bodily needs, as it is written (Avot 1), "Make your Torah permanent and your work temporary," by so doing, he makes the children of Israel soar upward in the internality and externality of the world, as well, and the nations of the world, which are the externality, to recognize and acknowledge the value of the children of Israel.

And if, God forbid, it is to the contrary, and an individual from Israel enhances and appreciates his externality, which is the nations of the world in him, more than the quality of Israel in him, as it is written (Deuteronomy 28), "The stranger that is in the midst of you," meaning the externality in him rises and soars, and you yourself, the internality, the Israel in you, plunges down. With these actions, he causes the externality of the world in general—the nations of the world—to soar ever higher, overcome Israel, degrade them to the ground, and the children of Israel—the internality in the world—will plunge deep down.

4. Baal HaSulam, "The Writings of the Last Generation"

I have already conveyed the basics of my views in 1933. I also spoke to the leaders of the generation but at the time, my words were not accepted, though I screamed like a crane and warned about the ruin of the world. Alas, it made no impression.
But now, after the atom and hydrogen bombs, I think the world will believe me that the end of the world is nearing rapidly, and Israel will be the first nation to be burned, as was in the previous war. Thus, today it is good to awaken the world to accept its only remedy so they may live and exist.

5. Baal HaSulam, "The Writings of the Last Generation"

I have already said that there are two ways to discover the completeness: the path of Torah or the path of suffering.
Hence, the Creator has given humanity technology, until they have invented the atom and the hydrogen bombs. If the total ruin that they are destined to bring upon the world is still not evident to the world, they can wait for a third world war, or a fourth one. The bombs will do their thing, and the relics who remain after the ruin will have no other choice but to take upon themselves this work where both individuals and nations will not work for themselves more than is necessary for their sustenance, while everything else they do will be for the good of others. If all the nations of the world agree to it, there will no longer be wars in the world, for no person will be concerned with his own good whatsoever, but only with the good of others.

This law of equivalence of form is the law of the Messiah. It was said about this, "But in the end of days, it shall come to pass, etc., and many nations shall go and say, 'Come, and let us go up, etc., for out of Zion shall go forth the law, etc., and He shall judge between many nations.'" That is, the Messiah will teach them the work of the Creator in equivalence of form, which is the teaching and the law of the Messiah. "And shall prove to mighty nations," meaning He will prove to them that if they do not take upon themselves the work of the Creator, all the nations will be destroyed by wars. But if they do accept His law, it is said about it, "And they shall beat their swords into shovels."

If you take the path of Torah and receive the spice, very well. And if you do not, you will tread the path of suffering, meaning that wars will break out with atom and hydrogen bombs, and all the nations of the world will seek advice how to escape the wars. Then they shall come to the Messiah, to Jerusalem, and He will teach them this law.

6. Baal HaSulam, "The Shofar of the Messiah"

Who better than I knows that I am not at all worthy of being even a messenger and a scribe for disclosing such secrets, much less to understand them down to their roots. So why has the Creator done so to me? It is only because the generation is worthy of it, as it is the last generation, which stands at the threshold of complete redemption. For this reason, it is worthy of beginning to hear the voice of the Shofar of the Messiah, which is the revealing of the secrets, as has been explained.

7. Baal HaSulam, "Time to Act"

For a long time now, my conscience has burdened me with a demand to come out and create a fundamental composition regarding the essence of Judaism, religion, and the knowledge of the authentic wisdom of Kabbalah, and spread it among the nation, so people will come to know and properly understand these exalted matters in their true meaning.

8. Baal HaSulam, "Introduction to the Book Panim Meirot uMasbirot," Item 5

Now you will understand what is written in *The Zohar*: "With this composition, the children of Israel will be redeemed from exile." Also, in many other places, only through the expansion of the wisdom of Kabbalah in the masses will we obtain complete redemption.

Our sages also said, "The light in it reforms him." They were intentionally meticulous about it, to show us that only the light enclosed within it, "like apples of gold in settings of silver," in it lies the *Segula* [power/cure] that reforms a person. Both the individual and the nation will not complete the aim for which they were created, except by attaining the internality of the Torah and its secrets.

9. Baal HaSulam, "Introduction to the Book Panim Meirot uMasbirot," Item 5

It is the great expansion of the wisdom of truth within the nation that we need first, so we may merit receiving the benefit from our Messiah. Consequently, the expansion of the wisdom and the coming of our Messiah are interdependent.

Therefore, we must establish seminaries and compose books to hasten the distribution of the wisdom throughout the nation.

10. Baal HaSulam, "Introduction to The Study of the Ten Sefirot," Item 30

Not only are these secrets not forbidden to disclose, but on the contrary, it is a great *Mitzva* [commandment] to disclose them (as it is written in *Pesachim* 119).

And one who knows how to disclose and discloses them, his reward is plentiful. This is because by disclosing these lights to many, particularly to the many, depends the coming of the Messiah, soon in our days, Amen.

11. Baal HaSulam, "Peace in the World"

In our generation, when each person is aided for his happiness by all the countries in the world, it is necessary that to that extent, the individual becomes enslaved to the whole world, like a wheel in a machine.

Therefore, the possibility of making good, happy, and peaceful conducts in one state is inconceivable when it is not so in all the countries in the world, and vice versa. In our time, the countries are all linked in the satisfaction of their needs of life, as individuals were in their families in earlier times. Therefore, we can no longer speak or deal with just conducts that guarantee the well-being of one country or one nation, but only with the well-being of the whole world, for the benefit or harm of each and every person in the world depends and is measured by the benefit of all the individuals the world over.

Although this is, in fact, known and felt, still the people in the world have not yet grasped it properly. Why? Because such is the conduct of development in nature: The act comes before the understanding, and only actions will prove and push humanity forward.

12. Baal HaSulam, "The Writings of the Last Generation"

First, there must be a small establishment, whose majority is willing to work as much as it can and receive as much as it needs for religious reasons. It will work as diligently as contract workers, even more than the eight-hour workday. It will contain all the forms of government of a complete state. In a word, the order of that small society will be sufficient for all the nations in the world, without adding or subtracting.

This institution will be like a global focal point for nations and states surrounding it to the farthest corners of the world. All who enter that framework shall assume the same leadership and the same agenda as the institution. Thus, the entire world will be a single nation, in profits, losses, and results.

13. Baal HaSulam, "The Writings of the Last Generation"

Life's direction is to attain adhesion with Him, strictly to benefit the Creator, or to reward the public with achieving adhesion with Him.

14. Baal HaSulam, "The Writings of the Last Generation"

It is impossible to have a stable democratic society except by means of a society whose majority is good and honest, since society is led by the majority, for better or for worse. Hence, the altruistic communist regime must not be established unless the majority of the public is ready to commit to it for generations. That can only be secured through religion because the nature of religion is that even though it begins coercively, it ends voluntarily.

15. Baal HaSulam, "The Teaching of the Kabbalah and Its Essence"

I am glad that I have been born in such a generation when it is permitted to disclose the wisdom of truth. And should you ask how I know that it is permitted, I will reply that it is because I have been given permission to disclose. That is, until now, the ways by which it is possible to publicly engage and to fully explain each word have not been revealed to any sage. And I, too, have sworn by my teacher not to disclose, as did all the disciples before me. However, this oath and this prohibition apply only to those manners that are given orally from generation to generation, back to the prophets and before. Had these ways been revealed to the public, they would have caused much harm, for reasons known only to us.

Yet, the way in which I engage in my books is a permitted way. Moreover, I have been instructed by my teacher to expand it as much as I can. We call it "the manner of clothing the matters." You will see in the writings of Rabbi Shimon Bar Yochai that he calls this way "giving permission," and this is what the Creator has given me to the fullest extent. We deem it as dependent not on the greatness of the sage, but on the state of the generation, as our sages said, "Little Samuel was worthy, etc., but his generation was unworthy." This is why I said that my being rewarded with the manner of disclosing the wisdom is only because of my generation.

16. Baal HaSulam, "The Shofar of the Messiah"

The disclosure of the wisdom of the hidden in great masses; it is a necessary precondition that must be met prior to the complete redemption.

And the books that have already been revealed through me in this wisdom will testify to it, that matters of the greatest importance have been spread out like a gown for all to see. This is a true testimony that we are already at the threshold of redemption, and the voice of the great Shofar has already been heard, though in the distance, for it still sounds very softly.

Indeed, every greatness requires prior smallness, and there is no great voice if it is not preceded by a soft sound. And this is the way of the Shofar: Its voice grows progressively. And who better than I knows that I am not at all worthy of being even a messenger and a scribe for disclosing such secrets, much less to understand them down to their roots. So why has the Creator done so to me? It is only because the generation is worthy of it, as it is the last generation, which stands at the threshold of complete redemption. For this reason, it is worthy of beginning to hear the voice of the Shofar of the Messiah, which is the revealing of the secrets, as has been explained.

17. Baal HaSulam, "The Prophecy of Baal HaSulam"

After all these days, I listened attentively to all the promises and destinies I have been chosen for by the Lord, yet I found in them neither satisfaction nor the words by which to speak to the dwellers of this world and lead them to God's will, as He had told me. I could not stride among the people, who are vain and slandering the Lord and His creation, while I was satiated and praising, and walking merrily as though mocking those wretched ones.

Matters have touched me to the bottom of my heart, and I resolved that come what may, even if I descend from my sublime degree, I must make a heartfelt prayer to the Lord to grant me attainment and knowledge of the prophecy and wisdom, and the words by which to help the forlorn people of the world, to raise them to the same degree of wisdom and pleasantness as mine.

18. Baal HaSulam, "One Commandment"

I say that the first and only *Mitzva* that guarantees the achievement of the aspiration to attain *Lishma* is to resolve not to work for oneself, apart for the necessary works—merely to provide for one's sustenance. In the rest of the time, he will work for the public: to save the oppressed, and every being in the world that needs salvation and benefit.

19. Baal HaSulam, Letter No. 4

You lack nothing but to go out to a field that the Lord has blessed, and collect all those flaccid organs that have drooped from your soul, and join them into a single body.

In that complete body, the Creator will instill His *Shechina* incessantly, and the fountain of intelligence and high streams of light will be as a never ending fountain. Each place on which you cast your eye will be blessed, and all will be blessed because of you, for they will bless you constantly.

20. Rav Shneur Zalman of Liadi, *Torah, Light*

The great length of this exile is in order to be rewarded with the revelation of the internality of the Torah that will take place in the future. In the giving of the Torah, it was the receiving of the revealed Torah. But the revelation of the internality of the flavors of Torah will be in the future, as was said about it, "I will show him wonders."

21. Rabbi Yaakov Tzemach, "Introduction to Tree of Life."

Studying *The Zohar* at this time is much needed to save and to protect us from all evil, since the disclosure of this wisdom now... in flawed generations, is to be a shield for us to wholeheartedly cling to our Father in Heaven. Previous generations were men of action and pious, and the good deeds saved them from the accusers. Now we are remote from the Upper Root like the yeast in the barrels. Who will protect us if not our study of this wondrous and profound wisdom? Especially, it is as the rav wrote, that the concealed has now become as the revealed.

22. Raaiah Kook, Letters the Raaiah 2, 34

I have agreed to disclose all the secrets of the world, since it is time to do unto the Creator, as it is required at this time. Greater and better than I have suffered slander from the nation for such matters, as their pure spirit pressured them for the sake of correcting the generation, to speak new words and to reveal the concealed, to which the intellect of the masses has not been accustomed.

23. Rav Kook, *Letters of the Raaiah*

I have agreed to disclose the secrets of the world since the time requires it. Greater and better than me have suffered the libel of the people for such matters, who pressed their pure spirits, for the correction of the generation, to say new things and reveal the concealed, to which the common mind has not been accustomed.

24. Raaiah Kook, *Arfiley Tohar*

To turn the hearts and engage the minds in noble thoughts whose origin is the secrets of Torah.

25. Rav Kook, *Letters of the Raaiah*

Have strength my friend to shine the light of the wisdom of the hidden in the world. Now the days are nearing when everyone will recognize and know that the salvation of Israel and the salvation of the whole world depend only on the emergence of the wisdom of Kabbalah in a clear language.

26. Rabbi Avraham Ben Mordechai Azulai, "Introduction to the Book Ohr HaChama," 81

What has been decreed above, not to engage openly in the wisdom of truth, was only for a time—until the end of the year, 1490. From then on it will be called "the last generation," the sentence has been lifted, and permission has been given to engage in *The Book of Zohar*. And from the year, 1540, it is has become praiseworthy to engage in public, great and small. And since it is by virtue of this that the Messiah King will come, and not by another virtue, we must not be negligent.

27. Rav Yitzhak HaCohen Kook (the Raaiah), *Otzrot HaRaaiah* [*Treasures of the Raaiah*], 2, 317

Before us is an obligation to expand and establish the engagement in the inner side of the Torah, in all its spiritual issues, which, in its broader sense, includes the broad wisdom of Israel, whose apex is the knowledge of God in truth, according to the depth of the secrets of Torah. These days, it requires elucidation, scrutiny, and explanation, to make it ever clearer and ever more expansive among our entire nation.

28. The Rav Kook, *Ikvey HaTzon* (Footsteps of the Flock), 54

The great spiritual questions that were previously known only to the greatest and most excellent, must know be known, in various degrees, to all the people. Sublime and lofty words must be brought down from their high fort to the depth of the common, ordinary level. This requires great wealth of spirit and constant practice. Only then will the mind expand and the language be clarified sufficiently to express even the deepest mattes in a light and popular style, to satiate thirsty souls.

29. Raaiah Kook, *Orot HaKodesh*

The tendency of revealing the secrets of Torah is the ideal goal in life and in reality. The darkness, with which the content of sanctity is covered, causes man's spirit to grow smaller and to minimize his aspirations. Thus, he is depleted, all of society is depleted by the depletion of the individuals, and the nation becomes impoverished in its spirit by the draining of its children's spirit.

30. RASHASH, *The Light of the RASHASH*, p 159

I know that by merit of *The Book of Zohar* and the writings of Kabbalah that will spread out in the world, the people of Israel will be freed. Our redemption depends on this learning.

31. The Baal Shem Tov, *Keter Shem Tov*

I asked the Messiah, "When will you come?" He replied to me, "By this you will know: When your teaching is made known and revealed in the world, and your fountains burst forth—what I had taught you and you have attained—and they, too, can make unifications and ascents like you, then all the *Klipot* [shells/peels] will vanish, and it will be a time of good will and salvation.

4

Our Generation – The Last Generation

1. Baal HaSulam, "A Speech for the Completion of The Zohar"

Our generation is the generation of the days of the Messiah. This is why we have been granted the redemption of our holy land from the hands of the foreigners. We have also been rewarded with the revelation of *The Book of Zohar*, which is the beginning of the realization of the verse, "For the earth will be full of the knowledge of the Lord." "And they will teach no more… for they will all know Me, from the least of them unto the greatest of them."

Yet, with those two, we have only been rewarded with giving from the Creator, but we have not received anything into our own hands. Instead, we have been given a chance to begin with the work of the Creator, to engage in Torah and *Mitzvot Lishma*. Then we will be granted the great success that is promised to the generation of the Messiah, which all the generations before us did not know. And then we will be rewarded with the time of reception of both the complete attainment and the complete redemption.

2. Baal HaSulam, "The Shofar of the Messiah"

The disclosure of the wisdom of the hidden in great masses; it is a necessary precondition that must be met prior to the complete redemption.

And the books that have already been revealed through me in this wisdom will testify to it, that matters of the greatest importance have been spread out like a gown for all to see. This is a true testimony that we are already at the threshold of redemption, and the voice of the great *Shofar* has already been heard, though in the distance, for it still sounds very softly.

Indeed, every greatness requires prior smallness, and there is no great voice if it is not preceded by a soft sound. And this is the way of the *Shofar*: Its voice grows progressively. And who better than I knows that I am not at all worthy of being even a messenger and a scribe for disclosing such secrets, much less to understand them down to their roots. So why has the Creator done so to me? It is only because the generation is worthy of it, as it is the last generation, which stands at the threshold of complete redemption. For this reason, it is worthy of beginning to hear the voice of the *Shofar* of the Messiah, which is the revealing of the secrets, as has been explained.

3. Baal HaSulam, "A Speech for the Completion of The Zohar"

All the interpretations of *The Book of Zohar* before ours did not clarify as much as ten percent of the difficult places in *The Zohar*. Even in the little they did clarify, their words are almost as abstruse as the words of *The Zohar* itself.

But in our generation, we have been rewarded with the *Sulam* [Ladder] commentary, which is a complete interpretation of all the words of *The Zohar*. Moreover, not only does it not leave an unclear matter in the whole of *The Zohar* without interpreting it, the clarifications are based on a straightforward analysis, which any intermediate examiner can understand. And since *The Zohar* appeared in our generation, it is a clear proof that we are already in the days of the Messiah, at the outset of that generation of which it was said, "for the earth will be full of the knowledge of the Lord."

4. Baal HaSulam, "A Speech for the Completion of The Zohar"

Rashbi and his generation, the authors of *The Zohar*, who were granted all 125 degrees in completeness, even though it was prior to the days of the Messiah. It was said about him and his disciples: "A sage is preferable to a prophet." Hence, we often find in *The Zohar* that there will be none like the generation of Rashbi until the generation of the Messiah King. This is why his composition made such a great impression in the world, since the secrets of the Torah in it occupy the level of all 125 degrees.

This is why it is said in *The Zohar* that *The Book of Zohar* will be revealed only at the End of Days, the days of the Messiah. This is so because we have already said that if the degrees of the examiners are not at the full measure of the degree of the author, they will not understand his intimations since they do not have a common attainment.

Since the degree of the authors of *The Zohar* is at the full level of the 125 degrees, they cannot be attained prior to the days of the Messiah. It follows that there will be no common attainment with the authors of *The Zohar* in the generations preceding the days of the Messiah. Hence, *The Zohar* could not be revealed in the generations before the generation of the Messiah.

5. Baal HaSulam, "Peace in the World"

There are already people among us who use their singularity in forms of bestowal upon others. Yet, they are still few, as we are still in the midst of the path of development. When we achieve the highest point of the degrees, we will all be using our singularity only in a form of bestowal upon others, and there will never be any case of any person using it in a manner of self-reception.

According to these words, we have found an opportunity to examine the conditions of life in the last generation—the time of world peace, when the whole of humanity achieves the level of the first side and will use their singularity only in a manner of bestowal upon others, and not at all in a manner of reception for oneself. And it is good to copy here the above-mentioned form of life so it will serve us as a lesson and a role model to settle our minds under the flood of the waves of our lives; perhaps it is worthwhile and possible in our generation, too, to experiment in resembling this above form of life.

6. Baal HaSulam, "The Writings of the Last Generation"

The basis of my entire commentary is the will to receive imprinted in every creature, and which is disparity of form to the Creator. Thus, the soul has separated from Him as an organ is separated from the body, since disparity of form in spirituality is like a separating axe in corporeality. It is therefore clear that what the Creator wants from us is equivalence of form, at which time we adhere to Him once more, as before we were created.

This is the meaning of the words, "Adhere to His attributes; as He is merciful, etc." It means that we are to change our attribute, which is the will to receive, and adopt the attribute of the Creator, which is only to bestow, so that all our actions will be only to bestow upon our fellow persons and benefit them as best as we can.

By this we come to the goal of adhering to Him, which is equivalence of form. What one is compelled to do for oneself, namely the necessary minimum for one's self and one's family's sustenance, is not considered disparity of form, as "Necessity is neither condemned nor praised." This is the great revelation that will be revealed in full only in the days of the Messiah. When this teaching is accepted, we will be rewarded with complete redemption.

7. Baal HaSulam, "The Teaching of the Kabbalah and Its Essence"

I am glad that I have been born in such a generation when it is permitted to disclose the wisdom of truth. And should you ask how I know that it is permitted, I will reply that it is because I have been given permission to disclose. That is, until now, the ways by which it is possible to publicly engage and to fully explain each word have not been revealed to any sage. And I, too, have sworn by my teacher not to disclose, as did all the disciples before me. However, this oath and this prohibition apply only to those manners that are given orally from generation to generation, back to the prophets and before. Had these ways been revealed to the public, they would have caused much harm, for reasons known only to us.

Yet, the way in which I engage in my books is a permitted way. Moreover, I have been instructed by my teacher to expand it as much as I can. We call it "the manner of clothing the matters." You will see in the writings of Rabbi Shimon Bar Yochai that he calls this way "giving permission," and this is what the Creator has given me to the fullest extent. We deem it as dependent not on the greatness of the sage, but on the state of the generation, as our sages said, "Little Samuel was worthy, etc., but his generation was unworthy." This is why I said that my being rewarded with the manner of disclosing the wisdom is only because of my generation.

8. *Zohar for All*, *Aharei Mot* [After the Death], "All the Streams Go to the See," Item 32

In the last generations that will come, the Torah will be forgotten from among them, and wiseh-earted will gather in their places and none will be found who will close and open the Torah. Woe to that generation. Henceforth there will not be as this generation until the arrival of the generation of the Messiah, the knowledge will awaken in the world, as it is written, "For they shall all know Me, from the least of them unto the greatest of them."

9. *Zohar for All*, *VaYera*, "A Calculation of the Time of the Messiah," Item 460

And when it is near the days of the Messiah, even infants in the world are destined to find the secrets of the wisdom, and know in them the ends and calculations of redemption, and at that time, it will be revealed to all.

10. Rabbi Avraham Ben Mordechai Azulai, "Introduction to the Book Ohr HaChama," 81

What has been decreed above, not to engage openly in the wisdom of truth, was only for a time—until the end of the year, 1490. From then on it will be called "the last generation," the sentence has been lifted, and permission has been given to engage in *The Book of Zohar*. And from the year, 1540, it is has become praiseworthy to engage in public, great and small. And since it is by virtue of this that the Messiah King will come, and not by another virtue, we must not be negligent.

11. Rav Kook, *Letters of the Raaiah*

I have agreed to disclose the secrets of the world since the time requires it. Greater and better than me have suffered the libel of the people for such matters, who pressed their pure spirits, for the correction of the generation, to say new things and reveal the concealed, to which the common mind has not been accustomed.

12. Raaiah Kook, *Arfiley Tohar*

Turning the hearts and engaging the minds in noble thoughts whose origin is the secrets of Torah has become an absolute must for the existence of Judaism in the last generation.

13. Rabbi Pinchas Eliyahu Ben Meir, *Sefer HaBrit* [*Book of the Covenant*], Part 2, Essay no. 12, Chapter 5

Know for certain, my brother, that the previous generations and the early days that were in the fifth millennium are not as these generations and these days. In those days, the gates of wisdom were closed and locked. Hence, Kabbalists were few then. Conversely, in this sixth millennium, when the gates of light, the gates of mercy, have been opened, since it is near the end of days, and there is joy of *Mitzva* [commandment] and great contentment in the eyes of the Creator to make the glory of His kingdom known forever. Especially now that the holy writings of the ARI have been printed, who opened for us the gates of light that have been sealed and locked by a thousand keys since days of old, and all his words are words of the living God, based on Prophet Elijah, and by whose permission he revealed what he revealed. Now there is no obstacle or peril before us, just as in the revealed.

14. Rav Chaim Vital, Introduction of Rav Chaim Vital to *Shaar HaHakdamot*

Until now, the words of the wisdom of *The Zohar* were concealed. In the last generation, this wisdom will be revealed and become known, and they will understand and become wise in secrets of Torah that the our predecessors did not attain.

15. *Zohar for All*, *VaYera*, "A Calculation of the Time of the Messiah," Item 460

And when it is near the days of the Messiah, even infants in the world are destined to find the secrets of the wisdom, and know in them the ends and calculations of redemption, and at that time, it will be revealed to all.

16. Rabbi Avraham Ben Mordechai Azulai, "Introduction to the Book Ohr HaChama," 81

What has been decreed above, not to engage openly in the wisdom of truth, was only for a time—until the end of the year, 1490. From then on it will be called "the last generation," the sentence has been lifted, and permission has been given to engage in *The Book of Zohar*. And from the year, 1540, it is has become praiseworthy to engage in public, great and small. And since it is by virtue of this that the Messiah King will come, and not by another virtue, we must not be negligent.

17. Rav Kook, *Letters of the Raaiah*

I have agreed to disclose the secrets of the world since the time requires it. Greater and better than me have suffered the libel of the people for such matters, who pressed their pure spirits, for the correction of the generation, to say new things and reveal the concealed, to which the common mind has not been accustomed.

18. Raaiah Kook, *Arfiley Tohar*

Turning the hearts and engaging the minds in noble thoughts whose origin is the secrets of Torah has become an absolute must for the existence of Judaism in the last generation.

19. Rabbi Pinchas Eliyahu Ben Meir, *Sefer HaBrit* [*Book of the Covenant*], Part 2, Essay no. 12, Chapter 5

Know for certain, my brother, that the previous generations and the early days that were in the fifth millennium are not as these generations and these days. In those days, the gates of wisdom were closed and locked. Hence, Kabbalists were few then. Conversely, in this sixth millennium, when the gates of light, the gates of mercy, have been opened, since it is near the end of days, and there is joy of *Mitzva* [commandment] and great contentment in the eyes of the Creator to make the glory of His kingdom known forever. Especially now that the holy writings of the ARI have been printed, who opened for us the gates of light that have been sealed and locked by a thousand keys since days of old, and all his words are words of the living God, based on Prophet Elijah, and by whose permission he revealed what he revealed. Now there is no obstacle or peril before us, just as in the revealed.

20. Rav Chaim Vital, Introduction of Rav Chaim Vital to *Shaar HaHakdamot*

Until now, the words of the wisdom of *The Zohar* were concealed. In the last generation, this wisdom will be revealed and become known, and they will understand and become wise in secrets of Torah that the our predecessors did not attain.

5

The Society in the Last Generation

1. Baal HaSulam, "The Writings of the Last Generation"

First, there must be a small establishment whose majority are altruists to the above-mentioned extent. This means that they will work as diligently as contract workers, ten to twelve hours a day and more. Each and every one will work according to his ability and receive according to his needs.

It will have all the forms of government of a state. In this manner, even if the framework of this institution contains the entire world, and the brute-force government will be revoked completely, nothing will need to change in governance or work.

This institution will be like a global focal point with nations and states surrounding it to the farthest corners of the world. All who enter this framework of communism will have the same program and the same leadership as the center. They will be as one nation in profits, losses, and results.

2. Baal HaSulam, "The Writings of the Last Generation"

Judgments relying on force will be completely revoked in this institution. Rather, all conflicts among the members of society will be resolved among the concerned parties. General public opinion shall condemn anyone who exploits the righteousness of his friend for his own good.

There will still be a courthouse, but it will only serve to sort out doubts that will come between people, but it will not rely on any force. One who rejects the court's decision will be condemned by public opinion, and nothing more.

We should not doubt its sufficiency, as it was unbelievable that children could be educated only by explanation, but only through the cane. However, today, the greater part of civilization has taken upon itself to refrain from beating children, and this upbringing is more successful than the previous method.

If there is one who is exceptional in society, he must not be brought before a court relying on force, but must be reformed through argumentation and explanation and public opinion. If all the counsels do not help him, the public will turn away from that person as though from an outcast. Thus, he will not be able to corrupt others in society.

3. Baal HaSulam, "The Writings of the Last Generation"

The religious form of all the nations should first obligate its members to bestowal upon each other to the extent that (the life of one's friend will come before one's own life), as in "Love your friend as yourself." One will not take pleasure in society more than a straggling friend.

This will be the collective religion of all the nations that will come within the framework of communism. However, besides this, each nation may follow its own religion and tradition, and one must not interfere in the other.

4. Baal HaSulam, "The Nation"

Briefly, we can say that we must set up such dissemination, scientifically and practically, that will be certain to install in the public opinion that any member who does not excel in altruism is like a predator that is unfit to be among humans, until one feels oneself within the society as a murderer and a robber.

If we systematically engage in circulating this matter using the appropriate manners, it will not require such a long process. Hitlerism proves that within a short period of time, an entire country has been turned upside down through propaganda and accepted his bizarre notion.

5. Baal HaSulam, "The Writings of the Last Generation"

The rules of the equal religion for the entire world are as follows:

1) One should work for the well-being of people as much as one can and even more than one's ability, if needed, until there is no hunger or thirst in the entire world.
2) One may be diligent, but no person shall benefit from the society more than the stragglers. There will be an equal standard of living for all.
3) Although there is religion, tokens of honors should be imparted according to the religion: The greater the benefit one contributes to society, the higher the decoration one shall receive.
4) Refraining from showing one's diligence toward the benefit of society will induce punishment according to the laws of society.
5) Each and every one is committed to the labor of raising ever higher the living standard of the world society, so all the people in the world will enjoy their lives and will feel more and more happiness.
6) The same applies for spirituality, though not everyone is obligated to engage in spirituality, but only special people, depending on the need.
7) There will be a sort of high court. Those who will want to dedicate their labor for spiritual life will have to be permitted to do so by this court.

Also, to elaborate on the other necessary laws.

6. Baal HaSulam, "The Writings of the Last Generation"

Neither bayonets nor education or public opinion can change human nature to work willingly without adequate fuel.

Hence, it is a curse for generations. When the compulsory government is revoked, the workers will no longer yield produce that will suffice for the sustenance of the state. There is no cure for this but to bring faith in spiritual reward and punishment from above into the hearts of the workers, from He who knows the mysteries.

Thus, through the right education and promotion, that spiritual reward and punishment will be sufficient fuel for the produce of their work. They will no longer need managers or supervisors over their shoulders, but each and every one will work willingly and wholeheartedly for society, to win his or her reward from Heaven.

7. Baal HaSulam, "The Writings of the Last Generation"

Each one of them fills his or her role in service of the public in the best way, albeit without seeing it, since public opinion presses a person even secretly, to the point where one feels that deceiving society by mistake is as grave as mistakenly killing a human being.

8. Baal HaSulam, "The Writings of the Last Generation"

1) They have many methodical books of wisdom and morals that prove the glory and sublimity of excellence in bestowing upon others, to a point where the entire nation, from small to great, engage in them wholeheartedly.
2) Each person who is appointed to an important position must first graduate a special training in the above-mentioned teaching.
3) Their courts are busy primarily with awarding accolades marking the level of each person's distinction in bestowal upon others. There is not a person without a medal on the sleeve, and it is a great offense to call a person not by one's title of honor. It is also a great offense for a person to forgive such an insult to one's title.
4) There is such fierce competition in the field of bestowal upon others that most people risk their lives, since public opinion tremendously appreciates and respects the accolades of the highest rank in bestowal upon others.
5) If a person is recognized as having done for oneself a little more than what was decided for him by society, society condemns it so much that it becomes a disgrace to speak with him, and he also gravely blemishes his family's reputation. The only remedy for his plight is to ask for the court's help, which has certain ways by which to help such miserable people who lost their position in society. But for the most part, they relocate him because of prejudice, since public opinion cannot be changed.

9. Baal HaSulam, "Peace in the World"

Do not be surprised if I mix together the well-being of a particular collective with the well-being of the whole world, because indeed we have already come to such a degree where the whole world is considered one collective and one society. That is, because each person in the world draws his life's marrow and his livelihood from all the people in the world, he thereby becomes enslaved, to serve and care for the well-being of the entire world.

10. Baal HaSulam, "The Writings of the Last Generation"

Even courthouses will not be necessary, unless some unusual event occurs, where the neighbors do not influence an exceptional individual. In that case, special pedagogues will be needed to turn that person around through argumentation and explanation of the benefit of society until that person is brought back in line.

If a person is stubborn, and it is all to no avail, the public will turn away from that person as though from an outcast until that person rejoins the rules of society.

11. Baal HaSulam, "Peace in the World"

In our generation, when each person is aided for his happiness by all the countries in the world, it is necessary that to that extent, the individual becomes enslaved to the whole world, like a wheel in a machine.

Therefore, the possibility of making good, happy, and peaceful conducts in one state is inconceivable when it is not so in all the countries in the world, and vice versa. In our time, the countries are all linked in the satisfaction of their needs of life, as individuals were in their families in earlier times. Therefore, we can no longer speak or deal with just conducts that guarantee the well-being of one country or one nation, but only with the well-being of the whole world, for the benefit or harm of each and every person in the world depends and is measured by the benefit of all the individuals the world over.

12. Baal HaSulam, "Peace in the World"

The collective and the individual are one and the same, and the individual is not harmed because of his enslavement to the collective, since the freedom of the collective and the freedom of the individual are one and the same, too, and as they share the good, they also share the freedom. Thus, good attributes and bad attributes, good deeds and bad deeds are evaluated only with respect to the benefit of the public.

Of course, the above words apply if all the individuals perform their role toward the public to the fullest and receive no more than they deserve, nor take from their friend's share. But if a part of the collective does not behave accordingly, as a result, they not only harm the collective, but they, too, are harmed.

We should not discuss further something that is known to all, and the aforesaid is only to show the drawback, the place that needs correction, namely that each and every individual will understand that his own benefit and the benefit of the collective are one and the same, and by this, the world will come to its full correction.

13. Baal HaSulam, "The Writings of the Last Generation"

The whole world is one family. The framework of communism should eventually encircle the entire world in an equal standard of living for all. However, the actual process is gradual. Each nation whose majority accepts these basic elements practically, and has a guaranteed fuel, may enter the framework of communism right away.

14. Baal HaSulam, "The Writings of the Last Generation"

First, there must be a small establishment, whose majority is willing to work as much as it can and receive as much as it needs for religious reasons. It will work as diligently as contract workers, even more than the eight-hour workday. It will contain all the forms of government of a complete state. In a word, the order of that small society will be sufficient for all the nations in the world, without adding or subtracting.

This institution will be like a global focal point for nations and states surrounding it to the farthest corners of the world. All who enter that framework shall assume the same leadership and the same agenda as the institution. Thus, the entire world will be a single nation, in profits, losses, and results.

15. Baal HaSulam, "The Writings of the Last Generation"

Ultimately, altruistic communism will encircle the entire world, and the entire world will have the same standard of living. However, the actual process is slow and gradual. Each nation whose majority of the public has been educated to bestowal upon one another will enter the international communist framework first.

All the nations that have already entered the international communist framework will have an equal standard of living.

16. Baal HaSulam, "The Nation"

Our planet is rich enough to provide for all of us, so why should we fight this tragic war to the death, which has been dimming our lives for generations? Let us share among us the labor and its produce equally, and the end to all the troubles! After all, what pleasure do even the millionaires among us derive from their possessions if not the security of their sustenance for them and for their progeny several generations on? But in a regime of just division they will also have the same certainty and even more.

And should you say that they will not have the respect that they had while they were property owners, that, too, is nothing, for all those strong ones who have gained the power to earn respect as property owners will certainly find the same amount of honor elsewhere, for the gates of competition will never be locked.

PART 4
Man's Relation to the Creator

1

If I am Not for Me, Who Is for Me?

1. Baal HaSulam, *Shamati*, Article No. 217, "If I Am Not for Me, Who Is for Me?"

"If I am not for me who is for me, and when I am for myself, what am I?" This is an inherent contradiction. The thing is that one should do all of one's work by way of "If I am not for me, who is for me," that no one can save him, but "by your mouth, and by your heart to do it," that is, a discernment of reward and punishment. However, to oneself, in private, one should know that "when I am for myself, what am I?" This means that everything is in private Providence and no one can do anything.

If you say that if everything is in private Providence, why is there the issue of working in the form of "If I am not for me, who is for me?" Yet, through working in the form of "If I am not for me, who is for me," one is awarded private Providence, meaning attains it. Thus, everything follows the path of correction, and the distribution of added fondness, called "children of the Creator," is not revealed unless it is preceded by work in the form of "If I am not for me, who is for me."

2. Baal HaSulam, Letter No. 16

I have already said in the name of the Baal Shem Tov that prior to making a *Mitzva* [commandment], one must not consider private Providence at all. On the contrary, one should say, "If I am not for me, who is for me?" But after the fact, one must reconsider and believe that it was not by "My power and the might of my hand" that I did the *Mitzva*, but only by the power of the Creator, who contemplated so about me in advance, and so I had to do.

It is likewise in worldly matters because spirituality and corporeality are equal. Therefore, before one goes out to make one's daily bread, he should remove his thoughts from private Providence and say, "If I am not for me, who is?" He should do all the tactics applied in corporeality to earn his living as do others.

But in the evening, when he returns home with his earnings, he must never think that he has earned this profit by his own innovations. Rather, even if he stayed all day in the basement of his home, he would still have earned his pay, for so the Creator contemplated for him in advance, and so it had to be.

Although the matters look the contrary on the surface, and are unreasonable, one must believe that so the Creator has determined for him in His law, from authors and from books.

3. Baal HaSulam, *Shamati*, Article No. 5, "Lishma Is an Awakening from Above, and Why Do We Need an Awakening From Below?"

In order to attain *Lishma* [for Her sake], it is not within one's hands to understand, as it is not for the human mind to grasp how such a thing can be in the world. This is so because one is only permitted to grasp that if he engages in Torah and *Mitzvot* [commandments] he will attain something. There must be self-benefit there for otherwise, one is unable to do anything. Rather, it is an illumination that comes from above, and only one who tastes it can know and understand. It is written about it, "Taste and see that the Lord is good."

Thus, we must understand why one should seek advice and counsels regarding how to achieve *Lishma*. After all, no counsels will help him, and if the Creator does not give him the second nature, called "the desire to bestow," no labor will help him to attain the matter of *Lishma*.

The answer is, as our sages said (*Avot*, Chapter 2, 21), "It is not for you to complete the work, and you are not free to idle away from it." This means that one must give the awakening from below, since this is regarded as a prayer.

A prayer is considered a deficiency, and without a deficiency there is no filling. Hence, when one has a need for *Lishma*, the filling comes from above, and the answer to the prayer comes from above, meaning he receives fulfillment for his lack.

4. RABASH, Assorted Notes, Article No. 845, "None as Holy as the Lord"

"There is none who is as holy as the Lord." But is there one who is worse than the Creator but holy? "There is no rock like our God." Does that mean that there is another rock, which is a little worse than the Creator? Rather, there are holy ones and angels and souls, and all receive *Kedusha* [holiness] from the Creator. This is not so "because there is none besides You." Rather, You will give them *Kedusha* [holiness] (*The Zohar*, *Tazria*, Item 37).

We should ask what this tells us in the work. One must believe how all the overcoming in the work, and did he labor in order to be rewarded with the Holy one, as it is written, "You will be holy, for I am holy." At that time, one must know that all of man's work does not help him whatsoever. Rather, it is all from the Creator.

In other words, all the *Kedusha* [holiness] that one feels he has comes to him from the Creator. This is what it means that there is no *Kedusha*, meaning no *Kedusha* in the world that one can obtain by himself. Rather, everything comes from the Creator. This is why it is written, "There is none as holy as the Lord," and "There is no rock like our God."

It is known that *Kelim* [vessels] are called by the name *Elokim* [God], and lights are called by the name of *HaVaYaH*. It is written, "there is no rock," which is when one sees that he has vessels of bestowal. This is regarded that a new thing was created for him, which is called a "rock," meaning that in a place where he had vessels of reception, vessels of bestowal have been depicted in him. One should not think that he helped the Creator in any way and by this obtained vessels of bestowal. Rather, everything came from above.

Baal HaSulam said that prior to working, one must say, "If I am not for me, who is for me?" After the work, he should believe in private Providence, meaning that the Creator does everything. This is the meaning of what is written there: "The Creator draws a picture within a picture." We should interpret that within the form of the *Kelim*, which is reception, He draws there the form of bestowal.

5. RABASH, Article No. 19 (1990), "Why Is the Torah Called "Middle Line" in the Work? - 2"

One should believe that "there is none else besides Him," that the Creator does everything. In other words, as Baal HaSulam said, before each action one should say that man was given only choice, since "If I am not for me, who is for me?" Thus, everything depends on one's choice. However, after the fact, one should say that everything is private Providence, and that one does nothing on his own.

6. RABASH, Assorted Notes, Article No. 659 "What Are Torah and Work?"

With regard to the Creator, we can speak of Torah, since work pertains specifically to the created beings.

Work applies only to the created beings. Hence, when we speak of work, it means that we learn what one should do. In that state, a person should say, "If I am not for me, who is for me?"

Afterward, we should extend the quality of Torah on this work, regarded as what the Creator does. That is, we must extend the discernment of private Providence and we must not say, "My strength and the might of my hand has gotten me these riches." This is the meaning of the Torah being called "the names of the Creator," meaning that the Creator does everything.

7. RABASH, Article No. 6 (1991), What Is, "The Herdsmen of Abram's Cattle and the Herdsmen of Lot's Cattle," in the Work?

As long as a person does not have the desire to bestow, he is unfit to receive delight and pleasure. Therefore, when a person suffers, he loses the faith. But once he has been rewarded with the desire to bestow, he receives delight and pleasure from the Creator and is rewarded with permanent faith. It follows that all those ascents and descents bring him to a state where the Creator helps him achieve the desire to bestow, and then all his works are for the sake of the Creator.

However, a person must know that when he comes to a state where he does not see how he will ever be able to emerge from self-love and he wants to escape the campaign, he must know that there are two matters here, which are opposite from one another, as our sages said (*Avot*, Chapter 2:21), "It is not for you to finish the work, nor are you free to idle away from it."

Thus, on one hand, a person must work and never idle away from it. That is, it is within man's power to attain, since he says, "nor are you free to idle away from it." This means that one should work because he is guaranteed to get what he wants, meaning to be able to work for the sake of the Creator in order to bring contentment to his Maker.

On the other hand, he says, "It is not for you to finish the work." This implies that it is not within man's hands, but rather, as it is written, "The Lord will finish for me." This means that it is not within man's ability to obtain the desire to bestow.

However, there are two matters here: 1) A person must say, "If I am not for me, who is for me?" Hence, he should not be alarmed by the fact that he has not been rewarded with obtaining the desire to bestow, although in his opinion, he has made great efforts. Nonetheless, he should believe that the Creator waits until he reveals what he must do. 2) Afterward, the Creator will finish for him, meaning that at that time, he will receive what he wants at once, as it is written, "The salvation of the Lord is as the blink of an eye."

8. RABASH, Article No. 6 (1989), "What Is Above Reason in the Work?"

This is the meaning of the words, "king of Israel and his redeemer." That is, once they have taken upon themselves the kingdom of heaven, called "king of Israel," they attain that the Creator is his redeemer, meaning that only the Creator redeemed them from the control of the evil, and they themselves were powerless to do so.

In this way, we should interpret the words "Lord of hosts." This name means, as Baal HaSulam interpreted, that as he said, *Tzevaot* [hosts] are two words: *Tze* [leave/go out] and *Ba* [comes]. That is, *Tzava* [army] are men of war. These are people who go each day to fight the evil inclination. They are called "army." Therefore, after they have been rewarded with redemption, meaning after they conquer the evil inclination and emerge from the control of the evil, their conduct in the work is by way of ascents and descents, which is called *Tzevaot* [plural of *Tzava* (army)]. Meaning, at times they emerge from their control, and then are under their control again. Thus, the name for ascents and descents is *Tzevaot*.

During the work, a person should say, "If I am not for me, who is for me?" At that time in the work, they think that they themselves are doing the ascents and descents, that they are men of war, called *Tzava*, "mighty men." Afterward, when they are redeemed, they attain that the Lord is of hosts [*Tzevaot*], meaning that the Creator made all the ups and downs they had.

In other words, even the descents come from the Creator. A person does not get so many ups and downs for no reason. Rather, the Creator caused all those exits. We can interpret "exit" as "exit from *Kedusha* [holiness]," and *Ba* [comes] as "coming to *Kedusha*. The Creator does everything. Hence, after the redemption, the Creator is called "Lord of Hosts." And who is He? "The king of Israel and his redeemer."

9. RABASH, Article No. 18 (1986), "Who Causes the Prayer"

One must not say, "I'm waiting for the Creator to give me an awakening from above, and then I will be able to work in the work of holiness." Baal HaSulam said that in regard to the future, a person must believe in reward and punishment, meaning he must say (*Avot*, Chapter 1), "If I am not for me who is for me, and when I am for me, what am I, and if not now, then when?"

Thus, one mustn't wait another moment. Instead, he should say, "If not now, then when?" And he must not wait for a better time, so "Then I will get up and do the work of holiness." Rather, it is as our sages said (*Avot*, Chapter 2), "Do not say, 'I will study when I have time,' lest you will not have time."

10. *Pirkei Avot*, 1:14

He (Old Hillel) would say, "If I am not for me, who is for me? And when I am for myself, what am I? And if not now then when?"

2

There Is None Else Besides Him

1. Baal HaSulam, *Shamati*, Article No. 1, "There Is None Else Besides Him"

It is written, "There is none else besides Him." This means that there is no other force in the world that has the ability to do anything against Him. And what one sees, that there are things in the world that deny the upper household, the reason is that this is His will.

This is deemed a correction called "the left rejects and the right pulls closer," meaning that what the left rejects is considered a correction. This means that there are things in the world that, to begin with, aim to divert a person from the right way, and by which he is rejected from *Kedusha* [holiness].

The benefit from the rejections is that through them a person receives a complete need and desire for the Creator to help him since he sees that otherwise he is lost; not only is he not progressing in the work, he even sees that he regresses. That is, he lacks the strength to observe Torah and *Mitzvot* [commandments] even *Lo Lishma* [not for Her sake], for only by genuinely overcoming all the obstacles, above reason, can he observe the Torah and *Mitzvot*. But he does not always have the strength to overcome above reason; otherwise, he is forced to deviate, God forbid, from the way of the Creator, even from *Lo Lishma*.

And he, who always feels that the shattered is greater than the whole, meaning that there are many more descents than ascents, and he does not see an end to these states, and he will forever remain outside of holiness, for he sees that it is difficult for him to observe even in the slightest bit, unless by overcoming above reason. But he cannot always overcome, so what will be in the end?

Then he comes to the decision that no one can help but the Creator Himself. This causes him to make a heartfelt demand that the Creator will open his eyes and heart and truly bring him closer to eternal *Dvekut* [adhesion] with the Creator. It therefore follows that all the rejections that he had were all from the Creator.

This means that it was not because he was at fault that he did not have the ability to overcome. Rather, for those people who truly want to draw near to the Creator, so they do not settle for little, meaning remain as senseless children, he is therefore given help from above so he will not be able to say, "Thank God, I have Torah and *Mitzvot* and good deeds, and what else do I need?"

Only if that person has a true desire will he receive help from above, and he will always be shown that he is at fault in the present state. Namely, he is sent thoughts and views that are against the work. This is in order for him to see that he is not in wholeness with the Creator. As much as he overcomes, he always sees that he is farther from holiness than others, who feel that they are in wholeness with the Creator.

But he, on the other hand, always has complaints and demands, and he cannot justify the Creator's behavior, the way He behaves with him. This pains him: Why is he not wholly with the Creator? Finally, he comes to feel that he has no part in holiness at all.

Although he occasionally receives an awakening from above, which momentarily revives him, soon after, he falls into the place of baseness. Yet, this is what causes him to come to realize that only the Creator can help and really bring him closer.

2. Baal HaSulam, *The Study of the Ten Sefirot*, "Inner Observation" Chapter 1, Item 1

The Ramban has already explained to us the matter of His uniqueness as expressed in the words, "One, Unique and Unified."

In his interpretation to *Sefer Yetzira* (Book of Creation), he explains the difference between One, Unique, and Unified: When He unites to act with One Force, He is called "Unified." When He divides to act His act, each part of Him is called Unique, and when He is in a single evenness, He is called One, thus far his pure words.

By saying, "unites to act with One Force," he wishes to say that He works to bestow, as worthy of His Oneness, and His operations are unchanging. When He "divides to act His act," meaning when His operations differ, and He seems to be doing good and bad, then He is called "Unique" because all His different operations have a single outcome: good.

We find that He is unique in every single act and does not change by His various operations. When He is in a single evenness He is called "One." One points to His Atzmut, where all the opposites are in a single evenness. It is as the Rambam wrote: "In Him, knower, known and knowledge are one, for His thoughts are far higher than our thoughts, and His ways higher than our ways".

3. Baal HaSulam, *Shamati*, Article No. 138, "Concerning Fear that Sometimes Comes Upon a Person"

When fear comes upon a person, he should know that there is none else but Him. And even witchcraft. And if he sees that fear overcomes him, he should say that there is no such thing as chance, but the Creator has given him a chance from above, and he must contemplate and study the end to which he has been sent this fear. It appears that it is so that he will overcome and say, "There is none else besides Him."

But if after all this, the fear has not departed him, he should take it as an example and say that his servitude of the Creator should be in the same measure of the fear, meaning that the fear of heaven, which is a merit, should be in the same manner of fear that he now has. That is, the body is impressed by this superficial fear, and exactly in the same way that the body is impressed, so should be the fear of heaven.

4. Baal HaSulam, "You Have Made Me in Behind and Before"

"You have made me in behind and before," meaning the revelation and concealment of the face of the Creator. This is because indeed, "His kingdom rules over all," and everything will return to its root because there is no place vacant of Him. But the difference is in the present or the future, because one who connects the two worlds discovers His clothing in the present, that everything that is done is a clothing for the revelation of the *Shechina* [Divinity].

This is deemed the present, meaning that now, too, he comes out in royal attire and evidently shows that the rider is not subordinate to the horse. But although it seemingly appears that the horse leads its rider, the truth is that the horse is provoked to any movement only by the sensation of the rider's bridle and headstall. This is called "The construction of the stature of the *Shechina*," and it is also called "face-to-face."

5. Baal HaSulam, *Shamati*, Article No. 67, "Depart from Evil"

Who thinks that he is deceiving his friend is really deceiving the Creator, since besides man's body there is only the Creator. This is because it is the essence of creation that man is called "creature" only with respect to himself. The Creator wants man to feel that he is a separate reality from Him; but other than this, it is all "The whole earth is full of His glory."

Hence, when lying to one's friend, one is lying to the Creator; and when saddening one's friend, one is saddening the Creator. For this reason, if one is accustomed to say the truth, it will help him with respect to the Creator.

6. Baal HaSulam, *Shamati*, Article No. 4, "What Is the Reason for the Heaviness One Feels when Annulling before the Creator in the Work?"

The essence of one's work is only to come to feel the existence of the Creator, meaning to feel the existence of the Creator, that "the whole earth is full of His glory," and this will be one's entire work. That is, all the energy one puts into the work will be only to achieve this, and nothing else.

One should not be misled into having to acquire anything. Rather, there is only one thing a person needs: faith in the Creator. He should not think of anything, meaning that the only reward that he wants for his work should be to be rewarded with faith in the Creator.

7. Baal HaSulam, "Introduction to A Sage's Fruit," Vol. 4 (Three Partners)

It is impossible to attribute the bad to the Creator since he is the absolute good. Hence, as long as one feels bad states, he must say that they come from elsewhere, from the environment. But in truth, when one is rewarded with seeing only good and that there is no bad in the world, and everything is turned to good, then he is shown the truth, that the Creator did everything because He is almighty, and He alone did, does, and will do all the deeds.

8. Baal HaSulam, "The Meaning of His Names"

Come and learn the real wisdom, the reason for this whole entanglement. In the Creator Himself, there is no thought or perception whatsoever, and the reason is simple: All the thoughts that come into one's mind are the very operations of the Creator. That is, it is not as one senses, that he extends them from some place or that they are born within him on the spot. This is a lie, the number one lie.

Rather, every thought, even the most slender, the Creator sends it to a person's mind, and this is the power of movement of man, beast, and every living thing. That is, when the Creator wishes to move the living being, He acts in it by sending a single thought, and that thought moves it according to its measure. It is as one who sends rain upon the ground but the ground cannot feel who sent it the rain. Likewise, man is utterly unable to feel who has sent him the thought, for he will not feel it before it comes into the domain of his imagining mind. And once it is in his domain, it seems to him as part of his self. By this you will understand that there is no thought or perception of Him, for the simple reason that the Creator did not wish to send us such a thought that will be capable of attaining Him.

However, He has arranged for us an procession of thoughts whereby this entire procession, one must ultimately attain Him to the real extent. This is the meaning of (2 Sam. 14:14), "No outcast shall be cast out from Him."

9. Baal HaSulam, Letter No. 1

Everyone believes in private Providence, but do not adhere to it at all.
The reason is that an alien and foul thought … cannot be attributed to the Creator, who is the epitome of the "good who does good." However, only to the true servants of the Creator does the knowledge of private Providence open, that He caused all the reasons that preceded it, both good and bad. Then they are adhered to private Providence, for all who are connected to the pure are pure.

Since the Guardian is united with His guarded, there is no apparent division between bad and good. They are all loved and are all clear, for they are all carriers of the vessels of the Creator, ready to glorify the revelation of His uniqueness. It is known by the senses, and to that extent, they have knowledge in the end that all the actions and the thoughts, both good and bad, are the carriers of the vessels of the Creator. He prepared them, from His mouth they emerged, and at the end of correction it will be known to all.

10. Baal HaSulam, *The Study of the Ten Sefirot*, "Inner Observation," Chapter 1, Item 8

This entire reality, *Elyonim* and *Tachtonim* as one in the final state of the end of correction, was emanated and created by a single thought. That single thought performs all the operations, is the essence of all the operations, the purpose and the essence of the labor. It is by itself the entire perfection and the sought-after reward.

11. Baal HaSulam, "Introduction to The Book of Zohar," Item 13

By the very thought to create the souls, His thought completed everything, for He does not need an act, as do we. Instantaneously, all the souls and worlds that were destined to be created emerged filled with all the delight and pleasure and the gentleness that He had planned for them, in the final perfection that the souls were destined to receive at the end of correction, after the will to receive in the souls has been fully corrected and has turned into pure bestowal, in complete equivalence of form with the Emanator.

This is so because in His eternalness, past, present, and future are as one. The future is as the present, and there is no such thing as time in Him (*The Zohar, Mishpatim*, Item 51, *New Zohar, Beresheet*, Item 243). Hence, there was never an issue of a corrupted will to receive in its separated state in *Ein Sof*.

On the contrary, that equivalence of form, destined to be revealed at the end of correction, appeared instantly in His eternalness. Our sages said about this (*Pirkei de Rabbi Eliezer*): "Before the world was created, there were He is one and His name One," for the separated form in the will to receive had not been revealed in the reality of the souls that emerged in the thought of creation. Rather, they were adhered to Him in equivalence of form by way of "He is one and His name One."

12. Baal HaSulam, *Shamati*, Article No. 50, "Two States"

There are two states to the world: 1) In the first state the world is called "pain." 2) In the second state, it is called "*Shechina* [Divinity]." It is so because before one is endowed with correcting his deeds to be in order to bestow, he feels the world only in the form of pains and torments.

However, afterward, he is rewarded with seeing that the *Shechina* is clothed in the whole world, and then the Creator is considered to be filling the world. Then the world is called "*Shechina*," who receives from the Creator. This is called "the unification of the Creator and His *Shechina*," for as the Creator gives, so the world is now occupied solely in bestowal.

13. Baal HaSulam, *Shamati*, Article No. 1, "There Is None Else Besides Him"

One must always try and adhere to the Creator, namely that all his thoughts will be about Him. That is to say, even if he is in the worst state, from which there cannot be a greater decline, he should not leave His domain, namely that there is another authority that prevents him from entering the *Kedusha* [holiness], that can bring benefit or harm.

That is, he must not think that there is a force of the *Sitra Achra* [other side] that does not let a person do good deeds and walk in the ways of the Creator. Rather, all is done by the Creator.

The Baal Shem Tov said that he who says that there is another force in the world, namely *Klipot* [shells], that person is in a state of "serving other gods." It is not necessarily the thought of heresy that is the transgression, but if he thinks that there is another authority and force apart from the Creator, he is committing a transgression.

Furthermore, one who says that man has his own authority, that is, he says that yesterday he himself did not want to follow the Creator's ways, this, too, is considered committing the transgression of heresy, meaning he does not believe that only the Creator is the leader of the world.

14. Baal HaSulam, Letter No. 18

One has no choice but to direct all the present and future moments to be offered and presented to His great name. One who rejects a moment before Him for it is difficult displays his folly openly, for all the worlds and all the times are not worthwhile for him because the light of His face is not clothed in the changing times and occasions although one's work certainly changes because of them. This is why thanks to our holy fathers, faith and confidence above reason have been prepared for us, which one uses in the tougher times effortlessly and tirelessly.

15. Baal HaSulam, Letter No. 16

The meaning of the unification of *HaVaYaH Elokim* [God]. *HaVaYaH* means private Providence, where the Creator is everything, and He does not need dwellers of material houses to help Him. *Elokim* in *Gematria* is *HaTeva* [the nature], where man behaves according to the nature that He instilled in the systems of the corporeal heaven and earth, and he keeps those rules as do the rest of the corporeal beings. And yet, he also believes in *HaVaYaH*, meaning in private Providence.

By this he unites them with one another, and "they became as one in his hand." In this way, he brings great contentment to his Maker and brings illumination in all the worlds.

This is the meaning of the three discernments—commandment, transgression, and permission. The commandment is the place of *Kedusha* [holiness], the transgression is the place of the *Sitra Achra* [other side], and permission, which is neither a *Mitzva* nor a transgression, is the place over which the *Kedusha* and the *Sitra Achra* fight.

When a person does permitted things but does not dedicate them to *Kedusha*, that entire place falls into the domain of the *Sitra Achra*. And when a person grows stronger and engages in permitted things to make unifications as much as he can, he returns the permission into the domain of *Kedusha*.

16. Baal HaSulam, *Shamati*, Article No. 15, "What Is Other Gods in the Work?"

It is known that when one begins to work more than one is used to, the body begins to kick and object to this work with all its might, since regarding bestowal, it is a load and a burden for the body. It cannot tolerate this work, and the resistance of the body appears in a person in the form of foreign thoughts. It comes and asks the questions of "who" and "what." Through these questions, a person says that all these questions are certainly sent to him by the *Sitra Achra* [other side] to obstruct him in the work.

It says that if, at that time, one says that they come from the *Sitra Achra*, one breaches what is written, "You shall make no other gods over Me." The reason is that one should believe that it comes to him from the *Shechina* [Divinity], since "There is none else besides Him." However, the *Shechina* shows one his true state, how he is walking in the ways of the Creator.

This means that by sending him these questions, called "foreign thoughts," meaning that through these foreign thoughts she sees how he answers the questions regarded as "foreign thoughts." And all this, one should know one's true state in the work so as to know what to do.

It is like an allegory about a friend who wanted to know how much his friend loved him. Certainly, when face to face, his friend hides himself because of shame. Therefore, he sends a person to speak badly about his friend. Then he sees his friend's reaction while he is away from his friend, and then one can know the true measure of his friend's love.

The lesson is that when the *Shechina* shows her face to a person, meaning when the Creator gives one vitality and joy, in that state, one is ashamed to say what he thinks about the work of bestowal without receiving anything for himself. However, when not facing her, meaning when the vitality and gladness cool down, which is considered not facing her, then one can see his true state regarding the aim to bestow.

If one believes that it is written that there is none else besides Him, and that the Creator sends all the foreign thoughts, meaning that He is the operator, he certainly knows what to do and how to answer all the questions. This seems as though she sends him messengers to see how he slanders it, his kingdom of heaven, and this is how we can interpret the above matter.

One can understand this, that everything comes from the Creator, for it is known that the beatings that the body beats a person with its foreign thoughts, since they do not come to a person when he does not engage in the work, but these beatings that come to a person in a complete sensation, to the point that these thoughts smash his mind, they come specifically after preceding Torah and work more than the usual. This is called stones to weigh with.

It means that these stones fall in one's mind when one wants to understand these questions. Afterward, one comes to weigh the purpose of one's work, if it is truly worthwhile to work in order to bestow, to work with all his might and soul, and that all his aspirations will be only to hope that what there is to acquire in this world is only in the purpose of his work to bring contentment to his Maker, and not in any corporeal matter.

At that time begins a bitter argument, since one sees that there are arguments both ways. The writings warn about this, "You shall make no other gods over Me." Do not say that another god gave you the stones with which to weigh your work, but "over Me."

Instead, one should know that this is considered "over Me." This is so that one will see the true form of the basis and the foundation upon which the structure of the work is built.

17. Baal HaSulam, Letter No. 8

Is written in the poem, "You surround everything and fill everything." During the attainment, abundance is felt. It appears and sits precisely on all those contradictions. This is the meaning of "more terrible than all terrors, prouder than all who are proud," and naturally, "He fills everything." The poet knew that He fills them abundantly, and none else perceived the pleasantness of unification with Him until it seemed to him, at the time of his wholeness, that the afflictions they had suffered had some merit, to value the savor and pleasantness of the abundance of unification with Him. His every organ and tendon will say and testify that each and every person in the world would chop off his hands and legs seven times a day for a single moment in their entire life, of tasting such a savor.

18. RABASH, Article No. 845, "None as Holy as the Lord"

"There is none who is as holy as the Lord." But is there one who is worse than the Creator but holy? "There is no rock like our God." Does that mean that there is another rock, which is a little worse than the Creator? Rather, there are holy ones and angels and souls, and all receive *Kedusha* [holiness] from the Creator. This is not so "because there is none besides You." Rather, You will give them *Kedusha* [holiness] (*The Zohar, Tazria*, Item 37).

We should ask what this tells us in the work. One must believe how all the overcoming in the work, and did he labor in order to be rewarded with the Holy one, as it is written, "You will be holy, for I am holy." At that time, one must know that all of man's work does not help him whatsoever. Rather, it is all from the Creator.

In other words, all the *Kedusha* [holiness] that one feels he has comes to him from the Creator. This is what it means that there is no *Kedusha*, meaning no *Kedusha* in the world that one can obtain by himself. Rather, everything comes from the Creator. This is why it is written, "There is none as holy as the Lord," and "There is no rock like our God."

It is known that *Kelim* [vessels] are called by the name *Elokim* [God], and lights are called by the name of *HaVaYaH*. It is written, "there is no rock," which is when one sees that he has vessels of bestowal. This is regarded that a new thing was created for him, which is called a "rock," meaning that in a place where he had vessels of reception, vessels of bestowal have been depicted in him. One should not think that he helped the Creator in any way and by this obtained vessels of bestowal. Rather, everything came from above.

Baal HaSulam said that prior to working, one must say, "If I am not for me, who is for me?" After the work, he should believe in private Providence, meaning that the Creator does everything. This is the meaning of what is written there: "The Creator draws a picture within a picture." We should interpret that within the form of the *Kelim*, which is reception, He draws there the form of bestowal.

19. RABASH, Article No. 19 (1990), "Why Is the Torah Called "Middle Line" in the Work? – 2"

One must believe as was said above, that "there is none else besides Him," meaning that it is the Creator who compels him to do the good deeds, but since he is still unworthy of knowing that it is the Creator who commits him, the Creator dresses Himself in dresses of flesh and blood, through which the Creator performs these actions. Thus, the Creator acts in the form of *Achoraim* [posterior].

In other words, the person sees people's faces but he should believe that behind the faces stands the Creator and performs these actions. That is, behind the man stands the Creator and compels him to do the deeds that the Creator wants. It follows that the Creator does everything, but the person regards what he sees and not what he should believe.

20. RABASH, Article No. 44 (1990), "What Is an Optional War, in the work - 2?"

A person must believe that this concealment, where a person does not feel that there is a King to the world, the Creator did this, and this is called "the correction of the *Tzimtzum* [restriction]." However, one must believe and make great efforts until he feels in his organs that the Creator is the leader of the world. And not just a leader! Rather, one must believe that His guidance is in the manner of good and doing good. A person must do all that he can to be able to attain this.

21. RABASH, Article No. 19 (1990), "Why Is the Torah Called "Middle Line" in the Work? – 2"

One should believe that "there is none else besides Him," that the Creator does everything. In other words, as Baal HaSulam said, before each action one should say that man was given only choice, since "If I am not for me, who is for me?" Thus, everything depends on one's choice. However, after the fact, one should say that everything is private Providence, and that one does nothing on his own.

22. RABASH, Article No. 5 (1987), "What Is the Advantage in the Work More than in the Reward?"

It is written in *The Zohar*, "For the whole of the Torah is the names of the Creator." Also, a complete man is one who has been rewarded with "The Torah and the Creator and Israel are one." Therefore, indeed, greeting the *Shechina* is very important because the purpose is for man to achieve this degree.

But to come to greet the *Shechina* requires prior preparation, for one to be fit for it. In the words of our sages, this is called "As He is merciful, so you are merciful." This is the interpretation of the verse, "and to cleave unto Him, cleave unto His attributes." It means, as explained in the book *Matan Torah* [*The Giving of the Torah*], that only by a person working in love of others can he achieve *Dvekut* [adhesion] with the Creator. There are many names to this: "Instilling of the *Shechina*," "attainment the Torah," "greeting the *Shechina*," etc.

The main preparation, which is called "labor," is that one must prepare oneself to annul one's authority, meaning one's self. We can call this hospitality [greeting guests], meaning that he cancels the view of landlords and craves the view of Torah, which is called "annulling of authority." Naturally, he becomes the guest of the Creator, who is the Host of the entire world.

23. RABASH, Letter No. 76

"If you walk in My statutes and keep My commandments so as to do them." The holy *Zohar* asks, "Since he already said, 'walk' and 'keep,' why also 'do'?" It replies, "One who does the *Mitzvot* [commandments] of the Torah and walks in His ways, it is as though he has made Him above. The Creator said, 'as though he had made Me.' This is the meaning of 'to do them,' as though you have made Me" (*Behukotai*, Item 18).

We should understand what it means that one who walks in the way of the Creator makes the Creator. How can one think such a thing?

It is known that "The whole earth is full of His glory." This is what every person should believe, as it is written, "I fill the heaven and the earth." However, the Creator has made a concealment so that we cannot see Him so as to have room for choice, and then there is room for faith—to believe that the Creator "fills all the worlds and encompasses all the worlds." And after a person engages in Torah and *Mitzvot* and keeps the commandment of choice, the Creator reveals Himself to him, and then he sees that the Creator is the ruler of the world.

Thus, at that time a person makes the king who will rule over him. That is, a person feels that the Creator is the ruler of the world, and this is regarded as a person making the Creator king over him.

24. RABASH, Article No. 14 (1985), "I Am the First and I Am the Last"

When a person wants to walk on the way to the goal of *Dvekut* with the Creator, which means to aim that everything will be in order to bestow, he must first have a deficiency, meaning dissatisfaction with the work in *Lo Lishma*.

At that time he begins to search for another order in the work, since the engagement in Torah and *Mitzvot* [commandments] he was used to was on the basis of the will to receive, called *Lo Lishma*. But now that he needs to replace his entire basis on which he built his entire life's order, it depends on the extent to which he sees that the state of *Lo Lishma* is the wrong way, does not let him rest, and he will not be at peace until he comes out of that state into a state of *Lishma*.

However, who is making him feel, while he is in the state of *Lo Lishma*, that this is still not the right way and he is still far from *Dvekut* with the Creator? When he looks at the rest of the people, they go by this path, so why does he need to be different? Another difficulty is that when he looks at the rest of the people he sees people who are more talented and more capable in the work than him. But they settle for the order of the work they had received when they were little, when the instructors taught them to work only in *Lo Lishma*, as in the above words of Maimonides. And then he sees about himself that although "a sorrow shared is a sorrow halved," he cannot accept the state of *Lo Lishma*. At that time comes the question: "If I am really less talented and less capable in the work, where did I get this restlessness in the state of *Lo Lishma*?"

To this comes the answer: "I am the first." That is, the Creator has given him this deficiency so he will not be able to continue on this path. One should not think that he has obtained this by his own wisdom. Rather, the Creator says, "I am the first," meaning "I have given you the first push, so you will begin to walk on the path of truth. By giving you a deficiency of feeling that with the respect to the truth, you are deficient."

Then begins the work that he begins to wait for a state where he repels self-love, and all his works are only in order to bestow. At that time he must dedicate to it all the thoughts and resources at his disposal, as in "Everything that you find within your power to do, that do."

Afterwards, when he is rewarded with *Dvekut* with the Creator, he thinks that it is through his labor in Torah and *Mitzvot*, and by overcoming his self-love. He thinks that he has been rewarded with it only through his work, that he was very persistent, and only he had the strength to make the most of his opportunities, which gave him this riches and he was rewarded what he was rewarded.

The verse says about that: "And I am the last. That is, as I was the first, giving you the deficiency, I am also the last, meaning I have given you the filling of the deficiency." The deficiency is called the *Kli* [vessel], and the filling is called "the light." Since there is no light without a *Kli*, the *Kli* is made first, and then the abundance is poured into the *Kli*. This is why the Creator first gives the *Kli*, which is called "I am the first," and then He gave the abundance, called "I am the last."

25. *Zohar for All*, *Lech Lecha*, "And It Came to Pass when Abraham Came to Egypt," Item 116

All that there is in the world is from the Creator, for He alone did, does, and will do all the deeds in the world. He knows in advance all that will unfold in the end, as it is written, "Declaring the end from the beginning." He watches and does things in the beginning in order to repeat them and to do them in wholeness after some time.

26. *Zohar for All, Beresheet* [Genesis], "Pure Marble Stones," Item 255

At the end of correction, when SAM is revoked, it will appear to all that SAM had never lived, but that unity was always ruling, as it is written, "There is none else besides Him."

27. *Zohar for All, Beresheet* [Genesis], "I, I am He," Item 175

The words, "See now that I, I am He" apply to the Creator and His Divinity, ZA and his *Nukva*. "I" is Divinity. "He" is the Creator, who is called *Vav-Hey-Vav*. In the future, at the end of correction, the *Nukva* will say, "See that I," *Vav-Hey-Vav* are one, as it is written, "And the light of the moon shall be as the light of the sun," meaning that the *Nukva* is equal to ZA.

"And there is no God with Me" refers to other gods, SAM and the serpent, for then it will be revealed that SAM and the serpent never separated between the Creator and His Divinity, as it is written, "By the mouth of two witnesses ... shall he that is to die be put to death," which applies to SAM, who was dead from his beginning and was but a servant to hurry the redemption of our souls.

This is the meaning of "I will put to death and make alive." I will put to death with My Divinity the one who is guilty, and I will make alive with my Divinity the one who is innocent. The Creator's guidance from the beginning will appear throughout the world, and then, as it is written, "Sinners will cease from the earth, and the wicked shall be no more." That is, unlike what it seems to us during the 6,000 years, that there is a governance that objects to *Kedusha*, which are SAM and the serpent, as it is written, "When man rules over man it is to his harm," then it will appear to all—"I will put to death and make alive" with My Divinity, and there is none else besides Him.

28. *Zohar for All, Nasso*, "The Holy Idra Rabah," Item 299

Everything is Godliness, above time, place, and change. All those degrees and corrections we discern in Godliness are only various concealments and covers toward the lower ones, since the ten *Sefirot* are ten kinds of covers of His *Atzmut* [self]. Likewise, all the imaginary images of time and place and actions are but various covers of His Godliness that seem that way to the lower ones.

As man is not affected or changes at all because of the covers that he covers in, and only his friends are affected by his disappearance or appearance, so His Godliness does not change and is not affected whatsoever by those degrees and corrections and names in time, place, and changes of actions that the lower ones discern in His covers. Rather, we must know that those covers also serve as disclosures.

Moreover, to the extent of the cover that there is in each name and correction, so is the extent of disclosure of the Creator that is in it. One who is rewarded with receiving the measure of the covers properly is then rewarded with the covers becoming for him measures of disclosure. One who learns must remember these things during the learning so he will not fail in his thought.

29. Deuteronomy 4:35

You have shown to know that the Lord, He is the God. There is none else besides Him.

30. Ramchal, *138 Doors to Wisdom*

The uniqueness of *Ein Sof* [infinity] is that only His will exists, and no other will exists but His. Therefore, He alone rules, and no other desire. This is the basis upon which the whole building is built.

The foundation and kernel of faith is His upper uniqueness. Therefore, this is the first thing we must clarify, since the whole of the wisdom of truth is but wisdom—showing the truthfulness of the faith, to understand all that was created or done in the world, how it emanates from the upper will, and how everything is conducted in the right way from the one God, to roll everything and finally bring it to complete wholeness. The details in this wisdom are only the details of knowing the guidance in all its rules and circumstances. It follows that the first concept in this wisdom is that everything we see, in created bodies or in instances that occur in time, all as one have only one Master. He is the one who does all this, who guides all this, and whose ways and conducts we explain and notify in this wisdom. Thus, this is what we should clarify first and foremost, especially since this matter is the basis of creation itself.

31. Rav Yitzhak Yehuda Yehiel of Komarno, *Trees of Eden*

The commandment of uniqueness of the Name is to believe and know that the Lord is the Master of everything, the Creator of everything, one, unique, and unified.

To believe and to know for certain that the Creator is the operator of reality, from the first emanation to the tiniest worm in the ocean, He is the master of everything, the Creator of everything, one, unique, and unified without any partner. He is unique and unified, as was said, "Hear, O Israel, the Lord our God, the Lord is one." One is from the literal meaning of the commandment and its root. All is one. One should know that there is a first one who is present there, and not an image or a body or any perception in the magnitude of His light and holiness, wisdom and understanding, mind and intellect whose depth is infinite and there are none like Him. "I am the first and I am the last, and there is no God besides Me." Nothing predates Him and nothing outlasts Him; He is the first and He is the last, and He is ever present—was, is, and will be. He watches over people's every action. The Champion of the world is in every single movement, and one must take upon oneself to dedicate oneself to this faith, the true faith, that the Creator is one, blessed be He and blessed be His name. The root of this commandment (commandment of uniqueness of the Creator), *The Book of Zohar*, the *Tikkunim* [corrections of *The Zohar*], the books of our teacher, and the books of the kabbalists were all based on this commandment.

32. Rav Yosef Albo, *Sefer HaIkarim* [*Book of Principles*]

It is written that wherever one pictures the Creator as the first, one should picture Him as the last. It implies that one title indicates both, and it is that He is independent of time. Isaiah said, "Thus says the Lord, the King of Israel and his Redeemer, the Lord of hosts: 'I am the first and I am the last, and there is no God besides Me.'" He wished to say that in all who are present, there is none who is described as the first and the last but Me, since all who are present besides Me, time came before them or after them, and this is why they were made possible in reality. But I, since I am independent of time, I am not made possible by reality, but I necessarily exist. This is why He concludes, "and there is no God besides Me." This means that among all who are present, there is none whose existence is mandatory, meaning superior to everything, but Me, since there is none among them for whom the titles "first" and "last" apply but Me. For this reason, it will be clarified that I alone am the God, meaning necessarily exist.

3

Adhesion

1. Baal HaSulam, "The Writings of the Last Generation"

Life's direction is to attain adhesion with Him, strictly to benefit the Creator, or to reward the public with achieving adhesion with Him.

2. Baal HaSulam, "The Writings of the Last Generation"

In every person, even in the secular, there is an unknown spark that demands unification with God. When it sometimes awakens, it awakens a passion to know God, or deny God, which is the same. If someone generates the satisfaction of this desire in that person, he will agree to anything.

3. Baal HaSulam, "Matan Torah [The Giving of the Torah]," Item 13

If indeed there are two parts in the Torah: 1) *Mitzvot* between man and the Creator, 2) *Mitzvot* between man and man, both aim for the same thing—to bring the creature to the final purpose of *Dvekut* with Him. Furthermore, even the practical side in both of them is really one and the same, for when one performs an act *Lishma*, without any mixture of self-love, meaning without drawing any benefit for himself, then one does not feel any difference whether one is working to love one's friend or to love the Creator.

4. Baal HaSulam, "A Speech for the Completion of The Zohar"

Spiritual *Dvekut* can only be depicted as equivalence of form. Hence, by equalizing our form with the form of His qualities, we become attached to Him.

This is why they said, "as He is merciful." In other words, all His actions are to bestow and benefit others, and not at all for His own benefit, since He has no deficiencies that require complementing. And also, He has no one from whom to receive. Similarly, all your actions will be to bestow and to benefit others. Thus, you will equalize your form with the form of the qualities of the Creator, and this is spiritual *Dvekut*.

There is a discernment of "mind" and a discernment of "heart" in the above-mentioned equivalence of form. The engagement in Torah and *Mitzvot* in order to bestow contentment upon one's Maker is equivalence of form in the mind. This is because the Creator does not think of Himself—whether He exists or whether He watches over His creations, and other such doubts. Similarly, one who wishes to achieve equivalence of form must not think of these things, as well, when it is clear to him that the Creator does not think of them, since there is no greater disparity of form than that. Hence, anyone who thinks of such matters is certainly separated from Him and will never achieve equivalence of form.

This is what our sages said, "Let all your actions be for the sake of the Creator," that is, *Dvekut* with the Creator. Do not do anything that does not yield this goal of *Dvekut*. This means that all your actions will be to bestow and to benefit your fellow person. At that time, you will achieve equivalence of form with the Creator—as all His actions are to bestow and to benefit others, so you, all your actions will be only to bestow and to benefit others. This is the complete *Dvekut*.

5. Baal HaSulam, "The Writings of the Last Generation"

The basis of my entire commentary is the will to receive imprinted in every creature, and which is disparity of form to the Creator. Thus, the soul has separated from Him as an organ is separated from the body, since disparity of form in spirituality is like a separating axe in corporeality. It is therefore clear that what the Creator wants from us is equivalence of form, at which time we adhere to Him once more, as before we were created.

This is the meaning of the words, "Adhere to His attributes; as He is merciful, etc." It means that we are to change our attribute, which is the will to receive, and adopt the attribute of the Creator, which is only to bestow, so that all our actions will be only to bestow upon our fellow persons and benefit them as best as we can.

By this we come to the goal of adhering to Him, which is equivalence of form. What one is compelled to do for oneself, namely the necessary minimum for one's self and one's family's sustenance, is not considered disparity of form, as "Necessity is neither condemned nor praised." This is the great revelation that will be revealed in full only in the days of the Messiah. When this teaching is accepted, we will be rewarded with complete redemption.

6. Baal HaSulam, "The Love of God and the Love of Man"

Our sages spoke only of the practical part of the Torah, which brings the world and the Torah to the desired goal. Therefore, when they say one *Mitzva*, they certainly mean a practical *Mitzva*. This is certainly as Hillel says, meaning "Love your friend as yourself." It is by this *Mitzva* alone that one attains the real goal, which is *Dvekut* [adhesion] with the Creator. Thus, you find that with this one *Mitzva*, one observes the entire goal and purpose.

Now there is no question about the *Mitzvot* between man and the Creator because the practical ones among them have the same purpose of cleansing the body, the last point of which is to love your friend as yourself, after which immediately comes the *Dvekut*.

7. Baal HaSulam, *Shamati*, Article No. 47, "In the Place Where You Find His Greatness"

"In the place where you find His greatness, there you find His humbleness." It means that one who is always in true *Dvekut* [adhesion] sees that the Creator lowers Himself, meaning the Creator is present in the low places.

One does not know what to do, and this is why it is written, "Who sits on high, who looks down on heaven and on earth." A person sees the greatness of the Creator and then "who looks down," meaning he lowers the heaven to the earth. The advice that is given to this is to think that if this desire is from the Creator, we have nothing greater than that, as it is written, "He raises the poor out of the litter."

First, one must see that he has a lack. If he does not, he should pray for it, why does one not have it? The reason he does not have a lack is due to the diminution of awareness.

Hence, in every *Mitzva* [commandment], one must pray, why does he not have awareness, for he is not keeping the *Mitzva* in wholeness. In other words, the will to receive covers so he will not see the truth.

If he would see that he is in such a lowly state, he would certainly not want to be in that state. Instead, one should exert in one's work every time until he comes to repentance, as it is written, "He brings down to the netherworld, and raises up."

This means that when the Creator wants the wicked one to repent, He makes the netherworld so low for him that the wicked one himself does not want to be so. Hence, one needs to pray pleadingly that the Creator will show him the truth by adding to him the light of the Torah.

8. Baal HaSulam, "The Freedom"

The children of Israel were rewarded with complete *Dvekut* on that holy occasion, their vessels of reception were completely emptied of any worldly possession and they were adhered to Him in equivalence of form. This means that they had no desire for any self-possession, but only to the extent that they could bestow contentment, so their Maker would delight in them.

And since their will to receive had clothed in an image of that object, it had clothed in it and bonded with it into complete oneness. Therefore, they were certainly liberated from the angel of death, for death is necessarily an absence and negation of the existence of something. But only while there is a spark that wishes to exist for its own pleasure is it possible to say about it that that spark does not exist because it has become absent and died.

However, if there is no such spark in man, but all the sparks of his selfness clothe in bestowal of contentment upon their Maker, then he neither becomes absent nor dies. For even when the body is annulled, it is only annulled with respect to self-reception, in which the will to receive is dressed and can only exist in it.

However, when he achieves the aim of creation and the Creator receives pleasure from him, since His will is done, man's essence, which clothes in His contentment, is granted complete eternity, like Him. Thus, he has been rewarded with freedom from the angel of death.

9. Baal HaSulam, *Ohr HaBahir*

The first restriction is the ascent of the desire of *Ein Sof* not to receive anymore in Phase Four. It is the great reception that is implemented in the world of *Ein Sof*, where there is disparity from His Self. This was in order to do good to His creations.

In other words, it is so that in the end, souls that are clothed in a body in this world will emerge from the ascent of this desire, so they will turn all of the great reception to be in order to bestow. At that time, they will have equivalence of form with His self and will be worthy of adhesion with Him. This is the meaning of doing good to His creations, since they will be able to receive the great lights that are received in Phase Four, who is called "His mate in *Ein Sof*." And yet, they will not be separated from Him because of it due to the disparity of form of reception, which does not occur in Him, since their whole intention in receiving from Him will be only because He wants it, and their sole aim is to bring contentment to their Maker. This is the meaning of "*Ein Sof* does not bring down his unification on her until He is given his mate."

10. Baal HaSulam, *Shamati*, Article No. 19, What Is "The Creator Hates the Bodies," in the Work?

One must always examine oneself, the purpose of one's work, meaning if the Creator receives contentment in every act that one performs, because he wants equivalence of form with the Creator. This is called "All your actions will be for the sake of the Creator," meaning that one wants the Creator to enjoy everything he does, as it is written, "to bring contentment to his Maker."

Also, one needs to conduct oneself with the will to receive and say to it, "I have already decided that I do not want to receive any pleasure because you want to enjoy, since with your desire I am forced to be separated from the Creator, for disparity of form causes separation and distance from the Creator."

11. Baal HaSulam, "The Writings of the Last Generation"

All of the anticipated reward from the Creator, and the purpose of the entire creation, are *Dvekut* [adhesion] with the Creator, as in, "A tower filled abundantly, but no guests." This is what they who cling to Him with love receive.
Naturally, first, one emerges from imprisonment, which is emerging from the skin of one's body by bestowal upon others. Subsequently, one comes to the king's palace, which is *Dvekut* with Him through the intention to bestow contentment upon one's maker.

Therefore, the bulk of commandments are between man and man. One who gives preference to the commandments between man and God is as one who climbs to the second step before he has climbed to the first step. Clearly, he will break his legs.

12. Baal HaSulam, *Shamati*, Article No. 3, "The Matter of Spiritual Attainment"

May we merit receiving His light and following the ways of the Creator, and to serve Him not in order to receive reward but to give contentment to the Creator and raise the *Shechina* [Divinity] from the dust. May we be rewarded with *Dvekut* [adhesion] with the Creator and the revelation of His Godliness to His creatures.

13. Baal HaSulam, *Shamati*, Article No. 1, "There Is None Else Besides Him"

One must always try and adhere to the Creator, namely that all his thoughts will be about Him. That is to say, even if he is in the worst state, from which there cannot be a greater decline, he should not leave His domain, namely that there is another authority that prevents him from entering the *Kedusha* [holiness], that can bring benefit or harm.

That is, he must not think that there is a force of the *Sitra Achra* [other side] that does not let a person do good deeds and walk in the ways of the Creator. Rather, all is done by the Creator.

The Baal Shem Tov said that he who says that there is another force in the world, namely *Klipot* [shells], that person is in a state of "serving other gods." It is not necessarily the thought of heresy that is the transgression, but if he thinks that there is another authority and force apart from the Creator, he is committing a transgression.

Furthermore, one who says that man has his own authority, that is, he says that yesterday he himself did not want to follow the Creator's ways, this, too, is considered committing the transgression of heresy, meaning he does not believe that only the Creator is the leader of the world.

14. Baal HaSulam, *Shamati*, Article No. 19, "What Is 'The Creator Hates the Bodies,' in the Work?"

One must especially try to have a strong desire to obtain the desire to bestow and overcome the will to receive. A strong desire means that a strong desire is measured by the increment of the in-between rests and the arrests, meaning the time gaps between each overcoming.

Sometimes one receives a cessation in the middle, meaning a descent. This descent can be a cessation of a minute, an hour, a day, or a month. Afterward, he resumes the work of overcoming the will to receive and the attempts to achieve the desire to bestow. A strong desire means that the cessation does not take him a long time and he is immediately reawakened to the work.

15. Baal HaSulam, *Shamati*, Article No. 5, "Lishma Is an Awakening from Above, and Why Do We Need an Awakening from Below?"

When the thief, meaning the will to receive, does not feel any flavor or vitality in the work of accepting the burden of the kingdom of heaven, in that state, if one works with faith above reason, coercively, and the body becomes accustomed to this work against the desire of his will to receive, then he has the means by which to come to work that will be with the purpose of bringing contentment to his Maker, since the primary requirement from a person is to come to *Dvekut* [adhesion] with the Creator through his work, which is discerned as equivalence of form, where all his actions are in order to bestow.

This is as it is written, "Then shall you delight in the Lord." The meaning of "Then" is that first, in the beginning of his work, he did not have pleasure. Instead, his work was coercive.

But afterward, when he has already accustomed himself to work in order to bestow and not examine himself—if he is feeling a good taste in the work—but believes that he is working to bring contentment to his Maker through his work, he should believe that the Creator accepts the work of the lower ones regardless of how and how much is the form of their work. In everything, the Creator examines the intention, and this brings contentment to the Creator. Then one is rewarded with "delight in the Lord."

Even during the work of the Creator he will feel delight and pleasure since now he really does work for the Creator because the effort he made during the coercive work qualifies him to be able to truly work for the Creator. You find that then, too, the pleasure he receives relates to the Creator, meaning specifically for the Creator.

16. Baal HaSulam, *Shamati*, Article No. 23, "You Who Love the Lord, Hate Evil"

In the verse, "You who love the Lord, hate evil; He preserves the souls of His followers; He will save them from the hand of the wicked," he interprets that it is not enough to love the Creator, and to want to be awarded *Dvekut* [adhesion] with the Creator. One should also hate evil.

Hatred is expressed by hating the evil, called "the will to receive." One sees that he has no way to get rid of it, and at the same time, he does not want to accept the situation. He feels the losses that the evil causes him, and also sees the truth, that one cannot annul the evil by himself, since it is a natural force from the Creator, who imprinted the will to receive in man.

In that state, the verse tells us what one can do is hate evil. And by this the Creator will keep him from that evil, as it is written, "He preserves the souls of His followers." What is preservation? "He will deliver them from the hand of the wicked." In that state, since he has some contact with the Creator, be it the smallest contact, he is already a successful person.

In truth, the matter of evil remains and serves as an *Achoraim* [posterior] to the *Partzuf*. But this is only through one's correction: Through sincere hatred of evil, it is corrected into a form of *Achoraim*. The hatred comes because if one wants to obtain *Dvekut* [adhesion] with the Creator then there is a conduct among friends: If two people realize that each of them hates what his friend hates, and loves what and whom his friend loves, they come into perpetual bonding like a stake that will never fall.

Hence, since the Creator loves to bestow, the lower ones should also adapt to want only to bestow. The Creator also hates to be a receiver, as He is completely whole and does not need anything. Thus, man, too, must hate the matter of reception for oneself.

It follows from all the above, that one must bitterly hate the will to receive, for all the ruins in the world come only from the will to receive. And through the hatred, one corrects it and surrenders under the *Kedusha* [holiness].

17. Baal HaSulam, *Shamati*, Article No. 61, "Round About Him It Storms Mightily"

Our sages say about the verse, "And round about Him it storms mightily," that the Creator is meticulous with the righteous as a hairsbreadth. He asked: If they are generally righteous, why do they deserve a harsh punishment?

The thing is that all the borders we speak of in the worlds are from the perspective of the receivers, meaning the lower ones limit and restrict themselves to some degree, and thus remain below, since above, they agree to everything that the lower ones do. Hence, to that extent the abundance extends below. Therefore, by their thoughts, words, and actions, the lower ones cause the abundance to come down from above in this manner.

It turns out that if the lower one regards a minor act or word as if it is an important act, such as considering a momentary pause in *Dvekut* [adhesion] with the Creator as breaking the gravest prohibition in the Torah, then there is consent above to the opinion of the lower one, and it is considered above as though he really broke a serious prohibition. Thus, the righteous says that the Creator is meticulous with him as a hairsbreadth, and as the lower one says, so it is agreed above.

When the lower one does not feel a slight prohibition as a serious one, from above they also do not regard the trifle things he breaks as great prohibitions. Hence, such a person is treated as though he is a small person, meaning his *Mitzvot* [commandments] are considered small, and his transgressions are considered small, too. They are regarded as having the same weight, and he is generally considered a small person.

However, one who regards the trifle things and says that the Creator is meticulous about them as a hairsbreadth is considered a great person, and both his transgressions and his *Mitzvot* are great.

One can suffer when committing a transgression to the extent that he feels pleasure when performing a *Mitzva* [commandment]. There is an allegory about this: A man did a terrible crime against the kingship and was sentenced to twenty years in prison with hard labor. The prison was outside the country in some desolate place in the world. The sentence was carried out right away and he was sent to the desolate place at the end of the world.

There, he found other people who were sentenced by the kingdom to be there like him, but he became sick with amnesia and forgot that he had a wife and children, friends and acquaintances. He thought that the whole world is nothing more than the desolate place with the people who are there, that he was born there, and he did not know of more than that. Thus, his truth is according to his present feeling and he has no regard for the actual reality, only according to his knowledge and sensations.

There he was taught rules and regulations so that he would not break the rules once more, and keep himself from the transgression written there, and know how to correct his actions so as to be brought out from there. In the books of the king, he learned that one who breaks this rule, for example, is sent to a punitive land far from any settlement. He is impressed by this harsh punishment and has grievances at why such harsh punishments are given.

Yet, he would never think that he himself is one of those who broke the rules of the state, that he has been sentenced harshly, and the verdict has been carried out. And since he became sick with amnesia, he will never feel his actual state.

This is the meaning of "and round about him it storms mightily": One must consider his every move, that he himself had already broken the king's commandment, and has already been banished from the world. Now, through many good deeds, his memory begins to work and he begins to feel how far he has become from the settled place of the world.

He begins to engage in repentance until he is taken out from there and brought back to the settled place, and this feeling comes specifically through one's work. He begins to feel that he has grown far from his origin and root until he is rewarded with *Dvekut* with the Creator.

18. Baal HaSulam, Letter No. 25

The Zohar also spoke about it, saying that one who is rewarded with repentance, the *Shechina* [Divinity] appears to him like a soft-hearted mother who has not seen her son for many days, and they made great efforts and experienced ordeals in order to see each other, because of which they both were in great dangers. But in the end, they came to that longed-for freedom and were rewarded with seeing one another. Then the mother fell on him, kissed him, comforted him, and spoke softly to him all day and all night. She told him of the longing and the dangers on the roads she has experienced until today, how she had always been with him, and that the *Shechina* never moved, but suffered with him in all the places, but he could not see it.

These are the words of *The Zohar*: "She says to him, 'Here we slept; here we were attacked by robbers and were saved from them; here we hid in a deep pit,' and so forth. What fool would not understand the great love and pleasantness and delight that burst from these comforting stories?"

19. Baal HaSulam, "This Is for Judah"

We find that the only need in man's wishes, which does not exist in the whole of the animate species, is the awakening toward Godly *Dvekut* [adhesion]. Only the human species is ready for it, and none other.

It follows that the whole issue of presence in the human species is in that preparation imprinted in him to crave His work, and in this he is superior to the beast.

20. Baal HaSulam, Letter No. 25

One who repents from love is rewarded with complete *Dvekut* [adhesion], meaning the highest degree, and one who is ready for sins is in the netherworld. These are the farthest two points in this entire reality.

It would seem that we should be meticulous with the word "repentance," which should have been called "wholeness," except it is to show that everything is preordained, and each and every soul is already established in all its light, goodness, and eternity. But for the bread of shame, the soul went out in restrictions until it clothed in the murky body, and only through it does it return to its root prior to the *Tzimtzum* [restriction], with its reward in its hand from all the terrible move it had made. The overall reward is the real *Dvekut*, meaning that she [the soul] got rid of the bread of shame because her vessel of reception has become a vessel of bestowal and her form is equal to her Maker.

21. Baal HaSulam, *Shamati*, Article No. 70, "With a Mighty Hand and with Fury Poured Out"

We should know that of those who want to come into the work of the Creator in order to truly adhere to Him and enter the King's palace, not everyone is admitted. Rather, he is tested: If he has no other desires but only a desire for *Dvekut* [adhesion], he is admitted.

And how is one tested if he has only one desire? He is given disturbances. This means that he is sent foreign thoughts and foreign messengers to obstruct him so he would leave this path and follow the path of all the people.

If one overcomes all the difficulties and breaks all the bars that block him, and little things cannot push him away, the Creator sends him great *Klipot* [shells/peels] and chariots to deflect one from entering into *Dvekut* with the Creator alone, and with nothing else. This is considered that the Creator is rejecting him with a mighty hand.

If the Creator does not show a mighty hand, it will be hard to push him away since he has a strong desire to adhere only to the Creator and to nothing else.

But when the Creator wants to reject one whose desire is not so strong, He pushes him away with a small thing. By giving him a great desire for corporeality, he already leaves the holy work entirely, and there is no need to repel him with a mighty hand.

Yet, when one overcomes all the hardships and the disturbances, one is not easily repelled, but with a mighty hand. And if one overcomes even the mighty hand and does not want to move from the place of *Kedusha* [holiness] whatsoever, but wants to adhere specifically to Him in truth, and sees that he is repelled, then one says that fury is poured out on him. Otherwise, he would be allowed inside. But because fury is poured out on him by the Creator, he is not admitted into the King's palace to adhere to Him.

It follows that before one wants to move from one's place, and breaks in and wants to enter, it cannot be said that he feels that fury is poured out on him. Rather, after all the rejections that he is rejected, and he does not move from his place, meaning when the mighty hand and the fury poured out have already been revealed upon him, then "I will be King over you" comes true. This is so because only through bursting and great efforts does the kingdom of heaven become revealed to him, and he is rewarded with entering the King's palace.

22. Baal HaSulam, Letter No. 8

There is a sublime purpose for all that happens in this world, and it is called "the drop of unification." When those dwellers of clay houses go through all those terrors, through all that totality, in His pride, which is removed from them, a door opens in the walls of their hearts, which are tightly sealed by the nature of creation itself, and by this they become fit for instilling that drop of unification in their hearts. Then they are inverted like an imprinted substance, and they will evidently see that it is to the contrary—that it was precisely in those dreadful terrors that they perceive the totality, which is removed by foreign pride. There, and only there, is the Creator Himself adhered, and there He can instill them with the drop of unification.

23. Baal HaSulam, "A Speech for the Completion of The Zohar"

Every time one equalizes one's form with one's rav, he adheres to him for a time. As a result, he obtains the knowledge and thoughts of the rav, according to his measure of *Dvekut*, as we explained in the allegory about the organ that has been cut off from the body and was reunited with it.

For this reason, the student can use his rav's attainment of the Creator's greatness, which inverts bestowal into reception and sufficient fuel to give one's heart and soul. At that time, the student, too, will be able to engage in Torah and *Mitzvot Lishma* with his very heart and soul, which is the remedy that yields eternal *Dvekut* with the Creator.

24. Baal HaSulam, Letter No. 1

Everyone believes in private Providence, but do not adhere to it at all.

The reason is that an alien and foul thought … cannot be attributed to the Creator, who is the epitome of the "good who does good." However, only to the true servants of the Creator does the knowledge of private Providence open, that He caused all the reasons that preceded it, both good and bad. Then they are adhered to private Providence, for all who are connected to the pure are pure.

Since the Guardian is united with His guarded, there is no apparent division between bad and good. They are all loved and are all clear, for they are all carriers of the vessels of the Creator, ready to glorify the revelation of His uniqueness. It is known by the senses, and to that extent, they have knowledge in the end that all the actions and the thoughts, both good and bad, are the carriers of the vessels of the Creator. He prepared them, from His mouth they emerged, and at the end of correction it will be known to all.

25. Baal HaSulam, *Shamati*, Article No. 218, "The Torah and the Creator Are One"

"The Torah and the Creator are one." Certainly, during the work they are two things. However, they contradict one another. The discernment of the Creator is *Dvekut* [adhesion], and *Dvekut* means equivalence, being canceled from reality. (And one should always depict how there was a time when he had a little bit of *Dvekut*, how he was filled with vitality and pleasure, and to always crave to be in *Dvekut*, for a spiritual matter is not divided in half. Moreover, if this is something fulfilling, he should always have the good thing. And one should depict the time he had since the body does not feel the negative, but the existing, that is, states he had already had. And the body can take these states as examples.)

The Torah is called "the light" in it. This means that during the study, when we feel the light, and want to give to the Creator with this light, as it is written, "One who knows the commandment the Master will serve Him." Hence, he feels that he exists, that he wants to bestow upon the Creator, and this is the sensation of oneself.

However, when one is awarded the discernment of "the Torah and the Creator are one," one finds that all is one. At that time, one feels the Creator in the Torah. One should always yearn for the light in it; and the light we can with what we learn, although it is easier to find the light in words of Kabbalah.

During the work, they are two ends. One is drawn to the discernment of the Creator, at which time he cannot study the Torah, and he yearns after the books of *Hassidim*. Then there is one who craves the Torah, to know the ways of the Creator, the worlds, their processes, and matters of guidance. These are the two ends. But in the future, "He shall smite the corners of Moab," that is, they are both included in the tree.

26. Baal HaSulam, *Shamati*, Article No. 17, "What Does It Mean that the Sitra Achra Is Called '*Malchut* without a Crown'?"

It is known that calculation is implemented only in *Malchut*, who calculates the height of the degree (through the *Ohr Hozer* [reflected light] in her). Also, it is known that *Malchut* is called "the will to receive for oneself."

When she annuls her will to receive before the Root, and does not want to receive but only to give to the Root, like the Root, which is a desire to bestow, then *Malchut*, called *Ani* [I], becomes *Ein* [nothing], with an *Aleph*. Only then does she extend the light of *Keter* to build her *Partzuf* and becomes twelve *Partzufim* of *Kedusha*.

However, when she wants to receive for herself, she becomes the evil *Ayin* [eye]. In other words, where there was a combination of *Ein*, meaning annulment before the root, which is *Keter*, it has become *Ayin* (meaning seeing and knowing within reason).

This is called "adding." It means that one wants to add knowing to faith, and work within reason. In other words, she says that it is more worthwhile to work within reason, and then the will to receive will not object to the work.

This causes a flaw, meaning that they were separated from the *Keter*, called "the desire to bestow," which is the Root. There is no longer the matter of equivalence of form with the Root, called *Keter*. For this reason, the *Sitra Achra* is called "*Malchut* without a Crown." It means that *Malchut* of the *Sitra Achra* does not have *Dvekut* [adhesion] with the *Keter*. For this reason, they have only eleven *Partzufim*, without *Partzuf Keter*.

This is the meaning of what our sages said, "ninety nine died of evil eye," meaning because they have no quality of *Keter*. It means that the *Malchut* in them, being the will to receive, does not want to annul before the Root, called *Keter*. This means that they do not want to make of the *Ani* [I], called "the will to receive," a quality of *Ein* [nothing], which is the annulment of the will to receive.

Instead, they want to add. And this is called "the evil *Ayin*" [eye]. That is, where there should be *Ein* with *Aleph* [the first letter in the word *Ein*], they insert the evil *Ayin* [eye, the first letter in the word]. Thus, they fall from their degree due to lack of *Dvekut* with the Root.

This is the meaning of what our sages said, "Anyone who is proud, the Creator says, 'He and I cannot dwell in the same abode,'" as he makes two authorities. However, when one is in a state of *Ein*, and annuls himself before the Root, meaning that one's sole intention is only to bestow, like the Root, you find that there is only one authority here—the authority of the Creator. Then, all that one receives in the world is only in order to bestow upon the Creator.

This is the meaning of what he had said, "The whole world was created only for me, and I, to serve my Maker." For this reason, I must receive all the degrees in the world so that I can give everything to the Creator, which is called "to serve my Maker."

27. Baal HaSulam, Letter No. 14

"Come to Pharaoh." It is the *Shechina* [Divinity] in disclosure, from the words, "and let the hair of the woman's head go loose," as it is written in *The Zohar*. The thing is that to the extent that the children of Israel thought that Egypt were enslaving them and impeding them from serving the Creator, they truly were in the exile in Egypt. Hence, the Redeemer's only work was to reveal to them that there is no other force involved here, that "I and not a messenger," for there is no other force but Him. This was indeed the light of redemption, as explained in the Passover Haggadah [story].

This is what the Creator gave to Moses in the verse, "Come to Pharaoh," meaning unite the truth, for the whole approaching the king of Egypt is only to Pharaoh, to disclose the *Shechina*. This is why He said, "For I have hardened his heart," etc., "that I may place these signs of Mine within him."

In spirituality, there are no letters, as I have already elaborated on before. All the multiplication in spirituality relies on the letters derived from the materiality of this world, as in, "And creator of darkness." There are no additions or initiations here, but the creation of darkness, the *Merkava* [chariot/structure] that is suited to disclose that the light is good. It follows that the Creator Himself hardened his heart. Why? Because it is letters that I need.

This is the meaning of "that I may place these signs of Mine within him, and that you may tell ... that you may know that I am the Lord." Explanation: Once you receive the letters, meaning when you understand that I gave and toiled for you, as in, do not move from "behind" Me, for you will thoroughly keep the *Achoraim* [posterior/back] for Me, for My name, then the abundance will do her thing and fill the letters. The qualities will become *Sefirot*, since before the filling they are called "qualities," and upon their fulfillment for the best, they are called *Sefirot*, sapphire, illuminating the world from one end to the other.

This is the meaning of "that you may tell." I need all this for the end of the matter, meaning "And you shall know that I am the Lord" "and not a messenger." This is the meaning of the fiftieth gate, which cannot appear unless the forty-nine faces of pure and impure appear in one opposite the other, in which the righteous falls [forty-nine in Gematria] before the wicked.

28. Baal HaSulam, *Shamati*, Article No. 38, "The Fear of God Is His Treasure"

Our sages said, "Everything is in the hands of heaven but the fear of heaven," is because He can give everything but fear. This is because what the Creator gives is more love, not fear.

Acquiring fear is through the *Segula* [power/remedy] of Torah and *Mitzvot*. It means that when one engages in Torah and *Mitzvot* with the intention to be rewarded with bringing contentment to one's Maker, that aim that rests on the acts of *Mitzvot* and the study of Torah brings one to attain it. Otherwise, one might remain—although he observes Torah and *Mitzvot* in every item and detail— he will still remain merely in the degree of still of *Kedusha* [holiness].

It follows that one should always remember the reason that obligates him to engage in Torah and *Mitzvot*. This is the meaning of what our sages meant by "that your *Kedusha* will be for My Name." It means that I will be your cause, meaning that all your work is in wanting to delight Me, meaning that all your actions will be in order to bestow.

Our sages said (*Berachot* 20), "Everything there is in keeping, there is in remembering." This means that all those who engage in observing Torah and *Mitzvot* with the aim to achieve "remembering," by way of "When I remember Him, He does not let me sleep." It follows, that the keeping is primarily in order to be awarded remembering.

Thus, one's desire to remember that the Creator is the cause for observing Torah and *Mitzvot*. This is so because it follows that the reason and the cause to observe the Torah and *Mitzvot* is the Creator, as without it one cannot adhere to the Creator, since "He and I cannot dwell in the same abode" due to the disparity of form.

29. Baal HaSulam, Letter No. 18

Keep away from suffering a man's jolt prematurely, for "Where one thinks is where one is." Therefore, when a person is certain that he will not lack abundance, he can focus his efforts on words of Torah because "the blessed adheres to the Blessed."

But lack of confidence behooves labor, and any labor is from the *Sitra Achra* [other side], and "The cursed does not adhere to the blessed," for he will not be able to focus all his efforts on words of Torah. And yet, if he wishes to travel overseas, he should not contemplate these things at all, but very quickly, as though the blink of an eye, and will return to normalcy, so as not to scatter his sparks in times and places that apart from this are still not sufficiently united.

Know that no flaw comes from the lower ones except in the permitted time and place, as it is now, meaning whether helpful or regretful, or God forbid despairs at the present moment, it is "rushing the end in all the times and in all the places in the world." This is the meaning of "a moment of His fury" and "How much is His fury? A moment."

Therefore, one has no choice but to direct all the present and future moments to be offered and presented to His great name. One who rejects a moment before Him for it is difficult displays his folly openly, for all the worlds and all the times are not worthwhile for him because the light of His face is not clothed in the changing times and occasions although one's work certainly changes because of them. This is why thanks to our holy fathers, faith and confidence above reason have been prepared for us, which one uses in the tougher times effortlessly and tirelessly.

This is the meaning of "By this comes lightly, ready for all His works on those six days." The letter *Hey*, which is the root of creation, is a light letter, and laboring to enhance its level does not help at all, for it is thrown, as in "no reason and no end." Therefore, one who assumes the complete burden of the kingdom of heaven finds no labor in the work of the Creator, and can therefore adhere to the Creator day and night, in light and in darkness. The *Geshem* ["rain," but also "corporeality"]—which is created in coming and going, changes and exchanges—will not stop him since the *Keter*, which is *Ein Sof*, illuminates to all completely equally. The fool—who walks under a flood of preventions that pour on him from before and from behind—says to all that he does not feel the cessation and the lack of *Dvekut* [adhesion] as a corruption or iniquity on his part.

Had he sensed it, he would certainly have strained to find some tactic to at least be saved from the cessation of *Dvekut*, whether more or less. This tactic has never been denied of anyone who sought it, either as in "the thought of faith" or as in "confidence," or as in "pleas of his prayer," which are suitable for a person specifically in the narrow and pressured places, for even a thief in hiding calls on the Creator. For this reason, it does not require *Mochin de Gadlut* to keep the branch from cutting from its root.

30. Baal HaSulam, *Shamati*, Article No. 121, "She Is Like Merchant-Ships"

"Man shall not live on bread alone, but on what proceeds out of the mouth of the Lord." This means that the life of *Kedusha* [holiness] in a person does not come specifically from drawing closer, from entries, meaning admissions into *Kedusha*, but also from the exits, from the removals. This is so because through the dressing of the *Sitra Achra* in one's body, and its claims, "She is all mine," with a just argument, one is awarded permanent faith by overcoming these states.

This means that one should dedicate everything to the Creator, that is, that even the exits stem from Him. When he is rewarded, he sees that both the exits and the entries were all from Him. This forces him to be humble, since he sees that the Creator does everything, the exits as well as the entries.

This is the meaning of what is said about Moses, that he was humble and patient—that one must tolerate the lowliness, meaning that in each degree one should keep the lowliness. The minute he leaves the lowliness, he immediately loses all the degrees of Moses he had already achieved.

This is the meaning of patience. Lowliness exists in everyone, but not every person feels that lowliness is a good thing. It turns out that we do not want to suffer. However, Moses tolerated the humbleness, which is why he was called "humble," since the lowliness made him glad.

31. Baal HaSulam, *Shamati*, Article No. 8, "What Is the Difference between a Shade of Kedusha and a Shade of Sitra Achra?"

There are two kinds of shadows, and this is the meaning of "and the shadows flee away," meaning that the shadows will pass away from the world.

The shade of Klipa [shell] is called "Another god is sterile and does not bear fruit." In *Kedusha* [holiness], however, it is called "Under its shadow I coveted to sit, and its fruit was sweet to my palate." In other words, he says that all the concealments and afflictions he feels are because the Creator has sent him these states so he would have a place for work above reason.

When one has the strength to say this—that the Creator causes him all this—it is to one's benefit. This means that through this he can come to work in order to bestow and not for his own sake. At that time, one realizes, meaning believes that the Creator enjoys specifically this work, which is built entirely on above reason.

It follows that at that time, one does not pray to the Creator that the shadows will flee from the world. Rather, he says, "I see that the Creator wants me to serve Him in this manner, entirely above reason." Thus, in everything he does he says, "The Creator certainly enjoys this work, so why should I care if I am working in a state of concealment of the face?"

Because one wants to work in order to bestow, meaning that the Creator will enjoy, he feels no humiliation in this work, meaning a sensation that he is in a state of concealment of the face, that the Creator does not enjoy this work. Instead, one agrees to the leadership of the Creator, meaning however the Creator wants him to feel the existence of the Creator during the work, he agrees wholeheartedly. This is so because one does not consider what can please him, but what can please the Creator. Thus, this shade brings him life.

This is called "Under its shadow I coveted," meaning one covets such a state where he can make some overcoming above reason.

32. Baal HaSulam, Letter No. 16

I have already said in the name of the Baal Shem Tov that prior to making a *Mitzva* [commandment], one must not consider private Providence at all. On the contrary, one should say, "If I am not for me, who is for me?" But after the fact, one must reconsider and believe that it was not by "My power and the might of my hand" that I did the *Mitzva*, but only by the power of the Creator, who contemplated so about me in advance, and so I had to do.

It is likewise in worldly matters because spirituality and corporeality are equal. Therefore, before one goes out to make one's daily bread, he should remove his thoughts from private Providence and say, "If I am not for me, who is?" He should do all the tactics applied in corporeality to earn his living as do others.

But in the evening, when he returns home with his earnings, he must never think that he has earned this profit by his own innovations. Rather, even if he stayed all day in the basement of his home, he would still have earned his pay, for so the Creator contemplated for him in advance, and so it had to be.

Although the matters look the contrary on the surface, and are unreasonable, one must believe that so the Creator has determined for him in His law, from authors and from books.

This is the meaning of the unification of HaVaYaH Elokim [God]. HaVaYaH means private Providence, where the Creator is everything, and He does not need dwellers of material houses to help Him. Elokim in Gematria is HaTeva [the nature], where man behaves according to the nature that He instilled in the systems of the corporeal heaven and earth, and he keeps those rules as do the rest of the corporeal beings. And yet, he also believes in HaVaYaH, meaning in private Providence.

By this he unites them with one another, and "they became as one in his hand." In this way, he brings great contentment to his Maker and brings illumination in all the worlds.

This is the meaning of the three discernments—commandment, transgression, and permission. The commandment is the place of *Kedusha* [holiness], the transgression is the place of the *Sitra Achra* [other side], and permission, which is neither a *Mitzva* nor a transgression, is the place over which the *Kedusha* and the *Sitra Achra* fight.

When a person does permitted things but does not dedicate them to *Kedusha*, that entire place falls into the domain of the *Sitra Achra*. And when a person grows stronger and engages in permitted things to make unifications as much as he can, he returns the permission into the domain of *Kedusha*.

Thus, I have interpreted what our sages said, "It follows that the physician has been given permission to heal." That is, although the healing is certainly in the hands of the Creator, and human tactics will not move Him from His place, the Torah still informs us, "and shall cause him to be thoroughly healed," to let you know that it is permitted, that this is the place of the campaign between *Mitzva* and transgression.

It follows that we ourselves are obliged to conquer that "permission" under the *Kedusha*. But how is it conquered? When a person goes to an expert physician who prescribes him a medication that has been tried and tested a thousand times, and after he takes the medicine he is cured, he must believe that without the doctor, the Creator would still cure him, for his longevity has been preordained. Thus, instead of singing and praising the human doctor, he thanks and praises the Creator. By so doing, he conquers the permitted under the domain of *Kedusha*.

It is likewise in the rest of the matters of "permission." By this he expands the boundaries of *Kedusha* so that the *Kedusha* expands to its fullest measure, and he suddenly sees himself and his full stature standing and living in the palace of holiness. Indeed, the boundaries of *Kedusha* have so expanded that it reached his own place.

33. Baal HaSulam, *Shamati*, Article No. 107, "Concerning the Two Angels"

Concerning the two angels that accompany one on the eve of Shabbat [Sabbath], a good angel and a bad angel, a good angel is called "right," by which one comes closer to serving the Creator. This is called "the right brings closer." And the bad angel is considered "left," pushing away. This means that it brings him foreign thoughts, whether in mind or in heart.

When one prevails over the bad and brings himself closer to the Creator, meaning that each time, he overcomes the evil and attaches himself to the Creator, it follows that through the two of them, he has come closer to *Dvekut* [adhesion] with the Creator. This means that both performed a single task—they have caused him to adhere to the Creator. In that state one says, "Come in peace."

And when one has completed all of one's work and has admitted all the left into *Kedusha* [holiness], as it is written, "There is no place to hide from You," the bad angel has nothing more to do, as the person has already overcome all the difficulties that the evil presented. At that time, the bad angel is idle. At that time, the person tells it, "Go in peace."

34. Baal HaSulam, Letter No. 11

All the good of the awakening from below concerns only our learning how to feel the deficiency, as it is set before us by the Creator. This is the meaning of "A prayer makes half," since as long as one does not feel the deficiency of the half—the part that was cut off from the whole, and the part does not feel as it should—one is incapable of complete *Dvekut* [adhesion] since this will not be considered advantageous for him, and one does not keep or sustain a needless thing.

Our sages told us that there is a remedy for this feeling by the power of the prayer. When one is persistent in praying and craving to adhere to Him perpetually, the prayer can do half, meaning that he will recognize that it is half. When the sparks multiply and become absorbed in the organs, he will certainly be rewarded with complete salvation and the part will be adhered to the whole forever.

35. Baal HaSulam, *Shamati*, Article No. 19, "What Is 'The Creator Hates the Bodies,' in the Work?"

If the Creator gives one some illumination from above, the will to receive surrenders and annuls like a candle before a torch. Then one has no labor anyhow, since he no longer needs to take upon himself the burden of the kingdom of heaven coercively as an ox to the burden and as a donkey to the load, as it is written, "You who love the Lord, hate evil."

This means that the love of the Creator extends only from the place of evil. In other words, to the extent that one has hatred for evil, meaning that he sees how the will to receive obstructs him from achieving the completeness of the goal, to that extent he needs to be imparted the love of the Creator. If one does feel that he has evil, he cannot be granted the love of the Creator since he has no need for it, as he already has satisfaction in the work.

As we have said, one must not be angry when he has work with the will to receive, that it obstructs him in the work. One would certainly be more satisfied if the will to receive were absent from the body, meaning that it would not bring its questions to a person, obstructing him in the work of observing Torah and *Mitzvot* [commandments].

However, one should believe that the obstructions of the will to receive in the work come to him from above. One is given the force to discover the will to receive from above because there is room for work precisely when the will to receive awakens.

Then one has close contact with the Creator to help him turn the will to receive to work in order to bestow. One must believe that from this extends contentment to the Creator, from his praying to Him to draw him near in the manner of *Dvekut* [adhesion], called "equivalence of form," discerned as the annulment of the will to receive, so it is in order to bestow. The Creator says about this, "My sons defeated Me." That is, I gave you the will to receive, and you ask Me to give you a desire to bestow instead.

36. Baal HaSulam, *Shamati*, Article No. 42, "What Is the Acronym Elul in the Work?"

Those who wish to work in order to bestow are admitted into the King's hall, and when one works in order to bestow, he does not mind what he feels during the work.

Rather, even in a state where he sees a shape of black, he is not impressed by it, but he only wants the Creator to give him strength to be able to overcome all the obstacles. It means that he does not ask the Creator to give him a shape of white, but to give him the strength to overcome all the concealments.

Hence, those people who want to work in order to bestow, if there is always a state of whiteness, the whiteness allows one to continue in the work. This is because, while it shines, one is able to work even in the form of reception for oneself.

Hence, one will never be able to know if his work is in purity or not, and this causes him never to be able to be awarded *Dvekut* [adhesion] with the Creator. For this reason, he is given from above a form of blackness, and then he sees if his work is in purity.

This means that if one can be in gladness in a state of blackness, too, it is a sign that his work is in purity, since one must be glad and believe that from above he was given an opportunity to be able to work in order to bestow.

37. Baal HaSulam, *Shamati*, Article No. 191, "The Time of Descent"

It is hard to depict the time of descent, when all the works and the efforts made from the beginning of the work until the time of descent are lost. To one who has never tasted the taste of servitude of the Creator, it seems as though this is outside of him, meaning that this happens to those of high degrees. But ordinary people have no connection to serving the Creator, only to crave the corporeal will to receive, present in the flow of the world, washing the whole world with this desire.

However, we must understand why they have come to such a state. After all, with or without one's consent, there is no change in the Creator of heaven and earth; He behaves in a manner of good and doing good. Thus, what is the outcome of this state?

We should say that it comes to announce His greatness. One does not need to act as though he does not want Her. Rather, one should behave in a manner of fearing the exaltedness, to know the merit and the distance between him and the Creator. It is difficult to understand this with a superficial mind, or have any possibility of connection between the Creator and creation.

During a descent he feels that it is impossible that he will have connection or belonging to the Creator by way of *Dvekut* [adhesion], since he feels that servitude is a foreign thing to the whole world.

In truth, this is so. But "In the place where you find His greatness, there you find His humbleness." This means that it is a matter that is above nature, that the Creator gave this gift to creation, to allow them to be connected and adhered to Him.

Hence, when one becomes reconnected, he should always remember his time of descent so as to know, understand, appreciate, and value the time of *Dvekut*, so he will know that now he has salvation above the natural way.

38. Baal HaSulam, Letter No. 18

First thing in the morning, when he rises from his sleep, he should sanctify the first moment with *Dvekut* with Him, pour out his heart to the Creator to keep him throughout the twenty-four hours of the day so that no idle thought will come into his mind, and he will not consider it impossible or above nature.

Indeed, it is the image of nature that makes an iron partition, and one should cancel nature's partitions that he feels. Rather, first he must believe that nature's partitions do not cut off from Him. Afterward, he should pray from the bottom of his heart, even for something that is above his natural desire.

Understand this always, even when forms that are not of *Kedusha* [holiness] traverse you, and they will instantly stop when you remember. See that you pour out your heart that henceforth the Creator will save you from cessations of *Dvekut* with Him. Gradually, your heart will grow accustomed to the Creator and will yearn to adhere to Him in truth, and the Lord's desire will succeed by you.

39. Baal HaSulam, *Shamati*, Article No. 211, "As Though Standing before a King"

One who is sitting at one's home is not as one who is standing before a King. This means that faith should be that he will feel all day as though he is standing before the King. Then his love and fear will certainly be complete. As long as he has not achieved this kind of faith, he should not rest, "for this is our lives and the length of our days," and we will accept no recompense.

And the lack of faith should be woven in his limbs until the habit becomes a second nature, to the extent that "When I remember Him, He does not let me sleep." But all the corporeal matters quench this lack, since he sees that anything that gives him pleasure, the pleasure cancels the deficiency and the pain.

Rather, he must want no consolation, and should be careful with any corporeal thing that he receives, so it does not quench his desire. This is done by regretting that by this pleasure, the sparks and powers of the *Kelim* [vessels] of *Kedusha* [holiness] are missing in him, meaning desires for *Kedusha*. Through the sorrow, he can keep from losing *Kelim* of *Kedusha*.

40. Baal HaSulam, "A Speech for the Completion of The Zohar"

The merit of one who has been rewarded with adhering to Him once more, meaning rewarded with equivalence of form with the Creator by inverting the will to receive imprinted in him through the power in Torah and *Mitzvot*. This was the very thing that separated him from His self. He turned it into a desire to bestow, and all of one's actions are only to bestow and to benefit others, as he has equalized his form with the Maker. It follows that he is just like the organ that was once cut off from the body and has reconnected to the body: It knows the thoughts of the rest of the body once again, just as it did prior to the separation from the body.

So is the soul: After it has acquired equivalence with Him, it knows His thoughts once more, as it knew prior to the separation from Him due to the will to receive's disparity of form. Then the verse, "Know the God of your father," comes true in him, as then he is rewarded with complete knowledge, which is Godly knowledge.

41. Baal HaSulam, *Shamati*, Article No. 16, "What Is the Day of the Lord and the Night of the Lord, in the Work?"

Is written, "Woe unto you who desire the day of the Lord! Why do you need the day of the Lord? It is darkness, and not light." The thing is that those who await the day of the Lord, it means that they are waiting to be imparted faith above reason, that faith will be so strong, as if they see with their eyes, with certainty, that it is so, that the Creator watches over the world in a manner of good and doing good.

In other words, they do not want to see how the Creator leads the world as The Good Who Does Good, since seeing is contradictory to faith. In other words, faith is precisely where it is against reason. And when one does what is against one's reason, this is called "faith above reason."

This means that they believe that the guidance of the Creator over the creatures is in a manner of good and doing good. While they do not see it with absolute certainty, they do not say to the Creator, "We want to see the quality of good and doing good as seeing within reason." Rather, they want it to remain in them as faith above reason, but they ask of the Creator to give them such strength that this faith will be so strong, as if they see it within reason, that there will be no difference between faith and knowledge in the mind. This is what they, those who want to adhere to the Creator, refer to as "the day of the Lord."

In other words, if they feel it as knowledge, the light of the Creator, called "the upper abundance," will go to the vessels of reception, called "*Kelim* [vessels] of separation." They do not want this since it will go to the will to receive, which is the opposite of *Kedusha* [holiness], which is against the will to receive for one's own sake. Instead, they want to adhere to the Creator.

42. Baal HaSulam, *Shamati*, Article No. 172, "The Matter of Preventions and Delays"

All the preventions and delays that appear before our eyes are but a form of nearing—the Creator wants to bring us closer, and all these preventions bring us only nearing, since without them we would have no possibility of approaching Him. This is so because, by nature, there is no greater distance, as we are made of pure matter while the Creator is higher than high. Only when one begins to approach does he begin to feel the distance between us. And any prevention one overcomes brings the way closer for that person.

This is so because one grows accustomed to moving on a line of growing farther

43. Baal HaSulam, Letter No. 19

In the beginning of one's nearing, he is given a soul in a manner of circles. This means that the Creator awakens toward him every time there is an opportunity on the part of man to cling to the man with longing and yearning. This is what the poet tells us, "Only goodness and mercy shall follow me all the days of my life." King David is the collective soul of the whole of Israel. Hence, he always longed, yearned, and craved true *Dvekut* [adhesion] with Him.

However, one must know in one's heart that the Creator chases him just as much as he chases the Creator. One must never forget that, even during the greatest longing. When remembering that the Creator misses and chases him to cling to him as intensely as one wishes for it himself, he then always goes from strength to strength, with yearning and longing, in a never-ending *Zivug* [coupling], the complete perfection of the soul, until he is rewarded with repentance from love, meaning the return of the *Vav* to the *Hey*, being the unification of the Creator with His *Shechina* [Divinity].

44. Baal HaSulam, "Introduction to The Study of the Ten Sefirot," Items 42-44

The reason for our great distance from the Creator, and that we are so prone to transgress His will, is for but one reason which became the source of all the torment and suffering we suffer, and for all the sins and the mistakes that we fail in. Clearly, by removing that reason, we will instantly be rid of any sorrow or pain. We will immediately be granted adhesion with Him in heart, soul, and might. And I tell you that that preliminary reason is none other than "our lack of understanding of His guidance over His creations," that we do not understand Him properly.

If, for example, the Creator were to establish open Providence with His creations in that, for instance, anyone who eats something forbidden would choke on the spot, and anyone who performs a *Mitzva* would discover such wonderful pleasures in it, like the finest pleasures in this corporeal world, then 1) what fool would even contemplate tasting something forbidden, knowing that he would immediately lose his life as a result, just as one does not contemplate jumping into a fire? 2) Also, what fool would leave any *Mitzva* without performing it as quickly as possible, just as one cannot retire from or linger with a great corporeal pleasure that comes into his hand, without receiving it as quickly as he can? Thus, if Providence were open to us, all the people in the world would be complete righteous.

Thus, you see that all we need in our world is open Providence. If we had open Providence, all the people in the world would be complete righteous and would also adhere to Him with absolute love, for it would certainly be a great honor for any one of us to befriend and love Him with our heart and soul, and always adhere to Him without losing even a minute.

45. Baal HaSulam, "The Essence of Religion and Its Purpose"

When one comes to love others, he is in direct *Dvekut*, which is equivalence of form with the Maker, and along with it man passes from his narrow world, filled with pain and impediments, to an eternal and broad world of bestowal upon the Creator and upon people.

46. Baal HaSulam, Letter No. 9

I know the great advantage with which the Creator has granted me over my contemporaries, for I have searched a long, long time why I have been chosen by God's will. And after all the lowliness emitted from that son of a wicked one, which is the *Klipa* [shell] that rules in my time, and after I have witnessed its true measure, I realize the Creator's kindness with me, to distract my heart today and always from hearing the above-mentioned question of the wicked.

I find myself committed and obligated, as today and as always, to be as an ox to the burden and as a donkey to the load, all day and all night. I will not rest from searching some place where I can bring some contentment to my Maker. Even in this day that I am in, I am happy to work under a great burden even seventy years, without any knowledge of its success (even my whole life), except that it is certainly the way that I have been commanded to walk in all His ways and to adhere to Him, which I have heard initially.

At the same time, I cannot excuse myself at all by any notion or contemplation from doing any work for His sake because of my lowliness. I crave and think all day about the sublimity of the work of God, in such sublimity that I cannot even write about it.

47. Baal HaSulam, Letter No. 2

I shall advise you to evoke within you fear of the coolness of the love between us. Although the intellect denies such a depiction, think for yourself—if there is a tactic by which to increase love and one does not increase it, that, too, is considered a flaw.

It is like a person who gives a great gift to his friend. The love that appears in his heart during the act is not like the love that remains in the heart after the fact. Rather, it gradually wanes each day until the blessing of the love can be entirely forgotten. Thus, the receiver of the gift must find a tactic every day to make it new in his eyes each day.

This is all our work—to display love between us, each and every day, just as upon receiving, meaning to increase and multiply the intellect with many additions to the core, until the additional blessings of now will be touching our senses like the essential gift at first. This requires great tactics, set up for the time of need.

48. Baal HaSulam, Letter No. 19

When one prepares to return to his root, he does not induce the complete *Zivug* at one time, but creates stimuli, which is the degree of *Nefesh*, by way of cycles, chasing the *Shechina* with all his might, quivering and sweating, until he mounts this extremity all day and all night, incessantly.

It is as the books write concerning the cycles. While one's soul is being completed in the degrees of *Nefesh*, he comes ever closer, and so his yearning and sorrow grow since the unsatisfied desire leaves behind it a great affliction according to the measure of the desire.

This is the meaning of "sound." The poet teaches us and says, "Awaken," meaning that you induce stimuli in the Shechina. "Sound," for you cause a great affliction, like no other, which is the meaning of "he groaned and moaned" because "What does the *Shechina* say when one is afflicted?" etc. And why do you do so? It is in order to "sever any shout."

This is the meaning of "The righteousness of the righteous will not save him on the day of his transgression." To Him who knows the mysteries, the desire in one's heart for His nearness is known, and that it might still be interrupted. Hence, He increases His stimuli, meaning the beginnings of the coituses, for if one listens to His voice, as in "The Lord of your shade," one does not fall and descend due to the increasing affliction of the stimuli since he sees and hears that the *Shechina* also suffers as he does by the increased longing. Thus, one's longing grows and intensifies each time until one's point in the heart is completed with complete will in a tight knot that will not crumble.

Rabbi Shimon Bar-Yochai said about this in the Idra: "I am for my beloved and upon me His desire. All the days I was connected to this world, I was connected to the Creator with one knot, and because of it, now, upon me His desire, etc." That is, "Until He who knows the mysteries shall testify that he shall not return to folly." Hence, he is granted the return of the *Hey* to the *Vav* for eternity, meaning the complete coitus and the restoration of past glory, which is the meaning of "the great Teki'a."

49. RABASH, Article No. 68, "The Order of the Work"

When one believes in the delight and pleasure that exists in above reason, he comes to consciously feel, to know the evil within him. That is, he believes that the Creator imparts such delight and pleasure, and although he sees all the good above reason, he achieves recognition. That is, he feels in all the organs the power of the evil that is found in receiving for oneself, which prevents him from receiving the abundance.

It follows that faith above reason causes him to feel his enemy within reason—who obstructs him from reaching the good. This is his standard. That is, to the extent that he believes in the delight and pleasure above reason, to that extent he can come to feel the recognition of evil.

Later, sensing the bad yields the sensation of delight and pleasure, since the recognition of evil in the sensation of the organs causes him to correct the bad.

This is done primarily through prayer, when he asks the Creator to give everything in bestowal, called *Dvekut* [adhesion]. Through these *Kelim* [vessels], the goal will be revealed in open Providence, meaning that there will be no need for the concealment because there will already be *Kelim* that are able to receive.

50. RABASH, Article No. 12 (1988), "What Are Torah and Work in the Way of the Creator?"

The meaning of "Torah and work" is that he learns Torah in order for the Torah to bring him the light of Torah. By this, he will be able to invert the vessels of reception to work in order to bestow, and with these *Kelim* he will be rewarded with *Dvekut* with the Creator, called "learning Torah *Lishma*."

51. RABASH, Article No. 12 (1988), "What Are Torah and Work in the Way of the Creator?"

We engage in the Torah in order to subdue the evil inclination, meaning to achieve *Dvekut* [adhesion] with the Creator, so that all our actions will be only in order to bestow. That is, by ourselves, we will never be able to go against nature, since the mind and heart that we must acquire require assistance, and the assistance is through the Torah. It is as our sages said, "I have created the evil inclination; I have created the Torah as a spice. By engaging in it, the light in it reforms them."

52. RABASH, Article No. 30 (1988), "What to Look for in the Assembly of Friends"

When a person makes the effort and judges him to the side of merit, it is a *Segula* [remedy/power/virtue], where by the toil that a person makes, which is called "an awakening from below," he is given strength from above to be able to love all the friends without exception.

This is called "Buy yourself a friend," that a person should make an effort to obtain love of others. And this is called "labor," since he must exert above reason. Reasonably thinking, "How is it possible to judge another person to the side of merit when his reason shows him his friend's true face, that he hates him?" What can he tell the body about that? Why should he submit himself before his friend?

The answer is that he wishes to achieve *Dvekut* [adhesion] with the Creator, called "equivalence of form," meaning not to think of his own benefit. Thus, why is subduing a difficult thing? The reason is that he must revoke his own worth, and the whole of the life that he wishes to live will be only with the consideration of his ability to work for others' benefit, beginning with love of others, between man and man, through the love of the Creator.

Hence, here is a place where he can say that anything he does is without any self-interest, since by reason, the friends are the ones who should love him, but he overcomes his reason, goes above reason, and says, "It is not worth living for myself." And although one is not always at a degree where he is able to say so, this is nonetheless the purpose of the work. Thus, he already has something to reply to the body.

53. RABASH, Article No. 12 (1988), "What Are Torah and Work in the Way of the Creator?"

Our sages said, that the Creator said to Israel, 'I have sold you My Torah. It is as though I have been sold with it.' This is the meaning of having a merchandise that one who sells it is sold with it."

This means that the Creator wants that when a person takes the Torah, he will seemingly take the Creator with him. Yet, a person does not feel he needs this. Primarily, a person takes after the majority. And since when beginning to teach women, children, and the general public, Maimonides says we should begin in *Lo Lishma*, and normally, everyone takes after the beginning, meaning that the reason they were given for why we need the Torah are reasons of *Lo Lishma*, and not because "I have created the evil inclination; I have created the Torah as a spice." Naturally, the majority of the world does not even understand that there is a reward called "*Dvekut* with the Creator."

For this reason, the view of the majority controls a person—that he does not need to study Torah so that by this he will be able to achieve the real intention. That is, that through the Torah he will be able to aim in order to bestow and not for his own benefit, that it will bring him *Dvekut*, to adhere to the Creator.

54. RABASH, Article No. 12 (1988), "What Are Torah and Work in the Way of the Creator?"

One who has faith in the Creator can believe that the giver of the Torah is clothed in the Torah. Conversely, a gentile, who has no faith in the Creator, how can he learn Torah, since he does not believe in the giver of the Torah? He can learn only from the clothing of the Torah, but not from the one who wears it, since he has no faith. The outer clothing is called "wisdom" and not "Torah," since Torah is specifically when he is connected to the giver of the Torah.

By this we understand what our sages said, "Should one tell you, 'There is wisdom in the gentiles,' believe." It is so because they can learn the clothing with the one who wears it, which is only called "wisdom," without any connection to the giver of the Torah. But "Should one tell you, 'There is Torah in the gentiles,' do not believe," since they have no connection to the giver of the Torah.

Since the essence of our work is to achieve *Dvekut* [adhesion] with the Creator, as it is written, "to cling unto Him," it follows that the Torah is the means to adhere to Him. That is, while learning Torah, we should aim to be rewarded with connecting to the one who wears it. This is done through the clothing, which is the Torah, in which the Creator is clothed.

55. RABASH, Article No. 875, "Three Lines – 4"

Before one is rewarded with emerging from self-love and doing everything in order to bestow, called *Lishma*, although he learns all these matters as they are, they are only names without any clarification, meaning that he has no attainment in those things that he is learning, since he has no knowledge about the material of the upper roots, called "the holy names," or *Sefirot* and *Partzufim* [pl. of *Partzuf*].

We can learn the upper matters, called "the wisdom of Kabbalah," only by way of *Segula* [remedy/power], since they can bring a person desire and yearning to adhere to the Creator because of the *Kedusha* [holiness] of the matters that speak of the holy names. Conversely, in the revealed Torah, he must believe that the whole Torah is the names of the Creator. It follows that these matters are more capable (as explained in the essay, "The Giving of the Torah").

When a person learns the upper matters in order for it to bring him closer to *Kedusha*, it causes a nearing of the lights. This means that this learning will cause him to thereby be rewarded with aiming all his actions in order to bestow. This is called "work in the manner of preparation," where he prepares himself to be worthy of entering the King's palace and to adhere to Him.

56. RABASH, Article No. 12 (1988), "What Are Torah and Work in the Way of the Creator?"

We see that the creation of the worlds and souls was primarily with one intention—to correct everything so that it works in order to bestow, which is called *Dvekut*, equivalence of form. The Creator said about the Torah, "I have created the evil inclination; I have created the Torah as a spice." That is, once man receives the Torah as a spice, the evil inclination will be corrected to work in order to bestow, as it is written in *The Zohar*, "The angel of death is destined to be a holy angel."

57. RABASH, Article No. 410, "Self-Love and Love of the Creator"

There is self-love and there is love of the Creator, and there is a medium, which is love of others. Through love of others we come to the love of the Creator. This is the meaning of what Rabbi Akiva said, "Love your neighbor as yourself is a great rule in the Torah."

As Old Hillel said to the gentile who told him, "Teach me the whole Torah on one leg." He said to him, "That which you hate, do not do to your friend. And the rest, go study." This is so because through love of others we come to love the Creator, and then the whole Torah and all the wisdom are in his heart.

It is written, "The Creator said to Israel, 'Be sure, the whole wisdom and the whole Torah are easy. Anyone who fears Me and performs the words of Torah, all the wisdom and all of the Torah are in his heart'" ("Introduction to The Study of the Ten Sefirot," where he references *Midrash Rabbah*, portion *VeZot HaBracha*). Concerning fear, it is explained in the *Sulam* [Ladder commentary on *The Zohar*], that it is fear that he might not be able to bestow upon the Creator, since it is the conduct of love that he wants to bestow upon the Creator.

Hence, one who has love of the Creator wants to bestow, and this is called *Dvekut* [adhesion], as in "And to cleave unto Him." By this the Creator passes onto him Torah and wisdom. It follows that he taught him on one leg, meaning that through love of others he will achieve the degree of love of the Creator, and then he will be rewarded with Torah and wisdom.

58. RABASH, Letter No. 66

It therefore follows that although he engages in Torah and *Mitzvot*, if it is not for the Creator, it is as one who has no God, for if he truly had the sensation of Godliness, he would certainly be engaging in order to bestow. But if he had engaged in doing good, then he would have the quality of love of others, by which he would also come to love the Creator, and would have the ability to observe Torah and *Mitzvot* for the Creator.

It turns out that a person should have the power and force to overcome his qualities, to turn them into being in favor of others, for by that he will later be rewarded with working with those qualities for the Creator.

Because once a person has already been corrected in his qualities so he can work in favor of others, he can work on the matter of faith in the Creator, for then he is fit to be rewarded with faith, for then he already has equivalence of form, called, "Cleave onto his attributes," as in, "As He is merciful, be you merciful."

59. RABASH, Article No. 19 (1984), "You Stand Today, All of You"

One should walk on the path of truth—to say, "My current state, being in utter lowliness, means that I was deliberately thrown out from above to know if I truly wish to do the holy work in order to bestow, or if I wish to be God's servant because I find it more rewarding than other things."

Then, if one can say, "Now I want to work in order to bestow and I do not want to do the holy work to receive some gratification in the work. Instead, I will settle for doing the work of holiness like any man of Israel—praying or taking a lesson on the daily portion. And I don't have time to think with which intent I study or pray, but I will simply observe the actions without any special intent." At that time, he will reenter the holy work because now he wishes to be God's servant without any preconditions.

This is the meaning of what is written, "You stand today, all of you," meaning everything you went through, all the states you have experienced—whether states of *Gadlut* or states of less than *Gadlut*, which were considered intermediate or so. You take all those details and you do not compare one degree to another because you do not care for any reward, but only for doing the Creator's will. He has commanded us to observe *Mitzvot* [commandments] and to study Torah, and this is what we do, like any common man of Israel. In other words, the state he is in right now is as important to him as when he thought he was in a state of *Gadlut*. At that time, "The Lord your God makes with you this day."

This means that then the Creator makes a covenant with him. In other words, precisely when one accepts His work without any conditions and agrees to do the holy work without any reward, which is called "unconditional surrender," this is the time when the Creator makes a covenant with him.

60. RABASH, Article No. 128, "Exalt the Lord Our God"

"Exalt the Lord our God and bow before His holy mountain, for the Lord our God is holy."

"Exalt" means that if one wants to know the exaltedness and greatness of the Creator, we can obtain this only through *Dvekut* [adhesion] and equivalence of form. Thus, what is "equivalence of form" and how does one achieve equivalence of form?

"Bow before His holy mountain." Bowing means surrendering. It is when one lowers his reason and says that what the reason understands or does not understand, I annul and subjugate it. Before which quality do I subjugate it? Before "His holy mountain."

Har [mountain] means *Hirhurim* [reflections], meaning thoughts. "His holy," for "holy" means separated from the matter. This means that he removes himself from the desire of reception. "Bow" means submitting the body, even though it disagrees, and taking upon oneself only thoughts of *Kedusha* [holiness]. This is the meaning "Bow before His holy mountain."

Why must we submit ourselves to thoughts of *Kedusha*, meaning retire from receiving in order to receive? It is because "The Lord our God is holy," for the Creator only bestows. For this reason, one must be in equivalence of form with the Creator, and by this we can obtain the exaltedness of the Creator. Afterward, we can achieve the attainment of the exaltedness of the Lord our God.

61. RABASH, Article No. 300, "A Land Where You Will Eat Bread without Scarcity"

One must engage in Torah day and night, that the night and the day should be equal for him, as written in *The Zohar* (*BeShalach*). In other words, the state of completeness called "day," and the state of incompleteness called "night," should be equal. That is, if his aim is for the sake of the Creator then he agrees that he wants to bring contentment to his Maker, and if the Creator wants him to remain in the state of incompleteness, he agrees to this, as well. The consent is expressed by doing his work as if he were rewarded with wholeness. This is regarded as "agreeing," when the day and the night are equal to him.

But if there is a difference, to the extent of the difference, there is separation, and on that separation there is a grip to the outer ones. Hence, if a person feels that to him there is a difference, he must pray to the Creator to help him so there will not be a difference for him, and then he will be rewarded with completeness.

62. RABASH, Letter No. 14

And one is rewarded with everything only by overcoming, called "strength," and each and every strength that a person elicits joins into a great amount. That is, even if a person overcomes once and gets an alien thought, and says, "But I already know from experience that soon I will not have this desire for the work, so what will I get now if I overcome it a little?" At that time, he must reply that many pennies join into a great amount, meaning to the general account, whether to the root of his soul or to the public.

Perhaps this is the meaning of "The gates of tears were not locked." *Shaarei* [gates] comes from the words, *Se'arot* ["hair," or "storms"], which is overcoming. "Tears" comes from the word "tearing," meaning that there is a mixture with other desires, and only in the middle of the desires there is a brief moment of a desire to overcome toward love and fear of heaven. "…not locked," but rather that moment joins into a great amount. When the amount is full, the person begins to feel the spiritual clothing.

This is the meaning of the importance of tears, meaning that even if he is in the lowest state and has base desires, but still has the strength to overcome, meaning that from the point in his heart he yearns and craves the Creator, then that force is very important. Thus, even when a person is in exile, when his point in the heart is placed under other governances, called "Divinity [*Shechina*] in exile" for that person, for one moment he overcomes and sanctifies the Creator. And even though he is already certain, because of all of his experiences, that afterwards he will fall again, it is still very important that a person can say the truth openly.

63. RABASH, Article No. 300, "A Land Where You Will Eat Bread without Scarcity"

Baal HaSulam said that because "The cursed does not cling to the Blessed," "The *Shechina* [Divinity] is present only out of joy," since he agrees to remain with all the bad if the Creator wants it this way, and in this way he engages in *Torah and Mitzvot* [commandments].

This is called "happy with his lot," and at that time, he is rich. This is the meaning of "As one blesses for the good, so one blesses for the bad." It means that if he were to be rewarded with the good that is concealed in *Torah and Mitzvot*, he would certainly work with joy and excitement and peace of mind. Likewise, now that he is deficient, he should also make his work be with joy and peace, and then he will be rewarded with food for humans, called "bread."

64. RABASH, Article No. 289, "The Creator Is Meticulous with the Righteous"

"It is very stormy around Him," meaning that the Creator is meticulous with the time of righteousness.

But when a person is in a state of lowliness, when he does not feel a good taste in the work, it is pointless to be meticulous with him because he is in lowliness anyhow, and he has work to approach the Creator. Hence, it cannot be said that He will deny him the flavor of the work because now he feels no flavor.

The blow that one receives from the Creator, when He takes from him the flavor of the work, by this itself He heals him because then he has no other way to serve the Creator but with faith above reason. It follows that the blow that he received from the Creator, from this itself he can be healed, for otherwise, he will remain in separation.

By this we understand what our sages said, that by the blows of the Creator, He heals (*Mechilta BeShalach*). In other words, this is the healing—that He gives him room to work with faith without any support.

65. RABASH, Article No. 10, "Jacob Went Out"

"Exit of the righteous from the place leaves an impression." It means that only then, through the exit of the righteous, when he thinks, "Now that I feel good taste in the work, I no longer need to work above reason," it causes him the exit of the righteous from the place. This creates in him an impression, so he will know how to keep himself from exiting the work of above reason from here on. As I heard from Baal HaSulam, when a person says, "Now that he has support and no longer stands between heaven and earth," he must fall from his degree because then he flaws the discernment of above reason.

It therefore follows that precisely the departure of the degree he had leaves an impression on him so he will know how to be careful next time and will not blemish the faith above reason, but always justify Providence.

66. RABASH, Article No. 6 (1990), "When Should One Use Pride in the Work?"

When a person engages in Torah and *Mitzvot*, this is the time to be in wholeness, as though the Creator has brought him close, to be among the King's servants. However, one must not lie to oneself and say that he feels that he is serving the King when he does not feel this way. Therefore, how can he be grateful to the Creator for drawing him near if he does not feel it?

Instead, at that time a person should say that although he is in utter lowliness, meaning he is still immersed in self-love, and still cannot do anything above reason, the Creator still gave him a thought and desire to engage in Torah and *Mitzvot*, and has also given him some strength to be able to overcome the spies who speak to him and poke his mind with their arguments. And still, he has some grip on spirituality.

At that time, a person should pay attention to this and believe that the Creator is tending to him and guides him on the track that leads to the King's palace. It follows that he should be happy that the Creator is watching over him and gives him the descents, as well.

67. RABASH, Article No. 17 (1989), "What Is the Prohibition to Greet Before Blessing the Creator, in the Work?"

A person must walk on the right line, regarded as wholeness, and pray to the Creator and thank Him, even if he does not find within him anything that desires spirituality. But accordingly, how can he thank the Creator and say that the Creator hears what he says to Him, which is the meaning of attributing the work to the Creator, and He accepts his work regardless of how the work seems?

However, if he relates only to the Creator and says, "I am turning to the Creator and I believe that He can answer my wishes," by this a person becomes happy and feels superior. That is, the rest of the people have no connection to spirituality, and he believes that the Creator has given him [a feeling] that he has no spirituality, in whatever way, but the fact that he has an interest in thinking about spirituality, it makes no difference if he has or hasn't, or that he is now in utter lowliness, meaning that he sees that now he has no desire to ascend in degree and emerge from the lowliness, but he thanks the Creator because at least he is thinking about spirituality, while the rest of the people do not have any thoughts of spirituality.

If he can thank the Creator, it gives him joy, and from *Lo Lishma* [not for Her sake] he comes to *Lishma* [for Her sake].

68. RABASH, Article No. 217, "Run My Beloved"

It is impossible to receive anything without equivalence. Rather, there must always be equivalence.

Hence, when he evokes mercy on himself, it follows that he is engaged in reception for himself. And the more he prays, not only is he not preparing the *Kli* [vessel] of equivalence, but on the contrary, sparks of reception form within him.

It turns out that he is going the opposite way: While he should prepare vessels of bestowal, he is preparing vessels of reception. "Cleave unto His attributes" is specifically "As He is merciful, so you are merciful."

Hence, when he prays for the public, through this prayer he engages in bestowal. And the more he prays, to that extent he forms vessels of bestowal, by which the light of bestowal, called "merciful," can be revealed.

69. RABASH, Letter No. 11

All these verses and saying of our sages advise us how to cling to Him, since our only flaw is that we do not feel His greatness. When we begin to criticize as in, "What is this work," we want to promptly receive everything as *Ohr Pnimi* (Inner Light). And you know that the Inner Light shines specifically when there are *Masach* and *Ohr Hozer* (Reflected Light), meaning clean *Kelim*. But *Behina Dalet* receives from the *Ohr Makif* (Surrounding Light), since *Ohr Makif* shines from afar, as it is written in *Tree of Life*.

This means that even if a person is still remote from the Creator and does not have equivalence of form, he can receive from the Surrounding Light. The ARI wrote that the Surrounding Light is greater than the Inner Light. That is, when can one receive when he is still remote? Only when he increases the greatness and importance of the Surrounding Light, meaning the exaltedness of the Creator and the importance of the light of Torah. Then he can receive illumination from afar.

We must believe that all the beauty of Creation is in the internality of the Torah. But faith requires great efforts. This is the meaning of, "Happy is the man who does not forget You." How is one rewarded with this? By "exerting in You."

70. RABASH, Article No. 159, "The Need and Importance of Teaching Faith"

Faith is called "clean and easy craft." It is "clean" because there must not be any mixture of self-benefit there, but only for the sake of the Creator, since when one believes in the greatness of the Creator, a person has no desire or yearning other than to adhere to Him all day and all night. This is why it is called "clean," meaning only for the sake of the Creator.

However, before a person is rewarded with his body's consent to the work of faith, this work is regarded as lowliness, since he does not see anyone respects him when he works only for the sake of the Creator.

At that time, he must see that his work is in concealment, since otherwise his work cannot be clean because while his work is with excitement, his actions will certainly be praised and by this, the matter of respect will interfere, that others will respect him for this.

Therefore, when he wants to have no mixtures, he must work in concealment and then he will not get any respect from this. This is why clean work is despicable in his eyes. Also, *Kalah* [easy/light] comes from the word *Nikleh* [despicable], meaning despised.

Also, clean work is despised because a person cannot tolerate faith above reason, since by nature, a person appreciates what he grasps in the mind when reason obligates him.

Conversely, going against reason is despicable because such work is called "gullible," as our sages said about the verse, "Who is gullible? Let him come here." This is Moses, pertaining to faith, since Moses is called "the faithful shepherd," who has faith and planted the faith in the whole of Israel.

In this way, we should interpret the words of Rabbi, "No craft passes from the world." As RASHI interpreted, whether it is loathsome or clean, since the view of Rabbi is that the whole world cannot do clean work, meaning that specifically one who is inclined to the work of truth is capable of doing clean work where there are no mixtures of *Lo Lishma* [not for Her sake] there.

71. RABASH, Article No. 557, "Concerning Ohr Hozer [reflected light]"

Why not everyone has the sensation of Godliness, since it is written, "I fill the heaven and the earth," and "The whole earth is full of His glory," and yet we do not feel anything.

The answer is that where there is no clothing called *Ohr Hozer*, the upper light is regarded as nonexistent from the perspective of the emanated being, and because the whole meaning of the *Ohr Hozer* is that he receives only according to the intention to bestow, as long as one has not emerged from self-reception, he does not have this *Ohr Hozer*. Thus, although "The whole earth is full of His glory," it is regarded as nonexistent from the perspective of the lower one.

It follows that the only thing that one must do in order to achieve the goal is to focus all of one's work on one point: to be able to dedicate all of one's free time for the sake of the Creator. This is the meaning of "Everything is in the hand of heaven but the fear of heaven." This means that the Creator gives everything. The upper lights are already prepared for a person, as in "More than the calf wants to suckle, the cow wants to nurse," and all we need is a *Kli* [vessel]. After the *Tzimtzum* [restriction], this *Kli* is called *Masach* and *Ohr Hozer*, and this is what connects the upper with the lower. That is, through it, the lower one connects to the upper one.

When this connector does not exist, the lower one cannot see the upper one, and the upper one is regarded as nonexistent from the perspective of the lower one. Hence, to the extent that one begins to work for the sake of the Creator, to that extent he acquires connection with the upper light. And by the measure of his connection, so is the measure of his attainment.

72. RABASH, Article No. 22 (1987), "What Is the Gift that a Person Asks of the Creator?"

The Creator created—existence from absence—a *Kli* called "desire and yearning to receive delight and pleasure." This means that what we see is as in "By Your actions we know You," meaning that we speak only of what we see that exists in the nature of creation. We see that it is impossible to enjoy anything, whatever it is, unless there is a yearning for it. For this reason, we learned that from the perspective of the light that created this *Kli*, called "will to receive," it underwent four *Behinot* [discernments], meaning four stages until the will to receive acquired the complete form of yearning. After the light created the *Kli*, this *Kli* received the delight and pleasure that He wished to give.

These two above-mentioned things, the light and the *Kli*, pertain to the Creator. We learn that in this respect, there was complete perfection and there is nothing to add to this.

However, afterwards, something new was born, which we attribute to the creature and not to the Creator. In other words, we attribute the matter of giving to the Creator, who is the giver, for His desire is to do good to His creations, which is to give abundance to the creatures and receive nothing from them. Yet, afterward, something new was made, as it is written in *The Study of the Ten Sefirot* (Part 1), that the first receiver, called *Malchut de Ein Sof*, craved a decoration called "decoration at the point of desire": to have equivalence of form called *Dvekut* [adhesion]. For this reason, the *Tzimtzum* [restriction] was made, meaning that she diminished her will to receive on the *Kli* called "will to receive," hence the light departed.

Malchut invented a new *Kli*, called "will to bestow," meaning not to receive delight and pleasure according to the level of the yearning for the light, but according to the level of her desire to bestow. This means that *Malchut* calculated how many percent of the abundance she could receive with the aim to bestow. On the part she would receive in order to receive, if she were to receive, she would not receive.

It follows that we attribute this *Kli*, which the lower one gives, to the lower one, since the *Kelim* [vessels] of the upper one, which the upper has made in order for the lower one to be able to enjoy the light, is only the will to receive. That *Kli* will never be revoked because what the Creator has created must always exist.

However, the lower one can add to the *Kli* of the Creator, as it is written, "Which God has created to do." This means that God has created the *Kli* called "desire to receive pleasure," and man must add to it a correction called "the intention to bestow," as was said above, that *Malchut de Ein Sof* decorated herself at the point of the desire. This means that her decoration was in that she placed on the will to receive the aim to bestow.

73. RABASH, Article No. 17 (1991), "What Is, "For I Have Hardened His Heart," in the work?"

A person must be glad that at least he has a need for spirituality, whereas the rest of the people have no interest in spirituality whatsoever.

When a person appreciates this, although it is not important to him, he does appreciate it and tries to thank the Creator for this. This causes him to acquire importance for spirituality, and from this a person can be happy. By this, a person can be rewarded with *Dvekut*, since as Baal HaSulam said, "The blessed clings to the Blessed." In other words, when a person is happy and thanks the Creator, he feels that the Creator has blessed him by giving him a little something of *Kedusha*, then "The blessed clings to the Blessed." Through this wholeness, one can achieve real *Dvekut*.

74. RABASH, Article No. 940, "The Point in the Heart"

It is written, "And let them make Me a Temple and I will dwell within them." This pertains to the point in the heart, which should be a Temple where the light of the Creator dwells, as it is written, "And I will dwell within them." Hence, one should try to build his structure of *Kedusha* [holiness], and the structure should be able to contain the upper abundance called "abundance poured from the Giver to the receiver." However, according to the rule, there must be equivalence of form between the Giver and the receiver so the receiver, too, must have the aim to bestow like the Giver.

This is called "action," as it is written, "Let them make Me a Temple," where the acting applies to the *Kli* [vessel] and not the light, since the light pertains to the Creator and only the action pertains to the creatures.

75. RABASH, Letter No. 8

At the end of the day, this is a group of people who have gathered in a certain place, under a certain leader, to be together. With superhuman courage they face up to all those who rise against them. Indeed, they are brave men with a strong spirit, and they are determined not to retreat one inch. They are first-class fighters, fighting the war against the inclination to their last drop of blood, and their only wish is to win the battle for the glory of His name.

76. RABASH, Article No. 27, "Three Lines – 1"

One should mainly walk on the right line, meaning do good deeds and feel himself as complete, and serving the king. One must believe that everything he does brings contentment to Him.

At the same time, he should dedicate time to walking on the left line, meaning to criticize, but the left should surrender before the right. That is, he walks on the left not because he wants the quality of the left, but in order to improve the right, to show that despite all his criticism and knowledge, he is going above reason, meaning in the "right," which is called "faith."

This is called the "middle line," which decides between the two lines and leans toward the right. This is also called *Achoraim* [posterior]. Through this unification, one is later rewarded with receiving the quality of *Panim* [face/anterior] of the degree. At that time there is clothing of *Hochma* in *Hassadim*, which cause a *Zivug* [coupling] *Panim be Panim* [face-to-face] above, in ZON.

77. RABASH, Article No. 44 (1990), "What Is an Optional War, in the work - 2?"

A person must believe that this concealment, where a person does not feel that there is a King to the world, the Creator did this, and this is called "the correction of the *Tzimtzum* [restriction]." However, one must believe and make great efforts until he feels in his organs that the Creator is the leader of the world. And not just a leader! Rather, one must believe that His guidance is in the manner of good and doing good. A person must do all that he can to be able to attain this.

78. RABASH, Article No. 195, "The Association of the Quality of Judgment with Mercy"

The main work is the choice, meaning "choose life," so there will be *Dvekut* [adhesion], which is *Lishma* [for Her sake]. By this, one is rewarded with *Dvekut* with the Life of Lives. When there is open Providence, there is no room for choice. For this reason, the upper one raised the *Malchut*, which is the quality of judgment, to the *Eynaim* [eyes]. This created a concealment, meaning that it seemed to the lower one that there was a drawback in the upper one, that there was no *Gadlut* [greatness/adulthood] in the upper one.

Subsequently, the qualities of the upper one are placed within the lower one, meaning they are deficient. It follows that these *Kelim* [vessels] have equivalence with the lower one, namely that as there is no vitality to the lower one, so there is no vitality in the upper qualities. In other words, he feels no taste in *Torah* and *Mitzvot* [commandments] for they are lifeless.

At that time, there is room for choice, for the lower one to say that this whole concealment that he feels is because the upper one restricted himself for the sake of the lower one. This is called "When Israel are in exile, the *Shechina* [Divinity] is with them," that whatever taste he feels, so he says. That is, it is not his fault that he does not feel the taste of vitality. Rather, in his view, there really is no vitality in spirituality.

If a person overcomes and says that the bitter taste he finds in these nourishments are only because he does not have the proper *Kelim* to receive the abundance because his *Kelim* are to receive and not to bestow, and he is sorry that the upper had to hide himself, for which the lower one can slander, this is regarded as *MAN* that the lower one raises.

By this, the upper raises his *AHP*. "Raising" means that the upper one can show the lower one the merit and the pleasure that exists in the *Kelim* of *AHP* that the upper one can reveal. Thus, from the perspective of the lower one, it follows that he raises the *Galgalta Eynaim* of the lower one, and by this itself, the lower one sees the merit of the upper one. It follows that the lower one ascends together with the *AHP* of the upper one.

79. RABASH, Article No. 1 (1984), "Purpose of Society – 2"

It is important to remain serious during the assembly so as not to lose the intention, as it is for this aim that they have gathered. And to walk humbly, which is a great thing, one should be accustomed to appear as though one is not serious. But in truth, a fire burns in their hearts.

Yet, to small people, during the assembly one should be wary of following words and deeds that do not yield the goal of the gathering—that thus they should achieve *Dvekut* with the Creator.

80. RABASH, Article No. 31, "Concerning *Yenika* [Suckling] and *Ibur* [Impregnation]"

The beginning of the entrance into the work of the Creator is regarded as *Ibur* [impregnation], when he cancels his self and becomes impregnated in the mother's womb, as it is written, "Hear, my son, your father's instruction, and do not forsake your mother's teaching." This comes from the verse, "For if you call the mother, 'understanding [*Bina*],'" meaning that he cancels self-love, called *Malchut*, whose original essence is called "will to receive in order to receive," and enters the vessels of bestowal, called *Bina*.

One should believe that before he was born, meaning before the soul descended into the body, the soul was adhered to Him, and now he longs to adhere to Him as prior to her descent. This is called *Ibur*, when he completely annuls his self.

81. RABASH, Article No. 14, "The Need for Love of Friends"

There is a special power in the adhesion of friends. Since views and thoughts pass from one to the other through the adhesion between them, each is mingled with the power of the other, and by that each person in the group has the power of the entire society. For this reason, although each person is an individual, he has the power of the entire group.

82. RABASH, Article No. 25 (1987), "What Is Heaviness of the Head in the Work?"

The primary goal should be to be rewarded with *Dvekut* [adhesion] with the Creator. Since the reason objects to this, he must go against reason, and this is very hard work.

Since he is asking the Creator to give him something to which all of his organs object, it follows that each and every prayer he makes to the Creator has its special work. This is why a prayer is called "work in the heart," meaning that he wants to go against the intellect and the mind, which tell him the complete opposite.

This is why it is not called "the work of the brain," since the work of the brain means that a person exerts to understand something with his mind and reason. But here he does not want to understand with his reason that we should serve the Creator in a state of knowing. Rather, he wants to serve the Creator specifically with faith above reason. This is why a prayer is called "work in the heart."

83. RABASH, Article No. 5 (1987), "What Is the Advantage in the Work More than in the Reward?"

It is written in *The Zohar*, "For the whole of the Torah is the names of the Creator." Also, a complete man is one who has been rewarded with "The Torah and the Creator and Israel are one." Therefore, indeed, greeting the *Shechina* is very important because the purpose is for man to achieve this degree.

But to come to greet the *Shechina* requires prior preparation, for one to be fit for it. In the words of our sages, this is called "As He is merciful, so you are merciful." This is the interpretation of the verse, "and to cleave unto Him, cleave unto His attributes." It means, as explained in the book *Matan Torah* [*The Giving of the Torah*], that only by a person working in love of others can he achieve *Dvekut* [adhesion] with the Creator. There are many names to this: "Instilling of the *Shechina*," "attainment the Torah," "greeting the *Shechina*," etc.

The main preparation, which is called "labor," is that one must prepare oneself to annul one's authority, meaning one's self. We can call this hospitality [greeting guests], meaning that he cancels the view of landlords and craves the view of Torah, which is called "annulling of authority." Naturally, he becomes the guest of the Creator, who is the Host of the entire world.

84. RABASH, Article No. 38 (1990), What Is, "A Cup of Blessing Must Be Full," in the Work?

When a person can go with his eyes shut, above reason, and believe in the sages and go all the way. This is called *Ibur*, when he has no mouth. *Ibur* means as it is written (*The Study of the Ten Sefirot*, Part 8, Item 17), "The level of *Malchut*, which is the most restricted *Katnut* [smallness/infancy] possible, is called *Ibur*. It comes from the words *Evra* [anger] and *Dinin* [Aramaic: judgments], as it is written, 'And the Lord was impregnated in me for your sake.'"

We should interpret the meaning of "anger and judgments." When a person must go with this eyes shut, above reason, the body resists this work. Hence, the fact that a person always has to overcome, this is called "anger, wrath, and trouble," since it is hard work to always overcome and annul before the upper one, for the upper one to do with him what the upper one wants. This is called *Ibur*, which is the most restricted *Katnut* possible.

85. RABASH, Article No. 21, "Sanctification of the Month"

A person must take upon himself the burden of the kingdom of heaven on the lowest quality, and say about it that to him, even that state, the lowest that can be, meaning one that is entirely above reason, when he has no support from the mind or the feeling, so he can build its foundations on it, and at that time, he is seemingly standing between heaven and earth and has no support, for then everything is above reason, then a person says that the Creator sent him this state, where he is in utter lowliness, since the Creator wants him to take upon himself the burden of the kingdom of heaven in this manner of lowliness.

At that time, because he believes above reason, he takes upon himself that the situation he is in now comes to him from the Creator, meaning that the Creator wants him to see the lowest possible state that can be in the world.

And yet, he must say that he believes in the Creator in all manners. This is considered that he has made an unconditional surrender. That is, a person does not say to the Creator, "If You give me a good feeling, to feel that 'The whole earth is full of His glory,' I will be willing to believe."

Rather, when he has no knowledge or sensation of spirituality, he cannot accept the burden of the kingdom of heaven and observe the *Torah and Mitzvot* [commandments]. Rather, he must accept the kingdom of heaven unconditionally.

This is what perplexed Moses: How could he come to the people of Israel with such lowliness? It is about this that the Creator showed him with the finger and said, "This you shall see and sanctify," meaning the moon at the time of its birth, when its merit is still not apparent.

Precisely accepting the kingdom of heaven in lowliness will reveal what our sages said, "Rabbi Elazar said, 'The Creator is destined to pardon the righteous and dwell among them in the Garden of Eden, and each one will point with his finger, as was said, 'And he said on that day, 'Behold, this is our God for whom we have waited and He will save us. This is the Lord for whom we have waited; let us rejoice and be glad in His salvation''''" (*Taanit* 31).

It follows that the hint that the Creator points to the moon with the finger and says, "This," by this we are rewarded with each one pointing with his finger, "Behold, this is our God."

86. RABASH, Article No. 496, "The Path of Truth"

It is written, "Wherever I mention My name, I will come to you and bless you." It should have said, "You mention My name." However, this means that to the same extent that I mention My name, to that same extent I will come to you.

It seems as though there is no answer to what he explains. But according to the above, it is thoroughly clear that to the same extent that he mentions, meaning what a person wants, this is what he is given. Those who walk on the path of truth, who want to bring contentment to the Maker, see that everything they do is not for the sake of the Creator, so they pray to the Creator to see that they can work for the sake of the Creator.

At that time, the Creator says, "Wherever I mention My name," meaning that you will give me the possibility to attribute My name to your actions. In other words, there will be an awakening from below, where I, says the Creator, will attribute My name to the actions. So how will you know that I am already attributing My name to them? You will see this if I "come to you and bless you."

In other words, the whole purpose of creation, which is to do good to His creations, cannot be revealed before you correct the matter of the bread of shame, meaning that you work in order to bestow. At that time, the purpose of creation will come true, which is to do good to His creations.

This is the meaning of what is written, "Wherever I mention My name," where I attribute My name to them, meaning that all your actions will be only to bestow. Then you will know if I "come to you and bless you." This is as Maimonides says, "How is repentance? Until He who knows the mysteries testifies to him."

87. RABASH, Article No. 21 (1988), "What Does It Mean that the Torah Was Given Out of the Darkness in the Work?'

When a person wants to draw near to the Creator, meaning use the vessels of bestowal, but he cannot because the body disagrees with it, since his body extends from vessels of reception, at that time a person feels that the world has grown dark on him, for he understands that if he cannot obtain vessels of bestowal, he will never be rewarded with the upper light, which is the light of "doing good to His creations."

It follows that the darkness he feels from not being able to obtain vessels of bestowal by himself gives him the need that someone will help him obtain those *Kelim* [vessels]. According to the rule, "There is no light without a *Kli* [vessel], no filling without a lack," it follows that now he has received a need for the light of Torah. It is as our sages said, "I have created the evil inclination; I have created the Torah as a spice."

Thus, the Torah is given specifically to the deficient, and that deficiency is called "darkness." This is the meaning of the words, "The Torah was given out of the darkness." That is, one who feels darkness in his life because he has no vessels of bestowal is fit to receive the Torah, so that through the Torah, the light in it will reform him and he will obtain the vessels of bestowal. Through them, he will be fit to receive the delight and pleasure, for those two are included in the Torah: 1) The *Kli*—that he wants to bestow. 2) Then he receives the delight and pleasure into the vessels of bestowal.

Conversely, the nations of the world did not receive the Torah, since it was given out of the darkness. In the work, "the nations of the world" means that the body comprises seventy nations that want the Torah not because they feel darkness when they have no vessels of bestowal. Rather, their only desire is the vessels of reception and they have no desire to emerge from that control. They want the Torah in order to add more light to themselves, meaning more pleasure than they receive from corporeal matters. That is, they also want the next world, as it is written in *The Zohar*, "They howl as dogs *Hav, Hav* [give, give], give us the wealth of this world, and give us the wealth of the next world." That is, the wealth of this world is not enough for them, but they also want the wealth of the next world.

It follows that the Torah was given specifically to those who feel that their will to receive controls them. They cry out from the darkness that they need the Torah in order to deliver them from the darkness that is the control of the vessels of reception, on which there was a *Tzimtzum* [restriction] and concealment so that no light will shine in that place. But that place is the cause for the need to receive the Torah.

88. RABASH, Article No. 15 (1986), "A Prayer of Many"

If there are a few people in the collective who can reach the goal of *Dvekut* with the Creator, and this will bring the Creator more contentment than if he himself were rewarded with nearing the Creator, he excludes himself. Instead, he wishes for the Creator to help them because this will bring more contentment above than from his own work. For this reason, he prays for the collective, that the Creator will help the entire collective and will give them that feeling—that they receive satisfaction from being able to bestow upon the Creator, to bring Him contentment.

And since everything requires an awakening from below, he gives the awakening from below, and others will receive the awakening from above, to whomever the Creator knows will be more beneficial for the Creator.

89. RABASH, Article No. 21 (1986), "Concerning Above Reason"

When he begins to do the holy work on the path of truth, meaning when he wishes to achieve *Dvekut* [adhesion] with the Creator, so all his actions will be for the Creator, by that he receives a little more light that shines for him each time, and then he begins to feel self-love as a bad thing.

It is a gradual process. Each time he sees that this is what obstructs him from achieving *Dvekut* with the Creator, he sees more clearly each time how it—the will to receive—is his real enemy, just as King Solomon referred to the evil inclination as "an enemy."

90. RABASH, Article No. 11 (1991), "What It Means that the Good Inclination and the Evil Inclination Guard a Person in the Work"

When a person wants to walk on the path of achieving *Dvekut* with the Creator and do all his work for the sake of the Creator, meaning to bestow contentment upon his Maker and not for his own sake, as it is against human nature, who was created with the will to receive for his own sake, and all of man's work is that he is told that he will not obtain this by his own strength, but only the Creator can give him this power called desire to bestow, and a person should only prepare the *Kli* to receive this power called "second nature," it follows that specifically through the evil inclination, which grows within him to its completion, a person sees his real deficiency—that he is unable to obtain the desire to bestow by himself. This brings him to a state where the Creator gives him the desire to bestow.

Thus, both the good inclination and the evil inclination lead a person to achieve the goal of equivalence of form, called "*Dvekut* with the Creator."

91. RABASH, Article No. 23 (1985), "On My Bed at Night"

"His father gives the white," as we said that wholeness is called "whiteness," where there is no dirt. There is a twofold gain here: 1) In this way he receives elation from being adhered to the Whole, meaning to the Creator, and we must believe that what He gives is wholeness. Wholeness makes a man whole, making him feel whole, too. Naturally, he derives nourishment from this, so he can live and persist and then have strength to do the holy work. 2) According to the importance he acquires during the work of wholeness, he will later have room to feel the deficiency with regard to his work, which is not truly pure. That is, at that time he can depict to himself how much he is losing by his negligence in the work, for he can compare between the importance of the Creator and his own lowliness, and this will give him energy to work.

However, one should also correct oneself, or he will remain in the dark and will not see the true light that shines on the *Kelim* [vessels] that are suitable for it, called "vessels of bestowal." The correction of the *Kelim* is called *Nukva*, deficiency, when he works on correcting his deficiencies. This is regarded as "His mother gives the red." That is, at that time he sees the red light, which are the barriers on his way, which prevent him from reaching the goal.

Then comes the time of prayer, since the man sees the measures of the work that he has in matters of "mind and heart," and how he has not progressed in the work of bestowal. He also sees how his body is weak, that he does not have great powers to be able to overcome his nature. For this reason, he sees that if the Creator does not help him, he is lost, as it is written (Psalms 127), "If the Lord does not build the house, they who build it labor in it in vain."

From those two, meaning from wholeness and deficiency, which are the "father and mother," it turns out that the Creator is the one who helps him, giving him a soul, which is the spirit of life. And then the newborn is born.

92. RABASH, Article No. 24 (1986), "The Difference between Charity and Gift"

In the work of the Creator, in the beginning of his work he had energy and confidence, and great importance for Torah and prayer because at that time he had grace of holiness, and felt that the work of the Creator is important. However, this was still not considered a "deficiency" that the Creator will satisfy, a deficiency is called *Dvekut* [adhesion] with the Creator, since the lack and pain of not having *Dvekut* with the Creator was still not felt in him as he has not exerted for it because he has just begun the work.

But after a long period of time of making efforts and not achieving satisfaction of his deficiency, torments and pain begin to form in him because he has made efforts but sees no progress in his work. At that time the thoughts begin to come one-by-one. Sometimes it is with sparks of despair, and sometimes he grows stronger, but then he sees once more that he has fallen from his state, and so on repeatedly. Finally, a real deficiency forms in him, which he has obtained through exertion in ascents and descents. These ascents and descents leave him with pain each time at not having been granted *Dvekut* with the Creator. Finally, when the cup of labor has been filled sufficiently, it is called a *Kli*. Then the filling of it comes from the Creator, since now he has a real *Kli*.

It follows that his seeing that now—after several years of work—he has retreated, this happens deliberately so he will ache at not having *Dvekut* with the Creator. It turns out that each time he must see that he is approaching the making of the *Kli*, called "real deficiency." That is, his gauge of *Katnut* [infancy/smallness] and *Gadlut* [adulthood/greatness] of the deficiency is to the extent of the suffering he feels at not having the filling, which is called here "*Dvekut* with the Creator," where all he wants is only to bring contentment to the Creator. Before the deficiency is completed, it is impossible for the filling to come in full.

93. RABASH, Article No. 7 (1991), What Is "Man" and What Is "Beast" in the Work?

When a person wants to work for the sake of the Creator and not for himself, then he sees that everything he does is not for the sake of the Creator but only for his own benefit. In that state, he feels that he has nothing and he is completely empty, and he can fill this place only with a pomegranate, meaning if he goes above reason, which is called "exaltedness of the Creator." In other words, he should ask the Creator to give him the power to believe above reason in the greatness of the Creator. That is, the fact that he wants the exaltedness of the Creator does not mean that he says, "If You let me attain the exaltedness and greatness of the Creator, I will agree to work." Rather, he wants the Creator to give him the power to believe in the greatness of the Creator, and with this he fills the emptiness in which he is in right now.

It follows that were it not for the emptiness, that is, if he did not work on the path toward achieving *Dvekut*, meaning in equivalence of form, called "in order to bestow," but rather like the general public, who suffice for the practices they observe, these people do not feel themselves as empty, but as full of *Mitzvot*.

However, specifically those who want to achieve bestowal feel the emptiness within them and need the greatness of the Creator. They can fill this emptiness specifically with exaltedness, called "full of *Mitzvot*," to the extent that they ask the Creator to give them the power to be able to go above reason, which is called "exaltedness.

94. RABASH, Article No. 39 (1991), "What Does It Mean that the Right Must Be Greater than the Left, in the Work?"

Is written (Sanhedrin 44b), "Rabbi Elazar said, 'One should always precede prayer to trouble.'" We should interpret that one does not go into the work of the left before he first worked in the manner of the right, which is regarded as wholeness, meaning that he does not lack anything and he thanks and praises the Creator for giving him some grip on the work of the Creator, and then he begins the work of the left. At that time, he sees that he is in trouble, that he has neither Torah nor work that is suitable for one who is serving the Creator. At that time, he feels how far he is from the work of the Creator, meaning from working for Him, namely working only with the aim to bestow contentment upon his Maker, and not at all for his own benefit. At that time, he sees how the body objects to this, and he does not see that he will ever be able to do anything only in order to bestow.

It follows that when he begins the path of the left, this is called "trouble," and he has no other choice but to pray to the Creator to help him and give him the desire to bestow, called "second nature." At that time, the prayer is from the bottom of the heart, and the Creator hears his prayer.

95. RABASH, Article No. 19 (1985), "Come unto Pharaoh – 1"

One should always overcome and not let thoughts of despair enter his mind, as our sages said (*Berachot*, 10), "Even if a sharp sword is placed on his neck he should not deny himself of mercy," as it was said (Job, 13), "Though He slay me, I will hope for Him."

We should interpret the "sharp sword placed on his neck" to mean that even though one's evil, called "self-love," is placed on his neck and wants to separate him from *Kedusha* by showing him that it is impossible to exit this authority, he should say that the picture he sees is the truth.

However, "He should not deny himself of mercy," for at that time he must believe that the Creator can give him the mercy, meaning the quality of bestowal. That is, by himself, it is true that one cannot exit the authority of self-reception. But from the perspective of the Creator, when the Creator helps him, of course He can bring him out. This is the meaning of what is written, "I am the Lord your God, who took you out from the land of Egypt to be your God."

96. RABASH, Article No. 645, "By Your Actions, We Know You"

It is written in *The Zohar*, "There is no place vacant of Him." Yet, we do not feel it for our lack of tools of sensation.

We can see that with a radio receiver, which receives all the signals in the world, the receiver does not create the sounds. Rather, the sound exists in the world, but before we had the receiving device, we did not detect the sounds although they did exist in reality.

Likewise, we can understand that "There is no place vacant of Him," but we need a receiving device. That receiving device is called *Dvekut* [adhesion] and "equivalence of form," which is a desire to bestow. When we have this machine, we will immediately feel that there is no place vacant of Him, but rather "The whole earth is full of His glory."

97. RABASH, Article No. 12 (1987), "What Is Half a Shekel in the Work – 1"

He should appreciate the service he is giving to the Creator by observing the commandments of the Creator. To the extent that he appreciates the greatness of the Creator, he rejoices in being rewarded with doing what the Creator commanded.

This matter of appreciating the great one is in our nature. We see that it is regarded as a great honor, if there is someone who is the greatest in the generation and people regard him as an important person. Everyone wants to serve him.

However, the satisfaction in the service depends on the greatness and importance that the world attributes to this great person. It follows that when one feels and depicts to himself that he is serving the Creator, he feels that he is blessed, and then comes the rule that the blessed clings to the blessed.

It follows that in such a state a person feels himself as the happiest in the world. This is the time when he needs to thank the Creator for giving him the little service that he served Him. It follows that in that state he is adhered to the Creator because there is joy in him, as our sages said, "The *Shechina* [Divinity] is present only out of joy."

98. RABASH, Article No. 29, (1987), "What Is 'According to the Sorrow, So Is the Reward'?"

Precisely when a person begins to walk on the path of bestowal, he comes to a state of pain and sorrow, and feels the labor that exists in serving the Creator. That is, the labor begins to work when one wants to work for the sake of the Creator. Only then do the arguments of the spies come to him. It is very difficult to overcome them, and many people escape the campaign and surrender to the argument of the spies.

But those who do not want to move, but rather say, "We have nowhere to go," suffer from not being able to always overcome them. They are in a state of ascending and descending, and every time they overcome, they see that they are farther from the goal that they want to be rewarded with *Dvekut* with the Creator, which is equivalence of form.

The measure of sorrow that they must tolerate is because in truth, a person cannot emerge from the control of self-reception by himself, as it is the nature in which the Creator created man, which only the Creator Himself can change. In other words, as He has given the created beings the desire to receive, He can later give them the desire to bestow.

However, according to the rule, "There is no light without a *Kli*, no filling without a lack," first one needs to obtain a deficiency. That is, he must feel that he is deficient of this *Kli* called "desire to bestow." And concerning feeling, it is impossible to feel any lack if one does not know what he is losing by not having the *Kli*, called "desire to bestow." For this reason, man must introspect on what causes him not to have the desire to bestow.

To the extent of the loss, he feels sorrow and suffering. When he has the real lack, meaning when he can pray to the Creator from the bottom of the heart for not having the strength to be able to work for the sake of the Creator, then, when he has the *Kli*, meaning the real lack, this is the time when his prayer is answered and he receives assistance from above. It is as our sages said, "He who comes to purify is aided."

99. RABASH, Article No. 5 (1968), "What Is, 'When Israel Are in Exile, the Shechina Is With Them,' in the Work?"

The Creator wants him to see his real state, how remote he is from working for the benefit of the Creator. For this reason, the Creator has taken from him the flavor he felt in *Lo Lishma* [not for Her sake], which leaves him lifeless. It follows that the Creator is tending to him and wants to admit him into *Kedusha*.

Therefore, now he must pray to the Creator to help him, since now he needs His help. Otherwise, he sees that he is completely lost. This is regarded as having obtained a *Kli* and a need for the Creator's help, since now he sees that he is truly separated from the Creator because he has no life, for one who adheres to the Creator has life, as it is written, "For with You is the source of life."

Now he can certainly pray from the bottom of the heart, for a real prayer is specifically from the bottom of the heart. Accordingly, he should be thankful to the Creator for letting him see his true state. Now he sees that he needs the Creator to give him the necessary assistance, as our sages said, "He who comes to purify is aided." And *The Zohar* asks, "With what is he aided?" and it replies, "With a holy soul."

Therefore, now the Creator has given him an opportunity to obtain a holy soul. He should be delighted about the state of descent and suffering that he feels in this state. For this reason, he should say that he is not in a state of descent, but on the contrary, he is in a state of ascent.

By this we can interpret what our sages said, "When torments come upon Israel, they surrender and pray." This means that when they come into a state of descent, they see their true state, that they are in lowliness. This is considered that they surrender, since they see their state—that they have parted from the Life of Lives, for one who has *Dvekut* with the Creator is alive. Otherwise, he feels only suffering. Therefore, it is clear to him that now is the time for prayer from the bottom of the heart. This is the meaning of the words, "They surrender and pray.

100. Zohar for All, BaHar [On Mount Sinai], "And If You Say, 'What Shall We Eat on the Seventh Year?'" Item 52

One should always be cautious with one's Master, and let his heart adhere to sublime faith, so he may be whole with his Master. When he is whole with his Master, no person in the world can harm him.

101. Zohar for All, VaYechi [Jacob Lived], "Serve the Lord with Fear," Item 414

Anyone who comes to serve the Creator should serve the Creator in the morning and in the evening.

102. Zohar for All, Truma [Donation], "And You, O Lord, Be Not Far Off," Items 224-225

Just as when a buck or a deer departs from its place, it promptly returns to that place, although the Creator departed upward to *Ein Sof*, He promptly returns to His place because Israel below cling to Him and do not leave Him to be forgotten and far off from them. This is why it is written, "O You my help, hasten to my assistance."

This is the reason why we must unite with the Creator and grip Him, as one who pulls from above to below, so that no one will be left from Him for even an hour.

103. Zohar for All, VaYechi [Jacob Lived], "A Lily and a Rose," Item 237

People do not look, do not know, and do not observe that when the Creator created man and cherished him with the upper *Mochin*, He asked of him to adhere to Him so he would be unique and would have one heart, and would adhere to a single place of *Dvekut* [adhesion], which does not change—in ZA. It was said about it, "I the Lord do not change," and which never inverts, and to which everything ties in a knot of unification.

104. Zohar for All, Yitro [Jethro], "You Shall Not Have," Items 421-422

"It is all one thing, and counts as a single degree. There are several faces within faces to the Creator. There are illuminating faces, faces that do not illuminate, lower faces, remote faces, near faces, faces within faces, faces without, faces of the right, and faces of the left."

Happy are Israel before the Creator, for they cling to the King's upper face, that face to which He and His name cling, and He and His name are one. The rest of the nations grip the remote faces, the lower faces. This is why they are remote from the King's body.

105. Zohar for All, Emor, "Raising the Right above the Left," Item 83

Happy are Israel in this world and in the next world, for they know how to adhere to the holy King, awaken the power of above, and extend the *Kedusha* [holiness] of their Master over them. This is why it is written, "Happy are you, Israel, who is like you, a people saved by the Lord," and also, "And you, who adhere to the Lord your God, are alive every one of you this day."

106. *Zohar for All, Truma* [Donation], The Watchman Says, "Morning Comes," Item 118

Happy are Israel, who are sanctified in the upper *Kedushot* because they cling above, as it is written, "And you that did cleave to the Lord your God are alive every one of you this day."

107. *Zohar for All, VaYikra* [The Lord Called], "How Good and How Pleasant," Items 99-101

"How good and how pleasant it is for brothers to dwell together, as well." Happy are Israel, for the Creator did not hand them over to a minister or to a messenger. Rather, Israel grip to Him and He to them. For their love, the Creator calls them, "servants," as it is written, "For unto Me the children of Israel are servants; they are My servants." Afterwards He calls them "sons," as it is written, "You are the children of the Lord your God." After that He calls them "brothers," as it is written, "My brothers and my friends." And because He called them "brothers," He wished to place His Divinity in them and He will not stray from them. Then it is written, "How good and how pleasant it is for brothers to dwell together, as well."

"How good and how pleasant it is for brothers to dwell together, as well" is as it is written, "And if a man shall take his sister ... and see her nakedness, and she sees his nakedness: it is a shameful thing." The "man" is the Creator. "Shall take his sister" refers to the assembly of Israel. Why is this so? Because "It is a shameful thing." Hence, How good and how pleasant it is for brothers to dwell together, as well," meaning the Creator, as well as the assembly of Israel. "As well" includes Israel below, for when the assembly of Israel is in unity, in *Zivug Panim be Panim* [face-to-face] with the Creator, Israel below are joyfully present in the Creator. This is why it writes, "Together, as well." "Together, as well" comes to join the *Tzadik*, meaning *Yesod*, with the assembly of Israel, who are one *Zivug*. This is why it says, "Together, as well," since *Yachad* [together] comes from the word, *Echad* [one].

108. *Zohar for All, Truma* [Donation], "They Will Take a Donation for Me," Item 151

Happy are the righteous who know how to aim their hearts' desire for the upper, holy King, and all their hearts' desire is not for this world and for its idle lust, but they know and exert to aim their desire for clinging above, to extend their Master's will in them from above downward.

109. *Zohar for All*, "Introduction of The Book of Zohar," "Two Points" Item 121

All the many contradictions to His uniqueness, which we taste in this world, separate us from the Creator. Yet, when exerting to keep Torah and *Mitzvot* with love, with our soul and might, as we are commanded—to bestow contentment upon our Maker—all those forces of separation do not affect us into subtracting any of the love of the Creator with all our souls and might. Rather, in that state, every contradiction we have overcome becomes a gate for attainment of His wisdom. This is so because there is a special quality in each contradiction—revealing a special degree in attaining Him. And those worthy ones who have been rewarded with it turn darkness into light and bitter into sweet, for all the powers of separation—from the darkness of the mind and the bitterness of the body—have become to them gates for obtainment of sublime degrees. Thus, the darkness becomes a great light and the bitter becomes sweet.

Hence, to the extent that they previously had all the conducts of His guidance toward the forces of separation, now they have all been inverted into forces of unification, and sentence the entire world to the side of merit.

110. *Zohar for All*, *Beresheet* [Genesis] – 1, "I, I am He," Item 175

The words, "See now that I, I am He" apply to the Creator and His Divinity, ZA and his *Nukva*. "I" is Divinity. "He" is the Creator, who is called *Vav-Hey-Vav*. In the future, at the end of correction, the *Nukva* will say, "See that I," *Vav-Hey-Vav* are one, as it is written, "And the light of the moon shall be as the light of the sun," meaning that the *Nukva* is equal to ZA.

"And there is no God with Me" refers to other gods, *SAM* and the serpent, for then it will be revealed that *SAM* and the serpent never separated between the Creator and His Divinity, as it is written, "By the mouth of two witnesses ... shall he that is to die be put to death," which applies to *SAM*, who was dead from his beginning and was but a servant to hurry the redemption of our souls.

This is the meaning of "I will put to death and make alive." I will put to death with My Divinity the one who is guilty, and I will make alive with my Divinity the one who is innocent. The Creator's guidance from the beginning will appear throughout the world, and then, as it is written, "Sinners will cease from the earth, and the wicked shall be no more." That is, unlike what it seems to us during the 6,000 years, that there is a governance that objects to *Kedusha*, which are *SAM* and the serpent, as it is written, "When man rules over man it is to his harm," then it will appear to all—"I will put to death and make alive" with My Divinity, and there is none else besides Him.

111. *Zohar for All*, *Ki Tazria* [When a Woman Inseminates], "Wisdom Excels over Folly," Item 105

"As the advantage of the light from within the darkness." The benefit of the light comes only out of the darkness. The correction of the white is black, for without the black, the white would be pointless. And because there is black, the white is elevated and respected. It is like sweet and bitter. A person cannot know the taste of sweetness before he has tasted bitterness. Thus, what makes it sweet is the bitter.

In things where there are opposites, the one reveals the other, such as in white and black, light and darkness, sick and healthy. If there were no sickness in the world, the term healthy would be unattainable, as it is written, "God has made the one opposite the other." And it is also written, "It is good that you grasp the one, and also not let go of the other."

112. *Zohar for All*, VaYera, "The Count of the Days of the Messiah," Item 453

Man is created in utter wickedness and lowliness, as it is written, "When a wild ass's foal is born a man." And all the vessels in one's body, meaning the senses and the qualities, and especially the thought serve him only wickedness and nothingness all day. And for one who is rewarded with adhering unto Him, the Creator does not create other tools instead, to be worthy and suitable for reception of the eternal spiritual abundance intended for him. Rather, the same lowly vessels that have thus far been used in a filthy and loathsome way are inverted to become vessels of reception of all the pleasantness and eternal gentleness.

Moreover, each *Kli* whose deficiencies had been the greatest has now become the most important. In other words, the measure that they reveal is the greatest.

113. *Zohar for All*, VaYetze [And Jacob Went Out], "The Two Rods," Item 250-352

King David always attached himself to the Creator. He did not worry about anything else in the world except to cling unto Him with his soul and his will, as it is written, "My soul cleaves unto You." And since he clung to the Creator, He supported him and He did not leave him, as it is written, "Your right hand holds me fast." We learn from this that when a person comes to cling to the Creator, the Creator holds him fast and does not leave him.

"My soul cleaves unto You," so that his degree would be crowned above. This is so because when his degree clings to the upper degrees, to rise after them, the right side, *Hassadim*, holds him so as to elevate him and connect him with the right in one bonding, as it should be. It is written about it, "Your right hand would hold me," and it is written, "And his right hand embrace me." This is why "Your right hand holds me fast."

When he grips to the Creator, it is written, "Let his left hand be under my head, and his right hand embrace me." This is one unification and one bonding with the Creator. And when it is one bonding with Him, his degree is filled and blessed.

114. *Likutey Moharan*, Last Edition, Mark 48

The work of the Creator requires great persistence, whatever happens to him. Remember this well for you will need it very much as you begin the work of the Creator. It requires great tenacity, and to be strong and brave, to brace oneself and stand still, even if you are dropped down every time. You must not allow yourself to fall off altogether, for it is necessary to experience all those falls, descents, and confusions prior to entering the gates of *Kedusha* [holiness], and the true righteous, too, have gone through all of it. Know, that man must cross and very, very narrow bridge, and the rule and the most important thing is not to be afraid at all.

115. The Holy Shlah, *Toldot Adam*

If one is attached above and resembles the Creator to walk in His ways, his name is called Adam [man], from the words *Adame LaElyon* [I will be like the upper one]. If one separates oneself from adhesion, the man is named after the earth from which he was taken, and dust he is and to dust he will return. However, the name Adam implies *Adame LaElyon* [I will be like the upper one]. This is the core purpose.

116. Martin Buber, *Ohr HaGanuz*

"Even if a sharp sword is placed on neck, let him not give up on mercy." Rabbi Shlomo of Karlin traveled with one of his disciples. Along the way, they stayed at an inn. They sat at the table and the rabbi asked for some mead [alcoholic beverage created by fermenting honey with water] to be warmed up for him, since he loved drinking hot mead. In the meanwhile, soldiers went in, and when they saw the Jews sitting at the table, they scolded them and ordered them to get out of the house at once.

"Has the mead been warmed yet?" the rabbi asked the owner of the inn. The soldiers thumped the table ferociously and screamed, "Get out of here or else…!"

"Is it still not warm?" asked the rabbi. The commander of the soldiers pulled his sword out of its sheath and placed it on his neck. "Indeed, it should not be too warm," said Rabbi Shlomo.
The soldiers left.

117. *Maor VaShemesh, Haazinu*

The whole purpose of creation was that bestowal would come down only through an awakening from below and raising of MAN that the assembly of Israel awakens. When they raise MAN, by this all the words ascend and add passion to adhere to their root. This is the main joy of the Creator, when Israel cleanse themselves from the depths of corporeality and yearn to adhere to their Creator.

118. Rabbi Menachem Mendel of Vitebsk, *Pri HaAretz*

The thing that guards from ignorance and cessation of adhesion is connection and love and true peace in adhesion of friends. Indeed, were it not for this, he would be in concealment of the face. And if, God forbid, he will rush to separate his heart from people due to some hate or envy, he should quickly run to his brothers, the friends who truly listen to the voice of the Creator saying, "My brothers, my soul, save me please and let me hear; the word of the Creator will heal my ruined heart." Let one accustom oneself to always install in his heart love of friends with all his might, and continue with it until his soul becomes adhered and they will adhere to one another. When they are all as one man, the One will dwell within them, they will be imparted from Him with many salvations and consolations, and they will rise in an ascent of body and soul.

119. Raaiah Kook, *Orot* [*Lights*]

When one sets one's heart and mind to adhere to the Godly light that shines in the assembly of Israel in general, by this he becomes adhered to the light of Godliness that dwells in the overall level of the overall man, of whom the assembly of Israel is the center and extract. By this, one also adheres to the general light of Godliness that is revealed in all of existence. By this, he willy-nilly connects his mind to adhesion with the upper Godliness above all of existence and his soul fills with vitality, sanctity, great glory, and might. By the addition to his strength, he adds strength to all the assembly of Israel since he is a part of it, and therefore adds power in the level of the man and in all the worlds.

120. Rav Chaim Vital, *Pri Etz Chaim*, Gate "Conducts of Learning," Chapter 1

My teacher would say that the heart of the intention of reading in the Torah depends on aiming to connect one's heart to its root through the Torah in order to complete the upper tree and complete the upper *Adam* [man] and correct him, for this is the whole purpose of man's creation and the purpose of his engagement in the Torah.

121. *Pri Tzadik*, *VaYeshev*, Item 3

The first *Hassidim* [adherents of the *Hassidut* movement] would spend one hour in prayer so as to aim their hearts to their Father in heaven. The word "aim" means the directness of the heart; it is to direct the heart so it is not scattered into the passions and lusts of worldly matters, but only to aim directly to his Father in heaven.

122. Ramchal, *Mesilat Yesharim*

Man's existence in this world is only to observe commandments and work and withstand trials. It is inappropriate that he should have worldly pleasures except as help and assistance, so he will have contentment and a sound mind so he can clear his heart to this work that is upon him. Indeed, his plea should be only to the Creator and not to have any other purpose in any act he does, small or great, but only to approach Him and break all the partitions that separate him from his Maker. These are all the material matters and what relates to them, until he is drawn after Him like iron after the magnet, and all that he can think of as a means for this closeness, he will pursue it and grip it and will not let go of it.

123. Meshulam Feibush Heler, *Yosher Divrei Emet*

The creation of the worlds was in order for the Creator to receive great pleasure from it, to emanate the souls of Israel from Him and they will cascade through several worlds until they come to this world and clothe in material clothing. From there, from that great distance, they will become refined and approach and adhere to Him with their thought, with their love for Him and their connection to Him, and they will resemble themselves to *Ein* [null], when they understand that indeed, without the creative force that has created them and sustains them, they are "null," as prior to creation. Thus, there is nothing in the world but the Creator. The Magid of Maazritch said that if they are "nulled" in their minds because of their adhesion with the Creator, it means that in their minds, they attach all their power to the Creator. It follows that they are very great because the branch has come to its root and is in one unity with its root, and the root is *Ein Sof* [infinity]. Thus, the branch, too, is *Ein*

Sof since its existence has been canceled like a drop that fell into the great sea and came to its root. Thus, it is one with the water of the sea and cannot be distinguished for itself.

124. *Degel Machaneh Ephraim, VaEtchanan*

It is written, "The Lord is one and Israel are one"; hence, they are adhered to the Creator, since it befits the One to cling to the one. And when is this? It is when Israel are bundled and attached together in complete unity. At that time, they are regarded as one, and the Creator is upon them, for He is one.

But when their hearts divide and they are apart from one another, they cannot be adhered to the One and the Creator is not on them. Rather, another God is on them. This is implied in the verse, "And you who are adhered," meaning when you are adhered and united with each other, "You are alive every one of you." When they are in one unity. Then it befits the One to cling to the one, and the one Creator is upon them.

4

By Your actions, We Know You

1. Baal HaSulam, "The Meaning of Conception and Birth"

Our entire development in creation is but emulation of it. All the flavors and beauty of colors that we innovate and devise are but emulation of the tasteful colors that we find in flowers. And so is a carpenter; from where does he know about making a four-legged table, if not by emulating the work of the Creator, who has made creations that stand on four legs? Or, from where would he know about combining two pieces of wood if not by emulating the organs of the body, which are joined together, so he went and built in the wood accordingly?

People observe and study the reality set before us in perfect reason and beauty. Afterward, when they understand it, they emulate it and do likewise. Subsequently, that example becomes a basis for another example, until man has created a handsome world full of inventions.

By looking at creation, planes were built with wings like birds. A radio was built to receive sound waves like the ears. In short, all of our successes are presented before us in creation and in reality as is, and all we need is to emulate it, and do.

2. Baal HaSulam, "Introduction to the Preface to the Wisdom of Kabbalah," Items 6-7

But in the Creator, there is no thought or perception whatsoever, and we cannot utter or say anything with regard to Him. But since we know You by Your actions, we should discern that He is a desire to bestow, since He created everything in order to delight His creatures and bestow His abundance upon us.

Thus, the souls are in oppositeness of form from Him, since He is all bestowal and has no will to receive anything, while the souls were imprinted with a will to receive for themselves. And we have already said that there is no greater oppositeness of form than this.

It follows that had the souls remained with the will to receive, they would forever remain separated from Him.

Now you will understand what is written (*The Tree of Life*, Branch 1), that the reason for the creation of the worlds was that He must be complete in all His actions and powers, and if He did not carry out His actions and powers in practice, He would seemingly not be considered whole. This seems perplexing, for how can incomplete actions emerge from a complete operator, to the extent that they would need correction?

From what has been explained, you can see that the essence of creation is only the will to receive. On one hand, it is very deficient since it is opposite in form from the Emanator, which is separation from Him, but on the other hand, this is the entire innovation and the existence from absence that He created, by which to receive from Him what He planned to delight them and bestow upon them.

Yet, had they remained separated from the Emanator, He would seemingly be incomplete, for in the end, complete operations must stem from the complete Operator.

For this reason, He restricted His light and created the worlds restriction after restriction down to this world, and clothed the soul in a worldly body. And through the practice of Torah and *Mitzvot*, the soul obtains the perfection it lacked prior to creation—the equivalence of form with Him. Thus, it will be fit to receive all the abundance and pleasure included in the thought of creation, and will also be in complete *Dvekut* [adhesion] with Him, in equivalence of form.

3. Baal HaSulam, "The Meaning of Conception and Birth"

All the flavor and contentment of the Creator who wanted to enjoy His work, meaning to fashion creations that can add, delight, and create like Him, but has no wish whatsoever to cook our food which is on the stove for us without our awareness, since we can do this by ourselves.

This is similar to a teacher and a student where the whole intention of the teacher is to give the student the strength to be like him, and to teach other students, like him. Likewise, the Creator is pleased when His creations create and innovate like Him. Yet, our whole power to innovate and develop is not real innovation. Rather, it is a type of emulation. And the more the emulation matches the work of nature, to that extent is our level of development measured.

From this we know that we have the power to correct ourselves, the existence of reality, like nature's pleasant example of reality. The proof of this is that had the Creator not worked His full Providence in that discernment, too, for "Is the Lord's hand short?" Rather, it is necessary that in this place, which is our own correction, we are able to correct ourselves.

4. Baal HaSulam, "A Speech for the Completion of The Zohar"

How right our sages were when they interpreted the verse, "and to adhere to Him," as *Dvekut* with His qualities—"As He is merciful, so you are merciful; as He is compassionate, so you are compassionate." They did not deflect the text from the literal meaning. Quite the contrary, they interpreted the text precisely according to its literal meaning, since spiritual *Dvekut* can only be depicted as equivalence of form. Hence, by equalizing our form with the form of His qualities, we become attached to Him.

This is why they said, "as He is merciful." In other words, all His actions are to bestow and benefit others, and not at all for His own benefit, since He has no deficiencies that require complementing. And also, He has no one from whom to receive. Similarly, all your actions will be to bestow and to benefit others. Thus, you will equalize your form with the form of the qualities of the Creator, and this is spiritual *Dvekut*.

There is a discernment of "mind" and a discernment of "heart" in the above-mentioned equivalence of form. The engagement in Torah and *Mitzvot* in order to bestow contentment upon one's Maker is equivalence of form in the mind. This is because the Creator does not think of

Himself—whether He exists or whether He watches over His creations, and other such doubts. Similarly, one who wishes to achieve equivalence of form must not think of these things, as well, when it is clear to him that the Creator does not think of them, since there is no greater disparity of form than that. Hence, anyone who thinks of such matters is certainly separated from Him and will never achieve equivalence of form.

This is what our sages said, "Let all your actions be for the sake of the Creator," that is, *Dvekut* with the Creator. Do not do anything that does not yield this goal of *Dvekut*. This means that all your actions will be to bestow and to benefit your fellow person. At that time, you will achieve equivalence of form with the Creator—as all His actions are to bestow and to benefit others, so you, all your actions will be only to bestow and to benefit others. This is the complete *Dvekut*.

5. RABASH, Letter No. 76

"If you walk in My statutes and keep My commandments so as to do them." The holy *Zohar* asks, "Since he already said, 'walk' and 'keep,' why also 'do'?" It replies, "One who does the *Mitzvot* [commandments] of the Torah and walks in His ways, it is as though he has made Him above. The Creator said, 'as though he had made Me.' This is the meaning of 'to do them,' as though you have made Me" (*Behukotai*, Item 18).

We should understand what it means that one who walks in the way of the Creator makes the Creator. How can one think such a thing?

It is known that "The whole earth is full of His glory." This is what every person should believe, as it is written, "I fill the heaven and the earth." However, the Creator has made a concealment so that we cannot see Him so as to have room for choice, and then there is room for faith—to believe that the Creator "fills all the worlds and encompasses all the worlds." And after a person engages in Torah and *Mitzvot* and keeps the commandment of choice, the Creator reveals Himself to him, and then he sees that the Creator is the ruler of the world.

Thus, at that time a person makes the king who will rule over him. That is, a person feels that the Creator is the ruler of the world, and this is regarded as a person making the Creator king over him. As long as one has not come to such a feeling, the Creator's kingship is concealed. This is why we say, "On that day, the Lord will be one and His name, 'One.'" That is, the glory of His kingship will appear over us.

This is the whole correction we must do in this world, and by that we extend abundance in the world, for all the bestowals from above are drawn by engaging in Torah and *Mitzvot* with the aim to extend His kingship on us.

6. RABASH, Article No. 645, "By Your Actions, We Know You"

The known rule, "By Your actions, we know You." It was interpreted that through the actions, we know His thoughts. Since the righteous of the world were rewarded with all the delight and pleasure, by this act they concluded that such was His intention: It is to do good to His creations.

It therefore follows that everything we say is only from the place where there is a connection between the Creator and the created beings, where the act is already apparent in the created beings, as in the verse, "You have made them all with wisdom." That is, we are speaking only from the perspective of actions, as it is written in the *Poem of Unification*, "By Your actions, we know You." However, we have no utterance or a word to speak of the Creator without His created beings, as was said, "There is no thought or perception of Him whatsoever."

Accordingly, why should we not ask why we say that Creation does not add anything to Him, so why did He create it if it does not add anything, since this question is asking whether the Creator had a need for Creation before He created it? It follows that we want to speak of Him prior to creation, meaning before there was a connection between the Creator and the created beings, and we said above that prior to this connection, "there is no thought or perception whatsoever."

However, we see that this was His intention. The proof of this is that He gives us abundance when we are ready to receive the King's gift, and there will not be any flaw in the gift, meaning when the bread of shame is not felt in the gift, namely when man's intention is only for the sake of the Creator.

At that time, when one receives from the Giver, it is also with the above-mentioned aim, meaning that he wants to receive the King's gift because he feels that this is His will, and not for the sake of self-benefit, and then he is rewarded with receiving all the delight and pleasure.

5

The Greatness of the Creator

1. Baal HaSulam, "Introduction to The Book of Zohar," Item 33

You should know that any contentment of our Maker from bestowing upon His creatures depends on the extent that the creatures feel Him—that He is the giver, and He is the one who delights them. Then He takes great pleasure in them, as a father playing with his beloved son, to the extent that the son feels and recognizes the greatness and exaltedness of his father, and his father shows him all the treasures he had prepared for him, as it is written (Jeremiah 31): "Ephraim, my darling son, is he a child of joy? For whenever I speak of him, I do remember him still. Hence, My heart yearns for him, I will surely have mercy on him, says the Lord."

Observe these words carefully and you can come to know the great delights of the Lord with those whole ones who have been granted feeling Him and recognizing His greatness in all those manners He has prepared for them, until they are like a father with his darling son, like a father with his child of joy. We need not continue about this, for it is enough for us to know that for this contentment and delight with those whole ones, it was worth His while to create all the worlds, higher and lower alike.

2. Baal HaSulam, "A Speech for the Completion of the Zohar"

Our sages said, "Make for yourself a rav and buy yourself a friend." This means that one can make a new environment for oneself. This environment will help him obtain the greatness of his rav through love of friends who appreciate his rav. Through the friends' discussing the greatness of the rav, each of them receives the sensation of his greatness. Thus, bestowal upon his rav becomes reception and sufficient motivation to an extent that will bring one to engage in Torah and *Mitzvot Lishma*.

It was said about this, "The Torah is acquired by forty-eight virtues, by serving of sages, and by meticulousness of friends." This is so because besides serving the rav, one needs the meticulousness of friends, as well, meaning the friends' influence, so they will influence him so he obtains the greatness of his rav. This is so because obtaining the greatness depends entirely on the environment, and a single person cannot do a thing about it whatsoever.

3. Baal HaSulam, *Shamati*, Article No. 191, "The Time of Descent"

It is hard to depict the time of descent, when all the works and the efforts made from the beginning of the work until the time of descent are lost. To one who has never tasted the taste of servitude of the Creator, it seems as though this is outside of him, meaning that this happens to those of high degrees. But ordinary people have no connection to serving the Creator, only to crave the corporeal will to receive, present in the flow of the world, washing the whole world with this desire.

However, we must understand why they have come to such a state. After all, with or without one's consent, there is no change in the Creator of heaven and earth; He behaves in a manner of good and doing good. Thus, what is the outcome of this state?

We should say that it comes to announce His greatness. One does not need to act as though he does not want Her. Rather, one should behave in a manner of fearing the exaltedness, to know the merit and the distance between him and the Creator. It is difficult to understand this with a superficial mind, or have any possibility of connection between the Creator and creation.

During a descent he feels that it is impossible that he will have connection or belonging to the Creator by way of *Dvekut* [adhesion], since he feels that servitude is a foreign thing to the whole world.

In truth, this is so. But "In the place where you find His greatness, there you find His humbleness." This means that it is a matter that is above nature, that the Creator gave this gift to creation, to allow them to be connected and adhered to Him.

Hence, when one becomes reconnected, he should always remember his time of descent so as to know, understand, appreciate, and value the time of *Dvekut*, so he will know that now he has salvation above the natural way.

4. Baal HaSulam, *Shamati*, Article No. 30, "The Most Important Is to Want Only to Bestow"

The most important is not to want anything except to bestow because of His greatness, since any reception is flawed. It is impossible to exit reception, but only to take the other extreme, meaning bestowal.

The moving force, meaning the extending force and the force that compels to work, is only greatness. One must think that, ultimately, the efforts and the labor must be made, but through these forces one can yield some benefit and pleasure. In other words, one can please a limited body with one's work and effort, which is either a passing guest or an eternal one, meaning that one's energy remains in eternity.

5. Baal HaSulam, *Shamati*, Article No. 33, "The Lots on Yom Kippurim and with Haman"

We must know that what appears to one as things that contradict the guidance of "The Good Who Does Good" is only to compel one to draw the upper light on the contradictions, when wanting to prevail over the contradictions. Otherwise, one cannot prevail. This is called "the exaltedness of the Creator," which one extends when having the contradictions, called *Dinim* [judgments].

This means that the contradictions can be annulled if one wants to overcome them, only if he extends the exaltedness of the Creator. You find that these *Dinim* cause the drawing of the exaltedness of the Creator. This is the meaning of what is written, "and cast his mantle upon him."

It means that afterward he attributed the whole mantle of hair to Him, to the Creator. That is, now he saw that the Creator gave him this mantle deliberately, in order to draw the upper light on them.

However, one can only see this later, after one has been granted the light that rests on these contradictions and *Dinim* that he had had in the beginning. This is so because he sees that without the hair, meaning the descents, there would not be a place for the upper light to be there, as there is no light without a *Kli* [vessel].

For this reason, he sees that all the exaltedness of the Creator he had obtained was because of the *Se'arot* and the contradictions he had had. This is the meaning of "The Lord on high is mighty." It means that the exaltedness of the Creator is awarded through the *Aderet*, and this is the meaning of "let the exaltedness of God be in their mouth."

This means that through the faults in the work of the Creator, it causes him to rise up, as without a push one is idle to make a movement and agrees to remain in the state he is in. But if one descends to a lower degree than he understands, this gives one the strength to overcome, for one cannot stay in such a bad state, since one cannot agree to remain like that, in the state to which he has descended.

For this reason, one must always prevail and emerge from the state of descent. In that state, he must draw upon himself the exaltedness of the Creator. This causes him to extend higher forces from above, or he remains in utter lowliness. It follows that through the *Se'arot*, one gradually discovers the exaltedness of the Creator until one finds the names of the Creator, called "the thirteen attributes of Mercy." This is the meaning of "and the elder shall serve the younger," and "the wicked will prepare and the righteous will wear," and also, "and you shall serve your brother."

This means that all the enslavement, meaning the contradictions that there were, which appeared to be obstructing the holy work, and were working against *Kedusha* [holiness]. Now, when granted the light of the Creator, which is placed over these contradictions, we see the opposite—that they were serving the *Kedusha*. That is, through them, there was a place for the *Kedusha* to clothe in their dresses. This is called "the wicked will prepare and the righteous will wear," meaning that they gave the *Kelim* [vessels] and the place for the *Kedusha*.

6. Baal HaSulam, *Shamati*, Article No. 26, "One's Future Depends and Is Tied to Gratitude for the Past"

It is written, "The Lord is high and the low will see," that only the low can see the exaltedness. The letters *Yakar* [precious] are the letters of *Yakir* [will know]. This means that one knows the exaltedness of a thing to the extent that it is precious to one.

One is impressed according to the importance of the thing. The impression brings one to a sensation in the heart, and according to the measure of one's recognition of the importance, to that extent, joy is born in him.

Thus, if one knows his lowliness, that he is not more privileged than his contemporaries, meaning he sees that there are many people in the world who were not given the strength to do the holy work even in the simplest way, even without the intention and in *Lo Lishma* [not for Her sake], even in *Lo Lishma* of *Lo Lishma*, and even in preparation for the preparation of the clothing of *Kedusha* [holiness], while he was imparted the desire and thought to at least occasionally do holy work, even in the simplest possible way, if one can appreciate the importance of this, according to the importance one attributes to the holy work, to that extent he should give praise and thanks for it.

This is so because it is true that we cannot appreciate the importance of being able to sometimes observe the *Mitzvot* [commandments] of the Creator, even without any intention. In that state, one comes to feel elation and joy in the heart.

The praise and the gratitude one gives for it expand the feelings, and one is elated by every single point in the holy work, he knows Whose servant he is, and thus soars ever higher. This is the meaning of what is written, "I thank You for the grace that You have made with me," meaning for the past, and by this one can confidently say, and he does say, "and that You are destined to do with me."

7. Baal HaSulam, *Shamati*, Article No. 14, "What Is the Exaltedness of the Creator?"

The *Romemut* [exaltedness/sublimity] of the Creator means that one should ask the Creator for the strength to go above reason. This means that there are two interpretations to the *Romemut* of the Creator:

A. To not be filled with knowledge, which is intellect with which one can answer one's questions. Rather, he wants the Creator to answer his questions. It is called *Romemut* because all the wisdom comes from above and not from man, meaning that man can answer his own questions.

Anything that one can answer is regarded as answering everything with the external mind. This means that the will to receive understands that it is worthwhile to observe Torah and *Mitzvot* [commandments]. However, if the above reason compels one to work, it is called "against the opinion of the will to receive."

B. The greatness of the Creator means that one becomes needy of the Creator to grant his wishes. Therefore:

1. One should go above reason. Then one sees that he is empty and becomes needy of the Creator.
2. Only the Creator can give him the strength to be able to go above reason. In other words, what the Creator gives is called "The *Romemut* of the Creator."

8. Baal HaSulam, "A Speech for the Completion of the Zohar"

When a person sees that the environment slights His work and does not properly appreciate His greatness, he cannot overcome the environment. Thus, he cannot obtain His greatness, and becomes negligent during his work, like them.

Since he does not have the basis for obtaining His greatness, he will obviously not be able to work in order to bring contentment to his Maker and not to himself, for he will have no motivation to exert, and "if you did not labor and find, do not believe." The only advice for this is either to work for oneself or not to work at all, since bestowing contentment upon his Maker will not be for him tantamount to reception.

Now you can understand the verse, "In the multitude of people is the king's glory," since the measure of the greatness comes from the environment under two conditions:

1. The extent of the appreciation of the environment.
2. The size of the environment. Thus, "In the multitude of people is the king's glory."

9. Baal HaSulam, *Shamati*, Article No. 13, "A Pomegranate"

There is emptiness only in a place where there is no existence, as in "The earth hangs on nothing." You find that what is the measure of the filling of the empty place? The answer is, according to one's elevation of oneself above reason.

This means that the emptiness should be filled with exaltedness, meaning with above reason, and to ask of the Creator to give him that strength. This will mean that all the emptiness was created, meaning it comes to a person to feel this way—that he is empty—only in order to fill it with the Romemut of the Creator. In other words, one is to take everything above reason.

This is the meaning of the verse, "God has made it that He will be feared." This means that these thoughts of emptiness come to a person in order for one to have a need to take upon himself faith above reason. And for this we need the help of the Creator. It follows that at that time, one must ask the Creator to give him the power to believe above reason.

It turns out that it is precisely then that one needs the Creator to help him, since the exterior mind lets him understand the opposite. Hence, at that time, one has no other choice but to ask the Creator to help him.

It is said about this, "One's desire overcomes him every day; and were it not for the Creator, he would not overcome it." It follows that only then is the state when one understands that no one will help him but the Creator. And this is "God has made it that He will be feared." The matter of fear is discerned as faith, and only then is one in need of the salvation of the Creator.

10. Baal HaSulam, *Shamati*, Article No. 47, "In the Place Where You Find His Greatness"

"In the place where you find His greatness, there you find His humbleness." It means that one who is always in true *Dvekut* [adhesion] sees that the Creator lowers Himself, meaning the Creator is present in the low places.

One does not know what to do, and this is why it is written, "Who sits on high, who looks down on heaven and on earth." A person sees the greatness of the Creator and then "who looks down," meaning he lowers the heaven to the earth. The advice that is given to this is to think that if this desire is from the Creator, we have nothing greater than that, as it is written, "He raises the poor out of the litter."

11. RABASH, Article No. 12 (1988), "What Are Torah and Work in the Way of the Creator?"

If a person wants to work and observe Torah and *Mitzvot* without any reward, only because he wants to serve the King, then he needs to know the greatness of the King, for the measure of his work depends on the extent of his faith in the greatness of the King, for only the greatness and importance of the King gives him fuel for work.

It is as it is written in *The Zohar* about the verse, "Her husband is known at the gates." It means that each according to what he assumes in his heart. By this, he tells us that to the extent that a person assumes in his heart the greatness and importance of the Creator, to that extent he dedicates himself to serving the King.

For this reason, people of this kind, who want to work only in order to bestow, and the whole reason that compels them to engage in Torah and *Mitzvot* is the importance and greatness of the Creator, as it is written in *The Zohar* that "The essence of fear is to work because He is great and ruling," when these people believe that the Creator is clothed in the Torah, and believe what the Creator said to Israel, "I sold you My Torah; it is as though I have been sold with it," when they learn Torah they want to elicit the light of the Torah that reforms him. This is the meaning of what our sages said, "He who comes to purify," through the Torah, "is aided," since the Creator is clothed in the Torah.

12. RABASH, Letter No. 62

It follows that man's primary work is to examine the greatness of the Creator. That is, one should delve in books that speak of the greatness of the Creator, and while delving, one should depict to oneself to what extent our sages, the Tanaaim and Amoraim, felt the greatness of the Creator.

One should pray to the Creator to shine so he may feel His greatness, so he can subdue his heart and annul before the Creator, and not follow the currents of the world, which is pursuing only the satisfaction of beastly lusts, but that the Creator will open his eyes so he may engage all his life in Torah and work, and "In all your ways, know Him." That is, even when engaging in corporeal matters, it will be for the purpose of *Kedusha* [holiness], as well.

But from *Lo Lishma*, we come to *Lishma*. That is, *Lishma* is already a high degree, and one must begin from *Lo Lishma*. In other words, one should be fully aware that pleasure is found primarily in Torah and work, and not in corporeality.

Although at the moment he feels more pleasure in corporeal things, more than he feels in spiritual things, it is because he lacks the qualification in Torah and work, which also depends on faith in the Creator. At that time, through Torah and faith in the Creator, one feels the light in the Torah, and that light reforms him.

13. RABASH, Article No. 128, "Exalt the Lord Our God"

"Exalt the Lord our God and bow before His holy mountain, for the Lord our God is holy."

"Exalt" means that if one wants to know the exaltedness and greatness of the Creator, we can obtain this only through *Dvekut* [adhesion] and equivalence of form. Thus, what is "equivalence of form" and how does one achieve equivalence of form?

"Bow before His holy mountain." Bowing means surrendering. It is when one lowers his reason and says that what the reason understands or does not understand, I annul and subjugate it. Before which quality do I subjugate it? Before "His holy mountain."

Har [mountain] means *Hirhurim* [reflections], meaning thoughts. "His holy," for "holy" means separated from the matter. This means that he removes himself from the desire of reception. "Bow" means submitting the body, even though it disagrees, and taking upon oneself only thoughts of *Kedusha* [holiness]. This is the meaning "Bow before His holy mountain."

Why must we submit ourselves to thoughts of *Kedusha*, meaning retire from receiving in order to receive? It is because "The Lord our God is holy," for the Creator only bestows. For this reason, one must be in equivalence of form with the Creator, and by this we can obtain the exaltedness of the Creator. Afterward, we can achieve the attainment of the exaltedness of the Lord our God.

14. RABASH, Article No. 223, "Entry into the Work"

Only after he achieves this degree called *Lo Lishma*, he is rewarded with other phenomena, when he comes to a higher state. That is, at that time he has no consideration of himself, and all his calculations and thoughts are the truth.

In other words, his aim is only to annul himself before the true reality, where he feels that he must only serve the King because he feels the exaltedness and greatness and importance of the King. At that time, he forgets, meaning he has no need to worry about himself, as his own self is annulled as a candle before a torch before the existence of the Creator that he feels. Then he is in a state of *Lishma* [for Her sake], meaning contentment to the Creator, and his concerns and yearnings are only about how he can delight the Creator, while his own existence, meaning the will to receive, does not merit a name whatsoever. Then he is regarded as "bestowing in order to bestow."

15. RABASH, Article No. 13 (1989), "What Is the 'Bread of an Evil-Eyed Man' in the Work?"

All our work in Torah and *Mitzvot* is in order to emerge from the exile of the will to receive for ourselves. In other words, we must aim—while engaging in Torah and *Mitzvot*—that our reward will be that by this we will be rewarded with emerging from the exile and enslavement in the will to receive for ourselves, and we will be able to work only in order to bring contentment to the Creator, and we will not demand any other reward for our work in Torah and *Mitzvot*.

In other words, we want to be rewarded with feeling—while engaging in Torah and *Mitzvot*—that we are serving a great and important king, and that by this there will be love of the Creator within us, from feeling His exaltedness. However, all of our pleasure will come from serving the Creator; this will be our reward, and not that He will somehow reward us for the work. Instead, we will feel that the work itself is the reward, and there is no greater reward in the world than the privilege of serving the Creator.

16. RABASH, Article No. 21 (1989), "What Is, 'A Drunken Man Must Not Pray,' in the Work?"

We see that in order to have fuel to work in order to bestow and not receive any reward, but the work itself will be the reward, we must believe in Him, meaning believe in His greatness. We must make great efforts to obtain faith in the greatness of the Creator. Without faith in the greatness of the Creator, there is no power to work in order to bestow. That is, precisely when we feel the greatness of the Creator, a person is ready to work without any reward.

Instead, the work itself is the reward, since serving a great King is more valuable to him than any fortune in the world, compared to this service, that the Creator permits him to come in and serve Him. Hence, we must focus all our thoughts on how to come to feel the greatness of the Creator, and then everything follows that point.

17. RABASH, Article No. 15 (1989), "What Is 'The Righteous Become Apparent through the Wicked,' in the Work?"

The work of the general public is in order to receive reward, and the work of individuals is for the sake of the Creator, and their reward is if they can serve the King. That is, their whole pleasure, which gives them fuel so they can work in order to bestow, is to feel that they are bringing contentment to the King and are praising and thanking the King for giving them the thought and desire to work for Him and not to receive any other reward for their work.

They say that in order to receive reward, "We do not need to feel the greatness of the King. Rather, we need to consider the greatness and importance of the reward we will receive if we observe the Torah and *Mitzvot*." But the Creator can stay for them at the same level of greatness and importance as He was for them at the beginning of their work.

However, if their intention is to bring contentment to the Creator, then if they want to increase the work, they must increase the greatness of the Creator, since to the extent of His greatness, to that extent they can annul before Him and do everything they do only for the sake of the Creator. It is as *The Zohar* says about the verse, "Her husband is known at the gates," each according to "what he assumes in his heart."

Therefore, in order to have fuel to work, those who want to work for the sake of the Creator must try each day to exert to obtain faith in the greatness of the Creator, since the greatness of the Creator is what compels them to work for Him, and this is all the pleasure they derive from their work.

18. RABASH, Article No. 42, "Serve the Creator with Joy"

The Zohar asks, It is written, "The Lord is near to the brokenhearted." A servant of the Creator, whose intention is to bestow, should be happy when he is serving the King. If he has no joy during this work, it is a sign that he lacks appreciation of the greatness of the King.

Therefore, if one sees that he has no joy he should make amendments, meaning think about the greatness of the King. If he still does not feel, he should pray to the Creator to open his eyes and heart to feel the greatness of the Creator.

Here the two discernments develop: 1) He should regret not having a sensation of the greatness of the King. 2) He should be happy that his regrets are about spirituality and not like the rest of the people, whose regrets are only in order to receive.

We should know who it is who gave us the awareness that our regrets should be over spirituality, and we should be happy that the Creator has sent us thoughts of spiritual deficiency, which in itself is regarded as the salvation of the Creator. For this reason, we should be happy.

19. RABASH, Article No. 30 (1988), "What to Look for in the Assembly of Friends"

The friends should primarily speak together about the greatness of the Creator, because according to the greatness of the Creator that one assumes, to that extent he naturally annuls himself before the Creator. It is as we see in nature that the small one annuls before the great one, and this has nothing to do with spirituality. Rather, this conduct applies even among secular people.

In other words, the Creator made nature this way. Thus, the friends' discussions of the greatness of the Creator awaken a desire and yearning to annul before the Creator because he begins to feel longing and desire to bond with the Creator. And we should also remember that to the extent that the friends can appreciate the importance and greatness of the Creator, we should still go above reason, meaning that the Creator is higher than any greatness of the Creator that one can imagine.

We should say that we believe above reason that He leads the world in a benevolent guidance, and if one believes that the Creator wants only man's best, it makes a person love the Creator until he is rewarded with "And you will love the Lord your God with all your heart and with all your soul." And this is what a person must receive from the friends.

20. RABASH, Article No. 17 (1986), "The Agenda of the Assembly-2"

The whole basis upon which we can receive delight and pleasure, and which is permitted for us to enjoy—and is even mandatory—is to enjoy an act of bestowal. Thus, there is one point we should work on—*appreciation of spirituality*. This is expressed in paying attention to whom I turn, with whom I speak, whose commandments I am keeping, and whose laws I am learning, meaning in seeking advice concerning how to appreciate the Giver of the Torah.

And before one obtains some illumination from above by himself, he should seek out like-minded people who are also seeking to enhance the importance of any contact with the Creator in whatever way. And when many people support it, everyone can receive assistance from his friend.

We should know that "Two is the least plural." This means that if two friends sit together and contemplate how to enhance the importance of the Creator, they already have the strength to receive enhancement of the greatness of the Creator in the form of awakening from below. And for this act, the awakening from above follows, and they begin to have some sensation of the greatness of the Creator.

According to what is written, "In the multitude of people is the King's glory," it follows that the greater the number of the collective, the more effective is the power of the collective. In other words, they produce a stronger atmosphere of greatness and importance of the Creator. At that time, each person's body feels that he regards anything that he wishes to do for holiness—meaning to bestow upon the Creator—as a great fortune, that he has been privileged with being among people who have been rewarded with serving the King. At that time, every little thing he does fills him with joy and pleasure that now he has something with which to serve the King.

To the extent that the society regards the greatness of the Creator with their thoughts during the assembly, each according to his degree originates the importance of the Creator in him. Thus, he can walk all day in the world of gladness and joy.

21. RABASH, Article No. 24, "The Main Thing We Need"

The main thing we need, and for which we have no fuel for the work, is that we are lacking importance of the goal. That is, we do not know how to appreciate our service so as to know to whom we are bestowing. Also, we are lacking the awareness of the greatness of the Creator, to know how happy we are that we have the privilege of serving the King, since we have nothing with which to be able to understand His greatness.

In the words of *The Zohar*, this is called "*Shechina* [Divinity] in the dust," meaning that bestowal upon Him is as important to us as dust. Naturally, we have no fuel to work, since without pleasure, there is no energy to work.

Where self-love shines, the body derives vitality from this. But in the work of bestowal, the body does not feel any pleasure in this and must naturally "collapse under its weight."

Conversely, when one feels that he is serving an important King, to the extent of the importance of the King, so is his delight and pleasure from serving Him. Hence, at that time he has fuel that can give him the power to go forward each time, since he feels that he is serving an important King.

Then, when he knows and feels to whom he bestows, to the extent that he had the strength to work with the intention of self-love, now he has the strength to work in order to bestow, since one who bestows upon an important person is regarded as receiving from him. And since the body has the strength to work for reception, in order to receive reward, likewise, in bestowing upon an important King he derives pleasure in this.

22. RABASH, Article No. 7 (1991), "What Is 'Man' and What Is 'Beast' in the Work?"

When one feels that he is empty, meaning that he feels that he has neither Torah nor *Mitzvot* [commandments/good deeds] or any good deeds, what can he do? At that time, he should ask the Creator to shine for him so he can obtain the greatness and exaltedness of the Creator above reason. In other words, although he is still unworthy of feeling the greatness and exaltedness of the Creator, since he has still not been rewarded with the quality of "man," and the *Tzimtzum* and concealment of the Creator are still on him, as it is written, "Do not hide Your face from me," he still asks the Creator to give him the strength to receive greatness and importance of the Creator above reason.

It is as Baal HaSulam says about what our sages said (*Iruvin* 19), "Even the empty ones among you are filled with *Mitzvot* like a pomegranate." He said that *Rimon* [pomegranate] comes from the word *Romemut* [exaltedness], which is above reason. Hence, the meaning of "Even the empty ones among you are filled with *Mitzvot* like a pomegranate" is that the measure of the filling is according to his ability to go above reason, which is called "exaltedness."

In other words, emptiness can be precisely where there is no presence and he feels that he is devoid of Torah, *Mitzvot*, and good deeds. When this continues over time when a person wants to work for the sake of the Creator and not for himself, then he sees that everything he does is not for the sake of the Creator but only for his own benefit. In that state, he feels that he has nothing and he is completely empty, and he can fill this place only with a pomegranate, meaning if he goes above reason, which is called "exaltedness of the Creator." In other words, he should ask the Creator to give him the power to believe above reason in the greatness of the Creator. That is, the fact that he wants the exaltedness of the Creator does not mean that he says, "If You let me attain the exaltedness and greatness of the Creator, I will agree to work." Rather, he wants the Creator to give him the power to believe in the greatness of the Creator, and with this he fills the emptiness in which he is in right now.

It follows that were it not for the emptiness, that is, if he did not work on the path toward achieving *Dvekut*, meaning in equivalence of form, called "in order to bestow," but rather like the general public, who suffice for the practices they observe, these people do not feel themselves as empty, but as full of *Mitzvot*.

However, specifically those who want to achieve bestowal feel the emptiness within them and need the greatness of the Creator. They can fill this emptiness specifically with exaltedness, called "full of *Mitzvot*," to the extent that they ask the Creator to give them the power to be able to go above reason, which is called "exaltedness." In other words, they ask the Creator to give them power in exaltedness that is above reason in greatness and importance of the Creator. They do not want the Creator to let them attain this, since they want to subjugate themselves with unconditional surrender, but they ask for help from the Creator, and to that extent they can fill the empty place with *Mitzvot*. This is the meaning of "filled with *Mitzvot* like a pomegranate."

23. RABASH, *Shamati*, Article No. 29 (1986), "Lishma and Lo Lishma"

There is only one way—to try to attain the greatness of the Creator. That is, in all that we do in Torah and *Mitzvot*, we want our reward to be the feeling of the greatness of the Creator, and all our prayers should be to "raise the *Shechina* [Divinity] from the dust," since the Creator is hidden from us due to the *Tzimtzum* that took place and we cannot appreciate His importance and greatness.

Therefore, we pray to the Creator to remove His concealment from us and to raise the glory of Torah. As we say in the Eighteen Prayer of *Rosh Hashanah* [New Year service], "Indeed, give glory to Your people." That is, "Give the glory of the Lord to Your people," so they will feel the glory of the King.

For this reason, one must try to remember the goal while studying Torah, so it will always be before his eyes what he wants to receive from the study, that the study will impart greatness and importance of the Creator. Also, while observing the *Mitzvot*, not to forget the intention that thanks to observing the *Mitzvot*, the Creator will lift the concealment on spirituality from him and he will receive a feeling of the greatness of the Creator.

24. RABASH, Article No. 12 (1987), "What Is Half a Shekel in the Work-1"

He should appreciate the service he is giving to the Creator by observing the commandments of the Creator. To the extent that he appreciates the greatness of the Creator, he rejoices in being rewarded with doing what the Creator commanded.

This matter of appreciating the great one is in our nature. We see that it is regarded as a great honor, if there is someone who is the greatest in the generation and people regard him as an important person. Everyone wants to serve him.

However, the satisfaction in the service depends on the greatness and importance that the world attributes to this great person. It follows that when one feels and depicts to himself that he is serving the Creator, he feels that he is blessed, and then comes the rule that the blessed clings to the blessed.

It follows that in such a state a person feels himself as the happiest in the world. This is the time when he needs to thank the Creator for giving him the little service that he served Him. It follows that in that state he is adhered to the Creator because there is joy in him, as our sages said, "The *Shechina* [Divinity] is present only out of joy."

25. RABASH, Article No. 468, "This Day, the Lord Your God Commands You"

"This day, the Lord your God commands you to do these statutes and ordinances, and you shall keep and do them with all your heart and with all your soul." RASHI interprets, each day they will be as new in your eyes, as if you were commanded them that day.

We should understand how one can make them be as new, as though he were commanded them that day, for it has been sworn and standing since Mt. Sinai. To understand this, we first need to know the rule that everything is measured by the greatness of the one who commands. That is, according to the greatness and importance of the giver of the Torah, so is the greatness of the Torah.

Hence, each day when one takes upon himself the kingdom of heaven, according to the measure of the faith in Him, the merit of the Torah increases. Therefore, according to what a person attains in the greatness of the Creator, so the Torah is renewed in him. It therefore follows that each time, he has a new Torah, meaning that each time he has a different Giver. Then, naturally, the Torah that extends from Him is regarded as a new Torah.

6

Contentment to the Creator

1. Baal HaSulam, "The Love of God and the Love of Man"

When one completes one's work in love of others and bestowal upon others through the final point, one also completes one's love for the Creator and bestowal upon the Creator. And there is no difference between the two, for anything that is outside one's body, meaning outside one's self-interest, is judged equally—either to bestow upon one's friend or to bestow contentment upon one's Maker.

2. Baal HaSulam, "The Peace"

From the perspective of empirical reason—out of the practical history unfolding before our very eyes—that there is no other cure for humanity but to assume the commandment of Providence to bestow upon others in order to bring contentment to the Creator in the measure of the two verses.

The first is "love your friend as yourself," which is the attribute of the work itself. This means that the measure of work to bestow upon others for the happiness of society should be no less than the measure imprinted in man to care for his own needs. Moreover, he should put his fellow person's needs before his own, as it written in the article, "Matan Torah," Item 4.

The other verse is, "And you will love the Lord your God with all your heart, with all your soul, and with all your might." This is the goal that must be before everyone's eyes when laboring for one's friend's needs. This means that he labors and toils only to be liked by the Creator, as He said, "and they do His will."

"And if you wish to listen, you will feed on the fruit of the land," for poverty and torment and exploitation will be no more in the land, and the happiness of each and every one will rise ever higher, beyond measure. But as long as you refuse to assume the covenant of the work for the sake of the Creator in the fullest measure, nature and its laws will stand ready to take revenge on you. And as we have shown, it will not let go until it defeats us and we accept its authority in whatever it commands.

3. Baal HaSulam, "Introduction to The Book of Zohar," Item 33

You should know that any contentment of our Maker from bestowing upon His creatures depends on the extent that the creatures feel Him—that He is the giver, and He is the one who delights them.

Then He takes great pleasure in them, as a father playing with his beloved son, to the extent that the son feels and recognizes the greatness and exaltedness of his father, and his father shows him all the treasures he had prepared for him, as it is written (Jeremiah 31): "Ephraim, my darling son, is he a child of joy? For whenever I speak of him, I do remember him still. Hence, My heart yearns for him, I will surely have mercy on him, says the Lord."

Observe these words carefully and you can come to know the great delights of the Lord with those whole ones who have been granted feeling Him and recognizing His greatness in all those manners He has prepared for them, until they are like a father with his darling son, like a father with his child of joy. We need not continue about this, for it is enough for us to know that for this contentment and delight with those whole ones, it was worth His while to create all the worlds, higher and lower alike.

4. Baal HaSulam, "One Commandment"

We have already explained the "practical" part of the one *Mitzva*: One should agree to dedicate all of one's free time to benefit the people in the world. The aspect of "thought" is more imperative in this *Mitzva* than in *Mitzvot* relating to man and the Creator since in *Mitzvot* between man and the Creator, the "act" in itself testifies that the intention is to benefit one's Maker, as there is no other room for such an action but Him.

Yet, with what concerns man and man, they are justified in and of themselves, since human conscience necessitates them. However, if one performs them from this perspective, he has not done a thing. In others words, these actions will not bring him closer to the Creator and to actual work *Lishma*.

Thus, each person should think that he is doing all this only to bring contentment to his Maker and to resemble His ways: As He is merciful, so I am merciful, and as He always imparts good, so do I. This image, coupled with good deeds, will bring him closer to the Creator in a way that will equalize his form with spirituality and with *Kedusha* [holiness], and he will become like a seal, fit to receive the true Higher Abundance.

5. Baal HaSulam, *Ohr HaBahir*

The first restriction is the ascent of the desire of *Ein Sof* not to receive anymore in Phase Four. It is the great reception that is implemented in the world of *Ein Sof*, where there is disparity from His Self. This was in order to do good to His creations.

In other words, it is so that in the end, souls that are clothed in a body in this world will emerge from the ascent of this desire, so they will turn all of the great reception to be in order to bestow. At that time, they will have equivalence of form with His self and will be worthy of adhesion with Him. This is the meaning of doing good to His creations, since they will be able to receive the great lights that are received in Phase Four, who is called "His mate in *Ein Sof*." And yet, they will not be separated from Him because of it due to the disparity of form of reception, which does not occur in Him, since their whole intention in receiving from Him will be only because He wants it, and their sole aim is to bring contentment to their Maker. This is the meaning of "*Ein Sof* does not bring down his unification on her until He is given his mate."

6. Baal HaSulam, *Shamati*, Article No. 81, "Concerning Raising MAN"

It is known that because of the breaking, sparks of *Kedusha* [holiness] fell into BYA. But there, in BYA, they cannot be corrected. Therefore, they must be raised to *Atzilut*. By doing *Mitzvot* [commandments] and good deeds with the aim to bring contentment to his Maker and not to himself, these sparks rise to *Atzilut*. Then they are included in the *Masach* [screen] of the upper one, at the *Rosh* [head/top] of the degree, where the *Masach* remains in its eternity. At that time, there is a *Zivug* [coupling] on the *Masach* by the *Hitkalelut* [mixture/integration] of the sparks, and the upper light spreads through all the worlds according to the measure of the sparks that they have raised.

7. Baal HaSulam, "The Meaning of Conception and Birth"

Know that the Creator needed the work of creation only to the extent that man was not given the strength to work there. Similar to digestion, the Creator created everything in such a way that the digestion of the food in our stomach happens without effort on our part.

However, from the point where one can work—as this is all the flavor and contentment of the Creator who wanted to enjoy His work, meaning to fashion creations that can add, delight, and create like Him, but has no wish whatsoever to cook our food which is on the stove for us without our awareness, since we can do this by ourselves.

This is similar to a teacher and a student where the whole intention of the teacher is to give the student the strength to be like him, and to teach other students, like him. Likewise, the Creator is pleased when His creations create and innovate like Him. Yet, our whole power to innovate and develop is not real innovation. Rather, it is a type of emulation. And the more the emulation matches the work of nature, to that extent is our level of development measured.

From this we know that we have the power to correct ourselves, the existence of reality, like nature's pleasant example of reality. The proof of this is that had the Creator not worked His full Providence in that discernment, too, for "Is the Lord's hand short?" Rather, it is necessary that in this place, which is our own correction, we are able to correct ourselves.

8. Baal HaSulam, "Introduction to The Study of the Ten Sefirot," Items 80-82

The reason for the concealment of the face from people has been explained: It is deliberately to give people room to labor and engage in His work in Torah and *Mitzvot* voluntarily, for then the contentment of the Creator from their work in His Torah and *Mitzvot* increases more than His contentment from the angels above, who have no choice and whose mission is compulsory. There are also other reasons, but this is not the place to elaborate on them.

Despite the above praise for concealment of face, it is still not considered wholeness, but only a "transition," as this is the place from which the longed-for wholeness is attained. This means that any reward for a *Mitzva* that is prepared for a person is acquired only through one's labor in Torah and good deeds during the concealment of the face, when he engages voluntarily. This is so because then one feels sorrow out of his strengthening in His faith in keeping His will. And one's whole reward is measured only according to the pain he suffers from keeping the Torah and the *Mitzva*, as in the words of Ben He He, "The reward is according to the pain."

Hence, every person must experience that transition period of concealment of the face. When he completes it, he is rewarded with open Providence, meaning the revelation of the face.

9. Baal HaSulam, *Shamati*, Article No. 12, "The Essence of Man's Work"

The essence of man's work should be how to come to feel taste in bestowing contentment to one's Maker, since all that one does for oneself removes him from the Creator due to the disparity of form. Conversely, if one acts in order to benefit the Creator, even if it is the smallest act, it is still considered a *Mitzva* [commandment].

Therefore, one's primary exertion should be to acquire the strength to feel taste in bestowing, which is through lessening the force that feels taste in self-reception. Then one slowly acquires the taste in bestowing.

10. Baal HaSulam, *Shamati*, Article No. 19, "What Is "The Creator Hates the Bodies," in the Work?"

One must always examine oneself, the purpose of one's work, meaning if the Creator receives contentment in every act that one performs, because he wants equivalence of form with the Creator. This is called "All your actions will be for the sake of the Creator," meaning that one wants the Creator to enjoy everything he does, as it is written, "to bring contentment to his Maker."

Also, one needs to conduct oneself with the will to receive and say to it, "I have already decided that I do not want to receive any pleasure because you want to enjoy, since with your desire I am forced to be separated from the Creator, for disparity of form causes separation and distance from the Creator."

One's hope should be that since he cannot break free from the power of the will to receive, he is therefore in perpetual ascents and descents. Hence, he awaits the Creator, to be rewarded with the Creator opening his eyes, and to have the strength to overcome and work only for the sake of the Creator. It is as it is written, "One have I asked of the Lord; her will I seek." "Her" means the *Shechina* [Divinity]. And one asks "that I may dwell in the house of the Lord all the days of my life."

11. Baal HaSulam, "The Writings of the Last Generation"

All of the anticipated reward from the Creator, and the purpose of the entire creation, are *Dvekut* [adhesion] with the Creator, as in, "A tower filled abundantly, but no guests." This is what they who cling to Him with love receive.

Naturally, first, one emerges from imprisonment, which is emerging from the skin of one's body by bestowal upon others. Subsequently, one comes to the king's palace, which is *Dvekut* with Him through the intention to bestow contentment upon one's maker.

Therefore, the bulk of commandments are between man and man. One who gives preference to the commandments between man and God is as one who climbs to the second step before he has climbed to the first step. Clearly, he will break his legs.

12. Baal HaSulam, *Shamati*, Article No. 38, "The Fear of God Is His Treasure"

Our sages said, "Everything is in the hands of heaven but the fear of heaven," is because He can give everything but fear. This is because what the Creator gives is more love, not fear.

Acquiring fear is through the *Segula* [power/remedy] of Torah and *Mitzvot*. It means that when one engages in Torah and *Mitzvot* with the intention to be rewarded with bringing contentment to one's Maker, that aim that rests on the acts of *Mitzvot* and the study of Torah brings one to attain it. Otherwise, one might remain—although he observes Torah and *Mitzvot* in every item and detail—he will still remain merely in the degree of still of *Kedusha* [holiness].

13. Baal HaSulam, *Shamati*, Article No. 19, What Is "The Creator Hates the Bodies," in the Work?

One must not be angry when he has work with the will to receive, that it obstructs him in the work. One would certainly be more satisfied if the will to receive were absent from the body, meaning that it would not bring its questions to a person, obstructing him in the work of observing Torah and *Mitzvot* [commandments].

However, one should believe that the obstructions of the will to receive in the work come to him from above. One is given the force to discover the will to receive from above because there is room for work precisely when the will to receive awakens.

Then one has close contact with the Creator to help him turn the will to receive to work in order to bestow. One must believe that from this extends contentment to the Creator, from his praying to Him to draw him near in the manner of *Dvekut* [adhesion], called "equivalence of form," discerned as the annulment of the will to receive, so it is in order to bestow. The Creator says about this, "My sons defeated Me." That is, I gave you the will to receive, and you ask Me to give you a desire to bestow instead.

14. Baal HaSulam, *Shamati*, Article No. 8, "What Is the Difference between a Shade of Kedusha and a Shade of Sitra Achra?"

The shade of *Klipa* [shell] is called "Another god is sterile and does not bear fruit." In *Kedusha* [holiness], however, it is called "Under its shadow I coveted to sit, and its fruit was sweet to my palate." In other words, he says that all the concealments and afflictions he feels are because the Creator has sent him these states so he would have a place for work above reason.

When one has the strength to say this—that the Creator causes him all this—it is to one's benefit. This means that through this he can come to work in order to bestow and not for his own sake. At that time, one realizes, meaning believes that the Creator enjoys specifically this work, which is built entirely on above reason.

It follows that at that time, one does not pray to the Creator that the shadows will flee from the world. Rather, he says, "I see that the Creator wants me to serve Him in this manner, entirely above reason." Thus, in everything he does he says, "The Creator certainly enjoys this work, so why should I care if I am working in a state of concealment of the face?"

Because one wants to work in order to bestow, meaning that the Creator will enjoy, he feels no humiliation in this work, meaning a sensation that he is in a state of concealment of the face, that the Creator does not enjoy this work. Instead, one agrees to the leadership of the Creator, meaning however the Creator wants him to feel the existence of the Creator during the work, he agrees wholeheartedly. This is so because one does not consider what can please him, but what can please the Creator. Thus, this shade brings him life.

This is called "Under its shadow I coveted," meaning one covets such a state where he can make some overcoming above reason.

15. Baal HaSulam, "The Freedom"

The children of Israel were rewarded with complete *Dvekut* on that holy occasion, their vessels of reception were completely emptied of any worldly possession and they were adhered to Him in equivalence of form. This means that they had no desire for any self-possession, but only to the extent that they could bestow contentment, so their Maker would delight in them.

And since their will to receive had clothed in an image of that object, it had clothed in it and bonded with it into complete oneness. Therefore, they were certainly liberated from the angel of death, for death is necessarily an absence and negation of the existence of something. But only while there is a spark that wishes to exist for its own pleasure is it possible to say about it that that spark does not exist because it has become absent and died.

However, if there is no such spark in man, but all the sparks of his selfness clothe in bestowal of contentment upon their Maker, then he neither becomes absent nor dies. For even when the body is annulled, it is only annulled with respect to self-reception, in which the will to receive is dressed and can only exist in it.

However, when he achieves the aim of creation and the Creator receives pleasure from him, since His will is done, man's essence, which clothes in His contentment, is granted complete eternity, like Him. Thus, he has been rewarded with freedom from the angel of death.

16. Baal HaSulam, *Shamati*, Article No. 5, Lishma Is an Awakening from Above, and Why Do We Need an Awakening from Below?

When the thief, meaning the will to receive, does not feel any flavor or vitality in the work of accepting the burden of the kingdom of heaven, in that state, if one works with faith above reason, coercively, and the body becomes accustomed to this work against the desire of his will to receive, then he has the means by which to come to work that will be with the purpose of bringing contentment to his Maker, since the primary requirement from a person is to come to *Dvekut* [adhesion] with the Creator through his work, which is discerned as equivalence of form, where all his actions are in order to bestow.

This is as it is written, "Then shall you delight in the Lord." The meaning of "Then" is that first, in the beginning of his work, he did not have pleasure. Instead, his work was coercive.

But afterward, when he has already accustomed himself to work in order to bestow and not examine himself—if he is feeling a good taste in the work—but believes that he is working to bring contentment to his Maker through his work, he should believe that the Creator accepts the work of the lower ones regardless of how and how much is the form of their work. In everything, the Creator examines the intention, and this brings contentment to the Creator. Then one is rewarded with "delight in the Lord."

Even during the work of the Creator he will feel delight and pleasure since now he really does work for the Creator because the effort he made during the coercive work qualifies him to be able to truly work for the Creator. You find that then, too, the pleasure he receives relates to the Creator, meaning specifically for the Creator.

17. Baal HaSulam, *Shamati*, Article No. 3, "The Matter of Spiritual Attainment"

May we merit receiving His light and following the ways of the Creator, and to serve Him not in order to receive reward but to give contentment to the Creator and raise the *Shechina* [Divinity] from the dust. May we be rewarded with *Dvekut* [adhesion] with the Creator and the revelation of His Godliness to His creatures.

18. Baal HaSulam, "The Essence of Religion and Its Purpose"

Through the subtle pleasantness we feel when working solely for Him, to bring Him contentment, there develops within us a relative recognition of the lowliness of these sparks of self-love—that they are obstacles on our way to receiving that subtle taste of bestowal upon the Creator.

19. Baal HaSulam, Letter No. 9

I know the great advantage with which the Creator has granted me over my contemporaries, for I have searched a long, long time why I have been chosen by God's will. And after all the lowliness emitted from that son of a wicked one, which is the *Klipa* [shell] that rules in my time, and after I have witnessed its true measure, I realize the Creator's kindness with me, to distract my heart today and always from hearing the above-mentioned question of the wicked.

I find myself committed and obligated, as today and as always, to be as an ox to the burden and as a donkey to the load, all day and all night. I will not rest from searching some place where I can bring some contentment to my Maker. Even in this day that I am in, I am happy to work under a great burden even seventy years, without any knowledge of its success (even my whole life), except that it is certainly the way that I have been commanded to walk in all His ways and to adhere to Him, which I have heard initially.

At the same time, I cannot excuse myself at all by any notion or contemplation from doing any work for His sake because of my lowliness. I crave and think all day about the sublimity of the work of God, in such sublimity that I cannot even write about it.

20. Baal HaSulam, "A Speech for the Completion of The Zohar"

The engagement in Torah and *Mitzvot* in order to bestow contentment upon one's Maker is equivalence of form in the mind. This is because the Creator does not think of Himself—whether He exists or whether He watches over His creations, and other such doubts. Similarly, one who wishes to achieve equivalence of form must not think of these things, as well, when it is clear to him that the Creator does not think of them, since there is no greater disparity of form than that. Hence, anyone who thinks of such matters is certainly separated from Him and will never achieve equivalence of form.

This is what our sages said, "Let all your actions be for the sake of the Creator," that is, *Dvekut* with the Creator. Do not do anything that does not yield this goal of *Dvekut*. This means that all your actions will be to bestow and to benefit your fellow person. At that time, you will achieve equivalence of form with the Creator—as all His actions are to bestow and to benefit others, so you, all your actions will be only to bestow and to benefit others. This is the complete *Dvekut*.

21. Baal HaSulam, *Shamati*, Article No. 17, "What Does It Mean that the Sitra Achra Is Called '*Malchut* without a Crown'?"

Our sages said, "Anyone who is proud, the Creator says, 'He and I cannot dwell in the same abode,'" as he makes two authorities. However, when one is in a state of *Ein*, and annuls himself before the Root, meaning that one's sole intention is only to bestow, like the Root, you find that there is only one authority here—the authority of the Creator. Then, all that one receives in the world is only in order to bestow upon the Creator.

This is the meaning of what he had said, "The whole world was created only for me, and I, to serve my Maker." For this reason, I must receive all the degrees in the world so that I can give everything to the Creator, which is called "to serve my Maker."

22. Baal HaSulam, *Shamati*, Article No. 175, "And If the Way Be Too Far for You"

Even though the craving is not up to man, if he has no desire for it, he cannot do a thing. Nevertheless, he should show the desire for the Kisufin, the desire to want (and perhaps VeTzarta [bind] comes from the word Ratzita [wanted]). One needs to show a desire for it, to show the desire and the craving to want the Creator, meaning to want to increase the glory of heaven, to bestow contentment upon Him, to be favored by Him.

23. Baal HaSulam, "Anyone Who Is Sorry for the Public"

"To the extent that one appreciates, so one is allotted" (*Megillah* 12, *Sotah* 8). That is, according to the size of the hole in the *Kli* [vessel], meaning the receptacle and its insides, that lack will always be filled, not less and not more. Therefore, a servant of the Creator who is not sorry for the public but feels only his own personal lack, his receptacle for abundance is also not greater. As a result, he will not be able to receive the collective revelation of Godliness in the form of the comfort of the public, since he did not prepare a *Kli* to receive this collective discernment, but only his individual discernment.

Conversely, one who is sorry for the public and feels the troubles of the public as his own trouble is rewarded with seeing the complete revelation of the *Shechina*, meaning the comfort of the whole of Israel. Because his lack is a collective lack, the abundance of *Kedusha* [holiness] is also collective.

By this you will understand the matter of "The righteous have no rest" (end of *Berachot*, end of *Moed Katan*). Interpretation: Since the abundance is blessed according to the level of the lack and longing of the righteous, to that extent, not less and not more, they always exert to deepen and expand their receptacle, for the Giver has no measure, only the receiver. "More than the calf wants to nurse," etc., (*Pesachim* 112) so their entire intention in life is to strengthen their yearning and make for themselves a receptacle in order to bring contentment by expanding the boundaries of *Kedusha* in the blessing of the Creator.

24. Baal HaSulam, "One Commandment"

It is hopeless to wait for a time when a solution is found that enables one to begin the work of the Creator in *Lishma*. As in the past, so is now, and so will it be: Every servant of the Creator must begin the work in *Lo Lishma*, and from that achieve *Lishma*.

The way to achieve this degree is not limited by time, but by his qualifiers, and by the measure of one's control over one's heart. Hence, many have fallen and will fall in the field of working *Lo Lishma*, and will die without wisdom. Yet, their reward is nevertheless great, since one's mind cannot appreciate the true merit and value of bringing contentment to one's Maker. Even if one works not under this condition, since one is not worthy of another way, one still brings contentment to one's Maker. This is called "unintentionally."

25. RABASH, Article No. 6 (1986), "Confidence"

Those who want to enter the path of truth, to achieve *Dvekut*, must accustom themselves to make every thought, word, and action have the aim to bring contentment to the Creator through the *Mitzvot* that they do and the Torah in which they engage. They must not consider what they can receive from the Creator for wanting to please Him. That is, they must not think, "What will the Creator give me?" meaning that they can extract from the Creator's authority into their own. This would cause them to create two authorities: an authority of the Creator and an authority of the creatures, which is the opposite of *Dvekut*.

26. RABASH, Letter No. 77

The whole foundation is that one should ask that all of one's thoughts and desires will be only to benefit the Creator, a depiction of lowliness, called *Shechina* in the dust, immediately appears. Hence, we must not be impressed by the descent, since many pennies join into a great amount.

This is as we learned, "there is no absence in spirituality," rather that it has temporarily departed in order to have room for work to advance. This is so because every moment that we scrutinize into holiness enters the domain of holiness, and a person descends only in order to sort out more sparks of holiness.

However, there is an advice that one should not wait until his degree is lowered for him, and when he feels his lowliness he goes up again, and that ascent is regarded as sorting a part into holiness. Instead, he himself descends and elevates other sparks, and raises them into the domain of holiness.

It is as our sages said, "Before I lose, I search" (Shabbat, 152), meaning before I lose the situation I am in, I start searching. It is as Baal HaSulam said about King David, who said, "I awaken the dawn." Our sages said, "I awaken the dawn and the dawn does not awaken me."

27. RABASH, Article No. 13 (1986), "Come unto Pharaoh – 2"

We should know that we were given love of friends to learn how to avoid blemishing the King's honor. In other words, if he has no other desire except to give contentment to the King, he will certainly blemish the King's honor, which is called "Passing on *Kedusha* [holiness/sanctity] to the external ones." For this reason, we mustn't underestimate the importance of the work in love of friends, for by that he will learn how to exit self-love and enter the path of love of others. And when he completes the work of love of friends, he will be able to be rewarded with love of the Creator.

28. RABASH, Article No. 283, "Be Mindful with a Minor Commandment as with a Major One – 3"

"Be mindful with a minor *Mitzva* [commandment] as with a major one, for you do not know the reward given for *Mitzvot* [commandments]."

A person thinks that receiving the reward is from something that gives contentment above. Hence, when he learns and finds success in his learning, meaning that he has vitality and can present innovations in the Torah, or feels while he prays that he has love and fear and *Dvekut* [adhesion] and excitement during the prayer, at that time he is mindful about the matter and wants to continue his work.

Although he sees that he has no time and he is preoccupied, he still has the strength to give even to the point of devotion so as not to rest from Torah and from prayer, since he feels in this knowledge, meaning he knows and feels on himself that these Torah and prayer give contentment above. Hence, at such a time he is mindful to do his work however he can.

This is not so with a minor *Mitzva*, which is only by acceptance of the burden of the kingdom of heaven, where he does not feel a flavor in the Torah, and where he has no vitality in the prayer. At such a time, it is regarded as "minor."

When he has no importance for such work, he does not want to be mindful and overcome the disturbances he has because he says that in any case, the engagement in *Torah and Mitzvot* is not so important above when he has no vitality. He wants to stop over a small disturbance because above it is also unimportant and he will not receive a great reward.

Therefore, they said, "You do not know the reward given for *Mitzvot*." In other words, the Creator derives contentment from his state of *Katnut* [smallness/infancy], which is only by acceptance of the burden of the kingdom of heaven without any knowledge, intellect, or other feeling from the time of *Gadlut* [greatness/adulthood], as his importance above is mainly the work during the *Katnut*, and not the *Gadlut*.

Because a person does not know which state gives more contentment above, "Be mindful with a minor *Mitzva*," meaning in the state of *Katnut*, "as with a major one," namely in the state of *Gadlut*.

29. RABASH, Article No. 24 (1991), "What Does It Mean that One Should Bear a Son and a Daughter, in the Work?"

If one decides that he wants to work as "dust," meaning even if he tastes the taste of dust in the work, he says that it is very important for him to be able to do something for the sake of the Creator, and for himself, he does not care which taste he feels, and says that this work, in which one tastes the taste of dust, meaning that the body mocks this work, he says to the body that in his view, this work is regarded as "raising the *Shechina* [Divinity] from the dust."

In other words, although the body tastes dust in this work, the person says that it is *Kedusha* and does not measure how much flavor he feels in the work. Rather, he believes that the Creator does enjoy this work, since there is no mixture of the will to receive here, since he has nothing to receive because there are no flavor or scent in this work, as there is only the taste of dust here. For this reason, he believes that this is the holy work, and he is delighted.

30. RABASH, Article No. 13 (1989), "What Is the 'Bread of an Evil-Eyed Man' in the Work?"

All our work in Torah and *Mitzvot* is in order to emerge from the exile of the will to receive for ourselves. In other words, we must aim—while engaging in Torah and *Mitzvot*—that our reward will be that by this we will be rewarded with emerging from the exile and enslavement in the will to receive for ourselves, and we will be able to work only in order to bring contentment to the Creator, and we will not demand any other reward for our work in Torah and *Mitzvot*.

In other words, we want to be rewarded with feeling—while engaging in Torah and *Mitzvot*—that we are serving a great and important king, and that by this there will be love of the Creator within us, from feeling His exaltedness. However, all of our pleasure will come from serving the Creator; this will be our reward, and not that He will somehow reward us for the work. Instead, we will feel that the work itself is the reward, and there is no greater reward in the world than the privilege of serving the Creator.

31. RABASH, Article No. 24 (1986), "The Difference between Charity and Gift"

When the cup of labor has been filled sufficiently, it is called a *Kli*. Then the filling of it comes from the Creator, since now he has a real *Kli*.

It follows that his seeing that now—after several years of work—he has retreated, this happens deliberately so he will ache at not having *Dvekut* with the Creator. It turns out that each time he must see that he is approaching the making of the *Kli*, called "real deficiency." That is, his gauge of *Katnut* [infancy/smallness] and *Gadlut* [adulthood/greatness] of the deficiency is to the extent of the suffering he feels at not having the filling, which is called here "*Dvekut* with the Creator," where all he wants is only to bring contentment to the Creator.

32. RABASH, Article No. 502, "If Man Wins, the Creator Is Happy"

If a person wants to receive the Torah with the Creator's intention—to do good to His creations—so the creatures will enjoy, it is called "the Torah of the Creator," when the Torah follows the line of the Creator. If a person takes the Torah so as to have the power to bestow, this is regarded as man's intention, where man wants to bestow contentment upon his Maker, and then it is regarded as his Torah.

33. RABASH, Article No. 5 (1990), "What It Means that the Land Did Not Bear Fruit before Man Was Created, in the Work"

In the work, man is regarded as one who has emerged from the control of the quality of a beast. A "beast" means one who is immersed in self-benefit, like a beast, and man means one in whom there is fear of heaven and works because of fear, which *The Zohar* calls "Because He is great and ruling," where he works only because of the greatness of the Creator and does not care for his own benefit, but for the benefit of the Creator. It is as our sages said about the verse, "In the end of the matter, fear God and observe His commandments, for this is the whole of man. What is 'for this is the whole of man'? Rabbi Elazar said, 'The whole world was created only for this'" (*Berachot* 6).

It follows that man is regarded as one in whom there is the fear of heaven. And what is the fear of heaven? That is, what is fear? It is as he says ("Introduction of The Book of Zohar," Item 191), "Both the first fear and the second fear are not for his own benefit, but only for fear that he will decline in bringing contentment to his Maker."

According to the above, we already know the meaning of Adam. It is one who has fear of heaven, who is afraid that perhaps he will not be able to do everything in order to bestow. This is called "man." A "beast" is the opposite: one who cares only for one's own benefit, as it is written (Ecclesiastes 3), "Who knows the spirit of man, whether it goes upward, and the spirit of the beast, whether it goes downward to the earth?" We should interpret that "spirit of man" goes upward means that everything he does is for the sake of the Creator. This is called "upward," when his intention is that everything will be only in order to bestow. From this man derives contentment.

34. RABASH, Article No. 15 (1989), "What Is, 'The Righteous Become Apparent through the Wicked,' in the Work?"

The Zohar says ("Introduction of The Book of Zohar," Item 190): "Fear that is *Lo Lishma* is not the main fear." (In Item 191) It says, "The main fear is that one should fear one's Master because He is great and ruling, and all is regarded as nothing before Him, and he should place his will in that place, which is called 'fear.'"

From this it follows that there are two kinds of intentions while performing actions, both in learning Torah and in performing *Mitzvot*. The work of the general public is in order to receive reward, and the work of individuals is for the sake of the Creator, and their reward is if they can serve the King. That is, their whole pleasure, which gives them fuel so they can work in order to bestow, is to feel that they are bringing contentment to the King and are praising and thanking the King for giving them the thought and desire to work for Him and not to receive any other reward for their work.

They say that in order to receive reward, "We do not need to feel the greatness of the King. Rather, we need to consider the greatness and importance of the reward we will receive if we observe the Torah and *Mitzvot*." But the Creator can stay for them at the same level of greatness and importance as He was for them at the beginning of their work.

However, if their intention is to bring contentment to the Creator, then if they want to increase the work, they must increase the greatness of the Creator, since to the extent of His greatness, to that extent they can annul before Him and do everything they do only for the sake of the Creator. It is as *The Zohar* says about the verse, "Her husband is known at the gates," each according to "what he assumes in his heart."

Therefore, in order to have fuel to work, those who want to work for the sake of the Creator must try each day to exert to obtain faith in the greatness of the Creator, since the greatness of the Creator is what compels them to work for Him, and this is all the pleasure they derive from their work.

35. RABASH, Article No. 18 (1989), "What Is, 'There Is No Blessing in That Which Is Counted,' in the Work?"

There are two discernments to make in this: 1) to have a desire to bestow contentment upon his Maker, that this will be his only aspiration, 2) to do things with the aim that the actions will bring him a desire to do things in order to please the Creator. In other words, he must work and toil extensively to obtain light and *Kli* [vessel]. Light means that he received from the Creator a desire where he craves all day to bring contentment to the Creator. A *Kli* is a desire, meaning that he wants to bestow upon the Creator. Those two, he should receive from the Creator, meaning both the light and the *Kli*.

However, a person should demand this, and it is written about this, "Zion, no one requires her." Our sages said, "This means that she ought to be sought," meaning that there must be a demand on the part of the lower ones that the Creator will give them both the light and the *Kli*.

36. RABASH, Article No. 295, "Anyone Who Sanctifies the Seventh – 1"

When one comes to a degree where he wants to bestow upon the Creator, meaning give contentment to his Maker, he begins to contemplate what the Creator needs so he can give it to Him, since all his concerns are to please the Creator. At that time, he realizes that the only reason He created the world was to receive pleasures from Him, and that more than this, the Creator does not need. Hence, he follows the Creator's will and receives the pleasures.

At that time, there is no issue of bread of shame because he is not receiving the pleasures because he wants to enjoy, but because he wants to bestow upon the Creator, for when one achieves the degree of wanting only to bestow upon the Creator, the *Tzimtzum* is lifted from him and he sees the world as full of His glory.

Then he sees that all this was revealed to him so he would enjoy it. Hence, once he has obtained the degree of bestowal, meaning obtained the degree where all he wants is only to bestow contentment upon the Creator, he fills himself with all the pleasures that his eyes see, as in the explanation, "The whole earth is full of His glory."

It follows that all that one needs to obtain that he can define as a reward after he has toiled several years is only one thing: the desire to bestow, meaning the degree of wanting to serve the rav not in order to receive reward.

All the labor where one needs to exert himself in *Torah and Mitzvot* [commandments] is only to obtain this. This is called "fear of heaven," as it is written, "What does the Lord your God ask of you? Only to fear Me."

37. RABASH, Article No. 300, "A Land Where You Will Eat Bread without Scarcity"

One must engage in Torah day and night, that the night and the day should be equal for him, as written in *The Zohar* (*BeShalach*). In other words, the state of completeness called "day," and the state of incompleteness called "night," should be equal. That is, if his aim is for the sake of the Creator then he agrees that he wants to bring contentment to his Maker, and if the Creator wants him to remain in the state of incompleteness, he agrees to this, as well. The consent is expressed by doing his work as if he were rewarded with wholeness. This is regarded as "agreeing," when the day and the night are equal to him.

But if there is a difference, to the extent of the difference, there is separation, and on that separation there is a grip to the outer ones. Hence, if a person feels that to him there is a difference, he must pray to the Creator to help him so there will not be a difference for him, and then he will be rewarded with completeness.

38. RABASH, Article No. 15 (1986), "A Prayer of Many"

The advice is to ask for the whole collective. In other words, everything that one feels that he is lacking and asks fulfillment for, he should not say that he is an exception or deserves more than what the collective has. Rather, "I dwell among my own people," meaning I am asking for the entire collective because I wish to come to a state where I will have no care for myself whatsoever, but only for the Creator to have contentment. Therefore, it makes no difference to me if the Creator takes pleasure in me or can receive the pleasure from others.

In other words, he asks the Creator to give us such an understanding, which is called, "entirely for the Creator." It means that he will be certain that he is not deceiving himself that he wants to bestow upon the Creator, that perhaps he is really thinking only of his own self-love, meaning that he will feel the delight and pleasure.

Therefore, he prays for the collective. This means that if there are a few people in the collective who can reach the goal of *Dvekut* with the Creator, and this will bring the Creator more contentment than if he himself were rewarded with nearing the Creator, he excludes himself. Instead, he wishes for the Creator to help them because this will bring more contentment above than from his own work. For this reason, he prays for the collective, that the Creator will help the entire collective and will give them that feeling—that they receive satisfaction from being able to bestow upon the Creator, to bring Him contentment.

39. RABASH, Article No. 502, "If Man Wins, the Creator Is Happy"

The intention of the Emanator is for the lower ones to receive pleasure. Yet, man uses the Torah in the opposite manner, wanting the Creator to receive pleasure. He receives this power from the Torah, from that spice. It follows that he is fighting with the Creator, meaning that the Creator wants man to receive pleasure, and man wants the Creator to receive pleasure.

Thus, he uses the Torah in the opposite direction from the seller. It was said about this that the Creator says, "My sons defeated Me." That is, they fight against the will to receive that the Creator imprinted in their hearts, where if the man wins, the Creator is happy.

40. RABASH, Article No. 16 (1989), "What Is the Prohibition to Bless on an Empty Table, in the Work?"

"Right line," meaning wholeness, in which there are no deficiencies. And what should one do when he engages in a manner of "right"? He should praise and thank the Creator, and engage in the Torah, for then is the time to receive the light of Torah, since he is in a state of wholeness, regarded as being a person who has blessing and no lacks. Naturally, this is the time for the blessing to be on him, as said above, "The blessed clings to The Blessed."

However, it is impossible to walk on one leg. That is, a person cannot progress on one leg. Since there is a rule, "There is no light without a *Kli*," meaning "No filling without a lack," and since on the right line he is in wholeness, it follows that he has nowhere to progress, no need for the Creator to satisfy his needs, since he has no needs at all.

For this reason, at that time a person must try to see his faults, so as to have room for prayer that the Creator will satisfy his needs. This is regarded as a person having to provide empty *Kelim* that the Creator may fill with upper abundance, which is called "a blessing." If there are no empty *Kelim*, meaning deficiencies, with what can he fill them?

This is regarded as a person walking on the "left line." In spirituality, "left" means something that requires correction. This means that a person should dedicate a small portion of his time to criticize himself and see how much effort he can put into working solely for the sake of the Creator, and not for his own sake, and if he can say that if he does not work in order to bring contentment to his Maker, he does not want to live, and so forth.

At that time he realizes that he cannot do this on his own, but only the Creator can help. It follows that now is the time when he can pray from the bottom of the heart. That is, he sees and feels that he is powerless to change the nature with which he was created, called "will to receive for himself and not to bestow."

41. RABASH, Article No. 5 (1991), "What Is, 'The Good Deeds of the Righteous Are the Generations,' in the Work?"

We ask the Creator to give us the strength so we can perform all our actions for You, meaning for the sake of the Creator. Otherwise, meaning if You do not help us, all our actions will be only for our own benefit. That is, "If not," meaning "If You do not help us, all our actions will be only for ourselves, for our own benefit, for we are powerless to overcome our will to receive. Therefore, help us be able to work for You. Hence, You must help us." This is called "Do for Your sake," meaning do this, give us the power of the desire to bestow. Otherwise, we are doomed; we will remain in the will to receive for our own sake.

42. RABASH, Article No. 16 (1984), "Concerning Bestowal"

It is said about that (Kidushin, 30), "Man's inclination overcomes him each day and seeks to kill him, as it is said, 'The wicked watches the righteous, and seeks to slay him.' And if the Creator did not help him, he would not overcome it, as it is said, 'The Lord will not leave him in his hand.'"

This means that first, one must see if he has the strength to come to be able to act with the aim to bestow contentment upon the Creator. Then, when he has already come to realize that he cannot achieve it by himself, that person focuses his Torah and *Mitzvot* on a single point, which is that "the light in it reforms him," that this will be the only reward that he wants from the Torah and *Mitzvot*. In other words, the reward for his labor will be for the Creator to give him this strength called "the power of bestowal."

43. RABASH, Article No. 223, "Entry into the Work"

The entry into the work must be in *Lo Lishma* [not for Her sake], meaning that by believing in the Creator he will have a life of pleasure. This means that if he does this action called "faith," it will give him elation and superior mental forces than when he does not perform this action.

It follows that this is a *Segula* [remedy/quality/power] by which he can taste greater flavors in quantity and quality than what he tastes while he is doing other things in order to receive pleasure. This means that there are many ways to obtain pleasure, such as eating, drinking, and sleeping, or impressive clothes, or by doing things that make people respect him. Such actions are means by which he obtains pleasure.

Yet, the pleasures that these actions yield for him are limited in quantity and quality. Conversely, the *Segula* of faith brings him greater pleasure in quantity and quality.

All this is called *Lo Lishma* because his intention is only to obtain a greater pleasure.

Only after he achieves this degree called *Lo Lishma*, he is rewarded with other phenomena, when he comes to a higher state. That is, at that time he has no consideration of himself, and all his calculations and thoughts are the truth.

In other words, his aim is only to annul himself before the true reality, where he feels that he must only serve the King because he feels the exaltedness and greatness and importance of the King. At that time, he forgets, meaning he has no need to worry about himself, as his own self is annulled as a candle before a torch before the existence of the Creator that he feels. Then he is in a state of *Lishma* [for Her sake], meaning contentment to the Creator, and his concerns and yearnings are only about how he can delight the Creator, while his own existence, meaning the will to receive, does not merit a name whatsoever. Then he is regarded as "bestowing in order to bestow."

44. *Zohar for All, Aharei Mot* [After the Death], "Behold, How Good and How Pleasant," Items 65-66

How good and how pleasant it is for brothers to also sit together." These are the friends as they sit together, and are not separated from each other. At first, they seem like people at war, wishing to kill one another. Then they return to being in brotherly love.

The Creator says about them, "Behold, how good and how pleasant it is for brothers to also sit together." The word, "also," comes to include the *Shechina* with them. Moreover, the Creator listens to their words and He has contentment and delights with them, as it is written, "Then those who feared the Lord spoke to one another, and the Lord listened and heard it, and a book of remembrance was written before Him."

And you, the friends who are here, as you were in fondness and love before, henceforth you will also not part until the Creator rejoices with you and summons peace upon you. And by your merit there will be peace in the world, as it is written, "For the sake of my brothers and my friends let me say, 'Let peace be in you.'"

45. *Zohar for All, Beresheet Bet* [Genesis 2], "Seven Palaces in the Garden of Eden," Item 103

The world was created only in bestowal, to engage in Torah and good deeds in order to bestow contentment to one's Maker, and not for one's own pleasure. It is written, "All the works of the Creator are for Him," so that people would bestow contentment upon Him.

But in the beginning, it is written, "A man is born a wild ass' colt," whose sole interest is his own delight and who has none of the desire to bestow. He argues, "All the works of the Creator are for me, for my own delight," since he wishes to devour the entire world for his own good and benefit.

Hence, the Creator has imprinted bitter and harsh afflictions in self-reception, instilled in man from the moment of his birth—bodily pains and pains of the soul—so that if he engages in Torah and *Mitzvot* even for his own pleasure, through the light in it he will still feel the lowliness and the terrible corruptness in the nature of receiving for oneself.

At that time he will resolve to retire from that nature of reception and completely devote himself to working only in order to bestow contentment upon his Maker, as it is written, "All the works of the Creator are for Him." Then the Creator will open his eyes to see before him a world filled with utter perfection without any deficiencies whatsoever.

Then he partakes in the joy as at the time of the creation of the world. Because he was rewarded, he has sentenced himself and the entire world to a scale of merit," for wherever he casts his eyes he sees only good and perfection. He sees no faults at all in the works of the Creator, only merits.

46. Elimelech of Lizhensk, *Noam Elimelech* [*The Pleasantness of Elimelech*]

Brace our ties of love to You, as it is known to You that all will be for bringing contentment to You, and this is our main intention. And should we not have the wit to aim our hearts to You, You will teach us, so we may truly know the aim of Your good will.

PART 5
Man's Work on the Spiritual Path

1

Faith Above Reason

1. Baal HaSulam, *Shamati*, Article No. 135, "Clean and Righteous Do Not Kill"

"The clean and righteous do not kill." A righteous is one who justifies the Creator: Whatever he feels, whether good or bad, he takes above reason. This is considered "right." Clean refers to the cleanness of the matter, the state as he sees it. This is so because "a judge has only what his eyes see." And if one does not understand the matter, or cannot attain the matter, he should not blur the forms as they seem to his eyes. This is considered "left," and he should nurture both.

2. Baal HaSulam, *Shamati*, Article No. 215, "Concerning Faith"

Faith, specifically, is pure work since the will to receive does not participate in this work. Moreover, the will to receive resists it. The nature of that desire is only to work in a place that it sees and knows. But above reason is not so. Hence, in this manner the *Dvekut* [adhesion] can be complete, since there is an element of equivalence here, meaning it is actually to bestow.

Therefore, when this basis is fixed and exists in him, even when receiving good influences, he considers it an *Atreia* [Aramaic: warning], which, in *Gematria*, is Torah. And there should be fear with this Torah, meaning he should see that he does not receive any support or assistance from the Torah, but from faith. And even when he already considers it superfluous because he is already receiving from the quality of "a pleasant land," he should believe that this is the truth. This is the meaning of "And all believe that He is a God of faith," since specifically through faith can he maintain the degree.

3. Baal HaSulam, *Shamati*, Article No. 13, "A Pomegranate"

There is emptiness only in a place where there is no existence, as in "The earth hangs on nothing." You find that what is the measure of the filling of the empty place? The answer is, according to one's elevation of oneself above reason.

This means that the emptiness should be filled with exaltedness, meaning with above reason, and to ask of the Creator to give him that strength. This will mean that all the emptiness was created, meaning it comes to a person to feel this way—that he is empty—only in order to fill it with the Romemut of the Creator. In other words, one is to take everything above reason.

This is the meaning of the verse, "God has made it that He will be feared." This means that these thoughts of emptiness come to a person in order for one to have a need to take upon himself faith above reason. And for this we need the help of the Creator. It follows that at that time, one must ask the Creator to give him the power to believe above reason.

It turns out that it is precisely then that one needs the Creator to help him, since the exterior mind lets him understand the opposite. Hence, at that time, one has no other choice but to ask the Creator to help him.

It is said about this, "One's desire overcomes him every day; and were it not for the Creator, he would not overcome it." It follows that only then is the state when one understands that no one will help him but the Creator. And this is "God has made it that He will be feared." The matter of fear is discerned as faith, and only then is one in need of the salvation of the Creator.

4. Baal HaSulam, *Shamati*, Article No. 108, "If You Leave Me One Day, I Will Leave You Two"

Right at the entrance (entrance is a constant thing because every time he has a descent he must begin anew. This is why it is called an "entrance." Naturally, there are many exits and many entrances) he tells his body, "Know that I want to begin to serve the Creator and my intention is only to bestow and not to receive any reward. You should not hope that you will receive anything for your efforts, but it is all in order to bestow."

And if the body asks, "What is your benefit from this work?" meaning, "Who receives this work, that I want to exert and toil?" Or he asks more simply, "For whose sake am I working so hard?" The reply should be, "I have faith in the sages, and they said that I should believe in abstract faith, above reason, that the Creator has so commanded us, to take upon ourselves faith, that He commanded us to keep Torah and *Mitzvot*. And we should also believe that the Creator derives pleasure when we keep the Torah and *Mitzvot* with faith above reason. Also, one should be glad at the Creator's pleasure from his work."

Thus, there are four things here:

1. Believing in the sages, that what they said is true.
2. Believing that the Creator commanded to engage in Torah and *Mitzvot* only through faith above reason.
3. There is joy when the creatures keep the Torah and *Mitzvot* on the basis of faith.
4. One should receive delight, pleasure, and gladness from having been rewarded with pleasing the King. And the measure of the greatness and the importance of man's work is measured by the measure of joy that one derives during his work. This depends on the measure of faith that one believes in the above.

5. Baal HaSulam, *Shamati*, Article No. 14, "What Is the Exaltedness of the Creator?"

The *Romemut* [exaltedness/sublimity] of the Creator means that one should ask the Creator for the strength to go above reason. This means that there are two interpretations to the *Romemut* of the Creator:

A. To not be filled with knowledge, which is intellect with which one can answer one's questions. Rather, he wants the Creator to answer his questions. It is called *Romemut* because all the wisdom comes from above and not from man, meaning that man can answer his own questions. Anything that one can answer is regarded as answering everything with the external mind. This means that the will to receive understands that it is worthwhile to observe Torah and *Mitzvot* [commandments]. However, if the above reason compels one to work, it is called "against the opinion of the will to receive."

B. The greatness of the Creator means that one becomes needy of the Creator to grant his wishes. Therefore:

1. One should go above reason. Then one sees that he is empty and becomes needy of the Creator.
2. Only the Creator can give him the strength to be able to go above reason. In other words, what the Creator gives is called "The *Romemut* of the Creator."

6. Baal HaSulam, *Shamati*, Article No. 129, "The Shechina in the Dust"

Suffering is primarily in a place that is above reason. And the measure of the suffering depends on the extent to which it contradicts the reason. This is called "faith above reason," and this work gives contentment to the Creator. It follows that the reward is that by this work there is contentment to one's Maker.

However, in between, before one can prevail and justify His guidance, the *Shechina* [Divinity] is in the dust. This means that the work by way of faith, called the *Shechina*, is in exile, canceled in the dust. And he said about that, "Neither they nor their reward." This means that he cannot stand the period in between. And this is the meaning of his reply to him, "I am crying for this and for that."

7. Baal HaSulam, *Shamati*, Article No. 200, "The Hizdakchut of the Masach"

The *Hizdakchut* [thinning/purification] of the *Masach* [screen], which occurs in the *Partzuf*, causes the departure of the light, too. And the reason is that after the *Tzimtzum* [restriction], the light is captured only in the *Kli* [vessel] of the *Masach*, which is the rejecting force. And this is the essence of the *Kli*.

When that *Kli* departs, the light departs, too. This means that a *Kli* is considered faith above reason. And then the light appears. When the light appears, its nature is to thin out the *Kli*, to cancel the *Kli* of faith. Because this is so, meaning that it comes into a form of knowing in him, the light immediately departs from him. Thus, he should see to increasing the *Kli* of faith, meaning the *Masach* over the knowing, and then the abundance will not stop from him.

This is the meaning of each *Kli* being deficient of light, that it is not filled by the light that it lacks. It follows that every place of lack becomes a place for faith. If it were filled, there would be no possibility for a *Kli*, a place for faith.

8. Baal HaSulam, *Shamati*, Article No. 96, "What Is Waste of Barn and Winery, in the Work?"

The purpose of the work is in the literal and nature, since in this work he no longer has room to fall lower down, since he is already placed on the ground. This is so because he does not need greatness because to him it is always like something new. That is, he always works as though he had just begun to work. And he works in the form of accepting the burden of the kingdom of heaven above reason. The basis, upon which he built the order of the work, was in the lowest manner, and all of it was truly above reason. Only one who is truly naïve can be so low as to proceed without any basis on which to establish his faith, literally with no support.

Additionally, he accepts this work with great joy, as though he had had real knowledge and vision on which to establish the certainty of faith. And to that exact measure of above reason, to that very measure as though he had reason. Hence, if he persists in this way, he can never fall. Rather, he can always be in gladness, by believing that he is serving a great King.

9. Baal HaSulam, *Shamati*, Article No. 207, "Receiving in order to Bestow"

It is only because he had had prior preparation by taking upon himself the above reason.
This means that through engagement in *Dvekut* [adhesion], he attached himself at the root. By this he was awarded reason, meaning that the reason he has obtained by the discernment of faith was a true revelation. It follows that he appreciates primarily the above reason, and also appreciates the reason, that he has now been rewarded with the revelation of His names to extend abundance.

This is why now he should strengthen further through reason, and take upon himself a greater above reason, as *Dvekut* in the root occurs primarily through faith, and this is his whole purpose. This is called "reception," the reason he extended in order to bestow, and by which he will be able to take upon himself faith above reason to the greatest extent in quantity and quality.

10. Baal HaSulam, *Shamati*, Article No. 19, "What Is 'The Creator Hates the Bodies,' in the Work?"

Sometimes one despises this work of assuming the burden of the kingdom of heaven, which is a time of a sensation of darkness, when one sees that no one can save him from the state he is in but the Creator. Then he takes upon himself the kingdom of heaven above reason, as an ox to the burden and as a donkey to the load. One should be glad that now he has something to give to the Creator, and the Creator enjoys him having something to give to the Creator. But one does not always have the strength to say that this is beautiful work, called "adornment," but he despises this work. This is a harsh condition for one to be able to say that he chooses this work over the work of whiteness, meaning that he does not sense a taste of darkness during the work, but then one feels a taste in the work. It means that then he does not have to work with the will to receive to agree to take upon himself the kingdom of heaven above reason. If he does overcome himself and can say that this work is pleasant to him that now he is observing the *Mitzva* [commandment] of faith above reason, and he accepts this work as beauty and adornment, this is called "A joy of *Mitzva*."

11. Baal HaSulam, *Shamati*, Article No. 40, "What Is the Measure of Faith in the Rav?"

When one is engaged in the right, the time is right to extend upper abundance, because "the blessed adheres to the Blessed." In other words, since one is in a state of completeness, called "blessed," in that respect one presently has equivalence of form, since the sign of completeness is if one is in gladness. Otherwise, there is no completeness.

It is as our sages said, "The *Shechina* [Divinity] is present only out of gladness of a *Mitzva* [commandment]." The meaning is that the reason that brings him joy is the *Mitzva*, meaning the fact that the rav had commanded him to take the right line.

It follows that he keeps the commandment of the rav, that he was allotted a special time to walk on the right and a special time to walk on the left. Left contradicts the right, since left means when one calculates for oneself and begins to examine what he has already acquired in the work of the Creator, and he sees that he is poor and indigent. Thus, how can he be in wholeness?

Still, one goes above reason because of the commandment of the rav. It follows that all his wholeness was built on above reason, and this is called "faith." This is the meaning of "In every place where I mention My Name, I will come to you and bless you." "In every place" means although he is still not worthy of a blessing, nonetheless, I gave My blessing because you make a place, meaning a place of gladness, in which the upper light can be.

12. Baal HaSulam, *Shamati*, Article No. 8, "What Is the Difference Between a Shade of Kedusha and a Shade of Sitra Achra?"

There are two kinds of shadows, and this is the meaning of "and the shadows flee away," meaning that the shadows will pass away from the world.

The shade of *Klipa* [shell] is called "Another god is sterile and does not bear fruit." In *Kedusha* [holiness], however, it is called "Under its shadow I coveted to sit, and its fruit was sweet to my palate." In other words, he says that all the concealments and afflictions he feels are because the Creator has sent him these states so he would have a place for work above reason.

When one has the strength to say this—that the Creator causes him all this—it is to one's benefit. This means that through this he can come to work in order to bestow and not for his own sake. At that time, one realizes, meaning believes that the Creator enjoys specifically this work, which is built entirely on above reason.

It follows that at that time, one does not pray to the Creator that the shadows will flee from the world. Rather, he says, "I see that the Creator wants me to serve Him in this manner, entirely above reason." Thus, in everything he does he says, "The Creator certainly enjoys this work, so why should I care if I am working in a state of concealment of the face?"

Because one wants to work in order to bestow, meaning that the Creator will enjoy, he feels no humiliation in this work, meaning a sensation that he is in a state of concealment of the face, that the Creator does not enjoy this work. Instead, one agrees to the leadership of the Creator, meaning however the Creator wants him to feel the existence of the Creator during the work, he agrees wholeheartedly. This is so because one does not consider what can please him, but what can please the Creator. Thus, this shade brings him life.

This is called "Under its shadow I coveted," meaning one covets such a state where he can make some overcoming above reason.

13. Baal HaSulam, *Shamati*, Article No. 83, "Concerning the Right Vav and the Left Vav"

In any state one is in, he can be a servant of the Creator since he does not need anything, but does everything above reason. It turns out that one does not need any *Mochin* with which to be the servant of the Creator.

Now we can interpret what is written, "Set up a table before me, against my enemies." A table means, as it is written, "and sent her out of his house, and she departed his house, and went" (Deuteronomy 24:1-2). A *Shulchan* [table] is like *VeShlacha* [and sent her], meaning exit from the work.

We should interpret that even during the exits from the work, meaning in a state of decline, one still has a place to work. This means that when one prevails above reason during the declines, and says that the descents, too, were given to him from above, by this the enemies are canceled. This is so because the enemies thought that through the declines the person will reach utter lowliness and escape the campaign, but in the end the opposite occurred—the enemies were canceled.

This is the meaning of what is written, "the table that is before the Lord," that precisely in this manner does he receive the face of the Creator. This is the meaning of subduing all the judgments, even the harshest judgments, since he assumes the burden of the kingdom of heaven at all times. That is, he always finds a place for work, as it is written that Rabbi Shimon Bar-Yochai said, "There is no place to hide from You."

14. Baal HaSulam, *Shamati*, Article No. 212, "Embrace of the Right, Embrace of the Left"

There is the embrace of the right and there is the embrace of the left, and both must be eternal. This means that when one is in the state of "right," he should think that there is no such quality as "left" in the world. And also, when one is in the left, he should think that there is no such quality as "right" in the world.

"Right" means private Providence, and "left" means guidance of reward and punishment. Although there is reason which says that there is no such thing as right and left together, he must work above reason, meaning that reason will not stop him.

The most important is the above reason. This means that one's whole work is measured by his work above reason. Although he later comes into within, it is nothing, since his basis is the above reason, so he always suckles from his root.

However, if, when he comes into within reason, he wants specifically to be fed within reason, at that time the light immediately departs. If he wants to extend, he must begin with above reason, as this is his whole root. Afterward, he comes to the reason of *Kedusha* [holiness].

15. Baal HaSulam, *Shamati*, Article No. 40, "What Is the Measure of Faith in the Rav?"

One should depict to oneself as if he has already been rewarded with whole faith in the Creator, and already feels in his organs that the Creator leads the whole world in the form of "The Good Who Does Good," meaning that the whole world receives only good from Him.

Yet, when one looks at oneself, he sees that he is poor and indigent. In addition, when he observes the world, he sees that the entire world is tormented, each according to his degree.

One should say about that, "They have eyes but they see not." "They" means that as long as one is in multiple authorities, called "they," they do not see the truth. What are the multiple authorities? As long as one has two desires, even though he believes that the entire world belongs to the Creator, but something belongs to man, too.

But in truth, one must annul one's authority before the authority of the Creator and say that one does not want to live for oneself, and the only reason that he wants to exist is in order to bring contentment to the Creator. Thus, by this one annuls his own authority completely, and then he is in the singular authority, the authority of the Creator. Only then can he see the truth, how the Creator leads the world by the quality of good and doing good.

As long as he is in multiple authorities, meaning when he still has two desires in both mind and heart, he is unable to see the truth. Instead, he must go above reason and say, "they have eyes," but they do not see the truth.

16. RABASH, *Shamati*, Article No. 16, "What Is the Day of the Lord and the Night of the Lord, in the Work?"

"Woe unto you who desire the day of the Lord! Why do you need the day of the Lord? It is darkness, and not light." The thing is that those who await the day of the Lord, it means that they are waiting to be imparted faith above reason, that faith will be so strong, as if they see with their eyes, with certainty, that it is so, that the Creator watches over the world in a manner of good and doing good.

In other words, they do not want to see how the Creator leads the world as The Good Who Does Good, since seeing is contradictory to faith. In other words, faith is precisely where it is against reason. And when one does what is against one's reason, this is called "faith above reason."

This means that they believe that the guidance of the Creator over the creatures is in a manner of good and doing good. While they do not see it with absolute certainty, they do not say to the Creator, "We want to see the quality of good and doing good as seeing within reason." Rather, they want it to remain in them as faith above reason, but they ask of the Creator to give them such strength that this faith will be so strong, as if they see it within reason, that there will be no difference between faith and knowledge in the mind. This is what they, those who want to adhere to the Creator, refer to as "the day of the Lord."

17. RABASH, Article No. 38 (1990), "What Is, 'A Cup of Blessing Must Be Full,' in the Work?"

We should discern between speech and mute in the work. Speech means revealing, when a person already has *Yenika* in spirituality, and he feels that he is suckling from *Kedusha*, for nursing on milk indicates *Hassadim*, for the quality of *Hesed* [mercy] is bestowal, when a person is rewarded with vessels of bestowal and all his actions are for the sake of the Creator and he has no concerns for his own benefit. This is regarded as the quality of *Hesed*.

However, before the *Yenika* there is *Ibur*, meaning that the upper one corrects him. This can be when a person is like an embryo in its mother's womb, where the embryo annuls before the mother and has no view of its own, but as our sages said, "An embryo is its mother's thigh, eats what its mother eats," and has no authority of its own to ask any questions. Rather, it does not merit a name. This is called "mute," when he has no mouth to ask questions.

This is so when a person can go with his eyes shut, above reason, and believe in the sages and go all the way. This is called *Ibur*, when he has no mouth. *Ibur* means as it is written (*The Study of the Ten Sefirot*, Part 8, Item 17), "The level of *Malchut*, which is the most restricted *Katnut* [smallness/infancy] possible, is called *Ibur*. It comes from the words *Evra* [anger] and *Dinin* [Aramaic: judgments], as it is written, 'And the Lord was impregnated in me for your sake.'"

We should interpret the meaning of "anger and judgments." When a person must go with this eyes shut, above reason, the body resists this work. Hence, the fact that a person always has to overcome, this is called "anger, wrath, and trouble," since it is hard work to always overcome and annul before the upper one, for the upper one to do with him what the upper one wants. This is called *Ibur*, which is the most restricted *Katnut* possible.

18. RABASH, Article No. 4 (1991), "What Is, 'The Saboteur Was in the Flood, and Was Putting to Death,' in the Work?"

When a person lowers himself, the question is, What is lowliness? How is it expressed that a person is in lowliness? The literal meaning is that lowliness is when one subdues oneself and works above reason. This is called "lowliness," when he lowers his reason and says that his reason is worthless.

In other words, man's reason dictates that if the Creator gives him all his needs, which the will to receive understands that it deserves, then he can love the Creator. That is, he loves Him because he satisfies all his needs. If He did not, he would not be able to lower himself and say that his reason is worthless. Rather, at that time he would depart from the Creator and say that it is not worthwhile to serve the Creator if He does not grant him his wishes. It follows that this is called "proud," since he wants to understand the ways of the Creator, in what is He regarded as good and doing good, if the body does not get what it demands. About such a proud person the Creator says, "He and I cannot dwell in the same abode."

But if he lowers himself and says, "I cannot understand the ways of the Creator," and he says that what his reason dictates is worthless, but he is going above reason, this is called "lowliness," and it was about him that the verse, "The Lord is high and the low will see" was said. He is rewarded with the Creator bringing him near Him.

19. RABASH, Article No. 401 (1981), "Hear, O Israel"

He has room for two opposite qualities. On one hand, he is regarded as complete, which is the "right," *Hesed* [mercy], happy with his share. He can praise and thank the Creator for letting him into a place of Torah and good deeds. On the other hand, he can pray to the Creator for remaining outside of the work of the Creator because everything was built on the basis of self-love.

At that time, the person is called "complete," and otherwise he is not considered "man" because if he sees his deficiencies he will soon run from the quality of the "right," as well.

But once he has seen his bad state and yet reinforces himself above reason that he has wholeness, and the sign of this is that he can thank the Creator for this, then he is called "complete." This is "Right and left, and a bride between them." By having the quality of male and female, he can be rewarded with the quality of "bride," meaning the real kingdom of heaven.

This is the meaning of "Serve the Lord with gladness." He asks there in *The Zohar*: But he cannot be happy because his heart is broken due to his sins! We learn about this, "One always enters through two doors: mercy and fear."

We can explain this in the above manner. The "right hand side" door is faith above reason, when he is complete. This is private Providence, and it is "for he desires mercy." The other door is fear, meaning *Gevura*, "left." On this door we must give labor and prayer. This is called "man," since he has two discernments, male and female, complete and lacking, and then his work is considered whole.

20. RABASH, Article No. 12 (1989), "What Is a Groom's Meal?"

A person should accept faith above reason even though he has no feeling and no excitement about taking upon himself the burden of the kingdom of heaven. Nevertheless, he should agree with that state and say that this must be the will of the Creator that he will work and serve Him in this lowliness, so he does not mind what elation he feels about this faith because about himself, meaning his own benefit, he has no concern, but only about the benefit of the Creator. If He wants him to remain in that state, he accepts this unconditionally. This is called "unconditional surrender."

21. RABASH, Article No. 21 (1986), "Concerning Above Reason"

Can be obtained by adhesion of friends—new qualities by which they will be qualified to achieve *Dvekut* with the Creator. And all this can be said while he sees the merits of the friends. At that time, it is relevant to say that he should learn from their actions. But when he sees that he is better qualified than they are, there is nothing he can receive from the friends.

This is why they said that when the evil inclination comes and shows him the lowliness of the friends, he should go above reason. But certainly, it would be better and more successful if he could see within reason that the friends are at a higher degree than his own. With that we can understand the prayer that Rabbi Elimelech had written for us, *"Let our hearts see the virtues of our friends, and not their faults."*

22. RABASH, Article No. 7 (1991), "What Is 'Man' and What Is 'Beast' in the Work?"

When one feels that he is empty, meaning that he feels that he has neither Torah nor *Mitzvot* [commandments/good deeds] or any good deeds, what can he do? At that time, he should ask the Creator to shine for him so he can obtain the greatness and exaltedness of the Creator above reason. In other words, although he is still unworthy of feeling the greatness and exaltedness of the Creator, since he has still not been rewarded with the quality of "man," and the *Tzimtzum* and concealment of the Creator are still on him, as it is written, "Do not hide Your face from me," he still asks the Creator to give him the strength to receive greatness and importance of the Creator above reason.

It is as Baal HaSulam says about what our sages said (*Iruvin* 19), "Even the empty ones among you are filled with *Mitzvot* like a pomegranate." He said that *Rimon* [pomegranate] comes from the word *Romemut* [exaltedness], which is above reason. Hence, the meaning of "Even the empty ones among you are filled with *Mitzvot* like a pomegranate" is that the measure of the filling is according to his ability to go above reason, which is called "exaltedness."

In other words, emptiness can be precisely where there is no presence and he feels that he is devoid of Torah, *Mitzvot*, and good deeds. When this continues over time when a person wants to work for the sake of the Creator and not for himself, then he sees that everything he does is not for the sake of the Creator but only for his own benefit. In that state, he feels that he has nothing and he is completely empty, and he can fill this place only with a pomegranate, meaning if he goes above reason, which is called "exaltedness of the Creator." In other words, he should ask the Creator to give him the power to believe above reason in the greatness of the Creator. That is, the fact that he wants the exaltedness of the Creator does not mean that he says, "If You let me attain the exaltedness and greatness of the Creator, I will agree to work." Rather, he wants the Creator to give him the power to believe in the greatness of the Creator, and with this he fills the emptiness in which he is in right now.

It follows that were it not for the emptiness, that is, if he did not work on the path toward achieving *Dvekut*, meaning in equivalence of form, called "in order to bestow," but rather like the general public, who suffice for the practices they observe, these people do not feel themselves as empty, but as full of *Mitzvot*.

However, specifically those who want to achieve bestowal feel the emptiness within them and need the greatness of the Creator. They can fill this emptiness specifically with exaltedness, called "full of *Mitzvot*," to the extent that they ask the Creator to give them the power to be able to go above reason, which is called "exaltedness." In other words, they ask the Creator to give them power in exaltedness that is above reason in greatness and importance of the Creator. They do not want the Creator to let them attain this, since they want to subjugate themselves with unconditional surrender, but they ask for help from the Creator, and to that extent they can fill the empty place with *Mitzvot*. This is the meaning of "filled with *Mitzvot* like a pomegranate."

23. RABASH, Article No. 11 (1985), "Concerning the Debate between Jacob and Laban"

Only one who observes Torah and *Mitzvot* because "He is Great and ruling," meaning because of the greatness and importance of the Creator, this is called *Lishma* (see The Book of Zohar, Item 190). This is called "in order to bestow and not to receive any reward for his work," and it is called "pure work."

Work in order to bestow can only be to the extent that one values the receiver of one's work. At that time one has the motivation. But if one cannot increase the importance of the one he serves, he has no energy to work. This is so because we see that in nature, the little one annuls itself before the great one as a candle before a torch. However, all the great work is to extol the receiver of the work, meaning to recognize His importance. If he has nothing with which to revere Him within reason, then our work is as Baal HaSulam said when he interpreted the verse, "Here is a place with Me," that the *Aleph* of *ETY* [with Me] implies faith above reason.

It follows that the essence of man's work is to work above reason, to appreciate the Creator.

24. RABASH, Article No. 2 (1987), "The Importance of Recognition of Evil"

The work that is the preparation to enter true spirituality. That is, when he takes upon himself to believe in the importance of the Creator above reason, he must take upon himself that he wants to go specifically with faith above reason. Even though he was given the reason to see the greatness of the Creator within reason, he prefers faith above reason due to "because of the honor of the Creator, conceal the matter."

This is regarded as wanting to go above reason. Precisely then he becomes a *Kli* [vessel] that is fit to receive spirituality, since he has no concern at all for himself, but all his intentions are only to bestow upon the Creator. For this reason there is no longer fear that should he be given some illumination it will go into the vessels of reception, since he is always trying to exit self-love.

Baal HaSulam said that as the will to receive wants only to receive and not bestow, even where it is told to work above reason it is only regarded as bestowing and not receiving because a person suffers where he has to go above reason. The evidence of this is that since the body is always concerned with receiving delight and pleasure in everything it does, and since if a person must work above reason, the body is dissatisfied with it, therefore, when a person is taught to go above reason he begins the work of bestowal. It therefore follows that when one prefers to go by way of above reason it is safeguarding that he will walk on the right path, which is the route for achieving *Dvekut* with the Creator.

25. RABASH, Assorted Notes, Article No. 236, "The Whole Earth Is Full of His Glory"

Before one is fit to attain the truth, he must believe that the truth is not as he knows or feels, but that it is as it is written, "They have eyes and they will not see; they have ears and they will not hear." This is only because of the correction, in order for man to achieve his wholeness, for he feels only himself and not another reality.

Hence, if one returns his heart to trying to walk in faith above the intellect, by this he qualifies it and establishes it so as to achieve the revelation of the face, as is presented in *The Zohar*, that the *Shechina* [Divinity] said to Rabbi Shimon Bar Yochai, "There is no place to hide from you," meaning that in all the concealments that he felt, he believed that here was the light of the Creator. This qualified him until he achieved the revelation of the face of His light.

This is the meaning of the measure of the faith that pulls one out of every lowliness and concealment if a person strengthens himself in this and asks the Creator to reveal Himself.

This is the meaning of what Baal HaSulam said, "Run my Beloved until she pleases," meaning that before one is fit to reveal His light, we ask of Him, "Run my Beloved," meaning that He will not reveal Himself to the created beings because the concealment is only the correction of creation.

Hence, one must brace oneself and pray for those two:

1) To be worthy of the revelation of the light of the Creator.
2) That the Creator will give him the power to grow stronger in faith above reason, for by this, he merges *Kelim* [vessels] that are fit for the revelation of the face, as in "The Lord will light up His face for you and will give you peace," as it is written, "I will hear what God will speak, for He will speak peace unto His people and unto His followers and let them not turn back to folly."

26. RABASH, Article No. 21 (1986), "Concerning Above Reason"

Between friends, if he can see his friend's virtue within reason, it is all the better.

And yet, the nature of the body is to the contrary—it always sees his friend's fault and not his virtues. This is why our sages said, "Judge every person favorably." In other words, although within reason you see that your friend is wrong, you should still try to judge him favorably. And this can be above reason. That is, although logically he cannot justify him, above reason he can justify him nonetheless.

However, if he can justify him within reason, this is certainly better.

27. RABASH, Article No. 572, "Two Labors"

The order of one's work in *Torah and Mitzvot* [commandments] when he wants to work for the sake of the Creator is that one must fight and defeat the evil inclination.

That is, it is human nature to toil when there is self-benefit. But when he sees that no self-benefit will emerge from this work, he cannot work. Instead, he complains and asks, "What is this work for you?" meaning what will you gain from exerting?

When a person overcomes it and says that he wants to work against nature and bestow upon the Creator, the evil inclination comes with a different argument, asking the question of wicked Pharaoh, "Who is the Lord that I should obey His voice?" It is possible to work for the sake of others only where I know that the other receives the labor.

However, when he has two labors, 1) He must overcome and go against nature, and work not for his own benefit but for the benefit of others, for the sake of the Creator. 2) He must believe that the Creator receives his labor.

These two questions are the main ones in the argument of the wicked one. The rest of the questions that come to a person are merely offspring of the two above questions.

It is possible to overcome these questions only by the power of faith, which is above reason. One must reply to the wicked one that from the perspective of the intellect, it makes sense to ask what he is asking. But above the intellect, in faith, when he believes in the words of the sages, this is the only way that is for the sake of the Creator.

That is, when one gives all his energy and efforts for the sake of the Creator, this is his only purpose, and the world was created for this purpose, as our sages said, "The whole world was created only for this" (*Berachot* 6b), meaning for the fear of heaven.

Hence, when he answers the wicked that he is going above reason, which is against the intellect, the intellect can no longer ask any questions because all the questions are within reason, whereas above the intellect there is no place for questions.

Hence, when the wicked one asks the questions, he is told that now is the time when I can do my work in faith. In other words, by the very fact that you are asking a question and I reply to you that I am going with faith, and I am not giving you an intellectual answer, this is a sign for you to know that my work is with faith above reason.

It follows that now you have caused me to make a *Mitzva* [commandment] in that only now does it become revealed to all that the path of the Creator is only faith.

28. RABASH, Article No. 5, "The Meaning of Sins Becoming as Merits"

We can understand the meaning of sins becoming as merits, that if a person has a question, which is certainly a great iniquity because this question might cause him to fall into the Klipa [shell/peel] called "pondering the beginning." If he repents from fear, meaning strengthens himself and is not impressed by this thought, then they become to him as mistakes. That is, it is not a sin but a mistake. In other words, it would be better had no foreign thought come to him, but now that it came, he did not have a choice but to strengthen himself with acceptance of the burden of the kingdom of heaven.

Also, there is repentance from love, when he receives the burden of faith anew because of love, meaning he accepts the work with love. That is, he is happy that the Creator has given him this foreign thought by which he can observe this *Mitzva* [commandment].

This is similar to a flame that is tied to the wick. The foreign thought is considered the wick, which wants to install a flaw in his work. That is, the foreign thought makes him think that from the perspective of the mind and reason, he has nothing to do in His work. And when he gets the foreign thought, he says that he does not want to make any excuses, but everything that the reason says is correct except he is walking on the path of faith, which is above reason.

It follows that the flame of faith is tied to the wick of the foreign thought. Thus, only now can he observe the *Mitzva* of faith properly. It follows that the questions have become to him as merits, since otherwise he would not be able to accept any merits from faith.

This is called "rejoicing in suffering." Although he suffers from the foreign thoughts that afflict him and cause him to slander and gossip and speak badly about His work, he is nonetheless happy about it for only now, at such a time, he can observe in a manner of faith above reason. This is called "the joy of *Mitzva*."

29. RABASH, Article No. 12 (1991), "These Candles Are Sacred"

And the most important is the prayer. That is, one must pray to the Creator to help him go above reason, meaning that the work should be with gladness, as though he has already been rewarded with the reason of *Kedusha*, and what joy he would feel then. Likewise, he should ask the Creator to give him this power, so he can go above the reason of the body. In other words, although the body does not agree to this work in order to bestow, he asks the Creator to be able to work with gladness, as is suitable for one who serves a great King. He does not ask the Creator to show the greatness of the Creator, and then he will work gladly. Rather, he wants the Creator to give him joy in the work of above reason, that it will be as important to a person as if he already has reason.

30. RABASH, Article No. 12 (1987), "What Is Half a Shekel in the Work-1"

One should not pray that the foreign thoughts will die but that they will repent.

This is done specifically by receiving help from above in the form of faith above reason. It follows that he is not asking the Creator that the thoughts will die so he will not have to overcome the thoughts, but rather to settle for the faith he has in the Creator, that to the extent of the faith he has before the evil inclination came with its correct arguments, and which could not be answered without the help of the Creator, he receives the strength to go above reason.

But one who is not walking on the path of truth, whose work is based entirely on a foundation of mind and heart, asks the Creator to take these thoughts away from him so they will not disrupt his work. It follows that he remains in his degree and cannot advance, since he has no need to advance. Instead, he wants to remain in the current state permanently, this is all he expects, and he has no need for greatness.

Although he wants higher degrees than the rest of the people, meaning, if he is a wise disciple and knows that there are people who are not nearly at his level, and of course he wants to be at the top in the work, for this reason he wants to rise to a higher level than where he feels he is right now. However, this is all in excess; it is not necessity. One who prays for surplus, his prayer cannot be from the bottom of the heart because he knows that his situation is not so bad. He sees that there are people who are worse than he, and he needs it only as a surplus.

The rule is that "There is no light without a *Kli* [vessel]," and a *Kli* means a lack and a need that he must satisfy. Surplus, however, is not regarded as a lack in spirituality, and for this reason a person stays where he is and cannot move at all.

However, it is not so for one who wishes to walk on the path of truth, who wants to work in mind and heart. When the body comes to him and begins to attack him over why he wants to veer off from the common way, that everyone works in order to receive, and after each time he overcomes it, it comes to him with stronger arguments, in that state he does not ask the Creator to take away its arguments, but rather asks the Creator to repent on all those arguments that the wicked one is presenting, meaning that the Creator will give him the strength to go above reason.

31. RABASH, Article No. 120, "Joy that Comes from Dancing"

In corporeality, we see that raising the feet off the ground implies vitality, for *Raglayim* [legs] imply *Meraglim* [spies], who went to tour the land. They went to see if it was worthwhile to make an effort to be rewarded with the land of *Kedusha* [holiness]. Within reason, there are always views that are opposite from *Kedusha*, but we need to believe above reason that it is a land flowing with milk and honey.

Therefore, when lifting the feet off the ground and going above reason, there can be joy, even though there are ups and downs.

However, the broken is not more than the standing; rather, the ascents and descents change rapidly, so the periods of joy never go away.

32. RABASH, Article No. 38 (1990), "What Is, 'A Cup of Blessing Must Be Full,' in the Work?"

A person needs great mercy in order not to escape the campaign. Although he uses the counsels that our sages said, "I have created the evil inclination; I have created the Torah as a spice," but the person says that he has already used this advice several times to no avail.

He also says that he has already used the advice "He who comes to purify is aided," and it is as though all the counsels are not for him. Thus, he does not know what to do. This is the worst state for a person, meaning he wants to escape from these states but has nowhere to run. At that time he suffers torments at being between despair and confidence. But then a person says, "Where will I turn?"

At that time, the only advice is prayer. Yet, this prayer is also without any guarantee, so it follows that then he must pray to believe that the Creator does hear a prayer, and everything that one feels in these states is to his benefit. But this can be only above reason, meaning although the mind tells him, "After all the calculations, you see that nothing can help you," he should believe this, too, above reason, that the Creator can deliver him from the will to receive for himself, in return for which he will receive the desire to bestow.

33. RABASH, Article No. 31 (1986), "Concerning *Yenika* [Suckling] and *Ibur* [Impregnation]"

Ibur means that a person temporarily *Maavir* [shifts/removes] his selfness and says, "Now I do not want to think of my own benefit whatsoever, and I also do not want to use my intellect, although to me it is the most important thing. That is, since I cannot do something that I do not understand—meaning I can do anything but I must understand the benefit of it—he still says, "Now I can temporarily say that I am taking upon myself at this time that I determine not to use my intellect. Rather, I believe above reason, believe in faith in the sages, believing that there is an overseer who is watching each and every one in the world in Private Providence."

34. RABASH, Article No. 3, "Against Your Will-1"

"Against your will you are born; against your will you live; and against your will you die."

Birth is as the verse, "A proselyte who converted is as a newly born child." That is, each time we reacquire the quality of faith, it is considered a "new birth." And the reception of the quality of "mind" is above reason.

Since the body cannot do anything that is against reason, he must accept the quality of "mind" against its will, meaning the body disagrees. But if one's work is in a manner of reception and knowledge, the body will obey any order.

This is the meaning of "Against your will you are born," that birth in *Kedusha* [holiness] is only against one's will.

35. RABASH, Article No. 1 (1990), "What Does 'May We Be the Head and Not the Tail' Mean in the Work?"

When a person wants to understand the path of the sages, they tell us that we must follow them with our eyes shut, or dust will enter. Something unimportant is called "dust," meaning that there cannot be greater lowliness than this.

Since man was given the reason and intellect in order to understand everything according to the intellect, and here we are told to walk by accepting faith in the sages, and a person wants to understand this path, and since as long as one is placed under the governance of the will to receive for himself, he cannot know what is good and what is bad, but must accept everything the way the sages determined for us, or dust and dirt will enter his eyes and he will not be able to move forward, but when we do not criticize the words of the sages and do not want to accept their words within reason, specifically by this we are rewarded with knowledge [reason] of *Kedusha* [holiness].

36. RABASH, Article No. 224, "The Reason for the Faith"

The reason for the faith is that there is no greater pleasure than to be rewarded with the revelation of Godliness and the instilling of the *Shechina* [Divinity].

In order for one to receive all this for the purpose of bestowal, there is a correction of concealment, where he engages in *Torah and Mitzvot* [commandments] even though he feels no pleasure. This is called "not in order to receive reward." When he has this *Kli* [vessel], his eyes soon open to welcome the face of the Creator.

When a desire awakens within him, that it is worthwhile to serve the Creator for the pleasure, he soon falls into concealment. This is regarded as death, meaning that previously, he was adhered to life, and he was rewarded with it only through the power of faith. Therefore, now that he is corrected and begins to work in faith once more, he receives back his breath of life. At that time, he says, "I thank You for returning my soul with compassion."

This is precisely when he assumes once more the work in the manner of faith above reason. When he had the concealment, he says, "Great is Your faith." The faith is so great that through it, he receives the soul once more.

37. RABASH, Article No. 4 (1989), "What Is a Flood of Water in the Work?"

The middle line is a merger of the two lines. Since the right line of *Kedusha* is wholeness, with respect to above reason, and the left line means that he sees within reason that he is incomplete, but quite the contrary, he is full of deficiencies.

For this reason, the middle line consists of two lines. That is, it is impossible to go above reason before he has reason that shows him the situation, how it seems to him within reason. Then it can be said that he is not looking at what the mind obligates him to do. Rather, he goes above the intellect and believes in the sages, in what the sages tell him, and does not use his own mind.

But if he has no mind and reason to tell him something, it cannot be said that he is going above reason. This is why the middle line is called "peace," since he needs the two lines. That is, by having two opposite lines and needing both.

But why is it called "peace"? We should interpret that when he has two lines together, he must raise the right line over the left line, as it is written in *The Zohar*. It means that the line of wholeness is built on the above reason, on the left line, and by this we acquire the desire to love the Creator. This is the *Segula* [virtue/remedy/quality] of above reason.

It is as Baal HaSulam said, that the fact that the Creator wants us to serve Him above reason, the Creator chose this way since this is the most successful way for the created beings to be rewarded with *Dvekut*, and then they are rewarded with peace. It is as it is written (Psalms 85), "I will hear what the Lord God shall speak, for He shall speak peace unto His people and unto His followers, and let them not turn back to folly." It follows that the merging of two lines is called "peace," and this is the middle line in *Kedusha*.

38. RABASH, Article No. 794, "The Place of Attainment"

In *GAR* there is no attainment, and all our attainment is in *VAK*.
We should interpret that *GAR* means mind, where it should be only by faith. We must believe that this was His will. *VAK* means "heart," meaning an impression in the heart, and here, it is apparent in one's quality of love and fear. This should be with clear attainment, meaning that the impression should be revealed in him, and not by faith.

However, to the extent that the impression is felt in the heart, so is the measure of one's attainment. Here it is a commandment to expand his feelings. Conversely, in the mind, his greatness depends on the extent to which he can work in the manner of above reason.

It follows that they are two opposite things. If his mind is above reason, and the impression he feels in the heart is in the mind, this is called *Gadlut* [greatness/adulthood]. That is, on one hand, it is above attainment, yet it is felt in the heart. The measure of *Gadlut* depends on this, on the measure of oppositeness between mind and heart, for then one must overcome above reason, and the heart is precisely within reason, meaning in the feeling.

Only one who has the quality of "Israel" can walk on this path, but a foreigner cannot work in two opposites. This requires great strengthening so as to be able to march forward on this path.

39. RABASH, Article No. 7 (1990), "What Are the Times of Prayer and Gratitude in the Work?"

A person must believe above reason that he is in wholeness, and so is the whole world.

It follows that in this way he can and should thank the Creator for giving us abundance. This is called the "right line," which is the complete opposite of the left line. That is, in the left line, we walk within reason, as was said, that "A judge has only what his eyes see." In other words, it is specifically with the intellect and not above the intellect. But when shifting to work with the "right," the left is the cause that the right is built on the basis of above reason.

This is as our sages said, "The left pushes away and the right pulls near." In other words, the state of "left" shows a person how he is rejected and separated from the work of the Creator. "The right pulls near" means that it shows him that he is close to the work of the Creator. This means that when he engages in the left, the left should bring him to see a state of rejection, that he is rejected and separated from the work. When he engages in the right, he should come to a state where he sees that he is close to the Creator. He should thank the Creator for the "right," and pray to the Creator for the "left," for only on two legs can a person walk in corporeality. This extends from spirituality, which shows that a person should walk on two lines.

40. RABASH, Article No. 6, (1989), "What Is Above Reason in the Work?"

The work, "faith above reason" means we must believe although the mind does not see that this is so, and it has several proofs that it is not as he wants to believe. This is called "faith above reason," meaning he says that he believes as though he sees it within reason. This is called "faith above reason" in the work.

In other words, it is a lot of work for a person to take this upon himself; it is against reason. This means that the body does not agree to this, yet he accepts it nonetheless as though it were within reason. Such faith requires help from the Creator. For this reason, for such faith, a person needs to pray that He will give him the power to be similar to Him as though he had attained it within reason.

In other words, a person should not pray to the Creator to help him understand everything within reason. Instead, he should pray to the Creator to give him the strength to assume faith above reason as though it were within reason.

41. RABASH, Article No. 6 (1989), "What Is Above Reason in the Work?"

In the work, "faith above reason" means we must believe although the mind does not see that this is so, and it has several proofs that it is not as he wants to believe. This is called "faith above reason," meaning he says that he believes as though he sees it within reason. This is called "faith above reason" in the work.

In other words, it is a lot of work for a person to take this upon himself; it is against reason. This means that the body does not agree to this, yet he accepts it nonetheless as though it were within reason. Such faith requires help from the Creator. For this reason, for such faith, a person needs to pray that He will give him the power to be similar to Him as though he had attained it within reason.

In other words, a person should not pray to the Creator to help him understand everything within reason. Instead, he should pray to the Creator to give him the strength to assume faith above reason as though it were within reason.

42. RABASH, Article No. 24 (1991), "What Does It Mean that One Should Bear a Son and a Daughter, in the Work?"

The work above reason should be unconditional surrender. That is, one should take upon himself the burden of the kingdom of heaven above reason. A person should say, "I want to be a servant of the Creator even though I have no idea about the work and I feel no flavor in the work. Nevertheless,

I am willing to work with all my might as though I have attainment and feeling and flavor in the work, and I am willing to work unconditionally." At that time, a person can go forward, and then there is no place for him to fall from his state, since he takes upon himself to work even when he is placed right in the earth, since it is impossible to be lower than the earth.

43. RABASH, Article No. 875, "Three Lines-4"

That sees his true state—that he has no grip on spirituality.
In other words, from the perspective of the intellect, he is in complete darkness, and now comes the time to go above reason and say "They have eyes but they will not see; they have ears but they will not hear." However, he is delighted that he has been rewarded with observing the *Mitzvot* of the Creator, who commanded us through Moses. Although he does not feel any flavor or understanding about it, above reason, he still believes that it is a great privilege that he can observe the commandments of the Creator in a simple manner, while others do not even have this. He believes that everything comes from above, and others were given only the enjoyment from nonsense that is suitable for beasts and animals, while he was given a thought and desire to see that their whole lives are nonsense and vanity.

Therefore, he regards this present as a great fortune and he is always elated because of this importance. It is as important to him as though he was awarded the highest degrees. At that time, it is called "right line," "wholeness," since precisely by being happy, one has *Dvekut* with the Creator, as our sages said, "The *Shechina* is present only out of joy." Since now he is in a state of wholeness, he has a reason for gladness.

44. RABASH, Article No. 24 (1991), "What Does It Mean that One Should Bear a Son and a Daughter, in the Work?"

That one yearns for knowledge, meaning he does not want to work above reason, but specifically within reason, meaning that he says that if the body understands the benefits of working and observing the *Mitzvot* [commandments/good deeds] of the King, he is willing to labor and work. But to believe above reason, to this the body does not agree. Instead, he stands and waits for the body to understand it, but otherwise, he cannot do the holy work. Sometimes, he does overcome these thoughts and desires, and this causes him the ascents and descents.

Yet, if one decides that he wants to work as "dust," meaning even if he tastes the taste of dust in the work, he says that it is very important for him to be able to do something for the sake of the Creator, and for himself, he does not care which taste he feels, and says that this work, in which one tastes the taste of dust, meaning that the body mocks this work, he says to the body that in his view, this work is regarded as "raising the *Shechina* [Divinity] from the dust."

In other words, although the body tastes dust in this work, the person says that it is *Kedusha* and does not measure how much flavor he feels in the work. Rather, he believes that the Creator does enjoy this work, since there is no mixture of the will to receive here, since he has nothing to receive because there are no flavor or scent in this work, as there is only the taste of dust here. For this reason, he believes that this is the holy work, and he is delighted.

45. RABASH, Article No. 875, "Three Lines-4"

He says that whatever he has, whatever he is given from above, even if he feels that he is in a worse state than what he received by education, he still regards it above reason as having great importance to him that he has been rewarded with having some contact with spirituality.

When he works on this, on settling for little and being happy with this share, and he wants to honor *Torah and Mitzvot* as if he felt the flavor as true knowing and feeling, when the body, too, agrees to this work, which is called "even his enemies make peace with him," but when he must work above reason, the body resists this work, this is called "true work." In other words, he sees his true state, yet overcomes it as though he had knowledge. This is called "right line."

All this is because he wants to glorify the Torah above reason. Although it seems as though he builds it on a structure of reason, when he says that many people have no connection to *Torah and Mitzvot*, so it makes sense that he already has something to be happy about because he has a possession that others do not have, this is true, but to say that this is something important and worth being happy about, he must have the quality of above reason. This is called "a joy of *Mitzva* [commandment]," meaning it is built on a basis of faith, and then he can sing and dance, and it is all true because it is above reason.

46. RABASH, Article No. 36 (1986), "What Is Preparation for Selichot [Forgiveness]"

One must believe that as there are corporeal pleasures, such as pleasures of eating, drinking, and respect, where each thing tastes differently, we must also believe that there is a special taste in each *Mitzva*. Accordingly, if he tasted the change of flavors during his engagement in Torah and *Mitzvot*, what excitement and vitality he would feel during his work? Reason would compel him to create for himself an image in the work that is suitable for a servant of the Creator. He would look at all the things that want to disrupt him from his work as inconsequential, unworthy of his attention.

According to the above-mentioned depiction, which he depicts to himself within reason, he should make the same depiction above reason. That is, although he does not feel that there will be something that reason supports, he still works precisely as if he has strong reason and feeling. When he does this, it is regarded as working above reason.

However, as long as he feels that if he had reason he would be serving the Creator more willingly and more consistently, then he is still working within reason, since there is still a difference between reason and above reason. Precisely when it makes no difference to him, it is regarded as "above reason."

47. RABASH, Article No. 3 (1985), "The Meaning of Truth and Faith"

He must believe above reason that the grip he has on the path of truth is great and very important, and he cannot even appreciate the importance of touching the path of truth for this is the entire *Kli* in which the Light of the Creator will be. However, this is in the *Kelim* of the upper one. That is, the Creator knows when a person should feel his *Dvekut* with the Creator.

In his own *Kelim* he feels the opposite—that now he is worse than when he walked on the path of the general public, where he felt that each day he was adding good deeds and Torah and *Mitzvot*. But now, since he has started walking on the path of the individual, to always keep the intention how much he can work in order to bestow and how much he can relinquish self-love, at that time he usually sees how much he is nearing the truth. At that time, he always sees more of the truth, that he is unable to exit self-love.

Still, in the *Kelim* of the upper one, meaning above reason, he can raise himself and say, "I don't care how I am bestowing upon the Creator. I want the Creator to bring me closer to Him, and the Creator certainly knows when the time will come when I feel that the Creator has brought me closer to Him. In the meantime, I believe that the Creator knows what is best for me, and this is why He makes me feel the feelings that I am feeling.

48. RABASH, Article No. 6 (1991), "What Is, 'The Herdsmen of Abram's Cattle and the Herdsmen of Lot's Cattle,' in the Work?"

Specifically through faith above reason, meaning even if he feels darkness on this path, and even though he understands that if *Malchut* had illuminated openly and not in concealment, and the body would feel the greatness of the Creator, it would be easier for him to move further and be rewarded with always being in a state of work and he would have no descents, he nonetheless chooses to go above reason. This is called "the herdsmen of Abram's cattle." This is called "west," meaning that even though it does not shine for him, he is still with all his might, as though everything illuminated for him openly.

49. RABASH, Article No. 36 (1989), "What Is 'For It Is Your Wisdom and Understanding in the Eyes of the Nations,' in the Work?"

He should tell the nations of the world within him, "Know that everything you say is true. Reasonably speaking, you are correct, and I have nothing to reply to you. However, we were given the work above reason—that we must believe above reason that you are incorrect. And since the work on faith must be above reason, I thank you very much for your correct arguments that you have brought me, since it cannot be said that a person goes above reason unless he has reason and intellect. Then, it can be said that he is going above the intellect.

But when there is no reason, it cannot be said that he is going above reason. That is, "above reason" means that this path is more important than the path within reason. However, when there is no other way to tell him, "Walk in this path!" it cannot be said that he chooses the path of faith above reason. For this reason, precisely through the power of faith above reason is it possible to defeat the views of the nations of the world within man.

50. RABASH, Article No. 914, "Two Opposites"

There are two opposites in above reason—in mind and in heart, which is regarded as "for he desires mercy." If foreign thoughts come to a person, he should remove them from him and not listen to them at all.

This is a hard work because Pharaoh king of Egypt afflicts them and throws foreign thoughts at them in mind and in heart, as it is written, "And the children of Israel sighed from the work, and their cry went up to God." This is one side by which they are rewarded with faith, meaning the exodus from Egypt, and this is regarded as a soul of *Kedusha* [holiness].

On the other hand, "a soul without knowledge is not good, too," and we need the knowledge of *Kedusha*, which is called "wealth," for there is no wealth except in *Daat* [reason/knowledge]. When the Creator wanted to enrich them, they did not have *Kelim* [vessels] because everything was for them above reason, so the Creator gave them the advice to borrow *Kelim* from the Egyptians.

The taking of the *Kelim* was only so they would be able to receive a filling for the *Kelim*, meaning answers to their questions. But once they took the answers, they immediately returned the *Kelim* to the Egyptians. Because they are going above reason, they have no questions and they took the questions of the Egyptians only temporarily and then returned them.

51. RABASH, Article No. 23 (1991), "What Is the Meaning of the Purification of a Cow's Ashes, in the Work?"

In faith, we should make three discernments:

1) For example, if a person gives to his friend $1,000, and the person accepts it, and he is completely sure and believes, since this man is my friend, and a meticulous person, so if he gives the money, there must be $1,000 there, and there is no need to count. This is called "faith below reason." In other words, he believes him because his reason does not object to what he believes, meaning there is no contradiction between believing him and the reason. It follows that to him, faith is below reason, and the reason is more important. That is, he believes him because reason does not object. However, if this is in contrast to reason, he will probably not believe. This is still not regarded as faith above reason.

2) He tells him, "Here is $1,000." The receiver counts it three times and sees that there is the stated amount there and says to the giver, "I believe you that there is that amount here, as you say." Certainly, this does not count as faith.

3) He counts the $1,000 three times and sees that one dollar is missing, but he says to the giver, "I believe you that there is $1,000 here. Even though the reason and the intellect say that there is less here, he says that he believes. This is called true "above reason."

52. RABASH, Article No. 13 (1988), "What Is 'the People's Shepherd Is the Whole People' in the Work?"

In that state, when he sees a dark world, and he wants to believe above reason that the Creator behaves with the world in Private Providence as good and doing good, he remains standing on this point, and all kinds of foreign thoughts come into his mind. Then, he must overcome above reason, that Providence is good and does good. At that time he receives a need for the Creator to give him the power of faith that he will have the strength to go above reason and justify Providence.

Then he can understand the meaning of "*Shechina* [Divinity] in the dust," since then he sees that where he should do something for the Creator and not for his own sake, the body promptly asks, "What is this work for you?" and does not want to give him strength to work. This is called "*Shechina* in the dust," meaning that what he wants to do for the sake of the *Shechina* tastes to him like dust and he is powerless to overcome his thoughts and desires.

At that time a person realizes that all he lacks in order to have strength to work is that the Creator will give him the power of faith, as said above (in the prayer of Rabbi Elimelech), that we must pray, "And do fix Your Faith in our hearts forever and ever." In that state, he comes to the realization that "If the Creator does not help him, he cannot overcome it."

53. RABASH, Article No. 16 (1989), "What Is the Prohibition to Bless on an Empty Table, in the Work?"

A person should establish the praise of the Creator, and then pray. Clearly, while he establishes the praises, he says that the Creator is good and does good to the bad and to the good, and that He is merciful and gracious. At that time, it cannot be said that a person is deficient, meaning that he lacks something whether in spirituality or in corporeality. Otherwise, it means that he is merely saying but his heart is not with him. That is, in his heart, he thinks differently from what he says with his mouth. For this reason, it is impossible to sing and thank the Creator and say His virtues, but a person says about himself that he has abundance and that he lacks nothing. Thus, how can one say so when he finds himself bare and destitute?

Baal HaSulam said about this that a person should depict to himself as though he has already been rewarded with complete faith in the Creator and already feels that the Creator leads the world in a manner of good and doing good. Although when he looks at himself and the world and sees that he and the whole world are deficient, each according to his degree, he should say about this, "They have eyes and see not," meaning above reason. In this way, he can say that he is a complete person and lacks nothing. Naturally, he can establish the praise of the Creator above reason.

54. RABASH, Article No. 31 (1987), "What Is Making a Covenant in the Work?"

As long as one has not been awarded permanent faith, there must be ascents and descents. It follows that there could be a time when the love between them cools. For this reason, now, in the beginning of his work, he takes upon himself the burden of the kingdom of heaven, to make a covenant, so that whether or not the body agrees to be a servant of the Creator, he takes upon himself not to change a thing. Instead, he will say, "I spoke once and I will not change." Instead, I will go above reason as I have taken upon myself when making the covenant in the beginning of the work.

55. RABASH, Article No. 3 (1987), "All of Israel Have a Part in the Next World"

Concerning Abraham and Avimelech, "And the two of them made a covenant." Baal HaSulam asked, "If two people understand that it is worthwhile for them to love each other, why should they make a covenant? How does an act of seemingly signing a contract help? What does it give us?" Then he said, "It gives us that when we make a covenant we mean that since it is possible that something might separate them, they are making a covenant now, so that just as now they understand that there is love and equivalence between them, this covenant will persist even if afterwards things will come that should separate them. Still, the connection they are establishing now will be permanent. Accordingly, we should say that if afterwards things will come that should separate them, we should say that each one should go above reason and say that they will not notice what they see within reason, but go above reason. Only in this way can the covenant hold and there will be no separation between them.

56. RABASH, Article No. 30 (1988), "What to Look for in the Assembly of Friends"

The friends should primarily speak together about the greatness of the Creator, because according to the greatness of the Creator that one assumes, to that extent he naturally annuls himself before the Creator. It is as we see in nature that the small one annuls before the great one, and this has nothing to do with spirituality. Rather, this conduct applies even among secular people.

In other words, the Creator made nature this way. Thus, the friends' discussions of the greatness of the Creator awaken a desire and yearning to annul before the Creator because he begins to feel longing and desire to bond with the Creator. And we should also remember that to the extent that the friends can appreciate the importance and greatness of the Creator, we should still go above reason, meaning that the Creator is higher than any greatness of the Creator that one can imagine.

We should say that we believe above reason that He leads the world in a benevolent guidance, and if one believes that the Creator wants only man's best, it makes a person love the Creator until he is rewarded with "And you will love the Lord your God with all your heart and with all your soul." And this is what a person must receive from the friends.

57. RABASH, Article No. 4 (1989), "What Is a Flood of Water in the Work?"

There is the matter of above reason. This is regarded as wanting to walk with his eyes shut, meaning that although reason and the senses do not understand what our sages tell us, they assume upon them faith in the sages and say that we must take upon ourselves faith in the sages, as it is written, "And they believed in the Lord and in His servant, Moses." Without faith, nothing can be achieved in spirituality.

58. RABASH, Article No. 17, Part 1, (1984), "Concerning the Importance of Friends"

How can one consider one's friend greater than himself when he can see that his own merits are greater than his friend's, that he is more talented and has better natural qualities? There are two ways to understand this:

1. He is going with faith above reason: once he has chosen him as a friend, he appreciates him above reason.
2. This is more natural—within reason. If he has decided to accept the other as a friend, and works on himself to love him, then it is natural with love to see only good things. And even

though there are bad things in one's friend, he cannot see them, as it is written, "love covers all transgressions."

59. RABASH, Article No. 23 (1990), "What Does It Mean that Moses Was Perplexed about the Birth of the Moon, in the Work?"

We must believe in the sages, who tell us that all our work, however we work, if the person attributes the work to the Creator, even if it is in utter lowliness, the Creator enjoys it. The person should be happy that he can do things while in a state of lowliness.

The person should tell himself that He enjoys this work, which is entirely above reason. Reasonably thinking, this work is not considered "work," meaning an important act that the Creator enjoys. Yet, he believes in the sages, who told us that the Creator does enjoy, but this is above reason.

60. RABASH, Article No. 136, "The Binding of Isaac"

The binding of Isaac, when Abraham, who is the right line, which is above reason, tied the left line, which is the mind that criticizes everything, it gave him a general picture of the situation he was in. He left all the "left" and took upon himself the quality of "right," which is above reason. By this he was later rewarded with the middle line.

That is, there is a difference between receiving the right line before he sees the left line, to a state where he renews the right line after he has seen the state of the left. "Right," which is above reason, is called "devotion," since he cancels all the reason he acquired from the left line and goes above reason, and then he is rewarded with the middle line.

61. RABASH, Article No. 25 (1987), "What Is Heaviness of the Head in the Work?"

A prayer should be with heaviness of the head, meaning when a person feels that he does not have faith above reason, meaning that the reason does not mandate him to work in order to bestow, yet the person understands the primary goal should be to be rewarded with *Dvekut* [adhesion] with the Creator. Since the reason objects to this, he must go against reason, and this is very hard work.

Since he is asking the Creator to give him something to which all of his organs object, it follows that each and every prayer he makes to the Creator has its special work. This is why a prayer is called "work in the heart," meaning that he wants to go against the intellect and the mind, which tell him the complete opposite.

This is why it is not called "the work of the brain," since the work of the brain means that a person exerts to understand something with his mind and reason. But here he does not want to understand with his reason that we should serve the Creator in a state of knowing. Rather, he wants to serve the Creator specifically with faith above reason. This is why a prayer is called "work in the heart."

62. RABASH, Article No. 68, "The Order of the Work"

In the beginning, one must believe above reason that the Creator wanted to do good to His creations. For this reason, He created His creations and installed in them the desire and yearning to receive pleasure. The reason is that this is the only *Kli* [vessel] to receive pleasure, since man enjoys only that for which he yearns. He can receive something to which he does not yearn, but he cannot enjoy it because the *Kli* for enjoyment is called "coveting," "yearning," etc.

However, this should be above reason, since when he looks within reason, he does not find His Providence over the world as benevolent. On the contrary, this is why it is said that we must believe above reason that this is so.

But in truth, if His guidance is only in a manner of good and doing good, why is this not felt within reason? We learned that it is because of the correction of the bread of shame. Therefore, as long as the created beings have no vessels of bestowal, they cannot see light and remain in the dark.

When one believes in the delight and pleasure that exists in above reason, he comes to consciously feel, to know the evil within him. That is, he believes that the Creator imparts such delight and pleasure, and although he sees all the good above reason, he achieves recognition. That is, he feels in all the organs the power of the evil that is found in receiving for oneself, which prevents him from receiving the abundance.

It follows that faith above reason causes him to feel his enemy within reason—who obstructs him from reaching the good. This is his standard. That is, to the extent that he believes in the delight and pleasure above reason, to that extent he can come to feel the recognition of evil.

Later, sensing the bad yields the sensation of delight and pleasure, since the recognition of evil in the sensation of the organs causes him to correct the bad.

This is done primarily through prayer, when he asks the Creator to give everything in bestowal, called *Dvekut* [adhesion]. Through these *Kelim* [vessels], the goal will be revealed in open Providence, meaning that there will be no need for the concealment because there will already be *Kelim* that are able to receive.

63. RABASH, Article No. 23 (1989), "What Is, 'If He Swallows the Bitter Herb, He Will Not Come Out,' in the Work?"

When one begins the work, he begins with faith, but the body resists this work, and then comes a state of labor, when he must overcome the body and seek all kinds of counsels, as our sages said, "In trickery shall you conduct war," since the body does not want to relinquish self-benefit. To the extent that he exerts, to that extent he begins to feel that he is incapable of doing anything since in his view, he has done everything he could. After the labor, he comes to know that only the Creator can help, and it is out of his hands. Then comes the third state—a prayer—and then the prayer is from the bottom of the heart, since it is utterly clear to him that no one can help him but the Creator.

However, even when he comes to know that the Creator can help him, and he understands that the real advice is only prayer, the body comes and makes him see that "You see how many prayers you have already prayed but you received no answer from above. Therefore, why bother praying that the Creator will help you? You see that you are not getting any help from above." At that time, he cannot pray. Then we need to overcome once more through faith, and believe that the Creator does hear the prayer of every mouth, and it does not matter if the person is adept and has good qualities, or to the contrary. Rather, he must overcome and believe above reason, although his reason dictates that since he has prayed many times but still received no answer from above, how can he come and pray once more? This, too, requires overcoming, meaning to exert above reason and pray that the Creator will help him overcome his view and pray.

64. RABASH, Article No. 21, "Sanctification of the Month"

A person must take upon himself the burden of the kingdom of heaven on the lowest quality, and say about it that to him, even that state, the lowest that can be, meaning one that is entirely above reason, when he has no support from the mind or the feeling, so he can build its foundations on it, and at that time, he is seemingly standing between heaven and earth and has no support, for then everything is above reason, then a person says that the Creator sent him this state, where he is in utter lowliness, since the Creator wants him to take upon himself the burden of the kingdom of heaven in this manner of lowliness.

At that time, because he believes above reason, he takes upon himself that the situation he is in now comes to him from the Creator, meaning that the Creator wants him to see the lowest possible state that can be in the world.

And yet, he must say that he believes in the Creator in all manners. This is considered that he has made an unconditional surrender. That is, a person does not say to the Creator, "If You give me a good feeling, to feel that 'The whole earth is full of His glory,' I will be willing to believe." Rather, when he has no knowledge or sensation of spirituality, he cannot accept the burden of the kingdom of heaven and observe the *Torah and Mitzvot* [commandments]. Rather, he must accept the kingdom of heaven unconditionally.

65. RABASH, Article No. 10 (1985), "Jacob Went Out"

We should also interpret regarding the above-mentioned verse, that the exit of a righteous from the place leaves an impression refers to a person, for when the righteous is in town, it means that a person can justify Providence. Then, when he overcomes the state he is in and says, "There is no doubt that the Creator, who is good and does good, is behaving benevolently with me. However, He wants me to feel as I do." It follows that he is justifying Providence. At that time he immediately sees the importance of the work of bestowal and above reason. This is called, "When the righteous is in town, he is its splendor, he is its brilliance, he is its majesty," for then he (sees) all the virtues.

"When he departs from there" means that he has departed from justifying Providence and wants to see everything within reason. At that time he feels no taste in the work in order to bestow. And then, "its splendor departs, its brilliance departs, and its majesty departs," and he falls once more into self-love. In other words, at that time he knows nothing but work that is built on a basis of within reason.

This is regarded as the "exit of the righteous from the place leaves an impression." It means that only then, through the exit of the righteous, when he thinks, "Now that I feel good taste in the work, I no longer need to work above reason," it causes him the exit of the righteous from the place. This creates in him an impression, so he will know how to keep himself from exiting the work of above reason from here on. As I heard from Baal HaSulam, when a person says, "Now that he has support and no longer stands between heaven and earth," he must fall from his degree because then he flaws the discernment of above reason.

It therefore follows that precisely the departure of the degree he had leaves an impression on him so he will know how to be careful next time and will not blemish the faith above reason, but always justify Providence.

66. RABASH, Article No. 3 (1985), "The Meaning of Truth and Faith"

We were given the path of faith, which is above reason, namely not to take our sensations and reason into account, but say, as it is written, "They have eyes and see not. They have ears and hear not." Rather, we should believe that the Creator is certainly the Overseer, and He knows what is good for me and what is not good for me. Therefore, He wants me to feel my state as I do, and for myself, I do not care how I feel myself because I want to work in order to bestow.

Therefore, the main thing is that I need to work for the Creator. And although I feel that there is no wholeness in my work, still, in the *Kelim* of the upper one, meaning from the perspective of the upper one, I am utterly complete, as it is written, "The cast out will not be cast out from Him." Hence, I am satisfied with my work—that I have the privilege of serving the King even at the lowest degree. That, too, I regard as a great privilege that the Creator has allowed me to come closer to Him at least to some degree.

67. RABASH, Article No. 638 (1965), "Man's Inclination"

"Man's inclination overcomes him every day, and unless the Creator helps him, he cannot overcome it." We should ask about this: It is known that everything is in the hands of heaven but the fear of heaven, so why did they say, "unless," etc.?

The thing is that faith is called above reason, meaning above nature, since everything that is within reason is called "within nature and reason," for that which a person understands, he can do, unless he is lazy. But above reason, he cannot do this. Therefore, anything that is above nature is regarded as a miracle.

All the miracles are attributed to the Creator, meaning regarded as an awakening from above and not as an awakening from below, since the lower one cannot do something that is above nature. But in order for a miracle to be done to him, a person should pray that a miracle be done to him.

Hence, the work from the perspective of the lower one, meaning that he will make a choice, was said only about the prayer, and then the Creator hears the prayer. Therefore, one is given one's wishes, and the rule is that a prayer pertains specifically to a deficiency.

For this reason, a person must create within him a need and a deficiency for faith, for only when one sees and feels that he is lacking faith, and to the extent that he needs it, since he sees that for himself he cannot receive the above-mentioned, then he makes a true prayer that the Creator will help him, and then the Creator makes a miracle for him and gives him the light of faith.

However, one must be careful not to enjoy this light, as our sages said, "One does not enjoy the work of miracles." This means that acceptance of faith should be only for the purpose of bestowal and not for the purpose of reception, for then there is room for the spirit of *Kedusha* [holiness] to be on him.

If he wants the above-mentioned light in order to have pleasure, since he feels that the corporeal pleasures are not eternal, so he wants an eternal pleasure, and this is why he asks for faith—he immediately loses the light of *Kedusha*.

Instead, one must ask because the *Shechina* [Divinity] is in exile, meaning that he wants to sanctify the name of heaven in him, and not to have foreign thoughts, since he cannot tolerate the slander that the body says about *Kedusha*, as it is written, "All day long, my enemies curse me." At that time, the Creator makes a miracle for him and gives him faith above reason, and he is rewarded with permanent faith.

68. RABASH, Article No. 24 (1991), "What Does It Mean that One Should Bear a Son and a Daughter, in the Work?"

When a person prevails and asks for help from the Creator, after he has decided that he has a harm-doer in his heart, called "will to receive," and that he cannot emerge from it, meaning after going through several ascents and descents, he finally sees that he has remained bare and destitute. At that time, his prayer is from the bottom of the heart. That is, he sees that if the Creator does not help him, he cannot overcome it.

Although one can say that he believes above reason that only the Creator helps him, within reason, he does not feel this, since he knows that he himself made the efforts and the labor to obtain something in spirituality. But when one sees that after all the exertions, he cannot emerge from the governance of the will to receive for himself, then he sees within reason that only the Creator can help him.

It follows that what our sages said, "Man's inclination overcomes him every day, and were it not for the help of the Creator, he would not be able to overcome it," he does not need to believe in this above reason, the way ordinary workers of the Creator who observe *Torah and Mitzvot* believe "above reason" that this is so, that the Creator helps them. Rather, those people who want to work in order to bestow, for them, it is within reason, to the point that they must believe above reason that the Creator can help them emerge from the governance of the will to receive.

69. RABASH, Article No. 71, "The Meaning of Exile"

"When Israel are in exile, the *Shechina* [Divinity] is with them." This means that if one falls into a descent, spirituality is also descended in him. But according to the rule, "a *Mitzva* [commandment] induces a *Mitzva*," why does he come into a descent? Answer: He is given a descent from above so as to feel that he is in exile and ask for mercy, to be delivered from exile. This is called "redemption," and there cannot be redemption if there is no exile there, first.

What is exile? It is that he is under the rule of self-love and cannot work for the sake of the Creator. When is self-love considered exile? It is only when he wants to emerge from this control because he suffers from not being able to do anything for the sake of the Creator.

It follows that when he began to work, there had to be some pleasure and reward for which the body agreed to this work. Afterward, when he was permitted to see that there is the matter of "for the sake of the Creator," because a *Mitzva* induces a *Mitzva*, and he had to ask to be delivered from exile, then he runs from the exile.

How does he run from the exile? It is by saying that he will not succeed in this work. Thus, what does he do? He commits suicide, meaning leaves the work and returns to corporeal life, which is regarded as "The wicked in their lives are called 'dead.'"

It follows that where he should have asked for redemption from exile, he runs from the exile and commits suicide. This is as it is written, "The ways of the Lord are straight; the righteous will walk in them, and transgressors will fail in them." However, he should go above reason.

A descent in spirituality does not mean that now he has no faith. Rather, now he must do more work, and the previous faith is considered a descent compared to this work.

70. RABASH, Article No. 438, "Save Your Servant, You, My God"

First, one must believe in the Creator above reason and praise his rav, meaning feel completely and utterly whole, for it is known that to the extent that a person feels that his friend is giving him gifts, to that extent he praises him. Also, to the extent that he feels his friend's greatness, to that extent he can praise. In other words, if he feels that he is lacking something and his friend can satisfy it, he immediately loses the power to praise and glorify his friend.

Therefore, when a person begins his work, he must go with faith above reason that he is not lacking anything, and that his rav has satisfied all his wishes. At that time, he is called "whole," and then the whole can connect to the whole. Conversely, when he is deficient, the deficient does not connect to the whole.

Afterward, he can establish deficiencies like a slave seeking a gift from his rav, when he asks for his needs, meaning that the judge has only what his eyes see and he must not ignore any deficiency that he has. On the contrary, to the extent that he feels his deficiency, so he can pray that his rav will satisfy his wishes. And then, the more the student asks, the better.

Finally, he must not stay deficient. He must go again on the path of faith above reason, that he is utterly and completely whole. This is the meaning of the words, "as a servant thanking his rav for the gift he has received from him, and he walks away." He should believe above reason that he has already received all his wishes, called a "gift."

He thanks his rav for this, for one must not live in separation, meaning that he has complaints against his rav that he is not giving him what he asks. For this reason, it is forbidden for man to be deficient and he must always be in joy. However, in order to have *Kelim* [vessels] to receive, he must evoke the deficiencies.

In the offering, this is regarded as ascending and descending, "Knowing in the beginning and knowing in the end, and concealment in between." That is, between knowing and knowing it is permitted to see the concealment, meaning that he has no revelation with respect to the truth, to feel that his work is desirable to his rav.

It follows that one must not disclose any lack in Torah and work for himself. Rather, he must always go above rhyme and reason that he is utterly and completely whole. In between, he can ask his wishes as his eyes see, that he has only faults. But afterward, he must believe as though he has already received all his wishes and he thanks his rav for this.

At that time, he can be happy that he is whole. It follows that all his wholeness is built on faith, and his deficiencies are built on knowledge, since "the judge has only what his eyes see."

71. RABASH, Article No. 28 (1987), "What Is 'Do Not Add and Do Not Take Away' in the Work?"

He must believe above reason and imagine that he has already been rewarded with faith in the Creator that is felt in his organs, and he sees and feels that the Creator leads the entire world as the good who does good. Although when he looks within reason he sees the opposite, he should still work above reason and it should appear to him as though he can already feel in his organs that so it really is, that the Creator leads the world as the good who does good.

Here he acquires the importance of the goal, and from here he derives life, meaning joy at being near to the Creator. Then a person can say that the Creator is good and does good, and feel that he has the strength to tell the Creator, "You have chosen us from among all nations, You have loved us and wanted us," since he has a reason to thank the Creator. And to the extent that he feels the importance of spirituality, so he establishes the praise of the Creator.

Once man has come to feel the importance of spirituality, which is called "One should always establish the praise of the Creator," then is the time when he must shift to the left line. He must criticize how he truly feels within reason the importance of the King, if he is truly willing to work only for the sake of the Creator.

When he sees within reason that he is bare and destitute, that state when he sees the importance of spirituality, but only above reason, that calculation can create in him deficiency and pain for being in utter lowliness. Then he can make a heartfelt prayer for what he lacks.

2

From Not for Her Sake to For Her Sake

1. Baal HaSulam, "Introduction to The Study of the Ten Sefirot," Item 11

We find and see in the words of the sages of the Talmud that they have made the path of Torah easier for us than the sages of the Mishnah. This is because they said, "One should always practice the Torah and *Mitzvot*, even *Lo Lishma*, and from *Lo Lishma* he will come to *Lishma*, since the light in it reforms him."

Thus, they have provided us with a new means instead of the penance presented in the above-mentioned Mishnah, *Avot*: the "light in the Torah." It bears sufficient power to reform one and bring him to practice Torah and *Mitzvot Lishma*.

They did not mention penance here, but only that engagement in Torah and *Mitzvot* alone provides one with that light that reforms, so one may engage in Torah and *Mitzvot* in order to bring contentment to his Maker and not at all for his own pleasure. And this is called *Lishma*.

2. Baal HaSulam, *Shamati*, Article No. 20, "Lishma [for Her sake]"

Do not be surprised that when one assumes the burden of the kingdom of heaven, when he wants to work in order to bestow upon the Creator, he still feels no vitality at all, and that this vitality would compel one to assume the burden of the kingdom of heaven. Rather, one should accept it coercively, against his better judgment. That is, the body does not agree to this enslavement, why the Creator does not shower him with vitality and pleasure.

The reason is that this is a great correction. Were it not for this, if the will to receive had agreed to this work, one would never have been able to achieve *Lishma*. Rather, he would always work for his own benefit, to satisfy his own desires. It is as people say, that the thief himself yells, "Catch the thief!" and then you cannot tell which is the real thief in order to catch him and reclaim the theft from him.

But when the thief, meaning the will to receive, does not find the work of accepting the burden of the kingdom of heaven tasteful, since the body accustoms itself to work against its will, one has the means by which to come to work only in order to bring contentment to his Maker, since his sole intention should be only for the Creator, as it is written, "Then shall you delight yourself in the Lord." Thus, when he served the Creator in the past, he did not sense any pleasure in the work. Rather his work was compulsory.

But now that he has accustomed himself to work in order to bestow, he is rewarded with delighting in the Creator, and the work itself renders him pleasure and vitality. This is considered that the pleasure, too, is specifically for the Creator.

3. Baal HaSulam, *Shamati*, Article No. 20, "Lishma [for Her sake]"

In order for a person to obtain *Lishma*, one needs an awakening from above, as it is an illumination from above and it is not for the human mind to understand. Rather, he who tastes, knows. It is said about this, "Taste and see that the Lord is good."

Because of this, upon assuming the burden of the kingdom of heaven, one needs it to be in utter completeness, meaning only to bestow and not at all to receive. If a person sees that the organs do not agree with this view, he has no other choice but prayer—to pour out his heart to the Creator to help him make his body consent to enslaving itself to the Creator.

Do not say that if *Lishma* [for Her sake] is a gift from above, what good is one's overcoming and efforts, and all the remedies and corrections that he does in order to achieve *Lishma*, if it depends on the Creator? Our sages said about it, "You are not free to rid yourself of it." Rather, one must give the awakening from below, and this is considered "prayer." Yet, there cannot be a real prayer if he does not know first that without prayer it cannot be obtained.

Therefore, the acts and remedies he does in order to obtain *Lishma* create the corrected *Kelim* [vessels] in him that want to receive the *Lishma*. Then, after all the actions and the remedies he can pray in earnest since he saw that all his actions did not help him whatsoever. Only then can he make an honest prayer from the bottom of his heart, and then the Creator hears his prayer and gives him the gift of *Lishma*.

4. Baal HaSulam, "Introduction to The Study of the Ten Sefirot," Item 12

Practicing Torah and *Mitzvot Lo Lishma* means that one believes in the Creator, in the Torah, and in reward and punishment, and engages in the Torah because the Creator commanded the engagement, but associates his own pleasure with bringing contentment to his Maker.

5. Baal HaSulam, *Shamati*, Article No. 79, "*Atzilut* and *BYA*"

Atzilut is considered from the *Chazeh* and above, which is only vessels of bestowal. *BYA* means reception in order to bestow, the ascent of the lower *Hey* to the place of *Bina*.

Because man is immersed in the will to receive in order to receive, he cannot do a thing without having reception for oneself there. This is why our sages said, "From *Lo Lishma* [not for Her sake], we come to *Lishma* [for Her sake]." This means that we begin the engagement in Torah and *Mitzvot* [commandments] in order to "Give us the wealth of this world," and afterward, "Give us the wealth of the next world."

When learning in this way, one should come to learn *Lishma*, for the sake of the Torah, meaning that the Torah will teach him the ways of the Creator. And then he should first make the sweetening of *Malchut* in *Bina*, which means that he elevates *Malchut*, called "will to receive," to *Bina*, which is considered bestowal. That is, that all his work will be only in order to bestow.

And then it becomes dark for him. He feels that the world has grown dark on him since the body gives strength to work only in the form of reception, and not in the form of bestowal. In that state, he has but one choice: to pray to the Creator to open his eyes so he can work in the manner of bestowal.

This is the meaning of "Who stands for the question?" It refers to *Bina*, called *Mi* [water] and the question comes from the verse, "asking about the rains," meaning prayer. Since they arrive to the state of "water of *Bina*," there is room to pray for it.

6. Baal HaSulam, "One Commandment"

It is hopeless to wait for a time when a solution is found that enables one to begin the work of the Creator in *Lishma*. As in the past, so is now, and so will it be: Every servant of the Creator must begin the work in *Lo Lishma*, and from that achieve *Lishma*.

The way to achieve this degree is not limited by time, but by his qualifiers, and by the measure of one's control over one's heart. Hence, many have fallen and will fall in the field of working *Lo Lishma*, and will die without wisdom. Yet, their reward is nevertheless great, since one's mind cannot appreciate the true merit and value of bringing contentment to one's Maker. Even if one works not under this condition, since one is not worthy of another way, one still brings contentment to one's Maker. This is called "unintentionally."

7. Baal HaSulam, *Shamati*, Article No. 5, "Lishma Is an Awakening from Above, and Why Do We Need an Awakening from Below?"

In order to attain *Lishma* [for Her sake], it is not within one's hands to understand, as it is not for the human mind to grasp how such a thing can be in the world. This is so because one is only permitted to grasp that if he engages in Torah and *Mitzvot* [commandments] he will attain something. There must be self-benefit there for otherwise, one is unable to do anything. Rather, it is an illumination that comes from above, and only one who tastes it can know and understand. It is written about it, "Taste and see that the Lord is good."

Thus, we must understand why one should seek advice and counsels regarding how to achieve *Lishma*. After all, no counsels will help him, and if the Creator does not give him the second nature, called "the desire to bestow," no labor will help him to attain the matter of *Lishma*.

The answer is, as our sages said (*Avot*, Chapter 2, 21), "It is not for you to complete the work, and you are not free to idle away from it." This means that one must give the awakening from below, since this is regarded as a prayer.

A prayer is considered a deficiency, and without a deficiency there is no filling. Hence, when one has a need for *Lishma*, the filling comes from above, and the answer to the prayer comes from above, meaning he receives fulfillment for his lack. It follows, that the need for man's work in order to receive the *Lishma* from the Creator is only in the form of a lack and a *Kli* [vessel]. Yet, one can never obtain the filling by himself; it is rather a gift from the Creator.

However, the prayer must be a complete prayer, from the bottom of the heart. This means that one knows one hundred percent that there is no one in the world who can help him but the Creator Himself.

Yet, how does one know this, that no one will help him but the Creator Himself? One can acquire that awareness precisely if he has exerted all the powers at his disposal and it did not help him. Thus, one must do every possible thing in the world to attain "for the sake of the Creator." Then one can pray from the bottom of the heart, and then the Creator hears his prayer.

However, one must know, when exerting to attain the *Lishma*, to take upon himself to want to work entirely to bestow, completely, meaning only to bestow and not to receive anything. Only then does one begin to see that the organs do not agree to this view.

From this one can come to clear awareness that he has no other choice but to pour out his heart to the Creator to help him so the body will agree to enslave itself to the Creator unconditionally, as he sees that he cannot persuade his body to annul itself completely. It turns out that precisely when one sees that there is no hope that his body will agree to work for the Creator by itself, one's prayer can be from the bottom of the heart, and then his prayer is accepted.

We must know that by attaining *Lishma*, one puts the evil inclination to death. The evil inclination is the will to receive, and acquiring the desire to bestow cancels the will to receive from being able to do anything. This is considered putting it to death. Since it has been removed from its office, and it has nothing more to do since it is no longer in use, when it is revoked from its function, this is considered putting it to death.

8. Baal HaSulam, *Shamati*, Article No. 28, "I Shall Not Die but Live"

In the verse, "I shall not die but live," in order for one to achieve the truth, there must be a sensation that if one does not obtain the truth, he feels himself as dead, since he wants to live. This means that the verse, "I shall not die but live" is said about one who wants to obtain the truth.

This is the meaning of "Jonah *Ben* [the son of] Amitai." Jonah comes from the [Hebrew] word *Honaa* [fraud], and *Ben* [son] comes from the word *Mevin* [understands]. One understands because one always examines the situation he is in and sees that he has deceived himself, and he is not walking on the path of truth.

Truth means to bestow, meaning *Lishma* [for Her sake], and the opposite of this is fraud and deceit, meaning only to receive, which is *Lo Lishma* [not for Her sake]. By this, one is later imparted the "Amitai," meaning *Emet* [truth].

9. RABASH, Article No. 12 (1988), "What Are Torah and Work in the Way of the Creator?"

Feeling the vitality in the Torah requires great preparation to prepare his body to be able to feel the life in the Torah. This is why our sages said we must begin in *Lo Lishma*, and through the light of Torah he obtains while still in *Lo Lishma*, it will bring him to *Lishma*, since the light in it reforms him. Then, he will be able to learn *Lishma*, meaning for the sake of the Torah, which is called "Torah [law] of life," as he has already attained the life in the Torah, for the light in the Torah will have given such qualification to a person as to be able to feel the life that is in the Torah.

10. RABASH, Article No. 12 (1988), "What Are Torah and Work in the Way of the Creator?"

Our sages said, that the Creator said to Israel, 'I have sold you My Torah. It is as though I have been sold with it.' This is the meaning of having a merchandise that one who sells it is sold with it."

This means that the Creator wants that when a person takes the Torah, he will seemingly take the Creator with him. Yet, a person does not feel he needs this. Primarily, a person takes after the majority. And since when beginning to teach women, children, and the general public, Maimonides says we should begin in *Lo Lishma*, and normally, everyone takes after the beginning, meaning that the reason they were given for why we need the Torah are reasons of *Lo Lishma*, and not because "I have created the evil inclination; I have created the Torah as a spice." Naturally, the majority of the world does not even understand that there is a reward called "*Dvekut* with the Creator."

For this reason, the view of the majority controls a person—that he does not need to study Torah so that by this he will be able to achieve the real intention. That is, that through the Torah he will be able to aim in order to bestow and not for his own benefit, that it will bring him *Dvekut*, to adhere to the Creator.

11. RABASH, Article No. 17 (1989), "What Is the Prohibition to Greet Before Blessing the Creator, in the Work?"

A person must walk on the right line, regarded as wholeness, and pray to the Creator and thank Him, even if he does not find within him anything that desires spirituality. But accordingly, how can he thank the Creator and say that the Creator hears what he says to Him, which is the meaning of attributing the work to the Creator, and He accepts his work regardless of how the work seems?

However, if he relates only to the Creator and says, "I am turning to the Creator and I believe that He can answer my wishes," by this a person becomes happy and feels superior. That is, the rest of the people have no connection to spirituality, and he believes that the Creator has given him [a feeling] that he has no spirituality, in whatever way, but the fact that he has an interest in thinking about spirituality, it makes no difference if he has or hasn't, or that he is now in utter lowliness, meaning that he sees that now he has no desire to ascend in degree and emerge from the lowliness, but he thanks the Creator because at least he is thinking about spirituality, while the rest of the people do not have any thoughts of spirituality.

If he can thank the Creator, it gives him joy, and from *Lo Lishma* [not for Her sake] he comes to *Lishma* [for Her sake].

12. RABASH, Article No. 223, "Entry into the Work"

The entry into the work must be in *Lo Lishma* [not for Her sake], meaning that by believing in the Creator he will have a life of pleasure. This means that if he does this action called "faith," it will give him elation and superior mental forces than when he does not perform this action.

It follows that this is a *Segula* [remedy/quality/power] by which he can taste greater flavors in quantity and quality than what he tastes while he is doing other things in order to receive pleasure.

This means that there are many ways to obtain pleasure, such as eating, drinking, and sleeping, or impressive clothes, or by doing things that make people respect him. Such actions are means by which he obtains pleasure.

Yet, the pleasures that these actions yield for him are limited in quantity and quality. Conversely, the *Segula* of faith brings him greater pleasure in quantity and quality.

All this is called *Lo Lishma* because his intention is only to obtain a greater pleasure.

Only after he achieves this degree called *Lo Lishma*, he is rewarded with other phenomena, when he comes to a higher state. That is, at that time he has no consideration of himself, and all his calculations and thoughts are the truth.

In other words, his aim is only to annul himself before the true reality, where he feels that he must only serve the King because he feels the exaltedness and greatness and importance of the King. At that time, he forgets, meaning he has no need to worry about himself, as his own self is annulled as a candle before a torch before the existence of the Creator that he feels. Then he is in a state of *Lishma* [for Her sake], meaning contentment to the Creator, and his concerns and yearnings are only about how he can delight the Creator, while his own existence, meaning the will to receive, does not merit a name whatsoever. Then he is regarded as "bestowing in order to bestow."

13. RABASH, Article No. 4 (1990), "What It Means that the Generations of the Righteous are Good Deeds, in the Work"

How can a person emerge from the tendencies that he is used to since birth? Intellectually, it is impossible to understand how it is possible that a person will think other than his inclinations. And there (in the introduction, Item 3) he says, "Because of this, we were given corrections, by which man must toil and labor. Otherwise, all creations would have been in a state of rest, since the root of the creatures, which is the Creator, is in a state of complete rest, and every branch wants to resemble its root."

These corrections, called "envy," "lust," and "honor," bring man out of the world (*Avot*, Chapter 4:28). He says there that through the envy and respect, it is possible to change the inclinations to lust into the degree of vegetative, where he begins to work for the sake of others for the purpose of *Lo Lishma* [not for Her sake]. Likewise, through envy, he can shift to the level of knowledge, as our sages said, "Authors' envy increases knowledge." And likewise, through *Lo Lishma* they can also shift from the animate level to the speaking.

Yet, how does the *Lo Lishma* help if one does not have the real inclination to the degree to which he enters? Our sages said about this, with respect to the Torah, "The light in it reforms him." It turns out that through *Lo Lishma*, we come to *Lishma* [for Her sake]. This is why they said, "One should always learn *Lo Lishma*, as from *Lo Lishma* we come to *Lishma*."

14. RABASH, Article No. 3 (1990), "What It Means that the World Was Created for the Torah"

The order of the work is that since we were born after the sin of the tree of knowledge, we are already immersed in the will to receive for our own sake, on which there were the *Tzimtzum* and concealment. For this reason, the order of our work begins in work *Lo Lishma* [not for Her sake]. That is, when we begin to observe Torah and *Mitzvot*, we must believe even if *Lo Lishma*, since without faith, even if *Lo Lishma*, we cannot work.

Wherever the work is on the basis of faith, it is hard work. That is, only where the reward and punishment are revealed, the work is called "within reason" because we immediately see the results.

But when the reward and punishment are covered and we must only believe in reward and punishment, even *Lo Lishma* is a great effort. However, this is still not so bad because it is not against the nature of the will to receive for oneself. But if we want to achieve *Dvekut*, called "in order to bestow," the body begins to resist with all its might, and it is impossible to emerge from the control of the will to receive without help from above.

It was said about this, "Were it not for the help of the Creator, he would not overcome it." The advice for this is Torah, since "the light in it reforms him."

15. RABASH, Article No. 23 (1987), "Peace After a Dispute Is More Important than Having No Disputes At All"

We should know that the degree of *Lo Lishma* is a very important degree, and we haven't the intellect to appreciate the importance of Torah and *Mitzvot Lo Lishma*. Baal HaSulam said that "as much as one may appreciate the work *Lishma*, which is important work, he should know that *Lo Lishma* is more important than the importance that a person attributes to *Lishma*, since one cannot properly assess the importance of observing Torah and *Mitzvot* even *Lo Lishma*, although observing Torah and *Mitzvot* should be *Lishma*.

16. RABASH, Article No. 269, "One Does Not Toil Over a Meal and Misses It"

Since one can only work *Lo Lishma* [not for Her sake], since his nature is the will to receive for himself, if one dedicates much time and effort over the intention *Lo Lishma*, in the end he will wonder what will he get out of all the work that he had done throughout his life. If the intention is not *Lishma* [for Her sake], then it will all go to waste, since *Lo Lishma* is a lie, and a lie can exist only in this world. Conversely, in the world of truth there is no room for lies.

It follows that all the efforts he has given throughout his life for Torah and work, who will take it, since there is no room for this in the world of truth, and there is a rule that one does not toil over a meal and misses it.

According to the above, it follows that he will lose at once all the efforts he had made in this world, for the moment one must go to the world of truth, he leaves all his toil in this world. It follows that this calculation causes him to repent in order to correct all his work so it is *Lishma*, since he does not want his work in this world to be in vain.

Therefore, the advice is that if a person sees that he still cannot work *Lishma*, he should increase his actions in *Lo Lishma*, since when he sees that he has done many actions in *Lo Lishma*, he will have no other choice but to repent and work *Lishma*, or his entire work will be in vain.

The rule is that a person does not toil over a meal and misses it. Hence, if one has done many actions in *Lo Lishma*, he will not want to lose all his trouble, so he will need to correct all his work so it enters the *Kedusha*.

But one who works *Lo Lishma* and did not do many works, meaning he did not dedicate much time to the Torah and work in *Lo Lishma*, he will not have such a need to repent, since he will not have that many actions to lose. For this reason, we must try to do many good deeds even in *Lo Lishma* because this is the reason he will have a need to repent and work *Lishma*.

17. RABASH, Article No. 587, "The Upper One Scrutinizes for the Purpose of the Lower One"

The upper one scrutinizes the GE for the purpose of the lower one (because "a prisoner does not free himself"). The upper one makes a *Masach* [screen] on the MAN of the lower one, meaning the rejecting force, until it is in the form of receiving in order to bestow, and only then is the light gripped in the MAN.

That is, MAN is a desire to receive. This is expressed through prayer, where prayer is regarded as raising MAN, and the answering of the prayer is called MAD, *Ohr Yashar* [direct light], upper abundance, bestowal. This prayer called MAN requires conditions, meaning that there will be the correction of a *Masach* in the prayer, namely that his intention will be for the sake of the Creator, called *Lishma* [for Her sake].

One must receive the power to work *Lishma* from the upper one, since the lower one is powerless to begin the work, but only in the form of *Lo Lishma* [not for Her sake], called "will to receive," for only the *Lo Lishma* gives the first moving force of the lower one, for when a person does not find sufficient flavor in corporeal pleasures, he begins to search for spiritual pleasures.

It follows that the root of the work of the lower one is the will to receive, and the prayer, called MAN, rises up, and then the upper one corrects this MAN and places on it the power of the *Masach*, which is a desire to delay the abundance before the lower one knows about himself that his aim is to bestow.

That is, the upper one bestows upon the lower one good taste and pleasure in the desire to bestow, by which the lower one feels His exaltedness. At that time, he begins to understand that it is worthwhile to annul before Him and cancel his existence before Him. Then, he feels that all that there is in reality is only because such is His will, that the Creator wants the lower one to exist, but for himself, he wants to annul his existence. It follows that then, all the vitality he feels is regarded as *Lishma* and not for himself.

When he feels this, it is considered that he already has the correction of the MAN, and then he is also fit to receive the MAD, as well, for there is no contradiction between them anymore, since the lower one, too, wants the benefit of the upper one and not his own benefit.

It is considered that when the upper one gives the lower one *Mochin*, he also gives him the clothing of the *Mochin*, meaning that he gives the lower one the abundance, as well as the power of the *Masach*, which is the desire to bestow. This is the meaning of "from *Lo Lishma*, we come to *Lishma*."

18. RABASH, Article No. 218, "Israel Are the Sons of Kings"

Wherever one retires from enjoying and causes unification, you find in it *Kedusha* [holiness], since the upper light can be there because the *Kelim* [vessels] can receive the light of the Creator called *Kedusha*, for the *Kedusha* is present only in a place of purity. "Purity" means purity of qualities, and then the *Kedusha* is present in a place of purity.

However, sometimes, "I the Lord, who dwells with them in the midst of their *Tuma'a* [impurity]," meaning that even when they still do not have *Kelim* that are ready to be in equivalence, in order to assist a person in achieving this, he must be aided from above. This is the meaning of *Lo Lishma*, that the light in it reforms him. That light is called "The Lord, who dwells with them in the midst of their *Tuma'a*."

This pertains specifically to one who wants to achieve *Lishma* but cannot overcome his body. Hence, he is given that light so he can defeat the will to receive and walk in the way of the Creator, which is bestowal.

19. RABASH, Letter No. 16

It is known that it is impossible to see a small object and it is easier to see a large object. Hence, when a person commits few lies, he cannot see the truth—that he is walking on a false path. Rather, he says that he is walking on the path of truth. But there is no greater lie than that. And the reason is that he does not have enough lies to see his true state.

But when a person has acquired many lies, the lies grow in him to the extent that he can see them if he wishes. Thus, now that he sees the lies—that he is walking on a false path—he sees his true state. In other words, he sees the truth in his soul and how to turn to the right path.

It follows that this point, which is a point of truth—that he is treading a false path—is the medium between truth and falsehood. This is the bridge that connects truth and falsehood. This point is also the end of the lie, and from here on begins the path of truth.

Thus, we can see that to be rewarded with *Lishma* (for Her Name), we first need to prepare the biggest *Lo Lishma* (not for Her Name), and then we can achieve *Lishma*. And similarly, *Lo Lishma* is called a "lie" and *Lishma* is called "truth."

When the lie is small and the *Mitzvot* and good deeds are few, he has a small *Lo Lishma*, and then he cannot see the truth. Hence, in that state, he says that he is walking on the good and true path, meaning working *Lishma*.

But when he engages in Torah all day and all night in *Lo Lishma*, then he can see the truth, since by the accumulation of lies, his lie increases and he sees that he is indeed walking on a false path.

And then he begins to correct his actions. In other words, he feels that everything he does is only *Lo Lishma*. From this point, one passes to the path of truth, to *Lishma*. Only here, at this point, does the issue of "from *Lo Lishma* one comes to *Lishma*" begins. But prior to that, he argues that he is working *Lishma*, and how can he change his state and his ways?

Hence, if a person is idle in the work, he cannot see the truth, that he is immersed in falsehood. But by increasing Torah in order to bestow contentment upon his Maker, one can then see the truth: that he is walking on a false path, called *Lo Lishma*. And this is the middle point between truth and falsehood. Hence, we must be strong and confident on our way, so every day will be as new to us, as we need to always renew our foundations, and then we shall march forward.

20. RABASH, Article No. 279, "Why Israel Are Compared to an Olive Tree"

"Rabbi Yochanan said, 'Why are Israel compared to an olive tree? It is to tell you that as the olive oozes its oil only by grinding, so Israel are reformed only by suffering'" (*Minchot* 53b).

Concerning the suffering that reforms a person, first one must know the meaning of being reformed. It is known that "The inclination of a man's heart is evil from his youth." This means that by nature, man cares only for his own sake. Naturally, it is impossible that he will be able to observe *Torah and Mitzvot* [commandments] for the sake of the Creator and not for his own sake.

However, through suffering, when he does not feel a good taste in corporeal things, meaning when they do not give him satisfaction in his life, since man was created with the aim to do good to His creations, he does not receive sufficient pleasure that will make it worthwhile to live in the world and tolerate everything in order to obtain the little pleasure that corporeality gives him.

To the extent that one feels torments in his life, when he has nothing from which to receive vitality, he is necessarily cancelled into working in the manner of bestowal. In other words, when he sees that he will not obtain vitality through acts of reception, he begins to perform acts of bestowal so that the acts of bestowal will give him pleasure.

It follows that the suffering reforms him, meaning the suffering he feels when he has nothing from which to derive pleasure makes him become reformed, meaning perform acts of bestowal, since "being reformed" means bestowal, as it is written, "My heart overflows with a good thing, I say, 'My work is for the King,'" meaning to bestow.

It follows that through the suffering he suffers from having no vitality, he chooses for himself a new way and begins to engage in bestowal.

Although this, too, is with the aim to receive, it is called *Lo Lishma* [not for Her sake] that is close to *Lishma* [for Her sake]. This is the meaning of "From *Lo Lishma* we come to *Lishma*," since "the light in it reforms him." Since he acts in order to bestow, by this he begins to feel light in the acts of bestowal, and that light can then make him bestow.

21. RABASH, Article No. 15 (1989), "What Is, 'The Righteous Become Apparent through the Wicked,' in the Work?"

It is known that there is the practice of *Mitzvot* [commandments/good deeds], and the intention of *Mitzvot*, meaning what one wants for one's work when exerting in Torah and *Mitzvot*. We learned that there are two manners of reward in this: 1) *Lo Lishma* [not for Her sake], 2) *Lishma* [for Her sake].

Lo Lishma means that one should be rewarded for his work both in this world and in the next world. As *The Zohar* says, this work is not considered the essence, as *The Zohar* says ("Introduction of The Book of Zohar," Item 190): "Fear that is *Lo Lishma* is not the main fear." (In Item 191) It says, "The main fear is that one should fear one's Master because He is great and ruling, and all is regarded as nothing before Him, and he should place his will in that place, which is called 'fear.'"

From this it follows that there are two kinds of intentions while performing actions, both in learning Torah and in performing *Mitzvot*. The work of the general public is in order to receive reward, and the work of individuals is for the sake of the Creator, and their reward is if they can serve the King. That is, their whole pleasure, which gives them fuel so they can work in order to bestow, is to feel that they are bringing contentment to the King and are praising and thanking the King for giving them the thought and desire to work for Him and not to receive any other reward for their work.

They say that in order to receive reward, "We do not need to feel the greatness of the King. Rather, we need to consider the greatness and importance of the reward we will receive if we observe the Torah and *Mitzvot*." But the Creator can stay for them at the same level of greatness and importance as He was for them at the beginning of their work.

However, if their intention is to bring contentment to the Creator, then if they want to increase the work, they must increase the greatness of the Creator, since to the extent of His greatness, to that extent they can annul before Him and do everything they do only for the sake of the Creator. It is as *The Zohar* says about the verse, "Her husband is known at the gates," each according to "what he assumes in his heart."

Therefore, in order to have fuel to work, those who want to work for the sake of the Creator must try each day to exert to obtain faith in the greatness of the Creator, since the greatness of the Creator is what compels them to work for Him, and this is all the pleasure they derive from their work.

22. RABASH, Article No. 27 (1985), "Repentance"

Our sages said, "One should always engage in Torah and *Mitzvot*, even if *Lo Lishma* [not for Her sake], since from *Lo Lishma* he comes to *Lishma* [for Her sake]" (*Pesachim*, 50b). Thus, in the act of *Mitzvot* and in the study of Torah there is a big difference between the revealed part, meaning the act, and the concealed part, meaning the intention, since no person can look at the intention, for the act that one does between man and God does not have a person in the middle who can criticize his intention. Normally, each one is busy with himself and does not have time to think of his friend's calculations. It follows that only he thinks of the intention.

That is, when he engages in *Lo Lishma*, meaning expects reward, the work and the reward are not in the same place and in the same time. But here, when we are speaking of punishments, the transgression and the punishment are not in the same place and in the same time, since he receives the punishment after he commits the transgression, and afterwards he suffers the punishment—a punishment in this world or a punishment in the next world. This applies only to the part of *Lo Lishma*.

However, in those who work on the intention—to be able to aim their actions only to bestow—the reward and the punishment are in the same place and the same time, since his inability to aim the act of bestowing contentment upon the Creator is his punishment, and he does not need to be given any other punishments, for nothing torments him more than seeing that he is still far from the Creator.

The evidence is that he does not have the love of the Creator, that he wants to respect Him. All this is because he is in a state of *Achoraim* [posterior] and concealment from the Creator. This is what pains him, and this is his punishment. But here is his reward—if he has love for the Creator and wants to bestow contentment upon him. However, all this concerns specifically those who want come to work only for the Creator, and not in *Lo Lishma*. It can be said about them that the punishment and the reward are in the same place and in the same time.

23. RABASH, Article No. 31 (1987), "What Is Making a Covenant in the Work?"

The work in Torah and *Mitzvot* [commandments] is primarily when beginning to walk on the path that leads to *Lishma* [for Her sake]. That is, when a person begins the work, he begins in *Lo Lishma* [not for Her sake], as our sages said, "One should always engage in Torah *Lo Lishma*, and from *Lo Lishma* we come to *Lishma*."

For this reason, the beginning of his work was with enthusiasm because he saw that by observing Torah and *Mitzvot* he would achieve happiness in life. Otherwise, he would not begin. Therefore, in the beginning of his work, when he is still working *Lo Lishma*, meaning that when he works, he constantly looks at the reward he will receive after his work, he has the strength to work.

As in corporeality, a person is used to working in a place where he knows he will be rewarded for his work. Otherwise, a person cannot work for free, if not for his own benefit. Only when he sees that self-benefit will come from this work does he have the strength to work enthusiastically and willingly, since he is looking at the reward and not at the work.

The work does not matter if a person understands that here he will receive from this employer twice as much as he would receive from working for the previous employer, before he came to the job where they pay twice as much. This means that according to the salary, so the work becomes easier and smaller.

Accordingly, we should interpret in the work that making a covenant means that when a person takes upon himself the work, even if in *Lo Lishma*, he must make a covenant with the Creator to serve Him whether he wants to or not.

Yet, we should understand on what the enthusiasm depends. It depends only on the reward. That is, when there is a big reward, the desire for the work does not stop. But when the reward is doubtful, the desire for the work vanishes and he shifts to rest. That is, at that time he feels more pleasantness in rest.

It is so much so that he says, "I relinquish the work, and anyone who wants can do this work because it is not for me." But making a covenant is when he begins to work even in *Lo Lishma*. And since now he wants the work, for who would force him to come into the work of the Creator, now he must make the covenant and say, "Even if there comes a time of descent," meaning that he will have no desire for the work, "I still take upon myself not to consider my desire but work as though I have a desire." This is called "making a covenant."

24. RABASH, Article No. 14 (1985), "I Am the First and I Am the Last"

When a person wants to walk on the way to the goal of *Dvekut* with the Creator, which means to aim that everything will be in order to bestow, he must first have a deficiency, meaning dissatisfaction with the work in *Lo Lishma*.

At that time he begins to search for another order in the work, since the engagement in Torah and *Mitzvot* [commandments] he was used to was on the basis of the will to receive, called *Lo Lishma*. But now that he needs to replace his entire basis on which he built his entire life's order, it depends on the extent to which he sees that the state of *Lo Lishma* is the wrong way, does not let him rest, and he will not be at peace until he comes out of that state into a state of *Lishma*.

However, who is making him feel, while he is in the state of *Lo Lishma*, that this is still not the right way and he is still far from *Dvekut* with the Creator? When he looks at the rest of the people, they go by this path, so why does he need to be different? Another difficulty is that when he looks at the rest of the people he sees people who are more talented and more capable in the work than him. But they settle for the order of the work they had received when they were little, when the instructors taught them to work only in *Lo Lishma*, as in the above words of Maimonides. And then he sees about himself that although "a sorrow shared is a sorrow halved," he cannot accept the state of *Lo Lishma*. At that time comes the question: "If I am really less talented and less capable in the work, where did I get this restlessness in the state of *Lo Lishma*?"

To this comes the answer: "I am the first." That is, the Creator has given him this deficiency so he will not be able to continue on this path. One should not think that he has obtained this by his own wisdom. Rather, the Creator says, "I am the first," meaning "I have given you the first push, so you will begin to walk on the path of truth. By giving you a deficiency of feeling that with the respect to the truth, you are deficient."

Then begins the work that he begins to wait for a state where he repels self-love, and all his works are only in order to bestow. At that time he must dedicate to it all the thoughts and resources at his disposal, as in "Everything that you find within your power to do, that do."

Afterwards, when he is rewarded with *Dvekut* with the Creator, he thinks that it is through his labor in Torah and *Mitzvot*, and by overcoming his self-love. He thinks that he has been rewarded with it only through his work, that he was very persistent, and only he had the strength to make the most of his opportunities, which gave him this riches and he was rewarded what he was rewarded.

The verse says about that: "And I am the last. That is, as I was the first, giving you the deficiency, I am also the last, meaning I have given you the filling of the deficiency." The deficiency is called the *Kli* [vessel], and the filling is called "the light." Since there is no light without a *Kli*, the *Kli* is made first, and then the abundance is poured into the *Kli*. This is why the Creator first gives the *Kli*, which is called "I am the first," and then He gave the abundance, called "I am the last."

25. Maimonides, *Mishneh Torah*

"Our sages said: 'One should always engage in Torah, even if *Lo Lishma* [not for Her sake], since from *Lo Lishma* he comes to *Lishma* [for Her sake].' Therefore, when teaching the young, the women, and the uneducated, they are taught to work only out of fear and to receive reward. Until they accumulate knowledge and gain wisdom, they are told that secret bit by bit, and are accustomed to that matter with ease until they attain Him and know Him and serve Him out of love."

3

Two Opposites in the Same Carrier

1. Baal HaSulam, Letter No. 51

The whole difficulty in serving Him is that in the worshipper, there are always two opposites in the same carrier, that His uniqueness is simple, but must clothe in man's body, which consists of a body and a soul, which are two opposites.

Therefore, in any spiritual concept that one attains, two opposite forms are immediately created in him—one form on the part of the body, and one form on the part of the soul. By nature, a person cannot scrutinize the body and the soul as two carriers. Rather, he is composed by the Creator as one, meaning as one carrier. For this reason, spiritual attainment is as difficult for him as two opposites that cannot properly clothe in one carrier.

It is similar to the binding of Isaac, when the Creator said to Abraham, "For in Isaac shall a seed be called to you," and the Creator said to him, "And offer him there for a burnt-offering." From the perspective of the Creator, it is as was written, "I the Lord do not change." But in the perception of the receiver, they are opposites.

2. Baal HaSulam, *Shamati*, Article No. 34, "The Advantage of a Land"

It is known that nothing appears in its true form, only through its opposite, "As the advantage of the light from within the darkness." This means that everything points to another, and by the opposite of something, the existence of its opposite can be perceived.

Hence, it is impossible to attain something in complete clarity if its parallel is absent. For example, it is impossible to estimate and say that something is good, if its opposite, pointing to the bad, is missing. It is the same with bitterness and sweetness, love and hate, hunger and satiation, thirst and saturation, separation and adhesion. It turns out that it is impossible to come to love adhesion prior to acquiring the hate of separation.

3. Baal HaSulam, Letter No. 52

In each and every movement in His work there are two opposites in the same carrier, as I have elaborated in previous letters, as the receiver consists of body and soul, which are opposites. Hence, in each attainment, great or small, He makes two opposite forms.

There are two concepts in the work of the Creator: 1) "prayer and plea," 2) "praise and gratitude." Naturally, both must be at their highest. To complete the prayer, a person must feel the Creator's closeness to him as mandatory, like an organ that is hanging loosely, for then he can complain and pour out his heart before Him.

But opposite that, regarding the complete praise and gratitude, a person must feel the Creator's closeness to him as an addition, a supplement, as something that does not belong to him at all, for "What is man that You should know him, the son of man that You should think of him?" Then he can certainly give complete praise and gratitude to His great name for choosing him from among all those who are standing ready to serve the Creator.

It is great work for the complex man to be completed in both those opposites, so they are set in his heart forever at the same time.

4. Baal HaSulam, "You Have Made Me in Behind and Before"

It is written, "Man and beast You save, O Lord." Our sages said, "These are people who are of cunning mind and pretend to be as beasts." This means that the whole path of creation that the Creator created is regarded as two opposites in one subject, and all the combinations in the world were made in this way, and this is the whole of the work of creation.

5. Baal HaSulam, "You Have Made Me in Behind and Before"

In the giving of the Torah, we were given the strength through "remember and keep were said in one utterance. What the mouth cannot say, and the ear hear and the heart think or contemplate." This means that it is written that "Remember" is the love and "Keep" is the fear, which are two opposites. They were said to us and given to us as one, to unite them. Although they are really opposite, and it is incomprehensible to the corporeal mind and heart how such a thing can exist in reality, it is the power of the Torah that one who adheres to it is rewarded with it—being connected and united in his heart, as in the quality of Jacob the Patriarch.

6. Baal HaSulam, *Ohr HaBahir*

Anything that is perceived in time is corporeality, and anything corporeal is complex. This means that there are two discernments that are unfit to come at once. For this reason, one sorts them out in the time given to him one at a time. After the scrutiny and the labor, the two discernments will come at once, and will not interfere or conceal each other whatsoever, and then it is considered removed of corporeality and removed also of time, and it comes to be defined as the eternity of the seventh millennium. This is what the poet implied by "Jerusalem that is built as a city that was joined together": The end of correction is called "Jerusalem that is built," meaning that the redeemed do not build it but are astonished by their attainment that it is already built and there was never any flaw in it, for any change of place, change of operation, and change of name, which is itself the moments of the time in exile, all those opposites have joined together, and it is complete simplicity, as the sum that is revealed when all its parts and details are revealed in it.

7. Baal HaSulam, *The Study of the Ten Sefirot*, "Inner Observation," Chapter 1, Part 1

The difference between One, Unique, and Unified: When He unites to act with One Force, He is called "Unified." When He divides to act His act, each part of Him is called Unique, and when He is in a single evenness, He is called One, thus far his pure words.

By saying, "unites to act with One Force," he wishes to say that He works to bestow, as worthy of His Oneness, and His operations are unchanging. When He "divides to act His act," meaning when His operations differ, and He seems to be doing good and bad, then He is called "Unique" because all His different operations have a single outcome: good.

We find that He is unique in every single act and does not change by His various operations. When He is in a single evenness He is called "One." One points to His Atzmut, where all the opposites are in a single evenness.

8. Baal HaSulam, *The Study of the Ten Sefirot*, "Inner Observation," Chapter 1, Part 2

We should learn from those who ate the manna. Manna is called "Bread off the sky" because it did not materialize when clothing in this world. Our sages said that each and every one tasted everything he or she wanted to taste in it.

That means that it had to have opposite forms in it. One person tasted sweet and the other tasted it as acrid and bitter. Thus, the manna itself had to have been contained of both opposites together, for can one give what is not in one? How can two opposites be contained in the same carrier?

It is therefore a must that it is simple, and devoid of both flavors, but only included in them in such a way that the corporeal receiver might discern the taste he or she wants. In the same way you can perceive anything spiritual: it is unique and simple in itself, but consists of the entire multiplicity of forms in the world. When falling in the hand of a corporeal receiver, it is the receiver who discriminates a separate form in it, unlike all other forms that unite in that spiritual essence.

9. RABASH, Article No. 19 (1986), "Concerning Joy"

As soon as the creature is created, he consists of two opposites: 1) vessels of reception, 2) vessels of bestowal. There is no greater oppositeness than this. These two opposites come in one carrier, but one at a time, and it seems as though there is a middle line that contains both of them: 1) the will to receive, 2) the will to bestow.

The middle line contains both of them when the will to receive is included in the will to bestow, called "receiving in order to bestow." It follows that the two forces are included in this middle line, meaning reception and bestowal together.

10. RABASH, Article No. 45 (1991), "What Does It Mean that a Judge Must Judge Absolutely Truthfully, in the Work?"

It is written, "'Peace, peace, to the far and to the near,' said the Lord, 'and I will heal him.'" We should interpret "far" and "near" in the work. "Far" means left line. That is, when a person places a judge to judge how he behaves in the work, he sees how far he is from the Creator. "To the near" means when a person returns to working on the right line, which is when he sees only wholeness. That is, he values the work and considers even a small grip on *Torah and Mitzvot* as a fortune, since he does not even deserve the little bit of nearness. Hence, in a state of "right," a person is considered "close to the Creator."

But those two lines are disputed with each other, since they contradict one another. At that time comes the middle line and decides and makes peace between them. This is regarded as the Creator making peace between them, as it is known that the Creator is called the "middle line."

4

Love Will Cover All Crimes

1. Baal HaSulam, Letter No. 47

Let me remind you the validity of love of friends in spite of everything at this time, for it is upon this that our right to exist depends, and upon this our near-to-come success is measured.

Hence, turn away from all the imaginary engagements and set your hearts on thinking thoughts and devising proper tactics to truly connect your hearts as one, so the words "Love your friend as yourself" will literally come true in you, for a verse does not reach beyond the literal, and you will be cleaned by the thought of love that will cover all crimes. Test me in that, and begin to truly connect in love, and then you will see, "the palate will taste,".

2. Baal HaSulam, Letter No. 5

I rejoice in those revealed corruptions and the ones that are being revealed.

I do, however, regret and complain about the corruptions that have still not appeared, but which are destined to appear, for a hidden corruption is hopeless, and its surfacing is a great salvation from heaven. The rule is that one does not give what he does not have. Hence, if it has appeared now, there is no doubt that it was here to begin with but was hidden. This is why I am happy when they come out of their holes because when you cast your eye on them, they become a pile of bones.

But I do not settle for it even for a moment, as I know that those who are with us are more numerous than those who are with them. But weakness stretches time, and those contemptible ants are hidden and their place is unknown. The sage says about this, "The fool folds his hands and eats his own flesh." Moses let down his hands, but when Moses lifts his hands of faith, all that should appear promptly appears, and then Israel triumphs "in all the mighty hand, and in all the great terror."

This is the meaning of "Whatever you find that your hand can do by your strength, do." When the cup is full, the verse, "The wicked are overthrown," comes true. And when the wicked are lost, light and gladness come to the world, and then they are gone.

3. RABASH, Article No. 8 (1985), "Make for Yourself a Rav and Buy Yourself a Friend – 2"

Those people agreed to unite into a single group that engages in love of friends is that each of them feels that they have one desire that can unite all their views, so as to receive the strength of love of others. There is a famous maxim by our sages, "As their faces differ, their views differ." Thus, those who agreed among them to unite into a group understood that there isn't such a great distance between them in the sense that they recognize the necessity to work in love of others. Therefore, each of them will be able to make concessions in favor of the others, and they can unite around that.

4. RABASH, Article No. 286, "Truth and Peace Loved"

Particularly in matters where there is hatred between them we can speak of something new, meaning that they love each other.

5. RABASH, Article No. 17, Part 1 (1984) "Concerning the Importance of Friends"

He should consider the friend as greater than himself.

But how can one consider one's friend greater than himself when he can see that his own merits are greater than his friend's, that he is more talented and has better natural qualities? There are two ways to understand this:

1. He is going with faith above reason: once he has chosen him as a friend, he appreciates him above reason.
2. This is more natural—within reason. If he has decided to accept the other as a friend, and works on himself to love him, then it is natural with love to see only good things. And even though there are bad things in one's friend, he cannot see them, as it is written, "love covers all transgressions."

6. RABASH, Article No. 273, "The Mightiest of the Mighty"

In ethics, we should interpret that "mighty" is "one who conquers his inclination" (*Avot*, Chapter 4). That is, he works with the good inclination and subdues the evil inclination.

The mightiest of the mighty is one who works also with the evil inclination, as our sages said, "With all your heart—with both your inclinations" (*Berachot* 54), where the evil inclination, too, serves the Creator. It follows that he makes his foe, the evil inclination, his friend. And since the evil inclination is also serving the Creator, it follows that here he has more work, for which he is called "the mightiest of the mighty."

7. RABASH, Letter No. 40

And in the matter of love, it is through "Buy yourself a friend." In other words, through actions, one buys one's friend's heart. And even if he sees that his friend's heart is like a stone, it is no excuse. If he feels that he is suitable for being his friend in the work, then he must buy him through deeds.

Each gift (and a gift is determined as such when he knows that his friend will enjoy it, whether in words, in thought, or in action. However, each gift must be out in the open, so that his friend will know about it, and with thoughts, one does not know that his friend was thinking of him. Hence, words are required, too, meaning he should tell him that he is thinking of him and cares about him. And that, too, should be about what his friend loves, meaning what his friend likes. One who doesn't like sweets, but pickles, cannot treat his friend to pickles, but specifically to sweets, since this is what his friend likes. And from that, we should understand that something could be unimportant to one, but more important than anything to another.) that he gives to his friend is like a bullet that makes a hollow in the stone. And although the first bullet only scratches the stone, when the second bullet hits the same place, it already makes a notch, and the third one makes a hole.

And through the bullets that he shoots repeatedly, the hole becomes a hollow in his friend's heart of stone, where all the presents gather. And each gift becomes a spark of love until all the sparks of love accumulate in the hollow of the stony heart and become a flame.

The difference between a spark and a flame is that where there is love, there is open disclosure, meaning a disclosure to all the peoples that the fire of love is burning in him. And the fire of love burns all the transgressions one meets along the way.

8. RABASH, Article No. 738, "A Covenant of Salt"

"On all your offerings you shall offer salt." This is the covenant of the salt, which is a covenant against the intellect, for when one takes good things from one's friend, they should make a covenant.

A covenant is needed precisely when each one has demands and complaints against the other, and they might come into anger and separation. At that time, the covenant they made obligates them to maintain the love and unity between them, for the rule is that whenever someone wishes to hurt the other, they have a cure—to remember the covenant that they had made between them.

This obligates them to maintain the love and peace. This is the meaning of "On all your offerings you shall offer salt," meaning that any nearing in the work of the Creator should be through a covenant of salt, as this is the whole foundation.

9. *Zohar for All*, *Aharei Mot* [After the Death], "Behold, How Good and How Pleasant," Items 65-66

"Behold, how good and how pleasant it is for brothers to also sit together." These are the friends as they sit together, and are not separated from each other. At first, they seem like people at war, wishing to kill one another. Then they return to being in brotherly love.

The Creator says about them, "Behold, how good and how pleasant it is for brothers to also sit together." The word, "also," comes to include the *Shechina* with them. Moreover, the Creator listens to their words and He has contentment and delights with them, as it is written, "Then those who feared the Lord spoke to one another, and the Lord listened and heard it, and a book of remembrance was written before Him."

And you, the friends who are here, as you were in fondness and love before, henceforth you will also not part until the Creator rejoices with you and summons peace upon you. And by your merit there will be peace in the world, as it is written, "For the sake of my brothers and my friends let me say, 'Let peace be in you.'"

10. The Holy Shlah, *Shaar HaOtiot*, Vol. 2

Although your friend's virtues are not equal to yours, you must tolerate him and love him, for so the Creator created him.

11. Babylonian Talmud, Masechet Kidushin

It is written, "They will not be ashamed when they speak with their enemies in the gate." What is "with their enemies in the gate"? Rabbi Hiya, son of Bar Aba, said, "Even father and son, teacher and disciple, when they engage in Torah in the same gate, become each other's enemies, but they do not move from there until they come to love each other."

12. Proverbs, 10:12

Hate stirs strife, and love will cover all crimes.

13. Rabbi Nachman of Breslov, *Likutei Halachot*

"Love will cover all crimes," meaning love that is of holiness that is present in the point covers all the crimes and cancels all the breaking of the heart and all the curses.

14. Rav Shneor Zalman of Liadi, *Likutei Torah*

By making the covenant, their love will be eternal love that will never fall. No prevention shall separate them since they make between them a strong and steadfast bond to unite and connect in their love in a wondrous connection and above rhyme or reason. Although rhyme or reason should have stopped the love or cause some hate, because of the making of the covenant, their love must exist forever. This love and this steadfast bond will cover all crimes, since they have made a covenant and bonded as though they have become one flesh. As one cannot stop loving oneself, so his love for his friend will not stop.

15. Raaiah Kook, *Orot* [*Lights*]

In each one from Israel there lives a spark of holy light inherited from his forefathers, from the holiness of the Torah and the greatness of the faith. It follows that any division between a person from Israel and his neighbor, between one collective and another, it, too, builds worlds. Since everything is improvement and construction, there is no reason to speak bitterly, but to announce the greatness that both sides are doing, and that together, they are perfecting the everlasting structure and are correcting the world. Then, according to the expansion of knowledge, the love will grow according to the intensity of the hate, and the connection will grow according to the size of the separation.

16. *Avot de Rabbi Natan*

Who is the strongest of the strong? He who makes his enemy his friend.

5

Make for Yourself a Rav [Teacher/Great One]

1. Baal HaSulam, "A Speech for the Completion of The Zohar"

Our sages said, "Make for yourself a rav and buy yourself a friend." This means that one can make a new environment for oneself. This environment will help him obtain the greatness of his rav through love of friends who appreciate his rav. Through the friends' discussing the greatness of the rav, each of them receives the sensation of his greatness. Thus, bestowal upon his rav becomes reception and sufficient motivation to an extent that will bring one to engage in Torah and *Mitzvot Lishma*.

It was said about this, "The Torah is acquired by forty-eight virtues, by serving of sages, and by meticulousness of friends." This is so because besides serving the rav, one needs the meticulousness of friends, as well, meaning the friends' influence, so they will influence him so he obtains the greatness of his rav. This is so because obtaining the greatness depends entirely on the environment, and a single person cannot do a thing about it whatsoever.

Yet, there are two conditions to obtaining the greatness:

1. Always listen and accept the appreciation of the environment to the extent of their greatness.
2. The environment should be great, as it is written, "In the multitude of people is the king's glory."

To receive the first condition, each student must feel that he is the smallest among all the friends. In that state, he will be able to receive the appreciation of the greatness from everyone, since the great cannot receive from a smaller one, much less be impressed by his words. Rather, only the small is impressed by the appreciation of the great.

For the second condition, each student must extol the virtues of each friend and cherish him as though he were the greatest in the generation. Then the environment will influence him as though it were a great environment, as it should be, since quality is more important than quantity.

2. Baal HaSulam, "A Speech for the Completion of The Zohar"

An environment that does not properly appreciate Him weakens the individual and prevents him from obtaining His greatness. This is certainly true concerning one's rav, as well. An environment that does not properly appreciate the rav prevents the student from being able to properly obtain the greatness of his rav.

3. Baal HaSulam, "The Freedom"

As far as spiritual life is concerned, there is no natural obligation on the individual to abide by society in any way. On the contrary, here applies a natural law over the collective, to subjugate itself to the individual.

4. Baal HaSulam, Letter No. 19

Even though one has a soul, he is not ready to know Him of his own "Until the spirit be poured upon him from on high." However, one must lend an ear and listen to the words of the sages and believe in them wholeheartedly.

5. Baal HaSulam, *Shamati*, Article No. 105, "A Bastard Wise Disciple Precedes a Commoner High Priest"

Through adhering to wise disciples, it is possible to receive some support.

In other words, only a wise disciple can help him, and nothing else. Even if he is great in the Torah, he will still be called "a commoner," if he has not been rewarded with learning from the Creator's mouth.

Hence, one must surrender before a wise disciple and accept what the wise disciple places on him without any arguments, but by way of above reason.

6. Baal HaSulam, *Shamati*, Article No. 99, "He Did Not Say Wicked or Righteous"

A person has the choice of going to a place where there are righteous. One can accept their authority, and then he will receive all the powers that he lacks by the nature of his own qualities. He will receive it from the righteous. This is the benefit in "planted them in each generation," so that each generation would have someone to turn to, adhere to, and from whom to receive the strength required to rise to the degree of a righteous. Thus, they, too, subsequently become righteous.

7. Baal HaSulam, "A Speech for the Completion of The Zohar"

Our sages advised us: "Make for yourself a rav [teacher/great person] and buy yourself a friend." This means that one should choose for oneself an important and renowned person to be his rav, and from him he will be able to come to engaging in Torah and *Mitzvot* in order to bring contentment to his Maker. This is so because there are two extenuations concerning one's rav:

1. Since he is an important person, the student can bestow contentment upon him, based on the sublimity of his rav, since bestowal becomes as reception for him. This is a natural fuel, so one can always increase his acts of bestowal. Once a person grows accustomed to engaging in bestowal upon the rav, he can transfer it to engaging in Torah and *Mitzvot Lishma* toward the Creator, too, since habit becomes a second nature.

2. Equivalence of form with the Creator does not help if it is not forever, "Until He who knows the mysteries will testify that he will not return to folly." This is not so with equivalence of form with his rav. Since the rav is in this world, within time, equivalence of form with him helps even if it is only temporary and he later turns sour again.

Thus, every time one equalizes one's form with one's rav, he adheres to him for a time. As a result, he obtains the knowledge and thoughts of the rav, according to his measure of *Dvekut*, as we explained in the allegory about the organ that has been cut off from the body and was reunited with it.

For this reason, the student can use his rav's attainment of the Creator's greatness, which inverts bestowal into reception and sufficient fuel to give one's heart and soul. At that time, the student, too, will be able to engage in Torah and *Mitzvot Lishma* with his very heart and soul, which is the remedy that yields eternal *Dvekut* with the Creator.

8. Baal HaSulam, *Shamati*, Article No. 187, "Choosing Labor"

The matter of the lower *Hey* in the *Eynaim* [eyes] means that there was a *Masach* [screen] and a cover over the eyes. The eyes mean Providence, when one sees hidden Providence.

A trial means that a person cannot decide either way, when one cannot determine the Creator's will and the will of his teacher. Although one can work devotedly, he is unable to determine if this devoted work is appropriate or not, that this hard work would be against his teacher's view, and the view of the Creator.

To determine, one chooses that which adds labor. This means that one should act according to one's teacher. Only labor is for man to do, and nothing else. Hence, there is no place for doubt in one's actions and thoughts and words. Instead, he should always increase labor.

9. Baal HaSulam, *Shamati*, Article No. 40, "What Is the Measure of Faith in the Rav?"

Only one who is already in the singular authority can discern and know the truth. Hence, one must trust the opinion of his rav and believe what his rav tells him. It means that one should go as his rav told him to do.

And although he sees many arguments and many teachings that do not go hand in hand with the opinion of his rav, he should nevertheless trust the opinion of his rav and say that what he understands and what he sees in other books that do not coincide with his rav's opinion, he should say that as long as he is in multiple authorities, he cannot understand the truth, and he cannot see what is written in other books, the truth that they say.

It is known that when one is still not rewarded, his Torah becomes to him a potion of death.

10. Baal HaSulam, "Introduction to the Book Panim Meirot uMasbirot," Item 8

Come and see how grateful we should be to our teachers, who impart us their sacred lights and dedicate their souls to do good to our souls. They stand in the middle between the path of harsh torments and the path of repentance. They save us from the netherworld, which is harder than death, and accustom us to reach the heavenly pleasures, the sublime gentleness and the pleasantness that is our share, ready and waiting for us from the very beginning, as we have said above. Each of them operates in his generation, according to the power of the light of his teaching and sanctity.

Our sages have already said, "You have not a generation without such as Abraham, Isaac, and Jacob."

11. Baal HaSulam, Talmud Eser Sefirot, "Histaklut Pnimit," Part 1, Chapter 2

Those whose eyes have not been opened to the sights of heaven, and have not acquired the proficiency in the connections of the branches of this world with their roots in the Upper Worlds are like the blind scraping the walls. They will not understand the true meaning of even a single word, for each word is a branch that relates to its *Shoresh*.

Only if they receive an interpretation from a genuine sage who makes himself available to explain it in the spoken language, which is necessarily like translating from one language to another, meaning from the language of the branches to the spoken language, only then he will be able to explain the spiritual term as it is.

12. Baal HaSulam, "The Teaching of the Kabbalah and Its Essence"

The most successful way for one who wishes to learn the wisdom is to search for a genuine Kabbalist and follow all his instructions, until one is rewarded with understanding the wisdom in one's own mind, meaning the first discernment. Afterward, one will be rewarded with its conveyance mouth to mouth, which is the second discernment, and after that, understand in writing, which is the third discernment. Then, one will have inherited all the wisdom and its instruments from his teacher with ease and will be left with all his time to develop and expand.

However, in reality there is a second way: Through one's great yearning, the sights of heaven will open before him and he will attain all the origins by himself. This is the first discernment. Yet, afterward, one must still labor and exert extensively until he finds a Kabbalist sage before whom he can bow and obey, and from whom to receive the wisdom by way of conveyance face to face, which is the second discernment.

Then comes the third discernment. Since he is not attached to a Kabbalist sage from the outset, the attainments come with great efforts and consume much time, leaving little time to develop in it. Also, sometimes the knowledge comes after the fact, as it is written, "and they shall die without wisdom." These are ninety-nine percent and what we call "entering but not exiting." They are as fools and ignorant in this world, who see the world set before them but do not understand any of it, except for the bread in their mouths.

Indeed, in the first way, too, not everyone succeeds, since after being rewarded with attainment, the majority of them become complacent and cannot subjugate themselves to their teacher sufficiently, as they are not worthy of the conveyance of the wisdom. In this case, the sage must hide the essence of the wisdom from them, and "they shall die without wisdom," "entering but not exiting."

This is so because there are harsh and strict conditions in conveying the wisdom, which stem from necessary reasons. Hence, very few are regarded highly enough by their teachers for them to find them worthy of this thing, and happy are the rewarded.

13. Baal HaSulam, Letter No. 45

You should believe that your teacher's bodily matters are truly engagements of the soul. This is why our sages said, "It did not say, 'learned,' but 'poured,' implying that serving is greater than learning."

A student should be in true annulment before the teacher, in the full sense of the word, for then he unites with him and he can perform salvations in his favor. A student cannot adhere to his teacher's soul, as it is above his attainment.

14. Baal HaSulam, *Shamati*, Article No. 25, "Things that Come from the Heart"

Regarding things that come from the heart, enter the heart. Hence, why do we see that even if things have already entered the heart, one still falls from his degree?

The thing is that when one hears the words of Torah from his teacher, he immediately agrees with his teacher and resolves to observe the words of his teacher with his heart and soul. But afterward, when he comes out to the world, he sees, covets, and is infected by the multitude of desires roaming the world. Then, he and his mind, his heart, and his will are annulled before the majority.

As long as he has no power to sentence the world to the side of merit, they subdue him, he mingles with their desires, and he is led like sheep to the slaughter. He has no choice; he is compelled to think, want, crave, and demand everything that the majority demands. Then he chooses their foreign thoughts and their loathsome lusts and desires, which are alien to the spirit of the Torah. In that state, he has no strength to subdue the majority.

Instead, there is only one counsel then: to cling to his teacher and to the books. This is called "From the mouth of books and from the mouth of authors." Only by clinging to them can he change his mind and will for the better. However, witty arguments will not help him change his mind, but only the remedy of *Dvekut* [adhesion], for this is a wondrous cure, as the *Dvekut* reforms him.

15. Baal HaSulam, "Introduction to The Book of Zohar," Item 57

The aridity and the darkness that have befallen us in this generation, such as we have never seen in all the generations preceding us. It is so because even the servants of the Creator have abandoned the engagement in the secrets of the Torah.

Maimonides has already given a true allegory about that. He said that if a line of a thousand blind people walks along the way and there is at least one leader amongst them who can see, they are guaranteed to walk on the right path and not fall in pits and obstacles since they follow the sighted one who leads them. But if that person is missing, they are certain to stumble over every hurdle on the way and will all fall into the pit.

So is the matter before us. If the servants of the Creator had, at least, engaged in the internality of the Torah and extended a complete light from *Ein Sof*, the whole generation would have followed them, and everyone would be certain of their way, that they would not fall. But if even the servants of the Creator have distanced themselves from this wisdom, it is no wonder the whole generation is failing because of them. And because of my great sorrow, I cannot elaborate on that!

16. Baal HaSulam, "The Freedom"

Since the more developed in the generation is certainly the individual, it follows that when the public wants to relieve themselves of the terrible agony and assume conscious and voluntary development, which is the path of Torah, they have no choice but to subjugate themselves and their physical freedom to the discipline of the individual, and obey the orders and remedies that he will offer them.

17. Baal HaSulam, Letter No. 43

Our sages have already said, "The fear of your teacher is as the fear of heaven." This, therefore, will be the measure of exaltedness that such a man obtains by his sanctity, for his exaltedness will by no means exceed the exaltedness of his teacher.

What the Rijnaar boasted about—that he was awarded a higher degree than all the sages in his generation because he acquired more faith in the sages than all of his contemporaries—we need to understand that faith does not come by lending. Such faith can be acquired by six-year-old children, too, but as a feeling of the exaltedness and the inspiration to his soul from the wisdom of the sages who have shared from His wisdom to those who fear Him.

I have already said and elaborated that the biggest *Masach* [screen] is in the work in the children of the land of Israel, since the domination of the Canaan *Klipa* [shell/peel] is in this place, and each one is as low as the ground, his friend is even lower than the ground, and his rav [teacher] is like him.

Allegorically, you can say the words of our sages about the verse, "Leave Me and keep My law"—"I wish they would leave Me" means that they were proud of the exaltedness. And although "he and I cannot dwell in the same place," still, "Keep My law," be attached to a genuine righteous with proper faith in the sages. Then there is hope that the righteous will reform them and will sentence them to the side of merit as is appropriate for the presence of the Creator. What could come out of their humbleness and lowliness so the Creator does not move His abode from them, if they have no genuine righteous [person] to guide them in His law and prayer, and lead them to a place of Torah and wisdom?

18. Baal HaSulam, *Shamati*, Article No. 40, "What Is the Measure of Faith in the Rav?"

It is known that there is a right path and a left path. Right comes from the words "to the right," referring to the verse, "And he believed in the Lord." The Targum says, "To the right, when the rav says to the disciple to take the right path."

Right is normally called "wholeness," and left, "incompleteness," that corrections are missing there. In that state the disciple must believe the words of his rav, who tells him to walk in the right line, called "wholeness."

And what is the "wholeness" by which the disciple should walk? It is that one should depict to oneself as if he has already been rewarded with whole faith in the Creator, and already feels in his organs that the Creator leads the whole world in the form of "The Good Who Does Good," meaning that the whole world receives only good from Him.

Yet, when one looks at oneself, he sees that he is poor and indigent. In addition, when he observes the world, he sees that the entire world is tormented, each according to his degree.

One should say about that, "They have eyes but they see not." "They" means that as long as one is in multiple authorities, called "they," they do not see the truth. What are the multiple authorities? As long as one has two desires, even though he believes that the entire world belongs to the Creator, but something belongs to man, too.

But in truth, one must annul one's authority before the authority of the Creator and say that one does not want to live for oneself, and the only reason that he wants to exist is in order to bring contentment to the Creator. Thus, by this one annuls his own authority completely, and then he is in the singular authority, the authority of the Creator. Only then can he see the truth, how the Creator leads the world by the quality of good and doing good.

As long as he is in multiple authorities, meaning when he still has two desires in both mind and heart, he is unable to see the truth. Instead, he must go above reason and say, "they have eyes," but they do not see the truth.

19. RABASH, Article No. 424, "The Dispute between Korah and Moses"

We must be strong in faith in the sages and submit ourselves, and be lowly in our eyes compared to the righteous.

20. RABASH, Article No. 1 (1990), "What Does 'May We Be the Head and Not the Tail' Mean in the Work?"

All the work of the created beings, that they must work above reason. It is impossible to do anything without faith in the sages, who arranged for us the order of the work. Once a person has accepted his work as "a tail to the lions," he follows the sages, to walk only as they had arranged for us.

This is as our sages said (*Avot*, Chapter 1:4), "Be dusted by the dust of their feet (of the sages)." The Bartenura interprets that you should follow them, for one who walks kicks up dust with his feet, and one who follows him fills up with the dust that they raise with their feet.

We should understand what our sages imply to us with this allegory. We should interpret that one who goes after faith in the sages looks at their way, and they say that we must go above reason. Then, a person begins to be as spies, to see if it is truly worthwhile to follow their path. This is regarded as the feet of the sages kicking up dust, which goes into the eyes of their followers. That is, when a person wants to understand the path of the sages, they tell us that we must follow them with our eyes shut, or dust will enter. Something unimportant is called "dust," meaning that there cannot be greater lowliness than this.

Since man was given the reason and intellect in order to understand everything according to the intellect, and here we are told to walk by accepting faith in the sages, and a person wants to understand this path, and since as long as one is placed under the governance of the will to receive for himself, he cannot know what is good and what is bad, but must accept everything the way the sages determined for us, or dust and dirt will enter his eyes and he will not be able to move forward, but when we do not criticize the words of the sages and do not want to accept their words within reason, specifically by this we are rewarded with knowledge [reason] of *Kedusha* [holiness].

This is so because the whole reason why we need to go above reason is that we are immersed in self-love. Hence, through faith above reason, we are rewarded with vessels of bestowal, and then the delight and pleasure in vessels of bestowal is revealed. In the words of *The Zohar*, this is called "Reason spreads and fills rooms and corridors." That is, when the *Kelim* [vessels] are proper, reason spreads both in the inner *Kelim* and in the outer *Kelim*.

21. RABASH, Article No. 10 (1989), "What Does It Mean that the Ladder Is Diagonal, in the Work?"

Is written (*Moed Katan* 17a), "If the Rav is similar to an angel of the Creator, let them seek to learn from him. If he is not, let them not seek to learn from him. They ask about it, Must one who wants to learn from a rav first see the angel of the Creator and then, after he has seen the form of the angel of the Creator, this is the time to go seek a rav who is similar to an angel of the Creator?"

According to the above, we should interpret that if the rav teaches the disciples the work that must be done in order to bestow, meaning why a person comes into this world, to do God's mission, to work for the sake of the Creator, that person is a messenger of the Creator and not a landlord in this world, but is a servant of the Creator. The meaning of "messenger of the Creator" is "angel of the Creator." This is the meaning of "If the rav is similar to an angel of the Creator, let them seek to learn from him."

22. RABASH, Article No. 4 (1989), "What Is a Flood of Water in the Work?"

There is the matter of above reason. This is regarded as wanting to walk with his eyes shut, meaning that although reason and the senses do not understand what our sages tell us, they assume upon them faith in the sages and say that we must take upon ourselves faith in the sages, as it is written, "And they believed in the Lord and in His servant, Moses." Without faith, nothing can be achieved in spirituality.

23. RABASH, Article No. 38 (1990), "What Is, 'A Cup of Blessing Must Be Full,' in the Work?"

Before the *Yenika* there is *Ibur*, meaning that the upper one corrects him. This can be when a person is like an embryo in its mother's womb, where the embryo annuls before the mother and has no view of its own, but as our sages said, "An embryo is its mother's thigh, eats what its mother eats," and has no authority of its own to ask any questions. Rather, it does not merit a name. This is called "mute," when he has no mouth to ask questions.

This is so when a person can go with his eyes shut, above reason, and believe in the sages and go all the way. This is called *Ibur*, when he has no mouth. *Ibur* means as it is written (*The Study of the Ten Sefirot*, Part 8, Item 17), "The level of *Malchut*, which is the most restricted *Katnut* [smallness/infancy] *possible*, is called *Ibur*. It comes from the words *Evra* [anger] and *Dinin* [Aramaic: judgments], as it is written, 'And the Lord was impregnated in me for your sake.'"

We should interpret the meaning of "anger and judgments." When a person must go with his eyes shut, above reason, the body resists this work. Hence, the fact that a person always has to overcome, this is called "anger, wrath, and trouble," since it is hard work to always overcome and annul before the upper one, for the upper one to do with him what the upper one wants. This is called *Ibur*, which is the most restricted *Katnut* possible.

24. RABASH, Article No. 438, "Save Your Servant, You, My God"

First, one must believe in the Creator above reason and praise his rav, meaning feel completely and utterly whole, for it is known that to the extent that a person feels that his friend is giving him gifts, to that extent he praises him. Also, to the extent that he feels his friend's greatness, to that extent he can praise. In other words, if he feels that he is lacking something and his friend can satisfy it, he immediately loses the power to praise and glorify his friend.

Therefore, when a person begins his work, he must go with faith above reason that he is not lacking anything, and that his rav has satisfied all his wishes. At that time, he is called "whole," and then the whole can connect to the whole. Conversely, when he is deficient, the deficient does not connect to the whole.

Afterward, he can establish deficiencies like a slave seeking a gift from his rav, when he asks for his needs, meaning that the judge has only what his eyes see and he must not ignore any deficiency that he has. On the contrary, to the extent that he feels his deficiency, so he can pray that his rav will satisfy his wishes. And then, the more the student asks, the better.

Finally, he must not stay deficient. He must go again on the path of faith above reason, that he is utterly and completely whole. This is the meaning of the words, "as a servant thanking his rav for the gift he has received from him, and he walks away." He should believe above reason that he has already received all his wishes, called a "gift."

He thanks his rav for this, for one must not live in separation, meaning that he has complaints against his rav that he is not giving him what he asks. For this reason, it is forbidden for man to be deficient and he must always be in joy. However, in order to have *Kelim* [vessels] to receive, he must evoke the deficiencies.

In the offering, this is regarded as ascending and descending, "Knowing in the beginning and knowing in the end, and concealment in between." That is, between knowing and knowing it is permitted to see the concealment, meaning that he has no revelation with respect to the truth, to feel that his work is desirable to his rav.

It follows that one must not disclose any lack in Torah and work for himself. Rather, he must always go above rhyme and reason that he is utterly and completely whole. In between, he can ask his wishes as his eyes see, that he has only faults. But afterward, he must believe as though he has already received all his wishes and he thanks his rav for this.

At that time, he can be happy that he is whole. It follows that all his wholeness is built on faith, and his deficiencies are built on knowledge, since "the judge has only what his eyes see."

25. RABASH, Article No. 680, "Annulment—the Baal Shem Tov Way "

The way to annul the body used to be through abstention. But there is another way, which is annulment before the rav [great one, teacher]. This is the meaning of "Make for yourself a rav." "Making" is clarified by force, without any intellect.

As abstention revokes the body only through action and not through the mind. Likewise, annulment before the rav is by force and not through intellect. That is, even in a place where one does not understand the view of one's rav, he annuls himself and the Torah and the work, and comes to the rav so he will guide him.

There is guidance in the manner of the general public, called *Ohr Makif* [surrounding light], which is light that shines only from outside, and is without words, but only by coming to the rav and sitting in front of him, sitting at his table during the meal or during the service. Yet, there is another way, which is internal, and this is specifically through "mouth-to-mouth."

26. *Zohar for All*, Yitro [Jethro], "You Shall Not Make for Yourself," Item 428

One should be so careful with words of Torah, and one should be so careful not to err in them and utter a word of Torah that he does not know, and which he did not receive from his teacher. Anyone who says words of Torah that he does not know or did not receive from his teacher, it is written about him, "You shall not make for yourself an idol or any likeness."

27. GRA (Vilna Gaon), *Aderet Eliyahu*

It is a grave warning not to learn the wisdom of Kabbalah by yourself from the books, for it is impossible to attain the depth of the intention of the Godly matters, which highly prevail over the human intellect, but rather through much sanctity and purity through a giver, an honest, faithful Kabbalist who had received from a renown Kabbalist.

28. Martin Buber, *Ohr HaGanuz*

Rabbi David Leykas, a disciple of the Baal Shem Tov, asked followers of his father-in-law, Rabbi Motel of Chernobyl: "Do you have complete faith in your Rav?" They kept silent, for who would dare to say that he has complete faith? "In that case," said Rabbi David, "I'd like to tell you what faith is. One Shabbat [Sabbath], the third meal [closing Sabbath meal] with the Baal Shem Tov stretched on until late in the evening, as would often happen. Afterwards, we said grace for the food and immediately proceeded to the evening service, did *Havdala* [marking the end of Shabbat and beginning of the week], and sat down for the *Melave Malka* [post Shabbat] meal. We were all very poor and did not have a penny, certainly not on Shabbat [when it's forbidden to carry money]. Even so, when the Baal Shem Tov told me after the *Melave Malka* meal, 'David, give money for mead [alcoholic beverage made of fermented honey and water],' I placed my hand in my pocket, although I knew I had nothing, and took out a *Zahuv* [coin]. I gave the coin to buy mead."

29. Rabbi Shmuel Di Ozida, *Midrash Shmuel*, Avot 1, 16

It is written "Make for yourself a Rav," meaning accept him as your Rav. In order to benefit from the Rav, the student must believe in him and trust his words, as was said, "Depart from doubt," namely do not doubt your Rav's words, but rather trust him, for without it, he will not help you.

30. Maimonides, *Mishneh Torah*

Who is the one who disputes his teacher? One who establishes a seminary and sits, explains, and teaches without his teacher's permission while his teacher lives, even if one's teacher is in another country. It is forbidden to ever teach in the presence of one's teacher, and whoever teaches a law in the presence of one's teacher must be put to death.

31. Rabbi Simcha Mordechai Ziskind, *Wisdom and Ethics*

It is known what educators said—that one who learns should know two things about his tutor, which will give him the courage to accept the teaching from his tutor gladly and willingly: 1) His tutor is wiser than him and knows what is best for him better than him. 2) His teacher truly seeks his benefit and not his own benefit or any other intention, but only to place the student on the ladder as he wants his son's best with success and wealth. When this is thoroughly clarified to him, that the tutor seeks his benefit and knows what is best for him better than himself, he will truly give himself over to his teacher to be his possession, and he will do anything that he commands him very gladly.

32. Rabbi Eliyahu Eliezer Desler, *A Letter from Eliyahu*

Rabbi Shlomo Elkabetz asked in the book *Brit HaLevi* why the disciples of Rabbi Akiva died specifically in the days of the [*Omer*] count. He explained that any rav who learns with the disciples gives them of his soul, meaning of his very spiritual essence. This is why disciples were called "sons." If the disciples unite properly, his bestowal achieves its goal, since only when all come together does all his bestowal illuminate in all of them. It is known that each disciple takes only one spark of the giving of his rav, the spark that pertains to the essence of the soul of the disciple. Naturally, only when they are all included together is his giving complete.

However, if the disciples part from one another in their conduct, they lose the bestowal of their rav and there remains a lone giving without achieving its goal. This is a dangerous situation. The disciples of Rabbi Akiva, for all their greatness, did not treat each other with respect, and by that they parted from each other. Naturally, they did not let the bestowal of Rabbi Akiva, their teacher, achieve its goal. When the days of the count arrived, in which the lights of the preparation for the giving of the Torah sparkle, they were put at risk and died, for one who sees the light of *Kedusha* [holiness] sparkles and does not exert to be rewarded with it and ascend by it, but rejects it and remains in his *Katnut* [smallness/infancy], it is certainly a great complaint that puts one in harm's way.

33. Rabbi Abraham Ben Rabbi Nachman of Toltshin, *Stars of Light*

"When I approached my Rav," said Rabbi Natan, "I abandoned my whole intellect as though I had no intellect, and when I heard from him some words, I received a little bit of intellect, a few more words—a little more intellect." It was said that this was the difference between our teacher Rabbi Natan and the rest of the disciples of Rabbi Nachman—that they knew that the rav was the most important, but they, too, had some merit, that they had some opinion. However, Rabbi Natan knew about himself that without the rav, he is nothing, nobody, truly null.

6

Labor

1. Baal HaSulam, Letter No. 38

The most important is the labor, meaning to crave to labor in His work, for the ordinary work does not count at all, only the bits that are more than usual, which is called "labor." It is like a person who must eat a pound of bread to be full. All his eating does not merit the title, "a satisfying meal," but only the last bit from the pound. That bit, for all its smallness, is what defines the meal as satisfying.

Similarly, out of every service, the Creator draws out only the bits beyond the ordinary, and they will be the letters and the *Kelim* [vessels] in which to receive the light of His face.

2. Baal HaSulam, Letter No. 57

Everything, small or great, is obtained only by the power of prayer. All the labor and work to which we are obliged are only to discover our lack of strength and our lowliness—that we are unfit for anything by our own strength—for then we can pour out a wholehearted prayer before Him.

We could argue about this, "So I can decide that I am unfit for anything, and why all the labor and exertion?" However, there is a natural law that there is none so wise as the experienced, and before one tries to actually do all he can do, he is utterly incapable of arriving at true lowliness, to the real extent, as said above.

This is why we must toil in *Kedusha* [holiness] and purity, as it is written, "Whatever you find that your hand can do by your strength, that do," and understand this for it is true and deep.

I revealed this truth to you only so you would not weaken or give up on mercy. Although you do not see anything, for even when the measure of labor is complete, it is the time of prayer, but until then, believe in our sages: "I did not labor and found, do not believe."

When the measure is full, your prayer will be complete and the Creator will grant generously, as our sages instructed us, "I labored and found, believe," for one is unfit for a prayer prior to this, and the Creator hears a prayer.

3. Baal HaSulam, "Introduction to The Study of the Ten Sefirot," Item 97

Our sages warned us in many places concerning the necessary condition in the practice of Torah, that it will be specifically *Lishma*, in a way that through it, one will be awarded life, for it is a Torah of life and this is why it was given to us, as it is written, "Therefore, choose life."

Hence, during the practice of Torah, every person must labor in it, and set his mind and heart to find "the light of the King's face" in it, meaning attainment of open Providence, called "light of the face." Any person is capable of it, as it is written, "those who seek Me shall find Me," and as it is written, "I labored and did not find, do not believe."

Thus, one needs nothing in this matter except the labor alone. It is written, "Anyone who practices Torah *Lishma*, his Torah becomes for him a potion of life" (*Taanit* 7a). It means that one should only set one's mind and heart to attain life, which is the meaning of *Lishma*.

4. Baal HaSulam, "Introduction to The Study of the Ten Sefirot," Item 18

The Creator, Who created it and gave the evil inclination its strength, evidently knew to create the remedy and the spice liable to wear off the power of the evil inclination and eradicate it altogether.

And if one practices Torah and fails to remove the evil inclination from himself, it is either that he has been negligent in giving the necessary labor and exertion in the practice of Torah, as it is written, "I did not labor and found, do not believe," or perhaps he did put in the necessary amount of labor, but has been negligent in the quality.

This means that while practicing Torah, they did not set their minds and hearts to draw the light in the Torah, which brings faith to one's heart. Rather, they have been absent-minded about the principal requirement demanded of the Torah, namely the light that yields faith. And although they initially aimed for it, their minds went astray during the study.

5. Baal HaSulam, *Shamati*, Article No. 20, "Lishma [for Her sake]"

If one considers what one receives for his work under the sun, he will find that it is not so difficult to submit himself to the Creator, for two reasons:

1. One must strain oneself in this world in any case, whether one wants to or not.
2. During the work, too, if one works *Lishma*, he receives pleasure from the work itself.

It is as the Sayer from Dubna said about the verse, "You did not call Me, Jacob, for you labored about Me, Israel." It means that he who works for the Creator has no labor. On the contrary, one has pleasure and elation.

But he who does not work for the Creator, but for other goals, cannot complain to the Creator that He is not giving him vitality in the work, since he is working for another goal. One can complain only to the one for whom he works, to give vitality and pleasure during his work. It is said about him: "They who make them shall be like them, every one who trusts them."

Do not be surprised that when one assumes the burden of the kingdom of heaven, when he wants to work in order to bestow upon the Creator, he still feels no vitality at all, and that this vitality would compel one to assume the burden of the kingdom of heaven. Rather, one should accept it coercively, against his better judgment. That is, the body does not agree to this enslavement, why the Creator does not shower him with vitality and pleasure.

The reason is that this is a great correction. Were it not for this, if the will to receive had agreed to this work, one would never have been able to achieve *Lishma*. Rather, he would always work for his own benefit, to satisfy his own desires. It is as people say, that the thief himself yells, "Catch the thief!" and then you cannot tell which is the real thief in order to catch him and reclaim the theft from him.

But when the thief, meaning the will to receive, does not find the work of accepting the burden of the kingdom of heaven tasteful, since the body accustoms itself to work against its will, one has the means by which to come to work only in order to bring contentment to his Maker, since his sole intention should be only for the Creator, as it is written, "Then shall you delight yourself in the Lord." Thus, when he served the Creator in the past, he did not sense any pleasure in the work. Rather his work was compulsory.

But now that he has accustomed himself to work in order to bestow, he is rewarded with delighting in the Creator, and the work itself renders him pleasure and vitality. This is considered that the pleasure, too, is specifically for the Creator.

6. Baal HaSulam, Letter No. 56

The iniquity of the Amorite is the *Klipa* [shell/peel] that keeps and surrounds the fruit, called "awakening from above," or "the land of Israel." That *Klipa* will not move from its place even as a hairsbreadth before Israel complement entirely the necessary measure of awakening from below, called "merit," meaning the labor and exertion beyond human capability.

Anything that one can do is merely called "work"; it is still not considered "labor." When Israel reach that point, they complement their amount, and then it is called "The iniquity of the Amorite is full." In other words, it is evident that the land of Israel and the glory of the Creator, being the *Shechina* [Divinity], do not belong to them.

Then they break that *Klipa* called "Amorite," and raise the *Shechina* from the dust, and not a moment sooner, as in the verse. This is the meaning of the explicit number, four hundred years, which shows the great precision in that matter, that there are no concessions here at all. As our sages said, the matter of skipping over the end, which was mandatory and obligatory for Israel, that skipping caused all the exiles to this day.

7. Baal HaSulam, *Shamati*, Article No. 187, "Choosing Labor"

The matter of the lower *Hey* in the *Eynaim* [eyes] means that there was a *Masach* [screen] and a cover over the eyes. The eyes mean Providence, when one sees hidden Providence.

A trial means that a person cannot decide either way, when one cannot determine the Creator's will and the will of his teacher. Although one can work devotedly, he is unable to determine if this devoted work is appropriate or not, that this hard work would be against his teacher's view, and the view of the Creator.

To determine, one chooses that which adds labor. This means that one should act according to one's teacher. Only labor is for man to do, and nothing else. Hence, there is no place for doubt in one's actions and thoughts and words. Instead, he should always increase labor.

8. Baal HaSulam, *Shamati*, Article No. 19, "What Is 'The Creator Hates the Bodies,' in the Work?"

We must know that during the work, when the will to receive comes to a person with its arguments, no arguments or rationalizations help with it. Though one thinks that they are just arguments, it will not help one defeat his evil.

Instead, as it is written, "Blunt its teeth." This means to advance only by actions, and not by arguments. This is considered that one must add powers coercively. This is the meaning of what our sages said, "He is coerced until he says 'I want.'" In other words, through persistence, habit becomes a second nature.

One must especially try to have a strong desire to obtain the desire to bestow and overcome the will to receive. A strong desire means that a strong desire is measured by the increment of the in-between rests and the arrests, meaning the time gaps between each overcoming.

Sometimes one receives a cessation in the middle, meaning a descent. This descent can be a cessation of a minute, an hour, a day, or a month. Afterward, he resumes the work of overcoming the will to receive and the attempts to achieve the desire to bestow. A strong desire means that the cessation does not take him a long time and he is immediately reawakened to the work.

It is like a person who wants to break a big rock. He takes a big hammer and hammers many times all day long, but they are weak. In other words, he does not hammer the rock with one swing but brings down the big hammer slowly. Afterward, he complains that this work of breaking the rock is not for him, that it must take a very strong man to be able to break this big rock. He says that he was not born with such great powers to be able to break the rock.

However, one who lifts this big hammer and strikes the rock with a big swing, not slowly but with a great effort, the rock immediately surrenders to him and breaks. This is the meaning of "like a strong hammer that shatters the rock."

Similarly, in the holy work, which is to bring the vessels of reception into *Kedusha* [holiness], we have a strong hammer, meaning words of Torah that give us good counsels. However, if it is not consistent, but with long intermissions in between, one escapes the campaign and says that he was not made for this, but this work requires one who was born with special skills for it. Nevertheless, one should believe that anyone can achieve the goal, but he should try to always increase his efforts to overcome, and then one can break the rock in a short time.

We must also know that for the effort to make contact with the Creator, there is a very harsh condition here: The effort must be in the form of adornment. "Adornment" means something that is important to a person. One cannot work gladly if the labor is not of importance, meaning that one is happy that now he has contact with the Creator.

9. Baal HaSulam, *Shamati*, Article No. 5, "Lishma Is an Awakening from Above, and Why Do We Need an Awakening from Below?"

When one comes and says that he exerted extensively in observing Torah and *Mitzvot*, the Creator tells him, "You did not call Me, Jacob." In other words, it is not My baggage that you took. Rather, this baggage belongs to someone else. Since you say that you had much effort in Torah and *Mitzvot*, you must have had a different landlord for whom you worked; so go to him to pay you.

This is the meaning of "for you labored about Me, Israel." This means that he who works for the Creator has no labor, but on the contrary, pleasure and elation. But one who works for other goals cannot come to the Creator with complaints that the Creator does not give him vitality in the work, since he did not work for the Creator, for the Creator to pay for his work.

10. Baal HaSulam, Letter No. 5

I rejoice in those revealed corruptions and the ones that are being revealed.

I do, however, regret and complain about the corruptions that have still not appeared, but which are destined to appear, for a hidden corruption is hopeless, and its surfacing is a great salvation from heaven. The rule is that one does not give what he does not have. Hence, if it has appeared now, there is no doubt that it was here to begin with but was hidden. This is why I am happy when they come out of their holes because when you cast your eye on them, they become a pile of bones.

But I do not settle for it even for a moment, as I know that those who are with us are more numerous than those who are with them. But weakness stretches time, and those contemptible ants are hidden and their place is unknown. The sage says about this, "The fool folds his hands and eats his own flesh." Moses let down his hands, but when Moses lifts his hands of faith, all that should appear promptly appears, and then Israel triumphs "in all the mighty hand, and in all the great terror."

This is the meaning of "Whatever you find that your hand can do by your strength, do." When the cup is full, the verse, "The wicked are overthrown," comes true. And when the wicked are lost, light and gladness come to the world, and then they are gone.

11. Baal HaSulam, *Shamati*, Article No. 4, "What Is the Reason for the Heaviness One Feels when Annulling before the Creator in the Work?"

One's work is only to come to feel the existence of the Creator, meaning to feel the existence of the Creator, that "the whole earth is full of His glory," and this will be one's entire work. That is, all the energy one puts into the work will be only to achieve this, and nothing else.

One should not be misled into having to acquire anything. Rather, there is only one thing a person needs: faith in the Creator. He should not think of anything, meaning that the only reward that he wants for his work should be to be rewarded with faith in the Creator.

12. Baal HaSulam, Letter No. 16

I have already said in the name of the Baal Shem Tov that prior to making a *Mitzva* [commandment], one must not consider private Providence at all. On the contrary, one should say, "If I am not for me, who is for me?" But after the fact, one must reconsider and believe that it was not by "My power and the might of my hand" that I did the *Mitzva*, but only by the power of the Creator, who contemplated so about me in advance, and so I had to do.

It is likewise in worldly matters because spirituality and corporeality are equal. Therefore, before one goes out to make one's daily bread, he should remove his thoughts from private Providence and say, "If I am not for me, who is?" He should do all the tactics applied in corporeality to earn his living as do others.

But in the evening, when he returns home with his earnings, he must never think that he has earned this profit by his own innovations. Rather, even if he stayed all day in the basement of his home, he would still have earned his pay, for so the Creator contemplated for him in advance, and so it had to be.

Although the matters look the contrary on the surface, and are unreasonable, one must believe that so the Creator has determined for him in His law, from authors and from books.

13. Baal HaSulam, *Shamati*, Article No. 35, "Concerning the Vitality of Kedusha"

If one extends some illumination and cannot sustain it permanently because his *Kelim* [vessels] are not yet clean to be fit for the light, meaning that he will receive it in vessels of bestowal like the light that comes from the Giver, the illumination must depart from him.

At that time, this illumination falls into the hands of the *Sitra Achra*. This continues several times, meaning that one extends, and then it departs from him.

Hence, the illuminations increase in the sea of the *Sitra Achra* until the cup is full. This means that after one reveals the full measure of the effort that one can reveal, the *Sitra Achra* gives him back everything she took into her own authority. This is the meaning of "He has swallowed down riches, and he shall vomit them up again." It follows that all that the *Sitra Achra* received into her own authority was only as a deposit, meaning that as long as she has control over man, and the matter of the control that she has is so that one will be able to scrutinize one's vessels of reception and admit them into *Kedusha* [holiness].

In other words, had she not controlled a person, he would settle for little. Then all of one's vessels of reception would remain separated, and he would never be able to gather all the *Kelim* that belong to the root of his soul, admit them into *Kedusha*, and extend the light that belongs to him.

Hence, it is a correction that each time one extends something and has a descent, he must start anew, meaning new scrutinies. And what one had from the past has fallen into the *Sitra Achra*, who holds it in her authority as a deposit. Afterward, one receives from her everything that she received from him the whole time.

14. Baal HaSulam, "Introduction to The Study of the Ten Sefirot," Item 133

Like a king who wished to select for himself the most loyal of his subjects in the country and bring them to work inside his palace. What did he do? He issued a decree that anyone who wished, young or old, would come to his palace to engage in the works inside his palace.

However, he appointed many of his servants to guard the palace gate and all the roads leading to it, and ordered them to cunningly deflect all those nearing his palace and divert them from the way that leads to the palace.

Naturally, all the people in the country began to run to the king's palace. But the diligent guards cunningly rejected them. Many of them overpowered them and came near the palace gate, but the guards at the gate were the most diligent, and if someone approached the gate, they diverted him and turned him away with great craftiness until one despaired and returned as he had come.

And so they came and went, and regained strength, and came and went again, and so on and so forth for several days and years until they grew weary of trying. Only the mighty ones among them, whose patience endured, defeated the guards and opened the gate. And they were instantly awarded seeing the king's face, who appointed each of them in his right place.

Of course, from that moment on, they had no further dealings with those guards, who diverted and mislead them and made their lives bitter for several days and years, running back and forth around the gate. This is because they have been rewarded with working and serving before the glory of the king's face inside his palace.

15. Baal HaSulam, "Introduction to The Study of the Ten Sefirot," Item 101

As long as one is not rewarded with a guidance of revelation of the face, the abundance of Torah and *Mitzvot* he has performed make his concealment of the face much heavier. This is the meaning of "The Creator hides Himself in the Torah."

Indeed, all that heaviness he feels through the Torah is but proclamations by which the Torah itself calls him, awakening him to hurry up and give the required measure of labor to promptly endow him with the revelation of the face, as God wills it.

16. Baal HaSulam, Letter No. 34

We rush our pleas above, knock by knock, tirelessly, endlessly, and do not weaken at all when He does not answer us. We believe He hears our prayer but waits for a time when we have the *Kelim* [vessels] to receive the faithful bounty, and then we will receive a reply to each and every prayer at once, since "the hand of the Lord will not be short," God forbid.

This is the meaning of the words, "Children in whom there was no blemish ... and who have the strength to stand in the King's palace." It teaches you that even those who have been rewarded with pardon for iniquities—which became as merits, by which the matter appears after the fact, and in whom there is no blemish—still need more strength to stand in the King's palace, meaning stand and pray, and wait tirelessly, knock by knock, until they elicit the complete desire from the Creator.

This is why we should learn this trade before we enter the King's palace, meaning muster power and might to stand as a pillar of iron until we elicit the desire from the Creator, as it is written, "Take no rest." Although the Creator seems silent and unresponsive, let it not cross your minds to be silent, too, "Take no rest." This is not what the Creator intended by His silence, but rather to give you power to stand afterward in the King's palace when you have no blemish. This is why, "and give Him no rest."

17. Baal HaSulam, Letter No. 2

Come and learn from the complete worker (complete even in awakening from above). Ask your elders and they will tell you that the Complete One is complete in everything and has complete knowledge in the "blessing in his future." And yet, it does not weaken him at all because of it—from the labor in Torah and the searching.

On the contrary, none exert in the Torah and in searching as much as he. This is for a simple reason: His labor is not so much to bring the good future to himself. Rather, all his labor is about displaying love between him and his Maker. This is why the feelings of love grow and multiply each day until the love is completed in the form of "absolute love." Afterward, it leads him to double his wholeness by way of awakening from below.

18. RABASH, Article No. 488, "The Garments of the Soul"

It is known that nothing can be attained in spirituality except by clothing, which is like a *Kli* [vessel] that is suitable for revealing light. Hence, if a person exerts, the exertion makes the *Kli* for him, meaning the desire and the need for the filling of light, since nothing is given from above before there is a need for that illumination.

The labor that a person exerts causes him a need and a desire, meaning he becomes needy of the Creator's help to emerge from the strait in which he finds himself during the labor. Were it not for the labor, he would have no need for His help. It follows that precisely the labor provides him with the clothing of the soul, so there will be revelation of Godliness.

19. RABASH, Article No. 844, "Labor Is the Reward"

"According to the labor, so is the reward." In other words, afterward, he sees that the labor he gave was his reward. To the extent of the labor, so is the reward, since the labor is the reward, and the Creator gave him the desire to labor.

20. RABASH, Article No. 21 (1989), "What Is, 'A Drunken Man Must Not Pray,' in the Work?"

In order to have fuel to work in order to bestow and not receive any reward, but the work itself will be the reward, we must believe in Him, meaning believe in His greatness. We must make great efforts to obtain faith in the greatness of the Creator. Without faith in the greatness of the Creator, there is no power to work in order to bestow. That is, precisely when we feel the greatness of the Creator, a person is ready to work without any reward.

Instead, the work itself is the reward, since serving a great King is more valuable to him than any fortune in the world, compared to this service, that the Creator permits him to come in and serve Him. Hence, we must focus all our thoughts on how to come to feel the greatness of the Creator, and then everything follows that point.

21. RABASH, Article No. 22 (1985), "The Whole of the Torah Is One Holy Name"

We must always consider the goal, which is to "do good to His creations." If the evil inclination comes to a person and asks him all of Pharaoh's questions, he should not reply with lame excuses, but say, "Now, with your questions, I can begin with the work of bestowal."

This means that we should not say about the questions of the evil inclination that it came to us in order to lower us from our degree. On the contrary, now it is giving us a place to work, by which we will ascend on the degrees of wholeness. That is, any overcoming in the work is called "walking in the work of the Creator," since each penny joins into a great amount." That is, all the times we overcome accumulate to a certain measure required to become a *Kli* for the reception of the abundance.

22. RABASH, Article No. 6 (1991), "What Is, 'The Herdsmen of Abram's Cattle and the Herdsmen of Lot's Cattle,' in the Work?"

Since in every beginning a person must start over the acceptance of the kingdom of heaven, it is not enough that yesterday he had faith in the Creator. For this reason, every acceptance of the kingdom of heaven is considered a new discernment. That is, now he receives a part of the vacant space that was devoid of the kingdom of heaven, and admits that empty place and fills it with the kingdom of heaven. It follows that now he sorted out a new thing, which did not exist before he took that empty place and filled it with the kingdom of heaven. This is regarded as elevating a new spark into the *Kedusha*. Finally, from all the ascents, he always raises sparks from the vacant space into the *Kedusha*.

It follows that from each descent he arrives at a new beginning and raises new sparks. Hence, when a person sees that he has descents, he should be careful not to escape from the campaign, even though he sees that he is not progressing. Rather, he must try to start anew each time. That is, the fact that he begins to ascend does not mean that he returned to his previous degree. This would mean that he did nothing by his work, since he thinks that he is now ascending to his previous level. Rather, he must believe that this is a new discernment, that each time, he raises different sparks, until he raises the sparks that pertain to his essence.

23. RABASH, Article No. 30 (1989), "What Is the Meaning of Lighting the Menorah in the Work?"

Only one who labors and works as much as he can, and goes through ups and downs, can say that he tastes the taste of darkness because he cannot overcome his will to receive for himself.

Thus, the descents that a person receives when he wants to walk on the path of truth are instruments for the sensation of the help he will receive. We must believe the words of our sages who said, "He who comes to purify is aided." A person must not escape the campaign when he sees that he is not making progress. Sometimes he gets thoughts of the spies, who said that this work is not for us and requires special people who can walk on the path of overcoming.

All this comes to him because he understands that each time, he must see how he is making progress. However, it does not occur to him that he must advance in obtaining darkness, that this is the only *Kli* he needs to acquire. A *Kli* is a need for a filling. That is, if he has no filling for the lack, he feels that he is in the dark. For this reason, a person must not say that he is not advancing in the work.

Hence, he wants to escape the campaign, for it is not the truth, since he sees each time how far he is from obtaining the light, meaning for the Creator to give him the *Kli* called "desire to bestow." He cannot obtain the desire to bestow by himself, and then he comes to feel that the world has grown dark on him. At that time, the light comes, meaning help from above, as it is written, "He who comes to purify is aided."

24. RABASH, Article No. 572, "Two Labors"

The order of one's work in *Torah and Mitzvot* [commandments] when he wants to work for the sake of the Creator is that one must fight and defeat the evil inclination.

That is, it is human nature to toil when there is self-benefit. But when he sees that no self-benefit will emerge from this work, he cannot work. Instead, he complains and asks, "What is this work for you?" meaning what will you gain from exerting?

When a person overcomes it and says that he wants to work against nature and bestow upon the Creator, the evil inclination comes with a different argument, asking the question of wicked Pharaoh, "Who is the Lord that I should obey His voice?" It is possible to work for the sake of others only where I know that the other receives the labor.

However, when he has two labors, 1) He must overcome and go against nature, and work not for his own benefit but for the benefit of others, for the sake of the Creator. 2) He must believe that the Creator receives his labor.

25. RABASH, Article No. 837, "*Ibur* [Conception] – 2"

Ibur Aleph [first conception] is done by the upper one, like a person who receives an awakening from above. *Ibur Bet* [second conception] means that the lower one must work by himself by the power of the awakening he had received. In other words, he must add, through the awakening he had received from the upper one, and work by his labor. Otherwise, he loses everything and returns to being a black dot, meaning that his spirituality is regarded as darkness that does not shine.

26. RABASH, Article No. 23 (1989), "What Is, 'If He Swallows the Bitter Herb, He Will Not Come Out,' in the Work?"

When one begins the work, he begins with faith, but the body resists this work, and then comes a state of labor, when he must overcome the body and seek all kinds of counsels, as our sages said, "In trickery shall you conduct war," since the body does not want to relinquish self-benefit. To the extent that he exerts, to that extent he begins to feel that he is incapable of doing anything since in his view, he has done everything he could. After the labor, he comes to know that only the Creator can help, and it is out of his hands. Then comes the third state—a prayer—and then the prayer is from the bottom of the heart, since it is utterly clear to him that no one can help him but the Creator.

However, even when he comes to know that the Creator can help him, and he understands that the real advice is only prayer, the body comes and makes him see that "You see how many prayers you have already prayed but you received no answer from above. Therefore, why bother praying that the Creator will help you? You see that you are not getting any help from above." At that time, he cannot pray. Then we need to overcome once more through faith, and believe that the Creator does hear the prayer of every mouth, and it does not matter if the person is adept and has good qualities, or to the contrary. Rather, he must overcome and believe above reason, although his reason dictates that since he has prayed many times but still received no answer from above, how can he come and pray once more? This, too, requires overcoming, meaning to exert above reason and pray that the Creator will help him overcome his view and pray.

27. RABASH, Letter No. 14

One is rewarded with everything only by overcoming, called "strength," and each and every strength that a person elicits joins into a great amount. That is, even if a person overcomes once and gets an alien thought, and says, "But I already know from experience that soon I will not have this desire for the work, so what will I get now if I overcome it a little?'" At that time, he must reply that many pennies join into a great amount, meaning to the general account, whether to the root of his soul or to the public.

28. RABASH, Article No. 1 (1986), "Moses Went"

One who has already begun the work, and is not saying that he will wait until the Creator gives him the desire to do the holy work and then he will begin to work. Rather, he does not want to wait because the craving to work and reach the truth pushes him forward though he does not see that he will have the ability to go forward alone, like Nahshon.

However, he sees that he cannot continue this work and is afraid that the burden of the kingdom of heaven, which he is now carrying, is beginning to fall off from him so he begins to call out for help, since he sees that each time, the burden he has taken on himself begins to fall. It is like a person carrying a sack on his back and sees that the sack is beginning to fall. We see that in corporeality, each one he asks for help helps him right away, and no one puts him off for later.

Similarly, in spirituality, one who begins to see that the burden and load are beginning to fall off from him, meaning the work he had previously assumed, to be "as an ox to the burden and as a donkey to the load," and he sees that soon he will be in descent, so he cries out to the Creator and receives help. It is as our sages said, "He who comes to purify is aided," as is written in *The Zohar*.

Conversely, Baal HaSulam said about one who waits for the Creator to help him first and then he will have the strength to work, that it is as it is written (Ecclesiastes, 11), "He who guards the wind will not sow and he who looks at the clouds…" meaning that he stands and waits for the Creator to send a spirit of repentance. This man will never reach the truth.

29. RABASH, Article No. 19 (1985), "Come unto Pharaoh – 1"

To keep from losing what he is given, one must first make great efforts, for something that comes to a person through labor causes him to keep the thing and not lose it. But during the exertion, when a person sees that the work is still far from finished, he sometimes escapes the campaign and falls into despair. At that time he needs great strengthening, to believe that the Creator will help him, and the fact that help has not arrived is because he has not given the required quantity and quality of labor for preparing the deficiency in order to receive the filing, as it is said ("Introduction to the Study of the Ten Sefirot," Item 18), "And if one practices Torah and fails to remove the evil inclination from himself, it is either that he has been negligent in giving the necessary labor and exertion in the practice of Torah, as it is written, 'I have not labored but found, do not believe,' or perhaps one did put in the necessary amount of labor, but has been negligent in the quality."

30. RABASH, Article No. 30 (1988), "What to Look for in the Assembly of Friends"

A person should make an effort to obtain love of others. And this is called "labor," since he must exert above reason. Reasonably thinking, "How is it possible to judge another person to the side of merit when his reason shows him his friend's true face, that he hates him?" What can he tell the body about that? Why should he submit himself before his friend?

The answer is that he wishes to achieve *Dvekut* [adhesion] with the Creator, called "equivalence of form," meaning not to think of his own benefit. Thus, why is subduing a difficult thing? The reason is that he must revoke his own worth, and the whole of the life that he wishes to live will be only with the consideration of his ability to work for others' benefit, beginning with love of others, between man and man, through the love of the Creator.

Hence, here is a place where he can say that anything he does is without any self-interest, since by reason, the friends are the ones who should love him, but he overcomes his reason, goes above reason, and says, "It is not worth living for myself."

31. RABASH, Article No. 24 (1991), "What Does It Mean that One Should Bear a Son and a Daughter, in the Work?"

When a person prevails and asks for help from the Creator, after he has decided that he has a harm-doer in his heart, called "will to receive," and that he cannot emerge from it, meaning after going through several ascents and descents, he finally sees that he has remained bare and destitute. At that time, his prayer is from the bottom of the heart. That is, he sees that if the Creator does not help him, he cannot overcome it.

Although one can say that he believes above reason that only the Creator helps him, within reason, he does not feel this, since he knows that he himself made the efforts and the labor to obtain something in spirituality. But when one sees that after all the exertions, he cannot emerge from the governance of the will to receive for himself, then he sees within reason that only the Creator can help him.

32. RABASH, Article No. 16 (1984), "Concerning Bestowal"

It is said about that (*Kidushin*, 30), "Man's inclination overcomes him each day and seeks to kill him, as it is said, 'The wicked watches the righteous, and seeks to slay him.' And if the Creator did not help him, he would not overcome it, as it is said, 'The Lord will not leave him in his hand.'"

This means that first, one must see if he has the strength to come to be able to act with the aim to bestow contentment upon the Creator. Then, when he has already come to realize that he cannot achieve it by himself, that person focuses his Torah and *Mitzvot* on a single point, which is that "the light in it reforms him," that this will be the only reward that he wants from the Torah and *Mitzvot*. In other words, the reward for his labor will be for the Creator to give him this strength called "the power of bestowal."

33. RABASH, Article No. 16 (1984), "Concerning Bestowal"

The only reward we need is the *Kli*, which is called "the power of bestowal." Thus, all we need are *Kelim* [plural of *Kli*], and not lights, and this is why the reward is primarily the power of bestowal.

However, to obtain that *Kli*, called "the desire to bestow," we need a desire, meaning to feel that we need this *Kli*. This is why we must first engage in Torah and *Mitzvot* in *Lo Lishma*, and this is our labor—to see that everything we do is for self-benefit, without any intention to bestow.

And then we see that we need the power of bestowal, and we want a reward for our work—that the Creator will give us this reward—the desire to bestow.

34. RABASH, Article No. 37 (1985), "Who Testifies to a Person?"

What can one do if, after all the efforts he has made, he still does not feel the lack of not being able to bestow as pain and suffering? The solution is to ask the Creator to give him the *Kli* called, "A lack from not feeling," and that he is unconscious, without any pain from being unable to bestow.

35. RABASH, Article No. 587, "The Upper One Scrutinizes for the Purpose of the Lower One"

The lower one is powerless to begin the work, but only in the form of *Lo Lishma* [not for Her sake], called "will to receive," for only the *Lo Lishma* gives the first moving force of the lower one, for when a person does not find sufficient flavor in corporeal pleasures, he begins to search for spiritual pleasures.

It follows that the root of the work of the lower one is the will to receive, and the prayer, called MAN, rises up, and then the upper one corrects this MAN and places on it the power of the *Masach*, which is a desire to delay the abundance before the lower one knows about himself that his aim is to bestow.

That is, the upper one bestows upon the lower one good taste and pleasure in the desire to bestow, by which the lower one feels His exaltedness. At that time, he begins to understand that it is worthwhile to annul before Him and cancel his existence before Him. Then, he feels that all that there is in reality is only because such is His will, that the Creator wants the lower one to exist, but for himself, he wants to annul his existence. It follows that then, all the vitality he feels is regarded as *Lishma* and not for himself.

When he feels this, it is considered that he already has the correction of the MAN, and then he is also fit to receive the MAD, as well, for there is no contradiction between them anymore, since the lower one, too, wants the benefit of the upper one and not his own benefit.

It is considered that when the upper one gives the lower one *Mochin*, he also gives him the clothing of the *Mochin*, meaning that he gives the lower one the abundance, as well as the power of the *Masach*, which is the desire to bestow. This is the meaning of "from *Lo Lishma*, we come to *Lishma*."

36. RABASH, Article No. 721, "The Segula of Torah and Mitzvot"

There is a *Segula* [power/cure] in *Torah and Mitzvot* [commandments] that if he learns with this intention, although his heart disagrees with it, and all that he does with this intention is against his will and heart, yet through compulsory work, he is rewarded with inverting his desire from self-love to love of others.

We should understand what is written, that it is harder to attain the concept of bestowal upon others as this is against nature. Nevertheless, through the power of *Torah and Mitzvot* in order to bestow, we can be rewarded with inverting our nature into aiming to bestow.

There is a question: When one is immersed in the nature of self-love, how can he engage in *Torah and Mitzvot* in order to bestow, since he has no desire or ability whatsoever to do anything unless it is for his own sake? Thus, how can one be educated into engaging in *Torah and Mitzvot* in order to bestow?

We should say that although man's nature is only self-love, and that which is against it is hard for him to do, to the point that all his organs go against him, but there is the matter of coercion, meaning that when he engages in *Torah and Mitzvot*, he learns against his will, meaning that he wants it to be only for the sake of the Creator, and then he learns and thinks only about things that speak of the matter of bestowal.

And although the body disagrees, through the labor in which he exerts himself, forcing his body to work with this intention, although his heart's desire disagrees with this intention, the light in it reforms him.

37. RABASH, Article No. 295, "Anyone Who Sanctifies the Seventh – 1"

When one comes to a degree where he wants to bestow upon the Creator, meaning give contentment to his Maker, he begins to contemplate what the Creator needs so he can give it to Him, since all his concerns are to please the Creator. At that time, he realizes that the only reason He created the world was to receive pleasures from Him, and that more than this, the Creator does not need. Hence, he follows the Creator's will and receives the pleasures.

At that time, there is no issue of bread of shame because he is not receiving the pleasures because he wants to enjoy, but because he wants to bestow upon the Creator, for when one achieves the degree of wanting only to bestow upon the Creator, the *Tzimtzum* is lifted from him and he sees the world as full of His glory.

Then he sees that all this was revealed to him so he would enjoy it. Hence, once he has obtained the degree of bestowal, meaning obtained the degree where all he wants is only to bestow contentment upon the Creator, he fills himself with all the pleasures that his eyes see, as in the explanation, "The whole earth is full of His glory."

It follows that all that one needs to obtain that he can define as a reward after he has toiled several years is only one thing: the desire to bestow, meaning the degree of wanting to serve the rav not in order to receive reward.

All the labor where one needs to exert himself in *Torah and Mitzvot* [commandments] is only to obtain this. This is called "fear of heaven," as it is written, "What does the Lord your God ask of you? Only to fear Me."

38. RABASH, Article No. 24 (1986), "The Difference between Charity and Gift"

In the work of the Creator, in the beginning of his work he had energy and confidence, and great importance for Torah and prayer because at that time he had grace of holiness, and felt that the work of the Creator is important. However, this was still not considered a "deficiency" that the Creator will satisfy, a deficiency is called *Dvekut* [adhesion] with the Creator, since the lack and pain of not having *Dvekut* with the Creator was still not felt in him as he has not exerted for it because he has just begun the work.

But after a long period of time of making efforts and not achieving satisfaction of his deficiency, torments and pain begin to form in him because he has made efforts but sees no progress in his work. At that time the thoughts begin to come one-by-one. Sometimes it is with sparks of despair, and sometimes he grows stronger, but then he sees once more that he has fallen from his state, and so on repeatedly. Finally, a real deficiency forms in him, which he has obtained through exertion in ascents and descents. These ascents and descents leave him with pain each time at not having been granted *Dvekut* with the Creator. Finally, when the cup of labor has been filled sufficiently, it is called a *Kli*. Then the filling of it comes from the Creator, since now he has a real *Kli*.

It follows that his seeing that now—after several years of work—he has retreated, this happens deliberately so he will ache at not having *Dvekut* with the Creator. It turns out that each time he must see that he is approaching the making of the *Kli*, called "real deficiency." That is, his gauge of *Katnut* [infancy/smallness] and *Gadlut* [adulthood/greatness] of the deficiency is to the extent of the suffering he feels at not having the filling, which is called here "*Dvekut* with the Creator," where all he wants is only to bring contentment to the Creator.

39. Rabbi Nachman of Breslov, *Likutey Moharan*, Last Edition, Mark 48

The work of the Creator requires great persistence, whatever happens to him. Remember this well for you will need it very much as you begin the work of the Creator. It requires great tenacity, and to be strong and brave, to brace oneself and stand still, even if you are dropped down every time. You must not allow yourself to fall off altogether, for it is necessary to experience all those falls, descents, and confusions prior to entering the gates of *Kedusha* [holiness], and the true righteous, too, have gone through all of it. Know, that man must cross and very, very narrow bridge, and the rule and the most important thing is not to be afraid at all.

7

Intention

1. Baal HaSulam, *Shamati*, Article No. 38, "The Fear of God Is His Treasure"

When one engages in Torah and *Mitzvot* with the intention to be rewarded with bringing contentment to one's Maker, that aim that rests on the acts of *Mitzvot* and the study of Torah brings one to attain it. Otherwise, one might remain—although he observes Torah and *Mitzvot* in every item and detail—he will still remain merely in the degree of still of *Kedusha* [holiness].

It follows that one should always remember the reason that obligates him to engage in Torah and *Mitzvot*. This is the meaning of what our sages meant by "that your *Kedusha* will be for My Name." It means that I will be your cause, meaning that all your work is in wanting to delight Me, meaning that all your actions will be in order to bestow.

Our sages said (*Berachot* 20), "Everything there is in keeping, there is in remembering." This means that all those who engage in observing Torah and *Mitzvot* with the aim to achieve "remembering," by way of "When I remember Him, He does not let me sleep." It follows, that the keeping is primarily in order to be awarded remembering.

Thus, one's desire to remember that the Creator is the cause for observing Torah and *Mitzvot*. This is so because it follows that the reason and the cause to observe the Torah and *Mitzvot* is the Creator, as without it one cannot adhere to the Creator, since "He and I cannot dwell in the same abode" due to the disparity of form.

2. Baal HaSulam, "Introduction to The Study of the Ten Sefirot," Item 18

The Creator, Who created it and gave the evil inclination its strength, evidently knew to create the remedy and the spice liable to wear off the power of the evil inclination and eradicate it altogether.

And if one practices Torah and fails to remove the evil inclination from himself, it is either that he has been negligent in giving the necessary labor and exertion in the practice of Torah, as it is written, "I did not labor and found, do not believe," or perhaps he did put in the necessary amount of labor, but has been negligent in the quality.

This means that while practicing Torah, they did not set their minds and hearts to draw the light in the Torah, which brings faith to one's heart. Rather, they have been absent-minded about the principal requirement demanded of the Torah, namely the light that yields faith. And although they initially aimed for it, their minds went astray during the study.

3. Baal HaSulam, "Introduction to The Study of the Ten Sefirot," Item 17

The student pledges, prior to the study, to strengthen himself in faith in the Creator and in His guidance in reward and punishment, as our sages said, "Your employer is liable to pay you the reward for your work." One should aim one's labor to be for the *Mitzvot* of the Torah, and in this way, he will be rewarded with enjoying the light in it, and his faith will strengthen and grow through the power in this light, as it is written, "It shall be health to your navel, and marrow to your bones" (Proverbs 3:8).

Then one can be certain that from *Lo Lishma* he will come to *Lishma*, in a way that even one who knows about himself that he has not been rewarded with faith still has hope through the practice of Torah, for if he sets his heart and mind to attain faith in the Creator through it, there is no greater *Mitzva* than this. It is as our sages said, "Habakkuk came and stressed only this: 'A righteous shall live by his faith'" (*Makkot* 24). Moreover, there is no other counsel but this.

4. Baal HaSulam, *Shamati*, Article No. 4, "What Is the Reason for the Heaviness One Feels when Annulling before the Creator in the Work?"

The essence of one's work is only to come to feel the existence of the Creator, meaning to feel the existence of the Creator, that "the whole earth is full of His glory," and this will be one's entire work. That is, all the energy one puts into the work will be only to achieve this, and nothing else.

One should not be misled into having to acquire anything. Rather, there is only one thing a person needs: faith in the Creator. He should not think of anything, meaning that the only reward that he wants for his work should be to be rewarded with faith in the Creator.

5. Baal HaSulam, *Shamati*, Article No. 19, "What Is 'The Creator Hates the Bodies,' in the Work?"

One must always examine oneself, the purpose of one's work, meaning if the Creator receives contentment in every act that one performs, because he wants equivalence of form with the Creator. This is called "All your actions will be for the sake of the Creator," meaning that one wants the Creator to enjoy everything he does, as it is written, "to bring contentment to his Maker."

Also, one needs to conduct oneself with the will to receive and say to it, "I have already decided that I do not want to receive any pleasure because you want to enjoy, since with your desire I am forced to be separated from the Creator, for disparity of form causes separation and distance from the Creator."

One's hope should be that since he cannot break free from the power of the will to receive, he is therefore in perpetual ascents and descents. Hence, he awaits the Creator, to be rewarded with the Creator opening his eyes, and to have the strength to overcome and work only for the sake of the Creator. It is as it is written, "One have I asked of the Lord; her will I seek." "Her" means the *Shechina* [Divinity]. And one asks "that I may dwell in the house of the Lord all the days of my life."

6. Baal HaSulam, Letter No. 17

The path of truth is a very thin line that one walks until one comes to the King's palace.

One who begins to walk in the beginning of the line needs great care so as not to deviate to the right or to the left of the line even as much as a hairsbreadth, for if at first the deviation is as a hairsbreadth, even if one continues completely straight, it is certain that he will no longer come to the King's palace, as he is not stepping on the true line.

7. Baal HaSulam, Letter No. 17

There are three discernments: 1) Israel is one who exerts to return to his root; 2) The Creator, namely the root he longs for; 3) The 613 ways of the Torah by which one purifies one's soul and body. This is the spice, as it is written, "I have created the evil inclination; I have created for it the Torah as a spice."

However, these three are actually one and the same. In the end, any servant of the Creator attains them as one, unique, and unified discernment, and they only appear to be divided into three because of one's incompleteness in the work of the Creator.

8. Baal HaSulam, *Shamati*, Article No. 5, "Lishma Is an Awakening from Above, and Why Do We Need an Awakening from Below?"

It is written, "Then shall you delight in the Lord." The meaning of "Then" is that first, in the beginning of his work, he did not have pleasure. Instead, his work was coercive.

But afterward, when he has already accustomed himself to work in order to bestow and not examine himself—if he is feeling a good taste in the work—but believes that he is working to bring contentment to his Maker through his work, he should believe that the Creator accepts the work of the lower ones regardless of how and how much is the form of their work. In everything, the Creator examines the intention, and this brings contentment to the Creator. Then one is rewarded with "delight in the Lord."

Even during the work of the Creator he will feel delight and pleasure since now he really does work for the Creator because the effort he made during the coercive work qualifies him to be able to truly work for the Creator. You find that then, too, the pleasure he receives relates to the Creator, meaning specifically for the Creator.

9. Baal HaSulam, *Shamati*, Article No. 3, "The Matter of Spiritual Attainment"

May we merit receiving His light and following the ways of the Creator, and to serve Him not in order to receive reward but to give contentment to the Creator and raise the *Shechina* [Divinity] from the dust. May we be rewarded with *Dvekut* [adhesion] with the Creator and the revelation of His Godliness to His creatures.

10. RABASH, Article No. 12 (1988), "What Are Torah and Work in the Way of the Creator?"

Prior to the study, a person should examine with which purpose does he want to observe the *Mitzva* [commandment] of learning Torah? That is, does he engage in Torah because of the Torah itself, in order to know how to observe the rules of doing the *Mitzvot*, or is the learning of Torah itself his whole intention, and knowing the rules of doing the *Mitzvot* is a completely different matter for him? meaning he is learning Torah for two reasons.

However, even while learning Torah for the sake of learning Torah, he should still distinguish with which intention he is learning. Is it to observe the commandments of the Creator, as it is written, "And you shall reflect on Him day and night," or is he learning in order to receive the light of Torah because he needs the light of Torah in order to cancel the evil within him, as our sages said, "I have created the evil inclination; I have created the Torah as a spice"? It turns out that he is learning in order to obtain the spice, as our sages said, "The light in it reforms him."

Certainly, prior to learning Torah, a person should examine the reason for which he is learning Torah, for any act needs to have some purpose that causes him to do the act. It is as our sages said, "A prayer without an aim is as a body without a soul."

11. RABASH, Article No. 27 (1985), "Repentance"

Our sages said, "One should always engage in Torah and *Mitzvot*, even if *Lo Lishma* [not for Her sake], since from *Lo Lishma* he comes to *Lishma* [for Her sake]" (Pesachim, 50b). Thus, in the act of *Mitzvot* and in the study of Torah there is a big difference between the revealed part, meaning the act, and the concealed part, meaning the intention, since no person can look at the intention, for the act that one does between man and God does not have a person in the middle who can criticize his intention. Normally, each one is busy with himself and does not have time to think of his friend's calculations. It follows that only he thinks of the intention.

That is, when he engages in *Lo Lishma*, meaning expects reward, the work and the reward are not in the same place and in the same time. But here, when we are speaking of punishments, the transgression and the punishment are not in the same place and in the same time, since he receives the punishment after he commits the transgression, and afterwards he suffers the punishment—a punishment in this world or a punishment in the next world. This applies only to the part of *Lo Lishma*.

However, in those who work on the intention—to be able to aim their actions only to bestow—the reward and the punishment are in the same place and the same time, since his inability to aim the act of bestowing contentment upon the Creator is his punishment, and he does not need to be given any other punishments, for nothing torments him more than seeing that he is still far from the Creator.

The evidence is that he does not have the love of the Creator, that he wants to respect Him. All this is because he is in a state of *Achoraim* [posterior] and concealment from the Creator. This is what pains him, and this is his punishment. But here is his reward—if he has love for the Creator and wants to bestow contentment upon him. However, all this concerns specifically those who want come to work only for the Creator, and not in *Lo Lishma*. It can be said about them that the punishment and the reward are in the same place and in the same time.

12. RABASH, Article No. 577, "Concerning the Goal"

Our sages said, "The Creator said, 'I have created the evil inclination; I have created the Torah as a spice.'" In other words, the *Torah and Mitzvot* spice up the evil inclination so it becomes tasty, for the evil inclination is called the "will to receive."

For itself, it is tasteless, for the *Tzimtzum* is on it and it remains in the vacant space. But through the *Torah and Mitzvot*, he achieves the intention to bestow. Then, with this *Kli*, called "will to receive," he receives all the delight and pleasure.

13. RABASH, Article No. 940, "The Point in the Heart"

It is written, "And let them make Me a Temple and I will dwell within them." This pertains to the point in the heart, which should be a Temple where the light of the Creator dwells, as it is written, "And I will dwell within them." Hence, one should try to build his structure of *Kedusha* [holiness], and the structure should be able to contain the upper abundance called "abundance poured from the Giver to the receiver." However, according to the rule, there must be equivalence of form between the Giver and the receiver so the receiver, too, must have the aim to bestow like the Giver.

This is called "action," as it is written, "Let them make Me a Temple," where the acting applies to the *Kli* [vessel] and not the light, since the light pertains to the Creator and only the action pertains to the creatures.

14. RABASH, Article No. 12 (1988), "What Are Torah and Work in the Way of the Creator?"

The purpose of the study is to come to feel the giver of the Torah. If a person does not place the goal of reaching the giver of the Torah in front of him, he is regarded as a gentile, meaning one who has no need for faith. That is, he should have the need to seek advice to achieve faith. This is why he is still considered a gentile and not "Israel."

16. RABASH, Article No. 502, "If Man Wins, the Creator Is Happy"

The intention of the Emanator is for the lower ones to receive pleasure. Yet, man uses the Torah in the opposite manner, wanting the Creator to receive pleasure. He receives this power from the Torah, from that spice. It follows that he is fighting with the Creator, meaning that the Creator wants man to receive pleasure, and man wants the Creator to receive pleasure.

Thus, he uses the Torah in the opposite direction from the seller. It was said about this that the Creator says, "My sons defeated Me." That is, they fight against the will to receive that the Creator imprinted in their hearts, where if the man wins, the Creator is happy.

It follows that the Torah of the Creator is according to the purpose of creation, and "His Torah" is when man uses the Torah with the aim of the spice, when he takes the Torah in order to please the Creator. This is why the Torah is named after man.

The Torah is named after its use: If a person wants to receive the Torah with the Creator's intention—to do good to His creations—so the creatures will enjoy, it is called "the Torah of the Creator," when the Torah follows the line of the Creator. If a person takes the Torah so as to have the power to bestow, this is regarded as man's intention, where man wants to bestow contentment upon his Maker, and then it is regarded as his Torah.

16. RABASH, Letter No. 8

At the end of the day, this is a group of people who have gathered in a certain place, under a certain leader, to be together. With superhuman courage they face up to all those who rise against them. Indeed, they are brave men with a strong spirit, and they are determined not to retreat one inch. They are first-class fighters, fighting the war against the inclination to their last drop of blood, and their only wish is to win the battle for the glory of His name.

17. RABASH, Article No. 1 (1984), "Purpose of Society – 1"

We gather here—to establish a society where each of us follows the spirit of bestowing upon the Creator. And to achieve bestowal upon the Creator, we must begin with bestowal upon man, which is called "love of others."

And love of others can only be through revoking of one's self. Thus, on the one hand, each person should feel lowly, and on the other hand, be proud that the Creator has given us the chance to be in a society where each of us has but a single goal: for The *Shechina* [Divinity] to be among us.

18. RABASH, Article No. 1 (1984), "Purpose of Society – 2"

There should be careful watch in the society, disallowing frivolity, since frivolity ruins everything.

19. RABASH, Article No. 29 (1989), "What Is the Preparation to Receive the Torah in the Work? – 2"

Our sages said, "The Torah exists only in one who puts himself to death over it." We should understand the word "exists." What does it tell us? We should interpret this according to what our sages said, "The Creator said, 'I have created the evil inclination; I have created the Torah as a spice.'" That is, the Torah should be a spice. In whom is this so, since "There is no light without a *Kli*, no filling without a lack"?

For this reason, they said that those who want to put their selves to death, meaning want to put to death the will to receive for their own sake, and want to do everything for the sake of the Creator, see that they cannot do this on their own. To them the Creator said, "I have created the evil inclination; I have created the Torah as a spice."

20. RABASH, Article No. 13 (1989), "What Is the Bread of an Evil-Eyed Man, in the Work?"

All our work in Torah and *Mitzvot* is in order to emerge from the exile of the will to receive for ourselves. In other words, we must aim—while engaging in Torah and *Mitzvot*—that our reward will be that by this we will be rewarded with emerging from the exile and enslavement in the will to receive for ourselves, and we will be able to work only in order to bring contentment to the Creator, and we will not demand any other reward for our work in Torah and *Mitzvot*.

In other words, we want to be rewarded with feeling—while engaging in Torah and *Mitzvot*—that we are serving a great and important king, and that by this there will be love of the Creator within us, from feeling His exaltedness. However, all of our pleasure will come from serving the Creator; this will be our reward, and not that He will somehow reward us for the work. Instead, we will feel that the work itself is the reward, and there is no greater reward in the world than the privilege of serving the Creator.

21. RABASH, Article No. 12 (1988), "What Are Torah and Work in the Way of the Creator?"

It is beneficial to elicit the light from the Torah—if he aims while engaging in the Torah, to learn in order to receive the reward of the Torah, called "light." At that time, the learning of Torah is good for him. But when he is distracted from the purpose of studying Torah, the Torah does not help complete the work of making the vessels of bestowal and not using the vessels of reception for one's own sake. Otherwise, his Torah vanishes from him. That is, the force of Torah and that should have subdued the evil inclination is cancelled. This is the meaning of the words, "Any Torah with which there is no work," meaning when he does not aim for the Torah to do the work of turning the vessels of reception to work in order to bestow, "is finally cancelled," meaning that that force is cancelled.

22. RABASH, Article No. 20 (1985), "He who Hardens His Heart"

One who wants to walk on the path of the Creator is called *Yashar-El* [straight to the Creator], which is directly to the Creator. This means that he wants all the actions that he does to rise straight to the Creator, and does not want to have any other intention.

23. RABASH, Article No. 721, "The Segula of Torah and Mitzvot"

There is a *Segula* [power/cure] in *Torah and Mitzvot* [commandments] that if he learns with this intention, although his heart disagrees with it, and all that he does with this intention is against his will and heart, yet through compulsory work, he is rewarded with inverting his desire from self-love to love of others.

We should understand what is written, that it is harder to attain the concept of bestowal upon others as this is against nature. Nevertheless, through the power of *Torah and Mitzvot* in order to bestow, we can be rewarded with inverting our nature into aiming to bestow.

There is a question: When one is immersed in the nature of self-love, how can he engage in *Torah and Mitzvot* in order to bestow, since he has no desire or ability whatsoever to do anything unless it is for his own sake? Thus, how can one be educated into engaging in *Torah and Mitzvot* in order to bestow?

We should say that although man's nature is only self-love, and that which is against it is hard for him to do, to the point that all his organs go against him, but there is the matter of coercion, meaning that when he engages in *Torah and Mitzvot*, he learns against his will, meaning that he wants it to be only for the sake of the Creator, and then he learns and thinks only about things that speak of the matter of bestowal.

And although the body disagrees, through the labor in which he exerts himself, forcing his body to work with this intention, although his heart's desire disagrees with this intention, the light in it reforms him.

24. RABASH, Article No. 496, "The Path of Truth"

Those who walk on the path of truth, who want to bring contentment to the Maker, see that everything they do is not for the sake of the Creator, so they pray to the Creator to see that they can work for the sake of the Creator.

At that time, the Creator says, "Wherever I mention My name," meaning that you will give me the possibility to attribute My name to your actions. In other words, there will be an awakening from below, where I, says the Creator, will attribute My name to the actions. So how will you know that I am already attributing My name to them? You will see this if I "come to you and bless you."

In other words, the whole purpose of creation, which is to do good to His creations, cannot be revealed before you correct the matter of the bread of shame, meaning that you work in order to bestow. At that time, the purpose of creation will come true, which is to do good to His creations.

25. *Zohar for All*, *Toldot* [Generations], "He called – I Do Not Know the Day of My Death," Item 125

One should engage in the Torah with the aim to extol the Creator and make Him respected and important in the world.
He tells us the meaning of Torah *Lishma* [for her name], which is highways in their hearts: to aim one's heart so his engagement in the Torah will draw abundance of knowledge for him and for the whole world. Thus, the name of the Creator will grow in the world, as it is written, "And the earth shall be filled of the knowledge of the Lord." Then the words, "And the Lord shall be king over all the earth" will come true.

26. RAMAK, *Know the God of Your Father*

One who learns Torah in order to know, as one who learns in a history book, this will certainly do him no good in his learning and no benefit will come to him from it, and I wish that he will not lose. Rather, when one comes to learn Torah, his intention must be to learn that matter because they are Godly words whose great depth is concealed from him. By this, the breath of Torah that comes out of his mouth before the Creator will be good.

27. Rav Yitzchak Safrin of Komarno, *The Path of Unification*

When you aim, with submission and fear, to awaken the surrounding lights and the *Mochin* above, although you do not know any essence or the surrounding lights or the *Mochin* of anything, still, by your knowledge, you awaken their existence. And although you do not know their essence, a great light is drawn over to you.

28. Elimelech of Lizhensk, Noam Elimelech [The Pleasantness of Elimelech]

Do save us from envy of one another, and let no envy of others come into our hearts, nor our envy of others. On the contrary, let our hearts see the virtues of our friends and not their faults, and let us speak to each other in a way that is seemly and worthy before You, and let no hatred rise in one towards another. Brace our ties of love to You, as it is known to You that all will be for bringing contentment to You, and this is our main intention. And should we not have the wit to aim our hearts to You, You will teach us, so we may truly know the aim of Your good will.

29. Rav Chaim Vital, Shaar HaGilgulim, Introduction, 38

To aim to love each one from Israel as his own soul, for by this his prayer would rise comprising all of Israel and will be able to ascend and make a correction above. Especially, our love of friends, each and every one of us should include himself as though he is an organ of those friends. My teacher sternly cautioned me about this matter.

30. The Baal Shem Tov, "The Will of RIBASH and Upright Guidance"

When learning, one should settle within him before Whom he is learning, for sometimes, he distances himself in his learning from the Creator. For this reason, he must settle himself at each time and at each hour.

31. Rav Chaim Vital, Pri Etz Chaim, Gate "Conducts of Learning," Chapter 1

My teacher would say that the heart of the intention of reading in the Torah depends on aiming to connect one's heart to its root through the Torah in order to complete the upper tree and complete the upper Adam [man] and correct him, for this is the whole purpose of man's creation and the purpose of his engagement in the Torah.

8

Yearning

1. Baal HaSulam, "Preface to the Wisdom of Kabbalah," Item 4

There is a great rule concerning the *Kelim* [pl. of *Kli*]: The expansion of the light and its departure make the *Kli* fit for its task. This means that as long as the *Kli* has not been separated from its light, it is included in the light and is annulled within it like a candle before a torch.

This annulment is because they are completely opposite from one another, on opposite ends. This is so because the light extends from His self, *existence from existence*. From the perspective of the thought of creation in *Ein Sof* [infinity], it is all toward bestowal and there is no trace of a will to receive in it. Its opposite is the *Kli*, the great will to receive that abundance, and is the root of the initiated creature, in which there is no bestowal whatsoever.

Hence, when they are bound together, the will to receive is annulled in the light within it, and can determine its form only once the light has departed from it once. Following the departure of the light from it, it begins to crave it, and this craving properly determines and sets the shape of the will to receive. Subsequently, when the light dresses in it once more, it is regarded as two separate matters: *Kli* and light, or *Guf* and life. Observe closely, for this is most profound.

2. Baal HaSulam, *Shamati*, Article No. 174, "Concealment"

Concerning the concealment, which is a correction, had it not been for that, man would have been unable to attain any completeness, since he would not be worthy of attaining the importance of the matter. However, when there is concealment, the thing becomes important to him. Even though one cannot appreciate the importance as it truly is, the concealment grants it merit. To the extent that one senses the concealment, a bedding of importance is formed within him.

It is like rungs. He climbs rung by rung until he comes to his designated place. This means that he achieves a certain measure of importance with which he can at least endure, though His true importance and sublimity are immeasurable, but nonetheless a measure that will suffice him to persist.

However, concealment in itself is not considered concealment. Concealment is measured by the demand. The greater the demand for something, the more the concealment is evident. And now we can understand the meaning of "The whole earth is full of His glory." Although we believe it, the concealment still fills the whole earth.

It is written about the future: "For I, ... will be unto her a wall of fire round about, and I will be the glory in the midst of her." Fire means concealment. But still, glory is in the midst of her, meaning that then the glory will be revealed. This is because then the demand will be so great, even though there will be concealment then, too. And the difference is that at this time there is concealment, but no demand. Hence, this is considered "exile." Then, however, although there will be concealment, there will also be demand, and this is what is important—only the demand.

3. Baal HaSulam, *Shamati*, Article No. 175, "And If the Way Be Too Far for You"

He interpreted, Why is the way so far? Because "you are not able to carry it." This is because he cannot carry the burden of Torah and *Mitzvot* [commandments], and hence he regards the way as far. The advice for it, says the verse, "Bind up the money in your hand." *Kesef* [silver/money] means *Kisufin* [longing], to draw longing in the work. Thus, through the desire, the craving for the Creator, he will be able to carry the burden of Torah and *Mitzvot*. *Kesef* also concerns shame. This is because one is created for the goal of glorifying heaven, as it is written, "Blessed is... who created us for His glory."

In general, Torah and *Mitzvot* are things that one does in order to be favored by Him. This is because it is the slave's nature to want to be liked by his master, since then his master's heart is for him. So it is here: The many actions and meticulousness that one becomes proficient in are but a means by which to be favored in His eyes, and then he will have the desired goal of Him.

And a person observes Torah and *Mitzvot* to be liked by people. And he turns the needs of heaven into a means. Meaning, through them he will be liked by people. And as long as one has not been rewarded with the Torah *Lishma* [for Her sake], he works for people.

Although one has no other choice but to work for people, he should still be ashamed of such servitude. Then, through this *Kesef*, he will be awarded the *Kesef* of *Kedusha* [holiness], meaning to want *Kedusha*.

4. Baal HaSulam, Letter No. 19

I have received all your letters, and may they please the Almighty. However, "Know the God of your father and serve Him." "Know" means recognition, because a soul without knowledge is not good. This means that one who yearns and longs to serve Him, for he has a soul, but he does not know his Master, this is not good.

Even though one has a soul, he is not ready to know Him of his own "Until the spirit be poured upon him from on high." However, one must lend an ear and listen to the words of the sages and believe in them wholeheartedly.

It has already been written, "Only goodness and mercy shall follow me all the days of my life." As The Baal Shem Tov interprets "The Lord is your shade"—like the shade that follows man's movements, and its inclinations lean every way the person does, so is man according to the Creator. This means that when love for the Creator awakens, one must see that the Creator has awakened toward him with intense longing, etc. This is the meaning of the words of Rabbi Akiva: "Happy are you Israel—before whom you purify, and who purifies you."

Hence, in the beginning of one's nearing, he is given a soul in a manner of circles. This means that the Creator awakens toward him every time there is an opportunity on the part of man to cling to the man with longing and yearning. This is what the poet tells us, "Only goodness and mercy shall follow me all the days of my life." King David is the collective soul of the whole of Israel. Hence, he always longed, yearned, and craved true *Dvekut* [adhesion] with Him.

However, one must know in one's heart that the Creator chases him just as much as he chases the Creator. One must never forget that, even during the greatest longing. When remembering that the Creator misses and chases him to cling to him as intensely as one wishes for it himself, he then always goes from strength to strength, with yearning and longing, in a never-ending *Zivug* [coupling], the complete perfection of the soul, until he is rewarded with repentance from love, meaning the return of the *Vav* to the *Hey*, being the unification of the Creator with His *Shechina* [Divinity].

However, a soul without knowledge and recognition of his Master is in great decline when the longing increases to a certain extent, for it seems to him that the Creator dislikes him. Woe to that shame and disgrace; not only does he not complete his yearning and longing to be filled with eternal love, he is even in a state of "A whisperer separates from the champion," since he thinks that only he wishes and longs and yearns for the Creator. He does not believe our sages that to the very same extent the Creator wishes, longs, and yearns for him.

5. Baal HaSulam, Letter No. 43

It is written, "And Moses will take the tent," etc. Why did he pitch his tent outside the camp? The fools believe that he did it to stop the flow of *Hochma* due to the sin. This is unthinkable, since after the sin they need the fountains of Torah and *Hochma* thousands of times more than before, as our sages said, "Had Israel not sinned, they would have been given only the Five Books of Moses and the book of Joshua."

However, it is to the contrary. It is a true remedy for opening the fountains of wisdom to a faithful source, since once Moses had pitched his tent outside the camp, the craving for him inside the camp increased, as "One who has bread in his basket is not like one who," etc., and along with it the adhesion with Him. Thus, they were rewarded with expansion of Moses' soul among them, for which they were called "the generation of knowledge."

I have already said and reminded you the words of teaching that I said on the festival of Shavuot [Feast of Weeks] prior to my departure from you about the verse, "Run My beloved, and be like a gazelle": "As the gazelle turns its face back when it runs," etc., for having no other way to make a *Panim* [face/anterior], they devise this tactic—bringing the *Panim* to the *Achoraim* [back/posterior]. It is as it is written, "So is the Creator when," etc., "He turns His face back," since the sensation of separation and *Achoraim*, and the inability to receive the *Panim* of *Kedusha* [holiness] increase the sparks of craving tremendously, until the *Achoraim* become *Panim*, since the tablets were written on both sides. You should be noticing these things by now.

6. Baal HaSulam, *Shamati*, Article No. 21, "When One Feels Oneself in a State of Ascent"

When one feels oneself in a state of ascent, that he is high-spirited, when he feels that he has no desire but only for spirituality, it is then good to delve in the secrets of the Torah in order to attain its internality.

Even if one sees that although he exerts to understand something, and still does not know anything, it is still worthwhile to delve in the secrets of the Torah even a hundred times in a single thing.

One should not despair, meaning say that it is useless since he does not understand anything. This is so for two reasons:

A) When one delves into something and yearns to understand it, that yearning is called a "prayer." This is because a prayer is a lack, meaning that one is craving what he lacks, that the Creator will satisfy his desire.

The extent of the prayer is measured by the desire, since the thing that one needs most, the desire for it is greater, for according to the measure of the need, so is the measure of the yearning.

There is a rule that in the thing that one makes the most effort, the exertion increases the lack, and he wants to receive filling for his deficiency. Also, a desire is called "a prayer," regarded as "the work in the heart," since "the Merciful One wants the hearts."

It turns out that then one can give a true prayer.

7. Baal HaSulam, "Anyone Who Is Sorry for the Public"

"To the extent that one appreciates, so one is allotted" (*Megillah* 12, *Sotah* 8). That is, according to the size of the hole in the *Kli* [vessel], meaning the receptacle and its insides, that lack will always be filled, not less and not more. Therefore, a servant of the Creator who is not sorry for the public but feels only his own personal lack, his receptacle for abundance is also not greater. As a result, he will not be able to receive the collective revelation of Godliness in the form of the comfort of the public, since he did not prepare a *Kli* to receive this collective discernment, but only his individual discernment.

Conversely, one who is sorry for the public and feels the troubles of the public as his own trouble is rewarded with seeing the complete revelation of the *Shechina*, meaning the comfort of the whole of Israel. Because his lack is a collective lack, the abundance of *Kedusha* [holiness] is also collective.

By this you will understand the matter of "The righteous have no rest" (end of *Berachot*, end of *Moed Katan*). Interpretation: Since the abundance is blessed according to the level of the lack and longing of the righteous, to that extent, not less and not more, they always exert to deepen and expand their receptacle, for the Giver has no measure, only the receiver. "More than the calf wants to nurse," etc., (*Pesachim* 112) so their entire intention in life is to strengthen their yearning and make for themselves a receptacle in order to bring contentment by expanding the boundaries of *Kedusha* in the blessing of the Creator.

8. Baal HaSulam, "The Writings of the Last Generation"

In every person, even in the secular, there is an unknown spark that demands unification with God. When it sometimes awakens, it awakens a passion to know God, or deny God, which is the same. If someone generates the satisfaction of this desire in that person, he will agree to anything.

9. Baal HaSulam, Letter No. 19

When one prepares to return to his root, he does not induce the complete *Zivug* at one time, but creates stimuli, which is the degree of *Nefesh*, by way of cycles, chasing the *Shechina* with all his might, quivering and sweating, until he mounts this extremity all day and all night, incessantly.

It is as the books write concerning the cycles. While one's soul is being completed in the degrees of *Nefesh*, he comes ever closer, and so his yearning and sorrow grow since the unsatisfied desire leaves behind it a great affliction according to the measure of the desire.

This is the meaning of "sound." The poet teaches us and says, "Awaken," meaning that you induce stimuli in the *Shechina*. "Sound," for you cause a great affliction, like no other, which is the meaning of "he groaned and moaned" because "What does the *Shechina* say when one is afflicted?" etc. And why do you do so? It is in order to "sever any shout."

This is the meaning of "The righteousness of the righteous will not save him on the day of his transgression." To Him who knows the mysteries, the desire in one's heart for His nearness is known, and that it might still be interrupted. Hence, He increases His stimuli, meaning the beginnings of the coituses, for if one listens to His voice, as in "The Lord of your shade," one does not fall and descend due to the increasing affliction of the stimuli since he sees and hears that the *Shechina* also suffers as he does by the increased longing. Thus, one's longing grows and intensifies each time until one's point in the heart is completed with complete will in a tight knot that will not crumble.

Rabbi Shimon Bar-Yochai said about this in the Idra: "I am for my beloved and upon me His desire. All the days I was connected to this world, I was connected to the Creator with one knot, and because of it, now, upon me His desire, etc." That is, "Until He who knows the mysteries shall testify that he shall not return to folly." Hence, he is granted the return of the *Hey* to the *Vav* for eternity, meaning the complete coitus and the restoration of past glory, which is the meaning of "the great *Teki'a*."

10. Baal HaSulam, Letter No. 2

By exerting the heart to display love between him and his Maker, the Creator instills His *Shechina* [Divinity] on him in remembrance, as in, "In every place where I mention My name, I will come to you and bless you."

When the remembrance increases by the very work, the desire and longing increase, as in "And spirit draws spirit and brings spirit," and so forth. Finally, the remembrance increases and grows by the craving and ascends in good deeds, for "All the pennies join into a great amount." This is the meaning of "Behold, this one comes and His reward is with Him, and His work is before Him."

11. Baal HaSulam, Letter No. 52

It is written about this: "Seek the Lord while He is found." That is, when the Creator presents Himself to you for asking, then you will necessarily seek Him, too, for it is man's way to move first. In other words, the Creator first gives you the heart to seek Him. When you know this, you will certainly grow stronger, as strong as you can ask, for the King is calling you.

So it says, "Call upon Him when He is near." That is, when you call on the Creator to bring you closer to Him, know that He is already near you, for otherwise there is no doubt you would not be calling Him. This is also the meaning of the verse, "Before they call, I will answer," meaning that if you are calling Him, then He has already turned to you to give you the awakening to call upon Him.

"While they speak, I listen," meaning the measure of the Creator's listening depends precisely on the measure of the longing that appears during the saying of the prayer. When one feels excessive longing, he should know at that time that the Creator is listening to him attentively.

Clearly, when he knows this, he pours his heart out even stronger, for there is no greater privilege than the King of the world being attentive to him. This is quite similar to what our sages said, "The Creator longs for the prayer of righteous," for the Creator's desire for a person to draw near Him awakens great power and longing in the person to crave for the Creator, for "As in water of the face to the face, so the heart of man to man."

It follows that the saying of the prayer and the hearing of the prayer go hand in hand until they accumulate to the full measure and he acquires everything.

12. Baal HaSulam, *Shamati*, Article No. 175, "And If the Way Be Too Far for You"

"And bind up the money in your hand." This means that even though the craving is not up to man, if he has no desire for it, he cannot do a thing. Nevertheless, he should show the desire for the *Kisufin*, the desire to want (and perhaps *VeTzarta* [bind] comes from the word *Ratzita* [wanted]). One needs to show a desire for it, to show the desire and the craving to want the Creator, meaning to want to increase the glory of heaven, to bestow contentment upon Him, to be favored by Him.

There is a discernment of *Zahav* [gold], and there is a discernment of *Kesef*. *Kesef* means having *Kisufin* [longing] in general, and *Zahav* [gold, made of the words "give this"] means that he wants only one thing, and all the longing and the craving that he had for several things are canceled in this desire. And he says "give this" only, meaning he does not want anything but to raise the *Shechina* [Divinity] from the dust. This is all that he wants.

It follows that even though one sees that he does not have the proper yearning and desire, he should still see and exert in deeds and thoughts to obtain the desire. This is called "And bind up the money in your hand." One should not think that if it is in the hands of man, it is a small thing. Rather, "for oxen (with grace), or for sheep," etc., for only by this will he be rewarded with the most sublime lights.

13. Baal HaSulam, Letter No. 19

"Grace is deceitful and beauty is vain; but a woman that fears the Lord, she shall be praised." This means that during the preparation, beauty and grace appear as the essence of perfection for which one yearns and longs. However, at the time of correction, when the earth is "full of the knowledge of the Lord," "I shall see an opposite world," as only fear and longing are the desired perfection. Then one feels that during the time of preparation they were lying to themselves.

14. RABASH, Article No. 22 (1990), "What Is the Order in Blotting Out Amalek?"

It is known that in every thing, we discern two discernments: light and *Kli* [vessel]. Even in corporeal things, we discern internality and externality in everything. The externality is called the *Kli*, and the internality is called the "light." For example, when a person yearns for bread, or for meat and fish, etc., a person does not yearn for the *Kli*, meaning the external part, which he sees. Rather, he yearns for the interior, which is not seen, meaning to the taste of bread, or meat, or fish.

Moreover, we see that enjoying the pleasure dressed in the *Kli* requires preparation. To the extent of one's preparation, so one can enjoy the light of pleasure clothed in the *Kli*, which is regarded as the externality. In other words, a person who comes to drink water when he is thirsty is not like one who drinks water when he is not thirsty, since the *Kli* for reception of pleasure is measured by the level of yearning for the pleasure.

For this reason, we see that when a person wants to enjoy drinks, he first eats acrid and salty foods in order to invoke in him the desire to drink. It is likewise in everything: Without yearning, it is impossible to enjoy anything. This stems from the beginning of creation, as we learn that the purpose of creation, which is His desire to do good to His creations, created a desire to receive delight and pleasure. Before the fourth phase—which is yearning—is revealed, it is still not regarded as a *Kli* that is fit to receive the light and pleasure.

15. RABASH, Article No. 18 (1987), "What Is Preparation for Reception of the Torah? – 1"

We must remember the known rule that there is no light without a *Kli* [vessel]. That is, there cannot be filling without a lack. It is impossible to enjoy something without yearning for it, and yearning for something is called "preparation," meaning a need. The need for something determines the yearning, and the level of the pleasure corresponds to the level of the yearning.

16. RABASH, Article No. 22 (1987), "What Is the Gift that a Person Asks of the Creator?"

The Creator created—existence from absence—a *Kli* called "desire and yearning to receive delight and pleasure." This means that what we see is as in "By Your actions we know You," meaning that we speak only of what we see that exists in the nature of creation. We see that it is impossible to enjoy anything, whatever it is, unless there is a yearning for it. For this reason, we learned that from the perspective of the light that created this *Kli*, called "will to receive," it underwent four *Behinot* [discernments], meaning four stages until the will to receive acquired the complete form of yearning. After the light created the *Kli*, this *Kli* received the delight and pleasure that He wished to give.

These two above-mentioned things, the light and the *Kli*, pertain to the Creator. We learn that in this respect, there was complete perfection and there is nothing to add to this.

17. RABASH, Article No. 409, "Concerning Suffering – 2"

It is known that the whole *Kli* [vessel] that receives pleasure is the yearning, a lack for the thing, meaning for the thing to which he has a great desire. To the extent that he desires it, to that extent he yearns. And the desire, great or small, is measured by the amount of suffering that he would feel if he did not obtain the matter.

As it is explained (in the "Introduction to The Study of the Ten Sefirot," Items 96-97), Torah *Lishma* [for Her sake] means for the sake of the life that he finds in the Torah, since when one finds His face in the Torah, so he finds the life in the Torah, as it is written, "For by the light of the King's face is life."

Thus, when one learns Torah and does not find the life in the Torah, he regrets it, and this is called "You will lead a life of sorrow." That is, he will regret not finding the light of His face, yet he does not stop learning Torah, as it is written, "And in the Torah you toil" although he does not find Him.

It follows that to the extent that he learns Torah and intends to find Him, so his suffering increases. At a certain extent called "labored," you "find," as is explained there, that this is the meaning of the existence of the light of the King's face in the Torah.

18. RABASH, Letter No. 33

Any pleasure, whether corporeal or spiritual, is called "light." And we have a rule about lights, that we have no attainment. That is, it is impossible to determine its final form unless through the *Kelim*. This means that we determine the shape of the lights according to the quality of the *Kelim*.

And regarding *Kelim* (vessels), it is known that it is regarded as yearning for something. It follows that the *Kelim* increase the light. This means that it is not the light that must be great, but the *Kelim* must be greater. Only if one has many *Kelim*, meaning a strong desire, one feels greater pleasure in the light.

Therefore, even in corporeality, the meal and the money do not determine the measure of the pleasure, but rather the labor and the yearning determine the measure of the pleasure.

19. RABASH, Article No. 17 (1989), "What Is the Prohibition to Greet Before Blessing the Creator, in the Work?"

A person must yearn to attain the Creator, meaning adhere to Him with complete recognition, that this is regarded as the Creator. This means that a person must walk on the right line, regarded as wholeness, and pray to the Creator and thank Him, even if he does not find within him anything that desires spirituality. But accordingly, how can he thank the Creator and say that the Creator hears what he says to Him, which is the meaning of attributing the work to the Creator, and He accepts his work regardless of how the work seems?

However, if he relates only to the Creator and says, "I am turning to the Creator and I believe that He can answer my wishes," by this a person becomes happy and feels superior. That is, the rest of the people have no connection to spirituality, and he believes that the Creator has given him [a feeling] that he has no spirituality, in whatever way, but the fact that he has an interest in thinking about spirituality, it makes no difference if he has or hasn't, or that he is now in utter lowliness, meaning that he sees that now he has no desire to ascend in degree and emerge from the lowliness, but he thanks the Creator because at least he is thinking about spirituality, while the rest of the people do not have any thoughts of spirituality.

If he can thank the Creator, it gives him joy, and from *Lo Lishma* [not for Her sake] he comes to *Lishma* [for Her sake]. By this he ascends from his state of wholeness and can thereby come to a state where even if he forgets the state of lowliness he was in prior to making the calculation and thanking the Creator, it appears to him as though he has always been in this state.

This extends from the discernment that "The blessed clings to the Blessed," since the thanks he gives to the Creator makes a person feel whole, and to the extent of the joy he extends, so he can ascend in degree. We must say that this path is true, meaning that man hasn't the power to assess the importance of *Kedusha*, but even touching anything of *Kedusha* is infinitely more important to the Creator than all the corporeal things.

20. RABASH, Article No. 44 (1990), "What Is an Optional War, in the work - 2?"

All those thoughts that the will to receive brings him are sent to him from above because he wants to walk on the path of bestowal, and in the meantime he is idle in the work, because he prayed for the Creator to bring him closer to being in *Dvekut* with the Creator, which is equivalence of form, when it is apparent that the person is idle in the work, he is sent the foreign thoughts that a person cannot agree to be under such a control. This, in turn, gives a person a push that he must overcome the state he is in.

It therefore follows that from this bad, when a person feels that he is in such a lowly state that he never imagined that he could be under such governance, for this reason, he should not be alarmed and escape the campaign. On the contrary, he should believe that the Creator is taking care of him now, and He is bringing him closer through a state of *Achoraim* [posterior].

This is as it is written in the book *A Sage's Fruit* (Vol. 1, p 139), "About the verse, 'My beloved is like a gazelle,' our sages said, 'As the gazelle looks back when he runs, when the Creator leaves Israel, He turns back His face.' Then the face returns to being in the *Achoraim*, meaning craving and longing to cling to Israel once more. This begets in Israel longing and craving to cling to the Creator, too, and the measure of the longing and craving is actually the face itself."

We should interpret that he means that when a person is in a state of lowliness, it is considered that the Creator has moved away from him, and he has no desire or yearning for the work, this is regarded as the Creator giving a person a shape of tastelessness about spirituality. Moreover, a person wants to escape and forget about the work altogether. This is regarded as the Creator showing him the *Achoraim*.

The *Panim* [face/anterior] of the Creator is His desire to do good to His creations, and the *Achoraim* is the complete opposite. Why does the Creator show a person the *Achoraim*? It is on purpose, for by this a person gets a thrust toward *Dvekut* with the Creator, for he cannot remain in a state of lowliness. It follows that here, within the *Achoraim* is the discernment of *Panim*.

21. Zohar for All, Shemot [Exodus], "Run, My Beloved," Item 235

He heard the voice of one of Rabbi Shimon's students saying, "Run, my beloved, and be like a gazelle or a young hart." Every yearning that Israel yearned for the Creator is the yearning of Israel that the Creator will not go and will not walk away, but run like a gazelle or a young hart.

22. Zohar for All, Truma [Donation], "As They," Item 168

There is no awakening above before Israel awaken below. Therefore, to evoke rest, it is forbidden to evoke *Din* for a holy nation who are crowned in holy crowns of souls, but rather everyone should be in good will, great love, evoking blessings above and below at once.

23. Rabbi Shmuel Bornstein, author of *Shem MiShmuel*

The difference between the word "gathering" and the word "grouping." It is written "Gather, purify," since gathering is more unification of the heart than the word "grouping." "Grouping" pertains only to the body, although the views are not united. But a gathering of people is also with one heart. It is a gathering from the outside in, where they become very unified.

Therefore, the word "gathering" applies mostly to the souls, since "soul" comes from the words "desire" and "yearning." If each and every one yearns for his own benefit, although they all want the same thing, it is still not one view, since one wants one's own benefit, and the other wants his own benefit.

However, if they are complete, and also many yearn to satisfy the Creator's will, this is certainly called "complete unification," and deserves the title "gathering," by everyone uniting with an immense feeling of the soul, to do the will of our Father in Heaven.

9

Devotion

1. Baal HaSulam, *Shamati*, Article No. 219, "Devotion"

The servitude that should primarily be in devotion is on the discernment of fear. At that time, the whole body disagrees with one's work, since it does not feel any taste in the servitude. And with each thing that he does, the body calculates that this servitude is not in completeness. Thus, what will you get out of working?

Then, because there is no validity or taste in this servitude, overcoming is only through devotion. This means that the servitude feels bitter, and each act causes him horrendous suffering, since the body is not accustomed to work in vain: either the work should benefit oneself, or others.

But during the *Katnut* [smallness/infancy], one does not feel any benefit for oneself, since he does not presently feel any pleasure in the servitude. And also, he does not believe that there will be benefit to others since it is not important to him, so what pleasure would others have from it? Then the suffering is harsh. And the more he works, the suffering increases proportionally. Finally, the suffering and the labor accumulate to a certain amount where the Creator has mercy on him and gives him a taste in the servitude of the Creator, as it is written, "Until the spirit be poured upon us from on high."

2. Baal HaSulam, *Shamati*, Article No. 208, "Labor"

The efforts that one makes are but preparations for achieving devotion. Hence, one should grow accustomed to devotion, since no degree can be achieved without devotion, as this is the only tool that qualifies one to be rewarded with all the degrees.

3. Baal HaSulam, *Shamati*, Article No. 201, "Spirituality and Corporeality"

Why do we see that there are many people who work so diligently for corporeality, even in life-threatening places, but in spirituality, each and every one examines one's soul very carefully? Moreover, one can exert in corporeality even when he is not given a great reward for his work. But in spirituality, one cannot agree to work unless he knows for certain that he will receive a good reward for his work.

The thing is that it is known that the body is worthless. After all, everyone sees that it is passing and leaves without a trace, so it is easy to abandon it, as it is worthless anyway.

But in spirituality, there are *Klipot* [shells] which guard the body and sustain it. This is why it is hard to abandon it. This is why we see that it is easier for secular people to abandon their body and they do not find heaviness in their body.

But this is not so in spirituality. This is the *Achoraim* [posterior] of *Kedusha* [holiness], called "devotion." It is specifically through this that one is awarded the light. And before one is completely devoted, he cannot achieve any degree.

4. RABASH, Article No. 12 (1985), "Jacob Dwelled in the Land Where His Father Had Lived"

With love of the Creator, we say that a person should work only for the Creator, meaning without any reward. This means that he is ready for complete devotion without any reward, without any return being born out of his devotion. Rather, this is the core—his purpose, that he wants to annul his self before the Creator, meaning (cancel) his will to receive, which is the existence of the creature. This is what he wants to annul before the Creator. It follows that this is his goal, meaning his goal is to give his soul to the Creator.

5. RABASH, Article No. 136, "The Binding of Isaac"

The binding of Isaac, when Abraham, who is the right line, which is above reason, tied the left line, which is the mind that criticizes everything, it gave him a general picture of the situation he was in. He left all the "left" and took upon himself the quality of "right," which is above reason. By this he was later rewarded with the middle line.

That is, there is a difference between receiving the right line before he sees the left line, to a state where he renews the right line after he has seen the state of the left. "Right," which is above reason, is called "devotion," since he cancels all the reason he acquired from the left line and goes above reason, and then he is rewarded with the middle line.

6. RABASH, Article No. 37 (1991), "What Is the Torah and What Is The Statute of the Torah, in the Work?"

When he wants to do everything for the sake of the Creator and not for his own sake. Here the body resists with all its might, since it argues, "Why do you want to put me and my domain to death? You come to me with having to work only for the sake of the Creator and not for one's own sake, which is truly annulment of the will to receive from everything. You tell me that our sages said, 'The Torah exists only in one who puts himself to death over it,' meaning to put to death all the domain of self-benefit and care only for the benefit of the Creator, and before this, a person cannot be rewarded with the Torah." Yet, a person sees that it is unrealistic that he will have the strength to go against nature.

At that time, one has no choice but to turn to the Creator and say, "Now I have come to a state where I see that unless You help me, I am lost. I will never have the strength to overcome the will to receive, as this is my nature. Rather, only the Creator can give another nature."

A person says that he believes that this was the exodus from Egypt, that the Creator delivered the people of Israel from under the governance of Egypt, as our sages said (in the Passover *Haggadah* [story/narrative]), "And the Lord brought us out from Egypt, not by an angel, and not by a messenger, but the Creator Himself; I am the Lord, it is I and not another."

Now, he, too, sees that only the Creator can deliver him from the governance of the will to receive and give him a second nature. In other words, just as the Creator gave the first nature, there is no one who can give the second nature but the Creator Himself. Therefore, at that time a person prays wholeheartedly, from the bottom of the heart, and this is the time for the reception of the prayer.

7. RABASH, Article No. 19 (1985), "Come unto Pharaoh – 1"

Our sages said (*Berachot*, 10), "Even if a sharp sword is placed on his neck he should not deny himself of mercy," as it was said (Job, 13), "Though He slay me, I will hope for Him."

We should interpret the "sharp sword placed on his neck" to mean that even though one's evil, called "self-love," is placed on his neck and wants to separate him from *Kedusha* by showing him that it is impossible to exit this authority, he should say that the picture he sees is the truth.

However, "He should not deny himself of mercy," for at that time he must believe that the Creator can give him the mercy, meaning the quality of bestowal. That is, by himself, it is true that one cannot exit the authority of self-reception. But from the perspective of the Creator, when the Creator helps him, of course He can bring him out. This is the meaning of what is written, "I am the Lord your God, who took you out from the land of Egypt to be your God."

8. *Zohar for All*, *VaYakhel* [And Moses Assembled], "The Intention of the Prayer," Items 112-117

Now that the upper King and *Malchut* are in bonding and joy in those kisses, he who needs to ask questions and make requests shall make them because then is a time of good will. Once the person has made his requests before the King and queen in the 12 middle blessings, he will set himself up in his will and heart for the last three blessings, to evoke joy in concealment. It is so because from these three blessings, he is blessed with another *Dvekut*, with a *Zivug*. And the man should correct himself to come out from before them and place them in hidden joy in those three blessings. For this reason, his desire should be that the lower ones will be blessed by these blessings of the hidden joy.

At that time he should fall on his face and give his soul when *Malchut* grips the souls and the spirits. That is the time for dedicating his soul among all those souls that she grips, for then the bundle of life, *Malchut*, is as it should be.

I heard this matter among the secrets of Rabbi Shimon and I was not given permission to disclose, except to you, the high pious ones. When *Malchut* grips people's souls and spirits in one desire for *Dvekut* [adhesion], the man places his heart and will on that and gives his soul in *Dvekut* with that desire, to include his soul in that *Dvekut*. If at that time his dedicating of his soul is accepted in the will of the souls [*Nefashot*, pl. of *Nefesh*] and spirits [*Ruchot*, pl. of *Ruach*] and souls [*Neshamot*, pl. of *Neshama*] that she grips, it is a man who was bundled in the bundle of life in this world and in the next world.

And while the King and queen, Torah and *Mitzvot*, must include all the sides above and below, and be crowned with *Neshamot* on all the sides, she is crowned in the *Neshamot* from above, and crowned in the *Neshamot* from below, of those who give her their souls [*Neshamot*]. If a person aims his heart and will to all that, and gives her his *Nefesh* from below willingly and in *Dvekut*, the Creator calls upon him peace below, such as the peace above, *Yesod*, who blesses the queen, and includes her and crowns her on all sides.

Likewise, the Creator calls this man Peace, as it is written, "And the Lord called him *Shalom* [peace]." All his days, this is what he is called above, "peace," because he included and crowned the queen from below, such as this peace above, *Yesod*.

When that person departs from this world, his soul rises and breaches all those firmaments and there is no one to stop her. The Creator calls her and says, "Let Peace come." And Divinity says, "Let them rest in their beds," and 13 mountains of pure persimmon shall open before her, and there will be no one to stop her. This is why happy is he who dedicates his heart and mind to that. And this is why it is written, "Whoever is of a generous heart, let him bring it as the Lord's donation" to the upper King.

9. Rabbi Nachman of Breslov, *Likutey Tefillot* [Assorted Prayers], Part 1, Prayer No. 16

Grant me with Your mercies, to pray with devotion and sincerity, that I may be awarded annulling all my being and my corporeality and will not pray for my own benefit at all, but rather be rewarded with complete annulment during the prayer as though I don't not exist in the world at all, and my whole intention in the prayer will be truly only for Your sake, to raise the *Shechina* [Divinity] from exile, to reveal Your Godliness in the world.

10

Overcoming

1. Baal HaSulam, *Shamati*, Article No. 99, "He Did Not Say Wicked or Righteous"

If one does not have any desire or craving for spirituality, if he is among people who have a desire and craving for spirituality, if he likes these people, he, too, will take their strength to prevail, and their desires and aspirations, although by his own quality, he does not have these desires and cravings and the power to overcome. But according to the grace and the importance he ascribes to these people, he will receive new powers.

2. Baal HaSulam, "Introduction to The Study of the Ten Sefirot," Item 133

A king who wished to select for himself the most loyal of his subjects in the country and bring them to work inside his palace. What did he do? He issued a decree that anyone who wished, young or old, would come to his palace to engage in the works inside his palace.

However, he appointed many of his servants to guard the palace gate and all the roads leading to it, and ordered them to cunningly deflect all those nearing his palace and divert them from the way that leads to the palace.

Naturally, all the people in the country began to run to the king's palace. But the diligent guards cunningly rejected them. Many of them overpowered them and came near the palace gate, but the guards at the gate were the most diligent, and if someone approached the gate, they diverted him and turned him away with great craftiness until one despaired and returned as he had come.

And so they came and went, and regained strength, and came and went again, and so on and so forth for several days and years until they grew weary of trying. Only the mighty ones among them, whose patience endured, defeated the guards and opened the gate. And they were instantly awarded seeing the king's face, who appointed each of them in his right place.

Of course, from that moment on, they had no further dealings with those guards, who diverted and mislead them and made their lives bitter for several days and years, running back and forth around the gate. This is because they have been rewarded with working and serving before the glory of the king's face inside his palace.

3. Baal HaSulam, Letter No. 14

One is rewarded with everything only by overcoming, called "strength," and each and every strength that a person elicits joins into a great amount. That is, even if a person overcomes once and gets an alien thought, and says, "But I already know from experience that soon I will not have this desire for the work, so what will I get now if I overcome it a little?'" At that time, he must reply that many pennies join into a great amount, meaning to the general account, whether to the root of his soul or to the public.

Perhaps this is the meaning of "The gates of tears were not locked." *Shaarei* [gates] comes from the words, *Se'arot* ["hair," or "storms"], which is overcoming. "Tears" comes from the word "tearing," meaning that there is a mixture with other desires, and only in the middle of the desires there is a brief moment of a desire to overcome toward love and fear of heaven. "…not locked," but rather that moment joins into a great amount. When the amount is full, the person begins to feel the spiritual clothing.

This is the meaning of the importance of tears, meaning that even if he is in the lowest state and has base desires, but still has the strength to overcome, meaning that from the point in his heart he yearns and craves the Creator, then that force is very important. Thus, even when a person is in exile, when his point in the heart is placed under other governances, called "Divinity [*Shechina*] in exile" for that person, for one moment he overcomes and sanctifies the Creator. And even though he is already certain, because of all of his experiences, that afterwards he will fall again, it is still very important that a person can say the truth openly.

This is similar to a person standing among criminals who are swearing and cursing the work of the Creator. And among them there are some who lecture eloquently and let you understand that there is no point to serving the Creator. But still there is someone there who cannot explain the value and the essence of the work so well, but he can make a few objections, meaning that he utters protests that what they're saying is not true. It is good that he disagrees, even though he is not as eloquent as the swearers. This is called the "gates of tears," and it is called "Many pennies join into a great amount."

4. RABASH, Article No. 22 (1985), "The Whole of the Torah Is One Holy Name"

We must always consider the goal, which is to "do good to His creations." If the evil inclination comes to a person and asks him all of Pharaoh's questions, he should not reply with lame excuses, but say, "Now, with your questions, I can begin with the work of bestowal."

This means that we should not say about the questions of the evil inclination that it came to us in order to lower us from our degree. On the contrary, now it is giving us a place to work, by which we will ascend on the degrees of wholeness. That is, any overcoming in the work is called "walking in the work of the Creator," since each penny joins into a great amount." That is, all the times we overcome accumulate to a certain measure required to become a *Kli* for the reception of the abundance.

Overcoming means taking a part of a vessel of reception and adding it to the vessels of bestowal. It is like the *Masach* [screen], which we must put on the *Aviut* [thickness/will to receive]. It follows that if one has no will to receive, one has nothing on which to place a *Masach*. For this reason, when the evil inclination brings us foreign thoughts, this is the time to take these thoughts and raise them above reason.

This is something one can do with everything one's soul desires. He should not say that now he has received rejection from the work. Rather, he should say that he was given thoughts and desires from above so as to have room to admit them into *Kedusha* [holiness]. It therefore follows that it is to the contrary: because he is brought closer from above, he was sent work.

It was said about this: "The ways of the Lord are straight; righteous walk in it and transgressors fail in it."

5. *Zohar for All*, "Introduction of The Book of Zohar," "Two Points," Item 121

Prior to being rewarded with inverting the desire to receive in us through Torah and *Mitzvot*, into reception in order to bestow, there are strong locks on those gates to the Creator, for then they have the opposite role: to drive us away from the Creator. This is why the forces of separation are called "locks," since they block the gates of approaching and drive us away from the Creator.

But if we overcome them so they do not affect us, cooling His love from our hearts, the locks become doors, the darkness becomes light, and the bitter becomes sweet. Over all the locks, we receive a special degree in His Providence, and they become openings, degrees of attainment of the Creator. And those degrees that we receive on the openings become halls of wisdom.

6. *Zohar for All*, *Kedoshim*, "Hybrid and Mixing," Item 108

When the Creator created the world, He established everything on its side, on the right or on the left, and appointed upper forces on them. You have not even a tiny grass on earth that does not have a higher force on it up in the worlds above. All that is done on each one, and all that each one does, is by increasing of the upper force that is appointed on it from above.

7. Rabbi Nachman of Breslov, *Likutey Moharan*

The work of the Creator requires great persistence, whatever happens to him. Remember this well for you will need it very much as you begin the work of the Creator. It requires great tenacity, and to be strong and brave, to brace oneself and stand still, even if you are dropped down every time. You must not allow yourself to fall off altogether, for it is necessary to experience all those falls, descents, and confusions prior to entering the gates of *Kedusha* [holiness], and the true righteous, too, have gone through all of it. Know, that man must cross and very, very narrow bridge, and the rule and the most important thing is not to be afraid at all.

11

Prayer

1. Baal HaSulam, *Shamati*, Article No. 209, "Three Conditions in Prayer"

There are three conditions in prayer:

1. Believing that He can save him. Although he has the worst conditions of all his contemporaries, still, "Will the Lord's hand be too short to save him?" If it is not so, then "the Landlord cannot save His vessels."
2. He no longer has any choice for he has already done all that he could but saw no cure to his plight.
3. If He does not help him, he will be better off dead than alive. Prayer means "lost in the heart." The more one is lost, so is the measure of his prayer. Clearly, one who lacks luxuries is not like one who has been sentenced to death, and only the execution is missing, and he is already tied with iron chains, and he is standing and pleading for his life. He will certainly not rest or sleep or be distracted for even a moment from praying for his life.

2. Baal HaSulam, *Shamati*, Article No. 122, "Understanding What Is Written in Shulchan Aruch"

When one cries "Write us to life," "life" means *Dvekut* [adhesion] with the Life of Lives, which is specifically by a person wanting to work entirely in the form of bestowal, and that all of one's thoughts of his own pleasure will be revoked. Then, when he feels what he is saying, his heart can fear that his prayer might be accepted, meaning that he will have no desire whatsoever for himself.

And concerning self-pleasure, there appears a state where it seems as though he leaves all the pleasures of this world, together with all the people, friends, his kin, all his possessions, and retires to the desert where there is nothing but wild beasts, without anyone knowing of him or of his existence. It seems to him as though he loses his world at once, and feels that he is losing a world filled with the joy of life, and takes upon himself death from this world. He feels as though he is committing suicide when he experiences this image.

Sometimes, the *Sitra Achra* [other side] helps him picture his state with all the dark colors. Then the body repels this prayer, and in such a state, his prayer cannot be accepted since he himself does not want his prayer to be accepted.

For this reason, there must be preparation for the prayer, to accustom oneself to the prayer, as though his mouth and heart are the same. And the heart can come to agree through accustoming, so it would understand that reception means separation, and that the most important is the *Dvekut* with the Life of Lives, which is bestowal.

One must always delve in the work of *Malchut*, called "writing," considered "ink" and *Shacharit* [blackness]. This means that one should not want one's work to be in the form of "Libni and Shimei,"[1] that only at the time of whiteness does he adhere to the Torah and *Mitzvot* [commandments], but unconditionally. Whether in white or in black, it will always be the same for him, and that come-what-may, he will adhere to the commandments of the Torah and *Mitzvot*.

3. Baal HaSulam, Letter No. 34

It is written, "Take no rest, and give Him no rest until He establishes, and until He makes Jerusalem a praise in the earth." So we rush our pleas above, knock by knock, tirelessly, endlessly, and do not weaken at all when He does not answer us. We believe He hears our prayer but waits for a time when we have the *Kelim* [vessels] to receive the faithful bounty, and then we will receive a reply to each and every prayer at once, since "the hand of the Lord will not be short," God forbid.

This is the meaning of the words, "Children in whom there was no blemish ... and who have the strength to stand in the King's palace." It teaches you that even those who have been rewarded with pardon for iniquities—which became as merits, by which the matter appears after the fact, and in whom there is no blemish—still need more strength to stand in the King's palace, meaning stand and pray, and wait tirelessly, knock by knock, until they elicit the complete desire from the Creator.

This is why we should learn this trade before we enter the King's palace, meaning muster power and might to stand as a pillar of iron until we elicit the desire from the Creator, as it is written, "Take no rest." Although the Creator seems silent and unresponsive, let it not cross your minds to be silent, too, "Take no rest." This is not what the Creator intended by His silence, but rather to give you power to stand afterward in the King's palace when you have no blemish. This is why, "and give Him no rest." Naturally, all the works are taught while one is still outside the palace, for afterward there will be no time to dedicate to crafts.

4. Baal HaSulam, Letter No. 52

In each and every movement in His work there are two opposites in the same carrier, as I have elaborated in previous letters, as the receiver consists of body and soul, which are opposites. Hence, in each attainment, great or small, He makes two opposite forms.

There are two concepts in the work of the Creator: 1) "prayer and plea," 2) "praise and gratitude." Naturally, both must be at their highest. To complete the prayer, a person must feel the Creator's closeness to him as mandatory, like an organ that is hanging loosely, for then he can complain and pour out his heart before Him.

But opposite that, regarding the complete praise and gratitude, a person must feel the Creator's closeness to him as an addition, a supplement, as something that does not belong to him at all, for "What is man that You should know him, the son of man that You should think of him?" Then he can certainly give complete praise and gratitude to His great name for choosing him from among all those who are standing ready to serve the Creator.

It is great work for the complex man to be completed in both those opposites, so they are set in his heart forever at the same time.

5. Baal HaSulam, Letter No. 57

There is no happier state in man's world than when he finds himself despaired with his own strength. That is, he has already labored and done all that he could possibly imagine he could do, but found no remedy. It is then that he is fit for a wholehearted prayer for His help because he knows for certain that his own work will not help him.

As long as he feels some strength of his own, his prayer will not be whole because the evil inclination rushes first and tells him, "First you must do what you can, and then you will be worthy of the Creator."

It was said about this, "The Lord is high and the low will see." For once a person has labored in all kinds of work, and has become disillusioned, he comes into real lowliness, knowing that he is the lowest of all the people, as there is nothing good in the structure of his body. At that time, his prayer is complete and he is granted by His generous hand.

6. Baal HaSulam, Letter No. 57

The writing says about this, "And the children of Israel sighed from the work, etc., and their cry went up." It is so because at that time they came into a state of despair from the work. It is as one who pumps into a punctured bucket. He pumps all day but does not have a drop of water to quench his thirst.

So were the children of Israel in Egypt: Everything they built was promptly swallowed in its place in the ground, as our sages said.

Similarly, one who has not been rewarded with His love, all that he has done in his work on purifying the soul the day before is as though completely burned the next day. And each day and each moment he must start anew as though he has not done a thing in his entire life.

Then, "The children of Israel sighed from the work," for they evidently saw that they were unfit to ever produce something by their own work. This is why their sigh and prayer were complete, as it should be, and this is why "Their cry went up," since the Creator hears the prayer, and He only awaits a wholehearted prayer.

7. Baal HaSulam, *Shamati*, Article No. 18, "My Soul Shall Weep In Secret – 1"

When concealment overpowers a person and he comes to a state where the work becomes tasteless, and he cannot picture or feel any love and fear, and he cannot do anything in *Kedusha* [holiness], his only counsel is to cry to the Creator to have mercy on him and remove the screen from his eyes and heart.

Crying is a very important matter. It is as our sages write: "All the gates were locked except for the gates of tears." The world asks about this: If the gates of tears are not locked, what is the need for the gates at all? He said that it is like a person who asks his friend for some necessary object. This object touches his heart, and he asks and begs him in every manner of prayer and plea. Yet, his friend pays no attention to all this. And when he sees that there is no longer reason for prayers and pleas then he raises his voice in weeping.

It is said about this: "All the gates were locked except for the gates of tears." That is, when were the gates of tears not locked? Precisely when all the gates were locked. It is then that there is room for the gates of tears, and then we see that they were not locked.

However, when the gates of prayer are open, the gates of tears and weeping are irrelevant. This is the meaning of the gates of tears being locked. Thus, when are the gates of tears not locked? Precisely when all the gates are locked, the gates of tears are open since one still has the choice of prayer and plea.

This is the meaning of "My soul shall weep in secret," meaning when one comes to a state of concealment, then "My soul shall weep," because one has no other option.

8. Baal HaSulam, Letter No. 56

The labor and exertion that appear in one's heart during the prayer is the most reliable and most guaranteed to reach its goal than any other matter in reality.

9. Baal HaSulam, *Shamati*, Article No. 5, "Lishma Is an Awakening from Above, and Why Do We Need an Awakening from Below?"

In order to attain *Lishma* [for Her sake], it is not within one's hands to understand, as it is not for the human mind to grasp how such a thing can be in the world. This is so because one is only permitted to grasp that if he engages in Torah and *Mitzvot* [commandments] he will attain something. There must be self-benefit there for otherwise, one is unable to do anything. Rather, it is an illumination that comes from above, and only one who tastes it can know and understand. It is written about it, "Taste and see that the Lord is good."

Thus, we must understand why one should seek advice and counsels regarding how to achieve *Lishma*. After all, no counsels will help him, and if the Creator does not give him the second nature, called "the desire to bestow," no labor will help him to attain the matter of *Lishma*.

The answer is, as our sages said (*Avot*, Chapter 2, 21), "It is not for you to complete the work, and you are not free to idle away from it." This means that one must give the awakening from below, since this is regarded as a prayer.

A prayer is considered a deficiency, and without a deficiency there is no filling. Hence, when one has a need for *Lishma*, the filling comes from above, and the answer to the prayer comes from above, meaning he receives fulfillment for his lack. It follows, that the need for man's work in order to receive the *Lishma* from the Creator is only in the form of a lack and a *Kli* [vessel]. Yet, one can never obtain the filling by himself; it is rather a gift from the Creator.

However, the prayer must be a complete prayer, from the bottom of the heart. This means that one knows one hundred percent that there is no one in the world who can help him but the Creator Himself.

Yet, how does one know this, that no one will help him but the Creator Himself? One can acquire that awareness precisely if he has exerted all the powers at his disposal and it did not help him. Thus, one must do every possible thing in the world to attain "for the sake of the Creator." Then one can pray from the bottom of the heart, and then the Creator hears his prayer.

However, one must know, when exerting to attain the *Lishma*, to take upon himself to want to work entirely to bestow, completely, meaning only to bestow and not to receive anything. Only then does one begin to see that the organs do not agree to this view.

From this one can come to clear awareness that he has no other choice but to pour out his heart to the Creator to help him so the body will agree to enslave itself to the Creator unconditionally, as he sees that he cannot persuade his body to annul itself completely. It turns out that precisely when one sees that there is no hope that his body will agree to work for the Creator by itself, one's prayer can be from the bottom of the heart, and then his prayer is accepted.

10. Baal HaSulam, *Shamati*, Article No. 20, "Lishma [for Her sake]"

In order for a person to obtain *Lishma*, one needs an awakening from above, as it is an illumination from above and it is not for the human mind to understand. Rather, he who tastes, knows. It is said about this, "Taste and see that the Lord is good."

Because of this, upon assuming the burden of the kingdom of heaven, one needs it to be in utter completeness, meaning only to bestow and not at all to receive. If a person sees that the organs do not agree with this view, he has no other choice but prayer—to pour out his heart to the Creator to help him make his body consent to enslaving itself to the Creator.

Do not say that if *Lishma* [for Her sake] is a gift from above, what good is one's overcoming and efforts, and all the remedies and corrections that he does in order to achieve *Lishma*, if it depends on the Creator? Our sages said about it, "You are not free to rid yourself of it." Rather, one must give the awakening from below, and this is considered "prayer." Yet, there cannot be a real prayer if he does not know first that without prayer it cannot be obtained.

Therefore, the acts and remedies he does in order to obtain *Lishma* create the corrected *Kelim* [vessels] in him that want to receive the *Lishma*. Then, after all the actions and the remedies he can pray in earnest since he saw that all his actions did not help him whatsoever. Only then can he make an honest prayer from the bottom of his heart, and then the Creator hears his prayer and gives him the gift of *Lishma*.

11. Baal HaSulam, Letter No. 52

When a person introspects and feels his poor state, he awakens to return to the Creator and pours out his prayer in great longing to adhere to the Creator. He thinks that all those prayers and all that awakening are by his own power. He sits and awaits the Creator's salvation, small or great. When time passes and he sees no sign of welcome from the Creator, he falls into despair because the Creator does not want him, since after all this longing, He did not turn to him at all.

It is written about this: "Seek the Lord while He is found." That is, when the Creator presents Himself to you for asking, then you will necessarily seek Him, too, for it is man's way to move first. In other words, the Creator first gives you the heart to seek Him. When you know this, you will certainly grow stronger, as strong as you can ask, for the King is calling you.

So it says, "Call upon Him when He is near." That is, when you call on the Creator to bring you closer to Him, know that He is already near you, for otherwise there is no doubt you would not be calling Him. This is also the meaning of the verse, "Before they call, I will answer," meaning that if you are calling Him, then He has already turned to you to give you the awakening to call upon Him.

"While they speak, I listen," meaning the measure of the Creator's listening depends precisely on the measure of the longing that appears during the saying of the prayer. When one feels excessive longing, he should know at that time that the Creator is listening to him attentively.

Clearly, when he knows this, he pours his heart out even stronger, for there is no greater privilege than the King of the world being attentive to him. This is quite similar to what our sages said, "The Creator longs for the prayer of righteous," for the Creator's desire for a person to draw near Him awakens great power and longing in the person to crave for the Creator, for "As in water of the face to the face, so the heart of man to man."

It follows that the saying of the prayer and the hearing of the prayer go hand in hand until they accumulate to the full measure and he acquires everything. This is the meaning of "spirit draws spirit and brings spirit." Note these words, for they are the first foundations in the ways of the Creator.

12. Baal HaSulam, *The Study of the Ten Sefirot*, Part 8, "Inner Light," Item 88

All our work in prayers and practical *Mitzvot* [commandments] is to sort once more and raise all those souls that fell from *Adam HaRishon* into the *Klipot* [shells] until they are brought to their first root as they were in it before he sinned with the tree of knowledge.

13. Baal HaSulam, *Shamati*, Article No. 113, "The Eighteen Prayer"

This is the meaning of "for You hear the prayer of every mouth." When does He hear every mouth? When Your people, Israel, pray with mercy, meaning simple mercy, when one prays to raise the *Shechina* from the dust, to receive faith.

It is similar to one who has not eaten in three days. Then, when he asks of another to be given something to eat, he is not asking for any luxuries or extras; he is simply asking to be given something to revive his soul.

Similarly, in the work of the Creator, when one finds himself standing between heaven and earth, he is not asking the Creator for something redundant, but only for the light of faith, for the Creator to open his eyes so he can take upon himself the quality of faith. This is called "raising the *Shechina* from the dust." This prayer is accepted from "every mouth." That is, whatever state a person is in, if he asks to revive his soul with faith, his prayer will be answered.

This is called "with mercy," when one's prayer is only to be pitied from above so he can sustain his vitality. This is the meaning of what is written in *The Zohar*, that a prayer for the poor is immediately accepted. That is, when it is for the *Shechina*, it is immediately accepted.

14. Baal HaSulam, *Shamati*, Article No. 47, "In the Place Where You Find His Greatness"

"In the place where you find His greatness, there you find His humbleness." It means that one who is always in true *Dvekut* [adhesion] sees that the Creator lowers Himself, meaning the Creator is present in the low places.

One does not know what to do, and this is why it is written, "Who sits on high, who looks down on heaven and on earth." A person sees the greatness of the Creator and then "who looks down," meaning he lowers the heaven to the earth. The advice that is given to this is to think that if this desire is from the Creator, we have nothing greater than that, as it is written, "He raises the poor out of the litter."

First, one must see that he has a lack. If he does not, he should pray for it, why does one not have it? The reason he does not have a lack is due to the diminution of awareness.

Hence, in every *Mitzva* [commandment], one must pray, why does he not have awareness, for he is not keeping the *Mitzva* in wholeness. In other words, the will to receive covers so he will not see the truth.

If he would see that he is in such a lowly state, he would certainly not want to be in that state. Instead, one should exert in one's work every time until he comes to repentance, as it is written, "He brings down to the netherworld, and raises up."

This means that when the Creator wants the wicked one to repent, He makes the netherworld so low for him that the wicked one himself does not want to be so. Hence, one needs to pray pleadingly that the Creator will show him the truth by adding to him the light of the Torah.

15. Baal HaSulam, Letter No. 57

Everything, small or great, is obtained only by the power of prayer. All the labor and work to which we are obliged are only to discover our lack of strength and our lowliness—that we are unfit for anything by our own strength—for then we can pour out a wholehearted prayer before Him.

We could argue about this, "So I can decide that I am unfit for anything, and why all the labor and exertion?" However, there is a natural law that there is none so wise as the experienced, and before one tries to actually do all he can do, he is utterly incapable of arriving at true lowliness, to the real extent, as said above.

This is why we must toil in *Kedusha* [holiness] and purity, as it is written, "Whatever you find that your hand can do by your strength, that do," and understand this for it is true and deep.

I revealed this truth to you only so you would not weaken or give up on mercy. Although you do not see anything, for even when the measure of labor is complete, it is the time of prayer, but until then, believe in our sages: "I did not labor and found, do not believe."

When the measure is full, your prayer will be complete and the Creator will grant generously, as our sages instructed us, "I labored and found, believe," for one is unfit for a prayer prior to this, and the Creator hears a prayer.

16. Baal HaSulam, Letter No. 11

All the good of the awakening from below concerns only our learning how to feel the deficiency, as it is set before us by the Creator. This is the meaning of "A prayer makes half," since as long as one does not feel the deficiency of the half—the part that was cut off from the whole, and the part does not feel as it should—one is incapable of complete *Dvekut* [adhesion] since this will not be considered advantageous for him, and one does not keep or sustain a needless thing.

Our sages told us that there is a remedy for this feeling by the power of the prayer. When one is persistent in praying and craving to adhere to Him perpetually, the prayer can do half, meaning that he will recognize that it is half. When the sparks multiply and become absorbed in the organs, he will certainly be rewarded with complete salvation and the part will be adhered to the whole forever.

17. Baal HaSulam, "Not the Time for the Livestock to Be Gathered"

This is the meaning of a prayer in public, that one must not exclude oneself from the public and ask for oneself, not even to bring contentment to one's maker, but only for the entire public. It is so because one cannot extend one's boundary while the boundaries of the rest of the buds of the flower remain where they are, for as smallness blemishes the beauty, so does greatness, since the boundaries of all the lines and circles of the flower must be related.

This is the meaning of (Psalms 22:21) "Save my soul from the sword, my only one from the dog." One who departs from the public to ask specifically for one's own soul does not build. On the contrary, he inflicts ruin upon his soul, as in (*Midrash Rabbah*, Chapter 7, Item 6) "All who is proud," etc., for there cannot be one who retires from the public unless with an attire of pride. Woe unto him, for he inflicts ruin on his soul.

18. Baal HaSulam, "Not the Time for the Livestock to Be Gathered"

Every one must gather with all of one's strength into the whole of Israel with every plea to the Creator in the prayer and in the work, for it is insolence and great disgrace to disclose one's nakedness before, etc.

This is the meaning of (Exodus 20:23) "And you shall not go up by steps to My altar," meaning as an individual, where one is above the other. And especially that he desires to boast over the seed of holiness, and a holy nation does not need him. He marches on the heads of the holy nation and demands greatness over them. This is a disgrace we must not mention henceforth.

Instead, he should include himself in the only one, the root of all of Israel.

19. RABASH, Article No. 18 (1986), "Who Causes the Prayer"

Baal HaSulam said about it, "It is written, 'And it shall come to pass that before they call, I will answer, and while they are still speaking, I will hear.'" He interpreted that when a person feels his fault and prays for the Creator to help him, it is not because a person feels his fault, and this gives him reason to pray. Rather, the reason is that *he is favored by the Creator, and the Creator wishes to bring him near*.

At that time, the Creator sends him the sensation of his own fault and calls upon him to join Him. In other words, *it is the Creator who brings him near by giving him a desire to turn to the Creator and to speak to the Creator*. It follows that he already had the granting of the prayer *even before he prayed*. That is, the Creator brought him closer by enabling him to speak to the Creator. This is called, "Before they call, I will answer." That is, the Creator brought that person near Him before the thought appeared in the man's mind that he should pray to the Creator.

But why did the Creator choose him and give him the call to come to Him and pray? To this, we have no answer. Instead, we must believe above reason that this is so. This is what we call, "Guidance of Private Providence." One must not say, "I'm waiting for the Creator to give me an awakening from above, and then I will be able to work in the work of holiness." Baal HaSulam said that in regard to the future, a person must believe in reward and punishment, meaning he must say (*Avot*, Chapter 1), "If I am not for me who is for me, and when I am for me, what am I, and if not now, then when?"

20. RABASH, Article No. 164, "What to Ask of the Creator—to Be His Servant"

When a person sees that he has disturbances in his work of the Creator and he wants to pray to the Creator to have the strength to work, what should he ask?

There are two options:

1) That the Creator will take away from him the disturbances. As a result, he will not need to make great efforts in order to walk in the ways of the Creator.
2) For the Creator to give him a greater taste for the Torah and prayer and good deeds, and by this the disturbances will not be able to detain him because when Torah and *Mitzvot* [commandments] are important, disturbances cannot rule.

For example, a person cannot say that he has many disturbances so he cannot save his life. That is, it is not true if he argued that because his relatives or his environment are disturbing him, he is unable to save his life. Rather, of course, a person will give all that he has for his life, and all the obstacles do not matter to him.

Therefore, he asks the Creator to give him the taste of life in *Torah and Mitzvot*, and against life, one cannot say that he has disturbances because the importance of life does not let him relate to the disturbances.

21. RABASH, Article No. 217, "Run My Beloved"

It is impossible to receive anything without equivalence. Rather, there must always be equivalence.

Hence, when he evokes mercy on himself, it follows that he is engaged in reception for himself. And the more he prays, not only is he not preparing the *Kli* [vessel] of equivalence, but on the contrary, sparks of reception form within him.

It turns out that he is going the opposite way: While he should prepare vessels of bestowal, he is preparing vessels of reception. "Cleave unto His attributes" is specifically "As He is merciful, so you are merciful."

Hence, when he prays for the public, through this prayer he engages in bestowal. And the more he prays, to that extent he forms vessels of bestowal, by which the light of bestowal, called "merciful," can be revealed.

22. RABASH, Article No. 29 (1986), "Lishma and Lo Lishma"

There is only one way—to try to attain the greatness of the Creator. That is, in all that we do in Torah and *Mitzvot*, we want our reward to be the feeling of the greatness of the Creator, and all our prayers should be to "raise the *Shechina* [Divinity] from the dust," since the Creator is hidden from us due to the *Tzimtzum* that took place and we cannot appreciate His importance and greatness.

Therefore, we pray to the Creator to remove His concealment from us and to raise the glory of Torah. As we say in the Eighteen Prayer of *Rosh Hashanah* [New Year service], "Indeed, give glory to Your people." That is, "Give the glory of the Lord to Your people," so they will feel the glory of the King.

For this reason, one must try to remember the goal while studying Torah, so it will always be before his eyes what he wants to receive from the study, that the study will impart greatness and importance of the Creator. Also, while observing the *Mitzvot*, not to forget the intention that thanks to observing the *Mitzvot*, the Creator will lift the concealment on spirituality from him and he will receive a feeling of the greatness of the Creator.

23. RABASH, Article No. 106, "The Ruin of Kedusha [Holiness]"

One must not ask the Creator to bring him closer to Him, as it is insolence on the part of man, for in what is he more important than others? However, when he prays for the collective—which is *Malchut*, called "assembly of Israel," the sum of the souls—that the *Shechina* [Divinity] is in the dust, and he prays that she will rise, meaning that the Creator will light up her darkness, then all of Israel will rise in degree, too, including the beseeching person, who is included in the collective.

24. RABASH, Article No. 18 (1989), "What Is, 'There Is No Blessing in That Which Is Counted,' in the Work?"

When a person should replace the goal, meaning where in the beginning of his work in Torah and *Mitzvot*, his goal—which he wanted to achieve through the labor—was self-benefit, now he replaces the goal. That is, where he thought, "When will I achieve the goal for my will to receive so I can enjoy?" now he yearns for the goal and says, "When will I be able to delight the Creator and relinquish self-benefit?"

Since this purpose is against nature, he needs more faith in the Creator, since he must always exert to obtain the greatness of the Creator. That is, to the extent that he believes in the greatness of the Creator, to that extent he can work with this intention. For this reason, it is upon a person to pray each day that the Creator will open his eyes so he will recognize the greatness and importance of the Creator, so he has fuel to labor with the aim to bestow.

There are two discernments to make in this: 1) to have a desire to bestow contentment upon his Maker, that this will be his only aspiration, 2) to do things with the aim that the actions will bring him a desire to do things in order to please the Creator. In other words, he must work and toil extensively to obtain light and *Kli* [vessel]. Light means that he received from the Creator a desire where he craves all day to bring contentment to the Creator. A *Kli* is a desire, meaning that he wants to bestow upon the Creator. Those two, he should receive from the Creator, meaning both the light and the *Kli*.

However, a person should demand this, and it is written about this, "Zion, no one requires her." Our sages said, "This means that she ought to be sought," meaning that there must be a demand on the part of the lower ones that the Creator will give them both the light and the *Kli*.

25. RABASH, Article No. 4 (1988), "What Is the Prayer for Help and for Forgiveness in the Work?"

Our sages said, "Man's inclination overcomes him every day. Were it not for the help of the Creator, he would not overcome it." Thus, why is it man's fault if he did not receive the required help from the Creator? And accordingly, why should one ask forgiveness from the Creator? The answer is simple: It is because he did not ask for help. Our sages said, "He who comes to purify is aided." It follows that the help comes from the Creator after he asks for help.

Thus, man's sin is that he did not ask the Creator for help. Had he asked for help, he would certainly get help from the Creator. But if a person says that he asked for help and the Creator did not help him, to this comes the answer that a person should believe that the Creator hears the prayers, as it is written, "For You hear the prayer of every mouth." If he truly believed, his prayer would be complete, and the Creator hears a complete prayer when a person yearns with all his heart that the Creator will help him.

But if his prayer is not constantly on his lips, it means that he does not have the real faith that the Creator can help him and that the Creator hears everyone who asks Him, and that small and great are equal before Him, meaning that He answers everyone. It follows that the prayer is incomplete. This is why he should ask forgiveness for his sins, for not asking for the required help from the Creator.

26. RABASH, Article No. 29 (1987), "What Is 'According to the Sorrow, So Is the Reward'?"

Precisely when a person begins to walk on the path of bestowal, he comes to a state of pain and sorrow, and feels the labor that exists in serving the Creator. That is, the labor begins to work when one wants to work for the sake of the Creator. Only then do the arguments of the spies come to him. It is very difficult to overcome them, and many people escape the campaign and surrender to the argument of the spies.

But those who do not want to move, but rather say, "We have nowhere to go," suffer from not being able to always overcome them. They are in a state of ascending and descending, and every time they overcome, they see that they are farther from the goal that they want to be rewarded with *Dvekut* with the Creator, which is equivalence of form.

The measure of sorrow that they must tolerate is because in truth, a person cannot emerge from the control of self-reception by himself, as it is the nature in which the Creator created man, which only the Creator Himself can change. In other words, as He has given the created beings the desire to receive, He can later give them the desire to bestow.

However, according to the rule, "There is no light without a *Kli*, no filling without a lack," first one needs to obtain a deficiency. That is, he must feel that he is deficient of this *Kli* called "desire to bestow." And concerning feeling, it is impossible to feel any lack if one does not know what he is losing by not having the *Kli*, called "desire to bestow." For this reason, man must introspect on what causes him not to have the desire to bestow.

To the extent of the loss, he feels sorrow and suffering. When he has the real lack, meaning when he can pray to the Creator from the bottom of the heart for not having the strength to be able to work for the sake of the Creator, then, when he has the *Kli*, meaning the real lack, this is the time when his prayer is answered and he receives assistance from above. It is as our sages said, "He who comes to purify is aided."

27. RABASH, Article No. 2 (1991), "What Is, 'Return, O Israel, Unto the Lord Your God,' in the Work?"

What it means that the Creator heals the brokenhearted. The thing is that it is known that the essence of man is the heart, as our sages said, "The Merciful one wants the heart." The heart is the *Kli* [vessel] that receives the *Kedusha* from above. It is as we learn about the breaking of the vessels, that if the *Kli* is broken, everything you put in it will spill out.

Likewise, if the heart is broken, meaning the will to receive controls the heart, abundance cannot enter there because everything that the will to receive receives will go to the *Klipot* [shells/peels]. This is called "the breaking of the heart." Hence, a person prays to the Creator and says, "You must help me because I am worse than everyone, since I feel that the will to receive controls my heart, and this is why nothing of *Kedusha* can enter my heart. I want no luxuries, only to be able to do something for the sake of the Creator, and I am utterly incapable of this, so only You can save me."

By this we should interpret what is written (Psalms 34), "The Lord is near to the brokenhearted." That is, those who ask the Creator to help them so their heart will not be broken and will be whole.

28. RABASH, Article No. 27 (1991), "What Is, 'If a Woman Inseminates First, She Delivers a Male Child,' in the Work?"

A request is what a person feels that he is lacking. This is specifically in the heart, meaning that it does not matter what he says with his mouth, since "requesting" means that a person asks for what he needs, and all of man's needs are not in the mouth, but in the heart. Therefore, it does not matter what a person says with his mouth. Rather, the Creator knows the thoughts. Hence, what is heard above is only what the heart demands and not what the mouth demands, since the mouth has no deficiency that must be satisfied.

29. RABASH, Article No. 16 (1988), "What Is the Foundation on which Kedusha [Holiness] Is Built?"

By being unable to emerge from his will to receive for himself, and by feeling that he needs the Creator's help, the need for assistance of the Creator is born within him.

His help is through Torah, since "The light in it reforms him," meaning he receives vessels of bestowal.

30. RABASH, Article No. 27 (1991), "What Is, 'If a Woman Inseminates First, She Delivers a Male Child,' in the Work?"

When a person comes to pray to the Creator to help him, he should first prepare and examine himself to see what he has and what he needs, and then he can know what to ask of the Creator to help him. It is written, "From the depths I have called upon You, Lord." "Depth" means that a person is at the very bottom, as was said, "at the bottom of Sheol," meaning that his lack is below and he feels that he is the lowliest of all humans.

In other words, he feels so far from *Kedusha*, more than everyone else, meaning that no one feels the truth, that his body has nothing to do with *Kedusha*. For this reason, those people, who do not see the truth of how far they are from *Kedusha*, can be content with their work in holiness, while he suffers from his situation.

31. RABASH, Article No. 268, "One Learns Only Where One's Heart Desires"

We also need to understand what our sages said, "One does not see one's own faults" (*Shabbat* 119). Accordingly, how can one correct his practices if he never sees that they are corrupt and require correction? According to this, a person should always remain corrupted.

The thing is that it is known that man was created with a nature that he wants to delight only himself. Hence, everything he learns, he wants to learn from this how he can enjoy. For this reason, if a person wants to enjoy, he will not learn other things that his heart desires because this is his nature.

Therefore, one who wants to come closer to the Creator and be able to learn things that show ways by which to bestow upon the Creator must pray to the Creator to give him a different heart, as it is written, "A pure heart, create for me, O God."

In other words, when there is another heart, and the desire in the heart is a desire to bestow, everything he learns will show ways of things that show only bestowal upon the Creator. However, he will never see against the heart, as was said about it, "And I will remove the stony heart from within you, and I will give you a heart of flesh."

32. RABASH, Article No. 528, "Prayer"

If he wants to know and asks the Creator to understand the connection, this is called a "prayer." This is a great and very important thing, since he has a connection with the Creator because he wants something from Him.

33. RABASH, Article No. 24, "Three Times in the Work"

A prayer is work in the heart. That is, since the root of man's heart is the will to receive, and he needs the opposite, meaning that it will work only to bestow and not to receive, it follows that he has a lot of work in inverting it.

And since this is against nature, he must pray to the Creator to help him come out of his nature and enter what is discerned as above nature. This is called a "miracle," and only the Creator can perform miracles. That is, for man to be able to exit self-love is a miraculous act.

34. RABASH, Article No. 37 (1985), "Who Testifies to a Person?"

We must study and scrutinize the books that discus the necessity of the work of bestowal until we understand and feel that if we don't have this *Kli*, we will not be able to enter the *Kedusha*. We should not look at the majority, who say that the most important thing is the act and here is where all the energy should go, and that the acts of *Mitzvot* and establishing of the Torah that we do are enough for us.

Instead, he must perform every act of Torah and *Mitzvot* in order to bring himself into the aim to bestow. Afterwards, when he has a complete understanding of how much he needs to engage in order to bestow, and he feels pain and suffering at not having this force, then it is considered that he already has something for which to pray—for work in the heart—since the heart feels what it needs.

For such a prayer comes the answer to the prayer. This means that he is given this strength from above so he will be able to aim in order to bestow, for then he already has the light and *Kli*. However, what can one do if, after all the efforts he has made, he still does not feel the lack of not being able to bestow as pain and suffering? The solution is to ask the Creator to give him the *Kli* called, "A lack from not feeling," and that he is unconscious, without any pain from being unable to bestow.

It follows that if he can regret and ache over not having the deficiency, for not feeling how remote he is from *Kedusha* [holiness].

This is called "work in the heart," as well. It is called, "a prayer." This means that for this deficiency, he already has a place in which to receive fulfillment from the Creator, to give him the sense of deficiency, which is the *Kli* that the Creator fills with a filling.

35. RABASH, Article No. 36, "Who Hears a Prayer"

"He hears a prayer." There is a question: Why is prayer written in singular form if the Creator hears prayers, as it is written, "For you hear the prayer of every mouth of Your people Israel with mercy"?

We should interpret that we have only one prayer to pray—to raise the *Shechina* [Divinity] from the dust, and by this all the salvations will come.

36. RABASH, Article No. 10 (1989), "What Does It Mean that the Ladder Is Diagonal, in the Work?"

Is written, "and behold, a ladder was set on the earth with its top reaching to heaven." That is, the ladder, by which we climb up to the King's palace, has two ends. 1) "A ladder was set on the earth." This is the left line, called "earth." One should see that he is placed in worldliness, immersed in self-love, as in, "the left pushes away." Then there is room to pray from the bottom of the heart, for then one looks within one's reason at how he cannot do anything for the sake of the Creator, and only He can deliver him from the governance of the evil in him. It is said about this, "Were it not for the help of the Creator, he would not be able to overcome it." 2) It is written, "its top reaching to heaven." The other end of the ladder is in "heaven," as though he has complete wholeness because he is content with his lot, in the little bit of contact that he has with the work of the Creator. He feels that he is happy with this, since it is a great privilege to be rewarded with serving the King and speaking with Him even one moment a day; this is enough for him to be in high spirits, and he thanks the King for this and praises Him.

37. RABASH, Article No. 38 (1990), "What Is, 'A Cup of Blessing Must Be Full,' in the Work?"

A person needs great mercy in order not to escape the campaign. Although he uses the counsels that our sages said, "I have created the evil inclination; I have created the Torah as a spice," but the person says that he has already used this advice several times to no avail.

He also says that he has already used the advice "He who comes to purify is aided," and it is as though all the counsels are not for him. Thus, he does not know what to do. This is the worst state for a person, meaning he wants to escape from these states but has nowhere to run. At that time he suffers torments at being between despair and confidence. But then a person says, "Where will I turn?"

At that time, the only advice is prayer. Yet, this prayer is also without any guarantee, so it follows that then he must pray to believe that the Creator does hear a prayer, and everything that one feels in these states is to his benefit. But this can be only above reason, meaning although the mind tells him, "After all the calculations, you see that nothing can help you," he should believe this, too, above reason, that the Creator can deliver him from the will to receive for himself, in return for which he will receive the desire to bestow.

38. RABASH, Article No. 16 (1989), "What Is the Prohibition to Bless on an Empty Table, in the Work?"

"Right line," meaning wholeness, in which there are no deficiencies. And what should one do when he engages in a manner of "right"? He should praise and thank the Creator, and engage in the Torah, for then is the time to receive the light of Torah, since he is in a state of wholeness, regarded as being a person who has blessing and no lacks. Naturally, this is the time for the blessing to be on him, as said above, "The blessed clings to The Blessed."

However, it is impossible to walk on one leg. That is, a person cannot progress on one leg. Since there is a rule, "There is no light without a *Kli*," meaning "No filling without a lack," and since on the right line he is in wholeness, it follows that he has nowhere to progress, no need for the Creator to satisfy his needs, since he has no needs at all.

For this reason, at that time a person must try to see his faults, so as to have room for prayer that the Creator will satisfy his needs. This is regarded as a person having to provide empty *Kelim* that the Creator may fill with upper abundance, which is called "a blessing." If there are no empty *Kelim*, meaning deficiencies, with what can he fill them?

This is regarded as a person walking on the "left line." In spirituality, "left" means something that requires correction. This means that a person should dedicate a small portion of his time to criticize himself and see how much effort he can put into working solely for the sake of the Creator, and not for his own sake, and if he can say that if he does not work in order to bring contentment to his Maker, he does not want to live, and so forth.

At that time he realizes that he cannot do this on his own, but only the Creator can help. It follows that now is the time when he can pray from the bottom of the heart. That is, he sees and feels that he is powerless to change the nature with which he was created, called "will to receive for himself and not to bestow."

39. RABASH, Article No. 401, "Hear, O Israel"

A person should begin the work of the Creator on the right, called "male," which is wholeness, called happy with his share, which is regarded as "desiring mercy." Whatever flavor and vitality he has in *Torah and Mitzvot* [commandments] is enough for him to labor in *Torah and Mitzvot* because he believes in private Providence, that such is the will of the Creator, and feels that he is a complete person, and thanks and praises the Creator for giving him a part in His work.

This is called a "male," when he feels himself as whole and he is always happy and observes, "Serve the Lord with gladness."

However, this is called "half a body"; he does not have the quality of female, which is a lack. From the perspective of the left, he begins to calculate to what extent his qualities and thoughts are whole, and then he sees the truth, that he is still immersed in the will to receive for his own benefit, and cannot work for the sake of others, whether between man and man or between man and the Creator.

To the extent that he has the recognition of evil, he can exert, meaning work, perform actions, as in "Everything that is in the power of your hand to do, that do." Also, he can pray from the bottom of the heart, since only to the extent that a person feels the bad, meaning feels that it is bad, to that extent he acts in order to be rid of the bad. This is called "female," meaning a lack.

It follows that he has room for two opposite qualities. On one hand, he is regarded as complete, which is the "right," *Hesed* [mercy], happy with his share. He can praise and thank the Creator for letting him into a place of Torah and good deeds. On the other hand, he can pray to the Creator for remaining outside of the work of the Creator because everything was built on the basis of self-love.

At that time, the person is called "complete," and otherwise he is not considered "man" because if he sees his deficiencies he will soon run from the quality of the "right," as well.

But once he has seen his bad state and yet reinforces himself above reason that he has wholeness, and the sign of this is that he can thank the Creator for this, then he is called "complete." This is "Right and left, and a bride between them." By having the quality of male and female, he can be rewarded with the quality of "bride," meaning the real kingdom of heaven.

40. RABASH, Article No. 16 (1988), "What Is the Foundation on which Kedusha [Holiness] Is Built?"

"I awaken the dawn" will mean "Whenever I want, I awaken the dawn." In other words, I myself awaken the darkness and the blackness within me—that I am still immersed in self-love and I still do not have love for the Creator. I am still without the glory of the Torah and I still do not have the importance of the Torah to know that it is worthwhile to do everything to obtain the light of Torah, as well as how to appreciate the importance of observing the *Mitzvot* that the Creator commanded for us.

When I need to perform some *Mitzva* and intend that it will be in order to bestow, the resistance in the body promptly awakens in full force. And he has a great struggle to do anything and he sees the ascents and descents each time. And then he has room for prayer. This is so because a person awakens himself at the right time, meaning when he feels that he will be able to pray instantaneously, and not that the black will bring him sadness and depression, that he will not have the ability to pray for the blackness.

One can see for himself whether it comes to him from the side of *Klipa* or not. The sign for this is that something that comes from *Kedusha* is always in the form of "increasing holiness and not decreasing." In other words, one always asks the Creator to elevate him to a higher degree than the one he is on. But when the blackness comes from the side of *Klipa*, a person cannot ask the Creator to raise him above his state.

"Rather, they bring down," meaning bring him down to the netherworld, and he loses the small portion of faith that he had and he remains seemingly dead.

41. RABASH, Letter No. 22,

That is, the fact that a person is permitted to learn and pray, and observe *Mitzvot* even one minute a day, that, too, is a gift from the Creator, for there are several billions in the world to whom the Creator did not give the chance to be able to think of the Creator for even one minute a year. Therefore, while engaging in the Torah, one must be glad, for only through joy is one rewarded with drawing the light of Torah.

42. RABASH, Article No. 10, "What Does 'The King Stands on His Field When the Crop Is Ripe' Mean in the Work?"

The correction of a person walking on the left line is because he does not wait to get a decline and fall, and then he will wait until an awakening from above comes to him. Instead, he draws upon him the left, and then he sees that he is in a state of descent, meaning that he does not have a single spark of desire to work in order to bestow and not for his own benefit. And then he can pray.

It is as Baal HaSulam said about what our sages said of David, who said, "I awaken the dawn, and the dawn does not awaken me." That is, King David did not wait for the dawn, which is called "black," which is darkness, meaning that the darkness awakens him. Instead, he awakens the darkness. He prays to the Creator to illuminate His face for him and thus he gains time from having the preparation for the darkness, and then it is easier to correct it.

And the two above-mentioned lines—right and left—beget a third line, the middle line. It is as our sages said, "And the Creator places the spirit and soul within him." Thus, after a person has completed the work in two lines, all the evil is revealed in him. This came to him because those two lines are as two verses that refute one another. And one sees that there is no end to the ups and downs, and then he makes an honest prayer for the Creator to help him receive the desire to bestow.

43. RABASH, Article No. 15 (1985), "And Hezekiah Turned His Face to the Wall"

The prayer should be primarily for the *Shechina* being in the dust. This means that work to bestow upon the Creator is despicable and contemptible, and we ask of the Creator to open our eyes and remove the darkness that is floating before our eyes.

We ask about this, as it is written (Psalms 113), "He raises the poor from the dust, and lifts the destitute from the trash." It is known that the holy *Shechina* is called poor and meager, as it is written in *The Zohar*, "and it is placed in the dust." "He lifts the poor from the trash" refers to those who want to cling to her but feel that they are lowly, and they do not see how they can emerge from this mud. At that time they ask of the Creator to lift them.

Where the body agrees with the work, where it is on the basis of the will to receive, since they have no clue about bestowal, their work is with pride, meaning they take pride in being servants of the Creator while others are in utter lowliness, and they always see others' faults.

But those who walk on the path of truth, who want to achieve bestowal, are lowly because they see that "Were it not for the Creator's help, he would not have overcome it." Thus, they find no special merit in themselves over others. These people are called "lowly" because they want to connect to bestowal, which is lowliness, and this is another reason why they are called "lowly."

At that time they can say what is written, "The Lord is high, great, and terrible. He lowers the proud to the ground, and raises the lowly to the heavens," for at that time they say that what was lowly before is now high and sublime, great and terrible. This is because now they feel that what was previously work in self-love, which is pride, when they felt proud about this work, has now become lowliness, since they are ashamed to work for self-love.

But who gave them the strength to feel this? It was the Creator who gave them. This is why at that time a person says, "Lowers the proud to the ground," while the work of bestowal, which was previously lowly, now the work of bestowal has become to him of the highest merit. And who did this for him? Only the Creator. At that time a person says, "And raises the lowly to the heaven."

44. RABASH, Article No. 20 (1990), "What Is Half a Shekel in the Work? – 2"

It is known that there is no light without a *Kli*, as there is no filling without a lack. Accordingly, a complete thing is called "light and *Kli*," which divides into two halves: The first half is the *Kli*, namely the lack. The second half is the light, namely the filling.

It follows that when a person prays to the Creator to satisfy his lack, it is called "half," meaning making a lack, which is the *Kli*, for the Creator to satisfy his lack. This is as our sages said (*VaYikra Rabbah* 18), "A prayer makes half." We should interpret that a prayer is when a person prays to the Creator to satisfy his lack. This is already regarded as "half," meaning the first half, which is in one's hand. The second half is in the hands of the Creator, meaning that the Creator must give the light, and then there will be a complete thing.

45. RABASH, Letter No. 9

One who sees one's lowliness sees that he is treading the path leading to the work *Lishma*. This gives one room for real prayer from the bottom of the heart, when he sees that no one will help him but the Creator himself, as Baal HaSulam interpreted concerning the redemption from Egypt, "I, and not a messenger," for everyone saw that only the Creator Himself redeemed them from the governance of evil.

And when rewarded with the work *Lishma* there is certainly nothing to be proud of because then one sees that it is only God's gift, and not "my power and the might of my hand," and there is no foreign hand that can help him. Therefore, he feels his lowliness—how serving the king is an immeasurable pleasure, and without His help he would not agree to it. Indeed, there is no greater lowliness than this.

46. RABASH, Article No. 10 (1986), "Concerning Prayer"

Before one knows that he cannot obtain the vessels of bestowal by himself, he does not ask the Creator to give them to him. It follows that he does not have a real desire for the Creator to answer his prayer.

For this reason, one must work to obtain the vessels of bestowal by himself, and after all the work that he has put into it without obtaining it begins the real prayer from the bottom of the heart. At that time he can receive help from above, as our sages said, "He who comes to purify is aided."

But since this prayer is against nature, since man was created with a desire to receive, which is self-love, how can he pray to the Creator to give him the force of bestowal while all the organs oppose this desire? This is why this work is called "prayer," meaning he must make great efforts to be able to pray to the Creator to give him the force of bestowal and annul man's force of reception.

This is why our sages said, "'And you shall work' is prayer, the work in the heart." By this we will understand why they refer to prayer as "work in the heart." It is because one must work a lot on himself to cancel self-love and assume the work of obtaining vessels of bestowal. It follows that on the desire to have vessels of bestowal he must work with himself to want to pray, to be given the force of bestowal.

47. RABASH, Article No. 3 (1989), "What Is the Difference between the Gate of Tears and the Rest of the Gates?"

A person must pray first, in order to know what he really needs. Then, he is notified from above that he does not need luxuries, but as *The Zohar* says about the verse "Or make his sin known to him," the Creator makes him know the sin. At that time he knows on what he needs to repent, meaning to restore what he is lacking.

It follows that when a person knows that he is wicked, as in "the wicked in their lives are called 'dead,'" when he has come to realize that the fact that he is placed under the control of the will to receive separates him from the Life of Lives, he knocks about this and wants to repent. That is, he wants to be given help from above so he can emerge from self-love and be able to love the Creator with all his heart. Thus, he feels that he is wicked, since where he should love the Creator, he loves himself.

It follows that his knocks, we understand that he does what he can to make the Creator bring him closer and take him out of the control of his own evil. This is called "real tears." This is the meaning of what we explained, "Open a gate for us, when a gate is locked." That is, since he sees that all the gates are closed, he begins to knock. It follows that at the time of the locking of the gate, when he has already prayed and was notified the reason for the sin, he begins to shed the real tears, meaning at that time he simply wants to be a Jew. At that time, his knocks are regarded as tears, and this is the meaning of "Who opens a gate to those who knock in repentance."

48. RABASH, Article No. 24 (1989), "What Is 'Do Not Slight the Blessing of a Layperson,' in the Work?"

Our sages said (*Yoma* 16), "Any turn you take should be only through the right." The meaning of "any" is "generally." That is, generally, a person should walk on the right line. It is permitted to walk on the left line only when he is certain he will be able to pray for his deficiencies. Otherwise, he must remain on the right until he feels that he is ready for it.

Therefore, if thoughts that he is at fault have awakened in him against his will, and how can he speak words of Torah and prayer to the Creator when his thoughts tell him, "You are filthy! How are you not ashamed to engage in matters of *Kedusha*?!" About this, a person (must) say that it is written, "I am the Lord, who dwells with them in the midst of their *Tuma'a* [impurity]." That is, even though I am in the lowest possible baseness, I still believe what is written, that the Creator dwells even in the worst lowliness.

However, He is not among the proud, as our sages said, "Anyone who is proud, the Creator says, 'I and he cannot dwell in the same abode.'" For this reason, when a person feels whole, according to the right line, when he appreciates his lowliness and says that nonetheless, the Creator has given him some grip on *Kedusha*, and that "some," compared to the *Kedusha* that a person should attain, that "some" is called "layperson."

But if he says according to his lowliness, "I thank and praise the Creator for this," it can be said about this what is written, "I am the Lord, who dwells with them in the midst of their *Tuma'a*." When he is happy about this, he can be rewarded with, "The *Shechina* [Divinity] is present only out of joy."

It follows that through this lowliness, that because the Creator has given him some grip on *Kedusha*, he can climb the rungs of holiness if he only takes from this the joy and appreciates it. Then, a person can say, "Raise the poor from the dust," "He will raise the destitute from the litter." That is, when a person feels his lowliness, that he is meager, meaning poor, as our sages said (*Nedarim* 41), "Abaye said, 'In our tradition, there is no poor but in knowledge.'" That is, it has been handed down from our father, a custom from our forefathers that "there is no poor but in knowledge."

This is why he says that he is meager, meaning poor, for he has no knowledge of *Kedusha*—he is called "poor and meager." Then, if there is any grip on *Kedusha*, even though he is poor, he says, "Raises the poor from the dust." That is, he says a prayer, for even though he is poor, the Creator still raised him. "He raises the destitute from the litter." Although he feels that he is destitute, the Creator still lifted him, and for this, he praises the Creator. If there is any grip on *Kedusha*, we can already praise and thank the Creator.

49. RABASH, Article No. 15 (1986), "A Prayer of Many"

If there are a few people in the collective who can reach the goal of *Dvekut* with the Creator, and this will bring the Creator more contentment than if he himself were rewarded with nearing the Creator, he excludes himself. Instead, he wishes for the Creator to help them because this will bring more contentment above than from his own work. For this reason, he prays for the collective, that the Creator will help the entire collective and will give them that feeling—that they receive satisfaction from being able to bestow upon the Creator, to bring Him contentment.

And since everything requires an awakening from below, he gives the awakening from below, and others will receive the awakening from above, to whomever the Creator knows will be more beneficial for the Creator.

It follows that if he has the strength to ask for such a prayer, then he will certainly face a true test—if he agrees to such a prayer. However, if he knows that what he is saying is only lip service, what can he do when he sees that the body disagrees with such a prayer to have pure bestowal without a hint of reception?

Here there is only the famous advice—to pray to the Creator and believe above reason that the Creator can help him and the whole collective.

50. RABASH, Article No. 39 (1991), "What Does It Mean that the Right Must Be Greater than the Left, in the Work?"

Is written (Sanhedrin 44b), "Rabbi Elazar said, 'One should always precede prayer to trouble.'" We should interpret that one does not go into the work of the left before he first worked in the manner of the right, which is regarded as wholeness, meaning that he does not lack anything and he thanks and praises the Creator for giving him some grip on the work of the Creator, and then he begins the work of the left. At that time, he sees that he is in trouble, that he has neither Torah nor work that is suitable for one who is serving the Creator. At that time, he feels how far he is from the work of the Creator, meaning from working for Him, namely working only with the aim to bestow contentment upon his Maker, and not at all for his own benefit. At that time, he sees how the body objects to this, and he does not see that he will ever be able to do anything only in order to bestow.

It follows that when he begins the path of the left, this is called "trouble," and he has no other choice but to pray to the Creator to help him and give him the desire to bestow, called "second nature." At that time, the prayer is from the bottom of the heart, and the Creator hears his prayer.

51. RABASH, Article No. 23 (1985), "On My Bed at Night"

This is called "his father gives the white," as we said that wholeness is called "whiteness," where there is no dirt. There is a twofold gain here: 1) In this way he receives elation from being adhered to the Whole, meaning to the Creator, and we must believe that what He gives is wholeness. Wholeness makes a man whole, making him feel whole, too. Naturally, he derives nourishment from this, so he can live and persist and then have strength to do the holy work. 2) According to the importance he acquires during the work of wholeness, he will later have room to feel the deficiency with regard to his work, which is not truly pure. That is, at that time he can depict to himself how much he is losing by his negligence in the work, for he can compare between the importance of the Creator and his own lowliness, and this will give him energy to work.

However, one should also correct oneself, or he will remain in the dark and will not see the true light that shines on the *Kelim* [vessels] that are suitable for it, called "vessels of bestowal." The correction of the *Kelim* is called *Nukva*, deficiency, when he works on correcting his deficiencies. This is regarded as "His mother gives the red." That is, at that time he sees the red light, which are the barriers on his way, which prevent him from reaching the goal.

Then comes the time of prayer, since the man sees the measures of the work that he has in matters of "mind and heart," and how he has not progressed in the work of bestowal. He also sees how his body is weak, that he does not have great powers to be able to overcome his nature. For this reason, he sees that if the Creator does not help him, he is lost, as it is written (Psalms 127), "If the Lord does not build the house, they who build it labor in it in vain."

From those two, meaning from wholeness and deficiency, which are the "father and mother," it turns out that the Creator is the one who helps him, giving him a soul, which is the spirit of life. And then the newborn is born.

52. RABASH, Article No. 15 (1989), "What Is, 'The Righteous Become Apparent through the Wicked,' in the Work?"

In order for a person to progress on the path of the Creator, to be rewarded with all his work being for the sake of the Creator, and now he feels that he is in a state of ascent, what more should he do? For this reason, the Creator leads His world with wicked. That is, at that time the Creator gives him thoughts of wicked—that it is not worthwhile to work for Him, but only for himself. By this, he suffers a descent and thinks that the descent he has received is not because it was given to him so he would advance in the path of the Creator, to be rewarded with knowledge of *Kedusha* [holiness]. Rather, he thinks that he regressed because he cannot work in the manner of individuals, but needs to work like the general public. And since he has departed from the general public, he is left empty handed from here and from there, since he cannot return to the general public.

For this reason, in that state, a person stands between heaven and earth, and feels that his situation is worse than that of the rest of the people. At that time, he can ask the Creator with all his heart, and pray as it is written, "Pardon me, O Lord, for I am wretched. Heal me, O Lord, for my bones are dismayed, and You, O Lord, how long?" That is, how long will I stay in a situation where I feel that my condition is worse than any other person, that I have no grip on spirituality.

For this reason, he has no other choice but to believe what is written, "For You hear the prayer of every mouth." Baal HaSulam explained that a person must believe that the Creator hears the prayer of every mouth, meaning even the worst mouth in the world, of which there cannot be lowlier and worse in the world. Still, the Creator hears him, as our sages said, "He who comes to purify is aided."

53. RABASH, Article No. 19 (1985), "Come unto Pharaoh – 1"

We should pay attention to "Come unto Pharaoh" and believe through the worst possible states, and not escape the campaign, but rather always trust that the Creator can help a person and give him, whether one needs a little help or a lot of help.

In truth, one who understands that he needs the Creator to give him a lot of help, because he is worse than the rest of the people, is more suitable for his prayer to be answered, as it is written, "The Lord is near to the brokenhearted, and saves the crushed in spirit."

Therefore, one should not say that he is unfit for the Creator to bring him closer, but that the reason is that he is idle in his work. Instead, one should always overcome and not let thoughts of despair enter his mind, as our sages said (*Berachot*, 10), "Even if a sharp sword is placed on his neck he should not deny himself of mercy," as it was said (Job, 13), "Though He slay me, I will hope for Him."

We should interpret the "sharp sword placed on his neck" to mean that even though one's evil, called "self-love," is placed on his neck and wants to separate him from *Kedusha* by showing him that it is impossible to exit this authority, he should say that the picture he sees is the truth.

However, "He should not deny himself of mercy," for at that time he must believe that the Creator can give him the mercy, meaning the quality of bestowal. That is, by himself, it is true that one cannot exit the authority of self-reception. But from the perspective of the Creator, when the Creator helps him, of course He can bring him out. This is the meaning of what is written, "I am the Lord your God, who took you out from the land of Egypt to be your God.

54. RABASH, Article No. 23 (1989), "What Is, 'If He Swallows the Bitter Herb, He Will Not Come Out,' in the Work?"

Even when he comes to know that the Creator can help him, and he understands that the real advice is only prayer, the body comes and makes him see that "You see how many prayers you have already prayed but you received no answer from above. Therefore, why bother praying that the Creator will help you? You see that you are not getting any help from above." At that time, he cannot pray. Then we need to overcome once more through faith, and believe that the Creator does hear the prayer of every mouth, and it does not matter if the person is adept and has good qualities, or to the contrary. Rather, he must overcome and believe above reason, although his reason dictates that since he has prayed many times but still received no answer from above, how can he come and pray once more? This, too, requires overcoming, meaning to exert above reason and pray that the Creator will help him overcome his view and pray.

55. RABASH, Article No. 24 (1991), "What Does It Mean that One Should Bear a Son and a Daughter, in the Work?"

When a person prevails and asks for help from the Creator, after he has decided that he has a harm-doer in his heart, called "will to receive," and that he cannot emerge from it, meaning after going through several ascents and descents, he finally sees that he has remained bare and destitute. At that time, his prayer is from the bottom of the heart. That is, he sees that if the Creator does not help him, he cannot overcome it.

Although one can say that he believes above reason that only the Creator helps him, within reason, he does not feel this, since he knows that he himself made the efforts and the labor to obtain something in spirituality. But when one sees that after all the exertions, he cannot emerge from the governance of the will to receive for himself, then he sees within reason that only the Creator can help him.

It follows that what our sages said, "Man's inclination overcomes him every day, and were it not for the help of the Creator, he would not be able to overcome it," he does not need to believe in this above reason, the way ordinary workers of the Creator who observe *Torah and Mitzvot* believe "above reason" that this is so, that the Creator helps them. Rather, those people who want to work in order to bestow, for them, it is within reason, to the point that they must believe above reason that the Creator can help them emerge from the governance of the will to receive.

56. RABASH, Article No. 5 (1988), "What Is, 'When Israel Are in Exile, the Shechina Is With Them,' in the Work?"

The Creator wants him to see his real state, how remote he is from working for the benefit of the Creator. For this reason, the Creator has taken from him the flavor he felt in *Lo Lishma* [not for

Her sake], which leaves him lifeless. It follows that the Creator is tending to him and wants to admit him into *Kedusha*.

Therefore, now he must pray to the Creator to help him, since now he needs His help. Otherwise, he sees that he is completely lost. This is regarded as having obtained a *Kli* and a need for the Creator's help, since now he sees that he is truly separated from the Creator because he has no life, for one who adheres to the Creator has life, as it is written, "For with You is the source of life."

Now he can certainly pray from the bottom of the heart, for a real prayer is specifically from the bottom of the heart. Accordingly, he should be thankful to the Creator for letting him see his true state. Now he sees that he needs the Creator to give him the necessary assistance, as our sages said, "He who comes to purify is aided." And *The Zohar* asks, "With what is he aided?" and it replies, "With a holy soul."

Therefore, now the Creator has given him an opportunity to obtain a holy soul. He should be delighted about the state of descent and suffering that he feels in this state. For this reason, he should say that he is not in a state of descent, but on the contrary, he is in a state of ascent.

By this we can interpret what our sages said, "When torments come upon Israel, they surrender and pray." This means that when they come into a state of descent, they see their true state, that they are in lowliness. This is considered that they surrender, since they see their state—that they have parted from the Life of Lives, for one who has *Dvekut* with the Creator is alive. Otherwise, he feels only suffering. Therefore, it is clear to him that now is the time for prayer from the bottom of the heart. This is the meaning of the words, "They surrender and pray."

57. RABASH, Article No. 28 (1987), "What Is 'Do Not Add and Do Not Take Away,' in the Work?"

He must believe above reason and imagine that he has already been rewarded with faith in the Creator that is felt in his organs, and he sees and feels that the Creator leads the entire world as the good who does good. Although when he looks within reason he sees the opposite, he should still work above reason and it should appear to him as though he can already feel in his organs that so it really is, that the Creator leads the world as the good who does good.

Here he acquires the importance of the goal, and from here he derives life, meaning joy at being near to the Creator. Then a person can say that the Creator is good and does good, and feel that he has the strength to tell the Creator, "You have chosen us from among all nations, You have loved us and wanted us," since he has a reason to thank the Creator. And to the extent that he feels the importance of spirituality, so he establishes the praise of the Creator.

Once man has come to feel the importance of spirituality, which is called "One should always establish the praise of the Creator," then is the time when he must shift to the left line. He must criticize how he truly feels within reason the importance of the King, if he is truly willing to work only for the sake of the Creator.

When he sees within reason that he is bare and destitute, that state when he sees the importance of spirituality, but only above reason, that calculation can create in him deficiency and pain for being in utter lowliness. Then he can make a heartfelt prayer for what he lacks.

58. RABASH, Article No. 22 (1986), "If a Woman Inseminates"

The only way to obtain a deficiency, that we are lacking the desire to bestow, is by prayer, which is a "medium" between man and the deficiency. That is, one prays for the Creator to give him something for which he has no deficiency, that he will lack it. It follows that the *Kli* that is called "deficiency" is a deficiency with respect to the feeling, meaning that he does not feel its lack, and the prayer is that the Creator will give him the light, which is the filling of his lack. It therefore follows that the filling is a lack. Thus, he has no other choice but to pray to the Creator to give him a deficiency.

59. RABASH, Article No. 42, "Serve the Creator with Joy"

The Zohar asks, It is written, "The Lord is near to the brokenhearted." A servant of the Creator, whose intention is to bestow, should be happy when he is serving the King. If he has no joy during this work, it is a sign that he lacks appreciation of the greatness of the King.

Therefore, if one sees that he has no joy he should make amendments, meaning think about the greatness of the King. If he still does not feel, he should pray to the Creator to open his eyes and heart to feel the greatness of the Creator.

Here the two discernments develop: 1) He should regret not having a sensation of the greatness of the King. 2) He should be happy that his regrets are about spirituality and not like the rest of the people, whose regrets are only in order to receive.

We should know who it is who gave us the awareness that our regrets should be over spirituality, and we should be happy that the Creator has sent us thoughts of spiritual deficiency, which in itself is regarded as the salvation of the Creator. For this reason, we should be happy.

60. RABASH, Article No. 25 (1987), "What Is Heaviness of the Head in the Work?"

A prayer should be with heaviness of the head, meaning when a person feels that he does not have faith above reason, meaning that the reason does not mandate him to work in order to bestow, yet the person understands the primary goal should be to be rewarded with *Dvekut* [adhesion] with the Creator. Since the reason objects to this, he must go against reason, and this is very hard work.

Since he is asking the Creator to give him something to which all of his organs object, it follows that each and every prayer he makes to the Creator has its special work. This is why a prayer is called "work in the heart," meaning that he wants to go against the intellect and the mind, which tell him the complete opposite.

This is why it is not called "the work of the brain," since the work of the brain means that a person exerts to understand something with his mind and reason. But here he does not want to understand with his reason that we should serve the Creator in a state of knowing. Rather, he wants to serve the Creator specifically with faith above reason. This is why a prayer is called "work in the heart."

61. RABASH, Article No. 12 (1991), "These Candles Are Sacred"

The most important is the prayer. That is, one must pray to the Creator to help him go above reason, meaning that the work should be with gladness, as though he has already been rewarded with the reason of *Kedusha*, and what joy he would feel then. Likewise, he should ask the Creator to give him this power, so he can go above the reason of the body.

In other words, although the body does not agree to this work in order to bestow, he asks the Creator to be able to work with gladness, as is suitable for one who serves a great King. He does not ask the Creator to show the greatness of the Creator, and then he will work gladly. Rather, he wants the Creator to give him joy in the work of above reason, that it will be as important to a person as if he already has reason.

62. RABASH, Article No. 1 (1991), "What Is, 'We Have No Other King But You,' in the Work?"

In order for a person to be able to receive a complete thing, he must have a complete lack. Hence, from above, he is shown his deficiencies each time, which were concealed within his body. It therefore follows that a person must say that the Creator was merciful with him in that He revealed to him his faults, just as He is giving him the filling, for "There is no filling without a lack."

By this we can interpret what is written (Psalms 89), "I will sing of the mercies of the Lord forever, generation after generation I will make known Your faith with my mouth." We should understand the meaning of "sing forever." How can one sing to the Creator when he sees that he is full of faults and his heart is not whole with the Creator, and he feels far from the Creator? And sometimes, he even wants to escape the campaign. How can he say that this is the Lord's mercies and he is singing about this to the Creator?

According to the above, a person should say that the fact that he in a lowly state is not because now he has become worse. Rather, now, since he wants to correct himself so that all his actions will be for the sake of the Creator, from above he is shown his true state—what is in his body, which until now was concealed and was not apparent. Now the Creator has revealed them, as it is written in the book *A Sage's Fruit*.

A person says about this that it is mercy that the Creator has revealed to him the bad in him so he would know the truth and would be able to ask of the Creator for a real prayer. It follows that on one hand, now he sees that he is far from the Creator. On the other hand, a person should say that the Creator is close to him and tends to him, and shows him the faults. Hence, he should say that they are mercies.

This is the meaning of the words, "I will sing of the mercies of the Lord forever." That is, on one hand, he is happy and is singing about this. On the other hand, he sees that he must repent. In other words, he must ask of the Creator to bring him closer and give him the desire to bestow, which is a second nature.

63. RABASH, Letter No. 65,

The main thing in the work is that there is no giving of half a thing from heaven. Otherwise, it could happen that if a person repented half way he would receive assistance from above for half the work. But since there is no giving of half a thing from heaven, a person must pray to the Creator to give him complete help. This means that during his prayer, a person sets what is in his heart in order, since prayer is work in the heart, so a person must decide that he wants the Creator to give him a desire to completely annul before Him, meaning not leave any desire under his own authority, but that all the desires in him will be only to give glory to the Creator.

Once he decides on complete annulment, he asks the Creator to help him execute it. This means that although in the mind and the desire he sees that the body disagrees with him annulling all his desires before the Creator instead of for his own sake, he should pray to the Creator to help him want to annul before Him with all the desires, leaving no desire for himself. This is called a "complete prayer," meaning that he wishes that the Creator will give him a complete desire without any compromises to himself, and he asks of the Creator to help him always be with his righteousness.

64. RABASH, Article No. 4 (1989), "What Is a Flood of Water in the Work?"

Bina, whose quality is desiring mercy, meaning that she does not need to receive anything, is therefore free, since only one who needs to receive is limited and dependent on the view of others. But one who goes with his eyes shut and does not need any greatness or anything else, this is called "freedom."

However, we must know that it is a lot of work before we attain the quality of *Bina*. That is, to be content with little with his feeling and his mind, and be happy with his share, with what he has. That person can always be in wholeness because he is happy with his share.

But what can one do if he has not yet obtained this quality, and he sees that he cannot overcome his will to receive. At that time, he must pray to the Creator to help him so he can go in the work with his eyes shut, and will not need anything, and will be able to do everything for the sake of the Creator despite the resistance of the body to this.

That is, he does not tell the Creator how He should help him. Rather, he must subjugate himself and annul before the Creator unconditionally. But since he cannot overcome his body, he asks the Creator to help him win the war against the inclination, since he understands his lowliness.

For this reason, he asks the Creator to have mercy on him.

65. RABASH, Article No. 23 (1989), "What Is, 'If He Swallows the Bitter Herb, He Will Not Come Out,' in the Work?"

When one begins the work, he begins with faith, but the body resists this work, and then comes a state of labor, when he must overcome the body and seek all kinds of counsels, as our sages said, "In trickery shall you conduct war," since the body does not want to relinquish self-benefit. To the extent that he exerts, to that extent he begins to feel that he is incapable of doing anything since in his view, he has done everything he could. After the labor, he comes to know that only the Creator can help, and it is out of his hands. Then comes the third state—a prayer—and then the prayer is from the bottom of the heart, since it is utterly clear to him that no one can help him but the Creator.

66. RABASH, Article No. 587, "The Upper One Scrutinizes for the Purpose of the Lower One"

The upper one scrutinizes the *GE* for the purpose of the lower one (because "a prisoner does not free himself"). The upper one makes a *Masach* [screen] on the *MAN* of the lower one, meaning the rejecting force, until it is in the form of receiving in order to bestow, and only then is the light gripped in the MAN.

That is, MAN is a desire to receive. This is expressed through prayer, where prayer is regarded as raising MAN, and the answering of the prayer is called MAD, *Ohr Yashar* [direct light], upper abundance, bestowal. This prayer called MAN requires conditions, meaning that there will be the correction of a *Masach* in the prayer, namely that his intention will be for the sake of the Creator, called *Lishma* [for Her sake].

One must receive the power to work *Lishma* from the upper one, since the lower one is powerless to begin the work, but only in the form of *Lo Lishma* [not for Her sake], called "will to receive," for only the *Lo Lishma* gives the first moving force of the lower one, for when a person does not find sufficient flavor in corporeal pleasures, he begins to search for spiritual pleasures.

It follows that the root of the work of the lower one is the will to receive, and the prayer, called MAN, rises up, and then the upper one corrects this MAN and places on it the power of the *Masach*, which is a desire to delay the abundance before the lower one knows about himself that his aim is to bestow.

That is, the upper one bestows upon the lower one good taste and pleasure in the desire to bestow, by which the lower one feels His exaltedness. At that time, he begins to understand that it is worthwhile to annul before Him and cancel his existence before Him. Then, he feels that all that there is in reality is only because such is His will, that the Creator wants the lower one to exist, but for himself, he wants to annul his existence. It follows that then, all the vitality he feels is regarded as *Lishma* and not for himself.

When he feels this, it is considered that he already has the correction of the MAN, and then he is also fit to receive the MAD, as well, for there is no contradiction between them anymore, since the lower one, too, wants the benefit of the upper one and not his own benefit.

It is considered that when the upper one gives the lower one *Mochin*, he also gives him the clothing of the *Mochin*, meaning that he gives the lower one the abundance, as well as the power of the *Masach*, which is the desire to bestow. This is the meaning of "from *Lo Lishma*, we come to *Lishma*."

67. *Zohar for All, VaYakhel* [And Moses Assembled], "The Ascent of the Prayer," No. 150

Happy is a man who knows how to set up his prayer properly. In this prayer, in which the Creator is crowned, he waits until all the prayers of Israel have concluded ascending and are included in the complete prayer, and then all is as perfect as it should be above and below.

68. *Zohar for All, Truma* [Donation], "In the Multitude of People Is the King's Glory," Items 692, 694-698

"In a multitude of people is a king's glory, and in the dearth of people is a prince's ruin."

When the Creator comes to the house of gathering and the whole people come together, pray, thank, and praise the Creator, it is the glory of the King, for the Creator is established with beauty and correction to rise up to *AVI*.

When the Creator comes to the house of gathering early and the people did not come to pray and to praise the Creator, the whole of the governance above and all those upper appointees and camps break from their rising, which they correct in the corrections of a King, the Creator.

The reason why they break from their rising is that when Israel below establish their prayers and litanies, and praise the high King, all those upper camps praise and become corrected in the holy correction, since all the upper camps are friends with Israel below, to praise the Creator together so the rising of the Creator will be above and below together.

And when the angels come to be friends with Israel, to praise the Creator together, and Israel below do not come to establish their prayers and litanies, and to praise their Master, all the holy camps in the upper government break from their corrections. It is so because they do not rise in rising, for they cannot praise their Master because the praises of the Creator must be above and below together, upper and lower at the same time. This is why it is written, "A prince's ruin," and not "A king's ruin," as it concerns only the camps of angels, not the King Himself.

And even though not many came to the house of gathering, but only ten, the upper camps come into these ten, to be friends with them and to praise the Creator, since all the King's corrections are in ten. Hence, ten is enough.

69. *Zohar for All, Hukat* [Constitution], "The Well," Item 78

Anyone who wishes to evoke things of above—in an act or in a word—if that act or that word is not done properly, nothing is evoked. All the people in the world go to the assembly-house to evoke a matter above, but few are the ones who know how to evoke. The Creator is near to all those who know how to call Him and to evoke a matter properly. But if they do not know how to call upon Him, He is not close, as it is written, "The Lord is near to all those who call upon Him, to all who call upon Him in truth." "In truth" means that they know how to properly evoke a true matter.

70. *Zohar for All, Truma* [Donation]," Three Colors in a Flame," Item 43

When Israel come to the synagogue and pray their prayer, when they come to redeem Israel and attach redemption to prayer, not stopping in the middle, by that they cause *Yesod*, which is called "redemption," to approach *Malchut*, which is called "prayer," that white color, *Netzah*, rises to the top of the chamber, *Malchut*, and becomes a *Keter* [crown] for it.

71. *Zohar for All, Shemot* [Exodus], "Sigh, Cry, and Outcry," Items 356-357

One who prays and cries and cries out until he can no longer move his lips, this is a complete prayer that is in the heart. It is never returned empty, but is accepted. Great is the cry for it tears a man's sentence from all his days.

Great is the cry that governs the quality of *Din* above. Great is the cry that governs this world and the next world. For a cry, man inherits this world and the next world, as it is written, "Then they cried unto the Lord in their trouble, and He delivered them out of their distresses."

72. *Zohar for All*, Balak, "A Prayer for Moses, a Prayer for David, a Prayer for the Poor," Items 187-188

Three are called "a prayer":

A prayer for Moses the man of God. This is a prayer of which there is none like it in another person.

A prayer for David. This is a prayer of which there is none like it in another king.

A prayer for the poor, the most important of all three. This prayer precedes Moses' prayer, precedes David's prayer, and precedes all the other prayers in the world.

It is so because the poor is brokenhearted, and it is written, "The Lord is near to the brokenhearted." The poor always quarrels with the Creator, and the Creator listens and hears his words. When the poor has prayed his prayer, He opens all the windows of the firmament and all the other prayers that rise up, the brokenhearted poor pushes them away. It is written, "A prayer for the poor for he will wrap." It should have said, "For he will wrap himself"; why is it written, "for he will wrap"? He causes delay, delaying all the prayers in the world, which do not enter until his prayer enters. Wrapping means delaying.

73. *Zohar for All*, Shemot [Exodus], "Sigh, Cry, and Outcry," Items 353-355

There are three things here: sigh, cry, and outcry, and they are not similar. With a sigh, it is written, "And the children of Israel sighed." With a cry, it is written, "And they cried." With an outcry, it is written, "And their outcry came up unto God." Each is interpreted separately, but Israel did all of them. However, another one said, "Israel did the cry and the outcry, but they did not do the sigh." This is implied by the words that they sighed but were not sighed, and that the sigh above was for them.

How are an outcry and a cry different? There is an outcry only in prayer, as it was said, "Hear my prayer, O Lord, and give ear to my outcry," and also, "Unto You, O Lord, is my outcry," and "My outcry is unto You, and You will heal me." Thus, an outcry means words of prayer. A cry means crying and not saying anything, without any words. The cry is greater than all of them, for the cry is in the heart. It is closer to the Creator than a prayer or a sigh, as it is written, "For if they cry unto Me, I will surely hear their cry."

A sigh, a cry, and an outcry are thought, voice, speech—*Bina*, ZA, and *Malchut*. Hence, a cry in which there is no speech is more acceptable to the Creator than a prayer in words, since the speech is revealed and there is gripping in it, but a cry, where there is no disclosure except in the crying heart, there is no hold for the accusers in it. It is also more acceptable than a sigh because it is revealed only in the thought of the one who sighs, which is *Bina*, and the lower one cannot properly adhere to the Creator through it. This is why a cry is more acceptable.

What does it say when the Creator said to Samuel, "It repents Me that I have set up Saul to be king"? "And it grieved Samuel; and he cried unto the Lord all night." He left everything—the sigh, the outcry—and took the cry, since it was closest to the Creator, as it is written, "And now, behold, the cry of the children of Israel has come unto Me."

74. *Zohar for All, Beresheet Bet* [Genesis 2], "Seven Palaces of *AVI de Beria*," Item 95

All those lights and camps travel with the rising of the prayer. They tie connections and become entirely mingled, as one, until the spirit of the bottom palace becomes tied to the spirit of that palace, and they become one. They all enter the pillar in the middle of the palace, and ascend by it to be included in the spirit in the fourth palace, above them. Happy is one who knows the secret of his Master and raises his banner where he should.

75. *Zohar for All, Toldot* [Generations], "And Isaac Entreated," Items 20-21

"And Rebecca his wife conceived." From the perspective of the system she was unworthy of conceiving, since she was barren from birth. But through his prayer, He subverted for him, meaning He changed the arrangement of the system, "And Rebecca his wife conceived."

For twenty years, Isaac waited on his wife and she did not deliver, until he prayed his prayer. This was so because the Creator desires the prayer of the righteous, when they ask before Him for their needs. And what is the reason? It is so that an ointment of holiness would grow and proliferate through the prayer of the righteous for anyone in need, for the righteous open the upper hose with their prayer, and then even those who are unworthy of being granted are granted.

76. *Zohar for All, VaYetze* [And Jacob Went Out], "His Thought Was of Rachel," Item 189

"If He set His heart upon man, He will gather his spirit and his breath unto Himself." The will and the thought draw the extension and do the deed with everything that is needed. This is why in prayer, a desire and a thought to aim in are required. Similarly, in all the works of the Creator, the thought and the contemplation does the deed and draw extensions to all that is needed.

77. *Zohar for All, VaYishlach* [And Jacob Sent], "The Prayer of the Righteous," Item 45

A prayer of many rises before the Creator and the Creator crowns Himself with that prayer, since it rises in several ways. This is because one asks for *Hassadim*, the other for *Gevurot*, and a third for *Rachamim*. And it consists of several sides: the right side, the left, and the middle. This is so because *Hassadim* extend from the right side, *Gevurot* from the left side, and *Rachamim* from the middle side. And because it consists of several ways and sides, it becomes a crown over the head of the Righteous One That Lives Forever, *Yesod*, which imparts all the salvations to the *Nukva*, and from her to the whole public.

But a prayer of one does not comprise all the sides; it is only on one way. Either one asks for *Hassadim* or *Gevurot* or *Rachamim*. Hence, a prayer of one is not erected to be received like the prayer of many, as it does not include all three lines like the prayer of many.

78. *Zohar for All, Shemot* [Exodus], "Twelve Mountains of Persimmon," Items 253-255

There is nothing that the Creator loves more than the prayer of the righteous. Even though He desires it, at times He does what they ask and at times He does not.

Our sages said, once the world needed rain. Rabbi Elazar came and declared forty fasts, but rain did not come. He prayed a prayer but rain did not come. Rabbi Akiva came and prayed and said, "The blower of wind," and a strong and harsh wind blew. He said, "He who brings down rain," and a torrent came down. Rabbi Elazar's mind was weak. Rabbi Akiva looked at his face and sensed the weakness of his mind.

Rabbi Akiva stood before the people and said, "I will give you an allegory. What is this like? Rabbi Elazar is like one who is loved by the king, whom the king loves more than anyone. When he comes before the king, he is welcome, so he does not wish to grant him his wish quickly, so he would not depart him, because he wishes for him to speak to him. I, however, am like the king's servant, who makes a request before him and the king does not wish that he will come into the palace, much less speak to him. The king says, 'Grant him his wish immediately lest he will enter.'

"Thus, Rabbi Elazar is the king's beloved one and I am a servant. The king wishes to speak to him everyday and to not part from him. But as for me, the king does not wish for me to come into the palace so he grants my wish immediately." Rabbi Elazar was appeased.

79. *Zohar for All*, *VaYishlach* [And Jacob Sent], "The Prayer of the Righteous," Item 66

The prayer of the righteous is joy for the assembly of Israel, *Nukva*, to be crowned with the prayer before the Creator. This is the reason why it is more loved by the Creator than the prayer of the poor. And for this reason, the Creator desires the prayer of the righteous, when they should pray, because they know how to appease their Master.

80. *Zohar for All*, *VaYishlach* [And Jacob Sent], "And God Went Up from Him," Item 164

How favored are Israel before the Creator, for you have not a nation or a tongue among all the idol worshipping nations in the world that has gods that will answer their prayers as the Creator is destined to answer the prayers and pleas of Israel any time they need the prayer answered. This is so because they pray only for their degree, which is Divinity. That is, each time they pray, it is for the correction of Divinity.

81. *Zohar for All*, *Miketz* [At the End], "And Saw Benjamin," Item 209

When one prays to the Creator, he should not look whether his salvation came or not, for when he looks, several litigants come to look at his actions.

82. *Zohar for All*, *Miketz* [At the End], "And Saw Benjamin," Items 211, 213

"Desire that comes is a tree of life." One who wishes for the Creator to grant his prayer should engage in Torah, which is the tree of life. And then desire comes. What is desire? It is a degree that all the prayers in the world are in its hands—the *Nukva*—and it brings them before the upper king, ZA. "Desire that comes," since it comes before the upper king for *Zivug*, to complement the wish of the invocator, to grant him his wish.

That does not extend among those appointees and the chariots from hand to hand. Rather, the Creator gives immediately because when it is extended among those appointees and chariots, several litigants are given permission to observe and to look at his sentence before they give him his salvation. But what comes out of the King's house and is given to man, whether he is worthy or unworthy, is given to him immediately. This is, "Desire that comes is a tree of life," which means that it is given to him immediately.

83. *Zohar for All, VaYechi* [Jacob Lived], "Dan Shall Judge His People," Items 713-714

"One should always praise one's Master and then pray his prayer." One whose heart is pure and wishes to pray his prayer, or is in trouble and cannot praise his Master, what is he?

Even though he cannot aim the heart and will, why should he diminish his Master's praise? Rather, he will praise his Master even though he cannot aim, and then he shall pray his prayer. It is written, "A prayer of David. Hear a just cause, O Lord, hear my singing, listen to my prayer." "Hear a just cause, O Lord," first, since he praised his Master. Afterwards, "Hear my singing, listen to my prayer." One who can praise his Master and does not do so, it is written about him, "Even if you pray profusely, I do not hear."

84. *Zohar for All, VaYechi* [Jacob Lived], "Dan Shall Judge His People," Item 717

What are MAN? In the craving below, lower waters rise, meaning MAN, to receive upper waters, MAD, from the degree atop them. This is so because lower waters, MAN, spring out only by an awakening of the desire of the lower one. At that time, the craving of the lower one and the upper one become attached, and lower waters spring out opposite the descending upper waters, the *Zivug* ends and the worlds are blessed, all the candles light up, and the upper ones and lower ones are in blessings.

85. *Zohar for All, VaYechi* [Jacob Lived], "The Terrible Mountain," Item 426

When a man goes out to the road, he should set up his prayer before his Master, to extend the light of Divinity on himself, and then set out. It turns out that the *Zivug* of Divinity is to redeem him on the way and to save him however is needed.

86. *Zohar for All, Shemot* [Exodus], "And the Daughter of Pharaoh Came Down," 203-204

All things in the world depend on repentance and on the prayer that a man prays to the Creator. It is all the more so with one who sheds tears during his prayer, for there is no gate through which these tears do not come. It is written, "She opened it and saw the child." "Opened" is Divinity, who stands over Israel like a mother over her children, opening, always in favor of Israel.

When she opened and saw the child, a delightful child, Israel, who always sin before their King and promptly plea before the Creator, repent and cry before Him as a son who cries before his father. It is written, "And behold a boy that wept." Since he wept, all the harsh decrees in the world were removed from him.

87. Zohar for All, Bo [Come unto Pharaoh], "The Tefillin [Phylacteries]," Item 235

"All the rivers flow into the sea." The rivers, which are the abundance from ZA, flow to *Malchut*, which is called, "a sea." And because she receives them from above, from *Malchut*, she is called, "prayer," and she is sanctified by their holiness, and she is called, "holy," since *Mochin de Malchut* is called, "holy," and it is called "prayer." Then, *Malchut* is called, "the complete kingdom of heaven."

88. Zohar for All, BeShalach [When Pharaoh Sent], "Your Right Hand, O Lord, Majestic in Power," Items 278-279

Any person who seeks to unite the holy Name and did not intend for it in heart, in desire, and in fear, so that upper and lower will be blessed in him, his prayer is thrown outside, everyone declares him bad, and the Creator calls upon him, "If you come to see My face."

"To see My face" means all those faces of the King, illumination of *Hochma*, as it is written, "A man's wisdom illuminates his face," hidden in the depth behind the dark, which are the *Dinim* in the left line. And all those who know how to properly unite the holy Name break all those walls of darkness and the King's face is seen and shines for all. And when it is seen and shines, all are blessed, upper and lower. Then there are blessings in all the worlds, and then it is written, "To see My face."

89. Zohar for All, BeShalach [When Pharaoh Sent], "The Story of Haman," Item 408

"A song of ascents. Out of the depths I have called You, O Lord." Why does it say, "A song of ascents," without saying who said it? A song of ascents means that all the people of the world are destined to say it because this song is destined to be said for all eternity.

90. Zohar for All, BeShalach [When Pharaoh Sent], "The Story of Haman," Items 409-410

"Out of the depths I have called You." Anyone who prays his prayer before the holy King must ask his pleas and pray from the bottom of the heart so that his heart will be wholly with the Creator, and he will aim his heart and will, as it is written, "Out of the depths I have called You." But it is written, "With all my heart I have sought You." This verse is sufficient, to pray with all of one's heart, so why the need for "From the bottom"?

Every person who asks his request of the King must aim his mind and will to the Root of Roots, to extend blessings from the depth of the pit, so that blessings will pour from the fountain of all. The place from which that river comes out is the concealed *Hochma*, as it is written, "And a river comes out of Eden. "Eden" is *Hochma*; "river" is *Bina* that went out of *Rosh AA*, which is the concealed *Hochma*. It is written, "There is a river whose streams make the city of God glad." This is called "Out of the depths," the depth of everything, the depth of the pit from which streams come out and extend from it to bless all. This is the beginning, to extend blessings from above downwards.

91. *Zohar for All*, *BeShalach* [When Pharaoh Sent], "The Story of Haman," Item 411

When Atik, who is more concealed than all that are concealed, wished to summon blessings for the world, He instilled everything and included everything in that high depth, which is the concealed *Hochma de AA* in relation to *Malchut* coming out of it. From here, a river, which is *Malchut*, draws and continues. Rivers and streams, which are the *Mochin*, come out of it and water everything from it, meaning that all the *Mochin* of ZON and BYA extend from there. And one who prays his prayer should aim one's heart and will to extend blessings from the depth of this everything, so his prayer will be accepted and his wish will be done.

92. *Zohar for All*, *BeShalach* [When Pharaoh Sent], "And Pharaoh Drew Near," Items 65-67

"And Pharaoh drew near" means that he sacrificed his whole army and vehicles to make war [*Hikriv* means both "brought closer" and "sacrificed"]. We also learn that Pharaoh brought Israel closer to repentance. This is why it is written, "And Pharaoh drew near" and not "And Pharaoh brought closer."

It is written, "O Lord, they sought You in distress; they could only whisper a prayer, Your chastening was upon them." "They sought You in distress" means that Israel do not visit the Creator in times of contentment, but when they are in distress, and then they all visit Him. "They could only whisper a prayer" means that they are all praying with prayers and litanies, and pour out prayers before Him. When? "Your chastening before them," when the Creator visits them in His strap. Then the Creator stands over them in *Rachamim* [mercies] and welcomes their voice, to avenge their enemies, and He fills with mercy over them.

Israel were nearing the sea and saw the sea before them becoming stormier, its waves straightening upward. They were afraid. They raised their eyes and saw Pharaoh and his army, and slings and arrows, and they were terrified. "And the children of Israel cried out." Who caused Israel to draw near to their father in heaven? It was Pharaoh, as it is written, "And Pharaoh drew near."

93. *Zohar for All*, *BeShalach* [When Pharaoh Sent], And Pharaoh Drew Near

"Stand by and see the salvation of the Lord." You need not make war, for the Creator will make war for you, as it is written, "The Lord will fight for you, and you will keep silent." On that night, the Creator assembled His company and sentenced the sentence of Israel. If the fathers did not pray for Israel first, they would not have been saved from the *Din* [judgment].

94. *Zohar for All*, *Truma* [Donation], "The Watchman Says, "Morning Comes," Item 86

"If you ask, ask." If you make your requests before the King in prayer, ask, pray and ask your requests and return to your Master. "Come," as one who invites, greeting his sons and having mercy on them. So is the Creator. In the morning and also at night, He calls out and says, "Come." Happy are the holy nation whose Master seeks them and calls for them to bring them near Him.

95. *Zohar for All*, *Truma* [Donation], "Lift Up a Song for Him Who Rides through the Prairies," Items 713-716

The great priest who stands before Him would enter the Temple only with joy, and to show joy because the place causes. It is written about it, "Serve the Lord with gladness,' for one must not show sadness in her.

Therefore, one who is in sorrow and distress, who cannot rejoice in his heart out of his distress, should ask for mercy before the high King. Therefore, he will not pray his prayer at all or come in with any sadness, for he cannot delight his heart and enter before Him with joy. What is the correction for such a person?

Rather, all the gates are locked and closed, and the gates of tears do not close. There is no tear except out of sorrow and sadness, and all those appointees over the gates break the turns of the roads and the locks, admit those tears, and that prayer enters before the holy King.

At that time, that place, *Malchut*, is pressured by the sadness and pressure of that man, as it is written, "In all their affliction He was afflicted." He called, "He was afflicted," for man's affliction moves Divinity. The craving of the upper world, ZA, to that place, *Malchut*, is as a male who always craves the female. Hence, when the King, ZA, enters the queen, *Malchut*, and finds her in sadness, then all she wants is handed to her, that man or that prayer are not returned empty, and the Creator takes pity on him. Happy is that man who sheds tears before the Creator in his prayer.

96. *Zohar for All*, *Sifra DeTzniuta* [The Book of Concealment], Chapter Three, Item 39

"Let the waters teem." Teeming is translated as murmuring, when his lips murmur, when his lips move with words of prayer in purity and cleanness of the mind. In the water that cleanses and purifies, the living soul is teeming.

When a person wishes to establish a prayer to his Master, his lips murmur in that manner from below upward, to raise the glory of his Master to the place of the potion of the deep well of *Bina*. Then he goes to draw from that potion of the stream, *Bina*, from above downward to each and every degree through the last degree, *Malchut*, to extend donations to all from above downward. Subsequently, he must make a connection through all, to unite all the degrees in *Ein Sof*, the connection of the aim of the faith, and all his wishes will be fulfilled, whether the wishes of the public or the wishes of an individual.

97. *Zohar for All*, *Sifra DeTzniuta* [The Book of Concealment], Chapter Three, Items 40-43

The prayer that one should ask of his Master is set up in nine manners:

1. In the order of the alphabet;
2. In mentioning the qualities of the Creator: Merciful, Gracious, and so forth;
3. In the honored names of the Creator: *EKYEH, Yod-Hey, Yod-Hey-Vav, El, Elokim, HaVaYaH*, Hosts, *Shadai*, and *ADNI*;

4. In ten *Sefirot*, KHB, HGT, NHYM;
5. In mentioning the righteous: the patriarchs, the prophets, and the kings;
6. In song and praise in which there is true reception;
7. Above them, one who knows how to properly correct corrections for his Master;
8. In knowing how to raise from below upward;
9. And there are those who know how to extend abundance from above downward.

In all those nine manners of prayer, great intention is required. If not, it is written about him, "They who despise Me will be despised." With Amen, he should intend to include the two names *HaVaYaH ADNI*, which are 91 in *Gematria*, and Amen is also 91 in *Gematria*. And the name *HaVaYaH*, ZA, conceals its abundance and blessings in the treasure, called "palace," which is ADNI, *Malchut*.

This is implied in the verse, "And the Lord is in the palace of His holiness, all the earth is silent before Him." It is also implied in what we learn, "Man's abundance is in his home." It is so because man [Adam] is 45 in *Gematria*, the name *HaVaYaH* filled with the letters *Aleph*. And "abundance is in his home" is ADNI, *Malchut*, as it is written, "In all My house he is trusted." It translates into "In all who are with Me," in *Malchut*.

And if he aims properly in all of these nine manners of prayer, it is a person who honors the name of his holy Master. It is written about it, "For I will honor those who honor Me, and those who despise Me will be despised." I will honor him in this world to keep and to do all his needs, and all the nations of the earth will see that the name of the Lord is called upon him and will fear him. In the next world, he will be rewarded with being with pious, in the realm of the pious, even though he did not read in the Torah sufficiently, but because he was rewarded with looking at knowing his Master and aimed in it properly.

One who does not know how to unify the holy Name and make the connection of faith, to extend to the place that is needed, and to honor the name of his Master, it is better for him not to be born, especially if he does not intend in the Amen. For this reason, anyone who murmurs with his lips with a clean heart, with cleansing waters, it is written about him, "And God said, 'Let us make man in our image, after our likeness,'" for a man who knows how to unite the image and the likeness properly, where ZA is *Tzelem* [image] and *Nukva* is the likeness, "and they will rule over the fish of the sea."

98. *Zohar for All*, *VaYakhel* [And Moses Assembled], "The Intention of the Prayer," Items 107, 108

Each day a herald calls upon all the people in the world, "This matter is up to you," as it is written, 'Take from among you a donation to the Lord.' And if you should say that the matter is hard for you, 'Whoever is of a generous heart, let him bring it.'"

Hence the meaning of the prayer: a person who fears his Master and aims his heart and will in a prayer corrects the upper correction, first by singing and praising that the upper angels say above. And in that order of praises that Israel say below, *Malchut* adorns herself in her corrections as a woman who adorns herself for her husband.

99. *Zohar for All, VaYakhel* [And Moses Assembled], "The Intention of the Prayer," Item 111

And before the high King, we must stand up with fear and quiver, for then He stretches out His right hand to her in the blessing, "Protector of Abraham," who is the right line. Afterwards, His left, which He puts under her head in the blessing, "You are mighty," is the left line. Then they both embrace together in kissing in the blessing, "The holy God," the middle line. From there up they are kisses until the last three. These are the first three blessings of the Eighteen Prayer. One must place his heart and will, and aim his mouth, heart, and will together in all those corrections and orders of the prayer.

100. *Zohar for All, New Zohar,* Noah, "Do Not Drink Wine or Ale," Items 93-97

Two things do not go together: wine and serving the Creator.
A drunk who prays is as one who performs idol-worship. Where is this from? From Hannah, as it is written, "And Eli thought that she was drunk." But she replied and said, "Do not regard your maidservant as a corrupt woman," an idol-worshipper.

No people are called holy except for those who abstain from wine, as it is written, "All the days when he abstained for the Lord, he will be holy." There is no wine that is called "good wine" like the wine of the land of Israel. And more than all of them is the wine of the Upper Galilee, from which no one can drink half a log [approx. half a liter].

Rabbi Elazar, son of Rabbi Shimon, went to see Rabbi Yosi, his father-in-law. They gave him a soft fine calf to eat and opened for him a barrel of wine. His father-in-law poured and he drank; he poured and he drank. Rabbi Yosi said to him, "Have you heard from your father what is the measure of the cup that is permitted to drink?"

He said to him, the measure of the cup is as it is. He should drink one cup if the drink is hot, and one cup if the drink is cold. But the sages did not imagine that your cup is small, your wine is good, and my belly is big."

101. *Zohar for All, Pekudei* [Accounts], "The Palace of Noga, Netzah," Items 574-577

The 12 wheels turning in this palace are called "seraphim" in two colors, white and red, *Rachamim* and *Din*. They are always poised to watch over the sorrowful, whom the rest of the nations afflict and oppress. They are called "windows," as it is written, "Watching over through the windows."

They stand to observe those who pray their prayer, and come early to the synagogue [house of gathering] to be counted among the first ten. Then the seraphim rise up and write them above because the first ten are considered their friends, as it is written, "Friends are listening to your voice, let me hear it."

Happy are the righteous who know how to set up their prayer properly because when that prayer begins to rise, those angels rise along with that prayer and enter the firmaments and palaces up to the gate to the upper door, and a prayer enters to be crowned before the King.

All those who pray prayers and sanctify their Master wholeheartedly, that prayer should elicit from the thought and by the will of speech and spirit. Then the name of the Creator is sanctified, and when the prayer reaches the angels, who are friends, they all take the prayer and go with it up to the seventh palace, to the door that is there. Those angels praise the Creator when Israel pray prayers and sanctify to the Creator. At daytime, they are the appointees during the day, who were appointed to praise along with the people of Israel, to be friends with them. At night, they are friends to those other ones, who say poems at night.

102. *Zohar for All, Pekudei* [Accounts], "The Palace of Holy of Holies," Items 824-825, 827

"Who esteem His name" are those who think and intend in His name, to unite palaces with palaces, to tie ties, and to unite everyone in one unification. They are the ones who esteem His name, as it is written, "And who esteem His name." Then he is written among those who esteem His name, and he is noted and becomes known above, and is completed above and below.

Anyone who comes near to his Master and prays his prayer, but does not complete the unification, and is not concerned with his Master's honor, tying ties, it is better for him if he were not born. The Creator says, "Write that man childless, a failure of a man in his life," as it is written, "Who robs his father and his mother," who are the Creator and His Divinity.

Happy is he who is sanctified in the prayer in this manner, ties connections, unifies unifications, properly intends in everything, and does not stray to the right or to the left. His prayer will not return denied; the Creator sentences and he revokes. It is written about it, "Your father and mother will be glad, the one who bore you shall rejoice." He has a portion in this world and in the next world.

103. *Zohar for All, Pekudei* [Accounts], "The Palace of Holy of Holies," Items 812-813

He must connect to the *Kedusha* of his Master and not part from Him. And when he asks, the beginning of the pleading should be to know his Master, to show his passion for Him, which is the first request, "Grant us from You wisdom, understanding, and intelligence." Henceforth, he will part a little and ask the pleas that he needs to ask.

All his questions will be after he arranges the order. Likewise, all his questions will be in litanies and requests before his Master, and He will not remove Himself from him, meaning will be angered. Happy is he who knows how to arrange that order, to go by the straight path as he should.

104. *Zohar for All, Pekudei* [Accounts], "The Palace of Holy of Holies," Item 832

Anyone who does not know how to establish the praise of his Master, it is better for him not to be born because the prayer must be complete above, out of thought, the will of the heart, the voice, and the word of the mouth, to make wholeness, connection, and unification above. As it is above, and as the wholeness comes out from above downward, so it should be from below upward, properly tying the connection.

105. *Zohar for All, VaYikra* [The Lord Called], "I Acknowledged My Sin unto You," Items 338-339

Anyone who covers his sins and does not acknowledge them before the holy King to ask for mercy for them, is not permitted to open the door of repentance, since it is covered from him. But if he details them before the Creator, the Creator has mercy on him and the *Rachamim* prevail over the *Din*.

It is even more so if he cries, since he opens all the hidden doors and his prayer is accepted. Hence, the confession of his sins is the glory of the King, to make *Rachamim* prevail over the *Din*.

106. *Zohar for All, VaYikra* [The Lord Called], "I Acknowledged My Sin unto You," Item 342

One who makes a request of the King must unite the holy Name in his will from below upwards, from *Malchut* to *Keter*, and from above downwards, from *Keter* to *Malchut*—uniting everything in one unification in *Ein Sof* [infinity], and in this unification he will include his plea. Who is so wise as to make his pleas like King David's, who was keeping the King's door? He was a *Merkava* [chariot/assembly] to *Malchut*, which is called "the King's door." So it is, and this is why the Torah teaches us the ways of the holy King, so we will know how to follow Him, as it is written, "After the Lord your God shall you walk."

107. *Zohar for All, Aharei Mot* [After the Death], "From the Depths I Have Called You, Lord," Items 244-245

Before the Creator created the world, He created repentance. The Creator said to repentance, *Bina*: "I wish to create man in the world provided that if they return to you from their iniquities you will be willing to pardon their iniquities and atone them." Each and every hour, repentance is ready for people. When people repent from their iniquities, this repentance, *Bina*, returns to the Creator giving *Mochin* to ZA and atones for everything. Then the *Dinim* surrender and all are perfumed, and the man is purified from his iniquities.

When is one purified from his iniquity? When he properly enters repentance. When he repents before the upper king and prays a prayer from the bottom of the heart, as it is written, "From the depths I have called You, O Lord."

108. *Zohar for All, BeHukotai* [In My Statutes], "Alms for the Poor," Item 21

The poor is gripped in *Din* and all his feeding is in *Din*, in a place called "justices," which is *Malchut*, as it is written, "A prayer for the poor when he is weakened." This prayer is the *Tefillin* of the hand, *Malchut*. When she is not in a *Zivug* with ZA, she is poor and she is called "justice," and one who gives *Tzedaka* [alms, but also righteousness in Hebrew] to the poor makes the Holy Name above properly whole, connecting her with ZA, which gives her everything. Because *Tzedaka* is the tree of life, ZA, and *Tzedaka* gives and bestows upon justice, *Malchut*, when she gives to justice, ZA and *Malchut* connect with one another and the Holy Name is complete.

One who evokes that awakening below, who gives *Tzedaka*, it is certainly as though he made the Holy Name in completeness. As one does below, so it awakens above. The one who does righteousness is the Creator, as though he made Him.

109. *Zohar for All, New Zohar, Nasso*, "The Blessing of the Priests," Items 3-4

Woe to one who comes to seduce his Master's heart with a distant heart and not with a complete desire, as it is written, "They deceived Him with their mouth and lied to Him with their tongue, and their heart was not steadfast with Him."

The unification of the prayer and the blessing depend on the speech and the words of the mouth, and everything depends on the root of the action. One who does not know the root of the action, his work is not work. If he blemishes the act of speaking, there is no place for the blessing to be in and his prayer is not a prayer. That person is blemished above and below.

110. *Zohar for All*, Zohar Hadash, Hukat, "To the Conductor [also: Winner] of Lilies," Items 119-121

Hear, daughter, and see, and lend your ear." "Hear," for hearing depends on you, since when Israel repent before Me, "Hear," bring their prayers before Me since the door to everything is in you. I have placed everything in your hand, to lead the lower world. Hence, "Hear, daughter, and see," since you are the vision of everything. *Hochma* is called "vision." It is revealed only in *Malchut*. This is why you are called Be'ar Lahai Roi. Therefore, each day, you must inquire about the deeds of the people of the world, to give to one according to one's deeds.

When the Creator created the world, He placed His hall in the hands of the queen to watch over the world. When people are worthy, joy is added above.

"Lend your ear," to receive the prayer of everyone. So she did with all the prayers, to bring the crown to the righteous, *Yesod*, since all the prayers are to bring the crown to the righteous. They are regarded as MAN so the righteous will pour on them MAD.

111. *Zohar for All*, Balak, "Sihon and Og," Item 7

We should pay attention to faith in the Creator, that all his words are words of truth and great faith. Once he says something, it is done entirely. A man with a narrow heart, if he says that this would be completed in several years and after so long, so it is. The Creator, according to His governance, and all the worlds are filled with His glory, is all the more so.

Man's words are small, and all his words are temporary. So is he, temporary, like a fleeting shadow. However, through repentance and prayer and good deeds with many tears, he is holy, since the Great One, who is superior to the entire world, shines His light and restricts His holiness for man to do His will.

112. *Zohar for All*, Balak, "A Prayer of Moses, a Prayer of David, a Prayer of the Poor," Items 190-191

All the hosts of heaven ask each other "What does the Creator do?" "In what does He exert?" They are told that He unites passionately with His *Kelim* [vessels], with the brokenhearted. Everyone does not know what was done with the prayer of the poor and all his grievances since the poor has no passion except when he sheds tears in grievances before the holy King, and the Creator has no passion except when He accepts them and they are poured down before Him. This prayer defers and delays all the prayers in the world.

Moses prayed his prayer and was delayed by several days in this prayer because of the prayer of the poor. David saw that all the windows and all the gates of Heaven were ready to open before the prayer of the poor. Of all the prayers in the world, there is none to which the Creator listens immediately as with the prayer of the poor.

113. *Zohar for All*, Balak, "A Prayer of Moses, a Prayer of David, a Prayer of the Poor," Item 192

One who prays should make himself poor so his prayer will be included in the prayers of all the poor, since all the guards of the gates do not let all the prayers in the world enter as they let the prayer of the poor, since they enter without permission.

If a person makes himself and makes his desire always as that of a poor, his prayer rises and meets the prayers of the poor, connects to them and ascends with them. It enters among them and is willingly accepted by the holy King.

114. *Zohar for All*, Yitro [Jethro], "You Shall Not Have," Items 414-416

"A prayer of the poor when he is weak and pours out his complaint before the Lord." All of Israel's prayers are prayer, and the prayer of the poor is the highest because it rises up to the throne of the King and crowns itself in His head and the Creator is praised in this prayer. This is why the prayer of the poor is called "a prayer."

"When he is weak ["weak" can also mean "wrap" in Hebrew]." This "weak" is not the wrapping of clothing, for he has no clothing. Rather, here it is written, "When he is weak," and there it is written, "Who are weak from hunger." Here, too, "When he is weak" is with hunger. "And pours out his complaint before the Lord," meaning that he cries out to his Master, and it pleases him before the Creator since the world exists in him when there are no others who sustain the world in the world. Woe unto one of whom that poor cries out to his Master, since the poor is closer to the King than anyone, as it is written, "And it shall come to pass, when he cries unto Me, that I will hear; for I am gracious."

As for the rest of the people in the world, at times He listens and at times He does not listen, since the tabernacle of the Creator is in those broken *Kelim*, as it is written, "And with the contrite and lowly of spirit." It is also written, "The Lord is near to those with a broken heart," and "A broken and a contrite heart, O God, You will not despise."

115. *Zohar for All*, VaEtchanan, "Midnight," Items 8-9

When one rises at midnight to engage in Torah, a herald calls out about him and says, "Here, bless the Lord all the servants of the Lord who stand in the house of the Lord at night." In the morning, when he stands in prayer before his Master, that herald calls out about him and says, "And I will let you walk among these who are standing here."

After he concludes his prayer willingly before his Master, he should willingly devote his soul to *Malchut*. A person has several counsels in everything. When he is in prayer, all those words that one utters from one's mouth in that prayer rise and break through airs and firmaments until they come to the place where they come, and are crowned on the head of the King, who makes from them a crown.

116. *Zohar for All*, *VaYelech* [And Moses Went], Answering "Amen," Items 37-39

When Israel below keep their answering of Amen and aim their hearts as they should, several doors of blessing open above, there is much goodness in all the world, and there is joy in everything. What is Israel's reward for causing it? Their reward is in this world and in the next world. In this world, when they are afflicted and they pray their prayer before their Master, the voice declares through all the worlds, "Open the gates and let in the righteous, loyal nation." Do not pronounce it "loyal," but Amens [a similar pronunciation in Hebrew], who observe their answering Amen. "Open the gates," as Israel opened the gates of blessings for them, now open the gates and let the prayer of those who are afflicted be answered.

This is their reward in this world. What is their reward in the next world? When a man who observed answering Amen departs this world, what does he observe—observe that blessing which the sayer blesses and he waits for him to answer after it, "Amen," as he should? At that time, his soul rises and declares before him, "Open the gates before him," as he opened the gates each day when he was loyal, meaning Amens.

What is Amen? Amen is the spring of the stream that extends, *Bina*. It is called Amen, as it is written, "And I was beside Him as an apprentice." Do not pronounce it *Amon* [apprentice], but Amen. Keeping all the degrees—that river that stretches out, *Bina*—is called "Amen," as it is written, "From the world and to the world," from the world above, *Bina*, to the world below, *Malchut*. Here, too, Amen and Amen, Amen of above, *Bina*, Amen of below, *Malchut*. Amen means keeping of them all.

117. *Zohar for All*, Ruth, "A Prayer, an Outcry, a Tear," Item 418

In the whole world, none stand before the Creator but man's repentance and prayer. There are three kinds of repentance: a prayer, an outcry, and a tear, and all of them are written in this verse, "Hear my prayer, Lord, and listen to my outcry; do not be silent at my tear."

All three are important to the Creator, but none are important as the tear, since through the tears, the heart, the desire, and the whole body awaken and come in thirteen gates before the Creator.

Hearing is written about a prayer, as it is written, "Hear my prayer, O Lord." It is written about the outcry, "Listen to my outcry." A prayer is not like them, but more than all of them, as it is written, "Do not keep silent to my tear."

With a prayer, sometimes a person prays his prayer and the Creator hears but does not want to do what he asks. He keeps silent to him and does not watch over him, for only hearing is written about it.

An outcry is more important than a prayer, since he cries out with his heart's will before his Master. And since he places more of his will, it is written about it, "Listen," as one who listens to the speaker. Nevertheless, He is silent and does not want to do what he wants.

But the tear is in the heart, and in the will of the entire body. This is why it is written about it, "Do not keep silent to my tear."

Not all the tears come before the King. Tears of anger and tears of one who complains about his friend do not come before the King. Rather, tears of prayer and repentance, when they pray the prayer out of their plight, they all break through firmaments and open gates and come before the King.

On the day when the Temple was ruined, all the gates were locked but the gates of tears were not locked. It is written about Hezekiah, "I heard your prayer, I saw your tear," truly seeing out of the tears.

118. *Zohar for All*, *Pekudei* [Accounts], "The Palace of the Sapphire Pavement, Yesod," Items 489-490

Above the door of the palace is another door, which the Creator dug out of *Dinim de Miftacha*, as it is written, "The well that the ministers dug." It opens three times a day, meaning that three lines illuminate in it, and it does not close. It stands open for those who repent, who have shed tears in their prayer before their Master. And all the gates and doors are closed until they come in by permission, except for these gates, which are called "the gates of tears." Those are open and require no permission.

This is so because the first door is as it is written, "Sin crouches at the door," where the *Malchut de Man'ula* is found, ten thousand. In that respect, repentance does not help because it is the quality of harsh *Din*. But the Creator dug another door above it, the *Miftacha*, *Malchut* that is mitigated in *Bina*, and from there the repentance helps.

When this prayer in tears rises through these gates, that *Ophan*, who is an angel from *Malchut*, called *Ophan* comes. He stands over 600 big animals, and his name is Yerachmiel. He takes the prayer in tears, the prayer enters and is connected above, and the tears remain here. They are written in a door that the Creator dug.

The prayer in tears raises MAN for correction of the *Miftacha*, to raise *Malchut* to *Bina*; hence, the prayer is accepted and the tears remain carved on the door, where they cause the mitigation of *Malchut* in *Bina*.

119. *Zohar for All*, *VaYechi* [Jacob Lived], "Be Gathered, that I May Tell You"

All the prayers in the world, prayers of many, are prayers. But a solitary prayer does not enter before the Holy King, unless with great force. This is so because before the prayer enters to be crowned in its place, the Creator watches it, observes it, and observes the sins and merits of that person, which He does not do with a prayer of many, where several of the prayers are not from righteous, and they all enter before the Creator and He does not notice their iniquities.

"He has regarded the prayer of the destitute." He turns the prayer and examines it from all sides, and considers with which desire the prayer was made, who is the person who prayed that prayer, and what are his deeds. Hence, one should pray one's prayer in the collective, since He does not despise their prayer, even though they are not all with intent and the will of heart, as it is written, "He has regarded the prayer of the destitute." Thus, He only observes the prayer of an individual, but with a prayer of many, He does not despise their prayer, even though they are unworthy.

"He has regarded the prayer of the destitute" means that He accepts his prayer, but it is an individual who is mingled with many. Hence, his prayer is as a prayer of many. And who is an individual who is mingled with many? It is Jacob, for he contains both sides—right and left, Abraham and Isaac, and he calls out to his sons and prays his prayer for them.

And what is the prayer that is fully granted above? It is a prayer that the children of Israel will not perish in the exile. This is because every prayer in favor of Divinity is received in full. And when Israel are in exile, Divinity is with them. This is why the prayer is regarded as being in favor of Divinity and is accepted in full.

120. *Zohar for All, VaYetze* [And Jacob Went Out], "Remembering and Visiting," Items 284-285

Wherever a person prays his prayer, he should incorporate himself in the public, in the manifold public, as it is written about Shunammite when Elisha told her, "Would you be spoken for to the king or to the captain of the army?" "Would you be spoken for to the king," since that day was the festival of the first day of the year, and the day when *Malchut* of the firmament rules and sentences the world. At that time, the Creator is called "The king of the sentence," and this is why he told her, "Would you be spoken for to the king," since he called the Creator "King."

And she said, "I dwell among my own people." In other words, she said, "I have no wish to be mentioned above, but to put my head among the masses and not leave the public. Similarly, man should be included in the public and not stand out as unique, so the slanderers will not look at him and mention his sins.

121. *Zohar for All, VaYakhel* [And Moses Assembled], "The Ascent of the Prayer," Items 121,123.

"And He said unto me, 'You are My servant, Israel, in whom I will be glorified.'" This concerns the prayer that one should pray before the Creator, which is one great work, more honored than the work of his Master. There is the work of the Creator that is in the work of the body, meaning the *Mitzvot* that depend on an act, and there is the work of the Creator that is more internal work—which is the most important—meaning *Mitzvot* that depend on speech and on the will of the heart.

A man's prayer is the work of the *Ruach* [spirit], work from *Behina Bet*, which depends on the speech. It is in high secrets and people do not know that a man's prayer breaches airs and breaches firmaments, opens doors and rises up.

122. *Zohar for All, VaYakhel* [And Moses Assembled], "The Meaning of the Book of Torah," Item 225

"Blessed is the name of the Master of the world. Blessed be Your crown and Your place. May Your favor remain with Your people Israel forever; may the redemption of Your right be shown to Your people in Your Temple, and impart upon us the best of Your light, and accept our prayers with mercy. May it be Your will that You extend our lives with goodness, that I, Your servant, be numbered among the righteous, that You have mercy on me, protect me, all that is mine, and that is of Your people Israel.

"It is You who nourishes all and sustains all. You control everything. It is You who rules over kings, and the kingship is Yours. I am a servant of the Creator, and I bow before Him and before the glory of His law [Torah] at all times. Not in man do I put trust, nor on any children of God do I rely, only on God in heaven, who is the true God, whose law is true, whose prophets are true, and who executes abundant kindness and truth. In him do I trust, and to His glorious and holy name do I declare praises. May it be Your will that You open my heart with Your law, and that You give me male sons who fulfill Your wish. May You fulfill my heart's wishes and the heart of Your entire people Israel for good, for life, and for peace. Amen."

123. *Zohar for All*, BeShalach [When Pharaoh Sent], "Your Right Hand, O Lord, Majestic in Power," Item 278

Any person who seeks to unite the holy Name and did not intend for it in heart, in desire, and in fear, so that upper and lower will be blessed in him, his prayer is thrown outside.

124. *Zohar for All*, Introduction of The Book of Zohar "Torah and Prayer," Item 183

The prayer that we pray is the correction of the Holy Divinity, to extend abundance to her, to satisfy all her deficiencies, for hence, all the requests are in plural form, such as "And grant us knowledge from You," or "Bring us back, our Father, into Your law."

This is so because the prayer is for the whole of Israel, since all that there is in the holy Divinity exists in the whole of Israel. And what is lacking in her is lacking in the whole of Israel. It follows that when we pray for the whole of Israel, we pray for the Holy Divinity, since they are the same. Thus, before the prayer, we must look into the deficiencies in Divinity, to know what needs to be corrected and filled in her.

125. *Zohar for All*, VaYishlach [And Jacob Sent], "The Prayer of the Righteous," Items 64-65

The prayer of the poor is always answered by the Creator before all other prayers in the world. A prayer for the poor, who is attached to his indigence as one who has nothing of his own.
Every man's prayer is a prayer. But the prayer of the poor is the prayer that stands before the Creator for it shatters gates and doors and enters and is admitted before Him. "…and pours out his complaint before the Lord," as one who complains about the judgments of the Creator.

126. *Zohar for All*, Truma [Donation], "The Watchman Says, "Morning Comes," Items 93-95

When Israel establish an order of songs and praises and the order of prayer in the synagogue, three camps of high angels gather. One camp is the holy angels who praise the Creator in the day. There are others who praise the Creator at night, but those are the ones who praise the Creator, and sing and praise with Israel during the day.

The second camp is the holy angels that are in each *Kedusha* that Israel sanctify below. Under their governance are all those who awaken in all the firmaments in the prayer of Israel. The third camp is the high maidens, which are seven spirits of seven palaces of *Beria*, which correct along with the *Malchut*. They correct the *Malchut* to bring her in before the King.

They all correct in the order of Israel that correct below, in those songs and praises and in the prayer that Israel pray. When these three camps gather, Israel begin to sing, and they chant before their Master. And the first camp, who are appointed on praising their Master during the day, congregate with them and sing together with them in those praises of King David.

127. Noam Elimelech, *Likutei Shoshana*

One must always pray for his friend, as one cannot do much for himself, for "One does not deliver oneself from imprisonment." But when asking for his friend, he is answered quickly. Therefore, each one should pray for his friend, and thus each works on the other's desire until all of them are answered. This is why it was said, "Israel are *Arevim* [responsible/sweet] for one another," where *Arevim* means sweetness, as they sweeten for each other by the prayers they pray for one another, and by this they are answered. And the essence of prayer is in the thought since in the thought, one's prayer can be accepted easily.

128. *Pri Tzadik*, *VaYeshev*, Item 3

The first *Hassidim* [adherents of the *Hassidut* movement] would spend one hour in prayer so as to aim their hearts to their Father in heaven. The word "aim" means the directness of the heart; it is to direct the heart so it is not scattered into the passions and lusts of worldly matters, but only to aim directly to his Father in heaven.

129. Rabbi Menachem Mendel of Kotzk, *There Is None More Whole than a Broken Heart*

The Creator is not called upon out loud, but secretly, in the heart, from its interior.

130. Babylonian Talmud, *Masechet Taanit*, 2a

To love the lord your God and to serve Him with all your hearts. Which is the work that is in the heart? Namely, it is a prayer.

131. Raaiah Kook, *Olat Raaiah*

The prayer is connecting the desire to the Creator.

132. Rav Menachem Mendel of Kosov, *Love of Peace*

One who prays for his friend is answered first. This means that one who prays for his friend becomes a pipeline of bestowal to bestow upon his friend. And since the abundance flows through him, he is answered first. By this we can understand the verse, "He who blesses is blessed," since one who blesses becomes a pipeline of bestowal and is therefore blessed. This is so because *bracha* [blessing] comes from the word *brecha* [pool], namely a pipeline of good bestowal. This is so specifically if the blessing and the blessed love one another and have true unity and are in wholeness. At that time, they awaken the upper pipeline which can impart through the righteous, who is the trail, as in, "The world is nourished because of Hanina, my son."

133. Maimonides, *Mishneh Torah*

How is there intention? One should clear his heart from all the thoughts and see himself as though he is standing before the *Shechina* [Divinity]. Therefore, one should settle oneself a little prior to the prayer, to aim his heart, and then pray. The first *Hassidim* [adherents of the *Hassidut* movement] would spend one hour prior to the prayer, one hour after the prayer, and extend the prayer by one hour.

134. *Likutey Halachot* [Assorted Rules], "Synagogue Rules," Rule One

The ascent of the soul and its completeness is mainly when all the souls merge and become one, for then they rise to the *Kedusha* [holiness], since the *Kedusha* is one. Therefore, the prayer, which is regarded as the soul, depends primarily on the unity of souls.

135. *Likutei Tefilot*, Part 1, Prayer 65

Help and save with Your great and plentiful mercies, so that each one from Israel who is far from the goal will be brought to his real purpose. May each one shut his eyes and mind completely to the imagination of this world until he is always included in utter annulment, back and forth, within the real purpose, which is all one, all good, so that each one in Israel is rewarded with including his prayer in the One. Give good help to all, so we merit annulling all our corporeality until we are rewarded with annulling ourselves completely, to truly be included in Your oneness, which is all good, always, until our prayer is utterly complete, included together from beginning to end with the complete unity.

136. *Meshivat Nefesh*, Item 40

The war against Amalek, which is the war against the inclination, is a very long war, and submitting it is mainly by strengthening. Through everything that one experiences in one's life, he should be very strong and not let himself fall under any circumstances, for as long as one does not despair oneself and strengthens oneself to somehow start over every time, he is regarded as winning the war, for it is impossible for man to defeat it by himself. It is as our sages said, "Were it not for the help of the Creator, he would not overcome it." Rather, man must only commit to strengthening himself each time anew, and not retreat from this war or cause oneself despair under any circumstances.

Certainly, in this war, it is impossible to evidently see who is the winner, since the war is still long, the exile is intensifying, and each one experiences what he experiences. Yet, as long as we are holding our weapons in our hands—and our main weapon is the prayer—and as long as we do not cause ourselves despair from this war and keep gripping to our weapons, we are winning for sure, since as long as one strengthens oneself in prayer and outcry to the Creator, he is winning the war, as this is essentially the victory.

137. Rabbi Menachem Mendel of Kotzk, *The Dawn Star*

When one has something to cry out about and wants to cry out but cannot cry out, this is the biggest outcry

12

A Prayer of Many

1. Baal HaSulam, "Not the Time for the Livestock to Be Gathered"

This is the meaning of the allegory in *The Zohar* (*The Sulam* [Ladder] commentary, *Nasso*, Item 19) about two who boarded a boat, and one was drilling under him. His friend admonished him, "Why are you drilling?" And that fool replied, "Why should you care? I am drilling under me!" But indeed, the individual spoils the beauty of the entire image.

From this we understand that in the ruin of the First Temple, the craftsman and the locksmith did not save the Temple from ruin because the majority of their contemporaries spoiled the beauty, though in them there was no flaw, for prophecy is not present in a flawed place, not even in the slightest.

This is the meaning of a prayer in public, that one must not exclude oneself from the public and ask for oneself, not even to bring contentment to one's maker, but only for the entire public. It is so because one cannot extend one's boundary while the boundaries of the rest of the buds of the flower remain where they are, for as smallness blemishes the beauty, so does greatness, since the boundaries of all the lines and circles of the flower must be related.

This is the meaning of (Psalms 22:21) "Save my soul from the sword, my only one from the dog." One who departs from the public to ask specifically for one's own soul does not build. On the contrary, he inflicts ruin upon his soul.

2. Baal HaSulam, "Not the Time for the Livestock to Be Gathered"

Even during work, when one prays alone, against his will he departs from the public and ruins his soul. That is, there was not even an awakening of anyone from the children of Israel to demand anything personal, for no one needed anything because they did not feel as separate selves, and this was their power to come out of Egypt with a mighty hand.

Thus, every one must gather with all of one's strength into the whole of Israel with every plea to the Creator in the prayer and in the work. He should include himself in the root of all of Israel, and will water all the herds from a well of water, for the previous boundary will be lifted from all the souls of Israel, both below him and above him. And the boundary of the holiness in general will be expanded greatly, for the light will appear from the *Chazeh* and below, for so is the nature of the light of the collective that is on the individual who has been annulled with regard to his own individuality and does not feel himself.

3. RABASH, Article No. 106, "The Ruin of Kedusha" [Holiness]

One should pray for the ruin of the Temple, that the *Kedusha* is ruined and in lowliness, and no one pays attention to this lowliness, that the *Kedusha* is placed in the earth and must be lifted from its lowliness.

In other words, each one recognizes his own benefit and knows that this is something very important and worth working for. But to bestow, this is not worthwhile. This is considered that the *Kedusha* is placed in the earth, unused and unwanted.

However, one must not ask the Creator to bring him closer to Him, as it is insolence on the part of man, for in what is he more important than others? However, when he prays for the collective—which is *Malchut*, called "assembly of Israel," the sum of the souls—that the *Shechina* [Divinity] is in the dust, and he prays that she will rise, meaning that the Creator will light up her darkness, then all of Israel will rise in degree, too, including the beseeching person, who is included in the collective.

4. RABASH, Article No. 251, "Concerning the Minyan" [Ten in the synagogue]

"When the Creator comes to the synagogue and does not find ten men there," meaning that there will be someone there who will pray for the quality of "ten," which is the *Shechina*, so she will rise from her exile, for by engaging with the desire to bestow, one raises the *Shechina* from the dust. But when each one cares for his personal needs, the Creator is angry.

He brings evidence from the verse, as was said, "Why have I come and there is no man" to care for the needs that pertain to the quality of "man," and cares only to satisfy the needs that pertain to the quality of a beast? Rather, one should always answer to himself for whom he spends his time and for whom he exerts, for he should be concerned only with the needs of the collective.

5. RABASH, Article No. 15 (1986), "A Prayer of Many"

We can interpret the words of *The Zohar*. It advises those people with an inner demand, who cannot accept the state they are in because they do not see any progress in the work of God, and believe what is written (Deuteronomy 30:20), "To love the Lord your God, to listen to His voice, and to cleave unto Him; for this is your life, and the length of your days." They see that they lack love and *Dvekut* [adhesion/cleaving], and they do not feel the life in the Torah or know how to find counsel for their souls to come to feel in their organs that which the text tells us.

The advice is to ask for the whole collective. In other words, everything that one feels that he is lacking and asks fulfillment for, he should not say that he is an exception or deserves more than what the collective has. Rather, "I dwell among my own people," meaning I am asking for the entire collective because I wish to come to a state where I will have no care for myself whatsoever, but only for the Creator to have contentment. Therefore, it makes no difference to me if the Creator takes pleasure in me or can receive the pleasure from others.

In other words, he asks the Creator to give us such an understanding, which is called, "entirely for the Creator." It means that he will be certain that he is not deceiving himself that he wants to bestow upon the Creator, that perhaps he is really thinking only of his own self-love, meaning that he will feel the delight and pleasure.

Therefore, he prays for the collective. This means that if there are a few people in the collective who can reach the goal of *Dvekut* with the Creator, and this will bring the Creator more contentment than if he himself were rewarded with nearing the Creator, he excludes himself. Instead, he wishes for the Creator to help them because this will bring more contentment above than from his own work. For this reason, he prays for the collective, that the Creator will help the entire collective and will give them that feeling—that they receive satisfaction from being able to bestow upon the Creator, to bring Him contentment.

And since everything requires an awakening from below, he gives the awakening from below, and others will receive the awakening from above, to whomever the Creator knows will be more beneficial for the Creator.

It follows that if he has the strength to ask for such a prayer, then he will certainly face a true test—if he agrees to such a prayer. However, if he knows that what he is saying is only lip service, what can he do when he sees that the body disagrees with such a prayer to have pure bestowal without a hint of reception?

Here there is only the famous advice—to pray to the Creator and believe above reason that the Creator can help him and the whole collective.

6. RABASH, Article No. 15 (1986), "A Prayer of Many"

We can understand the importance of a prayer of many, as it is written, "I dwell among my own people." *The Zohar* says, "One should never retire from the people because the mercy of the Creator is always on the whole people together." This means that if one asks the Creator to give him vessels of bestowal, as our sages said, "As He is merciful, you be merciful, too," one should pray for the whole collective. This is because then it is apparent that his aim is for the Creator to give him vessels of pure bestowal, as it was written, "The mercy of the Creator is always on the whole people together." It is known that there is no giving of half a thing from above. This means that when abundance is given from above to below, it is for the whole collective.

7. RABASH, Article No. 7 (1986), "The Importance of a Prayer of Many"

Baal HaSulam explained the matter of a prayer of many as a person praying for the many; this is called "a prayer of many." This is why a prayer of many is called "a time of good will." When a person prays for himself, he has slander and questions whether his prayer is truly worth acceptance. But when he prays for the public, it becomes irrelevant to scrutinize him and to see if he is worthy of his prayer being answered, since he is not asking for anything for himself, but only for the public.

This is why it was said that a prayer of many is called "a time of good will" and his prayer is answered.

8. RABASH, Article No. 217, "Run My Beloved"

It is a great rule that the person himself is called "a creature," meaning only he alone. Other than him it is already considered the holy *Shechina*. It follows that when he prays for his contemporaries, it is considered that he is praying for the holy Shechina, who is in exile and needs all the salvations. This is the meaning of eternity, and precisely in this manner, the light of mercy can be revealed.

Another reason we should pray only for the general public is the need to disclose the light of mercy, which is the light of bestowal. It is a rule that it is impossible to receive anything without equivalence. Rather, there must always be equivalence.

Hence, when he evokes mercy on himself, it follows that he is engaged in reception for himself. And the more he prays, not only is he not preparing the *Kli* [vessel] of equivalence, but on the contrary, sparks of reception form within him.

It turns out that he is going the opposite way: While he should prepare vessels of bestowal, he is preparing vessels of reception. "Cleave unto His attributes" is specifically "As He is merciful, so you are merciful."

Hence, when he prays for the public, through this prayer he engages in bestowal. And the more he prays, to that extent he forms vessels of bestowal, by which the light of bestowal, called "merciful," can be revealed.

By receiving the light of mercy, there is an ability to later reveal the quality of "gracious."

9. *Zohar for All*, "Introduction of The Book of Zohar," "Torah and Prayer," Item 183

The prayer that we pray is the correction of the Holy Divinity, to extend abundance to her, to satisfy all her deficiencies, for hence, all the requests are in plural form, such as "And grant us knowledge from You," or "Bring us back, our Father, into Your law."

This is so because the prayer is for the whole of Israel, since all that there is in the holy Divinity exists in the whole of Israel. And what is lacking in her is lacking in the whole of Israel. It follows that when we pray for the whole of Israel, we pray for the Holy Divinity, since they are the same. Thus, before the prayer, we must look into the deficiencies in Divinity, to know what needs to be corrected and filled in her.

10. *Zohar for All*, VaYetze [And Jacob Went Out], Remembering and Visiting," Items 284-285

Wherever a person prays his prayer, he should incorporate himself in the public, in the manifold public, as it is written about Shunammite when Elisha told her, "Would you be spoken for to the king or to the captain of the army?" "Would you be spoken for to the king," since that day was the festival of the first day of the year, and the day when *Malchut* of the firmament rules and sentences the world. At that time, the Creator is called "The king of the sentence," and this is why he told her, "Would you be spoken for to the king," since he called the Creator "King."

And she said, "I dwell among my own people." In other words, she said, "I have no wish to be mentioned above, but to put my head among the masses and not leave the public. Similarly, man should be included in the public and not stand out as unique, so the slanderers will not look at him and mention his sins.

11. *Zohar for All*, VaYechi [Jacob Lived], "Be Gathered, that I May Tell You," Items 514-516

All the prayers in the world, prayers of many, are prayers. But a solitary prayer does not enter before the Holy King, unless with great force. This is so because before the prayer enters to be crowned in its place, the Creator watches it, observes it, and observes the sins and merits of that person, which He does not do with a prayer of many, where several of the prayers are not from righteous, and they all enter before the Creator and He does not notice their iniquities.

"He has regarded the prayer of the destitute." He turns the prayer and examines it from all sides, and considers with which desire the prayer was made, who is the person who prayed that prayer, and what are his deeds. Hence, one should pray one's prayer in the collective, since He does not despise their prayer, even though they are not all with intent and the will of heart, as it is written, "He has regarded the prayer of the destitute." Thus, He only observes the prayer of an individual, but with a prayer of many, He does not despise their prayer, even though they are unworthy.

"He has regarded the prayer of the destitute" means that He accepts his prayer, but it is an individual who is mingled with many. Hence, his prayer is as a prayer of many. And who is an individual who is mingled with many? It is Jacob, for he contains both sides—right and left, Abraham and Isaac, and he calls out to his sons and prays his prayer for them.

And what is the prayer that is fully granted above? It is a prayer that the children of Israel will not perish in the exile. This is because every prayer in favor of Divinity is received in full. And when Israel are in exile, Divinity is with them. This is why the prayer is regarded as being in favor of Divinity and is accepted in full.

12. *Zohar for All, Pekudei* [Accounts], "The Palace of the Sapphire Pavement, Yesod," Items 485-487

The holy appointee stands over the door to all the prayers that breach airs and firmaments to come before the King. If it is a prayer of many, he opens the gate and lets her in, where she is detained until all the prayers of the world become a crown on the head of the righteous one who lives forever, *Yesod*.

If it is a prayer of one, it rises until it reaches the palace door, where that appointee stands. If the prayer is good for entering the holy King, he immediately opens a door and lets it in. If it is not good, he pushes it out and it descends and roams the world, standing at the bottom firmament from among those firmaments below, which lead the world. In that firmament is the appointee Sahadiel, who takes those rejected prayers, called "disqualified prayers," and conceals them until a person repents.

If he repents before his Master properly, and prays another prayer, a good one, when the prayer rises, the appointee, Sahadiel, takes that prayer, the disqualified one, and raises it until it meets the good prayer. Then they rise and mingle together, and come in before the holy King.

13. *Zohar for All, VaYishlach* [And Jacob Sent], "The Prayer of the Righteous," Item 45

A prayer of many rises before the Creator and the Creator crowns Himself with that prayer, since it rises in several ways. This is because one asks for *Hassadim*, the other for *Gevurot*, and a third for *Rachamim*. And it consists of several sides: the right side, the left, and the middle. This is so because *Hassadim* extend from the right side, *Gevurot* from the left side, and *Rachamim* from the middle side. And because it consists of several ways and sides, it becomes a crown over the head of the Righteous One That Lives Forever, *Yesod*, which imparts all the salvations to the *Nukva*, and from her to the whole public.

But a prayer of one does not comprise all the sides; it is only on one way. Either one asks for *Hassadim* or *Gevurot* or *Rachamim*. Hence, a prayer of one is not erected to be received like the prayer of many, as it does not include all three lines like the prayer of many.

14. Rabbi Nachman of Breslov, *Likutei Halachot*

The house of prayer is called "the house of assembly," for all the souls gather there through the prayer that they pray there, since the prayer is regarded as the soul. Hence, the prayer is mainly in the house of assembly and in public, since the ascent of the soul and its wholeness are mainly when all the souls are mingled and become one, for then they rise to the holiness, for holiness is one. For this reason, the prayer, which is regarded as the soul, depends mainly on the unity of the souls. Therefore, prior to the prayer, one must assume the commandment to-do of "Love your neighbor as yourself," for it is impossible to say the words of the prayer unless through peace, when one unites with all the souls of Israel. Hence, the prayer is mainly in public and not alone, so that one will not be isolated, by himself, as this is the opposite of holiness. Rather, we must only unite together the holy congregation and become one. This prayer is in public and specifically in the house of assembly, for there, the souls gather and unite. This is the completeness of the prayer.

15. Raaiah Kook, "Sermons of the Raaiah for the High Holidays"

It is known that everything is discerned by its opposite, as the advantage of the light that comes from recognizing the darkness. Likewise, one has more recognition of the benefit of the public and his mingling with them when he is alone on the road and feels how the collective complements his lacks, whether in corporeal matters or in spiritual matters. As a result, he installs more love of the collective in his heart. And when he unites with the public, his prayer acquires the merit of the prayer of the public.

Noam Elimelech, *Likutei Shoshana*

One must always pray for his friend, as one cannot do much for himself, for "One does not deliver oneself from imprisonment." But when asking for his friend, he is answered quickly. Therefore, each one should pray for his friend, and thus each works on the other's desire until all of them are answered. This is why it was said, "Israel are *Arevim* [responsible/sweet] for one another," where *Arevim* means sweetness, as they sweeten for each other by the prayers they pray for one another, and by this they are answered.

17. Rav Menachem Mendel of Kosov, *Love of Peace*

One who prays for his friend is answered first. This means that one who prays for his friend becomes a pipeline of bestowal to bestow upon his friend. Since the abundance flows through him, he is necessarily answered first, since the bestowal comes through him.

18. Rav Chaim Vital, *Shaar HaGilgulim*, Introduction, 38

My teacher cautioned me and all the friends who were with him in that society to take upon ourselves the commandment to-do of "Love your neighbor as yourself," and to aim to love each one from Israel as his own soul, for by this his prayer would rise comprising all of Israel and will be able to ascend and make a correction above. Especially, our love of friends, each and every one of us should include himself as though he is an organ of those friends. My teacher sternly cautioned me about this matter.

13

Gratitude

1. Baal HaSulam, *Shamati*, Article No. 26, "One's Future Depends and Is Tied to Gratitude for the Past"

It is written, "The Lord is high and the low will see," that only the low can see the exaltedness. The letters *Yakar* [precious] are the letters of *Yakir* [will know]. This means that one knows the exaltedness of a thing to the extent that it is precious to one.

One is impressed according to the importance of the thing. The impression brings one to a sensation in the heart, and according to the measure of one's recognition of the importance, to that extent, joy is born in him.

Thus, if one knows his lowliness, that he is not more privileged than his contemporaries, meaning he sees that there are many people in the world who were not given the strength to do the holy work even in the simplest way, even without the intention and in *Lo Lishma* [not for Her sake], even in *Lo Lishma* of *Lo Lishma*, and even in preparation for the preparation of the clothing of *Kedusha* [holiness], while he was imparted the desire and thought to at least occasionally do holy work, even in the simplest possible way, if one can appreciate the importance of this, according to the importance one attributes to the holy work, to that extent he should give praise and thanks for it.

This is so because it is true that we cannot appreciate the importance of being able to sometimes observe the *Mitzvot* [commandments] of the Creator, even without any intention. In that state, one comes to feel elation and joy in the heart.

The praise and the gratitude one gives for it expand the feelings, and one is elated by every single point in the holy work, he knows Whose servant he is, and thus soars ever higher. This is the meaning of what is written, "I thank You for the grace that You have made with me," meaning for the past, and by this one can confidently say, and he does say, "and that You are destined to do with me."

2. Baal HaSulam, *Shamati*, Article No. 4, "What Is the Reason for the Heaviness One Feels when Annulling before the Creator in the Work?"

We must know that there is no difference between a small illumination or a great illumination that a person obtains, since there are no changes in the light. Rather, all the changes are in the *Kelim* [vessels] that receive the abundance, as it is written, "I the Lord did not change." Hence, if one can magnify one's *Kelim*, to that extent he magnifies the illumination.

Yet, the question is, With what can one magnify one's *Kelim*? The answer is that to the extent to which he praises and thanks the Creator for having brought him closer to Him, so he would feel Him a little and think of the importance of the matter, meaning that he was rewarded with having some connection with the Creator.

To the extent of the importance that one pictures for oneself, so the illumination grows in him. One must know that he will never come to know the true measure of the importance of the connection between man and the Creator because one cannot assess its true value. Instead, as much as one appreciates it, so he attains its merit and importance. There is a *Segula* [power/remedy/virtue] in this, since by this he can be rewarded with this illumination staying permanently within him.

3. Baal HaSulam, Letter No. 52

In each and every movement in His work there are two opposites in the same carrier, as I have elaborated in previous letters, as the receiver consists of body and soul, which are opposites. Hence, in each attainment, great or small, He makes two opposite forms.

There are two concepts in the work of the Creator: 1) "prayer and plea," 2) "praise and gratitude." Naturally, both must be at their highest. To complete the prayer, a person must feel the Creator's closeness to him as mandatory, like an organ that is hanging loosely, for then he can complain and pour out his heart before Him.

But opposite that, regarding the complete praise and gratitude, a person must feel the Creator's closeness to him as an addition, a supplement, as something that does not belong to him at all, for "What is man that You should know him, the son of man that You should think of him?" Then he can certainly give complete praise and gratitude to His great name for choosing him from among all those who are standing ready to serve the Creator.

It is great work for the complex man to be completed in both those opposites, so they are set in his heart forever at the same time.

4. RABASH, Letter No. 36

"The left rejects." This requires a lot of work and toil to overcome all the obstacles and all the alien views and thoughts. However, we should also engage in the right, as our sages said, "Make your Torah (teaching) permanent and your work temporary." Torah is regarded as right, which is wholeness. A person should regard himself perfect with virtues and noble qualities. He should adapt the works in Torah and *Mitzva* as is suitable for a whole person as much as one can.

However, one must not regret it if one is unable to complete one's will. That is, if a person wishes to do plentiful good deeds and study of Torah, but cannot, he should not regret it but be happy while working in the right. He should be content with whatever he can do, and praise and thank His name for being able to do a small service to the King. Even a minute a day or a minute in two days should be to him like finding a great treasure.

And even if it is a simple deed, meaning without vitality, he should still try to be happy and derive vitality from being allowed to serve the King. This is how he should be during the study, meaning whole. This is regarded as Torah, which is right, as it is written, "On His right was a fiery law." For every opportunity, one must praise the Creator.

I heard from Baal HaSulam that with the praise and gratitude one gives to the Creator for nearing the Creator, one draws the light of His holiness below. A person should feel whole, and then he is regarded as blessed, and the blessed clings to the blessed. But when a person regards himself as cursed, the cursed does not cling to the cursed, as our sages said.

Therefore, you must regard yourselves as whole while performing Torah and *Mitzvot* (commandments). At that time you must not find any flaw in you, as it is written, "Anyone in whom there is a flaw shall not approach." This is called "Torah," meaning wholeness.

5. RABASH, Article No. 224, "The Reason for the Faith"

The reason for the faith is that there is no greater pleasure than to be rewarded with the revelation of Godliness and the instilling of the *Shechina* [Divinity].

In order for one to receive all this for the purpose of bestowal, there is a correction of concealment, where he engages in Torah and *Mitzvot* [commandments] even though he feels no pleasure. This is called "not in order to receive reward." When he has this *Kli* [vessel], his eyes soon open to welcome the face of the Creator.

When a desire awakens within him, that it is worthwhile to serve the Creator for the pleasure, he soon falls into concealment. This is regarded as death, meaning that previously, he was adhered to life, and he was rewarded with it only through the power of faith. Therefore, now that he is corrected and begins to work in faith once more, he receives back his breath of life. At that time, he says, "I thank You for returning my soul with compassion."

This is precisely when he assumes once more the work in the manner of faith above reason. When he had the concealment, he says, "Great is Your faith". The faith is so great that through it, he receives the soul once more.

6. RABASH, Article No. 15 (1991), "What Is the Blessing, 'Who Made a Miracle for Me in This Place,' in the Work?"

A person should accustom himself with anything to compare between the time of suffering and the time of pleasure, and to bless for the miracle of delivering him from suffering to a state of pleasure. By this, he will be able to thank the Creator and enjoy in the new *Kelim* that have been added to him now when he compares the two times to one another. From this, a person can advance in the work.

This is as Baal HaSulam said, that it does not matter whether a person receives from the Creator something great or small. What matters is how much a person thanks the Creator. To the extent of his gratitude, so grows the giving that the Creator gives. Therefore, we must take note to be grateful, to appreciate His gift, so we can approach the Creator. Hence, when a person always looks during the ascent at the state he was in while in descent, meaning how he felt during the descent, he can make a distinction as in, "as the advantage of the light from within the darkness," and he already has new *Kelim* in which to receive joy and be thankful to the Creator. This is the meaning of what is written, that a person should bless, "Blessed is He who made a miracle for me in this place," meaning in the place where he is now, during the ascent, since there cannot be an ascent if there was no prior state of descent.

7. RABASH, Article No. 18 (1989), "What Is, 'There Is No Blessing in That Which Is Counted,' in the Work?"

A person should be happy and praise and thank the Creator for rewarding him with some grip on *Kedusha*, however much he has, since he knows that this, too, he does not deserve.

This is regarded as being content with little. Thus, he has no reason to count him, to see how many qualities of Israel he has, meaning what percentage of his work can he say is *Yashar-El*, meaning how much effort he is willing to make for the *Kedusha*, called "for the sake of the Creator." This is not interesting at all because he says, "Whatever grip I have in Torah and *Mitzvot* is more important than all the pleasures in the world."

We could ask about this, If this is so important, why does he settle for little? To this he answers himself, "I probably do not deserve to be given by the Creator a bigger share than I have, and I also see that there are people who do not have even this." It follows that he is a person in whom there is blessing since he has something with which to be happy, and he sees that the rest of the people are joyful and happy over nonsense, while the Creator has given him the intellect and understanding to grasp that he should rejoice with the Creator.

8. RABASH, Article No. 401, "Hear, O Israel"

On the other hand, he can pray to the Creator for remaining outside of the work of the Creator because everything was built on the basis of self-love.

At that time, the person is called "complete," and otherwise he is not considered "man" because if he sees his deficiencies he will soon run from the quality of the "right," as well.

But once he has seen his bad state and yet reinforces himself above reason that he has wholeness, and the sign of this is that he can thank the Creator for this, then he is called "complete." This is "Right and left, and a bride between them." By having the quality of male and female, he can be rewarded with the quality of "bride," meaning the real kingdom of heaven.

9. RABASH, Article No. 463, "You Became Rich; You Are in the Evening; Light the Candle"

"You became rich; you are in the evening; light the candle." The king had two books of Torah—with one he comes out, and the other he leaves in his treasury.

It is known that there are two opposites in the work of the Creator: 1) A person must be happy in any state that he is in, even if it is the lowest possible state. He should praise and thank the Creator for letting him be among those who sit inside the seminary, as our sages said, "He who walks and does not do, the reward for walking is in his hand." This is called "You became rich," as in "wealth," for on the eve of Shabbat [Sabbath] he should be as one who is wealthy who does not lack a thing.

Afterward, one must shift to the other side, to see what he has—how much fear of heaven and greatness of the Creator he has, and how many good deeds and how much Torah, and understanding in the Torah. At that time, he sees that he is deficient. This is called "evening," as in "And there was evening and there was morning," and this is called "you are in the evening."

Once one has those two, then "Light the candle" of Shabbat. At that time, the middle line comes, namely the light of Shabbat.

10. RABASH, Article No. 24 (1989), "What Is 'Do Not Slight the Blessing of a Layperson' in the Work?"

Our sages said (*Yoma* 16), "Any turn you take should be only through the right." The meaning of "any" is "generally." That is, generally, a person should walk on the right line. It is permitted to walk on the left line only when he is certain he will be able to pray for his deficiencies. Otherwise, he must remain on the right until he feels that he is ready for it.

Therefore, if thoughts that he is at fault have awakened in him against his will, and how can he speak words of Torah and prayer to the Creator when his thoughts tell him, "You are filthy! How are you not ashamed to engage in matters of *Kedusha*?!" About this, a person (must) say that it is written, "I am the Lord, who dwells with them in the midst of their *Tuma'a* [impurity]." That is, even though I am in the lowest possible baseness, I still believe what is written, that the Creator dwells even in the worst lowliness.

However, He is not among the proud, as our sages said, "Anyone who is proud, the Creator says, 'I and he cannot dwell in the same abode.'" For this reason, when a person feels whole, according to the right line, when he appreciates his lowliness and says that nonetheless, the Creator has given him some grip on *Kedusha*, and that "some," compared to the *Kedusha* that a person should attain, that "some" is called "layperson."

But if he says according to his lowliness, "I thank and praise the Creator for this," it can be said about this what is written, "I am the Lord, who dwells with them in the midst of their *Tuma'a*." When he is happy about this, he can be rewarded with, "The *Shechina* [Divinity] is present only out of joy."

It follows that through this lowliness, that because the Creator has given him some grip on *Kedusha*, he can climb the rungs of holiness if he only takes from this the joy and appreciates it. Then, a person can say, "Raise the poor from the dust," "He will raise the destitute from the litter." That is, when a person feels his lowliness, that he is meager, meaning poor, as our sages said (*Nedarim* 41), "Abaye said, 'In our tradition, there is no poor but in knowledge.'" That is, it has been handed down from our father, a custom from our forefathers that "there is no poor but in knowledge."

This is why he says that he is meager, meaning poor, for he has no knowledge of *Kedusha*—he is called "poor and meager." Then, if there is any grip on *Kedusha*, even though he is poor, he says, "Raises the poor from the dust." That is, he says a prayer, for even though he is poor, the Creator still raised him. "He raises the destitute from the litter." Although he feels that he is destitute, the

Creator still lifted him, and for this, he praises the Creator. If there is any grip on *Kedusha*, we can already praise and thank the Creator.

11. RABASH, Article No. 28 (1987), "What Is 'Do Not Add and Do Not Take Away,' in the Work?"

He must believe above reason and imagine that he has already been rewarded with faith in the Creator that is felt in his organs, and he sees and feels that the Creator leads the entire world as the good who does good. Although when he looks within reason he sees the opposite, he should still work above reason and it should appear to him as though he can already feel in his organs that so it really is, that the Creator leads the world as the good who does good.

Here he acquires the importance of the goal, and from here he derives life, meaning joy at being near to the Creator. Then a person can say that the Creator is good and does good, and feel that he has the strength to tell the Creator, "You have chosen us from among all nations, You have loved us and wanted us," since he has a reason to thank the Creator. And to the extent that he feels the importance of spirituality, so he establishes the praise of the Creator.

Once man has come to feel the importance of spirituality, which is called "One should always establish the praise of the Creator," then is the time when he must shift to the left line. He must criticize how he truly feels within reason the importance of the King, if he is truly willing to work only for the sake of the Creator.

When he sees within reason that he is bare and destitute, that state when he sees the importance of spirituality, but only above reason, that calculation can create in him deficiency and pain for being in utter lowliness. Then he can make a heartfelt prayer for what he lacks.

14

The Perception of Reality

1. Baal HaSulam, "Introduction to The Book of Zohar," Items 39-40

The whole of the Creator's desired goal for the creation He had created is to bestow upon His creatures, so they would know His truthfulness and greatness, and receive all the delight and pleasure He had prepared for them, in the measure described in the verse: "Ephraim my darling son, is he a child of joy?" Thus, you clearly find that this purpose does not apply to the still and the great spheres, such as the earth, the moon, or the sun, however luminous they may be, and not to the vegetative or the animate, for they lack the sensation of others, even from among their own species. Therefore, how can the sensation of the Godly and His bestowal apply to them?

Humankind alone, having been prepared with the sensation of others of the same species, who are similar to them, after working in Torah and *Mitzvot*, when they invert their will to receive to a desire to bestow and achieve equivalence of form with their Maker, they receive all the degrees that have been prepared for them in the upper worlds, called NRNHY. By this they become qualified to receive the purpose of the thought of creation. After all, the purpose of the creation of all the worlds was for man alone.

And I know that it is completely unacceptable in the eyes of some philosophers. They cannot agree that man, who they regard as low and worthless, is the center of the magnificent creation. But they are like a worm that was born inside a radish. It lives there and thinks that the world of the Creator is as bitter, dark, and small as the radish in which it was born. But as soon as it breaks the peel of the radish and peeps out, it says in bewilderment: "I thought the whole world was like the radish I was born in, and now I see a grand, beautiful, and wondrous world before me!"

So, too, are those who are immersed in the *Klipa* [sing. of *Klipot*] of the will to receive they were born with, and did not try to take the unique spice, which are the practical Torah and *Mitzvot*, which can break this hard *Klipa* and turn it into a desire to bestow contentment upon the Maker. It is certain that they must determine according to their worthlessness and emptiness, as they truly are. They cannot comprehend that this magnificent reality had been created only for them.

Indeed, had they delved in Torah and *Mitzvot* to bestow contentment upon their Maker, with all the required purity, and would try to break the *Klipa* of the will to receive in which they were born, and would assume the desire to bestow, their eyes would promptly open to see and attain for themselves all the degrees of wisdom, intelligence, and clear mind that have been prepared for them in the spiritual worlds. Then they would say for themselves what our sages said, "What does a good guest say? 'Everything the host has done, he has done only for me.'"

2. Baal HaSulam, *The Study of the Ten Sefurot*, "Inner Observation," Part One, Chapter Ten, Item 36

We have no attainment and perception whatsoever in any substance, as our five senses are completely unfit for it. The sight, sound, smell, taste and touch, offer the scrutinizing mind merely abstract forms of "incidents" of the essence, formulating through the cooperation with our senses.

3. Baal HaSulam, "Introduction to the Preface to the Wisdom of Kabbalah," Item 1

It is written in *The Zohar*, *Vayikra*, Portion *Tazria*, "Come and see: All that exists in the world exists for man, and everything exists for him, as it is written, 'Then the Lord God formed man,' with a full name, as we have established, that he is the whole of everything and contains everything, and all that is above and below, etc., is included in that image."

Thus, it explains that all the worlds, upper and lower, are included in man. And also, the whole of reality within those worlds is only for man.

4. Baal HaSulam, "Foreword to The Book of Zohar," Item 34

Our sense of sight, for example: We see a wide world before us, wondrously filled. But in fact, we see all that only in our own interior. In other words, there is a sort of a photographic machine in our hindbrain, which portrays everything that appears to us and nothing outside of us.

He has made for us there, in our brain, a kind of polished mirror that inverts everything seen there, so we will see it outside our brain, in front of our faces. Yet, what we see outside of us is not a real thing. Nevertheless, we should be so grateful to His Providence for having created that polished mirror in our brains, enabling us to see and perceive everything outside of us, for by this He has given us the power to perceive everything with clear knowledge and attainment, and measure everything from within and from without.

Without it, we would lose most of our perception. The same is true with the Godly will, concerning Godly perceptions. Even though all these changes unfold in the interior of the receiving souls, they nevertheless see it all in the Giver Himself since only in this manner are they awarded all the perceptions and all the pleasantness in the thought of creation.

You can also deduce this from the above parable. Even though we see everything as being in front of us, every reasonable person knows for certain that all that we see is only in our own brains.

So are the souls: Although they see all the images in the Giver, they have no doubt that all those are only in their own interior and not at all in the Giver.

5. Baal HaSulam, "Foreword to The Book of Zohar," Item 12

The essence of the person in itself, without the matter. This is because our five senses and our imagination offer us only manifestations of the actions of the essence, but none of the essence itself. For example, the sense of sight offers us only shadows of the visible essence as they are formed opposite the light. Similarly, the sense of hearing is but a force of striking of some essence in the air.

The air that is rejected by it strikes the drum in our ear, and we hear that there is some essence in our proximity. The sense of smell is but air that emerges from the essence and strikes our nerves of scent, and we smell. Also, taste is but a result of the contact of some essence with our nerves of taste.

Thus, all that these four senses offer us are manifestations of the operations that stem from some essence and nothing of the essence itself.

Even the sense of touch, the strongest of the senses, separating hot from cold and solid from soft, all these are but manifestations of operations in the essence; they are but incidents of the essence. This is so because the hot can be chilled, the cold can be heated, the solid can be turned to liquid through chemical operations, and the liquid into air, meaning only gas where any discernment in our five senses has been expired. Yet, the essence still exists in it, since you can turn the air into liquid once again, and the liquid into solid.

Evidently, the five senses do not reveal to us any essence whatsoever, but only incidents and manifestations of operations from the essence. It is known that anything that we cannot grasp in our senses, we also cannot imagine. And what we cannot imagine will never appear in our thoughts and we have no way to perceive it.

6. Baal HaSulam, "The Essence of the Wisdom of Kabbalah"

As there is no perception of the Creator whatsoever, so is it impossible to attain the essence of any of His creatures, even the tangible objects that we feel with our hands.

Thus, all we know about our friends and relatives in the world of action before us are nothing more than "acquaintance with actions." These are prompted and born by the association of their encounter with our senses, which render us complete satisfaction although we have no perception whatsoever in the essence of the subject.

Furthermore, you have no perception or attainment whatsoever even in your own essence. Everything you know about your own essence is nothing more than a series of actions extending from your essence.

7. Baal HaSulam, *Shamati*, Article No. 66, "Concerning the Giving of the Torah – 1"

We cannot attain any reality as it is in itself. Rather, we attain everything only according to our sensations. And reality, as it is in itself, is of no interest to us at all. Hence, we do not attain the Torah as it is in itself; we attain only our sensations. Thus, all of our impressions follow only our sensations.

8. Baal HaSulam, *Shamati*, Article No. 3, "The Matter of Spiritual Attainment"

"There is no change in the light." Rather, all the changes are in the *Kelim*, meaning in our senses. We measure everything according to our imagination. From this it follows that if many people examine one spiritual thing, each will attain according to his imagination and senses, thereby seeing a different form.

In addition, the form itself will change in a person according to his ups and downs, as we have said above that the light is simple light and all the changes are only in the receivers.

9. Baal HaSulam, *Shamati*, Article No. 3, "The Matter of Spiritual Attainment"

For themselves, all the worlds are regarded as simple unity, and there is no change in Godliness. This is the meaning of "I the Lord did not change." There are no *Sefirot* or *Behinot* [discernments] in Godliness. Even the most subtle appellations do not refer to the light itself, as this is a discernment of *Atzmuto* where there is no attainment. Rather, all the *Sefirot* and the discernments speak only of what a person attains in them.

10. Baal HaSulam, *Shamati*, Article No. 3, "The Matter of Spiritual Attainment"

The proliferation of names is only with respect to the receivers. Hence, the first name that appeared, that is, the root for the creatures, is called *Ein Sof*. This name remains unchanged, and all the restrictions and the manifold changes unfold only with regard to the receivers, but He always shines in the first name called "His desire to do good to His creations," endlessly.

11. Baal HaSulam, *Shamati*, Article No. 3, "The Matter of Spiritual Attainment"

We can only speak from where our senses are impressed by the expanding light, which is "His desire to do good to His creations," which comes into the hands of the receivers in actual fact.

Similarly, when we examine a table, our sense of touch feels it as something hard, and its length and width, all according to our senses. However, that does not necessitate that the table will appear so to one who has other senses. For example, in the eyes of an angel, when it examines the table, it will see it according to its senses. For this reason, we cannot determine any form with regard to an angel since we do not know its senses.

Thus, since we have no attainment in the Creator, we cannot say which form the worlds have from His perspective. We only attain the worlds according to our senses and sensations.

12. Baal HaSulam, "Foreword to The Book of Zohar," Items 32-33

There is no change at all in the world *Atzilut* itself, whether the lower ones receive its great abundance lushly or receive nothing at all. The above-mentioned greatness lies solely on the lower ones.

Thus, why did the authors of *The Zohar* have to describe all those changes in the world of *Atzilut* itself? They should have spoken explicitly only with respect to the receivers in *BYA*, and not speak so elaborately of *Atzilut*, forcing us to provide answers.

Indeed, there is a very trenchant secret here: This is the meaning of "and by the hand of the prophets have I used similitudes" (Hosea 12). The truth is that there is a Godly will here, that these similitudes, which operate only in the souls of the receivers, will appear to the souls as He Himself participates in them to greatly increase the attainment of the souls.

It is like a father who constrains himself to show his little darling child a face of sadness and a face of contentment, although there is neither sadness nor contentment in him. He only does this to impress his darling child and expand his understanding so as to play with him.

Only when he grows will he learn and know that all that his father did was no more real than mere playing with him. So is the matter before us: All these images and changes begin and end only with the impression of the souls. Yet, by the will of God, they appear as though they are in Him Himself. He does that to enhance and expand the attainment of the souls to the utmost, in accordance with the thought of creation, to delight His creatures.

13. Baal HaSulam, "600,000 Souls"

It is said that there are 600,000 souls, and each soul divides into several sparks. We must understand how it is possible for the spiritual to divide, since initially, only one soul was created, the soul of *Adam HaRishon*.

In my opinion, there is indeed only one soul in the world, as it is written (Genesis 2:7), "and breathed into his nostrils the soul [also "breath" in Hebrew] of life." That same soul exists in all the children of Israel, complete in each and every one, as in *Adam HaRishon*, since the spiritual is indivisible and cannot be cut—which is rather a trait of corporeal things.

Rather, saying that there are 600,000 souls and sparks of souls appears as though it is divided by the force of the body of each person. In other words, first, the body divides and completely denies him of the radiance of the soul, and by the force of the Torah and the *Mitzva* [commandment], the body is cleansed, and to the extent of its cleansing, the common soul shines on him.

For this reason, two discernments were made in the corporeal body: In the first discernment, one feels one's soul as a unique organ and does not understand that this is the whole of Israel. This is truly a flaw; hence, it causes along with the above-mentioned.

In the second discernment, the true light of the soul of Israel does not shine on him in all its power of illumination, but only partially, by the measure he has purified himself by returning to the collective.

The sign for the body's complete correction is when one feels that one's soul exists in the whole of Israel, in each and every one of them, for which he does not feel himself as an individual, for one depends on the other. At that time, he is complete, flawless, and the soul truly shines on him in its fullest power, as it appeared in *Adam HaRishon*, as in "He who breathed, breathed from within Him." This is the meaning of the three times of a person:

1. A spark of a soul, the act by way of sparkling, as in prohibiting and permitting.
2. A particular soul, one part out of 600,000. It is permanently completed, but its flaw is with it. This means that his body cannot receive the whole of the soul, and feels himself as being distinct, which causes him a lot of pains of love.

Subsequently, he approaches wholeness, the common soul, since the body has been cleansed and is entirely dedicated to the Creator and does not pose any measures or screens and is completely included in the whole of Israel.

14. Baal HaSulam, *Shamati*, Article No. 36, "What Are the Three Bodies in Man?"

One must think only of the inner body, for it is a clothing for the soul of *Kedusha*. That is, one should think thoughts that are after one's skin. This means that after the body's skin is called "outside one's body," meaning outside one's own benefit, but only thoughts of benefiting others. This is called "outside one's skin."

This is so because after one's skin, there is no grip for the *Klipot* [pl. of *Klipa*], for the *Klipot* grip only that which is within one's skin, meaning that which belongs to one's body, and not outside one's body, called "outside one's skin." This means that they possess anything that is clothed in the body, and they cannot hold anything that is not clothed in the body.

When one persists with thoughts that are after one's skin, he will be rewarded with what is written, "And after my skin they broke this, and from my flesh shall I see God" (Job 19, 26). "This" is the *Shechina* [Divinity], and she stands after one's skin. "Broke" means that it has been corrected to be a pillar "after my skin." At that time, one is awarded "and from my flesh shall I see God."

It means that *Kedusha* comes and clothes the interior of the body specifically when one agrees to work outside one's skin, meaning without any clothing. The wicked, however, who want to work precisely when there is clothing in the body, called within the skin, they will die without wisdom. This is because then they have no clothing and they are not awarded anything. However, it is specifically the righteous who are rewarded with clothing in the body.

15. Baal HaSulam, "The Essence of the Wisdom of Kabbalah"

Each lower world is an imprint of the world above it. Hence, all the forms in the higher world are meticulously copied, in both quantity and quality, to the lower world.

Thus, there is not an element of reality or an occurrence of reality in a lower world that you will not find its likeness in the world above it, as identical as two drops in a pond. And they are called "root and branch." That means that the item in the lower world is deemed a branch of its pattern found in the higher world, which is the root of the lower element, as this is where that item in the lower world has been imprinted and made to be.

That was the intention of our sages when they said, "You have not a blade of grass below that has not a fortune and a guard above that strike it and tell it, 'Grow'!" (Omissions of *The Zohar*, p 251a [source in Hebrew], *Beresheet Rabbah*, Chapter 10). It follows that the root, called "fortune," compels it to grow and assume its attribute in quantity and quality, as with the seal and its imprint. This is the law of root and branch that applies to every detail and occurrence in reality, in every single world, in relation to the world above it.

16. Baal HaSulam, *The Study of the Ten Sefirot*, "Inner Light," Part One, Item 1

It is difficult for novice, for they perceive matters by means of corporeal boundaries of time, space, change and exchange. However, the authors only used those as signs to point to their Upper Roots.

17. Baal HaSulam, *Ohr HaBahir*

Spiritual revelation, whether emerging from concealment or some addition, extends and comes primarily through the power of the vessels and their quality, and does not depend at all on the upper light. It is so because the rule is that there is no change in the lights themselves from the beginning of the line to the bottom of *Assiya*. As it is in the beginning of the line, so it does not grow coarser or change when it is at the bottom of *Assiya*. It is also known that the upper light does not stop bestowing upon the lower ones even for a minute. Therefore, the whole matter of concealment, revelation, and changes, and any change, depend only on the merit of the vessels.

18. Baal HaSulam, Letter No. 14

"Come to Pharaoh." It is the *Shechina* [Divinity] in disclosure, from the words, "and let the hair of the woman's head go loose," as it is written in *The Zohar*. The thing is that to the extent that the children of Israel thought that Egypt were enslaving them and impeding them from serving the Creator, they truly were in the exile in Egypt. Hence, the Redeemer's only work was to reveal to them that there is no other force involved here, that "I and not a messenger," for there is no other force but Him. This was indeed the light of redemption, as explained in the Passover *Haggadah* [story].

This is what the Creator gave to Moses in the verse, "Come to Pharaoh," meaning unite the truth, for the whole approaching the king of Egypt is only to Pharaoh, to disclose the *Shechina*. This is why He said, "For I have hardened his heart," etc., "that I may place these signs of Mine within him."

In spirituality, there are no letters, as I have already elaborated on before. All the multiplication in spirituality relies on the letters derived from the materiality of this world, as in, "And creator of darkness." There are no additions or initiations here, but the creation of darkness, the *Merkava* [chariot/structure] that is suited to disclose that the light is good. It follows that the Creator Himself hardened his heart. Why? Because it is letters that I need.

This is the meaning of "that I may place these signs of Mine within him, and that you may tell ... that you may know that I am the Lord." Explanation: Once you receive the letters, meaning when you understand that I gave and toiled for you, as in, do not move from "behind" Me, for you will thoroughly keep the *Achoraim* [posterior/back] for Me, for My name, then the abundance will do her thing and fill the letters. The qualities will become *Sefirot*, since before the filling they are called "qualities," and upon their fulfillment for the best, they are called *Sefirot*, sapphire, illuminating the world from one end to the other.

This is the meaning of "that you may tell." I need all this for the end of the matter, meaning "And you shall know that I am the Lord" "and not a messenger." This is the meaning of the fiftieth gate, which cannot appear unless the forty-nine faces of pure and impure appear in one opposite the other, in which the righteous falls [forty-nine in *Gematria*] before the wicked.

19. Baal HaSulam, "The Writings of the Last Generation"

There is nothing more natural than coming into contact with one's Maker, for He has made nature. In fact, every creature has contact with his Maker, as it is written, "The whole earth is full of His glory," except we do not know or feel it.

Actually, one who is awarded contact with Him attains only the awareness. It is as though one has a treasure in his pocket, and he does not know it. Along comes another and lets him know what is in his pocket. Now he really has become rich.

Yet, there is nothing new here, no cause for excitement. In fact, nothing has been added in the actual reality.

20. Baal HaSulam, Letter No. 55

"This world," "the next [world]"—in the words of our sages. It is as presented in *The Zohar* in the title, *Sefer HaBahir* [*The Book of the Bright One*]: "Rabbi Rechimai was asked, 'What is 'the next world,' and what is 'in the future'?' He replied to them, 'In the next world and came.'" In other words, the abundance is still to come.

You can evidently see the difference between this world and the next world. This one is what we attain in the present or attained in the past. The next world, however, is what we have not attained, but which should come to us in the future, after some time. However, both speak of what one attains and receives in this world.

21. Baal HaSulam, "From My Flesh I Shall See God"

Spirituality does not depend on time or place, and there is no death there.

22. Baal HaSulam, "Introduction to The Book of Zohar, Item 13

By the very thought to create the souls, His thought completed everything, for He does not need an act, as do we. Instantaneously, all the souls and worlds that were destined to be created emerged filled with all the delight and pleasure and the gentleness that He had planned for them, in the final perfection that the souls were destined to receive at the end of correction, after the will to receive in the souls has been fully corrected and has turned into pure bestowal, in complete equivalence of form with the Emanator.

This is so because in His eternalness, past, present, and future are as one. The future is as the present, and there is no such thing as time in Him (*The Zohar*, *Mishpatim*, Item 51, *New Zohar*, *Beresheet*, Item 243). Hence, there was never an issue of a corrupted will to receive in its separated state in *Ein Sof*.

On the contrary, that equivalence of form, destined to be revealed at the end of correction, appeared instantly in His eternalness.

23. Baal HaSulam, Letter No. 32

The Creator is truly in the heart of each one from Israel. But this is on His part, so what does man need? Only to know it—the knowing changes, and the knowing finishes.

24. Baal HaSulam, "Foreword to The Book of Zohar," Item 35

When the light of *Malchut* descends and expands over the people. At that time, it appears to them, to each and every one, according to their own appearance, vision, and imagination, meaning only in the receivers and not at all in the *Sefira Malchut* herself.

25. Baal HaSulam, *The Study of the Ten Sefirot*, "Inner Observation," Part One, Chapter 9, Item 33

Know that spiritual movement is not like tangible motion from one location to another; it refers to a renewed Tzura.

We denominate every innovation of form by the title "movement."

26. Baal HaSulam, "The Peace"

There are no new souls the way bodies are renewed, but only a certain amount of souls that incarnate on the wheel of transformation of the form, for each time they clothe a new body and a new generation.

27. Baal HaSulam, "The Peace"

With regard to the souls, all generations since the beginning of creation to the end of correction are as one generation that has extended its life over several thousand years until it developed and became corrected as it should be. And the fact that in the meantime, each has changed his body several thousand times is completely irrelevant because the essence of the body's self, called "the soul," did not suffer at all by these changes.

28. Baal HaSulam, *The Study of the Ten Sefirot*, "Inner Observation," Part One, Chapter One, Item 8

This entire reality, *Elyonim* and *Tachtonim* as one in the final state of the end of correction, was emanated and created by a single thought. That single thought performs all the operations, is the essence of all the operations, the purpose and the essence of the labor. It is by itself the entire perfection and the sought-after reward.

29. Baal HaSulam, Letter No. 19

The Creator does nothing new at the end of correction, as the fools think. Rather, "And you shall eat old store long kept," meaning until he says, "I want."

30. Baal HaSulam, "You Have Made Me in Behind and Before"

"You have made me in behind and before," meaning the revelation and concealment of the face of the Creator. This is because indeed, "His kingdom rules over all," and everything will return to its root because there is no place vacant of Him. But the difference is in the present or the future, because one who connects the two worlds discovers His clothing in the present, that everything that is done is a clothing for the revelation of the *Shechina* [Divinity].

This is deemed the present, meaning that now, too, he comes out in royal attire and evidently shows that the rider is not subordinate to the horse. But although it seemingly appears that the horse leads its rider, the truth is that the horse is provoked to any movement only by the sensation of the rider's bridle and headstall. This is called "The construction of the stature of the *Shechina*," and it is also called "face-to-face."

31. Baal HaSulam, *Shamati*, Article No. 17, "What Does It Mean that the Sitra Achra Is Called '*Malchut* without a Crown'?"

Our sages said, "Anyone who is proud, the Creator says, 'He and I cannot dwell in the same abode,'" as he makes two authorities. However, when one is in a state of *Ein*, and annuls himself before the Root, meaning that one's sole intention is only to bestow, like the Root, you find that there is only one authority here—the authority of the Creator. Then, all that one receives in the world is only in order to bestow upon the Creator.

This is the meaning of what he had said, "The whole world was created only for me, and I, to serve my Maker." For this reason, I must receive all the degrees in the world so that I can give everything to the Creator, which is called "to serve my Maker."

32. Baal HaSulam, "Introduction to The Study of the Ten Sefirot," Items 68-69

All the inclinations, tendencies, and properties instilled in man, with which to serve one's friends, all these tendencies and natural properties are required for the work of the Creator.

To begin with, they were created and imprinted in man only because of their final role—the ultimate purpose of man, as it is written, "No outcast shall be cast out from Him." One needs them all so as to complement oneself in the ways of reception of the abundance and to complete the will of the Creator.

This is the meaning of "Everyone who is called by My name, I have created him for My glory" (Isaiah 43:7), and also "All that the Lord has worked was for His sake" (Proverbs 16:4). However, in the meantime, man has been given a whole world to develop and complete all these natural inclinations and qualities in him by engaging in them with people, thus yielding them suitable for their purpose.

It is as our sages said, "One must say, 'The world was created for me,'" for all the people in the world are required for a person, as they develop and qualify the attributes and inclinations of every individual to become a fit tool for His work.

Thus, we must understand the essence of the love of the Creator from the properties of love by which one person relates to another. The love of the Creator is necessarily given through these qualities, since they were only imprinted in man for His sake to begin with.

33. Baal HaSulam, "You Have Made Me in Behind and Before"

One who has not yet come to dedicate all his movements to the Creator alone, and the horse does not equalize its movements to the rider's bridle and headstall, but appears to do the opposite...

and crowns the handmaid on the mistress, this is discerned as "behind." That is, you should not think that you are drawing away from *Kedusha* [holiness], for "that which comes into your mind shall not be at all."

Thus says the Lord: "Surely with a mighty hand," etc., "For the outcast shall not be cast out from Him," and the whole wheel turns to come to the *Kedusha*, to its root. Therefore, although it seems that the horse leads the rider by its ignoble desire, the truth is not so. It is the rider who leads the horse to his destination. However, it is not apparent in the present, but in the future. Hence, in this way there is also contact, but it is back to back, meaning not according to the will of the one who dresses or the will of the dresser.

34. Baal HaSulam, "The Freedom"

The whole of reality seen in the nature of this world is only because they are extended and taken from laws and conducts of upper, spiritual worlds.

35. Baal HaSulam, "The Essence of the Wisdom of Kabbalah"

The lower is studied from the higher. Thus, one must first attain the upper roots the way they are in spirituality, above any imagination and with pure attainment. And once he has thoroughly attained the upper roots with his own mind, he may examine the tangible branches in this world and know how each branch relates to its root in the upper world, in all its orders, in quantity and quality.

36. Baal HaSulam, "Introduction to The Study of the Ten Sefirot," Item 156

There is a strict condition during the engagement in this wisdom not to materialize the matters with imaginary and corporeal issues. This is because thus they breach, "You shall not make unto you a statue or any image."
In that event, one is rather harmed instead of receiving benefit.

37. Baal HaSulam, *The Study of the Ten Sefirot*, Part Two, Chapter One, Item 5

The entire reality and all the creations that are destined to come into the *Olamot*, already exist in *Ein Sof*. Moreover, they exist there in their full glory and perfection, as it is destined to appear in the *Olamot*.

Thus you evidently see, that all the desires that are destined to appear, already appeared and were revealed in *Ein Sof*. They appear there in their perfect, complete state, and it is the completeness and the fulfillment, namely the *Ohr Elyon*, that fathered and created these desires.

38. Baal HaSulam, "Foreword to The Book of Zohar," Item 12

The thought has no perception whatsoever in the essence. Moreover, we do not even know our own essence. I feel and know that I take up space in the world, that I am solid, warm, and that I think, and other such manifestations of the operations of my essence. But if you ask me what is my own essence, from which all these manifestations stem, I do not know what to reply to you.

You therefore see that Providence has prevented us from attaining any essence. We attain only manifestations and images of operations that stem from the essences.

39. Baal HaSulam, *The Study of the Ten Sefirot*, "Inner Light," Part One, Chapter One, Item 1

Bear in mind, that the entire wisdom of Kabbalah is founded on spiritual matters that do not take up time or space.

40. Baal HaSulam, "Introduction to The Book of Zohar, Item 17

Our body, with all its trifle incidents and possessions, is not at all our real body. Our real, eternal, and complete body already exists in *Ein Sof*.

41. Baal HaSulam, "Introduction to The Book of Zohar, Item 17

This body does not blemish us in any way since it is destined to expire and die, and is only here for the time necessary for its cancellation and acquisition of our eternal form.

42. Baal HaSulam, *Shamati*, Article No. 4, "What Is the Reason for the Heaviness One Feels when Annulling before the Creator in the Work?"

The essence of one's work is only to come to feel the existence of the Creator, meaning to feel the existence of the Creator, that "the whole earth is full of His glory," and this will be one's entire work. That is, all the energy one puts into the work will be only to achieve this, and nothing else.

One should not be misled into having to acquire anything. Rather, there is only one thing a person needs: faith in the Creator. He should not think of anything, meaning that the only reward that he wants for his work should be to be rewarded with faith in the Creator.

43. Baal HaSulam, "Peace in the World"

Everything in reality, good or bad, and even the most harmful in the world, has a right to exist and must not be destroyed and eradicated from the world. We must only mend and reform it because any observation of the work of creation is enough to teach us about the greatness and perfection of its Operator and Creator. Therefore, we must understand and be very careful when casting a flaw on any item of creation, saying it is redundant and superfluous, as that would be slander about its Operator.

44. Baal HaSulam, "Peace in the World"

Because the Creator meticulously watches over all the elements in His creation, not letting anyone destroy a single thing in His domain, but only reform it and make it useful and good, all the reformers of the above-mentioned kind will vanish from the earth, and bad qualities will not vanish. They exist and count the degrees of development that they must still traverse until they complete their ripening.

At that time, the bad attributes themselves will turn to good and useful ones, as the Creator had initially planned for them.

45. Baal HaSulam, "The Essence of the Wisdom of Kabbalah"

Kabbalists have found that the form of the four worlds named *Atzilut*, *Beria*, *Yetzira*, and *Assiya*, beginning with the first, highest world, called *Atzilut*, down to this corporeal, tangible world, called *Assiya*, is exactly the same in every item and event. This means that everything that eventuates and occurs in the first world is found unchanged in the next world, below it, too. It is likewise in all the worlds that follow it, down to this tangible world.

There is no difference between them, but only a difference of degree perceived in the substance of the elements of reality in each and every world.

46. Baal HaSulam, *The Study of the Ten Sefirot*, "Inner Observation," Part One, Chapter Nine, Item 34

The spiritual definition of time, you must understand that time is essentially defined by us only as a sensation of movements. Our imagination pictures and devises a certain number of consecutive movements, which it discriminates one by one, and translates them like a certain amount of "time."

Thus, if one had been in a state of complete rest with one's environment, he would not even be aware of the concept of time.

47. Baal HaSulam, *Shamati*, Article No. 75, "There Is a Discernment of the Next World, and There Is a Discernment of This World"

There is a discernment of "the next world," and there is a discernment of "this world." The next world is called "faith," and this world is called "attainment."

It is written about the next world, "They shall be satiated and delighted," meaning that there is no end to the satiation. This is so because everything that is received by faith has no limits. Conversely, what is received through attainment already has limits since anything that comes in the *Kelim* [vessels] of the lower one, the lower one limits it. Hence, there is a limit to the discernment of this world.

48. Baal HaSulam, *Shamati*, Article No. 67, "Depart from Evil"

Who thinks that he is deceiving his friend is really deceiving the Creator, since besides man's body there is only the Creator. This is because it is the essence of creation that man is called "creature" only with respect to himself. The Creator wants man to feel that he is a separate reality from Him; but other than this, it is all "The whole earth is full of His glory."

Hence, when lying to one's friend, one is lying to the Creator; and when saddening one's friend, one is saddening the Creator.

49. RABASH, Article No. 19 (1990), "Why Is the Torah Called 'Middle Line' in the Work? – 2"

The Ari writes (*Talmud Eser Sefirot*, Part 13, Item 152), "There is the matter of *Se'arot* [hairs], which cover the light, so they do not enjoy the light as long as they are unworthy, since they might blemish." The thing is that we must believe that the Creator gave us a desire and yearning to do good deeds. And as long as one is unworthy, he must not feel that the Creator compels him to do good deeds. This is why the Creator hides Himself in dresses, and this dressing is called *Lo Lishma* [not for Her sake]. In other words, sometimes the Creator hides Himself in a clothing of friends.

50. RABASH, Article No. 11 (1990), "What Placing the Hanukkah Candle on the Left Means in the Work"

"Concealment of the face." In other words, the Creator hides Himself in the clothing of the friends, and in this way he does the Creator's will.

If he thanks the Creator for helping him through the concealment—meaning that now he has the choice to say that he is working because of the friends and he has no contact with the Creator, or that he believes that the Creator hid Himself in the clothing of the friends, and by that he engages in Torah and *Mitzvot*, and if he chooses and says that only the Creator helped him to be able to do good deeds by clothing in a clothing of friends, and he thanks the Creator for this—it brings upon him a great ascent: to be rewarded with the revelation of the face of the Creator. In other words, the Creator gives him a thought and desire to do the Creator's will, since now he has some illumination from above by sentencing above reason. This is why the Creator helped him, so that through the *Achoraim* [posterior], he will later be rewarded with the *Panim* [anterior/face] of the Creator. This means that he has been rewarded with being collected knowingly.

51. RABASH, Article No. 217, "Run My Beloved"

The Creator has prepared for us a whole world, as our sages said, "One must say, 'The world was created for me'" (Sanhedrin 37a), meaning that he should pray for the entire world. Therefore, when he comes to pray and has contact with the Creator, although he himself is not sick at the moment, he can pray for his contemporaries, meaning to extend mercies so that no one in his generation will lack abundance.

It is a great rule that the person himself is called "a creature," meaning only he alone. Other than him it is already considered the holy *Shechina*. It follows that when he prays for his contemporaries, it is considered that he is praying for the holy *Shechina*, who is in exile and needs all the salvations. This is the meaning of eternity, and precisely in this manner, the light of mercy can be revealed.

52. RABASH, Article No. 280, "This World and the Next World – 1"

This world is regarded as the state in which one is while he begins to enter the path of Torah, and this is the situation he is in now, in his beginning. This is why it is called "this world," and it is only a corridor.

Afterward, when he comes to the life of Torah itself, it is called "the next world," which is regarded as the next state, after he successfully went through the path of Torah, called "a corridor".

53. RABASH, Article No. 236, "The Whole Earth Is Full of His Glory"

There is no reality in the world besides Godliness, and all the concealment is only in one's sensations.

54. RABASH, Article No. 21, "Concerning Above Reason"

The whole matter of evil that is in man is not in finding the evil, since everyone has this evil, called "will to receive in order to receive," which is self-love. Instead, the difference is entirely in the disclosure of the evil. In other words, not every person sees and feels that self-love is bad and harmful, since a person doesn't see that engagement in satisfying his will to receive, called "self-love," will harm him.

Yet, when he begins to do the holy work on the path of truth, meaning when he wishes to achieve *Dvekut* [adhesion] with the Creator, so all his actions will be for the Creator, by that he receives a little more light that shines for him each time, and then he begins to feel self-love as a bad thing.

It is a gradual process. Each time he sees that this is what obstructs him from achieving *Dvekut* with the Creator, he sees more clearly each time how it—the will to receive—is his real enemy, just as King Solomon referred to the evil inclination as "an enemy."

55. RABASH, Article No. 17, Part 1 (1984) "Concerning the Importance of Friends"

If one has love of friends, the rule in love is that you want to see the friends' merits and not their faults. Hence, if one sees some fault in one's friend, it is not a sign that his friend is at fault, but that the seer is at fault, meaning that because his love of friends is flawed, he sees faults in his friend.

Therefore, now he should not see to his friend's correction. Rather, he himself needs correction. It follows from the above-said that he should not see to the correction of his friend's faults, which he sees in his friend, but he himself needs to correct the flaw he has created in the love of friends. And when he corrects himself, he will see only his friend's merits and not his faults.

56. RABASH, Article No. 645, "By Your Actions, We Know You"

It is written in *The Zohar*, "There is no place vacant of Him." Yet, we do not feel it for our lack of tools of sensation.

We can see that with a radio receiver, which receives all the signals in the world, the receiver does not create the sounds. Rather, the sound exists in the world, but before we had the receiving device, we did not detect the sounds although they did exist in reality.

Likewise, we can understand that "There is no place vacant of Him," but we need a receiving device. That receiving device is called *Dvekut* [adhesion] and "equivalence of form," which is a desire to bestow. When we have this machine, we will immediately feel that there is no place vacant of Him, but rather "The whole earth is full of His glory."

57. RABASH, Article No. 124, "To Serve Me"

"The whole world was created only to serve me." According to the interpretation of Baal HaSulam, it means that all the faults that a person sees in others, he believes that they are his. Therefore, he has what to correct. It follows that the whole world serves him by providing him with his faults, and he does not need to look by himself. Instead, they are doing him a big favor by providing him with his flaws.

58. RABASH, Letter No. 19

And if you wish to say, "What are the *Sefirot* and degrees themselves?" We say that this is unattainable because our attainment is only with respect to His desire to do good to His creations. Therefore, one should attain only that which is related to man's attainment, meaning a person's impression from the upper light that appears through the *Sefira* to the creatures, but not the *Sefira* itself.

The multiplication of *Sefirot* is only according to the attainment of the lower ones, depending on their attainment, and each one has a special skill according to one's labor. Besides that, everything is equal because there are no changes in spirituality. This is why we say about the *Sefirot* themselves that they are regarded as "there is no thought or perception in Him at all."

59. RABASH, Article No. 236, "The Whole Earth Is Full of His Glory"

The expansion of the upper light is clothed in the whole of reality and is called "the sustainer of reality." It appears in all the dresses that exist in the world, meaning in every corporeal thing before us. Everything is the light of the Creator, whether in dresses of Torah, meaning the letters of the Torah, or in the letters of the prayer, or in mundane things. The only difference is in the receiver, namely those who feel.

There are people who feel that the light of the Creator is dressed only in Torah and prayer. There are people who feel the light of the Creator also in combinations of letters of mundane things, and there are those who do not feel even in combinations of letters of Torah and prayer that it is the light of the Creator in the manner of "Who fills the whole of reality."

60. RABASH, Article No. 19 (1990), "Why Is the Torah Called 'Middle Line' in the Work? – 2"

One must believe that "There is none else besides Him," meaning that it is the Creator who compels him to do the good deeds. But since he is still unworthy of knowing that it is the Creator who commits him, the Creator dresses Himself in dresses of flesh and blood, through which the Creator performs these actions. Thus, the Creator acts in the form of *Achoraim* [posterior].

In other words, the person sees people's faces but he should believe that behind the faces stands the Creator and performs these actions. That is, behind the man stands the Creator and compels him to do the deeds that the Creator wants. It follows that the Creator does everything, but the person regards what he sees and not what he should believe.

61. *Zohar for All*, *VaYetze* [And Jacob Went Out], "Upper Righteous and Lower Righteous," Item 139

The Zohar speaks nothing of corporeal incidents, but of the upper worlds, where there is no sequence of times as it is in corporeality. Spiritual time is elucidated by change of forms and degrees that are above time and place.

62. *Zohar for All*, "Introduction of The Book of Zohar," "On the Night of the Bride," Item 138

It is a law that the creature cannot receive disclosed evil from the Creator, for it is a flaw in the glory of the Creator for the creature to perceive Him as an evildoer, for this is unbecoming of the complete Operator. Hence, when one feels bad, denial of the Creator's guidance lies upon him and the superior Operator is concealed from him to that same extent. This is the greatest punishment in the world.

Thus, the sensation of good and evil in relation to His guidance brings with it the sensation of reward and punishment, for one who exerts to not part from faith in the Creator is rewarded even when he tastes a bad taste in Providence. And if he does not exert, he will have a punishment because he is separated from faith in the Creator.

63. *Zohar for All*, *Lech Lecha* [Go Forth], "For Who Is God, Save the Lord? And Who Is a Rock, Save Our God?", Item 330

How great are the deeds of the Creator? The art and painting of a man are like the artisanship and the depiction of the world. In other words, man comprises the entire deed of the world, and he is called "a small world."

64. *Zohar for All*, *Toldot* [Generations], "These Are the Generations of Isaac," Item 3

Anyone who engages in Torah sustains the world and sustains each and every operation in the world in its proper way. Also, there is not an organ in a man's body that does not have a corresponding creation in the world.

This is so because as man's body divides into organs and they all stand degree over degree, established one atop the other and are all one body, similarly, the world, meaning all creations in the world are many organs standing one atop the other, and they are all one body. And when they are all corrected they will actually be one body. And everything, man and the world will be like the Torah because the whole of Torah is organs and joints standing one atop the other. And when the world is corrected they will become one body.

65. *Zohar for All*, *Pekudei* [Accounts], "These Are the Accounts of the Tabernacle," Item 17

"Which is being shown to you." "You" is the mirror that does not shine, *Malchut*, which showed him within her all those forms. And Moses saw each of them in its corrected form, as one who sees within a crystal lamp, within a mirror that shows all the forms. And when Moses looked into them, he found them perplexing, since there, in *Malchut*, everything stood in its spiritual form, but each form equalized its form to the imaginary form in this world, in the Tabernacle.

It follows that two forms were apparent in everything: the spiritual one and the imaginary one. This is why Moses was bewildered; he did not know which of them to grasp. The Creator told him, "You with your signs, and I with Mine," that Moses would perceive the imaginary signs in everything, and the Creator perceives the spiritual signs of everything, and then the spiritual form is placed over the imaginary form. Then Moses was reconciled in all the work of the Tabernacle.

66. *Zohar for All*, *Nasso*, "The Holy Idra Rabah," Item 297

The sum of all things, *Atik* of *Atikin* [pl. of *Atik*] and ZA, are all one, from the perspective of their *Atzmut* [self], and everything is above time from the perspective of their *Atzmut*. Was, is, and will be are the same in them, everything is, everything was, and everything will be. In Godliness, there is no matter of before or after. Also, there is no change of operation there from the perspective of their *Atzmut*, such as from mercy to judgment, since He will not change in the future, He did not change in the past, and He is not changing in the present. Rather, He is corrected in these corrections for the lower ones, and the form that contains all the forms, ZA, is completed. This is the form of Adam [man], who comprises male and female, the form that includes all the names, for ZA is called *HaVaYaH*, a name that contains all the names, the form in which all the forms are seen. It is not an actual form, but rather seemingly this form.

67. *Zohar for All*, *Nasso*, "The Holy Idra Rabah," Item 299

Everything is Godliness, above time, place, and change. All those degrees and corrections we discern in Godliness are only various concealments and covers toward the lower ones, since the ten *Sefirot* are ten kinds of covers of His *Atzmut* [self]. Likewise, all the imaginary images of time and place and actions are but various covers of His Godliness that seem that way to the lower ones.

As man is not affected or changes at all because of the covers that he covers in, and only his friends are affected by his disappearance or appearance, so His Godliness does not change and is not affected whatsoever by those degrees and corrections and names in time, place, and changes of actions that the lower ones discern in His covers. Rather, we must know that those covers also serve as disclosures.

Moreover, to the extent of the cover that there is in each name and correction, so is the extent of disclosure of the Creator that is in it. One who is rewarded with receiving the measure of the covers properly is then rewarded with the covers becoming for him measures of disclosure. One who learns must remember these things during the learning so he will not fail in his thought.

68. *Zohar for All*, *Mishpatim* [Ordinances], "The Grandfather," Item 165

It is written, "And God saw all that He has done, and behold, it was very good." "Good" is the good angel. "Very" is the angel of death. The Creator provides His corrections to all until even the angel of death returns to being very good.

69. Ramchal, "The Rules of the Book, *The Zeal of the Lord of Hosts*"

The whole world, in all its degrees, is a "great man," and man is a "small world," and there is in one only what is in the other.

70. Rabbi Abraham Yehoshua of Apt, *Ohev Ysrael, Beresheet*

A person sees all of the afflictions but his own. The advice for this is to look at the one who is in front of him. If he sees that another person did something wrong, he should think, "Why did the Creator make me see this thing if not because this affliction touches the walls of my own house, and because of the incitement of the inclination, my eyes could not see?"

71. Ecclesiastes 1:9

That which was is that which will be, and that which was done is that which will be done, and there is nothing new under the sun.

72. Rabbi Menachem Mendel of Kotzk, *The Dawn Star*

Death is nothing, like a person moving from one flat to another. However, the smart one chooses a nicer flat than the first.

73. Rabbi Tzadok HaCohen of Lublin, *Kometz HaMincha*

It is written in *The Zohar* that the next world is not renewed at that time, but has already been but was concealed. Interpretation: This world is called "the world of falsehood," and the next world is called "the world of truth." A lie is something that stops, that has no persistence; it is all the matters of this world, which have existence in the imagination but are not true and are destined to be revoked. Conversely, the next world, he wants to say, "is the abstraction of every thing from the imagination to the truth of that matter," that is, the force of that force that exists forever, and is eternal.

74. Rabbi Tzadok HaCohen of Lublin, *The Thoughts of the Diligent*

"When the Lord brought back the captive ones of Zion, we were as though dreaming." According to the truth that will be revealed then, all the matters that are regarded as true in this world, will also be only imagination, as this whole world is called "the world of falsehood." Although the truth in it is not real and it is impossible to attain the real truth in it. But one who reaches a degree where he tastes from the fruits of his actions in the next world in this world, meaning see his world in his life, it means that he will attain the world of truth in the physical life of this world.

75. Ramchal, *Adir BaMarom*, p 459

In truth, one who achieves real knowledge can see three things: the true, hidden guidance, the outer appearance of the guidance, which is not true, from where this appearance stems, and how it connects to the real guidance.

76. *Pirkei Avot*, 4:16

Rabbi Yaakov says, "This world is like a corridor to the next world. Prepare yourself in the corridor so you will enter the living room."

77. Rabbi Menachem Mendel of Kotzk

We make nothing new; our work is only to illuminate what is hidden within man.

78. Raaiah Kook, *Lights of Repentance*

In the heart of existence of the real life lies repentance, since it preceded the world, and before sin came, its repentance had already been prepared. Hence, there is nothing as certain in the world as repentance, and in the end, everything will return to correction.

79. *Degel Machaneh Ephraim, BeShalach* [When Jacob Sent]

One who truly wants to serve the Creator must include himself with all creations, connect himself with all the souls, include himself with them, and they with him. That is, you should leave for yourself only what is needed for connecting the *Shechina* [Divinity]. For this reason, one must include himself with all the people and with all creations, and raise everything to their root, to the correction of the *Shechina*.

80. Rabbi Nachman of Breslov, *Likutey Moharan*, First Edition, Mark 5

Every person should say, "The whole world was created only for me" (Sanhedrin 37). It follows that if the whole world has been created for me, I have to look and delve into the correction of the world at all times, satisfy the needs of the world, and pray for them.

81. *Degel Machaneh Ephraim, BeShalach* [When Jacob Sent]

One who wants to serve the Creator in truth must have two discernments:

1) The uniqueness of the deed, meaning as though he is alone in the world, and the Creator is revealed to him without clothing. It is as it is written, "No man is to come up with you." When he wants to serve the Creator, he will be alone and no one will come up with him.
2) There is another discernment: A servant of the Creator must include himself with all creations, connect himself with all the souls, include himself with them, and they with him. That is, you should leave for yourself only what is needed for connecting the *Shechina* [Divinity], so to speak. This requires closeness and many people, as it is written (Sanhedrin 70a), "Closeness of righteous is good for them and good for the world," for the more people serve the Creator, the more the light of the *Shechina* appears to them. For this reason, one

must include himself with all the people and with all creations, and raise everything to its root for the correction of the *Shechina*, so to speak.

82. Raaiah Kook, *Orot HaKodesh*

Past, present, and future are not divided by the truth of what there is. That which was is that which will be, and that which was done is that which will be done, and what was already done and what will be done in the future is ongoing and done in the present, always and promptly.

83. Raaiah Kook, *Letters*

Any content of time, even of the concept of past and future in general, is only one of the ways of human understanding. With regard to the upper one, it is irrelevant. Hence, from the perspective of the upper, absolute reality, there is no such reality as a potential that has no actual, since over time, anything that is in potential also becomes actual, and the extension of time is irrelevant with regard to the upper one. Therefore, we can say, "That which will be done is already present."

One who brings his desire and depth of his life to the height of the uppermost Godly adhesion, which stands at the top of the world, above the procession of times, to the extent of one's elevation, the differences between potential and actual—and therefore between future and present—become fainter until they form no partition at all.

PART 6
States on the Spiritual Path

1

The Preparation Period

1. Baal HaSulam, *Shamati*, Article No. 204, "The Purpose of the Work – 2"

During the preparation period, all the work is in the nos, that is, in the "no," as it is written, "and they shall be afflicted in a land that is not." However, with matters of the tongue, which is considered "me," one must first be awarded the discernment of love.

Yet, during the preparation, there is only work in the form of no's, regarded as "You shall not have," and by the profusion of no's, we come to the point of God[1] of *Hesed* [mercy]. But prior to that, there are many no's, which is other gods, many no's. This is so because from *Lo Lishma* [not for Her sake] we come to *Lishma* [for Her sake].

Since the *Sitra Achra* [other side] provides support, even afterwards, when we work and extend *Kedusha* [holiness], still, when she takes the support, we fall from the degree, and then she takes all the abundance that they extended. By this, the *Sitra Achra* has the power to control a person so he will be compelled to satisfy their wish. And he has no other choice but to raise himself to a higher degree.

Then the sequence begins anew, as before, with the forty-nine gates of *Tuma'a* [impurity]. This means that one walks in the degrees of *Kedusha* until the forty-nine gates. But there she has control to take all the vitality and abundance until a person falls each time into a higher gate of *Tuma'a*, since "God has made them one opposite the other."

When one comes into the 49th gate, he can no longer raise himself until the Creator comes and redeems him. And then "He has swallowed down riches, and he shall vomit them up again; God shall cast them out of his belly." This means that now one takes all the abundance and vitality that the *Klipa* [shell] was taking from all of the forty-nine gates of *Kedusha*. This is the meaning of "the looting of the sea."

Yet, it is impossible to be redeemed before we feel the exile. And when we walk on the forty-nine, we feel the exile, and the Creator redeems on the 50th gate. The only difference between *Gola* [exile] and *Ge'ula* [redemption] is in the *Aleph*, which is *Alupho Shel Olam* [Champion of the world]. Hence, if one does not properly attain the exile, too, he is deficient in the degree.

2. Baal HaSulam, Letter No. 19

"Grace is deceitful and beauty is vain, but a woman that fears the Lord, she shall be praised." This means that during the preparation, beauty and grace appear as the essence of perfection for which one yearns and longs. However, at the time of correction, when the earth is "full of the knowledge of the Lord," "I shall see an opposite world," as only fear and longing are the desired perfection. Then one feels that during the time of preparation they were lying to themselves.

3. Baal HaSulam, Letter No. 17

The purpose of the soul when it comes in the body is to be rewarded with returning to its root and with *Dvekut* [adhesion] with Him while clothed in the body, as it is written, "To love the Lord your God, to walk in all His ways, to keep His commandments, and to adhere to Him." You see that the matter ends with "to adhere to Him," meaning as it was prior to clothing in the body.

However, great preparation is required, which is to walk in all His ways. Yet, who knows the ways of the Creator? Indeed, this is the meaning of "Torah that has 613 ways." He who walks on them will finally be purified until his body no longer forms an iron partition between him and his Maker, as it is written, "And I will take away the stony heart from your flesh." Then he shall adhere to his Maker just as he was before the clothing of the soul in the body.

It turns out that there are three discernments: 1) Israel is one who exerts to return to his root; 2) The Creator, namely the root he longs for; 3) The 613 ways of the Torah by which one purifies one's soul and body. This is the spice, as it is written, "I have created the evil inclination; I have created for it the Torah as a spice."

However, these three are actually one and the same. In the end, any servant of the Creator attains them as one, unique, and unified discernment, and they only appear to be divided into three because of one's incompleteness in the work of the Creator.

4. RABASH, Article No. 28 (1991), "What Are Holiness and Purity, in the Work?"

We must observe the Torah and *Mitzvot* so it will bring us purity, where purity means purification of the *Kelim* from the will to receive for oneself, which is called "dirt," since it is in disparity of form from the Creator, who is all to bestow. For this reason, before we clean the *Kelim*, it is impossible to place within them anything good, for anything we might place in a dirty *Kli* [vessel] will be spoiled. Hence, we must receive good advice, things that will purify our *Kelim* [vessels], which is called "making kosher [fit to be eaten according to Jewish laws]" and "preparation" so we can receive the delight and pleasure. Because of this, we were given 613 *Mitzvot* [commandments/good deeds], which *The Zohar* calls "613 counsels".

5. RABASH, Article No. 2 (1987), "The Importance of Recognition of Evil"

The work that is the preparation to enter true spirituality. That is, when he takes upon himself to believe in the importance of the Creator above reason, he must take upon himself that he wants to go specifically with faith above reason. Even though he was given the reason to see the greatness of the Creator within reason, he prefers faith above reason due to "because of the honor of the Creator, conceal the matter."

This is regarded as wanting to go above reason. Precisely then he becomes a *Kli* [vessel] that is fit to receive spirituality, since he has no concern at all for himself, but all his intentions are only to bestow upon the Creator. For this reason there is no longer fear that should he be given some illumination it will go into the vessels of reception, since he is always trying to exit self-love.

Baal HaSulam said that as the will to receive wants only to receive and not bestow, even where it is told to work above reason it is only regarded as bestowing and not receiving because a person suffers where he has to go above reason. The evidence of this is that since the body is always concerned with receiving delight and pleasure in everything it does, and since if a person must work above reason, the body is dissatisfied with it, therefore, when a person is taught to go above reason he begins the work of bestowal. It therefore follows that when one prefers to go by way of above reason it is safeguarding that he will walk on the right path, which is the route for achieving *Dvekut* with the Creator.

6. RABASH, Article No. 875, "Three Lines – 4"

Even during the preparation, there is a place where he can receive illumination from above. Although this illumination cannot be permanent in him, even some connection with spirituality is a great profit because one cannot evaluate even the slightest contact with spirituality.

This right line is called "truth" because wholeness is built on the basis of truth. That is, he does not say that he has great possessions in *Torah and Mitzvot*, meaning feeling, attainment, and understanding. Rather, he says that whatever he has, whatever he is given from above, even if he feels that he is in a worse state than what he received by education, he still regards it above reason as having great importance to him that he has been rewarded with having some contact with spirituality.

7. RABASH, Article No. 5 (1987), "What Is the Advantage in the Work More than in the Reward?"

It is written in *The Zohar*, "For the whole of the Torah is the names of the Creator." Also, a complete man is one who has been rewarded with "The Torah and the Creator and Israel are one." Therefore, indeed, greeting the *Shechina* is very important because the purpose is for man to achieve this degree.

But to come to greet the *Shechina* requires prior preparation, for one to be fit for it. In the words of our sages, this is called "As He is merciful, so you are merciful." This is the interpretation of the verse, "and to cleave unto Him, cleave unto His attributes." It means, as explained in the book *Matan Torah* [*The Giving of the Torah*], that only by a person working in love of others can he achieve *Dvekut* [adhesion] with the Creator. There are many names to this: "Instilling of the *Shechina*," "attainment the Torah," "greeting the *Shechina*," etc.

The main preparation, which is called "labor," is that one must prepare oneself to annul one's authority, meaning one's self. We can call this hospitality [greeting guests], meaning that he cancels the view of landlords and craves the view of Torah, which is called "annulling of authority." Naturally, he becomes the guest of the Creator, who is the Host of the entire world.

2

Concealment and Revelation

1. Baal HaSulam, Letter No. 22

"My beloved is like a gazelle"? Our sages said, "As the gazelle turns his face back when he flees, when the Creator leaves Israel, He turns back His face." I interpreted for you that then the face returns to being in the *Achoraim* [back/posterior], meaning craving and longing to cling to Israel once more. This begets in Israel longing and craving to adhere to the Creator, too, and the measure of the longing and craving is actually the face itself, as it is written in "Bless My Soul," by Rabbi Yehuda HaLevi, "My face is to your prayer when you run to meet the Lord God."

Therefore, the most powerful at this time is only to persist and increase the longing and the yearning, for by this appears the face.

2. Baal HaSulam, "You Have Made Me in Behind and Before"

One who has not yet come to dedicate all his movements to the Creator alone, and the horse does not equalize its movements to the rider's bridle and headstall, but appears to do the opposite... and crowns the handmaid on the mistress, this is discerned as "behind." That is, you should not think that you are drawing away from *Kedusha* [holiness], for "that which comes into your mind shall not be at all."

Thus says the Lord: "Surely with a mighty hand," etc., "For the outcast shall not be cast out from Him," and the whole wheel turns to come to the *Kedusha*, to its root. Therefore, although it seems that the horse leads the rider by its ignoble desire, the truth is not so. It is the rider who leads the horse to his destination. However, it is not apparent in the present, but in the future. Hence, in this way there is also contact, but it is back to back, meaning not according to the will of the one who dresses or the will of the dresser.

3. Baal HaSulam, *Shamati*, Article No. 174, "Concealment"

Concerning the concealment, which is a correction, had it not been for that, man would have been unable to attain any completeness, since he would not be worthy of attaining the importance of the matter. However, when there is concealment, the thing becomes important to him. Even though one cannot appreciate the importance as it truly is, the concealment grants it merit. To the extent that one senses the concealment, a bedding of importance is formed within him.

It is like rungs. He climbs rung by rung until he comes to his designated place. This means that he achieves a certain measure of importance with which he can at least endure, though His true importance and sublimity are immeasurable, but nonetheless a measure that will suffice him to persist.

However, concealment in itself is not considered concealment. Concealment is measured by the demand. The greater the demand for something, the more the concealment is evident. And now we can understand the meaning of "The whole earth is full of His glory." Although we believe it, the concealment still fills the whole earth.

It is written about the future: "For I … will be unto her a wall of fire round about, and I will be the glory in the midst of her." Fire means concealment. But still, glory is in the midst of her, meaning that then the glory will be revealed. This is because then the demand will be so great, even though there will be concealment then, too. And the difference is that at this time there is concealment, but no demand. Hence, this is considered "exile." Then, however, although there will be concealment, there will also be demand, and this is what is important—only the demand.

4. Baal HaSulam, Letter No. 18

First thing in the morning, when he rises from his sleep, he should sanctify the first moment with *Dvekut* with Him, pour out his heart to the Creator to keep him throughout the twenty-four hours of the day so that no idle thought will come into his mind, and he will not consider it impossible or above nature.

Indeed, it is the image of nature that makes an iron partition, and one should cancel nature's partitions that he feels. Rather, first he must believe that nature's partitions do not cut off from Him. Afterward, he should pray from the bottom of his heart, even for something that is above his natural desire.

Understand this always, even when forms that are not of *Kedusha* [holiness] traverse you, and they will instantly stop when you remember. See that you pour out your heart that henceforth the Creator will save you from cessations of *Dvekut* with Him. Gradually, your heart will grow accustomed to the Creator and will yearn to adhere to Him in truth, and the Lord's desire will succeed by you.

5. Baal HaSulam, "Introduction to The Study of the Ten Sefirot," Item 107

After one is rewarded with the illumination of the face to such an extent that each sin he had committed, even the deliberate ones, is turned and becomes a *Mitzva* for him, one rejoices with all the torment and affliction he had ever suffered since the time he was placed in the two states of concealment of the face. This is because it is they that brought him all those sins, which have now become *Mitzvot* by the illumination of His face, Who performs wonders.

And any sorrow and trouble that drove him out of mind and he failed with mistakes, as in the first concealment, or failed with sins, as in the double concealment, has now become a cause and preparation for keeping a *Mitzva* and the reception of eternal and wondrous reward for it. Therefore, any sorrow has turned for him into a great joy and any evil to wonderful good.

6. Baal HaSulam, *Shamati*, Article No. 83, "Concerning the Right Vav and the Left Vav"

In any state one is in, he can be a servant of the Creator since he does not need anything, but does everything above reason. It turns out that one does not need any *Mochin* with which to be the servant of the Creator.

Now we can interpret what is written, "Set up a table before me, against my enemies." A table means, as it is written, "and sent her out of his house, and she departed his house, and went" (Deuteronomy 24:1-2). A *Shulchan* [table] is like *VeShlacha* [and sent her], meaning exit from the work.

We should interpret that even during the exits from the work, meaning in a state of decline, one still has a place to work. This means that when one prevails above reason during the declines, and says that the descents, too, were given to him from above, by this the enemies are canceled. This is so because the enemies thought that through the declines the person will reach utter lowliness and escape the campaign, but in the end the opposite occurred—the enemies were canceled.

This is the meaning of what is written, "the table that is before the Lord," that precisely in this manner does he receive the face of the Creator. This is the meaning of subduing all the judgments, even the harshest judgments, since he assumes the burden of the kingdom of heaven at all times. That is, he always finds a place for work, as it is written that Rabbi Shimon Bar-Yochai said, "There is no place to hide from You."

7. Baal HaSulam, "Introduction to The Study of the Ten Sefirot," Item 133

It is like a king who wished to select for himself the most loyal of his subjects in the country and bring them to work inside his palace. What did he do? He issued a decree that anyone who wished, young or old, would come to his palace to engage in the works inside his palace.

However, he appointed many of his servants to guard the palace gate and all the roads leading to it, and ordered them to cunningly deflect all those nearing his palace and divert them from the way that leads to the palace.

Naturally, all the people in the country began to run to the king's palace. But the diligent guards cunningly rejected them. Many of them overpowered them and came near the palace gate, but the guards at the gate were the most diligent, and if someone approached the gate, they diverted him and turned him away with great craftiness until one despaired and returned as he had come.

And so they came and went, and regained strength, and came and went again, and so on and so forth for several days and years until they grew weary of trying. Only the mighty ones among them, whose patience endured, defeated the guards and opened the gate. And they were instantly awarded seeing the king's face, who appointed each of them in his right place.

Of course, from that moment on, they had no further dealings with those guards, who diverted and mislead them and made their lives bitter for several days and years, running back and forth around the gate. This is because they have been rewarded with working and serving before the glory of the king's face inside his palace.

8. Baal HaSulam, *Shamati*, Article No. 181, "Honor"

Honor is something that stops the body, and to that extent it harms the soul. Hence, all the righteous who became famous and respected, it was a punishment. But the great righteous, when the Creator does not want them to lose by being famous as righteous, the Creator guards them from being honored, so as not to harm their souls.

Hence, to the extent that they are honored on one hand, on the other hand, they are faced with dissenters who degrade them with all kinds of degradations. To the extent that creates an equal weight to the honor given to a righteous, to that very extent the other side gives disgrace.

9. Baal HaSulam, Letter No. 39

Now they have defamed me in the eyes of the generation and have failed me on the path of my exalted work to bring contentment to my Maker. Who can forgive them this? Heaven will testify to my labor in all my strength to extend His holiness to that generation.

And yet, the *Sitra Achra* [other side] always finds her people, doers of her missions, setting obstacles before me wherever I turn to benefit others. Thus far are my words. "Those who are with us are more than those who are with them," and the Creator does not deny my reward. Bit by bit, I am paving the way, at times less, at times more, but always with profit (reward), until I am rewarded with taking down all the enemies of the Creator with the help of His great and terrible name.

As for you, do not fear the fear of fools. Those who slander, my little finger is bigger than their waist. So the Creator desired, and so He made me, and who will tell Him what to do and what to work? The merit of my law is greater than the merit of their fathers. Similarly, the contemporaries of Prophet Amos defamed him and said that the Creator had no one on whom to instill His *Shechina* [Divinity] but that stutterer, as it is written in the *Psikta* [a Midrash].

However, it is written, "A truthful lip shall be established forever, and a lying tongue is only momentary," for in the end, the truthful people are the winners. Amos remains alive and existing forever, and who has heard or knows what had happened to his adversaries?
So it is here. The sayers can harm only their own kind, so it follows that the storm swirls on the head of the wicked, the truth lives on and does not weaken by all the lies. Instead, it grows even stronger by them, like a sown field that is strengthened by the manure and dung that are thrown in. With the Creator's will, the blessing of the field increases and multiplies by them.

I still do not feel the harm that will come to me through them concerning the dissemination of my teaching, so I do not know how to calculate a way to instill light and save it from their evil. And yet, it is certain that if I feel any harm, I will take my revenge against them, as is the law of Torah, and I will contend forcefully with them. I will do all that is within the power of my hand to do, as it is the Creator I fear, and there is no other force but Him.

10. Baal HaSulam, "You Have Made Me in Behind and Before"

"You have made me in behind and before," meaning the revelation and concealment of the face of the Creator. This is because indeed, "His kingdom rules over all," and everything will return to its root because there is no place vacant of Him. But the difference is in the present or the future, because one who connects the two worlds discovers His clothing in the present, that everything that is done is a clothing for the revelation of the *Shechina [Divinity]*.

This is deemed the present, meaning that now, too, he comes out in royal attire and evidently shows that the rider is not subordinate to the horse. But although it seemingly appears that the horse leads its rider, the truth is that the horse is provoked to any movement only by the sensation of the rider's bridle and headstall. This is called "The construction of the stature of the *Shechina*," and it is also called "face-to-face."

11. Baal HaSulam, "You Have Made Me in Behind and Before"

Those who do His will, meaning reveal by themselves the royal attire in the present, are connected face to face through the good will of the one who dresses and the good will of the dresser, for precisely this is His wish.

This is the meaning of "Because you did not serve the Lord your God with gladness." You will serve Him anyhow, but the difference is that this way is "in siege and in distress," meaning unwillingly, and the other way is by reason of the abundance of all things, meaning willingly.

12. Baal HaSulam, *Shamati*, Article No. 42, "What Is the Acronym Elul in the Work?"

It is impossible to obtain disclosure before one receives the discernment of *Achoraim* [posterior], discerned as concealment of the Face, and to say that it is as important to him as the disclosure of the Face. It means that one should be as glad as though he has already acquired the disclosure of the Face.

However, one cannot persist and appreciate the concealment like the disclosure, except when one works in bestowal. At that time, one can say, "I do not care what I feel during the work because what is important to me is that I want to bestow upon the Creator. If the Creator understands that He will have more contentment if I work in a form of *Achoraim*, I agree."

However, if one still has sparks of reception, he comes to thoughts, and it is then hard for him to believe that the Creator leads the world in a manner of "good and doing good." This is the meaning of the letter *Yod* in the name *HaVaYaH*, which is the first letter, called "a black dot that has no white in it," meaning it is all darkness and concealment of the Face.

It means that when one comes to a state where one has no support, one's state becomes black, which is the lowest quality in the upper world, and that becomes the *Keter* to the lower one, as the *Kli* of *Keter* is a vessel of bestowal.

The lowest quality in the upper one is *Malchut*, which has nothing of its own, meaning that she does not have anything. Only in this manner is it called *Malchut*. It means that if one takes upon himself the kingdom of heaven—which is in a state of not having anything—gladly, afterward, it becomes *Keter*, which is a vessel of bestowal and the purest *Kli*. In other words, the reception of *Malchut* in a state of darkness subsequently becomes a *Kli* of *Keter*, which is a vessel of bestowal.

13. Baal HaSulam, "You Have Made Me in Behind and Before"

There are three discernments required of a man in the desirable path: surrender, division, sweetening, meaning "lights in deficient writing,"[1] since the light of this world was created out of darkness, "As the advantage of the light from within the darkness," and "What good is a candle during the day?" its light does not shine in the daytime. This is the meaning of the *Klipa* [shell/peel] that precedes the fruit. For this reason, he who becomes a partner to the Creator in the work of creation brings out the light from the darkness, meaning considers how lowly and ignoble one is compared to the *Kedusha* [holiness] of above, and how filthy are his clothes. Through it, the light becomes surrounded.

14. Baal HaSulam, Introduction to *A Sage's Fruit*, Vol. 4, "Three Partners"

It is impossible to attribute the bad to the Creator since he is the absolute good. Hence, as long as one feels bad states, he must say that they come from elsewhere, from the environment. But in truth, when one is rewarded with seeing only good and that there is no bad in the world, and everything is turned to good, then he is shown the truth, that the Creator did everything because He is almighty, and He alone did, does, and will do all the deeds.

15. Baal HaSulam, *Shamati*, Article No. 135, "Clean and Righteous Do Not Kill"

"The clean and righteous do not kill." A righteous is one who justifies the Creator: Whatever he feels, whether good or bad, he takes above reason. This is considered "right." Clean refers to the cleanness of the matter, the state as he sees it. This is so because "a judge has only what his eyes see." And if one does not understand the matter, or cannot attain the matter, he should not blur the forms as they seem to his eyes. This is considered "left," and he should nurture both.

16. Baal HaSulam, *Ohr HaBahir*

Spiritual revelation, whether emerging from concealment or some addition, extends and comes primarily through the power of the vessels and their quality, and does not depend at all on the upper light. It is so because the rule is that there is no change in the lights themselves from the beginning of the line to the bottom of *Assiya*. As it is in the beginning of the line, so it does not grow coarser or change when it is at the bottom of *Assiya*. It is also known that the upper light does not stop bestowing upon the lower ones even for a minute. Therefore, the whole matter of concealment, revelation, and changes, and any change, depend only on the merit of the vessels.

17. Baal HaSulam, "Introduction to The Study of the Ten Sefirot," Items 99-103

"Indeed You are a God who hides," that the Creator hides Himself in the Torah.

We asked above, "It makes sense that the Creator is hidden specifically in worldly matters and in the vanities of this world, which are outside the Torah, and not in the Torah itself, as only there is

Concealment and Revelation

the place of the disclosure. And we asked further: This concealment that the Creator hides Himself, to be sought and found, as it is written in *The Zohar*, "Why do I need all this?"

From the above explained you can thoroughly understand that this concealment that the Creator hides Himself so as to be sought is the concealment of the face, which He conducts with His creations in two manners: one concealment, and concealment within concealment.

The Zohar tells us that we should not even consider that the Creator wishes to remain in a guidance of concealed face from His creations. Rather, it is like a person who deliberately hides himself, so his friend will seek and find him.

Similarly, the Creator behaves in concealment of face with His creations only because He wants people to seek the disclosure of His face and find Him. In other words, there would be no way or inlet for people to attain the light of the King's face had He not first behaved with them in concealment of the face. Thus, the whole concealment is but a preparation for the disclosure of the face.

It is written that the Creator hides Himself in the Torah. Regarding the torments and pains one experiences during the concealment of the face, one who possesses transgressions and has done little in Torah and *Mitzvot* is unlike one who has engaged in Torah and good deeds extensively. The first is quite qualified to sentence his Maker to the side of merit, to think that the suffering came to him because of his sins and scarceness of Torah.

For the other, however, it is much harder to sentence his Maker to the side of merit since in his mind, he does not deserve such harsh punishments. Moreover, he sees that his friends, who are worse than him, do not suffer so, as it is written, "The wicked and the tranquil in the world gained riches," and also, "in vain have I cleansed my heart."

Thus, as long as one is not rewarded with a guidance of revelation of the face, the abundance of Torah and *Mitzvot* he has performed make his concealment of the face much heavier. This is the meaning of "The Creator hides Himself in the Torah."

Indeed, all that heaviness he feels through the Torah is but proclamations by which the Torah itself calls him, awakening him to hurry up and give the required measure of labor to promptly endow him with the revelation of the face, as God wills it.

This is why it is written that all who learn Torah *Lo Lishma*, their Torah becomes for them a potion of death. Not only do they not emerge from concealment of the face to disclosure of the face, since they did not set their minds to labor and attain it, the Torah that they accumulate greatly increases their concealment of the face. Finally, they fall into concealment within concealment, which is considered death, being completely detached from one's root. Thus, their Torah becomes for them a potion of death.

This clarifies the two names applied to the Torah: "revealed" and "concealed." We must understand why we need the concealed Torah, and why is not the whole Torah revealed?

Indeed, there is a profound intention here. The concealed Torah implies that the Creator hides in the Torah, hence the name, "the Torah of the hidden." Conversely, it is called "revealed" because the Creator is revealed by the Torah.

Therefore, the Kabbalists said, and we also find it in the prayer book of the Vilna Gaon [GRA], that the order of attainment of the Torah begins with the concealed and ends with the revealed. This means that through the appropriate labor, where one first delves in the Torah of the hidden, he is thus granted the revealed Torah, which is the literal. Thus, one begins with the concealed, called *Sod* [secret], and when he is rewarded, he ends in the literal.

18. Baal HaSulam, *Shamati*, Article No. 100, "The Written Torah and the Oral Torah – 1"

The written Torah is considered "awakening from above," and the oral Torah is an awakening from below. Together, they are called "Six years he shall serve, and in the seventh he shall go out free."

This is so because the essence of the work is specifically where there is resistance. And it is called *Alma* [Aramaic: world] from the word *He'elem* [concealment]. Then, when there is concealment, there is resistance, and then there is room for work. This is the meaning of the words of our sages, "Six thousand years the world, and one ruined." This means that the concealment will be ruined and there will be no more work. Rather, the Creator makes him wings, which are covers, so he would have work.

19. Baal HaSulam, *Shamati*, Article No. 8, "What Is the Difference between a Shade of Kedusha and a Shade of Sitra Achra?"

It is written (Song of Songs, 2), "Until the day breathes, and the shadows flee away." We must understand what are shadows in the work and what are two shadows. The thing is that when one does not feel His guidance, that He leads the world in a manner of "The Good Who Does Good," it is regarded as a shadow that hides the sun.

In other words, as the corporeal shadow that hides the sun does not change the sun in any way, and the sun shines in all its power, so one who does not feel the existence of His guidance does not induce any change above. Rather, there is no change above, as it is written, "I the Lord did not change."

Instead, all the changes are in the receivers. We must observe two discernments in this shade, meaning in this concealment:

1. When one still has the ability to overcome the darkness and concealments that one feels, justify the Creator, and pray to the Creator that the Creator will open his eyes to see that all the concealments that he feels come from the Creator, meaning that the Creator does all this to him so he may find his prayer and yearn to adhere to Him.
   This is so because only through the suffering that one receives from Him, wishing to break free from the trouble and flee from the torments, then he does everything he can. Hence, when receiving the concealments and afflictions, he is certain to take the known cure—to do much praying for the Creator to help him out of the state he is in. In that state, he still believes in His Providence.
2. When one comes to a state where he can no longer overcome and say that all the suffering and pains he feels are because the Creator sent them to him so as to have a reason to ascend in degree, he comes to a state of heresy, since he cannot believe in His guidance. Naturally, at that time, he cannot pray.

It follows that there are two kinds of shadows, and this is the meaning of "and the shadows flee away," meaning that the shadows will pass away from the world.

The shade of *Klipa* [shell] is called "Another god is sterile and does not bear fruit." In *Kedusha* [holiness], however, it is called "Under its shadow I coveted to sit, and its fruit was sweet to my palate." In other words, he says that all the concealments and afflictions he feels are because the Creator has sent him these states so he would have a place for work above reason.

When one has the strength to say this—that the Creator causes him all this—it is to one's benefit. This means that through this he can come to work in order to bestow and not for his own sake. At that time, one realizes, meaning believes that the Creator enjoys specifically this work, which is built entirely on above reason.

It follows that at that time, one does not pray to the Creator that the shadows will flee from the world. Rather, he says, "I see that the Creator wants me to serve Him in this manner, entirely above reason." Thus, in everything he does he says, "The Creator certainly enjoys this work, so why should I care if I am working in a state of concealment of the face?"

Because one wants to work in order to bestow, meaning that the Creator will enjoy, he feels no humiliation in this work, meaning a sensation that he is in a state of concealment of the face, that the Creator does not enjoy this work. Instead, one agrees to the leadership of the Creator, meaning however the Creator wants him to feel the existence of the Creator during the work, he agrees wholeheartedly. This is so because one does not consider what can please him, but what can please the Creator. Thus, this shade brings him life.

This is called "Under its shadow I coveted," meaning one covets such a state where he can make some overcoming above reason. It follows that if one does not exert in a state of concealment, when there is still room to pray for the Creator to bring him closer, and he is negligent in this, for this reason, he is sent a second concealment in which one cannot even pray. This is because of the sin of not exerting with all one's might to pray to the Creator. For this reason, one comes to a state of such lowliness.

However, after one comes to that state, he is pitied from above and is given another awakening from above. The same order begins anew until finally he strengthens in prayer, the Creator hears his prayer, brings him near, and reforms him.

20. Baal HaSulam, *Shamati*, Article No. 18, "My Soul Shall Weep In Secret – 1"

When concealment overpowers a person and he comes to a state where the work becomes tasteless, and he cannot picture or feel any love and fear, and he cannot do anything in *Kedusha* [holiness], his only counsel is to cry to the Creator to have mercy on him and remove the screen from his eyes and heart.

Crying is a very important matter. It is as our sages write: "All the gates were locked except for the gates of tears." The world asks about this: If the gates of tears are not locked, what is the need for the gates at all? He said that it is like a person who asks his friend for some necessary object. This object touches his heart, and he asks and begs him in every manner of prayer and plea. Yet, his friend pays no attention to all this. And when he sees that there is no longer reason for prayers and pleas then he raises his voice in weeping.

It is said about this: "All the gates were locked except for the gates of tears." That is, when were the gates of tears not locked? Precisely when all the gates were locked. It is then that there is room for the gates of tears, and then we see that they were not locked.

However, when the gates of prayer are open, the gates of tears and weeping are irrelevant. This is the meaning of the gates of tears being locked. Thus, when are the gates of tears not locked? Precisely when all the gates are locked, the gates of tears are open since one still has the choice of prayer and plea.

This is the meaning of "My soul shall weep in secret," meaning when one comes to a state of concealment, then "My soul shall weep," because one has no other option. This is the meaning of "All that your hand and strength can do, do."

21. Baal HaSulam, "Introduction to The Study of the Ten Sefirot," Items 80-82

The reason for the concealment of the face from people has been explained: It is deliberately to give people room to labor and engage in His work in Torah and *Mitzvot* voluntarily, for then the contentment of the Creator from their work in His Torah and *Mitzvot* increases more than His contentment from the angels above, who have no choice and whose mission is compulsory. There are also other reasons, but this is not the place to elaborate on them.

Despite the above praise for concealment of face, it is still not considered wholeness, but only a "transition," as this is the place from which the longed-for wholeness is attained. This means that any reward for a *Mitzva* that is prepared for a person is acquired only through one's labor in Torah and good deeds during the concealment of the face, when he engages voluntarily. This is so because then one feels sorrow out of his strengthening in His faith in keeping His will. And one's whole reward is measured only according to the pain he suffers from keeping the Torah and the *Mitzva*, as in the words of Ben He He, "The reward is according to the pain."

Hence, every person must experience that transition period of concealment of the face. When he completes it, he is rewarded with open Providence, meaning the revelation of the face.

22. Baal HaSulam, *Shamati*, Article No. 191, "The Time of Descent"

It is hard to depict the time of descent, when all the works and the efforts made from the beginning of the work until the time of descent are lost. To one who has never tasted the taste of servitude of the Creator, it seems as though this is outside of him, meaning that this happens to those of high degrees. But ordinary people have no connection to serving the Creator, only to crave the corporeal will to receive, present in the flow of the world, washing the whole world with this desire.

However, we must understand why they have come to such a state. After all, with or without one's consent, there is no change in the Creator of heaven and earth; He behaves in a manner of good and doing good. Thus, what is the outcome of this state?

We should say that it comes to announce His greatness. One does not need to act as though he does not want Her. Rather, one should behave in a manner of fearing the exaltedness, to know the merit and the distance between him and the Creator. It is difficult to understand this with a superficial mind, or have any possibility of connection between the Creator and creation.

During a descent he feels that it is impossible that he will have connection or belonging to the Creator by way of *Dvekut* [adhesion], since he feels that servitude is a foreign thing to the whole world.

In truth, this is so. But "In the place where you find His greatness, there you find His humbleness." This means that it is a matter that is above nature, that the Creator gave this gift to creation, to allow them to be connected and adhered to Him.

Hence, when one becomes reconnected, he should always remember his time of descent so as to know, understand, appreciate, and value the time of *Dvekut*, so he will know that now he has salvation above the natural way.

23. Baal HaSulam, *Shamati*, Article No. 172, "The Matter of Preventions and Delays"

All the preventions and delays that appear before our eyes are but a form of nearing—the Creator wants to bring us closer, and all these preventions bring us only nearing, since without them we would have no possibility of approaching Him. This is so because, by nature, there is no greater distance, as we are made of pure matter while the Creator is higher than high. Only when one begins to approach does he begin to feel the distance between us. And any prevention one overcomes brings the way closer for that person.

(This is so because one grows accustomed to moving on a line of growing farther. Hence, whenever one feels that he is distant, it does not induce any change in the process, since he knew in advance that he is moving on a line of growing farther, since this is the truth, that there are not enough words to describe the distance between us and the Creator. Hence, every time he feels that distance to a greater extent than he thought, it causes him no contention.)

24. Baal HaSulam, Letter No. 8

There is a sublime purpose for all that happens in this world, and it is called "the drop of unification." When those dwellers of clay houses go through all those terrors, through all that totality, in His pride, which is removed from them, a door opens in the walls of their hearts, which are tightly sealed by the nature of creation itself, and by this they become fit for instilling that drop of unification in their hearts. Then they are inverted like an imprinted substance, and they will evidently see that it is to the contrary—that it was precisely in those dreadful terrors that they perceive the totality, which is removed by foreign pride. There, and only there, is the Creator Himself adhered, and there He can instill them with the drop of unification.

25. Baal HaSulam, Letter No. 19

When one prepares to return to his root, he does not induce the complete *Zivug* at one time, but creates stimuli, which is the degree of *Nefesh*, by way of cycles, chasing the *Shechina* with all his might, quivering and sweating, until he mounts this extremity all day and all night, incessantly.

It is as the books write concerning the cycles. While one's soul is being completed in the degrees of *Nefesh*, he comes ever closer, and so his yearning and sorrow grow since the unsatisfied desire leaves behind it a great affliction according to the measure of the desire.

26. RABASH, Article No. 251, "Concerning the Minyan [Ten in the synagogue]"

It is known that we should pray mainly about the exile of the *Shechina* [Divinity], called *Malchut*, which is the tenth *Sefira* in the ten *Sefirot*, and whose essence is faith in His guidance, that He leads the world in a manner of good and doing good.

It is impossible to see the goodness of the Creator before a person purifies his desire from receiving for himself, since there is the *Tzimtzum* [restriction] on the will to receive, which is concealment on His guidance.

27. RABASH, Article No. 224, "The Reason for the Faith"

The reason for the faith is that there is no greater pleasure than to be rewarded with the revelation of Godliness and the instilling of the *Shechina* [Divinity].

In order for one to receive all this for the purpose of bestowal, there is a correction of concealment, where he engages in *Torah and Mitzvot* [commandments] even though he feels no pleasure. This is called "not in order to receive reward." When he has this *Kli* [vessel], his eyes soon open to welcome the face of the Creator.

When a desire awakens within him, that it is worthwhile to serve the Creator for the pleasure, he soon falls into concealment. This is regarded as death, meaning that previously, he was adhered to life, and he was rewarded with it only through the power of faith. Therefore, now that he is corrected and begins to work in faith once more, he receives back his breath of life. At that time, he says, "I thank You for returning my soul with compassion."

This is precisely when he assumes once more the work in the manner of faith above reason. When he had the concealment, he says, "Great is Your faith." The faith is so great that through it, he receives the soul once more.

28. RABASH, Article No. 236, "The Whole Earth Is Full of His Glory"

There are people who feel the light of the Creator also in combinations of letters of mundane things, and there are those who do not feel even in combinations of letters of Torah and prayer that it is the light of the Creator in the manner of "Who fills the whole of reality."

However, since there was a *Tzimtzum* [restriction], which is concealment, they do not feel that everything is the expanding light of the Creator.
That is, the measure that the creatures can attain, meaning the light that spreads into the sensation of the created beings, and besides the Creator wanting the lower ones to attain, it is certainly called "there is no thought or perception of Him whatsoever."

However, a person must believe in the *Tzimtzum*, meaning that it is only a concealment for man's benefit, while in truth, "The whole earth is full of His glory," and there is no reality in the world besides Godliness, and all the concealment is only in one's sensations.

29. RABASH, Article No. 3 (1985), "The Meaning of Truth and Faith"

We were given the path of faith, which is above reason, namely not to take our sensations and reason into account, but say, as it is written, "They have eyes and see not. They have ears and hear not." Rather, we should believe that the Creator is certainly the Overseer, and He knows what is good for me and what is not good for me. Therefore, He wants me to feel my state as I do, and for myself, I do not care how I feel myself because I want to work in order to bestow.

Therefore, the main thing is that I need to work for the Creator. And although I feel that there is no wholeness in my work, still, in the *Kelim* of the upper one, meaning from the perspective of the upper one, I am utterly complete, as it is written, "The cast out will not be cast out from Him." Hence, I am satisfied with my work—that I have the privilege of serving the King even at the lowest degree. That, too, I regard as a great privilege that the Creator has allowed me to come closer to Him at least to some degree.

30. RABASH, Article No. 11 (1990), "What Placing the Hanukkah Candle on the Left Means in the Work"

"Concealment of the face." In other words, the Creator hides Himself in the clothing of the friends, and in this way he does the Creator's will.

If he thanks the Creator for helping him through the concealment—meaning that now he has the choice to say that he is working because of the friends and he has no contact with the Creator, or that he believes that the Creator hid Himself in the clothing of the friends, and by that he engages in Torah and *Mitzvot*, and if he chooses and says that only the Creator helped him to be able to do good deeds by clothing in a clothing of friends, and he thanks the Creator for this—it brings upon him a great ascent: to be rewarded with the revelation of the face of the Creator.

31. RABASH, Article No. 18 (1990), "Why the Speech of Shabbat Must Not Be as the Speech of a Weekday, in the Work"

When the Creator generously bestows upon His creations, it is considered that His face is revealed to His creations, since then everyone knows and recognizes Him. Yet, when He behaves with His creations the opposite from the above mentioned, meaning when they suffer afflictions and torments in His world, it is considered the *Achoraim* of the Creator, for His face, meaning His complete attribute of goodness, is entirely concealed from them."

Therefore, in that state, if he can accept the *Achoraim*, which is called "exile," and does not run, but rather, "And they cried out to the Lord" to deliver him from the exile, then he accepts the *Achoraim* and says that it comes from the Creator, hence he asks Him that as He made him feel the taste of exile, so He will help him emerge from exile.

32. RABASH, Letter No. 76

It is known that "The whole earth is full of His glory." This is what every person should believe, as it is written, "I fill the heaven and the earth." However, the Creator has made a concealment so that we cannot see Him so as to have room for choice, and then there is room for faith—to believe that the Creator "fills all the worlds and encompasses all the worlds." And after a person engages in Torah and *Mitzvot* and keeps the commandment of choice, the Creator reveals Himself to him, and then he sees that the Creator is the ruler of the world.

Thus, at that time a person makes the king who will rule over him. That is, a person feels that the Creator is the ruler of the world, and this is regarded as a person making the Creator king over him. As long as one has not come to such a feeling, the Creator's kingship is concealed. This is why we say, "On that day, the Lord will be one and His name, 'One.'" That is, the glory of His kingship will appear over us.

This is the whole correction we must do in this world, and by that we extend abundance in the world, for all the bestowals from above are drawn by engaging in Torah and *Mitzvot* with the aim to extend His kingship on us.

33. RABASH, Article No. 236, "The Whole Earth Is Full of His Glory"

Before one is fit to attain the truth, he must believe that the truth is not as he knows or feels, but that it is as it is written, "They have eyes and they will not see; they have ears and they will not hear." This is only because of the correction, in order for man to achieve his wholeness, for he feels only himself and not another reality.

Hence, if one returns his heart to trying to walk in faith above the intellect, by this he qualifies it and establishes it so as to achieve the revelation of the face, as is presented in *The Zohar*, that the *Shechina* [Divinity] said to Rabbi Shimon Bar Yochai, "There is no place to hide from you," meaning that in all the concealments that he felt, he believed that here was the light of the Creator. This qualified him until he achieved the revelation of the face of His light.

This is the meaning of the measure of the faith that pulls one out of every lowliness and concealment if a person strengthens himself in this and asks the Creator to reveal Himself.

This is the meaning of what Baal HaSulam said, "Run my Beloved until she pleases," meaning that before one is fit to reveal His light, we ask of Him, "Run my Beloved," meaning that He will not reveal Himself to the created beings because the concealment is only the correction of creation.

Hence, one must brace oneself and pray for those two:

1) To be worthy of the revelation of the light of the Creator.
2) That the Creator will give him the power to grow stronger in faith above reason, for by this, he merges *Kelim* [vessels] that are fit for the revelation of the face, as in "The Lord will light up His face for you and will give you peace," as it is written, "I will hear what God will speak, for He will speak peace unto His people and unto His followers and let them not turn back to folly."

34. RABASH, Article No. 195, "The Association of the Quality of Judgment with Mercy"

Concerning the association of the quality of judgment with mercy, by which the lower one became worthy of *Mochin*, and concerning the *AHP* of the upper that fell into the lower one.

It is known that the main work is the choice, meaning "choose life," so there will be *Dvekut* [adhesion], which is *Lishma* [for Her sake]. By this, one is rewarded with *Dvekut* with the Life of Lives. When there is open Providence, there is no room for choice. For this reason, the upper one raised the *Malchut*, which is the quality of judgment, to the *Eynaim* [eyes]. This created a concealment, meaning that it seemed to the lower one that there was a drawback in the upper one, that there was no *Gadlut* [greatness/adulthood] in the upper one.

Subsequently, the qualities of the upper one are placed within the lower one, meaning they are deficient. It follows that these *Kelim* [vessels] have equivalence with the lower one, namely that as there is no vitality to the lower one, so there is no vitality in the upper qualities. In other words, he feels no taste in *Torah* and *Mitzvot* [commandments] for they are lifeless.

At that time, there is room for choice, for the lower one to say that this whole concealment that he feels is because the upper one restricted himself for the sake of the lower one. This is called "When Israel are in exile, the *Shechina* [Divinity] is with them," that whatever taste he feels, so he says. That is, it is not his fault that he does not feel the taste of vitality. Rather, in his view, there really is no vitality in spirituality.

If a person overcomes and says that the bitter taste he finds in these nourishments are only because he does not have the proper *Kelim* to receive the abundance because his *Kelim* are to receive and not to bestow, and he is sorry that the upper had to hide himself, for which the lower one can slander, this is regarded as MAN that the lower one raises.

By this, the upper raises his AHP. "Raising" means that the upper one can show the lower one the merit and the pleasure that exists in the *Kelim* of AHP that the upper one can reveal. Thus, from the perspective of the lower one, it follows that he raises the *Galgalta Eynaim* of the lower one, and by this itself, the lower one sees the merit of the upper one. It follows that the lower one ascends together with the AHP of the upper one.

Thus, when the lower one sees the greatness of the upper one, by this itself the lower one grows.

However, initially, the lower one is fit to receive only *Katnut* [smallness/infancy]. When *Gadlut* in the upper one appears to the lower one, a dispute between right and left emerges in the lower one, meaning between faith and knowledge.

However, the upper is also diminished later by the lower one. This is regarded as *Masach de Hirik*, meaning that for the lower one to be able to receive the degrees of the upper one, the lower one must receive knowledge only to the extent of the faith, and not more. This is regarded as the lower one restricting the left line of the upper one, meaning that the lower one is the cause.

At that time, the lower one can exist because he comprises knowledge and faith together. This is called "three lines," and specifically in this manner, the lower one acquires wholeness.

35. RABASH, Article No. 44, "Ruin by Elders—Construction; Construction by Youths—Ruin"

"Ruin by elders—construction; construction by youths—ruin" (Megillah 31b).

Elders are those who are accustomed to the work of the Creator. Youths are those who are in the beginning of their work. "Ruin" means a descent or a fall, where previously they had some ascent in the work, which is regarded as building, meaning that they appreciated the ascent, but the ruin is when they felt some fall, which comes from the concealment of the Creator, that the Creator hides Himself from them. This is called "ruin."

"Ruin by elders" means that they say that the Creator sent them the concealment. It follows that they are already building, since they believe that the Creator is tending to them, and from this they derive vitality.

Faith is apparent primarily during the descent, when it does not shine for a person. At that time, he faces a dilemma: Either he says, "I do not need any benefits. Rather, I want to bring contentment above and I do not care what I feel," or it is otherwise.

36. RABASH, Article No. 44 (1990), "What Is an Optional War, in the work - 2?"

All those thoughts that the will to receive brings him are sent to him from above because he wants to walk on the path of bestowal, and in the meantime he is idle in the work, because he prayed for the Creator to bring him closer to being in *Dvekut* with the Creator, which is equivalence of form, when it is apparent that the person is idle in the work, he is sent the foreign thoughts that a person cannot agree to be under such a control. This, in turn, gives a person a push that he must overcome the state he is in.

It therefore follows that from this bad, when a person feels that he is in such a lowly state that he never imagined that he could be under such governance, for this reason, he should not be alarmed and escape the campaign. On the contrary, he should believe that the Creator is taking care of him now, and He is bringing him closer through a state of *Achoraim* [posterior].

This is as it is written in the book *A Sage's Fruit* (Vol. 1, p 139), "About the verse, 'My beloved is like a gazelle,' our sages said, 'As the gazelle looks back when he runs, when the Creator leaves Israel, He turns back His face.' Then the face returns to being in the *Achoraim*, meaning craving and longing to cling to Israel once more. This begets in Israel longing and craving to cling to the Creator, too, and the measure of the longing and craving is actually the face itself."

We should interpret that he means that when a person is in a state of lowliness, it is considered that the Creator has moved away from him, and he has no desire or yearning for the work, this is regarded as the Creator giving a person a shape of tastelessness about spirituality. Moreover, a person wants to escape and forget about the work altogether. This is regarded as the Creator showing him the *Achoraim*.

The *Panim* [face/anterior] of the Creator is His desire to do good to His creations, and the *Achoraim* is the complete opposite. Why does the Creator show a person the *Achoraim*? It is on purpose, for by this a person gets a thrust toward *Dvekut* with the Creator, for he cannot remain in a state of lowliness. It follows that here, within the *Achoraim* is the discernment of *Panim*.

37. RABASH, Article No. 472, "The Concealed Things Belong to the Lord Our God"

"The concealed things belong to the Lord our God, and the revealed things belong to us and to our children forever, to do all the words of this Torah [law]."

By intimation, we should interpret that "revealed" means "practiced," and "concealed" means "intention." The intention—which is the reason that obligates a person to do the act—is concealed from people, for one does not know what is in one's friend's heart.

A person might even deceive himself with regard to the intention and think that the reason that obligates him to do the deed is the benefit of the Creator, when perhaps it is his own benefit that obligates him to do the deed. This is why "concealed" implies the intention.

We should make two discernments in regard to this: 1) the general public, 2) the individual. The general public normally thinks mainly about the action and not about the intention, since it is impossible to force the public to aim the true aim during the act. But with regard to the individual, we speak mainly about the intention. Hence, perhaps with respect to the general public, he is righteous, but with respect to the individual, he is wicked.

In that regard, it can be said, "Even if the whole world tells you that you are righteous, be wicked in your own eyes." That is, he should aim that it will be only for the Creator, meaning not in order to receive reward, and he is still regarded as wicked.

And when one sees that in terms of the concealed, he is completely removed from the goal, he must not despair. Rather, he must believe that "The concealed things belong to the Lord our God." This means that He will give the concealed part, and we will do the revealed part, namely the actions.

According to the increase in actions, so grows the need to increase intentions, meaning for the concealed part. Since there is a rule that there is no light without a *Kli* [vessel], meaning a desire, through increasing the actions we increase the lack until it reaches a certain measure, and then "The concealed things belong to the Lord our God," meaning that then He gives the concealed.

38. RABASH, Article No. 777, "A Prayer for the Exile of the Shechina"

From the perspective of the worlds, there are two states: the state of the first nine, regarded as vessels of bestowal, and *Malchut*, which is regarded as a *Kli* [vessel] for reception, from whom the *Klipot* [shells/peels] nurse. In spirituality, one does not mix with the other.

For this reason, there is the discernment of time for man, where until age thirteen he is under the governance of the *Klipot*, and from age thirteen onward he begins to obtain the first nine. At that time, because he consists of *Malchut* of reception, he can correct her so it will be reception in order to bestow, and then the verse, "The darkness will shine as light" will come true. This means that *Malchut* is called "reception and knowing." At that time, he inverts his *Kelim*. Conversely, if he consisted only of the first nine, he would not be able to correct anything.

This is why we need the work of the lower ones. This is the meaning of the Creator craving the prayer of the righteous, meaning those who pray and want to be righteous, meaning ask the Creator to help them invert the quality of *Malchut* to the quality of the upper nine.

39. *Zohar for All*, *Nasso*, "The Holy Idra Rabah," Item 299

Everything is Godliness, above time, place, and change. All those degrees and corrections we discern in Godliness are only various concealments and covers toward the lower ones, since the ten *Sefirot* are ten kinds of covers of His *Atzmut* [self]. Likewise, all the imaginary images of time and place and actions are but various covers of His Godliness that seem that way to the lower ones.

As man is not affected or changes at all because of the covers that he covers in, and only his friends are affected by his disappearance or appearance, so His Godliness does not change and is not affected whatsoever by those degrees and corrections and names in time, place, and changes of actions that the lower ones discern in His covers. Rather, we must know that those covers also serve as disclosures.

Moreover, to the extent of the cover that there is in each name and correction, so is the extent of disclosure of the Creator that is in it. One who is rewarded with receiving the measure of the covers properly is then rewarded with the covers becoming for him measures of disclosure. One who learns must remember these things during the learning so he will not fail in his thought.

40. *Zohar for All*, "Introduction of The Book of Zohar," "On the Night of the Bride," Item 138

It is a law that the creature cannot receive disclosed evil from the Creator, for it is a flaw in the glory of the Creator for the creature to perceive Him as an evildoer, for this is unbecoming of the complete Operator. Hence, when one feels bad, denial of the Creator's guidance lies upon him and the superior Operator is concealed from him to that same extent. This is the greatest punishment in the world.

Thus, the sensation of good and evil in relation to His guidance brings with it the sensation of reward and punishment, for one who exerts to not part from faith in the Creator is rewarded even when he tastes a bad taste in Providence. And if he does not exert, he will have a punishment because he is separated from faith in the Creator.

41. *Zohar for All*, "Introduction of The Book of Zohar," "Two Points," Item 121

All the many contradictions to His uniqueness, which we taste in this world, separate us from the Creator. Yet, when exerting to keep Torah and *Mitzvot* with love, with our soul and might, as we are commanded—to bestow contentment upon our Maker—all those forces of separation do not affect us into subtracting any of the love of the Creator with all our souls and might. Rather, in that state, every contradiction we have overcome becomes a gate for attainment of His wisdom. This is so because there is a special quality in each contradiction—revealing a special degree in attaining Him. And those worthy ones who have been rewarded with it turn darkness into light and bitter into sweet, for all the powers of separation—from the darkness of the mind and the bitterness of the body—have become to them gates for obtainment of sublime degrees. Thus, the darkness becomes a great light and the bitter becomes sweet.

Hence, to the extent that they previously had all the conducts of His guidance toward the forces of separation, now they have all been inverted into forces of unification, and sentence the entire world to the side of merit.

42. *Zohar for All*, *Beresheet* [Genesis], "Let Us Make Man," Item 159

According to the extent of the *Panim* of the degree, so is the extent of its *Achoraim*. The instilling of the *Achoraim* is a calling and an invitation to instill the *Panim*. This is why by the measure of the concealment of the *Achoraim* that they attained, they knew the measure of disclosure that they were about to attain.

As Rabbi Shimon heard, he was calling him Shimon and not Rabbi Shimon. This means that the instilling of the *Achoraim*, which is a calling, was so strong that he lost all his degrees and became a simple person, Shimon from the market. By that, he recognized that it was a calling and an invitation for very high attainment of *Panim*.

43. *Zohar for All,* "Introduction of The Book of Zohar," "Two Points," Item 121

Prior to being rewarded with inverting the desire to receive in us through Torah and *Mitzvot*, into reception in order to bestow, there are strong locks on those gates to the Creator, for then they have the opposite role: to drive us away from the Creator. This is why the forces of separation are called "locks," since they block the gates of approaching and drive us away from the Creator.

But if we overcome them so they do not affect us, cooling His love from our hearts, the locks become doors, the darkness becomes light, and the bitter becomes sweet. Over all the locks, we receive a special degree in His Providence, and they become openings, degrees of attainment of the Creator.

44. *Zohar for All, VaYera* [The Lord Appeared], "And the Lord Appeared unto Him"

And this applies in the upper worlds, as well, since no revelation is dispensed upon the worlds except through concealed discernments. And by the measure of concealment in a degree, so is the measure of revelations in it, which is given to the world. If there is no concealment in it, it cannot bestow a thing.

45. *Zohar for All, Beresheet*-1 [Genesis] "Let Us Make Man"

"And God said, 'Let us make man,'" there is a secret revealed only to those who fear Him. That elder of the elders started and said, "Shimon, Shimon, who is it who said, 'Let us make man,' and of whom is it written, 'And God said'? Who is that name 'God' here?" As Rabbi Shimon heard that he was calling him Shimon and not Rabbi Shimon, he said to his friends, "This must be the Creator, of whom it is written, 'And the ancient of days [*Atik Yomin*] is sitting.' Therefore, now is the time to disclose that secret, for there is a secret here that was not permitted to be disclosed, and now it means that permission to disclose has been given."

It is known that the secrets that were revealed to the sages of *The Zohar* were by attainment of the lights of the upper degrees by instilling. There are *Panim* and *Achoraim* [anterior and posterior respectively] in them, meaning concealment and disclosure. According to the extent of the *Panim* of the degree, so is the extent of its *Achoraim*. The instilling of the *Achoraim* is a calling and an invitation to instill the *Panim*. This is why by the measure of the concealment of the *Achoraim* that they attained, they knew the measure of disclosure that they were about to attain.

As Rabbi Shimon heard, he was calling him Shimon and not Rabbi Shimon. This means that the instilling of the *Achoraim*, which is a calling, was so strong that he lost all his degrees and became a simple person, Shimon from the market. By that, he recognized that it was a calling and an invitation for very high attainment of *Panim*.

This is why he promptly said to his friends, "This must be the Creator, of whom it is written, 'And the ancient of days [*Atik Yomin*] is sitting,'" of whose degree there is no higher.

46. Ramchal, *Daat Tevunot*

That deficiency was born only by the concealment of the face of the Master, who did not want to illuminate His face to His creations right away, so they would be complete from the beginning. On the contrary, He hid His face from them and left them lacking since the light of the King's face is life indeed, and His concealment is the source of all that is bad.

However, since the intended purpose in this concealment is not to be concealed, but rather to later be revealed and remove all the bad that was born only out of that concealment, He therefore set a law and ordinance to reveal His good hidden face. This is done either by deeds that people do, which are the ordinances and teachings He has given us, His law is the law of truth, which one who does them lives by them in eternal life, since the reward of a commandment is commandment, it is the illumination of His face, which He hid from man in the beginning of his creation.

For this reason, he was created for labor since the inclination governs him and his wickedness is great in all kinds of faults, and his distance from the light of life. And doing the commandments shines on him the hidden light until, when he completes his due commandments, he himself is completed with them to the light, in the light of this life.

3

Recognition of Evil

1. Baal HaSulam, Letter No. 21

Your letter from the thirteenth of *Tishrey* [the first Hebrew month]. What you write me about, "I recognize how much I need external mortifications to correct my externality," thus far your words, I say that you neither need mortifications nor to correct the externality. Who taught you this new law? It must be that you are not as attached to me as before, and are therefore learning other ways.

Know that you have no other trusted friend in your whole life, and I advise you not to correct your externality at all, but only your internality, for only your internality is destined to be corrected. And the main reason why the internality is corrupted due to the proliferation of sins is the filth, whose sign is pride and self-importance. That filth fears no mortification in the world. On the contrary, it relishes them because the self-importance and pride increase and strengthen by the mortification.

But if you do wish to cleanse the sins off you, you should engage in annulment of self-importance instead of the mortifications, meaning to feel that you are the lowest and the worst of all the people in the world. It requires much learning and education to understand this, and each time you should test yourself to see if you are not fooling and deceiving yourself. It also helps to lower yourself before your friend in practice.

However, you should be mindful that you lower yourself only before the right people. So if you wish to engage in it in practice, you can annul yourself before our group, and not before strangers, God forbid. However, you must know for certain that you are the worst and the lowest of all the people in the world, as this is the truth.

2. Baal HaSulam, "The Essence of Religion and Its Purpose"

When one detests any self-reception and his soul loathes the petite physical pleasures and respect, he finds himself roaming free in the Creator's world, and he is guaranteed that no damage or misfortune will ever come upon him, since all the damages come to a man only through the self-reception imprinted in him.

3. Baal HaSulam, "The Essence of Religion and Its Purpose"

The crass, undeveloped person does not recognize egoism as bad at all. Therefore, he uses it openly, without any shame or restraint, stealing and murdering in broad daylight wherever he can. The somewhat more developed sense some measure of their egoism as bad and are at least ashamed to use it in public, stealing and killing openly. But in secret, they still commit their crimes, but are careful that no one will see them.

The even more developed sense egoism as so loathsome that they cannot tolerate it in them and reject it completely, as much as they detect of it, until they cannot, and do not want to enjoy the labor of others. Then begin to emerge in them sparks of love of others, called "altruism," which is the general attribute of goodness.

But that, too, evolves gradually. First develops love and desire to bestow upon one's family and kin, as in the verse, "Do not ignore your own flesh." When one develops further, one's attribute of bestowal expands to all the people around him, being one's townspeople or one's nation. And so one adds until he finally develops love for the whole of humanity.

4. Baal HaSulam, *Shamati*, Article No. 107, "Concerning the Two Angels"

Concerning the two angels that accompany one on the eve of *Shabbat* [Sabbath], a good angel and a bad angel, a good angel is called "right," by which one comes closer to serving the Creator. This is called "the right brings closer." And the bad angel is considered "left," pushing away. This means that it brings him foreign thoughts, whether in mind or in heart.

When one prevails over the bad and brings himself closer to the Creator, meaning that each time, he overcomes the evil and attaches himself to the Creator, it follows that through the two of them, he has come closer to *Dvekut* [adhesion] with the Creator. This means that both performed a single task—they have caused him to adhere to the Creator. In that state one says, "Come in peace."

And when one has completed all of one's work and has admitted all the left into *Kedusha* [holiness], as it is written, "There is no place to hide from You," the bad angel has nothing more to do, as the person has already overcome all the difficulties that the evil presented. At that time, the bad angel is idle. At that time, the person tells it, "Go in peace."

5. Baal HaSulam, "The Essence of Religion and Its Purpose"

For engaging in *Mitzvot* and the work to bring contentment to our Maker rapidly develops in us that sense of recognition of evil.

6. Baal HaSulam, *Shamati*, Article No. 56, "Torah Is Called Indication"

When one engages in the Torah and sees the truth, meaning his measure of remoteness from spirituality, and sees that he is such a lowly being that there is not a worse person than him on earth.

7. Baal HaSulam, "The Essence of Religion and Its Purpose"

I would like to clear up the essence of that development, which is attained through engagement in Torah and *Mitzvot*.

Bear in mind that it is the recognition of the evil within us that engagement in *Mitzvot* can slowly and gradually purify those who delve in them. And the scale by which we measure the degrees of cleansing is the measure of the recognition of the evil within us.

8. Baal HaSulam, Letter No. 5

I rejoice in those revealed corruptions and the ones that are being revealed.

I do, however, regret and complain about the corruptions that have still not appeared, but which are destined to appear, for a hidden corruption is hopeless, and its surfacing is a great salvation from heaven. The rule is that one does not give what he does not have. Hence, if it has appeared now, there is no doubt that it was here to begin with but was hidden. This is why I am happy when they come out of their holes because when you cast your eye on them, they become a pile of bones.

9. Baal HaSulam, Letter No. 5

When buried wicked appear, although they have not been fully conquered, their very appearance is regarded as a great salvation and causes the *Kedusha* [holiness] of the day.

10. Baal HaSulam, *Shamati*, Article No. 52, "A Transgression Does Not Quench a Mitzva"

"A transgression does not quench a *Mitzva* [commandment], and a *Mitzva* does not quench a transgression." It is the conduct of the work that one must take the good path. But the bad in a person does not let him take the good path.

For this reason, evil has no existence on its own. Rather, the existence of evil depends on love for the evil or the hate for the evil. It means that if one has love for evil then one is caught in the authority of the evil. If one hates the evil, he exits their premises and one's evil has no dominion over that person.

It follows that the primary work is not in the actual evil, but in the measure of love and the measure of hate. For this reason, transgression prompts transgression. We must ask, "Why does he deserve such a punishment?" When one falls from one's work, he must be aided to rise from the fall. But here we see that more obstacles are added to him so he would fall lower than the first fall.

But in order to feel hatred for the evil, he is given more evil, so as to feel how the transgression removes him from the work of the Creator. Although he regretted the first transgression, he still did not feel regret enough to bring him hatred for the evil.

Hence, a transgression prompts a transgression, and every time he regrets, and each remorse certainly instigates hatred for the evil until the measure of his hatred for the evil is completed, and then he is separated from the evil, since hatred induces separation.

It therefore follows that if one finds a certain measure of hate at a level that prompts separation, he does not need a correction of transgression-prompts-transgression, and therefore saves time. When one has been rewarded, he is admitted to the love of the Creator. This is the meaning of "You who love the Lord, hate evil." They only hate the evil, but the evil itself remains in its place, and it is only hatred to the evil that we need.

11. Baal HaSulam, *Shamati*, Article No. 56, "Torah Is Called Indication"

Brought in Masechet Taanit (p 20), that Rabbi Elazar, son of Rabbi Shimon, came from a fenced tower from the house of his teacher. He was riding his donkey and strolling along the riverbank feeling great joy. And his mind was crude, as he had been studying much Torah.

A person who was very ugly came by his way. He told him, "Hello rabbi," but he did not reply. He told him, "Vain, how ugly is that man, are all your townspeople as ugly as you?" He replied, "I do not know, but go and tell the craftsman who made me, 'How ugly is this vessel that you have made.'" Because he knew that he had sinned, he descended from the donkey.

According to the above, we can see that since he learned much Torah, through it he was granted seeing the truth about the distance between himself and the Creator, meaning the measure of his remoteness and nearness. This is the meaning of his mind being crude, meaning that he saw the complete form of one who is proud, which is his will to receive, and then he could see the truth that it was he himself who was very ugly. How did he see the truth? By learning much Torah.

Thus, how will he be able to adhere to Him, since he is such an ugly person? This is why he asked if all the people were as ugly as him or was he the only ugly one and the rest of the people in the world were not ugly.

What was the answer? "I don't know." It means that they do not feel and therefore do not know. And why do they not feel? It is for the simple reason that they were not rewarded with seeing the truth, since they lack Torah, so the Torah will show them the truth.

To that Elijah replied to him, "Go to the craftsman who made me." Because he saw that he came to a state from which he could not ascend, Elijah appeared and told him, "Go to the craftsman who made me." In other words, since the Creator created you so ugly, He must have known that with these *Kelim* [vessels] it is possible to achieve the goal. So do not worry, go forward and succeed.

12. Baal HaSulam, *Shamati*, Article No. 23, "You Who Love the Lord, Hate Evil"

In the verse, "You who love the Lord, hate evil; He preserves the souls of His followers; He will save them from the hand of the wicked," he interprets that it is not enough to love the Creator, and to want to be awarded *Dvekut* [adhesion] with the Creator. One should also hate evil.

Hatred is expressed by hating the evil, called "the will to receive." One sees that he has no way to get rid of it, and at the same time, he does not want to accept the situation. He feels the losses that the evil causes him, and also sees the truth, that one cannot annul the evil by himself, since it is a natural force from the Creator, who imprinted the will to receive in man.

In that state, the verse tells us what one can do is hate evil. And by this the Creator will keep him from that evil, as it is written, "He preserves the souls of His followers." What is preservation? "He will deliver them from the hand of the wicked." In that state, since he has some contact with the Creator, be it the smallest contact, he is already a successful person.

In truth, the matter of evil remains and serves as an *Achoraim* [posterior] to the *Partzuf*. But this is only through one's correction: Through sincere hatred of evil, it is corrected into a form of *Achoraim*. The hatred comes because if one wants to obtain *Dvekut* [adhesion] with the Creator then there is a conduct among friends: If two people realize that each of them hates what his friend hates, and loves what and whom his friend loves, they come into perpetual bonding like a stake that will never fall.

Hence, since the Creator loves to bestow, the lower ones should also adapt to want only to bestow. The Creator also hates to be a receiver, as He is completely whole and does not need anything. Thus, man, too, must hate the matter of reception for oneself.

It follows from all the above, that one must bitterly hate the will to receive, for all the ruins in the world come only from the will to receive. And through the hatred, one corrects it and surrenders under the *Kedusha* [holiness].

13. Baal HaSulam, "Peace in the World"

Everything in reality, good or bad, and even the most harmful in the world, has a right to exist and must not be destroyed and eradicated from the world. We must only mend and reform it because any observation of the work of creation is enough to teach us about the greatness and perfection of its Operator and Creator. Therefore, we must understand and be very careful when casting a flaw on any item of creation, saying it is redundant and superfluous, as that would be slander about its Operator.

14. Baal HaSulam, "The Freedom"

The Torah and the *Mitzvot* were given only to purify Israel, to develop in us the sense of recognition of evil imprinted in us at birth, which is generally defined as our self-love, and to come to the pure good defined as "love of others," which is the one and only passage to the love of the Creator.

15. RABASH, Article No. 1 (1991), "What Is, 'We Have No Other King But You,' in the Work?"

Is written (Psalms 89), "I will sing of the mercies of the Lord forever, generation after generation I will make known Your faith with my mouth." We should understand the meaning of "sing forever." How can one sing to the Creator when he sees that he is full of faults and his heart is not whole with the Creator, and he feels far from the Creator? And sometimes, he even wants to escape the campaign. How can he say that this is the Lord's mercies and he is singing about this to the Creator?

According to the above, a person should say that the fact that he in a lowly state is not because now he has become worse. Rather, now, since he wants to correct himself so that all his actions will be for the sake of the Creator, from above he is shown his true state—what is in his body, which until now was concealed and was not apparent. Now the Creator has revealed them, as it is written in the book *A Sage's Fruit*.

A person says about this that it is mercy that the Creator has revealed to him the bad in him so he would know the truth and would be able to ask of the Creator for a real prayer. It follows that on one hand, now he sees that he is far from the Creator. On the other hand, a person should say that the Creator is close to him and tends to him, and shows him the faults. Hence, he should say that they are mercies.

This is the meaning of the words, "I will sing of the mercies of the Lord forever." That is, on one hand, he is happy and is singing about this. On the other hand, he sees that he must repent. In other words, he must ask of the Creator to bring him closer and give him the desire to bestow, which is a second nature.

16. RABASH, Article No. 18 (1987), "What Is Preparation for Reception of the Torah? – 1"

It is written, "And they stood at the foot of the mountain."

We must understand what is a "mountain." The word *Har* [mountain] comes from the word *Hirhurim* [thoughts], which is man's intellect. Anything that is in the intellect is regarded as "in potential." Afterward, it can expand into actual fact. Accordingly, we can interpret "And the Lord came down on Mount Sinai, to the top of the mountain," as the thought and intellect of man, meaning that the Creator informed all the people that the inclination of a man's heart is evil from his youth. After the Creator informed them in potential, meaning at the top of the mountain, that which was in potential expanded in actual fact.

For this reason, the people came to actually feel and everyone now sensed the need for the Torah, as it is written, "I have created the evil inclination; I have created the spice of Torah." Now they said that through actually feeling that they were forced to accept the Torah, meaning without choice, since they saw that if they received the Torah they would have delight and pleasure, and if not, there it would be their burial. In other words, if we remain in our current state, our lives will not be lives but they will be our burial place.

Accordingly, we should interpret "And the Lord came down to the top of the mountain" to mean that once the Creator informed them on the mountain, in the intellect, that the evil is man's heart, and once this has been set in their minds, in their thoughts and intellect, it immediately operated, as it is written, "And they stood at the foot of the mountain." In other words, the descent that was on the mountain operated on them and they stood at the foot of the mountain, meaning the above descents controlled them.

It follows that "forced the mountain on them like a vault" means the descent and the information they received on the mountain, meaning with the thought about them that now they will have to receive the Torah because this mountain, meaning this descent, causes them the need to receive the Torah, so they can overcome the evil in their hearts.

17. RABASH, Article No. 28 (1991), "What Are Holiness and Purity, in the Work?"

The beginning of his work is the recognition of evil, meaning that a person asks the Creator to feel how bad is the will to receive. This awareness that the will to receive is called "bad," only the Creator can make him feel. This is considered that through the Torah, a person can achieve recognition of evil, meaning to understand how much his will to receive is bad, and then he can ask to replace the will to receive and give him instead the desire to bestow.

18. RABASH, Article No. 68, "The Order of the Work"

When one believes in the delight and pleasure that exists in above reason, he comes to consciously feel, to know the evil within him. That is, he believes that the Creator imparts such delight and pleasure, and although he sees all the good above reason, he achieves recognition. That is, he feels in all the organs the power of the evil that is found in receiving for oneself, which prevents him from receiving the abundance.

It follows that faith above reason causes him to feel his enemy within reason—who obstructs him from reaching the good. This is his standard. That is, to the extent that he believes in the delight and pleasure above reason, to that extent he can come to feel the recognition of evil.

Later, sensing the bad yields the sensation of delight and pleasure, since the recognition of evil in the sensation of the organs causes him to correct the bad.

This is done primarily through prayer, when he asks the Creator to give everything in bestowal, called *Dvekut* [adhesion]. Through these *Kelim* [vessels], the goal will be revealed in open Providence, meaning that there will be no need for the concealment because there will already be *Kelim* that are able to receive.

19. RABASH, Article No. 143, "The Need for Recognition of Evil"

Why do we need recognition of evil, that we are submerged in the mud, unable to come out? This is the allegory. It is all because we must be very thankful. But there is a difference in how He helped him. To the extent of the favor that he received, so he comes to love Him and adhere to Him and can work for Him because He is great and ruling.

That is, the greatness of the Creator becomes evident to a person precisely if He made for him a great miracle. To the extent of the miracle, so the love awakens and His greatness is seen by His ability to help him out of the great trouble. Conversely, the spies said, "The Landlord cannot save His vessels." This is the meaning of the verse, "From the narrow place I called on the Lord; answer me in the broad space, Lord," meaning specifically when one is in a state of trouble.

20. RABASH, Article No. 22 (1985), "The Whole of the Torah Is One Holy Name"

We must always consider the goal, which is to "do good to His creations." If the evil inclination comes to a person and asks him all of Pharaoh's questions, he should not reply with lame excuses, but say, "Now, with your questions, I can begin with the work of bestowal."

This means that we should not say about the questions of the evil inclination that it came to us in order to lower us from our degree. On the contrary, now it is giving us a place to work, by which we will ascend on the degrees of wholeness. That is, any overcoming in the work is called "walking in the work of the Creator," since each penny joins into a great amount." That is, all the times we overcome accumulate to a certain measure required to become a *Kli* for the reception of the abundance.

21. RABASH, Article No. 401, "Hear, O Israel"

A person should begin the work of the Creator on the right, called "male," which is wholeness, called happy with his share, which is regarded as "desiring mercy." Whatever flavor and vitality he has in

Torah and Mitzvot [commandments] is enough for him to labor in *Torah and Mitzvot* because he believes in private Providence, that such is the will of the Creator, and feels that he is a complete person, and thanks and praises the Creator for giving him a part in His work.

This is called a "male," when he feels himself as whole and he is always happy and observes, "Serve the Lord with gladness."

However, this is called "half a body"; he does not have the quality of female, which is a lack. From the perspective of the left, he begins to calculate to what extent his qualities and thoughts are whole, and then he sees the truth, that he is still immersed in the will to receive for his own benefit, and cannot work for the sake of others, whether between man and man or between man and the Creator.

To the extent that he has the recognition of evil, he can exert, meaning work, perform actions, as in "Everything that is in the power of your hand to do, that do." Also, he can pray from the bottom of the heart, since only to the extent that a person feels the bad, meaning feels that it is bad, to that extent he acts in order to be rid of the bad. This is called "female," meaning a lack.

It follows that he has room for two opposite qualities. On one hand, he is regarded as complete, which is the "right," *Hesed* [mercy], happy with his share. He can praise and thank the Creator for letting him into a place of Torah and good deeds. On the other hand, he can pray to the Creator for remaining outside of the work of the Creator because everything was built on the basis of self-love.

At that time, the person is called "complete".

22. RABASH, Article No. 6 (1989), "What Is Above Reason in the Work?"

"King of Israel and his redeemer." That is, once they have taken upon themselves the kingdom of heaven, called "king of Israel," they attain that the Creator is his redeemer, meaning that only the Creator redeemed them from the control of the evil, and they themselves were powerless to do so.

In this way, we should interpret the words "Lord of hosts." This name means, as Baal HaSulam interpreted, that as he said, *Tzevaot* [hosts] are two words: *Tze* [leave/go out] and *Ba* [comes]. That is, *Tzava* [army] are men of war. These are people who go each day to fight the evil inclination. They are called "army." Therefore, after they have been rewarded with redemption, meaning after they conquer the evil inclination and emerge from the control of the evil, their conduct in the work is by way of ascents and descents, which is called *Tzevaot* [plural of *Tzava* (army)]. Meaning, at times they emerge from their control, and then are under their control again. Thus, the name for ascents and descents is *Tzevaot*.

During the work, a person should say, "If I am not for me, who is for me?" At that time in the work, they think that they themselves are doing the ascents and descents, that they are men of war, called *Tzava*, "mighty men." Afterward, when they are redeemed, they attain that the Lord is of hosts [*Tzevaot*], meaning that the Creator made all the ups and downs they had.

In other words, even the descents come from the Creator. A person does not get so many ups and downs for no reason. Rather, the Creator caused all those exits. We can interpret "exit" as "exit from *Kedusha* [holiness]," and *Ba* [comes] as "coming to *Kedusha*. The Creator does everything.

Hence, after the redemption, the Creator is called "Lord of Hosts." And who is He? "The king of Israel and his redeemer."

23. RABASH, Article No. 29 (1989), "What Is the Preparation to Receive the Torah in the Work? – 2"

Our sages said, "The Torah exists only in one who puts himself to death over it." We should understand the word "exists." What does it tell us? We should interpret this according to what our sages said, "The Creator said, 'I have created the evil inclination; I have created the Torah as a spice.'" That is, the Torah should be a spice. In whom is this so, since "There is no light without a *Kli*, no filling without a lack"?

For this reason, they said that those who want to put their selves to death, meaning want to put to death the will to receive for their own sake, and want to do everything for the sake of the Creator, see that they cannot do this on their own. To them the Creator said, "I have created the evil inclination; I have created the Torah as a spice."

24. RABASH, Article No. 273, "The Mightiest of the Mighty"

"Who is the mightiest of the mighty? He who makes his foe his friend" (*Avot de Rabbi Natan*, Chapter 23).

In ethics, we should interpret that "mighty" is "one who conquers his inclination" (*Avot*, Chapter 4). That is, he works with the good inclination and subdues the evil inclination.

The mightiest of the mighty is one who works also with the evil inclination, as our sages said, "With all your heart—with both your inclinations" (*Berachot* 54), where the evil inclination, too, serves the Creator. It follows that he makes his foe, the evil inclination, his friend. And since the evil inclination is also serving the Creator, it follows that here he has more work, for which he is called "the mightiest of the mighty."

25. RABASH, Article No. (1990), "Why the Speech of Shabbat Must Not Be as the Speech of a Weekday, in the Work"

The work on obtaining the vessels of bestowal comes by obtaining the state of *Gadlut* [greatness/adulthood] of the evil, as it is written, "For I have hardened his heart," meaning the attainment of the bad, then, when the people of Israel came to a state where they saw that they could not escape from the bad, meaning they saw that the power of the bad was on all sides and they did not see any salvation by nature, this is considered that the *Kli* of the bad has been completed.

At that time comes State 5), when the Creator gives them the light, and this light reforms them. In other words, by this they emerge from the governance of evil, called "vessels of self-reception," and are rewarded with vessels of bestowal. This is the meaning of "Stand by and see the salvation of the Lord, which He will do for you today." This means that once the *Kli* of the bad has been completed, there is room for disclosure of light on the part of the upper one. This is considered that the Creator is giving them the vessels of bestowal.

26. RABASH, Article No. 11 (1991), "What It Means that the Good Inclination and the Evil Inclination Guard a Person in the Work"

When a person wants to walk on the path of achieving *Dvekut* with the Creator and do all his work for the sake of the Creator, meaning to bestow contentment upon his Maker and not for his own sake, as it is against human nature, who was created with the will to receive for his own sake, and all of man's work is that he is told that he will not obtain this by his own strength, but only the Creator can give him this power called desire to bestow, and a person should only prepare the *Kli* to receive this power called "second nature," it follows that specifically through the evil inclination, which grows within him to its completion, a person sees his real deficiency—that he is unable to obtain the desire to bestow by himself. This brings him to a state where the Creator gives him the desire to bestow.

Thus, both the good inclination and the evil inclination lead a person to achieve the goal of equivalence of form, called "*Dvekut* with the Creator."

27. RABASH, Article No. 305, "The Meaning of Evil"

The evil in a person is regarded as evil only when one feels that it is evil. That is, the extent that the evil prevents him from receiving abundance determines the measure of the evil.

Normally, if one loses a penny to one's friend, he does not hate him for this, since a penny is not important enough to fight with the other over it. But to the extent that his friend causes him losses, the level of hatred forms in him until he cannot stand him.

It follows that to the extent that a person has importance of *Torah and Mitzvot* [commandments], to that extent he can determine the measure of hatred for the evil, which interferes with his engagement in *Torah and Mitzvot*. For this reason, if a person wants to come to hate the evil, he must increase the importance of spirituality.

At that time, he will receive such a measure of hatred that will remove him from befriending his evil, as it is written, "You who love the Lord hate evil." That is, to the extent that a person loves the Creator, so he hates those who interfere with loving the Creator.

28. RABASH, Article No. 21 (1986), "Concerning Above Reason"

If one does not do good deeds, does not engage in Torah and prayer, and wish to draw near the Creator, he has no light to illuminate his heart and to allow him to see the evil in his heart. It turns out that the reason why he is still not seeing that there is more evil in his heart than in all of the friends is that he needs more good. For this reason, he thinks that he is more virtuous than his friends.

It therefore turns out that his seeing that his friends are worse than he comes from his lack of the light that will shine for him, so he will see the evil in himself. Thus, the whole matter of evil that is in man is not in finding the evil, since everyone has this evil, called "will to receive in order to receive," which is self-love. Instead, the difference is entirely in the disclosure of the evil. In other words, not every person sees and feels that self-love is bad and harmful, since a person doesn't see that engagement in satisfying his will to receive, called "self-love," will harm him.

Yet, when he begins to do the holy work on the path of truth, meaning when he wishes to achieve *Dvekut* [adhesion] with the Creator, so all his actions will be for the Creator, by that he receives a little more light that shines for him each time, and then he begins to feel self-love as a bad thing.

It is a gradual process. Each time he sees that this is what obstructs him from achieving *Dvekut* with the Creator, he sees more clearly each time how it—the will to receive—is his real enemy, just as King Solomon referred to the evil inclination as "an enemy." It is written about it, "If your enemy is hungry, feed him bread, for you will heap burning coals on his head."

29. RABASH, Article No. 18 (1987), "What Is Preparation for Reception of the Torah? – 1"

After all the work that a person has put into awakening to achieve the truth, meaning to really know why he was born and what goal he should achieve, so now the Creator disclosed to him that the inclination of a man's heart, which is the receiver, is evil from his youth. That is, it cannot be said that now he sees that the inclination has become bad. Rather, it is evil from his youth. However, until now he could not determine that it was really evil; therefore, the person was in states of ascent and descent. In other words, at times he would listen to the inclination and say that from now on I will know that this is my enemy and everything it advises me to do is to my detriment.

But afterwards, the esteem of the inclination rises again and once again he listens to it and works for it wholeheartedly, and so on and so forth. He feels that he is as "a dog returning to its vomit." That is, he has already determined that it was unfit for him to listen to it because all the nourishments that the inclination gives him are but food fit for beasts and not for man. But all of a sudden, he returns to animal food and forgets all the decisions and views he had before.

Afterward, when he regrets, he sees that he has no other way but for the Creator to make him see that the inclination that is called "evil" really is evil. Then, once the Creator has given him this knowledge, he does not go astray again but asks the Creator to give him the strength to overcome it each and every time the inclination wants to fail him, so he will have the strength to overcome it.

It therefore follows that the Creator should give him both the *Kli* [vessel] and the light, meaning both the awareness that the inclination is evil and there is a need to emerge from under its reign, and the correction for this is the Torah, as it is written, "I have created the evil inclination, I have created the Torah as a spice." Accordingly, the Creator gave him both the need for the Torah, as well as the Torah. This is regarded as the Creator giving him the light, as well as the *Kli*.

30. RABASH, Article No. 12 (1985), "Jacob Dwelled in the Land Where His Father Had Lived"

One must believe that the Creator has created the world with benevolence, and the evil in his body removes him from all the good. That is, when he comes to learn Torah, he finds it utterly tasteless. And also, when he comes to perform some *Mitzva* [good deed/correction], he finds it utterly tasteless because the evil inclination in his body has the power not to let him believe in the Creator above reason by taking out every flavor. Whenever he begins to approach something spiritual, he feels that everything is dry without any moisture of life.

When the person began his work, he was told—and he believed what he was told—that the Torah is a Torah of life, as it is written, "For they are your life and the length of your days," and as it is written (Psalms 19), "More desirable than gold, than much fine gold, and sweeter than honey and the honeycomb."

But when one consider this and sees that the evil inclination is to blame for everything, and strongly feels the bad that it is causing him, then he feels on himself what is written (Psalms 34) "Many are the afflictions of the righteous." That is, that verse was said about him.

At that time he looks at what the verse says afterwards, "but the Lord delivers him out of them all." At that time he begins to cry out to the Creator to help him because he has already done everything that he could think of doing, but nothing helped, and he thinks that "Everything that you find within your power to do, that do," was said about him. At that time comes the time of salvation—the salvation of the Creator delivering him from the evil inclination—to the extent that from this day forth the evil inclination will surrender before him and will not be able to incite him into any transgression.

31. RABASH, Article No. 8 (1989), "What It Means, in the Work, that If the Good Grows, So Grows the Bad"

In the beginning of the work, during the *Ibur*, meaning when a person begins to shift from the work of the general public to the work of individuals, the bad immediately begins to appear in him. However, it is not so apparent. Yet, when he begins to ascend in the work and begins to grow, as it is written, "The boys grew," to the extent and order of the growth, so grows the evil. According to the measure of the good that he does, so grows the measure of the evil in him, as was said, so he will be half guilty, half innocent.

Now we can understand what RASHI explained, "Another interpretation: Struggling with each other and quarreling about the inheritance of two worlds." We should understand for what purpose there needs to be a quarrel between them. It is as our sages said (*Berachot* 5), "Rabbi Levi said, 'One should always vex the good inclination over the evil inclination.'" RASHI explains that he should wage war against the evil inclination. We need to understand what is the purpose of this war. Would it not be better if a person saw that the bad in him did not awaken? Why does he need to awaken it and fight it? It would be better if he did not risk himself, for he might not be able to defeat it, as our sages said, "One must not put oneself in danger."

In the work, when we want to achieve bestowal, we must say when we perform *Mitzvot* or engage in Torah, that we want to do everything with the aim to bestow. This is called vexing the good inclination over the evil inclination, since when a person says to his body, "We must work for the sake of the Creator and not for our own sake," the body immediately becomes angry and resists with all its might. It tells him, "You can do anything, but for the sake of the Creator and not for our own sake? This is out of the question." It follows that if he does not vex it, he will never be able to achieve the truth.

32. RABASH, Article No. 25 (1990), "What Is, 'Praise the Lord, All Nations,' in the Work?"

When a person is rewarded with vessels of bestowal, he is rewarded with the delight and pleasure that were in the thought of creation. This is called, "When the Lord favors a man's ways, even his enemies make peace with him." Rabbi Yehoshua Ben Levi interprets, "This is the serpent" (Jerusalem Talmud, *Terumot* 8:3). The serpent is the evil inclination, who is the appointee of the seventy nations. As was said, the quality of the nations of the world in one's body cause him not to be able to be rewarded with the delight and pleasure.

33. RABASH, Article No. 25 (1990), "What Is, 'Praise the Lord, All Nations,' in the Work?"

Man's enemies, which is the evil inclination, called "enemy," as it is written, "If your enemy is hungry, feed him bread," referring to the evil inclination, as our sages said, that King Solomon would call the evil inclination by the name "enemy," so he, too, will make peace with him. This is called, "And you shall love the Lord your God with all your heart, with both your inclinations," namely with the good inclination and with the evil inclination. When a person's vessels of reception obtain the force to receive in order to bestow, at that time he serves the Creator with the evil inclination, too. That is, the evil inclination also loves the Creator, for it, too, receives delight and pleasure.

This is why it is written, "and the truth of the Lord," as he interprets in *The Study of the Ten Sefirot* about the seventh correction of the thirteen corrections of *Dikna*, called "and truth," that it is called "and truth" because in this correction it becomes revealed to all that this is the truth, that such was the purpose of creation: to do good to His creations.

34. RABASH, Article No. 16 (1984), "Concerning Bestowal"

It is said about that (*Kidushin*, 30), "Man's inclination overcomes him each day and seeks to kill him, as it is said, 'The wicked watches the righteous, and seeks to slay him.' And if the Creator did not help him, he would not overcome it, as it is said, 'The Lord will not leave him in his hand.'"

This means that first, one must see if he has the strength to come to be able to act with the aim to bestow contentment upon the Creator. Then, when he has already come to realize that he cannot achieve it by himself, that person focuses his Torah and *Mitzvot* on a single point, which is that "the light in it reforms him," that this will be the only reward that he wants from the Torah and *Mitzvot*. In other words, the reward for his labor will be for the Creator to give him this strength called "the power of bestowal."

35. *Zohar for All*, "Introduction of The Book of Zohar," "On the Night of the Bride," Item 138

It is a law that the creature cannot receive disclosed evil from the Creator, for it is a flaw in the glory of the Creator for the creature to perceive Him as an evildoer, for this is unbecoming of the complete Operator. Hence, when one feels bad, denial of the Creator's guidance lies upon him and the superior Operator is concealed from him to that same extent. This is the greatest punishment in the world.

Thus, the sensation of good and evil in relation to His guidance brings with it the sensation of reward and punishment, for one who exerts to not part from faith in the Creator is rewarded even when he tastes a bad taste in Providence. And if he does not exert, he will have a punishment because he is separated from faith in the Creator.

36. *Zohar for All, VaYera* [The Lord Appeared], "Your Wife Shall Be As a Fruitful Vine," 453

Man is created in utter wickedness and lowliness, as it is written, "When a wild ass's foal is born a man." And all the vessels in one's body, meaning the senses and the qualities, and especially the thought serve him only wickedness and nothingness all day. And for one who is rewarded with adhering unto Him, the Creator does not create other tools instead, to be worthy and suitable for reception of the eternal spiritual abundance intended for him. Rather, the same lowly vessels that have thus far been used in a filthy and loathsome way are inverted to become vessels of reception of all the pleasantness and eternal gentleness.

37. Rabbi Nachman of Breslov, *Meshivat Nefesh*

It is a great merit when one has evil inclination, for then he can serve the Creator precisely with the evil inclination, meaning overcome out of the warmth of the evil inclination, to extend from it into some work out His work. If one has no evil inclination, his work is completely worthless. For this reason, the Creator lets the evil inclination expand over the person in this way, and especially over one who truly craves to draw near Him, although through its expansion and provocation, it brings one to great iniquities and flaws. Nevertheless, it is all worthwhile for Him, for the good movement, for by the intensification of the evil inclination, a person overcomes it through some movement and runs away from it. This is more precious to Him than if one served Him for a thousand years without the evil inclination, for all the worlds were created only for man, whose entire merit and importance are because he has such an evil inclination, and he braces himself against it.

4

The Burdening of the Heart

1. Baal HaSulam, *Shamati*, Article No. 4, "What Is the Reason for the Heaviness One Feels when Annulling before the Creator in the Work?"

We must know the reason for the heaviness one feels when he wants to work in annulling his self before the Creator and not worry about his own benefit. A person comes to a state as though the entire world stands still, and he alone is now seemingly absent from this world, and leaves his family and friends for the sake of annulling before the Creator.

There is but a simple reason for this, called "lack of faith." It means that one does not see before whom he nullifies, meaning he does not feel the existence of the Creator. This causes him heaviness.

But when he begins to feel the existence of the Creator, his soul immediately yearns to annul and connect with the root, to be contained in it like a candle in a torch, without any mind or reason. However, this comes naturally, as a candle is canceled before a torch.

It therefore follows that the essence of one's work is only to come to feel the existence of the Creator, meaning to feel the existence of the Creator, that "the whole earth is full of His glory," and this will be one's entire work. That is, all the energy one puts into the work will be only to achieve this, and nothing else.

One should not be misled into having to acquire anything. Rather, there is only one thing a person needs: faith in the Creator. He should not think of anything, meaning that the only reward that he wants for his work should be to be rewarded with faith in the Creator.

2. Baal HaSulam, *Shamati*, Article No. 121, "She Is Like Merchant-Ships"

"Man shall not live on bread alone, but on what proceeds out of the mouth of the Lord." This means that the life of *Kedusha* [holiness] in a person does not come specifically from drawing closer, from entries, meaning admissions into *Kedusha*, but also from the exits, from the removals. This is so because through the dressing of the *Sitra Achra* in one's body, and its claims, "She is all mine," with a just argument, one is awarded permanent faith by overcoming these states.

This means that one should dedicate everything to the Creator, that is, that even the exits stem from Him. When he is rewarded, he sees that both the exits and the entries were all from Him. This forces him to be humble, since he sees that the Creator does everything, the exits as well as the entries.

This is the meaning of what is said about Moses, that he was humble and patient—that one must tolerate the lowliness, meaning that in each degree one should keep the lowliness. The minute he leaves the lowliness, he immediately loses all the degrees of Moses he had already achieved.

This is the meaning of patience. Lowliness exists in everyone, but not every person feels that lowliness is a good thing. It turns out that we do not want to suffer. However, Moses tolerated the humbleness, which is why he was called "humble," since the lowliness made him glad.

3. Baal HaSulam, *Shamati*, Article No. 33, "The Lots on Yom Kippurim and with Haman"

We must know that what appears to one as things that contradict the guidance of "The Good Who Does Good" is only to compel one to draw the upper light on the contradictions, when wanting to prevail over the contradictions. Otherwise, one cannot prevail. This is called "the exaltedness of the Creator," which one extends when having the contradictions, called *Dinim* [judgments].

This means that the contradictions can be annulled if one wants to overcome them, only if he extends the exaltedness of the Creator. You find that these *Dinim* cause the drawing of the exaltedness of the Creator. This is the meaning of what is written, "and cast his mantle upon him."

It means that afterward he attributed the whole mantle of hair to Him, to the Creator. That is, now he saw that the Creator gave him this mantle deliberately, in order to draw the upper light on them.

However, one can only see this later, after one has been granted the light that rests on these contradictions and *Dinim* that he had had in the beginning. This is so because he sees that without the hair, meaning the descents, there would not be a place for the upper light to be there, as there is no light without a *Kli* [vessel].

For this reason, he sees that all the exaltedness of the Creator he had obtained was because of the *Se'arot* and the contradictions he had had. This is the meaning of "The Lord on high is mighty." It means that the exaltedness of the Creator is awarded through the *Aderet*, and this is the meaning of "let the exaltedness of God be in their mouth."

This means that through the faults in the work of the Creator, it causes him to rise up, as without a push one is idle to make a movement and agrees to remain in the state he is in. But if one descends to a lower degree than he understands, this gives one the strength to overcome, for one cannot stay in such a bad state, since one cannot agree to remain like that, in the state to which he has descended.

For this reason, one must always prevail and emerge from the state of descent. In that state, he must draw upon himself the exaltedness of the Creator. This causes him to extend higher forces from above, or he remains in utter lowliness. It follows that through the *Se'arot*, one gradually discovers the exaltedness of the Creator until one finds the names of the Creator, called "the thirteen attributes of Mercy." This is the meaning of "and the elder shall serve the younger," and "the wicked will prepare and the righteous will wear," and also, "and you shall serve your brother."

This means that all the enslavement, meaning the contradictions that there were, which appeared to be obstructing the holy work, and were working against *Kedusha* [holiness]. Now, when granted the light of the Creator, which is placed over these contradictions, we see the opposite—that they were serving the *Kedusha*. That is, through them, there was a place for the *Kedusha* to clothe in their dresses. This is called "the wicked will prepare and the righteous will wear," meaning that they gave the *Kelim* [vessels] and the place for the *Kedusha*.

4. Baal HaSulam, *Shamati*, Article No. 172 "The Matter of Preventions and Delays"

All the preventions and delays that appear before our eyes are but a form of nearing—the Creator wants to bring us closer, and all these preventions bring us only nearing, since without them we would have no possibility of approaching Him. This is so because, by nature, there is no greater distance, as we are made of pure matter while the Creator is higher than high. Only when one begins to approach does he begin to feel the distance between us. And any prevention one overcomes brings the way closer for that person.

(This is so because one grows accustomed to moving on a line of growing farther. Hence, whenever one feels that he is distant, it does not induce any change in the process, since he knew in advance that he is moving on a line of growing farther, since this is the truth, that there are not enough words to describe the distance between us and the Creator. Hence, every time he feels that distance to a greater extent than he thought, it causes him no contention.)

5. Baal HaSulam, *Shamati*, Article No. 42, "What Is the Acronym Elull in the Work?"

It is impossible to obtain disclosure before one receives the discernment of *Achoraim* [posterior], discerned as concealment of the Face, and to say that it is as important to him as the disclosure of the Face. It means that one should be as glad as though he has already acquired the disclosure of the Face.

However, one cannot persist and appreciate the concealment like the disclosure, except when one works in bestowal. At that time, one can say, "I do not care what I feel during the work because what is important to me is that I want to bestow upon the Creator. If the Creator understands that He will have more contentment if I work in a form of *Achoraim*, I agree."

However, if one still has sparks of reception, he comes to thoughts, and it is then hard for him to believe that the Creator leads the world in a manner of "good and doing good." This is the meaning of the letter *Yod* in the name *HaVaYaH*, which is the first letter, called "a black dot that has no white in it," meaning it is all darkness and concealment of the Face.

It means that when one comes to a state where one has no support, one's state becomes black, which is the lowest quality in the upper world, and that becomes the *Keter* to the lower one, as the *Kli* of *Keter* is a vessel of bestowal.

The lowest quality in the upper one is *Malchut*, which has nothing of its own, meaning that she does not have anything. Only in this manner is it called *Malchut*. It means that if one takes upon himself the kingdom of heaven—which is in a state of not having anything—gladly, afterward, it becomes *Keter*, which is a vessel of bestowal and the purest *Kli*. In other words, the reception of *Malchut* in a state of darkness subsequently becomes a *Kli* of *Keter*, which is a vessel of bestowal.

6. Baal HaSulam, *Shamati*, Article No. 70, "With a Mighty Hand and with Fury Poured Out"

We should know that of those who want to come into the work of the Creator in order to truly adhere to Him and enter the King's palace, not everyone is admitted. Rather, he is tested: If he has no other desires but only a desire for *Dvekut* [adhesion], he is admitted.

And how is one tested if he has only one desire? He is given disturbances. This means that he is sent foreign thoughts and foreign messengers to obstruct him so he would leave this path and follow the path of all the people.

If one overcomes all the difficulties and breaks all the bars that block him, and little things cannot push him away, the Creator sends him great *Klipot* [shells/peels] and chariots to deflect one from entering into *Dvekut* with the Creator alone, and with nothing else. This is considered that the Creator is rejecting him with a mighty hand.

If the Creator does not show a mighty hand, it will be hard to push him away since he has a strong desire to adhere only to the Creator and to nothing else.

But when the Creator wants to reject one whose desire is not so strong, He pushes him away with a small thing. By giving him a great desire for corporeality, he already leaves the holy work entirely, and there is no need to repel him with a mighty hand.

Yet, when one overcomes all the hardships and the disturbances, one is not easily repelled, but with a mighty hand. And if one overcomes even the mighty hand and does not want to move from the place of *Kedusha* [holiness] whatsoever, but wants to adhere specifically to Him in truth, and sees that he is repelled, then one says that fury is poured out on him. Otherwise, he would be allowed inside. But because fury is poured out on him by the Creator, he is not admitted into the King's palace to adhere to Him.

It follows that before one wants to move from one's place, and breaks in and wants to enter, it cannot be said that he feels that fury is poured out on him. Rather, after all the rejections that he is rejected, and he does not move from his place, meaning when the mighty hand and the fury poured out have already been revealed upon him, then "I will be King over you" comes true. This is so because only through bursting and great efforts does the kingdom of heaven become revealed to him, and he is rewarded with entering the King's palace.

7. Baal HaSulam, Letter No. 14

"Come to Pharaoh." It is the *Shechina* [Divinity] in disclosure, from the words, "and let the hair of the woman's head go loose," as it is written in *The Zohar*. The thing is that to the extent that the children of Israel thought that Egypt were enslaving them and impeding them from serving the Creator, they truly were in the exile in Egypt. Hence, the Redeemer's only work was to reveal to them that there is no other force involved here, that "I and not a messenger," for there is no other force but Him. This was indeed the light of redemption, as explained in the Passover *Haggadah* [story].

This is what the Creator gave to Moses in the verse, "Come to Pharaoh," meaning unite the truth, for the whole approaching the king of Egypt is only to Pharaoh, to disclose the *Shechina*. This is why He said, "For I have hardened his heart," etc., "that I may place these signs of Mine within him."

In spirituality, there are no letters, as I have already elaborated on before. All the multiplication in spirituality relies on the letters derived from the materiality of this world, as in, "And creator of darkness." There are no additions or initiations here, but the creation of darkness, the *Merkava* [chariot/structure] that is suited to disclose that the light is good. It follows that the Creator Himself hardened his heart. Why? Because it is letters that I need.

This is the meaning of "that I may place these signs of Mine within him, and that you may tell … that you may know that I am the Lord." Explanation: Once you receive the letters, meaning when you understand that I gave and toiled for you, as in, do not move from "behind" Me, for you will thoroughly keep the *Achoraim* [posterior/back] for Me, for My name, then the abundance will do her thing and fill the letters. The qualities will become *Sefirot*, since before the filling they are called "qualities," and upon their fulfillment for the best, they are called *Sefirot*, sapphire, illuminating the world from one end to the other.

This is the meaning of "that you may tell." I need all this for the end of the matter, meaning "And you shall know that I am the Lord" "and not a messenger." This is the meaning of the fiftieth gate, which cannot appear unless the forty-nine faces of pure and impure appear in one opposite the other, in which the righteous falls [forty-nine in *Gematria*] before the wicked.

8. Baal HaSulam, Letter No. 19

To Him who knows the mysteries, the desire in one's heart for His nearness is known, and that it might still be interrupted. Hence, He increases His stimuli, meaning the beginnings of the coituses, for if one listens to His voice, as in "The Lord of your shade," one does not fall and descend due to the increasing affliction of the stimuli since he sees and hears that the *Shechina* also suffers as he does by the increased longing. Thus, one's longing grows and intensifies each time until one's point in the heart is completed with complete will in a tight knot that will not crumble.

9. Baal HaSulam, *Shamati*, Article No. 19, "What Is "The Creator Hates the Bodies," in the Work?"

One must always examine oneself, the purpose of one's work, meaning if the Creator receives contentment in every act that one performs, because he wants equivalence of form with the Creator. This is called "All your actions will be for the sake of the Creator," meaning that one wants the Creator to enjoy everything he does, as it is written, "to bring contentment to his Maker."

Also, one needs to conduct oneself with the will to receive and say to it, "I have already decided that I do not want to receive any pleasure because you want to enjoy, since with your desire I am forced to be separated from the Creator, for disparity of form causes separation and distance from the Creator."

One's hope should be that since he cannot break free from the power of the will to receive, he is therefore in perpetual ascents and descents. Hence, he awaits the Creator, to be rewarded with the Creator opening his eyes, and to have the strength to overcome and work only for the sake of the Creator. It is as it is written, "One have I asked of the Lord; her will I seek." "Her" means the *Shechina* [Divinity]. And one asks "that I may dwell in the house of the Lord all the days of my life."

10. Baal HaSulam, "Introduction to The Study of the Ten Sefirot," Item 101

As long as one is not rewarded with a guidance of revelation of the face, the abundance of Torah and *Mitzvot* he has performed make his concealment of the face much heavier. This is the meaning of "The Creator hides Himself in the Torah."

Indeed, all that heaviness he feels through the Torah is but proclamations by which the Torah itself calls him, awakening him to hurry up and give the required measure of labor to promptly endow him with the revelation of the face, as God wills it.

11. Baal HaSulam, Letter No. 47

The nature of spirituality: One who is adhered to the Creator feels himself as not adhered. He worries and is insecure about it and does all that he can do by his strength to be rewarded with *Dvekut* [adhesion]. A wise one feels opposite from one who is not adhered to the Creator, who feels content and satisfied, and does not worry properly, except to keep the *Mitzvot* [commandments] of worry and longing, for "a fool does not feel."

12. Baal HaSulam, Letter No. 18

One who assumes the complete burden of the kingdom of heaven finds no labor in the work of the Creator, and can therefore adhere to the Creator day and night, in light and in darkness. The *Geshem* ["rain," but also "corporeality"]—which is created in coming and going, changes and exchanges—will not stop him since the *Keter*, which is *Ein Sof*, illuminates to all completely equally. The fool—who walks under a flood of preventions that pour on him from before and from behind—says to all that he does not feel the cessation and the lack of *Dvekut* [adhesion] as a corruption or iniquity on his part.

Had he sensed it, he would certainly have strained to find some tactic to at least be saved from the cessation of *Dvekut*, whether more or less. This tactic has never been denied of anyone who sought it, either as in "the thought of faith" or as in "confidence," or as in "pleas of his prayer," which are suitable for a person specifically in the narrow and pressured places.

13. RABASH, Article No. 1 (1989), "What Is the Measure of Repentance?"

We should know that when a person wants to emerge from merely performing actions, without the aim, and wants to begin the work of acting with the aim to bestow, there is much work in this, since when the body begins to hear about the aim to bestow, it immediately begins to resist and does not let one continue this work, showing him dark colors in this work.

In that state, a person should believe that only the Creator can help. Here is where a person can make a true prayer. It is called "true" because it is really the truth. That is, the Creator has made man unable to help himself, and the reason is that "There is no light without a *Kli*," as we have said several times. As Baal HaSulam says, the Creator made man unable to exit self-love by himself in order for man to need the Creator's help. How does the Creator help? With a holy soul, as it is written in *The Zohar*. Otherwise, a person does not have the need to receive the light of the Torah, and will settle for observing *Torah* and *Mitzvot* and not needing to receive the *NRNHY* of *Neshama* that have been prepared for him.

But when he sees that he cannot exit self-love and be rewarded with equivalence of form, he needs the Creator's help. How does He help a person? Through a holy soul, called "upper light" that is revealed within man, so he will feel that there is a soul within him that is "a part of God above." It follows that according to man's ability to overcome, he increases the disclosure of the light of the Creator. For this reason, the Creator has made the hardening of the heart, so that man will be unable to overcome the evil in him and will need the Creator. By this, man will need to be rewarded with the NRNHY of *Neshama*.

14. RABASH, Article No. 29 (1986), "Lishma and Lo Lishma"

A person who wishes to walk on the path of bestowal, he must understand that from above he is given a special treatment, that he was lowered from the previous state so he would begin to really contemplate the goal, meaning what is required of man and what man wants the Creator to give him. But when he is in a state of ascent, when he has desire for Torah and *Mitzvot*, he has no need to worry about spirituality. Instead, he sees that he will stay this way his whole life because he is happy this way.

It therefore follows that the descent he has received is for his own good, meaning that he is receiving special treatment, that he was lowered from his state where he thought that he had some wholeness. This is apparent in his agreeing to remain in the current state his whole life.

But now that he sees that he is far from spirituality, he begins to think, "What is really required of me? What should I do? What is the purpose I should achieve?" He sees that he has no power to work, and finds himself in a state of "between heaven and earth." Then, man's only strengthening is that only the Creator can help, but by himself, he is doomed.

It was said about this (Isaiah, 4:31): "Yet those who hope for the Lord will gain new strength," meaning those people who hope for the Creator. This means that they who see that there is no one else in the world who can help them regain strength each time. It follows that this descent is actually an ascent, meaning that this descent that they feel allows them to rise in degree, since "there is no light without a *Kli*."

15. RABASH, Article No. 38 (1985), "A Righteous Who Is Happy, a Righteous Who Is Suffering"

When one wants to go on the path of doing everything for the Creator, where in everything he does he thinks what benefit the Creator will derive from this, and does not think of his own benefit, then the body comes to him with arguments. It begins to slander this path, called "the path of bestowal and not for one's self-benefit," and argues the arguments of Pharaoh and the argument of the wicked, which are regarded as "mind and heart," namely "who and what."

When a person begins to listen to their arguments, he begins to wonder because he has never heard such strong arguments coming from his body as the ones he hears now. When he began the work he thought that each time he would advance further toward the goal, meaning that each time he would see that it is worthwhile to work for the Creator.

But suddenly he sees that where he should have had a greater desire to serve the Creator, he hears rejection from the body, which tells him now, "Why don't you want to go the way the whole world goes, where you should be meticulous with the nitty gritty actions, and concerning the intention you should say, 'May it be as though I intended.'" "But now," says the body, "I see that you are paying attention specifically to the intentions, meaning that you can aim that everything will be for the Creator and not for yourself. Can it be that you will be different? Don't you want to be like everyone else, who say that this is the safest way? And the evidence of this is to look at everyone else, how they behave."

At that time begins the work of overcoming. That is, he needs to overcome their arguments and not surrender to their demands. He must certainly give them clear answers to what they are making him see, that his desire to intend that all his works will be only to bestow and not for his own benefit is against reason, since reason mandates that since man was created with a will to receive delight and pleasure, and there is a natural demand to satisfy it—or else, why does he need life if not to enjoy it, to satisfy the body's demands—and so it lets him understand that this makes perfect sense, and there is no excuse to answer its arguments.

The clear reply should be that we believe in the words of the sages, who taught us that we must go above mind and reason. That is, true faith is specifically above reason, and what the mind understands is not all true, since with respect to the Creator, we learn that "My thoughts are not your thoughts, nor My ways your ways."

16. RABASH, Article No. 20 (1990), "What Is Half a Shekel in the Work? – 2"

There are two manners that cause a person to escape the campaign even when he enters the work of being adhered to the Creator. Once a person begins to walk on the path of truth, he is shown from above his lowliness, meaning that the more he overcomes, the more hardening of the heart he receives from above, because as it is written, "That I may set these signs of Mine within him." This means that by this, there will be room for the revelation of the light of Torah, called "letters," and this reforms him. That is, since there is no light without a *Kli*, through the hardening of the heart, the lack appears sufficiently, and the Creator knows when the measure is sufficient, when the *Kli* is completed.

Therefore, sometimes a person escapes the campaign when he sees that he has already prayed a lot in his opinion, but the Creator does not notice him. At that time, sometimes a person sentences the Creator to the side of merit for not granting his prayer, and says that it is because he has a poor character in every way, in virtues, and in good qualities, etc.

It was said about this, "The poor shall not give less," meaning that a person should not belittle himself and say that the Creator cannot help a lowly person such as him, for it was said about this, "The Lord is high and the low will see."

And sometimes, a person leaves the campaign because he knows that he is rich, meaning he has much Torah and many good deeds, and he knows that he is superior to others. Therefore, when he asks the Creator to help him be able to do everything in order to bestow, why is the Creator not granting him, for he knows that he has already given many prayers for it. Therefore, he says that the Creator does not want to answer him, and therefore he runs.

And yet, a person must always overcome.

17. RABASH, Article No. 18 (1990), "Why the Speech of Shabbat Must Not Be as the Speech of a Weekday, in the Work"

The first assistance he receives is the revelation of the evil in him. This is called "hardening of the heart," as it is written, "For I have hardened his heart." This is regarded as obtaining the *Achoraim* of *Kedusha*. *Kedusha* is called *Panim*, and *Panim* is considered something that illuminates, as he says ("Introduction to The Study of the Ten Sefirot," Item 47), "We must first understand what is the meaning of the 'face of the Creator,' about which the writing says, 'I will hide My face.' It can be thought of as a person who sees his friend's face and knows him right away. However, when he sees him from behind he is not certain of his identity. He might doubt, 'Perhaps he is another and not his friend?' So is the matter before us: Everyone knows and feels that the Creator is good and that it is the conduct of the good to do good. Hence, when the Creator generously bestows upon His creations, it is considered that His face is revealed to His creations, since then everyone knows and recognizes Him. Yet, when He behaves with His creations the opposite from the above mentioned, meaning when they suffer afflictions and torments in His world, it is considered the *Achoraim* of the Creator, for His face, meaning His complete attribute of goodness, is entirely concealed from them."

Therefore, in that state, if he can accept the *Achoraim*, which is called "exile," and does not run, but rather, "And they cried out to the Lord" to deliver him from the exile, then he accepts the *Achoraim* and says that it comes from the Creator, hence he asks Him that as He made him feel the taste of exile, so He will help him emerge from exile.

18. RABASH, Article No. 24 (1986), "The Difference between Charity and Gift"

In the work of the Creator, in the beginning of his work he had energy and confidence, and great importance for Torah and prayer because at that time he had grace of holiness, and felt that the work of the Creator is important. However, this was still not considered a "deficiency" that the Creator will satisfy, a deficiency is called *Dvekut* [adhesion] with the Creator, since the lack and pain of not having *Dvekut* with the Creator was still not felt in him as he has not exerted for it because he has just begun the work.

But after a long period of time of making efforts and not achieving satisfaction of his deficiency, torments and pain begin to form in him because he has made efforts but sees no progress in his work. At that time the thoughts begin to come one-by-one. Sometimes it is with sparks of despair, and sometimes he grows stronger, but then he sees once more that he has fallen from his state, and so on repeatedly. Finally, a real deficiency forms in him, which he has obtained through exertion in ascents and descents. These ascents and descents leave him with pain each time at not having been granted *Dvekut* with the Creator. Finally, when the cup of labor has been filled sufficiently, it is called a *Kli*. Then the filling of it comes from the Creator, since now he has a real *Kli*.

It follows that his seeing that now—after several years of work—he has retreated, this happens deliberately so he will ache at not having *Dvekut* with the Creator. It turns out that each time he must see that he is approaching the making of the *Kli*, called "real deficiency." That is, his gauge of *Katnut* [infancy/smallness] and *Gadlut* [adulthood/greatness] of the deficiency is to the extent of the suffering he feels at not having the filling, which is called here "*Dvekut* with the Creator," where all he wants is only to bring contentment to the Creator.

19. RABASH, Article No. 236, "The Whole Earth Is Full of His Glory"

Before one is fit to attain the truth, he must believe that the truth is not as he knows or feels, but that it is as it is written, "They have eyes and they will not see; they have ears and they will not hear."

This is only because of the correction, in order for man to achieve his wholeness, for he feels only himself and not another reality.

Hence, if one returns his heart to trying to walk in faith above the intellect, by this he qualifies it and establishes it so as to achieve the revelation of the face, as is presented in *The Zohar*, that the *Shechina* [Divinity] said to Rabbi Shimon Bar Yochai, "There is no place to hide from you," meaning that in all the concealments that he felt, he believed that here was the light of the Creator. This qualified him until he achieved the revelation of the face of His light.

This is the meaning of the measure of the faith that pulls one out of every lowliness and concealment if a person strengthens himself in this and asks the Creator to reveal Himself.

This is the meaning of what Baal HaSulam said, "Run my Beloved until she pleases," meaning that before one is fit to reveal His light, we ask of Him, "Run my Beloved," meaning that He will not reveal Himself to the created beings because the concealment is only the correction of creation.

Hence, one must brace oneself and pray for those two:

1) To be worthy of the revelation of the light of the Creator.
2) That the Creator will give him the power to grow stronger in faith above reason, for by this, he merges *Kelim* [vessels] that are fit for the revelation of the face.

20. RABASH, Article No. 19 (1985), "Come unto Pharaoh – 1"

We should pay attention to "Come unto Pharaoh" and believe through the worst possible states, and not escape the campaign, but rather always trust that the Creator can help a person and give him, whether one needs a little help or a lot of help.

In truth, one who understands that he needs the Creator to give him a lot of help, because he is worse than the rest of the people, is more suitable for his prayer to be answered, as it is written, "The Lord is near to the brokenhearted, and saves the crushed in spirit."

Therefore, one should not say that he is unfit for the Creator to bring him closer, but that the reason is that he is idle in his work. Instead, one should always overcome and not let thoughts of despair enter his mind, as our sages said (*Berachot*, 10), "Even if a sharp sword is placed on his neck he should not deny himself of mercy," as it was said (Job, 13), "Though He slay me, I will hope for Him."

We should interpret the "sharp sword placed on his neck" to mean that even though one's evil, called "self-love," is placed on his neck and wants to separate him from *Kedusha* by showing him that it is impossible to exit this authority, he should say that the picture he sees is the truth.

However, "He should not deny himself of mercy," for at that time he must believe that the Creator can give him the mercy, meaning the quality of bestowal. That is, by himself, it is true that one cannot exit the authority of self-reception. But from the perspective of the Creator, when the Creator helps him, of course He can bring him out. This is the meaning of what is written, "I am the Lord your God, who took you out from the land of Egypt to be your God."

21. RABASH, Article No. 44 (1990), "What Is an Optional War, in the work - 2?"

All those thoughts that the will to receive brings him are sent to him from above because he wants to walk on the path of bestowal, and in the meantime he is idle in the work, because he prayed for the

Creator to bring him closer to being in *Dvekut* with the Creator, which is equivalence of form, when it is apparent that the person is idle in the work, he is sent the foreign thoughts that a person cannot agree to be under such a control. This, in turn, gives a person a push that he must overcome the state he is in.

It therefore follows that from this bad, when a person feels that he is in such a lowly state that he never imagined that he could be under such governance, for this reason, he should not be alarmed and escape the campaign. On the contrary, he should believe that the Creator is taking care of him now, and He is bringing him closer through a state of *Achoraim* [posterior].

This is as it is written in the book *A Sage's Fruit* (Vol. 1, p 139), "About the verse, 'My beloved is like a gazelle,' our sages said, 'As the gazelle looks back when he runs, when the Creator leaves Israel, He turns back His face.' Then the face returns to being in the *Achoraim*, meaning craving and longing to cling to Israel once more. This begets in Israel longing and craving to cling to the Creator, too, and the measure of the longing and craving is actually the face itself."

We should interpret that he means that when a person is in a state of lowliness, it is considered that the Creator has moved away from him, and he has no desire or yearning for the work, this is regarded as the Creator giving a person a shape of tastelessness about spirituality. Moreover, a person wants to escape and forget about the work altogether. This is regarded as the Creator showing him the *Achoraim*.

The *Panim* [face/anterior] of the Creator is His desire to do good to His creations, and the *Achoraim* is the complete opposite. Why does the Creator show a person the *Achoraim*? It is on purpose, for by this a person gets a thrust toward *Dvekut* with the Creator, for he cannot remain in a state of lowliness. It follows that here, within the *Achoraim* is the discernment of *Panim*.

22. RABASH, Article No. 21 (1988), "What Does It Mean that the Torah Was Given Out of the Darkness in the Work?"

In the work, "the nations of the world" means that the body comprises seventy nations that want the Torah not because they feel darkness when they have no vessels of bestowal. Rather, their only desire is the vessels of reception and they have no desire to emerge from that control. They want the Torah in order to add more light to themselves, meaning more pleasure than they receive from corporeal matters. That is, they also want the next world, as it is written in *The Zohar*, "They howl as dogs *Hav, Hav* [give, give], give us the wealth of this world, and give us the wealth of the next world." That is, the wealth of this world is not enough for them, but they also want the wealth of the next world.

It follows that the Torah was given specifically to those who feel that their will to receive controls them. They cry out from the darkness that they need the Torah in order to deliver them from the darkness that is the control of the vessels of reception, on which there was a *Tzimtzum* [restriction] and concealment so that no light will shine in that place. But that place is the cause for the need to receive the Torah.

23. RABASH, Article No. 5 (1988), "What Is, 'When Israel Are in Exile, the Shechina Is With Them,' in the Work?"

What is the meaning of "When Israel are in exile, the *Shechina* is with them"? As Rabbi Shimon Ben Yochai said, "Wherever they exile, the *Shechina* is with them." What is the benefit from this in the work, that he says about it, "How beloved are Israel by the Creator"?

We should interpret that when a person feels that he is in exile, meaning feels the taste of exile in the work and wants to escape from the exile, the meaning will be that a person must believe that wherever they are exiled, the *Shechina* is with them. That is, the *Shechina* let him feel the taste of exile. "With them" means that the *Shechina* is attached to them and they are not separated from the *Shechina*, that they should say that it is a descent. On the contrary, now the *Shechina* is giving him a push so he will climb the degrees of *Kedusha* [holiness/sanctity], and dresses herself in a garment of descent.

When a person knows and believes that this is so, it will encourage him so he does not escape the campaign or say that the work of bestowal is not for him because he always sees that he is in states of ascents and descents, and he sees no end to these states and falls into despair.

But if he walks in the path of faith and believes in the words of our sage, then he must say the opposite.

24. RABASH, Article No. 30 (1989), "What Is the Meaning of Lighting the Menorah in the Work?"

Only one who labors and works as much as he can, and goes through ups and downs, can say that he tastes the taste of darkness because he cannot overcome his will to receive for himself.

Thus, the descents that a person receives when he wants to walk on the path of truth are instruments for the sensation of the help he will receive. We must believe the words of our sages who said, "He who comes to purify is aided." A person must not escape the campaign when he sees that he is not making progress. Sometimes he gets thoughts of the spies, who said that this work is not for us and requires special people who can walk on the path of overcoming.

All this comes to him because he understands that each time, he must see how he is making progress. However, it does not occur to him that he must advance in obtaining darkness, that this is the only *Kli* he needs to acquire. A *Kli* is a need for a filling. That is, if he has no filling for the lack, he feels that he is in the dark. For this reason, a person must not say that he is not advancing in the work.

Hence, he wants to escape the campaign, for it is not the truth, since he sees each time how far he is from obtaining the light, meaning for the Creator to give him the *Kli* called "desire to bestow." He cannot obtain the desire to bestow by himself, and then he comes to feel that the world has grown dark on him. At that time, the light comes, meaning help from above, as it is written, "He who comes to purify is aided."

25. RABASH, Letter No. 77

The whole foundation is that one should ask that all of one's thoughts and desires will be only to benefit the Creator, a depiction of lowliness, called *Shechina* in the dust, immediately appears. Hence, we must not be impressed by the descent, since many pennies join into a great amount.

This is as we learned, "there is no absence in spirituality," rather that it has temporarily departed in order to have room for work to advance. This is so because every moment that we scrutinize into holiness enters the domain of holiness, and a person descends only in order to sort out more sparks of holiness.

However, there is an advice that one should not wait until his degree is lowered for him, and when he feels his lowliness he goes up again, and that ascent is regarded as sorting a part into holiness. Instead, he himself descends and elevates other sparks, and raises them into the domain of holiness.

It is as our sages said, "Before I lose, I search" (Shabbat, 152), meaning before I lose the situation I am in, I start searching. It is as Baal HaSulam said about King David, who said, "I awaken the dawn." Our sages said, "I awaken the dawn and the dawn does not awaken me."

Therefore, the keeping is primarily during the ascent, and not during the descent.

26. RABASH, Article No. 44, "Ruin by Elders—Construction; Construction by Youths—Ruin"

"Ruin by elders—construction; construction by youths—ruin" (*Megillah* 31b).

Elders are those who are accustomed to the work of the Creator. Youths are those who are in the beginning of their work. "Ruin" means a descent or a fall, where previously they had some ascent in the work, which is regarded as building, meaning that they appreciated the ascent, but the ruin is when they felt some fall, which comes from the concealment of the Creator, that the Creator hides Himself from them. This is called "ruin."

"Ruin by elders" means that they say that the Creator sent them the concealment. It follows that they are already building, since they believe that the Creator is tending to them, and from this they derive vitality.

Faith is apparent primarily during the descent, when it does not shine for a person. At that time, he faces a dilemma: Either he says, "I do not need any benefits. Rather, I want to bring contentment above and I do not care what I feel," or it is otherwise.

27. RABASH, Article No. 6 (1991), "What Is, 'The Herdsmen of Abram's Cattle and the Herdsmen of Lot's Cattle,' in the Work?"

In every beginning a person must start over the acceptance of the kingdom of heaven, it is not enough that yesterday he had faith in the Creator. For this reason, every acceptance of the kingdom of heaven is considered a new discernment. That is, now he receives a part of the vacant space that was devoid of the kingdom of heaven, and admits that empty place and fills it with the kingdom of heaven. It follows that now he sorted out a new thing, which did not exist before he took that empty place and filled it with the kingdom of heaven. This is regarded as elevating a new spark into the *Kedusha*. Finally, from all the ascents, he always raises sparks from the vacant space into the *Kedusha*.

It follows that from each descent he arrives at a new beginning and raises new sparks. Hence, when a person sees that he has descents, he should be careful not to escape from the campaign, even though he sees that he is not progressing. Rather, he must try to start anew each time. That is, the fact that he begins to ascend does not mean that he returned to his previous degree. This would mean that he did nothing by his work, since he thinks that he is now ascending to his previous level. Rather, he must believe that this is a new discernment, that each time, he raises different sparks, until he raises the sparks that pertain to his essence.

28. RABASH, Article No. 289, "The Creator Is Meticulous with the Righteous"

The blow that one receives from the Creator, when He takes from him the flavor of the work, by this itself He heals him because then he has no other way to serve the Creator but with faith above reason. It follows that the blow that he received from the Creator, from this itself he can be healed, for otherwise, he will remain in separation.

By this we understand what our sages said, that by the blows of the Creator, He heals (*Mechilta BeShalach*). In other words, this is the healing—that He gives him room to work with faith without any support.

Also, we should understand what our sages said, "The Creator makes a decree and a righteous revokes it" (*Moed Katan*, 16). This means that the Creator makes a decree, taking from him the pleasure of the work, and there is no harsher decree than taking from someone the vitality in the work.

But the righteous revokes it. That is, if a person says he wants to work without any reward of vitality and pleasure, then the decree is revoked in any case. Moreover, now he rises to a higher degree, for now he is in a state of pure faith and is regarded as having no self-interest.

29. RABASH, Article No. 21, "Sanctification of the Month"

A person must take upon himself the burden of the kingdom of heaven on the lowest quality, and say about it that to him, even that state, the lowest that can be, meaning one that is entirely above reason, when he has no support from the mind or the feeling, so he can build its foundations on it, and at that time, he is seemingly standing between heaven and earth and has no support, for then everything is above reason, then a person says that the Creator sent him this state, where he is in utter lowliness, since the Creator wants him to take upon himself the burden of the kingdom of heaven in this manner of lowliness.

At that time, because he believes above reason, he takes upon himself that the situation he is in now comes to him from the Creator, meaning that the Creator wants him to see the lowest possible state that can be in the world.

And yet, he must say that he believes in the Creator in all manners. This is considered that he has made an unconditional surrender. That is, a person does not say to the Creator, "If You give me a good feeling, to feel that 'The whole earth is full of His glory,' I will be willing to believe."

Rather, when he has no knowledge or sensation of spirituality, he cannot accept the burden of the kingdom of heaven and observe the *Torah and Mitzvot* [commandments]. Rather, he must accept the kingdom of heaven unconditionally.

30. RABASH, Article No. 926, "Come unto Pharaoh"

They said that one should see oneself as half guilty, half innocent, since the Creator deliberately made it so that the good and the bad will always be of equal weight, so he can decide. Hence, if he performs one *Mitzva* [commandment] and has decided to the side of merit, he becomes great.

At that time, they say, "Anyone who is greater than his friend, his inclination is greater than him." In other words, the Creator deliberately hardens his heart so he would be able to make a choice once more, for in each choice, a person gains the letters of the Torah. Thus, the signs are not for the sake of the Creator but for the sake of man.

It therefore follows that the hardening of the heart is only for man's sake, for by this he will be rewarded with the letters of the Torah. Although during the fact, a person does not feel all that he is meant to feel, when he has completed his discernment, what he has done all that time is revealed to him at once.

Like the allegory that Baal HaSulam once gave, this is similar to a person earning nothing but zeros. Each time, he sees that he has earned only zero. After the first time, he has one zero. After the second time, two zeros, and after the third, three zeros, until he accumulates many zeros. But at the end of his work, he earns a one. Thus, he might have one zero with the one, which is only ten, or he might have one million, or more. It follows that each time, letters of the Torah are added in him. This is the meaning of "that I may set these signs of Mine within him."

31. RABASH, Article No. 38 (1990), "What Is, 'A Cup of Blessing Must Be Full,' in the Work?"

When a person is already standing near the place from which he will receive the help from above, and "near" means that the *Kli* [vessel], meaning the desire to bestow, is far away from him, then he sees that only the Creator can save him. As Baal HaSulam said, this is the most important point in man's work, for then he has close contact with the Creator because he sees one hundred percent that nothing can help him but the Creator Himself.

Although he believes this, still, this faith does not always illuminate for him that specifically now is the best time to receive the salvation of the Creator, that specifically now he can be saved and the Creator will bring him closer, meaning give him the desire to bestow and emerge from the control of self-love, which is called "exodus from Egypt." In other words, he comes out of the control of the Egyptians, who afflicted Israel and did not let them do the holy work. "And the children of Israel sighed from the work, and their cry rose up to God," and then the Creator brought them out from the exile in Egypt.

In other words, since the people of Israel felt the enslavement and wanted to escape from this exile that the Egyptians were enslaving them, when they came to this important point of feeling their lowliness, the Creator brought them out of Egypt. This is as the ARI says, that when the people of Israel were in Egypt, they were already in forty-nine gates of *Tuma'a* [impurity], and then the Creator brought them out from Egypt.

This means that they already came to the worst lowliness, the lowest that can be, and then the Creator brought them out.

32. RABASH, Article No. 16 (1988), "What Is the Foundation on which Kedusha [Holiness] Is Built?"

I am still immersed in self-love and I still do not have love for the Creator. I am still without the glory of the Torah and I still do not have the importance of the Torah to know that it is worthwhile to do everything to obtain the light of Torah, as well as how to appreciate the importance of observing the *Mitzvot* that the Creator commanded for us.

When I need to perform some *Mitzva* and intend that it will be in order to bestow, the resistance in the body promptly awakens in full force. And he has a great struggle to do anything and he sees the ascents and descents each time. And then he has room for prayer. This is so because a person awakens himself at the right time, meaning when he feels that he will be able to pray instantaneously, and not that the black will bring him sadness and depression, that he will not have the ability to pray for the blackness.

One can see for himself whether it comes to him from the side of *Klipa* or not. The sign for this is that something that comes from *Kedusha* is always in the form of "increasing holiness and not decreasing." In other words, one always asks the Creator to elevate him to a higher degree than the one he is on. But when the blackness comes from the side of *Klipa*, a person cannot ask the Creator to raise him above his state.

"Rather, they bring down," meaning bring him down to the netherworld, and he loses the small portion of faith that he had and he remains seemingly dead, without the spirit of life.

33. RABASH, Article No. 21 (1988), "What Does It Mean that the Torah Was Given Out of the Darkness in the Work?"

When a person wants to draw near to the Creator, meaning use the vessels of bestowal, but he cannot because the body disagrees with it, since his body extends from vessels of reception, at that time a person feels that the world has grown dark on him, for he understands that if he cannot obtain vessels of bestowal, he will never be rewarded with the upper light, which is the light of "doing good to His creations."

It follows that the darkness he feels from not being able to obtain vessels of bestowal by himself gives him the need that someone will help him obtain those *Kelim* [vessels]. According to the rule, "There is no light without a *Kli* [vessel], no filling without a lack," it follows that now he has received a need for the light of Torah. It is as our sages said, "I have created the evil inclination; I have created the Torah as a spice."

Thus, the Torah is given specifically to the deficient, and that deficiency is called "darkness." This is the meaning of the words, "The Torah was given out of the darkness." That is, one who feels darkness in his life because he has no vessels of bestowal is fit to receive the Torah, so that through the Torah, the light in it will reform him and he will obtain the vessels of bestowal. Through them, he will be fit to receive the delight and pleasure.

34. RABASH, Article No. 22 (1985), "The Whole of the Torah Is One Holy Name"

We must always consider the goal, which is to "do good to His creations." If the evil inclination comes to a person and asks him all of Pharaoh's questions, he should not reply with lame excuses, but say, "Now, with your questions, I can begin with the work of bestowal."

This means that we should not say about the questions of the evil inclination that it came to us in order to lower us from our degree. On the contrary, now it is giving us a place to work, by which we will ascend on the degrees of wholeness. That is, any overcoming in the work is called "walking in the work of the Creator," since each penny joins into a great amount." That is, all the times we overcome accumulate to a certain measure required to become a *Kli* for the reception of the abundance.

Overcoming means taking a part of a vessel of reception and adding it to the vessels of bestowal. It is like the *Masach* [screen], which we must put on the *Aviut* [thickness/will to receive]. It follows that if one has no will to receive, one has nothing on which to place a *Masach*. For this reason, when the evil inclination brings us foreign thoughts, this is the time to take these thoughts and raise them above reason.

This is something one can do with everything one's soul desires. He should not say that now he has received rejection from the work. Rather, he should say that he was given thoughts and desires from above so as to have room to admit them into *Kedusha* [holiness]. It therefore follows that it is to the contrary: because he is brought closer from above, he was sent work.

It was said about this: "The ways of the Lord are straight; righteous walk in it and transgressors fail in it."

35. RABASH, Article No. 71, "The Meaning of Exile"

"When Israel are in exile, the *Shechina* [Divinity] is with them." This means that if one falls into a descent, spirituality is also descended in him. But according to the rule, "a *Mitzva* [commandment] induces a *Mitzva*," why does he come into a descent? Answer: He is given a descent from above so as to feel that he is in exile and ask for mercy, to be delivered from exile. This is called "redemption," and there cannot be redemption if there is no exile there, first.

What is exile? It is that he is under the rule of self-love and cannot work for the sake of the Creator. When is self-love considered exile? It is only when he wants to emerge from this control because he suffers from not being able to do anything for the sake of the Creator.

It follows that when he began to work, there had to be some pleasure and reward for which the body agreed to this work. Afterward, when he was permitted to see that there is the matter of "for the sake of the Creator," because a *Mitzva* induces a *Mitzva*, and he had to ask to be delivered from exile, then he runs from the exile.

How does he run from the exile? It is by saying that he will not succeed in this work. Thus, what does he do? He commits suicide, meaning leaves the work and returns to corporeal life, which is regarded as "The wicked in their lives are called 'dead.'"

It follows that where he should have asked for redemption from exile, he runs from the exile and commits suicide. This is as it is written, "The ways of the Lord are straight; the righteous will walk in them, and transgressors will fail in them." However, he should go above reason.

A descent in spirituality does not mean that now he has no faith. Rather, now he must do more work, and the previous faith is considered a descent compared to this work.

36. RABASH, Article No. 4 (1998), "What Is a Flood of Water in the Work?"

We must know that it is a lot of work before we attain the quality of *Bina*. That is, to be content with little with his feeling and his mind, and be happy with his share, with what he has. That person can always be in wholeness because he is happy with his share.

But what can one do if he has not yet obtained this quality, and he sees that he cannot overcome his will to receive. At that time, he must pray to the Creator to help him so he can go in the work with his eyes shut, and will not need anything, and will be able to do everything for the sake of the Creator despite the resistance of the body to this.

That is, he does not tell the Creator how He should help him. Rather, he must subjugate himself and annul before the Creator unconditionally. But since he cannot overcome his body, he asks the Creator to help him win the war against the inclination.

37. RABASH, Article No. 16 (1985), "But the More They Afflicted Them"

"And the children of Israel sighed because of the labor, and they cried, and their cry came up unto God because of the labor. And God heard their groaning."

We should be precise about the words "because of the labor" being written twice. We should explain that all the sighs were from the labor, meaning that they could not work for the Creator. Indeed, their suffering was from not being able to make the work that they were doing be for the Creator, due to the *Klipa* of Egypt. This is why it is written, "Because of the labor" twice.

1) All the sighs were not because they were lacking anything. They lacked only one thing, meaning they did not wish for any luxuries or payment. Their only lack, for which they felt pain and suffering, was that of not being able to do anything for the Creator. In other words, they wished that they would have a desire to give contentment to the Creator and not to themselves, but they couldn't, and this afflicted them. This is called "wanting to have some grip in spirituality."

2) The second "Because of the labor" comes to teach that, "And their cry came up unto God," that God heard their groaning, was because their only request was work. This comes to imply to the other "because of the labor." It turns out that the whole exile that they felt was only because they were under the rule of the *Klipa* of Egypt and they could not do anything to make it only in order to bestow.

38. RABASH, Article No. 34 (1991), "What Is Eating Their Fruits in This World and Keeping the Principal for the Next World, in the Work?"

Those who say that they want to escape from the work but have nowhere else to go, since nothing satisfies them, those people do not walk out from the work. Although they have ups and downs, they do not give up. This is as it is written, "And the children of Israel sighed from the work, and they cried, and their cry went up to God from the work." In other words, they cried out from the work because they were not advancing in the work of the Creator, so they could work in order to bestow contentment upon the Maker. At that time, they were rewarded with the exodus from Egypt. In the work, this is called "emerging from the control of the will to receive and entry into the work of bestowal."

39. RABASH, Article No. 6 (1990), "When Should One Use Pride in the Work?"

A person should pay attention to this and believe that the Creator is tending to him and guides him on the track that leads to the King's palace. It follows that he should be happy that the Creator is watching over him and gives him the descents, as well. That is, a person should believe, as much as he can understand, that the Creator is giving him the ascents, since certainly, a person cannot say that he himself receives the ascents, but that the Creator wants to bring him closer; this is why He gives him the ascents.

Also, a person should believe that the Creator gives him the descents, as well, because He wants to bring him closer. Therefore, every single thing that he can do, he must do as though he is in a state of ascent. Therefore, when he overcomes a little during the descent, it is called an "awakening from below." Each act that he does, he believes that it is the Creator's will, and by this itself he is rewarded with greater nearing, meaning that the person himself begins to feel that the Creator has brought him closer.

40. *Zohar for All*, *Beresheet* [Genesis], "Let Us Make Man"

According to the extent of the *Panim* of the degree, so is the extent of its *Achoraim*. The instilling of the *Achoraim* is a calling and an invitation to instill the *Panim*. This is why by the measure of the concealment of the *Achoraim* that they attained, they knew the measure of disclosure that they were about to attain.

As Rabbi Shimon heard, he was calling him Shimon and not Rabbi Shimon. This means that the instilling of the *Achoraim*, which is a calling, was so strong that he lost all his degrees and became a simple person, Shimon from the market. By that, he recognized that it was a calling and an invitation for very high attainment of *Panim*.

41. *Zohar for All*, "Introduction of The Book of Zohar," "The Second Commandment," Item 201

Complete love is love on both sides, whether in *Din*, or in *Hesed* and successful ways. He will love the Creator even if He takes His soul away from Him. This love is complete, for it is on both sides, in *Hesed* and in *Din*. Hence, the light of the act of creation came out, and was then concealed. When it became concealed, the harsh *Din* came out and the two sides, *Hesed* and *Din*, were included together, becoming whole.

This is proper love, for the light that was created in the six days of creation, in the verse, "Let there be light," was concealed again, as it is written in *The Zohar*, "Let there be light for this world, and let there be light for the next world." The light from this world was concealed, and appears only for the righteous in the next world.

Why was it concealed? It is because with the concealing of the light, harsh *Din* came out in this world, by which the two sides, *Din* and *Rachamim*, were integrated, becoming whole. This gave room for the inclusion of the two ends as one. This is so because now it became possible to disclose the wholeness of His love even while He takes one's soul away from him. Thus, room was given to complement the love in a way that had it not been hidden and the harsh *Din* had not been revealed, this great love would have been devoid of the righteous, and it never would have been possible for it to become disclosed.

42. Rabbi Nachman of Breslov, *Likutey Moharan*

The work of the Creator requires great persistence, whatever happens to him. Remember this well for you will need it very much as you begin the work of the Creator. It requires great tenacity, and to be strong and brave, to brace oneself and stand still, even if you are dropped down every time. You must not allow yourself to fall off altogether, for it is necessary to experience all those falls, descents, and confusions prior to entering the gates of *Kedusha* [holiness], and the true righteous, too, have gone through all of it. Know, that man must cross and very, very narrow bridge, and the rule and the most important thing is not to be afraid at all.

5

Fear

1. Baal HaSulam, *Shamati*, Article No. 38, "The Fear of God Is His Treasure"

Our sages said, "Everything is in the hands of heaven but the fear of heaven," is because He can give everything but fear. This is because what the Creator gives is more love, not fear.

Acquiring fear is through the *Segula* [power/remedy] of Torah and *Mitzvot*. It means that when one engages in Torah and *Mitzvot* with the intention to be rewarded with bringing contentment to one's Maker, that aim that rests on the acts of *Mitzvot* and the study of Torah brings one to attain it. Otherwise, one might remain—although he observes Torah and *Mitzvot* in every item and detail— he will still remain merely in the degree of still of *Kedusha* [holiness].

It follows that one should always remember the reason that obligates him to engage in Torah and *Mitzvot*. This is the meaning of what our sages meant by "that your *Kedusha* will be for My Name." It means that I will be your cause, meaning that all your work is in wanting to delight Me, meaning that all your actions will be in order to bestow.

Our sages said (*Berachot* 20), "Everything there is in keeping, there is in remembering." This means that all those who engage in observing Torah and *Mitzvot* with the aim to achieve "remembering," by way of "When I remember Him, He does not let me sleep." It follows, that the keeping is primarily in order to be awarded remembering.

Thus, one's desire to remember that the Creator is the cause for observing Torah and *Mitzvot*. This is so because it follows that the reason and the cause to observe the Torah and *Mitzvot* is the Creator, as without it one cannot adhere to the Creator, since "He and I cannot dwell in the same abode" due to the disparity of form.

2. Baal HaSulam, Letter No. 2

There is none so wise as the experienced. Therefore, I shall advise you to evoke within you fear of the coolness of the love between us. Although the intellect denies such a depiction, think for yourself—if there is a tactic by which to increase love and one does not increase it, that, too, is considered a flaw.

It is like a person who gives a great gift to his friend. The love that appears in his heart during the act is not like the love that remains in the heart after the fact. Rather, it gradually wanes each day until the blessing of the love can be entirely forgotten. Thus, the receiver of the gift must find a tactic every day to make it new in his eyes each day.

3. Baal HaSulam, *Shamati*, Article No. 211, "As Though Standing before a King"

One who is sitting at one's home is not as one who is standing before a King. This means that faith should be that he will feel all day as though he is standing before the King. Then his love and fear will certainly be complete. As long as he has not achieved this kind of faith, he should not rest, "for this is our lives and the length of our days," and we will accept no recompense.

And the lack of faith should be woven in his limbs until the habit becomes a second nature, to the extent that "When I remember Him, He does not let me sleep."

4. Baal HaSulam, *Shamati*, Article No. 38, "The Fear of God Is His Treasure"

In His treasury, the Creator has only the treasure of fear of heaven (*Berachot* 33).

Yet, we should interpret what is fear: It is the *Kli*, and the treasure is made of this *Kli*, and all the important things are placed in it. He said that fear is as it is written about Moses: Our sages said (*Berachot*, p 7), "The reward for 'And Moses hid his face for he was afraid to look,' he was rewarded with 'the image of the Lord does he behold.'"

Fear refers to one's fear of the great pleasure that is there, that he will not be able to receive it in order to bestow. The reward for this, for having had fear, is that thus he had made for himself a *Kli* in which to receive the upper abundance. This is man's work, and besides that, we attribute everything to the Creator.

Yet, it is not so with fear, because the meaning of fear is not to receive. And what the Creator gives, He gives only to receive, and this is the meaning of "Everything is in the hands of heaven except the fear of heaven."

This is the *Kli* that we need. Otherwise, we will be considered fools, as our sages said, "Who is a fool? He who loses what he is given." This means that the *Sitra Achra* [other side] will take the abundance from us if we cannot aim in order to bestow, because then it goes to the vessels of reception, which is the *Sitra Achra* and *Tuma'a* [impurity].

This is the meaning of "And you shall observe the commandment of unleavened bread." Observing means fear. Although the nature of the light is that it keeps itself, meaning that the light leaves before one wants to receive the light into the vessels of reception, yet one must do it by himself, as much as he can, as our sages said, "You will keep yourselves a little from below, and I will keep you a lot from above."

The reason we attribute fear to people, as our sages said, "Everything is in the hands of heaven but the fear of heaven," is because He can give everything but fear. This is because what the Creator gives is more love, not fear.

5. Baal HaSulam, *Shamati*, Article No. 11, "Joy with Trembling"

Joy is considered love, which is existence. This is similar to one who builds for himself a house without making any holes in the walls. You find that he cannot enter the house, as there is no hollow place in the walls of the house by which to enter the house. Therefore, a hollow space must be made through which he will enter the house.

Therefore, where there is love, there should also be fear, as fear is the hollow. In other words, one must awaken the fear that one might not be able to aim to bestow.

It follows that when there are both, there is wholeness. Otherwise, each wants to revoke the other. For this reason, we must try to have both of them in the same place.

This is the meaning of the need for love and fear. Love is called existence, whereas fear is called a deficiency and a hollow. Only with the two of them together is there wholeness. This is called "two legs," where precisely when one has two legs can one walk.

6. Baal HaSulam, *Shamati*, Article No. 138, "Concerning Fear that Sometimes Comes Upon a Person"

When fear comes upon a person, he should know that there is none else but Him. And even witchcraft. And if he sees that fear overcomes him, he should say that there is no such thing as chance, but the Creator has given him a chance from above, and he must contemplate and study the end to which he has been sent this fear. It appears that it is so that he will overcome and say, "There is none else besides Him."

But if after all this, the fear has not departed him, he should take it as an example and say that his servitude of the Creator should be in the same measure of the fear, meaning that the fear of heaven, which is a merit, should be in the same manner of fear that he now has. That is, the body is impressed by this superficial fear, and exactly in the same way that the body is impressed, so should be the fear of heaven.

7. RABASH, Article No. 295, "Anyone Who Sanctifies the Seventh – 1"

Once he has obtained the degree of bestowal, meaning obtained the degree where all he wants is only to bestow contentment upon the Creator, he fills himself with all the pleasures that his eyes see, as in the explanation, "The whole earth is full of His glory."

It follows that all that one needs to obtain that he can define as a reward after he has toiled several years is only one thing: the desire to bestow, meaning the degree of wanting to serve the rav not in order to receive reward.

All the labor where one needs to exert himself in *Torah and Mitzvot* [commandments] is only to obtain this. This is called "fear of heaven," as it is written, "What does the Lord your God ask of you? Only to fear Me."

8. RABASH, Article No. 31, "How I Love Your Teaching"

"God has made it that He will be feared," that all the bad situation that we feel is only so that man will not remain in the state he is in. That is, unless a person rises on the degrees of greatness of the Creator, he will not be able to overcome, and only when one feels the greatness of the Creator does his heart surrender. This is regarded as having to climb the degrees of fear of the Creator.

It follows that these questions cause him to need the Creator to open his heart and eyes to be rewarded with the greatness for the Creator. Otherwise, he suffices for the fear of heaven he has acquired through his upbringing. But when the wicked one's question keeps coming to him, it is not enough for him and he needs to constantly ascend up the degrees of greatness of the Creator.

9. RABASH, Article No. 5 (1990), "What It Means that the Land Did Not Bear Fruit before Man Was Created, in the Work"

In the work, man is regarded as one who has emerged from the control of the quality of a beast. A "beast" means one who is immersed in self-benefit, like a beast, and man means one in whom there is fear of heaven and works because of fear, which *The Zohar* calls "Because He is great and ruling," where he works only because of the greatness of the Creator and does not care for his own benefit, but for the benefit of the Creator. It is as our sages said about the verse, "In the end of the matter, fear God and observe His commandments, for this is the whole of man. What is 'for this is the whole of man'? Rabbi Elazar said, 'The whole world was created only for this'" (*Berachot* 6).

It follows that man is regarded as one in whom there is the fear of heaven. And what is the fear of heaven? That is, what is fear? It is as he says ("Introduction of The Book of Zohar," Item 191), "Both the first fear and the second fear are not for his own benefit, but only for fear that he will decline in bringing contentment to his Maker."

According to the above, we already know the meaning of Adam. It is one who has fear of heaven, who is afraid that perhaps he will not be able to do everything in order to bestow. This is called "man." A "beast" is the opposite: one who cares only for one's own benefit, as it is written (Ecclesiastes 3), "Who knows the spirit of man, whether it goes upward, and the spirit of the beast, whether it goes downward to the earth?" We should interpret that "spirit of man" goes upward means that everything he does is for the sake of the Creator. This is called "upward," when his intention is that everything will be only in order to bestow. From this man derives contentment.

6

Shame

1. Baal HaSulam, Letter No. 25

Everything is preordained, and each and every soul is already established in all its light, goodness, and eternity. But for the bread of shame, the soul went out in restrictions until it clothed in the murky body, and only through it does it return to its root prior to the *Tzimtzum* [restriction], with its reward in its hand from all the terrible move it had made. The overall reward is the real *Dvekut*, meaning that she [the soul] got rid of the bread of shame because her vessel of reception has become a vessel of bestowal and her form is equal to her Maker.

2. Baal HaSulam, "Preface to the Wisdom of Kabbalah," Item 15

Man's nature is to cherish and favor the quality of bestowal, and to despise and loathe reception from one's friend. Hence, when one comes to one's friend's house and he [the host] invites him for a meal, he [the guest] will decline even if he is very hungry, since in his eyes it is humiliating to receive a gift from his friend.

Yet, when his friend sufficiently implores him until it is clear that he would do his friend a big favor by eating, he agrees to eat as he no longer feels that he is receiving a gift and that his friend is the giver. On the contrary, he [the guest] is the giver, doing his friend a favor by receiving this good from him.

Thus, you find that although hunger and appetite are vessels of reception designated to eating, and that that person had sufficient hunger and appetite to receive his friend's meal, he still could not taste a thing due to the shame. Yet, as his friend implored him and he rejected him, new vessels for eating began to form in him, since the power of his friend's pleading and the power of his own rejection, as they accumulated, finally accumulated into a sufficient amount that turned the measure of reception into a measure of bestowal.

In the end, he saw that by eating, he would do a big favor and bring great contentment to his friend by eating. In that state, new vessels of reception to receive his friend's meal were made in him. Now it is considered that his power of rejection has become the essential *Kli* in which to receive the meal, and not the hunger and appetite, although they are actually the usual vessels of reception.

3. Baal HaSulam, "Preface to the Wisdom of Kabbalah," Item 18

We must thoroughly understand that even though *Behina Dalet* was banned from being a vessel of reception for the ten *Sefirot* after the *Tzimtzum*, and the *Ohr Hozer* that rises from the *Masach* through the *Zivug de Hakaa* became the vessel of reception in its stead, it must still accompany the *Ohr Hozer* with its power of reception. Had it not been for that, the *Ohr Hozer* would have been unfit to be a vessel of reception.

You should also understand this from the allegory in Item 15. We demonstrated there that the power to reject and decline the meal became the vessel of reception instead of the hunger and appetite. This is because hunger and appetite, the usual vessels of reception, were banned from being vessels of reception in this case due to the shame and disgrace of receiving a gift from one's friend. Only the powers of rejection and refusal have become *vessels of reception* in their stead, as through the rejection and refusal, reception has been inverted into bestowal, and through them he achieved vessels of reception suitable to receive one's friend's meal.

Yet, it cannot be said that he no longer needs the usual vessels of reception, namely the hunger and the appetite, as it is clear that without appetite for eating he will not be able to satisfy his friend's wish and bring him contentment by eating at his place. But the thing is that the hunger and appetite, which were banned in their usual form, have now been transformed by the forces of rejection and decline into a new form—reception in order to bestow. Thus, the humiliation has become dignity.

It turns out that the usual vessels of reception are still as active as ever but have acquired a new form. You will also conclude, concerning our matter, that it is true that *Behina Dalet* has been banned from being a *Kli* for reception of the ten *Sefirot* because of its *Aviut*, meaning the difference of form from the Giver, which separates from the Giver. Yet, through correcting the *Masach* in *Behina Dalet*, which strikes the upper light and repels it, her previous, faulty form has been transformed and acquired a new form, called *Ohr Hozer*, like the transformation of the form of reception into a form of bestowal in the above allegory.

The content of its initial form has not changed; it still does not eat without appetite.

4. RABASH, Article No. 454, "He Who Prays for His Friend"

"To You Lord is the righteousness, and to us is the shame." "And he believed in the Lord and He considered it for him as righteousness." Concerning shame, it must be felt over the Giver, and then the shame comes by itself, as our sages said, "afraid to look at his face." However, when he does not feel the Giver, from whom will he be ashamed? Therefore, "To You Lord is the righteousness," meaning that he gives Him the faith. Then it can be said, "and to us is the shame."

This is as it is written in *The Zohar*: "It is known that no quality can rise above its degree before upper illumination is lowered down to it, so that afterward it will be able to grow and rise up".

7

Ascents and Descents

1. Baal HaSulam, *Shamati*, Article No. 191, "The Time of Descent"

It is hard to depict the time of descent, when all the works and the efforts made from the beginning of the work until the time of descent are lost. To one who has never tasted the taste of servitude of the Creator, it seems as though this is outside of him, meaning that this happens to those of high degrees. But ordinary people have no connection to serving the Creator, only to crave the corporeal will to receive, present in the flow of the world, washing the whole world with this desire.

However, we must understand why they have come to such a state. After all, with or without one's consent, there is no change in the Creator of heaven and earth; He behaves in a manner of good and doing good. Thus, what is the outcome of this state?

We should say that it comes to announce His greatness. One does not need to act as though he does not want Her. Rather, one should behave in a manner of fearing the exaltedness, to know the merit and the distance between him and the Creator. It is difficult to understand this with a superficial mind, or have any possibility of connection between the Creator and creation.

During a descent he feels that it is impossible that he will have connection or belonging to the Creator by way of *Dvekut* [adhesion], since he feels that servitude is a foreign thing to the whole world.

In truth, this is so. But "In the place where you find His greatness, there you find His humbleness." This means that it is a matter that is above nature, that the Creator gave this gift to creation, to allow them to be connected and adhered to Him.

Hence, when one becomes reconnected, he should always remember his time of descent so as to know, understand, appreciate, and value the time of *Dvekut*, so he will know that now he has salvation above the natural way.

2. Baal HaSulam, *Shamati*, Article No. 1, "There Is None Else Besides Him"

It is written, "There is none else besides Him." This means that there is no other force in the world that has the ability to do anything against Him. And what one sees, that there are things in the world that deny the upper household, the reason is that this is His will.

This is deemed a correction called "the left rejects and the right pulls closer," meaning that what the left rejects is considered a correction. This means that there are things in the world that, to begin with, aim to divert a person from the right way, and by which he is rejected from *Kedusha* [holiness].

The benefit from the rejections is that through them a person receives a complete need and desire for the Creator to help him since he sees that otherwise he is lost; not only is he not progressing in the work, he even sees that he regresses. That is, he lacks the strength to observe Torah and *Mitzvot* [commandments] even *Lo Lishma* [not for Her sake], for only by genuinely overcoming all the obstacles, above reason, can he observe the Torah and *Mitzvot*. But he does not always have the strength to overcome above reason; otherwise, he is forced to deviate, God forbid, from the way of the Creator, even from *Lo Lishma*.

And he, who always feels that the shattered is greater than the whole, meaning that there are many more descents than ascents, and he does not see an end to these states, and he will forever remain outside of holiness, for he sees that it is difficult for him to observe even in the slightest bit, unless by overcoming above reason. But he cannot always overcome, so what will be in the end?

Then he comes to the decision that no one can help but the Creator Himself. This causes him to make a heartfelt demand that the Creator will open his eyes and heart and truly bring him closer to eternal *Dvekut* [adhesion] with the Creator.

3. Baal HaSulam, *Shamati*, Article No. 33, "The Lots on Yom Kippurim and with Haman"

Through the faults in the work of the Creator, it causes him to rise up, as without a push one is idle to make a movement and agrees to remain in the state he is in. But if one descends to a lower degree than he understands, this gives one the strength to overcome, for one cannot stay in such a bad state, since one cannot agree to remain like that, in the state to which he has descended.

For this reason, one must always prevail and emerge from the state of descent. In that state, he must draw upon himself the exaltedness of the Creator. This causes him to extend higher forces from above, or he remains in utter lowliness. It follows that through the *Se'arot*, one gradually discovers the exaltedness of the Creator until one finds the names of the Creator, called "the thirteen attributes of Mercy." This is the meaning of "and the elder shall serve the younger," and "the wicked will prepare and the righteous will wear," and also, "and you shall serve your brother."

This means that all the enslavement, meaning the contradictions that there were, which appeared to be obstructing the holy work, and were working against *Kedusha* [holiness]. Now, when granted the light of the Creator, which is placed over these contradictions, we see the opposite—that they were serving the *Kedusha*. That is, through them, there was a place for the *Kedusha* to clothe in their dresses. This is called "the wicked will prepare and the righteous will wear," meaning that they gave the *Kelim* [vessels] and the place for the *Kedusha*.

4. Baal HaSulam, Letter No. 25

One who repents from love is rewarded with complete *Dvekut* [adhesion], meaning the highest degree, and one who is ready for sins is in the netherworld. These are the farthest two points in this entire reality.

It would seem that we should be meticulous with the word "repentance," which should have been called "wholeness," except it is to show that everything is preordained, and each and every soul is already established in all its light, goodness, and eternity. But for the bread of shame, the soul went out in restrictions until it clothed in the murky body, and only through it does it return to its root prior to the *Tzimtzum* [restriction], with its reward in its hand from all the terrible move it had made. The overall reward is the real *Dvekut*, meaning that she [the soul] got rid of the bread of shame because her vessel of reception has become a vessel of bestowal and her form is equal to her Maker, and I have often spoken to you about that.

By this you will see that if the descent is for the purpose of ascending, it is regarded as an ascent and not as a descent. Indeed, the descent itself is the ascent as the letters of the prayer themselves are filled with abundance, and with a short prayer, the abundance is small for lack of letters.

5. Baal HaSulam, *Shamati*, Article No. 19, "What Is 'The Creator Hates the Bodies,' in the Work?"

We must know that during the work, when the will to receive comes to a person with its arguments, no arguments or rationalizations help with it. Though one thinks that they are just arguments, it will not help one defeat his evil.

Instead, as it is written, "Blunt its teeth." This means to advance only by actions, and not by arguments. This is considered that one must add powers coercively. This is the meaning of what our sages said, "He is coerced until he says 'I want.'" In other words, through persistence, habit becomes a second nature.

One must especially try to have a strong desire to obtain the desire to bestow and overcome the will to receive. A strong desire means that a strong desire is measured by the increment of the in-between rests and the arrests, meaning the time gaps between each overcoming.

Sometimes one receives a cessation in the middle, meaning a descent. This descent can be a cessation of a minute, an hour, a day, or a month. Afterward, he resumes the work of overcoming the will to receive and the attempts to achieve the desire to bestow. A strong desire means that the cessation does not take him a long time and he is immediately reawakened to the work.

It is like a person who wants to break a big rock. He takes a big hammer and hammers many times all day long, but they are weak. In other words, he does not hammer the rock with one swing but brings down the big hammer slowly. Afterward, he complains that this work of breaking the rock is not for him, that it must take a very strong man to be able to break this big rock. He says that he was not born with such great powers to be able to break the rock.

However, one who lifts this big hammer and strikes the rock with a big swing, not slowly but with a great effort, the rock immediately surrenders to him and breaks. This is the meaning of "like a strong hammer that shatters the rock."

Similarly, in the holy work, which is to bring the vessels of reception into *Kedusha* [holiness], we have a strong hammer, meaning words of Torah that give us good counsels. However, if it is not consistent, but with long intermissions in between, one escapes the campaign and says that he was not made for this, but this work requires one who was born with special skills for it. Nevertheless, one should believe that anyone can achieve the goal, but he should try to always increase his efforts to overcome, and then one can break the rock in a short time.

We must also know that for the effort to make contact with the Creator, there is a very harsh condition here: The effort must be in the form of adornment. "Adornment" means something that is important to a person. One cannot work gladly if the labor is not of importance, meaning that one is happy that now he has contact with the Creator.

6. Baal HaSulam, *Shamati*, Article No. 42, "What Is the Acronym Elul in the Work?"

Those who wish to work in order to bestow are admitted into the King's hall, and when one works in order to bestow, he does not mind what he feels during the work.

Rather, even in a state where he sees a shape of black, he is not impressed by it, but he only wants the Creator to give him strength to be able to overcome all the obstacles. It means that he does not ask the Creator to give him a shape of white, but to give him the strength to overcome all the concealments.

Hence, those people who want to work in order to bestow, if there is always a state of whiteness, the whiteness allows one to continue in the work. This is because, while it shines, one is able to work even in the form of reception for oneself.

Hence, one will never be able to know if his work is in purity or not, and this causes him never to be able to be awarded *Dvekut* [adhesion] with the Creator. For this reason, he is given from above a form of blackness, and then he sees if his work is in purity.

This means that if one can be in gladness in a state of blackness, too, it is a sign that his work is in purity, since one must be glad and believe that from above he was given an opportunity to be able to work in order to bestow.

7. Baal HaSulam, Introduction to *A Sage's Fruit*, Vol. 4, "Three Partners"

It is impossible to attribute the bad to the Creator since he is the absolute good. Hence, as long as one feels bad states, he must say that they come from elsewhere, from the environment. But in truth, when one is rewarded with seeing only good and that there is no bad in the world, and everything is turned to good, then he is shown the truth, that the Creator did everything because He is almighty, and He alone did, does, and will do all the deeds.

8. Baal HaSulam, *Shamati* Article No. 83, "Concerning the Right Vav and the Left Vav"

In any state one is in, he can be a servant of the Creator since he does not need anything, but does everything above reason. It turns out that one does not need any *Mochin* with which to be the servant of the Creator.

Now we can interpret what is written, "Set up a table before me, against my enemies." A table means, as it is written, "and sent her out of his house, and she departed his house, and went" (Deuteronomy 24:1-2). A *Shulchan* [table] is like *VeShlacha* [and sent her], meaning exit from the work.

We should interpret that even during the exits from the work, meaning in a state of decline, one still has a place to work. This means that when one prevails above reason during the declines, and says that the descents, too, were given to him from above, by this the enemies are canceled. This is so because the enemies thought that through the declines the person will reach utter lowliness and escape the campaign, but in the end the opposite occurred—the enemies were canceled.

This is the meaning of what is written, "the table that is before the Lord," that precisely in this manner does he receive the face of the Creator. This is the meaning of subduing all the judgments, even the harshest judgments, since he assumes the burden of the kingdom of heaven at all times. That is, he always finds a place for work, as it is written that Rabbi Shimon Bar-Yochai said, "There is no place to hide from You."

9. Baal HaSulam, *Shamati*, Article No. 70, "With a Mighty Hand and with Fury Poured Out"

We should know that of those who want to come into the work of the Creator in order to truly adhere to Him and enter the King's palace, not everyone is admitted. Rather, he is tested: If he has no other desires but only a desire for *Dvekut* [adhesion], he is admitted.

And how is one tested if he has only one desire? He is given disturbances. This means that he is sent foreign thoughts and foreign messengers to obstruct him so he would leave this path and follow the path of all the people.

If one overcomes all the difficulties and breaks all the bars that block him, and little things cannot push him away, the Creator sends him great *Klipot* [shells/peels] and chariots to deflect one from entering into *Dvekut* with the Creator alone, and with nothing else. This is considered that the Creator is rejecting him with a mighty hand.

If the Creator does not show a mighty hand, it will be hard to push him away since he has a strong desire to adhere only to the Creator and to nothing else.

But when the Creator wants to reject one whose desire is not so strong, He pushes him away with a small thing. By giving him a great desire for corporeality, he already leaves the holy work entirely, and there is no need to repel him with a mighty hand.

Yet, when one overcomes all the hardships and the disturbances, one is not easily repelled, but with a mighty hand. And if one overcomes even the mighty hand and does not want to move from the place of *Kedusha* [holiness] whatsoever, but wants to adhere specifically to Him in truth, and sees that he is repelled, then one says that fury is poured out on him. Otherwise, he would be allowed inside. But because fury is poured out on him by the Creator, he is not admitted into the King's palace to adhere to Him.

It follows that before one wants to move from one's place, and breaks in and wants to enter, it cannot be said that he feels that fury is poured out on him. Rather, after all the rejections that he is rejected, and he does not move from his place, meaning when the mighty hand and the fury poured out have already been revealed upon him, then "I will be King over you" comes true. This is so because only through bursting and great efforts does the kingdom of heaven become revealed to him, and he is rewarded with entering the King's palace.

10. Baal HaSulam, *Shamati*, Article No. 121, "She Is Like Merchant-Ships"

"Man shall not live on bread alone, but on what proceeds out of the mouth of the Lord." This means that the life of *Kedusha* [holiness] in a person does not come specifically from drawing closer, from entries, meaning admissions into *Kedusha*, but also from the exits, from the removals. This is so because through the dressing of the *Sitra Achra* in one's body, and its claims, "She is all mine," with a just argument, one is awarded permanent faith by overcoming these states.

This means that one should dedicate everything to the Creator, that is, that even the exits stem from Him. When he is rewarded, he sees that both the exits and the entries were all from Him. This forces him to be humble, since he sees that the Creator does everything, the exits as well as the entries.

This is the meaning of what is said about Moses, that he was humble and patient—that one must tolerate the lowliness, meaning that in each degree one should keep the lowliness. The minute he leaves the lowliness, he immediately loses all the degrees of Moses he had already achieved.

This is the meaning of patience. Lowliness exists in everyone, but not every person feels that lowliness is a good thing. It turns out that we do not want to suffer. However, Moses tolerated the humbleness, which is why he was called "humble," since the lowliness made him glad.

11. Baal HaSulam, *Shamati*, Article No. 172, "The Matter of Preventions and Delays"

All the preventions and delays that appear before our eyes are but a form of nearing—the Creator wants to bring us closer, and all these preventions bring us only nearing, since without them we would have no possibility of approaching Him. This is so because, by nature, there is no greater distance, as we are made of pure matter while the Creator is higher than high. Only when one begins to approach does he begin to feel the distance between us. And any prevention one overcomes brings the way closer for that person.

(This is so because one grows accustomed to moving on a line of growing farther. Hence, whenever one feels that he is distant, it does not induce any change in the process, since he knew in advance that he is moving on a line of growing farther, since this is the truth, that there are not enough words to describe the distance between us and the Creator. Hence, every time he feels that distance to a greater extent than he thought, it causes him no contention.)

12. RABASH, Letter No. 24

You must always stand guard, all day and all night, when you feel a state of day or feel a state of night.

We say to the Creator, "Yours is the day, and Yours is also the night." Thus, the night, too, the darkness of night, comes from the Creator to man's favor, too, as it is written, "Day to day utters speech, and night to night expresses knowledge."

It follows that you must awaken the heart of the friends until the flame rises by itself, as our sages said about it, "When you mount the candles." By that, you will be rewarded with awakening the love of the Creator upon us.

13. RABASH, Article No. 44, "Ruin by Elders—Construction; Construction by Youths—Ruin"

"Ruin by elders—construction; construction by youths—ruin" (Megillah 31b).

Elders are those who are accustomed to the work of the Creator. Youths are those who are in the beginning of their work. "Ruin" means a descent or a fall, where previously they had some ascent in the work, which is regarded as building, meaning that they appreciated the ascent, but the ruin is when they felt some fall, which comes from the concealment of the Creator, that the Creator hides Himself from them. This is called "ruin."

"Ruin by elders" means that they say that the Creator sent them the concealment. It follows that they are already building, since they believe that the Creator is tending to them, and from this they derive vitality.

Faith is apparent primarily during the descent, when it does not shine for a person. At that time, he faces a dilemma: Either he says, "I do not need any benefits. Rather, I want to bring contentment above and I do not care what I feel," or it is otherwise.

14. RABASH, Article No. 71, "The Meaning of Exile"

"When Israel are in exile, the *Shechina* [Divinity] is with them." This means that if one falls into a descent, spirituality is also descended in him. But according to the rule, "a *Mitzva* [commandment] induces a *Mitzva*," why does he come into a descent? Answer: He is given a descent from above so as to feel that he is in exile and ask for mercy, to be delivered from exile. This is called "redemption," and there cannot be redemption if there is no exile there, first.

What is exile? It is that he is under the rule of self-love and cannot work for the sake of the Creator. When is self-love considered exile? It is only when he wants to emerge from this control because he suffers from not being able to do anything for the sake of the Creator.

It follows that when he began to work, there had to be some pleasure and reward for which the body agreed to this work. Afterward, when he was permitted to see that there is the matter of "for the sake of the Creator," because a *Mitzva* induces a *Mitzva*, and he had to ask to be delivered from exile, then he runs from the exile.

How does he run from the exile? It is by saying that he will not succeed in this work. Thus, what does he do? He commits suicide, meaning leaves the work and returns to corporeal life, which is regarded as "The wicked in their lives are called 'dead.'"

It follows that where he should have asked for redemption from exile, he runs from the exile and commits suicide. This is as it is written, "The ways of the Lord are straight; the righteous will walk in them, and transgressors will fail in them." However, he should go above reason.

A descent in spirituality does not mean that now he has no faith. Rather, now he must do more work, and the previous faith is considered a descent compared to this work.

15. RABASH, Article No. 8 (1991), "What Is, 'And Abraham Was Old, of Many Days,' in the Work?"

One who is clever and wants to save time does not wait until he suffers a descent from above. Rather, while he is in an ascent and wants to acquire the importance of the state of closeness to the Creator, he begins to depict to himself what is a state of descent, meaning how he suffered from being far from the Creator compared to how he feels now that he is close to the Creator. It follows that even during the ascent he learns from the discernments as though he were in a state of descent. At that time, he can calculate and discern between an ascent and a descent.

At that time he will get a picture of the advantage of light over darkness, since he can create a depiction of how he was back in the state of descent, and thought that the whole matter of the work of bestowal does not pertain to him, and how he suffered from these states when he wanted to escape the campaign, and only from one place he could get some relief, meaning only from one hope, that he thought, "When will I be able to go to sleep?" for then he would escape from all the states of impatience, when he felt that the world has grown dark on him.

Now, during the ascent, he sees everything differently. At that time, he wants to work only for the sake of the Creator, and he has no concern for his own benefit. From all those calculations that he will do during the ascent, it follows that now he has a place where he can discern between light and darkness, and he does not need to wait until he is given from above a state of descent.

16. RABASH, Article No. 9 (1991), "What Is, 'The Smell of His Garments,' in the Work?"

When a person is in a state of ascent, he must learn from his state during the descent in order to know the difference between light and darkness, as it is written, "as the advantage of the light from within the darkness." However, for the most part, a person does not want to remember the time of darkness because it pains him, and people do not want to suffer for no reason. Rather, a person wants to enjoy the state of ascent that he is in.

However, one must know that if he considers the descents while he is in an ascent, he will learn two things from this, which will benefit him and he will therefore not suffer from descents for no reason: 1) He must know how to keep himself as much as he can from falling into a descent. 2) "As the advantage of the light from within the darkness." At that time, he will have more vitality and joy from the state of ascent, and he will be able to thank the Creator for bringing him closer to Him. That is, now a person has a good feeling from being in a state where he understands that it is worthwhile to be a servant of the Creator, since now he feels the greatness and importance of the King.

But during the descent, it is the complete opposite. The body asks him, "What will you get out of wanting to annul before Him and cancel yourself from this entire world, and care only about how to bring contentment to the Creator?" When a person considers both extremes, he sees the differences between them. At that time he has the values of a different importance than he thought about the ascent. It follows that by looking at the descent, the ascent rises in him to a higher level than he feels without looking at the descent.

17. RABASH, Article No. 22 (1989), "Why Are Four Questions Asked Specifically on Passover Night?"

What it gives us to feel within reason that we are regressing instead of progressing. In other words, for what purpose does one need to feel that he is in decline? What is the benefit in that? We see that in a state of ascent, when one has a desire for spirituality and regards mundane pleasures—which the whole world chases so as to obtain these pleasures—as though they were created needlessly, meaning that it would be better if the Creator created all creations enjoying spiritual things.

Thus, regarding thoughts of declines, what does one gain by the fact that after each ascent he comes to a descent? As a result, a person always asks, "How many are the ascents and descents and why are they needed anyway? It would be better if I could stay in the state of ascent."

But the answer is that it is impossible to appreciate anything without knowing its importance. In other words, there is a rule that the joy that a person takes in something depends on the importance of the matter. Sometimes a person is given something important, and if he could appreciate it, he could receive great pleasure from it. But since he does not know the value of the thing, that person cannot enjoy it, except to the extent that he understands its importance.

For example, a person buys an object, a book, which is not so beautiful on the outside, and later that book is reprinted and costs more, but since he did not have much money, he bought this book. The seller, too, was not aware of the importance of the book and sold it to him for a low price. But sometime later, a man comes to his house, sees the book, and says, "Since this book was printed 300 years ago, this book is worth a fortune, as there are only three such books in the world." Now that he hears about the great value of the book, he begins to take pleasure in the book.

The lesson is that we do not know how to appreciate the ascent. That is, we do not understand the value of a single moment of having the power to believe in the Creator, and to have some sensation of the greatness of the Creator. In a state of ascent, we desire to annul before Him without any rhyme and reason, like a candle before a torch. Naturally, we cannot enjoy the fact that the Creator has brought us closer and has given us some nearness, from which we should derive the joy and elation that it should bring us. But since we haven't the importance to appreciate it, we can only enjoy according to the importance, as explained in the allegory.

This is why we were given descents: to be able to learn the importance of the ascents, as it is written, "as the advantage of the light from the darkness." Specifically through descents, one can come to know and appreciate ascents, and then he can enjoy the ascents and come to feel that "They are our lives and the length of our days."

18. RABASH, Article No. 15 (1991), "What Is the Blessing, 'Who Made a Miracle for Me in This Place,' in the Work?"

A person should accustom himself with anything to compare between the time of suffering and the time of pleasure, and to bless for the miracle of delivering him from suffering to a state of pleasure. By this, he will be able to thank the Creator and enjoy in the new *Kelim* that have been added to him now when he compares the two times to one another. From this, a person can advance in the work.

This is as Baal HaSulam said, that it does not matter whether a person receives from the Creator something great or small. What matters is how much a person thanks the Creator. To the extent of his gratitude, so grows the giving that the Creator gives. Therefore, we must take note to be grateful, to appreciate His gift, so we can approach the Creator. Hence, when a person always looks during the ascent at the state he was in while in descent, meaning how he felt during the descent, he can make a distinction as in, "as the advantage of the light from within the darkness," and he already has new *Kelim* in which to receive joy and be thankful to the Creator. This is the meaning of what is written, that a person should bless, "Blessed is He who made a miracle for me in this place," meaning in the place where he is now, during the ascent, since there cannot be an ascent if there was no prior state of descent.

19. RABASH, Article No. 6, 1991 "What Is, 'The Herdsmen of Abram's Cattle and the Herdsmen of Lot's Cattle,' in the Work?"

A person must believe that he has a point in the heart, which is a spark that shines. But sometimes, it is only a black dot and does not shine. We must always awaken that spark because at times that spark awakens by itself and reveals a lack in a person, where he feels that he needs spirituality, that he is too materialistic and he sees no purpose that enables him to emerge from these states.

That spark gives him no rest. That is, as a corporeal spark cannot illuminate, but using the spark, a person can light up things, so that through the things that the spark touches, a great fire can ignite. Likewise, the spark within man's heart cannot shine, but that spark can light up his actions so they will illuminate because the spark pushes him to work.

However, sometimes the spark quenches and does not shine. This can be in the middle of the work, and this is regarded as a person having a road accident. In other words, in the middle of the work, something happened to him and he descended from his state and was left unconscious. Now he does not know that there is spirituality in reality, he has forgotten everything, and he has entered the corporeal world with all of his senses.

Only after some time does he recover and sees that he is in the corporeal world and he begins to climb up once again, meaning to feel the spiritual lack. Then, once again, he receives a drive to approach the Creator.

Afterward, he descends from his degree once more, but he must believe that each time he raises his spark to *Kedusha* [holiness]. Although he sees that he has descended from his state and fell back to the place where he was at the beginning of his work, each time he nonetheless raises new sparks. That is, each time, he raises a new spark.

In the "Introduction to The Book of Zohar" (Item 43), he says, "When man is born, he immediately has a *Nefesh* [soul] of *Kedusha*. But not an actual *Nefesh*, but the *Achoraim* [posterior] of it, its last discernment, which, during its *Katnut* [smallness/infancy], is called a 'point,' and it dresses in man's heart."

We should interpret that this "point," which is still in the dark, reveals and shines each time according to one's work on purifying his heart. At that time, the point begins to shine. This means that each time a person begins to ascend once more after the descent, he should believe that this is a new discernment from what he had during the previous ascent, for he has already elevated it to *Kedusha*. Thus, each time he begins a new discernment.

20. RABASH, Article No. 18 (1988), "When Is One Considered 'A Worker of the Creator' in the Work?"

In the work, we should interpret that "a worker of the Creator" is one who wants to work for the sake of the Creator. Although he is not succeeding, since this requires a real prayer that the Creator will help him, if he began to walk on the right line, meaning that he already has a "left" that resists the right line, then the order of the path of the Creator begins. For this reason, he is already regarded as "a worker of the Creator," since his goal is to come to a state where all his works are for the sake of the Creator.

And although there are many descents and ascents along the way, everything follows the plan, meaning that the descents, too, a part of the work, since by this we acquire the need for the salvation of the Creator. Through the descents, a person comes to the decision that it is impossible to do anything by himself, but that only the Creator can help. This attainment, a person achieves specifically through the descents.

21. RABASH, Article No. 164, "What to Ask of the Creator—to Be His Servant"

When a person sees that he has disturbances in his work of the Creator and he wants to pray to the Creator to have the strength to work, what should he ask?

There are two options:

1) That the Creator will take away from him the disturbances. As a result, he will not need to make great efforts in order to walk in the ways of the Creator.
2) For the Creator to give him a greater taste for the Torah and prayer and good deeds, and by this the disturbances will not be able to detain him because when Torah and *Mitzvot* [commandments] are important, disturbances cannot rule.

For example, a person cannot say that he has many disturbances so he cannot save his life. That is, it is not true if he argued that because his relatives or his environment are disturbing him, he is unable to save his life. Rather, of course, a person will give all that he has for his life, and all the obstacles do not matter to him.

Therefore, he asks the Creator to give him the taste of life in *Torah and Mitzvot*, and against life, one cannot say that he has disturbances because the importance of life does not let him relate to the disturbances.

22. RABASH, Article No. 6 (1990), "When Should One Use Pride in the Work?"

When he engages in Torah and *Mitzvot*, since a person must walk on two lines—right and left—meaning a time of wholeness and a time of lack, on one hand we must thank the Creator, and one who feels he has received a lot of good from the Creator is more capable of giving more gratitude, so when a person engages in Torah and *Mitzvot*, this is the time to be in wholeness, as though the Creator has brought him close, to be among the King's servants. However, one must not lie to oneself and say that he feels that he is serving the King when he does not feel this way. Therefore, how can he be grateful to the Creator for drawing him near if he does not feel it?

Instead, at that time a person should say that although he is in utter lowliness, meaning he is still immersed in self-love, and still cannot do anything above reason, the Creator still gave him a thought and desire to engage in Torah and *Mitzvot*, and has also given him some strength to be able to overcome the spies who speak to him and poke his mind with their arguments. And still, he has some grip on spirituality.

At that time, a person should pay attention to this and believe that the Creator is tending to him and guides him on the track that leads to the King's palace. It follows that he should be happy that the Creator is watching over him and gives him the descents, as well. That is, a person should believe, as much as he can understand, that the Creator is giving him the ascents, since certainly, a person cannot say that he himself receives the ascents, but that the Creator wants to bring him closer; this is why He gives him the ascents.

Also, a person should believe that the Creator gives him the descents, as well, because He wants to bring him closer. Therefore, every single thing that he can do, he must do as though he is in a state of ascent. Therefore, when he overcomes a little during the descent, it is called an "awakening from below." Each act that he does, he believes that it is the Creator's will, and by this itself he is rewarded with greater nearing, meaning that the person himself begins to feel that the Creator has brought him closer.

23. RABASH, Article No. 24 (1991), "What Does It Mean that One Should Bear a Son and a Daughter, in the Work?"

That one yearns for knowledge, meaning he does not want to work above reason, but specifically within reason, meaning that he says that if the body understands the benefits of working and observing the *Mitzvot* [commandments/good deeds] of the King, he is willing to labor and work. But to believe above reason, to this the body does not agree. Instead, he stands and waits for the body to understand it, but otherwise, he cannot do the holy work. Sometimes, he does overcome these thoughts and desires, and this causes him the ascents and descents.

Yet, if one decides that he wants to work as "dust," meaning even if he tastes the taste of dust in the work, he says that it is very important for him to be able to do something for the sake of the Creator, and for himself, he does not care which taste he feels, and says that this work, in which one tastes the taste of dust, meaning that the body mocks this work, he says to the body that in his view, this work is regarded as "raising the *Shechina* [Divinity] from the dust."

In other words, although the body tastes dust in this work, the person says that it is *Kedusha* and does not measure how much flavor he feels in the work. Rather, he believes that the Creator does enjoy this work, since there is no mixture of the will to receive here, since he has nothing to receive because there is no flavor or scent in this work, as there is only the taste of dust here. For this reason, he believes that this is the holy work, and he is delighted.

24. RABASH, Article No. 34 (1991), "What Is Eating Their Fruits in This World and Keeping the Principal for the Next World, in the Work?"

When one sees that it is hard to get what he wants, he escapes from the work. He says, "I believe that there are people who have been rewarded and to whom the Creator gave the desire to bestow. But this was because they were more gifted than I am. But a person like me, with worse qualities than others, has no chance of meriting this." Hence, he escapes the campaign and begins to work like the general public.

Only those who say that they want to escape from the work but have nowhere else to go, since nothing satisfies them, those people do not walk out from the work. Although they have ups and downs, they do not give up. This is as it is written, "And the children of Israel sighed from the work, and they cried, and their cry went up to God from the work." In other words, they cried out from the work because they were not advancing in the work of the Creator, so they could work in order to bestow contentment upon the Maker. At that time, they were rewarded with the exodus from Egypt. In the work, this is called "emerging from the control of the will to receive and entry into the work of bestowal."

25. RABASH, Article No. 34 (1989), "What Is Peace in the Work?"

The Creator is good and does good, so why is He not behaving toward us as we understand? We understand the ascents and descents in such a way that sometimes, during the ascent, we are at peace with the Creator and say about Him that He leads the world as the good who does good. But during the descent, we haven't the strength to say that He behaves with a guidance of the good who does good. Hence, we are always in dispute.

Indeed, why is the order of the work so difficult that it requires ascents and descents? The known answer to this is what is written, "As the advantage of the light from within the darkness." In other words, it is impossible to receive light if he has no lack and need for the light.

For this reason, when a person sees that the nations of the world in him object to the Creator, and he cannot tolerate the enemy of Israel within him, he becomes jealous for his God and does not look at any descents he has, and does what he can and cries out to the Creator to help him be able to defeat the wicked ones within him.

By this he overcomes and does not escape the campaign. At that time, the Creator gives him the covenant. That is, he makes a covenant with Him that there will be peace between him and the Creator, by receiving a gift from the Creator, which is the vessels of bestowal. This is regarded as making the covenant, which is the *Klipa* [shell/peel], called "will to receive for himself," and instead of the foreskin, the Creator gives him vessels of bestowal, and by this they make a covenant, meaning peace.

26. RABASH, Article No. 29 (1986), "Lishma and Lo Lishma"

A person who wishes to walk on the path of bestowal, he must understand that from above he is given a special treatment, that he was lowered from the previous state so he would begin to really contemplate the goal, meaning what is required of man and what man wants the Creator to give him. But when he is in a state of ascent, when he has desire for Torah and *Mitzvot*, he has no need to worry about spirituality. Instead, he sees that he will stay this way his whole life because he is happy this way.

It therefore follows that the descent he has received is for his own good, meaning that he is receiving special treatment, that he was lowered from his state where he thought that he had some wholeness. This is apparent in his agreeing to remain in the current state his whole life.

But now that he sees that he is far from spirituality, he begins to think, "What is really required of me? What should I do? What is the purpose I should achieve?" He sees that he has no power to work, and finds himself in a state of "between heaven and earth." Then, man's only strengthening is that only the Creator can help, but by himself, he is doomed.

It was said about this (Isaiah, 4:31): "Yet those who hope for the Lord will gain new strength," meaning those people who hope for the Creator. This means that they who see that there is no one else in the world who can help them regain strength each time. It follows that this descent is actually an ascent, meaning that this descent that they feel allows them to rise in degree, since "there is no light without a *Kli*."

27. RABASH, Article No. 46 (1991), "What Is the Son of the Beloved and the Son of the Hated in the Work?"

The Zohar says (*VaYishlach*, Item 4), "If a man comes to be purified, the evil inclination surrenders before him and the right governs the left. And both the good inclination and the evil inclination join to keep man in all the roads he travels, as it is written, 'For He will give His angels charge over you, to keep you in all your ways.'"

We should understand how it can be said that the evil inclination keeps a person walking on the straight path. After all, it advises a person not to walk in the way of Torah, fails him in all his ways, and detains him from working for the sake of the Creator but only for his own sake. Thus, we should know how the evil inclination helps him.

The descents that a person receives, when the evil inclination gives him thoughts that are foreign to the spirit of Torah, cause him descents. According to a person's opinion, it must be that the evil inclination brought him the feeling that love of self is more important than love of the Creator, and that this is the cause of the descents.

But in truth, one should believe that the Creator does everything. In other words, the Creator sends these descents to a person in order for them to give man momentum in the work so he will not be content with little. When a person feels that he does all that he can in *Torah and Mitzvot*, and he cannot discern the matter of the intention for the sake of the Creator, or that he is working for his own benefit, since when one works in the manner of the general public, an illumination shines on a person as Surrounding Light, giving him satisfaction so he will not feel any lack in his work.

Only when one wants to work in the manner of individuals, meaning that the aim will also be for the sake of the Creator, and not specifically the act (as said in Article No. 45, *Tav-Shin-Nun-Aleph*), then he is notified from above that he is not all right, and from this he falls into a descent. At that time, one sees his real situation and begins to seek a way by which to emerge from the control of self-love.

It therefore follows that were it not for the evil inclination, which brings him the state of descents, he would remain in a state of ascent and would not need to achieve the goal of *Dvekut* with the Creator. It follows that the evil inclination is an angel of God, a messenger of the Creator to keep him from staying in a state of "still of *Kedusha* [holiness]," but rather needing to advance. This is why he says, "For He will give His angels charge over you, to keep you in all your ways." Thus, the evil inclination is also a messenger of the Creator to keep the person.

28. RABASH, Letter No. 77

The whole foundation is that one should ask that all of one's thoughts and desires will be only to benefit the Creator, a depiction of lowliness, called *Shechina* in the dust, immediately appears. Hence, we must not be impressed by the descent, since many pennies join into a great amount.

This is as we learned, "there is no absence in spirituality," rather that it has temporarily departed in order to have room for work to advance. This is so because every moment that we scrutinize into holiness enters the domain of holiness, and a person descends only in order to sort out more sparks of holiness.

However, there is an advice that one should not wait until his degree is lowered for him, and when he feels his lowliness he goes up again, and that ascent is regarded as sorting a part into holiness. Instead, he himself descends and elevates other sparks, and raises them into the domain of holiness.

It is as our sages said, "Before I lose, I search" (Shabbat, 152), meaning before I lose the situation I am in, I start searching. It is as Baal HaSulam said about King David, who said, "I awaken the dawn." Our sages said, "I awaken the dawn and the dawn does not awaken me."

Therefore, the keeping is primarily during the ascent, and not during the descent. During the ascent we need to extend fear, lest we are pushed out, God forbid. But after all these, all we need is to cry out to the King and ask for His mercy on us once and for all.

29. RABASH, Article No. 6 (1989), "What Is Above Reason in the Work?"

This is the meaning of the words, "king of Israel and his redeemer." That is, once they have taken upon themselves the kingdom of heaven, called "king of Israel," they attain that the Creator is his redeemer, meaning that only the Creator redeemed them from the control of the evil, and they themselves were powerless to do so.

In this way, we should interpret the words "Lord of hosts." This name means, as Baal HaSulam interpreted, that as he said, *Tzevaot* [hosts] are two words: *Tze* [leave/go out] and *Ba* [comes]. That is, *Tzava* [army] are men of war. These are people who go each day to fight the evil inclination. They are called "army." Therefore, after they have been rewarded with redemption, meaning after they conquer the evil inclination and emerge from the control of the evil, their conduct in the work is by way of ascents and descents, which is called *Tzevaot* [plural of *Tzava* (army)]. Meaning, at times they emerge from their control, and then are under their control again. Thus, the name for ascents and descents is *Tzevaot*.

During the work, a person should say, "If I am not for me, who is for me?" At that time in the work, they think that they themselves are doing the ascents and descents, that they are men of war, called *Tzava*, "mighty men." Afterward, when they are redeemed, they attain that the Lord is of hosts [*Tzevaot*], meaning that the Creator made all the ups and downs they had.

In other words, even the descents come from the Creator. A person does not get so many ups and downs for no reason. Rather, the Creator caused all those exits. We can interpret "exit" as "exit from *Kedusha* [holiness]," and *Ba* [comes] as "coming to *Kedusha*. The Creator does everything. Hence, after the redemption, the Creator is called "Lord of Hosts." And who is He? "The king of Israel and his redeemer."

30. RABASH, Article No. 6 (1991), "What Is, 'The Herdsmen of Abram's Cattle and the Herdsmen of Lot's Cattle,' in the Work?"

Since in every beginning a person must start over the acceptance of the kingdom of heaven, it is not enough that yesterday he had faith in the Creator. For this reason, every acceptance of the kingdom of heaven is considered a new discernment. That is, now he receives a part of the vacant space that was devoid of the kingdom of heaven, and admits that empty place and fills it with the kingdom of heaven. It follows that now he sorted out a new thing, which did not exist before he took that empty place and filled it with the kingdom of heaven. This is regarded as elevating a new spark into the *Kedusha*. Finally, from all the ascents, he always raises sparks from the vacant space into the *Kedusha*.

It follows that from each descent he arrives at a new beginning and raises new sparks. Hence, when a person sees that he has descents, he should be careful not to escape from the campaign, even though he sees that he is not progressing. Rather, he must try to start anew each time. That is, the fact that he begins to ascend does not mean that he returned to his previous degree. This would mean that he did nothing by his work, since he thinks that he is now ascending to his previous level. Rather, he must believe that this is a new discernment, that each time, he raises different sparks, until he raises the sparks that pertain to his essence.

31. RABASH, Article No. 24 (1986), "The Difference between Charity and Gift"

In the work of the Creator, in the beginning of his work he had energy and confidence, and great importance for Torah and prayer because at that time he had grace of holiness, and felt that the work of the Creator is important. However, this was still not considered a "deficiency" that the Creator will satisfy, a deficiency is called *Dvekut* [adhesion] with the Creator, since the lack and pain of not having *Dvekut* with the Creator was still not felt in him as he has not exerted for it because he has just begun the work.

But after a long period of time of making efforts and not achieving satisfaction of his deficiency, torments and pain begin to form in him because he has made efforts but sees no progress in his work. At that time the thoughts begin to come one-by-one. Sometimes it is with sparks of despair, and sometimes he grows stronger, but then he sees once more that he has fallen from his state, and so on repeatedly. Finally, a real deficiency forms in him, which he has obtained through exertion in ascents and descents. These ascents and descents leave him with pain each time at not having been granted *Dvekut* with the Creator. Finally, when the cup of labor has been filled sufficiently, it is called a *Kli*. Then the filling of it comes from the Creator, since now he has a real *Kli*.

It follows that his seeing that now—after several years of work—he has retreated, this happens deliberately so he will ache at not having *Dvekut* with the Creator. It turns out that each time he must see that he is approaching the making of the *Kli*, called "real deficiency." That is, his gauge of *Katnut* [infancy/smallness] and *Gadlut* [adulthood/greatness] of the deficiency is to the extent of the suffering he feels at not having the filling, which is called here "*Dvekut* with the Creator," where all he wants is only to bring contentment to the Creator. Before the deficiency is completed, it is impossible for the filling to come in full.

32. RABASH, Article No. 30 (1989), "What Is the Meaning of Lighting the Menorah in the Work?"

The advantage of the light is from within the darkness. By this we can see why the matter of choice, choosing the good, namely the desire to bestow, and loathing the bad, is so difficult. It is because we must taste the taste of darkness.

However, we must not be shown the darkness as it truly is. If we saw the measure of bad within us, we would immediately escape from the work. Then we would not feel darkness because he does not mind that the will to receive for himself is the ruler as he does not feel this as darkness. Only one who labors and works as much as he can, and goes through ups and downs, can say that he tastes the taste of darkness because he cannot overcome his will to receive for himself.

Thus, the descents that a person receives when he wants to walk on the path of truth are instruments for the sensation of the help he will receive. We must believe the words of our sages who said, "He who comes to purify is aided." A person must not escape the campaign when he sees that he is not making progress. Sometimes he gets thoughts of the spies, who said that this work is not for us and requires special people who can walk on the path of overcoming.

All this comes to him because he understands that each time, he must see how he is making progress. However, it does not occur to him that he must advance in obtaining darkness, that this is the only *Kli* he needs to acquire. A *Kli* is a need for a filling. That is, if he has no filling for the lack, he feels that he is in the dark. For this reason, a person must not say that he is not advancing in the work.

Hence, he wants to escape the campaign, for it is not the truth, since he sees each time how far he is from obtaining the light, meaning for the Creator to give him the *Kli* called "desire to bestow." He cannot obtain the desire to bestow by himself, and then he comes to feel that the world has grown dark on him. At that time, the light comes, meaning help from above, as it is written, "He who comes to purify is aided."

33. RABASH, Article No. 24 (1991), "What Does It Mean that One Should Bear a Son and a Daughter, in the Work?"

When a person prevails and asks for help from the Creator, after he has decided that he has a harm-doer in his heart, called "will to receive," and that he cannot emerge from it, meaning after going through several ascents and descents, he finally sees that he has remained bare and destitute. At that time, his prayer is from the bottom of the heart. That is, he sees that if the Creator does not help him, he cannot overcome it.

Although one can say that he believes above reason that only the Creator helps him, within reason, he does not feel this, since he knows that he himself made the efforts and the labor to obtain something in spirituality. But when one sees that after all the exertions, he cannot emerge from the governance of the will to receive for himself, then he sees within reason that only the Creator can help him.

34. RABASH, Article No. 27 (1989), "What Is the Meaning of Suffering in the Work?"

Our sages said (*Shabbat* 152), "What I did not lose, I seek." That is, an old man walking bent, always looking at the ground as though searching for something. He says, "I have lost nothing, yet I search." We should interpret "Old is he who has acquired wisdom." That is, he is "Wise, who sees the future." Since he can come to a descent in order acquire empty *Kelim*, so the Creator may fill them or he will remain in a state of lowliness because he will not feel deficient. Then, when he loses the state of ascent, he begins to seek advice how to ascent in spirituality once again.

Therefore, one who is old, meaning wise and sees the future, begins to search how to ascend in spirituality even before he loses the state of ascent. He begins to follow all the counsels about the ways to ascend on the spiritual degrees, and this is done by seeking deficiencies in the state he is in. In that case, there is no need to throw him down in importance so he will find and see deficiencies in himself, since he himself will be looking for deficiencies so as to have empty *Kelim* that the Creator may fill.

35. RABASH, Article No. 15 (1991), "What Is the Blessing, 'Who Made a Miracle for Me in This Place,' in the Work?"

During an ascent, he must remember and say, "In this place, where I now have an ascent, I had a descent and the Creator saved me and raised me from the netherworld, and I emerged from death, called 'removal from the Creator,' and I have been rewarded with some measure of nearing to the Creator, which is called 'some measure of *Dvekut* with the Life of Lives.'"

For this, a person should be thankful, for by this he has now come to a state where there he suffered, and now he is in a mood of delight and pleasure because the Creator bringing him closer has given him new *Kelim* of a lack that he can fill with the state of ascent that he is in now.

It follows that he extends a light of joy in new *Kelim* that he has obtained now by looking at the miracle that he has had, where the Creator saved him. Therefore, when he considers the suffering, it is as though now he is the recipient of the suffering, and now he fills them up with pleasure.

It follows that depicting to himself the state of descent causes him that the ascent he has received now will spread in new *Kelim* according to the rule "There is no light without a *Kli*." Hence, during the ascent, when he begins to contemplate the state of descent that he had, the suffering of the descent are regarded as *Kelim* in which the light of the ascent may spread.

36. RABASH, Article No. 43 (1990), "What Is, 'You Shall Not Plant for Yourself an Asherah by the Altar,' in the Work?"

Every descent is a trial. If a person can endure the trial, meaning that the thought that comes to a person causes him to see if he is under the governance of *Kedusha* or not, during the descent, a person can see that at the time of ascent, his whole structure was built on the will to receive for oneself.

During the descent, a person cannot make any calculations. But afterward, when he receives nearing from above once more, which comes to a person by what is written, "I am the Lord, who dwells with them in the midst of their impurity," meaning that even though a person is still in the authority of self-love, still, an illumination comes to him from above, called "an awakening from above." At that time, he must awaken the state of descent that he had by himself, and think what was the reason he received the descent, and what he must correct so as not to come into a descent once more. A person must believe that the fact that he suffered a descent is because he was thrown from above. This is why he fell into such lowliness. At that time, he can work on himself, correct corrections so he does not fall again, since he must believe that the descent is a correction for him.

37. RABASH, Article No. 29 (1988), "How to Recognize One Who Serves God from One Who Does Not Serve Him"

When does one learn and profit from the descent? Certainly not during the descent, for then he is dead. However, afterward, when the Creator revives him, meaning gives him an ascent, this is the time to learn what happened to him during the descent, meaning in what lowliness he was, what he craved and what he expected—that if he were to have it, he would feel like a complete human being. At that time he sees that his entire life of being in descent was nothing short of the life of an animal.

Let us take, for example, when trash is thrown in the garbage. When the cats in the area feel that there is some leftovers of an animal that was thrown in the trash, they find it and eat it. With the strength from eating, each of them runs to its place to obtain other pleasures. If a person observes during the ascent, he understands that it is not worthwhile to occupy his mind and heart in beastly lusts. In his current eyes, it is complete trash. When he looks at such a life, it makes him so nauseous that he wants to vomit.

It follows that the great benefit from this descent is that he sees his own lowliness, to what state he might come, and that only the Creator has brought him out of that lowliness. This is the time to see the greatness of the Creator, that He can bring a person "out of the miry clay," where he could drown and remain forever in the hands of the *Sitra Achra* [other side], and only the Creator has brought him out of there.

Accordingly, we can see that during the ascent, a person should read everything that is written about the time of descent. From this reading he will know how to ask the Creator for his soul so He will not throw him once again into the trash. Also, he will know how to thank the Creator for raising him from the bottomless pit, as it was said, "A king who puts to death and brings to life, and brings forth salvation." That is, salvation grows out of the descents and ascents.

38. RABASH, Article No. 23 (1987), "Peace after a Dispute Is More Important than Having No Disputes At All"

Only during the ascent, when he calculates what he gains and what he loses by being enslaved to the will to receive, that he cannot gain and only loses, that calculation that he does can make him feel how his inclination is harming him.

In each and every ascent, he must calculate what he lost from the descent. By this he sees that the inclination is causing him many harms. In order to set in his heart the need for the help of the Creator, many troubles come to him and he suffers from it, as in the words of *The Zohar*, which explained about the verse, "Many are the afflictions of the righteous," that the righteous suffers many troubles from the inclination.

According to what we explained, we should interpret the verse, "Many are the afflictions of the righteous." That is, after the righteous has suffered many afflictions, since "righteous" is named after the future, meaning one who wants to be righteous, who wants to work for the Creator, he suffers many afflictions until many afflictions are accumulated. This is why it is written, "from all of them," meaning that when he has many afflictions, the Creator will save him, since then he has a real need for the Creator's help and he will know how to appreciate the Creator's salvation, since there is no light without a *Kli*.

39. RABASH, Article No. 27 (1989), "What Is the Meaning of Suffering in the Work?"

The best advice in a state of ascent is that when a person feels that now there is a state of spirituality, and he wants to find deficiencies, in that state he should delve in the Torah and find the connection between the Torah and man. From this he will be able to take knowledge about how to serve the Creator, as it is written, "a soul without knowledge is also not good," and as it is written, "grant us wisdom, understanding, and knowledge from You." In that state, he will see the lack in him and will have empty *Kelim*. By this, he will be saved from coming into a real descent.

40. RABASH, Article No. 840, "Quick Nearing"

One does not enter the work of the left, called "trouble," unless during an ascent. At that time, he enters the left, meaning while he is still not in a descent.

"Rabbi Elazar said, 'One should always precede trouble with prayer'" (Sanhedrin 44b). This means that even when one is in a state of ascent, he must ask the Creator to bring him closer with another, greater nearing, so he will advance in the work. If he feels no deficiency, he cannot advance. This is why he is given a descent from above, so he will have a lack. A descent is called "trouble," and then he prays.

Hence, there is an advice: Before the trouble comes to him, he already prays.

41. RABASH, Article No. 34 (1988), "What Are Day and Night in the Work?"

At the end of correction it will be known to all that "Yours is the day; Yours is also the night." That is, since His will is to do good to His creations, and good means day, so how can it be said that the Creator gives darkness? It is against His purpose! However, the darkness, too, meaning the night, is regarded as "day," even though the person feels cessations in *Dvekut* with the Creator, which are called "darkness" and "night."

But at the end of correction, when it is known that He has given the darkness, too, this is certainly light, as well. The proof of it is that then the sins become as merits. Thus, at that time we know that "Yours is the day; Yours is also the night," since both belong to You, meaning that both are You, meaning the Creator has given both as "day."

Conversely, before the end of the work, it is impossible to attribute the cessations that a person has in *Dvekut* with the Creator to the Creator, that He has sent him this, since this contradicts the purpose of creation. This is the meaning of the words, "The darkness of the night will shine as the light of the day." That is, since the sins have then become to him has merits, everything becomes day.

Now we can understand what are day and night in the work. A person should know that he must feel what is darkness, or he will not be able to enjoy the light, since in anything that a person wants to taste any flavor, whether it is worth using, he must learn one from the other, as it is written, "as the advantage of the light out of the darkness." Likewise, a person cannot enjoy rest unless he knows what is fatigue.

For this reason, a person must go through a process of ascents and descents. However, he must not be impressed by the descents. Instead, he should exert not to escape the campaign. For this reason, although during the work he must know that they are two things, at the end of the work he sees that light and darkness are as two legs that lead a person to the goal.

42. RABASH, Article No. 5 (1988), "What Is, 'When Israel Are in Exile, the Shechina Is With Them,' in the Work?"

What is the meaning of "When Israel are in exile, the *Shechina* is with them"? As Rabbi Shimon Ben Yochai said, "Wherever they exile, the *Shechina* is with them." What is the benefit from this in the work, that he says about it, "How beloved are Israel by the Creator"?

We should interpret that when a person feels that he is in exile, meaning feels the taste of exile in the work and wants to escape from the exile, the meaning will be that a person must believe that wherever they are exiled, the *Shechina* is with them. That is, the *Shechina* let him feel the taste of exile. "With them" means that the *Shechina* is attached to them and they are not separated from the *Shechina*, that they should say that it is a descent. On the contrary, now the *Shechina* is giving him a push so he will climb the degrees of *Kedusha* [holiness/sanctity], and dresses herself in a garment of descent.

When a person knows and believes that this is so, it will encourage him so he does not escape the campaign or say that the work of bestowal is not for him because he always sees that he is in states of ascents and descents, and he sees no end to these states and falls into despair.

But if he walks in the path of faith and believes in the words of our sage, then he must say the opposite.

43. RABASH, Article No. 10 (1991), "What Does 'The King Stands on His Field When the Crop Is Ripe' Mean in the Work?"

The correction of a person walking on the left line is because he does not wait to get a decline and fall, and then he will wait until an awakening from above comes to him. Instead, he draws upon him the left, and then he sees that he is in a state of descent, meaning that he does not have a single spark of desire to work in order to bestow and not for his own benefit. And then he can pray.

It is as Baal HaSulam said about what our sages said of David, who said, "I awaken the dawn, and the dawn does not awaken me." That is, King David did not wait for the dawn, which is called "black," which is darkness, meaning that the darkness awakens him. Instead, he awakens the darkness. He prays to the Creator to illuminate His face for him and thus he gains time from having the preparation for the darkness, and then it is easier to correct it.

And the two above-mentioned lines—right and left—beget a third line, the middle line. It is as our sages said, "And the Creator places the spirit and soul within him." Thus, after a person has completed the work in two lines, all the evil is revealed in him. This came to him because those two lines are as two verses that refute one another. And one sees that there is no end to the ups and downs, and then he makes an honest prayer for the Creator to help him receive the desire to bestow.

44. RABASH, Article No. 255, "Words of a Dead Man"

"Dead" means during the fall. At that time, he is in a state of "The wicked in their lives are called 'dead.'" Then, when he is told words of Torah from others so he will wake up and return to work, it does not help him. It is called "Mocking the poor," since he is not impressed by others saying Torah.

However, if he is told the words of a dead man, meaning what he himself said when he was in ascent, regarded as when he was alive, and he is told, "Look what a great state you had," and that he had vitality of *Kedusha* [holiness], and "Look what words of Torah you said then," from this he can be resurrected. But if he is told words of Torah that others said, it does not impress him.

"Worldly matters do not belong here." "World [or worldly]" means faith. It is possible to speak with him about faith also from others, who encourage him and tell him, "Look, this and that person have fear of heaven, while you remain as still as dead." He might be inspired and come back to life when he hears matters of faith pertaining to others. Thus, even in worldly matters, only his own words should be said to him.

According to RASHI, this is perplexing. He says that everyone must speak words of Torah, and he is still. Therefore, it is regarded as mocking the poor. But with worldly matters, not everyone must speak, so why is it regarded as mocking the poor?

The reason it is forbidden to speak of worldly matters pertaining to faith, for faith is called "world" (as it is written in *The Zohar* in several places), since *Alma* [Aramaic: world] comes from the words *He'elem* [concealment] and *Hester* [hiding], which is faith. Therefore, they think, according to the view that some people say, that in matters of faith he will also not listen, that he will not be impressed by what others say.

But from the words of the dead, meaning from what he himself did in matters of faith during his life, it is possible that the *Reshimot* [recollections] will awaken in him and will revive him. But from others, even concerning faith, it will also not work.

Thus, when speaking to him of worldly matters that others do, he will not listen. Thus, he would be mocking the poor because all the words will be in vain. Hence, only his own *Reshimot* can awaken him. This is called "from the words of the dead himself," from when he was alive, when he was in a state of ascent.

45. RABASH, Article No. 16 (1988), "What Is the Foundation on which Kedusha [Holiness] Is Built?"

"I awaken the dawn" will mean "Whenever I want, I awaken the dawn." In other words, I myself awaken the darkness and the blackness within me—that I am still immersed in self-love and I still do not have love for the Creator. I am still without the glory of the Torah and I still do not have the importance of the Torah to know that it is worthwhile to do everything to obtain the light of Torah, as well as how to appreciate the importance of observing the *Mitzvot* that the Creator commanded for us.

When I need to perform some *Mitzva* and intend that it will be in order to bestow, the resistance in the body promptly awakens in full force. And he has a great struggle to do anything and he sees the ascents and descents each time. And then he has room for prayer. This is so because a person awakens himself at the right time, meaning when he feels that he will be able to pray instantaneously, and not that the black will bring him sadness and depression, that he will not have the ability to pray for the blackness.

One can see for himself whether it comes to him from the side of *Klipa* or not. The sign for this is that something that comes from *Kedusha* is always in the form of "increasing holiness and not decreasing." In other words, one always asks the Creator to elevate him to a higher degree than the one he is on. But when the blackness comes from the side of *Klipa*, a person cannot ask the Creator to raise him above his state.

"Rather, they bring down," meaning bring him down to the netherworld, and he loses the small portion of faith that he had and he remains seemingly dead.

46. RABASH, Article No. 15 (1989), "What Is, 'The Righteous Become Apparent through the Wicked,' in the Work?"

In order for a person to progress on the path of the Creator, to be rewarded with all his work being for the sake of the Creator, and now he feels that he is in a state of ascent, what more should he do? For this reason, the Creator leads His world with wicked. That is, at that time the Creator gives him thoughts of wicked—that it is not worthwhile to work for Him, but only for himself. By this, he suffers a descent and thinks that the descent he has received is not because it was given to him so he would advance in the path of the Creator, to be rewarded with knowledge of *Kedusha* [holiness]. Rather, he thinks that he regressed because he cannot work in the manner of individuals, but needs to work like the general public. And since he has departed from the general public, he is left empty handed from here and from there, since he cannot return to the general public.

For this reason, in that state, a person stands between heaven and earth, and feels that his situation is worse than that of the rest of the people. At that time, he can ask the Creator with all his heart, and pray as it is written, "Pardon me, O Lord, for I am wretched. Heal me, O Lord, for my bones are dismayed, and You, O Lord, how long?" That is, how long will I stay in a situation where I feel that my condition is worse than any other person, that I have no grip on spirituality.

For this reason, he has no other choice but to believe what is written, "For You hear the prayer of every mouth." Baal HaSulam explained that a person must believe that the Creator hears the prayer of every mouth, meaning even the worst mouth in the world, of which there cannot be lowlier and worse in the world. Still, the Creator hears him, as our sages said, "He who comes to purify is aided."

47. RABASH, Article No. 5 (1988), "What Is, 'When Israel Are in Exile, the Shechina Is With Them,' in the Work?"

The Creator wants him to see his real state, how remote he is from working for the benefit of the Creator. For this reason, the Creator has taken from him the flavor he felt in *Lo Lishma* [not for Her sake], which leaves him lifeless. It follows that the Creator is tending to him and wants to admit him into *Kedusha*.

Therefore, now he must pray to the Creator to help him, since now he needs His help. Otherwise, he sees that he is completely lost. This is regarded as having obtained a *Kli* and a need for the

Creator's help, since now he sees that he is truly separated from the Creator because he has no life, for one who adheres to the Creator has life, as it is written, "For with You is the source of life."

Now he can certainly pray from the bottom of the heart, for a real prayer is specifically from the bottom of the heart. Accordingly, he should be thankful to the Creator for letting him see his true state. Now he sees that he needs the Creator to give him the necessary assistance, as our sages said, "He who comes to purify is aided." And *The Zohar* asks, "With what is he aided?" and it replies, "With a holy soul."

Therefore, now the Creator has given him an opportunity to obtain a holy soul. He should be delighted about the state of descent and suffering that he feels in this state. For this reason, he should say that he is not in a state of descent, but on the contrary, he is in a state of ascent.

By this we can interpret what our sages said, "When torments come upon Israel, they surrender and pray." This means that when they come into a state of descent, they see their true state, that they are in lowliness. This is considered that they surrender, since they see their state—that they have parted from the Life of Lives, for one who has *Dvekut* with the Creator is alive. Otherwise, he feels only suffering. Therefore, it is clear to him that now is the time for prayer from the bottom of the heart. This is the meaning of the words, "They surrender and pray."

48. *Zohar for All*, "Introduction of the Book of Zohar," "On the Night of the Bride," Item 140

The guidance of good and evil causes us ascents and descents, each according to what he is. You should know that for this reason, each ascent is regarded as a separate day because due to the great descent that he had, doubting the beginning, during the ascent he is as a newly born child. Thus, in each ascent, it is as though he begins to serve the Creator anew. This is why each ascent is considered a specific day, and similarly, each descent is considered a specific night.

It is written, "Day to day pours forth speech," a holy day, from among those upper days of the King. In other words, on each ascent that a person had, when he clung to the upper days of the Creator, the friends are praised and each tells his friend that thing that he said. This is so because through the great *Zivug* at the end of correction they will be rewarded with repentance from love, for they will complete the correction of all the vessels of reception, so they will be only in order to bestow contentment upon the Creator. In that *Zivug*, all of the great delight and pleasure of the thought of creation will appear to us.

At that time, we will evidently see that all those punishments from the time of descents, which brought us into doubting the beginning, were the things that purified us and were the direct causes of all the happiness and goodness that have come to us at the time of the end of correction. This is so because were it not for those terrible punishments, we would never have come to this delight and pleasure. Then these sins will be inverted into actual merits.

"Day to day pours forth speech" means that each ascent prior to the end of correction is one of those upper days of the King, praising the friends. Thus, now it reappears in all the magnificence of its wholeness, which belongs to that day, and praises the friends who keep the Torah with that thing which each said to the friends, which is, "It is vain to serve God; and what profit is it that we have kept His charge," which at the time inflicted great punishments.

This is because now they have been turned into merits, since the entire wholeness and happiness of that day would not be able to appear now, in that grandeur and magnificence, were it not for those punishments. This is why those who speak those words are regarded as "Those who fear the Lord and who esteem His name," as actual good deeds. This is why it was said about them, too, "I will have compassion over them as a man has compassion for his own son who serves him."

It is said, "Day to day pours forth that speech" and praises it. This is so because all those nights are the descents, the suffering, and the punishments that arrested the *Dvekut* [adhesion] with the Creator until they became many days one after the other. Now, once the night and darkness have become merits and good deeds, as well, the night shines like the day and darkness like light, there are no more arrests, and all 6,000 years unite into a single great day.

Thus, all the *Zivugim* that came out one at a time and disclosed ascents and descents that were separate from one another have now assembled into a level of one, sublime, and transcendent level of *Zivug*, which shines from the end of the world through its end. It is written, "Day to day pours forth that speech" because the word that separated between one day and the next has now become a great praise and praises it, for it has become a merit. Thus, they all became one day for the Lord.

49. Talks with the ADMOR of Mogalintza

Once, a famous man confessed to the Rabbi of Lublin that all the restrictions and limitations he applies on himself do not save him from the evil inclination and there is hardly a day without a sin. The Rabbi of Lublin answered him: "It sounds from your words that you still have not begun the work of the Creator whatsoever, since anyone from Israel who does not find in himself 400 sins from the morning to the morning prayer, it is a sign that he has not begun to serve the Creator in holiness and purity."

50. Rabbi Nachman of Breslow, *Likutey Moharan*, Last Edition, Mark 48

The work of the Creator requires great persistence, whatever happens to him. Remember this well for you will need it very much as you begin the work of the Creator. It requires great tenacity, and to be strong and brave, to brace oneself and stand still, even if you are dropped down every time. You must not allow yourself to fall off altogether, for it is necessary to experience all those falls, descents, and confusions prior to entering the gates of *Kedusha* [holiness], and the true righteous, too, have gone through all of it. Know, that man must cross and very, very narrow bridge, and the rule and the most important thing is not to be afraid at all.

8

Despair with One's Own Strength

1. Baal HaSulam, Letter No. 57

There is no happier state in man's world than when he finds himself despaired with his own strength. That is, he has already labored and done all that he could possibly imagine he could do, but found no remedy. It is then that he is fit for a wholehearted prayer for His help because he knows for certain that his own work will not help him.

As long as he feels some strength of his own, his prayer will not be whole because the evil inclination rushes first and tells him, "First you must do what you can, and then you will be worthy of the Creator."

It was said about this, "The Lord is high and the low will see." For once a person has labored in all kinds of work, and has become disillusioned, he comes into real lowliness, knowing that he is the lowest of all the people, as there is nothing good in the structure of his body. At that time, his prayer is complete and he is granted by His generous hand.

The writing says about this, "And the children of Israel sighed from the work, etc., and their cry went up." It is so because at that time they came into a state of despair from the work. It is as one who pumps into a punctured bucket. He pumps all day but does not have a drop of water to quench his thirst.

So were the children of Israel in Egypt: Everything they built was promptly swallowed in its place in the ground, as our sages said.

Similarly, one who has not been rewarded with His love, all that he has done in his work on purifying the soul the day before is as though completely burned the next day. And each day and each moment he must start anew as though he has not done a thing in his entire life.

Then, "The children of Israel sighed from the work," for they evidently saw that they were unfit to ever produce something by their own work. This is why their sigh and prayer were complete, as it should be, and this is why "Their cry went up," since the Creator hears the prayer, and He only awaits a wholehearted prayer.

It follows from the above that everything, small or great, is obtained only by the power of prayer. All the labor and work to which we are obliged are only to discover our lack of strength and our lowliness—that we are unfit for anything by our own strength—for then we can pour out a wholehearted prayer before Him.

We could argue about this, "So I can decide that I am unfit for anything, and why all the labor and exertion?" However, there is a natural law that there is none so wise as the experienced, and before one tries to actually do all he can do, he is utterly incapable of arriving at true lowliness, to the real extent, as said above.

This is why we must toil in *Kedusha* [holiness] and purity, as it is written, "Whatever you find that your hand can do by your strength, that do," and understand this for it is true and deep.

I revealed this truth to you only so you would not weaken or give up on mercy. Although you do not see anything, for even when the measure of labor is complete, it is the time of prayer, but until then, believe in our sages: "I did not labor and found, do not believe."

When the measure is full, your prayer will be complete and the Creator will grant generously, as our sages instructed us, "I labored and found, believe," for one is unfit for a prayer prior to this, and the Creator hears a prayer.

2. Baal HaSulam, *Shamati*, Article No. 209, "Three Conditions in Prayer"

There are three conditions in prayer:

1. Believing that He can save him. Although he has the worst conditions of all his contemporaries, still, "Will the Lord's hand be too short to save him?" If it is not so, then "the Landlord cannot save His vessels."
2. He no longer has any choice for he has already done all that he could but saw no cure to his plight.
3. If He does not help him, he will be better off dead than alive. Prayer means "lost in the heart." The more one is lost, so is the measure of his prayer. Clearly, one who lacks luxuries is not like one who has been sentenced to death, and only the execution is missing, and he is already tied with iron chains, and he is standing and pleading for his life. He will certainly not rest or sleep or be distracted for even a moment from praying for his life.

3. Baal HaSulam, *Shamati*, Article No. 20, "Lishma [for Her sake]"

In order for a person to obtain *Lishma*, one needs an awakening from above, as it is an illumination from above and it is not for the human mind to understand. Rather, he who tastes, knows. It is said about this, "Taste and see that the Lord is good."

Because of this, upon assuming the burden of the kingdom of heaven, one needs it to be in utter completeness, meaning only to bestow and not at all to receive. If a person sees that the organs do not agree with this view, he has no other choice but prayer—to pour out his heart to the Creator to help him make his body consent to enslaving itself to the Creator.

Do not say that if *Lishma* [for Her sake] is a gift from above, what good is one's overcoming and efforts, and all the remedies and corrections that he does in order to achieve *Lishma*, if it depends on the Creator? Our sages said about it, "You are not free to rid yourself of it." Rather, one must give the awakening from below, and this is considered "prayer." Yet, there cannot be a real prayer if he does not know first that without prayer it cannot be obtained.

Therefore, the acts and remedies he does in order to obtain *Lishma* create the corrected *Kelim* [vessels] in him that want to receive the *Lishma*. Then, after all the actions and the remedies he can pray in earnest since he saw that all his actions did not help him whatsoever. Only then can he make an honest prayer from the bottom of his heart, and then the Creator hears his prayer and gives him the gift of *Lishma*.

4. Baal HaSulam, *Shamati*, Article No. 18, "My Soul Shall Weep In Secret – 1"

When concealment overpowers a person and he comes to a state where the work becomes tasteless, and he cannot picture or feel any love and fear, and he cannot do anything in *Kedusha* [holiness], his only counsel is to cry to the Creator to have mercy on him and remove the screen from his eyes and heart.

Crying is a very important matter. It is as our sages write: "All the gates were locked except for the gates of tears." The world asks about this: If the gates of tears are not locked, what is the need for the gates at all? He said that it is like a person who asks his friend for some necessary object. This object touches his heart, and he asks and begs him in every manner of prayer and plea. Yet, his friend pays no attention to all this. And when he sees that there is no longer reason for prayers and pleas then he raises his voice in weeping.

It is said about this: "All the gates were locked except for the gates of tears." That is, when were the gates of tears not locked? Precisely when all the gates were locked. It is then that there is room for the gates of tears, and then we see that they were not locked.

However, when the gates of prayer are open, the gates of tears and weeping are irrelevant. This is the meaning of the gates of tears being locked. Thus, when are the gates of tears not locked? Precisely when all the gates are locked, the gates of tears are open since one still has the choice of prayer and plea.

This is the meaning of "My soul shall weep in secret," meaning when one comes to a state of concealment, then "My soul shall weep," because one has no other option. This is the meaning of "All that your hand and strength can do, do."

5. Baal HaSulam, *Shamati*, Article No. 1, "There Is None Else Besides Him"

It is written, "There is none else besides Him." This means that there is no other force in the world that has the ability to do anything against Him. And what one sees, that there are things in the world that deny the upper household, the reason is that this is His will.

This is deemed a correction called "the left rejects and the right pulls closer," meaning that what the left rejects is considered a correction. This means that there are things in the world that, to begin with, aim to divert a person from the right way, and by which he is rejected from *Kedusha* [holiness].

The benefit from the rejections is that through them a person receives a complete need and desire for the Creator to help him since he sees that otherwise he is lost; not only is he not progressing in the work, he even sees that he regresses. That is, he lacks the strength to observe Torah and *Mitzvot* [commandments] even *Lo Lishma* [not for Her sake], for only by genuinely overcoming all the obstacles, above reason, can he observe the Torah and *Mitzvot*. But he does not always have the strength to overcome above reason; otherwise, he is forced to deviate, God forbid, from the way of the Creator, even from *Lo Lishma*.

And he, who always feels that the shattered is greater than the whole, meaning that there are many more descents than ascents, and he does not see an end to these states, and he will forever remain outside of holiness, for he sees that it is difficult for him to observe even in the slightest bit, unless by overcoming above reason. But he cannot always overcome, so what will be in the end?

Then he comes to the decision that no one can help but the Creator Himself. This causes him to make a heartfelt demand that the Creator will open his eyes and heart and truly bring him closer to eternal *Dvekut* [adhesion] with the Creator.

6. RABASH, Article No. 626, "Anything that the Merciful One Does, He Does for the Best"

Avid [Aramaic: do] comes from the word *Avud* [Hebrew: lost], for the *Ayin* and *Aleph* are interchangeable. In other words, when a person comes to a state where he is truly lost, when he does not see how he can exist in the world or that he has anything to hold on to, and he has exhausted all the tactics and ideas, and sees that after all the labor and exertions, everything is lost, he must brace himself and say, "Everything that the Merciful one does is for the best."

In other words, the Creator brought upon him all those states of being lost, and they are for the best. That is, through them he has come to a state where he is at the lowest degree, and by this he will be able to rise up, as it is written, "The Lord is high and the low will see," for there is no greater lowliness than when one feels completely lost.

This is the meaning of "Everything that the Merciful one does, He does for the best." Afterward, when he begins to work once more and correct his actions, and makes repentance from love, he says, "This, too, is for the best," meaning the states when he was lost, and there is no greater transgression than a person coming to a state of being lost.

When he repents from love, he sees that this, too, is for the best, that from the bad itself, the good was done. It follows that there is a difference between "Everything that the Merciful one does" and "this, too, is for the best."

7. RABASH, Article No. 38 (1990), "What Is, 'A Cup of Blessing Must Be Full,' in the Work?"

A person needs great mercy in order not to escape the campaign. Although he uses the counsels that our sages said, "I have created the evil inclination; I have created the Torah as a spice," but the person says that he has already used this advice several times to no avail.

He also says that he has already used the advice "He who comes to purify is aided," and it is as though all the counsels are not for him. Thus, he does not know what to do. This is the worst state for a person, meaning he wants to escape from these states but has nowhere to run. At that time he suffers torments at being between despair and confidence. But then a person says, "Where will I turn?"

At that time, the only advice is prayer. Yet, this prayer is also without any guarantee, so it follows that then he must pray to believe that the Creator does hear a prayer, and everything that one feels in these states is to his benefit. But this can be only above reason, meaning although the mind tells him, "After all the calculations, you see that nothing can help you," he should believe this, too, above reason, that the Creator can deliver him from the will to receive for himself, in return for which he will receive the desire to bestow.

8. RABASH, Letter No. 9

One who sees one's lowliness sees that he is treading the path leading to the work *Lishma*. This gives one room for real prayer from the bottom of the heart, when he sees that no one will help him but the Creator himself, as Baal HaSulam interpreted concerning the redemption from Egypt, "I, and not a messenger," for everyone saw that only the Creator Himself redeemed them from the governance of evil.

And when rewarded with the work *Lishma* there is certainly nothing to be proud of because then one sees that it is only God's gift, and not "my power and the might of my hand," and there is no foreign hand that can help him. Therefore, he feels his lowliness—how serving the king is an immeasurable pleasure, and without His help he would not agree to it. Indeed, there is no greater lowliness than this.

9. RABASH, Article No. 16 (1985), "But the More They Afflicted Them"

"And the children of Israel sighed because of the labor, and they cried, and their cry came up unto God because of the labor. And God heard their groaning."

We should be precise about the words "because of the labor" being written twice. We should explain that all the sighs were from the labor, meaning that they could not work for the Creator. Indeed, their suffering was from not being able to make the work that they were doing be for the Creator, due to the *Klipa* of Egypt. This is why it is written, "Because of the labor" twice.

1) All the sighs were not because they were lacking anything. They lacked only one thing, meaning they did not wish for any luxuries or payment. Their only lack, for which they felt pain and suffering, was that of not being able to do anything for the Creator. In other words, they wished that they would have a desire to give contentment to the Creator and not to themselves, but they couldn't, and this afflicted them. This is called "wanting to have some grip in spirituality."

2) The second "Because of the labor" comes to teach that, "And their cry came up unto God," that God heard their groaning, was because their only request was work. This comes to imply to the other "because of the labor." It turns out that the whole exile that they felt was only because they were under the rule of the *Klipa* of Egypt and they could not do anything to make it only in order to bestow.

10. RABASH, Article No. 2 (1991), "What Is, 'Return, O Israel, Unto the Lord Your God,' in the Work?"

The Creator heals the brokenhearted. The thing is that it is known that the essence of man is the heart, as our sages said, "The Merciful one wants the heart." The heart is the *Kli* [vessel] that receives the *Kedusha* from above. It is as we learn about the breaking of the vessels, that if the *Kli* is broken, everything you put in it will spill out.

Likewise, if the heart is broken, meaning the will to receive controls the heart, abundance cannot enter there because everything that the will to receive receives will go to the *Klipot* [shells/peels]. This is called "the breaking of the heart." Hence, a person prays to the Creator and says, "You must help me because I am worse than everyone, since I feel that the will to receive controls my heart, and this is why nothing of *Kedusha* can enter my heart. I want no luxuries, only to be able to do something for the sake of the Creator, and I am utterly incapable of this, so only You can save me."

By this we should interpret what is written (Psalms 34), "The Lord is near to the brokenhearted." That is, those who ask the Creator to help them so their heart will not be broken and will be whole.

11. RABASH, Article No. 37 (1991), "What Is the Torah and What Is The Statute of the Torah, in the Work?"

When he wants to do everything for the sake of the Creator and not for his own sake. Here the body resists with all its might, since it argues, "Why do you want to put me and my domain to death? You come to me with having to work only for the sake of the Creator and not for one's own sake, which is truly annulment of the will to receive from everything. You tell me that our sages said, 'The Torah exists only in one who puts himself to death over it,' meaning to put to death all the domain of self-benefit and care only for the benefit of the Creator, and before this, a person cannot be rewarded with the Torah." Yet, a person sees that it is unrealistic that he will have the strength to go against nature.

At that time, one has no choice but to turn to the Creator and say, "Now I have come to a state where I see that unless You help me, I am lost. I will never have the strength to overcome the will to receive, as this is my nature. Rather, only the Creator can give another nature."

A person says that he believes that this was the exodus from Egypt, that the Creator delivered the people of Israel from under the governance of Egypt, as our sages said (in the Passover *Haggadah* [story/narrative]), "And the Lord brought us out from Egypt, not by an angel, and not by a messenger, but the Creator Himself; I am the Lord, it is I and not another."

Now, he, too, sees that only the Creator can deliver him from the governance of the will to receive and give him a second nature.

12. RABASH, Article No. 19 (1985), "Come unto Pharaoh – 1"

We should pay attention to "Come unto Pharaoh" and believe through the worst possible states, and not escape the campaign, but rather always trust that the Creator can help a person and give him, whether one needs a little help or a lot of help.

In truth, one who understands that he needs the Creator to give him a lot of help, because he is worse than the rest of the people, is more suitable for his prayer to be answered, as it is written, "The Lord is near to the brokenhearted, and saves the crushed in spirit."

Therefore, one should not say that he is unfit for the Creator to bring him closer, but that the reason is that he is idle in his work. Instead, one should always overcome and not let thoughts of despair enter his mind, as our sages said (*Berachot*, 10), "Even if a sharp sword is placed on his neck he should not deny himself of mercy," as it was said (Job, 13), "Though He slay me, I will hope for Him."

We should interpret the "sharp sword placed on his neck" to mean that even though one's evil, called "self-love," is placed on his neck and wants to separate him from *Kedusha* by showing him that it is impossible to exit this authority, he should say that the picture he sees is the truth.

However, "He should not deny himself of mercy," for at that time he must believe that the Creator can give him the mercy, meaning the quality of bestowal. That is, by himself, it is true that one cannot exit the authority of self-reception. But from the perspective of the Creator, when the Creator helps him, of course He can bring him out. This is the meaning of what is written, "I am the Lord your God, who took you out from the land of Egypt to be your God."

13. RABASH, Article No. 12 (1985), "Jacob Dwelled in the Land Where His Father Had Lived"

One must believe that the Creator has created the world with benevolence, and the evil in his body removes him from all the good. That is, when he comes to learn Torah, he finds it utterly tasteless. And also, when he comes to perform some *Mitzva* [good deed/correction], he finds it utterly tasteless because the evil inclination in his body has the power not to let him believe in the Creator above reason by taking out every flavor. Whenever he begins to approach something spiritual, he feels that everything is dry without any moisture of life.

When the person began his work, he was told—and he believed what he was told—that the Torah is a Torah of life, as it is written, "For they are your life and the length of your days," and as it is written (Psalms 19), "More desirable than gold, than much fine gold, and sweeter than honey and the honeycomb."

But when one consider this and sees that the evil inclination is to blame for everything, and strongly feels the bad that it is causing him, then he feels on himself what is written (Psalms 34) "Many are the afflictions of the righteous." That is, that verse was said about him.

At that time he looks at what the verse says afterwards, "but the Lord delivers him out of them all." At that time he begins to cry out to the Creator to help him because he has already done everything that he could think of doing, but nothing helped, and he thinks that "Everything that you find within your power to do, that do," was said about him. At that time comes the time of salvation—the salvation of the Creator delivering him from the evil inclination—to the extent that from this day forth the evil inclination will surrender before him and will not be able to incite him into any transgression.

14. RABASH, Letter No. 28

I have already written you that there are mitigated judgments. To understand this in the preparation to entering the Creator's palace is that sometimes a person feels that he is in a state of lowliness, meaning that he has neither Torah nor work, and also thoughts of worldly vanities and so forth. At that time one becomes despaired saying, "'And I to serve my master' must have been said about someone else."

Rather, to people of high degrees, who have been born with good and upright qualities and a good mind, and desire and craving to persist with the study of Torah, and their only engagement since their arrival in the world, their minds and hearts are only about Torah and work. But a man of my value, I belong in the cowshed, and the verse, "For it is not a vain thing for you, for it is your life and the length of your days," was not said about me.

Sometimes there is mitigation during the awakening of the lowliness, and a person sees that "I did not know how immersed I was in transient things and my idle matters. I did not pay attention to being as one should be. And the psalm that is said, 'Will be glorified in me for He desires me,' I too should be saying that psalm because all of Israel have a part in the next world, as in 'He stood and concealed it for the righteous in the future.'

"But now that I am far from the whole thing, I must not despair and only trust the Creator, that 'You hear the prayer of every mouth.' 'Every' means that even though my mouth is not as proper as it should be, the thirteen qualities of mercy are bound to awaken on me, as well.

"From this day forth, I hope to be going forward, though I have already said this many times and in the end remained in my lowliness." At that time he replies that there are "world," "year," "soul," and these three must be united in same time, place, and soul together.

For this reason, he says, "It is now certainly the time for me to come out of all these bad states, and 'one who comes to purify is aided,'" and he promptly begins the work with renewed vigor and strength.

15. RABASH, Article No. 19 (1985), "Come unto Pharaoh – 1"

To keep from losing what he is given, one must first make great efforts, for something that comes to a person through labor causes him to keep the thing and not lose it. But during the exertion, when a person sees that the work is still far from finished, he sometimes escapes the campaign and falls into despair. At that time he needs great strengthening, to believe that the Creator will help him, and the fact that help has not arrived is because he has not given the required quantity and quality of labor for preparing the deficiency in order to receive the filing, as it is said ("Introduction to the Study of the Ten Sefirot," Item 18), "And if one practices Torah and fails to remove the evil inclination from himself, it is either that he has been negligent in giving the necessary labor and exertion in the practice of Torah, as it is written, 'I have not labored but found, do not believe,' or perhaps one did put in the necessary amount of labor, but has been negligent in the quality."

16. RABASH, Article No. 34 (1991), "What Is Eating Their Fruits in This World and Keeping the Principal for the Next World, in the Work?"

When one sees that it is hard to get what he wants, he escapes from the work. He says, "I believe that there are people who have been rewarded and to whom the Creator gave the desire to bestow. But this was because they were more gifted than I am. But a person like me, with worse qualities than others, has no chance of meriting this." Hence, he escapes the campaign and begins to work like the general public.

Only those who say that they want to escape from the work but have nowhere else to go, since nothing satisfies them, those people do not walk out from the work. Although they have ups and downs, they do not give up. This is as it is written, "And the children of Israel sighed from the work, and they cried, and their cry went up to God from the work." In other words, they cried out from the work because they were not advancing in the work of the Creator, so they could work in order to bestow contentment upon the Maker. At that time, they were rewarded with the exodus from Egypt. In the work, this is called "emerging from the control of the will to receive and entry into the work of bestowal."

17. RABASH, Article No. 23 (1989), "What Is, 'If He Swallows the Bitter Herb, He Will Not Come Out,' in the Work?"

When one begins the work, he begins with faith, but the body resists this work, and then comes a state of labor, when he must overcome the body and seek all kinds of counsels, as our sages said, "In trickery shall you conduct war," since the body does not want to relinquish self-benefit. To the extent that he exerts, to that extent he begins to feel that he is incapable of doing anything since in his view, he has done everything he could. After the labor, he comes to know that only the Creator can help, and it is out of his hands. Then comes the third state—a prayer—and then the prayer is from the bottom of the heart, since it is utterly clear to him that no one can help him but the Creator.

However, even when he comes to know that the Creator can help him, and he understands that the real advice is only prayer, the body comes and makes him see that "You see how many prayers you have already prayed but you received no answer from above. Therefore, why bother praying that the Creator will help you? You see that you are not getting any help from above." At that time, he cannot pray. Then we need to overcome once more through faith, and believe that the Creator does hear the prayer of every mouth, and it does not matter if the person is adept and has good qualities, or to the contrary. Rather, he must overcome and believe above reason, although his reason dictates that since he has prayed many times but still received no answer from above, how can he come and pray once more? This, too, requires overcoming, meaning to exert above reason and pray that the Creator will help him overcome his view and pray.

18. RABASH, Article No. 16 (1985), "But the More They Afflicted Them"

When he begins to scrutinize the quality of the deficiency, he sees that he feels no pain, that he is seemingly unconscious, unfeeling. And although remoteness from the Creator means not having life, it doesn't pain him that he has no life. Then he has no other choice but to pray to the Creator to give him some life, so he will feel that he is dangerously ill and needs to cure the soul.

And sometimes one comes to a state where he is in such a decline that he doesn't even have the strength to pray for it. Rather, he is in a state of complete indifference. This is called "being in a state of still," meaning he is completely motionless.

In that state, only his society can help him. In other words, if he comes among friends and does not criticize them in any way, testing if they, too, have the same obstructions and thoughts but have overcome them, or they just take no interest in introspection and this is why they can engage in Torah and *Mitzvot*, how can he be like them?

At that time, he cannot receive any assistance from society because he has no *Dvekut* [adhesion] with them at all, as they are too small to be his friends. Thus, naturally, he is not affected by them whatsoever.

But if he comes among his friends not with his head high, thinking that he is wise and the friends are fools—but rather tosses his pride away.

19. RABASH, Article No. 5 (1988), "What Is, 'When Israel Are in Exile, the Shechina Is With Them,' in the Work?"

What is the meaning of "When Israel are in exile, the *Shechina* is with them"? As Rabbi Shimon Ben Yochai said, "Wherever they exile, the *Shechina* is with them." What is the benefit from this in the work, that he says about it, "How beloved are Israel by the Creator"?

We should interpret that when a person feels that he is in exile, meaning feels the taste of exile in the work and wants to escape from the exile, the meaning will be that a person must believe that wherever they are exiled, the *Shechina* is with them. That is, the *Shechina* let him feel the taste of exile. "With them" means that the *Shechina* is attached to them and they are not separated from the *Shechina*, that they should say that it is a descent. On the contrary, now the *Shechina* is giving him a push so he will climb the degrees of *Kedusha* [holiness/sanctity], and dresses herself in a garment of descent.

When a person knows and believes that this is so, it will encourage him so he does not escape the campaign or say that the work of bestowal is not for him because he always sees that he is in states of ascents and descents, and he sees no end to these states and falls into despair.

But if he walks in the path of faith and believes in the words of our sage, then he must say the opposite.

9

Impregnation

1. Baal HaSulam, *Shamati*, Article No. 19, "What Is 'The Creator Hates the Bodies,' in the Work?"

The importance of the work is precisely when one comes to a state of zero, when one sees that he annuls his whole existence and being, for then the will to receive has no power. Only then does one enter the *Kedusha*.

2. Baal HaSulam, "One Commandment"

The focal point in the work of the Creator is the first footing.

3. Baal HaSulam, *The Study of the Ten Sefirot*, Part 9, "Inner Observation," Item 82

Our sages said concerning the conception (*Nidah* 30), that a candle is lit up on its head and it sees from the end of the world to its end, and it is taught the whole Torah in its entirety.

4. RABASH, Article No. 38 (1990), "What Is, 'A Cup of Blessing Must Be Full,' in the Work?"

We should discern between speech and mute in the work. Speech means revealing, when a person already has *Yenika* in spirituality, and he feels that he is suckling from *Kedusha*, for nursing on milk indicates *Hassadim*, for the quality of *Hesed* [mercy] is bestowal, when a person is rewarded with vessels of bestowal and all his actions are for the sake of the Creator and he has no concerns for his own benefit. This is regarded as the quality of *Hesed*.

However, before the *Yenika* there is *Ibur*, meaning that the upper one corrects him. This can be when a person is like an embryo in its mother's womb, where the embryo annuls before the mother and has no view of its own, but as our sages said, "An embryo is its mother's thigh, eats what its mother eats," and has no authority of its own to ask any questions. Rather, it does not merit a name. This is called "mute," when he has no mouth to ask questions.

This is so when a person can go with his eyes shut, above reason, and believe in the sages and go all the way. This is called *Ibur*, when he has no mouth.

5. RABASH, Article No. 799, "The Birth of the Moon"

The moon is called *Malchut*. It is called "the renewal of the moon" because we must accept the burden of the kingdom of heaven each day anew. Yesterday's acceptance is not enough, since each time, says the ARI, we must raise the sparks that fell to *BYA* and raise them to *Kedusha* [holiness]. It follows that when a person accepts a new burden each time, it is considered that each time, he takes a part of the separation and admits it into the unity of *Kedusha*.

This is the meaning of *Malchut* returning to being a dot each day, and in *The Zohar* a dot is called "a black dot in which there is no white." That is, it does not shine, since "white" means that it illuminates. This means that it must be renewed each time.

However, we must know that it is not the same quality as it was before. Rather, it is as it is written, there is no renewal of light that does not extend from *Ein Sof* [infinity/no end].

This is called "*Ibur* [impregnation] of the month." *Ibur* comes from the words "anger and rage." That is, a person must overcome while the kingdom of heaven is as a dot in him, meaning that the kingdom of heaven does not illuminate for him so he will be in gladness, as it is written, "Serve the Lord with gladness," but it is rather in sadness in him.

This is the meaning of *Ibur*. This is similar to an impregnation in corporeality, that the impregnation begins, and then, if the proper conditions are given, an offspring will emerge.

It follows that when one begins the work and sees how far he is from the Creator, and it hurts him, this is regarded as being rewarded with *Katnut* [smallness/infancy], meaning that he feels his own *Katnut*. This is called "a lack of a *Kli* [vessel]," and to that extent he can later obtain the light, called *Gadlut* [greatness/adulthood], according to the measure of the *Kli*.

A dot is called "*Shechina* [Divinity] in the dust," and rising is called "the sanctification of the month." That is, that which was in a state of "dust," he admitted this discernment into *Kedusha*. This is called "raising the *Shechina* from the dust."

6. RABASH, Article No. 31, "Concerning *Yenika* [Suckling] and *Ibur* [Impregnation]"

The beginning of the entrance into the work of the Creator is regarded as *Ibur* [impregnation], when he cancels his self and becomes impregnated in the mother's womb, as it is written, "Hear, my son, your father's instruction, and do not forsake your mother's teaching." This comes from the verse, "For if you call the mother, 'understanding [*Bina*],'" meaning that he cancels self-love, called *Malchut*, whose original essence is called "will to receive in order to receive," and enters the vessels of bestowal, called *Bina*.

One should believe that before he was born, meaning before the soul descended into the body, the soul was adhered to Him, and now he longs to adhere to Him as prior to her descent. This is called *Ibur*, when he completely annuls his self.

7. RABASH, Article No. 31 (1986), "Concerning *Yenika* [Suckling] and *Ibur* [Impregnation]"

Ibur [impregnation/conception] means that a person temporarily *Maavir* [shifts/removes] his selfness and says, "Now I do not want to think of my own benefit whatsoever, and I also do not want to use my intellect, although to me it is the most important thing. That is, since I cannot do something that I do not understand—meaning I can do anything but I must understand the benefit of it—he still says, "Now I can temporarily say that I am taking upon myself at this time that I determine not to use my intellect. Rather, I believe above reason, believe in faith in the sages, believing that there is an overseer who is watching each and every one in the world in Private Providence."

But why should I believe it and I cannot feel that this is so? It makes sense that if I could feel the existence of the Creator I could certainly work for Him and would desire to serve Him. Why then is this concealment? What does the Creator gain by hiding Himself from the creatures? Also, he does not provide any answer to this, but rather answers that with this question, too, he goes above reason and says that if the Creator knew that not making the concealment would be better for the creatures, He would not create concealment.

It turns out that to all the questions that come up in his mind he says that he is going above reason, and that now he is going with eyes shut and only with faith.

8. RABASH, Article No. 26 (1990), "What Is, 'There Is None as Holy as the Lord, for There Is None Besides You,' in the Work?"

The main thing that is hard for us is to enter the *Ubar*, meaning that the will to receive will receive within it a different desire called "desire to bestow." When a person is rewarded with the state of *Ubar*, meaning that within the desire to receive enters a desire to bestow, this is considered that the Creator forms a form within a form.

We should understand this wonder of forming a form within a form. According to what we interpreted, this is a great novelty, a real miracle, since it is against nature, for only the Creator can change nature, and it is out of man's hands. This is the novelty, that the Creator forms the form of bestowal within the form of the mother, which is the form of reception. This is called the *Kedusha* that the Creator gives.

It is said, "There is none as holy as the Lord, for there is none besides You," as there is no one in the world who can change nature and make within the *Kli* [vessel] that comes to a person by nature, the desire to receive, that it will later have a different nature, called "desire to bestow."

9. RABASH, Article No. 22 (1986), "If a Woman Inseminates"

Wanting to exit self-love and begin the work of bestowal is similar to leaving all the states in which he lived, dropping everything off, and entering an area where he has never been. For this reason, he must go through conception and months of pregnancy until he has the ability to acquire new qualities, which are foreign to the spirit he has received since birth.

10. RABASH, Article No. 38 (1990), "What Is, 'A Cup of Blessing Must Be Full,' in the Work?"

When a person can go with his eyes shut, above reason, and believe in the sages and go all the way. This is called *Ibur*, when he has no mouth. *Ibur* means as it is written (*The Study of the Ten Sefirot*, Part 8, Item 17), "The level of *Malchut*, which is the most restricted *Katnut* [smallness/infancy] possible, is called *Ibur*. It comes from the words *Evra* [anger] and *Dinin* [Aramaic: judgments], as it is written, 'And the Lord was impregnated in me for your sake.'"

We should interpret the meaning of "anger and judgments." When a person must go with this eyes shut, above reason, the body resists this work. Hence, the fact that a person always has to overcome, this is called "anger, wrath, and trouble," since it is hard work to always overcome and annul before the upper one, for the upper one to do with him what the upper one wants. This is called *Ibur*, which is the most restricted *Katnut* possible.

11. RABASH, Article No. 26 (1990), "What Is, 'There Is None as Holy as the Lord, for There Is None Besides You,' in the Work?"

We should interpret *Ubar* from the word *Over* [passing], which is the first state, when he passes from using the vessels of reception into the degree of *Kedusha*, where he uses only *Kelim* [vessels] that can aim to bestow. Otherwise, the *Kelim* are not used.

It follows that *Ibur* is the most important. As in corporeality, when a woman conceives, she is certain to also deliver. Thus, all the concern is for the woman to conceive. Afterward, the woman will usually deliver, too.

12. RABASH, Article No. 31 (1986), "Concerning *Yenika* and *Ibur*"

There are two forces in the *Ibur* [impregnation/conception]: 1) A depicting force, where the depiction of the fetus is *Katnut* [infancy/smallness], for in order to obtain *Katnut* there is an order, since *Katnut* is preparation for *Gadlut* [adulthood/greatness], and without *Katnut* in the degree there is no *Gadlut*. And as long as he is in *Katnut* he is still incomplete, and wherever there is a deficiency in *Kedusha* there is a grip to the *Sitra Achra*, who might spoil the *Ibur* so it cannot be completed. By this he is aborted, meaning that he is born before the state of *Ibur* has been completed.

It is so because there are twenty-five *Partzufim* [plural of *Partzuf*] in the *Ibur*, meaning NRNHY, and in each of them there is also NRNHY. Therefore, there must be a detaining force, meaning that even in *Katnut* there should be wholeness there. He receives this through his mother, although the fetus in itself has no *Kelim* [vessels] in which to receive *Gadlut* in order to bestow. Still, by annulling before the mother it can receive *Gadlut* from the *Kelim* of its mother. This is regarded as "An embryo is its mother's thigh; it eats what its mother eats."

That is, since it has no choice of its own but rather eats what its mother eats, meaning that what its mother knows is permitted to eat, it eats, as well, it means that he has shifted the choice of what is good and what is bad from himself. Rather, it is all attributed to the mother. This is called "its mother's thigh," meaning that he himself does not merit a name.

13. RABASH, Article No. 31 (1986), "Concerning *Yenika* [Suckling] and *Ibur* [Impregnation]"

The importance of the work by appreciating a small service in spirituality. By this we are later rewarded with enhancing the importance to a point where one can say that he has no way to appreciate the importance of serving the King. This is called *Ibur*.

14. RABASH, Article No. 31 (1986), "Concerning *Yenika* [Suckling] and *Ibur* [Impregnation]"

During the *Ibur*, when his force of depiction is only *Katnut*, when he can barely observe Torah and *Mitzvot* with any intention, he must believe that it is very important.

15. RABASH, Article No. 18 (1991), "What It Means that We Should Raise the Right Hand over the Left Hand, in the Work"

To have progress in the work, requires that one walks on two lines, which are called "right and left." We need the right because it is forbidden to reveal any deficiency, since where there is a deficiency in *Kedusha*, there is a grip to the *Sitra Achra* [other side], as the ARI says, "In *Ibur* [impregnation], we need the depicting force and the detaining force." *Ibur* means that this is the beginning of man's entrance into *Kedusha*. The depicting force shows the truth, meaning a depiction of the work, meaning if he has a good depiction about the situation he is in and the work shines for him, meaning what form he has when he looks at his work, whether he is in wholeness or not, whether he is working in order to bestow or does he want to nonetheless work in order to bestow.

The detaining force is considered that when the depicting force shows him the truth, that during *Ibur*, called "beginning of the work," he certainly sees deficiencies and there can be a grip to the *Sitra Achra* [other side]. Therefore, there must be a detaining force so the fetus is not aborted, meaning falls into the *Sitra Achra*. In order to prevent a miscarriage although there is a lack, as the depicting force indicates what is the form of this work, the detaining force is called "right" because he shifts to wholeness. That is, he believes in the sages who said that a person should be happy with his share, meaning whatever grip he has on Torah and *Mitzvot* he regards it as a great privilege, since he sees that there are people to whom the Creator did not give even the thought or desire for the little bit of grip that I have. This is called the "detaining force," so he will not fall off from the work and will also be born later, meaning that from this work of keeping himself in *Ibur* at the beginning of the work, he will have two lines, right and left, and he will be rewarded with birth and with being in *Yenika* [Suckling] of *Kedusha*. Thus, through the depicting force and the detaining force, a complete newborn will emerge in *Kedusha*.

16. RABASH, Article No. 26 (1990), "What Is, 'There Is None as Holy as the Lord, for There Is None Besides You,' in the Work?"

The first beginning, when a person enters the *Kedusha*, is the *Ubar*. This is the meaning of the Creator forming a form of bestowal within the previous form, which is the mother, who is called "vessels of reception." In the vessels of reception, the man is born. Afterward, the man shifts to *Kedusha*, which is that all his actions are for the sake of the Creator.

Thus, who gave him the vessels of bestowal? It is as we learn, that *Aviut* [thickness] *de Keter* is called *Aviut de Shoresh*, and is called *Aviut* of the *Ubar*. The *Shoresh* [root] is the Creator, whose desire is to do good to His creations. When a person receives the first quality of *Kedusha*, he receives vessels of bestowal, meaning he can aim to bestow in vessels of bestowal.

This is called that the Creator "forms a form," meaning the form of bestowal, which is that He gives him the power to be able to bestow within the form of his mother, who is the previous state, before he came to connect with the *Kedusha*. The previous state is called "mother," and the next state is called *Ibur*.

17. RABASH, Article No. 837, "*Ibur* [Conception] – 2"

Ibur Aleph [first conception] is done by the upper one, like a person who receives an awakening from above. *Ibur Bet* [second conception] means that the lower one must work by himself by the power of the awakening he had received. In other words, he must add, through the awakening he had received from the upper one, and work by his labor. Otherwise, he loses everything and returns to being a black dot, meaning that his spirituality is regarded as darkness that does not shine.

18. RABASH, Article No. 3 (1985), "The Meaning of Truth and Faith"

In spirituality, there are two discernments in the *Ibur*:

1. The shape of the *Ibur*, which is the degree of *Katnut* [smallness/infancy], which is its real shape. However, since it only has *Katnut*, it is regarded as a deficiency, and wherever there is a deficiency in holiness, there is a grip to the *Klipot* [shells/peels]. At that time the *Klipot* can cause a miscarriage—for the spiritual fetus to fall out before its stage of *Ibur* has been completed. For this reason, there should be a detaining element, which is that it is given wholeness, meaning *Gadlut* [adulthood/greatness].
2. However, we should understand how the newborn can be given *Gadlut* while it is still unfit to receive even *Katnut* sufficiently, since it still does not have the *Kelim* [vessels] in which to receive them in order to bestow. To that there is an answer there: Our sages said, "An embryo in its mother's abdomen eats what its mother eats." He also said, "A fetus is its mother's thigh." This means that since a fetus is its mother's thigh, the *Ibur* does not merit its own name. For this reason, the fetus eats what its mother eats. That is, the fetus receives everything that it receives in the mother's *Kelim*. For this reason, although the fetus has no *Kelim* that are fit to receive *Gadlut*, but in the *Kelim* of the upper one, which is its mother, it can receive because it is completely annulled before the mother and has no authority of its own. This is called *Ibur*, when it is completely annulled before the Upper One.

Then, when it receives *Gadlut*, it is in wholeness. This is why there is no grip to the *Klipot* there, and this is why it is called the "detaining force."

19. RABASH, Article No. 31 (1986), "Concerning *Yenika* [Suckling] and *Ibur* [Impregnation]"

It follows that when a person can annul himself a little bit and at that time says, "Now I want to annul myself before the *Kedusha*," meaning not to think about self-love. Rather, now he wants to bring contentment to the Creator, and believes above reason that although he still does not feel anything, he believes above reason, that the Creator hears the prayer of every mouth, and before Him, small and great are equal, and as He can deliver the greatest of the greatest, He can also help the smallest of the small.

This is called *Ibur*, meaning that he passes from his own domain into the domain of the Creator. However, it is temporary. That is, he truly wants to annul himself forever, but cannot believe that there will be annulling forever now since he has already thought many times that it would be so but then descended from his degree and fell to the place of garbage.

However, he does not need to worry about what to eat tomorrow, as was said above, that later he will probably fall from his degree, as this is for lack of faith. Rather, he must believe that the salvation of the Lord is as the blink of an eye. It follows that since he annuls himself for the time being and wants to remain this way forever, it follows that he has the value of *Ibur*.

20. RABASH, Article No. 9 (1985), "And the Children Struggled within Her"

Baal HaSulam said that this is the order of the work. The beginning of the work is called *Ibur* [impregnation], when a person begins to work on the path of truth. When he passes by the doors of Torah, the Jacob in a person awakens and wishes to walk on the path of Torah. When he walks by the doors of idol-worship, the Esau in a person awakens to come out.

We should interpret his words. Man consists of vessels of reception by nature, called "self-love," which is the evil inclination, and also consists of a point in the heart, which is his good inclination. When he begins to work in bestowal, it is regarded as *Ibur*, form the word, *Avra* [passed]. This is why he experiences ascents and descents and is unstable. He is influenced by the environment and is unable to overcome.

For this reason, when one moves to an environment where people engage in work that is alien to us, meaning self-love, the self-love in a person awakens and comes out from concealment to disclosure, and takes control over the body. At that time one is unable to do anything except that which concerns his receiver.

When he passes through an environment where people engage in work of bestowal, the Jacob in him awakens and comes out from concealment to disclosure. At that time works of bestowal govern the body. That is, at that time, when he looks back and sees how before he has reached the state he is in he was so immersed in self-love, he cannot understand how can one be so low and derive satisfaction from such base things that are inappropriate for an adult to build his house among lowly and despicable desires and thoughts. He is insulted by these desires and thoughts where his house once was.

But later, when he passes by the doors of idol-worship, meaning when he comes to an environment that engages in self-love, the Esau in him reawakens and wriggles to come out. This continues in the worker repeatedly, day after day. One who works harder may go through these changing states each and every hour.

21. RABASH, Article No. 8 (1989), "What It Means, in the Work, that If the Good Grows, So Grows the Bad"

In the beginning of the work, during the *Ibur*, meaning when a person begins to shift from the work of the general public to the work of individuals, the bad immediately begins to appear in him. However, it is not so apparent. Yet, when he begins to ascend in the work and begins to grow, as it is written, "The boys grew," to the extent and order of the growth, so grows the evil. According to the measure of the good that he does, so grows the measure of the evil in him, as was said, so he will be half guilty, half innocent.

Now we can understand what RASHI explained, "Another interpretation: Struggling with each other and quarreling about the inheritance of two worlds." We should understand for what purpose there needs to be a quarrel between them. It is as our sages said (*Berachot* 5), "Rabbi Levi said, 'One should always vex the good inclination over the evil inclination.'" RASHI explains that he should wage war against the evil inclination. We need to understand what is the purpose of this war. Would it not be better if a person saw that the bad in him did not awaken? Why does he need to awaken it and fight it? It would be better if he did not risk himself, for he might not be able to defeat it, as our sages said, "One must not put oneself in danger."

In the work, when we want to achieve bestowal, we must say when we perform *Mitzvot* or engage in Torah, that we want to do everything with the aim to bestow. This is called vexing the good inclination over the evil inclination, since when a person says to his body, "We must work for the sake of the Creator and not for our own sake," the body immediately becomes angry and resists with all its might. It tells him, "You can do anything, but for the sake of the Creator and not for our own sake? This is out of the question." It follows that if he does not vex it, he will never be able to achieve the truth.

PART 7
The Society as a Cause of Spiritual Attainment

1

The Choice of the Environment

1. Baal HaSulam, "The Freedom"

There is freedom for the will to initially choose such an environment, such books, and such guides that impart upon him good concepts. If one does not do this but is willing to enter any environment that appears before him and read any book that falls into his hands, he is bound to fall into a bad environment or waste his time on worthless books, which are abundant and more accessible. In consequence, he will be forced into foul concepts that make him sin and condemn. He will certainly be punished, not because of his evil thoughts or deeds, in which he has no choice, but because he did not choose to be in a good environment, for in this there is definitely a choice.

Therefore, he who strives to continually choose a better environment is worthy of praise and reward. But here, too, it is not because of his good thoughts or deeds, which come to him without his choice, but because of his effort to acquire a good environment, which brings him these good thoughts and actions. It is as Rabbi Yehoshua Ben Perachya said, "Make for yourself a rav and buy for yourself a friend."

2. Baal HaSulam, *Shamati*, Article No. 225, "Raising Oneself"

One cannot raise oneself above one's circle. Hence, one must nurse from one's environment, and he has no other way except through Torah and much work. Therefore, if one chooses for oneself a good environment, he saves time and efforts since he is drawn according to his environment

3. Baal HaSulam, "The Freedom"

All the praise and spirit depends on the choice of the environment.

4. Baal HaSulam, "The Freedom"

Rabbi Yosi Ben Kisma (*Avot*, Chapter 6), who replied to a person who offered him to live in his town, and he would give him millions of gold coins for it: "Even if you give me all the gold and silver and jewels in the world, I will live only in a place of Torah." These words seem inconceivable to our simple mind, for how could he relinquish millions of gold coins for such a small thing as living in a place where there are no disciples of Torah, while he himself was a great sage who needed to learn from no one? Indeed, a mystery.

The Choice of the Environment

But as we have seen, it is a simple thing and should be observed by each and every one of us. Although everyone has his own source, the forces are revealed openly only through the environment one is in. This is similar to the wheat sown in the ground, whose forces become apparent only through its environment, which is the soil, rain, and sunlight.

Thus, Rabbi Yosi Ben Kisma correctly assumed that if he were to leave the good environment he had chosen and fall into a harmful environment in a city where there is no Torah, not only would his former concepts be compromised, but all the other forces hidden in his source, which he had not yet revealed in action, would remain concealed. This is because they would not be subject to the right environment that would be able to activate them.

And as we have clarified above, only in the matter of the choice of environment is man's reign over himself measured, and for this he should receive reward or punishment. Therefore, one must not wonder that a sage such as Rabbi Yosi Ben Kisma chose the good and declined the bad, and was not tempted by material or corporeal things, as he deduces there: "When one dies, one does not take with him silver, gold, or jewels, but only Torah and good deeds."

And so our sages warned, "Make for yourself a rav and buy for yourself a friend." And there is also the choice of books, as we have mentioned, for only in this is one rebuked or praised—in his choice of the environment. But once he has chosen an environment, he is at its hands as clay in the hands of the potter.

5. Baal HaSulam, "A Speech for the Completion of the Zohar"

Our sages said, "Make for yourself a rav and buy yourself a friend." This means that one can make a new environment for oneself. This environment will help him obtain the greatness of his rav through love of friends who appreciate his rav. Through the friends' discussing the greatness of the rav, each of them receives the sensation of his greatness. Thus, bestowal upon his rav becomes reception and sufficient motivation to an extent that will bring one to engage in Torah and *Mitzvot Lishma*.

It was said about this, "The Torah is acquired by forty-eight virtues, by serving of sages, and by meticulousness of friends." This is so because besides serving the rav, one needs the meticulousness of friends, as well, meaning the friends' influence, so they will influence him so he obtains the greatness of his rav. This is so because obtaining the greatness depends entirely on the environment, and a single person cannot do a thing about it whatsoever.

6. Baal HaSulam, "A Speech for the Completion of The Zohar"

There are two conditions to obtaining the greatness:

1. Always listen and accept the appreciation of the environment to the extent of their greatness.
2. The environment should be great, as it is written, "In the multitude of people is the king's glory."

To receive the first condition, each student must feel that he is the smallest among all the friends. In that state, he will be able to receive the appreciation of the greatness from everyone, since the great cannot receive from a smaller one, much less be impressed by his words. Rather, only the small is impressed by the appreciation of the great.

For the second condition, each student must extol the virtues of each friend and cherish him as though he were the greatest in the generation. Then the environment will influence him as though it were a great environment, as it should be, since quality is more important than quantity.

7. Baal HaSulam, *Shamati*, Article No. 25, "Things that Come from the Heart"

When one hears the words of Torah from his teacher, he immediately agrees with his teacher and resolves to observe the words of his teacher with his heart and soul. But afterward, when he comes out to the world, he sees, covets, and is infected by the multitude of desires roaming the world. Then, he and his mind, his heart, and his will are annulled before the majority.

As long as he has no power to sentence the world to the side of merit, they subdue him, he mingles with their desires, and he is led like sheep to the slaughter. He has no choice; he is compelled to think, want, crave, and demand everything that the majority demands. Then he chooses their foreign thoughts and their loathsome lusts and desires, which are alien to the spirit of the Torah. In that state, he has no strength to subdue the majority.

Instead, there is only one counsel then: to cling to his teacher and to the books. This is called "From the mouth of books and from the mouth of authors." Only by clinging to them can he change his mind and will for the better. However, witty arguments will not help him change his mind, but only the remedy of *Dvekut* [adhesion], for this is a wondrous cure, as the *Dvekut* reforms him.

8. Baal HaSulam, "Introduction to The Study of the Ten Sefirot," Item 4

It is indeed true that the Creator Himself puts one's hand on the good fate by giving him a life of pleasure and contentment within the corporeal life that is filled with torment and pain, and devoid of any content. One necessarily departs and escapes them when he sees, even if it seemingly appears amidst the cracks, a tranquil place to escape there from this life, which is harder than death. Indeed, there is no greater placement of one's hand by Him than this.

And one's choice refers only to the strengthening. This is because there is certainly a great effort and exertion here before one purifies one's body to be able to keep the Torah and *Mitzvot* correctly, not for his own pleasure, but to bring contentment to his Maker, which is called *Lishma* [for Her sake]. Only in this manner is one endowed with a life of happiness and pleasantness that come with keeping the Torah.

Before one comes to that purification, there is certainly a choice to strengthen in the good way by all sorts of means and tactics. One should do whatever his hand finds the strength to do until he completes the work of purification and will not fall under his burden midway.

9. Baal HaSulam, *Shamati*, Article No. 99, "He Did Not Say Wicked or Righteous"

If one does not have any desire or craving for spirituality, if he is among people who have a desire and craving for spirituality, if he likes these people, he, too, will take their strength to prevail, and their desires and aspirations, although by his own quality, he does not have these desires and cravings and the power to overcome. But according to the grace and the importance he ascribes to these people, he will receive new powers.

Now we can understand the above words: "The Creator saw that the righteous were few," meaning that not any person can become a righteous, for lack of qualities for it, as it was written, that he is born a fool or a weakling; he, too, has a choice and his own qualities are no excuse. This is because the Creator planted the righteous in every generation.

10. RABASH, Article No. 37 (1985), "Who Testifies to a Person?"

We need an *environment*, meaning a group of people who are all of the view that they must achieve whole faith. This is the only thing that can save a person from the views of the collective. At that time, *everyone strengthens everyone else* to crave to achieve whole faith, that he can bestow contentment upon the Creator, and that this will be his only aspiration.

11. RABASH, Article No. 12 (1984), "Concerning the Importance of Society"

It is known that one is always among people who have no connection to the work on the path of truth, but to the contrary, always resist those who walk on the path of truth. And since people's thoughts mingle, the views of those who oppose the path of truth permeate those with some desire to walk on the path of truth.

Hence, there is no other solution but to establish a separate society for themselves, to be their framework, meaning a separate community that does not mingle with other people whose views differ from that society. And they should constantly evoke in themselves the issue of the purpose of society, so they will not follow the majority, because following the majority is our nature.

12. RABASH, Article No. 727, "The Most Important Is the Environment"

"And choose life." The most important is the environment. Man is always in an environment and necessarily follows them. Hence, if one is immersed in thoughts of Abaye and Raba, he is necessarily influenced by them. But if, for a brief moment, he places his thoughts on a different matter during the study, meaning thinks about something related to corporeal matters, he is necessarily immediately placed in a corporeal environment. This means that he begins to yearn for desires that the environment obligates him.

Also, concerning Abaye and Raba, if he regards them merely as great scholars, he will only be able to yearn for erudition. But if he regards them as sages with attainment, he will yearn for attainments.

13. RABASH, Article No. 9 (1984), "One Should Always Sell the Beams of His House"

If a society is established with certain people, and when they gathered, there must have been someone who wished to establish specifically this "bunch." Thus, he sorted out these people to see that they were suitable for each other. In other words, each of them had a spark of love of others, but the spark could not ignite the light of love to shine in each, so they agreed that by uniting, the sparks would become a big flame.

Hence, now, too, when he is spying on them, he should overcome and say, "As all of them were of one mind that they must walk on the path of love of others when the society was established, so it is now." And when everyone judges his friends favorably, all the sparks will ignite once more and again there will be one big flame.

14. RABASH, Article No. 21 (1986), "Concerning Above Reason"

Our sages said, "Counters' envy increases wisdom." In other words, when all the friends look at the society as being at a high level, both in thoughts and in actions, it is natural that each and every one must raise his degree to a higher level than he has by the qualities of his own body.

13. RABASH, Article No. 13 (1985), "Mighty Rock of My Salvation"

When he comes into a group where everyone is thirsty for the power to bestow, everyone receives this strength from everyone else. This is considered receiving strength from the outside in addition to the small power that he has within him.

16. RABASH, Article No. 17 (1986), "The Agenda of the Assembly-2"

The whole basis upon which we can receive delight and pleasure, and which is permitted for us to enjoy—and is even mandatory—is to enjoy an act of bestowal. Thus, there is one point we should work on—*appreciation of spirituality*. This is expressed in paying attention to whom I turn, with whom I speak, whose commandments I am keeping, and whose laws I am learning, meaning in seeking advice concerning how to appreciate the Giver of the Torah.

And before one obtains some illumination from above by himself, he should seek out like-minded people who are also seeking to enhance the importance of any contact with the Creator in whatever way. And when many people support it, everyone can receive assistance from his friend.

17. Raaiah Kook, *Lights*

A person from Israel who wants to be rewarded with the light of life in truth must agree to plant himself in the assembly of Israel with all his heart, with all his senses and corporeal and spiritual powers.

18. Israel Hopstein of Kozhnitz, *Avodat Israel* [The Work of Israel], Portion *Shlach*

Our sages said, "Dispersion is good for the wicked and gathering is good for the righteous." This is according to what the ARI said, that in the worlds of *Igulim* [circles], one *Igul* [circle] does not touch another, and there the breaking happened until it was corrected in the world of *Yosher* [straightness]. The meaning of the matter and the allegory is that the mind of the *Igulim* is that it is as one who surrounds and encircles himself, and becomes separated from his Maker. It seems to him that he will lead himself by his own will, and he is haughty and says, "I will rule," and this was the shattering.

Likewise, among the wicked, the heart of each one is haughty, saying "I will rule," which is why they are in the world of separation and cannot connect, like the circles, as we can evidently see, for they cannot sit together. To them, dispersion is good.

Conversely, although each of the righteous serves his Creator in a different style, they all aim at the same thing—their father in Heaven. They gather and assemble one by one, as one man with one heart, and each one diminishes himself and glorifies the work for the sake of the Creator, who gives him the strength and intelligence by which to serve Him. Hence, one will not be arrogant toward his friend, and they are in the world of straightness and unite with one another.

19. Babylonian Talmud, *Berachot*

The Torah is acquired only in company.

20. Rabbi Reuben Landa, *Shem Olam*

The very study, even when he studies alone, is also observing the commandment to-do of learning Torah. In any case, in the beginning, it is a commandment to glorify anything he can learn in company, for by this the name of the Creator is sanctified more, when many from among the children of Israel gather to serve the Creator. Also, our sages said in several places, "The King is glorified in the in the presence of many people."

21. Rabbi Nachman of Breslov, *Likutey Halachot*

It is written, "The Sanhedrin was as a round semicircle so they would see each other," for the love is mainly that they saw each other. They could not tolerate not seeing one another, for when they see each other, they receive from one another. This is the meaning of what our sages said, "Either company or death."

2

From Love of People to Love of the Creator

1. Baal HaSulam, "The Writings of the Last Generation"

All of the anticipated reward from the Creator, and the purpose of the entire creation, are *Dvekut* [adhesion] with the Creator, as in, "A tower filled abundantly, but no guests." This is what they who cling to Him with love receive.

Naturally, first, one emerges from imprisonment, which is emerging from the skin of one's body by bestowal upon others. Subsequently, one comes to the king's palace, which is *Dvekut* with Him through the intention to bestow contentment upon one's maker.

Therefore, the bulk of commandments are between man and man. One who gives preference to the commandments between man and God is as one who climbs to the second step before he has climbed to the first step. Clearly, he will break his legs.

2. Baal HaSulam, "The Peace"

From the perspective of empirical reason—out of the practical history unfolding before our very eyes—that there is no other cure for humanity but to assume the commandment of Providence to bestow upon others in order to bring contentment to the Creator in the measure of the two verses.

The first is "love your friend as yourself," which is the attribute of the work itself. This means that the measure of work to bestow upon others for the happiness of society should be no less than the measure imprinted in man to care for his own needs. Moreover, he should put his fellow person's needs before his own.

The other verse is, "And you will love the Lord your God with all your heart, with all your soul, and with all your might." This is the goal that must be before everyone's eyes when laboring for one's friend's needs. This means that he labors and toils only to be liked by the Creator, as He said, "and they do His will."

3. Baal HaSulam, "The Freedom"

The Torah and the *Mitzvot* were given only to purify Israel, to develop in us the sense of recognition of evil imprinted in us at birth, which is generally defined as our self-love, and to come to the pure good defined as "love of others," which is the one and only passage to the love of the Creator.

4. Baal HaSulam, "The Arvut [Mutual Guarantee]," Item 22

The impression he gets when engaging in *Mitzvot* between man and man, since one is obliged to perform all the *Mitzvot Lishma* [for Her sake], without any hope for self-love, meaning that no light or hope returns to him through his trouble in the form of reward or honor, etc. Here, at this exalted point, the love of the Creator and the love of his friend unite and actually become one.

5. Baal HaSulam, "Matan Torah [The Giving of the Torah]," Item 15

The words of Hillel HaNasi to the proselyte, that the essence of the Torah is "Love your friend as yourself," and the remaining six hundred and twelve *Mitzvot* are but an interpretation and preparation for it (see Item 2). And even the *Mitzvot* between man and the Creator are regarded as a preparation for that *Mitzva*, which is the final aim emerging from the Torah and *Mitzvot*, as our sages said, "The Torah and *Mitzvot* were given only so as to cleanse Israel" (Item 12), which is the cleansing of the body until one acquires a second nature defined as "love for others," meaning the one *Mitzva*: "Love your friend as yourself," which is the final aim of the Torah, after which one immediately obtains *Dvekut* with Him.

But one must not wonder why it was not defined in the words: "And you will love the Lord your God with all your heart and with all your soul and with all your might." He did this for the above reason that indeed, with respect to a person who is still within the nature of creation, there is no difference between the love of the Creator and the love of his fellow person, for anything that is from another is unreal to him.

And because that proselyte asked of Hillel HaNasi to explain to him the desired outcome of the Torah, so his goal would be near and he would not have to walk a long way, as he said, "Teach me the whole Torah while I am standing on one leg," he defined it for him as love of his friend since its aim is nearer and is revealed faster, since it is mistake-proof and is demanding.

6. Baal HaSulam, "Introduction to The Study of the Ten Sefirot," Items 68-69

To understand this we must first acquire a genuine understanding of the nature of the love of the Creator itself. We must know that all the inclinations, tendencies, and properties instilled in man, with which to serve one's friends, all these tendencies and natural properties are required for the work of the Creator.

To begin with, they were created and imprinted in man only because of their final role—the ultimate purpose of man, as it is written, "No outcast shall be cast out from Him." One needs them all so as to complement oneself in the ways of reception of the abundance and to complete the will of the Creator.

This is the meaning of "Everyone who is called by My name, I have created him for My glory" (Isaiah 43:7), and also "All that the Lord has worked was for His sake" (Proverbs 16:4). However, in the meantime, man has been given a whole world to develop and complete all these natural inclinations and qualities in him by engaging in them with people, thus yielding them suitable for their purpose.

It is as our sages said, "One must say, 'The world was created for me,'" for all the people in the world are required for a person, as they develop and qualify the attributes and inclinations of every individual to become a fit tool for His work.

Thus, we must understand the essence of the love of the Creator from the properties of love by which one person relates to another. The love of the Creator is necessarily given through these qualities, since they were only imprinted in man for His sake to begin with.

7. Baal HaSulam, "The Arvut [Mutual Guarantee]," Item 27

The work in Torah and *Mitzvot* is expressed in the words, "And you will be unto Me a kingdom of priests." A kingdom of priests means that all of you, from the youngest to the oldest, will be as priests. Just as the priests have no land or any corporeal possessions since the Creator is their lot, so will the entire nation be organized so that the whole earth and everything in it will be dedicated to the Creator. And no person should have any other engagement in it but to observe the *Mitzvot* of the Creator and satisfy the needs of his fellow person so his friend will lack none of his wishes, so that no person will need to have any worry about himself.

In this way, even secular works such as harvesting, sowing, etc., are considered to be precisely like the work with the sacrifices that the priests performed in the Temple. How is it different if I observe the *Mitzva* of making sacrifices to the Creator, which is a *Mitzva* "to do," or if I observe the *Mitzva* "to do," "Love your friend as yourself"? It follows that he who harvests his field in order to feed his fellow person is the same as one who sacrifices to the Creator. Moreover, it makes sense that the *Mitzva*, "Love your friend as yourself," is more important than one who makes the sacrifice.

Indeed, this is not the end of the matter, for the whole of the Torah and the *Mitzvot* were given for the sole purpose of cleansing Israel, which is the cleansing of the body, after which he will be granted the true reward of *Dvekut* with Him, which is the purpose of creation

8. Baal HaSulam, "The Love of God and the Love of Man"

Even if we see that there are two parts to the Torah—the first, *Mitzvot* between man and the Creator, and the second, *Mitzvot* between man and man—they are both one and the same thing. This means that the practice of them and the desired goal from them are one: *Lishma*.

It makes no difference if one works for one's friend or for the Creator, since it is engraved in the created being at birth that anything that comes from another appears empty and unreal.

Because of this, we are compelled to begin in *Lo Lishma*, as Nachmanides says, "Our sages said: 'One should always engage in Torah, even if *Lo Lishma*, since from *Lo Lishma* he comes to *Lishma*.' Therefore, when teaching the young, the women, and the uneducated, they are taught to work out of fear and to receive reward. Until they accumulate knowledge and gain wisdom, they are told that secret bit by bit, and are accustomed to that matter with ease until they attain Him and know Him and serve Him out of love."

…Thus, when one completes one's work in love of others and bestowal upon others through the final point, one also completes one's love for the Creator and bestowal upon the Creator. And there is no difference between the two, for anything that is outside one's body, meaning outside one's self-interest, is judged equally—either to bestow upon one's friend or to bestow contentment upon one's Maker.

This is what Hillel HaNasi assumed, that "Love your friend as yourself" is the ultimate goal in the practice, as it is the clearest nature and form to man.

We should not be mistaken about actions, since they are set before his eyes. He knows that if he puts the needs of his friend before his own needs, then he is in the quality of bestowal. For this reason, he does not define the goal as "And you will love the Lord your God with all your heart and with all your soul and with all your might," for indeed they are one and the same, since he should also love his friend with all his heart and with all his soul and with all his might, as this is the meaning of the words "as yourself." He certainly loves himself with all his heart and soul and might, and with the Creator, he may deceive oneself, but with his friend it is always spread out before his eyes.

9. Baal HaSulam, "Introduction to The Book of Zohar," Item 19

Bear in mind that the *Mitzvot* between man and man come before the *Mitzvot* between man and the Creator since bestowing upon one's friend brings one to bestow upon the Creator.

10. Baal HaSulam, "One Commandment"

There are two parts to the Torah: one concerns man and the Creator, and the other concerns man and man. And I call upon you, at any rate, to engage and assume that which concerns man and man, for by this you will also learn the part that concerns man and the Creator.

11. Baal HaSulam, "Matan Torah [The Giving of the Torah]," Item 14

The part of the Torah that deals with man's relationship with his friend is better capable of bringing one to the desired goal since the work in *Mitzvot* between man and God is fixed and specific, and is not demanding, and one becomes easily accustomed to it, and everything that is done out of habit is no longer useful. But the *Mitzvot* between man and man are changing and irregular, and demands surround him wherever he turns. Hence, their cure is much more certain and their aim is closer.

12. Baal HaSulam, *Shamati*, Article No. 67, "Depart from Evil"

Who thinks that he is deceiving his friend is really deceiving the Creator, since besides man's body there is only the Creator. This is because it is the essence of creation that man is called "creature" only with respect to himself. The Creator wants man to feel that he is a separate reality from Him; but other than this, it is all "The whole earth is full of His glory."

Hence, when lying to one's friend, one is lying to the Creator; and when saddening one's friend, one is saddening the Creator. For this reason, if one is accustomed to say the truth, it will help him with respect to the Creator.

13. Baal HaSulam, "Matan Torah [The Giving of the Torah]," Item 13

If indeed there are two parts in the Torah: 1) *Mitzvot* between man and the Creator, 2) *Mitzvot* between man and man, both aim for the same thing—to bring the creature to the final purpose of *Dvekut* with

Him. Furthermore, even the practical side in both of them is really one and the same, for when one performs an act *Lishma*, without any mixture of self-love, meaning without drawing any benefit for himself, then one does not feel any difference whether one is working to love one's friend or to love the Creator.

14. Baal HaSulam, "The Teaching of the Kabbalah and Its Essence"

Since there is no act without some purpose, it is certain that the Creator had a purpose in the creation set before us. The most important thing in this whole diverse reality is the sensation given to the animals—that each of them feels its own existence. And the most important sensation is the noetic sensation, given to man alone, by which one also feels what is in the other—others' pains and comforts. Hence, it is certain that if the Creator has a purpose in this creation, its subject is man. It is said about this, "All of the Lord's works are for him."

But we must still understand what was the purpose for which the Creator created this lot. Indeed, it is to elevate him to a higher and more important degree, to feel his Creator like the human sensation, which is already given to him. And as one knows and feels one's friend's wishes, so he will learn the ways of the Creator.

15. RABASH, Letter No. 24

Having to stand guard and evoke the love in the hearts of the friends, which you find unbecoming, I actually see that as necessary for you. You know what Baal HaSulam said, that from between man and man one learns how to behave between man and the Creator.

This is so because the upper light is in complete rest, and it is necessary to always evoke the love, "Until the love of our wedding pleases." In other words, you are being shown from above that on this way, you must always evoke the love of His name, since everyone awaits your awakening.

That is, as you see that in love of friends you have the rights as you see it, meaning as it is being shown to you from above, you are the evoker (although the truth is not necessarily so; if you ask the friends, I am not so sure they agree with your evidence that it is only you who desires them and not the other way around).

This is the meaning of "A judge has only what his eyes see." That is, as far as judgment goes, you must judge only by your evidence. This is why it is being shown to you from above that you have to keep awakening the love of the Creator in this way, that you must always stand guard, all day and all night, when you feel a state of day or feel a state of night.

We say to the Creator, "Yours is the day, and Yours is also the night." Thus, the night, too, the darkness of night, comes from the Creator to man's favor, too, as it is written, "Day to day utters speech, and night to night expresses knowledge."

It follows that you must awaken the heart of the friends until the flame rises by itself, as our sages said about it, "When you mount the candles." By that, you will be rewarded with awakening the love of the Creator upon us.

16. RABASH, Article No. 17 (1986), "The Agenda of the Assembly – 2"

As they speak of the importance of love of friends, and that its whole importance is that it leads us to the love of the Creator, they should also think that the love of friends should bring us into the importance of the love of the Creator.

17. RABASH, Article No. 13 (1986), "Come Unto Pharaoh 2"

We should know that we were given love of friends to learn how to avoid blemishing the King's honor. In other words, if he has no other desire except to give contentment to the King, he will certainly blemish the King's honor, which is called "Passing on *Kedusha* [holiness/sanctity] to the external ones." For this reason, we mustn't underestimate the importance of the work in love of friends, for by that he will learn how to exit self-love and enter the path of love of others. And when he completes the work of love of friends, he will be able to be rewarded with love of the Creator.

18. RABASH, Letter No. 40

It is about time that we started moving forward toward our sacred goal like mighty strong men. It is known that the paved road that leads to the goal is love of friends, by which one shifts to love of the Creator.

19. RABASH, Article No. 3 (1984), "Love of Friends – 1"

"And a certain man found him, and behold, he was wandering in the field. "And the man asked him, saying, 'What are you seeking?'" meaning, "How can I help you?" "And he said: 'I seek my brethren.'" By being together with my brothers, that is, by being in a group where there is love of friends, I will be able to mount the trail that leads to the house of God.

This trail is called "a path of bestowal," and this way is against our nature. To be able to achieve it, there is no other way but love of friends, by which everyone can help his friend.

20. RABASH, Article No. 10 (1987), "What Is the Substance of Slander and Against Whom Is It?"

Stage one is the love between a person and his friend, and then we can achieve the love of the Creator.

21. RABASH, Article No. 13 (1986), "Come unto Pharaoh – 2"

We should know that there is a virtue to love of friends. One cannot deceive himself and say that he loves the friends, if in fact he doesn't love them. Here he can examine whether he truly has love of friends or not. But with love of the Creator, one cannot examine oneself as to whether his intention is the love of the Creator, meaning that he wants to bestow upon the Creator, or his desire is to receive in order to receive.

22. RABASH, Article No. 7 (1984), "According to What Is Explained Concerning 'Love Your Friend as Yourself"

The advice for one to be able to increase his strength in the rule, "Love your friend," is by love of friends. If everyone is nullified before his friend and mingles with him, they become one mass where all the little parts that want the love of others unite in a collective force that consists of many parts. And when one has great strength, he can execute the love of others.

And then he can achieve the love of God. But the condition is that each will annul before the other. However, when he is separated from his friend, he cannot receive the share he should receive from his friend.

Thus, everyone should say that he is nothing compared to his friend.

23. RABASH, Article No. 7 (1984), "According to What Is Explained Concerning 'Love Your Friend as Yourself'"

We must remember that the matter of "Love your friend as yourself" should be kept because it is a *Mitzva*, since the Creator commanded to engage in love of friends. And Rabbi Akiva only interprets this *Mitzva* that the Creator commanded. He intended to make this *Mitzva* into a rule by which to be able to keep all the *Mitzvot* because of the commandment of the Creator, and not because of self-benefit.

In other words, it is not that the *Mitzvot* should expand our will to receive, meaning that by keeping the *Mitzvot* we would be generously rewarded. Quite the contrary; by keeping the *Mitzvot* we will reach the reward of being able to annul our self-love and achieve the love of others, and subsequently the love of God.

24. RABASH, Article No. 410, "Self-Love and Love of the Creator"

There is self-love and there is love of the Creator, and there is a medium, which is love of others. Through love of others we come to the love of the Creator. This is the meaning of what Rabbi Akiva said, "Love your neighbor as yourself is a great rule in the Torah."

As Old Hillel said to the gentile who told him, "Teach me the whole Torah on one leg." He said to him, "That which you hate, do not do to your friend. And the rest, go study." This is so because through love of others we come to love the Creator, and then the whole Torah and all the wisdom are in his heart.

It is written, "The Creator said to Israel, 'Be sure, the whole wisdom and the whole Torah are easy. Anyone who fears Me and performs the words of Torah, all the wisdom and all of the Torah are in his heart'" ("Introduction to The Study of the Ten Sefirot," where he references *Midrash Rabbah*, portion *VeZot HaBracha*). Concerning fear, it is explained in the *Sulam* [Ladder commentary on *The Zohar*], that it is fear that he might not be able to bestow upon the Creator, since it is the conduct of love that he wants to bestow upon the Creator.

Hence, one who has love of the Creator wants to bestow, and this is called *Dvekut* [adhesion], as in "And to cleave unto Him." By this the Creator passes onto him Torah and wisdom. It follows that he taught him on one leg, meaning that through love of others he will achieve the degree of love of the Creator, and then he will be rewarded with Torah and wisdom.

25. RABASH, Article No. 6 (1984), "Love of Friends – 2"

By which substance can one be brought to acquire a new quality that he must bestow, and that reception for self is faulty? This is against nature! Though at times, one receives a thought and desire that he must abandon self-love, which comes to us by hearing of it from friends and books, it is a very small force, which does not always shine for us so we can constantly appreciate it and say that this is the rule for all the *Mitzvot* in the Torah.

Thus, there is but one counsel: If several individuals come together with the force that it is worthwhile to abandon self-love, but without the sufficient power and importance of bestowal to become independent, without outside help, if these individuals annul before one another and all have at least potential love of the Creator, though they cannot keep it in practice, then by each joining the society and annulling oneself before it, they become one body.

For example, if there are ten people in that body, it has ten times more power than a single person does. However, there is a condition: When they gather, each of them should think that he has now come for the purpose of annulling self-love. It means that he will not consider how to satisfy his will to receive now, but will think as much as possible only of the love of others. This is the only way to acquire the desire and the need to acquire a new quality, called "the will to bestow."

And from love of friends one can reach love of the Creator, meaning wanting to give contentment to the Creator. It turns out that only in this does one obtain a need and understanding that bestowing is important and necessary, and this comes to him through love of friends. Then we can talk about fear, meaning that one is afraid that he will not be able to bestow contentment to the Creator, and this is called "fear."

Hence, the primary basis upon which the building of sanctity can be erected is the rule of "Love your friend." By that, one can acquire the need to bestow contentment upon the Creator. After that, there can be fear, meaning fear of perhaps not being able to give contentment to the Creator. When actually past that gate of fear, he can come to faith, because faith is the vessel for instilling the *Shechina*.

26. RABASH, Article No. 270, "Anyone with Whom the Spirit of the People Is Pleased – 2"

It is known that it is impossible to achieve love of the Creator before a person is rewarded with love of people through "love your neighbor as yourself," which Rabbi Akiva said is a great rule in the Torah. That is, by this a person accustoms himself to love people, which is love of others, and then he can achieve the degree of loving the Creator.

By this we should interpret the above-said, "Anyone with whom the spirit of the people is content," meaning that the spirit of the people is content with him, for he always engages in love of people, and always watches out for love of others. Then the spirit of the Creator is also pleased with him, meaning he enjoys making the spirit of the Creator, meaning bestowing upon the Creator. But it is not so with one who engages in love of self; then it is certain that the spirit of the Creator is also not pleased with him.

27. RABASH, Letter No. 66

The main thing that a person should do in the world is to make all his works be for the Creator. And since man was created with a quality of delighting only himself, to the point that it is impossible for him to do anything unless he sees that some good will come out of it for himself, then how can one work for the Creator?

But the Creator has given us commandments between man and man, by which man accustoms himself to work in favor of his neighbor. By that he comes to a higher degree, to having the ability to work for the Creator as well. Otherwise, even though a person engages in Torah and *Mitzvot*, he cannot engage for the Creator. It therefore follows that if he engages only in Torah, and not in doing good, he cannot work in order to bestow because he lacks the quality of love of others. It therefore follows that although he engages in Torah and *Mitzvot*, if it is not for the Creator, it is as one who has no God, for if he truly had the sensation of Godliness, he would certainly be engaging in order to bestow. But if he had engaged in doing good, then he would have the quality of love of others, by which he would also come to love the Creator, and would have the ability to observe Torah and *Mitzvot* for the Creator.

It turns out that a person should have the power and force to overcome his qualities, to turn them into being in favor of others, for by that he will later be rewarded with working with those qualities for the Creator.

Because once a person has already been corrected in his qualities so he can work in favor of others, he can work on the matter of faith in the Creator, for then he is fit to be rewarded with faith, for then he already has equivalence of form, called, "Cleave onto his attributes," as in, "As He is merciful, be you merciful."

28. The Holy Shlah, Proofreading on Shaar HaOtiot

Come let me show you that the love of your friend is interlaced with the love of the Creator, for the immenseness of the obligation to love the friend is for the sake of loving the Creator—to remember that he is made in the image and semblance of the upper one, and the part of the soul in him is a part of God above. This is why we are called the "assembly of Israel," for we are all assembled and unite in His uniqueness.

29. Rabbi Kalonymus Kalman Halevi Epstein, *Maor VaShemesh*

It is appropriate and correct to hold tight to love of friends and draw them closer to the path of the Creator for by this one can extend illumination for many days, by bringing them closer to the work of the Creator.

3

The Influence of the Environment on a Person

1. Baal HaSulam, "The Freedom"

He who strives to continually choose a better environment is worthy of praise and reward. But here, too, it is not because of his good thoughts or deeds, which come to him without his choice, but because of his effort to acquire a good environment, which brings him these good thoughts and actions. It is as Rabbi Yehoshua Ben Perachya said, "Make for yourself a rav and buy for yourself a friend."

2. Baal HaSulam, *Shamati*, Article No. 99, "He Did Not Say Wicked or Righteous"

If one does not have any desire or craving for spirituality, if he is among people who have a desire and craving for spirituality, if he likes these people, he, too, will take their strength to prevail, and their desires and aspirations, although by his own quality, he does not have these desires and cravings and the power to overcome. But according to the grace and the importance he ascribes to these people, he will receive new powers.

3. Baal HaSulam, *Shamati*, Article No. 225, "Raising Oneself"

One cannot raise oneself above one's circle. Hence, one must nurse from one's environment, and he has no other way except through Torah and much work. Therefore, if one chooses for oneself a good environment, he saves time and efforts since he is drawn according to his environment.

4. Baal HaSulam, "Introduction to The Study of the Ten Sefirot," Item 4

Now you can understand the words of our sages about the verse, "Therefore, choose life" (See RASHI's interpretation). It states, "I instruct you to choose the part of life, as one who says to his son: 'Choose for yourself a good part in my land.' He places him on the good part and tells him, 'Choose this for yourself.'" It was said about this, "Lord, the portion of my inheritance and of my cup, You support my lot. You placed my hand on the good fate, to say, 'Take this for you.'"

The words are seemingly perplexing. The verse says, "Therefore, choose life." This means that one makes the choice by himself. However, they say that He places him on the good part. Thus, is there no longer choice here? Moreover, they say that the Creator puts one's hand on the good fate. This is indeed perplexing, because if this is so, where then is man's choice?

Now you can see the true meaning of their words. It is indeed true that the Creator Himself puts one's hand on the good fate by giving him a life of pleasure and contentment within the corporeal life that is filled with torment and pain, and devoid of any content. One necessarily departs and escapes them when he sees, even if it seemingly appears amidst the cracks, a tranquil place to escape there from this life, which is harder than death. Indeed, there is no greater placement of one's hand by Him than this.

And one's choice refers only to the strengthening. This is because there is certainly a great effort and exertion here before one purifies one's body to be able to keep the Torah and *Mitzvot* correctly, not for his own pleasure, but to bring contentment to his Maker, which is called *Lishma* [for Her sake]. Only in this manner is one endowed with a life of happiness and pleasantness that come with keeping the Torah.

Before one comes to that purification, there is certainly a choice to strengthen in the good way by all sorts of means and tactics. One should do whatever his hand finds the strength to do until he completes the work of purification and will not fall under his burden midway.

5. Baal HaSulam, "The Freedom"

Rabbi Yosi Ben Kisma (*Avot*, Chapter 6), who replied to a person who offered him to live in his town, and he would give him millions of gold coins for it: "Even if you give me all the gold and silver and jewels in the world, I will live only in a place of Torah." These words seem inconceivable to our simple mind, for how could he relinquish millions of gold coins for such a small thing as living in a place where there are no disciples of Torah, while he himself was a great sage who needed to learn from no one? Indeed, a mystery.

But as we have seen, it is a simple thing and should be observed by each and every one of us. Although everyone has his own source, the forces are revealed openly only through the environment one is in. This is similar to the wheat sown in the ground, whose forces become apparent only through its environment, which is the soil, rain, and sunlight.

Thus, Rabbi Yosi Ben Kisma correctly assumed that if he were to leave the good environment he had chosen and fall into a harmful environment in a city where there is no Torah, not only would his former concepts be compromised, but all the other forces hidden in his source, which he had not yet revealed in action, would remain concealed. This is because they would not be subject to the right environment that would be able to activate them.

And as we have clarified above, only in the matter of the choice of environment is man's reign over himself measured, and for this he should receive reward or punishment. Therefore, one must not wonder that a sage such as Rabbi Yosi Ben Kisma chose the good and declined the bad, and was not tempted by material or corporeal things, as he deduces there: "When one dies, one does not take with him silver, gold, or jewels, but only Torah and good deeds."

And so our sages warned, "Make for yourself a rav and buy for yourself a friend." And there is also the choice of books, as we have mentioned, for only in this is one rebuked or praised—in his choice of the environment. But once he has chosen an environment, he is at its hands as clay in the hands of the potter.

6. Baal HaSulam, "The Freedom"

There is freedom for the will to initially choose such an environment, such books, and such guides that impart upon him good concepts. If one does not do this but is willing to enter any environment that appears before him and read any book that falls into his hands, he is bound to fall into a bad environment or waste his time on worthless books, which are abundant and more accessible. In consequence, he will be forced into foul concepts that make him sin and condemn. He will certainly be punished, not because of his evil thoughts or deeds, in which he has no choice, but because he did not choose to be in a good environment, for in this there is definitely a choice.

Therefore, he who strives to continually choose a better environment is worthy of praise and reward.

7. Baal HaSulam, "A Speech for the Completion of The Zohar"

Our sages said, "Make for yourself a rav and buy yourself a friend." This means that one can make a new environment for oneself. This environment will help him obtain the greatness of his rav through love of friends who appreciate his rav. Through the friends' discussing the greatness of the rav, each of them receives the sensation of his greatness. Thus, bestowal upon his rav becomes reception and sufficient motivation to an extent that will bring one to engage in Torah and *Mitzvot Lishma*.

It was said about this, "The Torah is acquired by forty-eight virtues, by serving of sages, and by meticulousness of friends." This is so because besides serving the rav, one needs the meticulousness of friends, as well, meaning the friends' influence, so they will influence him so he obtains the greatness of his rav. This is so because obtaining the greatness depends entirely on the environment, and a single person cannot do a thing about it whatsoever.

Yet, there are two conditions to obtaining the greatness:

1. Always listen and accept the appreciation of the environment to the extent of their greatness.
2. The environment should be great, as it is written, "In the multitude of people is the king's glory."

To receive the first condition, each student must feel that he is the smallest among all the friends. In that state, he will be able to receive the appreciation of the greatness from everyone, since the great cannot receive from a smaller one, much less be impressed by his words. Rather, only the small is impressed by the appreciation of the great.

For the second condition, each student must extol the virtues of each friend and cherish him as though he were the greatest in the generation. Then the environment will influence him as though it were a great environment, as it should be, since quality is more important than quantity.

8. Baal HaSulam, "A Speech for the Completion of the Zohar"

The measure of the greatness does not depend on the individual, but on the environment. For example, even if one is filled with virtues but the environment does not appreciate him as such, he will always be low-spirited and will not be able to take pride in his virtues, although he has no doubt that they are true. And conversely, a person with no merit at all, but the environment respects him as though he is virtuous, that person will be filled with pride, since the measure of importance and greatness is given entirely to the environment.

When a person sees that the environment slights His work and does not properly appreciate His greatness, he cannot overcome the environment. Thus, he cannot obtain His greatness, and becomes negligent during his work, like them.

Since he does not have the basis for obtaining His greatness, he will obviously not be able to work in order to bring contentment to his Maker and not to himself, for he will have no motivation to exert, and "if you did not labor and find, do not believe." The only advice for this is either to work for oneself or not to work at all, since bestowing contentment upon his Maker will not be for him tantamount to reception.

Now you can understand the verse, "In the multitude of people is the king's glory," since the measure of the greatness comes from the environment under two conditions:

1. The extent of the appreciation of the environment.
2. The size of the environment. Thus, "In the multitude of people is the king's glory."

9. Baal HaSulam, "The Freedom"

When we examine the acts of an individual, we will find them compulsory. He is compelled to do them and has no freedom of choice. In a sense, he is like a stew cooking on a stove; it has no choice but to cook, since Providence has harnessed life with two chains: pleasure and pain.

The living creatures have no freedom of choice—to choose pain or reject pleasure. And man's advantage over animals is that man can aim at a remote goal, meaning agree to a certain amount of current pain, out of choice of future benefit or pleasure to be attained after some time.

But in fact, there is no more than a seemingly commercial calculation here, where the future benefit or pleasure seems preferable and advantageous to the agony they are suffering from the pain they have agreed to assume presently. There is only a matter of deduction here—where they deduct the pain and suffering from the anticipated pleasure, and there remains some surplus.

Thus, only the pleasure is extended. And so it sometimes happens that we are tormented because the pleasure we received is not the surplus we had hoped for compared to the agony we suffered. Hence, we are in deficit, just as are merchants.

And when all is said and done, there is no difference here between man and animal. And if this is the case, there is no free choice whatsoever, but a pulling force drawing them toward any passing pleasure and rejecting them from painful circumstances. And Providence leads them to every place it chooses by means of these two forces without asking their opinion in the matter.

Moreover, even determining the type of pleasure and benefit are entirely out of one's own free choice, but follows the will of others, as they want, and not he. For example: I sit, I dress, I speak, and I eat. I do all these not because I want to sit that way, or talk that way, or dress that way, or eat that way, but because others want me to sit, dress, talk, and eat that way. It all follows the desire and fancy of society, and not my own free will.

Furthermore, in most cases, I do all these against my will. For I would be more comfortable behaving simply, without any burden. But I am chained with iron shackles, in all my movements, to the fancies and manners of others, which make up the society.

So tell me, where is my freedom of will?

10. Baal HaSulam, "Peace in the World"

We must thoroughly know the proportional value between the individual and the collective, between the individual and the collective that the individual lives in and nourishes from, in both matter and in spirit.

Reality shows us that an individual cannot exist in isolation without a sufficient number of people around him to serve him and help him provide for his needs. Hence, man is inherently born to lead a social life. Each and every individual in society is like a wheel that is linked to several other wheels placed in a machine. This single wheel has no freedom of movement in and of itself but continues with the motion of the rest of the wheels in a certain direction to qualify the machine to perform its general function.

And if there is some malfunction in the wheel, the malfunction is not evaluated relating to the wheel itself, but according to its service and role with respect to the whole machine.

11. RABASH, Article No. 13 (1985), "Mighty Rock of My Salvation"

A person has a desire within him, which comes from himself. In other words, even when he is alone and there are no people around him to affect him, or from whom to absorb some desire, he receives an awakening and craves to be a servant of the Creator. But his own desire is certainly not big enough for him not to need to enhance it so he can work with it to obtain the spiritual goal. Therefore, there is a way—just like in corporeality—to enhance that desire through people on the outside who will compel him to follow their views and their spirit.

This is done by bonding with people whom he sees that also have a need for spirituality. And the desire that those people on the outside have begets a desire in him, and thus he receives a great desire for spirituality. In other words, in addition to the desire that he has from within, he receives a desire for spirituality that they beget in him, and then he acquires a great desire with which he can reach the goal.

Hence, the issue of *love of friends* is where each person in the group, besides having a desire of his own, acquires desire from the friends. This is a great asset that can be obtained *only* through love of friends. However, one should take great care not to be among friends who have no desire to examine themselves, the basis of their work—whether it is to bestow or to receive—and to see if they are doing things in order to reach the path of truth, which is the way of nothing but bestowal.

Only in such a group is it possible to instill the friends with a desire to bestow, meaning that each will absorb a lack from the friends, which he himself lacks the power to bestow, and wherever he walks, he is eagerly searching for a place where perhaps someone will be able to give him the power to bestow.

Hence, when he comes into a group where everyone is thirsty for the power to bestow, everyone receives this strength from everyone else. This is considered receiving strength from the outside in addition to the small power that he has within him.

12. RABASH, Article No. 14 (1988), "The Need for Love of Friends"

There is a special power in the adhesion of friends. Since views and thoughts pass from one to the other through the adhesion between them, each is mingled with the power of the other, and by that each person in the group has the power of the entire society. For this reason, *although each person is an individual, he has the power of the entire group.*

13. RABASH, Article No. 727, "The Most Important Is the Environment"

"And choose life." The most important is the environment. Man is always in an environment and necessarily follows them. Hence, if one is immersed in thoughts of Abaye and Raba, he is necessarily influenced by them. But if, for a brief moment, he places his thoughts on a different matter during the study, meaning thinks about something related to corporeal matters, he is necessarily immediately placed in a corporeal environment. This means that he begins to yearn for desires that the environment obligates him.

Also, concerning Abaye and Raba, if he regards them merely as great scholars, he will only be able to yearn for erudition. But if he regards them as sages with attainment, he will yearn for attainments.

14. RABASH, Article No. 17 (1987), "The Meaning of the Strict Prohibition to Teach Idol Worshippers the Torah"

It is impossible to receive the influence of the society if he is not attached to the society, meaning *if he does not appreciate them*. To the extent that he does, he can receive from them the influence without any work, simply by adhering to the society.

15. RABASH, Article No. 21 (1986), "Concerning Above Reason"

If he sees that the friends are at a higher degree than his own, he sees within reason how he is in utter lowliness compared to the friends, that all the friends keep the schedule of arriving at the seminary, and take greater interest in all that is happening among the friends, to help anyone in any way they can, and immediately implement every advice for the work from the teachers in actual fact, etc., it certainly affects him and gives him strength to overcome his laziness, both when he needs to wake up before dawn and when he is awakened.

Also, during the lesson, his body is more interested in the lessons, since otherwise he will lag behind his friends. Also, with anything that concerns *Kedusha* [holiness/sanctity], he must take it more seriously because the body cannot tolerate lowliness. Moreover, when his body looks at the friends, it sees within reason that they are all working for the Creator, and then his body, too, lets him work for the Creator.

And the reason why the body helps him shift to in order to bestow is as mentioned—the body is unwilling to tolerate lowliness. Instead, everybody has pride, and he is unwilling to accept a situation where his friend is greater than him. Thus, when he sees that his friends are at a higher level than his own, this causes him to ascend in every way.

16. RABASH, Article No. 4 (1984), "They Helped Every One His Friend"

We must understand how one can help his friend. Is this matter specifically when there are rich and poor, wise and fools, weak and strong? But when all are rich, smart, or strong, etc., how can one help another?

We see that there is one thing that is common to all—the mood. It is said, "A concern in one's heart, let him speak of it with others." This is because with regard to feeling high-spirited, neither wealth nor erudition can be of assistance.

Rather, it is one person who can help another by seeing that one's friend is low. It is written, "One does not deliver oneself from imprisonment." Rather, it is one's friend who can lift his spirit.

This means that one's friend raises him from his state into a state of liveliness. Then, one begins to reacquire strength and confidence of life and wealth, and he begins as though his goal is now near him.

It turns out that each and every one must be attentive and think how he can help his friend raise his spirit, because in the matter of spirits, anyone can find a needy place in one's friend that he can fill.

17. RABASH, Assorted Notes, Article No. 759, "Man as a Whole"

One must know that love is bought by actions. By giving his friends gifts, each gift that he gives to his friend is like an arrow and a bullet that makes a hole in his friend's heart. Although his friend's heart is like a stone, still, each bullet makes a hole. And from many holes, a hollow is created, and the love of the giver of the gifts enters in this place.

The warmth of the love draws to him his friend's sparks of love, and then the two loves weave into a garment of love that covers both of them. This means that one love surrounds and envelops them, and then they two become one person because the clothing that covers them is a single garment. Hence, both are cancelled.

It is a rule that anything new is exciting and entertaining. Hence, after one receives the garment of love from another, he enjoys only the love of the other and forgets about self-love. At that time, each of them begins to receive pleasure only from caring for his friend, and they cannot worry about themselves because one can labor only where he can receive pleasure.

Since he is enjoying love of others and receives pleasure specifically from that, he will take no pleasure in caring for himself. If there is no pleasure, there is no concern and no place for labor.

18. RABASH, Article No. 17 (1986), "The Agenda of the Assembly-2"

The whole basis upon which we can receive delight and pleasure, and which is permitted for us to enjoy—and is even mandatory—is to enjoy an act of bestowal. Thus, there is one point we should work on—*appreciation of spirituality*. This is expressed in paying attention to whom I turn, with whom I speak, whose commandments I am keeping, and whose laws I am learning, meaning in seeking advice concerning how to appreciate the Giver of the Torah.

And before one obtains some illumination from above by himself, he should seek out like-minded people who are also seeking to enhance the importance of any contact with the Creator in whatever way. And when many people support it, everyone can receive assistance from his friend.

We should know that "Two is the least plural." This means that if two friends sit together and contemplate how to enhance the importance of the Creator, they already have the strength to receive enhancement of the greatness of the Creator in the form of awakening from below. And for this act, the awakening from above follows, and they begin to have some sensation of the greatness of the Creator.

According to what is written, "In the multitude of people is the King's glory," it follows that the greater the number of the collective, the more effective is the power of the collective. In other words, they produce a stronger atmosphere of greatness and importance of the Creator. At that time, each person's body feels that he regards anything that he wishes to do for holiness—meaning to bestow upon the Creator—as a great fortune, that he has been privileged with being among people who have been rewarded with serving the King. At that time, every little thing he does fills him with joy and pleasure that now he has something with which to serve the King.

To the extent that the society regards the greatness of the Creator with their thoughts during the assembly, each according to his degree originates the importance of the Creator in him. Thus, he can walk all day in the world of gladness and joy.

19. RABASH, Article No. 14 (1988), "The Need for Love of Friends"

Although the commandment to love your friend as yourself applies to the whole of Israel, the whole of Israel are not walking on the path of coming from love of others to love of the Creator. Also, there is a rule that when people unite they absorb each other's views, and the matter of *Lishma*—the essential aim of Torah and *Mitzvot*—has not yet been fixed in a man's heart, meaning that the main intention is that through observing Torah and *Mitzvot* they can achieve *Lishma*. Hence, by bonding with others, the views of the others weaken his view of *Lishma*. For this reason, it is better to serve and to bond with the kind of people who understand that "love your friend as yourself" is only *a means to achieve the love of the Creator*, and not because of self-love, but his whole aim will be to benefit the Creator. Hence, one should be careful in bonding and know with whom one bonds.

20. RABASH, Article No. 12 (1984), "Concerning the Importance of Society"

In matters of work on the path of truth, one should isolate oneself from other people. This is because the path of truth requires constant strengthening, since it is against the view of the world. The view of the world is knowing and receiving, whereas the view of Torah is faith and bestowal. If one strays from that, he immediately forgets all the work of the path of truth and falls into a world of self-love. Only from a society in the form of "They helped every man his friend" does each person in the society receive the strength to fight against the view of the world.

21. RABASH, Article No. 12 (1984), "Concerning the Importance of Society"

It is known that one is always among people who have no connection to the work on the path of truth, but to the contrary, always resist those who walk on the path of truth. And since people's thoughts mingle, the views of those who oppose the path of truth permeate those with some desire to walk on the path of truth.

Hence, there is no other solution but to establish a separate society for themselves, to be their framework, meaning a separate community that does not mingle with other people whose views differ from that society. And they should constantly evoke in themselves the issue of the purpose of society, so they will not follow the majority, because following the majority is our nature.

22. RABASH, Article No. 1 (1984), "Purpose of Society – 2"

There should be careful watch in the society, disallowing frivolity, since frivolity ruins everything.

23. RABASH, Article No. 13 (1985), "Mighty Rock of My Salvation"

A person alone will still want to eat, drink, sleep, and so on, even when there are no other people around him. However, if there are people around him, there is the matter of shame, where others compel him. Then he must eat and drink what people around him compel him to.

This is apparent primarily in clothing. At home, a person wears what is comfortable for him. But when he is among people, he must dress according to the way others see it. He has no choice, since shame compels him to follow their fancies.

24. RABASH, Article No. 8 (1985), "Make for Yourself a Rav and Buy Yourself a Friend – 2"

After he has bonded with a group of people who wish to achieve the degree of love of the Creator, and he wishes to take from them the strength to work in order to bestow and be moved by their words about the necessity for obtaining the love of the Creator, he must regard each friend in the group as greater than himself.

25. RABASH, Article No. 21 (1986), "Concerning Above Reason"

A person has qualities that his parents bequeathed to their children, and he has qualities that he acquired from the society, which is a new possession. And this comes to him only through bonding with the society and the envy that he feels toward the friends when he sees that they have better qualities than his own. It motivates him to acquire their good qualities, which he doesn't have and of which he is jealous.

Thus, through the society, he gains new qualities that he adopts by seeing that they are at a higher degree than his, and he is envious of them. This is the reason why now he can be greater than when he didn't have a society, since he acquires new powers through the society.

26. RABASH, Article No. 21 (1986), "Concerning Above Reason"

Our sages said, "Counters' envy increases wisdom." In other words, when all the friends look at the society as being at a high level, both in thoughts and in actions, it is natural that each and every one must raise his degree to a higher level than he has by the qualities of his own body.

27. Rabbi Kalonymus Kalman Halevi Epstein, *Maor VaShemesh*, Portion Yitro

One should depict his friend as serving the Creator more than him, and "authors' [also counters'] envy will increase wisdom." By this, he will grow increasingly stronger in the work of the Creator. This is the meaning of "Each one is burned by his friend's canopy," from the word "fervor." By seeing that his friend's canopy is bigger than his, a fire will burn in him and his soul will further ignite toward the work of the Creator, and he will attain more attainments of Godliness.

28. Raaiah Kook, *Lights*

A person who wants to be rewarded with the light of life in truth must agree to plant himself in the assembly of Israel with all his heart, with all his senses and corporeal and spiritual powers.

4

The Ten

1. RABASH, Article No. 2, (1984), "Concerning Love of Friends"

One must disclose the love in his heart towards the friends, since by revealing it he evokes his friends' hearts toward the friends so they, too, would feel that each of them is practicing love of friends. The benefit from that is that in this manner, one gains strength to practice love of friends more forcefully, since every person's force of love is integrated in each other's.

It turns out that where a person has one measure of strength to practice love of friends, if the group consists of ten members, then he is integrated with ten forces of the need, who understand that it is necessary to engage in love of friends.

2. RABASH, Article No. 2 (1984), "Concerning Love of Friends"

We must remember that the society was established on the basis of love of others, so each member would receive from the group the love of others and hatred of himself. And seeing that his friend is straining to annul his self and to love others would cause everyone to be integrated in their friends' intentions.

Thus, if the society is made of ten members, for example, each will have ten forces practicing self-annulment, hatred of self, and love of others.

3. RABASH, Article No. 5 (1984), "What Does the Rule, 'Love Your Friend as Thyself,' Give Us?"

"A sacred audience," we are referring to a number of individuals who have gathered and formed a unit. Afterwards, a head is appointed to the audience, etc., and this is called a *Minian* [ten/quorum] or a "congregation." At least ten people must be present, and then it is possible to say *Kedusha* (a specific part of a Jewish prayer) at the service.

The Zohar says about it: "Wherever there are ten, the *Shechina* [Divinity] dwells." This means that in a place where there are ten men, there is a place for the dwelling of the *Shechina*.

4. RABASH, Article No. 251, "Concerning the Minyan [Ten in the synagogue]"

Our sages said, "You are called 'man,' and not the nations of the world," since their sole aim is to receive for themselves. This is the meaning of "When the Creator comes to the synagogue and does not find ten men there," meaning that there will be someone there who will pray for the quality of "ten," which is the *Shechina*, so she will rise from her exile, for by engaging with the desire to bestow, one raises the *Shechina* from the dust. But when each one cares for his personal needs, the Creator is angry.

He brings evidence from the verse, as was said, "Why have I come and there is no man" to care for the needs that pertain to the quality of "man," and cares only to satisfy the needs that pertain to the quality of a beast? Rather, one should always answer to himself for whom he spends his time and for whom he exerts, for he should be concerned only with the needs of the collective.

5. RABASH, Article No. 28 (1986), "A Congregation Is No Less than Ten"

Our sages said (*Sanhedrin*, 39), "In every ten there is *Shechina*."

It is known that *Malchut* is called "tenth." It is also known that the receiving *Kli* is also called "the *Sefira Malchut*," who is the tenth *Sefira*, receiving the upper abundance. She is called "will to receive," and all the creatures extend only from her. For this reason, a congregation is no less than ten, since all the corporeal branches extend from the upper roots. Therefore, according to the rule, "There is no light that does not have ten *Sefirot*," in corporeality, something is not considered a congregation that can be regarded as important unless there are ten men there, such as the upper degrees.

6. *Zohar for All*, *Nasso*, "Why Have I Come and There Is No Man," Items 105-108

It is written, "Why have I come and there is no man." How beloved are Israel by the Creator, for wherever they are, the Creator is among them since He does not remove His love from them, as it is written, "And let them make Me a Temple and I will dwell among them." "Let them make Me a Temple" is any Temple, for any synagogue in the world is called "a Temple." "And I will dwell among them" since the *Shechina* [Divinity] is the first to come to the synagogue. Happy is the man who is among the first ten in the synagogue since they complete the congregation, which is no less than ten, and they are the first to be sanctified in the *Shechina*. There must be ten in the synagogue at once, and not come bit by bit so as not to delay the wholeness of the organs. All ten are as organs of one body in which the *Shechina* is present, for the Creator made man at once, and established all his organs together.

When all of one's organs are completed at that time, each organ is completed in itself properly. Likewise, when the *Shechina* comes to the synagogue first, there must be ten together there, and then it is completed since a congregation is no less than ten, corresponding to the ten *Sefirot* of *Malchut*. As long as there aren't ten there together, none of them is completed. Afterwards, the correction of the whole congregation is done, as it is written, "The king is glorified in the multitude of people." Hence, the people, who come after the first ten, are all a correction of that body, the correction of the congregation, since the increase of people increases the glory of the king.

When the *Shechina* comes first and people have not come ten together properly, the Creator calls out, "Why have I come and there is no man?" "There is no man" since the organs have not been corrected and the body, called "congregation," has not been completed. This is so because when the body is incomplete, there is no man, for the individual organs that have already come are incomplete.

When the body is completed below, when there are ten together, upper *Kedusha* [holiness] comes and enters that body, and the lower one becomes truly as the ten *Sefirot* of above. At that time, everyone must not open their mouths to speak of worldly matters since Israel are now in the wholeness of the upper one and are sanctified in the upper *Kedusha*.

7. *Zohar for All, Truma* [Donation], "In a Multitude of People Is a King's Glory," Items 692, 694-698

And when the angels come to be friends with Israel, to praise the Creator together, and Israel below do not come to establish their prayers and litanies, and to praise their Master, all the holy camps in the upper government break from their corrections. It is so because they do not rise in rising, for they cannot praise their Master because the praises of the Creator must be above and below together, upper and lower at the same time. This is why it is written, "A prince's ruin," and not "A king's ruin," as it concerns only the camps of angels, not the King Himself.

And even though not many came to the house of gathering, but only ten, the upper camps come into these ten, to be friends with them and to praise the Creator, since all the King's corrections are in ten. Hence, ten is enough.

8. *Pirkei Avot* [Ethics of the fathers], 3:6

Rabbi Halafta Ben Dossa says, "Ten who sit and engage in Torah, the *Shechina* [Divinity] is among them," as was said (Psalms 82), "God stands in the congregation of God."

9. Rav Shneor Zalman of Liadi, *The Tania*

The sages of the Mishnah said in their teaching, "Ten who sit and engage in Torah, the *Shechina* [Divinity] is among them," for "this is the whole of man." This was also all of his descent in this world, for the purpose of this ascent, of which there is none higher for the *Shechina* of His strength will dwell and grow within the children of Israel, as it is written, "For I the Lord dwell within the children of Israel," specifically through engagement in Torah and *Mitzvot* [commandments] in a ten. It was said about this, "holy in the midst of you," and there is nothing holy in less than ten since the installation is an enormous illumination from the light of the Creator that shines in it unboundedly and limitlessly. He cannot clothe in a limited soul, but rather surrounds it from above, as our sages said, "In any ten, the *Shechina* is present," meaning He is established and is present over us through the work of our hands in Torah and *Mitzvot* particularly in the collective.

10. *Tana de Bei Eliyahu Zuta*, Chapter 14

Israel are not redeemed by affliction or by enslavement, or by jolting, nor by madness or pressure or by absence of nourishment, but rather by ten people sitting with each other, and each of them reads and learns with his friend, and their voice is heard.

11. Exodus 18, 25-27

Moses chose able men out of all Israel and made them heads over the people, leaders of thousands, leaders of hundreds, leaders of fifties and leaders of tens. They judged the people at all times; the difficult dispute they would bring to Moses, and every minor thing they themselves would judge. Then Moses bade his father-in-law farewell, and he went his way into his own land.

12. Rabbi Abraham Chaim of Zlotshov, *Orach LaChaim*

In Israel, there were leaders of thousands, leaders of hundreds, leaders of fifties, and leaders of tens. Those who were from the leaders of tens, each had ten people from Israel under his hands. He was the head and bestowed upon them from his wisdom, while he himself submitted himself and lowered himself under the leader of fifty and received his wisdom among the fifty over whom was the leader of fifty. Likewise, the leader of fifty yielded and was lowered and received from the leader of hundred who was over him. And likewise, the leader of hundred received from the leader of thousand, and the leader of thousand from the president of the tribe. And the rule is that anyone who raises himself, the Creator lowers him, and anyone who lowers himself, the Creator raises him.

13. Rabbi Nachman of Breslov, *Likutey Halachot*

Wherever ten gather to pray, illumination from ten discernments is extended over them, as they are regarded as the world of correction. By this, all the bad factions in Israel are corrected. This is the heart of the correction of the ascent of the worlds and the qualities.

14. *Berachot*, 21b

Rabbi Yochanan said, "The verse says, 'I was sanctified among the children of Israel.' Anything of holiness shall be no less than ten."

15. Rabbi Kalonymus Kalman Halevi Epstein, *Maor VaShemesh, VaYechi*

The essence of the assembly is for everyone to be in one unity and for all to seek but one purpose: to find the Creator. In every ten there is the *Shechina* [Divinity]. Clearly, if there are more than ten then there is more revelation of the *Shechina*. Thus, each one should assemble with his friend and come to him to hear from him a word about the work of the Creator, and how to find the Creator. He should annul before his friend, and his friend should do the same toward him, and so should everyone do. Then, when the assembly is with this intention, then "More than the calf wants to suckle, the cow wants to nurse," and the Creator approaches them and He is with them, and great mercies and good and revealed kindness will be extended over the assembly of Israel.

16. Rabbi Kalonymus Kalman Halevi Epstein, *Maor VaShemesh*, *Ekev*

The most important is for each and every one to annul himself completely and not think of himself as righteous or that he counts at all among the friends. He should only see that his actions do not blemish the society. Although it seems as though he is a great person, he should nonetheless look into his actions and think, "What make me great?" and annul himself completely. It is known that in every ten there is *Shechina* [Divinity], and this is a complete level. In a complete level, there are head, hands, legs, and heels. It follows that when every person regards himself as nothing in society, then he regards himself as a heel compared to the society, while they are the head, the body, and the higher organs. When each one thinks of himself in this way, they make the gates of abundance and every lushness in the world open up to them, and it is drawn the most through the person who is more regarded as "nothing" and as "a heel."

5

The Center of the Group

1. Baal HaSulam, Letter No. 13

You should know that there are many sparks of holiness in each one in the group. When you assemble all the sparks of holiness to one place, as brothers, with love and friendship, you will certainly have a very high level of holiness for a while, from the light of life.

2. Baal HaSulam, "600,000 Souls"

The sign for the body's complete correction is when one feels that one's soul exists in the whole of Israel, in each and every one of them, for which he does not feel himself as an individual, for one depends on the other. At that time, he is complete, flawless, and the soul truly shines on him in its fullest power, as it appeared in *Adam HaRishon*, as in "He who breathed, breathed from within Him."

This is the meaning of the three times of a person:

1. A spark of a soul, the act by way of sparkling, as in prohibiting and permitting.
2. A particular soul, one part out of 600,000. It is permanently completed, but its flaw is with it. This means that his body cannot receive the whole of the soul, and feels himself as being distinct, which causes him a lot of pains of love.

Subsequently, he approaches wholeness, the common soul, since the body has been cleansed and is entirely dedicated to the Creator and does not pose any measures or screens and is completely included in the whole of Israel.

3. Baal HaSulam, "Not the Time for the Livestock to Be Gathered"

One must not exclude oneself from the public and ask for oneself, not even to bring contentment to one's maker, but only for the entire public. It is so because one who departs from the public to ask specifically for one's own soul does not build. On the contrary, he inflicts ruin upon his soul, as it is written, "All who is proud, he and I cannot dwell in the same abode," for there cannot be one who retires from the public unless with an attire of pride. Woe unto him, for he inflicts ruin on his soul.

Even during work, when one prays alone, against his will he departs from the public and ruins his soul. That is, there was not even an awakening of anyone from the children of Israel to demand anything personal for no one needed anything because they did not feel as separate selves, and this was their power to come out of Egypt with a mighty hand. Thus, every one must gather with all of one's strength into the whole of Israel with every plea to the Creator in the prayer and include himself in the only one, the root of all of Israel.

4. Baal HaSulam, "The Arvut [Mutual Guarantee]," Item 23

It is written, "And Israel camped there before the mountain," which our sages interpret as "as one man with one heart."

This is because each and every person from the nation completely detached himself from self-love, and wanted only to benefit his friend. It turns out that all the individuals in the nation had come together and became one heart and one man, for only then were they qualified to receive the Torah.

5. Baal HaSulam, Letter No. 8

There is a sublime purpose for all that happens in this world, and it is called "the drop of unification." When those dwellers of clay houses go through all those terrors, through all that totality, in His pride, which is removed from them, a door opens in the walls of their hearts, which are tightly sealed by the nature of creation itself, and by this they become fit for instilling that drop of unification in their hearts. Then they are inverted like an imprinted substance, and they will evidently see that it is to the contrary—that it was precisely in those dreadful terrors that they perceive the totality, which is removed by foreign pride. There, and only there, is the Creator Himself adhered, and there He can instill them with the drop of unification.

6. RABASH, Letter No. 42

It is written, "And the people encamped, as one man with one heart." This means that they all had one goal, which is to benefit the Creator. It follows…

We should understand how they could be as one man with one heart, since we know what our sages said, "As their faces are not similar to one another, their views are not similar to one another," so how could they be as one man with one heart?

Answer: If we are saying that each one cares for himself, it is impossible to be as one man, since they are not similar to one another. However, if they all annul their selves and worry only about the benefit of the Creator, they have no individual views, since the individuals have all been canceled and have entered the single authority.

7. RABASH, Letter No. 40

What can one do if he feels that he has a heart of stone toward his friend? The advice is very simple: The nature of fire is that when rubbing stones against each other, a fire starts. This is a great rule, since "From *Lo Lishma* [not for Her sake] one comes to *Lishma* [for Her sake]." And this is so particularly when the act is *Lishma*, meaning imparting a gift to one's friend, and the aim is *Lo Lishma*.

This is so because one gives a gift only to one that we know and recognize as someone we love. It follows that the aim of the gift is like gratitude for the love that his friend gives him. However, if one gives a gift to a stranger, meaning he doesn't feel that his friend is close to his heart, then he has nothing to be grateful for. It follows that the aim is *Lo Lishma*, meaning … the intention that should be.

Ostensibly, it could be said that this is called "charity," since he pities his friend when he sees that there is no one who is speaking to him and greets him, and this is why he does that to him. Indeed, there is a prayer for it—that the Creator will help him by making him feel the love of his friend and make his friend close to his heart. Thus, through the deeds, he is rewarded with the aim, as well.

But while at the time of doing the giver of the gift intended that the gift to his friends would only be as charity (even if he is giving his time for his friend, since it is sometimes more important to a person than his money, as it is said, "One cares for his lack of money but not for his lack of time." However, regarding time, each has his own value, since there are people who make one pound an hour, and there is more or less. And likewise with their spirituality—how much spirituality they make in an hour, etc.), then one is testifying about himself that he isn't aiming for love of friends, meaning that through the action, the love between them will increase.

And only when both of them intend for a gift and not for charity, through the wearing out of the hearts, even of the strongest ones, each will bring out warmth from the walls of his heart, and the warmth will ignite the sparks of love until a clothing of love will form. Then, both of them will be covered under one blanket, meaning a single love will surround and envelop the two of them, as it is known that *Dvekut* [adhesion] unites two into one.

And when one begins to feel the love of his friend, joy and pleasure immediately begin to awaken in him, for the rule is that a novelty entertains. His friend's love for him is a new thing for him because he always knew that he was the only one who cared for his own well-being. But the minute he discovers that his friend cares for him, it evokes within him immeasurable joy, and he can no longer care for himself, since man can toil only where he feels pleasure. And since he is beginning to feel pleasure in caring for his friend, he naturally cannot think of himself.

8. RABASH, Article No. 63, "You Stand Here Today – 1"

"You stand here today all of you." This means that he gathered them… to admit them into the covenant (RASHI). "All of you" means that everyone entered into the *Arvut* [mutual responsibility] (*Ohr HaChaim*).

There is a question why he begins with plural form, "all of you," then shifts to singular form, "every man from Israel." It means that "all of you" permeates everyone in Israel, meaning that every person from Israel will be included with "all of you," as it is written, "And the people camped at the bottom of the mountain," as one man with one heart. In other words, when there is love of Israel, they can succeed, as it is written, "Ephraim is joined to idols; let him be."

Man is a small world and comprises the entire world. He should achieve the degree of being singular, as it is written, "Rewarded, he sentences himself and the entire world to the side of merit" (*Kidushin* 40b).

Therefore, when a person admits all the individuals, "your heads and your tribes," for everyone must join in the covenant, meaning to come to be a worker of the Creator "with all your heart—with both your inclinations." In other words, even the lowly attributes in man should undergo correction.

"So that He may establish you today as His people and He will be a God unto you." That is, a person will achieve this attainment, that he is in the singular authority.

9. RABASH, Letter No. 8

Once I have acquired this above-mentioned clothing, sparks of love promptly begin to shine within me. The heart begins to long to unite with my friends, and it seems to me that my eyes see my friends, my ears hear their voices, my mouth speaks to them, the hands embrace, the feet dance in a circle, in love and joy together with them, and I transcend my corporeal boundaries. I forget the vast distance between my friends and me, and the outstretched land for many miles will not stand between us.

It is as though my friends are standing right within my heart and see all that is happening there, and I become ashamed of my petty acts against my friends. Then, I simply exit the corporeal vessels and it seems to me that there is no reality in the world except my friends and I. After that, even the "I" is cancelled and is immersed, mingled in my friends, until I stand and declare that there is no reality in the world—only the friends.

10. RABASH, Article No. 8 (1985), "Make for Yourself a Rav and Buy Yourself a Friend – 2"

Those people agreed to unite into a single group that engages in love of friends is that each of them feels that they have one desire that can unite all their views, so as to receive the strength of love of others. There is a famous maxim by our sages, "As their faces differ, their views differ." Thus, those who agreed among them to unite into a group understood that there isn't such a great distance between them in the sense that they recognize the necessity to work in love of others. Therefore, each of them will be able to make concessions in favor of the others, and they can unite around that.

11. RABASH, Article No. 28 (1986), "A Congregation Is No Less than Ten"

Our sages said (*Sanhedrin*, 39), "In every ten there is *Shechina*."

It is known that *Malchut* is called "tenth." It is also known that the receiving *Kli* is also called "the *Sefira Malchut*," who is the tenth *Sefira*, receiving the upper abundance. She is called "will to receive," and all the creatures extend only from her. For this reason, a congregation is no less than ten, since all the corporeal branches extend from the upper roots. Therefore, according to the rule, "There is no light that does not have ten *Sefirot*," in corporeality, something is not considered a congregation that can be regarded as important unless there are ten men there, such as the upper degrees.

12. RABASH, Article No. 9 (1984), "One Should Always Sell the Beams of His House"

Each of them had a spark of love of others, but the spark could not ignite the light of love to shine in each, so they agreed that by uniting, the sparks would become a big flame.

13. *Zohar for All*, Nasso, "Why Have I Come and There Is No Man," Items 105-108

It is written, "Why have I come and there is no man." How beloved are Israel by the Creator, for wherever they are, the Creator is among them since He does not remove His love from them, as it is written, "And let them make Me a Temple and I will dwell among them." "Let them make Me a Temple" is any Temple, for any synagogue in the world is called "a Temple." "And I will dwell among them" since the *Shechina* [Divinity] is the first to come to the synagogue. Happy is the man who is among the first ten in the synagogue since they complete the congregation, which is no less than ten, and they are the first to be sanctified in the *Shechina*. There must be ten in the synagogue at once, and not come bit by bit so as not to delay the wholeness of the organs. All ten are as organs of one body in which the *Shechina* is present, for the Creator made man at once, and established all his organs together.

When all of one's organs are completed at that time, each organ is completed in itself properly. Likewise, when the *Shechina* comes to the synagogue first, there must be ten together there, and then it is completed since a congregation is no less than ten, corresponding to the ten *Sefirot* of *Malchut*. As long as there aren't ten there together, none of them is completed. Afterwards, the correction of the whole congregation is done, as it is written, "The king is glorified in the multitude of people." Hence, the people, who come after the first ten, are all a correction of that body, the correction of the congregation, since the increase of people increases the glory of the king.

When the *Shechina* comes first and people have not come ten together properly, the Creator calls out, "Why have I come and there is no man?" "There is no man" since the organs have not been corrected and the body, called "congregation," has not been completed. This is so because when the body is incomplete, there is no man, for the individual organs that have already come are incomplete.

When the body is completed below, when there are ten together, upper *Kedusha* [holiness] comes and enters that body, and the lower one becomes truly as the ten *Sefirot* of above. At that time, everyone must not open their mouths to speak of worldly matters since Israel are now in the wholeness of the upper one and are sanctified in the upper *Kedusha*.

14. Rabbi Nachman of Breslov, *Likutey Halachot*

The work of the Creator is mainly in the desire. Each one, to the extent that he accustoms himself to strengthen his will and yearning and longing for the Creator, with a very strong desire, to that extent he is rewarded with nearing the Creator, His law, His commandments. Each one from Israel must rise in all the ascents from degree to degree, and it is all to the extent of the strengthening of the desire, for the heart of the purpose is to be willingly incorporated in the desire, for the beginning of nearing the Creator and the final purpose are all regarded as desire, and it is impossible to be incorporated in the desire unless through unity, and love, and peace, when all of Israel are included together in love and great unity.

15. *Maor VaShemesh*, Portion *Ekev*

It is a very great thing when the children of Israel assemble, but the most important is for each and every one to annul himself completely and not think of himself as righteous or that he counts at all among the friends. It is known that in every ten there is *Shechina* [Divinity], and this is a complete level. In a complete level, there are head, hands, legs, and heels. It follows that when every person regards himself as nothing in society, then he regards himself as a heel compared to the society, while they are the head, the body, and the higher organs. When each one thinks of himself in this way, they make the gates of abundance and every lushness in the world open up to them, and the most important is that righteous who can best grasp a discernment that is more "null" than all of them. Through him, all the abundance flows.

16. *Likutey Halachot* [Assorted Rules], "Synagogue Rules," Rule One

The ascent of the soul and its completeness is mainly when all the souls merge and become one, for then they rise to the *Kedusha* [holiness], since the *Kedusha* is one. Therefore, the prayer, which is regarded as the soul, depends primarily on the unity of souls. For this reason, prior to the prayer, he must take upon himself the to-do *Mitzva* [commandment] "Love your neighbor as yourself," for it is impossible to say the words of the prayer unless through peace, when we unite with all the souls of Israel. For this reason, the prayer is mainly in public and not alone, so that one will not be separated and alone, as this is the opposite of *Kedusha*. Rather, we must only unite the holy congregation together and become one. This is a prayer in public, when the souls assemble and unite, and this is the completeness of the prayer.

17. Ramchal, *Adir BaMarom*, Part 1

The *Nukva* [female], who leads all the worlds, is called "heart." Also, the *Nukva* feels the actions of all the worlds because she is the one who is impressed by the lower ones. It follows that the hearts in all the people are but parts of that heart. That is, all the souls are rooted in the *Nukva* and are therefore regarded as parts of her. Also, they are her MAN because she is not considered whole unless she is integrated with all her branches.

This matter of the heart also spreads through all the souls that are rooted in her. It follows that this heart is incomplete until it contains all the discernments of the heart that emerge from it in all the souls. Then, when it is inclusive, so he will understand, as in "the heart understands" all the guidance as a whole, as this is the order of bestowal, when the branches are included in the root, and then the root is comprised of all of them, receives what it needs for all of them, and returns and dispenses to everyone their rightful share.

18. *Maor VaShemesh*, Portion *Re'eh*

The main rule by which to come to the path of the Creator is through adhesion of friends, as it is written in *Pirkei Avot* [*Ethics of the Fathers*], "Acquiring the Torah, one of forty-eight things by which the Torah is acquired is adhesion of friends." And how is it adhesion of friends? By gathering together, where each one annuls before his friend when he sees his friend's merit, and he becomes lowly in his own eyes and his friend is greater than him. And he loves each and every one, and his desire is to truly permeate each one because of joy and love.

19. Raaiah Kook, *Lights*

A person from Israel who wants to be rewarded with the light of life in truth must agree to plant himself in the assembly of Israel with all his heart, with all his senses and corporeal and spiritual powers.

20. Rabbi Kalonymus Kalman Halevi Epstein, *Maor VaShemesh*

The advice and counsel for serving the Creator and the correct path of repentance is to unite our hearts in love of friends and look at the advantage of the other in serving the Creator and in knowing his Creator, and not to see his flaw. Repentance is mainly in uniting with each and every one in love and in one heart, to serve the Creator shoulder to shoulder. By this, the world of repentance and the world of mercy and the world of good will awaken. This is an intimation, as was said, "And all are reviewed in one review." This means that we should adhere and connect to one another and close into one another in the heart of each one. This is implied in the word "one," to become one bundle to serve the Creator wholeheartedly.

21. Rabbi Nachman of Breslov, *Likutey Halachot* [Assorted Rules], *Hoshen Mishpat*, "Rules of the Guarantor"

The essence of observance of the Torah, which is the desire, is through unity, anyone who wishes to take upon himself the burden of Torah and *Mitzvot*, which is primarily by overcoming the desire, must be included in the whole of Israel in great unity. For this reason, at the time of the reception of the Torah, they immediately became responsible for one another because they were regarded as one. Precisely by each being responsible for his friend, which is the quality of unity, specifically by this can they observe the Torah. Without it, it would not be possible to observe the Torah whatsoever, since the heart of observing the Torah, which is the desire, is through unity, when all are regarded as one. It follows that specifically through *Arvut*, which is when everyone are regarded as one, is the heart of observing the Torah, since the essence of love and unity is in the desire, when each one is pleased with his friend and there is no disparity of desire among them, and all are included in one desire, by which they are included in the upper desire, which is the purpose of the unity.

22. *Degel Machaneh Ephraim*, VaEtchanan

"The Lord is one and Israel are one"; hence, they are adhered to the Creator, since it befits the One to cling to the one. And when is this? It is when Israel are bundled and attached together in complete unity. At that time, they are regarded as one, and the Creator is upon them, for He is one.

The Center of the Group

But when their hearts divide and they are apart from one another, they cannot be adhered to the One and the Creator is not on them. Rather, another God is on them. This is implied in the verse, "And you who are adhered," meaning when you are adhered and united with each other, "You are alive every one of you." When they are in one unity. Then it befits the One to cling to the one, and the one Creator is upon them.

23. *Ohev Ysrael, Likutei Masachtot*

One should intend to love; the Creator is destined to pardon the righteous, and He sits among them. *Machol* [pardon/dancing in a circle] is in a circle, meaning that everyone will stand in a circle and the Creator is as the middle point of the circle. And each one points with his finger, "This is our God," meaning that each one will have great attainment equally from the upper *Hesed* [mercy].

24. The Holy Shlah, Proofreading on Shaar HaOtiot

Come let me show you that the love of your friend is interlaced with the love of the Creator, for the immenseness of the obligation to love the friend is for the sake of loving the Creator—to remember that he is made in the image and semblance of the upper one, and the part of the soul in him is a part of God above. This is why we are called the "assembly of Israel," for we are all assembled and unite in His uniqueness.

6

The Power in Connection

1. Baal HaSulam, Letter No. 4

You lack nothing but to go out to a field that the Lord has blessed, and collect all those flaccid organs that have drooped from your soul, and join them into a single body.

In that complete body, the Creator will instill His *Shechina* incessantly, and the fountain of intelligence and high streams of light will be as a never ending fountain.

2. Baal HaSulam, Letter No. 10

Do what you can and the salvation of the Lord is as the blink of an eye. The most important thing before you today is the unity of friends. Exert in that more and more, for it can recompense for all the faults.

3. Baal HaSulam, *Shamati*, Article No. 99, "He Did Not Say Wicked or Righteous"

If one does not have any desire or craving for spirituality, if he is among people who have a desire and craving for spirituality, if he likes these people, he, too, will take their strength to prevail, and their desires and aspirations, although by his own quality, he does not have these desires and cravings and the power to overcome. But according to the grace and the importance he ascribes to these people, he will receive new powers.

4. Baal HaSulam, "Matan Torah [The Giving of the Torah]," Item 15

If six hundred thousand men abandon their work for the satisfaction of their own needs and worry about nothing but standing guard so their friends will not lack a thing, and moreover, they will engage in this with great love, with their very heart and soul, in the full meaning of the *Mitzva*, "Love your friend as yourself," it is then beyond doubt that no one in the nation will need to worry about his own well-being.

Because of this, one becomes completely free of securing his own survival and can easily observe the *Mitzva*, "Love your friend as yourself," obeying all the conditions given in Items 3 and 4. After all, why would he worry about his own survival when six hundred thousand loyal lovers stand by, ready with great care to make sure he lacks nothing of his needs?

Therefore, once all the members of the nation agreed, they were immediately given the Torah, for now they were capable of observing it.

5. Baal HaSulam, "The Arvut [Mutual Guarantee]," Item 23

It is written, "And Israel camped there before the mountain," which our sages interpret as "as one man with one heart."

This is because each and every person from the nation completely detached himself from self-love, and wanted only to benefit his friend […]. It turns out that all the individuals in the nation had come together and became one heart and one man, for only then were they qualified to receive the Torah.

6. Baal HaSulam, Letter No. 13

You should know that there are many sparks of holiness in each one in the group. When you assemble all the sparks of holiness to one place, as brothers, with love and friendship, you will certainly have a very high level of holiness for a while, from the light of life.

7. Baal HaSulam, Letter No. 47

I have established for you conducts by which you can still hang on and not turn back.

And the single most special one among them is the *Dvekut* of friends. I sincerely promise that this love is able. And I shall remind you of every good thing that you need. And if you nonetheless braced yourselves in that, you would certainly go from strength to strength on the rungs of holiness.

8. Baal HaSulam, "A Speech for the Completion of The Zohar"

Our sages said, "Let all your actions be for the sake of the Creator," that is, *Dvekut* with the Creator. Do not do anything that does not yield this goal of *Dvekut*. This means that all your actions will be to bestow and to benefit your fellow person. At that time, you will achieve equivalence of form with the Creator—as all His actions are to bestow and to benefit others, so you, all your actions will be only to bestow and to benefit others. This is the complete *Dvekut*.

9. Baal HaSulam, "The Freedom"

The children of Israel were rewarded with complete *Dvekut* on that holy occasion, their vessels of reception were completely emptied of any worldly possession and they were adhered to Him in equivalence of form. This means that they had no desire for any self-possession, but only to the extent that they could bestow contentment, so their Maker would delight in them.

And since their will to receive had clothed in an image of that object, it had clothed in it and bonded with it into complete oneness. Therefore, they were certainly liberated from the angel of death.

10. Baal HaSulam, Letter No. 13

Indeed, I feel all of you together, that today has been replaced for you with tomorrow, and instead of "now," you say "later." There is no cure for this but to exert to understand that mistake and distortion—that one who is saved by the Creator is saved only if he needs salvation today. One who can wait for tomorrow will obtain his salvation after his years, God forbid.

This happened to you due to negligence in my request to exert in love of friends, as I have explained to you in every possible way that this cure is enough to recompense for all your faults.

11. Baal HaSulam, Letter No. 47

Let me remind you the validity of love of friends in spite of everything at this time, for it is upon this that our right to exist depends, and upon this our near-to-come success is measured. Hence, turn away from all the imaginary engagements and set your hearts on thinking thoughts and devising proper tactics to truly connect your hearts as one, so the words "Love your friend as yourself" will literally come true in you, for a verse does not reach beyond the literal, and you will be cleaned by the thought of love that will cover all crimes. Test me in that, and begin to truly connect in love, and then you will see, "the palate will taste".

12. Baal HaSulam, "Not the Time for the Livestock to Be Gathered"

One must not exclude oneself from the public and ask for oneself, not even to bring contentment to one's maker, but only for the entire public.

One who departs from the public to ask specifically for one's own soul does not build. On the contrary, he inflicts ruin upon his soul, as it is written, "All who is proud," etc., Woe unto him, for he inflicts ruin on his soul. Even during work, when one prays alone, against his will he departs from the public and ruins his soul. Thus, every one must gather with all of one's strength into the whole of Israel with every plea to the Creator in the prayer and include himself in the only one, the root of all of Israel.

13. RABASH, Article No. 14, "The Need for Love of Friends"

There is a special power in the adhesion of friends. Since views and thoughts pass from one to the other through the adhesion between them, each is mingled with the power of the other, and by that each person in the group has the power of the entire society. For this reason, although each person is an individual, he has the power of the entire group.

14. RABASH, Article No. 1 (1984),"Purpose of Society – 2"

Without annulling self-love, it is impossible to achieve *Dvekut* [adhesion)] with the Creator, meaning equivalence of form.

And since it is against our nature, we need a society that will form a great force so we can work together on annulling the will to receive, called "evil," as it hinders the achievement of the goal for which man was created.

For this reason, society must consist of individuals who unanimously agree that they must achieve it. Then, all the individuals become one great force that can fight against itself, since everyone is integrated in everyone else. Thus, each person is founded on a great desire to achieve the goal.

To be integrated in one another, each person should annul himself before the others. This is done by each seeing the friends' merits and not their faults. But one who thinks that he is a little higher than his friends can no longer unite with them.

15. RABASH, Letter No. 34

"And they shall all become one society." In that state, it will be easier "To do Your will wholeheartedly."

This is so because while there is not just one society, it is difficult to work wholeheartedly. Instead, part of the heart remains for its own benefit and not for the benefit of the Creator. It is said about it in Midrash Tanhuma, "'You stand today,' as the day at times shines and at times darkens, so it is with you. When it is dark for you, the light of the world will shine for you, as it is said, 'And the Lord shall be unto you an everlasting light.' When? When you are all one society, as it is written, 'Alive every one of you this day.'

Usually, if someone takes a pile of branches, can he break them all at once? But if taken one at a time, even a baby can break them. Similarly, you find that Israel will not be redeemed until they are all one society, as it is said, 'In those days and at that time, says the Lord, the children of Israel shall come, they and the sons of Judah together.' Thus, when they are united, they receive the face of Divinity."

I presented the words of the Midrash so that you don't think that the issue of a group, which is love of friends, relates to Hassidism. Rather, it is the teaching of our sages, who saw how necessary was the uniting of hearts into a single group for the reception of the face of Divinity.

16. RABASH, Article No. 17 (1986), "The Agenda of the Assembly – 2"

When one comes to the assembly of friends, he should always see whether or not the friends have the goal that he craves, that each of them has some grip on that goal. And he thinks that by everyone bonding together for one goal, each will have his own share, as well as the shares of the whole of society. It follows that each member of the society will have the same strength as the whole of society together.

17. RABASH, Article No. 9 (1984), "One Should Always Sell the Beams of His House"

If a society is established with certain people, and when they gathered, there must have been someone who wished to establish specifically this "bunch." Thus, he sorted out these people to see that they were suitable for each other. In other words, each of them had a spark of love of others, but the spark could not ignite the light of love to shine in each, so they agreed that by uniting, the sparks would become a big flame.

Hence, now, too, when he is spying on them, he should overcome and say, "As all of them were of one mind that they must walk on the path of love of others when the society was established, so it is now." And when everyone judges his friends favorably, all the sparks will ignite once more and again there will be one big flame.

18. RABASH, Article No. 13 (1985), "Mighty Rock of My Salvation"

The issue of *love of friends* is where each person in the group, besides having a desire of his own, acquires desire from the friends. This is a great asset that can be obtained *only* through love of friends. However, one should take great care not to be among friends who have no desire to examine themselves, the basis of their work—whether it is to bestow or to receive—and to see if they are doing things in order to reach the path of truth, which is the way of nothing but bestowal.

Only in such a group is it possible to instill the friends with a desire to bestow, meaning that each will absorb a lack from the friends, which he himself lacks the power to bestow, and wherever he walks, he is eagerly searching for a place where perhaps someone will be able to give him the power to bestow.

Hence, when he comes into a group where everyone is thirsty for the power to bestow, everyone receives this strength from everyone else. This is considered receiving strength from the outside in addition to the small power that he has within him.

19. RABASH, Article No. 21 (1986), "Concerning Above Reason"

Can be obtained by adhesion of friends—new qualities by which they will be qualified to achieve *Dvekut* with the Creator. And all this can be said while he sees the merits of the friends. At that time, it is relevant to say that he should learn from their actions. But when he sees that he is better qualified than they are, there is nothing he can receive from the friends.

This is why they said that when the evil inclination comes and shows him the lowliness of the friends, he should go above reason. But certainly, it would be better and more successful if he could see within reason that the friends are at a higher degree than his own. With that we can understand the prayer that Rabbi Elimelech had written for us, "*Let our hearts see the virtues of our friends, and not their faults.*"

20. RABASH, Article No. 3 (1984), "Love of Friends – 1"

"And a certain man found him, and behold, he was wandering in the field. And the man asked him, saying, 'What are you seeking?' And he said, 'I seek my brothers. Tell me, I pray you, where they are feeding the flock?'" (Genesis, 37).

A man "wandering in the field" refers to a place from which the crop of the field to sustain the world should spring. And the works of the field are plowing, sowing, and reaping. It is said about that: "They that sow in tears shall reap in joy," and this is called "a field which the Lord has blessed."

Baal HaTurim explained that a person wandering in the field refers to one who strays from the path of reason, who does not know the real way, which leads to the place he should reach, as in "an ass wandering in the field." And he comes to a state where he thinks that he will never achieve the goal he should achieve.

"And the man asked him, saying, 'What are you seeking?'" meaning, "How can I help you?" "And he said: 'I seek my brethren.'" By being together with my brothers, that is, by being in a group where there is love of friends, I will be able to mount the trail that leads to the house of God.

This trail is called "a path of bestowal," and this way is against our nature. To be able to achieve it, there is no other way but love of friends, by which everyone can help his friend.

21. RABASH, Letter No. 40

And when one begins to feel the love of his friend, joy and pleasure immediately begin to awaken in him, for the rule is that a novelty entertains. His friend's love for him is a new thing for him because he always knew that he was the only one who cared for his own well-being. But the minute he discovers that his friend cares for him, it evokes within him immeasurable joy, and he can no longer care for himself, since man can toil only where he feels pleasure. And since he is beginning to feel pleasure in caring for his friend, he naturally cannot think of himself.

22. RABASH, Letter No. 40

Each gift that he gives to his friend is like a bullet that makes a hollow in the stone. And although the first bullet only scratches the stone, when the second bullet hits the same place, it already makes a notch, and the third one makes a hole.

And through the bullets that he shoots repeatedly, the hole becomes a hollow in his friend's heart of stone, where all the presents gather. And each gift becomes a spark of love until all the sparks of love accumulate in the hollow of the stony heart and become a flame.

The difference between a spark and a flame is that where there is love, there is open disclosure, meaning a disclosure to all the peoples that the fire of love is burning in him. And the fire of love burns all the transgressions one meets along the way.

23. RABASH, Article No. 14 (1988), "The Need for Love of Friends"

When the friends unite into a single unit, they receive strength to appreciate the purpose of their work—to achieve *Lishma* [for Her sake].

24. RABASH, Article No. 7 (1984), "According to What Is Explained Concerning 'Love Your Friend as Yourself'"

The advice for one to be able to increase his strength in the rule, "Love your friend," is by love of friends. If everyone is nullified before his friend and mingles with him, they become one mass where all the little parts that want the love of others unite in a collective force that consists of many parts. And when one has great strength, he can execute the love of others.

And then he can achieve the love of God.

25. RABASH, Article No. 7 (1984), "According to What Is Explained Concerning 'Love Your Friend as Yourself'"

By assembling a few people who agree that they have to achieve the love of others, when they annul themselves before one another, they are all intermingled. Thus, in each person there accumulates a great force, according to the size of the association. And then each can execute the love of others in actual fact.

26. RABASH, Article No. 17 (1986), "The Agenda of the Assembly-2"

The whole basis upon which we can receive delight and pleasure, and which is permitted for us to enjoy—and is even mandatory—is to enjoy an act of bestowal. Thus, there is one point we should work on—*appreciation of spirituality*. This is expressed in paying attention to whom I turn, with whom I speak, whose commandments I am keeping, and whose laws I am learning, meaning in seeking advice concerning how to appreciate the Giver of the Torah.

And before one obtains some illumination from above by himself, he should seek out like-minded people who are also seeking to enhance the importance of any contact with the Creator in whatever way. And when many people support it, everyone can receive assistance from his friend.

We should know that "Two is the least plural." This means that if two friends sit together and contemplate how to enhance the importance of the Creator, they already have the strength to receive enhancement of the greatness of the Creator in the form of awakening from below. And for this act, the awakening from above follows, and they begin to have some sensation of the greatness of the Creator.

According to what is written, "In the multitude of people is the King's glory," it follows that the greater the number of the collective, the more effective is the power of the collective. In other words, they produce a stronger atmosphere of greatness and importance of the Creator. At that time, each person's body feels that he regards anything that he wishes to do for holiness—meaning to bestow upon the Creator—as a great fortune, that he has been privileged with being among people who have been rewarded with serving the King. At that time, every little thing he does fills him with joy and pleasure that now he has something with which to serve the King.

To the extent that the society regards the greatness of the Creator with their thoughts during the assembly, each according to his degree originates the importance of the Creator in him. Thus, he can walk all day in the world of gladness and joy.

27. RABASH, Article No. 30 (1988), "What to Look for in the Assembly of Friends"

The friends should primarily speak together about the greatness of the Creator, because according to the greatness of the Creator that one assumes, to that extent he naturally annuls himself before the Creator. It is as we see in nature that the small one annuls before the great one, and this has nothing to do with spirituality. Rather, this conduct applies even among secular people.

In other words, the Creator made nature this way. Thus, the friends' discussions of the greatness of the Creator awaken a desire and yearning to annul before the Creator because he begins to feel longing and desire to bond with the Creator. And we should also remember that to the extent that the friends can appreciate the importance and greatness of the Creator, we should still go above reason, meaning that the Creator is higher than any greatness of the Creator that one can imagine.

We should say that we believe above reason that He leads the world in a benevolent guidance, and if one believes that the Creator wants only man's best, it makes a person love the Creator until he is rewarded with "And you will love the Lord your God with all your heart and with all your soul." And this is what a person must receive from the friends.

28. RABASH, Article No. 17 (1987), "The Meaning of the Strict Prohibition to Teach Idol Worshipers the Torah"

It is impossible to receive the influence of the society if he is not attached to the society, meaning if he does not appreciate them. To the extent that he does, he can receive from them the influence without any work, simply by adhering to the society.

29. RABASH, Article No. 2 (1984), "Concerning Love of Friends"

One must disclose the love in his heart towards the friends, since by revealing it he evokes his friends' hearts toward the friends so they, too, would feel that each of them is practicing love of friends. The benefit from that is that in this manner, one gains strength to practice love of friends more forcefully, since every person's force of love is integrated in each other's.

It turns out that where a person has one measure of strength to practice love of friends, if the group consists of ten members, then he is integrated with ten forces of the need, who understand that it is necessary to engage in love of friends.

30. RABASH, Article No. 8 (1985), "Make for Yourself a Rav and Buy Yourself a Friend – 2"

Those people agreed to unite into a single group that engages in love of friends is that each of them feels that they have one desire that can unite all their views, so as to receive the strength of love of others. There is a famous maxim by our sages, "As their faces differ, their views differ." Thus, those who agreed among them to unite into a group understood that there isn't such a great distance between them in the sense that they recognize the necessity to work in love of others. Therefore, each of them will be able to make concessions in favor of the others, and they can unite around that.

31. RABASH, Article No. 21 (1986), "Concerning Above Reason"

Only through bonding with the society and the envy that he feels toward the friends when he sees that they have better qualities than his own. It motivates him to acquire their good qualities, which he doesn't have and of which he is jealous.

Thus, through the society, he gains new qualities that he adopts by seeing that they are at a higher degree than his, and he is envious of them. This is the reason why now he can be greater than when he didn't have a society, since he acquires new powers through the society.

32. *Zohar for All*, Nasso, "Why Have I Come and There Is No Man," Items 105-106

It is written, "And let them make Me a Temple and I will dwell among them." "Let them make Me a Temple" is any Temple, for any synagogue in the world is called "a Temple." "And I will dwell among them" since the *Shechina* [Divinity] is the first to come to the synagogue.

Happy is the man who is among the first ten in the synagogue since they complete the congregation, which is no less than ten, and they are the first to be sanctified in the *Shechina*. There must be ten in the synagogue at once, and not come bit by bit so as not to delay the wholeness of the organs. All ten are as organs of one body in which the *Shechina* is present.

33. *Zohar for All*, BeShalach [When Pharaoh Sent], "And Elisha Passed Over to Shunem," Item 11

"And she said, 'I dwell among my own people.'" What is she saying? When the *Din* hangs in the world, one should not part from the collective by himself. He will not be mentioned above and he will not be known alone. This is so because when the *Din* hangs in the world, those who are known and are inscribed alone, though they are righteous, they are caught first. Hence, one must never retire from the people because the Creator's mercies are always on the whole people together. This is why she said, "I dwell among my own people," and I do not wish to part from them, as I have been doing thus far.

34. *Zohar for All*, *Truma* [Donation], "Three Colors in a Flame," Item 44

A herald comes out and says, "Happy are you, holy nation, for you do good, you cause the unification of *Yesod* (called 'good') before the Creator." It is written, "And I have done what is good in Your eyes," attaching redemption to prayer, for at that time, when reaching "Praises to God above," that color, *Netzah*, rises to the top of the chamber, that righteous, *Yesod de* ZA, awakens to bond in the place that is needed in love, in fondness, in gladness, and in good will. And all the organs, all the *Sefirot*, willingly conjoin with one another, upper ones in lower ones.

Then all the candles, all the degrees illuminate and blaze, and they are all in a single bonding in this righteous who is called "good," as it is written, "Say, 'A righteous is good.'" This unites everyone in a single bonding, and then everything is in a whisper above and below, in kissing in good will, and the matter is in a bonding of the room, in an embrace.

35. *Zohar for All*, *VaYikra* [The Lord Called], "Eat, Friends; Drink, Drink Abundantly, O Beloved" Item 37

"Eat, friends" is above, and "Drink, drink abundantly, O beloved" is below. Above is a high place, where they are in unity and in joy, where they never part from one another, meaning upper *AVI*.

They are the ones called "friends," as it is written, "And a river comes out of Eden." Eden is *Aba* and the river is *Ima*. They never part and they are always willing, united, and joyful. "Drink, drink abundantly, O beloved" means the beloved below, which are ZON, which bond for a time during the prayer, on Sabbaths and on good days, but not always, as do upper AVI.

36. *Zohar for All*, Pinhas, "Let Us Make Man in Our Image, After Our Own Likeness," Item 497

After all the craftsmen completed their work, the Creator said to them: "I have one craft to make, in which we will all participate. Join together all of you to make in it each his share, and I will partake with you, to give it of My share." It is written about it, "Let us make man in our image, after our own likeness." Sages explained that there is no man but Israel, as it is written, "And you are My sheep, the sheep of My pasture, you are men." "You are men," and not the idol worshippers. This is why it is written, "Let Israel be glad with his Maker."

37. *Zohar for All*, VaYetze [And Jacob Went Out], "Remembering and Visiting," Item 285

And she said, "I dwell among my own people." In other words, she said, "I have no wish to be mentioned above, but to put my head among the masses and not leave the public. Similarly, man should be included in the public and not stand out as unique, so the slanderers will not look at him and mention his sins.

38. *Zohar for All*, VaYera [The Lord Appeared], "And the Lord Rained on Sodom," 278

When they all unite as one, by the power of the upper one, ZA, it is then called "And the Lord [*HaVaYaH*]," which means that all is included—ZA and *Nukva* and the seventy angels below her.

39. *Zohar for All*, Haazinu, "An Apple and a Lily," Item 9

"For I proclaim the name of the Lord." The end of the verse ties the connection of faith in what is written. It is as it is written, "He is righteous and upright." That is, He is everything. He is one, without separation. Should you say that all the names in the verse are many, he repeats and says, "He," that they all rise, connect, and unite in the One. He is everything; He was, He is, He will be, and He is one. Therefore, the matters connect and the holy words of the name of the Creator unite.

40. *Degel Machaneh Ephraim*, VaEtchanan

It is written, "The Lord is one and Israel are one"; hence, they are adhered to the Creator, since it befits the One to cling to the one. And when is this? It is when Israel are bundled and attached together in complete unity. At that time, they are regarded as one, and the Creator is upon them, for He is one.

But when their hearts divide and they are apart from one another, they cannot be adhered to the One and the Creator is not on them. Rather, another God is on them. This is implied in the verse, "And you who are adhered," meaning when you are adhered and united with each other, "You are alive every one of you." When they are in one unity. Then it befits the One to cling to the one, and the one Creator is upon them.

41. *Likutei Halachot, Hoshen Mishpat, Hilchot Arev*

It is impossible to observe Torah and *Mitzvot* [commandments] except through *Arvut* [mutual responsibility], when each one becomes responsible for his friend, since the essence of observing the Torah, which is the desire, is through unity. Therefore, anyone who wants to take upon himself the burden of Torah and *Mitzvot* should be included in the whole of Israel with great unity. For this reason, at the time of the reception of the Torah, they certainly became responsible for one another, since as soon as they want to receive the Torah they must all be included as one, in order to be incorporated in the desire. At that time, each one is certainly responsible for his friend because all are important as one. Precisely by each being responsible for his friend, which is the quality of unity, precisely by this they can observe the Torah. Without it, it would be utterly impossible to observe the Torah, since the essence of love and unity is in the desire, when each one is pleased with his friend, there is no disparity of form between them, and they are all included in one desire. By this they are incorporated in the upper desire, which is the end goal of the unity.

42. *Maor VaShemesh, Devarim*

It is known that the most important is the true connection among the friends. This causes all the salvations and the sweetening of the judgments. When you gather together in love, brotherhood, and friendship. By this, all the judgments are removed and sweetened with mercy, and through the connection, complete mercy and revealed kindness are revealed in the world.

43. *Adir BaMarom 24*

Rabbi Shimon Bar Yochai was revealing the secrets of the Torah, and the friends were listening to his voice and connected with him to be in this composition; each one answer his part.

44. Rabbi Moshe Chaim Ephraim of Sudilkov, *Degel Mahaneh Ephraim*

It is good for the people of the children of Israel to always unite together in one bundle. Then, even those who are of lesser degree help their friends sanctify with more *Kedusha* [holiness] and attain more. The upper one needs the one below it, and the lower one needs the one above it. Likewise, you should always be bundled in one bundle, and then your roots will unite, as well. This is the meaning of "You will be unto Me a *Segula* [virtue/remedy]," meaning that you will be a *Segula* in the upper world, as well, when you are in one unity below.

45. Rabbi Kalonymus Kalman Halevi Epstein, *Maor VaShemesh*

It is a great tenet, from among the tenets and the roots of the work, and an opening to repentance, to unite as one and connect in love of friends, to look at one's friend—his virtues and his serving of the Creator, and not to look at his blemishes. By this, he yearns and longs to resemble him in the good deeds, and he will return to the Creator with all his heart.

46. Rabbi Nachman of Breslov, *Likutey Halachot*

It is written, "The Sanhedrin was as a round semicircle so they would see each other," for the love is mainly that they saw each other. They could not tolerate not seeing one another, for when they see each other, they receive from one another. This is the meaning of what our sages said, "Either company or death."

47. *Shem MiShmuel, Yom Kippur Tav-Reish-Ayin-Gimel* (September 1912)

Creating unity in the collective is only through pulverizing, when each one pulverizes himself and removes from himself the shell of crassness. Through the battering and pulverizing, the light of the soul shines, and there is really all of Israel; all is one.

48. *Ohev Ysrael, Likutei Masachtot*

The Creator is destined to pardon the righteous, and He sits among them. *Machol* [pardon/dancing in a circle] is in a circle, meaning that everyone will stand in a circle and the Creator is as the middle point of the circle. And each one points with his finger, "This is our God," meaning that each one will have great attainment equally from the upper *Hesed* [mercy].

49. *Likutey Halachot* [Assorted Rules], "Blessings on Seeing and Personal Blessings," Rule No. 4

The vitality is mainly through unity, by all the changes being included in the source of the unity. For this reason, "Love your friend as yourself" is the great rule of the Torah, to include in unity and peace. The vitality, sustenance, and correction of the whole of creation is mainly by people of differing views becoming included together in love, unity, and peace.

Raaiah Kook, *Orot* [*Lights*]

In each one from Israel there lives a spark of holy light inherited from his forefathers, from the holiness of the Torah and the greatness of the faith. It follows that any division between a person from Israel and his neighbor, between one collective and another, it, too, builds worlds. Since everything is improvement and construction, there is no reason to speak bitterly, but to announce the greatness that both sides are doing, and that together, they are perfecting the everlasting structure and are correcting the world. Then, according to the expansion of knowledge, the love will grow according to the intensity of the hate, and the connection will grow according to the size of the separation.

51. Raaiah Kook, *Orot* [*Lights*]

Through the separations, each individual good acquires its own color, and one color that is in the other does not press it to blur its shape. Through this, the assembly of Israel is enriched by proliferation of lights, and that proliferation itself will cause the greater and more internal peace.

52. Martin Buber, "Education and World"

It is not neutrality for which we are demanded, but rather cohesion. We are demanded not to blur the boundaries between the fellowships, but rather recognize the common reality and sharing of the test of mutual responsibility. The separation of the hearts is an illness that afflicts the nations of our time, and one who comes to heal it through compulsory fusion is making a mistake. The unity in the organic structure is lacking. For the time being, there is no cure for this except for people from different circles of views who need each other with a pure heart to exert together to reveal the common basis.

53. Raaiah Kook, *Olat Raaiah*, Part One

Unity that comes through seeking to benefit each individual for the purpose of each individual loving himself is coincidental unity, whose origin is one's love for oneself. It is unsustainable as it has no real center. Even when the unity appears to grow, it will end in a flame of hatred and civil war since each one will pull toward his own benefit. Conversely, unity that comes by recognizing the value of the higher purpose, which comes only by peace among people, its basis is love of everyone and it will last. And the more it continues, the more it will grow and strengthen.

54. Raaiah Kook, *Orot* [*Lights*]

The love of Israel must be nourished. It is unlike the natural love in every nation, which is found in its members. The basis of every nation is natural and simple, a necessity of life and congregation, the satisfaction of natural and convenient desires through a group that has close ties to one another. That desire does not need to be awakened by means of education and learning.

However, connecting the assembly of Israel is built primarily on common spiritual aspirations, which themselves require much spiritual strengthening and reinforcement in the heart of every individual, and even more so in the life of the whole public.

55. *Shem MiShmuel*, Portion *Haazinu*

The intention of creation was for all to be one bundle, to do the Creator's will. But the matter was spoiled because of the sin of *Adam HaRishon*, until even the best in those generations could not unite together in order to serve the Creator. Rather, they were individuals, alone. The correction of this matter began in the generation of Babylon, when separation occurred in the human race, meaning the beginning of the correction of gathering and assembling people to serve the Creator, which started with Abraham and his descendants. Abraham would roam and call out the name of the Creator until a great community gathered unto him, who were called "the people of the house of Abraham." Thus, the matter grew until it became the assembly of the congregation of Israel. In the future, the end of correction will be when all become one bundle to do the Creator's will wholeheartedly.

56. *Maor VaShemesh*, *Ekev*

The most important is for each and every one to annul himself completely and not think of himself as righteous or that he counts at all among the friends. He should only see that his actions do not blemish the society. Although it seems as though he is a great person, he should nonetheless look into his actions and think, "What make me great?" and annul himself completely. It is known that in every ten there is *Shechina* [Divinity], and this is a complete level. In a complete level, there are head, hands, legs, and heels. It follows that when every person regards himself as nothing in society, then he regards himself as a heel compared to the society, while they are the head, the body, and the higher organs. When each one thinks of himself in this way, they make the gates of abundance and every lushness in the world open up to them, and it is drawn the most through the person who is more regarded as "nothing" and as "a heel."

57. Rabbi Shmuel Bornstein, *Shem MiShmuel*

It is written, "Gather, be purified," for the difference between the word "gathering" of people and the word "grouping," is that the word "gathering" is more unification of the heart and soul than the word "grouping." "Grouping" can also pertain only to the body, although the views are not united. But a gathering of people is also with one heart. It is a gathering from the outside in, where they unite the most.

Therefore, the word "gathering" applies mostly to the souls, since "soul" comes from the words "desire" and "yearning." If each and every one yearns for his own benefit, although everyone wants the same thing, it is still not one view since each one wants for one's own benefit.

However, if they are complete, and also many yearn to satisfy the Creator's will, this is certainly called "complete unification," and deserves the title "gathering."

58. *Likutey Halachot* [Assorted Rules], "Synagogue Rules," Rule One

The ascent of the soul and its completeness is mainly when all the souls merge and become one, for then they rise to the *Kedusha* [holiness], since the *Kedusha* is one. Therefore, the prayer, which is regarded as the soul, depends primarily on the unity of souls. For this reason, prior to the prayer, he must take upon himself the to-do *Mitzva* [commandment] "Love your neighbor as yourself," for it is impossible to say the words of the prayer unless through peace, when we unite with all the souls of Israel. For this reason, the prayer is mainly in public and not alone, so that one will not be separated and alone, as this is the opposite of *Kedusha*. Rather, we must only unite the holy congregation together and become one. This is a prayer in public, when the souls assemble and unite, and this is the completeness of the prayer.

59. Rabbi Menachem Mendel of Vitebsk, *Pri Haaretz*, Item 30

One should always accustom oneself to install love of friends in one's heart to the bottom of one's heart, and to persist with this until his soul is adhered and they adhere to one another. When they are all as one man, the One Creator will dwell within them and will impart upon them salvations and comforts aplenty, and they will ascend in the soaring of body and soul.

60. Rabbi Nachman of Breslov, *Likutey Halachot*

The work of the Creator is mainly in the desire. Each one, to the extent that he accustoms himself to strengthen his will and yearning and longing for the Creator, with a very strong desire, to that extent he is rewarded with nearing the Creator, His law, His commandments. Each one from Israel must rise in all the ascents from degree to degree, and it is all to the extent of the strengthening of the desire, for the heart of the purpose is to be willingly incorporated in the desire, for the beginning of nearing the Creator and the final purpose are all regarded as desire, and it is impossible to be incorporated in the desire unless through unity, and love, and peace, when all of Israel are included together in love and great unity.

PART 8
The Principles of Spiritual Work in the Group

1

The Purpose of the Society

1. Baal HaSulam, "The Essence of Religion and Its Purpose"

Our final aim is to be qualified for *Dvekut* with Him—for Him to reside within us.

2. Baal HaSulam, "Matan Torah [The Giving of the Torah]," Item 16

If six hundred thousand men abandon their work for the satisfaction of their own needs and worry about nothing but standing guard so their friends will not lack a thing, and moreover, they will engage in this with great love, with their very heart and soul, in the full meaning of the *Mitzva*, "Love your friend as yourself," it is then beyond doubt that no one in the nation will need to worry about his own well-being.

Because of this, one becomes completely free of securing his own survival and can easily observe the *Mitzva*, "Love your friend as yourself," obeying all the conditions given in Items 3 and 4. After all, why would he worry about his own survival when six hundred thousand loyal lovers stand by, ready with great care to make sure he lacks nothing of his needs?

Therefore, once all the members of the nation agreed, they were immediately given the Torah, for now they were capable of observing it.

3. Baal HaSulam, "A Speech for the Completion of The Zohar"

Our sages said, "Make for yourself a rav and buy yourself a friend." This means that one can make a new environment for oneself. This environment will help him obtain the greatness of his rav through love of friends who appreciate his rav. Through the friends' discussing the greatness of the rav, each of them receives the sensation of his greatness. Thus, bestowal upon his rav becomes reception and sufficient motivation to an extent that will bring one to engage in Torah and *Mitzvot Lishma*.

It was said about this, "The Torah is acquired by forty-eight virtues, by serving of sages, and by meticulousness of friends." This is so because besides serving the rav, one needs the meticulousness of friends, as well, meaning the friends' influence, so they will influence him so he obtains the greatness of his rav. This is so because obtaining the greatness depends entirely on the environment, and a single person cannot do a thing about it whatsoever.

4. RABASH, Article No. 14 (1988), "The Need for Love of Friends"

The benefit of love of friends in a special group, where everyone has a single goal—to achieve love of the Creator.

5. RABASH, Article No. 8 (1985), "Make for Yourself a Rav and Buy Yourself a Friend - 2"

Those people agreed to unite into a single group that engages in love of friends is that each of them feels that they have one desire that can unite all their views, so as to receive the strength of love of others. There is a famous maxim by our sages, "As their faces differ, their views differ." Thus, those who agreed among them to unite into a group understood that there isn't such a great distance between them in the sense that they recognize the necessity to work in love of others. Therefore, each of them will be able to make concessions in favor of the others, and they can unite around that.

6. RABASH, Article No. 8 (1985), "Make for Yourself a Rav and Buy Yourself a Friend - 2"

"Society," when people come together and wish to bond. This can happen through equivalence of form, by everyone caring in love of others. By that, they unite and become one.

7. RABASH, Article No. 12 (1984), "Concerning the Importance of Society"

The benefits of the society—it can introduce a different atmosphere—one of working only in order to bestow.

8. RABASH, Article No. 2 (1984), "Concerning Love of Friends"

One must always remind oneself of the purpose of the society. Otherwise, the body tends to blur the goal, since the body always cares for its own benefit. We must remember that the society was established solely on the basis of achieving love of others, and that this would be the springboard for the love of God.

9. RABASH, Article No. 13 (1984), "Sometimes Spirituality Is Called 'a Soul'"

We must always awaken what the heart forgets, what is needed for the correction of the heart—*Love of friends*—whose purpose is to achieve love of others.

This is not a pleasant thing for the heart, which is called "self-love." Hence, when there is a gathering of friends, we must remember to bring up the question, meaning everyone should ask himself how much we have advanced in love of others, and how much we have done to promote us in that matter.

10. RABASH, Article No. 6 (1984), "Love of Friends – 2"

If several individuals come together with the force that it is worthwhile to abandon self-love, but without the sufficient power and importance of bestowal to become independent, without outside help, if these individuals annul before one another and all have at least potential love of the Creator, though they cannot keep it in practice, then by each joining the society and annulling oneself before it, they become one body.

For example, if there are ten people in that body, it has ten times more power than a single person does. However, there is a condition: When they gather, each of them should think that he has now come for the purpose of annulling self-love. It means that he will not consider how to satisfy his will to receive now, but will think as much as possible only of the love of others. This is the only way to acquire the desire and the need to acquire a new quality, called "the will to bestow."

And from love of friends one can reach love of the Creator, meaning wanting to give contentment to the Creator.

11. RABASH, Letter No. 8

At the end of the day, this is a group of people who have gathered in a certain place, under a certain leader, to be together. With superhuman courage they face up to all those who rise against them. Indeed, they are brave men with a strong spirit, and they are determined not to retreat one inch. They are first-class fighters, fighting the war against the inclination to their last drop of blood, and their only wish is to win the battle for the glory of His name.

12. RABASH, Article No. 17 (1987), "The Meaning of the Strict Prohibition to Teach Idol Worshipers the Torah"

It is impossible to receive the influence of the society if he is not attached to the society, meaning if he does not appreciate them. To the extent that he does, he can receive from them the influence without any work, simply by adhering to the society.

13. RABASH, Article No. 17 (1986), "The Agenda of the Assembly – 2"

Is written, "In the multitude of people is the King's glory," it follows that the greater the number of the collective, the more effective is the power of the collective. In other words, they produce a stronger atmosphere of greatness and importance of the Creator. At that time, each person's body feels that he regards anything that he wishes to do for holiness—meaning to bestow upon the Creator—as a great fortune, that he has been privileged with being among people who have been rewarded with serving the King. At that time, every little thing he does fills him with joy and pleasure that now he has something with which to serve the King.

14. RABASH, Article No. 124, "To Serve Me"

"The whole world was created only to serve me." According to the interpretation of Baal HaSulam, it means that all the faults that a person sees in others, he believes that they are his. Therefore, he has what to correct. It follows that the whole world serves him by providing him with his faults, and he does not need to look by himself. Instead, they are doing him a big favor by providing him with his flaws.

15. RABASH, Article No. 3 (1984), "Love of Friends – 1"

I seek my brethren.'" By being together with my brothers, that is, by being in a group where there is love of friends, I will be able to mount the trail that leads to the house of God.

This trail is called "a path of bestowal," and this way is against our nature. To be able to achieve it, there is no other way but love of friends, by which everyone can help his friend.

16. RABASH, Article No. 1 (1984), "Purpose of Society – 1"

We have gathered here to establish a society for all who wish to follow the path and method of Baal HaSulam, the way by which to climb the degrees of man and not remain as a beast, as our sages said (*Yevamot*, 61a) about the verse, "And you My sheep, the sheep of My pasture, are men." And Rashbi said, "You are called 'men,' and idol worshipers are not called 'men.'"

17. RABASH, Article No. 1 (1984), "Purpose of Society – 1"

We gather here—to establish a society where each of us follows the spirit of bestowing upon the Creator. And to achieve bestowal upon the Creator, we must begin with bestowal upon man, which is called "love of others."

And love of others can only be through revoking of one's self. Thus, on the one hand, each person should feel lowly, and on the other hand, be proud that the Creator has given us the chance to be in a society where each of us has but a single goal: for The *Shechina* [Divinity] to be among us.

18. RABASH, Article No. 2 (1984), "Concerning Love of Friends"

We must remember that the society was established on the basis of love of others, so each member would receive from the group the love of others and hatred of himself. And seeing that his friend is straining to annul his self and to love others would cause everyone to be integrated in their friends' intentions.

Thus, if the society is made of ten members, for example, each will have ten forces practicing self-annulment, hatred of self, and love of others.

19. RABASH, Article No. 13 (1985), "Mighty Rock of My Salvation"

Each person in the group, besides having a desire of his own, acquires desire from the friends. This is a great asset that can be obtained *only* through love of friends. However, one should take great care not to be among friends who have no desire to examine themselves, the basis of their work—whether it is to bestow or to receive—and to see if they are doing things in order to reach the path of truth, which is the way of nothing but bestowal.

Only in such a group is it possible to instill the friends with a desire to bestow, meaning that each will absorb a lack from the friends, which he himself lacks the power to bestow.

20. RABASH, Article No. 30 (1988), "What to Look for in the Assembly of Friends"

The friends should primarily speak together about the greatness of the Creator, because according to the greatness of the Creator that one assumes, to that extent he naturally annuls himself before the Creator. It is as we see in nature that the small one annuls before the great one, and this has nothing to do with spirituality. Rather, this conduct applies even among secular people.

In other words, the Creator made nature this way. Thus, the friends' discussions of the greatness of the Creator awaken a desire and yearning to annul before the Creator because he begins to feel longing and desire to bond with the Creator. And we should also remember that to the extent that the friends can appreciate the importance and greatness of the Creator, we should still go above reason, meaning that the Creator is higher than any greatness of the Creator that one can imagine.

We should say that we believe above reason that He leads the world in a benevolent guidance, and if one believes that the Creator wants only man's best, it makes a person love the Creator until he is rewarded with "And you will love the Lord your God with all your heart and with all your soul." And this is what a person must receive from the friends.

21. RABASH, Article No. 21 (1986), "Concerning Above Reason"

Only through bonding with the society and the envy that he feels toward the friends when he sees that they have better qualities than his own. It motivates him to acquire their good qualities, which he doesn't have and of which he is jealous.

Thus, through the society, he gains new qualities that he adopts by seeing that they are at a higher degree than his, and he is envious of them. This is the reason why now he can be greater than when he didn't have a society, since he acquires new powers through the society.

22. RABASH, Article No. 1, Part 2 (1984), "Purpose of Society – 2"

There should be careful watch in the society, disallowing frivolity, since frivolity ruins everything.

23. RABASH, Letter No. 42

It is written, "And the people encamped, as one man with one heart." This means that they all had one goal, which is to benefit the Creator. It follows…

We should understand how they could be as one man with one heart, since we know what our sages said, "As their faces are not similar to one another, their views are not similar to one another," so how could they be as one man with one heart?

Answer: If we are saying that each one cares for himself, it is impossible to be as one man, since they are not similar to one another. However, if they all annul their selves and worry only about the benefit of the Creator, they have no individual views, since the individuals have all been canceled and have entered the single authority.

24. Rabbi Kalonymus Kalman Halevi Epstein, *Maor VaShemesh*, *VaYechi*

The essence of the assembly is for everyone to be in one unity and for all to seek but one purpose: to find the Creator. In every ten there is the *Shechina* [Divinity]. Clearly, if there are more than ten then there is more revelation of the *Shechina*. Thus, each one should assemble with his friend and come to him to hear from him a word about the work of the Creator, and how to find the Creator. He should annul before his friend, and his friend should do the same toward him, and so should everyone do. Then, when the assembly is with this intention, then "More than the calf wants to suckle, the cow wants to nurse," and the Creator approaches them and He is with them, and great mercies and good and revealed kindness will be extended over the assembly of Israel.

25. Rabbi Nachman of Breslov, *Likutey Halachot* [Assorted Rules], *Hoshen Mishpat*, "Rules of the Guarantor"

The essence of love and unity is in the desire, when each one is pleased with his friend and there is no disparity of desire among them, and all are included in one desire, by which they are included in the upper desire, which is the purpose of the unity.

2

The Importance of the Goal

1. RABASH, Article No. 24, "The Main Thing We Need"

The main thing we need, and for which we have no fuel for the work, is that we are lacking importance of the goal. That is, we do not know how to appreciate our service so as to know to whom we are bestowing. Also, we are lacking the awareness of the greatness of the Creator, to know how happy we are that we have the privilege of serving the King, since we have nothing with which to be able to understand His greatness.

In the words of *The Zohar*, this is called "*Shechina* [Divinity] in the dust," meaning that bestowal upon Him is as important to us as dust. Naturally, we have no fuel to work, since without pleasure, there is no energy to work.

Where self-love shines, the body derives vitality from this. But in the work of bestowal, the body does not feel any pleasure in this and must naturally "collapse under its weight."

Conversely, when one feels that he is serving an important King, to the extent of the importance of the King, so is his delight and pleasure from serving Him. Hence, at that time he has fuel that can give him the power to go forward each time, since he feels that he is serving an important King.

Then, when he knows and feels to whom he bestows, to the extent that he had the strength to work with the intention of self-love, now he has the strength to work in order to bestow, since one who bestows upon an important person is regarded as receiving from him. And since the body has the strength to work for reception, in order to receive reward, likewise, in bestowing upon an important King he derives pleasure in this.

By this we will understand what is written in the "Introduction to The Study of the Ten Sefirot" concerning the matter that if she gives, and he is an important person, she is sanctified because of the pleasure of receiving from him. We are seeing something new: Bestowing upon an important person is tantamount to receiving, although there he references the essay about matrimony in the context of reception in order to bestow, at which time reception means bestowal.

From this we can understand the other side of the coin—that bestowal is called reception, and because of this he already has fuel, for if he bestows upon an important person, it is to him as though he is receiving. Therefore, he already has the power to work.

It follows that all we need is to believe in the greatness of the Creator, and then we will have the energy to work in bestowal.

2. RABASH, Article No. 30 (1988), "What to Look for in the Assembly of Friends"

The matter of obtaining greatness, it should be obtained specifically through the society.

3. RABASH, Article No. 14 (1988), "The Need for Love of Friends"

When the friends unite into a single unit, they receive strength to appreciate the purpose of their work—to achieve *Lishma* [for Her sake].

4. RABASH, Article No. 28 (1987), "What Is Do Not Add and Do Not Take Away in the Work?"

He must believe above reason and imagine that he has already been rewarded with faith in the Creator that is felt in his organs, and he sees and feels that the Creator leads the entire world as the good who does good. Although when he looks within reason he sees the opposite, he should still work above reason and it should appear to him as though he can already feel in his organs that so it really is, that the Creator leads the world as the good who does good.

Here he acquires the importance of the goal, and from here he derives life, meaning joy at being near to the Creator. Then a person can say that the Creator is good and does good, and feel that he has the strength to tell the Creator, "You have chosen us from among all nations, You have loved us and wanted us," since he has a reason to thank the Creator. And to the extent that he feels the importance of spirituality, so he establishes the praise of the Creator.

5. RABASH, Article No. 17 (1986), "The Agenda of the Assembly-2"

There is one point we should work on—*appreciation of spirituality*.

6. RABASH, Article No. 28 (1987), "What Is Do Not Add and Do Not Take Away in the Work?"

Once man has come to feel the importance of spirituality, which is called "One should always establish the praise of the Creator," then is the time when he must shift to the left line. He must criticize how he truly feels within reason the importance of the King, if he is truly willing to work only for the sake of the Creator.

When he sees within reason that he is bare and destitute, that state when he sees the importance of spirituality, but only above reason, that calculation can create in him deficiency and pain for being in utter lowliness. Then he can make a heartfelt prayer for what he lacks.

3

Love of Friends

1. Baal HaSulam, Letter No. 11

I will also ask that you make great efforts in love of friends, to devise tactics that can increase the love among the friends and revoke the lust for bodily matters from among you, as this is what casts hate, and between those who give contentment to their Maker there shall be no hatred. Rather, there are great compassion and love between them.

2. Baal HaSulam, Letter No. 49

I order you to begin to love one another as yourselves with all your might, to ache with your friends' pains, and rejoice in your friends' joys as much as possible. I hope that you will keep these words of mine and execute this matter to the fullest.

3. Baal HaSulam, Letter No. 47

I have established for you conducts by which you can still hang on and not turn back.
    And the single most special one among them is the *Dvekut* of friends. I sincerely promise that this love is able. And I shall remind you of every good thing that you need. And if you nonetheless braced yourselves in that, you would certainly go from strength to strength on the rungs of holiness.

4. Baal HaSulam, Letter No. 47

Let me remind you the validity of love of friends in spite of everything at this time, for it is upon this that our right to exist depends, and upon this our near-to-come success is measured.
    Hence, turn away from all the imaginary engagements and set your hearts on thinking thoughts and devising proper tactics to truly connect your hearts as one, so the words "Love your friend as yourself" will literally come true in you, for a verse does not reach beyond the literal, and you will be cleaned by the thought of love that will cover all crimes. Test me in that, and begin to truly connect in love, and then you will see, "the palate will taste".

5. Baal HaSulam, Letter No. 13

Indeed, I feel all of you together, that today has been replaced for you with tomorrow, and instead of "now," you say "later." There is no cure for this but to exert to understand that mistake and distortion—that one who is saved by the Creator is saved only if he needs salvation today. One who can wait for tomorrow will obtain his salvation after his years, God forbid.

This happened to you due to negligence in my request to exert in love of friends, as I have explained to you in every possible way that this cure is enough to recompense for all your faults.

6. Baal HaSulam, "A Speech for the Completion of The Zohar"

Our sages said, "Make for yourself a rav and buy yourself a friend." This means that one can make a new environment for oneself. This environment will help him obtain the greatness of his rav through love of friends who appreciate his rav. Through the friends' discussing the greatness of the rav, each of them receives the sensation of his greatness. Thus, bestowal upon his rav becomes reception and sufficient motivation to an extent that will bring one to engage in Torah and *Mitzvot Lishma*.

It was said about this, "The Torah is acquired by forty-eight virtues, by serving of sages, and by meticulousness of friends." This is so because besides serving the rav, one needs the meticulousness of friends, as well, meaning the friends' influence, so they will influence him so he obtains the greatness of his rav. This is so because obtaining the greatness depends entirely on the environment, and a single person cannot do a thing about it whatsoever.

7. Baal HaSulam, Letter No. 2

I shall advise you to evoke within you fear of the coolness of the love between us. Although the intellect denies such a depiction, think for yourself—if there is a tactic by which to increase love and one does not increase it, that, too, is considered a flaw. It is like a person who gives a great gift to his friend. The love that appears in his heart during the act is not like the love that remains in the heart after the fact. Rather, it gradually wanes each day until the blessing of the love can be entirely forgotten. Thus, the receiver of the gift must find a tactic every day to make it new in his eyes each day. This is all our work—to display love between us, each and every day, just as upon receiving, meaning to increase and multiply the intellect with many additions to the core, until the additional blessings of now will be touching our senses like the essential gift at first. This requires great tactics, set up for the time of need.

8. Baal HaSulam, "The Arvut [Mutual Guarantee]," Item 17

This is to speak of the *Arvut* [mutual guarantee], when all of Israel became responsible for one another. Because the Torah was not given to them before each and every one from Israel was asked if he agreed to take upon himself the *Mitzva* [commandment] of loving others in the full measure expressed in the words "Love your friend as yourself," as explained in the article "Matan Torah," Items 2 and 3, examine it thoroughly there. This means that each and every one in Israel would take upon himself to care and work for each member of the nation, to satisfy all their needs, no less than the measure imprinted in him to care for his own needs.

Once the whole nation unanimously agreed and said, "We will do and we will hear," each member of Israel became responsible that no member of the nation will lack anything. Only then did they become worthy of receiving the Torah, and not before.

With this collective responsibility, each member of the nation was liberated from worrying about the needs of his own body and could observe the *Mitzva*, "Love your friend as yourself" in the fullest measure and give all that he had to any needy person since he no longer cared for the existence of his own body, as he knew for certain that he was surrounded by six hundred thousand loyal lovers standing ready to provide for him.

9. Baal HaSulam, "The Essence of Religion and Its Purpose"

When one comes to love others, he is in direct *Dvekut*, which is equivalence of form with the Maker, and along with it man passes from his narrow world, filled with pain and impediments, to an eternal and broad world of bestowal upon the Creator and upon people.

10. Baal HaSulam, "Introduction to The Book of Zohar," Item 19

Bear in mind that the *Mitzvot* between man and man come before the *Mitzvot* between man and the Creator since bestowing upon one's friend brings one to bestow upon the Creator.

11. Baal HaSulam, "Matan Torah [The Giving of the Torah]," Item 15

Our sages said, "The Torah and *Mitzvot* were given only so as to cleanse Israel," which is the cleansing of the body until one acquires a second nature defined as "love for others," meaning the one *Mitzva*: "Love your friend as yourself," which is the final aim of the Torah.

12. Baal HaSulam, "The Arvut [Mutual Guarantee]," Item 22

The impression he gets when engaging in *Mitzvot* between man and man, since one is obliged to perform all the *Mitzvot Lishma* [for Her sake], without any hope for self-love, meaning that no light or hope returns to him through his trouble in the form of reward or honor, etc. Here, at this exalted point, the love of the Creator and the love of his friend unite and actually become one.

13. Baal HaSulam, "Matan Torah [The Giving of the Torah]," Item 15

If six hundred thousand men abandon their work for the satisfaction of their own needs and worry about nothing but standing guard so their friends will not lack a thing, and moreover, they will engage in this with great love, with their very heart and soul, in the full meaning of the *Mitzva* [commandment],

"Love your friend as yourself," it is then beyond doubt that no one in the nation will need to worry about his own well-being.

Because of this, one becomes completely free of securing his own survival and can easily observe the *Mitzva*, "Love your friend as yourself." After all, why would he worry about his own survival when six hundred thousand loyal lovers stand by, ready with great care to make sure he lacks nothing of his needs?

Therefore, once all the members of the nation agreed, they were immediately given the Torah, for now they were capable of observing it.

14. Baal HaSulam, "The Essence of Religion and Its Purpose"

The crass, undeveloped person does not recognize egoism as bad at all. Therefore, he uses it openly, without any shame or restraint, stealing and murdering in broad daylight wherever he can. The somewhat more developed sense some measure of their egoism as bad and are at least ashamed to use it in public, stealing and killing openly. But in secret, they still commit their crimes, but are careful that no one will see them.

The even more developed sense egoism as so loathsome that they cannot tolerate it in them and reject it completely, as much as they detect of it, until they cannot, and do not want to enjoy the labor of others. Then begin to emerge in them sparks of love of others, called "altruism," which is the general attribute of goodness.

But that, too, evolves gradually. First develops love and desire to bestow upon one's family and kin, as in the verse, "Do not ignore your own flesh." When one develops further, one's attribute of bestowal expands to all the people around him, being one's townspeople or one's nation. And so one adds until he finally develops love for the whole of humanity.

15. Baal HaSulam, "The Writings of the Last Generation"

The religious form of all the nations should first obligate its members to bestowal upon each other to the extent that (the life of one's friend will come before one's own life), as in "Love your friend as yourself." One will not take pleasure in society more than a struggling friend. This will be the collective religion of all the nations that will come within the framework of communism. However, besides this, each nation may follow its own religion and tradition, and one must not interfere in the other.

16. Baal HaSulam, "Introduction to The Book of Zohar," Item 19

When all human beings agree to abolish and eradicate their will to receive for themselves and have no other desire but to bestow upon their friends, all worries and jeopardy in the world would cease to exist. We would all be assured of a whole and wholesome life, since each of us would have a whole world caring for us, ready to satisfy our needs.

Yet, while each of us has only a desire to receive for oneself, this is the source of all the worries, suffering, wars, and slaughter we cannot escape. They weaken our bodies with all sorts of sores and maladies.

17. Baal HaSulam, "The Peace"

There is no other cure for humanity but to assume the commandment of Providence to bestow upon others in order to bring contentment to the Creator in the measure of the two verses.

The first is "love your friend as yourself," which is the attribute of the work itself. This means that the measure of work to bestow upon others for the happiness of society should be no less than the measure imprinted in man to care for his own needs. Moreover, he should put his fellow person's needs before his own.

The other verse is, "And you will love the Lord your God with all your heart, with all your soul, and with all your might." This is the goal that must be before everyone's eyes when laboring for one's friend's needs. This means that he labors and toils only to be liked by the Creator, as He said, "and they do His will."

"And if you wish to listen, you will feed on the fruit of the land," for poverty and torment and exploitation will be no more in the land, and the happiness of each and every one will rise ever higher, beyond measure.

18. Baal HaSulam, "The Love of God and the Love of Man"

When one completes one's work in love of others and bestowal upon others through the final point, one also completes one's love for the Creator and bestowal upon the Creator. And there is no difference between the two, for anything that is outside one's body, meaning outside one's self-interest, is judged equally—either to bestow upon one's friend or to bestow contentment upon one's Maker. This is what Hillel HaNasi assumed, that "Love your friend as yourself" is the ultimate goal in the practice, as it is the clearest nature and form to man.

We should not be mistaken about actions, since they are set before his eyes. He knows that if he puts the needs of his friend before his own needs, then he is in the quality of bestowal. For this reason, he does not define the goal as "And you will love the Lord your God with all your heart and with all your soul and with all your might," for indeed they are one and the same, since he should also love his friend with all his heart and with all his soul and with all his might, as this is the meaning of the words "as yourself." He certainly loves himself with all his heart and soul and might, and with the Creator, he may deceive oneself, but with his friend it is always spread out before his eyes.

19. Baal HaSulam, Letter No. 13

You should know that there are many sparks of holiness in each one in the group. When you assemble all the sparks of holiness to one place, as brothers, with love and friendship, you will certainly have a very high level of holiness for a while, from the light of life.

20. Baal HaSulam, "The Freedom"

The Torah and the *Mitzvot* were given only to purify Israel, to develop in us the sense of recognition of evil imprinted in us at birth, which is generally defined as our self-love, and to come to the pure good defined as "love of others," which is the one and only passage to the love of the Creator.

21. RABASH, Article No. 8 (1985), "Make for Yourself a Rav and Buy Yourself a Friend – 2"

Those people agreed to unite into a single group that engages in love of friends is that each of them feels that they have one desire that can unite all their views, so as to receive the strength of love of others. There is a famous maxim by our sages, "As their faces differ, their views differ." Thus, those who agreed among them to unite into a group understood that there isn't such a great distance between them in the sense that they recognize the necessity to work in love of others. Therefore, each of them will be able to make concessions in favor of the others, and they can unite around that.

22. RABASH, Article No. 3 (1984), "Love of Friends – 1"

"And a certain man found him, and behold, he was wandering in the field. And the man asked him, saying, 'What are you seeking?' And he said, 'I seek my brothers. Tell me, I pray you, where they are feeding the flock?'" (Genesis, 37).

A man "wandering in the field" refers to a place from which the crop of the field to sustain the world should spring. And the works of the field are plowing, sowing, and reaping. It is said about that: "They that sow in tears shall reap in joy," and this is called "a field which the Lord has blessed."

Baal HaTurim explained that a person wandering in the field refers to one who strays from the path of reason, who does not know the real way, which leads to the place he should reach, as in "an ass wandering in the field." And he comes to a state where he thinks that he will never achieve the goal he should achieve.

"And the man asked him, saying, 'What are you seeking?'" meaning, "How can I help you?" "And he said: 'I seek my brethren.'" By being together with my brothers, that is, by being in a group where there is love of friends, I will be able to mount the trail that leads to the house of God.

This trail is called "a path of bestowal," and this way is against our nature. To be able to achieve it, there is no other way but love of friends, by which everyone can help his friend.

"And the man said: 'They are departed hence.'" And RASHI interpreted that they had departed themselves from the brotherhood, meaning they do not want to bond with you. This, in the end, caused Israel's exile in Egypt. And to be redeemed from Egypt, we must take it upon ourselves to enter a group that wants to be in love of friends, and by that we will be rewarded with exodus from Egypt and the reception of the Torah.

23. RABASH, Article No. 2 (1984), "Concerning Love of Friends"

We must remember that the society was established on the basis of love of others, so each member would receive from the group the love of others and hatred of himself. And seeing that his friend is straining to annul his self and to love others would cause everyone to be integrated in their friends' intentions.

Thus, if the society is made of ten members, for example, each will have ten forces practicing self-annulment, hatred of self, and love of others.

24. RABASH, Article No. 2, (1984), "Concerning Love of Friends"

One must disclose the love in his heart towards the friends, since by revealing it he evokes his friends' hearts toward the friends so they, too, would feel that each of them is practicing love of friends. The benefit from that is that in this manner, one gains strength to practice love of friends more forcefully, since every person's force of love is integrated in each other's.

It turns out that where a person has one measure of strength to practice love of friends, if the group consists of ten members, then he is integrated with ten forces of the need, who understand that it is necessary to engage in love of friends.

25. RABASH, Article No. 30 (1988), "What to Look for in the Assembly of Friends"

When a group of people gathers and wishes to work together on love of friends, they must all help one another as much as they can. And there are many discernments about that, since not everyone is the same, meaning that what one needs, the other does not. However, there is one thing in which all are equal: Each and every one of the friends needs high spirits. That is, when the friends are not in a good mood, they are not all the same in their needs. Rather, each has his own reason for being unhappy. Therefore, each one must contemplate how he can bring about a good mood to the other.

26. RABASH, Article No. 1 (1984), "Purpose of Society – 1"

When a person performs one of the *Mitzvot* [commandments] of the Creator, one should aim that this *Mitzva* will bring him pure thoughts that he will bestow upon the Creator by keeping God's *Mitzvot*. It is as our sages said, "Rabbi Hanania Ben Akashia says, 'The Creator wanted to cleanse Israel; hence, He gave them plentiful Torah and *Mitzvot*.'"

And this is why we gather here—to establish a society where each of us follows the spirit of bestowing upon the Creator. And to achieve bestowal upon the Creator, we must begin with bestowal upon man, which is called "love of others."

And love of others can only be through revoking of one's self. Thus, on the one hand, each person should feel lowly, and on the other hand, be proud that the Creator has given us the chance to be in a society where each of us has but a single goal: for The *Shechina* [Divinity] to be among us.

27. RABASH, Article No. 2 (1984), "Concerning Love of Friends"

If each of them does not show the society that he is practicing love of friends, then one lacks the force of the group.

This is so because it is very hard to judge one's friend favorably. Each one thinks that he is righteous and that only he engages in love of friends. In that state, one has very little strength to practice love of others.

28. RABASH, Article No. 13 (1984), "Sometimes Spirituality Is Called "a Soul"

We must always awaken what the heart forgets, what is needed for the correction of the heart—*Love of friends*—whose purpose is to achieve love of others.

This is not a pleasant thing for the heart, which is called "self-love." Hence, when there is a gathering of friends, we must remember to bring up the question, meaning everyone should ask himself how much we have advanced in love of others, and how much we have done to promote us in that matter.

29. RABASH, Article No. 30 (1988), "What to Look for in the Assembly of Friends"

The matter of the assembly of friends. When they gather, what should they discuss? First, the goal must be clear to everyone—this gathering must yield the result of love of friends, that each of the friends will be awakened to love the other, which is called "love of others." However, this is only a result. To beget this lovely offspring, actions must be taken to produce the love.

30. RABASH, Letter No. 5

You should do more in love of friends. It is impossible to achieve lasting love, unless through *Dvekut* [adhesion], meaning that the two of you will unite in a tight bond. This can be only if you try to "undress" the clothing in which the inner soul is placed. This clothing is called "self-love," for only this clothing separates two points. But if we walk on the straight path, the two points—which are discerned as two lines that refute one another—become a middle line that contains both lines together.

And when you feel that you are at war, each of you will know and feel that he needs the help of his friend, and without him, his own strength will wane, as well. Then, when you understand that you must save your life, each of you will forget he has a body he must preserve, and you will both be tied by the thought of how to defeat the enemy.

31. RABASH, Article No. 13 (1985), "Mighty Rock of My Salvation"

A person has a desire within him, which comes from himself. In other words, even when he is alone and there are no people around him to affect him, or from whom to absorb some desire, he receives an awakening and craves to be a servant of the Creator. But his own desire is certainly not big enough for him not to need to enhance it so he can work with it to obtain the spiritual goal. Therefore, there is a way—just like in corporeality—to enhance that desire through people on the outside who will compel him to follow their views and their spirit.

This is done by bonding with people whom he sees that also have a need for spirituality. And the desire that those people on the outside have begets a desire in him, and thus he receives a great desire for spirituality. In other words, in addition to the desire that he has from within, he receives a desire for spirituality that they beget in him, and then he acquires a great desire with which he can reach the goal.

Hence, the issue of *love of friends* is where each person in the group, besides having a desire of his own, acquires desire from the friends. This is a great asset that can be obtained *only* through love of friends. However, one should take great care not to be among friends who have no desire to examine themselves, the basis of their work—whether it is to bestow or to receive—and to see if they are doing things in order to reach the path of truth, which is the way of nothing but bestowal.

Only in such a group is it possible to instill the friends with a desire to bestow, meaning that each will absorb a lack from the friends, which he himself lacks the power to bestow, and wherever he walks, he is eagerly searching for a place where perhaps someone will be able to give him the power to bestow.

Hence, when he comes into a group where everyone is thirsty for the power to bestow, everyone receives this strength from everyone else. This is considered receiving strength from the outside in addition to the small power that he has within him.

32. RABASH, Letter No. 40

There is a prayer for it—that the Creator will help him by making him feel the love of his friend and make his friend close to his heart.

33. RABASH, Article No. 7 (1984), "According to What Is Explained Concerning 'Love Your Friend as Yourself'"

The advice for one to be able to increase his strength in the rule, "Love your friend," is by love of friends. If everyone is nullified before his friend and mingles with him, they become one mass where all the little parts that want the love of others unite in a collective force that consists of many parts. And when one has great strength, he can execute the love of others.

And then he can achieve the love of God. But the condition is that each will annul before the other.

34. RABASH, Letter No. 24

You must awaken the heart of the friends until the flame rises by itself, as our sages said about it, "When you mount the candles." By that, you will be rewarded with awakening the love of the Creator upon us.

35. RABASH, Article No. 13 (1986) "Come Unto Pharaoh 2"

We should know that we were given love of friends to learn how to avoid blemishing the King's honor. In other words, if he has no other desire except to give contentment to the King, he will certainly blemish the King's honor, which is called "Passing on *Kedusha* [holiness/sanctity] to the external ones." For this reason, we mustn't underestimate the importance of the work in love of friends, for by that he will learn how to exit self-love and enter the path of love of others. And when he completes the work of love of friends, he will be able to be rewarded with love of the Creator.

36. RABASH, Letter No. 40

It is about time that we started moving forward toward our sacred goal like mighty strong men. It is known that the paved road that leads to the goal is love of friends, by which one shifts to love of the Creator. And in the matter of love, it is through "Buy yourself a friend." In other words, through actions, one buys one's friend's heart. And even if he sees that his friend's heart is like a stone, it is no excuse. If he feels that he is suitable for being his friend in the work, then he must buy him through deeds.

Each gift (and a gift is determined as such when he knows that his friend will enjoy it, whether in words, in thought, or in action. However, each gift must be out in the open, so that his friend will know about it, and with thoughts, one does not know that his friend was thinking of him. Hence, words are required, too, meaning he should tell him that he is thinking of him and cares about him. And that, too, should be about what his friend loves, meaning what his friend likes. One who doesn't like sweets, but pickles, cannot treat his friend to pickles, but specifically to sweets, since this is what his friend likes. And from that, we should understand that something could be unimportant to one, but more important than anything to another.) that he gives to his friend is like a bullet that makes a hollow in the stone. And although the first bullet only scratches the stone, when the second bullet hits the same place, it already makes a notch, and the third one makes a hole.

And through the bullets that he shoots repeatedly, the hole becomes a hollow in his friend's heart of stone, where all the presents gather. And each gift becomes a spark of love until all the sparks of love accumulate in the hollow of the stony heart and become a flame.

The difference between a spark and a flame is that where there is love, there is open disclosure, meaning a disclosure to all the peoples that the fire of love is burning in him. And the fire of love burns all the transgressions one meets along the way.

37. RABASH, Article No. 1 (1985), "Make for Yourself a Rav and Buy Yourself a Friend – 1"

It is said, "*Make* for yourself a *rav* and *buy* yourself *a friend*"; both have to exist. In other words, each should regard the other as a friend, and then there is room for buying. This means that each must pay with concessions to the other, like a father concedes his rest, works for his son, spends money for his son, and all is because of the love.

However, there it is natural love. The Creator gave natural love for raising children so there would be persistence to the world. If, for instance, the father would raise the children because it is a *Mitzva* [commandment], his children would have food, clothing, and other things that are necessary for children to the extent that a person is committed to keep all the *Mitzvot* [plural of *Mitzva*]. At times he would keep the *Mitzvot*, and at times he would only do the very minimum, and his children could starve to death.

This is why the Creator gave parents natural love for their children, so there would be persistence to the world. This is not so with love of friends. Here everyone must make great efforts by himself to create the love of friends in his heart.

It is the same with "And buy yourself a friend." Once he understands, at least intellectually, that he needs help and he cannot do the holy work, to the extent that he understands it in his mind, he begins to buy, to make concessions for his friend's sake.

This is so because he understands that the work is primarily in bestowing upon the Creator. However, it is against his nature because man is born with a desire to receive only for his own benefit. Hence, we were given the *cure* by which to go from self-love to love of others, and by that he can arrive at the love of the Creator.

38. RABASH, Article No. 19 (1984), "You Stand Today, All of You"

"You stand today, all of you ...your heads, your tribes, your elders and your officers, every man of Israel." It begins with the plural form, "You" [plural form in Hebrew], and ends in singular form, "Every man of Israel." The author of the book, *Light and Sun*, explains that by using plural form and singular form, it points to the matter of love of friends. Although among you are "heads, tribes," etc., still no one sees greater merit in himself than in any man of Israel. Instead, everyone is equal in that no one complains about the other. For this reason, from above, too, they are treated accordingly, and this is why great abundance is imparted below.

39. RABASH, Article No. 7 (1984), According to What Is Explained Concerning 'Love Your Friend as Yourself'"

The meaning of "righteous"? It is those who want to keep the rule, "Love your friend as yourself." Their sole intention is to exit self-love and assume a different nature of love of others.

40. RABASH, Article No. 17, Part 1 (1984), "Concerning the Importance of Friends"

If one has love of friends, the rule in love is that you want to see the friends' merits and not their faults. Hence, if one sees some fault in one's friend, it is not a sign that his friend is at fault, but that the seer is at fault, meaning that because his love of friends is flawed, he sees faults in his friend.

Therefore, now he should not see to his friend's correction. Rather, he himself needs correction. It follows from the above-said that he should not see to the correction of his friend's faults, which he sees in his friend, but he himself needs to correct the flaw he has created in the love of friends. And when he corrects himself, he will see only his friend's merits and not his faults.

41. RABASH, Article No. 9 (1984), "One Should Always Sell the Beams of His House"

Each of them had a spark of love of others, but the spark could not ignite the light of love to shine in each, so they agreed that by uniting, the sparks would become a big flame.

42. RABASH, Letter No. 40

Through the wearing out of the hearts, even of the strongest ones, each will bring out warmth from the walls of his heart, and the warmth will ignite the sparks of love until a clothing of love will form. Then, both of them will be covered under one blanket, meaning a single love will surround and envelop the two of them, as it is known that *Dvekut* [adhesion] unites two into one.

And when one begins to feel the love of his friend, joy and pleasure immediately begin to awaken in him, for the rule is that a novelty entertains. His friend's love for him is a new thing for him because he always knew that he was the only one who cared for his own well-being. But the minute he discovers that his friend cares for him, it evokes within him immeasurable joy, and he can no longer care for himself, since man can toil only where he feels pleasure. And since he is beginning to feel pleasure in caring for his friend, he naturally cannot think of himself.

43. RABASH, Article No. 162, "Love of Others"

I look at one tiny dot, called "love of others," and I think about it: What can I do in order to benefit people? As I look at the general public, I see the suffering of individuals, illnesses and pains, and the suffering of individuals inflicted by the collective, meaning wars among nations. And besides prayer, there is nothing to give.

44. RABASH, Article No. 273, "The Mightiest of the Mighty"

Who is the mightiest of the mighty? He who makes his foe his friend" (*Avot de Rabbi Natan*, Chapter 23).
In ethics, we should interpret that "mighty" is "one who conquers his inclination" (*Avot*, Chapter 4). That is, he works with the good inclination and subdues the evil inclination.

The mightiest of the mighty is one who works also with the evil inclination, as our sages said, "With all your heart—with both your inclinations" (*Berachot* 54), where the evil inclination, too, serves the Creator. It follows that he makes his foe, the evil inclination, his friend. And since the evil inclination is also serving the Creator, it follows that here he has more work, for which he is called "the mightiest of the mighty."

45. RABASH, Letter No. 8

Once I have acquired this above-mentioned clothing, sparks of love promptly begin to shine within me. The heart begins to long to unite with my friends, and it seems to me that my eyes see my friends, my ears hear their voices, my mouth speaks to them, the hands embrace, the feet dance in a circle, in love and joy together with them, and I transcend my corporeal boundaries. I forget the vast distance between my friends and me, and the outstretched land for many miles will not stand between us.

It is as though my friends are standing right within my heart and see all that is happening there, and I become ashamed of my petty acts against my friends. Then, I simply exit the corporeal vessels and it seems to me that there is no reality in the world except my friends and I. After that, even the "I" is cancelled and is immersed, mingled in my friends, until I stand and declare that there is no reality in the world—only the friends.

46. RABASH, Article No. 21 (1986), "Concerning Above Reason"

The only thing that can help a person emerge from self-love and be rewarded with the love of the Creator is the love of friends.

47. RABASH, Article No. 13 (1986), "Come unto Pharaoh – 2"

We were given the *Mitzva* [commandment/good deed] of "love thy friend as thyself," and Rabbi Akiva said, "This is the great rule of the Torah" (*Beresheet* Rabba, *Parasha* 24). In other words, by working in love of friends, a person accustoms himself to exit self-love and achieve love of others.

48. RABASH, Assorted Notes, Article No. 759, "Man as a Whole"

One must know that love is bought by actions. By giving his friends gifts, each gift that he gives to his friend is like an arrow and a bullet that makes a hole in his friend's heart. Although his friend's heart is like a stone, still, each bullet makes a hole. And from many holes, a hollow is created, and the love of the giver of the gifts enters in this place.

The warmth of the love draws to him his friend's sparks of love, and then the two loves weave into a garment of love that covers both of them. This means that one love surrounds and envelops them, and then they two become one person because the clothing that covers them is a single garment.

49. RABASH, Assorted Notes, Article No. 759, "Man as a Whole"

After one receives the garment of love from another, he enjoys only the love of the other and forgets about self-love. At that time, each of them begins to receive pleasure only from caring for his friend, and they cannot worry about themselves because one can labor only where he can receive pleasure.

Since he is enjoying love of others and receives pleasure specifically from that, he will take no pleasure in caring for himself.

50. RABASH, Letter No. 34

It is said in Rosh Hashanah prayer [Hebrew New Year's Eve service], "And they shall all become one society." In that state, it will be easier "To do Your will wholeheartedly."

This is so because while there is not just one society, it is difficult to work wholeheartedly. Instead, part of the heart remains for its own benefit and not for the benefit of the Creator. It is said about it in Midrash Tanhuma, "'You stand today,' as the day at times shines and at times darkens, so it is with you. When it is dark for you, the light of the world will shine for you, as it is said, 'And the Lord shall be unto you an everlasting light.' When? When you are all one society, as it is written, 'Alive every one of you this day.'

Usually, if someone takes a pile of branches, can he break them all at once? But if taken one at a time, even a baby can break them. Similarly, you find that Israel will not be redeemed until they are all one society, as it is said, 'In those days and at that time, says the Lord, the children of Israel shall come, they and the sons of Judah together.' Thus, when they are united, they receive the face of Divinity."

51. RABASH, Article No. 17 (1984), "Concerning the Importance of Friends"

How can one consider one's friend greater than himself when he can see that his own merits are greater than his friend's, that he is more talented and has better natural qualities? There are two ways to understand this:

1. He is going with faith above reason: once he has chosen him as a friend, he appreciates him above reason.
2. This is more natural—within reason. If he has decided to accept the other as a friend, and works on himself to love him, then it is natural with love to see only good things. And even though there are bad things in one's friend, he cannot see them, as it is written, "love covers all transgressions."

52. *Zohar for All*, *Aharei Mot* [After the Death], "Behold, How Good and How Pleasant," Items 65-66

"Behold, how good and how pleasant it is for brothers to also sit together." These are the friends as they sit together, and are not separated from each other. At first, they seem like people at war, wishing to kill one another. Then they return to being in brotherly love.

The Creator says about them, "Behold, how good and how pleasant it is for brothers to also sit together." The word, "also," comes to include the *Shechina* with them. Moreover, the Creator listens to their words and He has contentment and delights with them, as it is written, "Then those who feared the Lord spoke to one another, and the Lord listened and heard it, and a book of remembrance was written before Him."

And you, the friends who are here, as you were in fondness and love before, henceforth you will also not part until the Creator rejoices with you and summons peace upon you. And by your merit there will be peace in the world, as it is written, "For the sake of my brothers and my friends let me say, 'Let peace be in you.'"

53. Rabbi Kalonymus Kalman Halevi Epstein, *Maor VaShemesh*, *Devarim*

It is known that the most important is the true connection among the friends. This causes all the salvations and the sweetening of the judgments. When you gather together in love, brotherhood, and friendship. By this, all the judgments are removed and sweetened with mercy, and through the connection, complete mercy and revealed kindness are revealed in the world.

54. Ramchal, *Mesilat Yesharim*

The Torah came and included made a rule in which everything is included: "Love your neighbor as yourself," as yourself, without any difference; as yourself, without any divisions, without ploys or machination, truly as yourself.

55. Rabbi Kalonymus Kalman Halevi Epstein, *Maor VaShemesh*

The advice and counsel for serving the Creator and the correct path of repentance is to unite our hearts in love of friends and look at the advantage of the other in serving the Creator and in knowing his Creator, and not to see his flaw. Repentance is mainly in uniting with each and every one in love and in one heart, to serve the Creator shoulder to shoulder. By this, the world of repentance and the world of mercy and the world of good will awaken. This is an intimation, as was said, "And all are reviewed in one review." This means that we should adhere and connect to one another and close into one another in the heart of each one. This is implied in the word "one," to become one bundle to serve the Creator wholeheartedly.

56. Rabbi Menachem Mendel of Vitebsk, *Pri Haaretz*, Item 30

By and large, the thing that leads to preserving and guarding from Him, to be saved from all the incidents of cessation of adhesion between him and his Maker, is connection, love, and true peace in adhesion of friends. Indeed, were it not for this, he would be in concealment of the face, may the Creator will save him from this. One should always accustom oneself to install love of friends in one's heart to the bottom of one's heart, and to persist with this until his soul is adhered and they adhere to one another. When they are all as one man, the One Creator will dwell within them and will impart upon them salvations and comforts aplenty, and they will ascend in the soaring of body and soul.

57. Rabbi Kalonymus Kalman Halevi Epstein, *Maor VaShemesh*, "Intimations of Song of Songs"

The heart and root of the work of the Creator is love of friends. Through it, one can come to the true work of the Creator. When one sees that his friends aspire and yearn to serve the Creator in Torah and prayer, it will excite his heart to connect with them, and all his friends' actions will seem to him as greater than his own actions.

5. Rav Chaim Vital, *Shaar HaGilgulim*, Introduction, 38

My teacher cautioned me and all the friends who were with him in that society to take upon ourselves the commandment to-do of "Love your neighbor as yourself," and to aim to love each one from Israel as his own soul, for by this his prayer would rise comprising all of Israel and will be able to ascend and make a correction above. Especially, our love of friends, each and every one of us should include himself as though he is an organ of those friends. My teacher sternly cautioned me about this matter.

59. Rabbi Kalonymus Kalman Halevi Epstein, *Maor VaShemesh*

It is appropriate and correct to hold tight to love of friends and draw them closer to the path of the Creator for by this one can extend illumination for many days, by bringing them closer to the work of the Creator.

60. Rabbi Kalonymus Kalman Halevi Epstein, *Maor VaShemesh*

It is a great tenet, from among the tenets and the roots of the work, and an opening to repentance, to unite as one and connect in love of friends, to look at one's friend—his virtues and his serving of the Creator, and not to look at his blemishes. By this, he yearns and longs to resemble him in the good deeds, and he will return to the Creator with all his heart.

61. Rabbi Kalonymus Kalman Halevi Epstein, *Maor VaShemesh*

You will find the tenet and the wedge on which everything depends, and the content of the paths of correct repentance, through love of friends and adhesion of friends, and drawing near to the righteous of the generation. By this he will come to complete surrender since he will see the work of his friends, the great burning in their hearts, and excitement to serve the Creator, and by this he will learn to do as they do. He will recognize his blemishes and will repent in complete repentance.

62. Rabbi Kalonymus Kalman Halevi Epstein, *Maor VaShemesh*

The main rule by which to truly come to the path of the Creator is through adhesion with friends. By gathering together, as each one annuls before his friend when he sees his friend's merit in Torah, *Mitzvot* [commandments], and good deeds, he becomes lowly in his own eyes, and his friend is greater than him, and he loves each and every one, and wishes and yearns to truly permeate each and every one out of joy and love. This is done by adhesion of friends.

63. Jerusalem Talmud, *Nedarim*

"Love your neighbor as yourself" is a great rule in the Torah.

64. Maimonides, *Mishneh Torah, Shoftim*, "Rules of Grieving," Chapter 14

"Love your neighbor as yourself." All the things you want others to do for you, do them to your brothers … This is the law that Abraham Our Father established and the way of mercy in which he behaved, giving food and drinks to passersby and accompanying them.

12. Rabbi Nachman of Breslov, *Likutey Halachot* [Assorted Rules]

"Love your friend as yourself" is the great rule of the Torah, to include in unity and peace. The vitality, sustenance, and correction of the whole of creation is mainly by people of differing views becoming included together in love, unity, and peace.

66. Maimonides, *The Book of Commandment*

The commandment we have been commanded, to love one another as we love ourselves, and for my compassion and love for my brothers with faith to be as my love and compassion for myself, with one's wealth and body and all that he has or desires, and all that I want for myself, I will likewise want for him, and all that I do not want for myself or for my friends, I will likewise not want for him, as was said, "Love your neighbor as yourself."

67. Rav Chaim Vital, *Shaarey Kedusha*, Part 2, Gate 4

Our sages said (*Yoma* 9b), "In the Second Temple, there were righteous and great sages, and it was ruined only because of unfounded hatred, and the end has been prolonged and concealed only because of unfounded hatred. Moreover, all other transgressions, he commits them only at that time, but unfounded hatred is always in the heart, and at every single moment he transgresses in 'Do not hate' and the cancelling of the commandment to-do of "Love your neighbor as yourself." Moreover, it was said about this commandment that it is a great rule in the Torah, that all of it depends on it, and that Moses was rewarded with all his merits only because he loved Israel and sympathized with their afflictions.

68. Raaiah Kook, "Israel's Destiny and Nationality"

We are obliged to have the measure of great and wondrous love for one another.

69. Raaiah Kook, *Letters*

If I had arms around the world, dear brothers, I would embrace you with love.

70. Rabbi Kalonymus Kalman Halevi Epstein, *Maor VaShemesh*

It is written in the *Midrash* (about Amalek), "Which *Karcha* [encountered] you along the way," from the word *Kerirut* [coolness], meaning he put out their fire of love and chilled it. At first, they were in warmth and excited about loving one another, but Amalek brought them into coolness and chilled their love from loving one another. How did he cool them? Through arrogance and pride, for Amalek has the *Gematria* of *Ram* [high], meaning arrogance, haughtiness, and pride.

The main thing that brings one to love another is by each one being lowly and despicable in his own eyes, always finding faults in everything he does, and seeing the righteousness and actions of one's friend as very great in his eyes. By this he comes to love his friend and be in unity with him. Conversely, if he is great in his own eyes and feels proud, he naturally sees his friend's faults and by this comes to hate him, since his friend is very lowly in his eyes. And Amalek chilled Israel from the warmth and excitement to love one another that they had before to love one another.

71. Rabbi Israel Meir HaCohen, *HaChafetz Chaim, Zachor LeMiriam*, 11

When is the Creator fond of creation? When Israel are united together and there is no envy, hatred, or competition among them whatsoever, when each one thinks only of his friend's benefit. At that time, the Creator is happy with His creation, and it was said about this, "The Lord will delight in

His deeds." By intimation, we can thereby explain the verse, "Love your neighbor as yourself; I am the Lord." That is, if you love your neighbor as yourself, I the Lord will be within you, and I will love you both.

72. Rabbi Menachem Mendel of Vitebsk, *Pri HaAretz* [*Fruit of the Land*], Letter No. 30

The thing that leads to keeping from ignorance and cessation of *Dvekut* [adhesion] is the connection and love, and true peace in *Dvekut* among friends.

4

Annulment and Subjugation

1. Baal HaSulam, "The Freedom"

The children of Israel were rewarded with complete *Dvekut* on that holy occasion, their vessels of reception were completely emptied of any worldly possession and they were adhered to Him in equivalence of form. This means that they had no desire for any self-possession, but only to the extent that they could bestow contentment, so their Maker would delight in them.

And since their will to receive had clothed in an image of that object, it had clothed in it and bonded with it into complete oneness. Therefore, they were certainly liberated from the angel of death, for death is necessarily an absence and negation of the existence of something. But only while there is a spark that wishes to exist for its own pleasure is it possible to say about it that that spark does not exist because it has become absent and died.

However, if there is no such spark in man, but all the sparks of his selfness clothe in bestowal of contentment upon their Maker, then he neither becomes absent nor dies. For even when the body is annulled, it is only annulled with respect to self-reception, in which the will to receive is dressed and can only exist in it.

However, when he achieves the aim of creation and the Creator receives pleasure from him, since His will is done, man's essence, which clothes in His contentment, is granted complete eternity, like Him. Thus, he has been rewarded with freedom from the angel of death.

2. Baal HaSulam, *Shamati*, Article No. 203, "Man's Pride Shall Bring Him Low"

"Man's pride shall bring him low." It is known that a man is born in utter lowliness. However, if the lowly one knows his place then he does not suffer for being low, as this is his place. For example, the legs are not at all degraded because they are always walking in the litter and must carry the full weight of the body, whereas the head is always above, since because they know their place. Hence, the legs are not at all degraded and do not suffer for being on a low degree.

Yet, if they had wanted to be on top but were forced to be below, they would feel the suffering. This is the meaning of "Man's pride shall bring him low." If one wants to remain in one's lowliness, he does not feel any lowliness, meaning no suffering that "Man is born a wild ass's colt." But when they want to be proud they feel the lowliness, and then they suffer.

Suffering and lowliness go hand in hand. If one feels no suffering, it is considered that he has no lowliness. It is precisely according to the measure of one's pride, or that he wants to be but is not, so he feels the lowliness. This lowliness later becomes a *Kli* [vessel] for pride, as it is written, "The Lord reigns; He wears pride." If they adhere to the Creator, they have a clothing of pride, as it is written, "Pride and glory are to the One who lives forever." Those who adhere to the One who lives forever have much pride. And to the extent that he feels the lowliness, and according to the measure of his suffering, so he is rewarded with the clothing of the Creator.

3. Baal HaSulam, *Shamati*, Article No. 42, "What Is the Acronym Elul in the Work?"

Is written, "Annul your will before His will," meaning annul the will to receive in you before the desire to bestow, which is the will of the Creator. This means that one will revoke self-love before the love of the Creator. This is called "annulling oneself before the Creator," and it is called *Dvekut* [adhesion]. Subsequently, the Creator can shine inside your will to receive because it is now corrected in the form of receiving in order to bestow.

This is the meaning of "so that He will annul His will before your will." It means that the Creator annuls His will, meaning the *Tzimtzum* that was because of the disparity of form. Now, however, when there is already equivalence of form, hence now there is expansion of the light into the desire of the lower one, which has been corrected in order to bestow, for this is the purpose of creation, to do good to His creations, and now it can be carried out.

Now we can interpret the verse, "I am my beloved's." It means that by the "I" annulling my will to receive before the Creator in the form of all to bestow, it obtains "and my beloved is mine." It means that My beloved, who is the Creator, "is mine," He imparts me the delight and pleasure found in the thought of creation.

4. Baal HaSulam, *Shamati*, Article No. 19, "What Is 'The Creator Hates the Bodies,' in the Work?"

One should believe that the obstructions of the will to receive in the work come to him from above. One is given the force to discover the will to receive from above because there is room for work precisely when the will to receive awakens.

Then one has close contact with the Creator to help him turn the will to receive to work in order to bestow. One must believe that from this extends contentment to the Creator, from his praying to Him to draw him near in the manner of *Dvekut* [adhesion], called "equivalence of form," discerned as the annulment of the will to receive, so it is in order to bestow. The Creator says about this, "My sons defeated Me." That is, I gave you the will to receive, and you ask Me to give you a desire to bestow instead.

5. Baal HaSulam, *Shamati*, Article No. 17, What Does It Mean that the Sitra Achra Is Called "*Malchut* without a Crown"?

It is known that calculation is implemented only in *Malchut*, who calculates the height of the degree (through the *Ohr Hozer* [reflected light] in her). Also, it is known that *Malchut* is called "the will to receive for oneself."

When she annuls her will to receive before the Root, and does not want to receive but only to give to the Root, like the Root, which is a desire to bestow, then *Malchut*, called *Ani* [I], becomes *Ein* [nothing], with an *Aleph*. Only then does she extend the light of *Keter* to build her *Partzuf* and becomes twelve *Partzufim* of *Kedusha*.

However, when she wants to receive for herself, she becomes the evil *Ayin* [eye]. In other words, where there was a combination of *Ein*, meaning annulment before the root, which is *Keter*, it has become *Ayin* (meaning seeing and knowing within reason).

This is called "adding." It means that one wants to add knowing to faith, and work within reason. In other words, she says that it is more worthwhile to work within reason, and then the will to receive will not object to the work.

This causes a flaw, meaning that they were separated from the *Keter*, called "the desire to bestow," which is the Root. There is no longer the matter of equivalence of form with the Root, called *Keter*. For this reason, the *Sitra Achra* is called "*Malchut* without a Crown." It means that *Malchut* of the *Sitra Achra* does not have *Dvekut* [adhesion] with the *Keter*. For this reason, they have only eleven *Partzufim*, without *Partzuf Keter*.

This is the meaning of what our sages said, "ninety nine died of evil eye," meaning because they have no quality of *Keter*. It means that the *Malchut* in them, being the will to receive, does not want to annul before the Root, called *Keter*. This means that they do not want to make of the *Ani* [I], called "the will to receive," a quality of *Ein* [nothing], which is the annulment of the will to receive.

Instead, they want to add. And this is called "the evil *Ayin*" [eye]. That is, where there should be *Ein* with *Aleph* [the first letter in the word *Ein*], they insert the evil *Ayin* [eye, the first letter in the word]. Thus, they fall from their degree due to lack of *Dvekut* with the Root.

This is the meaning of what our sages said, "Anyone who is proud, the Creator says, 'He and I cannot dwell in the same abode,'" as he makes two authorities. However, when one is in a state of *Ein*, and annuls himself before the Root, meaning that one's sole intention is only to bestow, like the Root, you find that there is only one authority here—the authority of the Creator. Then, all that one receives in the world is only in order to bestow upon the Creator.

This is the meaning of what he had said, "The whole world was created only for me, and I, to serve my Maker." For this reason, I must receive all the degrees in the world so that I can give everything to the Creator, which is called "to serve my Maker."

6. Baal HaSulam, *Shamati*, Article No. 27, "What Is 'The Lord Is High and the Low Will See'? – 1"

How can there be equivalence with the Creator when man is the receiver and the Creator is the Giver? The verse says about this, "The Lord is high and the low…"

If one annuls oneself, then one has no authority that separates him from the Creator. In that state, one "will see," meaning he is imparted *Mochin de Hochma*, "and the high will know from afar." However, someone with pride, meaning one who has his own authority, is distanced, since he lacks the equivalence.

Lowliness is not considered one's lowering oneself before others. This is humbleness, and one feels wholeness in this work. Rather, lowliness means that the world despises him. Precisely when people despise, it is considered lowliness, for then he does not feel any wholeness, for it is a law that what people think influences a person.

Therefore, if people respect him, he feels whole; and those whom people despise think of themselves as low.

7. Baal HaSulam, Letter No. 21

Your letter from the thirteenth of *Tishrey* [the first Hebrew month]. What you write me about, "I recognize how much I need external mortifications to correct my externality," thus far your words, I say that you neither need mortifications nor to correct the externality. Who taught you this new law? It must be that you are not as attached to me as before, and are therefore learning other ways.

Know that you have no other trusted friend in your whole life, and I advise you not to correct your externality at all, but only your internality, for only your internality is destined to be corrected. And the main reason why the internality is corrupted due to the proliferation of sins is the filth, whose sign is pride and self-importance. That filth fears no mortification in the world. On the contrary, it relishes them because the self-importance and pride increase and strengthen by the mortification.

But if you do wish to cleanse the sins off you, you should engage in annulment of self-importance instead of the mortifications, meaning to feel that you are the lowest and the worst of all the people in the world. It requires much learning and education to understand this, and each time you should test yourself to see if you are not fooling and deceiving yourself. It also helps to lower yourself before your friend in practice.

However, you should be mindful that you lower yourself only before the right people. So if you wish to engage in it in practice, you can annul yourself before our group, and not before strangers, God forbid. However, you must know for certain that you are the worst and the lowest of all the people in the world, as this is the truth.

Indeed, my advice is straightforward and easy, and even a weak person can keep it to the fullest, for it does not wear out the strength of the body, and it is the complete purity. Although I have not spoken to you about it, it was because you did not need it so, since while you were with me in the same place, you would gradually recognize your lowliness anyway, without any learning or actions. But now that you are not with me in my place, you must engage in annulment of the self-importance in the manner just mentioned.

8. Baal HaSulam, *Shamati*, Article No. 83, "Concerning the Right Vav and the Left Vav"

In any state one is in, he can be a servant of the Creator since he does not need anything, but does everything above reason. It turns out that one does not need any *Mochin* with which to be the servant of the Creator.

Now we can interpret what is written, "Set up a table before me, against my enemies." A table means, as it is written, "and sent her out of his house, and she departed his house, and went" (Deuteronomy 24:1-2). A *Shulchan* [table] is like *VeShlacha* [and sent her], meaning exit from the work.

We should interpret that even during the exits from the work, meaning in a state of decline, one still has a place to work. This means that when one prevails above reason during the declines, and says that the descents, too, were given to him from above, by this the enemies are canceled. This is so because the enemies thought that through the declines the person will reach utter lowliness and escape the campaign, but in the end the opposite occurred—the enemies were canceled.

This is the meaning of what is written, "the table that is before the Lord," that precisely in this manner does he receive the face of the Creator. This is the meaning of subduing all the judgments, even the harshest judgments, since he assumes the burden of the kingdom of heaven at all times. That is, he always finds a place for work, as it is written that Rabbi Shimon Bar-Yochai said, "There is no place to hide from You."

9. Baal HaSulam, *Shamati*, Article No. 40, "What Is the Measure of Faith in the Rav?"

It is known that there is a right path and a left path. Right comes from the words "to the right," referring to the verse, "And he believed in the Lord." The Targum says, "To the right, when the rav says to the disciple to take the right path."

Right is normally called "wholeness," and left, "incompleteness," that corrections are missing there. In that state the disciple must believe the words of his rav, who tells him to walk in the right line, called "wholeness."

And what is the "wholeness" by which the disciple should walk? It is that one should depict to oneself as if he has already been rewarded with whole faith in the Creator, and already feels in his organs that the Creator leads the whole world in the form of "The Good Who Does Good," meaning that the whole world receives only good from Him.

Yet, when one looks at oneself, he sees that he is poor and indigent. In addition, when he observes the world, he sees that the entire world is tormented, each according to his degree.

One should say about that, "They have eyes but they see not." "They" means that as long as one is in multiple authorities, called "they," they do not see the truth. What are the multiple authorities? As long as one has two desires, even though he believes that the entire world belongs to the Creator, but something belongs to man, too.

But in truth, one must annul one's authority before the authority of the Creator and say that one does not want to live for oneself, and the only reason that he wants to exist is in order to bring contentment to the Creator. Thus, by this one annuls his own authority completely, and then he is in the singular authority, the authority of the Creator. Only then can he see the truth, how the Creator leads the world by the quality of good and doing good.

As long as he is in multiple authorities, meaning when he still has two desires in both mind and heart, he is unable to see the truth. Instead, he must go above reason and say, "they have eyes," but they do not see the truth.

10. Baal HaSulam, Letter No. 45

A student should be in true annulment before the teacher, in the full sense of the word, for then he unites with him and he can perform salvations in his favor.

11. Baal HaSulam, *Shamati*, Article No. 96, "What Is Waste of Barn and Winery, in the Work?"

The purpose of the work is in the literal and nature, since in this work he no longer has room to fall lower down, since he is already placed on the ground. This is so because he does not need greatness because to him it is always like something new. That is, he always works as though he had just begun to work. And he works in the form of accepting the burden of the kingdom of heaven above reason. The basis, upon which he built the order of the work, was in the lowest manner, and all of it was truly above reason. Only one who is truly naïve can be so low as to proceed without any basis on which to establish his faith, literally with no support.

Additionally, he accepts this work with great joy, as though he had had real knowledge and vision on which to establish the certainty of faith. And to that exact measure of above reason, to that very measure as though he had reason. Hence, if he persists in this way, he can never fall. Rather, he can always be in gladness, by believing that he is serving a great King.

This is the meaning of the verse, "The one lamb you shall offer in the morning; and the other lamb you shall offer at dusk. ... according to the meal-offering of the morning, and according to the drink-offering thereof." This means that that gladness that he had while he was sacrificing his sacrifice, when it was a morning for him, as morning is called "light," meaning that the light of the Torah was shining for him in utter clarity. In that same gladness, he was making his sacrifice, meaning his work, even though for him it was like evening.

This means that even though he did not have any clarity in the Torah and the work, he still did everything gladly, since he worked above reason. Hence, he could not measure from which state the Creator derives more contentment.

12. Baal HaSulam, *Shamati*, Article No. 19, "What Is 'The Creator Hates the Bodies,' in the Work?"

Sometimes one despises this work of assuming the burden of the kingdom of heaven, which is a time of a sensation of darkness, when one sees that no one can save him from the state he is in but the Creator. Then he takes upon himself the kingdom of heaven above reason, as an ox to the burden and as a donkey to the load. One should be glad that now he has something to give to the Creator, and the Creator enjoys him having something to give to the Creator. But one does not always have the strength to say that this is beautiful work, called "adornment," but he despises this work. This is a harsh condition for one to be able to say that he chooses this work over the work of whiteness, meaning that he does not sense a taste of darkness during the work, but then one feels a taste in the work. It means that then he does not have to work with the will to receive to agree to take upon himself the kingdom of heaven above reason. If he does overcome himself and can say that this work is pleasant to him that now he is observing the *Mitzva* [commandment] of faith above reason, and he accepts this work as beauty and adornment, this is called "A joy of *Mitzva*."

13. Baal HaSulam, *Shamati*, Article No. 19, What Is "The Creator Hates the Bodies," in the Work?

The farther the thing is from clothing, the higher it is. One can feel in the most abstract thing, called "the absolute zero," since there man's hand does not reach.

This means that the will to receive can grip only in a place where there is some expansion of light. Before one purifies one's *Kelim* [vessels] so as to not blemish the light, he is unable for the light to come to him in a form of expansion in the *Kelim*. Only when one marches on the path of bestowal, in a place where the will to receive is not present, whether in mind or in heart, there the light can come in utter completeness. Then the light comes to him in a sensation that he can feel the exaltedness of the upper light.

However, when one has not corrected the *Kelim* to work in order to bestow, when the light expands, it must be restricted and shine only according to the purity of the *Kelim*. Hence, at that time, the light appears to be in utter smallness. Therefore, when the light is abstracted from clothing in the *Kelim*, the light can shine in utter completeness and clarity without any restrictions for the sake of the lower one.

It follows that the importance of the work is precisely when one comes to a state of zero, when one sees that he annuls his whole existence and being, for then the will to receive has no power. Only then does one enter the *Kedusha*.

14. Baal HaSulam, *Shamati*, Article No. 118, "To Understand the Matter of the Knees that Have Bowed to Baal"

There is the discernment of a wife, and there is the discernment of a husband. A wife is considered that "she has nothing but what her husband gives her," and a husband is considered extending abundance into his own aspect. Knees are considered "bowing," as it is written, "unto You every knee shall bow."

There are two discernments in bowing:

1. One who bows before one who is greater, and although he does not know his merit, but believes that he is great, he therefore bows before him;
2. When he knows his greatness and merit in utter clarity.
   There are also two discernments considering the faith in the greatness of the upper one:
3. He believes that he is great because he has no other choice, that is, he has no way to know his greatness.
4. He has a way to know his greatness in utter certainty, but he still chooses the path of faith because "It is the glory of God to conceal a thing." This means that although there are sparks in his body that want specifically to know His greatness, and not be as a beast, he still chooses faith for the above reason.

It follows that one who has no other choice, and chooses faith, is considered a woman, female—"he grew as weak as a female"—and she only receives from her husband. But one who has a choice yet struggles to go by the path of faith is called "a man of war." Hence, those who choose faith when they had the option of walking by the way of knowing, called *Baal* [husband/Canaanite god], are called "which have not bowed to Baal." This means that they did not surrender to the work of *Baal*, considered "knowing," but chose the path of faith.

15. Baal HaSulam, *Shamati*, Article No. 121, "She Is Like Merchant-Ships"

"Man shall not live on bread alone, but on what proceeds out of the mouth of the Lord." This means that the life of *Kedusha* [holiness] in a person does not come specifically from drawing closer, from entries, meaning admissions into *Kedusha*, but also from the exits, from the removals. This is so because through the dressing of the *Sitra Achra* in one's body, and its claims, "She is all mine," with a just argument, one is awarded permanent faith by overcoming these states.

This means that one should dedicate everything to the Creator, that is, that even the exits stem from Him. When he is rewarded, he sees that both the exits and the entries were all from Him. This forces him to be humble, since he sees that the Creator does everything, the exits as well as the entries.

This is the meaning of what is said about Moses, that he was humble and patient—that one must tolerate the lowliness, meaning that in each degree one should keep the lowliness. The minute he leaves the lowliness, he immediately loses all the degrees of Moses he had already achieved.

This is the meaning of patience. Lowliness exists in everyone, but not every person feels that lowliness is a good thing. It turns out that we do not want to suffer. However, Moses tolerated the humbleness, which is why he was called "humble," since the lowliness made him glad.

16. Baal HaSulam, *Shamati*, Article No. 5, "Lishma Is an Awakening from Above, and Why Do We Need an Awakening from Below?"

If one works with faith above reason, coercively, and the body becomes accustomed to this work against the desire of his will to receive, then he has the means by which to come to work that will be with the purpose of bringing contentment to his Maker, since the primary requirement from a person is to come to *Dvekut* [adhesion] with the Creator through his work, which is discerned as equivalence of form, where all his actions are in order to bestow.

This is as it is written, "Then shall you delight in the Lord." The meaning of "Then" is that first, in the beginning of his work, he did not have pleasure. Instead, his work was coercive.

But afterward, when he has already accustomed himself to work in order to bestow and not examine himself—if he is feeling a good taste in the work—but believes that he is working to bring contentment to his Maker through his work, he should believe that the Creator accepts the work of the lower ones regardless of how and how much is the form of their work. In everything, the Creator examines the intention, and this brings contentment to the Creator. Then one is rewarded with "delight in the Lord."

Even during the work of the Creator he will feel delight and pleasure since now he really does work for the Creator because the effort he made during the coercive work qualifies him to be able to truly work for the Creator. You find that then, too, the pleasure he receives relates to the Creator, meaning specifically for the Creator.

17. Baal HaSulam, *Shamati*, Article No. 143, "Only Good to Israel"

"Only good to Israel, God is to the pure in heart." It is known that "only" and "just" are diminutives. This means that in every place the Torah writes "only" and "just," it comes to diminish.

Therefore, in work matters we should interpret it as when one diminishes oneself and lowers himself. Lowering applies when one wants to be proud, meaning wants to be in *Gadlut* [greatness/adulthood]. This means that he wants to understand every single thing, that his soul craves seeing and hearing in everything, but he still lowers himself and agrees to go with his eyes shut and keep Torah and *Mitzvot* in utter simplicity. This is "good to Israel." The word *Yashar El* [Israel] is the letters of *Li Rosh* [the head (mind) is mine].

This means that he believes he has a mind of *Kedusha* [holiness] although he is only discerned as "just," meaning that he is in a state of diminution and lowliness. And he says about this "just" that it is absolute good. Then the verse, "God is to the pure in heart" comes true in him, meaning that he is awarded a pure heart. And this is the meaning of "and I will take away the stony heart from your flesh, and I will give you a heart of flesh." The heart of flesh is *Mochin de VAK*, called *Mochin* of clothing, which comes from the upper one. *Mochin de GAR*, however, should come from the lower one, through the scrutinies of the lower one.

The issue of *VAK de Mochin* and *GAR de Mochin* requires explanation: There are many discernments of *VAK* and *GAR* in each degree. And perhaps he is referring to what he wrote in several places, that the *Katnut*, called "*GE* of the lower one," rise to *MAN* through the *Kli* that raises *MAN*, called "*AHP* of the upper one." It therefore follows that the upper one raises the lower one. And then, to receive the *GAR* of the lights and the *AHP* of the *Kelim*, the lower one should rise by itself.

18. RABASH, Article No. 1 (1984), "Purpose of Society – 2"

We need a society that will form a great force so we can work together on annulling the will to receive, called "evil," as it hinders the achievement of the goal for which man was created.

For this reason, society must consist of individuals who unanimously agree that they must achieve it. Then, all the individuals become one great force that can fight against itself, since everyone is integrated in everyone else. Thus, each person is founded on a great desire to achieve the goal.

To be integrated in one another, each person should annul himself before the others. This is done by each seeing the friends' merits and not their faults. But one who thinks that he is a little higher than his friends can no longer unite with them.

19. RABASH, Article No. 128, "Exalt the Lord Our God"

"Exalt the Lord our God and bow before His holy mountain, for the Lord our God is holy."

"Exalt" means that if one wants to know the exaltedness and greatness of the Creator, we can obtain this only through *Dvekut* [adhesion] and equivalence of form. Thus, what is "equivalence of form" and how does one achieve equivalence of form?

"Bow before His holy mountain." Bowing means surrendering. It is when one lowers his reason and says that what the reason understands or does not understand, I annul and subjugate it. Before which quality do I subjugate it? Before "His holy mountain."

Har [mountain] means *Hirhurim* [reflections], meaning thoughts. "His holy," for "holy" means separated from the matter. This means that he removes himself from the desire of reception. "Bow" means submitting the body, even though it disagrees, and taking upon oneself only thoughts of *Kedusha* [holiness]. This is the meaning "Bow before His holy mountain."

Why must we submit ourselves to thoughts of *Kedusha*, meaning retire from receiving in order to receive? It is because "The Lord our God is holy," for the Creator only bestows. For this reason, one must be in equivalence of form with the Creator, and by this we can obtain the exaltedness of the Creator. Afterward, we can achieve the attainment of the exaltedness of the Lord our God.

20. RABASH, Article No. 19 (1984), "You Stand Today, All of You"

One should walk on the path of truth—to say, "My current state, being in utter lowliness, means that I was deliberately thrown out from above to know if I truly wish to do the holy work in order to bestow, or if I wish to be God's servant because I find it more rewarding than other things."

Then, if one can say, "Now I want to work in order to bestow and I do not want to do the holy work to receive some gratification in the work. Instead, I will settle for doing the work of holiness like any man of Israel—praying or taking a lesson on the daily portion. And I don't have time to think with which intent I study or pray, but I will simply observe the actions without any special intent." At that time, he will reenter the holy work because now he wishes to be God's servant without any preconditions.

This is the meaning of what is written, "You stand today, all of you," meaning everything you went through, all the states you have experienced—whether states of *Gadlut* or states of less than *Gadlut*, which were considered intermediate or so. You take all those details and you do not compare one degree to another because you do not care for any reward, but only for doing the Creator's will. He has commanded us to observe *Mitzvot* [commandments] and to study Torah, and this is what we do, like any common man of Israel. In other words, the state he is in right now is as important to him as when he thought he was in a state of *Gadlut*. At that time, "The Lord your God makes with you this day."

This means that then the Creator makes a covenant with him. In other words, precisely when one accepts His work without any conditions and agrees to do the holy work without any reward, which is called "unconditional surrender," this is the time when the Creator makes a covenant with him.

21. RABASH, Article No. 12 (1989), "What Is a Groom's Meal?"

A person should accept faith above reason even though he has no feeling and no excitement about taking upon himself the burden of the kingdom of heaven. Nevertheless, he should agree with that state and say that this must be the will of the Creator that he will work and serve Him in this lowliness, so he does not mind what elation he feels about this faith because about himself, meaning his own benefit, he has no concern, but only about the benefit of the Creator. If He wants him to remain in that state, he accepts this unconditionally. This is called "unconditional surrender."

22. RABASH, Article No. 6 (1984), "Love of Friends – 2"

If several individuals come together with the force that it is worthwhile to abandon self-love, but without the sufficient power and importance of bestowal to become independent, without outside help, if these individuals annul before one another and all have at least potential love of the Creator, though they cannot keep it in practice, then by each joining the society and annulling oneself before it, they become one body.

For example, if there are ten people in that body, it has ten times more power than a single person does. However, there is a condition: When they gather, each of them should think that he has now come for the purpose of annulling self-love. It means that he will not consider how to satisfy his will to receive now, but will think as much as possible only of the love of others. This is the only way to acquire the desire and the need to acquire a new quality, called "the will to bestow."

And from love of friends one can reach love of the Creator, meaning wanting to give contentment to the Creator.

23. RABASH, Article No. 1 (1984), "Purpose of Society – 1"

We gather here—to establish a society where each of us follows the spirit of bestowing upon the Creator. And to achieve bestowal upon the Creator, we must begin with bestowal upon man, which is called "love of others."

And love of others can only be through revoking of one's self. Thus, on the one hand, each person should feel lowly, and on the other hand, be proud that the Creator has given us the chance to be in a society where each of us has but a single goal: for The *Shechina* [Divinity] to be among us.

24. RABASH, Article No. 5 (1987), "What Is the Advantage in the Work More than in the Reward?"

It is written in *The Zohar*, "For the whole of the Torah is the names of the Creator." Also, a complete man is one who has been rewarded with "The Torah and the Creator and Israel are one." Therefore, indeed, greeting the *Shechina* is very important because the purpose is for man to achieve this degree.

But to come to greet the *Shechina* requires prior preparation, for one to be fit for it. In the words of our sages, this is called "As He is merciful, so you are merciful." This is the interpretation of the verse, "and to cleave unto Him, cleave unto His attributes." It means, as explained in the book Matan Torah [The Giving of the Torah], that only by a person working in love of others can he achieve *Dvekut* [adhesion] with the Creator. There are many names to this: "Instilling of the *Shechina*," "attainment the Torah," "greeting the *Shechina*," etc.

The main preparation, which is called "labor," is that one must prepare oneself to annul one's authority, meaning one's self. We can call this hospitality [greeting guests], meaning that he cancels the view of landlords and craves the view of Torah, which is called "annulling of authority." Naturally, he becomes the guest of the Creator, who is the Host of the entire world.

25. RABASH, Article No. 38 (1990), "What Is, 'A Cup of Blessing Must Be Full,' in the Work?"

We should discern between speech and mute in the work. Speech means revealing, when a person already has *Yenika* in spirituality, and he feels that he is suckling from *Kedusha*, for Nursing on milk indicates *Hassadim*, for the quality of *Hesed* [mercy] is bestowal, when a person is rewarded with vessels of bestowal and all his actions are for the sake of the Creator and he has no concerns for his own benefit. This is regarded as the quality of *Hesed*.

However, before the *Yenika* there is *Ibur*, meaning that the upper one corrects him. This can be when a person is like an embryo in its mother's womb, where the embryo annuls before the mother and has no view of its own, but as our sages said, "An embryo is its mother's thigh, eats what its mother eats," and has no authority of its own to ask any questions. Rather, it does not merit a name. This is called "mute," when he has no mouth to ask questions.

This is so when a person can go with his eyes shut, above reason, and believe in the sages and go all the way. This is called *Ibur*, when he has no mouth. *Ibur* means as it is written (*The Study of the Ten Sefirot*, Part 8, Item 17), "The level of *Malchut*, which is the most restricted *Katnut* [smallness/infancy] possible, is called *Ibur*. It comes from the words *Evra* [anger] and *Dinin* [Aramaic: judgments], as it is written, 'And the Lord was impregnated in me for your sake.'"

We should interpret the meaning of "anger and judgments." When a person must go with this eyes shut, above reason, the body resists this work. Hence, the fact that a person always has to overcome, this is called "anger, wrath, and trouble," since it is hard work to always overcome and annul before the upper one, for the upper one to do with him what the upper one wants. This is called *Ibur*, which is the most restricted *Katnut* possible.

26. RABASH, Article No. 136, "The Binding of Isaac"

The binding of Isaac, when Abraham, who is the right line, which is above reason, tied the left line, which is the mind that criticizes everything, it gave him a general picture of the situation he was in. He left all the "left" and took upon himself the quality of "right," which is above reason. By this he was later rewarded with the middle line.

That is, there is a difference between receiving the right line before he sees the left line, to a state where he renews the right line after he has seen the state of the left. "Right," which is above reason, is called "devotion," since he cancels all the reason he acquired from the left line and goes above reason, and then he is rewarded with the middle line.

27. RABASH, Letter No. 65

The main thing in the work is that there is no giving of half a thing from heaven. Otherwise, it could happen that if a person repented half way he would receive assistance from above for half the work.

But since there is no giving of half a thing from heaven, a person must pray to the Creator to give him complete help. This means that during his prayer, a person sets what is in his heart in order, since prayer is work in the heart, so a person must decide that he wants the Creator to give him a desire to completely annul before Him, meaning not leave any desire under his own authority, but that all the desires in him will be only to give glory to the Creator.

Once he decides on complete annulment, he asks the Creator to help him execute it. This means that although in the mind and the desire he sees that the body disagrees with him annulling all his desires before the Creator instead of for his own sake, he should pray to the Creator to help him want to annul before Him with all the desires, leaving no desire for himself. This is called a "complete prayer," meaning that he wishes that the Creator will give him a complete desire without any compromises to himself, and he asks of the Creator to help him always be with his righteousness.

28. RABASH, Article No. 821, "We Will Do and We Will Hear – 2"

How can an intelligent and knowledgeable person say that his mind will be annulled before each and every one, while he knows and feels that he is a hundred times higher than his friend?

However, there is a discernment of "part," and there is a discernment of "all." The collective is higher than the individual, and one must annul before each and every part, in that he is part of the "all." In other words, the whole of Israel, although they do not have such great importance individually, with respect to the collective, each one is very important from the perspective of the whole collective.

One must annul his personal needs before the needs of the collective, and since man must annul his view and thought before the Creator, he must accustom himself in externality, called "doing." This is called "We will do." All those annulments will influence him so he can annul his mind and thought before the Creator.

29. RABASH, Letter No. 42

It is written, "And the people encamped, as one man with one heart." This means that they all had one goal, which is to benefit the Creator. It follows…

We should understand how they could be as one man with one heart, since we know what our sages said, "As their faces are not similar to one another, their views are not similar to one another," so how could they be as one man with one heart?

Answer: If we are saying that each one cares for himself, it is impossible to be as one man, since they are not similar to one another. However, if they all annul their selves and worry only about the benefit of the Creator, they have no individual views, since the individuals have all been canceled and have entered the single authority.

This is the meaning of what is written, "The view of landlords is opposite from the view of Torah." It is so because the view of Torah is cancelling the authority, as our sages said, "'If a man dies in a tent,' the Torah exists only in one who puts himself to death," meaning he puts himself to death, namely his self-gratification, and does everything only for the Creator.

This is called "preparation for reception of the Torah."

30. RABASH, Article No. 223, "Entry into the Work"

After he achieves this degree called *Lo Lishma*, he is rewarded with other phenomena, when he comes to a higher state. That is, at that time he has no consideration of himself, and all his calculations and thoughts are the truth.

In other words, his aim is only to annul himself before the true reality, where he feels that he must only serve the King because he feels the exaltedness and greatness and importance of the King. At that time, he forgets, meaning he has no need to worry about himself, as his own self is annulled as a candle before a torch before the existence of the Creator that he feels. Then he is in a state of *Lishma* [for Her sake], meaning contentment to the Creator, and his concerns and yearnings are only about how he can delight the Creator, while his own existence, meaning the will to receive, does not merit a name whatsoever. Then he is regarded as "bestowing in order to bestow."

31. RABASH, Article No. 44 (1990), "What Is an Optional War, in the work - 2?"

A person should work on having a desire and yearning to want to annul his authority, as our sages said about the verse "If a man dies in a tent," since the Torah exists only in one who puts himself to death over it." This means that he wants to annul his self, meaning he must achieve a state where he has but one authority—the authority of the Creator. In other words, a person does not do anything for his own benefit, but sees only to the benefit of the Creator. This is called "singular authority," and it is called "optional war." In other words, he is fighting against himself to obtain this singular authority, and this is called "optional war" in the work.

32. RABASH, Article No. 587, "The Upper One Scrutinizes for the Purpose of the Lower One"

The lower one is powerless to begin the work, but only in the form of *Lo Lishma* [not for Her sake], called "will to receive," for only the *Lo Lishma* gives the first moving force of the lower one, for when a person does not find sufficient flavor in corporeal pleasures, he begins to search for spiritual pleasures.

It follows that the root of the work of the lower one is the will to receive, and the prayer, called *MAN*, rises up, and then the upper one corrects this *MAN* and places on it the power of the *Masach*, which is a desire to delay the abundance before the lower one knows about himself that his aim is to bestow.

That is, the upper one bestows upon the lower one good taste and pleasure in the desire to bestow, by which the lower one feels His exaltedness. At that time, he begins to understand that it is worthwhile to annul before Him and cancel his existence before Him. Then, he feels that all that there is in reality is only because such is His will, that the Creator wants the lower one to exist, but for himself, he wants to annul his existence. It follows that then, all the vitality he feels is regarded as *Lishma* and not for himself.

When he feels this, it is considered that he already has the correction of the *MAN*, and then he is also fit to receive the *MAD*, as well, for there is no contradiction between them anymore, since the lower one, too, wants the benefit of the upper one and not his own benefit.

It is considered that when the upper one gives the lower one *Mochin*, he also gives him the clothing of the *Mochin*, meaning that he gives the lower one the abundance, as well as the power of the *Masach*, which is the desire to bestow. This is the meaning of "from *Lo Lishma*, we come to *Lishma*."

33. RABASH, Article No. 2 (1984), "Concerning Love of Friends"

We must remember that the society was established on the basis of love of others, so each member would receive from the group the love of others and hatred of himself. And seeing that his friend is straining to annul his self and to love others would cause everyone to be integrated in their friends' intentions.

Thus, if the society is made of ten members, for example, each will have ten forces practicing self-annulment, hatred of self, and love of others.

34. RABASH, Article No. 31 (1986), "Concerning *Yenika* [Suckling] and *Ibur* [Impregnation]"

There are two forces in the *Ibur*: 1) A depicting force, where the depiction of the fetus is *Katnut* [infancy/smallness], for in order to obtain *Katnut* there is an order, since *Katnut* is preparation for *Gadlut* [adulthood/greatness], and without *Katnut* in the degree there is no *Gadlut*. And as long as he is in *Katnut* he is still incomplete, and wherever there is a deficiency in *Kedusha* there is a grip to the *Sitra Achra*, who might spoil the *Ibur* so it cannot be completed. By this he is aborted, meaning that he is born before the state of *Ibur* has been completed.

It is so because there are twenty-five *Partzufim* [plural of *Partzuf*] in the *Ibur*, meaning NRNHY, and in each of them there is also NRNHY. Therefore, there must be a detaining force, meaning that even in *Katnut* there should be wholeness there. He receives this through his mother, although the fetus in itself has no *Kelim* [vessels] in which to receive *Gadlut* in order to bestow. Still, by annulling before the mother it can receive *Gadlut* from the *Kelim* of its mother. This is regarded as "An embryo is its mother's thigh; it eats what its mother eats."

That is, since it has no choice of its own but rather eats what its mother eats, meaning that what its mother knows is permitted to eat, it eats, as well, it means that he has shifted the choice of what is good and what is bad from himself. Rather, it is all attributed to the mother. This is called "its mother's thigh," meaning that he himself does not merit a name.

35. RABASH, Article No. 31 (1986), "Concerning *Yenika* [Suckling] and *Ibur* [Impregnation]"

It follows that when a person can annul himself a little bit and at that time says, "Now I want to annul myself before the *Kedusha*," meaning not to think about self-love. Rather, now he wants to bring contentment to the Creator, and believes above reason that although he still does not feel anything, he believes above reason, that the Creator hears the prayer of every mouth, and before Him, small and great are equal, and as He can deliver the greatest of the greatest, He can also help the smallest of the small.

This is called *Ibur*, meaning that he passes from his own domain into the domain of the Creator. However, it is temporary. That is, he truly wants to annul himself forever, but cannot believe that there will be annulling forever now since he has already thought many times that it would be so but then descended from his degree and fell to the place of garbage.

However, he does not need to worry about what to eat tomorrow, as was said above, that later he will probably fall from his degree, as this is for lack of faith. Rather, he must believe that the salvation of the Lord is as the blink of an eye. It follows that since he annuls himself for the time being and wants to remain this way forever, it follows that he has the value of *Ibur*.

36. Baal HaSulam, Article No. 821, "We Will Do and We Will Hear – 2"

That person annuls himself before the other, not necessarily in external annulment, but also internally. Externality means that which is revealed outside, which is regarded as "revealed," when it is visible to everyone that he does not consider himself as anything, but that he regards his friend as being at a higher degree than his own. This is shown by the things he does before his friend.

But there is also internality, called "hidden." These are the thought and the mind, which he must also annul before his friend. This is the meaning of "My soul shall be as dust to all."

37. RABASH, Article No. 37 (1991), "What Is the Torah and What Is The Statute of the Torah, in the Work?"

When he wants to do everything for the sake of the Creator and not for his own sake. Here the body resists with all its might, since it argues, "Why do you want to put me and my domain to death? You come to me with having to work only for the sake of the Creator and not for one's own sake, which is truly annulment of the will to receive from everything. You tell me that our sages said, 'The Torah exists only in one who puts himself to death over it,' meaning to put to death all the domain of self-benefit and care only for the benefit of the Creator, and before this, a person cannot be rewarded with the Torah." Yet, a person sees that it is unrealistic that he will have the strength to go against nature.

At that time, one has no choice but to turn to the Creator and say, "Now I have come to a state where I see that unless You help me, I am lost. I will never have the strength to overcome the will to receive, as this is my nature. Rather, only the Creator can give another nature."

38. RABASH, Article No. 4 (1989), "What Is a Flood of Water in the Work?"

When a person does not feel the greatness of the Creator, the body cannot annul before Him "with all your heart and with all your soul." However, in truth, by presenting a condition that says, "I agree to work for You only on condition that I see Your importance and greatness," he already wants to receive from the Creator—the greatness of the Creator—or he will not want to work with all his heart. Thus, a person is already limited and placed under the governance of concealment, and he is not free to say that he wants nothing but to bestow. This is not true since he does want something before he observes "that all your works will be for the sake of the Creator." That is, he first wants to receive the greatness of the Creator, and then say that he will annul before the Creator. Certainly, this is not regarded as *Bina* because *Bina* desires mercy and wants nothing, for she does want.

39. RABASH, Article No. 30 (1988), "What to Look for in the Assembly of Friends"

When a person makes the effort and judges him to the side of merit, it is a *Segula* [remedy/power/virtue], where by the toil that a person makes, which is called "an awakening from below," he is given strength from above to be able to love all the friends without exception.

This is called "Buy yourself a friend," that a person should make an effort to obtain love of others. And this is called "labor," since he must exert above reason. Reasonably thinking, "How is it possible to judge another person to the side of merit when his reason shows him his friend's true face, that he hates him?" What can he tell the body about that? Why should he submit himself before his friend?

The answer is that he wishes to achieve *Dvekut* [adhesion] with the Creator, called "equivalence of form," meaning not to think of his own benefit. Thus, why is subduing a difficult thing? The reason is that he must revoke his own worth, and the whole of the life that he wishes to live will be only with the consideration of his ability to work for others' benefit, beginning with love of others, between man and man, through the love of the Creator.

Hence, here is a place where he can say that anything he does is without any self-interest, since by reason, the friends are the ones who should love him, but he overcomes his reason, goes above reason, and says, "It is not worth living for myself." And although one is not always at a degree where he is able to say so, this is nonetheless the purpose of the work. Thus, he already has something to reply to the body.

40. RABASH, Article No. 4 (1991), "What Is, 'The Saboteur Was in the Flood, and Was Putting to Death,' in the Work?"

When a person lowers himself, the question is, What is lowliness? How is it expressed that a person is in lowliness? The literal meaning is that lowliness is when one subdues oneself and works above reason. This is called "lowliness," when he lowers his reason and says that his reason is worthless.

In other words, man's reason dictates that if the Creator gives him all his needs, which the will to receive understands that it deserves, then he can love the Creator. That is, he loves Him because he satisfies all his needs. If He did not, he would not be able to lower himself and say that his reason is worthless. Rather, at that time he would depart from the Creator and say that it is not worthwhile to serve the Creator if He does not grant him his wishes. It follows that this is called "proud," since he wants to understand the ways of the Creator, in what is He regarded as good and doing good, if the body does not get what it demands. About such a proud person the Creator says, "He and I cannot dwell in the same abode."

But if he lowers himself and says, "I cannot understand the ways of the Creator," and he says that what his reason dictates is worthless, but he is going above reason, this is called "lowliness," and it was about him that the verse, "The Lord is high and the low will see" was said. He is rewarded with the Creator bringing him near Him.

41. RABASH, Article No. 21, "Sanctification of the Month"

A person must take upon himself the burden of the kingdom of heaven on the lowest quality, and say about it that to him, even that state, the lowest that can be, meaning one that is entirely above reason, when he has no support from the mind or the feeling, so he can build its foundations on it, and at that time, he is seemingly standing between heaven and earth and has no support, for then everything is above reason, then a person says that the Creator sent him this state, where he is in utter lowliness, since the Creator wants him to take upon himself the burden of the kingdom of heaven in this manner of lowliness.

At that time, because he believes above reason, he takes upon himself that the situation he is in now comes to him from the Creator, meaning that the Creator wants him to see the lowest possible state that can be in the world.

And yet, he must say that he believes in the Creator in all manners. This is considered that he has made an unconditional surrender. That is, a person does not say to the Creator, "If You give me a good feeling, to feel that 'The whole earth is full of His glory,' I will be willing to believe."

Rather, when he has no knowledge or sensation of spirituality, he cannot accept the burden of the kingdom of heaven and observe the *Torah and Mitzvot* [commandments]. Rather, he must accept the kingdom of heaven unconditionally.

This is what perplexed Moses: How could he come to the people of Israel with such lowliness? It is about this that the Creator showed him with the finger and said, "This you shall see and sanctify," meaning the moon at the time of its birth, when its merit is still not apparent.

Precisely accepting the kingdom of heaven in lowliness will reveal what our sages said, "Rabbi Elazar said, 'The Creator is destined to pardon the righteous and dwell among them in the Garden of Eden, and each one will point with his finger, as was said, 'And he said on that day, 'Behold, this is our God for whom we have waited and He will save us. This is the Lord for whom we have waited; let us rejoice and be glad in His salvation''" (*Taanit* 31).

It follows that the hint that the Creator points to the moon with the finger and says, "This," by this we are rewarded with each one pointing with his finger, "Behold, this is our God."

42. RABASH, Article No. 680, "Annulment—the Baal Shem Tov Way"

The way to annul the body used to be through abstention. But there is another way, which is annulment before the rav [great one, teacher]. This is the meaning of "Make for yourself a rav." "Making" is clarified by force, without any intellect.

As abstention revokes the body only through action and not through the mind. Likewise, annulment before the rav is by force and not through intellect. That is, even in a place where one does not understand the view of one's rav, he annuls himself and the Torah and the work, and comes to the rav so he will guide him.

There is guidance in the manner of the general public, called *Ohr Makif* [surrounding light], which is light that shines only from outside, and is without words, but only by coming to the rav and sitting in front of him, sitting at his table during the meal or during the service. Yet, there is another way, which is internal, and this is specifically through "mouth-to-mouth."

43. RABASH, Article No. 824, "Internality and Externality"

Humility means that in any manner, in action or in intellect, he annuls himself before the other, meaning that even his view he should annul before his friend.

There is "internality," and there is "externality." These are called "revealed" and "concealed," and "action" and "thought." Something that is revealed to all pertains to action, whereas a thought is not revealed; therefore, a thought is regarded as internal, meaning it is in man's internality. An act is called "externality," and within it there is an internal thought.

Therefore, when one must annul himself before his friend, it is not regarded as true annulment unless it is in two manners: in thought and in action.

It is not necessarily the action, but he should also annul his view and say that his friend's view is more important than his own. Otherwise, this is (not) regarded as "annulment." When he shows his friend an act of annulment, this is nothing but fawning, where on the outside he shows that his friend is more important, but deep inside he knows that his friend is not half as good as he is.

44. RABASH, Article No. 7 (1984), "According to What Is Explained Concerning 'Love Your Friend as Yourself'"

The advice for one to be able to increase his strength in the rule, "Love your friend," is by love of friends. If everyone is nullified before his friend and mingles with him, they become one mass where all the little parts that want the love of others unite in a collective force that consists of many parts. And when one has great strength, he can execute the love of others.

And then he can achieve the love of God. But the condition is that each will annul before the other. However, when he is separated from his friend, he cannot receive the share he should receive from his friend.

Thus, everyone should say that he is nothing compared to his friend. It is like writing numbers: If you first write "1" and then "0," it is ten times more. And when you write "00" it is a hundred times more. In other words, if his friend is number one, and the zero follows it, it is considered that one receives from his friend ten (10) times more. And if he says that he is double zero compared to his friend, he receives from his friend a hundred (100) times more.

However, if it is to the contrary, and he says that his friend is zero and he is one, then he is ten times less than his friend 0.1. And if he can say that he is one and he has two friends who are both zeros compared to him, then he is considered a hundred times less than them, meaning he is 0.01. Thus, his degree lessens according to the number of zeros he has from his friends.

Yet, even once he acquires that strength and can keep the love of others in actual fact, and feels his own gratification as bad for him, still, do not believe in yourself. There must be fear of falling into self-love in the middle of the work. In other words, should one be given a greater pleasure than he is used to receiving, although he can already work in order to bestow with small pleasures and is willing to relinquish them, he lives in fear of great pleasures.

This is called "fear," and this is the gate to receive the Light of faith, called "The inspiration of the *Shechina* [Divinity]," as it is written in *The Sulam* Commentary, "By the measure of fear is the measure of faith."

Hence, we must remember that the matter of "Love your friend as yourself" should be kept because it is a *Mitzva*, since the Creator commanded to engage in love of friends. And Rabbi Akiva only interprets this *Mitzva* that the Creator commanded. He intended to make this *Mitzva* into a rule by which to be able to keep all the *Mitzvot* because of the commandment of the Creator, and not because of self-benefit.

In other words, it is not that the *Mitzvot* should expand our will to receive, meaning that by keeping the *Mitzvot* we would be generously rewarded. Quite the contrary; by keeping the *Mitzvot* we will reach the reward of being able to annul our self-love and achieve the love of others, and subsequently the love of God.

45. RABASH, Article No. 3 (1985), "The Meaning of Truth and Faith"

There are two discernments in the *Ibur*:

1. The shape of the *Ibur*, which is the degree of *Katnut* [smallness/infancy], which is its real shape. However, since it only has *Katnut*, it is regarded as a deficiency, and wherever there is a deficiency in holiness, there is a grip to the *Klipot* [shells/peels]. At that time the *Klipot* can cause a miscarriage—for the spiritual fetus to fall out before its stage of *Ibur* has been completed. For this reason, there should be a detaining element, which is that it is given wholeness, meaning *Gadlut* [adulthood/greatness].
2. However, we should understand how the newborn can be given *Gadlut* while it is still unfit to receive even *Katnut* sufficiently, since it still does not have the *Kelim* [vessels] in which to receive them in order to bestow. To that there is an answer there: Our sages said, "An embryo in its mother's abdomen eats what its mother eats." He also said, "A fetus is its mother's thigh." This means that since a fetus is its mother's thigh, the *Ibur* does not merit its own name. For this reason, the fetus eats what its mother eats. That is, the fetus receives everything that it receives in the mother's *Kelim*. For this reason, although the fetus has no *Kelim* that are fit to receive *Gadlut*, but in the *Kelim* of the upper one, which is its mother, it can receive because it is completely annulled before the mother and has no authority of its own. This is called *Ibur*, when it is completely annulled before the Upper One.

46. RABASH, Article No. 654, "Who Despises the Day of Smallness"

"Who despises the day of smallness?" This means that one should be happy about work in *Katnut* [smallness/infancy] more than about work in *Gadlut* [greatness/adulthood] because the bigger the light, the more there is fear that the external ones will blemish it. Hence, it is covered so as to be seen, but only in the form of *Katnut*. Conversely, a smaller light can be revealed because there is less concern.

One should believe that there is more contentment from servitude in the time of *Katnut* than in the time of *Gadlut*.

47. RABASH, Article No. 31, "Concerning *Yenika* [Suckling] and *Ibur* [Impregnation]"

The beginning of the entrance into the work of the Creator is regarded as *Ibur* [impregnation], when he cancels his self and becomes impregnated in the mother's womb, as it is written, "Hear, my son, your father's instruction, and do not forsake your mother's teaching." This comes from the verse, "For if you call the mother, 'understanding [*Bina*],'" meaning that he cancels self-love, called *Malchut*, whose original essence is called "will to receive in order to receive," and enters the vessels of bestowal, called *Bina*.

One should believe that before he was born, meaning before the soul descended into the body, the soul was adhered to Him, and now he longs to adhere to Him as prior to her descent. This is called *Ibur*, when he completely annuls his self.

48. RABASH, Article No. 24 (1991) "What Does It Mean that One Should Bear a Son and a Daughter, in the Work?"

The work above reason should be unconditional surrender. That is, one should take upon himself the burden of the kingdom of heaven above reason. A person should say, "I want to be a servant of the Creator even though I have no idea about the work and I feel no flavor in the work. Nevertheless, I am willing to work with all my might as though I have attainment and feeling and flavor in the work, and I am willing to work unconditionally." At that time, a person can go forward, and then there is no place for him to fall from his state, since he takes upon himself to work even when he is placed right in the earth, since it is impossible to be lower than the earth.

49. RABASH, Article No. 40 (1990), "What Is, 'For You Are the Least of All the Peoples,' in the Work?"

How can one muster the strength to overcome the body when he feels that the *Shechina* is in the dust? What joy can he receive from this work? Even more perplexing, how can one need and want to work when he feels no taste in it? This would be understandable if he had no choice; we can understand when a person is forced to work. But how is it possible to want such a work, which feels tasteless? And since he does not have the strength to overcome and feel joy in such a work, how can he serve the King in such a lowly state, when he feels the taste of dust while serving the King?

Hence, in this regard, he does not ask the Creator to give him the revelation of His greatness, so he will feel a good taste in it. Rather, he asks the Creator to give him strength to be able to overcome the body and work gladly because now he can work only for the Creator, since the will to receive does not enjoy work that tastes like dust.

50. RABASH, Article No. 7 (1991), "What Is 'Man' and What Is 'Beast' in the Work?"

Specifically those who want to achieve bestowal feel the emptiness within them and need the greatness of the Creator. They can fill this emptiness specifically with exaltedness, called "full of *Mitzvot*," to the extent that they ask the Creator to give them the power to be able to go above reason, which is called "exaltedness." In other words, they ask the Creator to give them power in exaltedness that is above reason in greatness and importance of the Creator. They do not want the Creator to let them attain this, since they want to subjugate themselves with unconditional surrender, but they ask for help from the Creator, and to that extent they can fill the empty place with *Mitzvot*. This is the meaning of "filled with *Mitzvot* like a pomegranate."

51. RABASH, Article No. 4 (1989), "What Is a Flood of Water in the Work?"

We must know that it is a lot of work before we attain the quality of *Bina*. That is, to be content with little with his feeling and his mind, and be happy with his share, with what he has. That person can always be in wholeness because he is happy with his share.

But what can one do if he has not yet obtained this quality, and he sees that he cannot overcome his will to receive. At that time, he must pray to the Creator to help him so he can go in the work with his eyes shut, and will not need anything, and will be able to do everything for the sake of the Creator despite the resistance of the body to this.

That is, he does not tell the Creator how He should help him. Rather, he must subjugate himself and annul before the Creator unconditionally. But since he cannot overcome his body, he asks the Creator to help him win the war against the inclination, since he understands his lowliness.

For this reason, he asks the Creator to have mercy on him because he is worse than other people, who can be servants of the Creator, whereas he is worse than them. He sees that he has a desire to receive in self-love more than all of them. Therefore, he is ashamed of himself that he can be so lowly. For this reason, he asks the Creator to have mercy on him and deliver him from the governance of the evil inclination.

Yet, he does not ask for help because he is more important than other people. Rather, he is worse than the rest of the people because his will to receive is more developed and works within him more vigorously.

However, he is not asking to be given more knowledge about the greatness of the Creator, and then he will be able to emerge from the governance of evil. Although this is true, he does not want to tell the Creator that he wants to present Him with conditions and only then he will annul before the Creator. Rather, he agrees to remain with little understanding and little feeling, not more than he has now. But since he does not have the power to overcome, he asks the Creator to give him the power to overcome, and not brains, mind, or feeling.

Any advice that a person gives to the Creator seems as though he is setting conditions, as though he has a status and a view. But this is insolence of a person to present the Creator with conditions and say, "If You give me, for example, good taste in the work, I will be able to work for You. Otherwise, I cannot." Instead, one should say, "I want to annul myself and surrender unconditionally, just give me the strength to really be able to emerge from self-love and love the Lord 'with all your heart.'"

52. RABASH, Article No. 696, "Your Strength to the Torah"

A strong person is one who has a strong desire, and not one who has strong limbs, as in "Who is mighty? He who conquers his inclination," as is done with the powers of strong limbs.

For example, when one wants to go somewhere, but there are people who interfere with his walking on the path he wants to go, and each one pulls him to the place he wants, if he is drawn, he does not have the strength to subdue them, and then he is pulled away from the place where he wants to go to the place that the strongest one among them wants, since he subdues all the others because he is more powerful.

It is likewise with emotional strength. Man consists of many desires, and each of the desires wants to subdue the other desires and draw the body to go to its side. Here, too, the strongest among the desires prevails. And if there is a person whose desires are all equal, and none is more powerful than the others, he can be in a state of complete rest because he has no desire that overcomes the others, so they all stand and pull the body, and the body stands in the middle and does not move an inch, not here and not there, for all are pulling equally strong.

Then he naturally stays put without any movement. Even if he has great strength, they are all equally mighty forces, so no one can submit the other. Only when one desire is strong, that force can act, and the rest of the desires annul before it.

It therefore follows that if a person wants to succeed in the Torah, he must see that the desire to engage in Torah is stronger than the rest of the desires in him, and then they will surrender to it because the strong has the power to subdue the weak. Hence, the strong desire subdues the desire for idleness, for honor, and the rest of the lusts.

53. RABASH, Article No. 12, (1988), "What Are Torah and Work in the Way of the Creator?"

The Torah in order to subdue the evil inclination, meaning to achieve *Dvekut* [adhesion] with the Creator, so that all our actions will be only in order to bestow. That is, by ourselves, we will never be able to go against nature, since the mind and heart that we must acquire require assistance, and the assistance is through the Torah. It is as our sages said, "I have created the evil inclination; I have created the Torah as a spice. By engaging in it, the light in it reforms them."

54. RABASH, Article No. 18

When we hear the voice of the Creator speaking to the heart, as in "He who comes to purify is aided," and it was interpreted in the holy *Zohar* that he is aided by a holy soul, meaning that the heart hears the voice of the Creator and then specifically the voice of holiness receives the governance over all the desires, meaning the desire to bestow. And naturally, they will not turn back to folly, meaning he will not sin again because all the desires of reception have surrendered under the desire to bestow.

At that time all the good pleasantness appears on the heart, for then there is room in the heart for the instilling of the *Shechina* (Divinity), and the gentleness and pleasantness, and flavor and friendship spread, and fill up all of man's organs.

This applies specifically when hearing the voice of the Creator. At that time the whole body surrenders and enslaves itself to holiness.

55. Baal HaSulam, "The Dispute between Korah and Moses"

The matter of lowliness becomes revealed primarily when one must do something that his friend obligates him to do, while his own view indicates the opposite of his friend's view, and yet he subjugates himself. This is called "lowliness," when he lowers his own view.

56. RABASH, Article No. 3 (1985), "The Meaning of Truth and Faith"

We were given the path of faith, which is above reason, namely not to take our sensations and reason into account, but say, as it is written, "They have eyes and see not. They have ears and hear not." Rather, we should believe that the Creator is certainly the Overseer, and He knows what is good for me and what is not good for me. Therefore, He wants me to feel my state as I do, and for myself, I do not care how I feel myself because I want to work in order to bestow.

Therefore, the main thing is that I need to work for the Creator. And although I feel that there is no wholeness in my work, still, in the *Kelim* of the upper one, meaning from the perspective of the upper one, I am utterly complete, as it is written, "The cast out will not be cast out from Him." Hence, I am satisfied with my work—that I have the privilege of serving the King even at the lowest degree. That, too, I regard as a great privilege that the Creator has allowed me to come closer to Him at least to some degree.

57. RABASH, Letter No. 8

Once I have acquired this above-mentioned clothing, sparks of love promptly begin to shine within me. The heart begins to long to unite with my friends, and it seems to me that my eyes see my friends, my ears hear their voices, my mouth speaks to them, the hands embrace, the feet dance in a circle, in love and joy together with them, and I transcend my corporeal boundaries. I forget the vast distance between my friends and me, and the outstretched land for many miles will not stand between us.

It is as though my friends are standing right within my heart and see all that is happening there, and I become ashamed of my petty acts against my friends. Then, I simply exit the corporeal vessels and it seems to me that there is no reality in the world except my friends and I. After that, even the "I" is cancelled and is immersed, mingled in my friends, until I stand and declare that there is no reality in the world—only the friends.

58. *Zohar for All, Chayei Sarah* [The Life of Sarah], "One Who Diminishes Himself Is Great"

Happy is he who diminishes himself in this world; he is great and superior in the eternal world. One who is small in this world is great in the eternal world, and one who is great in this world is small in the eternal world, as it is written, "And the life of Sarah was…" 100, which is a great number, a year [in singular form] is written about it. This means that he diminished it into one year. And seven, which is a small number, he augmented it and increased it, for it writes "years" in regards to it.

The Creator augments only one who diminishes himself, and diminishes only one who magnifies himself. Happy is one who diminishes himself in this world; how great is he in the eternal world.

59. *Zohar for All, VaYishlach* [And Jacob Sent], "And Jacob Sent Messengers"

"Better is he that is ignoble and has a servant, than he that plays the man of rank and lacks bread." This verse is said about the evil inclination because it always complains against people. And the evil inclination raises man's heart and desire with pride, and man follows it, curling his hair and his head, until the evil inclination takes pride over him and pulls him to Hell.

One who does not follow the evil inclination and is not proud at all, who lowers his spirit, his heart, and his will toward the Creator, the evil inclination overturns and becomes his slave, since it cannot control him. On the contrary, that man controls it, as it is written, "and thou may rule over it."

60. Rabbi Kalonymus Kalman Halevi Epstein, *Maor VaShemesh, Ekev*

When the children of Israel join together, it is a very great thing, but the most important is for each and every one to annul himself completely and not think of himself as righteous or that he counts at all among the friends. He should only see that his actions do not blemish the society. Although it seems as though he is a great person, he should nonetheless look into his actions and think, "What make me great?" and annul himself completely. It is known that in every ten there is *Shechina* [Divinity], and this is a complete level. In a complete level, there are head, hands, legs, and heels. It follows that when every person regards himself as nothing in society, then he regards himself as a heel compared to the society, while they are the head, the body, and the higher organs. When each one thinks of himself in this way, they make the gates of abundance and every lushness in the world open up to them, and it is drawn the most through the person who is more regarded as "nothing" and as "a heel."

61. *Likutei Tefilot*, Part 1, Prayer No. 65

Help and save with Your great and plentiful mercies, so that each one from Israel who is far from the goal will be brought to his real purpose. May each one shut his eyes and mind completely to the imagination of this world until he is always included in utter annulment, back and forth, within the real purpose, which is all one, all good, so that each one in Israel is rewarded with including his prayer in the One. Give good help to all, so we merit annulling all our corporeality until we are rewarded with annulling ourselves completely, to truly be included in Your oneness, which is all good, always, until our prayer is utterly complete, included together from beginning to end with the complete unity.

62. *Shem MiShmuel, Yom Kippur Tav-Reish-Ayin-Gimel* (September 1912)

Creating unity in the collective is only through pulverizing, when each one pulverizes himself and removes from himself the shell of crassness. Through the battering and pulverizing, the light of the soul shines, and there is really all of Israel; all is one.

63. From the book, *Praises of the ARI*

One day, on the eve of *Shabbat* [Sabbath], the ARI went with his disciples for *Kabbalat Shabbat* [service beginning the Sabbath] as was his custom. He said to the friends: "Let us go now to Jerusalem … and build the Temple, and make an offering of Shabbat, for I see that this time is truly the time of redemption. Some of the friends said, 'How will we go to Jerusalem at this time, It is more than thirty parsas away (approx. 115 km)?' Others said, 'Very well, we are willing to go with you, but first we will go let our wives know so they will not worry about us, and then we will go.'" Then the Rav cried out and said to the friends, "How did the slandering of Satan succeed in revoking the redemption of Israel? I testify before Heaven and Earth that since the time of Rabbi Shimon Bar Yochai until today there has not been a better time for redemption than this time. Had you admitted this, we would have had the Temple, and the outcasts of Israel would have gathered into Jerusalem. Now the time had passed and Israel went into exile once again." When the friends heard this, they regretted what they had done, but it did not help them.

64. *Avodat Israel* [*The Work of Israel*], Portion *Shlach*

Our sages said, "Dispersion is good for the wicked and gathering is good for the righteous." This is according to what the ARI said, that in the worlds of *Igulim* [circles], one *Igul* [circle] does not touch another, and there the breaking happened until it was corrected in the world of *Yosher* [straightness]. The meaning of the matter and the allegory is that the mind of the *Igulim* is that it is as one who surrounds and encircles himself, and becomes separated from his Maker. It seems to him that he will lead himself by his own will, and he is haughty and says, "I will rule," and this was the shattering.

Likewise, among the wicked, the heart of each one is haughty, saying "I will rule," which is why they are in the world of separation and cannot connect, like the circles, as we can evidently see, for they cannot sit together. To them, dispersion is good.

Conversely, although each of the righteous serves his Creator in a different style, they all aim at the same thing—their father in Heaven. They gather and assemble one by one, as one man with one heart, and each one diminishes himself and glorifies the work for the sake of the Creator, who gives him the strength and intelligence by which to serve Him. Hence, one will not be arrogant toward his friend, and they are in the world of straightness and unite with one another.

5

Hitkalelut [Incorporation]

1. Baal HaSulam, *Shamati*, Article No. 99, "He Did Not Say Wicked or Righteous"

If one does not have any desire or craving for spirituality, if he is among people who have a desire and craving for spirituality, if he likes these people, he, too, will take their strength to prevail, and their desires and aspirations, although by his own quality, he does not have these desires and cravings and the power to overcome. But according to the grace and the importance he ascribes to these people, he will receive new powers.

2. Baal HaSulam, "Peace in the World"

Each and every individual in society is like a wheel that is linked to several other wheels placed in a machine. This single wheel has no freedom of movement in and of itself but continues with the motion of the rest of the wheels in a certain direction to qualify the machine to perform its general function.

And if there is some malfunction in the wheel, the malfunction is not evaluated relating to the wheel itself, but according to its service and role with respect to the whole machine.

3. Baal HaSulam, "Not the Time for the Livestock to Be Gathered"

And when the power of one part is missing, it causes weakness in the whole level. This is the meaning of (Braita de Rabbi Ishmael) an individual that requires a collective, and anything that was in the collective and has departed the collective, does not testify to itself, but departed in order to testify to the entire collective, since (Psalms 103:15) "As for man ... as a bud of the field, so he will bud."

The whole point of the buds rises into a single flower, the collective of Jacob and the tribes, a complete bed. This places a unique boundary for each and every soul, as in receiving light from above in this world, in the work, and one is greater than the other, one is higher than the other, and no face is like another.

The depiction of those boundaries is identical to the image of the lines and dots of the flower, where the boundaries in each part and dot on the flower form the beauty of the flower. But when the dot or the part in the flower extends its boundary, whether a little or a lot, it makes the whole flower unsightly. It is impossible to take only part of the flower and examine it alone, for then that part has neither beauty nor glory.

This is the meaning of the allegory in *The Zohar* (*The Sulam* [Ladder] commentary, *Nasso*, Item 19) about two who boarded a boat, and one was drilling under him. His friend admonished him, "Why are you drilling?" And that fool replied, "Why should you care? I am drilling under me!" But indeed, the individual spoils the beauty of the entire image.

4. Baal HaSulam, "The Teaching of the Kabbalah and Its Essence"

The greatest wonder about this wisdom is the integration in it: All the elements of the vast reality are incorporated in it until they come into a single thing—the Almighty, who contains them together.

5. Baal HaSulam, Letter No. 17

The Creator is the light of *Ein Sof*, clothed in the light of the Torah, which is found in the above 620 *Mitzvot*. Understand that thoroughly, for this is the meaning of their words, "The whole Torah is the names of the Creator." It means that the Creator is the whole, and the 620 names are parts and items. These items are according to degrees and steps of the soul that does not acquire its light at once, but gradually, one at a time.

From all the above, you find that the soul is destined to acquire all 620 holy names, its entire stature, which is 620 more than it had before it came. Its stature appears in the 620 *Mitzvot* where the light of the Torah is clothed, and the Creator in the collective light of the Torah. Thus, you see that "the Torah, the Creator, and Israel" are indeed one.

6. Baal HaSulam, "600,000 Souls"

It is said that there are 600,000 souls, and each soul divides into several sparks. We must understand how it is possible for the spiritual to divide, since initially, only one soul was created, the soul of *Adam HaRishon*.

In my opinion, there is indeed only one soul in the world, as it is written (Genesis 2:7), "and breathed into his nostrils the soul [also "breath" in Hebrew] of life." That same soul exists in all the children of Israel, complete in each and every one, as in *Adam HaRishon*, since the spiritual is indivisible and cannot be cut—which is rather a trait of corporeal things.

Rather, saying that there are 600,000 souls and sparks of souls appears as though it is divided by the force of the body of each person. In other words, first, the body divides and completely denies him of the radiance of the soul, and by the force of the Torah and the *Mitzva* [commandment], the body is cleansed, and to the extent of its cleansing, the common soul shines on him.

For this reason, two discernments were made in the corporeal body: In the first discernment, one feels one's soul as a unique organ and does not understand that this is the whole of Israel. This is truly a flaw; hence, it causes along with the above-mentioned.

In the second discernment, the true light of the soul of Israel does not shine on him in all its power of illumination, but only partially, by the measure he has purified himself by returning to the collective.

The sign for the body's complete correction is when one feels that one's soul exists in the whole of Israel, in each and every one of them, for which he does not feel himself as an individual, for one depends on the other. At that time, he is complete, flawless, and the soul truly shines on him in its fullest power, as it appeared in *Adam HaRishon*, as in "He who breathed, breathed from within Him."

This is the meaning of the three times of a person:

1. A spark of a soul, the act by way of sparkling, as in prohibiting and permitting.
2. A particular soul, one part out of 600,000. It is permanently completed, but its flaw is with it. This means that his body cannot receive the whole of the soul, and feels himself as being distinct, which causes him a lot of pains of love.

Subsequently, he approaches wholeness, the common soul, since the body has been cleansed and is entirely dedicated to the Creator and does not pose any measures or screens and is completely included in the whole of Israel.

7. Baal HaSulam, *Shamati*, Article No. 33, "The Lots on Yom Kippurim and with Haman"

Our sages wrote (*Hagigah* 15a), "Rewarded—a righteous. He takes his share and his friend's share in heaven. Convicted—a wicked. He takes his share and his friend's share in hell." It means that one takes the *Dinim* and the foreign thoughts of one's friend, which we should interpret over the whole world, meaning that this is why the world was created filled with so many people, each with his own thoughts and opinions, and all are present in the same world.

It is so deliberately, so that each and every one will be incorporated in all of one's friend's thoughts. Thus, when one repents, there will be benefit from this *Hitkalelut* [mingling/ incorporation].

It is so because when one wants to repent, he must sentence himself and the entire world to the side of merit, since he himself is incorporated in all the foreign notions and thoughts of the entire world. This is the meaning of "Convicted—a wicked. He takes his share and his friend's share in hell."

It follows that when he was still wicked, called "convicted," one's own share was of *Se'arot*, contradictions, and foreign thoughts. But also, he was mingled with one's friend's share in hell, meaning he was incorporated in all the views of all the people in the world.

Therefore, when later he becomes "Rewarded—a righteous," meaning after he repents, he sentences himself and the entire world "to the side of merit, he takes his share and his friend's share in heaven." This is because he must draw upper light for the foreign thoughts of all the people in the world, too, since he is mingled with them and must sentence them to the side of merit.

This is precisely through extending the upper light over these *Dinim* of the general public. Although they themselves cannot receive this light that he had drawn on their behalf because they do not have *Kelim* that are ready for this, but he drew it for them as well.

8. Baal HaSulam, "Not the Time for the Livestock to Be Gathered"

One must not exclude oneself from the public and ask for oneself, not even to bring contentment to one's maker, but only for the entire public. It is so because one cannot extend one's boundary while the boundaries of the rest of the buds of the flower remain where they are, for as smallness blemishes the beauty, so does greatness, since the boundaries of all the lines and circles of the flower must be related.

This is the meaning of (Psalms 22:21) "Save my soul from the sword, my only one from the dog." One who departs from the public to ask specifically for one's own soul does not build. On the contrary, he inflicts ruin upon his soul, as in (*Midrash Rabbah*, Chapter 7, Item 6) "All who is proud," etc., for there cannot be one who retires from the public unless with an attire of pride. Woe unto him, for he inflicts ruin on his soul.

Even during work, when one prays alone, against his will he departs from the public and ruins his soul. That is, there was not even an awakening of anyone from the children of Israel to demand anything personal for no one needed anything because they did not feel as separate selves, and this was their power to come out of Egypt with a mighty hand. Thus, every one must gather with all of one's strength into the whole of Israel with every plea to the Creator in the prayer and in the work, and include himself in the root of all of Israel.

9. Baal HaSulam, "A Speech for the Completion of The Zohar"

The body with its organs are one. The whole of the body exchanges thoughts and sensations with each of its organs. For example, if the whole body thinks that a certain organ should serve it and please it, this organ immediately knows that thought and provides the contemplated pleasure. Also, if an organ thinks and feels that the place it is in is narrow, the rest of the body immediately knows that thought and sensation and moves it to a comfortable place.

However, should an organ be cut off from the body, they become two separate entities; the rest of the body no longer knows the needs of the separated organ, and the organ no longer knows the thoughts of the body, to serve it and to benefit it. But if a physician came and reconnected the organ to the body as before, the organ would once again know the thoughts and needs of the rest of the body, and the rest of the body would once again know the needs of the organ.

10. Baal HaSulam, Letter No. 4

You lack nothing but to go out to a field that the Lord has blessed, and collect all those flaccid organs that have drooped from your soul, and join them into a single body.

In that complete body, the Creator will instill His *Shechina* incessantly, and the fountain of intelligence and high streams of light will be as a never ending fountain.

11. RABASH, Article No. 2 (1984), "Concerning Love of Friends"

If each of them does not show the society that he is practicing love of friends, then one lacks the force of the group.

This is so because it is very hard to judge one's friend favorably. Each one thinks that he is righteous and that only he engages in love of friends. In that state, one has very little strength to practice love of others. Thus, this work, specifically, should be public and not concealed.

But one must always remind oneself of the purpose of the society. Otherwise, the body tends to blur the goal, since the body always cares for its own benefit. We must remember that the society was established solely on the basis of achieving love of others, and that this would be the springboard for the love of God.

This is achieved specifically by saying that one needs a society to be able to give to one's friend without any reward. In other words, he does not need a society so the society would give him assistance and gifts, which would make the body's *vessels of reception* content. Such a society is built on self-love and prompts only the development of his *vessels of reception*, as now he sees an opportunity to gain more possessions by his friend assisting him to obtain corporeal possessions.

Instead, we must remember that the society was established on the basis of love of others, so each member would receive from the group the love of others and hatred of himself. And seeing that his friend is straining to annul his self and to love others would cause everyone to be integrated in their friends' intentions.

Thus, if the society is made of ten members, for example, each will have ten forces practicing self-annulment, hatred of self, and love of others.

12. RABASH, Letter No. 8

Once I have acquired this above-mentioned clothing, sparks of love promptly begin to shine within me. The heart begins to long to unite with my friends, and it seems to me that my eyes see my friends, my ears hear their voices, my mouth speaks to them, the hands embrace, the feet dance in a circle, in love and joy together with them, and I transcend my corporeal boundaries. I forget the vast distance between my friends and me, and the outstretched land for many miles will not stand between us.

It is as though my friends are standing right within my heart and see all that is happening there, and I become ashamed of my petty acts against my friends. Then, I simply exit the corporeal vessels and it seems to me that there is no reality in the world except my friends and I. After that, even the "I" is cancelled and is immersed, mingled in my friends, until I stand and declare that there is no reality in the world—only the friends.

13. RABASH, Article No. 14 (1988), "The Need for Love of Friends"

There is a special power in the adhesion of friends. Since views and thoughts pass from one to the other through the adhesion between them, each is mingled with the power of the other, and by that each person in the group has the power of the entire society. For this reason, *although each person is an individual, he has the power of the entire group.*

14. RABASH, Article No. 7 (1984), "According to What Is Explained Concerning 'Love Your Friend as Yourself'"

By assembling a few people who agree that they have to achieve the love of others, when they annul themselves before one another, they are all intermingled. Thus, in each person there accumulates a great force, according to the size of the association. And then each can execute the love of others in actual fact.

15. RABASH, Article No. 7 (1984), "According to What Is Explained Concerning 'Love Your Friend as Yourself'"

By assembling a few people who agree that they have to achieve the love of others, when they annul themselves before one another, they are all intermingled. Thus, in each person there accumulates a great force, according to the size of the association. And then each can execute the love of others in actual fact.

16. RABASH, Article No. 15 (1986), "A Prayer of Many"

We can interpret the words of *The Zohar*. It advises those people with an inner demand, who cannot accept the state they are in because they do not see any progress in the work of God, and believe what is written (Deuteronomy 30:20), "To love the Lord your God, to listen to His voice, and to cleave unto Him; for this is your life, and the length of your days." They see that they lack love and *Dvekut* [adhesion/cleaving], and they do not feel the life in the Torah or know how to find counsel for their souls to come to feel in their organs that which the text tells us.

The advice is to ask for the whole collective. In other words, everything that one feels that he is lacking and asks fulfillment for, he should not say that he is an exception or deserves more than what the collective has. Rather, "I dwell among my own people," meaning I am asking for the entire collective because I wish to come to a state where I will have no care for myself whatsoever, but only for the Creator to have contentment.

17. RABASH, Article No. 7 (1984), "According to What Is Explained Concerning 'Love Your Friend as Yourself'"

The advice for one to be able to increase his strength in the rule, "Love your friend," is by love of friends. If everyone is nullified before his friend and mingles with him, they become one mass where all the little parts that want the love of others unite in a collective force that consists of many parts. And when one has great strength, he can execute the love of others.

And then he can achieve the love of God. But the condition is that each will annul before the other.

18. RABASH, Article No. 875, "Three Lines – 4"

"Which is a dispute for the sake of the Creator … and one that is not for the sake of the Creator is the dispute of Korah and his congregation." There is a question: Why does it not say "Moses, and Korah and his congregation," as it is written about Hillel and Shammai?

To understand the above, we must know the meaning of "for the sake of the Creator." *The Zohar* interprets that "for the sake of the Creator" means *Zeir Anpin*. It is interpreted in the *Sulam* [Ladder commentary on *The Zohar*] that the dispute between Shammai and Hillel is the matter of the right line and the left line. Since the right line is incomplete by itself, since it does not contain *Hochma*, and the left line is also incomplete although it contains [*Hochma*], it still lacks *Hassadim*, which is the clothing on *Hochma*. Without this clothing, he is in the dark.

It follows that through the dispute, where each shows the other that there is no wholeness in it, and shows him the lack in the line of the other, it causes the two lines to merge with one another, meaning that both come into the middle line, called *Zeir Anpin*, which is the middle line in the *Partzufim* [pl. of *Partzuf*]. *Zeir Anpin* is called "for the sake of the Creator." This shows that if there weren't a dispute, each would remain in his line. Hence, the dispute was in order to achieve "for the sake of the Creator."

19. RABASH, Article No. 6 (1984), "Love of Friends – 2"

By each joining the society and annulling oneself before it, they become one body.

For example, if there are ten people in that body, it has ten times more power than a single person does. However, there is a condition: When they gather, each of them should think that he has now come for the purpose of annulling self-love. It means that he will not consider how to satisfy his will to receive now, but will think as much as possible only of the love of others. This is the only way to acquire the desire and the need to acquire a new quality, called "the will to bestow."

And from love of friends one can reach love of the Creator, meaning wanting to give contentment to the Creator.

20. RABASH, Letter No. 42

It is written, "And the people encamped, as one man with one heart." This means that they all had one goal, which is to benefit the Creator. It follows…

We should understand how they could be as one man with one heart, since we know what our sages said, "As their faces are not similar to one another, their views are not similar to one another," so how could they be as one man with one heart?

Answer: If we are saying that each one cares for himself, it is impossible to be as one man, since they are not similar to one another. However, if they all annul their selves and worry only about the benefit of the Creator, they have no individual views, since the individuals have all been canceled and have entered the single authority.

21. RABASH, Article No. 1 (1984),"Purpose of Society – 2"

Since man is created with a *Kli* called "self-love," where one does not see that an act will yield self-benefit, one has no motivation to make even the slightest motion. And without annulling self-love, it is impossible to achieve *Dvekut* [adhesion)] with the Creator, meaning equivalence of form.

And since it is against our nature, we need a society that will form a great force so we can work together on annulling the will to receive, called "evil," as it hinders the achievement of the goal for which man was created.

For this reason, society must consist of individuals who unanimously agree that they must achieve it. Then, all the individuals become one great force that can fight against itself, since everyone is integrated in everyone else. Thus, each person is founded on a great desire to achieve the goal.

To be integrated in one another, each person should annul himself before the others. This is done by each seeing the friends' merits and not their faults. But one who thinks that he is a little higher than his friends can no longer unite with them.

22. *Zohar for All, Toldot* [Generations], "These Are the Generations of Isaac," Item 3

There is not an organ in a man's body that does not have a corresponding creation in the world.

This is so because as man's body divides into organs and they all stand degree over degree, established one atop the other and are all one body, similarly, the world, meaning all creations in the world are many organs standing one atop the other, and they are all one body.

23. Rav Chaim Vital, *Shaar HaGilgulim*, Introduction, 38

My teacher cautioned me and all the friends who were with him in that society to take upon ourselves the commandment to-do of "Love your neighbor as yourself," and to aim to love each one from Israel as his own soul, for by this his prayer would rise comprising all of Israel and will be able to ascend and make a correction above. Especially, our love of friends, each and every one of us should include himself as though he is an organ of those friends. My teacher sternly cautioned me about this matter.

24. *Likutey Halachot* [*Assorted Rules*], "Synagogue Rules," Rule No. One

The ascent of the soul and its completeness is mainly when all the souls merge and become one, for then they rise to the *Kedusha* [holiness], since the *Kedusha* is one. Therefore, the prayer, which is regarded as the soul, depends primarily on the unity of souls. For this reason, a prayer is mainly in public and not alone, so that one will not be separated and alone, as this is the opposite of *Kedusha*. Rather, we must unite the holy congregation together and become one, and this is a prayer in public, and specifically in the synagogue, for there the souls gather. This is the completeness of the prayer.

25. Ramchal, *Adir BaMarom*

The *Nukva*, who leads all the worlds, is called "heart." This is why the heart was placed in man, and the heart is what understands and feels. It is likewise with all the operations of all the worlds; the feeling comes to the *Nukva* since she is operated by the lower ones. It follows that all the hearts in all the people are but parts of that heart. That is, all the souls are rooted in the *Nukva* and are therefore regarded as her parts, as well as her MAN, since she is regarded as complete only when she is with all her branches. This matter of the heart also spreads through all the souls that are rooted in her. It follows that this heart is incomplete until it contains all the discernments of the heart that emerge from it in all the souls. Then, when it is inclusive, so he will understand, as in "the heart understands" all the guidance as a whole, as this is the order of bestowal, when the branches are included in the root, and then the root is comprised of all of them, receives what it needs for all of them, and returns and dispenses to everyone their rightful share. This is the meaning of "He who fashions the hearts of them all, who understands all their works" (Psalms 33:15), for all the hearts gather in the *Nukva*, who is the upper, root heart. At that time, the heart does its work and dispenses its guidance properly to all the sides.

26. The Vilna Gaon (GRA), *The Voice of the Turtledove* [Kol HaTor]

Literally speaking, incorporation means that each one, every individual in Israel, must be incorporated in the collective. There is nothing in the individual except for what is found in the collective; all of Israel are responsible for one another. Each individual is part of the collective; there is no separate individual in Israel in any sense, both in raising the importance of the collective and in helping others, as well as in admonition of each other, since Jerusalem was ruined only because they did not admonish one another.

27. *Likutei Tefilot*, Part 1, Prayer 65

Help and save with Your great and plentiful mercies, so that each one from Israel who is far from the goal will be brought to his real purpose. May each one shut his eyes and mind completely to the imagination of this world until he is always included in utter annulment, back and forth, within the real purpose, which is all one, all good, so that each one in Israel is rewarded with including his prayer in the One. Give good help to all, so we merit annulling all our corporeality until we are rewarded with annulling ourselves completely, to truly be included in Your oneness, which is all good, always, until our prayer is utterly complete, included together from beginning to end with the complete unity.

28. Rabbi Moshe Chaim Ephraim of Sudilkov, *Degel Mahaneh Ephraim*

A person who wants to serve the Creator in truth must have two discernments: 1) uniqueness of the act, as though there is only him in the world and the Creator reveals to him without clothing, as it is written, "And no man shall go up with you." When one wants to serve the Creator, he should be alone and no one shall go up with him. There is another discernment for a servant of the Creator: He should incorporate himself with all created beings. Also, he should connect himself with all the souls, include himself with them, and they with him. That is, you should leave for yourself only what is needed for connecting the *Shechina* [Divinity], so to speak. This requires closeness and many people, as it is written (Sanhedrin 71), "Closeness of righteous, good for them and good for the world," for the more people serve the Creator, the more the light of the *Shechina* appears to them, and this requires incorporating oneself with all the people and with all creations, and raise everything to their root, for the correction of the *Shechina*, so to speak.

29. Raaiah Kook, "Sermons of the Raaiah for the High Holidays"

It is known that everything is discerned by its opposite, as the advantage of the light that comes from recognizing the darkness. Likewise, one has more recognition of the benefit of the public and his mingling with them when he is alone on the road and feels how the collective complements his lacks, whether in corporeal matters or in spiritual matters. As a result, he installs more love of the collective in his heart. And when he unites with the public, his prayer acquires the merit of the prayer of the public.

30. Simcha Bonim of Pshischa, *The Voice of Joy*

An individual who does not incorporate himself in all of Israel is not imparted from above by the love of the collective. The writing says about this, "Love your neighbor as yourself," truly, for the love of Israel is imparted by the abundance of the love of the Creator for Israel. If one does not incorporate himself in all of Israel, he might be in danger. It is about this that the Shunammite said, "I dwell among my own people."

31. Rabbi Kalonymus Kalman Halevi Epstein, *Maor VaShemesh*

Through love of friends and adhesion with the friends, one comes to complete submission since he will see his friends' work and the intensity of the fire in their hearts and their excitement in serving the Creator. By this, he, too, will learn to work like them, recognize his own deformation, and will repent in complete repentance.

32. Rabbi Nachman of Breslov, *Likutei Halachot* [Assorted Rules]

It is impossible to observe the Torah and *Mitzvot* [commandments] unless through *Arvut* [mutual responsibility], when each one becomes responsible for his friend. Since the essence of observance of the Torah, which is the desire, is through unity, each one must be included in the whole of Israel in great unity. For this reason, at the time of the reception of the Torah, they immediately became responsible for one another because when they want to receive the Torah, they must all be promptly incorporated together as one, in order to be incorporated in the desire. At that time, each one is certainly responsible for his friend, since all are regarded as one. Precisely by each being responsible for his friend, which is the quality of unity, specifically by this can they observe the Torah, since the essence of love and unity is in the desire, when each one pleases his friend, there is no disparity of desire among them, and all are incorporated in one desire, by which they are incorporated in the upper desire, which is the purpose of the unity.

6

Arvut [Mutual Responsibility]

1. Baal HaSulam, "Matan Torah [The Giving of the Torah]," Item 16

If six hundred thousand men abandon their work for the satisfaction of their own needs and worry about nothing but standing guard so their friends will not lack a thing, and moreover, they will engage in this with great love, with their very heart and soul, in the full meaning of the *Mitzva* [commandment], "Love your friend as yourself," it is then beyond doubt that no one in the nation will need to worry about his own well-being.

Because of this, one becomes completely free of securing his own survival and can easily observe the *Mitzva*, "Love your friend as yourself." After all, why would he worry about his own survival when six hundred thousand loyal lovers stand by, ready with great care to make sure he lacks nothing of his needs?

Therefore, once all the members of the nation agreed, they were immediately given the Torah, for now they were capable of observing it.

2. Baal HaSulam, "The Arvut [Mutual Guarantee]," Item 17

This is to speak of the *Arvut* [mutual guarantee], when all of Israel became responsible for one another. Because the Torah was not given to them before each and every one from Israel was asked if he agreed to take upon himself the *Mitzva* [commandment] of loving others in the full measure expressed in the words "Love your friend as yourself," This means that each and every one in Israel would take upon himself to care and work for each member of the nation, to satisfy all their needs, no less than the measure imprinted in him to care for his own needs.

Once the whole nation unanimously agreed and said, "We will do and we will hear," each member of Israel became responsible that no member of the nation will lack anything. Only then did they become worthy of receiving the Torah, and not before.

With this collective responsibility, each member of the nation was liberated from worrying about the needs of his own body and could observe the *Mitzva*, "Love your friend as yourself" in the fullest measure and give all that he had to any needy person since he no longer cared for the existence of his own body, as he knew for certain that he was surrounded by six hundred thousand loyal lovers standing ready to provide for him.

3. Baal HaSulam, "The Arvut [Mutual Guarantee]," Item 23

It is written, "And Israel camped there before the mountain," which our sages interpret as "as one man with one heart."

This is because each and every person from the nation completely detached himself from self-love, and wanted only to benefit his friend. It turns out that all the individuals in the nation had come together and became one heart and one man, for only then were they qualified to receive the Torah.

4. Baal HaSulam, "Not the Time for the Livestock to Be Gathered"

And when the power of one part is missing, it causes weakness in the whole level. This is the meaning of (Braita de Rabbi Ishmael) an individual that requires a collective, and anything that was in the collective and has departed the collective, does not testify to itself, but departed in order to testify to the entire collective, since (Psalms 103:15) "As for man... as a bud of the field, so he will bud."

The whole point of the buds rises into a single flower, the collective of Jacob and the tribes, a complete bed. This places a unique boundary for each and every soul, as in receiving light from above in this world, in the work, and one is greater than the other, one is higher than the other, and no face is like another.

The depiction of those boundaries is identical to the image of the lines and dots of the flower, where the boundaries in each part and dot on the flower form the beauty of the flower. But when the dot or the part in the flower extends its boundary, whether a little or a lot, it makes the whole flower unsightly. It is impossible to take only part of the flower and examine it alone, for then that part has neither beauty nor glory.

This is the meaning of the allegory in *The Zohar* about two who boarded a boat, and one was drilling under him. His friend admonished him, "Why are you drilling?" And that fool replied, "Why should you care? I am drilling under me!" But indeed, the individual spoils the beauty of the entire image.

This is the meaning of a prayer in public, that one must not exclude oneself from the public and ask for oneself, not even to bring contentment to one's maker, but only for the entire public. One who departs from the public to ask specifically for one's own soul does not build. On the contrary, he inflicts ruin upon his soul.

5. Baal HaSulam, "The Love of God and the Love of Man"

It is utterly impossible to observe Torah and *Mitzvot* unless the entire nation participates.

It follows that each one becomes responsible for his friend. This means that the reckless make the observers of the Torah remain in their filth, for they cannot be completed in bestowal upon others and love of others without their help. Thus, if some in the nation sin, they make the rest of the nation suffer because of them.

This is the meaning of what is written in the Midrash, "Israel, one of them sins and all of them feel." Rabbi Shimon said about this: "It is like people who were seated in a boat. One of them took a drill and began to drill under him. His friends told him, 'What are you doing?' He replied, 'Why do you care? Am I not drilling under me?' They replied, 'The water is rising and flooding the boat.'" As we have said above, because the reckless are immersed in self-love, their actions create an iron fence that prevents the observers of Torah from even beginning to observe the Torah and *Mitzvot* properly.

6. Baal HaSulam, "The Arvut [Mutual Guarantee]," Items 17-18

Israel are responsible for one another, both on the positive side and on the negative side. On the positive side, if they keep the *Arvut* to the point that each one cares and satisfies the needs of his friends, they can fully observe the Torah and *Mitzvot* [commandments], meaning to bring contentment to their Maker, as mentioned in "Matan Torah," Item 13. On the negative side, if a part of the nation does not want to keep the *Arvut*, but to wallow in self-love, they cause the rest of the nation to remain immersed in their filth and lowliness without finding a way out of their filth.

Therefore, the Tana described the *Arvut* as two people who were on a boat, and one of them began to drill a hole in the boat. His friend said, "Why are you drilling?" He replied, "Why should you mind? I am drilling under me, not under you." So he replied, "Fool! We will both drown together in the boat!"

7. Baal HaSulam, "The Arvut [Mutual Guarantee]," Item 19

Rabbi Elazar, son of Rashbi, clarifies the matter of *Arvut* even further. It is not enough for him that all of Israel be responsible for one another, but the whole world is included in the *Arvut*.

8. RABASH, Article No. 209, "A Groom and a Bride"

Israel are responsible for one another, meaning that all of Israel are one quality.

9. RABASH, Article No. 63, "You Stand Here Today – 1"

"You stand here today all of you." This means that he gathered them… to admit them into the covenant (RASHI). "All of you" means that everyone entered into the *Arvut* [mutual responsibility] (*Ohr HaChaim*).

There is a question why he begins with plural form, "all of you," then shifts to singular form, "every man from Israel." It means that "all of you" permeates everyone in Israel, meaning that every person from Israel will be included with "all of you," as it is written, "And the people camped at the bottom of the mountain," as one man with one heart.

10. Rabbi Simcha Bonim Bonhart of Pshischa, *Kol Mevaser*

Balaam wanted to curse Israel. Balak said to him, "You will see its very end, and you will not see all of it." If you look at individuals, you will "see its end," you will be able to see faults in the children of Israel. However, "You will not see all of it," (meaning) that when all of them are together, you see only good. This is also the mutual guarantee on which Moses worked so hard before his death, to unite the children of Israel, as it is written, "All of Israel are responsible for one another," meaning that when they are all together, they see only good.

11. Rabbi Nachman of Breslov, *Likutey Halachot* [Assorted Rules], *Hoshen Mishpat*, "Rules of the Guarantor"

It is impossible to observe the Torah and *Mitzvot* [commandments/good deeds] unless through *Arvut* [mutual responsibility], when each one becomes responsible for his friend. Since the essence of observance of the Torah, which is the desire, is through unity, anyone who wishes to take upon himself the burden of Torah and *Mitzvot*, which is primarily by overcoming the desire, must be included in the whole of Israel in great unity. For this reason, at the time of the reception of the Torah, they immediately became responsible for one another because they were regarded as one. Precisely by each being responsible for his friend, which is the quality of unity, specifically by this can they observe the Torah. Without it, it would not be possible to observe the Torah whatsoever, since the heart of observing the Torah, which is the desire, is through unity, when all are regarded as one. It follows that specifically through *Arvut*, which is when everyone are regarded as one, is the heart of observing the Torah, since the essence of love and unity is in the desire, when each one is pleased with his friend and there is no disparity of desire among them, and all are included in one desire, by which they are included in the upper desire, which is the purpose of the unity.

12. Elimelech of Lizhensk, *Noam Elimelech*

One must always pray for his friend, as one cannot do much for himself, for "One does not deliver oneself from imprisonment." But when asking for his friend, he is answered quickly. Therefore, each one should pray for his friend, and thus each works on the other's desire until all of them are answered. This is why it was said, "Israel are *Arevim* [responsible/sweet] for one another," where *Arevim* means sweetness, as they sweeten for each other by the prayers they pray for one another, and by this they are answered. And the essence of prayer is in the thought since in the thought, one's prayer can be accepted easily.

13. The RAMAK, *Conducts of Righteous*, "The Thirteen Attributes"

Israel are responsible for one another since in each one there is truly a part of his friend. When one sins, he blemishes himself and he blemishes the part that his friend has in him. It follows that as far as that part goes, his friend is responsible for him. Therefore, they are related to each other. For this reason, one should desire one's friend's benefit and look favorably upon one's friend's benefit, and his honor should be as dear to him as his own, for he is truly him. This is why we were commanded, "Love your friend as yourself."

One should want one's friend's purity and will not speak badly of him whatsoever, just as the Creator does not wish for our defamation or affliction or corruption. It should pain him just as though he were in the same affliction or the same joy.

14. Rav Chaim Vital, *Pri Etz Chaim*

One should speak in plural form, "we sinned," etc., and not "I sinned." The reason is that all of Israel are one body, and each one in Israel is one particular organ. This is the mutual responsibility, when one person is responsible for his friend, should he sin. Therefore, although he does not have that iniquity, he should still confess it since once he has made him his friend, it is as though he had committed it. This is why it is said in plural form. Even if one confesses at home alone, [he should] say that his sin is regarded as though he and I committed it together, because of the mutual responsibility of the souls.

15. *Likutei Halachot, Hilchot Arev*

The essence of the root of Arvut is extended from the reception of the Torah, when all of Israel were responsible for one another. And this is because at the root the souls of Israel all are considered as one, because they are extended from the source of unity. For this reason, all of Israel are responsible for one another in reception of the Torah.

16. Rabbi Menachem Mendel of Vitebsk, *Pri Haaretz*

The whole of Israel and their vitality sparkle in one another. Perhaps this is the meaning of "All of Israel are responsible for one another," meaning that their lights and vitality are mingled in each other's, which is why we, the children of Israel, are commanded and insist on the commandment to truly love our neighbor as ourselves.

17. Babylonian Talmud, *Shavuot*, 39a

That all of Israel are responsible for one another.

18. Ramchal, "Interpretations on the Twenty-Four Adornments of the Bride"

"You are all beautiful, my wife, and there is not a flaw in you" (Song of Songs, 4:7). to be complete, all the souls must connect in her and become one in her. At that time, the *Shechina* [Divinity] shines in a great correction, and then "You are all beautiful, my wife," and no flaw is left since by the power of mutual responsibility, each one corrects for the other and you find that everything is corrected.

19. *Sefat Emet, Shemot* [Exodus], Portion Yitro [Jethro]

The children of Israel became responsible for the correction of the entire world by the power of the Torah. This is the meaning of what was said to them, "For all the earth is Mine, and you will be unto Me a kingdom of priests and a holy nation." Everything depends on the children of Israel. As they correct themselves, so are all creations drawn after them.

20. The Vilna Gaon (GRA), *The Voice of the Turtledove* [*Kol HaTor*]

Literally speaking, incorporation means that each one, every individual in Israel, must be incorporated in the collective. There is nothing in the individual except for what is found in the collective; all of Israel are responsible for one another. Each individual is part of the collective; there is no separate individual in Israel in any sense, both in raising the importance of the collective and in helping others, as well as in admonition of each other, since Jerusalem was ruined only because they did not admonish one another.

7

The Agenda of the Assembly of Friends

1. Baal HaSulam, Letter No. 13

You should know that there are many sparks of holiness in each one in the group. When you assemble all the sparks of holiness to one place, as brothers, with love and friendship, you will certainly have a very high level of holiness for a while, from the light of life.

2. RABASH, Article No. 17 (1986), "The Agenda of the Assembly – 2"

One must praise the importance of the gathering, and then see what to acquire from that activity. It is as our sages said, "One should always praise the Creator, and then pray." In other words, the beginning of the assembly, meaning the beginning of the discussions, which is the beginning of the assembly, should be about praising the society. Each and every one must try to provide reasons and explanations for their merit and importance. They should speak of nothing but the praise of society.

Finally, its praise should be disclosed by all the friends. Then they should say, "Now we are through with Stage One of the assembly of friends, and Stage Two begins." Then each will state his mind about the actions we can take so that each and every one will be able to acquire the love of friends, *what each person can do to acquire love in his heart for each and every one in the society*.

And once Stage Two is completed—suggestions regarding what can be done in favor of society—begins Stage Three. This concerns *carrying out of the friends' decisions about what should be done*.

3. RABASH, Article No. 17 (1986), "The Agenda of the Assembly – 2"

When one comes to the assembly of friends, he should always see whether or not the friends have the goal that he craves, that each of them has some grip on that goal. And he thinks that by everyone bonding together for one goal, each will have his own share, as well as the shares of the whole of society. It follows that each member of the society will have the same strength as the whole of society together.

4. RABASH, Article No. 17 (1986), "The Agenda of the Assembly – 2"

Each one should seriously consider the purpose of the gathering—that it should bring about a sensation, following the assembly of friends, that each one has something in his hand which he can put in his vessels, and that he is not in the form of, "But do not put any in your vessels." Each one should consider that if he does not sit especially attentive during the assembly, not only does he himself lose, but he also corrupts the whole of society.

This is similar to what is written in the Midrash (*Vayikra Rabbah*, Chapter 4): "Two people went inside a boat. One of them began to drill beneath him making a hole in the boat. He told him, 'Why are you drilling?' And he replied, 'Why should you care; I am drilling under me, not under you?' So he replied, 'You fool! Both of us will drown together with the boat!'"

5. RABASH, Article No. 17 (1986), "The Agenda of the Assembly – 2"

And after they speak of the importance and necessity of the society, there begins the order of correction—how and with what can we reinforce the society to become one bloc, as it is written, "And there Israel camped before the mount" (Exodus 19), and it was explained, "as one man and one heart." The order should be that anyone with a suggestion that can improve the love of friends, it should be discussed, *but it must be accepted by all the friends, so there is no issue of coercion here.*

6. RABASH, Article No. 17 (1984), "The Agenda of the Assembly – 1"

In the beginning of the assembly, there should be an agenda. Everyone should speak of the importance of the society as much as he can, describing the profits that society will give him and the important things he hopes society will bring him, which he cannot obtain by himself, and how he appreciates the society accordingly.

7. RABASH, Article No. 17 (1984), "The Agenda of the Assembly – 1"

At the very beginning of the assembly, when gathering, we should praise the friends, the importance of each of the friends. To the extent that we assume the greatness of the society, one can appreciate the society.

"And then pray" means that everyone should examine himself and see how much effort he is giving to the society. Then, when he sees that he is powerless to do anything for society, there is room for prayer to the Creator to help him and give him strength and desire to engage in love of others.

8. RABASH, Article No. 17 (1984), "The Agenda of the Assembly – 1"

After examining ourselves and following the known advice of praying, we should think as though our prayer has been answered and rejoice with our friends, as though all the friends are one body. And as the body wishes for all its organs to enjoy, we, too, want all our friends to enjoy themselves now.

Hence, after all the calculations comes the time of joy and love of friends. At that time, everyone should feel happy, as though one had just sealed a very good deal that will earn him lots of money. And it is customary that at such a time he gives drinks to the friends.

Similarly, here everyone needs his friends to drink and eat cakes, etc. Because now he is happy, he wishes his friends to feel good, too. Hence, the dispersion of the assembly should be in a state of joy and elation.

9. RABASH, Article No. 17 (1986), "The Agenda of the Assembly – 2"

When the friends gather in one place, the assembly is certainly for a purpose, since when one allocates part of his time—which he would use for his own needs, relinquishing his engagements, and partaking in an assembly—he wishes to acquire something. Thus, it is important to try that when each of the friends goes home, he should see what he came to the assembly with, and what he has acquired now that he is going home.

10. RABASH, Article No. 30 (1988), "What to Look for in the Assembly of Friends"

In the matter of the assembly of friends, when they gather, what should they discuss? First, the goal must be clear to everyone—this gathering must yield the result of love of friends, that each of the friends will be awakened to love the other, which is called "love of others." However, this is only a result. To beget this lovely offspring, actions must be taken to produce the love.

11. RABASH, Article No. 1 (1984), "Purpose of Society – 2"

There should be careful watch in the society, disallowing frivolity, since frivolity ruins everything.

12. RABASH, Article No. 30 (1988), "What to Look for in the Assembly of Friends"

When a group of people gathers and wishes to work together on love of friends, they must all help one another as much as they can.

13. RABASH, Article No. 1 (1984), "Purpose of Society – 2"

It is important to remain serious during the assembly so as not to lose the intention, as it is for this aim that they have gathered. And to walk humbly, which is a great thing, one should be accustomed to appear as though one is not serious. But in truth, a fire burns in their hearts.

Yet, to small people, during the assembly one should be wary of following words and deeds that do not yield the goal of the gathering—that thus they should achieve *Dvekut* with the Creator.

14. RABASH, Article No. 30 (1988), "What to Look for in the Assembly of Friends"

Before each friend comes to the assembly of friends, he must contemplate what he can give to the society to uplift the spirit of life in it.

15. RABASH, Article No. 30 (1988), "What to Look for in the Assembly of Friends"

What can one do when he feels that he is in a state of sadness—both in terms of the corporeal state and the spiritual state—and the time when he must go to the society has come? And yet, our sages said, "A worry in a man's heart? Let him speak of it with others." In other words, he should tell his friends, and perhaps they can offer some help.

But if this is so, why do we say that everyone should bring high spirits into the society when one has none? Moreover, there is a rule that "one cannot give that which one does not have." Thus, what should he do to give something to the society that will give high spirits to the society?

Indeed, there is no other way but for man to walk on the right line. Thus, before he goes to the love of friends, he should read Baal HaSulam's essay (*Shamati*, No. 40) where he clarifies what is the right line, that this is the meaning of above reason. And he should draw strength from there so that when he comes to the society, each and every one will more or less be able to infuse a spirit of life, and by that, the whole of society will feel joy and strength, and confidence.

16. RABASH, Article No. 30 (1988), "What to Look for in the Assembly of Friends"

Each one should try to bring into the society a spirit of life and hopefulness, and infuse energy into the society. Thus, each of the friends will be able to tell himself, "Now I am starting a clean slate in the work." In other words, before he came to the society, he was disappointed with the progress in the work of the Creator, but now the society has filled him with life and hopefulness.

Thus, through society he obtained the confidence and strength to overcome because now he feels that he can achieve wholeness. And all his thoughts—that he was facing a high mountain that could not be conquered, and that these were truly formidable obstructions—now he feels that they are nothing. And he received it all from the power of the society because each and every one tried to instill a spirit of encouragement and the presence of a new atmosphere in the society.

17. RABASH, Article No. 30 (1988), "What to Look for in the Assembly of Friends"

During the assembly, it is forbidden to evoke the left line. Only when one is alone is he permitted to use the left line, but not more than half an hour a day. But the essence of man's work is to go specifically by the right line. But two people together must not speak of the left, for only thus can they receive assistance from the society.

18. RABASH, Article No. 30 (1988), "What to Look for in the Assembly of Friends"

When a person comes to the society and sees that the whole of society is in a state of decline, so how can he be strengthened by them? At that time, he must judge everyone to the side of merit.

19. RABASH, Article No. 30 (1988), "What to Look for in the Assembly of Friends"

What should a friend do if he needs help from his friends? We have said above that it is forbidden to speak of bad things that cause sadness at the assembly of friends. The answer is that one should tell a close friend, and that friend will speak to the society, but not at the time of the assembly of friends. In other words, he can speak to the whole of society together, but not during the regular assembly of friends. Instead, he can arrange for a special meeting in favor of the friend who needs assistance.

20. RABASH, Article No. 17 (1986), "The Agenda of the Assembly – 2"

We should know that "Two is the least plural." This means that if two friends sit together and contemplate how to enhance the importance of the Creator, they already have the strength to receive enhancement of the greatness of the Creator in the form of awakening from below. And for this act, the awakening from above follows, and they begin to have some sensation of the greatness of the Creator.

According to what is written, "In the multitude of people is the King's glory," it follows that the greater the number of the collective, the more effective is the power of the collective. In other words, they produce a stronger atmosphere of greatness and importance of the Creator. At that time, each person's body feels that he regards anything that he wishes to do for holiness—meaning to bestow upon the Creator—as a great fortune, that he has been privileged with being among people who have been rewarded with serving the King. At that time, every little thing he does fills him with joy and pleasure that now he has something with which to serve the King.

To the extent that the society regards the greatness of the Creator with their thoughts during the assembly, each according to his degree originates the importance of the Creator in him. Thus, he can walk all day in the world of gladness and joy.

21. RABASH, Article No. 13 (1984), "Sometimes Spirituality Is Called a 'Soul'"

We must always awaken what the heart forgets, what is needed for the correction of the heart—*Love of friends*—whose purpose is to achieve love of others.

This is not a pleasant thing for the heart, which is called "self-love." Hence, when there is a gathering of friends, we must remember to bring up the question, meaning everyone should ask himself how much we have advanced in love of others, and how much we have done to promote us in that matter.

22. Rabbi Shmuel Bornstein, author of *Shem MiShmuel*

It is written "Gather, purify," since gathering is more unification of the heart than the word "grouping." "Grouping" pertains only to the body, although the views are not united. But a gathering of people is also with one heart. It is a gathering from the outside in, where they become very unified.

Therefore, the word "gathering" applies mostly to the souls, since "soul" comes from the words "desire" and "yearning." If each and every one yearns for his own benefit, although they all want the same thing, it is still not one view, since one wants one's own benefit, and the other wants his own benefit.

However, if they are complete, and also many yearn to satisfy the Creator's will, this is certainly called "complete unification," and deserves the title "gathering," by everyone uniting with an immense feeling of the soul, to do the will of our Father in Heaven.

23. Rabbi Kalonymus Kalman Halevi Epstein, *Maor VaShemesh, VaYechi*

The essence of the assembly is for everyone to be in one unity and for all to seek but one purpose: to find the Creator. In every ten there is the *Shechina* [Divinity]. Clearly, if there are more than ten then there is more revelation of the *Shechina*. Thus, each one should assemble with his friend and come to him to hear from him a word about the work of the Creator, and how to find the Creator. He should annul before his friend, and his friend should do the same toward him, and so should everyone do. Then, when the assembly is with this intention, then "More than the calf wants to suckle, the cow wants to nurse," and the Creator approaches them and He is with them, and great mercies and good and revealed kindness will be extended over the assembly of Israel.

24. *Maor VaShemesh, Re'eh*

The main rule by which to come to the path of the Creator is through adhesion with friends, that by gathering together, as each one annuls before his friend when he sees his friend's merit in Torah, *Mitzvot* [commandments], and good deeds, he becomes lowly in his own eyes, and his friend is greater than him and loves each and every one, and his desire is to truly permeate each one because of joy. This is done by adhesion of friends.

25. Rabbi Kalonymus Kalman Halevi Epstein, *Maor VaShemesh*

When the children of Israel gather together, it is a very great thing. But the most important is for each and every one not think of himself at all, that he is regarded as righteous or that he counts at all among the friends. He should only see that his actions do not blemish the sacred society. Although it seems as though he is a great person, he should nonetheless look into his actions and think, and likewise each one in the sacred society will think, "What makes me great?" and annul himself completely. It is known that in every ten there is the *Shechina* [Divinity], and this is a complete level. In a complete level, there are head, hands, legs, and heels, as is known from the words of high and holy ones. It follows that when every person regards himself as nothing in the sacred society, then he regards himself as a heel compared to the society, while they are the head, the body, and the higher organs. When each one thinks of himself in this way, they make the gates of abundance and every lushness in the world open up to them, and it is drawn the most through the person who is more regarded as "nothing" and as "a heel."

8

The Covenant

1. Baal HaSulam, *Shamati*, Article No. 76, "On All Your Offerings You Shall Offer Salt"

"On all your offerings you shall offer salt," meaning the covenant of the salt. The covenant corresponds to the mind. Normally, when two people do good to one another, when there is love between them, they certainly do not need to make a covenant. But at the same time, we can see that precisely when there is love, this is the usual time for making covenants. Then he said that the making of the covenant is for later.

This means that the agreement is made now so that later, if there comes a state where each of them thinks that the other's heart is not whole with one's friend, they will have an agreement. This agreement will obligate them to remember the covenant that they had made between them, in order to continue the old love in this state, too.

This is the meaning of "On all your offerings you shall offer salt," meaning that all of the *Krevut*1 in the work of the Creator should be about the covenant of the King.

2. Baal HaSulam, "The Arvut [Mutual Guarantee]," Item 28

It is written, "Now, if you surely listen to My voice and keep My covenant," meaning make a covenant on what I am telling you here: to be My *Segula* from among all peoples. This means that you will be My *Segula*, and sparks of purification and cleansing of the body will pass through you onto all the peoples and the nations of the world, for the nations of the world are not yet ready for this, and at any rate, I need one nation to start with now, so it will be as a remedy for all the nations. For this reason, He ends, "for all the earth is Mine," meaning all the peoples of the earth belong to Me, as do you, and are destined to adhere to Me. But now, while they are still incapable of performing that task, I need a virtuous people. If you agree to be the remedy for all the nations, I command you to "be unto Me a kingdom of priests."

3. RABASH, Article No. 738, "A Covenant of Salt"

"On all your offerings you shall offer salt." This is the covenant of the salt, which is a covenant against the intellect, for when one takes good things from one's friend, they should make a covenant.

A covenant is needed precisely when each one has demands and complaints against the other, and they might come into anger and separation. At that time, the covenant they made obligates them to maintain the love and unity between them, for the rule is that whenever someone wishes to hurt the other, they have a cure—to remember the covenant that they had made between them.

This obligates them to maintain the love and peace. This is the meaning of "On all your offerings you shall offer salt," meaning that any nearing in the work of the Creator should be through a covenant of salt, as this is the whole foundation.

4. RABASH, Article No. 3 (1987), "All of Israel Have a Part in the Next World"

Concerning Abraham and Avimelech, "And the two of them made a covenant." Baal HaSulam asked, "If two people understand that it is worthwhile for them to love each other, why should they make a covenant? How does an act of seemingly signing a contract help? What does it give us?" Then he said, "It gives us that when we make a covenant we mean that since it is possible that something might separate them, they are making a covenant now, so that just as now they understand that there is love and equivalence between them, this covenant will persist even if afterwards things will come that should separate them. Still, the connection they are establishing now will be permanent. Accordingly, we should say that if afterwards things will come that should separate them, we should say that each one should go above reason and say that they will not notice what they see within reason, but go above reason. Only in this way can the covenant hold and there will be no separation between them.

5. RABASH, Article No. 9 (1984), "One Should Always Sell the Beams of His House"

The covenant that two friends make, as we find in the Torah (Gen 21:27), "And Abraham took sheep and oxen, and gave them unto Abimelech; and they two made a covenant." He asked, "If the two of them love each other, of course they do good to each other. And naturally, when there is no love between them because the love has waned for some reason, they do not do good to one another. So how does making a covenant between them help?"

He answered that the covenant that they do is not for now, since now when the love is felt between them, there is no need to make a covenant. Rather, the making of the covenant is done purposely for the future. In other words, it is possible that after some time, they will not feel the love as they do now, but they will still keep their relations as before. This is what the making of the covenant is for.

We can also see that although now they do not feel the love as it was when the society was established, everyone must still overcome his view and go above reason. By that, everything will be corrected and each will judge his friend favorably.

6. RABASH, Article No. 31 (1987), "What Is Making a Covenant in the Work?"

As long as one has not been awarded permanent faith, there must be ascents and descents. It follows that there could be a time when the love between them cools. For this reason, now, in the beginning of his work, he takes upon himself the burden of the kingdom of heaven, to make a covenant, so that whether or not the body agrees to be a servant of the Creator, he takes upon himself not to change a thing. Instead, he will say, "I spoke once and I will not change." Instead, I will go above reason as I have taken upon myself when making the covenant in the beginning of the work.

7. RABASH, Article No. 34 (1989), "What Is Peace in the Work?"

Is written, "As the advantage of the light from within the darkness." In other words, it is impossible to receive light if he has no lack and need for the light.

For this reason, when a person sees that the nations of the world in him object to the Creator, and he cannot tolerate the enemy of Israel within him, he becomes jealous for his God and does not look at any descents he has, and does what he can and cries out to the Creator to help him be able to defeat the wicked ones within him.

By this he overcomes and does not escape the campaign. At that time, the Creator gives him the covenant. That is, he makes a covenant with Him that there will be peace between him and the Creator, by receiving a gift from the Creator, which is the vessels of bestowal. This is regarded as making the covenant, which is the *Klipa* [shell/peel], called "will to receive for himself," and instead of the foreskin, the Creator gives him vessels of bestowal, and by this they make a covenant, meaning peace.

8. RABASH, Article No. 19 (1984) "You Stand Today, All of You"

Similarly, even though they currently do not feel the love as they did then, they still evoke the old love and do not look at the state they are currently in. Instead, they go back to doing things for each other. This is the benefit of the covenant. Thus, even when the love that was between them has lost its fancy, because they made the covenant, they have the strength to reawaken the shining love that they had before. In this way, they usher each other back into the future.

It follows that making the covenant is for the future. It is like a contract that they sign that they will not be able to regret when they see that the ties of love are not as they were, that this love gave them great pleasure while they were doing good to each other, but now that love has been corrupted, they are powerless and none can do anything for the other.

But if they do wish to do something for their friends, they must consider the making of the covenant that they had before, and out of that they should rebuild the love. It is like a person who signs a contract with his friend, and the contract connects them so they cannot part from one another.

9. RABASH, Article No. 471, "You Stand Today – 2"

Concerning the covenant, Baal HaSulam said why two people who love each other need the covenant if there is love and friendship between them. However, the covenant is because as now the love between them is complete, it is possible that after some time there will not be the same love and each one will imagine that the other is causing him harm. At that time, the covenant comes so that each one will keep the covenant that they had made while there was true love between them.

Thus, now, too, although they do not feel so, they will maintain the friendship between them as though now, too, they feel love.

Likewise, when a person feels the love of the Creator, he understands that it is worthwhile to leave other loves for the love of the Creator. But later, when the awakening passes away from him and he no longer feels the love of the Creator, he will want to return to the other loves that he had already decided to toss away.

At that time, a person needs the covenant and maintain the same conduct that he had while he felt the love of the Creator, although now he has no feeling whatsoever. Then, the work must be compulsory, to enslave himself to the covenant that he had made before. This is called "that you may enter into the covenant."

10. RABASH, Article No. 63, "You Stand Here Today – 1"

"You stand here today all of you." This means that he gathered them... to admit them into the covenant (RASHI). "All of you" means that everyone entered into the *Arvut* [mutual responsibility] (*Ohr HaChaim*).

There is a question why he begins with plural form, "all of you," then shifts to singular form, "every man from Israel." It means that "all of you" permeates everyone in Israel, meaning that every person from Israel will be included with "all of you," as it is written, "And the people camped at the bottom of the mountain," as one man with one heart. In other words, when there is love of Israel, they can succeed, as it is written, "Ephraim is joined to idols; let him be."

Man is a small world and comprises the entire world. He should achieve the degree of being singular, as it is written, "Rewarded, he sentences himself and the entire world to the side of merit" (*Kidushin* 40b).

Therefore, when a person admits all the individuals, "your heads and your tribes," for everyone must join in the covenant, meaning to come to be a worker of the Creator "with all your heart—with both your inclinations." In other words, even the lowly attributes in man should undergo correction.

"So that He may establish you today as His people and He will be a God unto you." That is, a person will achieve this attainment, that he is in the singular authority.

11. RABASH, Article No. 19 (1984), "You Stand Today, All of You"

One should walk on the path of truth—to say, "My current state, being in utter lowliness, means that I was deliberately thrown out from above to know if I truly wish to do the holy work in order to bestow, or if I wish to be God's servant because I find it more rewarding than other things."

Then, if one can say, "Now I want to work in order to bestow and I do not want to do the holy work to receive some gratification in the work. Instead, I will settle for doing the work of holiness like any man of Israel—praying or taking a lesson on the daily portion. And I don't have time to think with which intent I study or pray, but I will simply observe the actions without any special intent." At that time, he will reenter the holy work because now he wishes to be God's servant without any preconditions.

This is the meaning of what is written, "You stand today, all of you," meaning everything you went through, all the states you have experienced—whether states of *Gadlut* or states of less than *Gadlut*, which were considered intermediate or so. You take all those details and you do not compare one degree to another because you do not care for any reward, but only for doing the Creator's will. He has commanded us to observe *Mitzvot* [commandments] and to study Torah, and this is what we do, like any common man of Israel. In other words, the state he is in right now is as important to him as when he thought he was in a state of *Gadlut*. At that time, "The Lord your God makes with you this day."

This means that then the Creator makes a covenant with him. In other words, precisely when one accepts His work without any conditions and agrees to do the holy work without any reward, which is called "unconditional surrender," this is the time when the Creator makes a covenant with him.

12. RABASH, Article No. 31 (1987), "What Is Making a Covenant in the Work?"

The work in Torah and *Mitzvot* [commandments] is primarily when beginning to walk on the path that leads to *Lishma* [for Her sake]. That is, when a person begins the work, he begins in *Lo Lishma* [not for Her sake], as our sages said, "One should always engage in Torah *Lo Lishma*, and from *Lo Lishma* we come to *Lishma*."

For this reason, the beginning of his work was with enthusiasm because he saw that by observing Torah and *Mitzvot* he would achieve happiness in life. Otherwise, he would not begin. Therefore, in the beginning of his work, when he is still working *Lo Lishma*, meaning that when he works, he constantly looks at the reward he will receive after his work, he has the strength to work.

As in corporeality, a person is used to working in a place where he knows he will be rewarded for his work. Otherwise, a person cannot work for free, if not for his own benefit. Only when he sees that self-benefit will come from this work does he have the strength to work enthusiastically and willingly, since he is looking at the reward and not at the work.

The work does not matter if a person understands that here he will receive from this employer twice as much as he would receive from working for the previous employer, before he came to the job where they pay twice as much. This means that according to the salary, so the work becomes easier and smaller.

Accordingly, we should interpret in the work that making a covenant means that when a person takes upon himself the work, even if in *Lo Lishma*, he must make a covenant with the Creator to serve Him whether he wants to or not.

Yet, we should understand on what the enthusiasm depends. It depends only on the reward. That is, when there is a big reward, the desire for the work does not stop. But when the reward is doubtful, the desire for the work vanishes and he shifts to rest. That is, at that time he feels more pleasantness in rest.

It is so much so that he says, "I relinquish the work, and anyone who wants can do this work because it is not for me." But making a covenant is when he begins to work even in *Lo Lishma*. And since now he wants the work, for who would force him to come into the work of the Creator, now he must make the covenant and say, "Even if there comes a time of descent," meaning that he will have no desire for the work, "I still take upon myself not to consider my desire but work as though I have a desire." This is called "making a covenant."

13. *Zohar for All*, Yitro [Jethro], "You Shall Not Have," Items 405-406

Happy are Israel, whom the Creator names "man," as it is written, "And you, My sheep, the sheep of My pasture, you are men." It is also written, "When any man of you brings an offering." What is the reason that He calls them "men"? It is because it is written, "And you that cleave unto the Lord your God," meaning you, and not the rest of the idol-worshipping nations. This is the reason why you are men. You are called "man," and the idol-worshipping nations are not called "man."

When a person from Israel is circumcised, he enters the covenant that the Creator made with Abraham, as it is written, "And the Lord blessed Abraham in all." It is also written, "Mercy [*Hesed*] for Abraham." And he begins to enter in that place. When he has been rewarded with keeping the *Mitzvot* of the Torah, he comes into that man of the upper *Merkava* [chariot/assembly] and clings to the King's body, and then he is called "man."

14. *Zohar for All*, *Zohar Hadash*, *Hukat*, "I Drew Them with Cords of Man, with Bonds of Love," Item 60

It is written about it, "And the children of Israel sighted from the work." When they saw the hard work until the upper covenant remembered them, and upper *Ima*, *Bina*, remembered them and awoke with mercy for her children, as it is written, "and their outcry went up to the God." This is upper *Ima*, in whose hand is all the freedom. She opened for Israel the upper inlets, fifty gates, and brought them out from there. The lower *Ima*, *Malchut*, was filled with mercy for them and Moses went out to the world, an appointee and a father to shepherd Israel in the Torah.

15. The Constitution of the Members of Ramchal's Group

These are the words of the covenant that the undersigned friends have all taken upon themselves to uphold for the sake of the unification of the Creator and the *Shechina* [Divinity], for they have all become as one man, to do the work of the Creator, to regard each of them as all of them for all this work. This is what they have taken upon themselves: that this study will not be in order to receive reward in any manner of expectation of payment or any leaning toward a thought and another inclination, but solely for the purpose of correcting the *Shechina* and the correction of all of Israel, the Creator's people, to bring contentment to their Maker. They will have no reward from this, so that none of the friends will regard the learning as a personal correction, even for atonement of iniquities. Rather, all that will be in him is the complete intention to correct the *Shechina* and the correction of all of Israel.

16. Rav Shneor Zalman of Liadi, *Likutei Torah*

By making the covenant, their love will be eternal love that will never fall. No prevention shall separate them since they make between them a strong and steadfast bond to unite and connect in their love in a wondrous connection and above rhyme or reason. Although rhyme or reason should have stopped the love or cause some hate, because of the making of the covenant, their love must exist forever. This love and this steadfast bond will cover all crimes, since they have made a covenant and bonded as though they have become one flesh. As one cannot stop loving oneself, so his love for his friend will not stop.

9

They Helped Every Man His Friends

1. RABASH, Article No. 30 (1988), "What to Look for in the Assembly of Friends"

When a group of people gathers and wishes to work together on love of friends, they must all help one another as much as they can. And there are many discernments about that, since not everyone is the same, meaning that what one needs, the other does not. However, there is one thing in which all are equal: Each and every one of the friends needs high spirits. That is, when the friends are not in a good mood, they are not all the same in their needs. Rather, each has his own reason for being unhappy. Therefore, each one must contemplate how he can bring about a good mood to the other.

2. RABASH, Article No. 30 (1988), "What to Look for in the Assembly of Friends"

During the assembly, it is forbidden to evoke the left line. Only when one is alone is he permitted to use the left line, but not more than half an hour a day. But the essence of man's work is to go specifically by the right line. But two people together must not speak of the left, for only thus can they receive assistance from the society.

3. RABASH, Article No. 3 (1984), "Love of Friends – 1"

"And the man asked him, saying, 'What are you seeking?'" meaning, "How can I help you?" "And he said: 'I seek my brethren.'" By being together with my brothers, that is, by being in a group where there is love of friends, I will be able to mount the trail that leads to the house of God.

This trail is called "a path of bestowal," and this way is against our nature. To be able to achieve it, there is no other way but love of friends, by which everyone can help his friend.

4. RABASH, Article No. 12 (1984), "Concerning the Importance of Society"

In matters of work on the path of truth, one should isolate oneself from other people. This is because the path of truth requires constant strengthening, since it is against the view of the world. The view of the world is knowing and receiving, whereas the view of Torah is faith and bestowal. If one strays from that, he immediately forgets all the work of the path of truth and falls into a world of self-love.

Only from a society in the form of "They helped every man his friend" does each person in the society receive the strength to fight against the view of the world.

5. RABASH, Article No. 30 (1988), "What to Look for in the Assembly of Friends"

What can one do when he feels that he is in a state of sadness—both in terms of the corporeal state and the spiritual state—and the time when he must go to the society has come? And yet, our sages said, "A worry in a man's heart? Let him speak of it with others." In other words, he should tell his friends, and perhaps they can offer some help.

But if this is so, why do we say that everyone should bring high spirits into the society when one has none? Moreover, there is a rule that "one cannot give that which one does not have." Thus, what should he do to give something to the society that will give high spirits to the society?

Indeed, there is no other way but for man to walk on the right line. Thus, before he goes to the love of friends, he should read Baal HaSulam's essay (*Shamati*, No. 40) where he clarifies what is the right line, that this is the meaning of above reason. And he should draw strength from there so that when he comes to the society, each and every one will more or less be able to infuse a spirit of life, and by that, the whole of society will feel joy and strength, and confidence.

6. RABASH, Letter No. 5

When you feel that you are at war, each of you will know and feel that he needs the help of his friend, and without him, his own strength will wane, as well. Then, when you understand that you must save your life, each of you will forget he has a body he must preserve, and you will both be tied by the thought of how to defeat the enemy.

7. RABASH, Article No. 4 (1984)," They Helped Every One His Friend"

There is one thing that is common to all—the mood. It is said, "A concern in one's heart, let him speak of it with others." This is because with regard to feeling high-spirited, neither wealth nor erudition can be of assistance.

Rather, it is one person who can help another by seeing that one's friend is low. It is written, "One does not deliver oneself from imprisonment." Rather, it is one's friend who can lift his spirit.

This means that one's friend raises him from his state into a state of liveliness. Then, one begins to reacquire strength and confidence of life and wealth, and he begins as though his goal is now near him.

It turns out that each and every one must be attentive and think how he can help his friend raise his spirit, because in the matter of spirits, anyone can find a needy place in one's friend that he can fill.

8. *Meshivat Nefesh*, Item 3

Each one must strengthen his friend. They should awaken one another and strengthen one another in His work. Each one should remind his friend all the good counsels that each one knows and understands, as much as they had received from their teacher.

9. Noam Elimelech, *Likutei Shoshana*

One must always pray for his friend, as one cannot do much for himself, for "One does not deliver oneself from imprisonment." But when asking for his friend, he is answered quickly. Therefore, each one should pray for his friend, and thus each works on the other's desire until all of them are answered.

10

Envy, Lust, and Honor

1. Baal HaSulam, "Introduction to the Book Panim Meirot uMasbirot," Item 3

The Creator installed three inclinations in the masses, called "envy," "lust," and "honor." Due to them, the masses develop degree by degree to educe a face of a whole man.

The inclination for lust educes the wealthy. The selected among them have a strong desire, and also lust. They excel in acquiring wealth, which is the first degree in the evolution of the masses. Like the vegetative degree in reality, they are governed by an alien force that deviates them to their inclination, as lust is an alien force in the human species borrowed from the animate.

The inclination for honor educes the famous heroes from among them, who govern the synagogues, the town, etc. The most firm-willed among them, which also have an inclination for honor, excel in obtaining dominion. These are the second degree in the evolution of the masses, similar to the animate degree in reality, whose operating force is present in their own essence, as we have said above. This is because the inclination for honor is unique to the human species, and along with it the craving for governance, as it is written, "You have put all things under his feet" (Psalms 8:7).

The inclination for envy elicits the sages from among them, as our sages said, "Author's envy increases wisdom." The strong-willed, with an inclination for envy, excel in acquiring wisdom and knowledge. It is like the speaking degree in reality, in which the operating force is not limited by time or place, but is collective and encompasses every item in the world, throughout all times.

Also, it is the nature of the fire of envy to be general, encompassing all times and the whole reality. This is because it is the conduct of envy: If one had not seen the object in one's friend's possession, the desire for it would not have awakened in one at all.

You find that the sensation of absence is not for what one does not have, but for what one's friends have, who are the entire progeny of Adam and Eve throughout the generations. Thus, this force is unlimited and therefore fit for its sublime and elated role.

2. Baal HaSulam, *Shamati*, Article No. 9," What Are Three Things that Broaden One's Mind in the Work?"

When one takes upon himself faith in purity, in mind or in heart, he is imparted with a sightly woman, meaning that the *Shechina* appears to him in a form of grace and beauty, which broadens his mind.

In other words, through the pleasure and gladness he feels at that time, the *Shechina* appears within the organs, filling the outer and inner *Kelim*. This is called "broadening the mind."

This is obtained through envy, lust, and honor, which bring a person out of the world. Envy means through envy in the *Shechina*, regarded as zeal in "The zeal of the Lord of hosts." Honor means that he wants to increase the glory of heaven. Lust is by way of "You have heard the lust of the humble."

3. Baal HaSulam, "Introduction to the Book Panim Meirot uMasbirot," Item 4

The thing is that this careful watch and door-locking on the hall of wisdom is for fear of people in whom the spirit of writers' envy is mixed with the force of lust and honor. Their envy is not limited to wanting only wisdom and knowledge.

Hence, both texts are correct, and one comes and teaches of the other. The face of the generation is as the face of the dog, meaning they bark as dogs *Hav, Hav* [give, give] righteous are cast away and authors' wisdom went astray in them.

It follows that it is permitted to open the gates of the wisdom and remove the careful guard, since it is naturally safe from theft and exploitation. There is no longer fear lest indecent disciples might take it and sell it in the market to the materialistic plebs, since they will find no buyers for this merchandise, as it is loathsome in their eyes.

Since they have no hope of acquiring lust or honor through it, it has become safe and guarded by itself. No stranger will approach except for lovers of wisdom and counsel. Hence, any examination shall be removed from those who enter, until even the very young will be able to attain it.

4. Baal HaSulam, "Introduction to the Book Panim Meirot uMasbirot," Item 5

Our sages said, "Messiah, Son of David comes only in a generation that is all worthy…" meaning when everyone retires from pursuit of honor and lust. At that time, it will be possible to establish seminaries among the masses to prepare them for the coming of the Messiah Son of David. "…or in a generation that is all unworthy," meaning in such a generation when "the face of the generation is as the face of the dog, and righteous shall be cast away, and authors' wisdom shall go astray in them." At such a time, it will be possible to remove the careful guard and all who remain in the house of Jacob with their hearts pounding to attain the wisdom and the purpose, "Holy" will be said to them and they shall come and learn.

This is so because there will no longer be fear lest one might not sustain one's merit and trade the wisdom in the market, as no one in the mob will buy it. The wisdom will be so loathsome in their eyes that neither glory nor lust will be obtainable in return for it.

Hence, all who wish to enter may come and enter. Many will roam, and the knowledge will increase among the worthy of it. And by this we will soon be rewarded with the coming of the Messiah, and the redemption of our souls.

5. Baal HaSulam, "Introduction to the Book Panim Meirot uMasbirot," Item 15

We must thoroughly understand the sublimity of that man, the creation of the Creator, and also his wife, to whom the Creator administered greater intelligence than him, as they have written (*Nidah* 45) in the interpretation to the verse, "And the Lord made the rib."

Thus, how did they fail and became as fools, not knowing to beware of the serpent's cunningness? On the other hand, that serpent, of which the text testifies that it was more cunning than all the animals of the field, how did it utter such folly and emptiness that should they eat from the fruit of the Tree of Knowledge, they would be turned to God? Moreover, how did that folly settle in their hearts?

Also, it is said below that they did not eat because of their desire to become God, but simply because the tree is good to eat. This is seemingly a beastly desire!

6. Baal HaSulam, "Introduction to the Book Panim Meirot uMasbirot," Item 17

And the woman saw that the tree was good to eat and that it was a delight to the eyes." This means that she did not rely on His words, but went and examined with her own mind and understanding and sanctified herself with additional *Kedusha*, to bring contentment to the Creator in order to complete the aim desired of her, and not at all for herself. At that time, her eyes were opened, as the serpent had said, "And the woman saw that the tree was good to eat."

In other words, by seeing that "it was a delight to the eyes," before she even touched it, she felt great sweetness and lust, when her eyes saw by themselves that she had not seen such a desirable thing in all the trees of the garden.

She also learned that the tree is good for knowledge, meaning that there is far more to crave and covet in this tree than in all the trees of the garden. This refers to knowing that they were created for this act of eating, and that this is the whole purpose, as the serpent had revealed to her.

After all these absolute scrutinies, "she took of its fruit and ate, and gave also to her man with her, and he ate." The text accurately writes "with her," meaning with the pure intention only to bestow and not for her own sake. This is the meaning of the words "and gave to her man with her," with her in *Kedusha*.

7. RABASH, Assorted Notes, "From Lo Lishma to Lishma," No. 119

There must always be a beginning; otherwise, it is impossible to achieve *Lishma* [for Her sake]. That is, one must believe that in all the corporeal lusts, meaning eating, drinking, and the rest of the lusts, as well as in pleasures found in learning external teachings, control, vengeance, and so forth, as it is written in general, "Envy, lust, and honor take a person out of the world," in those pleasures there is nothing more than a thin light, as *The Zohar* says.

Conversely, great lights are deposited in *Torah and Mitzvot* [commandments], unlike corporeal pleasures, in which only sparks of the light of *Kedusha* fell.

Hence, *Klipot* [shells/peels] give one an awakening to enter *Kedusha* because they want to be rewarded with great lights. This is called *Lo Lishma* [not for Her sake]. Afterward, from this *Lo Lishma*, he can be rewarded with *Lishma*.

8. RABASH, Article No. 4 (1990), "What It Means that the Generations of the Righteous are Good Deeds, in the Work"

How can a person emerge from the tendencies that he is used to since birth? Intellectually, it is impossible to understand how it is possible that a person will think other than his inclinations. And there (in the introduction, Item 3) he says, "Because of this, we were given corrections, by which man must toil and labor. Otherwise, all creations would have been in a state of rest, since the root of the creatures, which is the Creator, is in a state of complete rest, and every branch wants to resemble its root."

These corrections, called "envy," "lust," and "honor," bring man out of the world (*Avot*, Chapter 4:28). He says there that through the envy and respect, it is possible to change the inclinations to lust into the degree of vegetative, where he begins to work for the sake of others for the purpose of *Lo Lishma* [not for Her sake]. Likewise, through envy, he can shift to the level of knowledge, as our sages said, "Authors' envy increases knowledge." And likewise, through *Lo Lishma* they can also shift from the animate level to the speaking.

Yet, how does the *Lo Lishma* help if one does not have the real inclination to the degree to which he enters? Our sages said about this, with respect to the Torah, "The light in it reforms him." It turns out that through *Lo Lishma*, we come to *Lishma* [for Her sake]. This is why they said, "One should always learn *Lo Lishma*, as from *Lo Lishma* we come to *Lishma*."

9. RABASH, Article No. 21 (1986), "Concerning Above Reason"

Our sages said, "Counters' envy increases wisdom." In other words, when all the friends look at the society as being at a high level, both in thoughts and in actions, it is natural that each and every one must raise his degree to a higher level than he has by the qualities of his own body.

This means that even if innately he has no craving for great desires or is not intensely attracted to honor, still, through envy, he can acquire additional powers that he doesn't have in his own nature. Instead, the force of the quality of envy in him has procreated new powers within him, which exist in the society. And through them, he has received those new qualities, meaning powers that were not installed in him by his progenitors. Thus, now he has new qualities that society has procreated in him.

It turns out that a person has qualities that his parents bequeathed to their children, and he has qualities that he acquired from the society, which is a new possession. And this comes to him only through bonding with the society and the envy that he feels toward the friends when he sees that they have better qualities than his own. It motivates him to acquire their good qualities, which he doesn't have and of which he is jealous.

Thus, through the society, he gains new qualities that he adopts by seeing that they are at a higher degree than his, and he is envious of them. This is the reason why now he can be greater than when he didn't have a society, since he acquires new powers through the society.

10. RABASH, Article No. 450, "Forces that Induce the Development of the Heart and the Mind"

"If a wise disciple gets into a rage, it is because the Torah inflames him." RASHI interpreted, that he has a big heart due to his Torah, and he becomes more attentive than other people. This means that we must sentence him to the side of merit" (*Taanit* 4a).

We should interpret that because of his big heart, he is moved by everything and he is sensitive to everything.

"Lust" is a demand from his own internality. "Envy" means that for himself he has no demand, but his externality invokes in him a demand. This is why it is considered a demand from his externality. Therefore, there are two forces in man that cause him to develop: the mind and the heart.

11. RABASH, Article No. 21 (1986), "Concerning Above Reason"

A person should feel that he is worse than others because this is indeed the truth. And we should also understand what our sages said, "Counters' envy increases wisdom." This is precisely within reason. But above reason, his friend's merit is not evident enough to say that he is envious of his friend, so it would cause him to work and toil because his friend compels him, due to envy.

Baal HaSulam interpreted a phrase by Rabbi Yohanan, "The Creator saw that righteous were few. He stood and planted them in each and every generation," as it is said, "For the pillars of the Earth are the Lord's, and He has set the world upon them." RASHI interprets, "Spread them through all the generations," to be a basis, sustenance, and a foundation for the existence of the world (*Yoma* 78b). "Few" means that they were growing fewer. Hence, what did He do? "He stood and planted them in each and every generation." Thus, by planting them in each generation, they would multiply.

We should understand how they would multiply if He planted them in each and every generation. We should understand the difference between all the righteous being in a single generation, and being scattered through all the generations, as is understood from the words of RASHI's commentary, that by spreading them throughout the generations the righteous would increase.

He, Baal HaSulam, said, "By having righteous in each generation, there will be room for people who do not have the innate qualities to achieve *Dvekut* with the Creator. However, by bonding with the righteous that will be in each generation, through adhering to them, they will learn from their actions and will be able to acquire new qualities through the righteous that will be in each generation. This is why He spread the righteous in each generation, so that in this way the righteous will increase."

12. RABASH, Article No. 21 (1986), "Concerning Above Reason"

When the evil inclination comes and shows him the lowliness of the friends, he should go above reason. But certainly, it would be better and more successful if he could see within reason that the friends are at a higher degree than his own. With that we can understand the prayer that Rabbi Elimelech had written for us, "*Let our hearts see the virtues of our friends, and not their faults.*"

13. RABASH, Article No. 21 (1986), "Concerning Above Reason"

If he sees that the friends are at a higher degree than his own, he sees within reason how he is in utter lowliness compared to the friends, that all the friends keep the schedule of arriving at the seminary, and take greater interest in all that is happening among the friends, to help anyone in any way they can, and immediately implement every advice for the work from the teachers in actual fact, etc., it certainly affects him and gives him strength to overcome his laziness, both when he needs to wake up before dawn and when he is awakened.

Also, during the lesson, his body is more interested in the lessons, since otherwise he will lag behind his friends. Also, with anything that concerns *Kedusha* [holiness/sanctity], he must take it more seriously because the body cannot tolerate lowliness. Moreover, when his body looks at the friends, it sees within reason that they are all working for the Creator, and then his body, too, lets him work for the Creator.

And the reason why the body helps him shift to in order to bestow is as mentioned—the body is unwilling to tolerate lowliness. Instead, everybody has pride, and he is unwilling to accept a situation where his friend is greater than him. Thus, when he sees that his friends are at a higher level than his own, this causes him to ascend in every way.

14. Elimelech of Lizhensk, *Noam Elimelech* [*The Pleasantness of Elimelech*]

Do save us from envy of one another, and let no envy of others come into our hearts, nor our envy of others. On the contrary, let our hearts see the virtues of our friends and not their faults, and let us speak to each other in a way that is seemly and worthy before You, and let no hatred rise in one towards another. Brace our ties of love to You, as it is known to You that all will be for bringing contentment to You, and this is our main intention. And should we not have the wit to aim our hearts to You, You will teach us, so we may truly know the aim of Your good will. Brace our ties of love to You, as it is known to You that all will be for bringing contentment to You, and this is our main intention. And should we not have the wit to aim our hearts to You, You will teach us, so we may truly know the aim of Your good will.

15. *Maor VaShemesh*, Intimations of Song of Songs

The heart and root of the work of the Creator is love of friends. Through it, one can come to the true work of the Creator. When one sees that his friends aspire and yearn to serve the Creator in

Torah and prayer, it will excite his heart to connect with them, and all his friends' actions will seem to him as greater than his own actions.

16. Rabbi Kalonymus Kalman Halevi Epstein, *Maor VaShemesh*

You will find the tenet and the wedge on which everything depends, and the content of the paths of correct repentance, through love of friends and adhesion of friends, and drawing near to the righteous of the generation. By this he will come to complete surrender since he will see the work of his friends, the great burning in their hearts, and excitement to serve the Creator, and by this he will learn to do as they do. He will recognize his blemishes and will repent in complete repentance.

17. Rabbi Kalonymus Kalman Halevi Epstein, *Maor VaShemesh*

One should depict his friend as serving the Creator more than him, and by this he strengthens himself more in the work of the Creator, for one should always say, "When will my work reach the work of my fathers?" This is the meaning of what they said in the Gemara, "In the future, each and every righteous will be burned by his friend's canopy." This seems perplexing, for is this the pleasure that will be in the future, to be burned by his friend's canopy? The thing is that as we said that in this world, it seems to each one that he is serving the Creator more than his friend, but in the future, when the Creator gives the righteous reward for their good deeds, He will give each one according to his actions. So He will give attainments of His Godliness, and he will see that his friend attained more than he, and he will understand that his friend intended by his good deeds in this world for the sake of the Creator more than he, which is why he attained more than he. Then "authors' [also counters'] envy will increase wisdom," by which he will grow increasingly stronger in the work of the Creator and will thereby attain more attainments of the Creator. This is the meaning of "Each one is burned by his friend's canopy," from the word "fervor." By seeing that his friend's canopy is bigger than his, a fire will burn in him and his soul will further ignite toward the work of the Creator, and he will attain more attainments of Godliness.

11

Buy Yourself a Friend

1. Baal HaSulam, "A Speech for the Completion of The Zohar"

Our sages said, "Make for yourself a rav and buy yourself a friend." This means that one can make a new environment for oneself. This environment will help him obtain the greatness of his rav through love of friends who appreciate his rav. Through the friends' discussing the greatness of the rav, each of them receives the sensation of his greatness. Thus, bestowal upon his rav becomes reception and sufficient motivation to an extent that will bring one to engage in Torah and *Mitzvot Lishma*.

It was said about this, "The Torah is acquired by forty-eight virtues, by serving of sages, and by meticulousness of friends." This is so because besides serving the rav, one needs the meticulousness of friends, as well, meaning the friends' influence, so they will influence him so he obtains the greatness of his rav. This is so because obtaining the greatness depends entirely on the environment, and a single person cannot do a thing about it whatsoever.

2. Baal HaSulam, Letter No. 2

I shall advise you to evoke within you fear of the coolness of the love between us. Although the intellect denies such a depiction, think for yourself—if there is a tactic by which to increase love and one does not increase it, that, too, is considered a flaw.

It is like a person who gives a great gift to his friend. The love that appears in his heart during the act is not like the love that remains in the heart after the fact. Rather, it gradually wanes each day until the blessing of the love can be entirely forgotten. Thus, the receiver of the gift must find a tactic every day to make it new in his eyes each day.

This is all our work—to display love between us, each and every day, just as upon receiving, meaning to increase and multiply the intellect with many additions to the core, until the additional blessings of now will be touching our senses like the essential gift at first. This requires great tactics, set up for the time of need.

3. RABASH, Article No. 1 (1985), "Make for Yourself a Rav and Buy Yourself a Friend – 1"

The order of the work is for one to begin with "Make for yourself a rav," and take upon himself the burden of the kingdom of heaven above logic and above reason. This is called "doing," meaning action only, despite the body's disapproval. Afterwards, "Buy yourself a friend." Buying is just as when a person wishes to buy something; he must let go of something that he has already acquired. He gives what he's had for some time and in return purchases a new object.

It is similar with the work of God. For one to achieve *Dvekut* [adhesion] with the Creator, which is equivalence of form, as in, "As He is merciful, so you are merciful," he must concede many things that he has in order to buy bonding with the Creator. This is the meaning of "Buy yourself a friend."

Before a person makes for himself a rav, meaning the kingdom of heaven, how can he buy himself a friend, meaning bond with the rav? After all, he has no rav yet. Only after he has made for himself a rav is there a point in demanding that the body make concessions to buy the bonding, that he wishes to give contentment to the Creator.

Moreover, we should understand that he has the strength to observe "buy yourself a friend" to the same extent as the greatness of the rav. This is so because he is willing to make concessions so as to bond with the rav to the very same extent that he feels the importance of the rav, since then he understands that obtaining *Dvekut* with the Creator is worth any effort.

4. RABASH, Article No. 1 (1985), "Make for Yourself a Rav and Buy Yourself a Friend – 1"

It turns out that real friendship—when each makes the necessary payment to buy his friend—is precisely when both are of equal status, and then both pay equally. It is like a corporeal business, where both of them give everything equally, or there cannot be a real partnership. Hence, "Buy yourself a friend," since there can be bonding—when each buys his friend—only when they are equal.

But on the other hand, it is impossible to learn from one another if one does not see that his friend is greater than he. But if the other one is greater, he cannot be his friend, but his rav [teacher/great], while he is considered a student. At that time, he can learn knowledge or virtues from him.

This is why it is said, "*Make* for yourself a *rav* and *buy* yourself *a friend*"; both have to exist. In other words, each should regard the other as a friend, and then there is room for buying. This means that each must pay with concessions to the other, like a father concedes his rest, works for his son, spends money for his son, and all is because of the love.

5. RABASH, Article No. 8 (1985), "Make for Yourself a Rav and Buy Yourself a Friend – 2"

"Make for yourself a rav [teacher/important person] and buy yourself a friend," are the path of correction, and another time, it is in the words, "And judge every person favorably" (*Avot*, Chapter 1). We should understand the difference between "make" and "buy," and the meaning of judging favorably.

We should interpret "make" as coming to exclude from reason. This is because when reason cannot understand if something is worth doing or not, how can it determine what is good for me? Or vice versa, if reason considers them as equal, who will determine for a person what he should do? Thus, the act can decide.

We should know that there are two ways before us: to work in order to bestow or to work in order to receive. There are parts in man's body that tell him, "You will succeed in life if you work in order to bestow, and this is the way you will enjoy life." This is the argument of the good inclination, as our sages said, "If you do so, you will be happy for this world and happy for the next world."

And the argument of the evil inclination is the opposite: It is better to work in order to receive. In that state, only the force called "action that is above reason" determines, not the intellect or emotion. This is why doing is called "above reason" and "above reasoning," and this is the force called "faith that is against the intellect."

"Buy" is within reason. Normally, people want to see what they want to buy, so the merchant shows them the goods and they negotiate whether or not it is worth the price that the merchant is asking. If they do not think it is worth it, they don't buy. Thus, "buy" is within reason.

6. RABASH, Article No. 8 (1985), "Make for Yourself a Rav and Buy Yourself a Friend – 2"

Between a man and his friend, we should begin with "Buy yourself a friend," and then "Make for yourself a rav." This is so because when a person looks for a friend, he should first examine him to see if he is really worth bonding with. After all, we see that a special prayer has been set up concerning a friend, which we say after the blessings in the prayer, "May it please ... Keep us away from an evil person and from a bad friend."

This means that before one takes a friend for himself, he must examine him in every possible way. At that time, he *must* use his reason. This is why it was not said, "Make yourself a friend," since "making" implies above reason. Therefore, concerning a man and his friend, he should go with his reason and examine as much as he can if his friend is okay, as we pray each day, "Keep us away from an evil person and from a bad friend."

7. RABASH, Article No. 8 (1985), "Make for Yourself a Rav and Buy Yourself a Friend – 2"

The Mishnah tells us, "Make for yourself a rav, buy for yourself a friend, and judge every person favorably" (*Avot*, Chapter 1).

We have explained that between a man and his friend the order is that first you go and buy yourself a friend—and we explained that buying is within reason—and then you must engage in "Make for yourself a rav." And between man and the Creator, the order is to first "Make for yourself a rav," and then "Buy yourself a friend."

8. RABASH, Letter No. 40

It is about time that we started moving forward toward our sacred goal like mighty strong men. It is known that the paved road that leads to the goal is love of friends, by which one shifts to love of the Creator. And in the matter of love, it is through "Buy yourself a friend." In other words, through actions, one buys one's friend's heart. And even if he sees that his friend's heart is like a stone, it is no excuse. If he feels that he is suitable for being his friend in the work, then he must buy him through deeds.

Each gift (and a gift is determined as such when he knows that his friend will enjoy it, whether in words, in thought, or in action. However, each gift must be out in the open, so that his friend will know about it, and with thoughts, one does not know that his friend was thinking of him. Hence, words are required, too, meaning he should tell him that he is thinking of him and cares about him. And that, too, should be about what his friend loves, meaning what his friend likes. One who doesn't like sweets, but pickles, cannot treat his friend to pickles, but specifically to sweets, since this is what his friend likes. And from that, we should understand that something could be unimportant to one, but more important than anything to another.) that he gives to his friend is like a bullet that makes a hollow in the stone. And although the first bullet only scratches the stone, when the second bullet hits the same place, it already makes a notch, and the third one makes a hole.

And through the bullets that he shoots repeatedly, the hole becomes a hollow in his friend's heart of stone, where all the presents gather. And each gift becomes a spark of love until all the sparks of love accumulate in the hollow of the stony heart and become a flame.

The difference between a spark and a flame is that where there is love, there is open disclosure, meaning a disclosure to all the peoples that the fire of love is burning in him. And the fire of love burns all the transgressions one meets along the way.

And should you ask, "What can one do if he feels that he has a heart of stone toward his friend?" Forgive me for writing, "Each and every one feels that he has a heart of stone," I mean except for the friends who feel and know that they have no objection that their friend will love them and will give them presents (not necessarily in action, but at least in good words and special attention only to him). I am referring only to those who feel that they have very cold hearts in regard to loving their friends, or those who had a heart of flesh but the coldness from the friends affected them, as well, and their hearts have frozen still.

The advice is very simple: The nature of fire is that when rubbing stones against each other, a fire starts. This is a great rule, since "From *Lo Lishma* [not for Her name] one comes to *Lishma* [for Her name]." And this is so particularly when the act is *Lishma*, meaning imparting a gift to one's friend, and the aim is *Lo Lishma*.

This is so because one gives a gift only to one that we know and recognize as someone we love. It follows that the aim of the gift is like gratitude for the love that his friend gives him. However, if one gives a gift to a stranger, meaning he doesn't feel that his friend is close to his heart, then he has nothing to be grateful for. It follows that the aim is *Lo Lishma*, meaning ... the intention that should be.

Ostensibly, it could be said that this is called "charity," since he pities his friend when he sees that there is no one who is speaking to him and greets him, and this is why he does that to him. Indeed, there is a prayer for it—that the Creator will help him by making him feel the love of his friend and make his friend close to his heart. Thus, through the deeds, he is rewarded with the aim, as well.

But while at the time of doing the giver of the gift intended that the gift to his friends would only be as charity (even if he is giving his time for his friend, since it is sometimes more important to a person than his money, as it is said, "One cares for his lack of money but not for his lack of time." However, regarding time, each has his own value, since there are people who make one pound an hour, and there is more or less. And likewise with their spirituality—how much spirituality they make in an hour, etc.), then one is testifying about himself that he isn't aiming for love of friends, meaning that through the action, the love between them will increase.

And only when both of them intend for a gift and not for charity, through the wearing out of the hearts, even of the strongest ones, each will bring out warmth from the walls of his heart, and the warmth will ignite the sparks of love until a clothing of love will form. Then, both of them will be covered under one blanket, meaning a single love will surround and envelop the two of them, as it is known that *Dvekut* [adhesion] unites two into one.

And when one begins to feel the love of his friend, joy and pleasure immediately begin to awaken in him, for the rule is that a novelty entertains. His friend's love for him is a new thing for him because he always knew that he was the only one who cared for his own well-being. But the minute he discovers that his friend cares for him, it evokes within him immeasurable joy, and he can no longer care for himself, since man can toil only where he feels pleasure. And since he is beginning to feel pleasure in caring for his friend, he naturally cannot think of himself.

9. RABASH, Article No. 31 (1990), "What 'There Is No Blessing in That Which Is Counted' Means in the Work"

The purpose of creation to do good to His creations. If they do not know and do not feel the delight and pleasure, what benefit is it? This is why this light is called *Hochma* [wisdom] and "seeing," and is named "light of *Panim* [face/anterior]," as in, "A man's wisdom illuminates his face."

In the work, this is called "something that is counted," meaning something that is received in the *vessels of reception*. This means that if he receives it, he will see what he has received and will be able to count what he has.

It is also called "a gift." Usually, when someone gives his friend a gift, he wants his friend to count and appreciate the value of the present for the simple reason that he gives the present to his friend because he wants to show his love for him. According to the value of the gift, a person can appreciate the measure of the love. It follows that if one does not look at the gift, to see the greatness of the gift, he blemishes the measure of the love.

Therefore, when a person receives a gift, if he does not see or does not try to see the importance of the gift, he blemishes the measure of love that the giver wants to show by it. For instance, our sages said, "Buy yourself a friend." And that person wants to buy his friend by sending him gifts. If that person does not see or appreciate the greatness and importance of the gift that he receives from him, how can he come to a state of "Buy yourself a friend"? It follows that with the gift, one should count and measure what he has received from his friend.

10. RABASH, Article No. 31 (1990), "What 'There Is No Blessing in That Which Is Counted' Means in the Work"

The light that is received in the vessels of bestowal is called "light of *Hassadim* [mercy]." *Hesed* [mercy/grace] means that he is giving, like a person who performs an act of mercy or grace toward his friend. This is called "covered *Hassadim*," meaning that the *Hassadim*—what he receives in vessels of bestowal, meaning what he gives—the light has the same value as the *Kli*.

In other words, it is known that there is charity and there is a gift. With a gift, we explained above that a person must see what he received and not simply receive a gift from his friend. If a person says, "It doesn't matter what he gave me," he is blemishing his friend's gift. Thus, the purpose for which he sent him the gift is not realized. The gift was meant to buy him a friend, as was said above, "Buy yourself a friend," but if he does not see the importance of the gift, he cannot buy him as a friend. Hence, he must count and measure the gift.

11. *Zohar for All*, *Truma* [Donation], "And They Shall Take a Donation for Me"

And how do we know that the Creator desires him and places His abode within him? When we see that man's will is to chase and to exert after the Creator with his heart, soul, and will, we know for certain that Divinity is present there. Then we need to buy that man for the full cost, bond with him and learn from him. We learn about that, "And buy yourself a friend." He should be bought for the full price to be rewarded with the Divinity that is in him. This is how far we must chase a righteous man and buy him.

12

Seeing the Friend's Merit

1. Baal HaSulam, Letter No 13

Make an effort to see the merits of the friends and not their faults at all, and connect in true love, together, until "Love will cover all crimes."

2. Baal HaSulam, *Shamati*, Article No. 62, "Descends and Incites, Ascends and Complains"

One who works in purity, cannot complain about others and always complains about himself, and sees others in a better degree than he feels himself.

3. RABASH, Article No. 30 (1988), "What to Look for in the Assembly of Friends"

There are two conditions to obtaining the greatness: 1) Always listen and assume appreciation of the environment to the extent that they exaggerate. 2) The environment should be great, as it is written, 'In the multitude of people is the king's glory.'
  "To receive the first condition, each student must feel that he is the smallest among all the friends. In that state, one can receive the appreciation of the greatness from everyone, since the great cannot receive from a smaller one, much less be impressed by his words. Rather, only the small is impressed by the appreciation of the great.
  "And for the second condition, each student must extol the virtues of each friend and cherish him as though he were the greatest in the generation. Then the environment will affect him as a sufficiently great environment, since quality is more important than quantity."

4. RABASH, Article No. 17 (1984), "Concerning the Importance of Friends"

If one has love of friends, the rule in love is that you want to see the friends' merits and not their faults. Hence, if one sees some fault in one's friend, it is not a sign that his friend is at fault, but that the seer is at fault, meaning that because his love of friends is flawed, he sees faults in his friend.
  Therefore, now he should not see to his friend's correction. Rather, he himself needs correction. It follows from the above-said that he should not see to the correction of his friend's faults, which

he sees in his friend, but he himself needs to correct the flaw he has created in the love of friends. And when he corrects himself, he will see only his friend's merits and not his faults.

5. RABASH, Article No. 21 (1986), "Concerning Above Reason"

Between friends, if he can see his friend's virtue within reason, it is all the better.

And yet, the nature of the body is to the contrary—it always sees his friend's fault and not his virtues. This is why our sages said, "Judge every person favorably." In other words, although within reason you see that your friend is wrong, you should still try to judge him favorably. And this can be above reason. That is, although logically he cannot justify him, above reason he can justify him nonetheless.

However, if he can justify him within reason, this is certainly better.

6. RABASH, Article No. 1 (1985), "Make for Yourself a Rav and Buy Yourself a Friend – 2"

After he has bonded with a group of people who wish to achieve the degree of love of the Creator, and he wishes to take from them the strength to work in order to bestow and be moved by their words about the necessity for obtaining the love of the Creator, he must regard each friend in the group as greater than himself.

It was written that one is not impressed by the society or takes their appreciation of something unless he regards the society as greater than himself. This is the reason why each one must feel that he is the smallest of them all, since one who is great cannot receive from one who is smaller than himself, much less be impressed by his words. Rather, it is only the smaller one who is impressed through appreciating the greater one.

7. RABASH, Article No. 21 (1986) "Concerning Above Reason"

The envy that he feels toward the friends when he sees that they have better qualities than his own. It motivates him to acquire their good qualities, which he doesn't have and of which he is jealous.

Thus, through the society, he gains new qualities that he adopts by seeing that they are at a higher degree than his, and he is envious of them. This is the reason why now he can be greater than when he didn't have a society, since he acquires new powers through the society.

8. RABASH, Article No. 17, (1984), "Concerning the Importance of Friends"

How can one consider one's friend greater than himself when he can see that his own merits are greater than his friend's, that he is more talented and has better natural qualities? There are two ways to understand this:

1. He is going with faith above reason: once he has chosen him as a friend, he appreciates him above reason.

2. This is more natural—within reason. If he has decided to accept the other as a friend, and works on himself to love him, then it is natural with love to see only good things. And even though there are bad things in one's friend, he cannot see them, as it is written, "love covers all transgressions."

9. RABASH, Article No. 21 (1986), "Concerning Above Reason"

Can be obtained by adhesion of friends—new qualities by which they will be qualified to achieve *Dvekut* with the Creator. And all this can be said while he sees the merits of the friends. At that time, it is relevant to say that he should learn from their actions. But when he sees that he is better qualified than they are, there is nothing he can receive from the friends.

This is why they said that when the evil inclination comes and shows him the lowliness of the friends, he should go above reason. But certainly, it would be better and more successful if he could see within reason that the friends are at a higher degree than his own. With that we can understand the prayer that Rabbi Elimelech had written for us, *"Let our hearts see the virtues of our friends, and not their faults."*

10. *Likutey Etzot*, "Peace," Item 10

One must not look at one's friend unfavorably, finding in him precisely that which is not good and searching for flaws in his friend's work. On the contrary, one must only look at the good and always search and find in him merit and good, and by this there will be peace with everything.

11. Rabbi Kalonymus Kalman Halevi Epstein, *Maor VaShemesh*

The main thing that brings one to love another is by each one being lowly and despicable in his own eyes, always finding faults in everything he does, and seeing the righteousness and actions of one's friend as very great in his eyes. By this he comes to love his friend and be in unity with him. Conversely, if he is great in his own eyes and feels proud, he naturally sees his friend's faults and by this comes to hate him, since his friend is very lowly in his eyes.

13

Joy on the Path

1. Baal HaSulam, *Shamati*, Article No. 58, "Joy Is a Reflection of Good Deeds"

Joy is a "reflection" of good deeds. If the deeds are of *Kedusha* [holiness], hence joy appears. However, we must know that there is also a discernment of a *Klipa* [shell]. In order to know if it is *Kedusha*, the scrutiny is in the reason. In *Kedusha*, there is reason, and in the *Sitra Achra* [other side] there is no reason, since another god is sterile and does not bear fruit. Hence, when gladness comes to a person, he should delve in words of Torah in order to discover the mind of the Torah.

We must also know that gladness is discerned as upper illumination that appears by MAN, which is good deeds. The Creator sentences one where one is. In other words, if one takes upon himself the burden of the kingdom of heaven for eternity, there is an immediate upper illumination on this, which is considered eternity, too.

Even if one evidently sees that he will soon fall from his degree, He still sentences one where one is. It means that if a person has now made up his mind to take upon himself the burden of the kingdom of heaven for eternity, it is considered wholeness.

2. Baal HaSulam, *Shamati*, Article No. 40, "What Is the Measure of Faith in the Rav?"

When one is engaged in the right, the time is right to extend upper abundance, because "the blessed adheres to the Blessed." In other words, since one is in a state of completeness, called "blessed," in that respect one presently has equivalence of form, since the sign of completeness is if one is in gladness. Otherwise, there is no completeness.

It is as our sages said, "The *Shechina* [Divinity] is present only out of gladness of a *Mitzva* [commandment]." The meaning is that the reason that brings him joy is the *Mitzva*, meaning the fact that the rav had commanded him to take the right line.

It follows that he keeps the commandment of the rav, that he was allotted a special time to walk on the right and a special time to walk on the left. Left contradicts the right, since left means when one calculates for oneself and begins to examine what he has already acquired in the work of the Creator, and he sees that he is poor and indigent. Thus, how can he be in wholeness?

Still, one goes above reason because of the commandment of the rav. It follows that all his wholeness was built on above reason, and this is called "faith."

3. Baal HaSulam, Letter No. 5

I rejoice in those revealed corruptions and the ones that are being revealed.

I do, however, regret and complain about the corruptions that have still not appeared, but which are destined to appear, for a hidden corruption is hopeless, and its surfacing is a great salvation from heaven. The rule is that one does not give what he does not have. Hence, if it has appeared now, there is no doubt that it was here to begin with but was hidden. This is why I am happy when they come out of their holes because when you cast your eye on them, they become a pile of bones.

But I do not settle for it even for a moment, as I know that those who are with us are more numerous than those who are with them. But weakness stretches time, and those contemptible ants are hidden and their place is unknown. The sage says about this, "The fool folds his hands and eats his own flesh." Moses let down his hands, but when Moses lifts his hands of faith, all that should appear promptly appears, and then Israel triumphs "in all the mighty hand, and in all the great terror."

This is the meaning of "Whatever you find that your hand can do by your strength, do." When the cup is full, the verse, "The wicked are overthrown," comes true. And when the wicked are lost, light and gladness come to the world, and then they are gone.

I remember you shared with me very sad things that you saw that morning during the service [prayer]. I was filled with joy before you and you asked me, "Why this joy?" I replied to you the same, that when buried wicked appear, although they have not been fully conquered, their very appearance is regarded as a great salvation and causes the *Kedusha* [holiness] of the day.

4. Baal HaSulam, *Shamati*, Article No. 1, "There Is None Else Besides Him"

When one feels some closeness to *Kedusha*, when he feels joy at having been favored by the Creator. Then, too, he must say that his joy is primarily because now there is joy above, in the *Shechina*, at being able to bring her private organ near her, and that she did not have to send her private organ out.

And one derives joy from being rewarded with pleasing the *Shechina*. This is in accord with the above calculation that when there is joy to the part, it is only a part of the joy of the whole. Through these calculations, he loses his individuality and avoids being trapped by the *Sitra Achra*, which is the will to receive for his own benefit.

5. Baal HaSulam, "Introduction to The Study of the Ten Sefirot," Items 106-107

Our sages. They said, "One who repents from love, his sins become as merits." It means that not only does the Creator forgive his sins, He also turns each sin and transgression he had made into a *Mitzva*.

Hence, after one is rewarded with the illumination of the face to such an extent that each sin he had committed, even the deliberate ones, is turned and becomes a *Mitzva* for him, one rejoices with all the torment and affliction he had ever suffered since the time he was placed in the two states of concealment of the face. This is because it is they that brought him all those sins, which have now become *Mitzvot* by the illumination of His face, Who performs wonders.

And any sorrow and trouble that drove him out of mind and he failed with mistakes, as in the first concealment, or failed with sins, as in the double concealment, has now become a cause and preparation for keeping a *Mitzva* and the reception of eternal and wondrous reward for it. Therefore, any sorrow has turned for him into a great joy and any evil to wonderful good.

6. Baal HaSulam, *Shamati*, "One's Future Depends and Is Tied to Gratitude for the Past," Article No. 26

It is written, "The Lord is high and the low will see," that only the low can see the exaltedness. The letters *Yakar* [precious] are the letters of *Yakir* [will know]. This means that one knows the exaltedness of a thing to the extent that it is precious to one.

One is impressed according to the importance of the thing. The impression brings one to a sensation in the heart, and according to the measure of one's recognition of the importance, to that extent, joy is born in him.

Thus, if one knows his lowliness, that he is not more privileged than his contemporaries, meaning he sees that there are many people in the world who were not given the strength to do the holy work even in the simplest way, even without the intention and in *Lo Lishma* [not for Her sake], even in *Lo Lishma* of *Lo Lishma*, and even in preparation for the preparation of the clothing of *Kedusha* [holiness], while he was imparted the desire and thought to at least occasionally do holy work, even in the simplest possible way, if one can appreciate the importance of this, according to the importance one attributes to the holy work, to that extent he should give praise and thanks for it.

This is so because it is true that we cannot appreciate the importance of being able to sometimes observe the *Mitzvot* [commandments] of the Creator, even without any intention. In that state, one comes to feel elation and joy in the heart.

The praise and the gratitude one gives for it expand the feelings, and one is elated by every single point in the holy work, he knows Whose servant he is, and thus soars ever higher. This is the meaning of what is written, "I thank You for the grace that You have made with me," meaning for the past, and by this one can confidently say, and he does say, "and that You are destined to do with me."

7. Baal HaSulam, *Shamati*, Article No. 42, "What Is the Acronym Elul in the Work?"

If one can be in gladness in a state of blackness, too, it is a sign that his work is in purity, since one must be glad and believe that from above he was given an opportunity to be able to work in order to bestow.

This is as our sages said, "All who are gluttonous are angry." It means that one who is immersed in self-reception is angry, since he is always lacking. He forever needs to satisfy his vessels of reception.

However, those who want to walk in the path of bestowal should always be in gladness. This means that in any shape that comes upon him he should be in gladness since he has no intention to receive for himself. This is why he says that either way, if he is really working in order to bestow, he should certainly be glad that he has been granted bringing contentment to his Maker. And if he feels that his work is still not to bestow, he should also be glad because for himself, he says that he does not want anything for himself. He is happy that the will to receive cannot enjoy this work, and that should give him joy.

8. Baal HaSulam, *Shamati*, Article No. 1, "What Is 'The Creator Hates the Bodies,' in the Work?"

Sometimes one despises this work of assuming the burden of the kingdom of heaven, which is a time of a sensation of darkness, when one sees that no one can save him from the state he is in but the Creator. Then he takes upon himself the kingdom of heaven above reason, as an ox to the burden and as a donkey to the load. One should be glad that now he has something to give to the Creator, and the Creator enjoys him having something to give to the Creator. But one does not always have the strength to say that this is beautiful work, called "adornment," but he despises this work. This is a harsh condition for one to be able to say that he chooses this work over the work of whiteness, meaning that he does not sense a taste of darkness during the work, but then one feels a taste in the work. It means that then he does not have to work with the will to receive to agree to take upon himself the kingdom of heaven above reason. If he does overcome himself and can say that this work is pleasant to him that now he is observing the *Mitzva* [commandment] of faith above reason, and he accepts this work as beauty and adornment, this is called "A joy of *Mitzva*."

9. Baal HaSulam, *Shamati*, Article No. 96, "What Is Waste of Barn and Winery, in the Work?"

The purpose of the work is in the literal and nature, since in this work he no longer has room to fall lower down, since he is already placed on the ground. This is so because he does not need greatness because to him it is always like something new. That is, he always works as though he had just begun to work. And he works in the form of accepting the burden of the kingdom of heaven above reason. The basis, upon which he built the order of the work, was in the lowest manner, and all of it was truly above reason. Only one who is truly naïve can be so low as to proceed without any basis on which to establish his faith, literally with no support.

Additionally, he accepts this work with great joy, as though he had had real knowledge and vision on which to establish the certainty of faith. And to that exact measure of above reason, to that very measure as though he had reason. Hence, if he persists in this way, he can never fall. Rather, he can always be in gladness, by believing that he is serving a great King.

10. Baal HaSulam, *Shamati*, Article No. 42, "What Is the Acronym Elul in the Work?"

Those who wish to work in order to bestow are admitted into the King's hall, and when one works in order to bestow, he does not mind what he feels during the work.

Rather, even in a state where he sees a shape of black, he is not impressed by it, but he only wants the Creator to give him strength to be able to overcome all the obstacles. It means that he does not ask the Creator to give him a shape of white, but to give him the strength to overcome all the concealments.

Hence, those people who want to work in order to bestow, if there is always a state of whiteness, the whiteness allows one to continue in the work. This is because, while it shines, one is able to work even in the form of reception for oneself.

Hence, one will never be able to know if his work is in purity or not, and this causes him never to be able to be awarded *Dvekut* [adhesion] with the Creator. For this reason, he is given from above a form of blackness, and then he sees if his work is in purity.

11. Baal HaSulam, *Shamati*, Article No. 42, "What Is the Acronym Elul in the Work?"

It is impossible to obtain disclosure before one receives the discernment of *Achoraim* [posterior], discerned as concealment of the Face, and to say that it is as important to him as the disclosure of the Face. It means that one should be as glad as though he has already acquired the disclosure of the Face.

However, one cannot persist and appreciate the concealment like the disclosure, except when one works in bestowal. At that time, one can say, "I do not care what I feel during the work because what is important to me is that I want to bestow upon the Creator. If the Creator understands that He will have more contentment if I work in a form of *Achoraim*, I agree."

However, if one still has sparks of reception, he comes to thoughts, and it is then hard for him to believe that the Creator leads the world in a manner of "good and doing good." This is the meaning of the letter *Yod* in the name *HaVaYaH*, which is the first letter, called "a black dot that has no white in it," meaning it is all darkness and concealment of the Face.

It means that when one comes to a state where one has no support, one's state becomes black, which is the lowest quality in the upper world, and that becomes the *Keter* to the lower one, as the *Kli* of *Keter* is a vessel of bestowal.

The lowest quality in the upper one is *Malchut*, which has nothing of its own, meaning that she does not have anything. Only in this manner is it called *Malchut*. It means that if one takes upon himself the kingdom of heaven—which is in a state of not having anything—gladly, afterward, it becomes *Keter*, which is a vessel of bestowal and the purest *Kli*. In other words, the reception of *Malchut* in a state of darkness subsequently becomes a *Kli* of *Keter*, which is a vessel of bestowal.

12. Baal HaSulam, *Shamati*, Article No. 11, "Joy with Trembling"

Joy is considered love, which is existence. This is similar to one who builds for himself a house without making any holes in the walls. You find that he cannot enter the house, as there is no hollow place in the walls of the house by which to enter the house. Therefore, a hollow space must be made through which he will enter the house.

Therefore, where there is love, there should also be fear, as fear is the hollow. In other words, one must awaken the fear that one might not be able to aim to bestow.

It follows that when there are both, there is wholeness. Otherwise, each wants to revoke the other. For this reason, we must try to have both of them in the same place.

This is the meaning of the need for love and fear. Love is called existence, whereas fear is called a deficiency and a hollow. Only with the two of them together is there wholeness. This is called "two legs," where precisely when one has two legs can one walk.

13. RABASH, Article No. 22 (1985), "The Whole of the Torah Is One Holy Name"

During the study we must always pay attention to the purpose of the study of Torah, meaning what we should demand from the study of Torah. At that time we are told that first we must ask for *Kelim*, meaning to have vessels of bestowal, called "equivalence of form," by which the restriction and concealment that were placed on the creatures are removed. To the extent that this is so he begins to feel the holiness and begins to have a taste for the work of the Creator. At that time he can be happy because *Kedusha* [holiness] yields joy, for the light of doing good to His creations shines there.

But if he has not yet decided that he should always walk on the path of bestowal, as our sages said, "all your works will be for the Creator," this is regarded as "preparation of the *Kelim*" to be fit for reception of the upper abundance. He wants to be rewarded with vessels of bestowal through the study, as our sages said, "The light in it reforms him."

And once he has been rewarded with vessels of bestowal, he comes to a degree called "attainment of the Torah," which is the "names of the Creator," as *The Zohar* calls it: "The Torah, the Creator, and Israel are one."

14. RABASH, Article No. 799, "The Birth of the Moon"

The moon is called *Malchut*. It is called "the renewal of the moon" because we must accept the burden of the kingdom of heaven each day anew. Yesterday's acceptance is not enough, since each time, says the ARI, we must raise the sparks that fell to *BYA* and raise them to *Kedusha* [holiness]. It follows that when a person accepts a new burden each time, it is considered that each time, he takes a part of the separation and admits it into the unity of *Kedusha*.

This is the meaning of *Malchut* returning to being a dot each day, and in *The Zohar* a dot is called "a black dot in which there is no white." That is, it does not shine, since "white" means that it illuminates. This means that it must be renewed each time.

However, we must know that it is not the same quality as it was before. Rather, it is as it is written, there is no renewal of light that does not extend from *Ein Sof* [infinity/no end].

This is called "*Ibur* [impregnation] of the month." *Ibur* comes from the words "anger and rage." That is, a person must overcome while the kingdom of heaven is as a dot in him, meaning that the kingdom of heaven does not illuminate for him so he will be in gladness, as it is written, "Serve the Lord with gladness," but it is rather in sadness in him.

This is the meaning of *Ibur*. This is similar to an impregnation in corporeality, that the impregnation begins, and then, if the proper conditions are given, an offspring will emerge.

It follows that when one begins the work and sees how far he is from the Creator, and it hurts him, this is regarded as being rewarded with *Katnut* [smallness/infancy], meaning that he feels his own *Katnut*. This is called "a lack of a *Kli* [vessel]," and to that extent he can later obtain the light, called *Gadlut* [greatness/adulthood], according to the measure of the *Kli*.

A dot is called "*Shechina* [Divinity] in the dust," and rising is called "the sanctification of the month." That is, that which was in a state of "dust," he admitted this discernment into *Kedusha*. This is called "raising the *Shechina* from the dust."

15. RABASH, Article No. 24 (1989), "What Is 'Do Not Slight the Blessing of a Layperson' in the Work?"

Our sages said, "Anyone who is proud, the Creator says, 'I and he cannot dwell in the same abode.'" For this reason, when a person feels whole, according to the right line, when he appreciates his lowliness and says that nonetheless, the Creator has given him some grip on *Kedusha*, and that "some," compared to the *Kedusha* that a person should attain, that "some" is called "layperson."

But if he says according to his lowliness, "I thank and praise the Creator for this," it can be said about this what is written, "I am the Lord, who dwells with them in the midst of their *Tuma'a*." When he is happy about this, he can be rewarded with, "The *Shechina* [Divinity] is present only out of joy."

It follows that through this lowliness, that because the Creator has given him some grip on *Kedusha*, he can climb the rungs of holiness if he only takes from this the joy and appreciates it. Then, a person can say, "Raise the poor from the dust," "He will raise the destitute from the litter." That is, when a person feels his lowliness, that he is meager, meaning poor, as our sages said (*Nedarim* 41), "Abaye said, 'In our tradition, there is no poor but in knowledge.'" That is, it has been handed down from our father, a custom from our forefathers that "there is no poor but in knowledge."

This is why he says that he is meager, meaning poor, for he has no knowledge of *Kedusha*—he is called "poor and meager." Then, if there is any grip on *Kedusha*, even though he is poor, he says, "Raises the poor from the dust." That is, he says a prayer, for even though he is poor, the Creator still raised him. "He raises the destitute from the litter." Although he feels that he is destitute, the Creator still lifted him, and for this, he praises the Creator. If there is any grip on *Kedusha*, we can already praise and thank the Creator.

16. RABASH, Article No. 875, "Three Lines-4"

That sees his true state—that he has no grip on spirituality.

In other words, from the perspective of the intellect, he is in complete darkness, and now comes the time to go above reason and say "They have eyes but they will not see; they have ears but they will not hear." However, he is delighted that he has been rewarded with observing the *Mitzvot* of the Creator, who commanded us through Moses. Although he does not feel any flavor or understanding about it, above reason, he still believes that it is a great privilege that he can observe the commandments of the Creator in a simple manner, while others do not even have this. He believes that everything comes from above, and others were given only the enjoyment from nonsense that is suitable for beasts and animals, while he was given a thought and desire to see that their whole lives are nonsense and vanity.

Therefore, he regards this present as a great fortune and he is always elated because of this importance. It is as important to him as though he was awarded the highest degrees. At that time, it is called "right line," "wholeness," since precisely by being happy, one has *Dvekut* with the Creator, as our sages said, "The *Shechina* is present only out of joy." Since now he is in a state of wholeness, he has a reason for gladness.

17. RABASH, Article No. 401, "Hear, O Israel"

A person should begin the work of the Creator on the right, called "male," which is wholeness, called happy with his share, which is regarded as "desiring mercy." Whatever flavor and vitality he has in *Torah and Mitzvot* [commandments] is enough for him to labor in *Torah and Mitzvot* because he believes in private Providence, that such is the will of the Creator, and feels that he is a complete person, and thanks and praises the Creator for giving him a part in His work.

This is called a "male," when he feels himself as whole and he is always happy and observes, "Serve the Lord with gladness."

However, this is called "half a body"; he does not have the quality of female, which is a lack. From the perspective of the left, he begins to calculate to what extent his qualities and thoughts are whole, and then he sees the truth, that he is still immersed in the will to receive for his own benefit, and cannot work for the sake of others, whether between man and man or between man and the Creator.

To the extent that he has the recognition of evil, he can exert, meaning work, perform actions, as in "Everything that is in the power of your hand to do, that do." Also, he can pray from the bottom of the heart.

18. RABASH, Article No. 438, "Save Your Servant, You, My God"

He should believe above reason that he has already received all his wishes, called a "gift."
He thanks his rav for this, for one must not live in separation, meaning that he has complaints against his rav that he is not giving him what he asks. For this reason, it is forbidden for man to be deficient and he must always be in joy. However, in order to have *Kelim* [vessels] to receive, he must evoke the deficiencies.

In the offering, this is regarded as ascending and descending, "Knowing in the beginning and knowing in the end, and concealment in between." That is, between knowing and knowing it is permitted to see the concealment, meaning that he has no revelation with respect to the truth, to feel that his work is desirable to his rav.

It follows that one must not disclose any lack in Torah and work for himself. Rather, he must always go above rhyme and reason that he is utterly and completely whole. In between, he can ask his wishes as his eyes see, that he has only faults. But afterward, he must believe as though he has already received all his wishes and he thanks his rav for this.

At that time, he can be happy that he is whole. It follows that all his wholeness is built on faith, and his deficiencies are built on knowledge, since "the judge has only what his eyes see."

19. RABASH, Article No. 6 (1990), "When Should One Use Pride in the Work?"

When a person engages in Torah and *Mitzvot*, this is the time to be in wholeness, as though the Creator has brought him close, to be among the King's servants. However, one must not lie to oneself and say that he feels that he is serving the King when he does not feel this way. Therefore, how can he be grateful to the Creator for drawing him near if he does not feel it?

Instead, at that time a person should say that although he is in utter lowliness, meaning he is still immersed in self-love, and still cannot do anything above reason, the Creator still gave him a thought and desire to engage in Torah and *Mitzvot*, and has also given him some strength to be able to overcome the spies who speak to him and poke his mind with their arguments. And still, he has some grip on spirituality.

At that time, a person should pay attention to this and believe that the Creator is tending to him and guides him on the track that leads to the King's palace. It follows that he should be happy that the Creator is watching over him and gives him the descents, as well.

20. RABASH, Article No. 6 (1990), "When Should One Use Pride in the Work?"

A person should believe, as much as he can understand, that the Creator is giving him the ascents, since certainly, a person cannot say that he himself receives the ascents, but that the Creator wants to bring him closer; this is why He gives him the ascents.

Also, a person should believe that the Creator gives him the descents, as well, because He wants to bring him closer. Therefore, every single thing that he can do, he must do as though he is in a state of ascent. Therefore, when he overcomes a little during the descent, it is called an "awakening from below." Each act that he does, he believes that it is the Creator's will, and by this itself he is rewarded with greater nearing, meaning that the person himself begins to feel that the Creator has brought him closer.

It is as Baal HaSulam said, that when a person is happy, when he feels that he is privileged that he has some grip on spirituality, that person is called "blessed," and "The blessed clings to the Blessed."

21. RABASH, Article No. 30 (1988), "What to Look for in the Assembly of Friends"

When a group of people gathers and wishes to work together on love of friends, they must all help one another as much as they can.

And there are many discernments about that, since not everyone is the same, meaning that what one needs, the other does not. However, there is one thing in which all are equal: Each and every one of the friends needs high spirits. That is, when the friends are not in a good mood, they are not all the same in their needs. Rather, each has his own reason for being unhappy.

Therefore, each one must contemplate how he can bring about a good mood to the other.

22. RABASH, Article No. 28 (1987), "What Is Do Not Add and Do Not Take Away in the Work?"

He must believe above reason and imagine that he has already been rewarded with faith in the Creator that is felt in his organs, and he sees and feels that the Creator leads the entire world as the good who does good. Although when he looks within reason he sees the opposite, he should still work above reason and it should appear to him as though he can already feel in his organs that so it really is, that the Creator leads the world as the good who does good.

Here he acquires the importance of the goal, and from here he derives life, meaning joy at being near to the Creator. Then a person can say that the Creator is good and does good, and feel that he has the strength to tell the Creator, "You have chosen us from among all nations, You have loved us and wanted us," since he has a reason to thank the Creator. And to the extent that he feels the importance of spirituality, so he establishes the praise of the Creator.

23. RABASH, Article No. 805, "Concerning Joy"

Joy is a testimony. If a person becomes stronger in the matter of faith, to believe that the Creator is good and does good, that there is none above Him, although in the situation he is in right now he has nothing to rejoice with, meaning to be happy about, and yet he reinforces himself and says that the Creator watches over him in a manner of good and doing good, if his faith is sincere, it stands to reason that he should be happy and delighted. And the measure of joy testifies to the level of sincerity in his faith.

By this we can interpret what is said about Rabbi Elimelech, who would say that when he passes away and is told to go to hell, he will say, "If this is what the Creator wants, I will jump in." That is, this is regarded as Providence of good and doing good. Thus, he is always happy.

24. RABASH, Article No. 12 (1991), "These Candles Are Sacred"

The most important is the prayer. That is, one must pray to the Creator to help him go above reason, meaning that the work should be with gladness, as though he has already been rewarded with the reason of *Kedusha*, and what joy he would feel then. Likewise, he should ask the Creator to give him this power, so he can go above the reason of the body.

In other words, although the body does not agree to this work in order to bestow, he asks the Creator to be able to work with gladness, as is suitable for one who serves a great King. He does not ask the Creator to show the greatness of the Creator, and then he will work gladly. Rather, he wants the Creator to give him joy in the work of above reason, that it will be as important to a person as if he already has reason.

25. RABASH, Article No. 507, "What Is Joy?"

One who sees he has no joy the way other people have, it is because he is at a higher degree. Therefore, he should know that the Creator is giving him a chance to begin to engage in Torah and work, and this will bring him the real joy called "the joy of *Mitzva* [commandment]."

26. RABASH, Article No. 120, "Joy that Comes from Dancing"

In corporeality, we see that raising the feet off the ground implies vitality, for *Raglayim* [legs] imply *Meraglim* [spies], who went to tour the land. They went to see if it was worthwhile to make an effort to be rewarded with the land of *Kedusha* [holiness]. Within reason, there are always views that are opposite from *Kedusha*, but we need to believe above reason that it is a land flowing with milk and honey.

Therefore, when lifting the feet off the ground and going above reason, there can be joy, even though there are ups and downs.

However, the broken is not more than the standing; rather, the ascents and descents change rapidly, so the periods of joy never go away.

27. RABASH, Letter No. 22

While engaging in Torah, one should draw light, and then is the time for wholeness.

We must believe what our sages said, "From Mattanah to Nahaliel." The Torah is called *Mattanah* (gift). That is, the fact that a person is permitted to learn and pray, and observe *Mitzvot* even one minute a day, that, too, is a gift from the Creator, for there are several billions in the world to whom the Creator did not give the chance to be able to think of the Creator for even one minute a year. Therefore, while engaging in the Torah, one must be glad, for only through joy is one rewarded with drawing the light of Torah.

28. RABASH, Letter No. 40

"What can one do if he feels that he has a heart of stone toward his friend?" Forgive me for writing, "Each and every one feels that he has a heart of stone," I mean except for the friends who feel and know that they have no objection that their friend will love them and will give them presents (not necessarily in action, but at least in good words and special attention only to him). I am referring only to those who feel that they have very cold hearts in regard to loving their friends, or those who had a heart of flesh but the coldness from the friends affected them, as well, and their hearts have frozen still.

The advice is very simple: The nature of fire is that when rubbing stones against each other, a fire starts. This is a great rule, since "From *Lo Lishma* [not for Her name] one comes to *Lishma* [for Her name]." And this is so particularly when the act is *Lishma*, meaning imparting a gift to one's friend, and the aim is *Lo Lishma*.

This is so because one gives a gift only to one that we know and recognize as someone we love. It follows that the aim of the gift is like gratitude for the love that his friend gives him. However, if one gives a gift to a stranger, meaning he doesn't feel that his friend is close to his heart, then he has nothing to be grateful for. It follows that the aim is *Lo Lishma*, meaning ... the intention that should be.

Ostensibly, it could be said that this is called "charity," since he pities his friend when he sees that there is no one who is speaking to him and greets him, and this is why he does that to him.

Indeed, there is a prayer for it—that the Creator will help him by making him feel the love of his friend and make his friend close to his heart. Thus, through the deeds, he is rewarded with the aim, as well.

But while at the time of doing the giver of the gift intended that the gift to his friends would only be as charity (even if he is giving his time for his friend, since it is sometimes more important to a person than his money, as it is said, "One cares for his lack of money but not for his lack of time." However, regarding time, each has his own value, since there are people who make one pound an hour, and there is more or less. And likewise with their spirituality—how much spirituality they make in an hour, etc.), then one is testifying about himself that he isn't aiming for love of friends, meaning that through the action, the love between them will increase.

And only when both of them intend for a gift and not for charity, through the wearing out of the hearts, even of the strongest ones, each will bring out warmth from the walls of his heart, and the warmth will ignite the sparks of love until a clothing of love will form. Then, both of them will be covered under one blanket, meaning a single love will surround and envelop the two of them, as it is known that *Dvekut* [adhesion] unites two into one.

And when one begins to feel the love of his friend, joy and pleasure immediately begin to awaken in him, for the rule is that a novelty entertains. His friend's love for him is a new thing for him because he always knew that he was the only one who cared for his own well-being. But the minute he discovers that his friend cares for him, it evokes within him immeasurable joy, and he can no longer care for himself, since man can toil only where he feels pleasure. And since he is beginning to feel pleasure in caring for his friend, he naturally cannot think of himself.

29. RABASH, Letter No. 36

"The left rejects." This requires a lot of work and toil to overcome all the obstacles and all the alien views and thoughts. However, we should also engage in the right, as our sages said, "Make your Torah (teaching) permanent and your work temporary." Torah is regarded as right, which is wholeness. A person should regard himself perfect with virtues and noble qualities. He should adapt the works in Torah and *Mitzva* as is suitable for a whole person as much as one can.

However, one must not regret it if one is unable to complete one's will. That is, if a person wishes to do plentiful good deeds and study of Torah, but cannot, he should not regret it but be happy while working in the right. He should be content with whatever he can do, and praise and thank His name for being able to do a small service to the King. Even a minute a day or a minute in two days should be to him like finding a great treasure.

And even if it is a simple deed, meaning without vitality, he should still try to be happy and derive vitality from being allowed to serve the King. This is how he should be during the study, meaning whole. This is regarded as Torah, which is right, as it is written, "On His right was a fiery law." For every opportunity, one must praise the Creator.

I heard from Baal HaSulam that with the praise and gratitude one gives to the Creator for nearing the Creator, one draws the light of His holiness below. A person should feel whole, and then he is regarded as blessed, and the blessed clings to the blessed. But when a person regards himself as cursed, the cursed does not cling to the cursed, as our sages said.

Therefore, you must regard yourselves as whole while performing Torah and *Mitzvot* (commandments). At that time you must not find any flaw in you, as it is written, "Anyone in whom there is a flaw shall not approach." This is called "Torah," meaning wholeness.

30. RABASH, Article No. 12 (1987), "What Is Half a Shekel in the Work – 1"

He should appreciate the service he is giving to the Creator by observing the commandments of the Creator. To the extent that he appreciates the greatness of the Creator, he rejoices in being rewarded with doing what the Creator commanded.

This matter of appreciating the great one is in our nature. We see that it is regarded as a great honor, if there is someone who is the greatest in the generation and people regard him as an important person. Everyone wants to serve him.

However, the satisfaction in the service depends on the greatness and importance that the world attributes to this great person. It follows that when one feels and depicts to himself that he is serving the Creator, he feels that he is blessed, and then comes the rule that the blessed clings to the blessed.

It follows that in such a state a person feels himself as the happiest in the world. This is the time when he needs to thank the Creator for giving him the little service that he served Him. It follows that in that state he is adhered to the Creator because there is joy in him, as our sages said, "The *Shechina* [Divinity] is present only out of joy."

31. RABASH, Article No. 42, "Serve the Creator with Joy"

The Zohar asks, It is written, "The Lord is near to the brokenhearted." A servant of the Creator, whose intention is to bestow, should be happy when he is serving the King. If he has no joy during this work, it is a sign that he lacks appreciation of the greatness of the King.

Therefore, if one sees that he has no joy he should make amendments, meaning think about the greatness of the King. If he still does not feel, he should pray to the Creator to open his eyes and heart to feel the greatness of the Creator.

Here the two discernments develop: 1) He should regret not having a sensation of the greatness of the King. 2) He should be happy that his regrets are about spirituality and not like the rest of the people, whose regrets are only in order to receive.

We should know who it is who gave us the awareness that our regrets should be over spirituality, and we should be happy that the Creator has sent us thoughts of spiritual deficiency, which in itself is regarded as the salvation of the Creator. For this reason, we should be happy.

32. RABASH, Article No. 300, "A Land Where You Will Eat Bread without Scarcity"

"As one blesses for the good, so one blesses for the bad." It means that if he were to be rewarded with the good that is concealed in *Torah and Mitzvot*, he would certainly work with joy and excitement and peace of mind. Likewise, now that he is deficient, he should also make his work be with joy and peace, and then he will be rewarded with food for humans, called "bread."

33. RABASH, Article No. 17 (1986), "The Agenda of the Assembly – 2"

According to what is written, "In the multitude of people is the King's glory," it follows that the greater the number of the collective, the more effective is the power of the collective. In other words, they produce a stronger atmosphere of greatness and importance of the Creator. At that time, each person's body feels that he regards anything that he wishes to do for holiness—meaning to bestow upon the Creator—as a great fortune, that he has been privileged with being among people who have been rewarded with serving the King. At that time, every little thing he does fills him with joy and pleasure that now he has something with which to serve the King.

To the extent that the society regards the greatness of the Creator with their thoughts during the assembly, each according to his degree originates the importance of the Creator in him. Thus, he can walk all day in the world of gladness and joy.

34. RABASH, Article No. 40 (1990), "What Is, 'For You Are the Least of All the Peoples,' in the Work?"

How can one muster the strength to overcome the body when he feels that the *Shechina* is in the dust? What joy can he receive from this work? Even more perplexing, how can one need and want to work when he feels no taste in it? This would be understandable if he had no choice; we can understand when a person is forced to work. But how is it possible to want such a work, which feels tasteless? And since he does not have the strength to overcome and feel joy in such a work, how can he serve the King in such a lowly state, when he feels the taste of dust while serving the King?

Hence, in this regard, he does not ask the Creator to give him the revelation of His greatness, so he will feel a good taste in it. Rather, he asks the Creator to give him strength to be able to overcome the body and work gladly because now he can work only for the Creator, since the will to receive does not enjoy work that tastes like dust.

35. RABASH, Article No. 386, "This Is the Day that the Lord Has Made"

"This is the day which the Lord has made; we will rejoice and be glad in it." "This is the day" means that "this" is called "day," and not something else. What is it when the Lord "makes"? It is that each one will attain that "we will rejoice and be glad in it." "In it" means in the Creator, in *Dvekut* [adhesion] with the Creator, which is called "equivalence of form," which is that each and every one will understand that there is no greater joy than to bestow contentment upon one's Maker. This is what we hope for. When the general public achieves this degree, it will be called "the end of correction."

36. RABASH, Article No. 17 (1991), "What Is, 'For I Have Hardened His Heart,' in the work?"

A person must be glad that at least he has a need for spirituality, whereas the rest of the people have no interest in spirituality whatsoever.

When a person appreciates this, although it is not important to him, he does appreciate it and tries to thank the Creator for this. This causes him to acquire importance for spirituality, and from this a person can be happy. By this, a person can be rewarded with *Dvekut*, since as Baal HaSulam said, "The blessed clings to the Blessed." In other words, when a person is happy and thanks the Creator, he feels that the Creator has blessed him by giving him a little something of *Kedusha*, then "The blessed clings to the Blessed." Through this wholeness, one can achieve real *Dvekut*.

37. RABASH, Article No. 23 (1990), "What Does It Mean that Moses Was Perplexed about the Birth of the Moon, in the Work?"

We must believe in the sages, who tell us that all our work, however we work, if the person attributes the work to the Creator, even if it is in utter lowliness, the Creator enjoys it. The person should be happy that he can do things while in a state of lowliness.

The person should tell himself that He enjoys this work, which is entirely above reason. Reasonably thinking, this work is not considered "work," meaning an important act that the Creator enjoys. Yet, he believes in the sages, who told us that the Creator does enjoy, but this is above reason.

38. RABASH, Article No. 463, "You Became Rich; You Are in the Evening; Light the Candle"

"You became rich; you are in the evening; light the candle." The king had two books of Torah—with one he comes out, and the other he leaves in his treasury.

It is known that there are two opposites in the work of the Creator: 1) A person must be happy in any state that he is in, even if it is the lowest possible state. He should praise and thank the Creator for letting him be among those who sit inside the seminary, as our sages said, "He who walks and does not do, the reward for walking is in his hand." This is called "You became rich," as in "wealth," for on the eve of Shabbat [Sabbath] he should be as one who is wealthy who does not lack a thing.

Afterward, one must shift to the other side, to see what he has—how much fear of heaven and greatness of the Creator he has, and how many good deeds and how much Torah, and understanding in the Torah. At that time, he sees that he is deficient. This is called "evening," as in "And there was evening and there was morning," and this is called "you are in the evening."

Once one has those two, then "Light the candle" of Shabbat. At that time, the middle line comes, namely the light of Shabbat.

39. RABASH, Article No. 5, "The Meaning of Sins Becoming as Merits"

We can understand the meaning of sins becoming as merits, that if a person has a question, which is certainly a great iniquity because this question might cause him to fall into the *Klipa* [shell/peel] called "pondering the beginning." If he repents from fear, meaning strengthens himself and is not impressed by this thought, then they become to him as mistakes. That is, it is not a sin but a mistake. In other words, it would be better had no foreign thought come to him, but now that it came, he did not have a choice but to strengthen himself with acceptance of the burden of the kingdom of heaven.

Also, there is repentance from love, when he receives the burden of faith anew because of love, meaning he accepts the work with love. That is, he is happy that the Creator has given him this foreign thought by which he can observe this *Mitzva* [commandment].

This is similar to a flame that is tied to the wick. The foreign thought is considered the wick, which wants to install a flaw in his work. That is, the foreign thought makes him think that from the perspective of the mind and reason, he has nothing to do in His work. And when he gets the foreign thought, he says that he does not want to make any excuses, but everything that the reason says is correct except he is walking on the path of faith, which is above reason.

It follows that the flame of faith is tied to the wick of the foreign thought. Thus, only now can he observe the *Mitzva* of faith properly. It follows that the questions have become to him as merits, since otherwise he would not be able to accept any merits from faith.

This is called "rejoicing in suffering." Although he suffers from the foreign thoughts that afflict him and cause him to slander and gossip and speak badly about His work, he is nonetheless happy about it for only now, at such a time, he can observe in a manner of faith above reason. This is called "the joy of *Mitzva*."

40. RABASH, Article No. 15 (1991), "What Is the Blessing, 'Who Made a Miracle for Me in This Place,' in the Work?"

A person should accustom himself with anything to compare between the time of suffering and the time of pleasure, and to bless for the miracle of delivering him from suffering to a state of pleasure. By this, he will be able to thank the Creator and enjoy in the new *Kelim* that have been added to him now when he compares the two times to one another. From this, a person can advance in the work.

This is as Baal HaSulam said, that it does not matter whether a person receives from the Creator something great or small. What matters is how much a person thanks the Creator. To the extent of his gratitude, so grows the giving that the Creator gives. Therefore, we must take note to be grateful, to appreciate His gift, so we can approach the Creator. Hence, when a person always looks during the ascent at the state he was in while in descent, meaning how he felt during the descent, he can make a distinction as in, "as the advantage of the light from within the darkness," and he already has new *Kelim* in which to receive joy and be thankful to the Creator. This is the meaning of what is written, that a person should bless, "Blessed is He who made a miracle for me in this place," meaning in the place where he is now, during the ascent, since there cannot be an ascent if there was no prior state of descent.

41. *Zohar for All, New Zohar,* Song of Songs, "Twenty-Two Letters and MANTZEPACH," Item 290

We will rejoice and delight in You; we will remember Your love more than wine." Since it was connected together in our joy, each was given a part from our joy, and we will satiate them, as it is written, "He will remember all Your gifts." "From wine," from our joy from the side of the wine, illumination of *Hochma*, which delights everyone.

42. *Zohar for All*, BaMidbar [In the Desert], "Be Joyful with Jerusalem," Items 24-25

When Jerusalem rejoices, man should rejoice, and not during the exile. "Be joyful with Jerusalem," as it is written, "Serve the Lord with gladness." Jerusalem, meaning Divinity, should be served and delighted.

One verse says, "Serve the Lord with gladness," and one verse says, "Serve the Lord with fear, and rejoice with trembling." When Israel are in the holy land, they serve before the Lord with gladness. When Israel are in another land, they should serve with fear and rejoice with trembling. "Serve the Lord with fear" is the assembly of Israel, *Malchut*, when she is in exile among the nations.

43. *Zohar for All*, VaYetze [And Jacob Went Out], "The Trees of the Lord Have Their Fill," Item 340

It is written about the *Nukva*, "And it repented the Lord ... and it grieved Him," since *Dinim* and sadness are in this place. However, in everything that is above, in *Bina*, it is all in light and life to all directions, and there is no sadness before the place, which indicates to the inner one, *Bina*, who is the only one in whom there is no sadness. But the external one, the *Nukva*, there is sadness in her. This is why it is written, "Serve the Lord with gladness; come before His presence with singing." "Serve the Lord with gladness" corresponds to the upper world. "Come before His presence with singing" corresponds to the lower world.

44. *Zohar for All*, VaYeshev (And Jacob Sat), "For He Pays a Man According To His Work," Item 29

Divinity does not dwell in a place of sadness, but in a place of joy. And if one has no joy, Divinity will not be in that place.

45. *Zohar for All*, Zohar Hadash, Hukat, "To the Conductor [also: Winner] of Lilies," Item 111

He has no joy from all His *Merkavot* [chariots/structures] as the joy of the souls of the righteous who are close to Him.

46. *Zohar for All*, Zohar Hadash, Hukat, "To the Conductor [also: Winner] of Lilies," Item 112

He had no joy as when Solomon made The Song of Songs and sang the praises of the Queen to the King.

47. *Zohar for All*, *New Zohar*, Song of Songs, "He Shall Walk and Weep," Items 105-106

When Solomon built the Temple and the lower world, *Malchut*, was completed similar to the upper world, *Bina*, Israel were all worthy and ascended by several sublime degrees. At that time, the throne, *Malchut*, ascended with joy, with several joys and in several values.

At that time, The Song of Songs that is of Solomon rose in joy and descended in joy, and all the worlds were in joy, and the connection was in joy. A song to the Creator is when *Malchut* sings to the Creator. The songs are to the upper ones and to the lower ones, to the connection of ZA and *Malchut* through *Yesod*, which unites them with one another. "That is for Solomon," the connection of all the worlds in joy, to the king that peace is all his, *Bina*.

48. *Zohar for All*, *New Zohar*, Song of Songs, "I see a gold lampstand, seven lamps on it with seven spouts," Items 87-88

The Song of Songs is the praise of praises to the King that peace is his, *Bina*, since this is the place that needs joy, where there are no anger or judgment, since the next world, *Bina*, which is all joy, delights everyone. For this reason, it sends joy and merriment to all the degrees.

As the joy must be awakened from this world upward, merriment must be awakened from the world of the moon to the upper world, *Bina*. For this reason, the worlds stand in one way and the awakening ascends only from below upward.

49. *Zohar for All*, *New Zohar*, Song of Songs, "The King Brought Me to His Rooms," Item 232

I do not take notice of it. Rather, I want to be with You in lowliness and You will control me. Therefore, although I will be in more lowliness with You, I and the hosts will rejoice and delight in You. We have joy and good will to be with You and not part from You, for any joy and good will are only in You, since a woman has joy and good will only with her husband, and not with her mother or father. Therefore, the King brought me to His rooms and I received joy and good will only with You.

50. *Zohar for All*, *New Zohar*, Song of Songs, "Explaining the Verses according to the Aleph-Bet of Aleph-Tav Bet-Shin," Item 318

Wherever there is joy, we must increase efforts so the *Sitra Achra* [other side] cannot slander. Also, wherever there is mourning, the *Sitra Achra* is there and we should increase efforts so he cannot slander and break his strength.

51. *Zohar for All*, *VaYikra* [The Lord Called], "Serve the Lord with Gladness," Item 109

"Serve the Lord with gladness." Any work that a person wishes to do for the Creator should be done with gladness, willingly, so that his work will be whole.

52. *Zohar for All, VaYikra* [The Lord Called], "Serve the Lord with Gladness," Items 114-115

Joy is the assembly of Israel, *Malchut*, which is called "joy." It is also written, "For you shall go out with joy," meaning that Israel are destined to come out of exile with joy. And who is she? The assembly of Israel, *Malchut*. It is written, "Serve the Lord with gladness," in the quality of *Malchut*, as it is written, "With this shall Aaron come into the holy place," with the quality of *Malchut*. Here, too, serve the Lord with *Malchut*, called "joy," and called, "this."

"Come before His presence with singing." This is her perfection, since gladness is in the heart and singing is in the mouth. In the mouth, she is more perfect, and the perfection of this gladness is known; it is known what it is—that it is man's correction, who needs to be corrected before his Master, to be rewarded with that. And when he is rewarded with that, then, "Know that the Lord He is God," when he unites that unification of "*HaVaYaH* [the Lord] He is *Elokim* [God]."

And everything, the two interpretations, come in one thing—that afterwards the Holy Name should be properly united and tied to one another, so all will be one. This is the work of the Creator. Happy are the righteous who engage in the Torah and know the ways of the Creator.

53. *Zohar for All, Tetzaveh* [Command], "Blow the Horn [Shofar] on the New Moon," Item 94

"Serve the Lord with gladness," since man's joy draws another joy, the higher one. Similarly, the lower world, *Malchut*, as it is crowned, so it extends from above.

54. *Zohar for All, Truma* [Donation], "Lift Up a Song for Him Who Rides through the Prairies," Items 712-713

It is written, "And rejoice before Him." Before Him, who is *Bina*, who rides in the prairies. He who comes in before Me in this firmament should enter with joy, and not at all with sadness, since this firmament causes that there will not be any sadness or anger there at all, for there everything is in joy.

For this reason, the great priest who stands before Him would enter the Temple only with joy, and to show joy because the place causes.

55. *Zohar for All, VaYechi* [Jacob Lived], "Jacob," Items 116-117

Divinity is present only in a whole place, and not in a deficient place or a flawed place or a place of sadness, but in a proper place—a place of joy. For this reason, all those years when Joseph was separated from his father and Jacob was sad, Divinity was not on him.

"Serve the Lord with gladness; come before Him with singing." There is no service of the Creator unless out of joy. Divinity is not present in sadness, as it is written, "'And now bring me a player.' And it came to pass that when the player played." It writes "Play" three times, to evoke the spirit from the source of wholeness, ZA, which includes three lines, which is the complete spirit. The threefold "play" corresponds to his three lines.

56. *Zohar for All*, Pinhas, "Hear, My Son, Your Father's Reproof," Item 2

Anyone who engages in Torah in this world is rewarded with several gates being opened to him, several lights to that world. Hence, when he passes away from this world, the Torah walks before him and goes to all the gate-keepers, declares and says, "Open the gates and let the righteous gentile in, set up a chair for so and so, the King's servant," for there is no joy to the Creator except in one who engages in the Torah.

57. *Zohar for All*, *Aharei Mot* [After the Death], "Therefore Maidens Love You," Item 50

"The king has brought me to his chambers; we will be glad and rejoice in you." If the King brings me to His chambers, "We will be glad and rejoice in you," I and all My hosts. All the hosts, when the Assembly of Israel is glad and blessed, everyone is glad. At that time there is no *Din* [judgment] in the world. This is why it is written, "Let the heavens be glad, and let the earth rejoice."

58. *Zohar for All*, *VaEra* [And I Appeared], "And They May Become Blood"

"Go then, eat your bread in happiness" means that when a person goes in the ways of the Creator, the Creator brings him closer and gives him peace and tranquility. Then the bread and wine that a man eats and drinks are with joy in the heart since the Creator desires his works.

Where is the wisdom in this verse?

Solomon warned people to crown the assembly of Israel, *Malchut*, with joy on the right side, meaning with light of *Hassadim*, which is bread. This is so because bread implies to the light of *Hassadim*. Afterwards he will be crowned with wine, left side, illumination of *Hochma* in the left of *Bina*, so that the faith of all, meaning *Malchut*, would be in complete joy on the right and on the left. And when she is between the two of them, all the blessings will be in the world, since this is the complete perfection of *Malchut*, that the illumination of the left, *Hochma*, will clothe in the light of *Hassadim* on the right, at which time both shine in her, which are bread and wine. And this is the meaning of the Creator wanting people's actions.

59. *Zohar for All*, *Miketz* (At the End), "They Brought Him Hastily out of the Dungeon," Item 55

Hence, everything is given to people's will, as it is written, "So that man will not find out the work which God has done from the beginning even to the end." And because these deeds were not done so as to be corrected in their degree—as they should have—for this deed to be included in its corresponding degree, it is all in correction. Instead, they were done according to man's will, by his arbitrary heart, as it is written, "I know that there is nothing good about them but to rejoice and to get pleasure so long as they live." "I know that there is nothing good about them," about those deeds that were not done with the proper intention for correction. But to rejoice with everything that comes to him, both good and bad, and to give thanks to the Creator, "And to get pleasure so long as they live."

Why should one rejoice with the bad? If the deed he has done harmed him because of the degree that was appointed over it from the left, he should be happy and thankful for this bad that has come to him, for he caused that himself, since he went without knowledge, like a trapped bird. And now, since he has obtained knowledge through the punishment, he will know how to do good in his life. Hence, he should be happy and thankful for the punishment.

60. *Zohar for All*, Yitro [Jethro], "And You Will Behold the Secret of the Eyes," Item 86

There are four colors in the eyes. 1) The white that surrounds the eye, as every person has. This is the same for all people. 2) In front of it is the surrounding black. White and black are mingled, implying to *HG*, which are included in one another. 3) In front of it is the green, which implies to *Tifferet* and is included in the black. 4) In front of it is the pupil, which is a black point that implies to *Malchut*. This is a person who is always laughing, always joyful, and thinks positive thoughts. And the thoughts are not completed because he always elevates them from his will. He engages in mundane matters, and when he engages in heavenly matters he succeeds. Such a person should be encouraged to engage in Torah, as he will succeed in it.

61. *Zohar for All*, VaYakhel [And Moses Assembled], "An Added Neshama [Soul]," Items 183-184

When that lowermost point, *Malchut*, rises and appears, meaning when she receives *Hochma*—called "vision"—and is adorned in the upper *Mochin*, there is every joy above and below, and all the worlds are in joy. On that night of the Sabbath, that point expands in its lights and spreads its wings on the whole world, all the other rulers pass away, and there is watching over the world.

At that time the spirit of *Neshama* is added in Israel, on each and every one, and in that added *Neshama* they forget every sadness and wrath, and there is only joy above and below. When that spirit that came down and was added in the people of the world comes down, it bathes in the perfumes of the Garden of Eden, descends, and stays over the holy people. Happy are they when that spirit awakens.

62. *Zohar for All*, VaYikra [The Lord Called], "Tell Me, You Whom My Soul Loves," Item 288

As long as the assembly of Israel is with the Creator, the Creator is in wholeness and willingly pastures Himself and to others. To Himself means that He nurtures Himself by sucking the milk of upper *Ima*. He receives the abundance of *Bina* and from that nursing that He suckles, He waters all the others and nurtures them.

When the assembly of Israel is with the Creator, the Creator is in wholeness and joy, and there are blessings in Him, which come out from Him to all the others, to all the worlds. And any time when the assembly of Israel is not with the Creator, the blessings are devoid of Him and of all the others.

63. *Zohar for All*, *Tzav* [Command], "The Fire of the Altar Crouches like a Lion," Item 130

It is similar to a king whose people sent him a gift which he welcomed. He said to his servant, "Go and take that gift that they brought me." This is what the Creator said to Angel Uriel, "Go and receive the gift that My sons have sacrificed before Me." What joy was there in everything, and what sweetness was in all when the priest and the Levite, and the one who made the offering, would aim to make the offering as it should be, in complete unification.

64. *Zohar for All*, *Hukat* [The Statute], "Who Sends Forth Springs in the Streams," Item 31

After all that, when all the upper ones and lower ones are filled with abundance from AVI, it is written, "The land shall be satiated from the fruits of Your works." This is the upper holy land, *Malchut*. When she is blessed, all the worlds are blessed and rejoice. It is when the blessings are found from the potion of the stream, the spring, AVI, the deepest of all, for illumination of *Hochma* from the left does not appear in *Malchut*, being the abundance that is dedicated to her, except after the upper ones and all the lower ones are filled with abundance of ample *Hassadim* from upper AVI.

65. *Zohar for All*, *New Zohar*, Song of Songs, "The King Brought Me to His Rooms," Item 288

Rabbi Shimon wept as before and said, "May we be able to reveal the upper secrets, which is joy before the Creator, for He wishes to reveal high secrets in this generation."

66. Rabbi Nachman of Breslov, *Likutei Moharan*

The rule is that one should overcome with all of one's might to always be only happy, since man's nature is to drag himself to melancholy and sadness due to the afflictions and incidents of time, and every person is full of suffering. For this reason, one must force oneself with great force to always be happy and delight himself wherever he can, even with words of nonsense. Although a broken heart is also good, it is so only for a certain time, so one should dedicate some time during the day to break his heart and pour out his words before Him, as is customary for us. However, throughout the day, one must be glad.

67. Rabbi Nachman of Breslov, *Likutei Moharan*

One should delight and reinforce himself and not stay in his place even if he fell where he fell. Nevertheless, one should reinforce himself with the littlest of the little good that he still finds in himself until he is rewarded with returning by this to the Creator, and all the sins will become merits.

From this you will understand how much you must grow stronger and not despair yourself whatever happens. And the most important is to always be happy. One should delight himself however he can, even with words of nonsense, to pretend he is a fool and perform follies and laughter or jump and dance in order to come to joy, which is a very great thing.

68. Rav Yitzchak Safrin of Komarno, *The Path of Unification*

When you aim, with submission and fear, to awaken the surrounding lights and the *Mochin* above, although you do not know any essence or the surrounding lights or the *Mochin* of anything, still, by your knowledge, you awaken their existence. And although you do not know their essence, a great light is drawn over to you, and you serve the Creator with true joy and merriment from all the great light that shines on you.

14

Judge Every Person to the Side of Merit

1. Baal HaSulam, *Shamati*, Article No. 25, "Things that Come from the Heart"

When one hears the words of Torah from his teacher, he immediately agrees with his teacher and resolves to observe the words of his teacher with his heart and soul. But afterward, when he comes out to the world, he sees, covets, and is infected by the multitude of desires roaming the world. Then, he and his mind, his heart, and his will are annulled before the majority.

As long as he has no power to sentence the world to the side of merit, they subdue him, he mingles with their desires, and he is led like sheep to the slaughter. He has no choice; he is compelled to think, want, crave, and demand everything that the majority demands. Then he chooses their foreign thoughts and their loathsome lusts and desires, which are alien to the spirit of the Torah. In that state, he has no strength to subdue the majority.

Instead, there is only one counsel then: to cling to his teacher and to the books. This is called "From the mouth of books and from the mouth of authors." Only by clinging to them can he change his mind and will for the better. However, witty arguments will not help him change his mind, but only the remedy of *Dvekut* [adhesion], for this is a wondrous cure, as the *Dvekut* reforms him.

2. RABASH, Article No. 30 (1988), "What to Look for in the Assembly of Friends"

When a person comes to the society and sees that the whole of society is in a state of decline, so how can he be strengthened by them? At that time, he must judge everyone to the side of merit.

3. RABASH, Article No. 30 (1988), "What to Look for in the Assembly of Friends"

It is a great effort when one should judge the friends to the side of merit, and not everyone is ready for it.

Sometimes, it is even worse. At times, a person sees that his friend is disrespectful toward him. Even worse, he heard a slanderous rumor, meaning he heard from a friend that that friend, who is called so and so, said about him things that are not nice for friends to say about each other. Now he must subdue himself and judge him to the side of merit. This, indeed, is a great effort. It follows that through the exertion, he gives the payment, which is even more important than a payment of money.

However, if that person slanders him, where will his friend muster the strength to love him? He knows for certain that he hates him, or he would not slander him, so what is the point in subduing himself and judging him to the side of merit?

The answer is that Love of friends that is built on the basis of love of others, by which they can achieve the love of the Creator, is the opposite of what is normally considered love of friends. In other words, love of others does not mean that the friends will love me. Rather, it is I who must love the friends. For this reason, it makes no difference if the friend slanders him and must certainly hate him. Instead, a person who wishes to acquire love of others needs the correction of loving the other. Therefore, when a person makes the effort and judges him to the side of merit, it is a *Segula* [remedy/power/virtue], where by the toil that a person makes, which is called "an awakening from below," he is given strength from above to be able to love all the friends without exception.

4. RABASH, Article No. 1 (1985), "Make for Yourself a Rav and Buy Yourself a Friend – 1"

Rabbi Yehoshua Ben Perachia says about it, "Judge every person favorably," meaning one should judge everyone favorably.

This means that the fact that he does not find merits in them is not their fault. Rather, it is not in his power to be able to see the merits of the general public. For this reason, he sees according to the qualities of his own soul. This is true according to his attainment, but not according to the truth.

5. RABASH, Article No. 9 (1984), "One Should Always Sell the Beams of His House"

If a society is established with certain people, and when they gathered, there must have been someone who wished to establish specifically this "bunch." Thus, he sorted out these people to see that they were suitable for each other. In other words, each of them had a spark of love of others, but the spark could not ignite the light of love to shine in each, so they agreed that by uniting, the sparks would become a big flame.

Hence, now, too, when he is spying on them, he should overcome and say, "As all of them were of one mind that they must walk on the path of love of others when the society was established, so it is now." And when everyone judges his friends favorably, all the sparks will ignite once more and again there will be one big flame.

6. RABASH, Article No. 21 (1986), "Concerning Above Reason"

Between friends, if he can see his friend's virtue within reason, it is all the better.

And yet, the nature of the body is to the contrary—it always sees his friend's fault and not his virtues. This is why our sages said, "Judge every person favorably." In other words, although within reason you see that your friend is wrong, you should still try to judge him favorably. And this can be above reason. That is, although logically he cannot justify him, above reason he can justify him nonetheless.

However, if he can justify him within reason, this is certainly better.

7. RABASH, Article No. 561, "The Soul of Israel"

Anyone who destroys one soul from Israel, the text says about him that it is as though he destroyed a whole world. Likewise, anyone who sustains one soul from Israel, the text says about him that it is as though he sustained a whole world" (Sanhedrin 37).

We should say, Why did the writing say this? After all, we have divisions in the Torah between individuals and the collective where the collective takes precedence over the individual, and it also stands to reason that the individual is one, and not many. Thus, what is the reason that the writing says that the individual is like the collective?

Our sages said, "He who performs one *Mitzva* [commandment], happy is he for he has sentenced himself and the entire world to the side of merit" (*Kidushin* 40). Why is this so? After all, we see that there are wicked in the world, and it is known that in each generation, we have righteous, as our sages said, "There is no generation that has none such as Abraham," etc.

Thus, the merit that the righteous caused should have been apparent to the collective. Yet, we see that someone who invents some invention in science, this wisdom that the wise extended is enough for the whole collective. That is, one who wants to delve in the wisdom can benefit from what the wise person extended to the collective. But clearly, one who does not engage in science has no connection to that innovation that the wise person extended.

It is likewise in spirituality: "He who performs one *Mitzva* sentences himself and the entire world to the side of merit." That is, one who engages in the work of the Creator can benefit from the lights he has obtained through his sentencing.

Accordingly, "One who sustains one soul from Israel," who made the sentencing to the side of merit, sustains his soul, since "The wicked in their lives are called 'dead.'" It follows that without sentencing, he is "half and half," like a person hanging between life and death. By sentencing, he becomes alive. It follows that the lights that he drew suffice for the whole collective.

This is the meaning of "The world stands on one righteous," meaning that the light that he extended is as in "A candle for one, a candle for one hundred." Hence, he who loses his soul, by sentencing to the side of fault, loses a whole world, meaning that he denied the revelation of the light that was enough for the entire world. This is the meaning of the words, "One must say, 'The world was created for me.'"

8. *Zohar for All, Beresheet Bet* [Genesis 2], "Seven Palaces in the Garden of Eden" Item 103

All the people of the world are in utter wholeness, to such an extent that there has never been such joy before the Creator as on the day when heaven and earth were created. However, a person cannot take part in His great joy unless he has made complete repentance from love. Before that, he will not rejoice at all with himself or with the people of the world. On the contrary, he feels before him a world full of sorrow and pain until he says, "The earth is given into the hand of the wicked," both pains of the body and pains of the soul, which are the sins he commits.

All of that came to him because he is going against the nature of creation, since the world was created only in bestowal, to engage in Torah and good deeds in order to bestow contentment to one's

Maker, and not for one's own pleasure. It is written, "All the works of the Creator are for Him," so that people would bestow contentment upon Him.

But in the beginning, it is written, "A man is born a wild ass' colt," whose sole interest is his own delight and who has none of the desire to bestow. He argues, "All the works of the Creator are for me, for my own delight," since he wishes to devour the entire world for his own good and benefit.

Hence, the Creator has imprinted bitter and harsh afflictions in self-reception, instilled in man from the moment of his birth—bodily pains and pains of the soul—so that if he engages in Torah and *Mitzvot* even for his own pleasure, through the light in it he will still feel the lowliness and the terrible corruptness in the nature of receiving for oneself.

At that time he will resolve to retire from that nature of reception and completely devote himself to working only in order to bestow contentment upon his Maker, as it is written, "All the works of the Creator are for Him." Then the Creator will open his eyes to see before him a world filled with utter perfection without any deficiencies whatsoever.

Then he partakes in the joy as at the time of the creation of the world. Because he was rewarded, he has sentenced himself and the entire world to a scale of merit," for wherever he casts his eyes he sees only good and perfection. He sees no faults at all in the works of the Creator, only merits.

9. *Zohar for All*, "Introduction of The Book of Zohar," "Two Points," Item 121

All the many contradictions to His uniqueness, which we taste in this world, separate us from the Creator. Yet, when exerting to keep Torah and *Mitzvot* with love, with our soul and might, as we are commanded—to bestow contentment upon our Maker—all those forces of separation do not affect us into subtracting any of the love of the Creator with all our souls and might. Rather, in that state, every contradiction we have overcome becomes a gate for attainment of His wisdom. This is so because there is a special quality in each contradiction—revealing a special degree in attaining Him. And those worthy ones who have been rewarded with it turn darkness into light and bitter into sweet, for all the powers of separation—from the darkness of the mind and the bitterness of the body—have become to them gates for obtainment of sublime degrees. Thus, the darkness becomes a great light and the bitter becomes sweet.

Hence, to the extent that they previously had all the conducts of His guidance toward the forces of separation, now they have all been inverted into forces of unification, and sentence the entire world to the side of merit. This is because now each force serves for them as a gate of righteousness, by which they will come to receive from the Creator everything that He has contemplated for them, to delight them with the thought of creation, as it is written, "This is the gate of the Lord; the righteous will enter through it."

However, prior to being rewarded with inverting the desire to receive in us through Torah and *Mitzvot*, into reception in order to bestow, there are strong locks on those gates to the Creator, for then they have the opposite role: to drive us away from the Creator. This is why the forces of separation are called "locks," since they block the gates of approaching and drive us away from the Creator.

But if we overcome them so they do not affect us, cooling His love from our hearts, the locks become doors, the darkness becomes light, and the bitter becomes sweet. Over all the locks, we receive a special degree in His Providence, and they become openings, degrees of attainment of the Creator.

www.ingramcontent.com/pod-product-compliance
Lightning Source LLC
Chambersburg PA
CBHW080536230426
43663CB00015B/2612